SO-EJV-259

PLEASE STAMP DATE DUE, BOTH BELOW AND ON CARD

DATE DUE	DATE DUE	DATE DUE	DATE DUE

GL-15(3/71)

WITHDRAWN
CALTECH LIBRARY SERVICES

J
80
A283
INDEX
1977/81

HUMS

The Cumulated Indexes
to the
Public Papers of the Presidents
of the
United States

Jimmy Carter
1977–1981

KRAUS INTERNATIONAL PUBLICATIONS
Millwood, New York • London, England • Schaan, Liechtenstein
A Division of Kraus-Thomson Organization Limited
1983

Copyright © Kraus International Publications 1983

All rights reserved. No part of this work covered by the copyright hereon may be reproduced or used in any form or by any means—graphic, electronic, or mechanical, including photocopying, recording, or taping, or information storage and retrieval systems—without written permission of the publisher.

ISBN 0-527-20757-8

Composition by Vance Weaver Composition, Inc., New York

First Printing
Printed in the United States of America

PREFACE

Although the words spoken by a president during the course of his administration are directed to the citizens of his own time, they become invaluable to future generations of Americans who look to the past for help in understanding their present world. As Jimmy Carter wrote in the Foreword to the 1978 *Public Papers of the Presidents of the United States*, "The Presidential papers . . . document our concerns as a nation, both the transitory and the passing, and the deep and lasting questions that will occupy our attention and affect our lives for generations." *The Cumulated Indexes to the Public Papers of the Presidents of the United States* provide, for the first time in one volume, full access to the papers of each presidential administration published in the government series.

The *Public Papers* for the Carter years chronicle events both historic and mundane; also in his 1978 Foreword, Jimmy Carter states: "These papers reflect the variety of a President's role, from ceremonial leader to party chieftain, from partner with Congress in the making of laws to representative of the Nation in the building of a more peaceful world." The papers document the administration's accomplishments, aspirations, and disappointments, ranging from the Camp David Middle East treaty, attempted ratification of the SALT II treaty, and the Energy Security Act, to the American reaction against the Soviet invasion of Afghanistan, the Summer Olympics boycott, the Iran hostage situation, and the failed hostage rescue mission, described by Carter in the 1980–81 Foreword as "the most agonizing point in my Presidency."

Thus, the Carter volumes of the *Public Papers*, like the other volumes in the series, offer a unique view of the American presidents and of American history. The character of a president, the individuals with whom a president interacts, the historical events that are shaped by a president and that, in turn, shape his presidency, are all to be found within the pages of the *Public Papers*.

A resolution passed by the United States Congress on July 17, 1894, provided that a compilation of "all the annual, special, and veto messages, proclamations, and inaugural addresses" of all the presidents from

1789 to 1894 be printed. The publication was to be prepared by James D. Richardson, a representative from Tennessee, under the direction of the Joint Committee on Printing, of which Richardson was a member. The official set was issued in two series of ten volumes each. A joint resolution of May 2, 1896, provided for the distribution of the set to members of Congress, with the remainder to be delivered to the compiler, James Richardson. An act passed about a year later provided that the plates for *A Compilation of the Messages and Papers of the Presidents* be delivered to Richardson "without cost to him." Representative Richardson then made arrangements for the commercial publication of the set. Several other compilations of presidential papers were commercially published in the first half of the nineteenth century; these usually contained only selected documents.

The Richardson edition of the *Messages and Papers*, however, was the only set authorized by Congress and published by the government until 1957, when the official publication of the public messages and statements of the presidents, the *Public Papers of the Presidents of the United States*, was initiated based on a recommendation made by the National Historical Publications Commission (now the National Historical Publications and Records Commission). The Commission suggested that public presidential papers be compiled on a yearly basis and issued in a uniform, systematic publication similar to the *United States Supreme Court Reports* and the *Congressional Record*. An official series thus began in which presidential writings and statements of a public nature could be made promptly available. These presidential volumes are compiled by the Office of the Federal Register of the General Services Administration's National Archives and Record Service.

As might be expected, the "public papers" vary greatly in importance and content; some contain important policy statements while others are routine messages. They include, in chronological order, texts of such documents as the president's messages to Congress, public addresses, transcripts of news conferences and speeches, public letters, messages to heads of state, remarks to informal groups, etc. Executive orders, proclamations, and similar documents that are required by law to be published in the *Federal Register* and *Code of Federal Regulations* are not reprinted, but are listed by number and subject in an appendix in each volume.

The *Public Papers of the Presidents* are kept in print, and are available from the Superintendent of Documents, United States Government Printing Office. The *Papers* for each year are published in a single- or multi-volume work; these volumes contain indexes for that calendar year. *The Cumulated Indexes to the Public Papers of the Presidents* combines and integrates the separate indexes for a president's administration into one alphabetical listing.

References to all of the volumes of a president's public papers can thus be found by consulting this one-volume cumulated index. *See* and *see also*

references have been added and minor editorial changes have been made in the process of cumulating the separate indexes.

References in this *Index* are to page numbers. Individual volumes are identified in the *Index* by year, as are the actual volumes of the *Papers*. The year identifying the volume in which a paper is located appears in boldface type.

Other volumes in the set of *The Cumulated Indexes to the Public Papers of the Presidents* include Herbert Hoover, 1929–1933; Harry S. Truman, 1945–1953; Dwight D. Eisenhower, 1953–1961; John F. Kennedy, 1961–1963; Lyndon B. Johnson, 1963–1969; Richard M. Nixon, 1969–1974; and Gerald R. Ford, 1974–1977. Forthcoming volumes will index the papers of Ronald Reagan, as well as those of future presidents when their administrations are completed.

Kraus International Publications

JIMMY CARTER
1977–1981

A7E aircraft, **1977:** 866

Aamodt, Gary Jay Northrop, **1979:** 464

Aaron, David L., **1977:** 86, 1126, 1210, 1382, 1699, 1930, 2005, 2036, 2049, 2128; **1978:** 232, 415, 503, 934, 1009, 1110, 1154, 1344, 1345, 1571, 1668, 1722, 1723, 2209

Meetings with the President (Digest), **1979:** 327, 401, 467, 841, 1882, 1975, 2081, 2206; **1980–81:** 103, 267, 268, 291, 292, 333, 607, 653, 891, 930, 1013, 1469, 1564, 1598, 1846, 2726, 2740

Stealth bomber classification, **1980–81:** 1770

Aaron, Henry (Hank), **1978:** 1406, 1457, 2036

Aaron, Henry Jacob, **1977:** 372

ABC.

See American Broadcasting Company.

'Abd al-Ghani, 'Abd al-'Aziz, **1978:** 1485

Abdelkader Braik al-Ameri, **1980–81:** 1564

Abel, Elie, **1980–81:** 1713, 1847

Abelson, Neva Martin, **1977:** 196

Abernathy, Ralph, **1980–81:** 2328, 2441

Abernathy, Walter, **1980–81:** 1302n.

Abilene, Tex., **1980–81:** 2627, 2699

Ablard, Charles David, **1980–81:** 56, 218

Abortion, **1977:** 392, 898, 1062, 1236, 1324, 1341, 1997; **1978:** 355, 362, 464; **1979:** 478; **1980–81:** 2256, 2325, 2354, 2435

Abourezk, Sen. James, **1977:** 706, 1826, 2181; **1978:** 549, 575, 770, 1194, 1425, 1787, 2000

Abraham, **1980–81:** 528

Abraham, Philip T., **1980–81:** 2107

Abrahamson, John, **1980–81:** 948

Abrahamson, Shirley Schlanger, **1980–81:** 2612

Abram, Morris, **1979:** 1263, 1294

Abram, Ruth J., **1977:** 525

Abram, Sam F., **1978:** 696

Abramowitz, Morton I., **1978:** 1030, 1034; **1980–81:** 2999

Abrams, Harvey A., **1980–81:** 192

Abrams, Mike, **1977:** 882

Abrams, Rosalie, **1978:** 1799

Abruzzo, Ben, **1978:** 1449

Absaroka-Beartooth Wilderness, **1978:** 575

Abscam investigation, **1980–81:** 2355

Abu Daoud, **1977:** 60

Abzug, Bella S., **1977:** 194, 525; **1978:** 553, 554, 1134; **1979:** 26, 52

Academy.

See other part of title.

Academy of Television Arts and Sciences, **1979:** 1615

Accident Compensation and Insurance Issues, Interagency Council on, **1979:** 339

Accounting firms, **1980–81:** 825

Accounting Office, General, **1977:** 277, 279, 653, 1498

Aceves, Jose, **1980–81:** 218

Acid rain, **1980–81:** 448, 473, 1253

Acid Rain Coordination Committee, **1979:** 1372, 1389

Acid rain programs, Federal, **1979:** 1372, 1389

Ackerman, Harold Arnold, **1979:** 1786, 1787

Acosta, Raymond L., **1980–81:** 269

Acosta, Salvador A., **1980–81:** 928

ACTION

Annual report, **1978:** 1345; **1979:** 2248; **1980–81:** 2752, 3049

Assistant Directors, **1977:** 1243, 1266

Associate Directors, **1979:** 666, 667; **1977:** 1243, 1266, 1540, 1568

Civil service rule, **1977:** 2062

Cooperative volunteers, **1978:** 51

Deputy Director, **1977:** 216, 253, 375, 608

Director, **1977:** 193, 266, 272, 273, 608, 1305; **1978:** 457, 2075; **1979:** 878, 881, 1388; **1980–81:** 281, 291, 328, 2822

Domestic volunteer service programs, **1979:** 2237

Handicapped persons program, **1980–81:** 2610

Interagency Coordinating Council, **1978:** 1434

National Voluntary Action Program, **1979:** 880

Peace Corps, **1977:** 272, 1699, 1701

Programs, organizational review, **1979:** 396

ACTION — *continued*
  Review project, **1977:** 608
  Urban policy functions, **1978:** 592
  VISTA, **1977:** 272
  Volunteer programs, **1980–81:** 696
  World forest preservation programs, **1979:** 1388
  See also Peace Corps.
Ad Hoc Coalition for Women, **1977:** 355
Ad Hoc Committee on Tax Reform, **1978:** 769
Ad Hoc Leadership Council of Aging Organizations, **1978:** 930
Adams, Ansel, **1980–81:** 751, 1058, 1404
Adams, Brock, **1977:** 10, 14, 31, 35, 86, 231–234, 248, 280, 286, 389, 396, 508, 745, 778, 806 949, 989, 1084, 1134, 1210, 1306, 1527, 1533, 1648, 1668, 1731, 1916, 2036, 2165; **1978:** 232, 516, 553, 1471, 1484, 1573, 1669, 1827, 1839, 2077, 2146, 2269
  See also Transportation, Secretary of.
Adams, Harmon H., **1980–81:** 19
Adams, J.M.G., **1980–81:** 824
Adams, John, **1979:** 1565; **1980–81:** 809
Adams, William P., **1977:** 2079, 2089; **1978:** 231, 1438; **1980–81:** 1547
Adamson, Terrance B., **1979:** 1591
Addabbo, Repr. Joseph P., **1978:** 1808, 1848; **1980–81:** 1281, 2194, 2381
Addams, Jane, **1980–81:** 630
Addiction Research Center, **1977:** 1405
Addison, Ill., **1980–81:** 2080
Addresses to the Nation
  Energy and national goals, **1979:** 609, 1235
  Farewell address, **1980–81:** 2889
  Foreign policy, **1980–81:** 2336
  Iran, rescue attempt for American hostages in, **1980–81:** 772
  National economy, **1980–81:** 2189
  SALT II treaty, **1979:** 1087
  Soviet combat troops in Cuba and the SALT II treaty, **1979:** 1802
  Soviet invasion of Afghanistan, **1980–81:** 21, 64
  State of the Union
    1979, **1979:** 103
    1980, **1980–81:** 194
Addresses and Remarks
  Academy of Television Arts and Sciences, Emmy Award show, **1979:** 1615
  ACTION review project, **1977:** 608
  Administration policies, White House briefing for civic and community leaders, **1980–81:** 458
  Advertising Council, Inc., **1977:** 1143
  Afghanistan
    Soviet intervention in, **1979:** 2287
    White House briefing for Congressmen, **1980–81:** 38

Addresses and Remarks — *continued*
  AFL-CIO
    Building and Construction Trades Departments
      Convention, San Diego, Calif., **1979:** 1866
      National conference, **1980–81:** 577
    Constitutional Convention, **1979:** 2122
    General Board meeting, **1980–81:** 1647
  Agriculture Department, **1977:** 167
  Air Force One
    Briefing for reporters, **1979:** 1211
    Question-and-answer session with reporters, **1980–81:** 1085
  Alaska land legislation, White House Briefing, **1980–81:** 1386
  Alaska public lands briefing, **1979:** 773
  Albuquerque, N. Mex.
    Meeting with civic and community leaders, **1979:** 1863
  Aliquippa, Pa.
    Atkinson, Gene, reception, **1978:** 1617
    Town meeting, **1978:** 1603
  Alma, Wis., **1979:** 1470
  American Committee on Italian Migration, **1980–81:** 1063
  American Convention on Human Rights, signing, **1977:** 1050
  American Federation of Teachers, Detroit, Mich., **1980–81:** 1556
  American Film Institute, **1977:** 2041
  American Heart Month, proclamation presentation, **1978:** 289
  American Legion
    Annual conference, **1980–81:** 344
    Annual Convention, Boston, Mass., **1980–81:** 1549
  American Newspaper Publishers Association, New York, N.Y., **1979:** 693
  American Public Transit Association, New York, N.Y., **1979:** 1739
  American Retail Federation, **1979:** 832
  American Society of Newspaper Editors, **1977:** 789
  American Textile Manufacturers Institute, **1977:** 120
  Anti-inflation program
    Accord between labor leaders and administration, **1979:** 1777
    Address to the Nation, **1978:** 1839
    Administration policy, **1978:** 721, 1060
    Federal sub-Cabinet officials briefing, **1978:** 2028
    President's announcement of new initiatives, **1980–81:** 476
    White House briefing for community leaders, **1980–81:** 511
    White House briefing for State and local officials, **1979:** 306

Addresses and Remarks — *continued*

Apollo 11, Moon landing anniversary observance, **1979:** 1276

Archbishop Iakovos of the Greek Orthodox Church, White House reception, **1979:** 1688

Armenian Americans, reception, **1978:** 916

Asheville, N.C.
Ingram, John, reception for, **1978:** 1579
President's arrival, **1978:** 1575

Asian/Pacific American Democratic Caucus, **1980–81:** 962

"Ask President Carter" telephone call-in program, **1977:** 291; **1979:** 1885

Atlanta, Ga.
Exchange with reporters, **1978:** 2285
Georgia campaign volunteers reception, **1978:** 154
Southern Baptist Brotherhood Commission, **1978:** 1113
Southern Salute to the President dinner, **1978:** 155

Atlantic City, N.J.
Democratic campaign luncheon, **1978:** 1550
National Aviation Facilities Experimental Center, groundbreaking ceremony, **1978:** 1542
United Steelworkers of America convention, **1978:** 1544, 1573

Awards and citations
Congressional Medal of Honor, **1980–81:** 1379, 1708
Conservationist of the Year Award, **1979:** 217
International Human Rights Award, **1979:** 2009
Martin Luther King, Jr. Nonviolent Peace Award, Atlanta, Ga., **1979:** 27
National Caucus on the Black Aged Living Legacy awards, **1979:** 317
National Medal of Science, **1980–81:** 80
National Small Business Person of the Year, **1979:** 868
Presidential Medal of Freedom, **1980–81:** 1057, 2922
Presidential Rank Awards for Senior Executive Service, **1980–81:** 1697
President's Award for Energy Efficiency, **1980–81:** 1452, 2875
President's Environmental Youth Awards, **1979:** 2075

Baltimore, Md., neighborhood revitalization projects tour, **1979:** 1406

Bangor, Maine
Hathaway, Sen. William D., reception, **1978:** 341
Town meeting, **1978:** 344

Bardstown, Ky., town meeting, **1979:** 1340

Beame, Abraham D., fundraising dinner, **1978:** 2160

Addresses and Remarks —*continued*

Beaumont, Tex., Jack Brooks Federal Building, dedication ceremonies, **1978:** 1173

Black business executives, reception, **1978:** 1103

Black colleges and universities, Executive order signing ceremony, **1980–81:** 1514

Black ministers, White House reception, **1980–81:** 2425

Black Music Association, **1979:** 1014

B'nai B'rith International, **1980–81:** 1654

Boise, Idaho, President's arrival, **1978:** 1473

Bonn Economic Summit Conference.
See Bonn Economic Summit Conference.

Boston, Mass., President's arrival, **1980–81:** 1548

Boys Nation, **1980–81:** 1412

Brown v. Board of Education, anniversary observance, **1979:** 883

Brunswick, Ga., **1977:** 1033, 1042

Budget
1979, message signing ceremony, **1979:** 95
1981, message signing ceremony, **1980–81:** 225
1982, message signing ceremony, **1980–81:** 2893
Revisions, **1980–81:** 568

Buffalo, N.Y., arrival, **1978:** 1883

Burlington, Iowa, **1979:** 1493, 1494

Business Council, **1977:** 2106
Defense policy address, **1979:** 2232
Question-and-answer session, **1978:** 2235

Byrd, Sen. Robert, dinner honoring, **1978:** 924

Byrne, Mayor Jane, fundraising dinner in Chicago, Ill., **1979:** 1932

Cabinet changes, **1979:** 1291

Calhoun, Ga., **1977:** 604

Camp David agreements, first anniversary, **1979:** 1684

Camp David Meeting on the Middle East
Conclusion remarks, **1978:** 1519
Joint Session of Congress, address, **1978:** 1533
President's Departure from the White House, **1978:** 1496

Capitol Page School, **1977:** 1061; **1978:** 1081

Caribbean/Central American Action, **1980–81:** 624

Carter, Billy, activities with Libyan Government, **1980–81:** 1439

Carter, Lillian, exchange with reporters following visit in Americus, Ga., **1980–81:** 2068

Carter/Mondale congressional supporters, **1980–81:** 1030

Carter/Mondale convention delegates, **1980–81:** 1380, 1424, 1463

Carter/Mondale Presidential Committee, Inc., **1980–81:** 937, 1024

Cedar of Lebanon tree-planting ceremony, **1978:** 794

Central Intelligence Agency, **1978:** 1434

Addresses and Remarks — *continued*
  Chanukah
    National Menorah lighting ceremony, **1979:**
      2263
    Torch relay, **1977:** 2084
  Charleston, W.Va., energy panel discussion,
      1977: 402
  Cherry Blossom Festival, **1977:** 546
  Cheyney State College, Pa., commencement
      excercises, **1979:** 908
  Chicago, Ill., Cook County Democratic dinner,
      1978: 979
  Children's Hospital National Medical Center,
      1977: 327
  China, People's Republic of, diplomatic relations
      with U.S., **1978:** 2264, 2266
  China-U.S. agreements, signing ceremony,
      1980–81: 1771
  Christmas Pageant of Peace, **1977:** 2125; **1978:**
      2246; **1979:** 2244; **1980–81:** 2817
  Cleveland, Ohio
    Carter/Mondale fundraising dinner, **1980–81:**
      1005
    Olivet Institutional Baptist Church, **1980–81:**
      1001
  Clinton, Mass., town meeting, **1977:** 382
  CLOSE-UP program, **1977:** 693
  Columbia, Mo., Midcontinent Farmers Associ-
      ation, **1978:** 1419
  Columbus Day, proclamation signing ceremony,
      1977: 1674
  Columbus, Ohio
    Carter/Mondale campaign rally, **1980–81:** 992
    Carter/Mondale fundraising luncheon, **1980–
      81:** 995
    Community and civic leaders, White House
      briefings, **1980–81:** 801, 976
    Mount Vernon Plaza, dedication ceremonies,
      1978: 1619
    Ohio State Democratic Party, reception, **1978:**
      1620
  Commerce Department, **1977:** 110
  Communications Workers of America, Detroit,
      Mich., **1979:** 1247
    Reception, **1978:** 685
  Community Investment Fund program, **1978:**
      1058
  Conference on Security and Cooperation in
      Europe, commemorative ceremony of Fi-
      nal Act signing in Helsinki, **1980–81:** 1434
  Congressional Black Caucus, **1978:** 1679; **1980–
      81:** 1927
    Dinner, **1977:** 1661
  Congressional Christmas Ball, **1978:** 2228
  Congressional Hispanic Caucus, **1980–81:** 1835
    Dinner, **1979:** 1662
  Consumer Federation of America, **1980–81:** 278
  Consumer protection agency, proposal, **1977:**
      1048

Addresses and Remarks — *continued*
  Country Music Gala, **1979:** 1816
  Cranston, R.I., Governors' reception for civic
      and community leaders, **1979:** 2059
  Cuban refugee policy, **1980–81:** 912
  Dallas County, Tex., Democratic Committee
      vote registration rally, **1980–81:** 1391
  Davenport, Iowa
    Arrival, **1979:** 1478
    Radio telephone question-and-answer session,
      1979: 1479
  Defense Department, **1977:** 259
  Democratic congressional campaign dinner,
      1978: 511; **1977:** 1013
  Democratic National Committee, **1979:** 1766
    Executive Finance Committee, breakfast
      meeting, **1977:** 189
    Fundraising dinner, **1977:** 1153; **1978:** 1645
    Fundraising events.
      See under Democratic National Committee.
    'Get Out the Vote' campaign, **1978:** 1733
    Meeting with leaders in New York City,
      1980–81: 1541
  National Finance Council
    Breakfast, **1978:** 2195
    Luncheon, **1977:** 734
    Platform committee reception, **1980–81:** 1100
    Quarterly meeting, **1977:** 1745
    Special meeting of the Committee, **1978:** 224
    White House briefing, **1978:** 2092
  Democratic National Convention.
    See under Elections, 1980: Democratic Na-
      tional Convention.
  Democratic Party
    Congressional campaign dinner, **1980–81:** 538
    State Chairman, White House reception,
      1980–81: 1043
  Democratic Party activities
    Congressional campaign dinner, **1979:** 827
    Dinners and receptions
      Bedford, N.H., **1979:** 714
      Des Moines, Iowa, **1979:** 804
      Los Angeles, Calif., **1979:** 372
      Manchester, N.H., **1979:** 713
      Wausau, Wis., **1979:** 567
    Jefferson-Jackson Day dinners
      Indianapolis, Ind., **1979:** 988, 989
      Milwaukee, Wis., **1979:** 573
      Richmond, Va., **1979:** 630
    Kennedys-King Day dinner, **1979:** 1920
    National Committee spring meeting, **1979:** 948
  Denver, Colo.
    Environmental, community, and governmen-
      tal leaders, meeting, **1978:** 832
    Governor's Annual Prayer Breakfast, **1978:**
      829
    Haskell, Sen. Floyd K., reception, **1978:** 827
    Panama Canal treaties briefing, **1977:** 1884

Addresses and Remarks — *continued*
  Denver, Colo. — *continued*
    Western water policy, panel discussion, **1977:** 1861
  Des Moines, Iowa
    Democratic Party Jefferson-Jackson Day dinner, **1977:** 1855
    International Airport, President's arrival, **1977:** 1853
  Detroit, Mich.
    Public policy forum, **1977:** 1829
    Remarks following meeting with automobile industry representatives, **1980–81:** 1329
  Distributive Education Clubs of America, **1978:** 888
  Dobbins Air Force Base, Ga., **1977:** 599; **1978:** 153
  Dollar, U.S., value, **1978:** 1908, 1955
  Dolton, Ill., town meeting, **1979:** 1940
  Drug abuse, **1977:** 1399
  Domestic issues, Camp David, Md., **1979:** 1329
  Dubs, Adolph, memorial ceremony, **1979:** 295
  Dubuque, Iowa, **1979:** 1474
  East Rutherford, N.J., Democratic State legislative candidates fundraising dinner, **1979:** 2024
  Economic renewal program, **1980–81:** 1585
  Economic Report and tax and budget messages, **1978:** 123
  Economic stimulus package, **1977:** 618–622
  Economy, national
    National Press Club, question-and-answer session, **1980–81:** 2219
    Renewal program, **1980–81:** 1585
  Education Department, inauguration ceremonies, **1980–81:** 850, 855
  Education legislation
    Elementary and secondary, **1978:** 422
    Higher, **1978:** 288
  Egypt, President's trip, **1979:** 394, 405, 407, 410, 412, 415, 430
  Egypt-U.S. Business Council, dinner honoring President Sadat, **1979:** 546
  Egyptian-Israeli peace negotiations, **1978:** 1757
  Egyptian-Israeli peace treaty
    First anniversary reception, **1980–81:** 525
    Signing ceremonies, **1979:** 517, 522
  Election campaign.
    See Elections.
  Elk City, Okla., town meeting, **1979:** 469
  Elkins, W.Va., Mountain State Forest Festival, **1978:** 1729
  Ellington Air Force Base, Tex., **1978:** 1164
  Elmendorf Air Force Base, Alaska, **1979:** 1161; **1980–81:** 1342
  Emergency agricultural legislation, **1978:** 738
  Emergency Board to investigate a railway labor dispute, establishment, **1979:** 1695

Addresses and Remarks — *continued*
  Emergency Natural Gas Act of 1977, proposal, **1977:** 21
  Emory University, Atlanta, Ga., **1979:** 1561
  Employment seminar, **1978:** 1341
  Energy
    White House briefings, **1979:** 862, 2161
      For community and religious leaders, **1980–81:** 49, 367, 511, 845
  Energy conservation in transportation
    White House briefing, **1980–81:** 787
  Energy crisis, Cabinet meeting, **1977:** 34
  Energy Department, **1977:** 257, 1582
  Energy program
    Address to Congress, **1977:** 663
    Addresses to the Nation, **1977:** 656, 1981
    Conference with Governors, **1977:** 1225
    Legislation, **1977:** 740
  Equal employment opportunity enforcement (Reorganization Plan No. 1 of 1978), **1978:** 398
  Equal rights amendment
    Fundraising dinner, **1980–81:** 1133
    Supporters reception, **1979:** 2008
    White House briefing, **1980–81:** 921
  Ethnic and fraternal organization leaders, White House briefing, **1980–81:** 648
  European trip
    President's departure, **1980–81:** 1135
    President's return, **1980–81:** 1234
    See also specific country.
  Executive branch reorganization studies, **1977:** 1191
  Executive Office of the President, reorganization, **1977:** 1253
  Export policy, United States, **1978:** 1630
  Fayetteville, N.C., radio interview, **1977:** 2132
  Federal agency consumer programs, **1980–81:** 1054
  Federal civil justice system legislation, **1979:** 340
  Federal civil service reform
    Question-and-answer session, **1978:** 1361
    Reorganization Plan No. 2 of 1978, **1978:** 435
  Federal consumer programs, Executive order signing, **1979:** 1761
  Federal Emergency Management Agency (Reorganization Plan No. 3 of 1978), **1978:** 1128
  Federal employees, question-and-answer session, **1979:** 916
  Federal grants-in-aid, **1977:** 1557
  Federal initiatives in rural areas, **1978:** 2106
  Federal paperwork reduction, Executive order signing, **1977:** 2176
  First Lady's trip to the Caribbean
    Central and South America, **1977:** 1041, 1098
  Ford, Gerald R. and Betty, portraits unveiling ceremony, **1978:** 963

Addresses and Remarks — *continued*
  Ford's Theatre, 10th anniversary, **1978:** 242
  Foreign Ambassadors, White House ceremony
    for, **1979:** 2161
  Foreign Intelligence Surveillance Act, proposal,
    1977: 921
  Foreign leaders, U.S. visits
    Australia, Prime Minister J. Malcolm Fraser,
      1980–81: 284
    Bangladesh, President Ziaur Rahman, **1980–
      81:** 1577
    Belgium, King Baudouin I and Queen
      Fabiola, **1980–81:** 757
    Canada, Prime Minister Trudeau, **1979:** 379
    China, People's Republic of, Vice Premier
      Deng, **1979:** 189, 192, 195, 198, 211
    Egypt
      President Anwar al-Sadat, **1980–81:** 617,
        622
      Vice President Muhammad Husni
        Mubarak, **1980–81:** 2764
    Germany, Federal Republic of, Chancellor
      Helmut Schmidt, **1980–81:** 435, 441
    Ireland, Prime Minister Lynch, **1979:** 2093,
      2095, 2098
    Israel, Prime Minister Menahem Begin, **1980–
      81:** 686, 694
    Italy, Prime Minister Francesco Cossiga,
      1980–81: 200, 207
    Japan, Prime Minister Ohira, **1979:** 761, 768
    Jordan, King Hussein, **1980–81:** 1121, 1125,
      1129
    Kenya, President Daniel T. arap Moi, **1980–
      81:** 352, 357
    Mexico, President López Portillo, **1979:** 1781,
      1789
    Nigeria, President Alhaji Shehu Shagari,
      1980–81: 2095, 2108
    Pakistan, President Mohammad Zia ul-Haq,
      1980–81: 2056
    Thailand, Prime Minister Kriangsak, **1979:**
      221, 225
    United Kingdom, Prime Minister Thatcher,
      1979: 2257, 2259, 2264
    Vatican City, Pope John Paul II, **1979:** 1827,
      1830
    Zimbabwe, Prime Minister Robert Mugabe,
      1980–81: 1579
  Fort Benning, Ga., **1978:** 2286
  Fort Hood, Tex., **1978:** 1176
  Fort Worth, Tex., civic organizations luncheon,
    question-and-answer session, **1978:** 1157
  Frances Perkins Building, Labor Department,
    dedication ceremony, **1980–81:** 629
  Fresno, Calif., **1977:** 915
  Friends of Carter/Mondale, **1979:** 2015
  Friendship Force, reception for South American
    participants, **1980–81:** 944

Addresses and Remarks — *continued*
  Friendship Force from Berlin, **1978:** 1966
  Future Farmers of America, **1977:** 1303; **1978:**
    1318, 1994; **1979:** 1267
  Gasoline
    Conservation fee on imported oil, **1980–81:**
      1027
    Shortages in California, **1979:** 872
  Georgia General Assembly, Atlanta, **1979:** 297,
    328
  Georgia Institute of Technology, Atlanta, **1979:**
    300, 328
  Girls Nation, **1980–81:** 1369
  Golden, Colo., Solar Energy Research Institute,
    1978: 824
  Gospel Music Association, **1979:** 1614
  Government regulations, Executive order sign-
    ing, **1978:** 556
  Grand Island, Nebr., **1980–81:** 1089, 1090
  Grand Teton National Park, Wyo., **1978:** 1476
  Great Plains coal gasification plant, N.Dak.,
    1980–81: 1371
  Guadeloupe, meeting with Western European
    leaders, **1979:** 17
  Hannibal, Mo., **1979:** 1508
  Hartsfield Atlanta International Airport, Ga.,
    dedication ceremonies, **1980–81:** 1755
  Health, Education, and Welfare Department,
    1977: 158
  Health care legislation, **1977:** 717
  Health and Human Services Department, in-
    auguration ceremonies, **1980–81:** 908
  Heavy crude oil decontrol, Executive order sign-
    ing, **1979:** 1449
  Hispanic Democratic Victory Dinner, **1980–81:**
    1939
  Holocaust, Capitol commemorative ceremony,
    1979: 684
  Home heating oil supplies, **1979:** 1877
  Hospital cost containment legislation, **1979:** 383,
    603
  House-Senate bipartisan senior citizen intern
    program, **1979:** 837
  Housing and Urban Development Department,
    1977: 132
  Houston, Tex., Democratic fundraising dinners,
    1978: 1165, 1221
  Hubert H. Humphrey North-South Scholarship
    program, **1978:** 2158
  Hubert H. Humphrey tribute in New England,
    telephone remarks to Worcester, Mass.,
    1980–81: 935
  Humphrey, Sen. Hubert H.
    Dinner honoring, **1977:** 2073
    And Dirksen, Sen. Everett M., institutes hon-
      oring, **1978:** 784
    Memorial services
      Capitol, **1978:** 78
      St. Paul, Minn., **1978:** 80

[References are to page numbers except as otherwise indicated]

Addresses and Remarks — *continued*
  Inauguration
    Address, **1977:** 1
    Portfolio presentation, **1977:** 1117
    Remarks to other nations, **1977:** 4
  Independence, Mo., townhall meeting, **1980–81:**
    1610
  Industrial innovation initiatives, program an-
    nouncement, **1979:** 2068
  Inflation, White House briefing for community
    leaders, **1980–81:** 845
  Interior Department, **1977:** 197
  International economic summit meeting, **1977:**
    814, 816–819, 825–828
  International Nuclear Fuel Cycle Evaluation,
    first plenary session, **1977:** 1812
  International Solvent Refined Coal II Agree-
    ment, signing ceremony, **1980–81:** 1447
  International trade functions, Executive order
    signing, **1980–81:** 5
  International Transport Workers Federation,
    Hollywood, Fla., **1980–81:** 1360
  International Year of the Child, 1979, **1978:** 1191
  Interstate 75, dedication ceremony, **1977:** 2165
  Interviews with news media
    ABC News, **1978:** 2247
    American Jewish Press Association, **1980–81:**
      1113
    American Press Institute, **1978:** 233, 517;
      1979: 557
    American Society of Magazine Editors, **1978:**
      1409
    American Society of Newspaper Editors,
      1980–81: 631
    Associated Press, **1980–81:** 2319
    Black media associations, **1978:** 318; **1979:** 33
    Black Perspective on the News, **1978:** 688
    Cable News Network, **1980–81:** 1017
    CBS News, **1978:** 2275
    Chancellor, John, NBC News, **1980–81:** 34,
      2233
    China, People's Republic of, Central TV,
      1979: 163
    Der Spiegel Magazine, **1978:** 1272
    Detroit Free Press, **1980–81:** 2009
    Editors, news directors, publishers, and broad-
      casters, **1978:** 67, 305, 459, 713, 805, 937,
      1073, 1225, 1347, 1588, 1775, 2061, 2149;
      1979: 181, 243, 621, 845, 901, 1321, 1425,
      1578, 1607, 1707, 1855; **1980–81:** 87, 239,
      337, 385, 658, 900
    Egyptian television, **1979:** 455
    Florida News Network, **1980–81:** 2155
    Foreign correspondents, **1980–81:** 668
    Foreign Policy Conference for editors and
      broadcasters, **1979:** 310
    Gannett newspapers and broadcast executives,
      1979: 2239

Addresses and Remarks — *continued*
  Interviews with news media — *continued*
    German reporters, **1978:** 1258
    Harte-Hanks Communications, **1980–81:** 761
    Hispanic media, **1978:** 901
    International Labor Press Association, **1978:**
      1490
    Israeli television, **1979:** 453; **1980–81:** 1670
    Italian reporters, **1980–81:** 1102
    Japanese Broadcasting Corporation, **1979:**
      1107
    Japanese reporters, **1979:** 1145; **1980–81:** 1339
    KNBC-TV, Los Angeles, Calif., **1980–81:** 1889
    KOMO-TV, Tacoma, Wash., **1980–81:** 1905
    Latin American affairs, senior editors, **1978:**
      1596
    "Meet the Press," **1980–81:** 107
    Mexican television, **1979:** 235, 252
    Minnesota editors and broadcasters, **1979:**
      2047
    National Association of Farm Broadcasting,
      1978: 1671
    NBC News, **1979:** 47, 985
    New Jersey news editors, **1980–81:** 1679
    Newhouse Newspaper editors, **1980–81:** 984
    Newspaper and television reporters, **1979:**
      1982
    Pennsylvania reporters, **1980–81:** 723, 742
    Portuguese news agency, **1980–81:** 1223
    Public Broadcasting Service, **1978:** 2014
    RKO General Broadcasting, **1980–81:** 2430
    Spanish news agency, **1980–81:** 1213
    United Press International Newspaper Advi-
      sory Board, **1979:** 735
    WCAU-TV, Philadelphia, Pa., **1980–81:** 2047
    Western European and Japanese reporters,
      1978: 1252
    Westinghouse Broadcasting Co., Inc., **1980–
      81:** 233
    White House Correspondents Association,
      1978: 2039, 2171
    WNET-TV, East Rutherford, N.J., **1979:** 2027
    WPIV-TV, Philadelphia, Pa., **1980–81:** 1635
    WTMJ-TV, Milwaukee, Wis., **1980–81:** 2080
    WTVT-TV, St. Petersburg, Fla., **1980–81:** 2166
    Yugoslavian reporters, **1980–81:** 1204
    See also under News media.
  Iowa State Association of Counties, **1979:** 789
  Iran, American hostage situation
    Economic sanctions imposition, **1979:** 2277
    Informal exchanges with reporters, **1980–81:**
      1722, 2288, 2451, 2659, 2847, 2868, 2875
    Oil imports discontinuance, **1979:** 2107
    President's remarks to:
      Reporters, **1979:** 2287
      State Department employees, **1979:** 2205
      State Governors, **1979:** 2131

[References are to page numbers except as otherwise indicated]

Addresses and Remarks — *continued*
  Iran, American hostage situation — *continued*
    Release agreement, **1980–81:** 3019
    Release conditions, **1980–81:** 2650
    Rescue mission
      Eulogy for servicemen killed in attempt,
        1980–81: 864
      Visit with injured servicemen, **1980–81:** 786
    Return of American citizens, telephone con-
      versation with Canadian Prime Minister
      Clark, **1980–81:** 255
    Transfer of hostages from militants to Iranian
      Government, possibility of, **1980–81:** 576
    U.S. sanctions, **1980–81:** 611
    Vice President's remarks, **1979:** 2194
    White House briefing for Congressmen,
      1980–81: 38
  Iraq-Iran conflict, **1980–81:** 1900, 1921
  Israel
    President's visit, **1979:** 394, 415, 417, 419, 424,
      428, 430
    30th anniversary, reception, **1978:** 812
  Israel-U.S. oil agreement, signing ceremony,
    1980–81: 2313
  Italian-American Heritage Week, proclamation
    signing ceremony in New York City,
    1980–81: 2198
  Italy, President's visit, **1980–81:** 1153, 1162, 1170
  Jackson, Miss., Allen C. Thompson Airport,
    President's arrival, **1977:** 1315
  Jacksonville, Fla.
    Community and civic leaders, meeting with,
      1980–81: 1349
    Exchange with reporters, **1980–81:** 1360
    Public reception, **1980–81:** 1347
  Japan, President's visit, **1979:** 1162–1197; **1980–
    81:** 1339
  Japan-U.S. Agreement on Cooperation in Re-
    search and Development in Science and
    Technology, signing ceremony, **1980–81:**
    816
  John F. Kennedy Center for the Performing Arts
    African Room, dedication, **1977:** 709
    Corporate Fund for the Performing Arts,
      reception, **1977:** 987
  John F. Kennedy Library dedication ceremo-
    nies, Boston, Mass., **1979:** 1979
  Joint Chiefs of Staff, **1978:** 1218
  Jordan, Vernon E., Jr., President's visit with in:
    Fort Wayne, Ind., **1980–81:** 1019
    New York City, N.Y., **1980–81:** 1506
  Justin, Tex., tour of heat- and drought-affected
    areas, **1980–81:** 1390
  Kampuchea
    U.S. relief efforts, **1979:** 2011, 2112
    Visit by Senators, **1979:** 2036
  Kansas City, Mo., business and civic leaders
    reception, **1979:** 1931

Addresses and Remarks — *continued*
  King, Martin Luther, Jr., visit to assassination
    site, **1978:** 2218
  Kirtland Air Force Base, N. Mex., **1979:** 1851
  Knoxville, Tenn., Tennessee Valley Authority,
    1978: 945
  Korea, Republic of, President's visit, **1979:** 1201,
    1202
  Labor Council for Latin American Advance-
    ment, **1980–81:** 857
  Labor Day, White House picnic, **1979:** 1593;
    1980–81: 1605
  Labor Department, **1977:** 102
  Labor leaders, White House dinner honoring,
    1980–81: 2883, 2887
  Lance, Thomas Bertram, investigation of fi-
    nances, **1977:** 1480, 1481, 1483
  Law Day, U.S.A., White House reception, **1979:**
    757
  Law enforcement assistance reorganization and
    Department of Housing and Urban De-
    velopment program, **1978:** 1241
  Lawyers' Committee for Civil Rights Under
    Law, **1978:** 1149
  Leadership Conference on Civil Rights, Hubert
    H. Humphrey Award dinner, **1980–81:**
    221
  League of Women Voters, **1979:** 771; **1980–81:**
    828
  Los Angeles, Calif., Cinco de Mayo celebration,
    1979: 810
    Democratic fundraising dinner, **1977:** 1893
    KNXT-TV question-and-answer session,
      1977: 895
    Los Angeles County Bar Association, **1978:**
      834
    Placita de Dolores dedication, **1979:** 809
    Remarks with reporters, **1977:** 915
    Senior Citizens Nutrition Center, **1978:** 841
  Louisville Gas and Electric Company, Ky., **1979:**
    1337
  Martin Luther King, Jr. Center for Social
    Change, **1978:** 1702
  McGregor, Iowa, **1979:** 1473
  McIntyre, James T., Jr., nomination announce-
    ment, **1977:** 2176
  Mental health systems legislation, **1979:** 857
  Merced, Calif., townhall meeting, **1980–81:** 1305
  Mexican-United States Interparliamentary Con-
    ference, reception, **1978:** 1042
  Mexico, President's visit, **1979:** 272, 273, 277,
    280, 281, 284
  Miami, Fla.
    Hispanic-American community, **1980–81:**
      1072
    Remarks to reporters following meeting with
      community leaders, **1980–81:** 1074
  Miami Conference on the Caribbean, **1979:** 2159

Addresses and Remarks — *continued*

Middle East, Air Force One, question-and-answer session, **1978:** 151

Middle East peace talks, role of Robert Strauss, **1979:** 687

Military Selective Service Act, proclamation signing ceremony, **1980–81:** 1274

Miller, G. William, nomination announcement, **1977:** 2183

Minneapolis, Minn., International Airport, President's arrival, **1977:** 1898

Minnesota City, Minn., exchange with reporters, **1979:** 1471

Mobile, Ala., tour of areas damaged by Hurricane David, **1979:** 1672

Moscone, George, memorial tribute in San Francisco, Calif., **1979:** 807

Mount St. Helens, Wash., eruption
Portland, Oreg., inspection tour of damaged areas, **1980–81:** 950
Spokane, Wash., remarks following meeting with State and community leaders, **1980–81:** 956

Muscatine, Iowa, **1979:** 1492

MX missile system, **1979:** 1599

Nashua, N.H., town meeting, **1978:** 364

National Academy of Sciences, **1979:** 677

National Afro-American (Black) History Month, message signing ceremony, **1980–81:** 84

National Association for the Advancement of Colored People, Miami, Fla., **1980–81:** 1322

National Association of Counties, Kansas City, Mo., **1979:** 1241

National Association of Development Organizations, Albuquerque, N. Mex., **1979:** 1853

National Association for Equal Opportunity in Higher Education, **1979:** 742

National Association of Women Judges, **1980–81:** 2057

National Bible Week
Dinner, **1978:** 2070
White House reception for ministers and religious leaders, **1980–81:** 2747

National Cable Television Association, **1979:** 932

National Commission on the International Year of the Child, 1979, final report reception, **1980–81:** 752

National Commission on the Observance of International Women's Year, 1975, reception, **1978:** 553

National Commission for the Review of Antitrust Laws and Procedures, **1978:** 1140

National Conference of Artists, **1980–81:** 600

National Conference of Catholic Charities, Kansas City, Mo., **1979:** 1925

Addresses and Remarks — *continued*

National Conference of Christians and Jews, **1979:** 969

National Conference on Fraud, Abuse and Error, **1978:** 2228

National Conference on Physical Fitness and Sports for All, **1980–81:** 259

National Conference of State Legislatures, **1980–81:** 552

National Convention of the Order of the Sons of Italy, Baltimore, Md., **1979:** 1408

National Council of Negro Women, **1979:** 2136

National Council of Senior Citizens, **1978:** 1062

National Democratic Party Conference
Opening session, **1978:** 2189
Workshops, **1978:** 2198, 2209

National Education Association, **1978:** 296

National Education Association, Los Angeles, Calif., **1980–81:** 1295

National Energy Education Day, proclamation signing ceremony, **1980–81:** 509

National energy efficiency program, **1980–81:** 1399

National energy plan, **1978:** 763

National Federation of Democratic Women, **1978:** 797

National 4-H Club, **1980–81:** 701

National Gallery of Art, East Building dedication ceremony, **1978:** 1027

National Governors' Association, **1979:** 330

National Governors' Association, **1980–81:** 397

National Governors' Conference, **1977:** 268; **1978:** 431

National health plan, **1979:** 1024

National Hispanic Heritage Week, **1977:** 1600
Proclamation signing ceremony, **1980–81:** 1457

National Issue Forum of the National Retired Teachers Association and the American Association of Retired Persons, Hartford, Conn., **1979:** 1630

National Italian-American Foundation, **1980–81:** 1718

National League of Cities, **1980–81:** 495
Board of Directors budget briefing, question-and-answer session, **1978:** 2080
1978 Congress of Cities, **1978:** 2075, 2147

National Mental Health Association's salute to Rosalynn Carter, **1980–81:** 1091

National Newspaper Association, question-and-answer session, **1977:** 1921

National Prayer Breakfast, **1977:** 24; **1978:** 263; **1979:** 58; **1980–81:** 275

National Religious Broadcasters, **1980–81:** 180

National Rural Electric Cooperative Association, **1978:** 1101
Youth Tour, **1977:** 1119

[References are to page numbers except as otherwise indicated]

Addresses and Remarks — *continued*
  National security, White House briefing for
      community leaders, **1980–81:** 367
  National Urban League, **1977:** 1347
    Annual convention, New York City, **1980–81:**
      1499
  National urban policy, **1978:** 577, 1427
  National Women's Political Caucus, **1977:** 544
  National YMCA Youth Governors Conference,
      1978: 1210
  NATO ministerial meeting, **1977:** 848, 852
  Natural gas
    Legislation, **1978:** 1452, 1644
    Prices, **1977:** 1671
    U.S.-Canadian pipeline agreement, **1977:** 1547
  Neighborhood development, **1980–81:** 1094
  New Brunswick, N.J., energy conservation meet-
      ing, **1979:** 2020
  New congressional Members dinner, **1978:** 2167
  New Hampshire Democratic Party primary,
      1980–81: 399
  New Hampshire political supporters, White
      House reception, **1978:** 420
  New Orleans, La., question-and-answer session,
      1977: 1334
  New Year's Day, **1980–81:** 2847
  New York, N.Y.
    Community leaders reception **1979:** 1745
    Democratic National Convention.
      See under Elections, 1980.
    Exchange with reporters, **1977:** 1728
    Picasso exhibit at Museum of Modern Art,
        remarks following visit, **1980–81:** 1540
    Town meeting at Queens County, **1979:** 1746
  Newark, N.J.
    College of Medicine and Dentistry of New
        Jersey, **1977:** 1574
    Fundraising breakfast for Gov. Brendan
        Byrne, **1977:** 1571
  Newspaper Farm Editors of America, **1977:** 1703
  Nimitz Battle Group return to U.S., Norfolk, Va.
    Address to crew members, **1980–81:** 969
    Address to families awaiting return, **1980–81:**
      972
  1980 Democratic Presidential nomination, can-
      didacy announcement, **1979:** 2192, 2193
  North Atlantic Alliance Summit
    Delegation heads, dinner honoring, **1978:** 1016
    Final session, **1978:** 1024
    NATO defense policy, **1978:** 1019
    Opening ceremonies, **1978:** 1011
  Northeast Summit on Energy, Providence, R.I.,
      1979: 2055
  Nuclear power policy, **1977:** 581
  Oak Ridge, Tenn., Oak Ridge National Labo-
      ratory, **1978:** 948
  Oakland, Calif., reception for East Bay area
      leaders, **1980–81:** 1299

Addresses and Remarks — *continued*
  Offutt Air Force Base, Nebr., **1977:** 1860
  Olympics, 1980
    Summer games, White House briefing for
        team representatives, **1980–81:** 517
    Winter team, White House reception, **1980–
      81:** 379
  O'Neill, Repr. Thomas P., Jr., dinner honoring,
      1978: 286
  Opportunities Industrialization Centers of Amer-
      ica, Miami, Fla., **1980–81:** 1066
  Order of the American Hellenic Educational
      Progressive Association, **1980–81:** 381
  Organization of American States, **1978:** 1141
    General Assembly session, **1980–81:** 2733
    Permanent Council, **1977:** 611
  Orlando, Fla., International Chamber of Com-
      merce
    Reception, **1978:** 1688
    26th Conference, opening session, **1978:** 1689
  Panama Canal treaties
    Address to the Nation, **1978:** 258
    Agreement in principle, **1977:** 1462
    Briefings, **1977:** 1525, 1884
    President's trip to Panama, **1978:** 1118–1127
    Senate ratifications
      Neutrality treaty, **1978:** 516
      Panama Canal treaty, **1978:** 758
    Signing ceremonies, **1977:** 1542, 1544
    Telephone question-and-answer sessions
      Albuquerque, N.Mex., **1978:** 85
      Hattiesburg, Miss., **1978:** 82
  Parma, Ohio, question-and-answer session with
      community leaders and senior citizens,
      1980–81: 997
  Pascagoula Miss., tour of areas damaged by
      Hurricane Frederic, **1979:** 1674
  Pell, Sen. Claiborne, reception in Providence,
      R.I., **1978:** 339
  Pensacola, Fla., tour of areas damaged by Hur-
      ricane David, **1979:** 1675
  Performing Arts Company of the People's Re-
      public of China, **1978:** 1321
  Philadelphia, Pa.
    Town meeting at Temple University, **1980–81:**
      874
    World Affairs Council, **1980–81:** 867
  Pittsburgh, Pa., **1977:** 37, 45
  Pittsburgh Pirates and Steelers, White House
      reception, **1980–81:** 369
  Placita de Dolores dedication, Los Angeles,
      Calif., **1979:** 809
  Plains, Ga., **1978:** 944, 2286; **1979:** 1589
    Allie Smith's home, **1977:** 2172
    Alton Carter's home, **1977:** 2174
    Carter's Warehouse, **1977:** 1459
    Exchange with reporters, **1980–81:** 2832, 2839,
      2840, 2873

Addresses and Remarks — *continued*
  Plains, Ga. — *continued*
    Exchanges with reporters, **1977:** 1044, 2169, 2170
    Hugh Carter's Antique Shop, **1977:** 2169
    Poland, agricultural commodity credit guarantees to, **1980–81:** 1711
    Polish Americans, reception, **1978:** 281
    Port Canaveral, Fla., **1977:** 1036
    Portland, Maine, Jefferson-Jackson dinner, **1978:** 1897
    Portland, Oreg.
      Community leaders reception, **1978:** 853
      Exchange with reporters, **1978:** 855
    Portsmouth, N.H., town meeting, **1979:** 699
    Portugal, President's visit, **1980–81:** 1230, 1231
    Prairie du Chien, Wis., **1979:** 1472
    Presidential Commission on Americans Missing and Unaccounted for in Southeast Asia, **1977:** 489
    Presidential Energy Technology Seminar, Atlanta, Ga., **1979:** 1533
    Presidential Management Intern Program, **1977:** 1498, 1499
    Presidential Scholars, **1977:** 1074
    Presidential Task Force on the District of Columbia, Vice President's remarks, **1977:** 1635
    Presidential transition, **1980–81:** 2702
    President's campaign appearances.
      See Elections.
    President's Commission on the Accident at Three Mile Island
      Establishment, **1979:** 657
      Final report, **1979:** 2062, 2202
      Members, meeting with the President, **1979:** 691
    President's Commission on the Coal Industry, **1978:** 1002
      Reports reception, **1980–81:** 471
    President's Commission on the Holocaust, final report reception, **1979:** 1773
    President's Commission on Mental Health, **1977:** 185; **1978:** 791
    President's Commission on Military Compensation, **1977:** 1178
    President's Commission for a National Agenda for the Eighties, final report reception, **1980–81:** 2917
    President's Committee on the Employment of the Handicapped, **1980–81:** 808
    President's Committee on HIRE, **1977:** 1115
    President's Export Council, final report reception, **1980–81:** 2827
    President's overseas trips
      Air Force One
        Briefing remarks, **1978:** 667
        Question-and-answer session, **1978:** 41

Addresses and Remarks — *continued*
  President's overseas trips — *continued*
    England, **1977:** 810, 811, 813, 816, 817, 825, 826, 847, 848, 857
    Iran, **1977:** 2217, 2218
    Poland, **1977:** 2203, 2205, 2212
    President's departures, **1977:** 809, 2202; **1978:** 610, 1267
    President's returns, **1978:** 39, 678
    Switzerland, **1977:** 841, 842, 844
    See also specific countries.
  President's portrait unveiling, Atlanta, Ga., **1979:** 296
  Private Sector Initiative program in employment, **1978:** 959
  Project Head Start, 15th anniversary reception, **1980–81:** 462
  Public debt limit extension bill, veto signing, **1980–81:** 1037
  Public works bill, **1978:** 1702, 1706
  Randolph, A. Philip, memorial services, **1979:** 996
  Randolph, Sen. Jennings, reception in Charleston, W. Va., **1978:** 999
  Ravenel, Charles, fundraising reception in Columbia, S.C., **1978:** 1582
  Reagan, President-elect Ronald, meeting with, **1980–81:** 2739
  Recording Industry Association of America, **1979:** 446
  Red Cross Month, **1977:** 210
  Reedley, Calif., **1977:** 917
  Reorganization plan authority legislation, **1977:** 84
  Report to the American people, **1977:** 69, 87
  Retiring Congressmen, White House dinner, **1980–81:** 1570
  Retiring Members of Congress, dinner, **1978:** 393
  Rochester, Minn., President's arrival, **1978:** 1822
  St. Louis, Mo., **1979:** 1511
  St. Patrick's Day, White House celebration, **1980–81:** 500
  St. Paul, Minn., energy briefing by citizens, **1979:** 1457
  Salmon River, Idaho, raft trip conclusion, **1978:** 1475
  Salt Lake City, Utah, ceremony honoring American family, **1978:** 2084
  SALT negotiations with the Soviet Union, **1977:** 538
  San Diego, Calif.
    County Board of Supervisors, **1979:** 1872
    President's departure, **1979:** 1876
  San Francisco, Calif., memorial tribute to George Moscone, **1979:** 807
  Sapelo Island, Ga., **1979:** 669

Addresses and Remarks — *continued*
  Savannah, Ga.
    Hibernian Society dinner, **1978:** 539
    U.S.S. *Dwight D. Eisenhower,* President's visit,
      1978: 538
    Scripps-Howard National Spelling Bee, **1980–81:**
      1008
  Second environmental decade, 10th anniversary
    celebration, **1980–81:** 414
  Secret Service and military aides office employ-
    ees, White House reception, **1980–81:**
    2829
  Shippingport, Pa., light water breeder reactor,
    1977: 2130
  Small business leaders, **1980–81:** 515
  Small community and rural development policy,
    1979: 2273
  Solar energy, **1979:** 1095
  Southern Baptist Convention, Baptist Brother-
    hood Commission, **1977:** 877
  Southern Legislative Conference, **1977:** 1309
  Soviet combat troops in Cuba, **1979:** 1602
  Spain, President's visit, **1980–81:** 1220, 1227
  Spokane, Wash.
    Riverfront Park, **1978:** 857
    Town meeting, **1978:** 860
  Springfield, Ill.
    Bakalis, Michael J., fundraising breakfast,
      1978: 996
    Illinois State legislature, question-and-answer
      session, **1978:** 987
  Standby gasoline rationing plan, **1979:** 840
  State, Secretary of (Muskie, Edmund)
    Selection as Secretary, **1980–81:** 791
    Trip to People's Republic of China, **1977:** 1519
    Trip to Soviet Union, **1977:** 559
    Trip to Vienna, Austria, **1980–81:** 896
  State attorneys general, district attorneys, and
    police chiefs, White House reception,
    1980–81: 412
  State Department, **1977:** 235
  State of Israel Bond Organization, dinner hon-
    oring Lane Kirkland, **1980–81:** 2766
  State and local government officials, White
    House dinner, **1980–81:** 2861
  State of the Union address, **1978:** 90
  Steel industry revitalization program, **1980–81:**
    1959
  Stetson Junior High School, West Chester, Pa.,
    meeting with students, **1977:** 27
  Steubenville, Ohio, town meeting, **1979:** 1640
  Strategic arms limitation talks, **1978:** 1029
  Strategy Council, **1977:** 1976
  Strauss, Robert S., dinners honoring, **1980–81:**
    2790, 2791
  Student leaders, question-and-answer session,
    1980–81: 324

Addresses and Remarks — *continued*
  Swearing-in ceremonies
    ACTION
      Deputy Director, **1977:** 576
      Director, **1977:** 272
    Agency for International Development, Ad-
      ministrator, **1977:** 533
    Agriculture Department, Assistant Secretary,
      1977: 511
    Cabinet and Cabinet-level officers, **1977:** 12,
      16, 19, 26, 46
    Central Intelligence Agency, Director, **1977:**
      350
    Commerce Department
      Secretary and Deputy Secretary, **1980–81:**
        43
      Under Secretary, **1977:** 691
    Community Services Administration, Direc-
      tor, **1977:** 871; **1980–81:** 1457
    Council on Environmental Quality, Chairman,
      1977: 375
    Education Department, Secretary, **1979:** 2199
    Energy Department, Secretary, **1977:** 1441;
      1979: 1514
    Environmental Protection Agency, Adminis-
      trator and Deputy Administrator, **1977:**
      376
    Equal Employment Opportunity Commission,
      Chairman, **1977:** 1131
    Federal Bureau of Investigation, Director,
      1978: 396
    Federal Council on the Aging, members, **1979:**
      2212
    Federal Reserve System, Board of Governors,
      Chairman, **1978:** 481; **1979:** 1402
    Federal Trade Commission, Commissioner,
      1977: 691
    General Services Administration, Administra-
      tor, **1977:** 871
    Health, Education, and Welfare Department,
      Secretary, **1979:** 1391
    Housing and Urban Development Depart-
      ment, Secretary, **1979:** 1718
    Immigration and Naturalization Service,
      Commissioner, **1977:** 871
    Justice Department, Attorney General, **1979:**
      1440
    National Science Foundation, Director, **1977:**
      1046
    Office of Drug Abuse Policy, Director, **1977:**
      1046
    Office of Management and Budget
      Deputy Director, **1977:** 511
      Director, **1978:** 568
    Office of Science and Technology Policy,
      Director, **1977:** 1046
    President's Export Council, Chairman and
      members, **1979:** 943

Addresses and Remarks — *continued*
  Swearing-in ceremonies — *continued*
    Securities and Exchange Commission, member, **1977**: 691
    Small Business Administration, Administrator, **1977**: 691
    Small Business Conference Commission, members, **1979**: 368
    Special Representative for Trade Negotiations, **1977**: 533; **1979**: 1807
    State Department
      Chief of Protocol, **1977**: 272
      Coordinator for Human Rights and Humanitarian Affairs, **1977**: 1131
      Secretary, **1980–81**: 861
    Transportation Department, Secretary, **1979**: 1718
    Treasury Department, Secretary, **1979**: 1402
    United Nations, U.S. Representative, **1979**: 1715
    United States Arms Control and Disarmament Agency, Director, **1977**: 379
    United States Civil Service Commission, Commissioner, **1977**: 871
    United States Information Agency, Director, **1977**: 512
    Veterans Administration, Administrator, **1977**: 272
  Synthetic fuels, Executive order signing ceremony, **1980–81**: 1971
  Synthetic Fuels Corporation, nomination announcement of Board of Directors Chairman, **1980–81**: 1700
  Tampa, Fla., town meeting, **1979**: 1566
  Task Force on Women Business Owners, **1978**: 1188
  Tax reduction and reform, **1978**: 754
  Tchaikovsky Competition in Moscow, reception honoring gold medal winners, **1978**: 1356
  Telecommunications minority assistance program, **1980–81**: 1703
  Thailand, Rosalynn Carter's trip, **1979**: 2090, 2112
  Thanksgiving, departure for Camp David, **1977**: 2049
  Thomas P. O'Neill Chair at Boston College, fundraising dinner, **1979**: 2210
  Three Mile Island nuclear plant, Pa., President's visit, **979**: 578
  Titan missile site explosion in Arkansas, **1980–81**: 1844
  Tokyo Economic Summit Conference.
    See Tokyo Economic Summit Conference.
  Transportation Department, **1977**: 231
  Treasury Department, **1977**: 126
  Treaty of Tlatelolco, Protocol I, signing, **1977**: 1027
  Trenton, N.J., **1977**: 1566

Addresses and Remarks — *continued*
  Truckers' strikes, independent, **1979**: 1129
  Trucking industry deregulation, **1979**: 1114
  Undocumented aliens, **1977**: 1415
  United Auto Workers, **1977**: 887
  United Food and Commercial Workers International Union, **1979**: 1008
  United Jewish Appeal, National Young Leadership Conference, **1980–81**: 377
  United Mine Workers strike, **1978**: 316, 419, 469
  United Nations
    African nations luncheon, **1977**: 1723
    Asian nations luncheon, **1977**: 1735
    European nations dinner, **1977**: 1727
    General Assembly address, **1977**: 444, 1715
    International covenants on human rights, **1977**: 1734
    Secretariat, U.S. delegation, **1977**: 1725
    Secretary General Kurt Waldheim's visit, **1977**: 245
  United Negro College Fund, **1977**: 2003
  United Service Organizations, reception, **1978**: 965
  United States Conference of Mayors, **1977**: 1100; **1980–81**: 212, 1078
  United States foreign intelligence activities, Executive order signing, **1978**: 189
  United States Jaycees, **1979**: 1723
  United States-Mexico Agreement on Natural Gas, announcement of framework, **1979**: 1703
  United States Naval Academy commencement exercises, **1978**: 1052
  United States Senate Youth Program, **1977**: 79
  United States Summer Olympic team Medals presentation ceremony, **1980–81**: 1440
    Swim team, medal presentation ceremony, **1980–81**: 1493
    White House reception, **1980–81**: 1444
  United Steelworkers of America, **1980–81**: 1510
  Universal Declaration of Human Rights, 30th anniversary, **1978**: 2161
  University of Notre Dame, **1977**: 954
  Urban Development Action Grant program, second anniversary reception, **1979**: 1965
  U.S. Ambassador to Mexico, meeting with, **1980–81**: 755
  U.S. foreign assistance, congressional briefing, **1980–81**: 941
  U.S.S. *Mississippi,* commissioning ceremony, **1978**: 1383, 1407
  Vance, Cyrus R., State Department reception honoring, **1980–81**: 2732
  Vatican City, President's visit, **1980–81**: 1164, 1168
  Venice Economic Summit Conference
    Concluding statements, **1980–81**: 1174

[References are to page numbers except as otherwise indicated]

Addresses and Remarks — *continued*
  Venice Conference — *continued*
    Exchange with reporters following first two
      sessions, **1980–81:** 1173
    Interview with reporters following conclusion
      of Conference, **1980–81:** 1191
  Veterans Administration, 50th anniversary pro-
    gram, **1980–81:** 1383
  Veterans Day ceremony, **1977:** 1900; **1978:** 2012
  Vice President's trips
    Europe and Japan, departure, **1977:** 11, 57, 58
    Nordic countries and Netherlands, **1979:** 639
  Vienna Summit Meeting.
    See Vienna Summit Meeting.
  Vietnam veterans reception, **1979:** 972
  Virginia, campaign for Democratic candidates,
    1977: 1653–1661
  Visit of Egyptian President Anwar al-Sadat to
    Israel, exchange with reporters, **1977:**
    2042
  Wabasha, Minn., **1979:** 1468
  Warner Robins Air Force Base, Ga., **1977:** 2175
  Washington Bullets basketball team, reception,
    1978: 1069
  Washington Press Club, **1977:** 22
  Water policy, **1978:** 1043
  Weizmann Institute of Science, reception of
    honorary degree, **1980–81:** 646
  Welfare reform, **1977:** 770
  White House barbecue for Georgians, **1980–81:**
    1512
  White House Commission on Small Business,
    1980–81: 916
  White House Conference on Aging, **1980–81:**
    534
  White House Conference on Balanced National
    Growth and Economic Development,
    1979: 65
  White House Conference on Coal Exports,
    1980–81: 2810
  White House Conference on the Family, **1979:**
    1286; **1980–81:** 1032
  White House Conference on Handicapped In-
    dividuals, **1977:** 988
  White House Conference on Libraries and In-
    formation Services, **1979:** 2129
  White House Conference on Regulatory Reform,
    1980–81: 57
  White House Conference on Religion and Peace,
    1979: 1598
  White House Conference on Small Business,
    1980–81: 68
  White House Correspondents Association, **1977:**
    758; **1979:** 743
  White House Fellows, **1977:** 1142
  White House Forums on Inflation, telephone
    question-and-answer sessions
    Hartford, Conn., **1978:** 1967
    St. Louis, Mo., **1978:** 1910

Addresses and Remarks — *continued*
  White House Promenade, reception for con-
    gressional Members and their families,
    1978: 944
  White House "Salute to Congress", **1980–81:**
    1096
  Wiesenthal, Simon, congressional gold medal
    presentation ceremony, **1980–81:** 1495
  Wilmington, Del.
    Biden, Sen. Joseph R., Jr., dinner honoring,
      1978: 385
    State Democratic fundraising dinner, **1978:**
      386
  Wilson, N.C.
    Growers Cooperative Warehouse, Inc., **1978:**
      1390
    Ingram, John, campaign rally, **1978:** 1386
  Windfall profits tax and energy security trust
    fund, message signing ceremony, **1979:**
    728
  Windfall profits tax legislation, telephone con-
    versation with congressional leaders,
    1980–81: 542
  Winston-Salem, N.C.
    Question-and-answer session with reporters,
      1978: 535
    Wake Forest University, **1978:** 529
  Women's business enterprise, **1979:** 887
  Women's Equality Day, **1977:** 1502
    Proclamation signing ceremony, **1980–81:**
      1572
  Women's organizations, representatives, **1977:**
    355
  World Bank Group and International Monetary
    Fund, **1977:** 1669; **1978:** 1627; **1980–81:**
    1972
  World Jewish Congress, **1977:** 1952
  Yazoo City, Miss., public meeting, **1977:** 1316
  Youth education and employment programs,
    1980–81: 52
  Yugoslavia, President's visit, **1980–81:** 1208,
    1210, 1211
  Zablocki, Repr. Clement J., reception in Mil-
    waukee, Wis., **1979:** 572
  Zimbabwe-Rhodesia, U.S. trade sanctions, **1979:**
    1012
  See also Awards and Citations; Bill Signings;
    Meetings with Foreign Leaders; News
    Conferences.
Addressing the President, President's preference,
  1979: 1888
Adkins, Charles M., Jr., **1977:** 1438, 1439
Adler, Kurt Herbert, **1979:** 807ftn.; **1980–81:** 1440,
  1470
Administration.
  See other part of title.
Administration, Office of, **1979:** 3, 337, 824

Administration's accomplishments and goals, **1977:** 791, 1146, 1155, 1165, 1171, 1237, 1269, 1348, 1473, 1509, 1808, 1809, 1913, 1933, 1934, 2009, 2010, 2057, 2110 **1978:** 233, 371, 685, 686, 693, 713, 727, 798, 805, 861, 864, 901, 937, 988, 1168, 1226, 1227, 1347, 1380, 1409, 1490, 1577, 1589, 1597, 1603, 1604, 1623, 1648, 1671, 1776, 1911, 1931, 1934, 1945, 1948, 1951, 1996, 2024, 2026, 2061, 2062, 2077, 2093, 2107, 2108, 2151, 2169, 2190, 2221, 2222, 2238

Administration's first-year accomplishments, **1977:** 2136

Administrative Conference of the United States, **1978:** 1652; **1979:** 494, 886

   Council of the, **1980–81:** 2726, 2801

Admiralty Island National Monument, Alaska, **1978:** 2112; **1979:** 855

Adoption Assistance and Child Welfare Act, **1980–81:** 1124

Adsit, Col. John Miley, **1978:** 1639, 1669

Adult Education, National Advisory Council on, **1978:** 570; **1979:** 1524; **1980–81:** 267, 844, 2558, 3022

Advertising Agencies, American Association of, **1978:** 254

Advertising Council, Inc., **1977:** 1143; **1979:** 786

Advertising lighting restrictions, **1979:** 370

Advisor to the President on Inflation.

   See Kahn, Alfred E.

Advisory Commission on Intergovernmental Relations, **1977:** 549, 1476, 1477, 1563; **1979:** 463, 886, 1034, 1876, 2081

   Chairman, **1978:** 422; **1980–81:** 422

   Meeting with the President, **1978:** 750

   Members, **1978:** 748, 1836, 2165; **1980–81:** 104, 273, 1335, 1770, 3021

   Vice Chairman, **1978:** 748

Advisory Committee on the Arts, **1977:** 1767, 1771

Advisory Committee on Federal Pay, **1978:** 823, 1457; **1979:** 64, 1529; **1980–81:** 468, 1399, 1596, 2730

Advisory Committee on Housing, **1980–81:** 2559

Advisory Committee on Intergovernmental Relations.

   See Advisory Commission on Intergovernmental Relations.

Advisory Committee on Oceans and Atmosphere, National, **1979:** 2187

Advisory Committee on Reactor Safeguards, **1980–81:** 504, 547, 549, 837–840

Advisory Committee on Small and Minority Business Ownership, **1980–81:** 262, 305, 2849

Advisory Committee for Trade Negotiations, **1977:** 1541; **1978:** 454, 759, 1030, 2069, 2264; **1979:** 1705

   Members, **1980–81:** 1048, 1447, 2117, 2609, 2832, 3022

Advisory committees, Federal, **1977:** 249, 528, 753, 1012, 1494, 1495, 1507, 2067; **1978:** 577, 612, 2301; **1979:** 463, 468; **1980–81:** 507, 2849, 2914

Advisory Council on Historic Preservation, **1978:** 228, 1060, 1343; **1979:** 1432, 1704; **1980–81:** 1292, 1935, 2302

Advisory Panel on Financing Elementary and Secondary Education, **1979:** 1524

Aegis cruiser, **1980–81:** 475

Aeronautics Board, Civil.

   See Civil Aeronautics Board.

Aeronautics and Space Administration, National.

   See National Aeronautics and Space Administration.

Aeronautics and Space Report of the President, **1978:** 1516

Aerospace & Agricultural Implement Workers of America, United Automobile, **1980–81:** 1598

Affirmative action, **1977:** 1344, 1376

   Programs, **1978:** 1230, 1320

Afghanistan

   Afghan army desertions, **1980–81:** 2833

   Alignment with Soviet Union, **1979:** 316, 565, 1612

   Ambassador to U.S., **1977:** 1383; **1978:** 1380

   Babrak Karmal regime, **1980–81:** 1193, 2835

   Former President Hafizullah Amin, **1980–81:** 672, 2835

   Freedom-fighters, **1980–81:** 663, 747, 1304, 1308, 1327, 1414, 2292

   Refugees

      Mentions, **1980–81:** 971, 1007

      Pakistan and Iran, flight tc, **1980–81:** 256, 964, 1139, 1327, 2056, 2565

      U.S. assistance, **1980–81:** 256, 1139

   Soviet intervention in, **1979:** 2287

   Soviet invasion

      Address to the Nation, **1980–81:** 21, 25

      American leadership, responsibility for, **1980–81:** 641

      Brzezinski, Zbigniew, question-and-answer session (Checklist) **1980–81:** 1246

      Chemical warfare, **1980–81:** 2021

      Conditions of withdrawal, **1980–81:** 309

      Effect on:

         Presidential campaign, **1980–81:** 90, 243, 310, 729, 733, 746

         SALT II treaty.

            See SALT II treaty

            under Strategic arms limitation.

         U.S.-Soviet relations, **1980–81:** 111, 406, 1207

   International reaction

      Australia, **1980–81:** 259, 285

      Bangladesh, **1980–81:** 1579

Afghanistan — *continued*
  Soviet invasion — *continued*
    International reaction — *continued*
      Commission on European Communities,
        1980–81: 189
      European Communities, **1980–81:** 238, 900
      France, **1980–81:** 292, 313
      German Democratic Republic, **1980–81:** 41
      Germany, Federal Republic of, **1980–81:**
        189, 292, 313, 437, 439, 470, 719, 920, 1170
      Islamic nations, **1980–81:** 88, 284, 325, 329,
        390, 398, 459, 579, 642, 1308, 2292, 2324,
        2835
      Italy, **1980–81:** 208, 210, 211, 1160
      Jordan, **1980–81:** 1126
      Kenya, **1980–81:** 353, 355, 358
      Libya, **1980–81:** 1478
      Mention, **1980–81:** 2338
      Olympics, 1980 Summer, boycott.
        See International boycott
        under Olympics, 1980 Summer
      Pakistan, **1980–81:** 68
      Portugal, **1980–81:** 1233
      Spain, **1980–81:** 83, 1229
      United Nations.
        See under United Nations.
      U.S. allies, **1980–81:** 338, 712, 987, 1103,
        1113, 1225
      Venice Economic Summit Conference,
        1980–81: 1170, 1173, 1192, 1194, 1200,
        1202, 1235
      Yugoslavia, **1980–81:** 1205
    Mentions, **1980–81:** 52, 194, 216, 367, 382, 553,
      625, 649, 659, 685, 702, 867, 875, 938, 962,
      1301, 1640
    1-year anniversary statement, **1980–81:** 2835
    Prior knowledge of invasion, **1980–81:** 244,
      672
    Public opinion, **1980–81:** 90
    Threat to:
      Iran, **1980–81:** 40, 195
      Oil supplies, **1980–81:** 26, 36, 108, 111, 183,
        197, 346, 976
      Persian Gulf, **1980–81:** 511, 871, 971, 1554
      World peace, **1980–81:** 196, 634, 639, 669,
        1364, 1414
    Troop withdrawal, **1980–81:** 1194, 1199, 1203,
      1211
    U.S. leadership role in international reaction,
      1980–81: 330, 386
    U.S. retaliatory actions
      Agricultural exports suspension.
        See Agricultural trade.
      Draft registration.
        See Draft registration
        under Selective Service System.
      Fishing restrictions in American waters,
        1980–81: 23, 41, 196, 278, 634, 747, 1193,
        1308

Afghanistan — *continued*
  Soviet invasion — *continued*
    U.S. retaliatory actions — *continued*
      Labor support, **1980–81:** 1653
      Mentions, **1980–81:** 796, 804, 889
      Military capabilities improvement in Per-
        sian Gulf area.
        See Persian Gulf area.
      Olympics, 1980 Summer, boycott
        See U.S. boycott *under* Olympics, 1980
        Summer.
      Phosphate shipments suspension, **1980–81:**
        560, 2470
      President's commitment to peaceful mea-
        sures, **1980–81:** 308, 325, 386, 398, 459,
        2131, 2292, 2323, 2566
      Reagan, Ronald, policy differences with the
        President, **1980–81:** 1534, 1728, 2470,
        2473, 2555
      Technology and other strategic items trans-
        fer restrictions.
        See under Science and technology.
      White House briefings, **1980–81:** 38, 63, 64
      White House statement, **1980–81:** 11
    Trade beneficiary developing country designa-
      tion, suspension and withdrawal, **1980–**
      81: 429, 550
    U.S. Ambassador, **1978:** 1022, 1034; **1979:** 271,
      295
    U.S. development and military assistance pro-
      grams, **1979:** 310
AFL-CIO, **1977:** 31, 219, 508, 706, 1210, 1825,
    1892, 1965
  Building and Construction Trades Department,
    1979: 732, 1866, 1883
    National Conference, **1980–81:** 577
    President (Robert A. Georgine), **1977:** 706;
      1979: 1866, 1868
      Advisory Committee on Housing, member,
        1980–81: 2559
    Mentions, **1980–81:** 577, 589, 1372, 1718
    National Institute of Building Sciences,
      member, **1980–81:** 1595, 1599
    U.S. assistance for earthquake victims in
      Italy, U.S. delegation member, **1980–81:**
      2807
  Constitutional Convention, **1979:** 2120
  Executive council, **1979:** 26 (Digest), 1870;
    1980–81: 1557
  Industrial Union Department, **1980–81:** 930
  International Labor Organization, support of,
    1980–81: 307
  Meany, George, role in, **1980–81:** 56, 222
  Members, meetings with the President, **1978:**
    802, 848
  Pension funds proposal, **1980–81:** 2166
  President's address to:
    California State Convention, **1980–81:** 1883
    General Board meeting, **1980–81:** 1647, 1663

AFL-CIO — *continued*
  President's assessment, **1980–81:** 1361
  President's Committee on International Labor
      Organization, member, **1980–81:** 1128
  President's Council for Energy Efficiency, mem-
      ber, **1980–81:** 1405
  Sprik, Dale, fundraising reception for,**1980–81:**
      2451
  State of Israel Bond Organization's dinner hon-
      oring, **1980–81:** 2766
  Synthetic Fuels Corporation, Board of Directors,
      members, **1980–81:** 1717, 1848, 2726,
      2727, 2867, 2874
  United Food and Commercial Workers Inter-
      national Union, **1979:** 1008
  Voluntary wage controls, **1978:** 1912
  White House dinner remarks, **1980–81:** 2883,
      2886
  See also specific union.
AFL-CIO, President (Lane Kirkland)
  Chrysler Corporation Loan Guarantee Act of
      1979, support **1980–81:** 27
  Economic renewal program, consultations with
      the President, **1980–81:** 1607
  Economic Revitalization Board, Co-chairman,
      1980–81: 1589, 1650
  Federal Prison Industries, Inc., member, **1980–
      81:** 452
  Meany, George
      Civil rights award, acceptance for, **1980–81:**
          224n.
      Commemorative stamp ceremony, remarks,
          1980–81: 1608
AFL-CIO, President (George Meany), **1978:** 66,
      236, 710, 1344, 1591
  Anti-inflation accord with administration, sup-
      port, **1979:** 1778
  Meeting with the President (Digest), **1979:** 26
  Mention, **1979:** 2098
  President's assessment, **1979:** 1595, 1869, 2125
AFL-CIO, Secretary-treasurer, **1980–81:** 2766ftn.
AFL-CIO, Secretary-treasurer (Lane Kirkland),
      1978:217, 230, 1134
  Anti-inflation accords with administration, news
      conference, **1979:** 1778n., 1787
  Energy crisis, meeting with the President at
      Camp David, **1979:** 1594, 1867, 2123
  Mention, **1979:** 1008
  Pay Advisory Committee, member, **1979:** 1954
Africa
  Administration's accomplishments and goals,
      1980–81: 2986
  Congressional Black Caucus, remarks, **1978:**
      1682
  Congressional visit, **1978:** 229
  Forged document on U.S. black movement and
      black Africa, **1980–81:** 1846

Africa — *continued*
  International Exchange-of-Persons program,
      1979: 324
  Interview remarks, **1978:** 1257, 1348, 2177
  News conference remarks, **1978:** 56, 57, 442,
      975–979
  Ohio State Democratic Party, reception remarks,
      1978: 1624
  Portuguese relations, **1980–81:** 1234
  Presidential travel, possibility of, **1979:** 39
  Soviet and Cuban intervention, **1978:** 903, 904,
      940, 941, 1013, 1056, 1092, 1094, 1275;
      1979: 160, 1092, 1754; **1980–81:** 93, 108,
      111, 1105, 1225
  Spokane, Wash., town meeting remarks, **1978:**
      871
  Trade with U.S., **1979:** 1786
  U.S. food assistance, **1980–81:** 1333
  U.S. policy, **1977:** 457, 497, 646, 709, 782, 785,
      953, 961, 1382, 1433, 1723, 1724, 1748,
      2011; **1978:** 120, 374, 651, 670, 688, 694,
      1075, 1163
  U.S. relations, **1979:** 39, 565, 1013, 1996, 2033,
      2047, 2137
      Administration's accomplishments, **1980–81:**
          2147, 2148, 2301, 2406
      Economic development role, **1980–81:** 172,
          1683
      Majority rule policy, **1980–81:** 673, 870, 1604,
          1683, 1929, 2095, 2339, 2428
      United Nations Representatives, role in im-
          proved relations, **1980–81:** 1501, 1929,
          2366, 2428
  U.S. Representative to the United Nations, trip,
      1977: 33
  Vice President's visit, **1980–81:** 1501
  See also specific country.
Africa, southern
  Foreign intervention, **1979:** 1013
  Peace negotiations, **1980–81:** 198
  Racial situation, U.S. policy, **1979:** 39, 157, 160,
      357, 576, 909, 910, 1050, 2018, 2138
  U.S. policy, **1980–81:** 172
African American national historic sites, Boston,
      Mass., **1980–81:** 2172, 2179
African-American Visual Artists Week, **1980–81:**
      601
African Art, Museum of, **1978:** 1712
African Development Bank, **1977:** 456
African Development Fund, **1977:** 380, 509, 943;
      1979: 1454, 1455
African Methodist Episcopal Zion Church, **1979:**
      618, 1422
African Unity, Organization of, **1977:** 1720, 1825,
      1827; **1980–81:** 1928
  Interview remarks, **1978:** 325, 903, 940, 1257
  News conference remarks, **1978:** 442, 490, 1095
  Role in Africa, **1978:** 669, 1056

Afro-American (Black) History Month, National,
    1978: 224; **1980–81:** 84, 85
  Afro-American Life and History, Association for
    the study of, **1980–81:** 85
Age Discrimination in Employment Act, **1979:**
    1633
  Amendments, **1978:** 698
Aged.
  See Older persons.
Agee, James, **1979:** 1982ftn.
Agency.
  See other part of title.
Agent Orange, **1980–81:** 2464, 2509
Aggregate Report on Personnel, **1979:** 2187
Aggrey, O. Rudolph, **1977:** 1673, 1700
Aging, Administration on, **1977:** 1190, 1825, 2082,
    2089; **1979:** 441; **1980–81:** 291, 824
Aging, Council of Organizations on, **1979:** 2081
Aging, Federal Council on the.
  See Federal Council on the Aging.
Aging, White House Conference on, **1978:** 1792,
    1794; **1979:** 1445, 2212, 2249; **1980–81:**
    462, 534, 539, 2280
Aging Organizations, Ad Hoc Leadership Council
    of, **1978:** 930
Agnew, Harold M., **1977:** 196; **1978:** 217, 230
Agreement.
  See other part of title.
Agreement on Government Procurement, **1980–81:**
    2854
Agricultural, space, and educational agreement
    with China, **1979:** 204
Agricultural Act, **1980–81:** 2770
Agricultural Adjustment Act, **1980–81:** 503
Agricultural areas.
  See Rural areas.
Agricultural Credit Act, **1978:** 1375, 1376, 1422
Agricultural Credit Adjustment Act
  Amendments, Emergency, **1980–81:** 567
Agricultural Development, Board for International
    Food and, **1980–81:** 323
Agricultural Development, International Fund for,
    1979: 63; **1980–81:** 1190
Agricultural Editors' Association, American,
    1980–81: 563
Agricultural Foreign Investment Disclosure Act,
    1978: 1783
Agricultural Implement Workers of America, Unit-
    ed Automobile, Aerospace &, **1980–81:**
    1598
Agricultural Marketing Service, **1977:** 2168
Agricultural Organization, Food and, **1980–81:**
    1190
Agricultural research and development, **1979:** 533
Agricultural Sciences, Inter-American Institute of,
    1979: 2118
Agricultural Stabilization and Conservation Ser-
    vice, **1977:** 488

Agricultural trade
  Administration's accomplishments and goals,
    1980–81: 2468
  International negotiations and agreements, **1979:**
    6, 152, 438, 946, 1312
  Levels increase, **1980–81:** 125, 661, 904, 1546,
    1868, 1904, 1917, 2119, 2148, 2192, 2203,
    2205, 2209, 2224, 2400, 2402, 2407, 2416,
    2468, 2514, 2551, 2588, 2600, 2607, 2619,
    2632, 2638, 2669, 2828
  Past export embargoes, **1980–81:** 2467
  Upland cotton imports, **1980–81:** 575
  U.S. and:
    China, People's Republic of.
      See Trade with U.S. *under* China, People's
        Republic of.
    Japan, **1979:** 152, 767, 1177
    Korea, Republic of, **1980–81:** 2587, 2601, 2607
    Mexico.
      See Trade with U.S. *under* Mexico.
    Nigeria, **1980–81:** 2587, 2601, 2607
    OPEC nations, **1979:** 802, 1251, 1910, 1944
    Poland, **1980–81:** 1711, 1905, 2537
    Soviet Union sales suspension
      Presidential election, effect on, **1980–81:**
        675, 740, 2710
      Prices, effect on, **1980–81:** 2203
      Effectiveness of suspension, **1980–81:** 661,
        747, 1727, 2712
      Farmer-owned reserves legislation, **1980–81:**
        652
      Letter to Speaker of House and President of
        Senate transmitting report, **1980–81:**
        183–188
      Memorandum to Department Secretaries,
        1980–81: 32
      News conference (Checklist), **1980–81:** 219
      President's comments, **1980–81:** 23, 41, 92,
        196, 391, 634, 1193, 1308, 1530, 2324,
        2351, 2407, 2409, 2472, 2566, 2828, 2833
      Reagan, Ronald, position on, **1980–81:**
        1535, 2470, 2473, 2555
      State of the Union, **1980–81:** 160
    U.S. exports, **1978:** 1375, 1387, 1390, 1391, 1421,
      1624, 1632, 1819, 1826
    Effect on:
      Farm income, **1979:** 152
      Trade balance of payments, **1979:** 152
    Embargoes, **1979:** 570, 805, 1910, 1945
    Levels increases, **1979:** 66, 152, 307, 534, 570,
      802, 806, 924, 1252, 1312, 1481, 1495,
      1710, 1936, 1944, 2031
    Revenues pay for farmers' energy use, **1979:**
      791
    See also specific commodity.
  U.S. imports
    Cheese and chocolate crumbs, **1979:** 2227
    Meat, **1979:** 336, 2292
    Sugar, syrup, molasses, **1979:** 153, 946

Agricultural Trade Act, **1978:** 1818
Agriculture, Convention on the Inter-American
    Institute for Cooperation on, **1979:** 2118
Agriculture, Department of
  Acid rain research programs, **1979:** 1389
  Agricultural commodity credit guarantees to
    Poland, **1980–81:** 1711
  Agricultural Economics, Director, **1977:** 1534
  Agricultural exchange agreement with China,
    1979: 200
  Agricultural exports to Soviet Union, suspension
    actions, **1980–81:** 161, 187
  Alaska Natural Gas Transportation System,
    transfer of functions, **1979:** 595
  Alcohol fuel production plants, loan guarantees,
    1979: 1502ftn.
  Assistant Secretaries, **1977:** 331, 372, 461, 465,
    495, 505, 510, 535, 557, 1709, 1906; **1978:**
    326, 416, 457, 2147; **1979:** 1779, 1824,
    1865; **1980–81:** 271, 1938, 1941
  Beef imports, **1978:** 1074
  Budget deferrals and rescission, **1978:** 502, 895,
    1041, 2183; **1979:** 200, 1772; **1980–81:**
    355, 1129
  Civil land remote-sensing activities, **1979:** 2150
  Consumer Affairs Council membership, **1979:**
    1763
  Dam inspection program, **1977:** 2072
  Deputy Secretary.
    See Agriculture, Deputy Secretary of (James
      H. Williams).
  Diesel fuel shortages responsibilities, **1979:** 945,
    987, 1140
  Disaster loans, **1978:** 472
  Emergency Livestock Feed program, **1977:** 488
  Employees, President's assessment, **1979:** 924
  Endangered plant species activities, **1979:** 2288
  Energy crisis, **1977:** 35
  Environmental message, **1977:** 789, 978, 981, 982
  Environmental protection activities, **1980–81:**
    352
  Export policy functions, **1978:** 1633
  Export promotion centers, **1979:** 1710
  Farm lending, **1978:** 1852
  Federal Grain Inspection Service, **1977:** 1079,
    1085
  Feed grain program, **1978:** 2011
  Food nutritional value testing, **1980–81:** 1936
  Food transportation system, **1977:** 2168
  Forest Service, Chief, **1979:** 1044
  Fort Worth Civic Organizations, remarks, **1978:**
    1158
  Fuel oil management group membership, **1979:**
    2056
  Gasohol research, **1979:** 792
  General Counsel, **1977:** 1251, 1266; **1979:** 980,
    984
  Grain set-aside and reserve programs, **1978:** 293

Agriculture, Department of — *continued*
  Hauling contract standardization, **1979:** 1625
  Heat- and drought-affected areas, assistance
    functions, **1980–81:** 1423
  Heating oil management group, **1979:** 1631
  Inspector General, **1979:** 366, 377
  Integrated pest management programs, **1979:**
    1383
  Interagency Coordinating Council, **1978:** 1434
  International trade functions, **1979:** 1731
  Juvenile delinquency programs, **1980–81:** 1273
  Market news service for truckers, **1979:** 1624
  National Forest System, roadless areas evalua-
    tion, **1979:** 151, 671
  National water policy, **1978:** 1048–1050
  Office of Economics, Policy Analysis and Bud-
    get, Director, **1978:** 2064; **1980–81:** 219
  Office for Small Community and Rural Devel-
    opment, creation, **1980–81:** 1920
  Peanut price support program, **1980–81:** 2775
  President's visit, question-and-answer session,
    1977: 167
  Public lands, grazing fees, **1978:** 1331, 1876
  Rabbit meat inspection, **1977:** 1993
  Research Apprenticeship Program, **1979:** 2064
  Rural development activities, **1979:** 75, 77
  Rural water system contracts, **1980–81:** 1429
  Secretary.
    See Agriculture, Secretary of.
  Sikes Act activities, **1978:** 1250
  Soil and conservation policy appraisal, **1979:**
    1367, 1382
  Solar energy programs, **1979:** 1105
  Sugar industry and imports, **1977:** 2019; **1978:**
    145, 146, 2289, 2290
  Tahoe Federal Coordinating Council member-
    ship, **1980–81:** 2235, 2236
  Task Force on Global Resources and Environ-
    ment, functions, **1980–81:** 1416
  Timber harvests, **1978:** 725
  Tobacco import determination, **1980–81:** 2144
  Trucking rates for transportation of exempt
    commodities, **1979:** 1122, 1136, 1139
  Tuolumne River, Calif., wild and scenic river
    study, **1979:** 1814
  Under Secretaries, **1980–81:** 145, 219, 2430, 2726,
    2727, 2751, 2870, 2873; **1978:** 2157; **1979:**
    218
  Under Secretary for small communities and
    rural development, proposed, **1979:** 2275
  Watershed projects, evaluation, **1977:** 494
  Wildlife law enforcement, **1979:** 1364, 1377
  World forest protection support, **1979:** 1388
  See also specific constituent agencies.
Agriculture, Deputy Secretary of (James H. Wil-
    liams), **1977:** 339, 372, 373, 508, 1534;
    1978: 1158

Agriculture, Deputy Secretary — *continued*
  Commodity Credit Corporation, Board of Directors member, **1979:** 110, 179
  Diesel fuel allocations for farmers, **1979:** 945
  Mentions,**1980–81:** 703n., 1920n.
  News conference (Checklist), **1980–81:** 65
  Nomination, **1979:** 42, 91
  President's assessment, **1980–81:** 2149, 2400
  President's Commission on Executive Exchange, member, **1979:** 977
  Soviet grain sales suspension actions, **1980–81:** 42
Agriculture, energy use and needs
  Alcohol fuels production, **1980–81:** 61, 1899, 2588
  Conservation measures, **1980–81:** 790, 904, 1400
  Development of alternatives to oil, **1979:** 534, 792–794, 1102, 1103, 1105
  Food production, development of energy conservation techniques, **1979:** 1268
  Fuel requirements guarantee, **1979:** 791, 803, 846, 937, 945, 951, 987, 1495, 1496, 1502, 1858
    Rule No. 9, **1979:** 1135, 1136, 1139, 1140
Agriculture, farmers and farm sector
  Administration's accomplishments, **1979:** 570; **1980–81:** 160, 748, 1619, 2973
  Administration's policy address, **1980–81:** 2466–2471
  Commodities transportation costs, **1979:** 1122
  Credit
    Legislation, **1980–81:** 567, 706, 2837
    Seasonal loans, **1980–81:** 702
  Crop insurance, **1980–81:** 161
  Democratic Congressmen, discussions with the President (Digest), **1980–81:** 774
  Demonstrations in Washington, D.C., **1979:** 186, 249, 353
  Disaster payment program, **1980–81:** 504
  Economic distress programs, **1979:** 74, 153
  Elk City, Okla., farmers, invitation to visit President, **1979:** 473
  Energy use and needs.
    See Agriculture, energy use and needs.
  Exports.
    See under Agricultural trade.
  Farm organization representatives, meetings with the President, **1980–81:** 1468
  Fertilizer supplies, **1979:** 2221, 2222
  Grain reserves, **1979:** 1497; **1980–81:** 253, 652, 2224, 2588, 2619, 2631, 2669
  Harvests, future controls over, **1979:** 307, 806
  Heat- and drought-affected areas, Federal assistance for, **1980–81:** 1346, 1422
  Impact of:
    Inflation, **1980–81:** 723, 762
    Mount St. Helens eruption, **1980–81:** 951, 957

Agriculture, farmers — *continued*
  Impact of — *continued*
    Soviet grain shipments suspension, **1980–81:** 23, 161, 183, 230, 391, 519, 661, 740, 1728
  Income, **1979:** 152, 186, 307, 570, 806, 1433, 1572; **1980–81:** 253, 701, 903, 904, 2119, 2205, 2224, 2400, 2416, 2589, 2600, 2607, 2619, 2632, 2669
  Milk price supports, **1979:** 2163
  1977 farm bill, **1979:** 186, 249, 570
  Parity demands, **1979:** 249, 353
  President's comments on attitudes and values, **1980–81:** 701
  Prices, **1980–81:** 706, 2619
  Production industry representatives, meeting with the President, **1980–81:** 893
  Productivity, **1979:** 152, 307, 534, 1495
  Progress during Administration, **1979:** 152, 805
  Reagan, Ronald, policy differences with the President, **1980–81:** 2469, 2470, 2601
  Soil conservation incentives, **1979:** 1382
  See also Food.
Agriculture, Inter-American Board of, **1979:** 2120
Agriculture, National Association of State Departments of, **1979:** 239; **1980–81:** 492
Agriculture, Secretary of (Bob Bergland), **1977:** 9, 13, 167, 168, 170, 175, 248, 298, 356, 488, 510, 553, 595, 626, 635, 648, 662, 676, 705, 723, 797–801, 805, 807, 920, 998, 1135, 1210, 1222, 1265, 1348, 1506, 1622, 1680, 1695, 1704, 1705, 1761, 1857, 1879, 1921, 2013, 2060, 2076, 2096, 2121, 2168, 2171; **1978:** 293, 327, 384, 409, 456, 570, 594, 700, 733, 811, 881, 914, 1061, 1062, 1072, 1234, 1331, 1376, 1391, 1420, 1422, 1424, 1442, 1674, 1771, 1783, 2000, 2109, 2111
  Agricultural imports decisions, **1979:** 336, 946
  Agriculture exports to Soviet Union, suspension actions, **1980–81:** 32, 42, 161, 187
  Alaska national monuments designation, **1979:** 1356
  Alaska Natural Gas Transportation System, Executive Policy Board member, **1979:** 1126
  Aquaculture research and development functions, **1980–81:** 1938
  Beef and veal import responsibilities, **1979:** 2299
  China, People's Republic of, Secretary's visit to, **1979:** 205
  Combined Federal Campaign, Chairman, **1979:** 1231, 1234; **1980–81:** 1098
  Council on Wage and Price Stability, advisermember, **1980–81:** 967
  Diesel fuel supply responsibilities for farmers, **1979:** 791, 803, 945, 1135, 1136
  Economic assistance actions for pollution control, **1979:** 1384
  Emergency credit loan functions, **1980–81:** 567

Agriculture, Secretary — *continued*
  Energy conservation responsibilities, **1980–81:** 788
  Farmer-owned grain reserve authority, **1980–81:** 652
  Federal public resources policy coordination, **1979:** 1364, 1375
  Food Security Wheat Reserve responsibilities, **1980–81:** 2911
  Foreign ownership of U.S. real estate, report preparation, **1980–81:** 1924
  Forest Service, recommended programs for, **1980–81:** 1141–1146
  Grain supplies shipment actions, **1979:** 1609
  Heat- and drought-affected areas, assistance functions, **1980–81:** 1346, 1390, 1422
  Idaho wilderness legislation sponsorship, **1980–81:** 1408
  Independent truckers' strike progress reports, **1979:** 1624
  International Sugar Agreement implementation functions, **1980–81:** 1271
  Lake Tahoe region protection responsibilities, **1980–81:** 1013, 2236
  Land conversion for agricultural uses study, **1979:** 1368
  Meetings with the President (Digest), **1979:** 1453, 1678, 1704; **1980–81:** 267, 423, 492, 825, 1427
  Mentions, **1979:** 1494–1496, 1501; **1980–81:** 391, 1101
  Milk price supports authority, **1979:** 2164
  Mount St. Helens eruption, disaster assistance responsibilities, **1980–81:** 951, 955, 956, 958, 961
  National Forest System functions, **1979:** 672
    Land conveyance, **1980–81:** 2845
  National trails designation, **1979:** 1366, 1380
  National Wilderness Preservation System, reports preparation, **1979:** 240, 1966
  News conferences (Checklist), **1979:** 1044, 1143; **1980–81:** 2615
  Peanut imports analysis, **1980–81:** 2776
  President's assessment, **1980–81:** 2467, 2588, 2600, 2607, 2619, 2631, 2669, 2672
  President's Award for Energy Efficiency, ceremony participation, **1980–81:** 2877n.
  Relations with farmers, **1979:** 353, 789, 805
  Rock Island Railroad strike actions, **1979:** 1696, 1787
  Rural development responsibilities, **1979:** 2275; **1980–81:** 1916, 1920
  Soil conservation incentives study, **1979:** 1382
  Strategic and critical materials functions (EO 12155), **1979:** 1621
  Task Force on Global Resources and Environment, duties, **1980–81:** 1417

Agriculture, Secretary — *continued*
  Trade functions, **1980–81:** 8, 10, 1237
  Trip to Iowa, report to President, **1980–81:** 92
  Upland cotton import determinations, **1980–81:** 575, 2745
  Urban noise abatement program development, **1979:** 1385
  World forest preservation responsibilities, **1979:** 1387
  For functions of the Department in general, see Agriculture, Department of.
Agriculture and agricultural programs
  American farming, **1978:** 1353, 1815, 1861, 1900, 1933, 1950
  Des Moines, Iowa, Jefferson-Jackson Day dinner remarks, **1977:** 1857, 1858
  Enforcement of 1902 law concerning land holdings, **1977:** 1705, 1926
  Exports, **1978:** 722, 723, 995, 1632, 1819, 1826
  Farm legislation, **1978:** 700, 738, 914
  Farm prices, **1978:** 724
  Farm program, President's letter to Mrs. Eston Luke, **1977:** 2166, 2169
  Farmers
    Income, **1977:** 298
    Meeting with representatives, **1977:** 2170
  Food and Agriculture Act of 1977, **1977:** 1679, 1703–1705, 1879
  Future Farmers of America, President's remarks, **1978:** 1319, 1995
  Grain set-aside and reserve programs, **1978:** 292, 2064
  Growers Cooperative Warehouse, Inc., President's remarks, **1978:** 1392
  Interview remarks, **1977:** 1705, 1709, 1710, 1921, 2013, 2096, 2097; **1978:** 240, 718, 719, 1494, 1495, 1672–1678
  Legislation, **1977:** 1017, 1019
  Meat imports, **1978:** 2010
  Midcontinent Farmers Association, remarks, **1978:** 1420, 1421
  National Democratic Party Conference, remarks, **1978:** 2192
  News conference remarks, **1977:** 2120, 2121; **1978:** 250, 1986, 1991, 1992
  Ohio State Democratic Party, reception remarks, **1978:** 1624
  President's campaign remarks, **1978:** 1387, 1576
  Prices, **1977:** 298, 309, 514, 632, 635, 648
  Representatives of farm organizations, meeting with the President, **1978:** 1484
  Research, **1977:** 170
  State of the Union, **1978:** 93, 94, 101
  Subsidies, **1977:** 2111
  Tax message, **1978:** 171
  Working Group on Food and Agricultural Policy, **1977:** 1695
  World Hunger Working Group, **1977:** 1696

Agriculture Day, American, **1977:** 508
Agriculture Day, National, **1980–81:** 2145n.
Agriculture Stabilization and Conservation Service,
    1979: 1502
Aguilar, Robert P., **1980–81:** 608
Aguirre, Pedro, **1980–81:** 2559
Ahearne, John F., **1978:** 929, 935; **1979:** 2203;
    1980–81: 131
Ahlberg, Clark D., **1979:** 464
Ahmadou Sallah, Ousman, **1979:** 842
Ahoua, Timothé, **1977:** 710
Aid to Families with Dependent Children, **1977:**
    1445, 1451, 1455; **1978:** 104; **1979:** 940;
    1980–81: 806, 836, 892, 1499
Aiello, Stephen R., **1980–81:** 13, 2372
Ailes, Stephen, **1977:** 801
Air Act, Clean, **1980–81:** 449, 1966, 2201
    Amendments of 1977, **1980–81:** 416
Air Force, Department of the
    American hostages in Iran, servicemen killed in
        rescue attempt, **1980–81:** 780n.
    Assistant Secretaries, **1977:** 1031, 1952, 1967;
        1978: 231; **1979:** 1128, 1142, 2271, 2281;
        1980–81: 449, 453
    Labor-Management Relations Program exemp-
        tions, **1979:** 2145
    Secretary, **1977:** 474, 510; **1979:** 1127, 1142, 1280
    Under Secretary, **1977:** 966, 1031; **1979:** 1128,
        1142
Air Force Academy, United States, **1978:** 569;
    1979: 435; **1980–81:** 606, 757, 2802
Air Force One, **1980–81:** 654, 1085
Air Line Pilots Association, **1978:** 1924, 2033;
    1979: 293
Air pollution.
    See Pollution.
Air Quality, National Commission on, **1978:** 762,
    1178; **1979:** 1353; **1980–81:** 508, 1966
Air Quality Planning Grant program, **1979:** 74
Air Transportation Competition Act, International,
    1980–81: 332
Airborne Warning and Control System (AWACS),
    1977: 1377, 1568
Aircraft, Agreement on Trade in Civil, **1979:** 2224,
    2225, 2227, 2253, 2255
Aircraft and aviation
    Air services agreement with United Kingdom,
        1977: 1346, 1365, 1482; **1978:** 442, 471,
        525, 527
    Airline companies mergers, **1979:** 1587
    China-U.S. agreement, **1980–81:** 1772, 1774
    Emergency Board to investigate labor dispute,
        1978: 1924, 2033, 2158
    Environmental standards, **1977:** 322
    Hijacking, **1978:** 1308, 1310, 1676; **1979:** 63,
        1188; **1980–81:** 1172

Aircraft and aviation — *continued*
    Industry Deregulation, **1977:** 256, 508, 748, 757,
        1137, 1379, 1916, 1988; **1978:** 346, 725,
        762, 840, 1424, 1549, 1553, 1562, 1648,
        1692, 1798, 1817, 1831, 1824, 1849, 1861,
        1867, 1886, 2192, 2237, 2243
        Competition increase, **1979:** 130, 935
        Consumer prices reduction, **1979:** 127, 484,
            719, 834, 935, 1115, 1699, 1874, 1951;
            1980–81: 50, 281, 1261
        Industry profits increase, **1979:** 105, 484, 1115,
            1699, 1874, 1951
        Mentions, **1980–81:** 71, 215, 573, 918, 1357,
            1537
        U.S. exports, international agreement, **1979:** 6
    Industry reform, **1977:** 1133, 1161
    International and domestic routes, competition,
        1978: 153
    International transportation negotiations, **1978:**
        1462, 1471, 1549
    Service with China and United Kingdom, **1980–
        81:** 2651
    "Skytrain" airline service, **1977:** 1112
    Small airplane construction business, **1980–81:**
        666
    State of the Union, **1978:** 106, 107, 109
    Transatlantic service, **1977:** 748, 757, 1668, 1669,
        1952, 2158
    White House military passenger lists, **1980–81:**
        267
Airline Deregulation Act of 1978, **1978:** 1837, 1879;
    1980–81: 332
Airline labor dispute, Emergency Board to inves-
    tigate an, **1979:** 89, 293
Airport and Airway Development Act functions,
    1978: 1532
Akaka, Repr. Daniel K., **1979:** 1218; **1980–81:** 962
Akins, Charlie, **1979:** 1439
Akinyemi, Bolaji, **1978:** 645
Akron, Ohio, **1980–81:** 2655–2659
Al-Azhar, **1977:** 2076
Al Fatah, **1978:** 505
Alabama
    Cahaba River, wild and scenic river study, **1979:**
        2245
    Civic and community leaders, meetings with the
        President (Digest), **1979:** 842, 2104
    Democratic Party primary, **1980–81:** 461
    Disaster assistance, **1977:** 640; **1980–81:** 1422
    Disaster declarations, **1978:** 1470; **1979:** 675,
        1678; **1980–81:** 774
    Emergency declaration, **1977:** 1306; **1978:** 802
    Energy emergency, **1978:** 507
    Gov. Forrest H. James, Jr., **1980–81:** 1423n.
    President's visit, **1979:** 1672; **1980–81:** 1601
    U.S. attorneys, **1977:** 1059, 1128, 1613, 1614
    U.S. district judges, **1980–81:** 64, 218, 1846, 1847
    U.S. marshals, **1978:** 1407; **1977:** 1569, 1755

Alabama Democratic Black Caucus, **1979:** 2104
Alamosa, Cole, **1980–81:** 1453
Alarcon, Arthur L., **1979:** 1531, 1532
Alarcon, Terry Q., **1980–81:** 2701
Alaska
  Airplane crash, **1978:** 2158
  Democratic Party caucuses, **1980–81:** 461
  Domestic oil supplies, **1979:** 185, 723, 725, 1345
  Federal-State Land Use Planning Commission, **1977:** 1072, 1085
  Interview remarks, **1978:** 715, 716
  Lands protection
    Administration's accomplishments and goals, **1980–81:** 2970
    Legislation.
      See Alaska National Interest Lands Conservation Act.
  National Monuments, **1979:** 151, 766, 855
    Designation, **1978:** 2111–2144, 2147
  National Petroleum Reserves, **1977:** 1127, 1128; **1978:** 1345; **1980–81:** 63, 232, 233, 269
  Natural gas transportation system, **1977:** 1212, 1494, 1533, 1620, 1645, 1978, 1980
  Oil production, **1977:** 657
  Oil supplies, **1980–81:** 369
  Pipeline, **1977:** 534
  President's visit, **1979:** 1161; **1980–81:** 1342
  Public lands
    Energy exploration on, **1979:** 444, 1899
    Legislation, **1979:** 444, 855, 877, 1356, 1995, 2067
    White House briefing, **1979:** 773
  U.S. attorney, **1977:** 1931, 1932
  Wilderness lands, **1977:** 202, 979; **1978:** 116, 409
Alaska National Interest Lands Conservation Act
  Fact sheet (Checklist), **1980–81:** 2782
  House approval, **1980–81:** 2718
  Offshore energy exploration proposal, **1980–81:** 2494
  President's support, **1980–81:** 1343, 1408, 1411
  Senate approval, **1980–81:** 1548
  Signing ceremony, **1980–81:** 2756
  White House briefing, **1980–81:** 1386
Alaska Natural Gas Transportation System
  Administration's efforts to expedite construction, **1979:** 1245, 1327
  Canadian Government approval of first 4,800 miles, **1980–81:** 1372, 1375
  Federal Inspector, **1979:** 1016, 1019; **1980–81:** 617
  News conference (Checklist), **1980–81:** 1377
  President's Letter to Canadian Prime Minister Trudeau, **1980–81:** 1367
  Reorganization Plan No. 1 of 1979
    Enactment of plan (EO 12142), **1979:** 1126
    Message transmittal to Congress, **1979:** 591
  Statement by the President, **1980–81:** 1368
Alaska Pipeline Company, Northwest, **1979:** 591

Alaska Railroad, **1977:** 1030; **1978:** 1279; **1979:** 1785; **1980–81:** 2726, 2845
Alaska Resources, Organization for Management of, **1978:** 802
Albee, Sarah J., **1980–81:** 929
Alberger, William R., **1977:** 1666, 1700; **1978:** 1154; **1980–81:** 948, 1330
Albers, William E., **1978:** 687, 711
Albert, Margo, **1980–81:** 1440, 1470
Albosta, Repr. Donald Joseph, **1980–81:** 2344
Albright, Harry, **1980–81:** 2560
Albright, Horace Marden, **1980–81:** 1598
Albright, Madeleine, **1978:** 2003
Albright, Dr. Tenley, **1980–81:** 381
Albuquerque, N. Mex., **1978:** 85; **1979:** 1853, 1854, 1863
ALCOA.
  See Aluminum Company of America.
Alcohol, Drug Abuse, and Mental Health Administration, **1977:** 1779, 1796; **1979:** 1596
Alcohol, Education Commission of the States Task Force on Responsible Decisions about, **1977:** 641
Alcohol fuels
  Increased production, **1979:** 1896
  New initiatives program, **1980–81:** 61, 65, 2468
  Production
    Corn reserves utilization, **1980–81:** 652
    Foreign, **1980–81:** 2560
  Proposed legislation, **1979:** 1502ftn.
Alcohol Fuels Commission, National, **1979:** 1007, 1445; **1980–81:** 235, 899
Alcoholic beverages, **1979:** 2224, 2226
Alcoholism, **1980–81:** 2753
Alcoholism and Other Alcohol-Related Problems, National Commission on, **1980–81:** 2609, 2801
Alden, Robert A., **1977:** 642
Aldrete, Cristobal P., **1977:** 1069, 1085; **1980–81:** 1942
Aldrich, Ann, **1980–81:** 564
Aldrich, George H., **1977:** 276, 277, 1667, 1795, 1826
Aldrin, Edwin (Buzz) E., Jr., **1979:** 1276
Aleutian-Pribilof Island Association, **1980–81:** 1455
Alexander, Repr. Bill, **1979:** 943
Alexander, Clifford L., Jr., **1977:** 65, 87, 207, 490, 1345, 2076; **1978:** 1682, 1725; **1979:** 837, 1280, 1715, 1921; **1980–81:** 955, 956, 1004, 1071
Alexander, Kelly, **1980–81:** 1322
Alexander, Gov. Lamar, **1980–81:** 1423n.
Alexander, Lee A., **1978:** 570, 641; **1979:** 402
Alexander, Margaret Walker, **1979:** 318
Alexander, Sadie T. M., **1979:** 2213; **1980–81:** 534, 537, 1634
Alexander Hamilton Award, **1978:** 125

Alexandria, La., **1979:** 1817
Alexandrides, C. G., **1977:** 1126
Alexis, Marcus, **1979:** 885, 886, 900
Alfred E. Smith Memorial Dinner, **1980–81:** 2309
Algeria
    Ambassador to U.S., **1977:** 1163; **1979:** 2162n.
    American hostages in Iran
        Intermediary role in release negotiations,
            1980–81: 2683, 2703, 2833, 2840, 2856,
            3019
        Release agreement implementation role,
            1980–81: 3027
        President Houari Boumediene, **1978:** 2288
        Revolution celebrations, U.S. delegation, **1979:**
            2043
    U.S. Ambassador, **1977:** 727, 745
Alhegelan, Faisal, **1979:** 1318
Ali, Kamal Hassan.
    See Egypt, Foreign Minister.
Ali, Muhammad, **1977:** 1544; **1978:** 2288; **1980–81:**
    63, 333, 2074, 2364
Alia, Queen, **1977:** 147
Alien Property, Office of, **1978:** 1221; **1979:** 217;
    1980–81: 1291, 2726
Aliens, undocumented, **1977:** 632, 644, 901, 1030,
    1101, 1415, 1416, 1438, 1802, 1923; **1978:**
    112, 249, 838, 904, 908; **1980–81:** 1726
    Human rights, **1979:** 1662, 1664, 1667
    Select Commission on Immigration and Refugee
        Policy, permanent solution recommenda-
        tion, **1979:** 564, 812
    U.S. consultations with Mexico, **1979:** 145, 184,
        185, 236, 253, 806, 907
Aliquippa, Pa., **1978:** 1603, 1617
'All in the Family', cast members and others,
    meeting with the President, **1978:** 1571
All-volunteer armed force, **1977:** 267, 314, 388
Allan, Virginia R., **1977:** 1502, 1503
Allara, Michael A., **1979:** 842
Allen, Bryan, **1979:** 2079
Allen, Mrs. Clifford R., **1978:** 1857
Allen, Repr. Clifford R., **1978:** 1133
Allen, Dr. Ethel D., **1977:** 2153
Allen, H. K., **1977:** 2128, 2130; **1978:** 150
Allen, Ivan, **1980–81:** 1756
Allen, Sen. James B., **1978:** 263, 328, 512, 1029
Allen, Jimmy, **1978:** 1117
Allen, Gen. Lew, Jr., **1978:** 684, 1219, 1220
Allen, Sen. Maryon, **1978:** 1110
Allen, Peter J., **1979:** 1775
Allen, Priscilla, **1977:** 529
Allen, Richard R., **1979:** 215, 241
Allen, Susan, **1977:** 304
Allen-Spilka, Janet, **1980–81:** 192
Alliance to Save Energy, **1977:** 126, 128, 134; **1979:**
    1976
Allied Chemicals, **1979:** 2022
Allison, Thomas G., **1980–81:** 643, 775

Allison, William W., **1977:** 1053, 1059
Allon, Yigal, **1977:** 836
Alloy tool steel imports, **1977:** 1121
Alm, Alvin L., **1977:** 1584, 1613; **1979:** 733, 1294
Alma, Wis., **1979:** 1470
Almond, Lincoln, **1978:** 335
Alpers, Helmut A., **1979:** 2277, 2281
Alpharetta, Ga., **1980–81:** 1744
Alspach, Gretchen, **1980–81:** 1468
Alston, Philip Henry Jr., **1977:** 576, 597, 744, 805,
    873, 883; **1978:** 231; **1979:** 46, 91; **1980–**
    81: 2806
Altman, Roger C., **1977:** 460, 465; **1979:** 240, 1221,
    1223
Altmayer, Jay P., **1979:** 782
Aluminum Company of America (ALCOA),
    1980–81: 552, 581
Alumni Association of the School of International
    Affairs, **1979:** 1787
Alvarado, Jeanette, **1980–81:** 452
Alvarez, Edmund, **1978:** 409
Alvarez del Castillo, Enrique, **1978:** 1043
Alverson, Dayton L., **1980–81:** 2774
Amado, Juan Jose, **1980–81:** 1564
Amalgamated Clothing and Textile Workers, **1978:**
    750; **1980–81:** 563
Amalgamated Clothing Workers of America, **1979:**
    1421
Amaraich, Andon L., **1980–81:** 2611
Amateur Sports Act, **1978:** 1976
Ambach, Gordon M., **1980–81:** 1445, 1470
Ambassadorial Appointments, Presidential Advi-
    sory Board on, **1977:** 78, 86, 89, 90, 148,
    576; **1979:** 552, 2042; **1980–81:** 1420, 2849
Ambassadors
    Foreign
        Presentation of credentials (Digest), visits, etc.,
            1977: 194, 464, 822, 942, 1163, 1383, 1754;
            1978: 148, 328, 710, 1070, 1380, 2059;
            1979: 25, 376, 377, 554, 842, 1318, 1453,
            1802; **1980–81:** 268, 1051, 1564, 1598,
            2752, 2807
        White House ceremony for, **1979:** 2161
    United States
        Ambassadors at Large.
            See under State Department.
    See also under Appointments and Nominations;
        (country to which assigned.)
Ambler, Ernest, **1977:** 1760, 2001, 2006; **1978:** 231
Ambrosio, Gabe, **1980–81:** 2265ftn.
Ambrus, Clara M., **1977:** 196
Amerada Hess Oil Company, **1979:** 1583
America, President's views on
    Achievements and strengths, **1980–81:** 806, 890,
        976, 1305, 1317, 1369, 1394, 1425, 1640
    Challenges of the 1980's **1980–81:** 995, 1413,
        1539, 1655

America, President's views on — *continued*
Challenges of the past, **1980–81:** 649, 702, 1007, 2034, 2123, 2139, 2394
Founding principles, **1980–81:** 2018
Commitment to, **1979:** 1715, 1873
Government system, **1979:** 2060
Intangible values, **1979:** 1563; **1980–81:** 828, 874, 971
Nation of immigrants and refugees, **1979:** 1409, 2026, 2060; **1980–81:** 648, 963, 997, 1306, 1616, 1876, 2123, 2146, 2152, 2368, 2382, 2458, 2485
News media influence, **1980–81:** 890
Societal divisions, **1980–81:** 2299
Spirit and unity revival, **1980–81:** 51, 180, 200, 242, 1395
Strengths, **1979:** 1467, 1472, 1473, 1917, 2173
America Alliance for Health, Physical Education, Recreation and Dance, **1979:** 955
American Academy of Family Practice, **1977:** 1221; **1978:** 934
American Agricultural Editors' Association, **1980–81:** 563
American Agriculture Day, **1977:** 508
American Agriculture Movement, **1978:** 1820
American Arbitration Association, **1979:** 1454
American Association of Advertising Agencies, **1978:** 254
American Association of Editorial Cartoonists, **1978:** 1771
American Association of Retired People, **1979:** 1630; **1980–81:** 589
American Bar Association, **1978:** 839, 840, 2059; **1979:** 760
American Battle Monuments Commission, **1978:** 28, 2089; **1979:** 81; **1980–81:** 1596
American Bible Society, **1977:** 1612
American Broadcasting Company (ABC), **1978:** 2247; **1979:** 1586, 1591, 1678
American Bureau of Shipping, **1980–81:** 1628
American Cancer Society, **1977:** 566; **1978:** 710; **1979:** 553
American Committee on Italian Migration, **1980–81:** 1063
American Convention on Human Rights, **1977:** 1050; **1978:** 395, 1144; **1980–81:** 2735
American Education Week, **1977:** 1694; **1978:** 1651
(Proc. 4692), **1979:** 1698
(Proc. 4797), **1980–81:** 1969
American Enterprise Day (Proc. 4778), **1980–81:** 1519
American Farm Bureau, **1980–81:** 334
American Farm Bureau Federation, **1979:** 1318
American Federation of Government Employees, **1978:** 802, 1366, 1765, 1766; **1979:** 2247
American Federation of Grain Millers, **1979:** 1452, 1467

American Federation of Labor and Congress of Industrial Organizations.
See AFL-CIO.
American Federation of State, County, and Municipal Employees, **1980–81:** 1662
American Federation of Teachers, **1977:** 1222; **1980–81:** 1549, 1556
American Film Institute, **1977:** 2036, 2041
American Folklife Center, **1977:** 2036
American Forestry Association, **1978:** 1234; **1980–81:** 2822
American Foundation for Negro Affairs, **1978:** 328
American Heart Association, **1978:** 289; **1980–81:** 190
American Heart Month, **1978:** 89, 289
(Proc. 4633), **1979:** 21
(Proc. 4716), **1980–81:** 190
(Proc. 4816), **1980–81:** 2914
American Hellenic Educational Progressive Association, Order of the, **1979:** 618; **1980–81:** 381
American Indian Religious Freedom Act, **1978:** 1417
American Institute of Architects, **1979:** 1537
American Islamic community, **1979:** 2206
American Jewish Committee, **1977:** 788, 1136
American Jewish Congress, **1977:** 788, 1136
American Jewish Press Association, **1980–81:** 1113
American Lebanese League, **1978:** 794
American Legion, **1977:** 509; **1978:** 277, 770, 1771; **1979:** 1824; **1980–81:** 344, 375, 1549, 1565
American Lung Association, **1978:** 2073; **1979:** 2042
American Medical Association, **1978:** 864, 1345
American National Red Cross, **1977:** 210, 249, 250, 1665; **1978:** 770; **1979:** 376, 552, 1678; **1980–81:** 951, 1292
American Newspaper Publishers Association, **1979:** 693, 733; **1980–81:** 720
American Press Institute, **1978:** 229, 233, 517; **1979:** 557
American Public Gas Association, **1979:** 793
American Public Transit Association, **1979:** 1739, 1787; **1980–81:** 589
American Retail Federation, **1978:** 898; **1979:** 832
American Samoa
Congressional delegate, **1978:** 1907
Disaster assistance, **1979:** 2106
U.S. policy, **1980–81:** 317
American Society of Association Executives, **1977:** 706
American Society of Magazine Editors, **1978:** 1407, 1409
American Society of Newspaper Editors, **1977:** 789; **1978:** 721, 727; **1979:** 788; **1980–81:** 631

American spirit revival, President's commitment to, **1979:** 1240, 1241, 1248, 1258, 1303, 1332, 1426, 1480, 1484, 1565, 1842, 1852, 1862, 1865, 1867, 1930, 1991, 2026, 2035, 2058
   President's initial statement, **1979:** 1237
American States, Organization of, **1979:** 279, 644, 1794, 2120; **1980–81:** 455, 914, 2733, 2741
   Address, **1977:** 611, 642
   Convention for Nature Protection and Wildlife Preservation in the Western Hemisphere, **1977:** 984
   Dominican Republic elections, **1978:** 931, 942
   General Assembly, opening session remarks, **1978:** 1141
   Human rights treaties, **1978:** 395
   Interview remarks, **1978:** 1598
   Panama Canal treaties signing ceremony, **1977:** 1542–1544
   Secretary General, **1978:** 570
   United Nations address, **1977:** 1720
   U.S. Permanent Representative, **1977:** 465
   U.S. support, **1978:** 1056
American Stock Exchange, **1980–81:** 64
American Telephone and Telegraph Company (AT&T), **1979:** 2022; **1980–81:** 653
American Textile Manufacturers Institute, **1977:** 120
American Train Dispatchers Association, **1979:** 818, 984
American Trucking Association, **1980–81:** 1402
American Veterans of World War II, Korea and Vietnam, **1978:** 1879
Americans Missing and Unaccounted for in Southeast Asia, Presidential Commission on, **1977:** 316, 377, 489, 499
Americas, Council of the, **1978:** 148
Americas, Partners of the, **1980–81:** 628
Americus, Ga., **1980–81:** 2068
Amiar, Jose-Joseph, **1979:** 25
Amin, Hafizullah, **1980–81:** 40, 41, 672, 2835
Amin Dada, Idi, **1977:** 220, 269, 292, 315; **1979:** 867
Amiotte, Arthur D., **1979:** 464
Ammonia industry, anhydrous, **1979:** 2221, 2222; **1980–81:** 102
Amnesty International, **1978:** 768, 1330; **1979:** 1914
Amos, Harold, **1980–81:** 1292
Amoss, W. James, Jr., **1978:** 454; **1980–81:** 1048
Amtrak.
   See National Railroad Passenger Corporation.
Amtrak Improvement Act, **1978:** 1718
Andersen, Edward, **1980–81:** 1428
Anderson, Arvin, **1979:** 1954
Anderson, Bernard E., **1978:** 52, 150
Anderson, Bette Beasley, **1977:** 275, 280; **1978:** 1407
Anderson, C. Joseph, **1978:** 1193; **1980–81:** 3022

Anderson, Charlotte N., **1980–81:** 1507
Anderson, Claud, **1977:** 1070, 1085
Anderson, Maj. Gen. Earl O., **1978:** 710
Anderson, Eric E., **1980–81:** 929
Anderson, Frank J., **1977:** 1163
Anderson, Fred E., **1978:** 748; **1980–81:** 3021
Anderson, George M., **1977:** 1127, 1128
Anderson, George Ross, Jr., **1980–81:** 721
Anderson, Gerald, **1977:** 318
Anderson, Repr. Glenn M., **1977:** 1134, 1988; **1978:** 1563, 1669, 1827, 1838; **1980–81:** 333
Anderson, Jack, **1980–81:** 1545, 1851
Anderson, Repr. John B., **1979:** 776, 2085
   Campaign debates, President's opposition to inclusion in, **1980–81:** 988, 1636, 1702, 1733, 1871, 1873, 1911, 2138, 2272
   Mention, **1980–81:** 1085
   President's appeal to supporters of, **1980–81:** 2640, 2658, 2663, 2671, 2676
   Third party candidacy, President's assessment of impact on Presidential election, **1980–81:** 729, 738
   TV political commercial on Jesus Christ amendment, **1980–81:** 2037
Anderson, John F., **1979:** 1614n.
Anderson, Joseph B., **1977:** 986
Anderson, Marian, **1978:** 1787
Anderson, Max, **1978:** 1449
Anderson, Owanah, **1978:** 1134
Anderson, Mrs. Owanah, **1980–81:** 1438n.
Anderson, Philip S., **1978:** 734
Anderson, R. E., **1980–81:** 2751
Anderson, R. Lanier, III, **1979:** 675
Anderson, Robert O., **1978:** 53, 1723; **1979:** 1614n.
Anderson, Sen. Wendell R., **1977:** 1612; **1978:** 784, 1713, 1823, 1824, 1827, 1832, 1953
Anderson, William, **1980–81:** 516
Andrade, Jose Manuel Pita, **1980–81:** 1244
Andrawes, Adib, **1979:** 455
Andreas, Martin Lowell, **1980–81:** 1946
Andrei, Stefan, **1978:** 1032
Andreotti, Giulio, **1977:** 767, 824, 881, 884, 1264, 1353, 1358, 1363, 1383; **1978:** 1019, 1310, 1334; **1979:** 1193, 1197n., 1415
Andréas Peréz, Carlos, **1977:** 640, 1098, 1180, 1183, 1188, 1190, 1207, 1208, 1211, 1542, 1568
Andrew, Robert F., **1977:** 806; **1978:** 885
Andrew Mellon Foundation, **1978:** 1028
Andrews, Repr. Ike, **1980–81:** 2733
Andrews, Judy, **1980–81:** 753
Andrews, Mike, **1980–81:** 2605
Andrews, Robert C., **1978:** 1340
Andrews, Rupert E., **1980–81:** 1342
Andrews, Sydney D., **1977:** 196, 1944, 1966; **1978:** 231
Andrews Air Force Base, Md., **1977:** 595; **1978:** 611, 1457, 1506, 1507, 2004, 2302; **1979:** 842; **1980–81:** 1234

Andrus, Cecil D.
  See Interior, Secretary of the.
Andrus, Mrs. Cecil D., **1979:** 554
Andrus, Tracy, **1979:** 554
Angel, Ronald E., **1977:** 1507, 1534
Angel, Sam Epstein, **1979:** 1129, 1143
Angelou, Maya, **1977:** 525
Anglada, Mario A., **1980–81:** 2608
Anglim, Philip, **1978:** 394
Angola, **1977:** 173, 647
  Alignment with Soviet Union, **1979:** 316
  Cuban troops in, **1979:** 1754
  News conference remarks, **1978:** 972, 1092, 1184, 1185
  South African raid, **1978:** 851, 855
  Soviet and Cuban involvement, **1980–81:** 93, 108, 111, 674, 1105, 1225
Anhydrous ammonia industry, **1979:** 2221, 2222 (Proc. 4714), **1980–81:** 102
Aniakchak National Monument, **1978:** 2114
Ankeny, V. Scott, **1980–81:** 919
Annapolis, Md., **1977:** 2035
Anne, Princess, **1977:** 1127
Annual Assay Commission, **1980–81:** 483
Annunzio, Repr. Frank, **1977:** 1628; **1978:** 933, 1808; **1979:** 1935, 1937
Antarctica, environmental protection, **1977:** 984
Anthony, Susan B., **1979:** 2008; **1980–81:** 412, 1575, 2057
  Coin authorization bill, **1978:** 1737
Anti-arson program, Federal, **1979:** 2249
Antiballistic missiles, **1977:** 1807
Anti-Ballistic Missile Treaty, **1979:** 1038
Antiboycott laws and regulations, **1980–81:** 402, 1656
Anti-Defamation League, **1977:** 788, 1136
Antigua, U.S. Special Representative, **1977:** 1530; **1979:** 980
Anti-inflation program
  Accord between administration and labor leaders.
    See under Labor.
  Administration briefing for black ministers (Digest), **1980–81:** 825
  Administration's accomplishments and goals, **1980–81:** 743, 3009
  Antitrust laws enforcement, **1979:** 105, 234
  Business and industry stability, **1979:** 2041
  Competition policy, **1979:** 234, 242
  Comprehensive energy plan, **1979:** 2041, 2046
  Congressional actions, **1979:** 105
  Consumer involvement, **1979:** 620
  Consumer prices
    News conference (Checklist), **1980–81:** 453
    Monitoring, **1979:** 635
  Economic productivity rate increases, **1980–81:** 249, 1832

Anti-inflation program — *continued*
  Economic renewal program, relationship with, **1980–81:** 1504, 1512, 1537, 1586, 1675, 2217, 2433
  Energy prices deregulation, **1979:** 611, 622
  Federal budget restraint.
    See Deficit reduction *under* Budget, Federal.
  Federal civilian and military pay increase levels, **1979:** 1529
  Federal Reserve System actions, **1979:** 1835, 1909; **1980–81:** 2040
  Hospital cost containment, **1979:** 105, 123, 256, 383, 386, 569, 603, 838, 846, 951, 2111; **1980–81:** 388
  Import relief determinations, **1980–81:** 420, 532
  Labor accord with administration.
    See under Labor.
  March initiatives
    Administration's goals, **1980–81:** 1079
    Announcement remarks, **1980–81:** 476
    Budget revisions, 1981.
      See Fiscal Year 1981 *under* Budget, Federal.
    Credit controls.
      See Credit controls.
    Economic productivity, savings, and innovation encouragement, **1980–81:** 498, 513, 554, 2128, 2165, 2270, 2515
    Fact sheet (Checklist), **1980–81:** 494
    Gasoline conservation fee on imported oil.
      See under Gasoline.
    Initial results, **1980–81:** 994, 1354, 1637, 1879, 1895
    Interest rate reduction.
      See Interest rates.
    Mentions, **1980–81:** 536, 723, 748, 802, 804, 859, 978, 1066
    News conference statement, **1980–81:** 484
  Mentions, **1979:** 741, 902, 2122
  Oil imports reduction.
    See Reduction *under* Oil imports.
  Partnership with American people to control, **1979:** 576, 650, 796, 933, 934, 1010, 1247
  Real wage insurance, **1979:** 115, 124, 256, 951
  Regulatory reform, **1979:** 115, 650, 701, 935, 1607, 1985; **1980–81:** 120, 215, 573, 604
  Second year supplement (EO 12161), **1979:** 1778
  Small business support, **1980–81:** 516
  Solar energy use increase, **1979:** 1358
  State and local governments cooperation, **1979:** 124
  Supply and demand balance, **1980–81:** 250
  Targeted fiscal assistance to State and local governments, **1979:** 1247
  Tax proposals, **1980–81:** 122, 1880
  U.S. exports increase, **1979:** 65O, 736, 796, 935, 944, 1607, 2041
  Vetoes of inflationary legislation, **1980–81:** 280, 456

Anti-inflation program — *continued*
    Voluntary wage and price guidelines.
        See under Wages and prices.
    White House briefing for State and local offi-
        cials, **1979:** 306, 378
    See also Inflation.
Anti-inflationary procurement practices, **1978:**
    1919
Antiochian Orthodox Church, **1977:** 1265
Anti-Recession Fiscal Assistance, **1978:** 100, 589
Antitrust laws, **1978:** 1610, 1634; **1979:** 2071
Antitrust Laws and Procedures, National Commis-
        sion for the Review of, **1977:** 2064, 2177,
        1978: 112, 707, 1139, 1140, 1878; **1979:**
        132, 178, 875; **1980–81:** 2850
Antoine, Valerie, **1977:** 196
Antonio del Rosario Ceballos, Enriquillo, **1979:**
    1882
Aoki, Yoshio, **1979:** 1180n.
Apel, Hans, **1978:** 1292
Apodaca, Gov. Jerry, **1978:** 1341, 1345, 1506, 1725;
        1980–81: 261, 262, 1420, 1939
Apodaca, Patrick V., **1979:** 1976; **1980–81:** 1942
Apollo 11, **1979:** 1259, 1276
Aponte, Mari C., **1978:** 696; **1979:** 914
Appalachian migrants, **1977:** 1840
Appalachian Regional Commission, **1977:** 1026,
        1031, 2104; **1978:** 687, 711, 1006, 2154;
        1979: 79, 81, 2231
Appalachian Trail, **1978:** 549; **1979:** 1367
Apparel industry, **1977:** 1210
Appeals, Court of, **1980–81:** 45
Appeals, Special Panel on, **1980–81:** 1051
Appeals Review Board, **1978:** 955
Appleby, Tom, **1979:** 270
Applegate, Repr. Douglas, **1979:** 1006, 1640, 1646,
    1648
Applegate, Harry A., **1978:** 890
Applewhaite, Leon B., **1979:** 784, 843
Appointments and Nominations
    ACTION
        Assistant Directors, **1977:** 1243, 1266
        Associate Directors, **1979:** 666, 667; **1977:**
            1243, 1266, 1540, 1568
        Deputy Director, **1977:** 253
        Director, **1977:** 193, 266
        Peace Corps
            Deputy Director, **1979:** 1692, 1706
            Director, **1979:** 551, 554
    Administrative Conference of the United States
        Chairman, **1980–81:** 1147
        Council members, **1978:** 1652; **1979:** 886;
            1980–81: 1146, 2726, 2801
        Vice-Chair, **1980–81:** 1146
    Advisory Commission on Intergovernmental Re-
        lations
        Chairman, **1978:** 422; **1980–81:** 422

Appointments and Nominations — *continued*
    Advisory Commission — *continued*
        Members, **1977:** 549, 1476, 1477, 1563; **1978:**
            748, 1836, 2165; **1979:** 463, 886, 1034,
            1876, 2081; **1980–81:** 104, 273, 1336, 1770,
            3021
        Vice Chairperson, **1978:** 748
    Advisory Committee on Federal Pay, Chairman,
        1978: 823
        Member, **1980–81:** 1399
    Advisory Committee on Housing, Chairman and
        members, **1980–81:** 2559
    Advisory Committee on Small and Minority
        Business Ownership, members, **1980–81:**
        305
    Advisory Committee for Trade Negotiations,
        members, **1977:** 1541; **1978:** 454, 759,
        1030, 2069, 2264; **1979:** 1705; **1980–81:**
        1048, 1447, 2117, 2609, 2832, 3022
    Advisory Council on Historic Preservation
        Members, **1978:** 228, 1060, 1343; **1979:** 1432,
            1704; **1980–81:** 1935
        Vice Chairman, **1980–81:** 1292
    Advisory Panel on Financing Elementary and
        Secondary Education, members, **1979:**
        1524
    African Development Bank, U.S. Governor,
        1979: 1454, 1455; **1977:** 509, 943
    Agency for International Development
        Administrator, **1977:** 337, 372
        Assistant Administrators, **1977:** 739, 746, 804,
            807, 933, 943, 944, 1064, 1068, 1081, 1085,
            1086
        Deputy Administrator, **1977:** 933, 943
    Agriculture Department
        Assistant Secretaries, **1977:** 331, 372, 461, 465,
            495, 505, 510, 535, 557; **1978:** 326, 416;
            1979: 1779, 1824; **1980–81:** 1938
        Commodity Credit Corporation
            Board of Directors, member, **1979:** 110, 179
            Member, **1977:** 1228, 1266
        Deputy Secretary, **1977:** 339, 372, 373; **1979:**
            43, 91
        Federal Grain Inspection Service, Adminis-
            trator, **1977:** 1079, 1085
        General Counsel, **1977:** 1252, 1266; **1979:** 980,
            984
        Inspector General, **1979:** 366, 377
        Rural Telephone Bank, Board of Directors,
            members, **1978:** 506; **1980–81:** 293
        Secretary, **1977:** 9
        Under Secretary, **1978:** 2157; **1979:** 218;
            1980–81: 2453, 2870, 2873
    Air Force Department
        Assistant Secretaries, **1977:** 1031, 1952, 1967;
            1978: 231; **1979:** 1128, 1142, 2271, 2281;
            1980–81: 449, 453
        Secretary, **1977:** 474, 510; **1979:** 1127, 1142

Appointments and Nominations — *continued*
  Air Force Department — *continued*
    Under Secretary, **1977:** 966, 1031; **1979:** 1128, 1142
  Alaska Natural Gas Transportation System, Federal Inspector, **1979:** 1016, 1019
  Ambassadors, U.S.
    Afghanistan, **1978:** 1022, 1034
    Algeria, **1977:** 727, 745
    Ambassadors at Large, **1977:** 17, 252; **1978:** 452, 458, 1704, 1723; **1979:** 42, 91, 364, 377, 1134, 1143, 1221, 1222, 2182, 2189; **1980–81:** 868
    Argentina, **1977:** 1481; **1980–81:** 1710, 1715
    Australia, **1977:** 576, 597, 873, 883
    Austria, **1977:** 1124, 1128; **1980–81:** 191
    Bahamas, **1977:** 1475, 1483
    Bahrain, **1979:** 101, 179; **1980–81:** 1106, 1112
    Bangladesh, **1977:** 1977, 2006; **1978:** 231
    Barbados, **1977:** 1189, 1212; **1979:** 664, 667
    Belgium, **1977:** 577, 597
    Bolivia, **1977:** 1505, 1507; **1980–81:** 287, 293
    Botswana, **1977:** 714, 745; **1979:** 1616, 1679
    Brazil, **1978:** 295, 304
    Bulgaria, **1977:** 1220, 1223; **1979:** 1262, 1293
    Burma, **1977:** 1474, 1483; **1979:** 2066, 2082
    Burundi, **1977:** 1977, 2006; **1978:** 231; **1980–81:** 1025, 1051
    Cameroon, **1977:** 713, 745; **1980–81:** 1107, 1111
    Canada, **1979:** 1616, 1679
    Cape Verde, **1977:** 1398, 1438; **1980–81:** 1411, 1428
    Central African Empire, **1978:** 1562, 1572
    Central African Republic, **1980–81:** 1700
    Chad, **1979:** 1676, 1705
    Chile, **1977:** 1588
    China, People's Republic of, **1979:** 41, 91
      U.S.Liaison Office, Chief, **1977:** 1132, 1163
    Colombia, **1977:** 1646, 1650; **1980–81:** 1710, 1715
    Comoros, **1980–81:** 2752
    Congo, **1979:** 580, 619
    Costa Rica, **1977:** 935, 943; **1980–81:** 900, 932
    Cyprus, **1978:** 295, 304
    Czechoslovakia, **1979:** 383, 402; **1980–81:** 1926, 1947
    Denmark, **1978:** 1008, 1010
    Djibouti, **1980–81:** 1025, 1051
    Dominica, **1979:** 664, 667
    Dominican Republic, **1978:** 567, 641
    Ecuador, **1978:** 1029, 1034
    Egypt, **1979:** 819, 843
    El Salvador, **1977:** 1539, 1568; **1980–81:** 191
    Ethiopia, **1978:** 1023, 1034
    Equatorial Guinea, **1979:** 2147; **1980–81:** 1107, 1111
    Fiji, **1978:** 286, 304

Appointments and Nominations — *continued*
  Ambassadors, U.S. — *continued*
    Fiji, Tonga, and Tuvalu, **1980–81:** 1107, 1111
    Finland, **1977:** 783, 807; **1980–81:** 405, 423
    France, **1977:** 873, 875, 883
    Gabonese Republic, **1978:** 88, 149
    Gambia, **1977:** 1081, 1086; **1978:** 232; **1980–81:** 983, 1014
    German Democratic Republic, **1977:** 1218, 1223; **1980–81:** 1025, 1052
    Ghana, **1979:** 1658, 1680
    Greece, **1977:** 1152, 1163; **1978:** 270, 303
    Grenada, **1977:** 1189, 1212; **1979:** 664, 667
    Guatemala, **1979:** 783, 842
    Guinea, **1977:** 1791, 1796; **1980–81:** 983, 1015
    Guinea-Bissau, **1977:** 1152, 1192; **1980–81:** 1411, 1428
    Guyana, **1977:** 1219, 1223; **1979:** 1617, 1679
    Haiti, **1977:** 1356, 1384; **1980–81:** 1473, 1524
    Honduras, **1977:** 1474, 1483; **1980–81:** 1442, 1470
    Hungary, **1977:** 901, 1140, 1163; **1980–81:** 236, 268
    Iceland, **1978:** 1710, 1724
    India, **1977:** 578, 597
    Indonesia, **1977:** 1811, 1826
    Iran, **1977:** 580, 597; **1979:** 685, 732
    Ireland, **1977:** 1133, 1163
    Israel, **1977:** 579, 597
    Italy, **1977:** 280
    Ivory Coast, **1979:** 1617, 1679
    Jamaica, **1977:** 936, 943; **1979:** 220, 241
    Japan, **1977:** 579, 597
    Jordan, **1978:** 1397, 1407
    Kenya, **1977:** 578, 597; **1980–81:** 843, 893
    Korea, Republic of, **1978:** 1023, 1034
    Kuwait, **1979:** 1446, 1455
    Lebanon, **1977:** 81, 87; **1978:** 1513, 1572
    Lesotho, **1977:** 714, 745; **1979:** 1446, 1455
    Liberia, **1979:** 579, 619
    Luxembourg, **1977:** 873, 875, 883
    Madagascar, **1980–81:** 1577, 1599
    Malawi, **1978:** 1320, 1333; **1980–81:** 1860, 1946
    Malaysia, **1977:** 873, 876, 883; **1980–81:** 1334, 1336
    Maldives, **1977:** 1196, 1212; **1978:** 231; **1979:** 2097, 2107
    Mali, **1979:** 1849, 1883
    Malta, **1977:** 714, 745; **1979:** 215, 241
    Mauritania, **1977:** 1792, 1796; **1980–81:** 1289
    Mauritius, **1978:** 1711, 1724; **1980–81:** 369, 375
    Mexico, **1977:** 589, 943; **1980–81:** 434, 452
    Morocco, **1978:** 1700, 1724; **1979:** 2077, 2082
    Mozambique, **1980–81:** 1699
    Nauru, **1977:** 873, 883; **1978:** 231; **1979:** 46, 91
    Nepal, **1977:** 783, 807; **1980–81:** 843, 893
    Netherlands, **1978:** 1100, 1111

Appointments and Nominations — *continued*
  Ambassadors, U.S. — *continued*
    New Zealand, **1979:** 1040, 1043
    Nicaragua, **1977:** 1219, 1223; **1979:** 686, 733
    Niger, **1979:** 979, 984
    Nigeria, **1979:** 1451, 1519
    Norway, **1977:** 1206, 1213; **1979:** 2217
    Oman, **1978:** 1557, 1572
    Pakistan, **1977:** 581, 597, 807, 964, 1031
    Panama, **1978:** 1512, 1517, 1723
    Papua New Guinea, **1979:** 1228, 1232
    Paraguay, **1977:** 1763, 1795; **1980–81:** 1290
    Peru, **1977:**873, 876, 883; **1980–81:** 1711, 1715
    Philippines, **1977:** 1673, 1700; **1978:** 888, 899
    Poland, **1978:** 87, 149; **1980–81:** 1703
    Portugal, **1977:** 2161; **1978:** 149
    Principe, **1978:** 88, 149
    Qatar, **1977:** 1355, 1384; **1980–81:** 718, 720
    Romania, **1977:** 1673, 1700
    Rwanda, **1979:** 1726, 1785
    Saint Lucia, **1980–81:** 1860, 1947
    Sao Tome, **1978:** 88, 149
    Saudi Arabia, **1977:** 993, 1031
    Senegal, **1977:** 1081, 1086; **1980–81:** 1143, 1246
    Seychelles, **1977:** 578, 597; **1980–81:** 843, 869
    Sierra Leone, **1977:** 986, 1030; **1980–81:** 899, 932
    Singapore, **1978:** 821, 881; **1980–81:** 1834, 1847
    Solomon Islands, **1978:** 1188, 1222; **1979:** 1228, 1232
    Somali Democratic Republic, **1978:** 1562, 1572
    South Africa, **1978:** 745, 750
    Spain, **1978:** 887, 899
    Sri Lanka, **1977:** 1196, 1212; **1979:** 2097, 2107
    Sudan, **1977:** 873, 874, 883; **1980–81:** 843, 893
    Suriname, **1978:** 760, 771; **1980–81:** 1108, 1111
    Swaziland, **1977:** 714, 745; **1979:** 2062, 2081
    Sweden, **1977:** 1356, 1384
    Switzerland, **1977:** 1026, 1031; **1979:** 1618, 1679
    Syria, **1978:** 1252, 1279
    Tanzania, **1979:** 1618, 1679
    Thailand, **1978:** 1030, 1034
    Tobago, **1977:** 886, 943; **1979:** 1156, 1159
    Togo, **1978:** 1451, 1458
    Tonga, **1979:** 1523, 1531
    Trinidad, **1977:** 886, 943; **1979:** 1156, 1159
    Tunisia, **1979:** 101, 179
    Turkey, **1977:** 617, 642; **1979:** 2238
    Tuvalu, **1979:** 1523, 1531
    Uganda, **1980–81:** 629, 720
    Union of Soviet Socialist Republics, **1977:** 715, 745; **1979:** 1284, 1293
    United Arab Emirates, **1979:** 1300, 1319
    United Kingdom, **1977:** 576, 577, 597
    Upper Volta, **1978:** 1109, 1111

Appointments and Nominations — *continued*
  Ambassadors, U.S. — *continued*
    Uruguay, **1977:** 1206, 1213; **1979:** 1132, 1143; **1980–81:** 1334, 1336
    U.S. negotiator for textile matters, **1978:** 1809
    Venezuela, **1978:** 1465, 1471
    Western Samoa, **1979:** 1040, 1043
    Yemen, **1978:** 1266, 1279
    Yugoslavia, **1977:** 873, 874, 883
    Zaire, **1979:** 1848, 1883
    Zambia, **1979:** 1263, 1293
    Zimbabwe, **1980–81:** 717, 720
  American Battle Monuments Commission, members, **1980–81:** 1596; **1978:** 2089
  American Folklife Center, Board of Trustees, members, **1977:** 2036
  American National Red Cross
    Board of Directors, members, **1979:** 376, 1678
    Board of Governors
      Chairman, **1979:** 552
      Members, **1977:** 1665; **1978:** 770, **1980–81:** 1292
  Antigua, Dominica, St. Christopher-Nevis-Anguilla, St. Lucia, and St. Vincent, U.S. Representative, **1977:** 1530
  Antigua, U.S. Special Representative, **1979:** 980
  Appalachian Regional Commission, Alternate Federal Cochairman, **1978:** 687, 711; **1979:** 2231
  Architectural and Transportation Barriers Compliance Board, Chairman and members, **1979:** 2191
  Architectural and Transportation Compliance Board, members, **1980–81:** 2730
  Army Department
    Assistant Secretaries, **1977:** 591, 596, 712, 745, 934, 944; **1979:** 109, 179; **1980–81:** 304
    Chief of Staff, U.S. Army, **1979:** 763
    Secretary, **1977:** 65, 87
    Under Secretary, **1977:** 1174, 1212; **1980–81:** 98
  Asian Development Bank
    U.S. Director, **1977:** 795, 807
    U.S. Governors, **1977:** 509, 943; **1979:** 1454, 1455
  Auto Industry Committee, Executive Committee, members, **1980–81:** 1669
  Bilateral air services agreement, U.S.-United Kingdom, President's Special Representative for negotiations, **1977:** 256
  Board of Foreign Scholarships, members, **1978:** 408, 2264; **1980–81:** 272, 2608
  Board for International Broadcasting
    Chairman, **1977:** 1073, 1085; **1980–81:** 1376
    Members, **1977:** 2024, 2037; **1978:** 231; **1979:** 1659, 1680; **1980–81:** 218, 1376, 1847, 2870, 2872

Appointments and Nominations — *continued*
  Board for International Food and Agricultural
    Development
    Chairman and members, **1980–81:** 323
    Members, **1978:** 218, 1652; **1979:** 437
  California Debris Commission, members, **1977:**
    1553, 1569 **1978:** 1639, 1669; **1979:** 43, 91;
    1980–81: 237
  Canada-U.S. maritime boundary negotiations,
    President's Special Representative, **1977:**
    1362
  Canadian River Commission, Federal Represen-
    tative and Chairman, **1980–81:** 2747
  Carter-Mondale Presidential Committee, Inc.,
    campaign staff director, **1979:** 1967
  Central Intelligence Agency
    Deputy Director, **1977:** 2161; **1978:** 150
    Director, **1977:** 91, 148
  Chief of Protocol, **1977:** 148; **1978:** 1458
  Civil Aeronautics Board
    Chairman, **1977:** 806, 933, 944; **1978:** 1850;
      1979: 2176, 2188; **1980–81:** 2841
    Members, **1977:** 1218, 1223; **1978:** 1270, 1279,
      1511, 1517; **1979:** 1395, 1398, 2176, 2188;
      1980–81: 1419, 1428
    Vice Chairman, **1977:** 1124, 1128
  Civil Rights Commission, Vice Chairman, **1980–
    81:** 892
  Coastal Plains Regional Commission, Federal
    Cochairman, **1977:** 1070, 1085
  Commerce Department
    Assistant Secretaries, **1977:** 229, 248, 252, 253,
      280, 381, 465, 554, 596, 618, 642, 2025,
      2037; **1978:** 554, 571; **1979:** 1036, 1044;
      1980–81: 48, 255, 374, 522
    Associate Deputy Secretary, **1980–81:** 25
    Bureau of the Census, Director, **1977:** 617,
      642; **1979:** 981, 1019
    General Counsel, **1977:** 338, 373; **1979:** 2231
    Inspector General, **1979:** 398, 402
    National Bureau of Standards, Director, **1977:**
      2001, 2006; **1978:** 231
    National Oceanic and Atmospheric Admin-
      istration
      Administrator, **1977:** 1196, 1213
      Associate Administrator, **1978:** 576, 641
      Commissioned Officers Corps, Director,
        1980–81: 2746, 2782
      Deputy Administrator, **1978:** 285, 304
      National Ocean Survey, Director, **1980–81:**
        1432, 1470
    Patent and Trademark Office
      Assistant Commissioner, **1979:** 196, 218;
        1980–81: 237
      Commissioner, **1979:** 1938, 2081
    Secretary, **1977:** 9; **1979:** 2135, 2140, 2249
    Under Secretaries, **1977:** 465; **1979:** 782, 842;
      1980–81: 188, 654

Appointments and Nominations — *continued*
  Commerce Department — *continued*
    United States Fire Administration, Adminis-
      trator, **1979:** 22, 91
  Commission on Civil Rights
    Members, **1980–81:** 605, 608, 968
    Staff Director, **1978:** 2219; **1979:** 91
  Commission on Executive, Legislative, and Ju-
    dicial Salaries, Chairman and members,
    1980–81: 1412
  Commission on Fine Arts, Chairman and mem-
    bers, **1980–81:** 2701
  Commission on Presidential Scholars, members,
    1978: 696; **1979:** 598, 1034; **1980–81:** 606,
    774, 1444
  Commission on Proposals for the National
    Academy of Peace and Conflict Resolu-
    tion, members, **1979:** 2195
  Commission on the Review of the Federal Im-
    pact Aid Program, members, **1979:** 1439
  Commission on Security and Cooperation in
    Europe, member, **1980–81:** 1292
  Commission on Wartime Relocation and In-
    ternment of Civilians, members, **1980–81:**
    2870
  Committee on Disarmament, U.S. Representa-
    tive, **1980–81:** 204
  Committee for the Preservation of the White
    House, members, **1977:** 2182; **1978:** 1500;
    1979: 782; **1980–81:** 1047, 1935
  Committee for Purchase from the Blind and
    Other Severely Handicapped, members,
    1978: 408, 770, 2069; **1979:** 163, 437;
    1980–81: 37, 521, 931, 1292
  Committee on Selection of the Director of the
    Federal Bureau of Investigation, Chair-
    man and members, **1977:** 182
  Committee on Selection of Federal Judicial
    Officers, members, **1977:** 1528
  Commodity Credit Corporation, Board of Di-
    rectors, members, **1977:** 368, 373, 461,
    465, 495, 505, 510, 535, 557, 745; **1978:**
    457, 458
  Commodity Futures Trading Commission
    Chairman, **1979:** 41, 93
    Commissioner, **1978:** 886, 899; **1979:** 598, 619
  Communications Satellite Corporation, Board of
    Directors, members, **1978:** 2146; **1979:** 91,
    271, 294; **1980–81:** 515, 894, 1220, 1246,
    2870, 2873
  Community Services Administration
    Assistant Directors, **1977:** 1262, 1263, 1267,
      1439, 1458; **1980–81:** 979, 1015, 1423,
      1469, 1653, 1715, 2332, 2726, 2727, 2870,
      2873
    Deputy Director, **1977:** 1053, 1059
    Director, **1977:** 86, 564, 596; **1980–81:** 769,
      1015

Appointments and Nominations — *continued*
  Community Services Admin. — *continued*
    General Counsel, **1977:** 1458
    Inspector General, **1979:** 1042, 1044
  Comprehensive Test Ban Negotiations, U.S.
    Representative, rank of Ambassador,
    1979: 215, 1129, 1143
  Conference of the Committee on Disarmament,
    U.S. Representative, **1977:** 879, 883
  Conference on Security and Cooperation in
    Europe
    U.S. delegation, **1977:** 994, 1031, 1085
      Chairman and Cochairman, **1980–81:** 848
    U.S. Representative, **1977:** 1541, 1568
  Consultative Group on U.S.-Japan Economic
    Relations, Cochairmen, **1979:** 1165
  Consumer Affairs Council, Chairperson, **1979:**
    1766
  Consumer Product Safety Commission
    Chairman, **1978:** 1208
    Commissioners, **1977:** 1945, 1966; **1978:** 84,
      149, 1666, 1670; **1979:** 1041, 1044
    Member, **1978:** 1666, 1670
  Copyright Royalty Tribunal, Commissioners,
    1977: 1666, 1667, 1700, 1755
  Corporation for Public Broadcasting, Board of
    Directors, members, **1977:** 1713, 1755,
    1817, 1826; **1978:** 1426, 1458, 1744, 1772;
    1979: 46, 91, 435, 441, 1001, 1019; **1980–
    81:** 1467, 1524, 2429, 2727, 2859, 2870,
    2873
  Council of Economic Advisers
    Chairman, **1977:** 10
    Members, **1977:** 372, 373; **1979:** 599, 619;
      1980–81: 1148, 1151
  Council on Environmental Quality
    Chairman, **1979:** 1353
    Members, **1977:** 229, 253, 332, 372, 885, 943;
      1978: 1270, 1279; **1979:** 2077, 2082
  Council on Wage and Price Stability
    Chairman, **1978:** 1849 1880; **1980–81:** 2726
    Chairman and members, **1977:** 712, 1437
    Director, **1977:** 1220, 1223; **1979:** 1333, 1604
    Members and adviser-members, **1980–81:** 967
  Cyprus, President's personal emissary, **1977:** 77
  Defense Department
    Assistant Secretaries, **1977:** 151, 195, 246, 247,
      253, 549, 558, 706, 707, 745; **1980–81:**
      1093, 1111
    Defense Research and Engineering, Director,
      1977: 368, 465
    Deputy Assistant Secretary, **1977:** 1823, 1931
    Deputy Secretary, **1977:** 31; **1979:** 1290, 1319
    General Counsel, **1977:** 549, 558; **1979:** 2165,
      2188
    Secretary, **1977:** 9
    Under Secretary, **1977:** 1824, 1931; **1978:**
      1265, 1279; **1979:** 1774, 1786

Appointments and Nominations — *continued*
  Delaware River Basin Commission
    Alternate Federal member, **1977:** 2080
    Member, **1977:** 251
  District of Columbia
    Commission on Judicial Disabilities and Ten-
      ure, member, **1980–81:** 392
    Court of Appeals, Associate Judge, **1977:** 940,
      944; **1979:** 957
    Judicial Nominating Commission, member,
      1980–81: 1292
    Law Revision Commission, member, **1979:**
      2065; **1980–81:** 521
    Superior Court, Associate Judges, **1977:** 465,
      1438, 1439; **1978:** 1533, 1572; **1979:** 46,
      91, 665, 667, 980, 984, 1624, 2117; **1980–
      81:** 458, 493, 1823, 1824, 1847, 2871, 2872
    U.S. marshal, **1977:** 707
  Education Department
    Assistant Secretaries, **1980–81:** 203, 204, 219,
      425, 426, 608, 751, 759, 768, 775, 840, 841,
      967, 1015, 1052
    Deputy Under Secretaries, **1980–81:** 493
    General Counsel, **1980–81:** 315
    Inspector General, **1980–81:** 841, 1096, 1112
    National Institute of Education
      Deputy Director, **1980–81:** 949
      Director, **1980–81:** 651, 825
    National Council on Educational Research,
      members, **1980–81:** 96, 508, 522, 1335,
      1336, 2752, 2870, 2872, 2873
    Secretary, **1979:** 2063, 2139
    Under Secretaries, **1980–81:** 426, 522
  Emergency board in railway labor dispute, mem-
    bers, **1978:** 1663; **1979:** 819, 1697, 2247;
    1980–81: 684
  Endangered Species Committee, members, **1979:**
    23, 376
  Energy Department
    Administration, Director of, **1977:** 1585
    Assistant Secretaries, **1977:** 1584, 1585, 1613,
      1646, 1650, 2062, 2077; **1978:** 218, 230–
      232, 884, 898, 1268, 1279; **1979:** 1652–
      1654, 1883, 2064, 2065, 2107, 2183, 2187,
      2207
    Controller, **1977:** 1585
    Deputy Assistant Secretaries, **1977:** 1585, 1586
    Deputy Inspector General, **1978:** 1560, 1572
    Deputy Secretary, **1977:** 1584, 1613; **1979:**
      1653, 1680; **1980–81:** 2841, 2870, 2873
    Economic Regulatory Administration, Ad-
      ministrator, **1977:** 1584, 1613; **1979:** 1654,
      2044
    Energy Information Administration, Admin-
      istrator, **1977:** 2047, 2050
    Energy Research, Office of, Director, **1977:**
      1585, 1613; **1979:** 1655, 2044
    Executive Secretariat, Director, **1977:** 1586

Appointments and Nominations — *continued*
  Energy Department — *continued*
    Federal Energy Regulatory Commission
      Acting Chairman, **1980–81:** 2807
      Chairman and member, **1979:** 1879, 1977
      Member, **1980–81:** 813, 1246
    General Counsel, **1977:** 1646, 1650; **1978:** 231
    Inspector General, **1978:** 760, 771
    Military Liaison Committee, Chairman, **1978:** 1090, 1111
    Office of Minority Economic Impact, Director, **1979:** 1040, 1044
    Procurement and Contracts Management, Director, **1977:** 1586
    Secretary, **1977:** 1412, 1438; **1979:** 1290, 1319
    Special Assistant, **1977:** 1585
    Under Secretary, **1977:** 1584, 1613; **1979:** 955, 983
  Energy-Expo '82, U.S. Commissioner General, **1980–81:** 1277, 1292
  Environmental Protection Agency
    Administrator, **1977:** 176, 195; **1980–81:** 1975, 2070
    Assistant Administrators, **1977:** 1051, 1059, 1175, 1212, 1531, 1534, 1975, 2006; **1978:** 231; **1979:** 1726, 1785; **1980–81:** 1975, 2070
    Deputy Administrator, **1977:** 176, 195
    Inspector General, **1979:** 1691, 1706
  Equal Employment Opportunity Commission
    Chairman, **1977:** 885
    General Counsel, **1979:** 1157, 1159
    Members, **1977:** 885, 943; **1978:** 1510, 1517, 1539, 1572; **1979:** 1259, 1293; **1980–81:** 1125, 1150
    Vice Chairman, **1977:** 1473; **1979:** 1259
  European Communities, U.S. Representative, **1979:** 1821, 1824
  Executive Committee on Reorganization, members, **1977:** 1052
  Executive Office of the President
    Office of Administration, Director, **1977:** 2182
  Export-Import Bank of the United States
    Board of Directors, members, **1977:** 1751, 1755, 1975, 2006
    First Vice President, **1977:** 2128, 2130; **1978:** 150
    President, **1977:** 536, 557
  Farmers Home Administration
    Administrator, **1977:** 879, 943
  Federal Aviation Administration
    Administrator, **1977:** 536, 537, 557
    Deputy Administrator, **1977:** 557
  Federal Bureau of Investigation, Director, **1977:** 1478, 1479, 1483, 1701; **1978:** 150
  Federal Communications Commission, members, **1977:** 1580, 1612, 1793, 1826; **1978:** 1719, 1724; **1979:** 46, 91, 1021, 1043

Appointments and Nominations — *continued*
  Federal Council on the Aging
    Chairman, **1977:** 1066, 1085
    Members, **1978:** 702, 711, 1279; **1979:** 1682, 1706; **1980–81:** 816, 826, 1051, 1419, 1428
  Federal Council on the Arts and Humanities, Chairman, **1977:** 1825
  Federal Deposit Insurance Corporation, Board of Directors, members, **1977:** 1974, 2006; **1978:** 230, 2058; **1979:** 91
  Federal Election Commission, members, **1977:** 1665, 1700, 1824, 1931; **1978:** 703, 750, 1418, 1458, 1744, 1773, 1851; **1979:** 45, 46, 90, 91, 757, 788; **1980–81:** 2856, 2870, 2873
  Federal Emergency Management Agency
    Acting Associate Director, **1979:** 599
    Acting Director, **1979:** 567
    Associate Directors, **1979:** 1601, 1604, 1879, 1977, 2091, 2107, 2127, 2139
    Director, **1979:** 781
  Federal Energy Administration
    Administrator, **1977:** 56, 87
    Assistant Administrators, **1977:** 590, 597, 939, 944, 1250, 1266
    Deputy Administrator, **1977:** 547, 558
  Federal Energy Regulatory Commission, members, **1977:** 1585, 1613, 1647, 1650, 1676, 1701
  Federal Farm Credit Administration
    Farm Credit Board, members, **1977:** 1629, 1650; **1978:** 919, 935; **1979:** 1418, 1423; **1980–81:** 1291
  Federal Highway Administration, Administrator, **1977:** 548, 558
  Federal Home Loan Bank Board
    Chairman, **1977:** 1153, 1163; **1979:** 1336, 1531; **1980–81:** 2007
    Members, **1978:** 703, 711; **1979:** 981, 984, 1336, 1531, 2216; **1980–81:** 268
  Federal Labor Relations Authority
    General Counsel, **1979:** 528, 554
    Members, **1979:** 24, 46, 90, 784, 843; **1980–81:** 468, 493
  Federal Maritime Commission
    Chairman, **1977:** 1437
    Commissioners, **1977:** 1358, 1384, 1683, 1701; **1978:** 299, 329, 1211, 1222; **1979:** 1395, 1398 **1980–81:** 428, 452
  Federal Mediation and Conciliation Service, Director, **1977:** 616, 642
    Federal Service Impasses Panel, members, **1978:** 411
  Federal Mine Safety and Health Review Commission
    Chairman, **1980–81:** 2107
    Members, **1978:** 971, 1010, 1270, 1279, 1343, 1346; **1980–81:** 1654, 1715

Appointments and Nominations — *continued*
  Federal National Mortgage Association
    Board of Directors, members, **1977:** 706, 934;
      1978: 920; **1979:** 931
    Members, **1977:** 934
  Federal Power Commission
    Chairman, **1977:** 1250, 1436
    Members, **1977:** 1381, 1384
  Federal Prison Insustries, Inc., Board of Direc-
    tors, members, **1979:** 1961; **1980–81:** 452
  Federal Railroad Administration, Administrator,
    1977: 740, 746
  Federal Regional Councils, Chairpersons, **1977:**
    1816; **1979:** 269
  Federal Reserve System
    Board of Directors, member, **1980–81:** 421,
      522, 523
    Board of Governors
      Chairman, **1977:** 2183; **1979:** 1300, 1320
      Members, **1978:** 230, 1478, 1485; **1979:** 663,
        664, 899, 1044, 1320
      Vice Chairman, **1979:** 1043, 1044
  Federal Service Impasses Panel, members,
    1980–81: 83
  Federal-State Land Use Planning Commission
    for Alaska, member, **1977:** 1072, 1085
  Federal Trade Commission
    Chairman, **1977:** 486, 510
    Commissioner, **1979:** 1394, 1397; **1980–81:**
      1066, 1111
    Member, **1978:** 971, 1010
  Fish and wildlife matters, international confer-
    ences, U.S. Representative, **1977:** 1220,
    1223
  Foreign Claims Settlement Commission of the
    United States, members, **1978:** 2184;
    1980–81: 534, 564, 1595, 1599, 1926, 1947,
    2857, 2870, 2873
  Four Corners Regional Commission, Federal
    Cochairman, **1977:** 1070, 1085; **1980–81:**
    372, 453
  General Services Administration
    Administrator, **1977:** 589, 596; **1979:** 458, 619
    Inspector General, **1979:** 198, 378
  Geneva Conference on Kampuchean Relief,
    U.S. delegation head, **1980–81:** 933
  Government National Mortgage Association,
    President, **1977:** 591, 596
  Government Printing Office, Public Printer,
    1977: 1676; **1980–81:** 1672, 1715
  Government Red Cross Programs, Associate
    Director, **1980–81:** 1292
  Great Lakes Basin Commission, Chairman,
    1978: 408
  Great Lakes Fishery Commission, U.S. Section,
    Commissioner,
  Greece, President's personal emissary, **1977:** 77
    1978: 1986

Appointments and Nominations — *continued*
  Harry S Truman Scholarship Foundation, Board
    of Trustess, members, **1977:** 2101, 2130;
    1978: 88, 232, 596, 641
  Health, Education, and Welfare Department
    Aging, Commissioner on, **1977:** 2082, 2089;
      1978: 231
    Alcohol, Drug Abuse, and Mental Health
      Administration, Administrator, **1977:**
      1779, 1796
    Assistant Secretaries, **1977:** 252, 253, 372, 373,
      465, 1080, 1085; **1979:** 339, 377, 1157,
      1159, 1319, 1775, 1786, 1820, 1824
    Children's Bureau, Chief, **1977:** 1139, 1163;
      1979: 2184, 2207
    Deputy Inspector General, **1977:** 1195, 1213;
      1979: 616, 667
    Education, Commissioner of, **1979:** 2276, 2281
    General Counsel, **1977:** 369, 373; **1979:** 1000,
      1019, 1960, 1977
    Inspector General, **1977:** 230, 252
    National Cancer Institute, Director, **1977:**
      1378
    National Institute of Education
      Deputy Director, **1977:** 1780
      Director, **1977:** 1253, 1266
    Office of Consumer Affairs
      Deputy Director, **1978:** 2280
      Director, **1978:** 1418
    Office of Education, Commissioner, **1977:** 382,
      465
    Public Health Service, Medical Director, Reg-
      ular Corps and Surgeon General, **1977:**
      1080, 1085
    Public Health Service, National Library of
      Medicine, Board of Regents, members,
      1978: 275, 303
    Rehabilitation Services Administration, Com-
      missioner, **1977:** 1644, 1650
    Secretary, **1977:** 10; **1979:** 1270, 1293
    Social Security, Commissioner of, **1978:** 1468,
      1471
    Under Secretary, **1977:** 252; **1979:** 1851, 1883
  Health and Human Services Department
    Assistant Secretaries, **1980–81:** 316, 334
    Education, Commissioner of, **1980–81:** 25
    Inspector General, **1980–81:** 1494, 1524
    Social Security Administration, Commission-
      er, **1980–81:** 12, 25, 217, 218
  Housing and Urban Development Department
    Assistant Secretaries, **1977:** 366, 367, 373, 470,
      471, 506, 509, 510, 712, 745; **1979:** 42, 61,
      93; **1980–81:** 192
    Federal Insurance Administration, Adminis-
      trator, **1978:** 298, 329
    Federal National Mortgage Association
      Board of Directors, members, **1977:** 1264;
      1980–81: 911

Appointments and Nominations — *continued*
  Housing and Urban Development — *continued*
    President, **1979:** 1677, 1705
    General Counsel, **1977:** 576, 596; **1979:** 1221, 1223
    Inspector General, **1979:** 365, 377
    New Community Development Corporation, Board of Directors, member, **1980–81:** 752, 775
    Secretary, **1977:** 10; **1979:** 1315, 1320, 1397
    Under Secretary, **1977:** 275, 280; **1979:** 2078, 2249
  Immigration and Naturalization Service, Commissioner, **1977:** 590, 597
  India, President's Personal Emissary to, **1980–81:** 188
  Indian claims dispute in Maine, President's special representative to coordinate negotiations, **1977:** 363
  Institute of Museum Services, Director, **1977:** 2072, 2077
  Intelligence Oversight Board, Chairman and members, **1977:** 801
  Interagency Committee on Emergency Medical Services, members, **1978:** 1187; **1979:** 2158; **1980–81:** 1936
  Interagency Committee on Women's Business Enterprise, Chairperson, **1980–81:** 1569
  Inter-American Council for Education, Science, and Culture, U.S. delegation head, rank of Ambassador, **1978:** 1516; **1979:** 1334
  Inter-American Development Bank
    U.S. Alternate Governor, **1977:** 943
    U.S. Executive Director and Alternate U.S. Executive Director, **1977:** 796, 807
    U.S. Governor, **1977:** 509; **1979:** 1454, 1455
  Inter-American Economic and Social Council, U.S. delegation head, rank of Ambassador, **1978:** 1516; **1979:** 1334
  Inter-American Foundation, Board of Directors, members, **1978:** 884, 899, 1072; **1980–81:** 522, 1446, 1469, 1524
  Inter-American Tropical Tuna Commission, Commissioners, **1977:** 1764
  Intergovernmental Advisory Council on Education, members, **1980–81:** 1432
  Interior Department
    Assistant Secretaries, **1977:** 273, 280, 535, 557, 804, 807, 1239, 1266; **1978:** 1666, 1670; **1979:** 46, 91; **1980–81:** 1129, 1151, 1418, 1428, 2859, 2870, 2873
    Bureau of Indian Affairs, Commissioner, **1979:** 1775, 1786
    Bureau of Land Management, Director, **1978:** 223, 232
    Bureau of Mines, Director, **1978:** 1269, 1279; **1980–81:** 1065, 1111

Appointments and Nominations — *continued*
  Interior Department — *continued*
    Bureau of Reclamation, Commissioner, **1977:** 565
    Geological Survey, Director, **1978:** 407, 416
    Inspector General, **1979:** 365, 377
    Office of Surface Mining Reclamation and Enforcement, Director, **1977:** 1810, 1826
    Secretary, **1977:** 9
    Solicitor, **1977:** 227, 252; **1980–81:** 718, 775
    Under Secretary, **1977:** 226, 252
  Internal Revenue Service, Commissioner, **1977:** 470, 509
  International Atomic Energy Agency
    General Conference, U.S. Representative and Alternate Representatives, **1977:** 1501, 1502, 1507, 1565, 1569; **1978:** 1426, 1458; **1980–81:** 1572, 1848, 1859
    U.S. Deputy Representative, **1978:** 317, 329
    U.S. Representative, **1977:** 1182, 1212
    U.S. Representative and Alternate Representatives, **1979:** 2148
  International Bank for Reconstruction and Development
    U.S. Alternate Executive Director, **1977:** 1377, 1384; **1979:** 2269, 2281
    U.S. Alternate Governor, **1977:** 943
    U.S. Executive Director, **1977:** 1067, 1085; **1979:** 2269, 2281
    U.S. Governor, **1977:** 509; **1979:** 1455
  International Boundary Commission
    United States and Canada, U.S. Commissioner, **1977:** 1407
  International Centre for the Settlement of Investment Disputes, Panel of Conciliators and Panel of Arbitrators, members, **1980–81:** 2731
  International Civil Aviation Organization
    Alternate U.S. Representative, **1979:** 1451
    U.S. Representative on the Council, **1977:** 1779, 1795
  International Commission for the Conservation of Atlantic Tunas, U.S. Commissioner, **1979:** 436
  International Communication Agency
    Associate Directors, **1978:** 434, 457, 1178, 1222, 1400, 1407; **1980–81:** 236, 1845, 1848
    Deputy Director, **1978:** 277, 303
    Director, **1978:** 277, 303
  International Joint Commission—United States and Canada, U.S. Commissioner, **1978:** 681, 711, 761, 803; **1979:** 1395, 1398
  International Labor Office, Governing Body, U.S. Representative, **1980–81:** 930
  International Mediation Group for Nicaragua, U.S. Representative, **1978:** 1694

Appointments and Nominations — *continued*
  International Monetary Fund
    U.S. Alternate Executive Director, **1977:** 1025,
      1031; **1979:** 446, 468
    U.S. Alternate Governor, **1978:** 1515, 1517;
      1979: 1455, 1518
    U.S. Executive Director, **1977:** 967, 1030
    U.S. Governor, **1977:** 509; **1979:** 1454, 1455
  International North Pacific Fisheries Commis-
    sion, U.S. Section, Commissioners, **1979:**
    1001; **1980–81:** 2774
  International Pacific Salmon Fisheries Commis-
    sion, member, **1977:** 1485
  International Whaling Commission
    Deputy U.S. Commissioner, **1977:** 1532
    U.S. Commissioner, **1977:** 1135, 2077
  Interstate Commerce Commission
    Chairman, **1977:** 571; **1979:** 1880
    Members, **1979:** 871, 886, 899, 900, 1702, 2249
  Interstate Commission on the Potomac River
    Basin, member, **1978:** 85, 325; **1979:** 399
  John F. Kennedy Center for the Performing Arts
    Advisory Committee on the Arts, members,
      1979: 464, 2015; **1980–81:** 273, 304
    Board of Trustees, members, **1979:** 23; **1980–
      81:** 2871, 3023
  Joint Chiefs of Staff
    Chairman, **1978:** 684; **1980–81:** 1014, 1015
    Chief of Naval Operations, **1978:** 684
    Chief of Staff of the Air Force, **1978:** 684
  Justice Department
    Assistant Attorneys General, **1977:** 155, 195,
      803, 807, 1054, 1059, 1217, 1222; **1978:**
      893, 899; **1979:** 975, 976, 983, 984, 2038,
      2044, 2175, 2188
    Associate Attorney General, **1977:** 1821, 1826;
      1979: 2038, 2044
    Attorney General, **1977:** 9; **1979:** 1272, 1293
    Bureau of Statistics, Director, **1980–81:** 1290
    Community Relations Service, Director, **1978:**
      784, 803
    Deputy Attorneys General, **1977:** 336, 373,
      2083, 2090; **1978:** 231; **1979:** 2148
    Drug Enforcement Administration, Deputy
      Administrator, **1979:** 1961, 1977
    Immigration and Naturalization Service,
      Commissioners, **1980–81:** 1149, 1292
    Law Enforcement Assistance Administration
      Administrator, **1979:** 268, 294, 2207; **1980–
        81:** 288, 293
      Administrator and Deputy Administrators,
        1978: 1538, 1572
      Assistant Administrator, **1977:** 1079, 1085;
        1979: 2183
    National Institute of Justice, Advisory Board,
      members, **1980–81:** 2612, 2701, 2875
    Office of Justice Assistance, Research, and
      Statistics, **1980–81:** 288, 293

Appointments and Nominations — *continued*
  Justice Department — *continued*
    Solicitor General, **1977:** 155, 195
  Kiribati, U.S. Minister to, **1980–81:** 1107, 1111
  Labor Department
    Assistant Secretaries, **1977:** 228, 252, 364, 365,
      373; **1978:** 218, 230; **1979:** 1259, 1293
    Bureau of Labor Statistics, Commissioner,
      1977: 1665, 1700; **1979:** 527, 554
    Deputy Assistant Secretary, **1977:** 1065, 1085;
      1979: 339, 377
    Inspector General, **1979:** 365, 377
    Secretary, **1977:** 10
    Solicitor, **1977:** 227, 252
    Under Secretary, **1977:** 227, 252; **1979:** 1836,
      1883
    Wage and Hour Administration, Administra-
      tor, **1977:** 965, 1031
    Women's Bureau, Director, **1977:** 366, 373
  Lake Tahoe Regional Planning Agency, U.S.
    Government Representative, **1980–81:**
    1946
  Law of the Sea Conference
    President's Special Representative, **1977:** 17,
      252
    U.S. Deputy Special Representative, **1977:**
      1667, 1795, 1826
  Legal Services Corporation, Board of Directors,
    members, **1977:** 2101, 2130; **1978:** 88, 232,
    1753, 1772; **1979:** 46, 91, 92; **1980–81:**
    1149
  Library of Congress, Trust Fund Board, mem-
    bers, **1980–81:** 1047, 2883
  Maine Indian land claims dispute, working
    group, **1977:** 1759
  Marine Mammal Commission, members, **1979:**
    2116
  Merit Systems Protection Board
    Acting Special Counsel, **1980–81:** 62
    Chairman, **1979:** 46, 90
    Members, **1979:** 2, 46, 90, 1019, 1302, 1319
    Special Counsel, **1979:** 46; **1980–81:** 62, 374
  Middle East peace negotiations
    Deputy to the Personal Representative, **1979:**
      852
    Personal Representatives of the President,
      1979: 687, 2105
    U.S. Mission chief, **1979:** 1706
  Mississippi River Commission
    Members, **1977:** 1542, 1569; **1978:** 511, 898,
      1279; **1979:** 44, 92, 1129, 1143; **1980–81:**
      1432, 1470, 2070, 2916, 3050
    President, **1977:** 1375, 1384, 3050
  Missouri River Basin Commission, Chairman,
    1978: 1837
  Motor Carrier Ratemaking Study Commission,
    members, **1980–81:** 2731

Appointments and Nominations — *continued*
  Mutual and Balanced Force Reductions
    Minister, **1978**: 1516
    U.S. Representative, **1979**: 110, 179
  National Advisory Committee for Juvenile Justice and Delinquency Prevention, members, **1977**: 1713; **1978**: 1193; **1980–81**: 1097, 3022
  National Advisory Committee on Oceans and Atmosphere
    Chairman, **1979**: 1628
    Members, **1978**: 217; **1979**: 2116; **1980–81**: 1023, 2242
    Vice Chairman, **1979**: 2187
  National Advisory Committee for Women, members, **1978**: 1134; **1980–81**: 2613, 2882
  National Advisory Community Investment Board, members, **1979**: 1815
  National Advisory Council on Adult Education, members, **1979**: 1524; **1980–81**: 844, 2558, 3022
  National Advisory Council on Economic Opportunity
    Chairman, **1977**: 1477
    Members, **1978**: 709; **1979**: 1447, 1727; **1980–81**: 2609
  National Advisory Council on the Education of Disadvantaged Children
    Chairman and members, **1979**: 1727
    Members, **1980–81**: 257, 1839
  National Advisory Council on Extension and Continuing Education, members, **1978**: 913; **1979**: 1023; **1980–81**: 1669, 2817
  National Advisory Council on Indian Education, members, **1978**: 1418; **1979**: 446, 932; **1980–81**: 849, 2883
  National Advisory Council on Vocational Education, members, **1979**: 1447; **1980–81**: 2817
  National Advisory Council on Women's Educational Programs, members, **1978**: 1086, 1111; **1979**: 339, 377, 2039, 2044; **1980–81**: 508, 1023, 1051, 1569
  National Aeronautics and Space Administration
    Administrator, **1977**: 965, 1031
    Inspector General, **1979**: 398, 402
  National Alcohol Fuels Commission, members, **1979**: 1007
  National Cancer Advisory Board, Chairman and members, **1979**: 686; **1980–81**: 911
  National Cancer Institute, Director, **1980–81**: 1332
  National Capital Planning Commission, member, **1979**: 687; **1980–81**: 1412
  National Commission on Air Quality, members, **1978**: 762, 1178; **1979**: 1353; **1980–81**: 508

Appointments and Nominations — *continued*
  National Commission on Alcoholism and Other Alcohol-Related Problems, members, **1980–81**: 2609, 2801
  National Commission for Employment Policy
    Chairman and members, **1980–81**: 1981
    Members, **1979**: 947
  National Commission on Employment and Unemployment Statistics, members, **1977**: 1175, 1212; **1978**: 52, 150
  National Commission on the International Year of the Child
    Chairman, **1978**: 815
    Member, **1979**: 229; **1978**: 1190
  National Commission on Libraries and Information Science
    Chairman and members, **1980–81**: 1445, 1470
    Members, **1978**: 919, 935, 1454, 1458; **1979**: 196, 218, 2277, 2281
  National Commission for Manpower Policy, members, **1978**: 697
    President, **1977**: 1375, 1384
  National Commission on Neighborhoods
    Chairman **1977**: 1905
    Members, **1977**: 2153
  National Commission on the Observance of International Women's Year, 1975, members and presiding officer, **1977**: 525, 2025
  National Commission for the Review of Antitrust Laws and Procedures
    Business advisory panel, members, **1978**: 1878
    Members, **1978**: 1139
  National Commission on Social Security, members, **1978**: 1720, 1772; **1979**: 23, 45, 46, 90, 92
  National Commission on Student Financial Assistance, Chairman and members, **1980–81**: 2751, 2812
  National Commission on Unemployment Compensation, members, **1978**: 257, 1051
  National Consumer Cooperative Bank, Board of Directors
    Members, **1979**: 1220, 1223, 1317, 1319; **1980–81**: 605, 608, 844, 893, 2614
    Office of Self-Help Development and Technical Assistance, Director, **1980–81**: 1419, 1428
  National Corporation for Housing Partnerships, Board of Directors, members, **1978**: 1500, 1506; **1980–81**: 1048, 1111
  National Council on the Arts, members, **1977**: 2024, 2037; **1978**: 252, 277; **1979**: 45, 92, 435, 441; **1980–81**: 237, 268
  National Council on Educational Research
    Chairman, **1979**: 1820
    Members, **1978**: 54, 149, 895, 935; **1979**: 44, 91

Appointments and Nominations — *continued*
  National Council on the Handicapped
    Chairman and member, **1979:** 2089
    Members, **1980–81:** 812, 826, 1596, 1599
  National Council on the Humanities, members,
    1978: 1706, 1724, 2049; **1979:** 45, 46, 90,
    91, 231, 241; **1980–81:** 264, 269
  National Credit Union Administration
    Administrator, **1977:** 1376, 1384
    National Credit Union Board
      Chairman, **1977:** 1375, 1384
      Members, **1979:** 397, 402, 1041, 1044, 1299,
        1319
  National Endowment for the Arts, Chairman,
    1977: 1946, 1966
  National Endowment for the Arts, National
    Council on the Arts, member, **1980–81:**
    1439, 1470, 1927, 1947
  National Endowment for the Humanities
    Chairman, **1977:** 1398, 1438
    Members, **1980–81:** 1332, 1337
  National Health Resources Advisory Council,
    member, **1978:** 325
  National Highway Safety Advisory Committee,
    members, **1977:** 2028; **1978:** 1467, 1564;
    1979: 1775; **1980–81:** 1845, 2107, 2815,
    3022
  National Highway Traffic Safety Administra-
    tion, Administrator, **1977:** 461, 465
  National Historical Publications and Records
    Commission, members, **1978:** 2274;
    1980–81: 1424
  National Institute of Building Sciences,
    Board of Directors, members, **1979:** 44, 92,
      607, 619; **1980–81:** 533, 564
    Members, **1980–81:** 1595, 1599
  National Institute of Handicapped Research,
    Director, **1979:** 2089, 2106
  National Labor Relations Board
    Acting General Counsel, **1979:** 1976
    Chairman, **1977:** 618
    General Counsel, **1979:** 2166, 2300; **1980–81:**
      217, 218
    Members, **1977:** 1666, 1700, 1752, 1755; **1978:**
      1468, 1471; **1980–81:** 1026, 1052, 1494,
      1524, 2453, 2726, 2727, 2870, 2873
  National Library of Medicine, members, **1978:**
    275
  National Mediation Board, members, **1977:**
    1293, 1307; **1978:** 1701, 1724; **1979:** 1299,
    1319; **1980–81:** 1125, 1150
  National Museum Services Board, members,
    1977: 1780, 1796; **1979:** 269, 1157, 1159;
    1980–81: 2859, 2870, 2873
  National Railroad Passenger Corporation, Board
    of Directors, members, **1977:** 1810, 1826;
    1978: 230, 275, 881, 1512, 1517, 2184;
    1979: 92, 397, 402; **1980–81:** 296, 1823,
    1847, 1969, 2070

Appointments and Nominations — *continued*
  National Science Foundation
    Assistant Directors, **1977:** 1475, 1483, 1529,
      1534, 1929, 1931
    Associate Directors, **1979:** 1619
    Deputy Director, **1977:** 1475, 1483; **1980–81:**
      1022, 1051
    Director, **1977:** 689, 707; **1980–81:** 1289, 1292
    National Science Board, members, **1977:** 2002,
      2006; **1978:** 1760, 1773; **1979:** 46, 92, 93,
      196, 218, 528, 554; **1980–81:** 1149, 1246
  National Security Council, staff members, **1979:**
    984, 1045
  National Task Force on Ridesharing, members,
    1979: 2023
  National Transportation Policy Study Commis-
    sion, member, **1978:** 930
  National Transportation Safety Board
    Chairman, **1978:** 277, 303; **1980–81:** 493
    Members, **1977:** 1286, 1307; **1978:** 223, 232,
      795, 881; **1979:** 437, 441, 1007, 1019, 1964,
      2043; **1980–81:** 1975, 2070
    Vice Chairman, **1978:** 1669
  Navy Department
    Assistant Secretaries, **1977:** 472, 509, 550, 558,
      1779, 1795; **1979:** 2232
    Secretary, **1977:** 90, 148; **1979:** 1659, 1976
    Under Secretary, **1977:** 207, 252; **1980–81:** 98
  Negotiations for Combatting Terrorism, U.S.
    Representative, **1979:** 1158, 1159
  New Community Development Corporation,
    Board of Directors, **1977:** 575, 596
  New England Regional Commission, Federal
    Cochairman, **1977:** 1071, 1085
  New England River Basins Commission, Chair-
    man, **1978:** 822
  1979 World Administrative Radio Conference,
    U.S. delegation Chairman, rank of Am-
    bassador, **1979:** 1334
  Non-Proliferation Matters, U.S. Special Repre-
    sentative, **1977:** 1182, 1212
  Non-Proliferation Treaty Review Conference,
    U.S. delegation head, rank of Ambas-
    sador, **1979:** 685; **1980–81:** 932
  North Atlantic Treaty Organization
    Committee on the Challenges of Modern So-
    ciety
      Alternate U.S. Representative, **1980–81:** 493
      U.S. Representative and Alternate Repre-
      sentative, **1977:** 744
    Supreme Allied Commander, Europe, and
      Commander in Chief of U.S. Forces in
      Europe, **1979:** 363
    U.S. Permanent Representative, **1977:** 589,
      597
  North Pacific Fisheries Commission, U.S. Com-
    missioner, **1978:** 216

Appointments and Nominations — *continued*
  Northern Mariana Islands Commission on Federal Laws, members, **1980–81:** 343, 930
  Nuclear Regulatory Commission
    Chairman, **1977:** 1240, 1266
    Chairman and member, **1980–81:** 1331, 1377
    Members, **1977:** 1152, 1163, 1189, 1213, 1240, 1266; **1978:** 929, 935; **1979:** 855, 899
  Nuclear Safety Oversight Committee, members, **1980–81:** 849
  Occupational Safety and Health Commission, member, **1978:** 231
  Occupational Safety and Health Review Commission
    Chairman, **1977:** 1529; **1979:** 552
    Members, **1977:** 1541, 1569; **1979:** 552, 619
  Office of Drug Abuse Policy, Director and Deputy Director, **1977:** 92, 148
  Office of Management and Budget
    Administrator for Federal Procurement Policy, **1977:** 607, 642
    Deputy Director, **1977:** 157, 195; **1978:** 1665, 1772, 1921
    Director, **1977:** 10, 2176; **1978:** 149
    Federal Procurement Policy, Administrator for, **1980–81:** 371, 375
  Office of Personnel Management
    Deputy Director, **1979:** 3, 46, 90
    Director, **1979:** 3, 46, 90
    Office of Government Ethics, Director, **1979:** 41, 2153
  Office of Rail Public Counsel, Director, **1977:** 1961, 1967
  Office of Science and Technology Policy, Director, **1977:** 459, 465
  Office of the Special Representative for Trade Negotiations
    Acting Special Representative, **1979:** 1418, 1678
    Deputy Special Representatives, **1977:** 795, 807, 1305, 1308; **1979:** 2065, 2066, 2082
    Special Representative, **1977:** 370, 373; **1979:** 1418, 1423
  Ohio River Basin Commission, Chairman, **1979:** 607
  Ohio River Valley Water Sanitation Commission, U.S. Commissioner, **1977:** 1486; **1978:** 556; **1980–81:** 654
  Old West Regional Commission, Federal Cochairman, **1977:** 1071, 1085
  Organization of American States, Permanent Representative, **1977:** 465
  Organization for Economic Cooperation and Development
    Development Assistance Committee, Chairman, **1979:** 224, 241
    U.S. Representative, **1977:** 965, 1030

Appointments and Nominations — *continued*
  Overseas Private Investment Corporation
    Board of Directors, members, **1978:** 314, 329, 1037, 1071; **1979:** 783, 842, 899, 1022, 1043; **1980–81:** 521, 1446, 1926, 1947
    Executive Vice President, **1980–81:** 605, 608
    Members, **1977:** 805
    President, **1978:** 1701, 1724
  Ozarks Regional Commission, Federal Cochairman, **1977:** 1070, 1085
  Pacific Northwest Regional Commission, Federal Cochairman, **1977:** 1071, 1085
  Pacific Northwest River Basin Commission, Federal Chairman, **1978:** 481
  Pan American Railway Congress Association, U.S. National Commission, Chairman, **1978:** 898
  Panama Canal Commission
    Administrator, **1979:** 1333, 1786
    Deputy Administrator, **1979:** 2074
    Supervisory Board, members, **1980–81:** 32
  Panama Canal Consultative Committee, members, **1980–81:** 33
  Panama Canal Joint Commission on the Environment, members, **1980–81:** 33
  Panama Canal negotiations, Special Representative for, **1977:** 101
  Panama Canal Treaty Affairs, deputy to Ambassador Bunker, **1977:** 1581
  Pay Advisory Committee, members, **1979:** 1953
  Peace Corps, Director, **1977:** 1701
  Peace Corps Advisory Council
    Cochairperson, **1980–81:** 2074
    Members, **1980–81:** 1240, 2074
  Pennsylvania Avenue Development Corporation
    Acting Chairman, **1980–81:** 95
    Board of Directors
      Chairman, **1980–81:** 1346
      Members, **1978:** 2050; **1980–81:** 1346, 1981
  Pension Benefit Guaranty Corporation
    Advisory Committee
      Chairman, **1978:** 898; **1980–81:** 2789
      Members, **1978:** 1760; **1979:** 781; **1980–81:** 2789, 3021
    Members, **1978:** 317
  Permanent Committee for the Oliver Wendell Holmes Devise, member, **1979:** 746
  Permanent Joint Board on Defense—United States and Canada, U.S. Section, Chairman, **1978:** 453
  Postal Rate Commission
    Chairman, **1979:** 856
    Commissioners, **1977:** 1352, 1384, 2105, 2130; **1978:** 231; **1979:** 372, 378, 856, 899; **1980–81:** 979, 1015
  Poznan International Technical Fair, Representative of the President, **1977:** 936

Appointments and Nominations — *continued*
  Presidential Advisory Board on Ambassadorial
      Appointments
    Chairman, **1979:** 2042
    Chairman and members, **1977:** 90
    Members, **1979:** 552; **1980–81:** 1420
  Presidential Commission on World Hunger,
      members, **1978:** 1511, 2069; **1979:** 214
  Presidential Scholars, **1980–81:** 925
  President's Advisory Committee for Women
    Chair and Vice-Chairs, **1979:** 826
    Members, **1979:** 826, 1697, 2159; **1980–81:** 814
  President's Cancer Panel, members, **1977:** 1587;
      1979: 2196; **1980–81:** 1292
  President's Commission on the Accident at
      Three Mile Island, members, **1979:** 660,
      856
  President's Commission on the Coal Industry
    Coordinator of Labor Relations Programs,
      1978: 1500
    Members, **1978:** 1500
    Staff Director, **1978:** 1500
  President's Commission on Executive Exchange,
      members and representatives, **1979:** 976,
      1679; **1980–81:** 272, 1332, 2533
  President's Commission on Foreign Language
      and International Studies, members,
      1978: 1514
  President's Commission on the Holocaust, mem-
      bers and advisers, **1978:** 1973
  President's Commission on Mental Health,
      members, **1977:** 528; **1978:** 2070
  President's Commission on Military Compen-
      sation, members, **1977:** 1178
  President's Commission for a National Agenda
      for the Eighties
    Chairman, **1979:** 2014
    Members, **1980–81:** 263
  President's Commission on Pension Policy
    Chairman and member, **1978:** 1502
    Members, **1979:** 271
  President's Commission on Personnel Inter-
      change
    Executive Director, **1978:** 1466
    Members, **1978:** 968
  President's Commission for the Study of Ethical
      Problems in Medicine and Biomedical
      and Behavioral Research
    Chairman, **1979:** 1263, 1294
    Members, **1979:** 1263; **1980–81:** 896, 1723
  President's Commission on United States-
      Liberian Relations, members, **1980–81:**
      508
  President's Commission on White House Fel-
      lowships
    Chairman and members, **1977:** 941
    Members, **1978:** 737; **1979:** 931; **1980–81:** 949,
      1823

Appointments and Nominations — *continued*
  President's Committee on Employment of the
      Handicapped
    Members, **1979:** 463
    Vice Chairman, **1978:** 216
  President's Committee on Mental Retardation,
      members, **1978:** 407; **1980–81:** 192, 2242
  President's Committee on the National Medal of
      Science, members, **1979:** 448; **1980–81:**
      3023
  President's Council for Energy Efficiency, mem-
      bers, **1980–81:** 1404
  President's Council on Physical Fitness and
      Sports
    Chairman, **1978:** 1341, 1345; **1980–81:** 1440
    Members, **1978:** 2036, 2280; **1979:** 1226, 1815;
      1980–81: 1823, 2814
  President's Council on Spinal Cord Injury, mem-
      bers, **1980–81:** 3025
  President's Export Council, members, **1978:** 892;
      1979: 942, 1727; **1980–81:** 1570, 2610,
      2736
  President's Management Improvement Council
    Cochairpersons, **1979:** 1670
    Members, **1979:** 1670, 2154
  President's Special Summit Representative,
      1978: 758
  Price Advisory Committee, members, **1979:** 2218
  Railroad Retirement Board, members, **1977:**
      1239, 1266, 1664, 2079, 2089; **1978:** 231,
      1720, 1724; **1979:** 1037, 1044
  Red River Compact Commission, Federal rep-
      resentative and nonvoting Chairman,
      1977: 1462
  Regulatory Council
    Chairman, **1980–81:** 63
    Vice Chairman, **1980–81:** 1050
  Renegotiation Board
    Chairman, **1977:** 337
    Members, **1977:** 367, 465; **1979:** 375, 402
  Rural Electrification Administration, Adminis-
      trator, **1978:** 1666, 1670
  Sabine River Compact Administration, Federal
      Representative, **1978:** 1466
  Saint Christopher-Nevis-Anguilla, U.S. Special
      Representative, **1979:** 980
  Saint Lawrence Seaway Development Corpora-
      tion, members, **1980–81:** 237, 269
  Saint Lucia, U.S. Minister, **1979:** 664, 667
  Saint Vincent, U.S. Special Representative, **1979:**
      980
  Securities and Exchange Commission
    Chairman, **1977:** 537, 557
    Members, **1977:** 1395, 1438; **1979:** 1021, 1022,
      1398; **1980–81:** 235, 564, 1434, 1470
  Securities Investor Protection Corporation, Di-
      rectors, **1977:** 2183; **1978:** 150, 506, 571,
      1483, 1485; **1979:** 1022, 1043

Appointments and Nominations — *continued*
  Select Commission on Immigration and Refugee
      Policy
    Chairman, **1979:** 1876
    Members, **1979:** 450, 1876
  Selective Service System, Director, **1979:** 1419,
      1604
  Small Business Administration
    Administrator, **1977:** 475, 510
    Chief Counsel for Advocacy, **1978:** 451, 457
    Inspector General, **1979:** 399, 402
  Small Business Conference Commission, mem-
      bers, **1978:** 1836; **1979:** 229
  Smithsonian Institution, National Armed Forces
      Museum Advisory Board, members,
      1980–81: 913, 1047
  Solar Energy and Energy Conservation Bank,
      President, **1980–81:** 2016, 2782, 2870,
      2873
  South Pacific Commission
    Alternate U.S. Representatives, **1978:** 88, 1266
    U.S. Representative, **1978:** 898
    U.S. Representative and Alternate Represen-
        tatives, **1980–81:** 893, 1700
  Southwest Border Regional Commission, Fed-
      eral Cochairman, **1977:** 1069, 1085
  Spain-U.S. Treaty of Friendship and Coopera-
      tion, U.S. Special Negotiator for a suc-
      cessor agreement, rank of Ambassador,
      1980–81: 1860, 1947
  Special Panel on Appeals, Chairman, **1980–81:**
      1051
  Special Panel for Employment Discrimination
      Cases, Chairman, **1980–81:** 567
  State Department
    Agency for International Development
      Administrator, **1979:** 1271, 1293
      Assistant Administrators, **1978:** 703, 711,
          1343, 1346; **1979:** 1880, 1976
      Assistant Secretaries, **1977:** 7, 280, 372, 465,
          510, 804, 807, 1054, 1059; **1978:** 434, 452,
          457, 458, 1060, 1072, 1509, 1516; **1979:** 21,
          91, 1292, 1294, 1524, 1531, 1960, 2151,
          2204, 2207; **1980–81:** 991, 1015, 1096,
          1398, 1428
    Bureau of Intelligence and Research, Director,
        1977: 7
    Bureau of Security and Consular Affairs,
        Administrator, **1977:** 510
    Career Ministers, **1978:** 230
    Chief of Protocol, **1977:** 101
    Coordinator for Mexican Affairs, **1979:** 1134,
        1143
    Coordinator for Population Affairs, **1979:** 377,
        378
    Coordinators for Refugee Affairs, **1979:** 364,
        377, 2189, 2249
      Deputy Coordinator, rank of Ambassador,
          1980–81: 217

Appointments and Nominations — *continued*
  State Department — *continued*
    Counselor, **1977:** 509; **1979:** 2270; **1980–81:**
        334
    Deputy Assistant Secretary, **1980–81:** 893
    Deputy Secretary, **1977:** 148
    Deputy Under Secretary, **1977:** 280, 1353,
        1384
    Executive Secretary, **1977:** 7
    Foreign Service, Director General, **1977:** 7
    Human Rights and Humanitarian Affairs,
        Coordinator, **1977:** 327, 746
    Legal Adviser, **1977:** 471, 509; **1979:** 1697,
        1706
    Office for Liaison with State and Local Gov-
        ernments, head officials, **1978:** 2049
    Officials, **1977:** 7
    Secretary, **1977:** 9
    Secretary, **1980–81:** 791, 893
    Special Adviser for Soviet Affairs, **1977:** 1376,
        1384
    Under Secretary, **1977:** 373, 557; **1978:** 508,
        571; **1979:** 2270; **1980–81:** 219
    U.S. Representative, **1977:** 1485, 1507
  State Planning Council on Radioactive Waste
      Management, members, **1980–81:** 303
  Strategic arms limitation talks
    Chairman, U.S. Delegation, **1978:** 1857
    Minister, **1978:** 1697, 1723
    Special negotiator, **1977:** 66
    U.S. Delegation, Alternate Chairman, **1977:**
        740, 746
  Strategy Council, Executive Director and mem-
      bers, **1977:** 1963
  Strategy Council on Drug Abuse, members,
      1980–81: 1440
  Student Loan Marketing Association, Board of
      Directors
    Chairman, **1978:** 2053
    Members, **1978:** 1208, 2053
  Summit meeting preparations, President's per-
      sonal representative, **1977:** 332
  Supplemental Health Insurance Panel, members,
      1980–81: 2558
  Susquehanna River Basin Commission
    Alternate Federal member, **1977:** 1916
    U.S. Representative, **1977:** 251
  Synthetic Fuels Corporation, Board of Directors
    Advisory Committee, Chairman and Vice
        Chairman, **1980–81:** 2752
    Chairman, **1980–81:** 1700, 1715, 2726, 2727,
        2870, 2873
    Members, **1980–81:** 1717, 1848, 2071, 2074,
        2179, 2726, 2727, 2870, 2874
  Tennessee Valley Authority, Board of Directors,
      members, **1977:** 1284, 1307; **1978:** 1449,
      1458; **1979:** 877, 957

Appointments and Nominations — *continued*
  Transportation Department
    Acting Secretary, **1979:** 1285
    Assistant Secretaries, **1977:** 84, 148, 1752,
      1755; **1979:** 2089, 2107, 2126, 2139
    Deputy Secretary, **1977:** 84, 148; **1979:** 2039,
      2044; **1980–81:** 22
    Federal Highway Administration, Administra-
      tor, **1978:** 1357, 1381; **1980–81:** 842, 893
    General Counsel, **1977:** 84, 148; **1980–81:** 643,
      775
    Inspector General, **1979:** 398, 402
    Secretary, **1977:** 10; **1979:** 1317, 1320, 1679
    Urban Mass Transportation Association, Ad-
      ministrator, **1979:** 1744
  Treasury Department
    Assistant General Counsel (Chief Counsel for
      the Internal Revenue Service), **1977:** 803,
      807
    Assistant Secretaries, **1977:** 181, 252, 377, 460,
      465, 547, 557; **1978:** 569, 641; **1979:** 1000,
      1018; **1980–81:** 434, 453
    Bureau of the Mint
      U.S. Assay Office at New York, Assayer,
        1978: 569, 641
      U.S. Assay Office at New York, Superin-
        tendent, **1978:** 390, 416
      U.S. Mint at Denver, Assayer, **1979:** 2040,
        2044
      U.S. Mint at Denver, Superintendent, **1978:**
        325, 329
      U.S. Mint at Philadelphia, Superintendent,
        1978: 408, 416
    Comptroller of the Currency, **1977:** 1025, 1031
    Deputy Secretary, **1977:** 487, 510
    Deputy Under Secretary, **1977:** 148, 280
    Director of the Mint, **1977:** 1907, 1931
    General Counsel, **1977:** 1119, 1128
    Internal Revenue Service, Chief Counsel,
      1979: 1962, 1977
    Secretary, **1977:** 9; **1979:** 1273, 1294, 1320
    Treasurer of the United States, **1977:** 1066,
      1085
    Under Secretary, **1977:** 275, 280
  Truckee, Carson and Walker Rivers and Lake
    Tahoe Compact, U.S Federal Represen-
    tative, **1978:** 1466
  Trust Territory of the Pacific Islands
    High Commissioner, **1977:** 705, 745
    U.S. Representative, **1977:** 1303, 1308
  Turkey, President's personal emissary, **1977:** 77
  Uniformed Services University of the Health
    Sciences, Board of Regents, members,
    1980–81: 1445, 1470, 1927, 1947
  United Nations
    Alternate U.S. Representative for Special Po-
      litical Affairs, **1978:** 1528, 1572; **1979:**
      2196

Appointments and Nominations — *continued*
  United Nations — *continued*
    Commission on the Status of Women, U.S.
      Representative, **1977:** 1176
    Conference on Science and Technology for
      Development
      Coordinator for U.S. Preparations, **1977:**
        1230, 1266
      U.S. Delegation, Chairman, **1977:** 1751,
        1755, 1795
    Deputy U.S. Representatives, **1977:** 505, 510,
      527, 557; **1979:** 1298, 1319, 1396, 1725,
      2043
    Economic and Social Council
      Commission on Narcotic Drugs, Deputy
        U.S. Representative, **1978:** 2157
      Commission on Narcotic Drugs, U.S. Rep-
        resentative, **1978:** 64
      Commission for Social Development, U.S.
        Representative, **1977:** 1587
      Deputy U.S. Representative, **1977:** 1587;
        1980–81: 606
      U.S. Representative, **1977:** 994, 1031;
        1980–81: 507, 522
    European Office, U.S. Representative, **1977:**
      1123, 1128; **1979:** 2147
    General Assembly
      Special Session on Disarmament, Special
        Adviser, **1978:** 757
      Special Session on Disarmament, U.S. Rep-
        resentatives and Alternate Representa-
        tives, **1978:** 919, 935
      U.S. Representatives and Alternate Repre-
        sentatives, **1977:** 1625, 1626, 1650; **1978:**
        1509, 1516; **1979:** 1667, 1680; **1980–81:**
        1859, 1946, 2070, 2726, 2727
    Human Rights Commission, U.S. Represen-
      tative, **1977:** 1252
    Outer Space Conference, U.S. delegation
      head, rank of Ambassador, **1980–81:**
      1846, 1847
    Security Council, Deputy U.S. Representative,
      1979: 2038, 2044
    Special Political Affairs, Alternate U.S. Rep-
      resentative, **1977:** 1252, 1266
    Trusteeship Council, U.S. Representative,
      1978: 895
    U.S. Representative, **1977:** 10; **1979:** 1588,
      1679
  United Nations Children's Fund, Executive
    Board
    Alternate Representative, **1978:** 318
    U.S. Representative, **1978:** 296; **1979:** 1602
  United Nations Commission on Human Rights,
    U.S. Representative, **1979:** 2217
  United Nations Day, U.S. National Chairman,
    1980–81: 653

Appointments and Nominations — *continued*
United Nations Educational, Scientific and Cultural Organization
Executive Board, U.S. member, **1977:** 1486
General Conference, U.S. delegates and alternates, **1980–81:** 1713, 1847
U.S. Permanent Representative, **1977:** 1540, 1568; **1979:** 1819, 1824
U.S. Representatives and Alternate Representatives, **1978:** 1630, 1669
United Nations Industrial Development Organization, Third General Conference, U.S. Representative, **1979:** 2187
United Nations Pledging Conference on Refugee Relief, U.S. delegation, **1979:** 2085
United Service Organizations, Inc.
Board of Governors, members, **1978:** 1340, 1653
Corporation, members, **1978:** 1340
United States Advisory Commission on International Communication, Cultural and Educational Affairs, members, **1978:** 510, 571, 1720, 1772; **1979:** 729, 787
United States Advisory Commission on Public Diplomacy, member, **1980–81:** 1445, 1470
United States Air Force Academy, Board of Visitors, members, **1978:** 569; **1979:** 435; **1980–81:** 606, 757, 2802
United States Arms Control and Disarmament Agency
Assistant Directors, **1977:** 1135, 1163, 1528, 1534, 1676, 1680; **1980–81:** 428, 452, 866, 894
Deputy Director, **1977:** 733, 745
Director, **1977:** 66, 87, 148; **1978:** 1807, 2053; **1979:** 45, 2270; **1980–81:** 25
General Advisory Committee
Chairman, **1979:** 1820
Members, **1978:** 217, 230, 1706, 1724; **1980–81:** 25
Special Representative for Arms Control and Disarmament Negotiations, **1977:** 1607
United States attorneys
Alabama, **1977:** 1059, 1128, 1613, 1614
Alaska, **1977:** 1931, 1932
Arizona, **1977:** 642
Arkansas, **1977:** 2006, 2007; **1979:** 1786, 1787
California, **1977:** 1613, 1614, 1755, 1796, 1967
Colorado, **1977:** 1211, 1212
Connecticut, **1977:** 1059
Delaware, **1977:** 746
District of Columbia, **1979:** 1883
Florida, **1977:** 1613, 1614; **1979:** 241, 242; **1980–81:** 1715
Georgia, **1977:** 1127, 1128, 1211, 1212
Guam, **1977:** 1827, 1931
Hawaii, **1978:** 899
Idaho, **1977:** 1569

Appointments and Nominations — *continued*
United States attorneys — *continued*
Illinois, **1977:** 943, 1059, 1827, 1931
Indiana, **1977:** 1031, 1613, 1614
Iowa, **1977:** 1613, 1614
Kansas, **1977:** 1128
Kentucky, **1977:** 1059, 1222, 1266
Louisiana, **1977:** 1222, 1266, 1569; **1978:** 66, 149; **1979:** 667, 668
Maine, **1977:** 597; **1980–81:** 375
Maryland, **1978:** 935, 936
Massachusetts, **1977:** 1266, 1307
Michigan, **1977:** 1031, 1755
Minnesota, **1979:** 2281; **1980–81:** 25
Mississippi, **1978:** 1222, 1223
Missouri, **1977:** 1163, 1164, 1650, 1651
Montana, **1977:** 1701
Nebraska, **1977:** 1650. 1651
Nevada, **1977:** 1931, 1932
New Hampshire, **1977:** 1266, 1307
New Jersey, **1977:** 1613
New Mexico, **1978:** 899
New York, **1977:** 1211, 1212, 1569; **1978:** 771, 803, 1333; **1980–81:** 523, 564, 1470, 1471
North Carolina, **1977:** 1127, 1128, 1211, 1213; **1980–81:** 1715
North Dakota, **1977:** 883
Northern Mariana Islands, **1978:** 149, 150
Ohio, **1978:** 416, 457, 458
Oklahoma, **1977:** 1266, 1307, 1613, 1614, 1931, 1932; **1978:** 231
Pennsylvania, **1977:** 2089, 2090; **1978:** 899, 1222, 1223; **1979:** 93
Puerto Rico, **1980–81:** 269
Rhode Island, **1978:** 1035, 1071
South Carolina, **1977:** 557, 558
South Dakota, **1977:** 746; **1979:** 1883, 1884
Tennessee, **1977:** 1086, 2037
Texas, **1977:** 883, 884, 1211, 1212, 1222, 1266
Utah, **1977:** 1569
Vermont, **1977:** 1266, 1307
Virgin Islands, **1978:** 899
Virginia, **1980–81:** 269
Washington, **1977:** 1211, 1212
West Virginia, **1977:** 1163
Wisconsin, **1977:** 707; **1978:** 457, 458
Wyoming, **1977:** 1211, 1212
United States Circuit Judge Nominating Commission, panels, **1977:** 815, 1053, 1055, 1127, 1242
United States Circuit Judge Nominating Panel for the Eighth Circuit, members, **1978:** 734
United States circuit judges
District of Columbia, **1979:** 733, 787, 958, 983; **1980–81:** 654, 720
1st circuit, **1977:** 1650, 1651; **1980–81:** 2727
2d circuit, **1979:** 733, 787, 788; **1980–81:** 1599

Appointments and Nominations — *continued*
  United States circuit judges — *continued*
    3d circuit, **1977:** 1650, 1651; **1979:** 619
    4th circuit, **1978:** 1333; **1979:** 843, 1223;
      1980–81: 608
    5th circuit, **1977:** 1483, 1484, 1967; **1979:** 93,
      555, 619, 675, 733, 787, 899, 900, 1397,
      1398, 1423, 1531, 1532, 1883; **1980–81:**
      654, 720
    6th circuit, **1977:** 1507, 1534, 1701; **1979:** 441,
      620, 667, 1018, 1019, 1531, 1532
    7th circuit, **1979:** 957; **1980–81:** 1715
    8th circuit, **1978:** 1381; **1979:** 2249; **1980–81:**
      1470, 1471
    9th circuit, **1977:** 1507, 1534; **1979:** 788, 1043,
      1044, 1232, 1233, 1786, 1787, 1883, 2188,
      2189; **1980–81:** 423, 608, 968
    10th circuit, **1977:** 1967; **1979:** 1531, 1532
  United States Civil Service Commission
    Commissioners, **1977:** 570, 596, 807
    Vice Chairman, **1977:** 793
  United States Court of Claims
    Associate Judge, **1978:** 1218, 1222
    Chief Judge, **1978:** 550, 571
  United States Court of Customs and Patent
    Appeals, associate judge, **1980–81:** 866,
    894
  United States Court of Military Appeals, judge,
    1980–81: 317
  United States Court of Military Appeals Nom-
    inating Commission, members, **1979:**
    1451
  United States Customs Court, Chief Judge, **1977:**
    372
  United States District Courts
    Louisiana, **1978:** 231, 771, 803
    Massachusetts, **1978:** 231
    Michigan, **1978:** 1345, 1346
    Nevada, **1978:** 1346
    New Hampshire, **1978:** 935, 936
    New Mexico, **1978:** 1034, 1035
    New York, **1978:** 329, 330, 711, 712, 898, 899
    Northern Mariana Islands, **1978:** 712, 750
    Pennsylvania, **1978:** 231, 571, 711, 712, 1010,
      1071, 1072, 1381
    Tennessee, **1978:** 1381
    Utah, **1978:** 1485
    Virgin Islands, **1978:** 66, 149
    Washington, **1978:** 149, 150
  United States district judges
    Alabama, **1980–81:** 64, 1846, 1847
    Arizona, **1979:** 733, 787, 1018, 1019; **1980–81:**
      608, 1015, 1051
    Arkansas, **1977:** 1827, 1931; **1978:** 1458, 1459;
      1979: 402, 403, 2249; **1980–81:** 1015, 1051
    California, **1978:** 1407; **1979:** 1018, 1019, 1786,
      1787, 2081, 2082, 2207, 2208, 2249; **1980–**
      81: 608, 894, 1151

Appointments and Nominations — *continued*
  United States district judges — *continued*
    Canal Zone, **1978:** 1154, 1155
    Colorado, **1977:** 1967; **1979:** 984
    Connecticut, **1977:** 1211, 1212; **1978:** 329;
      1979: 1018, 1019, 2106, 2107
    District of Columbia, **1977:** 1613, 1614; **1978:**
      571, 1572; **1979:** 93, 378, 402, 2207, 2208;
      1980–81: 423, 424
    Florida, **1977:** 557, 558, 596, 2050, 2051; **1978:**
      1239; **1979:** 957, 1018, 1019, 1232, 1233,
      1293, 1294, 1319, 1423, 1531, 1532; **1980–**
      81: 1847
    Georgia, **1977:** 1222; **1978:** 1669, 1670; **1979:**
      1018, 1019, 1043, 1044, 1293, 1294, 1786,
      1787, 2081, 2082
    Guam, **1978:** 711, 712
    Hawaii, **1980–81:** 423, 424, 2857, 2870, 2873
    Illinois, **1977:** 1307; **1978:** 1407; **1979:** 733,
      787, 957, 1397, 1398; **1980–81:** 608, 1015,
      1051, 1052
    Indiana, **1979:** 1319, 1320
    Iowa, **1978:** 1670; **1979:** 441
    Kansas, **1979:** 1786, 1787; **1980–81:** 720
    Kentucky, **1977:** 1507, 1700, 1701; **1979:** 1531,
      1532, 1883, 2281
    Louisiana, **1977:** 1307, 1967; **1979:** 957, 958,
      1018, 1019, 1043, 1044, 1883; **1980–81:**
      608
    Maine, **1979:** 1397, 1398; **1980–81:** 1599
    Maryland, **1979:** 957, 958; **1980–81:** 1428,
      1429
    Massachusetts, **1977:** 2050, 2051; **1979:** 179,
      180
    Michigan, **1979:** 899, 900, 1232, 1233, 2188;
      1980–81: 968
    Minnesota, **1977:** 1438, 1439; **1979:** 2188, 2189
    Mississippi, **1979:** 1883
    Missouri, **1977:** 1127, 1128, 1163, 1164; **1979:**
      899, 900, 957, 958; **1980–81:** 608
    Montana, **1979:** 441
    Nevada, **1979:** 667, 668
    New Hampshire, **1979:** 241, 242
    New Jersey, **1979:** 1786, 1787
    New Mexico, **1979:** 1293, 1294
    New York, **1977:** 1483, 1484, 1826, 1827; **1979:**
      93, 1786, 1787; **1980–81:** 1015, 1051, 1847
    North Carolina, **1979:** 554, 555; **1980–81:** 654,
      720, 1111, 1112, 1598, 1599
    Ohio, **1980–81:** 564, 654, 720, 1599
    Oklahoma, **1979:** 1786, 1787
    Oregon, **1979:** 2207
    Pennsylvania, **1977:** 2050, 2051; **1979:** 958,
      983, 1398, 1883
    Puerto Rico, **1979:** 2044, 2188; **1980–81:** 932,
      1470, 1471
    Rhode Island, **1977:** 807

Appointments and Nominations — *continued*
  United States district judges — *continued*
    South Carolina, **1979:** 1018, 1019, 1223;
      1980–81: 721
    South Dakota, **1979:** 441
    Tennessee, **1980–81:** 423, 424
    Texas, **1977:** 944; **1979:** 241, 294, 327, 328,
      377, 378, 402, 403, 1397, 1398, 1883, 2281;
      1980–81: 104, 1599
    Utah, **1979:** 2081, 2082
    Virgin Islands, **1980–81:** 1715
    Virginia, **1979:** 667, 668, 899, 900; **1980–81:**
      654
    Washington, **1979:** 2105, 2106, 2207; **1980–81:**
      894
    West Virginia, **1979:** 1044, 2188
    Wisconsin, **1979:** 1294, 1319
  United States Foreign Claims Settlement Com-
    mission, member, **1979:** 46, 90
  United States Holocaust Memorial Council,
    members, **1980–81:** 820
  United States Information Agency
    Deputy Director, **1977:** 732, 745
    Director, **1977:** 372
  United States International Development Co-
    operation Agency
    Agency for International Development
      Assistant Administrator, **1980–81:** 1108,
      1150
      Deputy Administrator, **1980–81:** 427, 452
    Associate Director, **1980–81:** 51
    Deputy Director, **1980–81:** 296
  United States International Trade Commission
    Chairman, **1979:** 2285; **1980–81:** 948
    Chairman and Vice Chairman, **1978:** 1154
    Director, **1979:** 1272, 1293
    Members, **1977:** 1666, 1700; **1978:** 1453, 1458;
      1979: 2166, 2188; **1980–81:** 1975, 2070,
      2071
    Vice Chairman, **1980–81:** 1150
  United States-Japan Economic Relations Group,
    1979: 2126
  United States Marine Corps
    Brigadier General, **1978:** 697
    Commandant, **1979:** 672
  United States marshals
    Alabama, **1977:** 1569, 1755; **1978:** 1407
    Arizona, **1977:** 1086
    Arkansas, **1977:** 2089, 2090; **1978:** 230, 232
    California, **1977:** 1613, 1614, 2090; **1978:** 711,
      712; **1980–81:** 269
    Colorado, **1977:** 1613
    Connecticut, **1977:** 745, 746
    Delaware, **1978:** 711, 712; **1979:** 1293, 1294
    Florida, **1977:** 1128, 1437, 1438
    Georgia, **1977:** 1059, 1507, 1534; **1978:** 416
    Guam, **1977:** 1437, 1438
    Hawaii, **1977:** 1211, 1212

Appointments and Nominations — *continued*
  United States marshals — *continued*
    Idaho, **1977:** 1569
    Illinois, **1977:** 883, 884, 1384, 1755; **1979:** 788
    Indiana, **1977:** 1163, 1931, 1932
    Iowa, **1977:** 1796; **1978:** 416
    Kansas, **1977:** 1437, 1438
    Kentucky, **1977:** 943, 1163
    Louisiana, **1978:** 329, 330; **1980–81:** 1292
    Maine, **1977:** 1650, 1651
    Maryland, **1980–81:** 269
    Massachusetts, **1977:** 1437, 1438
    Michigan, **1978:** 1111, 1346
    Minnesota, **1977:** 1266, 1307
    Mississippi, **1977:** 2037, 2038; **1978:** 1572
    Missouri, **1977:** 1128, 1483, 1484
    Montana, **1977:** 1308
    Nebraska, **1979:** 468; **1980–81:** 775, 1715
    Nevada, **1977:** 1483, 1484
    New Hampshire, **1977:** 1384
    New Jersey, **1980–81:** 423, 424
    New Mexico, **1977:** 1222, 1266
    New York, **1977:** 1384, 1437, 1438; **1978:** 1072,
      1222, 1223
    North Carolina, **1977:** 1384, 1796, 2050, 2051
    North Dakota, **1977:** 883
    Northern Mariana Islands, **1978:** 149, 150
    Ohio, **1977:** 1569, 2130, 2131
    Oklahoma, **1977:** 1437, 1438, 1569, 2089, 2090;
      1978: 231
    Oregon, **1977:** 1437, 1438
    Pennsylvania, **1977:** 1438, 1439, 1483, 1484;
      1979: 733, 787
    Puerto Rico, **1979:** 899, 900
    Rhode Island, **1979:** 2249
    South Carolina, **1977:** 596
    South Dakota, **1977:** 2050, 2051
    Tennessee, **1977:** 1266, 1307, 1650, 1651, 1931,
      1932
    Texas, **1977:** 943, 1222, 1266; **1978:** 1222, 1223
    Utah, **1978:** 1407
    Vermont, **1977:** 1266, 1307
    Virginia, **1977:** 1483, 1484, 1755
    Washington, **1977:** 943, 1701
    West Virginia, **1977:** 1211, 1212, 1438, 1439
    Wisconsin, **1977:** 1569, 2077, 2078
    Wyoming, **1977:** 745, 746
  United States Metric Board
    Chairman, **1978:** 230
    Chairman and members, **1977:** 1944, 1966
    Members, **1978:** 230, 484, 504, 1069, 1072;
      1980–81: 940, 967, 1443, 1470
  United States Military Academy, Board of Vis-
    itors, members, **1978:** 510; **1979:** 687
  United States Naval Academy, Board of Visi-
    tors, members, **1978:** 515; **1979:** 730;
      1980–81: 769, 2613, 2847
  United States Navy, Supreme Allied Command-
    er, Atlantic, **1978:** 1407

Appointments and Nominations — *continued*
  United States Negotiator on Textile Matters, rank of Ambassador, **1980–81:** 2752, 2753
  United States Office of Consumer Affairs, Deputy Director, **1980–81:** 83
  United States Parole Commission, Commissioners, **1977:** 1644, 1650, 1824, 1931; **1978:** 1083, 1111, 1503, 1506; **1980–81:** 1411, 1428
  United States Postal Service, Board of Governors, members, **1979:** 24, 46, 90, 215, 241; **1980–81:** 940, 968, 2781, 2782, 2857
  United States Railway Association, Board of Directors
    Chairman, **1978:** 1269, 1333; **1980–81:** 392, 423
    Members, **1978:** 1360, 1381; **1979:** 43, 93; **1980–81:** 1824, 1847
  United States Sinai Support Mission, Special Representative and Director, **1980–81:** 1547
  United States-Soviet Standing Consultative Commission, U.S. Commissioner, **1978:** 63, 149
  United States Special Negotiator for Economic Matters, rank of Ambassador, **1980–81:** 1468, 1470
  United States Tax Court, judges, **1978:** 481, 504; **1979:** 820, 843; **1980–81:** 683, 720, 756, 775
  United States Tax Court Nominating Commission, members, **1978:** 1711
  Upper Great Lakes Regional Commission, Federal Cochairman, **1977:** 1070, 1085
  Upper Mississippi River Basin Commission, Chairman, **1977:** 1917
  Urban Mass Transportation Administration, Administrator, **1977:** 1100, 1127
  Vatican, President's personal representative, **1977:** 1215; **1978:** 1795
  Veterans Administration
    Administrator, **1977:** 192, 252
    Inspector General, **1979:** 367, 377
  Veterans Federal Coordinating Committee, Executive Director and Deputy Director, **1980–81:** 1591
  White House Coal Advisory Council, members, **1980–81:** 1643
  White House Conference on Balanced National Growth and Economic Development, Advisory Committee, members, **1978:** 53
  White House Conference on Families, Chairman, **1978:** 748; **1979:** 667
  White House Conference on Library and Information Services, Advisory Committee, members, **1979:** 400, 746
  White House Fellows, **1977:** 986; **1978:** 1026; **1979:** 914; **1980–81:** 948

Appointments and Nominations — *continued*
  White House staff
    Adviser to the President, **1978:** 1849, 1880
    Appointments Secretary, **1978:** 892
    Assistant Press Secretary, **1979:** 1017
    Assistants, **1978:** 770, 771, 803; **1979:** 1422, 1423
    Associate Assistant, **1977:** 184
    Associate Counsels, **1977:** 184; **1979:** 1976
    Chief of Protocol, **1979:** 1659, 1976
    Chief Speechwriter, **1977:** 30
    Chief of Staff, **1979:** 1292
    Counsel to the President, **1979:** 1448, 1455
    Counselor to the President on Aging, **1980–81:** 718
    Deputy Appointments Secretary, **1978:** 893
    Deputy Assistants, **1977:** 184, 806; **1979:** 7
    Deputy Counsels, **1977:** 184; **1979:** 1976
    Deputy Press Secretary, **1979:** 1017
    Presidential Personnel Office, Director, **1978:** 1787
    Senior Adviser, **1979:** 1300
    Senior Associate Counsel, **1979:** 1976
    Special Adviser to the President, **1980–81:** 651
    Special Assistant to the President for Ethnic Affairs, **1980–81:** 13
    Special Assistants, **1977:** 9, 30, 565; **1978:** 1407, 1484; **1979:** 377, 378, 1422, 1518
    Staff Secretary, **1977:** 184
    White House Projects, Director, **1977:** 9
  Wien Air Alaska emergency board, members, **1978:** 2033, 2158
  Withdrawal of prior nominations, **1977:** 195, 373, 707, 745, 806, 807, 1714, 1755, 2037, 2087, 2090
  Woodrow Wilson International Center for Scholars
    Board of Trustees, members, **1977:** 2036; **1980–81:** 2732, 3023
    Chairman, **1979:** 2248
    Members, **1979:** 2118
  World Health Assembly, 30th, U.S. delegation, **1977:** 806
Aquaculture Act, National, **1980–81:** 1937
Aquaculture bill, U.S. memorandum of disapproval, **1978:** 1799
Aquino Herrera, Francisco, **1980–81:** 775
Arab-American community leaders, **1977:** 2130
Arab boycott, **1977:** 116
Arab Emirates, United, **1979:** 1300, 1319
Aragon, Joseph W., **1977:** 35, 86; **1978:** 906
Arantes do Nascimento, Edson (Pelé), **1977:** 556
Arbitration Association, American, **1979:** 1454
Arce Alvarez, Roberto, **1979:** 554
Arce, Carlos Humberto, **1980–81:** 2613
Arceneaux, George, Jr., **1979:** 1043, 1044
Archbold, John D., **1978:** 1879
Archer, Repr. William R., **1979:** 666

Architects, American Institute of, **1979:** 1537
Architectural Barrier Awareness Week, National, **1978:** 774, 933; **1979:** 641
Architectural and Transportation Barriers Compliance Board, **1978:** 933; **1979:** 2191; **1980–81:** 2730
Arciniega, Tomas A., **1980–81:** 96
Arctic Marine Living Resources, Convention on the Conservation of, **1980–81:** 2765
Arctic National Monument, Gates of the, **1978:** 2123
Arctic Wildlife Range, William O. Douglas, Alaska, **1979:** 855, 1356; **1980–81:** 416, 419
Areco, Jorge Pacheco, **1980–81:** 1051
Arel, Maurice, **1978:** 364
Argentina
 Grain exports, **1980–81:** 42
 President Jorge Rafael Videla, **1977:** 1555, 1568
 Trade with U.S., **1979:** 1791
 U.S. Ambassador, **1977:** 1481; **1980–81:** 1710, 1715
Argetsinger, Elizabeth S., **1980–81:** 926
Arias-Schreiber, Alfonso, **1979:** 554
Aristotle, **1980–81:** 842
Ariyoshi, Gov. George R., **1979:** 1217, 1222, 1223
Ariyoshi, Mrs. George R., **1979:** 1222
Arizona
 Disaster declarations, **1978:** 503, 2281; **1980–81:** 374
 Emergency declaration, **1977:** 642
 Gov. Bruce Babbitt, **1980–81:** 849, 3021
 U.S. attorney, **1977:** 642
 U.S. district judges, **1979:** 733, 787, 1018, 1019; **1980–81:** 608, 1015, 1051
 U.S. marshal, **1977:** 1086
 Water projects, **1980–81:** 88
Arizzi, Rocco, **1980–81:** 492
Arkansas
 Disaster assistance, **1980–81:** 1345, 1421
 Disaster declarations, **1978:** 1571; **1979:** 667, 674; **1980–81:** 720
 Emergency declarations, **1978:** 149, 801
 Gov. Bill Clinton, **1980–81:** 1404, 1423n., 2154
 President's visit, **1980–81:** 2417, 2418
 Titan missile silo explosion, **1980–81:** 1844, 1894
 U.S. attorney, **1977:** 2006, 2007; **1979:** 1786, 1787
 U.S. district judges, **1977:** 1827, 1931; **1978:** 1458, 1459; **1979:** 402, 403, 2249; **1980–81:** 1015, 1051
 U.S. marshal, **1977:** 2089, 2090; **1978:** 230, 232
Arky, Marlin, **1979:** 464
Arline, Ron, **1978:** 1860
Armacost, Michael, **1978:** 2281
Armed Conflicts, Diplomatic Conference on International Law in, **1977:** 276
Armed forces, United States
 Administration's accomplishments and goals, **1980–81:** 2978

Armed forces, United States — *continued*
 All-volunteer forces, **1977:** 267, 314, 388; **1979:** 1344; **1980–81:** 290, 328, 1392, 1875, 2028, 2292
 Benefits, **1980–81:** 969, 971, 2007, 2387
 Caribbean joint task force to monitor Cuban activities, **1979:** 1804
 Code of Conduct, amendment, **1977:** 1958
 Commissaries, **1977:** 905
 Courts-martial manual amendments, **1977:** 1958; **1980–81:** 493, 1626
 Defense Department visit, question-and-answer session, **1977:** 259
 Draft registration.
  See Draft registration *under* Selective Service System.
 East Asia, military capabilities in, **1979:** 764
 Fiscal year 1982 budget allocations, **1980–81:** 2897
 Fort Hood, Tex., firepower demonstration, **1978:** 1176
 Inaugural reception, **1977:** 9
 Indian Ocean buildup.
  See U.S. military capabilities improvement *under* Indian Ocean.
 Interview remarks, **1978:** 76
 Iran, rescue mission for American hostages.
  See Iran, American hostages in, rescue mission.
 Memorial Day observance, **1980–81:** 814
 Mentions, **1979:** 311; **1980–81:** 164
 Middle East, U.S. intervention in, possibility, **1979:** 1839
 Military awards program, **1979:** 363; **1980–81:** 475, 2921
 Military construction legislation, **1980–81:** 2185
 Military installations, **1977:** 389, 1018; **1979:** 906
 Military organizations, leaders, meeting with the President, **1977:** 1126
 Military personnel, **1978:** 2207
  Taxation of, **1979:** 479
 Military personnel and compensation legislation, **1980–81:** 1665, 1686
 Military Selective Service Act violations, pardon, **1977:** 5, 6, 299, 321, 399, 1409
 Minority discrimination, **1977:** 1345
 Missing in action, **1977:** 173, 377, 489
 National Guard and Reserve, **1977:** 267, 1694
 North Atlantic Treaty Organization forces, **1978:** 1289
 Northern Mariana Islands citizens enlistment, **1980–81:** 1722
 Pay increases, **1977:** 1681, 1682; **1978:** 1480, 1485, 1732; **1979:** 64, 1481, 1529, 1532, 1848; **1980–81:** 467, 468, 1596, 2312, 2729, 3001

Armed forces, United States — *continued*
  Persian Gulf buildup.
    See U.S. military capabilities improvement
      under Persian Gulf area.
  Physical training, **1977:** 320
  Physician shortage, **1980–81:** 456
  President's commitment to strength of, **1980–81:**
    971, 1163, 1550
  President's endorsement of military career,
    1980–81: 2360
  Prisoners of war, **1977:** 1958, 1959
  Promotion and disability separation limitations,
    1978: 1541
    Suspension, **1980–81:** 1857
  Proportion of officers, **1979:** 1253
  Rapid deployment forces, **1979:** 1805; **1980–81:**
    166, 197, 248, 348, 1535, 1555, 1725, 2213,
    2304, 2447
  Recruitment goals, **1980–81:** 167, 340, 2387, 2446
  Reserve Officers' Training Corps, **1980–81:** 2292
  Reserves personnel, **1977:** 267, 314, 319, 388;
    1980–81: 167
  Retirement pay for Marine Corps Sergeants
    Major, **1978:** 1929
  Retirement system, **1977:** 262, 390
  South Korea, withdrawal of troops, **1979:** 247
  Soviet Union
    Military strength comparison with, **1980–81:**
      660
    Presence in countries bordering, **1979:** 1757
  State of the Union, **1978:** 123
  Strategic Air Command facilities, **1977:** 1860
  Taxes, withholding, **1977:** 56, 1138
  Thailand, military equipment airlift to, **1980–81:**
    1267
  U.S.S. *Dwight D. Eisenhower,* remarks, **1978:** 538
  U.S.S. *Mississippi,* remarks, **1978:** 1383
  Variable housing allowances, **1980–81:** 2065
  Veterans.
    See Veterans.
  Wake Forest University, address, **1978:** 534
  White House military aides office employees,
    1980–81: 2829
  Women's role, **1980–81:** 922
  See also specific service; Arms and Weapons;
    Defense and national security; Veterans.
Armed Forces Day, **1977:** 476; **1978:** 912
Armed Forces Museum Advisory Board, National,
  1980–81: 1047
Armed Forces physicians pay act, proposed, **1980–**
  81: 456
Armenian Americans, **1978:** 916, **1979:** 1017
Arms Control and Disarmament Act Amendments
  of 1977, **1977:** 1480
Arms Control and Disarmament Agency, United
  States.
  See United States Arms Control and Disar-
    mament Agency.

Arms Export Control Act, **1980–81:** 2813
Arms and weapons systems
  Administration's accomplishments and goals,
    1980–81: 2126, 2582, 2600, 2624, 2639
  Chemical warfare, **1980–81:** 2021
  Control and disarmament, **1977:** 28, 93, 94, 172,
    358, 447, 496, 498, 538, 560, 613, 1017,
    1038, 1043; **1978:** 702; **1979:** 108, 158;
    1980–81: 1438
  Conventional forces modernization, **1980–81:**
    348
  Defense budget allocations, **1979:** 1629
  Democratic workshop on defense, remarks,
    1978: 2201
  Export controls administration, **1980–81:** 696
  Fiscal year 1982 budget allocations, **1980–81:**
    2899
  Interview remarks, **1977:** 1807, 2134; **1978:** 2018
  Munitions export licensing, **1980–81:** 403
  Mutual and balanced force reductions, **1977:**
    849, 866; **1978:** 38, 122, 875, 1014
  National Democratic Party Conference, re-
    marks, **1978:** 2194
  News conference remarks, **1977:** 1197, 1231,
    1232, 1367, 1692, 2211; **1978:** 1658, 2096,
    2097
  North Atlantic Alliance Summit, remarks, **1978:**
    1013
  North Atlantic Treaty Organization equipment,
    1978: 1290, 1292, 1297
  Nuclear nonproliferation, **1977:** 496, 540, 582–
    586, 613, 728, 730, 763, 779, 817, 818,
    825–834, 960, 1027, 1145
  Nuclear test ban, **1978:** 96, 122, 875, 1075
    Treaty, **1977:** 61, 96, 358, 496, 539, 1107
  On-site inspections, **1977:** 543
  Sales to foreign counties, **1977:** 93, 289, 496, 523,
    539, 556, 848, 931, 960; **1978:** 245, 256,
    324, 333, 335, 338, 359, 368, 777, 778, 782,
    801, 806, 807, 848, 849, 857, 866, 867, 896,
    901, 910, 915, 1593; **1979:** 51, 53, 106, 184,
    563, 902, 1023, 1130, 2299; **1980–81:** 1267,
    2170, 2431, 2447, 2542
  Science and technology development, **1979:** 542
  Soviet levels, comparison with, **1979:** 2235
  State of the Union, **1978:** 96, 122, 123
  Strategic forces strengthening, **1980–81:** 1535,
    1551, 1552
  United Nations address, **1977:** 1715
  U.S. Naval Academy, remarks, **1978:** 1055
  U.S. tranfer levels, **1978:** 2094
  Wake Forest University, address, **1978:** 532, 533
  See also specific weapons system; Nuclear weap-
    ons; Strategic arms limitation talks.
Armstrong, Ben, **1980–81:** 183
Armstrong, Neil A., **1978:** 1687; **1979:** 1276
Armstrong, Peggy Sue, **1979:** 1447
Armstrong, Richard C., **1977:** 1486

Army, Department of the
    Assistant Secretaries, **1977:** 591, 596, 712, 745,
      934, 944; **1979:** 109, 179; **1980–81:** 304
    Chief of Engineers, **1979:** 1126
    Chief of Staff, United States Army, **1980–81:**
      1686
    Chief of Staff, U.S. Army, **1979:** 763
    Cross-Florida Barge Canal, **1977:** 981
    Hydroelectric power projects, **1979:** 1509 1510
    Labor-Management Relations Program exemp-
      tions, **1979:** 2145
    Michigan missile plant, conveyance of, **1980–81:**
      769
    Secretary, **1977:** 65, 87, 207, 490, 723, 1345, 2076;
      1978: 1682, 1725; **1979:** 83, 1280, 1715,
      1921; **1980–81:** 955, 956, 1004, 1071
    Under Secretary, **1977:** 1174, 1207; **1980–81:** 98
    Water policy functions, **1978:** 1050
    See also specific constituent agencies.
Army Corps of Engineers.
    See Corps of Engineers, Army.
Arnold, Richard S., **1978:** 1458, 1459
Arnold, S. Gerald, **1980–81:** 1598, 1599
Arnowitt, Michael P., **1980–81:** 927
Arns, Paulo Evaristo Cardinal, **1978:** 632, 640
Arntz, Bill, **1977:**7 1817; **1979:** 270
Aron, William, **1977:** 1135
Arrangement Regarding Bovine Meat, **1979:** 2253
Arrington, Richard, Jr., **1980–81:** 1500, 2875
Art, National Gallery of, **1980–81:** 340
Art award, Women's Caucus for, **1979:** 217
Arthur, John, **1977:** 2070
Arthur, Neal, **1979:** 1451
Articles of Confederation, anniversary proclama-
    tion, **1977:** 2027
Artificial baits and flies industry, **1978:** 2071
Artists, National Conference of, **1980–81:** 600
Artists Week, African-American Visual, **1980–81:**
    601
Arts, Advisory Committee on the, **1977:** 1767, 1771
Arts, Commission on Fine, **1980–81:** 2701
Arts, John F. Kennedy Center for the Performing.
    See John F. Kennedy Center for the Performing
      Arts.
Arts, National Council on the, **1977:** 1264, 2024,
    2037; **1978:** 252, 277; **1980–81:** 237, 452
Arts, National Endowment for the, **1977:** 1264,
    1522, 1534, 1744, 1946, 1966; **1978:** 590;
    1979: 2280
Art and humanities, **1978:** 107, 605, 606
    Administration's accomplishments and goals,
      1980–81: 147, 2963
    President's favorite painters, **1980–81:** 340
Arts and Humanities, Federal Council on the,
    1977: 1825; **1979:** 956; **1980–81:** 3004
Arts and Humanites, National Endowment for the,
    1979: 142

Arts and Humanities, National Foundation on the,
    1978: 2059; **1980–81:** 754
Art and Humanities acts, 1979 White House Con-
    ferences on the, **1978:** 823
Arvizu, Steven F. **1980–81:** 1935
Asad, Hafiz al-, **1977:** 835, 841, 842, 844, 884, 1433,
    1434, 2044, 2059, 2098, 2119, 2120, 2172,
    2175, 2189, 2190, 2206; **1978:** 46, 71, 1554,
    1678; **1979:** 456
Asencio, Diego C., **1977:** 1646, 1650; **1978:** 1380;
    1980–81: 781, 825, 1398, 1428
Ashari, Danudirdjo, **1978:** 328
Asher, John, **1980–81:** 821
Asheville, N.C., **1978:** 1575, 1579
Ashley, Ivan, **1977:** 1816
Ashley, Repr. Thomas L., **1977:** 744, 806, 1297,
    1396, 1825; **1978:** 769, 1980, 1981; **1979:**
    1973; **1980–81:** 217, 2113, 2463
Ashton, Al., **1980–81:** 380
Ashworth, George William, **1980–81:** 856, 894
Asia Foundation, **1978:** 749
Asian Americans, **1978:** 1380
Asian Development Bank, **1977:** 456, 509, 795, 807,
    943; **1979:** 1454, 1455
Asian Pacific American Committee, **1980–81:** 2368
Asian/Pacific American Democratic Caucus,
    1980–81: 962
Asian/Pacific American Heritage Week
    (Proc. 4650), **1979:** 549
    (Proc. 4727), **1980–81:** 405
Asian/Pacific Americans, **1979:** 786
Asian-Pacific nations.
    See specific country.
"Ask the President" telephone call-out program,
    1979: 1885
Askanase, Reuben W., **1980–81:** 1467, 1524, 2859,
    2870, 2873
Askew, Gov. Reubin, **1977:** 78, 79, 90, 194, 280,
    356, 1225, 1265, 1476, 1534, 1622, 1937;
    1978: 1506, 1689, 1865, 2155
    See also Select Committee on Immigration and
      Refugee Policy, Chairman; Special Rep-
      resentative for Trade Negotiations; Unit-
      ed States Trade Representative.
Aspen, Marvin E., **1979:** 733, 787
Aspin, Repr. Les, **1979:** 1327
Assassination
    Hearings, **1978:** 1780
    Investigation, **1979:** 37
Assay Commission, Annual, **1980–81:** 483
Assay Office, United States, **1978:** 390, 416, 569,
    641
Associated Electric Cooperative, Inc., **1978:** 1770
Associated Press, **1980–81:** 2319
Association.
    See also other part of title.
Association Executives, American Society of,
    1977: 706

[References are to page numbers except as otherwise indicated]

Association of South-East Asian Nations
    (ASEAN), **1978:** 1378; **1979:** 303, 304,
    765
Astin, Helen S., **1979:** 44, 91
Atchafalaya River, La., **1977:** 208
Athanasakos, Elizabeth, **1977:** 525
Athanson, George, **1979:** 2280
Athens, Andrew A., **1980–81:** 218
Atherton, Alfred L., Jr., **1977:** 1283, 2054; **1978:**
    189, 280, 305, 441, 452, 458, 494, 2059,
    2268; **1979:** 669, 819, 843, 955; **1980–81:**
    86, 930
Atherton, Mrs, Alfred L., Jr., **1979:** 955
Athletic Boosters Week, National, **1980–81:** 1131
Athletics, President's views on, **1979:** 1170
Atiyeh, Gov. Victor, **1979:** 2286; **1980–81:** 323
Atkins, C. Clyde, **1978:** 1139, 1140
Atkins, Chet, **1979:** 447; **1980–81:** 1846
Atkins, Hannah D., **1980–81:** 1859, 1946, 2070,
    2726, 2727
Atkins, Orin E., **1979:** 1614n.
Atkinson, Gene, **1978:** 1617
Atkinson, Richard C., **1977:** 689, 707, 1046; **1978:**
    1187; **1979:** 205, 1388, 1389; **1980–81:**
    3023
Atlanta, Ga., **1978:** 154, 155, 228, 1113, 2285
    Martin Luther King, Jr., national historic site,
        1980–81: 2172, 2184
    Mayor Maynard Jackson
        Campaign appearances with the President,
            1980–81: 1750, 1755
        Mention, **1977:** 86, 2153; **1978:** 53; **1980–81:**
            1500
        President's Council on Energy Efficiency;
            member, **1980–81:** 1405
        Zimbabwe independence, U.S. delegation
            member, **1980–81:** 719
    President's visits, **1979:** 296–306, 328, 1533–1565,
        1605; **1980–81:** 1749–1758, 1848
Atlantic City, N.J., **1977:** 1572; **1978:** 1542–1555
Atlantic Richfield Company, **1979:** 1586; **1980–81:**
    1401
Atlantic Treaty Association, **1977:** 1520
Atmosphere, National Advisory Committee on
    Oceans and, **1979:** 1628, 2187; **1980–81:**
    1023, 2242
Atmospheric Administration, National Oceanic
    and.
    See National Oceanic and Atmospheric Admin-
        istration.
Atmospheric Research Project, Global, **1979:** 538
Atomic energy.
    See Nuclear energy.
Atomic Energy Agency, International.
    See International Atomic Energy Agency.
Atomic Energy Commission, **1978:** 272, 273
Atomic Energy Community, European, **1980–81:**
    286, 304

Atomic Energy for Mutual Defense Purposes
    amendment, U.S.-United Kingdom
    Agreement for Cooperation on the Uses
    of, **1979:** 2164
Atomic Safety and Licensing Appeal Panel, **1980–
    81:** 838–840
AT&T.
    See American Telephone and Telegraph Com-
        pany.
Attneave, Carolyn L., **1979:** 2039, 2044
Attorney General (Griffin B. Bell), **1977:** 9, 19, 234,
        242, 248, 503, 712, 862, 873, 882, 922,
        1126, 1210, 1238, 1280, 1305, 1345, 1347,
        1383, 1442, 1465, 1504, 1533, 1649, 1691,
        1912, 1963, 1996, 2077, 2094, 2130; **1978:**
        65, 66, 77, 148, 150, 245, 363, 397, 488,
        489, 734, 802, 841, 1155, 1181, 1223, 1242,
        1328, 1610, 1854; **1980–81:** 848, 1434,
        1479
    Electronic surveillance orders review, **1979:** 585
    Federal Bureau of Investigation, operational
        guidelines review, **1979:** 1336
    Federal Legal Council, Chairman, **1979:** 1265
    Federal legal resources management, **1979:** 1264,
        1266
    Offshore oil spill pollution, study responsibilities,
        1979: 339
    President's assessment, **1979:** 1440
    Resignation, **1980–81:** 1272, 1401
    Spanish-speaking Americans civil rights viola-
        tions, corrective program establishment,
        1979: 847
    Standby gasoline rationing plan recommenda-
        tions, **1979:** 814, 821
    Swearing in of Attorney General Benjamin
        Civiletti, remarks, **1979:** 1441
    Vesco, Robert, extradition actions, **1979:** 1592
    Weber case position, **1979:** 847
    Wood, Judge John H., Jr., investigation of
        murder, **1979:** 959
    For functions of the Department in general, see
        Justice, Department of.
Attorney General (Benjamin R. Civiletti), **1977:**
        156, 195, 1971, 2083, 2090; **1978:** 460, 802,
        1098, 1182, 1280, 1505
    Advisory Council on Historic Preservation, rul-
        ing on, **1980–81:** 2803
    Carter, Billy, investigation of activities with
        Libyan Government, **1980–81:** 1479,
        1481, 1489, 1491, 1492, 2017
    Clark, Ramsey, investigation of, **1980–81:** 1087–
        1089
    Congressional veto of executive branch action
        ruling, examination of, **1980–81:** 2835,
        2836, 2882
    Council on Wage and Price Stability, member,
        1980–81: 1427

Attorney General — *continued*
Cuban refugees
Exclusion proceedings against criminals, **1980–81:** 913, 914, 1055
Meeting with the President, **1980–81:** 780
News conferences, **1980–81:** 916n., 932
Demarcation lines dividing high seas and inland water, determination, **1980–81:** 1522
Environmental damage response activities, **1980–81:** 3045
Fair housing laws enforcement, **1980–81:** 2853
Farm Credit Administration regulation, consideration, **1980–81:** 2837
Federal employees ruling, **1980–81:** 1981
Foreign Corrupt Practices Act review, **1980–81:** 402, 1694
Forged document on Africa and U.S. black movement, investigation, **1980–81:** 1846
Grain industry labor dispute actions, **1979:** 1708
Greensboro, N.C., shooting of demonstrators, discussions with the President (Digest), **1979:** 2104
Handicapped persons antidiscrimination, regulations enforcement, **1980–81:** 809
Interagency Employee Benefit Council, member, **1980–81:** 2864
Iran
American hostages release agreement implementation functions, **1980–81:** 3028, 3029, 3031, 3033–3035, 3037, 3038, 3043
International, Court of Justice, U.S. position on American hostages in Iran presentation, **1979:** 2209, 2240
Sanctions against, duties, **1980–81:** 611, 612
Iranian aliens, entry into U.S. authority, **1979:** 2154
Iranian student visas, examination responsibilities, **1979:** 2107, 2286
Lawsuits authority against public institutions, **1980–81:** 965
Meetings with the President (Digest), **1979:** 1222, 1293, 2248
Membership on:
Oil Policy Committee, **1980–81:** 10
Trade Policy Committee, **1980–81:** 8
Mentions, **1979:** 1335, 1408, 1410, 1416, 1609; **1980–81:** 413
Miami, Fla., court system investigation, **1980–81:** 1075
National Petroleum Reserves in Alaska, report, **1980–81:** 232
News conference (Checklist), **1979:** 2281
Nomination, **1979:** 1272, 1293
Nondiscrimination laws enforcement, **1980–81:** 2652, 2654
Privacy protection responsibilities, **1980–81:** 2218

Attorney General — *continued*
Private school tax credit exemption position, **1980–81:** 2052
Puerto Rican Nationalists, prison sentences commutation recommendations, **1979:** 1597
Refugee admission functions, **1980–81:** 684, 685
Swearing-in ceremony, **1979:** 1440–1442
Task Force on Global Resources and Environment, duties, **1980–81:** 1417
U.N. Representative Young's apartment, investigation of bugging of, **1979:** 1586, 1591
For functions of the Department in general, see Justice, Department of.
Attorneys, U.S.
See U.S. attorneys *under* Appointments and Nominations.
Attorneys General, National Association of State, **1977:** 251; **1979:** 618
Attwood, William, **1978:** 1630, 1669
Atwood, J. Brian, **1979:** 1292, 1294
Atwood, Robert, **1979:** 2218
Auburn-Folsom South, Central Valley Project, Calif., **1977:** 208
AuCoin, Repr. Les, **1978:** 1944; **1980–81:** 1661, 1938, 2672
Audiovisual programs, Federal, **1977:** 1112; **1978:** 785
Audits, Federal grants-in-aid, **1977:** 1561, 1563
Audubon Society, National, **1980–81:** 415
Auguste, Barry Bertrand Lucas, **1980–81:** 775
Aukofer, Frank, **1978:** 438
Ausley, DuBose, **1977:** 816
Austen, Dr. William, **1978:** 289
Austin, J. Paul, **1977:** 1084
Austin, Thomas S., **1980–81:** 86
Australia
Ambassador to U.S. **1977:** 194; **1979:** 2162n.
Australia-American Week celebrations, **1979:** 376
Defense Minister, **1980–81:** 422
Foreign Minister, **1980–81:** 422
Former Prime Minister Sir Robert Menzies, **1978:** 913
Grain exports, **1980–81:** 42
Nuclear energy agreement with U.S., **1979:** 1314
Nuclear fuel supplies, **1977:** 585
Prime Minister J. Malcolm Fraser, **1977:** 1127, 1140; **1979:** 2, 1231; **1980–81:** 103
U.S. Ambassador, **1977:** 576, 597, 744, 805, 873, 883; **1980–81:** 2806
U.S. relations, **1980–81:** 169, 2984
Vice President's visit, **1978:** 327
Australian-American Association, **1979:** 376
Austria
Ambassador to U.S. **1977:** 508
Chancellor Bruno Kreisky, **1977:** 463, 785; **1979:** 1047, 1142, 2036

Austria — *continued*
  Jewish Documentation Center in Vienna, **1980–81:** 1495
  President Rudolph Kirchschläger, **1979:** 1047, 1142
  U.S. Ambassador, **1977:** 1124, 1128; **1979:** 1048; **1980–81:** 191, 1765, 1770n.
  Vice President's visit, **1977:** 785
  Vienna Summit Meeting.
    See Vienna Summit Meeting.
Auto Industry Committee, **1980–81:** 1650, 1669, 1826, 2187
Auto Workers, United.
  See United Auto Workers.
Automobile, Aerospace & Agricultural Implement Workers of America, United, **1980–81:** 1598
Automobile Fuel Efficiency Act, **1980–81:** 2186
Automobile Manufacturers Association, **1979:** 900
Automobiles and automobile industry
  Air pollution control **1979:** 183
  Chief executives, meeting with the President (Digest), **1980–81:** 931
  Chrysler Corporation loan.
    See Chrysler Corporation.
  Emission standards, **1977:** 286, 1072, 1460
  Employment
    Federal assistance for high unemployment areas, **1980–81:** 2187
    Impact of:
      Foreign automakers plant construction, **1980–81:** 706, 711
      Inflation rates, **1980–81:** 705
      Oil imports reduction, **1980–81:** 2457
    Statistics, **1980–81:** 1632, 2009, 2257, 2268, 2362
  Energy legislation, lobbyists, **1977:** 1082, 1092, 1103
  Energy program, impact, **1977:** 753
  Energy-saving measures, **1977:** 665, 674, 891, 896
  Federal impact assistance, **1980–81:** 1040
  Ford Motor Co., assembly plant, President's remarks at, **1980–81:** 1984
  Foreign competition, **1977:** 891
  Foreign manufacturers plant construction in U.S., **1980–81:** 706, 711, 1676
  Fuel-efficient cars, domestic production increases, **1980–81:** 664, 665, 711, 1618, 1637, 1638, 1830, 1908, 2039, 2045, 2085, 2192, 2206, 2209, 2462, 2515, 2547
  Gasoline consumption, **1977:** 660, 1299
  Impact of:
    Interest rates, **1980–81:** 723, 994, 1114
    OPEC price increases, **1980–81:** 1987, 2009, 2048
  Imports, **1979:** 1488
    Japanese export levels, **1980–81:** 1826, 1908, 1990

Automobiles — *continued*
  Imports — *continued*
    Unemployment compensation for workers affected by, **1980–81:** 923, 2009
    United States International Trade Commission's investigation, **1980–81:** 1330
  Industry employees' health care costs, **1979:** 838
  Industry representatives, meeting with the President (Digest), **1979:** 899; **1980–81:** 1329
  Industry revitalization, **1980–81:** 1607, 1619, 1987, 2009, 2048, 2087
  Innovative initiatives, **1979:** 2070
  Michigan Army Missile Plant, conveyance of, **1980–81:** 769
  No-fault insurance, **1978:** 840; **1979:** 131
  Plant closings, **1980–81:** 705
  President's appeal for support of American industry, **1980–81:** 2143
  Research initiatives technology, **1979:** 900
  Safety requirements, **1977:** 1210; **1980–81:** 1617, 2880
  Sales, **1980–81:** 902, 1511
  State of the Union, **1978:** 106, 107
  Tariff suspensions, **1979:** 2226
  Tax and rebate schedule, proposed, **1977:** 688
  Technical developments for fuel efficiency, **1979:** 797, 1488, 1504, 1549, 1651, 1949
Automotive Engineers, Society of, **1980–81:** 1404
Automotive Products Trade Act of 1965, Operation of the, **1977:** 464, 2077; **1979:** 178; **1980–81:** 653
Avant, Clarence, **1978:** 1406
Aviation.
  See Aircraft and aviation.
Aviation Administration, Federal, **1977:** 536, 537, 557
Aviation, Convention on International Civil, **1979:** 449; **1980–81:** 3024
Aviation Facilities Experimental Center, National, **1978:** 1542
Aviation Organization, International Civil, **1979:** 449
Aviation Year and Wright Brothers Day, National, **1978:** 1396
Avila, Edward, **1980–81:** 1404
AWACS (Airborne Warning and Control System), **1977:** 1377, 1568
Awards and Citations
  Alexander Hamilton Award, **1978:** 125
  American Cancer Society Cancer Courage Award, **1977:** 566; **1978:** 710; **1979:** 554; **1980–81:** 607
  Armand Hammer Conference human rights award medal, **1979:** 1521
  Boy Scouts of America Silver Buffalo award, **1978:** 328
  Boy of the Year award, **1980–81:** 1846
  Cancer Research Foundation awards, **1979:** 786

Awards and Citations — *continued*
  Christian Service Award, **1980–81:** 333
  Congressional Medal of Honor, **1980–81:** 1379, 1565, 1708
  Congressional Space Medal of Honor Awards, **1978:** 1684, 1724
  Conservationist of the Year Award, **1979:** 443
  Environmental Industry Council national leadership award, **1980–81:** 415
  Federal Incentive Awards Program, **1977:** 930
  Friend of Education award, **1980–81:** 1299n.
  Goddard Memorial Trophy, **1980–81:** 563, 564
  Golda Meir Leadership Award, **1980–81:** 2768
  Hubert H. Humphrey Award, **1980–81:** 221
  International Human Rights Award, **1979:** 2009
  International Mediation Medal, **1979:** 1454
  Kennedy Center Honors, **1978:** 2186; **1980–81:** 2785
  Martin Luther King, Jr. Nonviolent Peace Award, **1979:** 27
  Military awards program, **1980–81:** 475
  National Caucus on the Black Aged Living Legacy awards, **1979:** 317
  National Medal of Science, **1977:** 2044; **1979:** 2289; **1980–81:** 80
  National Security Award, **1979:** 1515
  National Security Medal, **1979:** 179
  National Small Business Person of the Year, **1978:** 819; **1979:** 868
  National Teacher of the Year Award, **1977:** 477; **1978:** 546; **1979:** 598
  Nobel Prize winners, **1979:** 1962, 1963; **1980–81:** 2740
  Outdoor Life magazine award, **1979:** 2186
  Pepperdine University Tyler Ecology Award, **1977:** 642
  Presidential energy efficiency award, **1980–81:** 790
  Presidential Management Improvement awards, **1978:** 950; **1980–81:** 18, 19, 1507
  Presidential Medal of Freedom, **1977:** 1215, 1228; **1978:** 1338; **1979:** 87; **1980–81:** 751, 1057, 1598, 2922
  Presidential Physical Fitness Award, **1979:** 955
  Presidential Rank Awards for the Senior Executive Service, **1980–81:** 1697, 1715
  Presidential Scholars medallions, **1978:** 968
  President's Award for Distinguished Federal Civilian Service, **1980–81:** 86, 2999
  President's Award for Energy Effciency, **1980–81:** 1399, 1401, 1452, 2875
  President's Environmental Youth Awards, **1978:** 787; **1979:** 2075
  Public Health Service Award, **1979:** 983
  Recording for the Blind, Inc., scholarship achievement awards, **1978:** 925
  Scott Newman Drug Abuse Prevention Award, **1980–81:** 1715

Awards and Citations — *continued*
  Small Business Person Awards, **1977:** 995; **1980–81:** 921
  Special Congressional Medal, **1978:** 1787
  Special Conservation Award of the Florida Wildlife Federation, **1979:** 1604
  Special Country Music Association Award, **1979:** 898
  United States Summer Olympic team medals, **1980–81:** 1440
  Wiezmann Institute of Science honorary degree, **1980–81:** 646
  Women's Caucus for Art awards, **1979:** 217
Axtell, Dean R., **1980–81:** 605, 608
Ayalew, Mandefro, **1977:** 2050
Ayers, H. Brandt, **1980–81:** 2608
Ayres, Richard E., **1978:** 762
Ayuso-Planes, Damaris, **1980–81:** 928
Azeredo da Silveira, Antonoio Francisco, **1979:** 1318

B-1 bomber, **1977:** 28, 96, 106, 224, 1084, 1110, 1197, 1199, 1210, 1693, 1854, 2118; **1978:** 307, 472; **1979:** 1052, 1062
  Effectiveness comparison with cruise missile, **1980–81:** 348, 1309, 1551, 1870, 2011, 2304
  Mention, **1980–81:** 1688
B-52 bomber, **1977:** 1199; **1978:** 123; **1979:** 1052, 1062; **1980–81:** 1552, 1870
Babalas, Peter K., **1980–81:** 218
Babbitt, Gov. Bruce E., **1978:** 1836; **1979:** 660; **1980–81:** 849, 3021
Babcock, Barbara, **1977:** 156, 195
Babcock, David E., **1980–81:** 940 968
Babione, Dale R., **1979:** 437
Babrak Karmal, **1980–81:** 1193, 2835
Baca-Barragan, Polly, **1979:** 1439
Backfire bomber, **1977:** 96, 348, 538, 540, 542, 1017; **1979:** 1079, 1090, 1587, 1845
Backhaus, Mack A., **1980–81:** 1715
Backley Richard V., **1978:** 1270, 1279; **1980–81:** 2107
Badillo, Repr. Herman, **1977:** 1826
Baez, Joan, **1979:** 2081
Baffour-Senkyire, Joseph Kingsley, **1980–81:** 1598
Bagley, Vicki I., **1977:** 2182
Bahamas
  Ambassador to U.S. **1980–81:** 775
  Prime Minister Lynden O. Pindling, **1977:** 1568
  U.S. Ambassador, **1977:** 195, 1475, 1483
Bahamonde, Jose, **1980–81:** 1404
Bahrain, U.S. Ambassador, **1979:** 101, 179; **1980–81:** 1106, 1112
Bailar, Benjamin F., **1977:** 1084; **1978:** 504
Bailey, Elizabeth E., **1977:** 1218, 1223

Bailey, Mrs. John, **1978:** 1887
Bailey, Patricia Price, **1979:** 1394, 1397; **1980–81:** 1066, 1111
Baily, R. E., **1979:** 1614n.
Bailly, Jacques, **1980–81:** 1008, 1009
Bair, Ron, **1980–81:** 961
Baird, Hannah Hume, **1978:** 709; **1979:** 1447
Baits and flies industry, artificial, **1978:** 2071
Bakalis, Michael J., **1978:** 710, 982, 983, 996 1937; **1980–81:** 493
Baker, Harold A., **1978:** 1407
Baker, Sen. Howard H., Jr., **1977:** 251, 1280, 1700, 1794; **1978:** 148, 303, 311, 517, 526, 758, 785, 1458, 1477, 2003; **1980–81:** 2106, 2726, 2797, 2822
Baker, Rev. James, **1977:** 312
Baker, James E., **1977:** 1587; **1979:** 1396
Baker, Louis, **1980–81:** 1438n.
Baker, Richard, **1980–81:** 1008, 1009
Baker, Russell T., Jr., **1978:** 935, 936, 1937
Bakhtiar, Shahpour, **1979:** 50, 259
Bakke case, **1978:** 111, 322, 1223, 1230, 1320; **1979:** 847
Bakke, Capt. Richard L., **1980–81:** 780n., 864
Balaguer, Joaquín, **1977:** 1551, 1568; **1978:** 932, 942
Balcomb, Douglas, **1979:** 1534, 1537
Baldazo, Noelia G., **1980–81:** 844
Baldus, Repr. Alvin, **1978:** 1237
Baldwin, Robert E., **1979:** 2166, 2188; **1980–81:** 2071
Baldwin, Roger Nash, **1980–81:** 2930
Ball, George, **1979:** 1823
Ball, Gordon, **1978:** 1860
Ball, Ralph M., **1980–81:** 1595, 1599
Ball, Robert, **1980–81:** 2585, 2615
Ballantine, Thomas A., Jr., **1977:** 1700, 1701
Balloon crossing, transatlantic, **1978:** 1449
Baltimore, David, **1980–81:** 3023
Baltimore, Md., **1978:** 1795; **1979:** 1406, 1408
Baltimore Orioles, **1979:** 1975
Bamberger, Clinton, **1979:** 1451
Bangladesh
    Ambassador to U.S., **1978:** 1722
    Iran, abstention from voting on U.N. sanctions against, **1980–81:** 39
    Joint statement, **1980–81:** 1579
    President Ziaur Rahman, **1980–81:** 1564, 1577, 1579
    Taxation convention with U.S., **1980–81:** 2762
    U.S. Ambassador, **1977:** 1977, 2006; **1978:** 231
    U.S. relations, **1980–81:** 172
Bangor, Maine, **1978:** 341, 344, 414, 1009
Bani-Sadr, Abol Hassan.
    See Iran, President.
Bank.
    See other part of title.
Bank, National Development, **1978:** 2193; **1979:** 99, 137

Bank for Reconstruction and Development, International, **1979:** 1454, 1801, 2269, 2281
Bankers Association, National, **1977:** 744
Banks, Fred L., Jr., **1979:** 1727
Banks and banking
    Credit controls.
        See Credit controls.
    Deposit interest rate controls, **1979:** 132
    Farm loans, **1980–81:** 652, 2837
    Federal access to bank records, **1979:** 583
    Federal institutions deregulation legislation, **1979:** 928, 1728, 2078, 2288
        Congressional consideration, **1980–81:** 252
        Mentions, **1980–81:** 118, 121, 215, 918, 1537
        Purposes, **1980–81:** 151
        Signing ceremony, **1980–81:** 572
    Federal Reserve membership decline, **1979:** 2289
    Interest rate reform, **1979:** 928
    Interest rates.
        See Interest rates.
    Iran, prohibition on U.S. business with, **1980–81:** 613, 615
    Iranian assets blockage, **1979:** 2118
    Small business credit financing, **1980–81:** 76
Banner, Donald W., **1978:** 292, 304
Bannerman, Charles, **1979:** 2276
Banzer Suarez, Hugo, **1977:** 1550, 1568
Baptist Brotherhood Commission, Southern, **1978:** 1113
Baptist Radio and Television Commission, Southern, **1980–81:** 333
Baptista de Oliveira Figueiredo, João, **1979:** 239, 401
Baptists, Southern, **1977:** 877, 1084
Barabba, Vincent P., **1979:** 981, 1019
Baranski, Tibor, **1980–81:** 821
Barbados
    Ambassador to U.S., **1977:** 942
    Prime Minister J. M. G. Adams, **1980–81:** 824
    U.S. Ambassador, **1977:** 1189, 1212; **1978:** 1879; **1979:** 293, 664
    U.S. arms sales, **1979:** 1130
Barber, Chip, **1978:** 1082
Barber, Randolph L., **1979:** 2076
Barbour, Elaine, **1978:** 546, 696
Barcelo, Gov. Carlos Romero, **1978:** 1336
Barco, Virgilio, **1977:** 1163
Bardin, David J., **1977:** 547, 558, 1584, 1613
Bardstown, Ky., **1979:** 1340, 1398
Bare, Bobby, **1980–81:** 1404
Barfield, Claude, **1980–81:** 264
Bario, Patricia Y., **1978:** 1496, 1596; **1980–81:** 94, 245, 343, 392, 665, 767, 906, 991, 1120
    Deputy Press Secretary to the President, appointment, **1979:** 1017
    Mentions, **1979:** 252n., 852n., 908n., 1329n., 1613n., 1715n., 1863n.

Barker, Norma C., **1978:** 696
Barnes, Arthur H., **1979:** 2195
Barnes, Iraline, **1979:** 2116, 2138
Barnes, Repr. Michael D., **1980–81:** 16
Barnett, James E., **1980–81:** 237, 268
Barnstable Middle School, Hyannis, Mass, **1979:** 1908
Barnum, Thomas F., **1980–81:** 2610
Barnwell, S.C., plutonium reprocessing plant, **1977:** 582, 588
Baron, Frederick, **1977:** 944
Baroni, Geno Charles, **1977:** 510, 1675, 1833, 1836, 1841, 1848; **1979:** 1221, 1223, 1408, 1921; **1980–81:** 281, 1095
Barre, Maj. Gen. Mohamed Siad, **1978:** 490
Barre, Raymond, **1977:** 1383, 1390, 1603, 1607, 1609, 1612, 1613
Barreaux, Theodore C., **1979:** 2117
Barrett, Thomas Joseph, **1980–81:** 2074
Barrie, Robert, **1980–81:** 2832
Barringer, John W., **1979:** 942
Barron, Gary, **1978:** 1223
Barrow, Gen. Robert H., **1979:** 672; **1980–81:** 1710n.
Barry, Marion S., Jr., **1979:** 25, 144, 1920; **1980–81:** 13, 601
Barry, Robert, **1979:** 1143
Bartalan, Imre, **1980–81:** 1438n.
Bartels, Elmer, **1980–81:** 3025
Bartelt, Leland E., **1977:** 1079, 1085
Barthe, Richmond, **1980–81:** 602
Bartlett, Sen. Dewey, **1978:** 393, 1808; **1979:** 374
Bartley, Anne, **1977:** 2153
Barton, James G., **1977:** 943
Baruch, Jordan, **1979:** 2070n., 2082
Baruch, Jordan A., **1978:** 1188
Baruch, Jordan J., **1977:** 554, 596
Baryshnikov, Mikhail, **1979:** 376; **1980–81:** 2787
Basic Educational Opportunity Grants, **1977:** 2088; **1978:** 425
Basketball Association, National, **1978:** 1070; **1980–81:** 268
Baskette, F. Kenneth, Jr., **1977:** 1070, 1085
Bass, Jack, **1978:** 1586
Bass, Mary P., **1979:** 398, 402
Batoff, Bill, **1980–81:** 2046
Battaglia, Frank J., **1979:** 1417
Battan, Louis J., **1978:** 217
Battle Monuments Commission, American, **1978:** 2089; **1979:** 81; **1980–81:** 1596
Baucus, Sen. Max, **1979:** 2036, 2044, 2085, 2110; **1980–81:** 1063, 1936
Baudouin I, King, **1978:** 32–34; **1980–81:** 757
Baum, Werner A., **1978:** 217
Baum, William Cardinal, **1980–81:** 1168
Bauman, Jim, **1978:** 1627
Bauman, Repr. Robert E., **1979:** 667
Baumann, Carol E., **1978:** 1514

Baxley, Ga., **1977:** 2126
Baxter, Elaine, **1978:** 734
Baxter, Harry Y., **1977:** 1855, 1860; **1978:** 510
Bayh, Sen. Birch, **1977:** 527, 925, 1712; **1978:** 191, 277, 802, 1719, 1801, 1854
    Carter, Billy, investigation of activities with Libyan Government, **1980–81:** 2647
    Gasohol production legislation sponsorship, **1979:** 993
    Jefferson-Jackson Day dinner, Indianapolis, Ind., remarks, **1979:** 988
    Legislation passage leadership
        Dispute Resolution Act, **1980–81:** 303
        Intelligence Authorization Act for fiscal year 1981, **1980–81:** 2233
        Judicial Councils Reform and Judicial Conduct and Disability Act, **1980–81:** 2241
        Privacy Protection Act, **1980–81:** 2218
    Meeting with the President (Digest), **1979:** 956
    Mention, **1979:** 990
    President's assessment, **1979:** 989
    SALT II treaty consideration, **1979:** 994, 1822
Bayh, Marvella, **1979:** 691, 989, 991
Bazargan, Mehdi, **1979:** 257, 259, 352
Bazelon, David L., **1977:** 377, 1048
Beach, William O., **1978:** 748
Beall, C. E. Campbell, **1979:** 400
Beall, Donald R., **1979:** 241
Beals, Alan L., **1978:** 2080
Beals, Melba P., **1980–81:** 2429, 2727, 2859, 2870, 2873
Beame, Abraham, **1977:** 148, 263, 1154, 1729, 1755, 2006; **1978:** 422, 2160; **1979:** 1746; **1980–81:** 422, 2370
Bean, Maurice D., **1977:** 1474, 1483
Beard, Repr. Edward P., **1977:** 1758
Beard, Repr. Robin L., **1978:** 1695
Beard, Thomas V., **1977:** 1117; **1980–81:** 1466
Bearden, Romare, **1980–81:** 602
Beattie, Richard I., **1979:** 1000, 1019
Beatty, Otto, Jr., **1980–81:** 2613
Beatty, William L., **1979:** 1397, 1398
Beaumont, Dina G., **1979:** 552
Beaumont, Tex., **1978:** 1173; **1980–81:** 2408, 2409
Beauregard, Pierre, **1980–81:** 1602
Beaver Castle Girl Scouts, **1978:** 1608
Beaver Falls, Pa., **1980–81:** 2344
Becharof National Monument, **1978:** 2116
Bechily, Maria C., **1980–81:** 508, 1023, 1051
Bechtel, William R., **1977:** 1070, 1085
Bechtol, Terryl, **1979:** 1725
Beck, Carl A., **1977:** 196, 1944, 1966; **1978:** 230
Beck, Eckardt C., **1977:** 1817; **1979:** 1726, 1785
Beck, Gordon, **1979:** 2042
Beckel, Robert G., meetings with the President (Digest), **1979:** 618, 666, 731, 842, 956
Becker, Ernest, **1978:** 1240
Becker, Sylvia, **1978:** 1974

Becker, William H., **1977:** 372

Beckham, William J., Jr., **1977:** 460, 465; **1978:** 1682; **1979:** 2039, 2044; **1980–81:** 25, 493, 2877n.

Beckman, Aldo B., **1979:** 746n.

Beckner, Donald L., **1977:** 1222, 1266

Bedell, Repr. Berkley W., **1977:** 1855; **1978:** 1237; **1979:** 2299

Bedell, Catherine May, **1979:** 2285; **1980–81:** 102

Bedford, N.H., **1979:** 714, 733

Bee Gees, meeting with the President (Digest), **1979:** 1784

Beebe, William, **1980–81:** 1404

Beef industry
    Imports, **1978:** 1061, 1062, 1072, 1074, 1080, 1158, 1421, 1494, 1672; **1979:** 2299
    Prices and price controls, **1979:** 475, 705, 754, 796, 849, 850
    Representatives, meeting with the President, **1978:** 1345

Beer, Peter Hill, **1979:** 1883

Begay, Nelson R., **1980–81:** 928

Begin, Menahem.
    See Israel, Prime Minister.

Begin, Mrs. Menahem, **1979:** 417n., 430n., 522n.; **1980–81:** 686

Behavioral Research, President's Commission for the Study of Ethical Problems in Medicine and Biomedical and, **1979:** 1263, 1294; **1980–81:** 896, 1723

Behavioral Research, President's Special Commission for the Study of Ethical Problems in Medicine and Biomedical and, **1979:** 2260

Behen, John V., **1978:** 1380

Beigel, Alan, **1977:** 529

Beilenson, Repr. Anthony C., **1980–81:** 433

Belew, David O., Jr., **1979:** 241, 242

Belgium,
    Ambassador to U.S., **1979:** 1882
    King Baudouin I and Queen Fabiola, **1980–81:** 757
    President's visit, **1977:** 1649, 1983, 2077; **1978:** 32–39
    Prime Minister Leo Tindemans, **1977:** 882, 1506, 1532, 1533, 1634, 1814, 1818, 1827
    U.S. Ambassador, **1977:** 576, 577, 597

Belgrade meeting, Conference on Security and Cooperation in Europe, **1977:** 994, 1031, 2037, 2038, 2208

Belgrade Review Conference, **1978:** 453

Belitsos, George P., **1977:** 1713

Bell, Griffin B.
    See Attorney General.

Bellamy, Carol, **1977:** 1805; **1980–81:** 2074

Bellamy, G. Thomas, **1980–81:** 192

Belli. Lia Triff, **1980–81:** 272

Bellmon, Sen. Henry L., **1977:** 1648; **1978:** 521, 2110; **1979:** 2257n.; **1980–81:** 2778

Belloni, Pete, **1977:** 292

Bellotti, Francis X., **1978:** 1723

Benacerraf, Baruj, **1980–81:** 2740

Bender, Michael W., **1980–81:** 927

Bendixen, Sergio, **1977:** 882

Benedick, Richard Elliot, **1979:** 377, 378

Benedict, Al, **1980–81:** 1629

Benedict, Robert C., **1977:** 2082, 2089; **1978:** 231

Benet, Stephen Vincent, **1979:** 1930

Bengelloun, Ali, **1977:** 1163

Benjamin. Repr. Adam, Jr., **1979:** 990; **1980–81:** 966

Benjamin, Judah P., **1980–81:** 1602

Bennet, Douglas Joseph, Jr., **1977:** 8, 280, 2181; **1979:** 1271, 1293

Bennett, Brian R., **1980–81:** 927

Bennett. Carolyn M., **1978:** 696

Bennett, Repr. Charles E., **1977:** 2076

Bennett, Jack, **1978:** 1293

Bennett, W. Tapley, Jr., **1977:** 589, 597

Benoit, Joan, **1979:** 770

Benovitz, Madge, **1977:** 1053

Bensen, Robert S., **1980–81:** 263

Bensinger, Peter B., **1977:** 1161; **1978:** 1599

Benson, Charles S., **1979:** 1525

Benson, Dale, **1979:** 1468n.

Benson, Lucy Wilson, **1977:** 373

Benti, Joseph, **1977:** 895

Benton, Charles W., **1978:** 1454, 1458; **1979:** 2128; **1980–81:** 1445, 1470

Benton, George S., **1978:** 576, 641

Benton, Marjorie Craig, **1977:** 1626, 1650; **1978:** 919, 935, 1190; **1979:** 1602, 2085

Bentsen, Sen. Lloyd M., **1977:** 1507, 1612, 1825; **1978:** 415, 1164–1166, 1672, 1673, 1782; **1979:** 376, 1397, 2257n., 2299
    Campaign appearances with the President, **1980–81:** 2413, 2622, 2627
    Meetings with the President (Digest), **1980–81:** 374, 1523
    Mentions, **1980–81:** 1395, 2081
    National Aquaculture Act, passage leadership, **1980–81:** 1938

Bere, James, **1980–81:** 1670

Berenbaum. Michael, **1978:** 1974

Berg, Harold E., **1979:** 1614n.

Berg, Thomas K., **1979:** 2281; **1980–81:** 25

Bergen, Dr. Stanley S., **1977:** 1575

Berger, Stephen, **1980–81:** 392, 423

Bergin, Thomas P., **1979:** 435, 441

Bergland, Bob, **1977:** 9, 13, 35, 167, 168, 170, 175, 248, 299, 356, 508, 648, 705, 797–801, 805, 807, 920, 1210, 1222, 1265, 1506, 1622, 1680, 1704, 1705, 1857, 1879, 2013, 2076, 2096, 2121, 2168, 2178; **1978:** 145, 293,

Bergland, Bob — *continued*
>327, 409, 456, 570, 700, 733, 811, 881, 914, 1062, 1072, 1376, 1391, 1420, 1422, 1424, 1674, 2109, 2111
>*See also* Agriculture, Secretary of.
Bergman, Barbara E., **1979:** 1976
Bergmann, Barbara, **1979:** 2218
Bergold, Harry E., Jr., **1977:** 1584, 1613; **1980–81:** 236, 268
Bergsten, C. Fred, **1977:** 86, 148, 805; **1978:** 1155
Bergus, Donald C., **1977:** 873, 874, 883
Bering Land Bridge National Monument, **1978:** 2117
Berkeley, Norborne, Jr., **1978:** 759; **1980–81:** 1048
Berlin
>Airlift Memorial, **1978:** 1293
>Four Powers meeting, **1978:** 1308
>Friendship Force, **1978:** 1966
>Protest of President's visit, **1978:** 1283
>Town meeting, **1978:** 1295
>U.S. policy, **1977:** 51, 767, 828, 840
Berlioux, Monique, **1980–81:** 929
Berman, Jason S., **1979:** 293, 976
Berman, Joan F., **1978:** 696
Bermuda, Prime Minister John David Gibbons, **1980–81:** 931
Bermudez-Milla, Jose Antonio, **1979:** 25
Bernalillo County, N. Mex., **1979:** 1817
Bernardin, Archbishop Joseph L., **1977:** 1611
Bernstein, Irving, **1978:** 411, 1974; **1979:** 23; **1980–81:** 84, 821
Bernstein, Joan Zeldes, **1978:** 1652; **1979:** 1960, 1977; **1980–81:** 1146, 2870
Bernstein, Leonard, **1979:** 281, 282ftn., 2102; **1980–81:** 2341, 2786
Bernstein, Marver, **1980–81:** 821
Bernstein, Samuel, **1980–81:** 2817
Berrios, Gonzalo, **1978:** 623
Berry, Chuck, **1979:** 1015
Berry, Mary Frances, **1977:** 252, 2036; **1978:** 971, 1681, 1917, 1919; **1979:** 742, 886n.; **1980–81:** 605, 608, 892
Berry, Max N., **1980–81:** 1346
Bertelsman, William O., **1979:** 1883
Bertoni, Anthony, **1978:** 1111
Beshar, Robert P., **1978:** 1878
Bessinger, B.L., **1980–81:** 1946
Best, Dave, **1980–81:** 2397
Betancourt, Romulo, **1978:** 640
Bethesda Naval Hospital, Md., **1977:** 296
Bethlehem Steel Corporation, **1978:** 1111; **1980–81:** 2409
Bethune, Mary McCloud, **1979:** 2135
Better Hearing and Speech Month, **1977:** 743; **1978:** 822
>Poster Child, **1980–81:** 824
Better Jobs and Income program, **1977:** 1443, 1451, 1844, 2000; **1978:** 133, 138, 579, 1643

Better Way Club, **1979:** 568
Betz, Gary Louis, **1979:** 241, 242
Beverly Hills, Calif., **1980–81:** 1887
Beverly Hills School, Concord, N.C., **1977:** 740
Bevill, Repr. Tom, **1977:** 744; **1978:** 302, 1571, 2003
Bey, Shallie M., Jr., **1978:** 408, 416
Beyer, Gordon R., **1980–81:** 355, 629, 720
Beyers, Staff Sgt. Joseph, **1980–81:** 786
Biaggi, Repr. Mario, **1978:** 289, 304; **1979:** 1410
>Campaign appearance with the President, **1980–81:** 2194
>Heat- and drought-affected areas, assistance legislation sponsorship, **1980–81:** 1422
>Legislation passage leadership
>>Comprehensive Environmental Response, Compensation, and Liability Act, **1980–81:** 2797
>>Illegal drug trafficking on the high seas prevention, **1980–81:** 1722
>>Inland Navigational Rules Act, **1980–81:** 2837
>Meetings with the President (Digest), **1980–81:** 1523, 1946
>U.S. assistance for earthquake victims in Italy, activities, **1980–81:** 2807, 2889
Bible Society, American, **1977:** 1612
Bible Week, National, **1978:** 2070; **1980–81:** 2747
Bicentennial functions, **1977:** 1190
Bicycle tire and tube industry, **1978:** 1903, 1904
Bicycling Day, National, **1980–81:** 562
Biddle, Livingston L., Jr., **1977:** 1946, 1966; **1978:** 2059; **1980–81:** 601, 754
Biden, Frank, **1978:** 385
Biden, Sen. Joseph R., Jr., **1977:** 1126; **1978:** 276, 385, 386, 1194; **1979:** 293, 1587; **1980–81:** 662
Biemiller, Andrew, **1977:** 1948
Biernacki, Lorilee J., **1980–81:** 927
Bieszczat, Mathew W., **1978:** 1808
Big Thompson River, Colo., **1979:** 1814
Biggs, John A., **1978:** 217
Bighorse, Bobby, **1980–81:** 2883
Bigjim, Frederick S., **1978:** 1419
Bikel, Theodore, **1977:** 2024, 2037; **1978:** 252, 277
Bilandic, Michael A., **1977:** 147, 1804; **1978:** 641, 974, 980, 982, 983, 985, 1940, 1952
Bilby, Richard M., **1979:** 1018, 1019
Bildner, Albert, **1978:** 1380
Bilingual education, **1978:** 428
Bill of Rights Day, **1977:** 2086; **1978:** 2089
>(Proc. 4705), **1979:** 2198
>(Proc. 4804), **1980–81:** 2724
Bill signings
>Absaroka-Beartooth Wilderness, Montana, statement, **1978:** 575
>Adoption Assistance and Child Welfare Act, statement, **1980–81:** 1124
>Age Discrimination in Employment Act Amendments, remarks, **1978:** 698

Bill signings — *continued*
  Agricultural Act, statement, **1980–81:** 2770
  Agricultural Adjustment Act, statement, **1980–81:** 503
  Agricultural Credit Act, remarks and statement, **1978:** 1375, 1376
  Agricultural Foreign Investment Disclosure Act, statement, **1978:** 1783
  Agricultural Trade Act, remarks, **1978:** 1818
  Air cargo deregulation, remarks, **1977:** 1987
  Airline Deregulation Act, remarks, **1978:** 1837
  Alaska National Interest Lands Conservation Act, remarks, **1980–81:** 2756
  Alaska natural gas transportation system, remarks and statement, **1977:** 1978, 1980
  Amateur Sports Act, statement, **1978:** 1976
  American Indian Religious Freedom Act, statement, **1978:** 1417
  Amtrak Improvement Act, statement, **1978:** 1718
  Appalachian Trail, statement, **1978:** 548
  Arms Control and Disarmament Act Amendments of 1977, statement, **1977:** 1480
  Automobile Fuel Efficiency Act, statement, **1980–81:** 2186
  Beef and veal imports, statement, **1979:** 2299
  Black Lung Benefits Reform Act of 1977, remarks, **1978:** 432
  Career Education Incentive Act, statement, **1977:** 2104
  Central Idaho Wilderness Act, remarks and statement, **1980–81:** 1407, 1410
  Central Valley Project, San Luis Unit, authorization, statement, **1977:** 1124
  Child Nutrition Amendments statement, **1978:** 2000
  Chrysler Corporation Loan Guarantee Act of 1979, remarks, **1980–81:** 27
  Civil Rights of Institutionalized Persons Act, statement, **1980–81:** 965
  Civil Service Reform Act, remarks and statement, **1978:** 1761, 1765
  Civil service retirement credit for Japanese Americans interned during World War II, statement, **1978:** 1569
  Clean Air Act Amendments of 1977, statement, **1977:** 1460
  Clean Water Act of 1977, statement, **1977:** 2179
  Coastal Zone Management Improvement Act, statement, **1980–81:** 2335
  Commission on Wartime Relocation and Internment of Civilians Act, remarks, **1980–81:** 1455
  Community Emergency Drought Relief Act of 1977, remarks, **1977:** 962
  Comprehensive Employment and Training Act Amendments
    Remarks, **1978:** 1871
    Statement, **1977:** 1123

Bill signings — *continued*
  Comprehensive Environmental Response, Compensation, and Liability Act, remarks, **1980–81:** 2797
  Comprehensive Older Americans Act Amendments, remarks and statement, **1978:** 1792, 1793
  Congressional delegate for American Samoa, statement, **1978:** 1907
  Congressional Reports Elimination Act, statement, **1980–81:** 2344
  Consumer Credit Protection Act amendments, remarks, **1977:** 1628
  Consumer Product Safety Commission, continuing authorization, statement, **1978:** 2001
  Contract Disputes Act, statement, **1978:** 1922
  Council on Wages and Price Stability appropriations, statement, **1980–81:** 2789
  Cow Creek Band of the Umpqua Indian Tribe Claims, statement, **1980–81:** 980
  Crude Oil Windfall Profit Tax Act, remarks, **1980–81:** 584
  Customs Court Act, statement, **1980–81:** 2185
  Customs Procedural Reform and Simplification Act, statement, **1978:** 1705
  Davis, Jefferson F., restoration of citizenship rights, statement, **1978:** 1786
  Days of rememberance of victims of the Holocaust, statement, **1978:** 1529
  Deep Seabed Hard Mineral Resources Act, White House statement, **1980–81:** 1284
  Demarcation lines dividing the high seas and inland waters, statement, **1980–81:** 1521
  Department of Defense Authorization Act, **1980–81:** 1667
  Department of Education Organization Act, remarks and statement, **1979:** 1955, 1958
  Department of Energy National Security and Military Applications of Nuclear Energy Authorization Act of 1980, statement, **1979:** 2298
  Department of Energy Organization Act, remarks, **1977:** 1410
  Department of Transportation and Related Agencies Appropriations Act, 1980, statement, **1979:** 2185
  Departments of Labor and Health, Education and Welfare continuing appropriations bill, statement, **1977:** 2087
  Departments of State, Justice, and Commerce, the Judiciary, and Related Agencies Appropriation Act
    1978, statement, **1977:** 1409
    1979, statement, **1978:** 1735
  Depository institutions, amendment of regulatory authority, statement, **1977:** 662
  Depository Institutions Deregulation and Monetary Control Act, remarks, **1980–81:** 572

Bill signings — *continued*

Diplomatic Relations Act, statement, **1978:** 1694

Disaster Relief Act amendments, statement, **1977:** 1134

Dispute Resolution Act, statement, **1980–81:** 303

District and circuit judges, additional appointments, statement, **1978:** 1803

District of Columbia Appropriations Act, statement, **1978:** 1531

District of Columbia housing revenue bonds, statement, **1980–81:** 666

District of Columbia Retirement Reform Act, statement, **1979:** 2144

Domestic Volunteer Service Act amendments, statement, **1979:** 2237

Drought relief, remarks and statement, **1977:** 592, 593

Earthquake in southern Italy, U.S. assistance, statement, **1980–81:** 2804

Education Amendments, remarks and statement, **1978:** 1916, 1918; **1980–81:** 2060

Eleanor Roosevelt National Historic Site, statement, **1977:** 1028

Emergency agricultural assistance, statement, **1978:** 914

Emergency Agricultural Credit Adjustment Act Amendments, statement, **1980–81:** 567

Emergency Energy Conservation Act, remarks, **1979:** 2085

Emergency Natural Gas Act of 1977, remarks, **1977:** 66

Endangered American Wilderness Act, remarks, **1978:** 409

Endangered Species Act amendments, statement, **1978:** 2002; **1979:** 2288

Energy Research and Development Administration, appropriations, statement, **1977:** 1057

Energy Security Act, remarks, **1980–81:** 1252

Energy and Water Development Appropriation Act, 1980, statement, **1979:** 1760; **1980–81:** 1983

Equal Rights Amendment, remarks, **1978:** 1800

Ethics in Government Act of 1978
Amendments, statement, **1979:** 1131
Remarks, **1978:** 1854, 1880

Export Administration Amendments of 1977, remarks and statement, **1977:** 1136, 1164

Fair Labor Standards Amendments of 1977, remarks, **1977:** 1947

Farm Credit Act Amendments, statement, **1980–81:** 2837

Farmer-owned grain reserve, statement, **1980–81:** 652

Federal agency reorganization, statement, **1980–81:** 483

Federal District Court Organization Act, statement, **1980–81:** 2241

Bill signings — *continued*

Federal Election Campaign Act Amendments of 1979, statement, **1980–81:** 37

Federal Employees' Flexible and Compressed Work Schedules Act, statement, **1978:** 1667

Federal Employees' Group Life Insurance Act, statement, **1980–81:** 2187

Federal Employees' Part-Time Career Employment Act, statement, **1978:** 1736

Federal Insecticide, Fungicide, and Rodenticide Act extension, statement, **1980–81:** 2814

Federal Magistrate Act, statement, **1979:** 1849

Federal Mine Safety and Health Amendments Act of 1977, remarks and statement, **1977:** 1987, 1989

Federal Pesticide Act, statement, **1978:** 1696

Federal recreation and historic sites in Georgia and Kansas, remarks, **1978:** 1424, 1471

Federal-State cooperative forestry programs, statement, **1978:** 1234

Federal-State social services claims, statement, **1978:** 1082

Federal-State-local government funding simplification, statement, **1980–81:** 2814

Federal Trade Commission authorization, statement, **1980–81:** 562

Federal Trade Commission Improvements Act, statement, **1980–81:** 982

Fifth Circuit Court of Appeals Reorganization Act, statement, **1980–81:** 2237

Financial institutions deregulation, statement, **1979:** 2288

Fiscal year 1981 continuing appropriations, statement, **1980–81:** 2015

Fish and Wildlife Conservation Act, statement, **1980–81:** 1958

Fishery Conservation and Management Act of 1976 amendments, statements, **1978:** 1479; **1979:** 1435

Food and Agriculture Act of 1977, remarks, **1977:** 1679

Food Stamp Act of 1977 amendments, statements, **1979:** 1432; **1980–81:** 975

Foreign Assistance Act amendment, statement, **1980–81:** 1522

Foreign corrupt practices and investment disclosure bill, statement, **1977:** 2157

Foreign Intelligence Surveillance Act, statement, **1978:** 1853

Foreign Relations Authorization Act, Fiscal Year 1979, statement, **1978:** 1734

Foreign Service Act, statement, **1980–81:** 2328

Full Employment and Balanced Growth Act, remarks, **1978:** 1871

Futures Trading Act, statement, **1978:** 1696

General Accounting Office Act, statement, **1980–81:** 603

Bill signings — *continued*
GI Bill Improvement Act of 1977, statement, **1977:** 2048
Great Bear and Bob Marshall Wildernesses, Montana, statement, **1978:** 1902
Health Planning and Resources Development Amendments, statement, **1979:** 1818
Hostage Relief Act, statement, **1980–81:** 2231
Household Goods Transportation Act, statement, **1980–81:** 2239
Housing and Community Development Act of 1977, remarks, **1977:** 1777; **1980–81:** 2112
Hubert H. Humphrey Fellowship, statement, **1978:** 1011
Humphrey, Hubert H., gold medal, statement, **1979:** 1036
Illegal drug traffic on the high seas, statement, **1980–81:** 1722
Indochina refugees, remarks, **1977:** 1918
Infant Formula Act, remarks and statement, **1980–81:** 1936, 1937
Inland Navigational Rules Act, statement, **1980–81:** 2836
Inland waterways authorization, remarks and statement, **1978:** 1826, 1827
Inspector General Act, remarks and statement, **1978:** 1754, 1757
Installment Sales Revision Act, statement, **1980–81:** 2343
Intelligence Authorization Act for Fiscal Year 1981, statement, **1980–81:** 2232
Intelligence and Intelligence-Related Activities Authorization Act, of 1979, statement, **1978:** 1529
Interim Reciprocal Fisheries Agreement with Canada, statement, **1978:** 1234
Interior Department appropriations, remarks, **1979:** 2154
International Air Transportation Competition Act, statement, **1980–81:** 332
International Development and Food Assistance Act, statement, **1978:** 1721
International Monetary Fund quota increase, statement, **1980–81:** 2105
International Navigational Rules Act of 1977, statement, **1977:** 1374
International Security Assistance Act of 1977, statements, **1977:** 1431; **1978:** 1636
International Security and Development and Cooperation Act, statement, **1980–81:** 2813
Interstate Commerce Act codification, statement, **1978:** 1794
John Fitzgerald Kennedy Library, statement, **1977:** 1028
Judicial Reform and Judicial Conduct and Disability Act, statement, **1980–81:** 2240

Bill signings — *continued*
Justice William O. Douglas, Federal Building, statement, **1978:** 1877
Juvenile Justice Amendments of 1977
Remarks, **1977:** 1711
Statement, **1980–81:** 2787
Knoxville International Energy Exposition of 1982, statement, **1979:** 2298
Land and Water Conservation Fund, authorization, statement, **1977:** 1097
Lowell National Historical Park, statement, **1978:** 1037
Magnetic Fusion Energy Engineering Act, statement, **1980–81:** 2105
Maine Indian Claims Settlement Act, remarks and statements, **1980–81:** 2176, 2185
Marine Protection, Research, and Sanctuaries Act amendments
Remarks, **1977:** 1961
Statement, **1980–81:** 1592
Maritime training and appropriation authorization, statement, **1980–81:** 2238
Martin Luther King, Jr., and Boston African American national historic sites, remarks and statement, **1980–81:** 2172, 2184
Medicare-Medicaid Anti-Fraud and Abuse Amendments, remarks, **1977:** 1902
Medicare renal disease program, amendments, **1978:** 1086
Mental Health Systems Act, remarks, **1980–81:** 2098
Michigan Army Missile Plant, conveyance of, remarks, **1980–81:** 769
Middle Income Student Assistance Act, remarks and statement, **1978:** 1916, 1918
Military Construction Authorization Act, statement, **1980–81:** 2185
Military Personnel and Compensation Amendments, remarks, **1980–81:** 1665
Milk price supports, statement, **1979:** 2163
Minority and disadvantaged small business assistance, statement, **1978:** 1848
Motor Carrier Act, remarks and statement, **1980–81:** 1261, 1265
Museum of African Art, acquisition by the Smithsonian Institution, statement, **1978:** 1712
Moapa Band of Paiutes, statement, **1980–81:** 2781
National Agriculture Day, remarks, **1980–81:** 2145n.
National Aquaculture Act, statement, **1980–81:** 1937
National Capital Transportation Amendments of 1979, remarks and statement, **1980–81:** 13, 17
National energy, remarks, **1978:** 1978

[References are to page numbers except as otherwise indicated]

Bill signings — *continued*
National Forest Management Act of 1976, amendment, statement, **1978:** 384
National Historic Preservation Act Amendments, statement, **1980–81:** 2802
National Labor Relations Act amendments, statement, **1980–81:** 2856
National Parks and Recreation Act of 1978, statements, **1978:** 1999; **1980–81:** 432
National P.O.W.-M.I.A. Recognition Day, statement, **1978:** 1453
National Science Foundation Authorization and Science and Technology Equal Opportunity Act, statement, **1980–81:** 2804
New York City Loan Guarantee Act, remarks, **1978:** 1397
New York and New Jersey economic compact, statement, **1979:** 2290
1979 White House Conferences on the Arts and Humanities, statement, **1978:** 823
North Atlantic Alliance Summit, joint resolution, statement, **1978:** 1014
Northeast corridor appropriations, remarks, **1980–81:** 1009
Northern Mariana Islands citizens, military service for, statement, **1980–81:** 1722
Nuclear Non-Proliferation Act, remarks and statement, **1978:** 498, 500
Nuclear Regulatory Commission, appropriations, statements, **1978:** 1971; **1980–81:** 1257
Occupational discrimination based on pregnancy, statement, **1978:** 1906
Ocean Thermal Energy Conversion Act, statement **1980–81:** 1473
Ocean Thermal Energy Conversion Research, Development, and Demonstration Act, statement, **1980–81:** 1375
Office of Federal Procurement Policy Act amendments, statement, **1979:** 1850
Omnibus Reconciliation Act, remarks, **1980–81:** 2778
Outer Continental Shelf Lands Act Amendments, statement, **1978:** 1530
Paiute Indian Tribe of Utah Restoration Act, statement, **1980–81:** 604
Panama Canal Act, statement, **1979:** 1776
Paperwork Reduction Act, remarks, **1980–81:** 2794
Patent and trademark system reform, statement, **1980–81:** 2803
Pennsylvania Avenue Development Corporation, appropriations authorization, statement, **1978:** 2001
Presidential Records Act, statement, **1978:** 1965
Presidential war powers bill, statement, **1977:** 2186

Bill signings — *continued*
Prisoner transfers with Mexico and Canada, remarks, **1977:** 1918
Privacy Protection Act, statement, **1980–81:** 2218
Psychotropic Substances Act, statement, **1978:** 2003
Public lands grazing fee moratorium, statement, **1978:** 1331
Public Rangelands Improvement Act, statement, **1978:** 1875
Public Telecommunications Financing Act, statement, **1978:** 1927
Public works appropriations, statement, **1977:** 1461
Public works employment and economic stimulus appropriations bills, remarks, **1977:** 870
Rail worker pension benefits, statement, **1980–81:** 2830
Rape victims, protection, statement, **1978:** 1902
Reclamation Safety of Dams Act, statement, **1978:** 1928
Redwood National Park expansion, statement, **1978:** 575
Refuge Education Assistance Act, remarks, **1980–81:** 2152
Refugee Act, statement, **1980–81:** 503
Regulatory Flexibility Act, remarks and statement, **1980–81:** 1839, 1843
Reorganization Act of 1977
  Extension, statement, **1980–81:** 616
  Remarks and statement, **1977:** 571
Retirement Pay for Marine Corps Sergeants Major, statement, **1978:** 1929
Rhode Island Indian Claims Settlement Act, statement, **1978:** 1695
Rhodesian chrome legislation, remarks and statement, **1977:** 451–453
Rural Development Policy Act, remarks and statement, **1980–81:** 1916, 1920
Rural health clinic services bill, statement, **1977:** 2104
Ship pollution prevention, statement, **1980–81:** 2378
Sikes Act Amendment, statement, **1978:** 1717
Siletz Indian tribes of Oregon, statement, **1980–81:** 1661
Small Business Administration Act amendments, remarks, **1977:** 1410
Small Business Administration authorization, remarks, **1980–81:** 1277
Small Business Energy Loan Act, statement, **1978:** 1237
Small Business Investment Incentive Act, statements, **1980–81:** 2377, 2380
Social Security Amendments of 1977, remarks and statement, **1977:** 2153, 2155

[References are to page numbers except as otherwise indicated]

Bill signings — *continued*

Social Security Disability Amendments, statement, **1980–81:** 1062

Soft Drink Interbrand Competition Act, statement, **1980–81:** 1334

Solar Photovoltaic Energy Research, Development, and Demonstration Act, statement, **1978:** 1964

Solid Waste Disposal Act Amendments, statement, **1980–81:** 2381

Southwestern Power Administration, power rate charges, statement, **1978:** 1770

Special Central American Assistance Act of 1979, statement, **1980–81:** 1017

Staggers Rail Act, remarks and statement, **1980–81:** 2226, 2229

State Department, International Communication Agency, and Board for International Broadcasting, appropriations, statement, **1979:** 1434

Stevenson-Wydler Technology Innovation Act, statement, **1980–81:** 2379

Supplemental Appropriations Act, statement, **1978:** 472

Surface Mining Control and Reclamation Act of 1977, remarks, **1977:** 1407

Susan B. Anthony dollar coin authorization, statement, **1978:** 1737

Taiwan Relations Act, statement, **1979:** 640

Tax Reduction and Simplification Act of 1977, remarks, **1977:** 962

Tinicum National Environmental Center, remarks, **1977:** 1961

Tinicum National Environmental Center and Sailors' Snug Harbor, statement, **1980–81:** 1431

Trade Agreements Act, remarks, **1979:** 1311

Tribally Controlled Community College Assistance Act, statement, **1978:** 1786

Uniformed Services Health Professionals Special Pay Act, statement, **1980–81:** 1251

Uniformed Services University of the Health Sciences, statement, **1978:** 1964

United States Holocaust Memorial Commission, statement, **1980–81:** 2106

United States International Trade Commission, appropriations, statement, **1977:** 1479

United States territories administration, statement, **1980–81:** 466

United States Travel Service appropriations, statement, **1979:** 1850

Urban Mass Transportation Act of 1964 amendments, statement, **1977:** 2033

Veterans, discharge review and benefit eligibility, statement, **1977:** 1757

Veterans' Disability Compensation and Survivors' Benefits Act of 1977

Bill signings — *continued*

Veterans' Disability — *continued*

Remarks and statement, **1978:** 1789, 1791

Statement, **1977:** 1712

Amendments, statement, **1979:** 2165; **1980–81:** 2097

Veteran's Health Care Amendments, statement, **1979:** 1039

Veterans' Housing Benefits Act, remarks and statement, **1978:** 1789, 1791

Veterans' Rehabilitation and Education Amendments, remarks and statement, **1980–81:** 2315, 2318

Veterans' and Survivors' Pension Improvement, statement, **1978:** 1965

Vietnam veterans memorial, remarks, **1980–81:** 1268

Warren Grant Magnuson Clinical Center, statement, **1980–81:** 2806

Water Research and Development Act, statement, **1978:** 1786

Wayne, John, gold medal, statement, **1979:** 959

West Valley Demonstration Project Act, remarks, **1980–81:** 2001

Wind Energy Systems Act, statement, **1980–81:** 1668

Wood Residue Utilization Act, statement, **1980–81:** 2821

Wyoming, extension of Federal oil and gas leases, statement, **1977:** 1395

Youth Employment and Demonstration Projects Act of 1977, remarks, **1977:** 1427

See also last page of text of each issue for acts approved.

Biller, Robert P., **1979:** 1670

Billings, K., LeMoyne, **1979:** 24

Bimes, Beverly Joyce, **1980–81:** 1444

Bingaman, Anne K., **1977:** 1055

Binger, James H., **1978:** 454; **1980–81:** 1048

Bingham, Barry, Sr., **1977:** 941

Bingham, Charles, **1979:** 1671

Bingham, Eula, **1977:** 365, 373, 2109; **1978:** 820, 1492, 1594

Bingham, Repr. Jonathan B., **1977:** 251, 265, 650, 788, 1136; **1978:** 328, 498–500

Bingham, Rebecca T., **1979:** 400

Binns, Jack Robert, **1980–81:** 1442, 1470

Biomass energy, **1979:** 1105, 1541, 1650, 1724; **1980–81:** 470, 2192

Biomedical and Behavioral Research, President's Commission for the Study of Ethical Problems in Medicine and, **1979:** 1263, 1294, **1980–81:** 896, 1723

Biomedical and Behavioral Research, President's Special Commission for the Study of Ethical Problems in Medicine and, **1979:** 2260

Birch River, W. Va., **1980–81:** 433

Bird, Sandra, **1980–81:** 1847

Birds protection convention, U.S.-Canada migratory, **1980–81:** 2743

Birlew, Michael, **1979:** 2076

Birmingham, Ala., **1979:** 1817

Bishop, Charles E., **1978:** 53, 268

Bishop, Isabel, **1979:** 217

Bishop, James, Jr., **1977:** 1585

Bishop, James Keough, **1979:** 979, 984

Bishop, Ralph C., **1977:** 1569

Bissell, A. K., **1978:** 948, 1859

Bissell, Jean Galloway, **1977:** 1242

Bitterman, Mary G. F., **1980–81:** 236, 268, 452

Bituminous Coal Operators Association of America, **1978:** 328, 415, 419, 1007, 2243

Biwott, Nicholas K., **1980–81:** 355

Black, Harold Alonza, **1979:** 1299, 1319

Black, Marilyn W., **1979:** 598

Black, Norman W., **1979:** 327, 328

Black, Susan H., **1979:** 957

Black, Theodore M., Sr., **1979:** 1525

Black Aged, National Caucus on the, **1979:** 317

Black Caucus, Congressional, **1977:** 1568, 1661, 1938, 2005; **1978:** 319, 1230, 1668, 1669, 1678, 1679, 1871; **1979:** 911; **1980–81:** 1110, 1580, 1927, 1947

Black Caucus of State Legislators, National, **1980–81:** 334

Black Enterprise Magazine, **1978:** 1106

Black History Month, **1978:** 224

Black Leadership Forum, **1978:** 2187

Black Lung Benefits Reform Act of 1977, **1978:** 432, 1006

Black lung disease, **1977:** 419, 425

Black Mayors, National Conference of, **1977:** 1945; **1980–81:** 720

Black Music Association, **1979:** 1014

Black Press Day, **1977:** 1099

Black Press Week, **1979:** 440

Black Radio Network, National, **1977:** 1340

Blackburn, James Leslie, **1980–81:** 1715

Blacks
  Briefing for Southern leaders, **1978:** 1879
  Business assistance, **1979:** 847
  Business executives, reception, **1978:** 1103
  Civil rights, **1979:** 884, 970; **1980–81:** 85, 222, 1322, 2058, 2173, 2184
  Democratic National Convention delegates, meeting with the President, **1980–81:** 1540
  Desegregation of Southern universities, **1978:** 309, 537
  Economic recession, impact on, **1980–81:** 798
  Education
    College institutions, **1978:** 1356, 1514, 1518, 1561
    Past segregation, **1978:** 1003, 2128
  Employment, **1979:** 126, 1936

Blacks — *continued*
  Employment — *continued*
    Federal Government, **1980–81:** 1003
    Statistics, **1980–81:** 123, 249, 1323, 1531, 1752, 2020, 2484
    Youth initiatives program.
      See Employment *under* Children and youth.
  Federal appointments, **1980–81:** 1325, 1493, 1633
  Forged document on black Africa and U.S. movement, **1980–81:** 1846
  Higher education, **1979:** 48, 140, 173, 742, 911
  Judicial appointments, **1979:** 36, 131, 759, 847, 885, 2138; **1980–81:** 887, 1071
  Leaders, meetings with the President, **1978:** 66; **1979:** 810, 841; **1980–81:** 2872(Digest)
  Martin Luther King, Jr., and Boston national historic sites, **1980–81:** 2172, 2184
  Media interviews, **1978:** 318, 688
  Media representatives, interview with the President, **1979:** 33
  Miami, Fla., community, **1980–81:** 1076
  Ministers, meetings with the President, **1980–81:** 522, 825, 2425, 2524
  National Afro-American History Month, **1980–81:** 84
  National Urban League address, **1980–81:** 1499–1506
  Political endorsements, **1980–81:** 2441
  Relationship with Jewish Americans, **1979:** 1563, 1860, 1997
  Representatives of Houston, Tex., meeting with the President **1978:** 1221
  Southern leaders, meeting with the President, **1980–81:** 1750
  See also Minorities.

Blacks to the Federal Judiciary in the Fifth Circuit, Committee for the Appointment of, **1977:** 1210

Blackwell, Unita, **1978:** 1134, 1190

Blake, Robert O., **1980–81:** 34

Blakeley, Gary, **1980–81:** 372, 453

Blanchard, Repr. James J., **1979:** 942, 1773; **1980–81:** 27, 29, 770, 823

Blango, Antoinette, **1979:** 913

Blanton, Betty, **1977:** 525

Blas, Juan G., **1977:** 1437, 1438; **1978:** 149, 150

Blass, Elizabeth W., **1979:** 464

Blatnik, John, **1979:** 293

Blaustein, Arthur I., **1977:** 1477; **1979:** 1447

Blaylock, Kenneth, **1978:** 802, 1366, 1367, 1765, 1766; **1979:** 931, 2247

Blecher, Maxwell M., **1978:** 1139, 1140

Blechman, Barry M., **1977:** 1676, 1700

Bleckstein, William L., **1980–81:** 2817

Bleicher, Michael M., **1979:** 578n.

Bleier, Rocky, **1980–81:** 371

Bleiweis, Phyllis R., **1980–81:** 949

Blind and Other Severely Handicapped, Committee for Purchase from the, **1978:** 408, 770, 2069; **1979:** 163, 437; **1980–81:** 37, 521, 931, 1292
Blind, Inc., Recording for the, **1978:** 925
Bloch, Alan N., **1979:** 1398
Block, Charlene M., **1979:** 1007
Block, Paul, Jr., **1977:** 1944, 1966; **1978:** 231
Blood Institute, National Heart, Lung, and, **1980–81:** 190
Bloodmobile, Red Cross, **1977:** 252
Bloom, Floyd E., **1980–81:** 2609
Bloomfield, Lincoln P., **1979:** 984, 1522n. 2183n., 2189
Bloomfield, Richard J., **1977:** 2161; **1978:** 149; **1980–81:** 1245
Bloomington, Ind., **1979:** 1817
Blouin, Repr. Michael T., **1977:** 1855; **1978:** 1723, 1787; **1980–81:** 979, 1015
Blountville, Tenn., **1980–81:** 2122
Bluestone, Irving, **1979:** 1447
Blum, Barbara, **1977:** 176, 195, 376; **1978:** 787; **1979:** 1222, 2075
Blum, Richard C., **1980–81:** 2614
Blume, Sheila Bierman, **1980–81:** 2609
Blumenfeld, Michael, **1979:** 109, 179; **1980–81:** 33
Blumenthal, Richard, **1977:** 1059
Blumenthal, W. Michael.
  See Treasury, Secretary of the.
Blumenthal, Mrs. W. Michael, **1978:** 2288
Blythe, Ronald, **1979:** 2216
B'nai B'rith International, **1980–81:** 1654, 1663
Bo Yibo.
  See China, People's Republic of, Vice Premier.
Board.
  See other part of title.
Boating Week, National Safe, **1977:** 1080
Bock, Paul, **1980–81:** 1023
Bodde, William, Jr., **1980–81:** 1107, 1111, 1700
Bodine, William W., Jr., **1980–81:** 867, 874n.
Boe, Jason, **1979:** 1876
Boeker, Paul H., **1977:** 1505, 1507
Boggs, Elizabeth Monroe, **1980–81:** 812, 826
Boggs, Repr. Lindie, **1977:** 1340; **1978:** 1713; **1980–81:** 2401
Boggs, Thomas Hale, **1979:** 976
Bogosian, Betty, **1980–81:** 2560
Boise, Idaho, **1978:** 1473
Bokoko, Aboubacar, **1980–81:** 1564
Boland, Repr. Edward P., **1978:** 191, 1194, 1854
Bole, Filipe Nagera, **1980–81:** 1598
Bolen, David B., **1977:** 1218, 1223; **1979:** 2210; **1980–81:** 2233
Bolger, William F., **1978:** 934; **1980–81:** 1608
Bolin, Gov. Wesley, **1978:** 468
Bolivia
  Ambassador to U.S., **1978:** 710; **1979:** 554

Bolivia — *continued*
  Penal sentences treaty, **1978:** 748
  President Hugo Banzer Suarez, **1977:** 1550, 1568
  U.S. Ambassador, **1977:** 1505, 1507; **1980–81:** 287, 293
Bolling, Repr. Richard, **1978:** 148, 1345; **1979:** 840, 942; **1980–81:** 2781
Bolstad, Edward C., **1979:** 1439
Bolt, nut, and large screw industry, **1978:** 299–301, 2283, 2284; **1979:** 3
Bolter, Arthur, **1980–81:** 58
Bolton, Peggy, **1979:** 1432
Bomar, James L., Jr., **1980–81:** 334
Bombeck, Erma, **1978:** 1134; **1980–81:** 1404
Bommarito, Peter, **1980–81:** 1670
Bond, Langhorne McCook, **1977:** 536, 557
Bond, Maj. Gen. Robert, **1980–81:** 780n.
Bonda, Alva T., **1980–81:** 218, 2074
Boner, Bill, **1978:** 1860
Bongo, El Hadj Omar, **1977:** 279, 1825, 1827
Bonifay, Fla., **1979:** 1615
Bonilla, Ruben, **1980–81:** 563
Bonior, Repr. David E., **1980–81:** 374, 770, 1268
Bonker, Repr. Don, **1978:** 229; **1979:** 867; **1980–81:** 961
Bonn Economic Summit Conference, **1979:** 160, 1187, 1188, 1197
  Concluding remarks, **1978:** 1309, 1333
  Exchange with reporters, **1978:** 1307
  Joint declaration, **1978:** 1310
  Meeting with Members of Congress, **1978:** 1332
  Post-conference comments, **1978:** 1316
  Pre-conference comments, **1978:** 1154, 1171, 1267, 1282, 1284, 1287, 1292
  Terrorism statement, **1978:** 1308
  White House statement, **1978:** 1360
Bonneville Power Administration, **1978:** 272
Bonyun, William L., **1979:** 464
Boochever, Robert, **1980–81:** 968
Bookbinder, Hyman, **1978:** 1973; **1980–81:** 821
Bookout, John F., Jr., **1979:** 1614n.
Bookstein, Kenneth H., **1980–81:** 926
Boone, Daniel, **1979:** 2098
Booth, Patricia, **1977:** 1055
Bordallo, Ricardo J., **1978:** 1722
Bordeaux, Lionel R., **1978:** 1419
Borders, William A., Jr., **1980–81:** 218, 1292, 1438n.
Boren, Gov. David, **1977:** 744, 1941
Boren, Sen. David L., **1979:** 2257n.
Borg, C. Arthur, **1977:** 8
Borge, Victor, **1980–81:** 821
Borja, Jesus, **1980–81:** 344
Bork, Norman, **1978:** 1947
Borkowski, Francis T., **1979:** 464
Borlaug, Norman E., **1978:** 1511
Borman, Col. Frank, **1978:** 1687, 1867

Borsting, Jack R., **1980–81:** 1093, 1111
Boschwitz, Sen. Rudolph E., **1979:** 2251n.; **1980–81:** 823
Bossie, Robert F., **1979:** 2042
Boster, Davis Eugene, **1978:** 1111
Boston, Mass., **1979:** 1817, 1979, 1982, 2044
   African American national historic sites, **1980–81:** 2172, 2179
   Mayor Kevin White, **1980–81:** 2889
   President's visits, **1980–81:** 1548, 1549, 1565, 2243, 2251, 2333
Bosworth, Barry P.
   See Wage and Price Stability, Council on, Director.
Bosworth, Stephen W., **1979:** 101, 179
Botbol, Joseph M., **1978:** 952
Botha, Pieter, **1978:** 1776
Botha, Roelof F., **1977:** 508; **1978:** 2146, 2149, 2178
Botswana
   Ambassador to U.S. **1977:** 194, 195, 714, 745; **1980–81:** 2807
   U.S. Ambassador, **1979:** 1616
Botts, Leila L., **1978:** 408
Boucher, Bob, **1980–81:** 2559
Boucher, Paul R., **1979:** 399, 402
Bouchet, Margo, **1977:** 816
Boulding, Elise, **1979:** 2195
Boumediene, Houari, **1978:** 2288
Bouna Ould Sidi, Sidi, **1979:** 376
Boundary and Water Commission, International, U.S. Section, **1977:** 723
Bourguiba, Habib, Jr., **1980–81:** 423
Bourne, Dr. Peter G., **1977:** 92, 290, 306, 378, 595, 840, 941, 954, 1047, 1383, 1399, 1437, 1696, 1963, 1976, 2037; **1978:** 277, 770, 873, 1322, 1326, 1329, 1334, 1779; **1980–81:** 1486ftn.
Bournias, Nicholas, **1980–81:** 1507
Boutros, Fuad, **1977:** 1730, 1754
Boutte, Alvin J., **1980–81:** 2117
Bovine Meat, Arrangement Regarding, **1979:** 2253
Bowden, Henry L., **1977:** 816; **1979:** 271, 1562
Bowden, Katherine R., **1977:** 816
Bowdler, William G., **1978:** 1694, 1993, 2059; **1979:** 1960, 2151; **1980–81:** 522, 933
Bowe, Frank, **1980–81:** 1432
Bowen, Repr. David R., **1977:** 1533; **1978:** 2003; **1979:** 1125, 1777
Bowen, Dudley H., Jr., **1979:** 1293, 1294
Bowen, Gov. Otis, **1979:** 2131
Bowen, Roger W., **1978:** 952
Bowen, Wallace P., **1977:** 1437, 1438
Bowers, Darralyn C., **1980–81:** 911
Bowers, Karl Smith, **1978:** 1357, 1381
Bowers, Shellie F., **1979:** 665, 667
Bowie, Robert R., **1977:** 1611; **1978:** 1154, 1879; **1979:** 25, 1396
Bowker, Albert H., **1980–81:** 425, 775

Bowmer, Jim, **1977:** 816
Bownes, Hugh H., **1977:** 1650, 1651
Boxing team, United States amateur, **1980–81:** 482, 517, 564
Boy Scouts of America, **1977:** 194, 1437; **1978:** 328; **1979:** 240; **1980–81:** 292
Boy of the Year Award, **1979:** 1705
Boyatt, Thomas D., **1978:** 1109, 1111; **1980–81:** 1710, 1715
Boycotts, foreign, **1977:** 116, 650, 788, 898, 918, 1136; **1978:** 111
Boyd, Alan, **1977:** 256, 508, 748, 1137, 1482
Boyd, Howard T., **1978:** 2288
Boyd, Jamie C., **1977:** 883, 884
Boyer, Ernest LeRoy, **1977:** 382, 465; **1978:** 1514, 1917, 1919
Boyer, George, **1980–81:** 2453
Boyer, Neil A., **1979:** 815
Boyer, Dr. Robert E., **1977:** 1221
Boyle, Clayton T., **1980–81:** 1508
Boyle, Francis J., **1977:** 807
Boyle, John J., **1977:** 1676; **1978:** 1955
Boyle, Patricia J. E., **1978:** 1345, 1346
Boys' Clubs of America, **1978:** 526; **1979:** 1705; **1980–81:** 1846
Boys Nation, **1980–81:** 1412
Bracewell, Joseph S., **1980–81:** 2016, 2782, 2856, 2870, 2873
Bracy, Terrence L., **1977:** 84, 148
Brademas, Repr. John, **1977:** 595; **1978:** 237, 289, 304, 327, 823, 1792–1794, 1966; **1979:** 1125; **1980–81:** 383, 2822
Bradenton, Fla., **1979:** 1817
Bradford, O.G., **1980–81:** 1605n.
Bradford, Peter A., **1977:** 1240, 1266
Bradley, Amelia Jane, **1980–81:** 948
Bradley Sen. Bill, **1978:** 1551; **1979:** 2021, 2039
   Campaign appearances with the President, **1980–81:** 1672, 1677, 1680, 1682, 2276
   Legislation passage leadership
      Comprehensive Environmental Response, Compensation, and Liability Act, **1980–81:** 1684, 2797
      Crude Oil Windfall Profit Tax Act, **1980–81:** 588
   Meeting with the President (Digest) **1980–81:** 2752
Bradley, James A., **1980–81:** 2747
Bradley, Tom, **1977:** 182, 744; **1978:** 748, 762, 842, 1333; **1980–81:** 789, 1299n.
   California gasoline shortages actions, **1978:** 872, 876
   National Task Force on Ridesharing, chairman, **1979:** 2023
   1984 Summer Olympics, meeting with the President (Digest), **1979:** 2206
   Ridesharing programs support, **1979:** 2022, 2024
Bradshaw, T.F., **1979:** 2024

Bradshaw, Thomas W., Jr., **1979:** 2024
Bradshaw, Thornton, **1980–81:** 789
Brady, James S., **1977:** 1755
Bragg, John T., **1979:** 271
Bramberg, Rudolph William, Jr., **1980–81:** 533, 564
Branch, Jana L., **1980–81:** 927
Branch, Joseph, **1980–81:** 47
Branch Line Railroad Investments, **1979:** 76
Branchina, Lisa, **1979:** 955
Branchina, Minnie, **1979:** 955, 956
Brandon, Eddie Lee, **1978:** 1190
Brandt, Willy, **1977:** 371; **1980–81:** 334
Branigin, Roger, **1979:** 990
Branscomb, Lewis M., **1978:** 1760, 1773; **1979:** 528, 554
Branton, Wiley, **1979:** 1921
Bray, Charles W., III, **1977:** 148, 732, 745; **1978:** 277, 303, 2038
Brazil
    Ambassador to U.S., **1977:** 806; **1979:** 1318
    Inaugural ceremonies, U.S. delegation, **1979:** 239, 241, 401
    Interview remarks, **1977:** 764
    President's visit, **1977:** 1649, 1938, 2077; **1978:** 416, 417, 626–636, 670
    President's visit while Governor of Georgia, **1980–81:** 945
    Science and technology cooperation with U.S., **1980–81:** 407
    U.S. Ambassador, **1978:** 295, 304
    Vice President Adalberto Pereira dos Santos, **1977:** 1567
Breathitt, Francis H., **1979:** 24
Breaux, Repr. John B., **1977:** 1073; **1980–81:** 1938
Brebbia, John H., **1977:** 941
Breckinridge, Repr. John, **1977:** 252
Breeder reactors, **1977:** 503, 505, 507, 583, 585, 588, 1170, 1237, 1461, 1707, 1972, 2012, 2068; **1978:** 72, 114, 473, 501, 939, 1469, 1471, 1473, 1477
    Clinch River breeder reactor plant.
        See Clinch River Breeder Reactor Demonstration Plant.
    Federal research and development programs, **1979:** 149
Brement, Marshall, **1979:** 1045
Brennan, Donald G., **1979:** 976
Brennan, Gov. Joseph E., **1980–81:** 2177
Brennan, Thomas C., **1977:** 1666, 1667, 1700
Brennan, William J., Jr., **1977:** 17, 692
Brett, George, **1980–81:** 1610
Brett, Thomas Rutheford, **1979:** 1786, 1787
Brewer, Harper, Jr., **1980–81:** 2107
Brewer, Herbert Richard Wright, **1980–81:** 268
Brewer, Col. Margaret A., **1978:** 697
Brewster, Kingman, Jr., **1977:** 576, 577, 597, 942, 1382; **1979:** 1603
Breyer, Stephen G., **1980–81:** 2727

Brezhnev, L.I.
    See Union of Soviet Socialist Republics, President.
Bright, Simeon M., **1977:** 1352, 1384
Brightwell, Juanita, **1979:** 2128
Brill, Daniel H., **1977:** 377, 465; **1979:** 1233
Brimmer, Andrew F., **1979:** 976; **1980–81:** 373, 509
Brinkley, Repr. Jack, **1978:** 1791
Briscoe, Gov. Dolph, Jr., **1977:** 31, 1389, 1941; **1978:** 1173; **1979:** 1670
Britt, Mr. and Mrs. Travis O., **1977:** 744
Britt, W. Earl, **1980–81:** 654, 720
Britton, James R., **1977:** 833
Broadcast System, Emergency, **1979:** 567
Broadcasters, National Association of, **1978:** 254; **1979:** 482, 490; **1980–81:** 1050
Broadcasting, Board for International, **1977:** 1073, 1085, 2024, 2037; **1978:** 231, 1735; **1979:** 1434, 1659, 1680
    Chairman, **1980–81:** 1376
    Members, **1980–81:** 56, 218, 1376, 1847, 2870, 2872
Broadcasting, Corporation for Public, **1977:** 195, 1713, 1738, 1754, 1817, 1826, 2000; **1978:** 613, 1426, 1458, 1744, 1772, 1927
    Annual report, **1979:** 609; **1980–81:** 913
    Board of Directors, members, **1979:** 46, 91, 435, 441, 1001, 1019; **1980–81:** 1467, 1524, 2429, 2727, 2859, 2870, 2873
Broadcasting industry.
    See Communications and telecommunications.
Broadcasting, international, **1977:** 478, 1073, 1085
Broadcasting Service, Public, **1977:** 327, 1738
Brock, Lou, **1979:** 1784
Brockington, Melanie, **1978:** 2274
Brockman, Norbert, **1980–81:** 1424
Broder, David, **1980–81:** 107
Brodhead, Repr. William M., **1977:** 2105; **1980–81:** 1124
Brodie, Jay, **1979:** 1408
Brokaw, Tom, **1977:** 2187
Bronheim, David, **1978:** 703, 711; **1980–81:** 51, 522, 1469, 1524
Brooke, Sen. Edward W., **1977:** 396; **1978:** 504, 717, 1038
Brooks, David W., **1978:** 454, 1511; **1979:** 1562; **1980–81:** 1048
Brooks, Gene E., **1979:** 1319, 1320
Brooks, Gwendolyn, **1980–81:** 263
Brooks, Herb, **1980–81:** 379, 388
Brooks, Repr. Jack, **1977:** 99, 1183, 1306, 1411, 1412; **1978:** 327, 400, 1173, 1317, 1406, 1570, 1754–1756, 1763, 1765, 1782, 1966
    Bipartisan visit to China, delegation head, **1979:** 666
    Campaign appearances with the President, **1980–81:** 2414, 2603

Brooks, Repr. Jack — *continued*
  Communications from the President, **1980–81:** 267
  Federal paperwork reduction efforts, **1979:** 2176, 2178, 2182
  Foreign assistance programs reorganization, proposal support, **1979:** 1230
  Legislation passage leadership
    Congressional Reports Elimination Act, **1980–81:** 2344
    Department of Education, **1979:** 1776, 1957, 1959
    Federal agency reorganization, **1980–81:** 483, 616
    General Accounting Office Act, **1980–81:** 603
    Paperwork Reduction Act, **1980–81:** 2795, 2796
    State and local governments fiscal assistance, **1979:** 2196
  Meetings with the President (Digest), **1979:** 217, 2186
  White House military aircraft passenger list reception, **1979:** 240
Brooks, Jesse Roscoe, **1977:** 1059
Brooks, John Wood, **1979:** 942
Brooks, Roger, **1980–81:** 928
Broome, Homer F., Jr., **1978:** 1538, 1572; **1980–81:** 288, 293
Broomfield, Repr. William S., **1978:** 897
Brosby, Elizabeth C., **1979:** 2289
Brotherhood of Railway Carmen of the United States and Canada, **1980–81:** 667, 684, 930
Brotherhood Week, National, **1978:** 326; **1980–81:** 343
Broussard, Flo L., **1978:** 1188
Brown, A. Omie, **1980–81:** 2242
Brown, B. Mahlon, III, **1977:** 1931, 1932
Brown, Bailey, **1979:** 441
Brown, Ben, **1977:** 1436
Brown, Chris, **1979:** 1865, 1986
Brown, Clanzel Thornton, **1979:** 1815; **1980–81:** 2614
Brown, Repr. Clarence J., **1979:** 2086
Brown, Cynthia G., **1980–81:** 768, 841, 1052
Brown, Edmund (Jerry) G., Jr.
  See Governor *under* California.
Brown, Edwin C., Jr., **1977:** 196
Brown, Gabrielle A., **1980–81:** 928
Brown, Repr. George E., Jr., **1980–81:** 761, 2380
Brown, Gen. George S., **1977:** 85, 86, 261, 1021, 1029, 1084, 1221, 1483, 1526, 2036, 2089; **1978:** 1110, 2165
Brown, Harold.
  See Defense, Secretary of.
Brown, Mrs. Harold, **1979:** 1155
Brown, Herbert C., **1979:** 1962; **1980–81:** 3023

Brown, J. Carter, **1978:** 1028; **1980–81:** 2701, 2748
Brown, John, **1980–81:** 2238
Brown, Gov. John Y., **1980–81:** 422, 1388, 1390n., 1423n.
Brown, June Gibbs, **1979:** 365, 377
Brown, Ken, **1980–81:** 1609
Brown, Les, **1978:** 1620
Brown, Matthew, **1977:** 1483
Brown, Pat, **1980–81:** 1319
Brown, Reagan V., **1980–81:** 1391n.
Brown, Robert, **1978:** 2068; **1979:** 1615
Brown, Robert Joseph, **1977:** 227, 252, 1930; **1979:** 1299, 1319
Brown, Robert McAfee, **1978:** 1973; **1980–81:** 821
Brown, Sam W., Jr., **1977:** 9, 193, 252, 272, 273, 608, 1305; **1978:** 457, 2075; **1979:** 1221, 1223; **1980–81:** 281, 291, 328, 2822
Brown, Tyrone, **1977:** 1793, 1826; **1979:** 977, 1021, 1043, 1921
Brown, William L., **1977:** 1569
Brown v. *Board of Education*, **1979:** 883, 909–911
Browning, Chauncey H., Jr., **1978:** 1139, 1140
Browning, Robert, **1979:** 1277
Brownstein, Phil, **1980–81:** 2559
Brownsville, Tex., **1980–81:** 2617
Broyhill, Repr. James T.
  Legislation passage leadership
    Dispute Resolution Act, **1980–81:** 303
    Federal Trade Commission Improvements Act, **1980–81:** 983
    Ship pollution prevention, **1980–81:** 2378
    Staggers Rail Act, **1980–81:** 1699, 2227, 2230
  Meeting with the President (Digest), **1980–81:** 1598
Bruce, Ailsa Mellon, **1978:** 1028
Bruce, David K.E., **1977:** 2083
Bruce, Sandra, **1979:** 1217
Brumby rockers, **1977:** 600
Brumidi Day, Constantino, **1980–81:** 1834
Bruneau River, Idaho, **1979:** 1813
Brunswick, Ga., **1977:** 1033, 1042
Bruzda, Francis J., **1979:** 976
Bryan, Morris M., Jr., **1979:** 942
Bryant, Hubert H., **1977:** 1266, 1307
Bryant, John E., **1978:** 885
Bryant, John H., **1979:** 815
Bryant, Milton F., **1977:** 1963
Bryant, Reginald, **1978:** 688
Bryant, Thomas E., **1977:** 186, 187, 529, 1612; **1978:** 792, 793, 878; **1979:** 857, 858; **1980–81:** 2099
Bryner, Alexander O., **1977:** 1931, 1932
Brzezinski, Zbigniew, **1977:** 8, 15, 30, 31, 46, 85, 86, 194, 243, 248, 251, 252, 279, 371, 463, 464, 507, 508, 555–558, 595, 596, 640–642, 705, 706, 743–745, 805, 806, 882–884, 942, 943, 951, 1029, 1030, 1058, 1083, 1084, 1126,

Brzezinski, Zbigniew — *continued*
    1127, 1137, 1161–1163, 1210, 1211, 1221,
    1263–1265, 1283, 1305, 1306, 1382, 1383,
    1436, 1437, 1482, 1506, 1532, 1567, 1611,
    1612, 1648, 1649, 1651, 1699, 1753, 1754,
    1794, 1795, 1825, 1826, 1930, 1931, 1965,
    1966, 2005, 2006, 2035, 2036, 2050, 2088,
    2089, 2129, 2130, 2162, 2207, 2223; **1978:**
    45, 50, 65, 66, 148, 149, 229, 232, 276, 277,
    281, 302, 303, 327, 328, 414, 415, 456, 457,
    503, 504, 525, 526, 570, 610, 641, 710,
    711,749, 750, 769, 770, 801–803, 880, 881,
    897, 898, 933, 934, 936, 1034, 1070, 1071,
    1110, 1153, 1154, 1159, 1160, 1183, 1221,
    1222, 1278, 1279, 1332, 1333, 1379, 1380,
    1405, 1406, 1457, 1459, 1484, 1485, 1505,
    1506, 1515, 1516, 1538, 1571, 1668, 1669,
    1722, 1723, 1771, 1772, 1807–1809, 1879,
    1954, 1955, 2004, 2058, 2059, 2072, 2073,
    2146, 2147, 2156, 2186, 2187, 2269, 2270,
    2280, 2281
  Agricultural trade development functions,
    1980–81: 1238
  Algerian revolution celebrations, U.S. delegation
    head, **1979:** 2043
  Alumni Association of the School for Interna-
    tional Affairs, remarks (Checklist), **1979:**
    1787
  American Society of Newspaper Editors address,
    1980–81: 631
  Canadian Club address (Checklist), **1980–81:**
    2782
  Carter, Billy, involvement in activities with Lib-
    yan Government, **1980–81:** 1406, 1483,
    1976n., 2016, 2648
  Chicago Council on Foreign Relations, remarks
    (Checklist), **1979:** 619
  Council on Foreign Relations, remarks (Check-
    list), **1980–81:** 2615
  Fordham University commencement address
    (Checklist) **1979:** 944
  Foreign policy role, **1980–81:** 881, 2135, 2174
  General Pulaski memorial dinner remarks
    (Checklist), **1979:** 1884
  Institut Francais des Relations Internationales,
    remarks (Checklist) **1980–81:** 3050
  International Platform Association, remarks
    (Checklist) **1979:** 1398
  Interviews with editors and broadcasters (Check-
    list), **1979:** 1680, 1786
  Iraq-Iran conflict, consultations with the Pres-
    ident, **1980–81:** 1890, 1900, 1902, 1906
  Meetings with:
    Bavarian Minister President Franz Josef
      Strauss, **1980–81:** 470
    Kenyan President Daniel T. arap Moi, **1980–
      81:** 355

Brzezinski, Zbigniew — *continued*
  Meetings with the President (Digest), **1979:** 14,
    25, 26, 89, 177–179, 217, 239–241, 293,
    327, 329, 375–377, 400, 440, 467, 468, 553,
    554, 617, 618, 666, 667, 731, 732, 786–788,
    841, 842, 897–899, 955–957, 982, 983,
    1017, 1018, 1042, 1043, 1142, 1159, 1222,
    1292, 1318, 1319, 1396, 1397, 1422, 1454,
    1455, 1603, 1604, 1678, 1679, 1704, 1705,
    1784, 1785, 1823, 1824, 1881, 1882, 1975,
    1976, 2042, 2043, 2081, 2104–2106, 2138,
    2139, 2151, 2186, 2206, 2247, 2248, 2279,
    2280, 2300; **1980–81:** 24, 25, 63, 64, 103,
    217, 267, 268, 292, 293, 333, 334, 373, 374,
    422, 423, 452, 492, 493, 521, 563, 606, 607,
    631, 653, 654, 719, 720, 773–775, 824, 825,
    891–893, 930–932, 966, 967, 1013, 1014,
    1049, 1050, 1110, 1111, 1150, 1291, 1376,
    1427, 1428, 1468, 1469, 1846, 1945, 1946,
    2069, 2070, 2178, 2179, 2332, 2453, 2726,
    2740, 2741, 2752, 2781, 2782, 2806, 2807,
    2822, 2823, 2841, 2857, 2872, 3048, 3049
  Membership on:
    President's Committee on the International
      Labor Organization, **1980–81:** 1127
    Trade Policy Committee, **1980–81:** 8
  Mentions, **1979:** 329n., 744, 1155n., 1607; **1980–
    81:** 324, 367, 459, 1101, 1852
  Middle East, visit to, **1979:** 436, 468
  News conference (Checklist), **1980–81:** 1429
  Olympics, 1980 Summer, briefing for U.S. team
    representatives, **1980–81:** 518
  Pakistan and Saudi Arabia, trip to (Digest),
    1980–81: 267
  Presidential Medal of Freedom recipient, **1980–
    81:** 2923
  President's assessment, **1980–81:** 797
  President's trip to Europe, interviews on (Check-
    list), **1980–81:** 1246
  SALT II treaty briefing for U.S. Jaycees, **1979:**
    1723
  Soviet-Cuban relations, remarks to editors, **1979:**
    1605
  Soviet invasion of Afghanistan, question-and-
    answer session (Checklist), **1980–81:** 1246
  Task Force on Global Resources and Environ-
    ment, duties, **1980–81:** 1417
  United States Sinai Support Mission, supervi-
    sion, **1980–81:** 1397
  U.S. troop withdrawal from Republic of Korea,
    announcement, **1979:** 1276n., 1294
  Vance, Cyrus R., relationship with, **1980–81:** 876
  Vienna Summit statement, **1979:** 839
  World Jewish Congress, remarks (Checklist),
    1979: 1706
Bua, Nicholas J., **1977:** 1307; **1980–81:** 1715
Buchele, James P., **1977:** 1128

Buchmeyer, Jerry L., **1979:** 1398
Buckley, William F., **1977:** 1513
Bucy, J. Fred, Jr., **1980–81:** 263
Budget, Federal
  Administration's accomplishments and goals,
    1980–81: 2934, 3009
  Advisers, meetings with the President (Digest),
    1980–81: 1428, 1469, 2752
  Anti-inflation program, **1978:** 1840, 1841, 1845
  Briefings and meetings, **1977:** 748, 805, 1030,
    1059, 1083, 1087, 1094, 1127, 1162, 1931,
    2006, 2050, 2076, 2077, 2088, 2089, 2129,
    2130, 2162, 2223
  Business Council, question-and-answer session,
    1978: 2236
  Caribbean area assistance, **1980–81:** 627
  Chrysler Corporation, loan effect on, **1980–81:**
    32
  Constitutional amendment for balanced budget,
    1979: 57, 562
  Consumer program exhibits, **1979:** 1765
  Defense spending.
    See under Defense and national security.
  Deferrals and rescissions, **1977:** 352, 495, 739,
    931, 1217, 1285, 1286, 1357, 1477, 1647,
    1714, 2002, 2125; **1978:** 223, 407, 502, 895,
    1041, 1321, 1652, 1699, 2095, 2183, 2227;
    1979: 200, 272, 433, 603, 720, 1299, 1445,
    1522, 1772, 1780, 1801, 2121, 2285; **1980–**
    81: 235, 355, 428, 695, 898, 948, 1128,
    1440, 1577, 1981, 2763
  Deficits
    Federal budget restraint, **1979:** 55, 95, 97, 104,
      111, 114, 123, 255, 300, 471, 487, 489, 650,
      701, 704, 790, 796, 833, 935, 1247, 1403,
      1566, 1607, 1985, 1987, 2040
    Legislation, **1980–81:** 2778
    Reduction, **1979:** 114, 307, 571, 577, 635, 653,
      704, 716, 790, 830, 833, 935, 1750, 1768,
      1841, 1874, 1892, 1936, 1943, 1951, 1985,
      2020, 2026, 2028
    Reductions during administration, **1980–81:**
      71, 76, 120, 121, 126, 215, 246, 247, 280,
      388, 389, 456, 558, 639, 978, 2129, 2186,
      2220, 2270, 2358, 2893, 2895
    Relationship with inflation, **1980–81:** 2029,
      2085, 2114
  Democratic National Committee, remarks, **1978:**
    2196
  Democratic workshop on inflation, remarks,
    1978: 2215
  Economic development allocations, **1980–81:**
    1589, 1964
  Economic Report, **1978:** 132
  Education program allocations, **1980–81:** 1295,
    1560
  Efforts to balance, **1977:** 47, 391, 441, 497, 728,
    890, 1016, 1298, 1318, 1883, 2170, 2194;

Budget, Federal — *continued*
  Efforts to balance — *continued*
    1978: 338, 369, 723, 1352, 1388, 1409,
    1423, 1549, 1552, 1581, 1587, 1589, 1590,
    1649, 1732, 1798, 1816, 1861, 1868, 1885,
    1890, 1894, 1913, 1934, 1938, 1945, 1951,
    1969, 2192; **1979:** 57, 562
  Federal spending, **1978:** 1233, 1318, 1707
  Fiscal Year 1978 revisions, **1977:** 214
  Fiscal Year 1980
    Deficit figure decision, **1979:** 54
    Export-Import Bank allocation, **1979:** 331
    First resolution, congressional approval, **1979:**
      947
    Mentions, **1979:** 40, 104, 111, 123, 306
    Message to Congress, **1979:** 95, 96
    Mid-session review, **1979:** 1233
    News conference statement, **1979:** 50
    Second resolution, **1979:** 1707
    Social programs allocations, **1979:** 34, 116,
      123, 177, 187
  Fiscal Year 1981
    Administration officials, meetings with the
      President to discuss (Digest), **1979:** 898,
      1017, 1018, 2138, 2187, 2207, 2248, 2279,
      2280
    Congressional briefing (Digest), **1980–81:** 824
    Continuing appropriations, **1980–81:** 1981,
      2015
    Critical programs spending increases, **1980–**
      81: 122
    Deficit estimates, **1980–81:** 2026, 2216, 2327
    Employment programs, **1980–81:** 806
    Federal territories, **1980–81:** 320
    First resolution, **1980–81:** 857, 985, 1015, 1113
    Inflation control measure, **1980–81:** 121, 247
    International science and technology pro-
      grams, **1980–81:** 408
    Message transmittal to Congress, **1980–81:**
      225, 227
    President's assessment, **1980–81:** 239
    President's revisions to balance
      Announcement remarks, **1980–81:** 477
      Congressional consideration, **1980–81:** 497,
        512, 517, 539, 586, 705, 761, 1067
      Defense spending, **1980–81:** 978, 994, 1079
      Formal request to implement (Digest),
        1980–81: 719
      Mentions, **1980–81:** 486, 724, 737, 1637
      Message transmittal to Congress and sign-
        ing ceremony, **1980–81:** 568, 569
      News conference (Checklist), **1980–81:** 608
      News conference statement, **1980–81:** 484
      Purposes, **1980–81:** 489, 554, 581, 639, 713,
        994
      Review session, **1980–81:** 1429
      Social program allocations, **1980–81:** 536,
        554, 767, 829, 835, 909, 978, 994, 1079

Budget, Federal — *continued*
   Fiscal Year 1981 — *continued*
      Radiation protection program, **1980–81:** 364
      Tax relief rejection, **1980–81:** 247
      Youth programs, **1980–81:** 53
   Fiscal Year 1982
      Advisers, meetings with the President (Digest),
         1980–81: 1050, 2806, 2807, 2823
      Message transmittal to Congress, **1980–81:**
         2895
      Signing ceremony, **1980–81:** 2893
   Foreign spending, **1980–81:** 627
   Forestry programs, **1980–81:** 1145
   General revenue sharing reductions, **1980–81:**
      698
   Government travel costs, **1978:** 1483
   Growth decrease, **1980–81:** 1586
   Growth in total expenditures, **1977:** 1062
   Interview remarks, **1978:** 2149, 2182
   Library services allocations, **1980–81:** 1931
   Low-level radiation research funding, **1979:** 2007
   Meetings, **1978:** 934, 1009, 1034, 1070, 1071,
      1879, 1954, 2186, 2187, 2269, 2270, 2281
   Mention, **1979:** 1739
   Message to Congress, **1978:** 125, 185
   Migration and refugee appropriations for fiscal
      1980 and 1981 (Checklist), **1979:** 2139
   Multi-year planning, **1978:** 62
   National League of Cities budget briefing, re-
      marks, **1978:** 2081, 2082
   Navy shipbuilding programs, **1980–81:** 475
   News conference remarks, **1978:** 1327, 1441,
      1657, 1752, 1988
   1980 projections, **1978:** 1914, 2042, 2078, 2079
   Policy, **1978:** 899, 1091, 1170
   Reagan, Ronald, policy comparison with the
      President, **1980–81:** 2026
   Real terms spending increase, **1980–81:** 244
   Republican tax cut proposal, **1979:** 1304
   Scientific and technological research allocations,
      1979: 2146
   Social programs allocation increase during ad-
      ministration, **1980–81:** 1632
   Solar energy allocations, **1980–81:** 1882, 1898,
      1931
   State of the Union, **1978:** 93
   Unspent appropriations, **1977:** 2001
   Women's organization allocations, **1980–81:** 923
   Zero-base budgeting, **1977:** 154, 160, 169, 174,
      190, 394, 728, 1030, 1087; **1978:** 125, 133,
      187, 753, 815, 882, 1422; **1979:** 75, 97,
      100; **1980–81:** 115, 1357, 2902
Budget Committee, Congressional, **1980–81:** 2025
Budig, Gene A., **1980–81:** 1432
Buena Vista, Ga., **1980–81:** 463
Buergenthal, Thomas, **1978:** 1974
Buffalo, N.Y., **1977:** 86, 295; **1978:** 1883
Buffalo River, Tenn., **1979:** 1813

Buffington, Ulysses, **1977:** 1161
Bugotu, Francis, **1979:** 554
Building Sciences, National Institute of.
   See National Institute of Building Sciences.
Building temperature restrictions, emergency,
      1979: 370, 690, 797, 1227, 1246, 1327;
      1980–81: 685, 2877
Bukovsky, Vladimir, **1977:** 279
Bulgaria
   Ambassador to U.S., **1978:** 328; **1980–81:** 2752
   U.S. Ambassador, **1977:** 1220, 1223; **1979:** 1262,
      1293
Bull, Bartle, **1978:** 408
Bullard, Betty M., **1978:** 1514
Bullets basketball team, Washington, **1978:** 1069
Bullitt County, Ky., **1979:** 1343
Bullock, J. Jerome, **1977:** 707
Bumpers, Sen. Dale, **1977:** 1264, 1408, 1612, 1826,
      2018; **1978:** 519, 769, 770, 2110; **1979:**
      887; **1980–81:** 1050, 1268, 2803
Bumpers, Mrs. Dale, **1978:** 2259
Bund, Bill, **1978:** 1512
Bundy, McGeorge, **1978:** 217, 230; **1979:** 1820,
      1823
Bunker, Ellsworth, **1977:** 148, 279, 1383, 1463–
      1465, 1493, 1544, 1749; **1978:** 148, 1066
Bunton, Lucius Desha, III, **1979:** 1883
Buonomo, Joseph A., **1980–81:** 2242
Burch, Betsy, **1979:** 2248
Burdick, Sen. Quentin, **1977:** 963, 1753; **1978:** 456,
      1278; **1980–81:** 1372
Bureau.
   See other part of title.
Burciaga, Cecilia, **1978:** 1134
Bureaucracy, Federal.
   See Government reform and reorganization.
Burg, Mary Lou, **1977:** 1667, 1700
Burg, Yosef, **1980–81:** 378, 1292, 1303
Burger, Warren E., **1977:** 4, 13, 15, 19, 26, 27, 396,
      1700; **1978:** 398, 482; **1979:** 760n., 1441,
      2201n.
Burgess, James R., Jr., **1977:** 1059
Burke, Colman, **1977:** 1612
Burke, Repr. James A., **1977:** 2050, 2155, 2157
Burke, James E., **1978:** 1360, 1381
Burke, John R., 1219, 1223
Burke, Selma, **1979:** 217
Burke, Repr. Yvonne Brathwaite, **1978:** 1683, 1736,
      1946
Burkhalter, William M., **1979:** 375, 402
Burkhardt, Francis X., **1977:** 364, 373
Burleson, Repr. Omar, **1977:** 750
Burlington, Iowa, **1979:** 1493, 1494
Burlison, Repr. Bill D., **1980–81:** 2233
Burma
   Ambassador to U.S., **1978:** 1380; **1979:** 2066,
      2082; **1980–81:** 2752

Burma — *continued*
    Drug traffic, **1977:** 1399, 1401
    U.S. Ambassador, **1977:** 1474, 1483
Burnet, Alastair, **1978:** 1252, 1255, 1258
Burns, Arthur F., **1977:** 105, 371, 630, 744, 747, 942,
        1162, 1382, 1383, 1699, 1709, 1909, 1999,
        2006, 2011, 2058, 2183–2185, 2192, 2193,
        2223; **1978:** 57, 64, 66, 277, 354, 415, 482,
        977; **1980–81:** 1427
Burns, Bill, **1980–81:** 742n.
Burns, Ellen B., **1978:** 329
Burns, Robert W., Jr., **1978:** 920, 935
Burris, Robert Harza, **1979:** 2289; **1980–81:** 82n.
Burroughs, John A., Jr., **1980–81:** 1860, 1946
Burroughs, Margaret T., **1980–81:** 601, 602
Bursley, G.H. Patrick, **1979:** 1007, 1019, 1964, 2043
Burtis, Theodore A., **1979:** 1614n.
Burton, Glenn W., **1980–81:** 2999
Burton, Repr. John L., **1978:** 1947; **1979:** 667
Burton, Mack, **1977:** 2089, 2090
Burton, Repr. Phillip, **1977:** 556; **1978:** 549, 575,
        1425, 1947, 2000
    Federal territorial policy development, **1980–81:**
        318
    Lake Tahoe region protection support, **1980–81:**
        1013, 2237
    Legislation passage leadership
        Alaska National Interest Lands Conservation
            Act, **1980–81:** 2756
        National Parks and Recreation Act Amend-
            ments, **1980–81:** 433
    Northern Mariana Islands Commission on Fed-
        eral Laws, member, **1980–81:** 932
Burundi
    Ambassador to U.S, **1980–81:** 268
    U.S. Ambassador, **1977:** 1977, 2006; **1978:** 231;
        1980–81: 1025, 1051
Burwell, David, **1980–81:** 1404
Bus Fuel Economy Advisory Committee, Truck
        and, **1980–81:** 1404
Bus industry, **1979:** 1742
Busbee, Gov. George D., **1977:** 595, 599, 1513,
        2165; **1980–81:** 1423n., 1749, 1756, 2828
    Committee on international trade and foreign
        relations, chairman, **1979:** 66, 330, 334
    Mention, **1979:** 1809
    President's Export Council, member, **1979:** 942,
        943
Busby, Morris D., **1980–81:** 892, 893
Bush, Bob, **1977:** 882
Bush, Dorothy, **1980–81:** 1541
Bush George, **1977:** 352; **1980–81:** 1538, 1640,
        2023, 2078, 2144, 2420, 2433, 2450, 2480,
        2607
Bushnell, John A., **1980–81:** 33, 269
Business, Inc., National Alliance of, **1978:** 1772;
        1980–81: 422

Business, White House Conference on Small.
    See White House Conference on Small Business.
Business Administration, Small.
    See Small Business Administration.
Business Council, **1977:** 2106; **1978:** 2235; **1979:**
        2232, 2240, 2249
Business development agency, minority, proposed,
        1980–81: 77, 127
Business Enterprise, Interagency Council for Mi-
        nority, **1980–81:** 76, 77
Business and Industry
    Administration's accomplishments and goals,
        1979: 561, 634
    Air and water pollution standards, **1980–81:** 352
    Anti-inflation program, **1978:** 1381, 1843, 1844,
        1846, 1880, 1990, 2054
    Corporate officials, meeting with the President,
        1977: 1127
    Economic Report, **1978:** 135, 138
    Energy conservation measures, **1979:** 1535, 1568,
        2050
    Environmental protection, **1977:** 985
    Export policy, **1978:** 1630, 1631
    Export promotion policies, **1980–81:** 402, 1692
    Federal Government, relationship with, **1980–81:**
        1349
    Federal procurement policy, **1980–81:** 72
    Federal regulations, **1977:** 108, 109, 2015, 2113;
        1978: 346; **1980–81:** 2510
    Federal stabilization actions, **1979:** 2041
    Foreign boycotts, **1977:** 788, 1136
    Foreign business investments, **1980–81:** 1118
    Foreign corrupt practices and investment dis-
        closure bill, **1977:** 2157
    Foreign manufacturers, competition with, **1979:**
        1488
    Forest products development, **1979:** 670
    Free enterprise system, relationship with Federal
        Government, **1980–81:** 44
    Government ban of Tris in sleepwear, **1978:**
        1977, 1978
    HIRE program, **1977:** 53, 944, 1115, 1482, 1611
    Industrial goods export, **1980–81:** 125
    Industrial innovation initiatives program, **1979:**
        680, 2068, 2070; **1980–81:** 121
    International trade responsibilities, **1979:** 1733
    Interview remarks, **1978:** 1416
    Investment growth, **1979:** 112
    Investment plans, **1977:** 636, 888
    Iran, prohibition on transactions with, **1980–81:**
        613, 615
    Japanese leaders, meeting with the President,
        1977: 595
    Labor law reform, **1977:** 1277, 1332
        Legislation, **1978:** 990, 993, 1079
    Leaders, meeting with the President, **1978:** 1380
    Minority ownerships.
        See Business ownerships *under* Minorities.

Business and Industry — *continued*
 Natural gas legislation, **1978:** 1452, 1484
 Northwest corridor railroad legislation, effect on, **1980–81:** 1011
 Occupational safety and health programs, **1977:** 200, 398
 Oil use reduction, **1979:** 1239, 1244
 Powerplant conversions and construction restrictions, **1980–81:** 1131
 Presidential Management Intern Program, **1977:** 1498-1500
 Privacy rights, **1979:** 582
 Private sector, job creation, **1977:** 240, 295
 Private Sector Initiative Program, **1978:** 960, 961
 Productivity
  Growth, **1980–81:** 3005
  Inflation, relationship with, **1980–81:** 748
  Research and development allocations, **1980–81:** 121, 226
  Statistics, **1980–81:** 3010
  Worldwide comparison, **1980–81:** 748, 992, 1083
 Profits increase, **1979:** 2040
 Prohibition on transactions with Soviet Union with respect to 1980 Summer Olympics, **1980–81:** 560, 565
 Reagan, Ronald, proposals for, **1980–81:** 2221
 Relationship with the President, **1977:** 775, 1095
 Representatives, meetings with the President, **1978:** 66, 770, 994, 1154
 Research and development legislation, **1980–81:** 2379
 Revitalization program
  Computer technology development, **1980–81:** 1537
  Declining industries assistance, **1980–81:** 1505, 1603, 1607, 1631, 1676, 1885, 1959, 2192, 2205
  Facilities modernization, **1980–81:** 1505, 1512, 1615, 1659, 1674, 1734, 1743, 1768, 1879, 1884, 1952, 1986, 1987, 2077, 2081, 2166, 2191, 2217, 2221, 2252, 2434
  Investment tax credits, **1980–81:** 1973, 2077, 2084, 2191, 2220, 2481, 2514, 2547, 2568, 2897, 3011
  Mentions, **1980–81:** 1678, 1726, 1729, 1870
  New energy industries creation.
   See National program *under* Energy.
 Science and technology development, **1979:** 530, 545
 Small business, **1977:** 397
 State of the Union, **1978:** 92, 100, 102, 111
 Taxation, **1977:** 55, 618–622, 642, 695, 1397, 1621; **1978:** 160, 162, 165, 172, 174, 346
 Urban rehabilitation, **1978:** 1428
 U.S. human rights positions, effect on, **1979:** 2010
 South African investments, **1980–81:** 2300

Business and Industry — *continued*
 Voluntary wage and price guidelines, **1978:** 723, 977, 1074, 1155, 1222, 1223, 1327, 1352, 1423, 1910, 1912, 2066, 2239; **1980–81:** 120, 247, 248, 581
  See also under Wages and prices
 Wage and price increases, **1977:** 51, 219
 Wage rate comparability surveys, **1979:** 1003
 White House conference for business community, **1977:** 120
 White House Forum on Inflation, **1978:** 1914, 1915
 Women's enterprises, **1979:** 888, 890, 894; **1980–81:** 70
  See also specific business or industry; Corporations; Small businesses.
Business Leadership Conference, Junior Achievement Program's National, **1977:** 86
Business League, National, **1980–81:** 63, 1281
Business Ownership, Advisory Committee on Small and Minority, **1980–81:** 262
Business Roundtable, **1977:** 650, 788, 1136; **1978:** 1110, 1222; **1980–81:** 1281
Business Utilization, Office of Small and Disadvantaged, **1980–81:** 73
Businessmen, National Alliance of, **1977:** 1611; **1978:**, 961, 973, 994; **1979:** 1976
Busing, school, **1977:** 1210; **1980–81:** 2809
Bussiere, Emile R., **1978:** 892; **1979:** 942
Bustamante, John H., **1977:** 816
Butcher, Clara, **1980–81:** 850
Butcher, Goler T., **1977:** 1068; **1980–81:** 719
Butcher, Jake, **1978:** 1859, 1860, 1864
Butchman, Alan A., **1977:** 84, 774
Buthelezi, Gatsha, **1977:** 371
Butkovitz, Dale, **1977:** 308, 309
Butler, Landon, **1977:** 1965; **1979:** 1785, 2043
Butler, Merrill, **1980–81:** 2560
Buttimer, Toby, **1978:** 539, 540, 543
Butz, Earl L., **1979:** 1710; **1980–81:** 2619
Buzbee, Kenneth V., **1980–81:** 1644
Byrd, Sen. Harry F., Jr., **1978:** 2175; **1979:** 36
Byrd, James W., **1977:** 745, 746
Byrd, Sen. Robert C., **1977:** 23, 402, 435, 586, 619, 650, 1013, 1016, 1063, 1084, 1092, 1162, 1410, 1506, 1583, 1672, 1694, 1700, 1746, 1794, 1823, 1888, 1972, 2000, 2016, 2064, 2154, 2196; **1978:** 66, 282, 284, 432, 457, 511, 512, 517, 700, 720, 758, 924, 1005, 1222, 1278, 1467, 1468, 1570, 1644, 1647, 1654, 1656, 1665, 1679, 1719, 1729, 1730, 1732, 1758, 1771, 1871, 1885, 1947, 1979, 1982, 1983, 2059, 2073, 2254
 Communications from the President, **1980–81:** 1012, 2066, 2774
 Congressional energy and inflation task forces, membership recommendations to President, **1979:** 1216

Byrd, Sen. Robert C. — *continued*
  Democratic Presidential candidates debate, advocacy for, **1980–81:** 907
  International coal agreement support, **1980–81:** 1448, 1450, 1451
  Legislation passage leadership
    Chrysler Corporation Loan Guarantee Act, **1980–81:** 27
    Crude Oil Windfall Profit Tax Act, **1980–81:** 542, 585, 587
    Department of Education, **1979:** 756
    Department of Interior appropriations, **1979:** 2156
    Emergency Energy Conservation Act, **1979:** 2086
    Energy Security Act, **1980–81:** 1257
    Omnibus Reconciliation Act, **1980–81:** 2780
    Standby gasoline rationing plan, **1979:** 840, 1213
  Meetings with the President (Digest), **1979:** 178, 293
  Mentions, **1979:** 1609, 1776; **1980–81:** 538, 569
  President's assessment, **1979:** 829
  Relationship with the President, **1980–81:** 907
  SALT II treaty consideration, **1980–81:** 12, 488, 831
  Telephone conversation with the President (Digest), **1980–81:** 2822
Byrne, Gov. Brendan T.
  See Governor *under* New Jersey.
Byrne, Jane, **1979:** 1603, 1932, 1977; **1980–81:** 342, 833, 1852
Byrne, Patricia M., **1979:** 2066, 2082
Byron, Repr. Goodloe E., **1978:** 549, 1761

Cabinet
  Anti-inflation program briefing, **1978:** 2028
  Camp David meetings, **1978:** 755, 769
  Changes in, **1979:** 1291, 1304, 1308, 1322, 1332, 1748
  Meetings with the President, **1977:** 9, 30, 34, 85, 194, 251, 371, 463, 507, 555, 595, 640, 705, 706, 743, 942, 1030, 1083, 1126, 1161, 1210, 1263, 1305, 1382, 1436, 1532, 1611, 1648, 1753, 1825, 1965, 2005, 2036, 2050, 2076, 2088, 2129; **1978:** 65, 148, 276, 302, 327, 456, 503, 749, 802, 897, 1009, 1070, 1153, 1278, 1344, 1405, 1406, 1668, 1772, 1878, 2072, 2269; **1979:** 89, 239, 617, 731, 841, 842, 955, 1678, 2042; **1980–81:** 291, 493, 563, 1468, 2782
  Members, selection of, **1978:** 2258
  Members, swearing-in ceremonies, **1977:** 12, 16, 19, 26, 46
  Oil portraits of Secretaries, **1977:** 662

Cabinet — *continued*
  Percentage of former mayors in, **1979:** 1972
  Personal statements, **1977:** 248
  Presidential campaign role, **1979:** 1986
  President's assessment, **1978:** 70, 227
  Relationship with the President, **1977:** 110, 748, 1253, 2100, 2113, 2114; **1978:** 938
  Secretary, **1977:** 34–37, 86, 226, 278, 485, 943, 944, 1100, 1162; **1978:** 1110
  White House Christmas reception, **1979:** 2280
  White House dinner, **1980–81:** 2822
  See also specific departments.
Cable, William H., **1977:** 806; **1978:** 1154, 2083, 2084; **1980–81:** 2071
  Meetings with the President (Digest) **1979:** 467, 553, 618, 731, 732, 786, 842, 898, 956, 1142
Cable News Network, **1980–81:** 1017, 1246
Cable television, **1979:** 932, 933, 938
Cable Television Association, National, **1979:** 932
Cabranes, Jose A., **1977:** 529; **1980–81:** 1823
Cache Basin, Ark., **1977:** 208
Caddell, Pat, **1977:** 864, 1914; **1980–81:** 2688, 2829
Cafferty, Pastora San Juan, **1979:** 730
Cagney, James, **1980–81:** 502, 2786
Cahaba River, Ala., **1979:** 2245
Cahill, Clyde S., Jr., **1980–81:** 608
Cahill, William T., **1980–81:** 1823, 1847
Cain, Glen G., **1978:** 52, 150
Calaway, Jim, **1980–81:** 1738
Caldera, Manuel R., **1980–81:** 305
Caldwell, John, **1977:** 323
Caldwell, Philip, **1979:** 900; **1980–81:** 1670, 1986n., 2117
Calhoun, Ga., **1977:** 596, 604, 640; **1979:** 731
Calhoun, John A., III, **1979:** 2184, 2207
Calhoun, Michael J., **1979:** 2166, 2188; **1980–81:** 1150
Califano, Joseph A., Jr., **1980–81:** 329, 2161, 2284
  See also Health, Education, and Welfare, Secretary of.
California
  Central Valley Project, San Luis Unit, **1977:** 1124
  Channel Islands National Park and Marine Sanctuary, **1980–81:** 432, 1856
  Crude oil production, **1979:** 874
  Disaster declarations, **1978:** 328; **1979:** 1319, 2042; **1980–81:** 291, 374, 2070, 2753
  Drought, **1977:** 916
  Emergency declaration, **1978:** 1954, 2004
  Gasoline shortages, **1979:** 800, 808, 862, 872, 875, 898, 900, 985, 986
  Gov. Edmund G. (Jerry) Brown, Jr., **1977:** 31, 67, 196, 864, 944, 1894; **1978:** 857, 1078, 1096, 1946, 1947
    Balanced Federal budget, proposed constitutional amendment, **1979:** 562

California — *continued*
  Gov. Edmund Brown, Jr. — *continued*
    California gasoline shortage actions, **1979:**
      800, 872, 876, 898, 986
    Channel Islands Marine Sanctuary support,
      1980–81: 1857
    Democratic platform positions presentation,
      1980–81: 1029
    Iranian oil imports discontinuance support,
      1979: 2131
    Maine Democratic primary results, **1980–81:**
      295
    Meetings with the President (Digest), **1980–81:**
      1305n., 2752
    Mentions, **1979:** 350, 1582; **1980–81:** 1039,
      1299n., 1532, 1887
    Support of President's candidacy, **1980–81:**
      1912
    United States Air Force Academy, Board of
      Visitors, member, **1980–81:** 2802
  High sulfur crude oil, **1978:** 1112, 1771
  Lake Tahoe region legislation, **1980–81:** 2235,
    2237
  Natural gas, **1977:** 67, 1620
  Point Reyes-Farallon Islands National Marine
    Sanctuary, **1980–81:** 2997
  President's visits, **1977:** 887, 895, 915, 1893;
    1978: 834, 841, 1946; **1979:** 787, 807, 809,
    810, 841, 843, 1866, 1872, 1876; **1980–81:**
    1295–1322, 1868–1900
  Proposition 13, **1978:** 1077, 1093, 1096, 1229,
    1353
  Tuolumne River, **1979:** 1815
  U.S. attorney Herman Sillas, Jr., **1980–81:** 1346,
    1412, 1661
  U.S. attorneys, **1977:** 1613, 1614, 1755, 1796,
    1967
  U.S. district judges, **1978:** 1407; **1979:** 1018,
    1019, 1786, 1787, 2081, 2082, 2207, 2208,
    2249; **1980–81:** 608, 894, 1151
  U.S. marshals, **1977:** 1613, 1614, 2090; **1978:** 711,
    712; **1980–81:** 269
  White House briefing for civic and community
    leaders, **1980–81:** 563
California, U.S.S., **1980–81:** 972, 976
California Chicano Caucus, **1979:** 810
California Debris Commission, **1977:** 1307, 1323;
    1978: 1639, 1669; **1979:** 43, 91; **1980–81:**
    237
California Institute of Technology, **1980–81:** 664
Caliguri, Richard S., **1980–81:** 369
Calkins, David Ross, **1978:** 1026
Callaghan, James.
  See United Kingdom, Prime Minister.
Callaghan, Mrs. James, **1979:** 25
Calloway, DeVerne Lee, **1978:** 734
Calogero, Paul, **1979:** 1720
Camacho, Andy, **1980–81:** 2614

Camacho, Carlos S., **1980–81:** 1723
Camacho, Ernest M., **1979:** 229, 811
Camara, Ibrahima, **1977:** 1754
Cambodia.
  See Kampuchea.
Cambridge, Mass., **1979:** 1817
Camden County, N.J., **1979:** 1817
Cameroon, U.S. Ambassador, **1977:** 713, 745;
    1980–81: 1107, 1111
Camicia, Nicholas Thomas, **1980–81:** 1644
Camm, Frank A., **1978:** 1879, 1977
Camp, George W., **1979:** 215, 241
Camp David, Md., **1977:** 252, 304, 323, 509, 555,
    883, 942, 1211, 1221, 1265, 1305, 1483,
    1505, 1533, 1567, 1612, 1700, 1753, 1754,
    1804, 1931, 2049, 2089, 2129; **1978:** 66,
    275, 277, 279, 303, 457, 503, 570, 640, 710,
    749, 750, 755, 769, 803, 880, 898, 933,
    1034, 1070, 1071, 1110, 1222, 1239, 1278,
    1333, 1344, 1345, 1379, 1407, 1505, 1515,
    1656, 1723, 1771, 1807, 1878, 1954, 1964,
    2004, 2059, 2073, 2146, 2280, 2302
  Domestic issues meetings, **1979:** 1221, 1222,
    1232, 1329; **1980–81:** 23, 62, 104, 216, 267,
    291, 333, 374, 451, 493, 521, 563, 603, 653,
    825, 891, 932, 966, 967, 1013, 1049, 1051,
    1110, 1111, 1150, 1245, 1428, 1468, 1523,
    1524, 1544, 1564, 1598, 1662, 1714, 1847,
    1945, 1946, 2069, 2178, 2179, 2332, 2453,
    2614, 2699, 2741, 2751, 2781, 2782, 2806,
    2807, 2823, 2841, 3049
  Foreign policy advisers, meeting with the Pres-
    ident (Digest) **1979:** 2151
  Mentions, **1979:** 1226, 1340
  Middle East peace negotiations, meetings of
    Egyptian and Israeli Ministers, **1979:** 303,
    329, 346
  President's visits (Digest), **1979:** 14, 89, 177, 179,
    216, 217, 239, 241, 292, 327, 440, 467, 619,
    666, 899, 957, 982, 983, 1292, 1319, 1396,
    1423, 1453, 1518, 1531, 1679, 1704, 1823,
    2042, 2043, 2080, 2081, 2104, 2151, 2186,
    2187, 2206, 2248, 2279, 2280, 2300
Camp David, Md., summit meeting.
  See under Middle East.
Camp Hoover, Va., **1978:** 1879; **1979:** 842, 897
Campaign Act Amendments of 1979, Federal Elec-
    tion, **1980–81:** 38
Campaign, 1980 Presidential.
  See Elections, 1980: campaign.
Campaign financing, **1977:** 482, 737
Campbell Alan K., **1977:** 570, 596, 872, 941, 1052,
    1463, 1499, 1535; **1978:** 316, 802, 897, 952,
    953, 1138, 1158, 1362, 1407, 1765, 1773,
    1972
  See also Personnel Management, Office of, Di-
    rector.

Campbell, Don, **1979:** 2242n
Campbell, Ed, **1979:** 804ftn.
Campbell, James, **1980–81:** 19
Campbell, Thomas John, **1980–81:** 948
Campobello Conference on Peace and Human
    Rights, **1979:** 1521
Campos, Santiago E., **1978:** 1034, 1035
Canada
    Agreements and treaties with U.S.
        Fisheries, **1977:** 256; **1978:** 812, 1234; **1979:**
            776, 1420
        Maritime boundary, **1979:** 776
        Penal sentences, **1977:** 655
        Pipelines, **1977:** 534, 1546, 1547, 1569
    Ambassador to U.S., **1977:** 1383, 1978, 1980
    American citizens in Iran, rescue of, **1980–81:**
        255
    Bonn Economic Summit Conference, **1978:**
        1310, 1311
    Conventions with U.S.
        Migratory birds protection, **1980–81:** 2743
        Nuclear energy, **1980–81:** 782
        Taxation, **1980–81:** 2715
    Cyprus conflict actions, **1979:** 191
    Energy projects with U.S., **1979:** 591, 1245, 1327
    Grain exports, **1980–81:** 42
    International Dairy Arrangement exception,
        1979: 2255
    Joint statement, **1979:** 381
    Maritime boundary negotiations with U.S., Pres-
        ident's Special Representative, **1977:** 1362
    Natural gas and oil, **1977:** 7, 283
    Natural gas transportation system, **1980–81:**
        1367, 1368, 1372
    Nuclear fuel supplies, **1977:** 585
    Oil supplies, **1979:** 2050
    President's visit, **1979:** 1882, 2106, 2170
    Prime Minister.
        See Canada, Prime Minister
    Prisoner transfers with U.S., **1977:** 1919
    Royal Standard, return of, **1980–81:** 988
    St. Lawrence Seaway navigation clearance, **1979:**
        2037
    Saint Lawrence Seaway operation, **1980–81:**
        1418
    Tar sands conversion to oil, **1979:** 1185
    Tokyo Summit
        Attendance announcement, **1979:** 550
        Joint statement, **1979:** 1197
        Oil imports ceiling, **1979:** 1198
    Trade with U.S., **1980–81:** 1248, 1734
    U.S. advertising in broadcasting industries,
        1980–81: 1671
    U.S. Ambassador, **1979:** 1616
    U.S. border States, relationship with, **1979:** 335
    U.S. policy, **1977:** 223
    U.S. relations, **1980–81:** 1312, 1743, 1995
    Vice President's visit, **1977:** 2073

Canada — *continued*
    West-to-east crude oil transportation system,
        1980–81: 100
Canada, International Boundary Commission,
    United States and, **1977:** 1407
Canada, International Joint Commission-United
    States and, **1978:** 681, 711, 761, 803; **1979:**
    1395, 1398
Canada, Permanent Joint Board on Defense-Unit-
    ed States and, **1978:** 453
Canada, Prime Minister (Joe Clark), **1980–81:** 255
    Invitation to President to visit Canada, **1979:**
        1882
    Mention, **1979:** 2050
    Tokyo Summit
        Conclusion remarks, **1979:** 1196, 1197n.
        Meeting with the President, **1979:** 1181
Canada, Prime Minister (Pierre Elliott Trudeau),
    1977: 31, 149, 208, 210, 223, 251, 283, 313,
    824, 1546, 1547, 1568, 1978, 1980; **1978:**
    228, 244, 1310, 1334, 1599; **1979:** 327, 376,
    379, 381
    Alaska Natural Gas Transportation System,
        completion expedition, **1980–81:** 1367,
        1368
    Mention, **1980–81:** 861
    Venice Economic Summit Conference
        Concluding remarks, **1980–81:** 1182
        Meeting with the President (Digest), **1980–81:**
        1243
Canadian Club, **1980–81:** 2782
Canadian Energy Board, **1980–81:** 99
Canadian River Commission, **1980–81:** 2747
Canal Zone, U.S district judge, **1978:** 1154, 1155
Canal Zone Government, **1979:** 102
Canales, Jose A., **1977:** 1222, 1266
Canavan, Gregory H., **1977:** 987
Canby, William Cameron, Jr., **1980–81:** 608
Cancer Advisory Board, National, **1979:** 675, 686,
    1975, 2151; **1980–81:** 911
Cancer Control Month, **1977:** 338; **1978:** 509
    (Proc. 4643), **1979:** 389
    (Proc. 4731), **1980–81:** 450
Cancer Courage Award, **1977:** 566; **1978:** 710;
    1979: 554
Cancer Institute, National, **1977:** 1378; **1980–81:**
    1332
Cancer Panel, President's, **1977:** 1587; **1979:** 2196;
    1980–81: 1292
Cancer Program, National, **1977:** 556, 706; **1979:**
    675, 2105
Cancer Research Foundation awards, General
    Motors, **1979:** 786
Cancer Society, American, **1977:** 566; **1979:** 553
Cannon, Sen. Howard W., **1977:** 389, 485, 1134,
    1380, 1916, 1988; **1978:** 148, 302, 762,
    1009, 1669, 1838, 1927, 2110

Cannon, Sen. Howard W. — *continued*
  Legislation passage leadership
    Household Goods Transportation Act, **1980–81:** 2240
    International Air Transportation Competition Act, **1980–81:** 333
    Moapa Band of Paiutes, **1980–81:** 2781
    Motor Carrier Act, **1980–81:** 461, 694, 1262, 1263, 1267
    National Aquaculture Act, **1980–81:** 1938
    Northeast corridor rail transportation, **1980–81:** 1009, 1011
    Small business, **1980–81:** 2380
    Staggers Rail Act, **1980–81:** 584, 2230
  Telecommunications industry regulatory reform efforts, **1979:** 1702
  Trucking industry deregulation legislation support, **1979:** 1115, 1116, 1143, 2185
Cannon, William R., **1979:** 1562
Cannon, Wilson P., Jr., **1979:** 942
Cano, Sylvia, **1977:** 816
Cantor, Joe, **1980–81:** 1362
Cantu, Alfredo A., **1980–81:** 1443, 1470
Cantwell, Bernal D., **1977:** 1437, 1438
Cape Krusenstern National Mounument, **1978:** 2119
Cape Verde
  Ambassador to U.S., **1980–81:** 1564
  U.S. Ambassador, **1980–81:** 1411, 1428; **1977:** 1398, 1438
Capital gains tax, **1978:** 1178, 1185, 1230, 1323, 1354, 1989
Capital Planning Commission, National, **1979:** 687; **1980–81:** 1412
Capitol Hill Page School, **1977:** 1061; **1978:** 1081; **1980–81:** 1150
Capp, Lincoln W., II, **1979:** 914
Capper-Volstead Act, **1980–81:** 2468
Captioning Institute, National, **1980–81:** 811
Captive Nations Week, **1977:** 1292; **1978:** 1251
  (Proc. 4666), **1979:** 1141
  (Proc. 4761), **1980–81:** 940
Capture, George Horse, **1977:** 1781, 1796
Caputo, Philip, **1979:** 974; **1980–81:** 1269, 2316
Caramanlis, Constantine, **1977:** 712, 721, 869, 881, 1137; **1978:** 1026, 1152
Carazo Odio, Rodrigo, **1978:** 1119, 1122, 1123; **1980–81:** 904, 2781
Carbanes, Jose A., **1979:** 2106, 2107
Carbon ferrochromium industry, high, **1978:** 1940, 1941, 2037
Carbone, Nicholas R., **1977:** 2153
Carbray, James, **1978:** 1067
Cardenas, Blandina, **1977:** 1139, 1163, 1844
Cardenas, Jose A., **1978:** 1190
Cardoza, Michael H., **1980–81:** 3050
Cardozo, Michael H., **1979:** 1976

Career Education Incentive Act, **1977:** 2104
Carey, Barbara M., **1980–81:** 1023, 1051
Carey, Gov. Hugh L.
  See Governor *under* New York.
Carey, John M., **1978:** 1771
Cargas, Harry James, **1980–81:** 821
Caribbean
  Administration's accomplishments and goals, **1980–81:** 2373, 2988
  Cuban influence, **1980–81:** 173, 626, 1017
  Hurricane David, U.S. relief efforts, **1979:** 1679
  Illegal drug trafficking, **1980–81:** 1722
  United States
    Assistance, **1979:** 2103
    Foreign relations, **1980–81:** 173, 626, 1215
    Nongovernmental volunteer programs, **1980–81:** 64
    Policy, **1979:** 1665
    Science and technology cooperation, **1980–81:** 407
  See also Latin America; *specific country*.
Caribbean/Central American Action, **1980–81:** 624, 654
Caribbean Development Group, **1979:** 2104
Caribbean Group, **1978:** 1601; **1980–81:** 173
Caribbean, Miami Conference on the, **1979:** 2159
Carl, Beverly May, **1980–81:** 272
Carlin, Gov. John, **1980–81:** 1423n.
Carlin, John, **1978:** 1813, 1820
Carlock, David, **1980–81:** 1393n.
Carlson, Jack W., **1978:** 52, 150
Carlucci, Frank C., **1977:** 252, 2161; **1978:** 66, 150, 570, 1436, 1668; **1979:** 553; **1980–81:** 24, 422
Carnegie Commission on the Future of Public Broadcasting, **1977:** 1739; **1979:** 199
Carnegie, Pa., **1979:** 1232
Carnesale, Albert, **1980–81:** 1331, 1377
Carney, Eliza Macaulay, **1978:** 1086, 1111
Carp, Bertram W., **1979:** 1294
Carpenter, Cyril Hilary, **1979:** 1682, 1706, 2214
Carpenter, Elizabeth S., **1977:** 525; **1979:** 2008, 2009n.; **1980–81:** 203, 219, 1133
Carpenter, Todd C., **1980–81:** 926
Carr, Repr. Bob, **1978:** 1380; **1980–81:** 770, 825, 1843
Carr, George C., **1977:** 1804, 1805
Carr, John, **1980–81:** 1032, 2423
Carr, Patrick E., **1979:** 1044
Carrier Wing Seven, **1980–81:** 2827n.
Carrigan, Jim R., **1979:** 984
Carrillo, Yolanda H., **1978:** 951
Carrington, Lord, **1979:** 2259, 2264; **1980–81:** 892
Carrington, Walter C., **1980–81:** 1148, 1246
Carroll, Constance M., **1980–81:** 2817
Carroll, Earl H., **1980–81:** 1015, 1051
Carroll, Gov. Julian, **1977:** 86, 1225, 1265, 1507; **1978:** 415, 416, 1480, 1485

Carroll, Gov. Julian — *continued*
  Camp David, Md., meeting with the President (Digest), **1979:** 1222
  Mention, **1979:** 1343
  National Governors' Association, Chairman, **1979:** 330, 334, 361, 362n.
Carroon, Lamar E., **1978:** 1466
Carson, Rachel, **1980–81:** 751, 1058
Carson and Walker Rivers and Lake Tahoe Compact, Truckee, **1978:** 1466
Carswell, Robert, **1977:** 487, 510, 1930; **1979:** 977; **1980–81:** 324, 774
Cartegena Agreement countries, trade with U.S., **1980–81:** 20
Cartella De Rubin, Pilar, **1980–81:** 334
Carter, Alton (Buddy), **1977:** 2174; **1978:** 228
Carter, Amy, **1977:** 326, 328, 757, 1061, 1062, 1064; **1978:** 1008, 1293, 1295, 1296, 1300, 1829, 2059
  Educational training, **1979:** 1175, 1923
  European trip, **1980–81:** 1234, 1241–1245
  Friends' visits to White House, **1980–81:** 2133
  Japan, visit to, **1979:** 1108, 1155
  Luncheon with the President (Digest), **1979:** 240
  Mentions, **1979:** 745, 1595, 2128; **1980–81:** 703n., 1371, 1561
  Mississippi River trip, mentions, **1979:** 1472, 1474, 1478, 1491, 1492, 1494, 1509, 1513
  Musical training, **1979:** 1505; **1980–81:** 850
  Relationship with the President, **1979:** 710, 1171
  13th birthday, **1980–81:** 2297
Carter, Annette, **1978:** 2270
Carter, Beverly, **1979:** 2085
Carter, Billy, **1977:** 143, 759, 1013, 1855, 1893, 1942; **1978:** 540, 1008, 2179; **1979:** 47, 348, 1325
  Libyan Government, activities with
    Administration actions disclosure, **1980–81:** 1439
    Congressional investigation, **1980–81:** 1468, 1564
    Exchange with reporters, **1980–81:** 1360
    News conference (Checklist), **1980–81:** 1429
    President's news conference, **1980–81:** 1477–1491
    Report to Congress, **1980–81:** 1523
    Statement by the President, **1980–81:** 1407
    White House Press Secretary statement, **1980–81:** 1466
    White House statements on:
      Department of Justice investigation, **1980–81:** 1406, 2557, 2647
      Senate Judiciary Committee inquiry, **1980–81:** 1420, 1976, 2016
      State Department cables, **1980–81:** 1443, 1471
  Mentions, **1980–81:** 1032, 2840
Carter, Calvin W., **1978:** 228

Carter, Chip, **1979:** 436, 804, 1872, 2054n.; **1980–81:** 1541
Carter, Chip and Caron, **1977:** 86, 148, 295, 595, 648, 1062; **1978:** 2259, 2288
Carter, Hodding, III, **1977:** 280
Carter, Hugh A., Jr., **1977:** 9; **1978:** 1670; **1979:** 1670, 1679; **1980–81:** 2835n.
Carter, Mr. and Mrs. Hugh A., Sr., **1977:** 2036, 2169
Carter, Jack, **1977:** 596; **1979:** 731, 1872
Carter, Jana Kae, **1978:** 1008
Carter, Jeffrey, **1980–81:** 2287
Carter, Jeffrey and Annette, **1977:** 1061
Carter, Jimmy, Personal Assets Trust, **1977:** 140–143; **1979:** 1422
Carter, Jimmy, Presidential Library, **1979:** 1422, 1823
Carter, John Mack, **1977:** 525
Carter, Judy, **1978:** 2285; **1979:** 731
Carter, June, **1977:** 1115; **1978:** 1859
Carter, Kathleen, **1977:** 1242
Carter, Lillian, **1977:** 148, 1894; **1978:** 48, 1067, 1279, 1280, 1645, 1722, 1724
  Broken hip accident, **1980–81:** 2054, 2357
  Campaign efforts for the President, **1980–81:** 1541
  International representative role, **1980–81:** 1488
  Israel, 32d anniversary of, U.S. representative, **1980–81:** 687
  Medical problem, **1979:** 1325
  Mentions, **1979:** 804, 839, 2015, 2214; **1980–81:** 585, 2243
  1976 Presidential campaign efforts, **1980–81:** 382
  Peace Corps Advisory Council, honorary Chair, **1980–81:** 2075
  Peace Corps Service, **1979:** 1982; **1980–81:** 276, 2280
  President's visit, **1980–81:** 2068
  Registered nurse experience, **1980–81:** 908
Carter, Lisle C., Jr., **1979:** 271
Carter, Maybelle, **1978:** 1859; **1979:** 1816
Carter, Rosalynn, **1977:** 86, 146, 185–187, 268, 270, 329, 528, 529, 757, 758, 822, 942, 1030, 1041–1046, 1060, 1098, 1210, 1222, 1265, 1306, 1383, 1437, 1506, 1533, 1568, 1612, 1620, 1649, 1699, 1754, 1795, 1825, 1931, 1966, 2005, 2035, 2036, 2050, 2053, 2077, 2089, 2130, 2207; **1978:** 45, 48, 66, 148, 155, 229, 234, 267, 276, 281, 302, 328, 349, 415, 457, 504, 526, 570, 710, 750, 769, 770, 791, 800, 802, 880, 917, 1008, 1034, 1071, 1110, 1153, 1154, 1221, 1293, 1296, 1344, 1380, 1393, 1406, 1412, 1413, 1429, 1457, 1506, 1668, 1722, 1772, 1793, 1807, 1954, 1955, 1966, 2059, 2073, 2146, 2187, 2274, 2280, 2281
  Advisory role to President, **1980–81:** 1940

Carter, Rosalynn — *continued*
  American hostages in Iran, release efforts,
    1980–81: 1487
  Campaign efforts for the President, **1979:** 2194;
    1980–81: 400, 1465, 1541, 2688
  Christmas, 1980, comments, **1980–81:** 2840
  Congressional wives briefings (Digest), **1980–81:**
    291, 422
  Democratic National Convention delegates, re-
    marks to, **1980–81:** 1466
  Dinner host for:
    Congressmen, **1979:** 1781
    Israeli Prime Minister Begin, **1979:** 400
    Mexican President López Portillo, **1979:** 1782
  District of Columbia activities, **1979:** 1923
  Equal rights amendment support, **1979:** 1897,
    2008; **1980–81:** 833
  European trip, **1980–81:** 1234, 1241–1245
  Family life importance, **1980–81:** 1033
  Family programs interest, **1979:** 1930
  First Lady's staff, size and salaries, **1979:** 1580
  Friendship Force in Georgia, establishment,
    1980–81: 628, 944
  Income tax return, **1980–81:** 719
  Jogging schedule, **1979:** 1747; **1980–81:** 766
  Kentucky Democratic Party fund-raiser atten-
    dance, **1979:** 1223
  Luncheons with the President (Digest), **1979:** 25,
    89, 179, 217, 240, 241, 327, 377, 467, 553,
    787, 898, 955, 983, 1397, 1454, 1705, 1824,
    2042, 2186, 2248; **1980–81:** 63, 217, 522,
    893, 1051, 1523, 1714
  Mental health programs support and involve-
    ment, **1979:** 858, 1350, 1983; **1980–81:**
    2035, 2098, 2100, 2361
  Mentions, **1979:** 745, 842, 1566, 1595, 1615, 1627,
    1767, 1872, 1934, 2015, 2136, 2183n.,
    2189; **1980–81:** 84, 257, 306, 384, 397, 500,
    534, 754, 850, 858, 1005, 1382, 1444, 1654
  Middle East, visit to, **1979:** 417, 428
  Mississippi River trip
    Mentions, **1979:** 1472, 1474, 1478, 1491, 1492,
      1494, 1500
    Remarks, **1979:** 1470, 1473, 1513
  National Mental Health Association salute,
    1980–81: 1091
  National Volunteer Week support, **1980–81:** 695
  Presidential Medal of Freedom, presentation
    ceremony remarks, **1980–81:** 1061
  President's Commission on Mental Health,
    Chairman, **1980–81:** 811
  Public role, President's assessment, **1979:** 1843,
    1872
  Queen, Richard, telephone conversation with
    (Digest), **1980–81:** 1376
  Reagan, Nancy, meeting with, **1980–81:** 2739
  Thailand, visit to, **1979:** 2090, 2099, 2112, 2115
  U.S. Embassy in Mexico, remarks, **1979:** 278

Carter, Rosalynn — *continued*
  Vietnam Memorial Fund sponsor, **1980–81:** 1268
  Volunteer organizations conference sponsorship,
    1980–81: 2285
  White House receptions hostess, **1980–81:** 381n.,
    857n., 1386n., 1514n., 1570, 2829
Carter, Sarah, Rosemary, **1978:** 2286; **1979:** 731
Carter, Sybil, **1979:** 1325
Carter, Repr. Tim Lee, **1978:** 2003; **1980–81:** 1936,
    1937, 1976, 2099
Carter, W. Beverly, Jr., **1978:** 2049; **1979:** 42, 91
Carter family peanut warehouse, **1979:** 652, 1954;
    1980–81: 1487
Carter/Mondale, Friends of, **1979:** 2015
Carter/Mondale, New York Business/Labor for,
    1980–81: 1953, 2071
Carter/Mondale Presidential Committee, Inc.,
    1979: 1865, 1976, 1985ftn., 2194
  Campaign workers party, **1980–81:** 1024
  Chairman, **1980–81:** 932, 1030, 1544
  National Campaign Headquarters remarks,
    1980–81: 937
Carter/Mondale Re-election Committee, **1980–81:**
    1707, 1977, 2340, 2502
Carter/Mondale transition team
  Conflict of interest and financial guidelines,
    1977: 124
  Funds, return to Treasury, **1977:** 226
Carver, Richard E., **1978:** 748; **1980–81:** 1084n.,
    1085
Cary, Frank T., **1978:** 1031; **1980–81:** 1717, 1848,
    2071
Cary, Harold F., **1979:** 436
Cary, John H., **1977:** 2037
Casamento, Anthony, **1980–81:** 1565, 1708, 1720,
    2295
Casco Montenegro, Rita Delia, **1980–81:** 2752
Case, Sen. Clifford P., **1977:** 1794; **1978:** 1543,
    1856; **1980–81:** 1438n.
Casey, Kimberly A., **1980–81:** 929
Casey, Patrick C., **1979:** 2191
Casey, Robert, **1980–81:** 2251
Casey, Thomas R., **1980–81:** 819
Cash, Sgt. David, **1977:** 319
Cash, Johnny, **1977:** 1115
Cash management, Federal, **1977:** 2025
Cashett, Marianne J., **1980–81:** 3026
Cassatt, Mary, **1980–81:** 340
Cassidy, Lee, **1978:** 1466
Castagna, William J., **1979:** 1018, 1019
Castillo, Leonel J., **1977:** 590, 597, 872, 1416, 1438;
    1978: 1158, 1393; **1979:** 812, 1663; **1980–
    81:** 1460, 1943
Castle Air Force Base, Calif., **1980–81:** 1309
Castro, Fidel.
  See Cuba, Premier.
Castro, Nash, **1978:** 963, 964
Castro, Raul H., **1977:** 1481, 1507

Catalino, Judith Ann Koch, **1980–81:** 2614
Catholic Bishops, National Conference of, **1977:** 1611; **1978:** 2059
Catholic Charities, National Conference of, **1979:** 1925, 1977
Catholic Conference, U.S., **1977:** 1611; **1980–81:** 2841
Catterton, Brenda L., **1978:** 1208
Cattle imports (Proc. 4808), **1980–81:** 2801
Cattle industry.
  See Beef industry.
Cattlemen's Association, National, **1980–81:** 521
Cauas, Jorge, **1977:** 447
Caution-Lebby, Gael, **1980–81:** 949
Cavanaugh, Gordon, **1977:** 879, 943
Cavanaugh, Repr. John J., **1980–81:** 522
Cavazos, Lauro F., **1980–81:** 1445, 1470
CBS.
  See Columbia Broadcasting System.
Cease, Jane, **1980–81:** 2107
Ceausescu, Nicolae, **1977:** 251, 327; **1978:** 570, 734, 735, 738, 740, 743, 753, 1032, 2187
Cedano, Blanca, **1979:** 44, 92
Cedeño, Blanca, **1980–81:** 533, 564
Cedronio, Paolo Pansa, **1980–81:** 1241
Celarie, André, **1980–81:** 682n.
Celebrezze, Anthony J., Jr., **1980–81:** 769
Celeste, Dagmar I., **1980–81:** 1669
Celeste, Richard F.
  See Peace Corps, Director.
Celeste, Lt. Gov. and Mrs. Richard F., **1978:** 1278, 1620
Census, Bureau of the, **1977:** 556, 617, 642; **1979:** 239, 981, 1019, 1665; **1980–81:** 2383, 2812, 2872
Census 1980 (Proc. 4701), **1979:** 2086
Center.
  See other part of title.
Central African Republic
  Ambassador to U.S, **1980–81:** 1051
  Generalized System of Preferences, **1979:** 2229
  U.S. Ambassador, **1978:** 1562, 1572; **1980–81:** 1700
Central America.
  See Latin America.
Central American Action, Caribbean, **1980–81:** 624, 654
Central American Assistance Act of 1979, Special, **1980–81:** 1017
Central Arizona Project, Ariz., **1977:** 208
Central Bank of Iran, **1980–81:** 614
Central Freight Lines, **1980–81:** 1402
Central Idaho Wilderness Act, **1980–81:** 1407–1411
Central Intelligence Agency
  Acting Director, **1977:** 37, 85
  Activities, assessment, **1977:** 218, 220, 242, 283, 344

Central Intelligence Agency — *continued*
  Civil land remote-sensing activities, **1979:** 2150
  Deputy Directors, **1977:** 1611, 2161; **1978:** 66, 150, 570, 1154, 1436, 1668, 1879; **1979:** 179, 553, 1396; **1980–81:** 22, 422
  Drug experiments, **1977:** 1265
  Energy report, **1977:** 649, 707
  Gasoline shortages prediction, **1979:** 1997
  Intelligence activities, Executive order, **1978:** 201
  Intelligence report requirements, **1980–81:** 241
  President's remarks to employees, **1978:** 1434
  Retirement and disability system, **1977:** 2066; **1980–81:** 431, 2749, 3001
Central Intelligence Agency, Director (Stansfield Turner), **1977:** 91, 194, 218, 344, 350, 371, 378, 464, 508, 641, 649, 706, 744, 745, 806, 882, 942, 943, 1030, 1059, 1084, 1126, 1162, 1163, 1264, 1265, 1306, 1387, 1421, 1436, 1506, 1533, 1568, 1649, 1691, 1699, 1754, 1794, 1825, 1930, 1966, 1998, 2005, 2036, 2050, 2076, 2088, 2163; **1978:** 65, 66, 148, 190, 198, 214, 276, 327, 372, 415, 456, 525, 710, 750, 769, 802, 897, 934, 1009, 1034, 1071, 1110, 1185, 1201, 1203, 1221, 1278, 1333, 1344, 1380, 1435, 1436, 1457, 1571, 1722, 1747, 1772, 1807, 1854, 1954, 2004, 2058, 2073, 2146, 2187, 2281
  Intelligence sources and methods protection, **1980–81:** 397
  Meetings with the President (Digest), **1979:** 25, 89, 178, 217, 240, 293, 327, 401, 467, 618, 666, 732, 787, 842, 898, 956, 982, 1017, 1043, 1142, 1454, 1604, 1824, 1975, 2081, 2186, 2248; **1980–81:** 103, 267, 333, 422, 492, 563, 774, 892, 967, 1110, 1427, 1598, 1846, 1945
  Mention, **1979:** 37
  Newsmen as agents, policy toward using, **1980–81:** 659
  SALT II treaty role, **1979:** 753
  Task Force on Global Resources and Environment, duties, **1980–81:** 1417
Central Utah project, **1978:** 520
  Bonneville Unit, Utah, **1977:** 208
Ceramic tableware imports, **1978:** 1699
Cerda, Maria B., **1979:** 229; **1980–81:** 1335–1337
Cerda, Rafael Solis, **1979:** 2162n.
Cerel, Sylvia L., **1980–81:** 926
Cerezo, Carmen Consuelo, **1980–81:** 932
CETA.
  See Comprehensive Employment and Training Act programs.
Chabot, Herbert L., **1978:** 481, 504
Chad
  Ambassador to U.S, **1977:** 822
  U.S. Ambassador, **1979:** 1676, 1705
Chadha v. *Immigration and Naturalization Service,* **1980–81:** 2836, 2842, 2882

Chafee, Sen. John H., **1977:** 1753; **1978:** 1071, 1695; **1980–81:** 1548

Chaffee, Roger, **1980–81:** 2443

Chai Zemin, **1978:** 1538; **1979:** 377, 787; **1980–81:** 1821, 1822

Chaikin, Sol G.
    See President *under* International Ladies' Garment Workers Union.

Challandes-Angelini, Frederica P., **1979:** 914

Chalmers, Thomas C., **1978:** 275, 303

Chamber of Commerce, International, **1978:** 1688; **1980–81:** 307, 1127

Chamber of Commerce, United States, **1977:** 251, 1048; **1978:** 1223; **1980–81:** 522, 1281

Chamberlain, Charles J., **1977:** 1664; **1978:** 1438; **1979:** 1037, 1044

Chamberlain, Mr, and Mrs. Lynne, **1979:** 1491n.

Chamberlin, Mary Ellen, **1980–81:** 1097, 3022

Chambers, Anne Cox, **1977:** 576, 577, 597

Chambers, Marjorie Bell, **1978:** 1134; **1979:** 88, 217, 827

Chambers, Mary P., **1980–81:** 812, 826

Chamie, Alfred P., **1978:** 2089

Champ, Norman B., Jr., **1977:** 2182; **1979:** 45, 92

Champion, Hale, **1977:** 252, 706; **1978:** 1630, 1669

Champion Spark Plug Co., **1980–81:** 1402

CHAMPUS.
    See Civilian Health and Medical Program for the Uniformed Services.

Chan, Tom, **1979:** 229

Chancellor, John, **1979:** 47, 410n.; **1980–81:** 34, 1246, 2233

Chand, Prem, **1978:** 667

Chandler, Marilyn B., **1977:** 941

Chaney, Mary Louise, **1979:** 464

Chang, Andrew I.T., **1978:** 2070

Channel Islands, Calif., **1980–81:** 432, 1856

Channing, Carol, **1980–81:** 1747, 2341

Chan-Palay, Victoria L., **1979:** 914

Chanukah, **1979:** 2263
    Torch relay, **1977:** 2084

Chao, Rose Fong, **1980–81:** 2817

Chapa, Amanzio, **1980–81:** 2559

Chapel of the Four Chaplains, Pa., **1980–81:** 292

Chapin, Frederic L., **1978:** 1023, 1034

Chapin, Harry, **1978:** 277, 1511

Chaplin, George, **1978:** 1266

CHAPS program, **1977:** 1840, 1850

Char, Kenneth F. C., **1980–81:** 273

Charles, Serge Elie, **1980–81:** 775

Charleston, S.C., **1977:** 1309

Charleston, W. Va., **1977:** 402; **1978:** 999, 1002

Charlesworth, Susan, **1980–81:** 380

Charter Company, **1980–81:** 581

Chartrand, Robert Lee, **1979:** 400

Chase, Goodwin, **1977:** 337

Chase, Harold W., **1977:** 1823, 1911

Chase, John S., **1980–81:** 2701

Chase, Lucia, **1980–81:** 752, 1058

Chase, Nadine H., **1980–81:** 2883

Chase, Robert, **1977:** 86

Chasen, Robert E., **1980–81:** 98, 102

Chasis, Sarah, **1978:** 217

Chassler, Seymour M., **1977:** 525; **1978:** 1134

Chavez, Fabian, Jr., **1977:** 618, 642; **1979:** 1865

Chavez, Nelba R., **1980–81:** 812, 826

Chavis, Rev. Ben, **1977:** 1105; **1978:** 1328, 1330

Chayes, Antonia Handler, **1977:** 1031; **1979:** 1128, 1142, 1451

Cheek, James, **1980–81:** 1946

Cheese imports (Proc. 4811), **1980–81:** 2846

Chemical industry
    Hazardous waste disposal. **1980–81:** 1353, 1683
    Representatives, meeting with the President (Digest), **1980–81:** 654
    Voluntary price standards compliance, **1980–81:** 659

Chemical warfare, **1980–81:** 2021

Chemical weapons storage, **1979:** 1711

Chemistry, 1979 Nobel Prize in, **1979:** 1962

Chen, Lily Lee, **1979:** 1524

Cheng, Margaret Y., **1980–81:** 927

Chernyayev, Rudolf, **1979:** 731

Cherry, Horace Dicken, **1980–81:** 192, 218

Cherry Blossom Festival, **1977:** 546

Cherry Blossom princesses, **1979:** 618

Cheslaw, Irving G., **1979:** 1156, 1157, 1159

Chesonis, Ray, **1980–81:** 1438n.

Chesser, Jenny, **1979:** 2042

Cheyney State College, Pa., **1979:** 742, 908, 913, 957

Chicago, Ill., **1978:** 972, 980, 1009; **1979:** 1817, 1932
    Grand Park armory construction, **1980–81:** 483
    Mayor Jane Byrne, **1979:** 1603, 1932, 1977; **1980–81:** 342, 726, 736
    President's visits, **1980–81:** 2089, 2091, 2646

Chicago Council on Foreign Relations, **1979:** 619

Chicano Caucus, California, **1979:** 810

Chien-Shiung Wu, **1980–81:** 3023

Child, 1979 International Year of the, **1978:** 1191

Child, 1979, National Commission on the International Year of the, **1978:** 746, 815, 963, 1190, 1191; **1979:** 229; **1980–81:** 752

Child Abuse and Maltreatment, National Alliance for the Prevention and Treatment of, **1980–81:** 267

Child Abuse Prevention Month, National, **1979:** 2153

Child Health Assessment Act of 1977 proposed, **1977:** 717, 720

Child Health Assessment Program, **1978:** 103

Child Health Day, **1977:** 1631; **1978:** 1450
    (Proc. 4683), **1979:** 1627
    (Proc. 4780), **1980–81:** 1520

Child Nutrition Amendments, **1978:** 2000

Child Welfare Act, Adoption Assistance and,
  1980–81: 1124
Children, Aid to Families With Dependent, **1979:**
  940; **1980–81:** 806, 836, 892, 1499
Children, National Advisory Council on the Edu-
  cation of Disadvantaged, **1980–81:** 257
Children, National Center of Economic Education
  for, **1979:** 842
Children and youth
  Administration's accomplishments and goals,
    1980–81: 2943, 2948
  Athletic programs, **1980–81:** 261, 1131
  Child welfare reform, **1979:** 138
  Day care programs, **1977:** 164; **1979:** 1903
  Disease immunization program, **1977:** 605, 892,
    896
  Drug abuse, **1977:** 378
  Education, **1980–81:** 859
  Employment, **1978:** 268, 315, 583, 586, 1872;
    1979: 126, 187, 836, 910, 1936
    Budget allocations increase during adminis-
      tration, **1980–81:** 124, 249, 1324, 1503,
      1561
    Employment and training programs, **1977:** 47,
      241, 295, 340, 342, 349, 645, 646, 819, 861,
      889, 1427, 1838, 1842
    Federal initiatives program
      Announcement remarks, **1980–81:** 52
      Budget allocations, **1980–81:** 226, 239, 248,
        249, 290
      Education and Labor Department roles,
        1980–81: 125, 313, 337, 1068, 1081, 1706,
        1731, 1874, 1998, 2021, 2061, 2133, 2517
      Goals of program, **1980–81:** 117, 252, 342,
        1876
      House of Representatives actions, **1980–81:**
        847, 1585
      Legislative proposal commitment, **1980–81:**
        116
      Major domestic program for 1980, **1980–81:**
        1590
      Mentions, **1980–81:** 555, 724, 833, 1886,
        2568
      News conference (Checklist, **1980–81:** 64
      President's appeal for passage, **1980–81:**
        1003, 1296, 1324, 1503, 1561, 1730
      Private sector involvement, **1980–81:** 2027,
        2360
      Senate consideration, **1980–81:** 1754, 1929,
        1998, 2360, 2364, 2426, 2481
    Federal programs expansion, President's com-
      mitment to, **1980–81:** 1607
    Statistics, **1980–81:** 123, 124, 214
    Summer program, **1980–81:** 805, 815, 832, 835,
      878, 1000, 1040, 1074, 2000, 2360
    Targeted tax credits, **1980–81:** 124
  Federal budget allocations, **1980–81:** 1499

Children and youth — *continued*
  Federal programs, **1980–81:** 836
    Increase, **1979:** 1872
  Health programs, **1979:** 117, 134, 862, 1030;
    1980–81: 118, 754, 811, 1310, 2900
  Juvenile delinquency programs, **1980–81:** 1273
  Leadership role, **1979:** 1172
  Learning disabilities, **1977:** 1850
  Legislation, **1979:** 1928
  Mental health programs, **1980–81:** 1654
  Public service alternative to military draft, **1977:**
    314
  Scouting programs, **1979:** 2209
  State of the Union, **1978:** 93, 100, 103, 105
  United States Senate Youth Program, **1977:** 79
  Voter registration, **1977:** 30, 224
  Welfare programs, **1980–81:** 1355
Children's Bureau, **1977:** 1139, 1163; **1979:** 2184,
  2207
Children's Fund, United Nations.
  See United Nations Children's Fund.
Children's Hospital National Medical Center,
  1977: 327
Children's Television Workshop, **1977:** 1740
Chile
  Ambassador to U.S., **1977:** 508; **1978:** 1070
  President Augusto Pinochet Ugarte, **1977:** 1538,
    1567; **1978:** 2257
  U.S. Ambassador, **1977:** 1588
  U.S. policy, **1977:** 341
  Whaling operations, **1979:** 266–268
Chiles, Sen. Lawton, 1755, 1756, 1922; **1979:** 2176,
  2177, 2182, 2257n.
  Legislation passage leadership
    Paperwork Reduction Act, **1980–81:** 2795,
      2796
    Refugee Education Assistance Act, **1980–81:**
      2154, 2157
  Meeting with the President (Digest), **1980–81:**
    869
Chin, Carolyn Sue, **1978:** 1026
China, People's Republic of
  Agreements with U.S.
    Consular relations and Consulates General,
      1979: 209
    Culture, **1979:** 207
    High energy physics, **1979:** 205
    Science and technology, **1979:** 200, 539;
      1980–81: 407
    Space, agriculture, and education, **1979:** 202
  Air service with U.S., **1980–81:** 2651
  Ambassador to U.S., **1979:** 377
  Aquaculture development, **1980–81:** 1938
  Arms control and disarmament, **1977:** 95
  Central TV, interview with the President, **1979:**
    163
  Clothespin industry, **1978:** 1698; **1979:** 233

China, People's Republic of — *continued*
  Congressional visits, **1977:** 595, 2180; **1978:** 2003,
    2110; **1979:** 666
  Embargo regulations, **1978:** 1504
  Foreign Minister Huang Hua, **1977:** 1487, 1517,
    1520; **1979:** 14, 212, 248
  International Exchange-of-Persons program,
    1979: 324
  Interview remarks, **1978:** 942, 1257, 1263, 1276,
    2260
  Japan, relationship with, **1979:** 764; **1980–81:**
    1341
  Joint statement, **1979:** 212
  Liaison Office with U.S., Chief, **1977:** 147, 1203;
    1978: 1538
  Mention, **1979:** 576
  Muhammad Ali's visit, **1980–81:** 63
  News conference remarks, **1977:** 1203; **1978:**
    732, 1180, 1444, 2097, 2099
  Office of Science and Technology Policy, Direc-
    tor's visit, **1978:** 1278
  Overseas Private Investment Corporation, op-
    erations with, **1980–81:** 1522
  Performing Arts Company, **1978:** 1321
  Premier Hua Guofeng, **1979:** 1, 1112; **1980–81:**
    1341, 1342n., 1377
  President's Assistant for National Security Af-
    fairs, visit, **1978:** 803
  Rabbit meat exports to U.S., **1977:** 1994
  Science and technology matters, U.S. delegation,
    1978: 1187, 1280
  Science and technology programs with U.S.,
    1979: 539; **1980–81:** 407
  Secretary of State's visit, **1977:** 1288, 1516, 1517,
    1519, 1520, 1532, 1534
  Secretary of the Treasury's visit, **1979:** 348
  Settlement claims agreement with U.S., **1979:**
    1655, 1656
  Soviet relations, **1980–81:** 807, 1995
  Taiwan, agreement to peacefully resolve differ-
    ences, **1979:** 52, 257
  Trade with U.S., **1977:** 1708, 1921; **1978:** 1691,
    1819, 2224, 2225
    Agreement on Trade Relations, **1979:** 2000,
      2005–2007; **1980–81:** 119
    Agricultural products, **1979:** 152, 205
    Cotton, **1980–81:** 2587, 2601, 2607, 2619, 2632,
      2638
    Credit availability with U.S., **1979:** 332, 358
    Export-Import Bank financing, **1980–81:** 607
    Grain agreement
      Fact sheet (Checklist), **1980–81:** 2433
      President's comments, **1980–81:** 2203, 2352,
        2402, 2407, 2416, 2587, 2601, 2607, 2619,
        2632, 2638, 2672, 2678
      White House statement, **1980–81:** 2424
    Levels increase during administration, **1980–**
      81: 1728, 2416, 2469, 2828

China, People's Republic of — *continued*
  Trade with U.S. — *continued*
    Most Favored Nation status, **1979:** 332, 358,
      749
    Science and technology products, **1979:** 1150
    State governments trade missions, **1979:** 334
    Steel imports, **1980–81:** 1674, 1678, 1697, 1740,
      1749, 1753, 1769, 2039, 2142, 2205, 2293,
      2406, 2411
    Textile products, **1980–81:** 1759, 1769, 1794
    U.S. exports increase, **1980–81:** 126, 1915
    Waiver authority extension, **1980–81:** 980, 982
  University control, **1980–81:** 81
  U.S. arms sales, **1979:** 184
  U.S. Liaison Office, Chief, **1977:** 863, 888, 1132,
    1163, 1222; **1978:** 302
  U.S. mission, **1978:** 2281
  U.S. policy, **1977:** 648, 702, 863, 1517
  U.S. relations, **1978:** 122, 1257, 1263, 1276, 1322,
    2264–2268, 2275–2279; **1979:** 2, 107, 157,
    248, 257, 356, 640, 1111, 1205, 1612, 1769,
    1916, 2033, 2047, 2053, 2244
  Congressional resolutions, **1979:** 170, 257
  Soviet reaction to normalization, **1979:** 57,
    173, 259
  U.S. relations normalization
    Administration's accomplishment, **1980–81:**
      91, 170, 197, 338, 345, 399, 579, 673, 870,
      891, 906, 963, 987, 1207, 1300, 1304, 1321,
      1341, 1554, 1604, 1619, 1682, 1740, 1743,
      1753, 1913, 1995, 2124, 2147, 2277, 2415,
      2424, 2449, 2531, 2607, 2983
    Agreements
      Advance text, **1980–81:** 1848
      Civil air transport, **1980–81:** 1774
      Consular relations, **1980–81:** 1807, 3019
      Maritime transport, **1980–81:** 1801
      Signing ceremony, **1980–81:** 1771
      Textile products, **1980–81:** 1794
    Fact sheet, **1980–81:** 1848
    Pacific region responsibilities sharing, **1980–**
      81: 1902, 1904, 2339, 2368, 2406, 2446,
      2566
    Vice Premier Bo Yibo, **1977:** 1271, 1274; **1980–**
      81: 1771, 1773, 1783, 1797, 1804, 1807,
      1821
    Vice Premier of the State Council, **1979:** 982;
      1980–81: 1013
    Vice President's visit, **1979:** 1125
China, People's Republic of, U.S. Ambassador
    (Leonard Woodcock), **1980–81:** 1013
  China-U.S. trade agreement, authorized U.S.
    representative, **1979:** 2005
  Nomination, **1979:** 41, 91, 348
  President's assessment, **1979:** 1590
  Vice Premier Deng's visit to U.S., escort for,
    1979: 881

China, People's Republic of, Vice Premier (Deng Xiaoping), **1977:** 1487, 1517, 1520; **1978:** 2261, 2265–2267; **1979:** 53, 248, 359; **1980–81:** 181, 407
  New Year's message from the President, **1979:** 2
  Visit to U.S.
    Agreements with U.S., **1979:** 200, 202, 205, 207, 209, 211, 212
    Announcement, **1979:** 88
    Joint statement, **1979:** 213
    Kennedy Center for the Performing Arts, **1979:** 195
    Meetings with the President, **1979:** 191, 198, 218
    Postvisit comments, **1979:** 259, 356, 640
    Previsit comments, **1979:** 54, 107, 164, 165, 172, 174, 181, 186
    State dinner, **1979:** 192
    Welcoming ceremony, **1979:** 189
China, Republic of.
  See Taiwan.
China-U.S. Joint Commission on Scientific and Technological Cooperation, **1979:** 203
China-U.S. Joint Economic Committee, **1979:** 1454
Chinese New Year, **1978:** 257; **1979:** 109; **1980–81:** 257
Chinese People's Institute of Foreign Affairs, **1977:** 595
Ching-Chung, Priscilla, **1978:** 1514
Chippewa Indians, **1978:** 1344; **1980–81:** 2189
Chisholm, Alex, **1978:** 454; **1980–81:** 1048
Chisholm, Robert L., **1979:** 1439
Chisholm, Repr. Shirley, **1977:** 99, 1264, 1343; **1978:** 1684: **1980–81:** 2364, 2366
Chishom, Andrew J., **1977:** 576
Choi Kyu Ha, **1979:** 2054
Chona, Mark, **1977:** 2089
Chookasian, Lili, **1978:** 917
Chou Pei-yuan, **1979:** 205
Christensen, Carrie Lynn, **1978:** 1333
Christensen, Thomas G. S., **1980–81:** 684
Christian, Almeric L., **1978:** 66, 149
Christian Leadership Conference, Southern, **1980–81:** 2453
Christian Methodist Episcopal Church, **1980–81:** 775
Christian Service Award, **1980–81:** 333
Christians and Jews, National Conference of, **1979:** 969; **1980–81:** 343
Christianson, Capt. J. C., **1977:** 1041
Christmas, 1977
  Message, **1977:** 2171
  White House receptions, **1977:** 2129, 2130, 2162, 2163
Christmas, 1978, **1978:** 2274
Christmas, 1979
  National Community Christmas Tree lighting ceremony, **1979:** 2244

Christmas, 1979 — *continued*
  Statement by the President, **1979:** 2245
  White House receptions (Digest), **1979:** 2248, 2280
Christmas, 1980
  Congressional Ball, **1980–81:** 2823
  National Community Christmas Tree lighting ceremony, **1980–81:** 2817
  Plains, Ga., exchange with reporters, **1980–81:** 2839
  Statement by the President, **1980–81:** 2764
  White House receptions, **1980–81:** 2823, 2829
Christmas Pageant of Peace, **1977:** 2125; **1978:** 2246
Christmas Seals Campaign, **1978:** 2073; **1979:** 2042
Christmas Tree, National Community, lighting ceremony, **1978:** 2246; **1979:** 2244
Christopher, Warren M.
  See State, Deputy Secretary of.
Christy, Arthur A., **1980–81:** 984n.
Christy, Roger, **1980–81:** 1061n.
Chrome imports, **1977:** 451–453
Chrone, Leo, **1977:** 801
Chrysler Corporation, **1979:** 1430, 1499, 1651, 2250
  K-car production, **1980–81:** 2548, 2567
  Reagan, Ronald, position comparison with President on Federal loan, **1980–81:** 1994, 2007, 2010, 2164, 2354, 2473, 2547, 2567
Chrysler Corporation Loan Guarantee Act of 1979, **1980–81:** 28, 311, 1831
Chun Doo Hwan, **1980–81:** 1618
Chung, Connie, **1977:** 895
Church, Sen. Frank, **1977:** 882, 1465, 1794, 1979; **1978:** 149, 409, 410, 698, 802
  Alaska lands legislation support, **1980–81:** 1548
  Communications from the President, **1979:** 191, 240, 462, 997, 1301, 1522, 1738
  Foreign assistance program reorganization proposals, passage leadership, **1979:** 1230
  Legislation passage leadership
    Central Idaho Wildernesses Act, **1980–81:** 1408
    Mental Health Systems Act, **1980–81:** 2106
  Letters from the President on Cyprus conflict settlement, **1980–81:** 205, 947, 1397, 1923, 2739, 3020
  SALT II treaty support, **1979:** 2102
Church, Mrs. Frank, **1979:** 240
Church, Richard, **1978:** 2158
Church, Sam, Jr.
  See United Mine Workers, President.
Church of Jesus Christ of Latter-day Saints, **1977:** 372, 1059; **1978:** 2088
Churches of Christ of America, National Council of, **1978:** 415
Churchill, Winston, **1979:** 2257; **1980–81:** 80, 579, 1539
Cincinnati, Ohio, **1979:** 1817

Cinco de Mayo celebration, **1979:** 810, 843
Cincotta, Gayle, **1977:** 2153; **1980–81:** 2560
Cindrich, Robert J., **1978:** 1222, 1223
Cini Foundation, **1980–81:** 1162
Circuit Court of Appeals Reorganization Act,
      Fifth, **1980–81:** 2237
Circuit Judge Nominating Commission, United
      States, **1977:** 179, 815, 1010, 1053, 1055,
      1127, 1242; **1980–81:** 2849
Circuit judges, U.S.
      See U.S. circuit judges *under* Appointments and
      Nominations.
Cire, George E., **1979:** 294
Cissell, James C., **1978:** 457, 458
Cities.
      See Urban areas.
Cities, National League of, **1978:** 2075, 2080, 2188;
      1980–81: 103, 495, 523
Citizens' Advisory Committee on Environmental
      Quality, **1977:** 1494
Citizens' Advisory Council, **1979:** 2275
Citizens band radio, **1978:** 607–609, 707, 1697
Citizens' Coalition for the Windfall Profits Tax,
      National, **1979:** 1705
Citizens Committee on Conscience, **1979:** 2041
Citizenship Day
      (Proc. 4670), **1979:** 1297
      (Proc. 4773), **1980–81:** 1279
Citizenship Day and Constitution Week, **1977:**
      1521; **1978:** 1317
Civil Aeronautics Board
      Acting Chairman, **1977:** 806
      Airline industry, reduced Federal regulation,
            1977: 277, 278
      Airline industry deregulation, consumer savings
            statistics, **1980–81:** 1261
      Chairman, **1977:** 933, 944, 1134, 1365, 2223;
            1978: 471, 564, 1849, 1850; **1979:** 2176,
            2188, 2283; **1980–81:** 103, 2651, 2841
      China-U.S. civil air transport agreement author-
            ity, **1980–81:** 1774
      Competitive advocacy program, **1979:** 235
      Members, **1977:** 1218, 1223, 1381, 1698, 1714,
            1755, 1946; **1978:** 724, 1270, 1279, 1511,
            1517; **1979:** 1395, 1398, 2176, 2188;
            1980–81: 1419, 1428
      Mention, **1980–81:** 1705
      National Airlines merger recommendation,
            1979: 1587
      News conference (Checklist), **1979:** 843
      News conference remarks, **1978:** 442
      Passenger fares, **1978:** 800
      "Skytrain" airline service decision, **1977:** 1112
      Termination, possibility, **1978:** 1831, 1861
      Termination legislation, **1980–81:** 332
      Transatlantic air service, **1977:** 1668, 1669, 1952,
            2158
      Vice Chairman, **1977:** 1124, 1128; **1978:** 255, 277

Civil Aircraft, Agreement on Trade in, **1979:** 2224,
      2225, 2227, 2253, 2255
Civil Aviation, Convention on International,
      1980–81: 3024
Civil Aviation Organization, International, **1979:**
      1451
Civil Defense Administration, Federal, **1979:** 1281
Civil justice reform, Federal, **1980–81:** 303
Civil justice system, Federal, **1979:** 340–346, 378
Civil and Political Rights, Covenant on, **1977:** 1734
Civil and Political Rights, International Covenant
      on, **1978:** 395
Civil rights.
      See Human rights, domestic.
Civil Rights, Commission on, **1977:** 1190, 1222,
      1629; **1978:** 2219; **1979:** 91; **1980–81:** 605,
      608, 892, 968
Civil Rights, Leadership Conference on, **1980–81:**
      221, 720
Civil Rights Act, Title VI, enforcement, **1977:** 1293
Civil Rights Act of 1964, **1980–81:** 1500
Civil Rights of Institutionalized Persons Act,
      1980–81: 965
Civil Service Commission, United States.
      See United States Civil Service Commission.
Civil Service Employees Association, **1980–81:**
      2003, 2071
Civil service reform.
      See Federal civil service reform.
Civil Service Reform Act, **1978:** 1761, 1765, 1773;
      1979: 462; **1980–81:** 898
Civil service retirement credit for Japanese Amer-
      icans interned during World War II,
      1978: 1569
Civiletti, Benjamin R.
      See Attorney General.
Civilian Health and Medical Program for the
      Uniformed Services (CHAMPUS),
      1980–81: 972, 1355
Civilian Service, President's Award for Distin-
      guished Federal, **1980–81:** 86
Civitan International, **1977:** 31
Claiborne, Harry E., **1978:** 1346
Claims, United States Court of, **1980–81:** 980
Clark, Carolyn G., **1979:** 464
Clark, Cheryl, **1977:** 294
Clark, Dennis Dale, **1980–81:** 1654, 1715
Clark, Dick.
      See Coordinator for Refugee Affairs *under* State,
      Department of.
Clark, Sen. Dick, **1977:** 1855, 2105; **1978:** 802,
      1185, 1278
Clark, Ed., **1980–81:** 1654, 1872, 2272
Clark, James, Jr., **1979:** 271
Clark, Joan M., **1979:** 215, 241
Clark, Joe.
      See Canada, Prime Minister.
Clark, John W., **1980–81:** 33, 269

[References are to page numbers except as otherwise indicated]

Clark, Kenneth B., **1979:** 401; **1980–81:** 2732
Clark, Leroy D., **1979:** 1157, 1159
Clark, Mamie P., **1977:** 1781, 1796
Clark, Ramsey, **1979:** 2105; **1980–81:** 1087–1089
Clark, Russell G., **1977:** 1127, 1128
Clark, Septima Poinsettia, **1979:** 318
Clark, Stephen, **1980–81:** 1328n.
Clark, Thomas A., **1979:** 1531, 1532
Clark, Tom C., **1977:** 1102
Clarke, Mrs. Athalie Irvine, **1977:** 2182
Clarke, Gary K., **1977:** 1781, 1796
Classen, Ann E., **1980–81:** 929
Classification Review Committee, Interagency,
    1978: 1207
Clausen, A. W., **1979:** 2128; **1980–81:** 2561
Clausen, Repr. Don H., **1980–81:** 318
Clauss, Carin Ann, **1977:** 227, 252, 1306; **1978:**
    1572
Clawson, Repr. Dale, **1978:** 526
Clay, A. Stephens, **1977:** 1265, 1759
Clay, Gen. Lucius D., **1978:** 757
Claybrook, Joan Buckler, **1977:** 461, 465, 1533;
    1980–81: 281, 2612
Clayman, Jacob, **1980–81:** 1418, 1428
Claypoole, Richard L., **1978:** 1955
Claytor, W. Graham, Jr., **1977:** 90, 930; **1978:** 809;
    1979: 1285, 1290, 1319, 1670; **1980–81:**
    641, 775, 1740
Clean Air Act of 1977, **1979:** 1354, 1359; **1980–81:**
    449, 1966, 2201
  Amendments, **1977:** 439, 707, 1072, 1082, 1460,
    1465; **1978:** 115; **1980–81:** 416
Clean Water Act of 1977, **1977:** 2179; **1978:** 115;
    1979: 702, 1354, 1359; **1980–81:** 416
Clearinghouse for Community Energy Efficiency,
    President's, **1979:** 1457
Cleary, Catherine B., **1980–81:** 1717, 1848, 2074n.,
    2726, 2727, 2870, 2874
Cleary, Timothy F., **1977:** 1529; **1979:** 552, 619
Cleburne, Pat, **1980–81:** 1602
Cleland, Max.
    See Veterans Administration, Administrator.
Clemens, Samuel.
    See Twain, Mark.
Clement, Alfred W., **1978:** 913
Clement, Robert N., **1978:** 1858; **1979:** 877, 957
Clement, William A., Jr., **1979:** 1317, 1319
Clemente, Roberto, **1980–81:** 370
Clements, Gov. William P., Jr., **1980–81:** 1423n.
Clemmons, N.C., **1980–81:** 2145
Clemon, U. W., **1980–81:** 64
Clergy Week, International, **1977:** 33
Cleveland, Harlan, **1980–81:** 2074
Cleveland, Ohio, **1979:** 1817
  Mayors from surrounding suburbs, meeting with
    the President (Digest), **1980–81:** 452
  President's visits, **1980–81:** 1001, 1005, 1762,
    1765, 2476, 2502

Cleveland Electric Company, **1979:** 1645
Clifford, Clark M., **1977:** 77, 194, 638, 1137, 1501,
    1637, 1966; **1978:** 1110, 2288; **1979:** 553,
    1823, 2042; **1980–81:** 188, 217, 382
Clifford, Maurice C., **1979:** 464
Climate program, national, **1978:** 1907; **1980–81:**
    2723
Clinard, David Marion, **1980–81:** 428, 452
Clinch River Breeder Reactor Demonstration
    Plant, **1977:** 585, 1972, 2012; **1978:** 72,
    114, 473, 939, 1473, 1477
  Congressional actions
    House Science and Technology Committee,
      1979: 730, 795
    Senate Energy and Natural Resources Com-
      mittee, **1979:** 887
  President's opposition to project, **1979:** 149, 741,
    795, 1324
Clingerman, John R., **1979:** 1446, 1455
Clinton, Gov. Bill, **1980–81:** 1404, 1423n., 2154
Clinton, Mass., **1977:** 382
Clinton County, Mich., **1979:** 1452
Clodfelter, Mark Alan, **1980–81:** 948
Cloherty, Patricia M., **1977:** 1438; **1979:** 888–890
CLOSE-UP program, **1977:** 693
Clothespin industry, **1978:** 1698; **1979:** 232–234,
    325
Clothing and Textile Workers, Amalgamated,
    1978: 750; **1979:** 1421; **1980–81:** 563
Cloud, Sanford, Jr., **1980–81:** 2107
Clough, Susan S., **1979:** 751; **1980–81:** 1466
Clower, Jerry, **1977:** 1330
Clusen, Ruth C., **1977:** 525; **1978:** 1268, 1279
Cmarik, Joan L., **1980–81:** 928
Coal
  Alternative fuel source, **1977:** 34, 44, 284, 403,
    413, 519, 659, 660, 669, 683; **1978:** 1312
  Anthracite production, tax credit incentive,
    1979: 1714
  Charleston, W. Va., panel discussion, **1977:** 406,
    408, 416, 437, 441
  Conversion to:
    Natural gas, **1979:** 793, 1610
    Synthetic fuels, **1979:** 1538, 1715; **1980–81:**
      831, 2086, 2258
  Environmental message, **1977:** 974
  Environmental standards, **1979:** 841, 905, 1325,
    1338n., 1346, 1648; **1980–81:** 2262, 2474,
    2493, 2511
  Exports, **1979:** 1643
    Inflation control measure, **1980–81:** 2358
    Policy development, **1980–81:** 2953
    U.S. levels increase, **1980–81:** 1588, 1639,
      1898, 2254, 2410
    See also Transportation system improvement.
  Federal installations conversion, **1980–81:** 2702
  Federal mine safety and health reports, **1979:**
    103, 1396, 1445

Coal — *continued*
  Great Plains, N. Dak., gasification plant, **1980–81:** 1371, 1448
  Hauling price rates, **1979:** 1709
  High-sulfur plants, **1979:** 1644
  Illinois State legislature, remarks, **1978:** 989
  Increased production
    Federal Government recommendation, **1979:** 905
    Mentions, **1979:** 1325, 1327
    Relationship with:
      Oil imports reduction, **1979:** 864, 1098, 1338, 1641, 1715, 1891
      Windfall profits tax, **1979:** 1181, 1457, 1715
    Tokyo Summit commitment, **1979:** 1190, 1199
  Industry
    Revitalization, **1979:** 633; **1980–81:** 1537, 2192, 2253
    Unemployment, **1979:** 1646
  Interview remarks, **1978:** 1414
  Legislation, **1978:** 1979
  Liquefaction and gasification, **1979:** 1185, 1211
  Mine health activities, Federal, **1978:** 576, 1271
  Natural reserves, **1979:** 1337
  New technologies development, **1979:** 553, 622, 905, 1150
  Ohio resources, **1979:** 1641
  Oil companies ownership, **1980–81:** 883
  President's Commission on the Coal Industry, recommendations for future production, **1980–81:** 471
  Production, **1977:** 1146, 1169; **1978:** 1349
  Production increases
    National energy program goal, **1980–81:** 470, 480, 586
    1980 statistics, **1980–81:** 1253, 1701, 1733, 1768, 1864, 1870, 1884, 1888, 1915, 1974, 2019, 2040, 2045, 2047, 2082, 2119, 2142, 2166, 2191, 2205, 2277, 2297, 2345, 2349, 2406, 2416, 2437, 2457, 2474, 2493, 2532, 2540, 2589, 2601, 2607, 2630, 2811
  Slurry pipeline, **1977:** 2093
  Strip mining, **1979:** 150
  Transportation system improvement
    Rail system, **1980–81:** 2298, 2402, 2475
    Shiploading, **1980–81:** 2258, 2298, 2402, 2406, 2475, 2811
    U.S. exports increase, relationship with, **1980–81:** 1588, 1639, 1898, 2254, 2410
  United Mine Workers strike
    Board of Inquiry, **1978:** 469
    Contract approval, **1978:** 573, 641
    Court decision on temporary restraining order, **1978:** 539
    Government officials, meetings with the President, **1978:** 327, 328, 414–416
    Interview remarks, **1978:** 235, 308, 320, 366, 379
    Letter to Attorney General, **1978:** 488

Coal — *continued*
  United Mine Workers strike — *continued*
    Negotiations, **1978:** 316, 419, 508
    News conference remarks, **1978:** 248, 331, 333, 336, 337, 439, 489, 490, 493, 495
    Statement by the President, **1978:** 313
    Taft-Hartley Act invocation, **1978:** 469, 535
  Utilities conversion to.
    See under Utilities.
  Venice Economic Summit statement, **1980–81:** 1188
  West Frankfort, Ill., Old Ben Coal Mine No. 25, President's remarks to employees, **1980–81:** 2199
Coal Advisory Council, White House, **1980–81:** 473, 1433, 1643
Coal Caucus, Congressional, **1979:** 2280
Coal Exports, White House Conference on, **1980–81:** 2810
Coal Industry, President's Commission on the.
  See President's Commission on the Coal Industry.
Coal Industry Advisory Board, International, **1980–81:** 1188
Coal Mine Health and Safety Act of 1969, Federal, **1977:** 339
Coal Mining Museum, National, **1980–81:** 2199
Coal Operators Association of America, Bituminous, **1978:** 328, 415, 419, 1006, 2243
Coal Regulation Project, **1979:** 1339n.
Coal Research, Office of, **1980–81:** 1451
Coal Study, World, **1980–81:** 931
Coal II Agreement, International Solvent Refined, **1980–81:** 1447, 1471
Coalition for a Fair Minimum Wage, **1977:** 942
Coalition of Northeastern Governors, **1979:** 2060
Coast Guard, United States.
  See United States Coast Guard.
Coast Guard Academy, U.S., **1980–81:** 607
Coastal barrier islands, **1977:** 977
Coastal Plains Regional Commission, Federal Cochairman, **1977:** 1070, 1085
Coastal protection, national, **1979:** 1362, 1373
Coastal Zone management, **1979:** 178
Coastal Zone Management Act of 1972, **1979:** 1362, 1373
  Report, **1977:** 745; **1979:** 178
Coastal Zone Management Improvement Act, **1980–81:** 2335
Coats and Clark, Inc., **1980–81:** 1928
Cobb, Jewel Plummer, **1978:** 408, 2264
Cobb, Montague, **1979:** 319; **1980–81:** 1322
Cobbi, Hugo, **1980–81:** 1397
Coca-Cola Co., **1977:** 1084
Cocaine, **1978:** 1600
Cochran, Sen. Thad, **1979:** 2081; **1980–81:** 1938
Cody, Iron Eyes, **1978:** 771, 830
Cody, W. J. Michael, **1977:** 373
Coe, Douglas E., **1978:** 1668

Coelho, Repr. Tony, **1980–81:** 1305, 1310, 1315, 1319
Coerr, Wymberley DeR., **1977:** 1764
Cofer, H. J., Jr., **1978:** 217
Coffee, Richard, **1979:** 2027n.
Coffee imports, **1977:** 309
Coffee industry, **1980–81:** 2991
Coffee Study Group, International, **1978:** 51
Coffin, Frank M., **1980–81:** 862
Coggleshall, Susanna and Tomlin, **1980–81:** 631n.
Cogo, Father Joseph A., **1980–81:** 1065
Cohan, George M., **1979:** 2098; **1980–81:** 502
Cohen, David, **1978:** 1766
Cohen, Edward B., **1980–81:** 83
Cohen, Esther, **1980–81:** 821
Cohen, Rabbi Gerson, **1978:** 1973
Cohen, Gerson D., **1980–81:** 821
Cohen, Herbert J., **1978:** 770, 2070
Cohen, Herman J., **1977:** 1081, 1085, 1086; **1978:** 232
Cohen, Kelley, **1979:** 464
Cohen, Marvin S., **1978:** 1511, 1517, 1850; **1979:** 843, 2176, 2188, 2283; **1980–81:** 103, 2558, 2841
Cohen, Morris, **1977:** 2046
Cohen, N. Jerold, **1979:** 1962, 1977
Cohen, Saul, **1979:** 1760
Cohen, Vincent H., **1980–81:** 392
Cohen, Wilbur J., **1977:** 2155; **1978:** 257, 748; **1980–81:** 2585, 2615
Cohen, Sen. William S., **1979:** 178
Cohn, Anne H., **1979:** 914
Cohn, Avern, **1979:** 899, 900
Cohn, Marcus, **1980–81:** 1332, 1337
Coker, Ed, **1979:** 270
Colbert, Evelyn, **1979:** 1222
Coleman, Beatrice, **1978:** 257
Coleman, Repr. E. Thomas, **1980–81:** 2788
Coleman, Henry R., **1980–81:** 1407
Coleman, Julia, **1977:** 991; **1980–81:**1746
Coleman, Lynn R., **1977:** 1646, 1650; **1978:** 231; **1980–81:** 2841, 2870, 2873
Coleman, Stock, **1977:** 31
Coleman, William T., Jr., **1977:** 178
Coleman/Goff, Inc., **1980–81:** 1402
Coles, Bishop Joseph C., **1978:** 2269
Collazo, Oscar, **1979:** 1597
Colleges and universities
    Black institutions, **1979:** 48, 140, 173, 742, 911; **1980–81:** 328, 1356, 1514, 1518, 1561
    Developing institutions program, **1979:** 140
    Federal budget allocations for research and development, **1980–81:** 2087
    Federal programs, **1980–81:** 1004
    Graduates, job opportunities, **1977:** 392, 910
    Legislation, **1978:** 1786; **1980–81:** 2061
    Science and technology programs, **1979:** 544, 2070

Colleges and universities — *continued*
    Southern universities desegregation, **1978:** 309, 537
    Student aid programs, **1980–81:** 2617
    Student loans, **1978:** 357, 382, 2230; **1979:** 140, 711, 1948
    Tuition tax credits, **1978:** 462, 730, 868, 874, 1061, 1444, 1609, 1724; **1979:** 625, 1948; **1980–81:** 1560, 2019
    University presidents, meeting with the President, **1977:** 251
    Work-study programs, **1978:** 425; **1980–81:** 2360
    See also Education.
Collet, John C., **1979:** 976
Colley, George, **1977:** 1671
Collins, Repr. Cardiss, **1978:** 1009; **1979:** 666; **1980–81:** 1573, 1928
Collins, Jon R., **1977:** 816
Collins, Lt. Gov. Martha Lynn, **1980–81:** 1388, 1390n.
Collins, Michael, **1979:** 1276
Collins, Paul, **1979:** 464
Collins, Priscilla B., **1977:** 941
Collins, Robert F., **1977:** 1967; **1978:** 231
Colloff, Roger D., **1977:** 1585
Colodzin, Robert S., **1980–81:** 1404
Cologne Food Fair, **1977:** 1704
Colom, Audrey Rowe, **1977:** 525
Colombia
    Ambassador to U.S., **1977:** 1163; **1980–81:** 2807
    Dominican Embassy in Bogotá, release of hostages, **1980–81:** 780, 781
    Drug control, **1978:** 1600
    Drug traffic, **1977:** 1399, 1401
    Foreign Minister, **1978:** 1146
    Inaugural ceremonies, U.S. delegation, **1978:** 1380
    Nuclear energy agreement with U.S., **1980–81:** 2878
    Peace Corps volunteer Richard Starr, terrorists release of, **1980–81:** 306
    President Julio César Turbay Ayala, **1980–81:** 780
    President Alfonso López Michelsen, **1977:** 1537, 1567; **1978:** 1119, 1122, 1123
    U.S. Ambassador, **1977:** 1646, 1650; **1978:** 1380; **1980–81:** 781, 825, 1710, 1715
Colombo, Emilio, **1980–81:** 1110
Colon, Gilbert, **1979:** 1664
Color television receiver subassemblies (Proc. 4759), **1980–81:** 920
Colorado
    Disaster declaration, **1977:** 35, 85
    Interview remarks, **1978:** 715, 807
    President's visit, **1977:** 1861, 1884; **1978:** 824, 827, 829, 832
    U.S. attorney, **1977:** 1211, 1212
    U.S. district judge, **1977:** 1967; **1979:** 984
    U.S. marshal, **1977:** 1613

Colorado — *continued*
  Ute Mountain Ute Tribe, **1980–81:** 1043
Columbia, Md., **1980–81:** 1722n.
Columbia, Mo., **1978:** 1419
Columbia, S.C., **1978:** 1582; **1980–81:** 2563, 2577
Columbia Broadcasting System (CBS), **1978:** 2275;
    1979: 1678, 2194; **1980–81:** 1049, 1732
  CBS radio network, telephone call-in program,
    1977: 291
  CBS record album of 1977 Inaugural Concert,
    1977: 806
Columbia River Treaty, **1978:** 272
Columbus, Ohio, **1978:** 1619, 1620; **1980–81:** 992
Columbus Day, **1977:** 1674, 1675; **1978:** 1437
    (Proc. 4676), **1979:** 1526
    (Proc. 4788), **1980–81:** 1593
Colvill, Jacqueline, **1980–81:** 1051
Comaneci, Nadia, **1980–81:** 380
Combined Federal Campaign, **1977:** 1464; **1978:**
    1235, 1236; **1979:** 1231, 1678; **1980–81:**
    1098
Combs, Bert T., **1978:** 217, 230
Come, Norton J., **1979:** 1976
Comer, Larry, **1977:** 996
Comerford, John Paul, **1980–81:** 2882
Commager, Henry Steele, **1980–81:** 1432
Commemorative Presidential proclamations, **1978:**
    1532
Commerce, Department of
  Acid rain research program, **1979:** 1389
  Antiboycott programs, **1980–81:** 402
  Appropriations, **1977:** 1163; **1978:** 1735; **1980–**
    81: 2774, 2809
  Assistant Secretaries, **1977:** 229, 248, 252, 253,
    381, 465, 554, 596, 618, 642, 1649, 2025,
    2037; **1978:** 554, 571, 611, 2263; **1979:**
    619, 2070n., 2082; **1980–81:** 48, 255, 374,
    522, 1706n., 1805, 1806
  Associate Deputy Secretary, **1980–81:** 25
  Banned or significantly restricted substances
    exports, duties, **1980–81:** 2907, 2909
  Board to consider Pittston Company's proposed
    oil refinery, member, **1979:** 1017(Digest)
  Budget deferrals and rescissions, **1977:** 567, 739,
    1357; **1978:** 407, 895, 1041, 2095, 2228;
    1979: 200, 1772, 2122, 2285; **1980–81:**
    235, 899, 1577, 2916
  Census statistics for legal immigrants, **1980–81:**
    2812
  Channel Islands Marine Sanctuary, Calif., des-
    ignation, **1980–81:** 1856
  China-U.S. maritime transport agreement au-
    thority, **1980–81:** 1804
  Civil land remote-sensing activities, **1979:** 2149
  Consumer Affairs Council membership, **1979:**
    1763
  Counselor on Labor Management Relations,
    1979: 3

Commerce, Department of — *continued*
  Cuban and Haitian refugee assistance respon-
    sibilities, **1980–81:** 2383
  Deputy Assistant Secretary, **1978:** 2281
  Deputy Secretary, **1979:** 2135, 2140, 2201, 2249;
    1980–81: 25, 43, 73
  Deputy Under Secretary, **1978:** 770, 771
  Director of International Fisheries, **1980–81:**
    1938
  Economic development plan requirements, **1979:**
    75
  Elimination possibility, **1978:** 2239, 2240
  Energy crisis, **1977:** 36
  Environmental message, **1977:** 973, 977, 982, 984
  Export development programs, **1978:** 1632–1634;
    1980–81: 1546, 1690, 1691, 2380
  Federal emergency management, transfer of
    functions, **1979:** 566, 1278
  Foreign technical information dissemination,
    1979: 2070
  General Counsel, **1977:** 338, 373; **1979:** 2231
  Industrial innovation initiatives study, **1979:** 2068
  Inspector General, **1979:** 398, 402
  Integrated pest management program, **1979:**
    1383
  Interagency Coordinating Council, **1978:** 1434
  International Exposition on Energy, financing
    legislation proposal, **1979:** 1525
  International trade functions, **1979:** 1730
  Labor/Technology Forecasting System, **1979:**
    2073
  Marine protection and research functions,
    1980–81: 1592
  Maritime industry relations with Federal offi-
    cials, **1978:** 1926
  Minority business development agency, pro-
    posed, **1980–81:** 77
  Minority business programs, **1977:** 1322; **1980–**
    81: 73, 78, 1280
  Minority Business Enterprise, Office of, **1977:**
    517
  National climate program, **1978:** 1907, 1908
  National Marine Sanctuaries designation, **1980–**
    81: 2997
  National Productivity Council, **1978:** 1833, 1835,
    1836
  National water policy functions, **1978:** 1048,
    1050
  Nuclear nonproliferation functions, **1978:** 894
  Patents and Trademarks, Commissioner of,
    1978: 292, 304
  Public works program, **1977:** 51, 97
  Radiation Policy Council membership, **1980–81:**
    363
  Reorganization, **1977:** 114
  Science and technology programs, **1979:** 140
  Secretary.
    See Commerce, Secretary of.

Commerce, Department of — *continued*
  Shoe industry, trade adjustment assistance program, **1977:** 1296, 1307
  Small businesses
    Foreign trade opportunities, **1977:** 398
    Patent counsels for, **1980–81:** 78
  Soviet trade restrictions enforcement, **1980–81:** 184
  State and regional development programs, **1979:** 78
  Statistical policy functions, **1977:** 1759
  Steel industry
    Antidumping suits, **1980–81:** 732, 736, 905
    Community assistance, **1980–81:** 1968
  Tahoe Federal Coordinating Council membership, **1980–81:** 2235, 2236
  Task Force on Global Resources and Environment, functions, **1980–81:** 1417
  Telecommunications functions, **1978:** 253, 598–605, 611
  Telecommunications minority assistance program, **1980–81:** 1703
  Title V Regional Commissions, **1979:** 78–80
  Transfer of certain programs to proposed Energy Department, **1977:** 258
  Trigger price mechanism enforcement, **1980–81:** 1964
  Under Secretaries, **1977:** 465, 691, 1296, 1307, 1579, 1613, 1649, 1930; **1978:** 1753; **1979:** 782, 842; **1980–81:** 188, 654, 2071
  Urban noise abatement program development, **1979:** 1371, 1385
  Urban programs, **1978:** 585, 588
  Veterans' Federal Coordinating Committee, **1978:** 1743
  Visit, question-and-answer session, **1977:** 110
  Weather programs, **1979:** 2150
  Wildlife law enforcement, **1979:** 1364, 1377
  Women and minorities, employment, **1977:** 114, 117
  See also specific constituent agencies.
Commerce, international
  Administration's accomplishments and goals, **1979:** 118, 160; **1980–81:** 175, 1696, 2834, 2937
  Antiboycott laws, **1980–81:** 1656
  Antiprotectionist policy, **1980–81:** 1206, 1964, 2358, 2828
  Balance of payments, **1980–81:** 3005
  Commission of the European Communities, remarks, **1978:** 34, 35
  Competition in world markets study, **1980–81:** 1695
  Economic Report, **1978:** 130–132, 137, 142, 143
  Embargo regulations, **1978:** 1504
  Exports, U.S.
    Administrative functions, **1980–81:** 827
    Agricultural products.
      See Agricultural trade.

Commerce, international — *continued*
  Exports, U.S. — *continued*
    Arms and weapons systems, **1980–81:** 696
    Banned or significantly restricted substances, **1980–81:** 2903, 2909
    Coal.
      See under Coal.
    Foreign policy controls, **1979:** 2290
    International credit negotiations, **1979:** 438
    Levels increase, **1980–81:** 125, 1546, 1586, 1588, 1734, 1988, 2828
    Nuclear materials, **1980–81:** 403, 1137
    Policy statement, **1980–81:** 400
    Promotion policies, **1980–81:** 1689
    Steel.
      See under Steel industry.
    Technology controls, **1979:** 543
    Textile products, **1980–81:** 1759
    U.S. policy, **1978:** 1630, 1631, 1633–1635, 1668, 1670
  Federal functions reorganization, **1980–81:** 5, 7, 23
  Foreign investments in U.S., **1980–81:** 1118, 1924
  Imports, U.S.
    Alloy tool steel, **1977:** 1121
    Anhydrous ammonia, **1979:** 2221, 2222; **1980–81:** 101, 102
    Artificial baits and flies, **1978:** 2070, 2071
    Automobiles.
      See Imports *under* Automobiles and automobile industry.
    Beef, **1978:** 1061, 1062, 1072, 1074, 1080, 1158, 1421, 1494, 1672
    Bicycle tires and tubes, **1978:** 1903, 1904
    Bolts, nuts, and large screws, **1978:** 300, 301, 2283, 2284; **1979:** 4
    Cheese, **1979:** 2227; **1980–81:** 2846
    Clothespins, **1978:** 1698, 1699; **1979:** 232–234, 325
    Chocolate crumbs, **1979:** 2227
    Chrome, **1977:** 451–453
    Coffee, **1977:** 309
    Copper, **1978:** 1804, 1805
    Educational, scientific, and cultural materials, **1980–81:** 2920
    Generalized System of Preferences, **1977:** 255, 1346, 1671, 1950, 2181
    High carbon ferrochromium, **1978:** 1940, 1941
    Lead products, **1980–81:** 1723, 3000
    Leather wearing apparel, **1980–81:** 531, 532
    Live cattle, **1980–81:** 2801
    Meat, **1978:** 1236, 1988, 2009, 2011, 2212; **1979:** 336, 2299; **1980–81:** 2750
    Mushrooms, **1977:** 362; **1980–81:** 2329, 2331, 2562
    Natural gas, **1979:** 58, 182, 183, 236, 737
    Nonrubber footwear, **1980–81:** 420
    Nuclear waste material, **1979:** 1483

Commerce, international — *continued*
  Imports, U.S. — *continued*
    Oil.
      See Oil imports.
    Papermaking machinery, **1978:** 2271, 2272
    Peanuts, **1980–81:** 2772, 2775
    Porcelain-on-steel cookware, **1980–81:** 2, 3, 97
    Regulations, **1977:** 43
    Relief **1977:** 550–554, 558
    Shoes, **1977:** 283, 550–554, 558, 644, 755, 1113, 1128, 1148
    Stainless steel table flatware, **1978:** 1216, 1217
    Steel, **1977:** 1789; **1978:** 682, 1545, 1546, 1613, 1625, 1661, 2153, 2288; **1979:** 1032, 1228, 1429; **1980–81:** 723, 732, 902, 1961
    Sugars, sirups, and molasses, **1977:** 797–801, 807, 1705; **1978:** 145, 1154, 2104; **1979:** 153, 946; **1980–81:** 265, 1272
    Television receiver subassemblies, color, **1977:** 644, 755, 936, 944, 1157; **1979:** 166; **1980–81:** 920, 1257
    Textiles, **1977:** 755
    Unemployment adjustment assistance for workers affected by, **1980–81:** 823, 1999, 2352
    Upland cotton, **1980–81:** 575, 2745
  Inflation, impact on, **1979:** 2031
  International Chamber of Commerce, remarks, **1978:** 1691, 1693
  International monetary system interrelationship, **1979:** 1840
  Interview remarks, **1978:** 518, 1253–1255, 1277, 1416, 1601
  Legislation, **1980–81:** 1300
  Multilateral trade institutions, **1979:** 1800
  News conference remarks, **1978:** 438
  Organization of American States, remarks, **1978:** 1145
  Relationship with:
    Foreign policy, **1980–81:** 2208
    Tourism, **1980–81:** 2838
  State of the Union, **1978:** 94, 102, 118, 119
  Trade, U.S.
    Africa, **1979:** 1786
    Argentina, **1979:** 1791
    Balance of payments, **1978:** 55, 722, 1255, 1262, 1284, 1314, 1441, 1487–1489, 2065; **1979:** 330, 736, 944, 1216
    Canada, **1980–81:** 1248
    Cartegena Agreement countries, **1980–81:** 20
    China, People's Republic of.
      See Trade with U.S. *under* China, People's Republic of.
    Communist countries, **1978:** 2224
    Countervailing duties' waiver, **1979:** 46
    Democratic workshop on inflation, remarks, **1978:** 2210

Commerce, international — *continued*
  Trade, U.S. — *continued*
    Developing countries, **1980–81:** 429, 549, 942, 2208
    Dominican Republic, **1980–81:** 1247
    European Communities, **1980–81:** 1247, 1824
    Federal trade functions reorganization, **1979:** 1729, 1786, 2201
    Foreign boycotts, U.S. position on, **1979:** 146
    General Agreement on Tariffs and Trade, Geneva Protocol to, **1979:** 2223
    Generalized System of Preferences, **1978:** 421; **1979:** 367
    Hungary, **1980–81:** 980, 982
    India, **1980–81:** 1137, 2848
    Indonesia, **1980–81:** 20, 1247
    International agreements, **1979:** 6, 7
    Iran, **1980–81:** 113, 611, 612, 614
    Italy, **1980–81:** 421
    Japan, agreement with U.S., **1978:** 67
    Korea, Republic of, **1980–81:** 420, 1258
    Legislation, **1979:** 1311
    Mexico.
      See Trade with U.S. *under* Mexico.
    Philippines, **1980–81:** 1251
    Romania, **1980–81:** 980, 982
    Switzerland, **1980–81:** 1247
    Taiwan, **1980–81:** 420, 1258
    Tariff and nontariff barriers, **1978:** 1145
    Thailand, **1980–81:** 1251
    Tobago, **1980–81:** 20
    Trinidad, **1980–81:** 20
    Uganda, **1979:** 224, 225
    Union of Soviet Socialist Republics.
      See Trade with U.S. *under* Union of Soviet Socialist Republics.
    United Kingdom, **1980–81:** 1343, 1344
    U.S. human rights positions, effect on, **1979:** 2010
    Zimbabwe-Rhodesia.
      See under Zimbabwe-Rhodesia.
  Treaties and other international agreements
    Customs Valuation Agreement, **1980–81:** 94, 1247, 1463
    International agreements program for 1979, **1980–81:** 1545
    International Natural Rubber Agreement, 1979, **1980–81:** 591
    International Sugar Agreement, **1980–81:** 1271
    International Trade in Endangered Fauna and Flora Convention, **1980–81:** 590
  Venice Economic Summit Conference statement, **1980–81:** 1191
  World Bank Group and International Monetary Fund, remarks, **1978:** 1628
  See also Bonn Economic Summit Conference; Economy, international; Multilateral

Commerce, international — *continued*
　　See also — *continued*
　　　　trade negotiations; Tokyo Economic
　　　　　Summit Conference.
Commerce, Secretary of (Philip M. Klutznick)
　　Antiboycott laws enforcement, **1980–81:** 1656
　　Aquaculture research and development func-
　　　tions, **1980–81:** 1938
　　Auto Industry Committee, Executive Committee
　　　member, **1980–81:** 1670
　　Coastal zone management, **1980–81:** 2335
　　Council on Wage and Price Stability, member,
　　　1980–81: 967
　　Energy conservation responsibilities, **1980–81:**
　　　788
　　Export promotion and administration respon-
　　　sibilities, **1980–81:** 401, 824, 1689, 1692,
　　　1694
　　Foreign Corrupt Practices Act review, **1980–81:**
　　　402
　　Gasoline conservation fee support, **1980–81:** 593,
　　　598
　　Import relief determinations, **1980–81:** 3, 4, 532,
　　　533
　　Interagency Employee Benefit Council, member,
　　　1980–81: 2864
　　International Convention for the Safety of Life
　　　at Sea, enforcement functions, **1980–81:**
　　　1268
　　International trade functions, **1980–81:** 6, 8–10
　　Labor/Technology Forecasting System devel-
　　　opment, **1979:** 2073
　　Marine sanctuaries protection, **1980–81:** 1856
　　Meetings with the President (Digest), **1980–81:**
　　　63, 423, 825
　　Nomination, **1979:** 2135, 2140, 2249
　　Olympics, 1980 Summer, prohibition against
　　　transactions with Soviet Union, **1980–81:**
　　　559, 560
　　President's Committee on the International La-
　　　bor Organization, member, **1980–81:** 1127
　　President's Export Council, final report prepa-
　　　ration, **1980–81:** 2828
　　Soviet trade restriction functions, **1980–81:** 32,
　　　43, 184
　　Steel imports antidumping suits study, **1980–81:**
　　　736
　　Steel industry revitalization program responsi-
　　　bilities, **1980–81:** 1960, 1964, 2071
　　Swearing-in ceremony, **1980–81:** 43
　　Task Force on Global Resources and Environ-
　　　ment, functions, **1980–81:** 1417
　　Zimbabwe-Rhodesia trade functions (EO 12183),
　　　1979: 2252
　　For functions of the Department in general, see
　　　Commerce, Department of.
Commerce, Secretary of (Juanita M. Kreps), **1977:**
　　9, 13, 86, 97, 248, 252, 399, 485, 549,

Commerce, Secretary of — *continued*
　　551–554, 627, 662, 676, 712, 745, 806, 870,
　　1084, 1087, 1101, 1216, 1415, 1532, 1648,
　　1690, 1759, 1761, 1930, 2001, 2089, 2102,
　　2112, 2162; **1978:** 66, 265, 527, 530, 553,
　　554, 587, 594, 682, 723, 770, 771, 850, 880,
　　892, 961, 985, 1010, 1104, 1188, 1234,
　　1630, 1631, 1635, 1670, 1808, 2065, 2238,
　　2240, 2242
　　China, People's Republic of, visit to, **1979:** 174,
　　　213, 331
　　Credit application functions (EO 12166), **1979:**
　　　1965
　　Federal emergency management functions (EO
　　　12127), **1979:** 566
　　Foreign assistance functions (EO 12163), **1979:**
　　　1795
　　Industrial innovation initiatives actions, **1979:**
　　　531, 680, 2070
　　International trade study, **1979:** 332–334
　　Meetings with the President (Digest), **1979:** 467,
　　　666, 1705, 1824
　　Mentions, **1979:** 96, 548, 1216
　　National coastal protection, programs review,
　　　1979: 1363, 1373
　　News conference (Checklist), **1979:** 2082
　　Offshore oil spill pollution functions (EO 12123),
　　　1979: 338
　　President's assessment, **1979:** 2070
　　President's Export Council, administrative re-
　　　sponsibilities (EO 12131), **1979:** 785
　　Resignation, **1979:** 1818
　　Ugandan trade actions, **1979:** 867
　　Urban noise abatement program development,
　　　1979: 1385
　　Whale protection, investigation of foreign vio-
　　　lations, **1979:** 265, 1435
　　White House Conference on Economic Devel-
　　　opment, executive agency representative,
　　　1979: 65, 68
　　For functions of the Department in general, see
　　　Commerce, Department of.
Commerce Commission, Interstate.
　　See Interstate Commerce Commission.
Commission.
　　See other part of title.
Committee.
　　See other part of title.
Commodity Credit Corporation, **1978:** 457, 458,
　　914, 1279; **1979:** 110, 179, 898
　　Annual report, **1980–81:** 1662
　　Board of Directors, **1977:** 368, 373, 461, 465, 495,
　　　505, 510, 535, 557, 745, 1228, 1266
　　Poland, agricultural credit guarantees to, **1980–
　　　81:** 1711
　　Report transmittal, **1977:** 2089

Commodity Credit Corporation — *continued*
  Soviet grain shipments suspension, contractual
    obligations assumption, **1980–81:** 161,
    391, 652
  U.S. balance of trade and payments, **1977:** 2160
Commodity Futures Trading Commission, **1978:**
    564, 886, 899, 1182; **1979:** 41, 93, 598, 619
Common Cause, **1977:** 706; **1980–81:** 2823
Common Fund, **1978:** 1315
Common Market, European.
  See European Economic Community.
Common situs picketing bill, **1977:** 516
Commoner, Barry, **1980–81:** 1636, 1733, 1872, 2272
Commons, D. L., **1979:** 942
Communication Agency, International.
  See International Communication Agency.
Communications, wireless, **1978:** 87
Communications Commission, Federal.
  See Federal Communications Commission.
Communications Satellite Corporation, **1978:**
    2146; **1979:** 91, 271, 294, 1253
  Board of Directors, members, **1980–81:** 515, 870,
    1220, 1246, 2870, 2873
Communications satellite system, **1978:** 599
Communications and telecommunications
  Administration's accomplishments and goals,
    1980–81: 152
  Cable television, **1979:** 932, 933, 938
  Electromagnetic spectrum, **1979:** 541
  Handicapped persons programs, **1980–81:** 811
  Industry deregulation
    Congressional consideration, **1979:** 1699;
      1980–81: 252, 573
    Legislative proposal commitment for 1980,
      1980–81: 118, 121, 152
    Mentions, **1980–81:** 215, 918
    Purposes, **1980–81:** 151, 1934
  Minority assistance program, **1978:** 252, 277,
    324; **1980–81:** 1703
  Public broadcasting.
    See Public broadcasting.
  Rural areas systems, **1979:** 270
  Submarine systems, **1980–81:** 1996
  Transfer of functions, **1978:** 598
  U.S. advertising in foreign broadcasting indus-
    tries, **1980–81:** 1671
  U.S. international policy, **1979:** 240
Communications Workers of America, **1979:** 1247,
    1252, 1294; **1978:** 685
Communism, **1978:** 1302
Communist Workers Party, **1980–81:** 1392, 1500
Community action programs, **1977:** 1838, 1849,
    1852
Community College Assistance Act, Tribally Con-
    trolled, **1978:** 1786
Community development
  Administration's accomplishments and goals,
    1980–81: 2960

Community development — *continued*
  Block grants, **1980–81:** 1082
  Federal programs, **1980–81:** 650, 1095, 2116
  Rebuilding projects for economic dislocation
    areas, **1980–81:** 1607, 1615, 1631, 1650,
    1676, 1986
Community Development Act of 1974, Housing
    and, **1980–81:** 1469
Community Development Act of 1980, Housing
    and, **1980–81:** 2112, 2179
Community Development Block Grant program,
    1979: 136; **1978:** 100, 579, 583
Community Development Corporation, New,
    1977: 575, 596; **1980–81:** 752, 775
Community Development Corporations, **1978:** 588
Community Development Credit Unions, **1978:**
    592
Community Emergency Drought Relief Act of
    1977, **1977:** 962
Community Health Centers, National Association
    of, **1979:** 983
Community impact analyses, urban and, **1978:**
    1428, 1429, 1433
Community Investment, Institute for, **1978:** 589
Community Investment Board, National Advisory,
    1979: 1815; **1980–81:** 2613, 2770, 2882
Community Investment Fund, **1978:** 1058, 1072
Community Mental Health System, **1979:** 134, 135,
    860
Community programs, **1978:** 1605
Community Relations Service, **1978:** 784, 803
Community Services Administration, **1978:** 588,
    594, 1094, 1434
  Alcohol fuels production plants construction,
    1979: 1502ftn.
  Annual report, **1980–81:** 492
  Appropriations, **1977:** 2087
  Assistant Directors, **1977:** 1262, 1263, 1267,
    1439, 1458; **1980–81:** 979, 1015, 1423,
    1469, 1653, 1715, 2332, 2726, 2727, 2870,
    2873
  Budget rescission, **1980–81:** 2916
  Civil service rule, **1977:** 2062
  Deputy Director, **1977:** 1053, 1059
  Director, **1977:** 86, 564, 596, 871, 1127, 1829,
    1837, 1844, 1852
  Fuel bill payments, **1977:** 1732
  General Counsel, **1977:** 1458
  Handicapped persons programs, **1980–81:** 2610
  Hard-core unemployed jobs program, **1979:** 2158
  Heat- and drought-affected areas, assistance ac-
    tions, **1980–81:** 1345, 1421, 1423
  Hydroelectric power projects, **1979:** 1511
  Inspector General, **1979:** 1042, 1044
  Miami, Fla., programs, **1980–81:** 1492
Community Services Administration, Director
    (Graciela Olivarez), **1979:** 337, 1865;
    1980–81: 281

Community Services Administration, Director (Richard J. Rios)
  Heat- and drought-affected areas, assistance actions, **1980–81:** 1422
  National Advisory Community Investment Board, support services, **1980–81:** 2771
  National Consumer Cooperative Bank, Board of Directors member, **1980–81:** 2614
  Nomination, **1980–81:** 769, 1015
  President's assessment, **1980–81:** 1941
  Swearing-in ceremony, **1980–81:** 1457, 1461
Comoros, U.S. Ambassador, **1980–81:** 2752
Compensation reform act, Federal employees, proposed, **1979:** 1002
Comprehensive Employment and Training Act (CETA) programs, **1977:** 51, 52, 349, 1123, 1838; **1978:** 318, 332, 390, 416, 506, 959, 960, 1009, 1242, 1643, 2227
  Abuses elimination, **1980–81:** 2516
  Administration's accomplishments and goals, **1979:** 126; **1980–81:** 124, 213, 1000, 1003, 1069, 1081
  Amendments, **1978:** 1739, 1871, 1880, 2063, 2076, 2077
  Annual report, **1980–81:** 2721
  Civil service status for participants, **1980–81:** 2820
  Department of Labor youth employment program, **1980–81:** 125
  Federal budget allocations increase, **1980–81:** 1324, 1499, 1968, 1998, 2009
  Mention, **1979:** 1756
  Miami, Fla., programs, **1980–81:** 1074
  Michigan projects, **1980–81:** 1993
  Opportunities Industrialization Centers funds, **1980–81:** 1068
  Private Sector Initiatives program, **1979:** 73, 99, 126, 601, 2158
  Programs preservation in 1981 budget, **1980–81:** 808, 832, 909, 1000, 1040
  Progress during administration, **1979:** 1969
  Summer youth programs, **1980–81:** 2000
Comprehensive Environmental Response, Compensation, and Liability Act
  Congressional consideration, **1980–81:** 1353, 1683
  Executive order implementing, **1980–81:** 3044
  Fact sheet, **1980–81:** 2807
  Signing ceremony, **1980–81:** 2797
Comprehensive Older Americans Act, **1979:** 1633
  Amendments, **1978:** 1792, 1793
Comprehensive Test Ban negotiations, **1979:** 215, 1129, 1143
Compton, W. Dale, **1979:** 448, 1549
Computer industry, **1980–81:** 1537, 1897
Computers, use in Government, **1977:** 115
Conable, Repr. Barber B., Jr., **1978:** 802, 1783; **1979:** 1312; **1980–81:** 585, 2344

Conaboy, Richard P., **1979:** 958, 983
Concord, N.C., **1977:** 740
Concorde aircraft, **1977:** 178, 321, 765, 1607, 1648, 1649
Concussion bombs, **1977:** 93
Condominiums, **1980–81:** 2162
Condon, John P., **1978:** 286, 304, 898, 1668; **1979:** 1222, 1523, 1531; **1980–81:** 893
Coney, Theddis R., **1977:** 1222, 1266
Conference.
  See other part of title.
Conflicts of interest, **1977:** 124, 195, 370, 786, 893, 1244, 1245
Conger, Clement, **1978:** 916
Conger, John, **1977:** 529
Congo
  Ambassador to U.S., **1979:** 25
  Brazzaville Centennial celebrations, U.S. delegation, **1980–81:** 1946
  U.S. Ambassador, **1979:** 580, 619
Congress
  Abscam investigation, **1980–81:** 2355
  Action on administration's proposals, **1977:** 1082, 1318, 1509, 1583, 1672, 1686, 1703, 1784, 1799, 1981, 1982, 1999, 2009, 2095, 2108, 2117, 2135, 2161, 2188, 2201; **1978:** 55, 56, 74, 91, 311, 369, 713, 729, 780, 806, 937, 938, 950, 972, 988, 1060, 1061, 1063, 1064, 1074, 1092, 1274, 1317, 1318, 1324–1327, 1337, 1351, 1375, 1377, 1378, 1409, 1424, 1441, 1487–1489, 1492, 1493, 1551, 1576, 1589, 1622, 1745, 1752, 1784, 1912, 1914, 2024
  Administration's percentage of success, **1979:** 1855, 2017, 2033, 2052, 2053; **1980–81:** 114, 2433
  Alaska public lands, **1979:** 877, 2067; **1980–81:** 1343, 1548, 2718
  Budget, **1979:** 947
  Clinch River breeder reactor, **1979:** 730, 795, 887
  Department of Education.
    See under Education, Department of.
  Employment programs, **1979:** 1975
  Energy.
    See Energy legislation.
  Fair housing, **1980–81:** 1098, 1113, 1325, 1503, 1771
  Financial institutions deregulation, **1979:** 1728, 2079
  Fiscal Year 1981 budget, **1980–81:** 835, 857, 1981
  Five Year Defense Program, **1980–81:** 197
  Food stamps provisions, **1979:** 1432
  Gasoline conservation fee on imported oil, **1980–81:** 1027, 1090, 1113
  Hazardous waste disposal, **1980–81:** 1353

Congress — *continued*
  Action on proposals — *continued*
    Hospital cost containment, **1979:** 952, 963, 1772, 2129
    India, nuclear fuel shipment from U.S., **1980–81:** 1922
    Labor law reform, **1979:** 1870, 2047
    Mass transit, **1979:** 1326
    Mental health systems, **1979:** 1982; **1980–81:** 1976
    Multilateral trade agreements, **1980–81:** 2828
    New York City loan guarantees, **1980–81:** 1954
    Nuclear Regulatory Commission reorganization, **1980–81:** 617
    Panama Canal treaties.
      See under Panama Canal treaties.
    Public works projects, **1979:** 2049
    Railroad deregulation, **1979:** 1696; **1980–81:** 1699
    Real wage insurance, **1979:** 951
    Regulatory reform, **1979:** 2071, 2271; **1980–81:** 604, 785
    SALT II treaty.
      See under Strategic arms limitation.
    Small business regulatory reform, **1980–81:** 1508, 1697
    Standby gasoline rationing, **1980–81:** 116
    State and local governments fiscal assistance, **1979:** 2196
    Tax reform, **1979:** 2044
    Trucking industry deregulation, **1980–81:** 693, 920
    United States International Development Cooperation Agency, **1979:** 1230
    U.S. foreign assistance loans, **1980–81:** 941
    Water projects, **1979:** 2049
    Welfare system reform, **1979:** 1661, 1928, 2044, 2092
    Windfall profits tax.
      See Windfall profits tax.
    Youth employment and training programs.
      See Employment *under* Children and youth.
  Administration's support of legislation
    Alcohol fuels production plants, **1979:** 1502ftn.
    Trucking standards, **1979:** 1625
  Assassination hearings, **1978:** 1780
  Balanced budget for Fiscal Year 1981, consultations with the President, **1980–81:** 478, 484, 539, 556, 568, 570, 705
  Bipartisan senior citizen intern program, **1979:** 837
  Budget Committee, **1980–81:** 2025
  Budget process, **1979:** 100
  Camp David meeting on the Middle East, Joint Session of Congress, **1978:** 1533
  Campaign financing, public, **1977:** 221, 224, 482

Congress — *continued*
  Capitol Hill Page School, **1977:** 1061
  Carter, Billy, investigation of activities with Libyan Government, **1980–81:** 1420, 1439, 1648, 1564
  Carter/Mondale campaign supporters, **1980–81:** 1030
  China, People's Republic of
    Consultation with President on diplomatic relations, **1978:** 2277, 2278
    Visit of bipartisan delegation, **1977:** 2180; **1978:** 2003, 2110; **1979:** 666
  Christmas Ball, **1978:** 2228
  Christmas Ball at the White House, **1980–81:** 2823
  Coal utilization promotion, **1980–81:** 472
  Congressional elections, public financing of, **1980–81:** 153
  Democratic congressional dinner, **1977:** 1013
  District of Columbia representation, **1978:** 1465, 1467
  Energy and inflation task forces, **1979:** 1211, 1216
  Equal rights amendment support, **1980–81:** 923
  Ethics legislation, **1977:** 97, 318, 786; **1978:** 110, 1603, 1615, 1622, 1644, 1797, 1854, 1866, 1885, 1890, 1894, 1938
  Federal Government reorganization, survey, **1977:** 1378
  Foreign policy briefings, **1978:** 1154, 1278
  House of Representatives
    Interstate and Foreign Commerce Committee, **1977:** 1191
    Majority leader, **1977:** 595
    Minority leader, **1977:** 251, 595
    Social security financing bill, **1977:** 1917
    Speaker, **1977:** 97–99, 357, 508, 672, 800, 882, 1058, 1063, 1158, 1198, 1202, 1500, 1540
    Ways and Means Committee, **1977:** 1082, 1092, 1103
  Inflationary legislation, President's commitment to veto, **1980–81:** 568, 572
  Intelligence committees, **1978:** 211
  International convention advisory commission on endangered species, **1979:** 2288
  Interview remarks, **1978:** 1227, 1775, 1776, 1778, 1779, 1781, 2046
  Iran crisis, meeting with the President, **1980–81:** 577
  Kampuchea, Senatorial delegation's visit, **1979:** 2036, 2044
  Legislative veto of executive branch actions, Ninth Circuit Court of Appeals ruling, **1980–81:** 2836, 2882
  Legislative vetoes, **1978:** 1146
  Lobbyists' influence, **1980–81:** 1044, 1054
  Members
    Economic status, **1977:** 297

Congress — *continued*
  Members — *continued*
    Meeting with the President.
      See Digest of Other White House An-
      nouncements *at the end of each issue.*
    Members' term of office, President's assessment,
      1979: 739
    Mount St. Helens eruption, disaster assistance
      appropriations, **1980–81:** 960
    National agenda for the eighties, consultations
      with the President, **1979:** 2014
    National Conference of Negro Women, rela-
      tionship with, **1979:** 2137
    New Members dinner, **1978:** 2167
    95th Session, President's statement on, **1978:**
      1784
    96th Session, President's assessment of perform-
      ance, **1980–81:** 2066
    Public financing of congressional elections,
      1978: 1079, 2046
    Refugee admission consultations, **1980–81:** 684,
      685
    Relationship with the President, **1977:** 98, 99,
      221, 281, 750, 775, 1061, 1082, 1092, 1093,
      1103, 1106, 1155, 1171, 1237, 1370, 1447,
      1472, 1688, 1786, 1943, 2058, 2099, 2202;
      1978: 69, 811, 943, 1414, 1442, 1445, 1778,
      2027, 2028; **1979:** 121, 963, 1014, 1323,
      2033; **1980–81:** 906, 1031, 1530, 2122
    Retiring Members, White House dinner, **1978:**
      393; **1980–81:** 1570
  Salary
    Increase, **1977:** 97, 191, 238, 318
    Recommendations, **1980–81:** 2865, 2874
  Senate
    Commerce, Science, and Transportation Com-
      mittee, **1977:** 1916
    Election campaign financing, **1977:** 1366
    Foreign Assistance Subcommittee, **1977:** 1377
    Government Operations Committee, **1977:**
      1567
    Judiciary Committee, **1977:** 1941
    Majority leader, **1977:** 97, 99, 251, 586, 650,
      1063
    President, **1977:** 357, 800
    Select Committee on Intelligence, **1977:** 882
    Youth program, **1977:** 79
  Summer Olympics, 1980, boycott support,
    1980–81: 356, 616, 664, 678
  Sunset legislation, **1977:** 395
  Taxation responsibilities, **1979:** 1837
  Tellico Dam, Fla., construction project approval,
    1979: 1995
  Urban and community impact analyses, **1978:**
    1428, 1429
  Water projects legislation, **1980–81:** 88
  White House briefings on:
    Foreign assistance, **1980–81:** 941

Congress — *continued*
  White House Christmas reception, **1979:** 2247
  White House Promenade, **1978:** 944
  White House "Salute to Congress" dinner,
    1980–81: 1096
  White House survey of constituent problems,
    1977: 1960
Congress, Communications to
  ACTION, report, **1978:** 1345; **1979:** 2248; **1980–
    81:** 2752, 3049
  Activity of Korean agents in the United States,
    letter to congressional leaders, **1977:** 1280,
    1969
  Addresses
    SALT II treaty, **1979:** 1087
    State of the Union, **1979:** 103; **1980–81:** 194
    Iran and Afghanistan situations, **1980–81:** 38
  Administration on Aging, report, **1979:** 441;
    1980–81: 291, 824
  Administration of the Radiation Control for
    Health and Safety Act of 1968, report,
    1979: 2035
  Aeronautics and Space Report of the President,
    1978: 1516
  Agency for International Development, person-
    nel system, message, **1979:** 760
  Aggregate Report on Personnel, report, **1979:**
    2187
  Agricultural commodity shipments to Soviet
    Union, reports, **1980–81:** 183
  Airline industry regulation
    Letter to members of Senate Committee on
      Commerce, Science, and Transportation,
      1977: 1379
    Message, **1977:** 277
  Alaska natural gas transportation system
    Letter to Speaker of House and President of
      Senate, **1977:** 1530
    Message, **1977:** 1645
  Alaska Naval Petroleum Reserve, report, **1977:**
    1127, 1128
  Alaska public lands legislation, letter, **1979:** 855
  Alaska Railroad
    Report, **1978:** 1279; **1979:** 1785; **1980–81:** 2726
    Report transmittal, **1977:** 1030
  Alcoholic health hazards, reports, **1980–81:** 2753
  Anhydrous ammonia industry, reports, **1979:**
    2221, 2222
  Artificial baits and flies industry, letter to Speak-
    er of House and President of Senate,
    1978: 2071
  Automotive Products Trade Act of 1965, report,
    1977: 464
  Automotive Products Trade Act of 1965, Oper-
    ation of the, reports, **1977:** 2077; **1979:**
    178; **1980–81:** 653

Congress, Communications to — *continued*
  Bicycle tire and tube industry, letter to Speaker
      of House and President of Senate, **1978:**
      1903
  Bolt, nut, and large screw industry, letters to
      Speaker of House and President of Sen-
      ate, **1978:** 301, 2283
  Broadcasting, United States international, re-
      port, **1977:** 478
  Budget
    Deferrals and rescissions, messages, **1977:** 352,
        495, 739, 931, 1217, 1285, 1286, 1357,
        1477, 1647, 1714, 2002, 2125; **1978:** 223,
        407, 502, 895, 1041, 1321, 1652, 1699,
        2095, 2183, 2227; **1979:** 200, 272, 433, 603,
        720, 1299, 1445, 1522, 1772, 1780, 1801,
        2121
    Message, **1978:** 185
    1978 revisions, message, **1977:** 214
  Budget, 1980, message, **1979:** 96
  Budget, 1981, message
    Rescissions and deferrals, **1980–81:** 235, 355,
        428, 695, 898, 948, 1128, 1440, 1577, 1981,
        2763, 2916
    Revisions, **1980–81:** 569
    Text, **1980–81:** 227
  Budget, 1982, message, **1980–81:** 2895
  Cahaba River in Alabama, report, **1979:** 2245
  Cancer program, national, report and plan, **1977:**
      556, 706
  Carter, Billy, activities with Libyan Government,
      report, **1980–81:** 1523
  Census statistics, report, **1980–81:** 2872
  Central America and the Caribbean, U.S. assis-
      tance to, message, **1979:** 2103
  Citizens band radio transceivers, letter to Speak-
      er of House and President of Senate,
      1978: 607
  Clean Air Act amendments, letter to Senators
      Muskie, Randolph, and Stafford, **1977:**
      1072
  Clothespin industry
    Letter, **1979:** 232, 233
    Report, **1978:** 1698
  Coal mine health and safety, report, **1977:** 339;
      1979: 103
  Coastal Zone Management Act of 1972, report,
      1977: 745; **1979:** 178
  Commodity Credit Corporation, reports, **1977:**
      2089; **1978:** 1279; **1980–81:** 1662
  Commodity Services Administration, report,
      1980–81: 492
  Comprehensive Employment and Training Act
      (CETA)
    Message, **1978:** 390
    Report, **1980–81:** 2721

Congress, Communications to — *continued*
  Consumer agency legislation
    Letter from Bert Lance to Speaker of House
        and President of Senate, **1977:** 1396
    Message, **1977:** 573
  Copper industry, letter to Speaker of House and
      President of Senate, **1978:** 1804
  Corporation for Public Broadcasting, reports,
      1978: 613; **1979:** 609; **1980–81:** 912
  Cotton program, upland, report, **1977:** 279;
      1978: 1571
  China-U.S. trade relations, message, **1979:** 2006
  Council on Environmental Quality, reports,
      1978: 430; **1979:** 119; **1980–81:** 351, 3018
  Council on Wage and Price Stability, reports,
      1977: 706, 1771; **1978:** 252, 422, 701,
      1559; **1979:** 178, 393, 815, 1683, 2272;
      1980–81: 645, 1446, 2701, 2922
  Countervailing duties' waiver, message, **1979:** 46
  Crude oil transportation system, letter, **1979:**
      2174
  Cuba, U.S. policy, report, **1979:** 240
  Cyprus conflict
    Letters, **1979:** 191, 461, 997, 1301, 1738, 2162
    Messages, **1977:** 143, 144, 638, 1137, 1500,
        1501, 1928; **1978:** 127, 555, 1151, 1481,
        2103
    Settlement, letter, **1980–81:** 205, 551, 947,
        1397, 1923
  Defense appropriations, letter to Speaker of
      House and Senate Majority Leader, **1977:**
      1693
  Defense budgets for fiscal years 1980 and 1981,
      message, **1979:** 1628
  Defense Department, Military Award Program,
      reports, **1978:** 1345; **1979:** 363
  Departments of State, Justice, and Commerce,
      the Judiciary, and related agencies ap-
      propriations bill, letter, **1980–81:** 2774
  Disease control programs, report, **1979:** 1604,
      1705
  District of Columbia
    Budget, message, **1979:** 217
    Budget transmittal, **1977:** 557; **1978:** 640
    Report, **1980–81:** 292
  Drought in Western and Plains States, message,
      1977: 487
  Drug abuse, message, **1977:** 1400
  Economic recovery program, message, **1977:** 47
  Economic Report of the President
    Message, **1978:** 129
    Report, **1979:** 110; **1980–81:** 245, 3004
  Education, Department of, proposed
    Letter to Speaker of House, **1978:** 1754
    Message, **1979:** 264
  Education Department, report, **1980–81:** 2882
  Egypt and Israel, scientific and technological
      cooperation with, report, **1980–81:** 1957

Congress, Communications to — *continued*
  Egyptian-Israeli peace treaty, letters, **1979:** 590, 638
  Election reform, message, **1977:** 481, 509
  Elementary and secondary education, message, **1978:** 424
  Embargo regulations under the Trading With the Enemy Act, letter, **1979:** 1656
  Emergency building temperature restrictions, message, **1980–81:** 2877
  Emergency Natural Gas Act of 1977, letter to Speaker of House and President of Senate, **1977:** 20
  Emergency weekend gasoline sales restrictions, message, **1979:** 608
  Employee Retirement Income Security Act of 1974, report, **1980–81:** 295
  Employment and training, report, **1979:** 1523
  Energy, letters
    Chairman of House Ad Hoc Committee on Energy, **1977:** 1297
    Speaker of House and President of Senate, **1977:** 742
  Energy conservation contingency plans, message, **1979:** 370–372
  Energy conservation programs, report, **1978:** 704
  Energy Department Authorization bill, veto message to Senate, **1977:** 1972
  Energy Department proposal, message, **1977:** 257
  Energy Department, report, **1980–81:** 292
  Energy management legislation, letter, **1979:** 895
  Energy security trust fund, message, **1979:** 721
  Energy supplies shortage, message, **1979:** 1228
  Environment, message, **1977:** 967
  Environmental priorities and programs, message, **1979:** 1353
  Equal rights amendment, letter to House Judiciary Committee members, **1978:** 1266
  Ethics in Government, message, **1977:** 786
  Executive, legislative, and judicial salary recommendations, message, **1980–81:** 2865
  Executive Office of the President
    Amendments to Plan No. 1 of 1977, **1977:** 1592
    Plan No. 1 of 1977, **1977:** 1253, 1255
  Export controls for foreign policy purposes, letter, **1979:** 2290
  Export financing negotiations, report, **1979:** 438
  Export of special nuclear material to India, Executive order transmittal, **1978:** 790
  Farm legislation, letter to congressional leaders, **1978:** 700
  Federal advisory committees, reports, **1977:** 528; **1978:** 577; **1979:** 463; **1980–81:** 507
  Federal Bureau of Investigation legislation, message, **1979:** 1334

Congress, Communications to — *continued*
  Federal civil justice system, message, **1979:** 342
  Federal civil service reform
    Letter to Members, **1978:** 936
    Message, **1978:** 444
    Reorganization Plan No. 2 of 1978, amendment, **1978:** 1251
  Federal civilian and military pay increases
    Messages, **1977:** 1682; **1979:** 64, 1529; **1980–81:** 468, 1596
    Report, **1980–81:** 2729
  Federal coal mine health activities, reports, **1978:** 576, 1271
  Federal Council on the Aging, reports, **1977:** 596; **1978:** 818; **1979:** 2043; **1980–81:** 1291
  Federal drug program, report, **1980–81:** 1859
  Federal employees pay raise, message, **1978:** 1480
  Federal energy conservation program, report, **1980–81:** 274, 2722
  Federal Labor Relations Authority, report, **1980–81:** 1647
  Federal law enforcement assistance programs, message, **1978:** 1246
  Federal Mine Health and Safety Act of 1977, report, **1979:** 1445
  Federal mine safety and health activities, report, **1980–81:** 564, 1049
  Federal pay system reform, message, **1979:** 1002
  Federal Prevailing Rate Advisory Committee, reports, **1978:** 216; **1980–81:** 1292
  Federal Railroad Safety Act of 1970, administration of, report, **1980–81:** 2872
  Federal territorial policy, message, **1980–81:** 317
  Floodplain management, letter, **1980–81:** 36
  Food for Peace program, letter to committee chairmen, **1978:** 315
  Foreign assistance
    Letter to Speaker of House and President of Senate, **1977:** 522
    Message, **1977:** 455
  Foreign ownership of U.S. real estate, report, **1980–81:** 1924
  Freight rail industry deregulation legislation, message, **1979:** 459
  Fuel assurances, initial, report, **1979:** 326
  Gasoline conservation fee on imported oil, letter, **1980–81:** 1012
  General revenue sharing legislation, message, **1980–81:** 698
  Generalized System of Preferences for developing countries
    Afghanistan, designation suspension, letter, **1980–81:** 429
    New beneficiary designations, letter, **1980–81:** 429
    Report, **1980–81:** 703

[References are to page numbers except as otherwise indicated]

Congress, Communications to — *continued*
  Genetic diseases program, report, **1980–81:** 1049
  Great Lakes Basin Commission, report, **1978:** 1807
  Guam, proposed constitution, message, **1978:** 795
  Handicapped persons programs, report, **1980–81:** 2726
  Hazardous materials control, reports, **1977:** 1483; **1979:** 178; **1980–81:** 2872, 3049
  Hazardous waste disposal, letter, **1979:** 1034
  Health, Education, and Welfare Department, occupational safety and health, report, **1980–81:** 1051
  Health care legislation, message, **1977:** 717
  Health information and promotion, reports, **1979:** 467, 1704; **1980–81:** 1714
  High carbon ferrochromium industry, letter to Speaker of House and President of Senate, **1978:** 1940
  Highway Safety and National Motor Vehicle and Traffic Safety Acts of 1966, reports, **1977:** 1210; **1978:** 1237; **1979:** 1881; **1980–81:** 2880
  Hospital cost containment legislation
    Committee chairmen, **1977:** 1772
    Letters, **1979:** 2111
    Members of House Interstate and Foreign Commerce Committee, **1978:** 961
    Message, **1979:** 386
  Housing and Community Development Act of 1974, reports, **1977:** 464; **1980–81:** 1469
  Housing and Urban Development, Department of, reports, **1977:** 744; **1978:** 1807; **1980–81:** 824, 1714
  Hungary-U.S. trade relations
    Letter to Speaker of House and President of Senate, **1978:** 704
    Messages, **1978:** 706, 1031
  India, export of U.S. nuclear materials to, message, **1980–81:** 1137
  Indochina refugees
    Letter to committee chairmen, **1977:** 1744
    Reports, **1977:** 504, 1151
  Industrial innovation initiatives program, message, **1979:** 2070
  Interest rates, message, **1979:** 928
  Intergovernmental fiscal assistance legislation, message, **1979:** 391
  International communications policy, report, **1979:** 240
  International development cooperation agency, proposed, message, **1979:** 395
  International Emergency Economic Powers Act, message, **1980–81:** 2772
  International Exchange-of-Persons program, report, **1979:** 324
  International exhibitions, report, **1978:** 229

Congress, Communications to — *continued*
  International Exposition on Energy, message, **1979:** 1525
  International journalistic freedom, report, **1979:** 240
  International science and technology programs, message, **1980–81:** 406
  International Security Assistance Act of 1977, report, **1978:** 1471
  International transport of goods, customs convention, message, **1977:** 1357
  International Whaling Commission, report, **1979:** 265
  International Women's Year, 1975, report, **1978:** 1640
  Iran
    American hostage release agreement, message, **1980–81:** 3040
    Assets blockage, message, **1979:** 2118
    Economic sanctions against, message, **1980–81:** 614, 716
    Rescue attempt for American hostages, letter, **1980–81:** 777
  Japan, cooperative medical science program with U.S., reports, **1977:** 1382; **1978:** 1278; **1979:** 732; **1980–81:** 493
  John Day River in Oregon, wild and scenic river study, message, **1980–81:** 323
  Justice Department, Office of Alien Property, report, **1980–81:** 1291
  Juvenile delinquency, Federal programs, report, **1980–81:** 1273
  Labor law reform legislation, message, **1977:** 1277
  Labor surplus area procurement program, report, **1980–81:** 1427
  Leather wearing apparel industry, letter, **1980–81:** 532
  Legislative vetoes, message, **1978:** 1146
  Libraries and information services, message, **1980–81:** 1930
  Marine pollution protocol, message, **1977:** 1352
  Memorandums of disapproval
    District of Columbia retirement program, **1978:** 1961
    Government ban on Tris in sleepwear, **1978:** 1977
    Legionville National Historic Site, Pennsylvania, **1978:** 1926
    Maritime industry relations with Federal officials, **1978:** 1926
    Meat imports, **1978:** 2009
    Navajo and Hopi relocation, **1978:** 1925
    Nurse training programs, **1978:** 2007
    Shipping rebating laws, **1978:** 1962
    Small Business Act and Small Business Investment Act amendments, **1978:** 1851

Congress, Communications to — *continued*
  Memorandums of disapproval — *continued*
    Tax structure in United States territories, **1978:** 1971
    Textile and apparel items exemptions from tariff reductions, **1978:** 2008
    U.S. aquaculture, **1978:** 1799
  Mental health systems legislation, message, **1979:** 859
  Middle distillate fuels situation during the winter of 1979–1980, report, **1980–81:** 25
  Middle East arms sales, letter to Members, **1978:** 896
  Military awards program, Defense and Transportation Departments, report, **1980–81:** 474, 2921
  Mining Enforcement Safety Administration and Bureau of Mines, report, **1977:** 706
  Missouri River Basin Commission, report, **1978:** 1807
  Multilateral Export Controls, report, **1978:** 1278
  Multilateral Trade Negotiations, messages, **1978:** 1663; **1979:** 1092
  Mushroom industry, report, **1977:** 361
  National Advisory Council on Adult Education, report, **1980–81:** 267
  National Advisory Council on Economic Opportunity, reports, **1977:** 1030; **1978:** 1278; **1980–81:** 274, 1925
  National Advisory Council on Extension and Continuing Education, report, **1977:** 2063
  National aeronautics and space programs, report, **1979:** 1421
  National Cancer Advisory Board, report, **1979:** 675, 1966, 2151
  National Cancer Program, report, **1979:** 675, 2105
  National climate program, message, **1980–81:** 2723
  National Commission on the International Year of the Child, 1979, letter to Speaker of House and President of Senate, **1978:** 963
  National Commission for the Review of Antitrust Laws and Procedures, letter to Speaker of House and President of Senate, **1977:** 2177
  National Corporation for Housing Partnerships and the National Housing Partnership, report, **1978:** 1279
  National Council on the Arts, reports, **1979:** 2280; **1980–81:** 452, 1428
  National Credit Union Administration, reports, **1977:** 744; **1978:** 1772
  National Earthquake Hazards Reduction program, report, **1978:** 1150
  National Endowment for the Arts, reports, **1979:** 2280; **1980–81:** 452, 1428

Congress, Communications to — *continued*
  National Endowment for the Arts and the National Council on the Arts, report, **1977:** 1264
  National Endowment for the Humanities, reports, **1977:** 1465; **1980–81:** 521
  National energy plan, message, **1979:** 816
  National health plan, message, **1979:** 1028
  National Heart, Blood Vessel, Lung, and Blood Program, report, **1977:** 1209
  National Heart, Lung, and Blood Institute, report, **1979:** 178
  National Housing Goal, report, **1978:** 1723
  National Institute for Building Sciences, reports, **1978:** 1154; **1980–81:** 422
  National Outdoor Recreation Plan, message, **1979:** 2220
  National Petroleum Reserve in Alaska, reports, **1978:** 1345; **1980–81:** 63
  National Science Board, reports, **1978:** 128, 1358; **1979:** 2146
  National Science Foundation, reports, **1977:** 1475, 1476; **1978:** 1378; **1979:** 1272; **1980–81:** 1287
  National Science and Technology Policy, Organization, and Priorities Act of 1976, report, **1978:** 1639
  National Sickle Cell Anemia, Cooley's Anemia, Tay-Sachs, and Genetic Diseases Act, reports, **1978:** 897; **1979:** 1705, 2106
  National urban policy
    Message, **1978:** 581
    Report, **1980–81:** 1861
  National Wild and Scenic Rivers and National Trails Systems, message, **1979:** 1813
  National Wilderness Preservation System, report, **1977:** 1264; **1979:** 240, 1966
  Natural gas legislation, Conference committee report, letter to members of the Senate, **1978:** 1487
  Natural Gas Pipeline Safety Act of 1968, report, **1980–81:** 291
  Navy shipbuilding programs, letter, **1980–81:** 475
  New England River Basins Commission, report, **1978:** 1807
  1959 Geneva Radio Regulations, partial revision transmittal, message, **1980–81:** 225
  1980 national housing production, report, **1980–81:** 521
  96th Congress, letter, **1980–81:** 2066
  Nuclear fuel exports, letter, **1980–81:** 286
  Nuclear nonproliferation
    Message, **1977:** 728
    Report, **1980–81:** 403
  Nuclear Non-Proliferation Act of 1978, **1979:** 452
  Nuclear Regulatory Commission, reports, **1978:** 1457; **1980–81:** 2722

Congress, Communications to — *continued*
  Occupational safety and health activities in Federal Government, report, **1978:** 1031
  Occupational safety and health for 1976, 1977, and 1978, report, **1979:** 2105
  Office of Alien Property, reports, **1978:** 1221; **1979:** 217; **1980–81:** 2726
  Office of Personnel Management, **1980–81:** 1569
  Ohio River Basin Commission, report, **1978:** 1807
  Oil import reduction program, letter to Members of Congress, **1979:** 1316
  Oil spills, message, **1977:** 458
  Owyhee River in Idaho and Oregon, message, **1979:** 1814
  Panama Canal treaties
    Letter to Members of Congress, **1979:** 102
    Letter to Sen. Richard Stone, **1978:** 227
    Message, **1977:** 1625
  Paperwork reduction, message, **1979:** 2180
  Pipeline safety, reports, **1980–81:** 2869
  Porcelain-on-steel cookware industry, report, **1980–81:** 2
  Postsecondary education in Micronesia, letter to Sen. Jackson and Repr. Udall transmitting report, **1977:** 1294
  Powerplant and industrial fuel use, report, **1980–81:** 2702
  President's 1978 Employment and Training Report, **1978:** 1009
  President's 1978 National Urban Policy Report, **1978:** 1430
  Privacy Act of 1974
    Reports, **1977:** 1211; **1979:** 1446; **1980–81:** 1462
    Letter to Speaker of House and President of Senate, **1978:** 1321
  Privacy rights, message, **1979:** 581
  Public broadcasting system, message, **1977:** 1737
  Public works bill, letter to Members of Congress, **1978:** 1710
  Public works and economic development legislation, message, **1979:** 599
  Rabbit meat, mandatory inspection, veto message to the House of Representatives, **1977:** 1993
  Radiation Control for Health and Safety Act, reports, **1977:** 609; **1978:** 1560; **1979:** 2043; **1980–81:** 1014
  Radioactive waste management program, message, **1980–81:** 296
  Railroad Retirement Board, reports, **1977:** 84, 85; **1978:** 1438; **1979:** 1683; **1980–81:** 1547
  Railroad Safety Act of 1970, report, **1977:** 1465
  Railroad Safety Report, **1978:** 1772; **1980–81:** 292

Congress, Communications to — *continued*
  Refugee resettlement grants program, letter, **1980–81:** 2879
  Regulatory reform, message, **1979:** 491
  Renewable resources of the United States, letter **1980–81:** 1141
  Reorganization of Federal audit and investigation functions, letter to Sen. Robert C. Byrd **1978:** 1570
  Reorganization plan authority
    Letter to Speaker of House and President of Senate, **1977:** 81
    Message, **1977:** 81
  Reorganization plans
    Alaska Natural Gas Transportation System (No. 1 of 1979), **1979:** 591
    Amendments, **1979:** 915
    International trade functions (No. 3 of 1979), **1979:** 1729
    Nuclear Regulatory Commission (No. 1 of 1980), **1980–81:** 543
      Amendment, **1980–81:** 836
    United States International Development Cooperation Agency (No. 2 of 1979), **1979:** 642
    See also Reorganization Plans.
  River basin commissions, reports, **1978:** 737; **1979:** 2248
  River of No Return Wilderness, letter to Speaker of House and President of Senate, **1978:** 2279
  Romania and Hungary, U.S. trade, message, **1979:** 978
  Romania, Hungary, and People's Republic of China, trade with U.S., message, **1980–81:** 980
  Romania-U.S. trade relations, message, **1978:** 1031
  Saint Lawrence Seaway Development Corporation, reports, **1977:** 1306; **1978:** 1333; **1980–81:** 1418
  SALT II treaty, letter to Members of Congress, **1979:** 2256
  SALT II treaty delay, letter, **1980–81:** 12
  Science and technology, report, **1980–81:** 2702, 3024, 3049
  Science and technology policy, message, **1979:** 529
  Scientific and technological cooperation with Egypt and Israel, report, **1980–81:** 1957
  Selective Service System reform, report, **1980–81:** 333
  Small business, message, **1980–81:** 73
  Social security
    Letter to congressional leaders, **1977:** 2063
    Message, **1977:** 836
  Social security financing, letter to congressional leaders, **1978:** 720

Congress, Communications to — *continued*
  Solar energy, message, **1979:** 1097
  Solar energy development bank legislation, letter to Members of Congress, **1979:** 1315
  Soviet Union, trade with U.S., letter, **1980–81:** 2471
  Space and aeronautics, report, **1980–81:** 2726
  Stainless steel table flatware industry, report, **1978:** 1215
  Standby gasoline rationing plan, messages, **1979:** 371; **1980–81:** 1099
    Amendment, **1979:** 813,820
  State of the Union, 1978
    Address, **1978:** 90
    Message, **1978:** 98
  State of the Union, 1979, message, **1979:** 121
  State of the Union, 1980, message, **1980–81:** 114
  State of the Union, 1981, message, **1980–81:** 2931
  Sugar industry, report, **1977:** 800
  Taiwan, U.S. relations, message, **1979:** 165
  Tax reduction and reform, message, **1978:** 158
  Telecommunications industry deregulation legislation, message, **1979:** 1699
  Television industry, letter to Speaker of House and President of Senate, **1977:** 937
  Trade agreements program, report, **1977:** 1163
  Trade agreements program for 1979, report, **1980–81:** 1545
  Trading With the Enemy Act, embargo regulations, letter to Speaker of House and President of Senate, **1978:** 1504
  Transfer of certain defense articles to the Republic of Korea, letter to Speaker of House, President of Senate, and Senate Majority Leader, **1977:** 1822
  Transportation, message, **1978:** 220
  Transportation Department
    Annual report, **1978:** 1345
    Military Award Program, report, **1978:** 1345; **1979:** 363
    Report, **1980–81:** 423, 3049
  Treaties and other international agreements
    Agreement on Importation of Educational, Scientific, and Cultural Materials, **1980–81:** 2920
    Agreement on International Carriage of Perishable Foodstuffs, **1979:** 83
    American Convention on Human Rights, **1977:** 1050
    Australia, nuclear energy agreement, **1979:** 1314
    Bangladesh, taxation convention, **1980–81:** 2762
    Bolivia, penal sentences, message to Senate, **1978:** 748
    Canada
      Execution of penal sentences, message, **1977:** 655

Congress, Communications to — *continued*
  Treaties — *continued*
    Fishery agreement, message, **1977:** 256
    Fishery treaty, **1979:** 776
    Maritime boundary treaty, **1979:** 776
    Migratory birds protection convention, **1980–81:** 2743
    Northern Pacific Halibut fishery convention, **1979:** 1420
    Taxation convention, **1980–81:** 2715
    Transit pipeline agreement, message, **1977:** 534, 1546, 1547, 1569
  China, People's Republic of, consular convention, **1980–81:** 3019
  China-U.S. trade relations agreement, **1979:** 2005
  Colombia, nuclear energy agreement, **1980–81:** 2878
  Convention on the Conservation of Antarctic Marine Living Resources, **1980–81:** 2765
  Convention on the Elimination of All Forms of Discrimination Against Women, **1980–81:** 2715
  Convention on the Inter-American Institute for Cooperation on Agriculture, **1979:** 2120
  Convention on International Civil Aviation, **1979:** 449; **1980–81:** 3024
  Convention on International Trade in Endangered Species of Wild Fauna and Flora, **1980–81:** 590
  Convention on the Physical Protection of Nuclear Material, **1980–81:** 867
  Convention on Pollution from Ships, **1979:** 85
  Convention on the Prevention of Marine Pollution, **1979:** 224
  Convention on the Prevention and Punishment of the Crime of Genocide, message, **1977:** 450, 997
  Convention on Psychotropic Substances, **1977:** 1402
  Convention for the Safety of Life at Sea, **1979:** 86
  Cook Islands, maritime boundary treaty, **1980–81:** 1625
  Customs Valuation Agreement amendments, **1980–81:** 94, 1463
  Cyprus, taxation and fiscal evasion convention, **1980–81:** 925
  Denmark
    Fishery agreement, **1979:** 1850
    Taxation and fiscal evasion convention, **1980–81:** 1646
  Egypt, taxation and fiscal evasion convention, **1980–81:** 2714
  European region, education convention, **1980–81:** 2721

Congress, Communications to — *continued*
  Treaties — *continued*
    Finland, extradition treaty, message, **1977:** 655
    Fishery agreements, messages
      Canada, **1977:** 256; **1978:** 812
      Cuba, **1977:** 886
      European Economic Community, **1977:** 205
      Japan, **1977:** 205, 1052
      Korea, Republic of, **1977:** 206
      Mexico, **1977:** 1752
      North Pacific fisheries convention, **1978:** 1041
      Portugal, **1980–81:** 2755
      Sockeye salmon fisheries, convention protocol, **1977:** 548
      Spain, **1977:** 206
      United Kingdom, **1977:** 1753
    Food Aid Convention, **1980–81:** 865
    France
      Income and property taxes, **1979:** 239
      Taxation and fiscal evasion, **1979:** 238
    German Democratic Republic, consular convention, **1980–81:** 783
    Germany, Federal Republic of
      Extradition treaty, **1979:** 85
      Social security agreement, **1978:** 1559; **1979:** 362
      Taxation and fiscal evasion convention, **1980–81:** 2915
    Hostile use of environmental modification techniques, convention, message to the Senate, **1978:** 1564
    Human rights treaties, message to Senate, **1978:** 395
    Hungary, taxation and fiscal evasion convention, **1979:** 822
    Indonesia, nuclear energy agreement, **1980–81:** 1281
    Intergovernmental Maritime Consultative Organization Convention, **1979:** 778; **1980–81:** 945
    Interim Convention on the Conservation of North Pacific Fur Seals, **1980–81:** 2716
    International Atomic Energy Agency, nuclear safeguards agreement, message to the Senate, **1978:** 293
    International Atomic Energy Agency Cooperation Agreement, **1980–81:** 266
    International Convention Against the Taking of Hostages, **1980–81:** 1475
    International Convention on Load Lines, 1966, amendment, **1979:** 1954
    International Convention on Maritime Search and Rescue, 1979, **1980–81:** 946
    International Convention for the Prevention of Pollution from Ships, **1977:** 458, 476
    International environmental agreements, **1977:** 984

Congress, Communications to — *continued*
  Treaties — *continued*
    International Natural Rubber Agreement, 1979, **1980–81:** 591
    International Seafarers Convention, **1979:** 1419
    International Sugar Agreement, 1977, message to the Senate, **1978:** 219
    International transport of goods, customs convention, **1977:** 1357
    International Wheat Agreement, 1971, **1979:** 434, 1625
    Israel, income tax convention, **1980–81:** 1285
    Italy, social security agreement, message to the Senate, **1978:** 429
    Jamaica, taxation and fiscal evasion convention, **1980–81:** 1476
    Japan
      Extradition treaty, **1979:** 598
      Trade agreement, message to the Senate, **1978:** 67
    Kiribati, friendship treaty, **1980–81:** 206
    Malta, income taxes treaty, **1980–81:** 756
    Marine pollution protocol, **1977:** 1352
    Maritime boundary treaties with Mexico, Venezuela, and Cuba, **1979:** 86
    Mexico
      Execution of penal sentences, message, **1977:** 156
      Extradition treaty, **1979:** 450
    Morocco
      Nuclear energy agreement, **1980–81:** 1026
      Taxation and fiscal evasion convention, message to the Senate, **1978:** 818
    Nice Agreement on International Trademarks, **1979:** 84
    Northwest Atlantic Fisheries Convention, **1979:** 777
    Norway
      Extradition treaty, **1979:** 1420
      Taxation convention, **1980–81:** 2763
    Nuclear Weapons in Latin America, Treaty for the Prohibition of, message to the Senate, **1978:** 962, 1143
    Panama, penal sentences treaty, **1979:** 1329
    Peru
      Nuclear energy agreement, **1980–81:** 1239
      Penal sentences treaty, **1979:** 2272
    Portugal, fishery agreement, **1980–81:** 2755
    Romania, trade agreement, **1977:** 1055, 1057
    Switzerland, social security agreement, **1980–81:** 264
    Treaty for the Elimination of All Forms of Racial Discrimination, **1977:** 450
    Treaty on the Limitation of Strategic Offensive Arms and related documents, **1979:** 1155

Congress, Communications to — *continued*
  Treaties — *continued*
    Treaty of Tlatelolco, **1977:** 613, 1027
    Turkey
      Extradition treaty, **1979:** 1390
      Penal judgments treaty, **1979:** 1391
    Tuvalu, friendship treaty, **1979:** 822
    Union of Soviet Socialist Republics
      Migratory bird convention, **1977:** 1279
      Science and technology agreement, **1977:** 1222
    United Kingdom
      Air services agreement, **1977:** 256, 1137, 1346
      Atomic energy agreement, **1979:** 2164
      Taxation and fiscal evasion convention, **1977:** 1066; **1979:** 663, 778
      Reciprocal fisheries agreement, **1980–81:** 1022
  Trucking industry deregulation legislation, message, **1979:** 1117
  Tuolumne River in California, message, **1979:** 1815
  Turkey, U.S. economic assistance, letter to Members of Congress, **1979:** 647
  Undocumented aliens, message, **1977:** 1416
  United Nations, U.S. participation in
    Message, **1977:** 1950
    Reports, **1978:** 449; **1979:** 62; **1980–81:** 1286, 2863
  United Nations Joint Inspection Unit, report, **1979:** 1531, 2186
  United States Arms Control and Disarmament Agency
    Letter to Speaker of House and President of Senate, **1977:** 358; **1978:** 451
    Report, **1978:** 549; **1979:** 682; **1980–81:** 450, 2879
  United States citizens living abroad, letter to Members of Congress, **1979:** 1522; **1980–81:** 206
  United States Civil Service Commission, reports, **1977:** 556, 1162
  United States Sinai Support Mission, reports, **1977:** 734, 1820; **1978:** 773; **1979:** 64, 756, 1821; **1980–81:** 697, 1957
  Upper Mississippi River Basin Commission, report, **1978:** 1807
  Uranium enrichment capacity, report, **1979:** 1822
  U.S. advertising in foreign broadcasting industries, message, **1980–81:** 1671
  U.S. competition in world markets, report, **1980–81:** 1695
  U.S. export promotion policies, **1980–81:** 1689
  Utility companies, oil and natural gas use reduction legislation, letter, **1980–81:** 448

Congress, Communications to — *continued*
  Veterans preference in civil service reform, letter to House Post Office and Civil Service Committee Chairman, **1978:** 1138
  Veto messages
    Department of Defense appropriation and authorization bill, message to House, **1978:** 1447
    Departments of State, Justice, and Commerce, the Judiciary, and related agencies appropriation, **1980–81:** 2809
    Dioxin exposure, health effects study, **1980–81:** 4
    Federal employees' death benefit, **1980–81:** 2830
    Federal firefighters' work week reduction, message to House, **1978:** 1133
    Hulver, Isaac, relief for, **1980–81:** 2846
    Mille Lacs Band of the Minnesota Chippewa Indians, **1980–81:** 2189
    National Forest System lands conveyance, **1980–81:** 2845
    National tourism policy, **1980–81:** 2838
    Oveson, Mr. and Mrs. Clarence, relief for, **1980–81:** 2839
    Public debt limit extension bill, **1980–81:** 1041
    Public works bill, message to House, **1978:** 1707
    Sikes Act amendments, message to House, **1978:** 1250
    Uniformed services health professionals special pay bill, **1980–81:** 456
    Ute Mountain Ute Tribe benefits bill, **1980–81:** 1043
    Veterans Administration health care, **1980–81:** 1563
  Vietnam era veterans, message, **1978:** 1737
  Virgin Islands, proposed constitution, **1978:** 1556
  Water policy, message, **1978:** 1044
  Water resource projects
    Letter, **1977:** 453
    Message, **1977:** 207
  Weatherization assistance program, **1980–81:** 492, 3049
  Welfare reform, message, **1977:** 1451; **1979:** 938
  White House Conference on Balanced National Growth and Economic Development, **1979:** 69
  White House Conference on Small Business, letter to Sen. Gaylord Nelson, **1978:** 695
  White House personnel, report, **1980–81:** 2782
  Wild and Scenic River designation, letter to Speaker of House and President of Senate, **1978:** 1771
  Windfall profits tax, message, **1979:** 721
  Windfall profits tax revenues, letter, **1980–81:** 1287

Congress, Communications to — *continued*
  Wiretapping and electronic surveillance, message, **1979:** 587
  World Weather Program
    Message, **1980–81:** 2725
    Report, **1977:** 1957
  Youth employment programs, message, **1977:** 349
  See also Reorganization Plans.
Congress, Library of, **1980–81:** 1933
Congress, National Committee for an Effective, **1978:** 770
Congressional Black Caucus, **1977:** 1568, 1661, 1938, 2005; **1978:** 319, 1230, 1678, 1679; **1979:** 911; **1980–81:** 1110, 1580, 1927, 1947
Congressional Budget Office, **1977:** 1235; **1979:** 1609
Congressional Campaign Committee
  Democratic, **1980–81:** 1529
Congressional Coal Caucus, **1979:** 2280; **1978:** 898
Congressional Hispanic Caucus, **1979:** 1661; **1980–81:** 1835, 1848
Congressional Liaison, Office of, **1979:** 179
Congressional Medal of Honor, **1980–81:** 1379, 1565, 1708
Congressional Reports Elimination Act, **1980–81:** 2344
Congressional Space Medal of Honor Awards, **1978:** 1684
Congressional Steel Caucus, **1979:** 1018
Conlan, Thomas, **1977:** 529
Conley, Michael A., **1980–81:** 928
Conlin, Roxanne Barton, **1977:** 1613, 1614
Connally, John, **1979:** 744, 1147, 1767, 1996
Connecticut
  Administration briefing for community and civic leaders, **1980–81:** 334
  Democratic Party primary, **1980–81:** 538, 564
  Department of Education, **1980–81:** 1402
  Disaster declaration, **1979:** 1824
  Emergency declaration, **1978:** 302
  Governor Ella Grasso, **1978:** 1506, 1723, 1887, 1891; **1979:** 1632, 2024, 2157
    Campaign appearances with the President, **1980–81:** 2283, 2286
    Northeast corridor rail system, legislation support, **1980–81:** 1010
    Resignation, **1980–81:** 2771
    Ridesharing programs development, **1980–81:** 789
  State Planning Council on Radioactive Waste Management, member, **1980–81:** 303
  President's visits, **1978:** 1887, 1891; **1979:** 1630; **1980–81:** 2279, 2289
  SALT II treaty briefing for community and civic leaders by administration officials (Digest), **1979:** 2106

Connecticut — *continued*
  U.S. attorney, **1977:** 1059
  U.S. district judges, **1977:** 1211, 1212; **1978:** 329; **1979:** 1018, 1019, 2106, 2107
  U.S. marshal, **1977:** 745, 746
Connell, John, **1980–81:** 2859, 2870, 2873
Connell, Lawrence, Jr., **1977:** 1376, 1384; **1979:** 397, 402, 1221, 1223
Connelly, John F., **1978:** 1808
Conner, Doyle, **1980–81:** 2397
Conner, John T., **1979:** 1954
Conner, Robert Kenneth, **1978:** 890
Connolly, Brig. Gen. Joseph H., **1980–81:** 37
Connor, Joseph E., **1979:** 1670
Conrad, C. Carson, **1980–81:** 261
Conrad, Capt. Charles, Jr., **1978:** 1687
Conroy, Catherine, **1980–81:** 814
Conscience, Citizens Committee on, **1979:** 2041
Conservation
  Agricultural resources, **1979:** 1367, 1382; **1980–81:** 2468
  Alaska lands, **1980–81:** 2718, 2756
  Coastal resources, **1979:** 1362, 1373
  Energy.
    See Energy conservation.
  Environmental message, **1977:** 967
  Fish and wildlife, **1980–81:** 1958, 2716, 2765
  Natural resources, **1980–81:** 418, 590
  Soil and water, **1978:** 943, 944, 1043–1051
  200-mile fishery conservation zone, **1977:** 215, 388
  Water, **1977:** 287, 302, 487, 592, 593, 751, 754, 912, 916–988, 1862; **1979:** 150
  Whales, **1979:** 1359, 1435
Conservation Act, Emergency Energy, **1979:** 2085
Conservation Award of the Florida Wildlife Federation, Special, **1979:** 1604
Conservation Month, International Energy, **1979:** 1622
Conservation Voters, League of, **1978:** 302
Conservationist of the Year Award, **1979:** 443
Considine, Frank W., **1979:** 548n.
Constantino Brumidi Day (Proc. 4794), **1980–81:** 1834
Constitution Week
  (Proc. 4670), **1979:** 1297
  (Proc. 4773), **1980–81:** 1279
Constitutional Convention for balanced Federal budget, proposed, **1979:** 350, 562
Construction Coordinating Councils, **1980–81:** 1649
Construction industry
  Employment
    Appropriations legislation, **1979:** 1971
    Full employment, administration's goal, **1979:** 1869
    Private sector responsibilities for new job creation, **1979:** 1988

Construction industry — *continued*
  Employment — *continued*
    Unemployment rate reduction, **1979:** 1755, 1866, 1936, 1937, 1949, 1988, 2028, 2030, 2051
    Energy technologies development, job creation by, **1980–81:** 580
    Interest rates, effect on, **1979:** 1869, 1876, 1949, 2051; **1980–81:** 1114, 2053
    New energy technologies, job creation in, **1979:** 1868
    New home construction, **1979:** 1984, 2047
Consular Convention, China-U.S., **1980–81:** 1772, 1807, 3019
Consular relations and Consulates General agreement with China, **1979:** 211
Consultative Group on U.S.-Japan Economic Relations, **1979:** 1165
Consulting services, use by Federal Government, **1977:** 878
Consumer Advisory Council, **1977:** 1495
Consumer Affairs, United States Office of, **1978:** 1418, 2280; **1979:** 1765; **1980–81:** 83
Consumer Affairs Council, **1979:** 1763, 1766; **1980–81:** 2910
Consumer Cooperative Bank, National.
  See National Consumer Cooperative Bank.
Consumer Credit Protection Act amendments, **1977:** 1628
Consumer Education Week, National, **1980–81:** 621
Consumer Federation of America, **1980–81:** 293
Consumer interests
  Administration's accomplishments and goals, **1980–81:** 2961
  Agricultural products, prices, **1977:** 298
  Anti-inflation competition policy, **1979:** 234
  Boycotts, **1978:** 2224
  Consumer protection agency, proposed, **1977:** 162, 312, 573, 597, 893, 1048, 1396
  Credit control, **1980–81:** 639
  Educational programs, **1980–81:** 621
  Federal agency programs, **1980–81:** 1054–1057
  Federal Government, representation, **1978:** 789, 804; **1979:** 131; **1980–81:** 145
  Federal programs, **1979:** 1761, 1762, 1787
  Federal Trade Commission protection, **1980–81:** 562
  Meetings with the President:
    Advocates (Digest), **1980–81:** 1846
    Organization leaders (Digest), **1980–81:** 1014
    Representatives, **1977:** 194, 1826; **1978:** 148, 750
  Services information, **1980–81:** 146
  Special Assistant to the President for Consumer Affairs, **1977:** 162, 565, 575
  State of the Union, **1978:** 110

Consumer Price Index, **1978:** 1035, 1353, 1489; **1979:** 1739, 2052
  Cost-of-living increase measure, deficiency as, **1980–81:** 2901, 3010
  Impact of:
    Oil import conservation fee, **1980–81:** 1042
    Trucking industry deregulation, **1980–81:** 694
  Mention, **1980–81:** 917
  1979 and 1980 statistics, **1980–81:** 479, 555
  Statistics validity, **1980–81:** 2444
Consumer Product Safety Commission, **1979:** 1041, 1044, 1921; **1980–81:** 281, 2907
  Chairman, **1978:** 564, 1208
  Commissioners, **1977:** 195, 1407, 1945, 1966; **1978:** 84, 149
  Legislation, **1978:** 2001
  Member, **1978:** 1666, 1670
Consumers Opposed to Inflation in the Necessities, **1978:** 2279
Consumers Resources Handbook, **1980–81:** 1055
Conte, Repr. Silvio O., **1979:** 983
Continental Shelf, Outer, **1977:** 973; **1980–81:** 233
Contract Disputes Act, **1978:** 1922
Convention.
  See other part of title.
Conway, Jack T., **1979:** 1698
Conway, James V. P., **1979:** 972
Conway, Kiernan, **1980–81:** 1414, 1415n.
Conyers, Repr. John, Jr., **1978:** 1656, 1668
Cook, Frances D., **1980–81:** 1025, 1051
Cook, Henry G., **1980–81:** 926
Cook, Julian A., Jr., **1978:** 1345, 1346
Cook, Samuel Dubois, **1980–81:** 1332, 1337
Cook, Thomas H., Jr., **1980–81:** 492
Cook, Vern, **1978:** 1946
Cook County Democratic organization, **1978:** 979
Cook Islands, maritime boundary treaty with U.S., **1980–81:** 1625
Cooke, Goodwin, **1978:** 1562, 1572
Cooke, John W., **1979:** 631
Cooke, Terence Cardinal, **1977:** 1436; **1978:** 1400, 2059; **1980–81:** 1168
Cooks, Stoney, **1977:** 34; **1978:** 895
Cookware industry, porcelain-on-steel, **1980–81:** 2, 3, 97
Cooley's anemia, **1978:** 897
Cooley's Anemia, Tay-Sachs, and Genetic Diseases Act, National Sickle Cell Anemia, **1979:** 1705, 2106
Cooney, Joan Ganz, **1978:** 454; **1980–81:** 263
Coons, John E., **1979:** 1525
Cooper, Deani L., **1980–81:** 928
Cooper, Owen, **1977:** 1629, 1650
Cooper, Richard N., **1977:** 62, 86, 557, 943, 2089, 2162; **1978:** 1351; **1980–81:** 775
Coopersmith, Esther L., **1979:** 464, 1668, 1680
Coordinating Council on Juvenile Justice and Delinquency Prevention, **1980–81:** 1273

Coordinating Council for North American Affairs, **1979:** 640, 1133, 2223; **1980–81:** 1258

Copeland, Mr. Lammot duPont, **1977:** 2182

Copland, Aaron, **1980–81:** 2786

Copper industry, **1978:** 1804, 1805

Copyright Royalty Tribunal, **1977:** 1666, 1667, 1700, 1755

Corcoran, Thomas J., **1977:** 1977, 2006; **1978:** 231, 1467

Cordero, Andres Figueroa, **1977:** 1745

Cordova, Valdemar A., **1979:** 733, 787

Core, Jesse, **1978:** 1500

Corey, Paul A., **1978:** 794

Corless, Patrick J., **1980–81:** 928

Corley, Ernest L., **1978:** 952

Cormack, Allan McCleod, **1979:** 1962

Corman, Adam, **1979:** 1975

Corman, Repr. James C., **1977:** 892, 942, 1013, 2005, 2077; **1978:** 504, 512, 1452, 1733, 1947; **1980–81:** 1063, 1124, 1896, 2069
　China, People's Republic of, visit to, **1979:** 666
　Meeting with the President (Digest), **1979:** 1975
　National health plan support, **1979:** 1025, 1637
　Welfare reform legislation, passage leadership, **1979:** 1661, 2092

Corn, Robert K., **1978:** 1340

Corning, Peter E., **1977:** 1211, 1212, 1569

Cooper, L. Owen, Sr., **1978:** 217, 230

Corning Glass Factory, Sunderland, England, **1977:** 881

Corporate Fund for the Performing Arts at the Kennedy Center, **1977:** 987

Corporation.
　See other part of title.

Corporations
　Profits, **1979:** 473, 1943; **1980–81:** 110
　Voluntary wage and price guidelines.
　　See under Wages and prices.

Corporations for Innovative Development, **1980–81:** 77

Corps of Engineers, Army, **1978:** 895, 1044, 1045
　Alaska Natural Gas Transportation System, transfer of functions, **1979:** 594
　Budget deferral, **1977:** 495
　Dam safety inspection, **1977:** 1977, 2060, 2071
　Energy and water development programs, **1980–81:** 1983
　Environmental research and development activities, **1980–81:** 352
　Flood assessment, **1977:** 42
　Fuel oil management group, **1979:** 1631, 2057
　Hydroelectric power projects, **1979:** 793, 1510, 1511
　Mount St. Helens eruption, disaster assistance responsibilities, **1980–81:** 951, 953
　Water resource projects, review, **1977:** 208, 287, 454, 490, 500, 1135, 1329; **1980–81:** 88, 239

Corpus Christi, Tex., **1980–81:** 1725, 1848

Corr, Edwin Gharst, **1980–81:** 1711, 1715

Corrada, Baltasar, **1978:** 458, 934; **1979:** 1664; **1980–81:** 1835

Corrections, National Institute of, **1978:** 1249

Corrigan, Mairead, **1978:** 526

Cortines, Ramon C., **1980–81:** 1432

Corvino, Anthony, **1979:** 1468n.

Cory, Kenneth, **1978:** 1112

Cosby, Bill, **1978:** 1190

Cossiga, Francesco.
　See Italy, Prime Minister.

Costa Rica
　Ambassador to U.S., **1978:** 1070
　Cuban refugee assistance, **1980–81:** 682
　President Rodrigo Carazo Odio, **1978:** 1119, 1122, 1123; **1980–81:** 904, 2781
　President Daniel Oduber Quirós, **1977:** 1566, 1568
　Refugee conference, **1980–81:** 874
　U.S. Ambassador, **1977:** 806, 935, 943; **1980–81:** 900, 932

Costa Rican National Youth Symphony, **1978:** 1071

Costanza, Margaret (Midge), **1977:** 86, 1119, 1303, 1438; **1978:** 459, 464, 553, 771, 1335, 1336, 1358, 1443

Costle, Douglas M.
　See Environmental Protection Agency, Administrator; Regulatory Council, Chairman.

Costley, Cheryl I., **1979:** 1448

Cost-of-living allowances, Federal, **1978:** 1220

Cota-Robles, Eugene H., **1978:** 1760, 1773; **1979:** 46, 92

Cotter, Repr. William R., **1978:** 1889; **1979:** 956

Cottine, Bertram R., **1977:** 1541, 1569; **1978:** 231

Cotton, Alonza H., **1980–81:** 2999

Cotton, upland, program, **1977:** 279; **1978:** 1571; **1979:** 786; **1980–81:** 575, 2745

Cotton dust regulations, **1978:** 1061, 1072, 1074, 1674

Cottrell, William, **1977:** 882

Coughlin, Roy, **1979:** 2024

Coulson, Richard, **1977:** 1055

Coulter, Douglas, **1977:** 1667, 1700, 1755

Council.
　See other part of title.

Counties, National Association of, **1977:** 1794; **1979:** 1241, 1294; **1980–81:** 1846

Country music, White House luncheon for performers, **1979:** 1823

Country Music Association, **1978:** 769

Country Music Association Award, Special, **1979:** 898

Country Music Gala, **1979:** 1816

Country Music Month, **1977:** 1679, 1697; **1978:** 1653; **1979:** 1728; **1980–81:** 1927

Court.
See other part of title.
Courts, United States
Appointments and nominations.
See specific group under Appointments and
Nominations.
Appropriations, **1977:** 1409; **1980–81:** 2774, 2809
Committee on Selection of Federal Judicial
Officers, **1977:** 1009, 1528
Congressional veto of executive branch actions,
Ninth Circuit Court of Appeals ruling,
1980–81: 2835, 2836
Courts-martial manual amendments, **1980–81:**
493, 1626
Disadvantaged persons, treatment of, **1980–81:**
1753
District and circuit judges, additional appoint-
ments, **1978:** 1803
District of Columbia
Court of Appeals
Associate Judge, **1977:** 940, 944
Chief Judge, **1977:** 377, 1048
Superior Court, Associate Judges, **1977:** 465,
940, 1439; **1978:** 1533, 1572
U.S. District Court, Judge, **1977:** 380
Federal civil justice reform, **1980–81:** 303
Federal civil justice system, **1979:** 340
Federal district court organization, **1980–81:**
2241
Federal judge appointments, **1978:** 1803, 2174
Federal judgeships, merit selection, **1979:** 131,
171, 759
Federal magistrates, **1979:** 1849
Federal officers, selection, **1977:** 396, 1803; **1978:**
324, 335, 460, 465, 497, 524, 535, 838
Fifth Circuit Court of Appeals reorganization,
1980–81: 2237
Foreign intelligence activities, review, **1977:** 922,
928
Judges
Minority appointments, **1979:** 36, 131, 759,
772, 847, 885, 2138; **1980–81:** 223, 887,
1071, 1459, 1493, 1501, 1573, 1633, 1705,
1726, 1837, 1877, 1942, 1952, 2059, 2233,
2250, 2302, 2367, 2426, 2435, 2618, 2685,
2693
President's criteria for selection, **1980–81:**
2326
Reagan, Ronald, criteria for selection, **1980–**
81: 2197, 2543
Salaries, **1977:** 238, 318; **1980–81:** 467, 2863,
2871
Legislation, **1980–81:** 154
Reform legislation, **1980–81:** 2240
Supreme Court of the United States.
See Supreme Court of the United States.

Courts, United States — *continued*
U.S. attorneys
Alabama, **1977:** 1059, 1128, 1613, 1614
Alaska, **1977:** 1931, 1932
Arizona, **1977:** 642
Arkansas, **1977:** 2006, 2007
California, **1977:** 1613, 1614, 1755, 1796, 1967
Colorado, **1977:** 1211, 1212
Connecticut, **1977:** 1059
Delaware, **1977:** 746
Florida, **1977:** 1613, 1614
Georgia, **1977:** 1127, 1128, 1211, 1212
Guam, **1977:** 1827, 1931
Hawaii, **1978:** 899
Idaho, **1977:** 1569
Illinois, **1977:** 943, 1059, 1827, 1931
Indiana, **1977:** 1031, 1613, 1614
Iowa, **1977:** 1613, 1614
Kansas, **1977:** 1128
Kentucky, **1977:** 1059, 1222, 1266
Louisiana, **1977:** 1222, 1266, 1569; **1978:** 149
Maine, **1977:** 597
Maryland, **1978:** 935, 936
Massachusetts, **1977:** 1266, 1307
Michigan, **1977:** 1031, 1755
Mississippi, **1978:** 1222, 1223
Missouri, **1977:** 1163, 1164, 1650, 1651
Montana, **1977:** 1701
Nebraska, **1977:** 1650, 1651
Nevada, **1977:** 1931, 1932
New Hampshire, **1977:** 1266, 1307
New Jersey, **1977:** 1613
New Mexico, **1978:** 899
New York, **1977:** 965, 966, 1211, 1212, 1569;
1978: 771, 803, 1333
North Carolina, **1977:** 1127, 1128, 1211, 1213
Northern Mariana Islands, **1978:** 149, 150
North Dakota, **1977:** 883
Ohio, **1978:** 416, 457, 458
Oklahoma, **1977:** 1266, 1307, 1613, 1614, 1931
1932; **1978:** 231
Oregon, **1978:** 881, 882
Pennsylvania, **1977:** 2089, 2090; **1978:** 899,
1222, 1223
Rhode Island, **1978:** 1035, 1071
South Carolina, **1977:** 557, 558
South Dakota, **1977:** 746
Tennessee, **1977:** 373, 1086, 2037
Texas, **1977:** 883, 884, 1211, 1212, 1222, 1266
Utah, **1977:** 1569
Vermont, **1977:** 1266, 1307
Virgin Islands, **1978:** 899
Washington, **1977:** 883, 884, 1211, 1212
West Virginia, **1977:** 1163
Wisconsin, **1977:** 707; **1978:** 457, 458
Wyoming, **1977:** 1211, 1212
U.S. Circuit Judge Nominating Commission,
1977: 179, 815, 1010, 1053, 1055, 1127,
1242; **1978:** 910

Courts, United States — *continued*
  U.S. Circuit Judge Nominating Panel for the
      Eighth Circuit, members, **1978:** 734
  U.S. circuit judges
    1st circuit, **1977:** 1650, 1651
    3d circuit, **1977:** 1650, 1651
    4th circuit, **1978:** 1333, 1334
    5th circuit, **1977:** 1967
    6th circuit, **1977:** 1507, 1534, 1701
    8th circuit, **1978:** 1381
    9th circuit, **1977:** 1507, 1534
    10th circuit, **1977:** 1967
  U.S. Court of Claims
    Associate Judge, **1978:** 1218, 1222
    Chief Judge, **1978:** 457, 458
  U.S. Court of Military Appeals Nominating
      Commission, **1978:** 1038
  U.S. Customs Court, Chief Judge, **1977:** 372
  U.S. district judges
    Arkansas, **1977:** 1827, 1931; **1978:** 1458, 1459
    California, **1978:** 1407
    Canal Zone, **1978:** 1154, 1155
    Colorado, **1977:** 1967
    Connecticut, **1977:** 1211, 1212; **1978:** 329
    District of Columbia, **1977:** 1613, 1614; **1978:**
        571, 1572
    Florida, **1977:** 557, 558, 596, 2050, 2051; **1978:**
        1239
    Georgia, **1977:** 1222; **1978:** 1669, 1670
    Guam, **1978:** 711, 712
    Illinois, **1977:** 1307; **1978:** 1407
    Iowa, **1978:** 1670
    Kentucky, **1977:** 1507, 1700, 1701
    Louisiana, **1977:** 1307, 1967; **1978:** 231, 771,
        803
    Massachusetts, **1977:** 2050, 2051; **1978:** 231
    Michigan, **1978:** 1345, 1346
    Minnesota, **1977:** 1438, 1439
    Missouri, **1977:** 372, 1127, 1128, 1163, 1164
    Nevada, **1978:** 1346
    New Hampshire, **1978:** 935, 936
    New Mexico, **1978:** 1034
    New York, **1977:** 1483, 1484, 1826, 1827; **1978:**
        329, 330, 711, 712, 898, 899
    Northern Mariana Islands, **1978:** 712, 750
    Pennsylvania, **1977:** 463, 1132, 2050, 2051;
        1978: 231, 571, 711, 712, 1010, 1071, 1072,
        1381
    Rhode Island, **1977:** 807
    Tennessee, **1978:** 1381
    Texas, **1977:** 944
    Utah, **1978:** 1485
    Virgin Islands, **1978:** 149
    Washington, **1978:** 149, 150
  U.S. district judges, merit selection, **1978:** 1975
  U.S. marshals
    Alabama, **1977:** 1569, 1755; **1978:** 1407
    Arizona, **1977:** 1086

Courts, United States — *continued*
  U.S. marshals — *continued*
    Arkansas, **1977:** 2089, 2090; **1978:** 230, 232
    California, **1977:** 1613, 1614, 2090; **1978:** 711,
        712
    Colorado, **1977:** 1613
    Connecticut, **1977:** 745, 746
    Delaware, **1978:** 711, 712
    District of Columbia, **1977:** 707
    Florida, **1977:** 1128, 1437, 1438
    Georgia, **1977:** 1059, 1507, 1534; **1978:** 416
    Guam, **1977:** 1437, 1438
    Hawaii, **1977:** 1211, 1212
    Idaho, **1977:** 1569
    Illinois, **1977:** 883, 884, 1384, 1755
    Indiana, **1977:** 1163, 1931, 1932
    Iowa, **1977:** 1796; **1978:** 416
    Kansas, **1977:** 1437, 1438
    Kentucky, **1977:** 943, 1163
    Louisiana, **1978:** 329, 330
    Maine, **1977:** 1650, 1651
    Massachusetts, **1977:** 1437, 1438
    Michigan, **1978:** 1111, 1346
    Minnesota, **1977:** 1266, 1307
    Mississippi, **1977:** 2037, 2038; **1978:** 1572
    Missouri, **1977:** 1128, 1483, 1484
    Montana, **1977:** 1308
    Nevada, **1977:** 1483, 1484
    New Hampshire, **1977:** 1384
    New Mexico, **1977:** 1222, 1266
    New York, **1977:** 1384, 1437, 1438; **1978:** 1072,
        1222, 1223
    North Carolina, **1977:** 1384, 1796, 2050, 2051
    North Dakota, **1977:** 883
    Northern Mariana Islands, **1979:** 149, 150
    Ohio, **1977:** 1569, 2130, 2131
    Oklahoma, **1977:** 1437, 1438, 1569, 2089, 2090;
        1978: 231
    Oregon, **1977:** 1437, 1438
    Pennsylvania, **1977:** 1438, 1439, 1483, 1484
    South Carolina, **1977:** 596
    South Dakota, **1977:** 2050, 2051
    Tennessee, **1977:** 1266, 1307, 1650, 1651, 1931,
        1932
    Texas, **1977:** 883, 884, 943, 1222, 1266; **1978:**
        1222, 1223
    Utah, **1978:** 1407
    Vermont, **1977:** 1266, 1307
    Virginia, **1977:** 1483, 1484, 1755
    Washington, **1977:** 943, 1701
    West Virginia, **1977:** 1211, 1212, 1438, 1439
    Wisconsin, **1977:** 1569, 2077
    Wyoming, **1977:** 745, 746
  U.S. Tax Court, judge, **1978:** 481, 504
  U.S. Tax Court Nominating Commission, **1978:**
      1039, 1711
Cow Creek Band of the Umpqua Indian Tribe,
    1980–81: 980

[*References are to page numbers except as otherwise indicated*]

Cowan, Finis E., **1977:** 944
Cowan, Geoffrey, **1978:** 1426, 1458; **1979:** 46, 91
Cowley, R. Adams, **1978:** 1467
Cox, William Meredith, **1977:** 548, 558
Coyne, Marshall B., **1979:** 24
Crabb, Barbara B., **1979:** 1294, 1319
Craft, Chris, **1980–81:** 1693
Craig, Col. James C., **1979:** 710
Craig, James D., **1980–81:** 1404
Craig, John M., **1979:** 1679
Craig, Lois A., **1979:** 44, 92
Craig, Sara, **1977:** 1817; **1979:** 270
Cramer, Jim, **1978:** 1820
Crane, Repr. Philip M., **1978:** 460
Cranston, Sen. Alan, **1977:** 485, 586, 620, 1016,
     1583, 1794, 1965, 2181; **1978:** 575, 1333,
     1647, 1790, 1947, 1965; **1979:** 1040, 1875,
     2238, 2279
  Channel Islands Marine Sanctuary support,
     1980–81: 1857
  Lake Tahoe protection legislation sponsorship,
     1980–81: 1013
  Legislation passage leadership
    Adoption Assistance and Child Welfare Act,
       1980–81: 1124
    Alaska National Interest Lands Conservation
       Act, **1980–81:** 1548, 2756
    National Parks and Recreation Act Amend-
       ments, **1980–81:** 433
    Veteran's Rehabilitation and Education
       Amendments, **1980–81:** 2315
  Mention, **1980–81:** 539
Cranston, R. I., **1979:** 2059
Crawford, Edwin S., **1980–81:** 2882
Crawford, Francis Jay, **1978:** 1180
Crawford, Michael E., **1980–81:** 844
Crawford, Reva, **1979:** 1524
Craxi, Bettino, **1980–81:** 1241
Creal, James B., **1979:** 1007; **1980–81:** 1404
Credit controls
  Announcement remarks, **1980–81:** 477, 478
  Federal programs, **1980–81:** 479, 571, 2902
  Federal Reserve System authority, **1980–81:** 478,
     485, 497, 513, 571, 666, 961
  Investment exceptions, **1980–81:** 479, 485, 497,
     513, 662
  Mentions, **1980–81:** 761, 884, 2128, 2165, 2270
  Private investment, **1980–81:** 554, 571, 890
  Revocation, **1980–81:** 1282, 1283, 1637
Credit Union Administration, National.
  See National Credit Union Administration.
Creighton, Jack, **1980–81:** 2559
Creswell, Thomas J., **1980–81:** 1508
Cribbins, Joseph P., **1979:** 922, 927
Crichlow, Ernest, **1980–81:** 602
Crim, Alonzo A., **1978:** 896, 935
Crim, Bobby D., **1978:** 1936

Crime.
  See Law enforcement and crime.
Crime index, national, **1977:** 1976
Criminal Code, Federal, **1978:** 112, 837; **1979:** 146
Crinkley, Richmond, **1980–81:** 2871
Crisp, Mary, **1978:** 1134
Critical energy facility program (EO 12129), **1979:**
     614
Crocetti, Annemarie F., **1979:** 762
Cronin, James W., **1980–81:** 2740
Cronkite, Walter, **1977:** 166, 291, 2013; **1978:** 2275;
     1979: 410n.; **1980–81:** 2924
Crosby, Bing, **1977:** 1794; **1979:** 2098
Crosby, Elizabeth C., **1980–81:** 82n.
Crosby, Oliver S., **1977:** 1791, 1796
Crosland, Anthony, **1977:** 251
Cross, Sam Y., Jr., **1977:** 967, 1030
Crossley, Mary A., **1980–81:** 930
Crotts, Marcus B., **1980–81:** 941, 967
Crouch, Andrae, **1979:** 1015; **1980–81:** 1404
Crowley, Dave, **1980–81:** 2560
Crowley, John J., Jr., **1980–81:** 1108, 1111
Crowley, Steven J., **1979:** 2150, 2186, 2187
Crown Central Petroleum, **1980–81:** 581
Crude oil equalization tax, **1978:** 968
Crude Oil Windfall Profit Tax Act
  Budget 1981, sole revenue proposal in, **1980–81:**
     227
  Congressional consideration
    House of Representatives approval **1980–81:**
       470
    House-Senate Conference Committee, **1980–
       81:** 117, 128, 251, 279, 368, 400
    Mentions, **1980–81:** 71, 75, 121, 225
    Senate approval, **1980–81:** 542
  Human resource service revenues, possibility of,
     1980–81: 1356
  Mentions, **1980–81:** 788, 804, 1318, 1365, 1373
  National energy policy, relationship with, **1980–
     81:** 279, 480, 579, 888, 1083
  Purposes, **1980–81:** 1117, 2191, 2210
  Reagan, Ronald, position on, **1980–81:** 1865,
     1886, 2045, 2142, 2221, 2261, 2307, 2493
  Revenues allocation proposal, letter to congres-
     sional leaders, **1980–81:** 1287
  Signing ceremony, **1980–81:** 584
  See also Energy Security Trust Fund.
Cruikshank, Nelson H., **1977:** 1066, 1085, 2155;
     1978: 702, 711, 819, 933, 1062, 1066, 1067,
     1793; **1979:** 1633, 1635, 2081; **1980–81:**
     534
Cruise missile, **1977:** 95, 96, 348, 538, 540–542,
     1017, 1043, 1197, 1199, 1313; **1978:** 123,
     533; **1979:** 155, 156, 695, 2235
  Effectiveness comparison with B–1, **1980–81:**
     348, 1309, 1551 1870
  Features, **1980–81:** 2213

Cruise missile — *continued*
  Long range development program, **1980–81:**
      1309, 1535, 1552, 1725, 1740, 1871, 1909,
      2126, 2336, 2415, 2639
Crum, Tom, **1980–81:** 1386, 1388n.
Crutchfield, Charles H., **1977:** 195
Cruz, Miriam I., **1978:** 1134
Cruz Velez, David F., **1979:** 2191
Cuadra, Carlos, A., **1979:** 2277, 2281
Cuba
  Africa, involvement in, **1977:** 2011; **1978:** 903,
      904, 907, 940, 941, 972, 977, 979, 1013,
      1056, 1092, 1094, 1275; **1980–81:** 94, 108,
      111, 674
  Embargo regulations, **1978:** 1505
  Fishery agreement, **1977:** 886
  Guantanamo Naval Base, **1979:** 1890; **1980–81:**
      1073
  Latin America, influence in, **1980–81:** 1017,
      1216, 1712
  Maritime boundary treaty with U.S., **1979:** 86
  Nicaraguan conflict, influence on, **1979:** 1307,
      1308
  Premier Fidel Castro.
      See Cuba, Premier.
  Prisoner exchanges, **1978:** 1600
  Refugees.
      See Cuban refugees.
  Soviet combat troops presence, **1980–81:** 2594
      Address to the Nation, **1979:** 1802
      Meetings with the President (Digest)
          Advisory panel, **1979:** 1823
          Congressmen, **1979:** 1705
          National Security Council, **1979:** 1704
      Mention, **1979:** 1707
      Remarks to reporters, **1979:** 1602
      SALT II treaty, effect on, **1979:** 1756, 1836
      Secretary of State's statement, **1979:** 1589,
          1714
      Status quo unacceptable to U.S., **1979:** 1714,
          1754, 1756
  Soviet MIG–23's, **1978:** 2176
  Soviet Union, relationship with, **1979:** 1754,
      1943; **1980–81:** 93, 625, 642, 674, 876,
      1007, 1105
  Travel restrictions on American citizens, remov-
      al, **1977:** 340
  United Nations Mission, bombing of, **1979:** 2231
  U.S. blockade, President's opposition to, **1980–
      81:** 94
  U.S. policy, **1977:** 173, 222, 293, 614, 647, 946,
      1043, 1046, 1112, 1388, 1409; **1979:** 240
  U.S.-Soviet relations, effect on, **1979:** 316, 1092,
      1943
  U.S. trade restrictions, **1979:** 1656, 2292, 2295
Cuba, Premier (Fidel Castro), **1977:** 1046, 1389;
      1978: 1092; **1979:** 1804, 1890, 1943
  Mention, **1980–81:** 873

Cuba, Premier — *continued*
  Refugee evacuation actions, **1980–81:** 780, 834,
      912–915, 989, 999, 1053, 1072, 1314, 1944
Cuban refugees
  Census statistics, **1980–81:** 2812
  Indiantown Gap, Pa., disturbances at
      resettlement camp, **1980–81:** 1498
  International assistance, **1980–81:** 682, 874, 1165
  Mentions, **1980–81:** 964, 971
  Peruvian Embassy in Havana, asylum in, **1980–
      81:** 625, 647
  Presidential election, effect on, **1980–81:** 2693
  Reagan, Ronald, position on, **1980–81:** 2156
  U.S. assistance
      Administration's policy
          Announcement remarks, **1980–81:** 912
          News conferences (Checklist), **1980–81:** 934,
              1848
          White House statement, **1980–81:** 912
      Announcement to accept one-third of asylees,
          1980–81: 682
      Coast Guard and Navy patrols, **1980–81:**
          1880, 1989, 2154, 2211, 2383, 2393, 2458
      Congressional response, **1980–81:** 2156
      Criminals exclusion, **1980–81:** 1072
      Education legislation, **1980–81:** 2152, 2155,
          2382
      Federal emergency actions, **1980–81:** 819, 833
      Fort Chaffee, Ark., use as temporary housing
          site, **1980–81:** 849
      President's meetings with:
          Congressional Members, **1980–81:** 892, 931
          Florida delegation, **1980–81:** 845
      President's position on:
          Emergency assistance legislation, **1980–81:**
              2155
          Equitable treatment, **1980–81:** 1075, 1838,
              2210
          Immigration laws enforcement, **1980–81:**
              901, 904, 989, 990, 1072, 1314, 1838, 1989,
              2210, 2458
      Resettlement
          Cuban-American community efforts, **1980–
              81:** 1073, 2210
          Health and Human Services, Secretary of,
              duties, **1980–81:** 2729
          Private sector sponsorship, **1980–81:** 1880,
              2387
          Puerto Rico, **1980–81:** 1943, 2068, 2178
          Religious groups' efforts, **1980–81:** 2387
          State, Secretary of, duties, **1980–81:** 2183
          States with low unemployment rates, pref-
              erence for, **1980–81:** 2209, 2387, 2393
      Screening process, **1980–81:** 1075, 1091
      Transport boats, refusal to allow additional,
          1980–81: 999, 1031

Cuban refugees — *continued*
  U.S. assistance — *continued*
    U.S. Emergency Refugee and Migration As-
      sistance Fund allocations, **1980–81:** 1523,
      1945
    Vice President's statement, **1980–81:** 780
    White House statements, **1980–81:** 1053
Cudahy, Richard D., **1979:** 957
Culbreth, Jane, **1977:** 525
Cultural agreement with China, **1979:** 209
Cultural Organization, United Nations Education-
  al, Scientific and, **1980–81:** 2721
Culver, Sen. John C., **1977:** 1855; **1978:** 472, 2003,
  2187, 2199, 2202, 2204, 2209
  Comprehensive energy plan support, **1979:** 1479,
    1498
  Legislation passage leadership
    Alaska public lands, **1980–81:** 1548
    Small business, **1980–81:** 1509, 1839, 1841,
      1844, 2331
  Meeting with the President (Digest), **1979:** 956
  Mentions, **1979:** 1495, 1496, 1504, 2179
  President's assessment, **1979:** 1474, 1494
  President's efforts for 1980 reelection, **1979:** 804
  Regulatory reform legislation support, **1979:**
    2143, 2271
Cunningham, George W., **1979:** 2064, 2187
Cunningham, Neil L., **1978:** 968
Cuomo, Lt. Gov. Mario M., **1978:** 1932; **1980–81:**
  821, 1037n., 2807
Cupit, Danny E., **1977:** 816
Curran, Paul J., **1979:** 1954
Current, Gloster, **1979:** 319
Curry, Susanne Shutz, **1979:** 464
Curtis, Charles B., **1977:** 1381, 1384, 1436, 1585,
  1613; **1979:** 1879, 1977
Curtis, Kenneth M., **1977:** 86, 192, 734, 738, 942,
  1161, 1264, 1506, 1612, 1795, 2036, 2179,
  2223; **1978:** 156, 158, 224, 229, 234, 341,
  761, 803, 2198; **1979:** 1616, 1679
Customs Court Act, **1980–81:** 2185
Customs and Patent Appeals, United States Court
  of, **1980–81:** 866, 894
Customs Procedural Reform and Simplification
  Act, **1978:** 1705
Customs Service, United States.
  See United States Customs Service.
Customs Valuation Agreement amendments,
  1980–81: 94, 1247, 1463
Customs Valuation Code, **1980–81:** 2815
Cuthbertson, John W., **1980–81:** 927
Cutler, Eliot, **1978:** 337, 351
Cutler, Elliot R., **1979:** 733, 1294
Cutler, Henry, **1979:** 464
Cutler, Jonathan D., **1980–81:** 927
Cutler, Lloyd N., **1977:** 941, 1362; **1978:** 1235
  American hostages in Iran, release negotiations
    activities, **1980–81:** 3019

Cutler, Lloyd N. — *continued*
  Appointments to the staff of, **1979:** 1976, 1977
  Carter, Billy, activities with Libyan Government,
    involvement in, **1980–81:** 1406, 1467,
    1480, 1485, 1488, 1489, 2648
  Counsel to the President, appointment, **1979:**
    1448, 1454
  Meetings with the President (Digest), **1979:** 1785,
    2043, 2105, 2138, 2207; **1980–81:** 25, 64,
    104, 217, 268, 293, 374, 423, 493, 522, 563,
    720, 775, 825, 932, 967, 1014, 1112, 1662,
    1714, 1846, 1946, 2070, 2332, 2453, 2740
  News conference (Checklist), **1980–81:** 2333
  Official dealings between Federal employees and
    President's family, duties, **1980–81:** 1982
  Resignation, **1980–81:** 2750
  U.S. attorney Herman Sillas, Jr., investigation of,
    1980–81: 1346, 1412, 1661
  U.S. participation in 1980 Summer Olympics,
    meetings and news conference, **1980–81:**
    104, 107, 219
Cutler, Lynn G., **1977:** 1477; **1979:** 789, 794, 795n.,
  2276; **1980–81:** 1335
Cutler, M. Rupert, **1977:** 461, 465; **1978:** 1187, 2147
Cutler, Mitchell S., **1979:** 464
Cutler, Walter L., **1979:** 685, 733
Cutter, W. Bowman, **1978:** 1573, 1596, 2082–2084
Cuyahoga County, Ohio, **1979:** 1817
Cyprus
  Ambassador to U.S., **1979:** 1318
  Archbishop Makarios III, **1977:** 1409
  Conflict, **1977:** 638, 1137, 1500, 1501, 1928;
    1978: 121, 127, 361, 555, 1151, 1331, 1481,
    2103
  Conflict settlement
    Progress reports for negotiated solution, **1979:**
      191, 461, 997, 1301, 1738, 2162; **1980–81:**
      205, 382, 551, 947, 1397, 1923, 2739, 3020
    U.S. support of U.N. negotiating efforts, **1979:**
      648, 1332
  Democratic National Committee, remarks, **1978:**
    2197
  Interview remarks, **1978:** 2067
  Meeting with administration officials, **1977:** 1966
  Mention, **1979:** 357
  News conference remarks, **1978:** 1091, 1098,
    1327
  President Spyros Kyprianou, **1977:** 1501, 1754;
    1978: 1719; **1979:** 998, 2163; **1980–81:** 382
  President's personal emissary, **1977:** 77, 194, 638,
    1501, 1966; **1978:** 1110
  Taxation and fiscal evasion convention with
    U.S., **1980–81:** 925
  Turkey, relationship, **1978:** 1337, 1357, 1590,
    1636
  United Nations Peacekeeping Force, **1980–81:**
    205
  U.S. Ambassador, **1978:** 295, 304

Cyprus — *continued*
  U.S. policy, **1977:** 225, 847
Cystic Fibrosis Poster Child, National, **1977:** 1084;
  1980–81: 720
Cystic Fibrosis Week, National, **1980–81:** 1395
Czaplicki, Hilary, **1980–81:** 1851
Czechoslovakia
  Embargo regulations, **1978:** 1505; **1979:** 1657
  Iran, abstention from voting on sanctions
    against, **1980–81:** 39
  Soviet suppression of 1969 uprising, **1980–81:** 91
  U.S. Ambassador, **1979:** 383, 402; **1980–81:**
    1926, 1947

Dabney, Seth M., **1978:** 1878
Dade County, Fla., **1979:** 1817
Dairy Arrangement, International, **1979:** 2253,
  2255
Dalberth, Louis, **1978:** 1543
Dale, Clamma, **1980–81:** 2748
Daley, Richard J., **1978:** 980, 983; **1979:** 1934;
  1980–81: 2089
Daley, Mrs. Richard M., **1980–81:** 1110
Daley, Richard M., Jr., **1980–81:** 833, 1110
Daley, William M., **1978:** 709; **1979:** 1447
Dall, Bob, **1980–81:** 2560
Dallas, Tex., **1979:** 482
Dalley, George A., **1979:** 1395, 1398
Dalton, Gene, **1977:** 1084
Dalton, John, **1980–81:** 2807
Dalton, John H., **1977:** 591, 596; **1979:** 1034, 2216;
  1980–81: 268, 303
Daly, T. F. Gilroy, **1977:** 1211, 1212
Dam safety inspection, **1977:** 723, 1997, 2060, 2071,
  2076, 2078
Dambrell, Frank, **1980–81:** 1322
D'Amours, Repr. Norman E., **1978:** 366
  Civil service reform support, **1979:** 719
  Meeting with the President (Digest), **1979:** 1396
  Mention, **1979:** 699
  1974 election to House, **1979:** 713, 715
Damman, Lt. Gov. James L., **1977:** 1162
Dancy, John, **1979:** 985–987
Dansforth, Sen. John C., **1978:** 1530; **1980–81:** 303,
  823, 983
  Communication from the President, **1979:**
    2257n.
  Kampuchea, visit to, **1979:** 2036, 2044, 2110
  United Nations Pledging Conference on Refugee
    Relief, member, **1979:** 2085
Daniel, Alice, **1979:** 2038, 2044
Daniels, Charlie, **1980–81:** 1601
Daniels, Thomas, **1977:** 1059
Daniels, Wilbur, **1978:** 257
Danielson, Andrew W., **1977:** 883

Danielson, Repr. George E., **1978:** 784, 1644, 1855;
  1979: 1130
Danks, Dale, **1979:** 670
Danner, Patsy Ann, **1977:** 1070, 1085
Dantin, Maurice, **1978:** 1963
Danzansky, Joseph B., **1978:** 2050
Danzansky, Stephen I., **1979:** 2065
Darden, W. Boone, **1978:** 1467
Darling, Martha A., **1977:** 987
Darman, Morton H., **1978:** 454
D'Arms, John, **1980–81:** 1241
Daschbach, Richard J., **1977:** 1358, 1384, 1437
Daschle, Repr. Thomas A., **1980–81:** 1268, 1920,
  1921
Datsun Motor Co.
  See Nissan Motor Co.
Datt, John, **1980–81:** 334
Daudelin, Roland G., **1980–81:** 1508
Davenport, Chester, **1977:** 84, 148
Davenport, Iowa, **1979:** 1478, 1479
Davenport, Joan M., **1977:** 535, 557
Davidson, Evelyn T., **1978:** 325, 329
Davidson, Ira, **1980–81:** 892
Davidson, Michael, **1980–81:** 2647
Davies, Don, **1979:** 1727
Davies, Joseph J., Jr., **1980–81:** 1335, 1336
Davies, Nicholas E., **1978:** 275, 303
Davin, Frances M., **1979:** 1023
Davis, A. Arthur, **1978:** 734
Davis, Allen Clayton, **1980–81:** 983, 1015
Davis, Ann M., **1978:** 1836
Davis, Anselm G., Jr., **1979:** 1439
Davis, Arthur, **1980–81:** 821
Davis, Lt. Gen. Benjamin O., **1977:** 1178, 1179,
  1527, 1533
Davis, Gen. Benjamin O., Jr., **1978:** 2089
Davis, Calif., **1979:** 1452
Davis, Edward B., **1979:** 1423
Davis, F. Tread, Jr., **1977:** 1612; **1980–81:** 2613
Davis, Mr. and Mrs. G. C., Jr., **1978:** 2270
Davis, Jefferson F., **1978:** 1786
Davis, Jeffrey W., **1980–81:** 926
Davis, Lewis, **1977:** 1780, 1796
Davis, Marjorie Fry, **1980–81:** 1935
Davis, Paul W., **1980–81:** 926
Davis, Richard J., **1979:** 637n.
Davis, Russell, **1977:** 1315
Davis, Ruth M., **1979:** 1653, 1882
Davis, Timothy S., **1977:** 1713
Davis, Tom, **1977:** 508
Davis, W. Jack, **1977:** 1506
Davis, Walter G., **1977:** 941
Davis-Bacon Act, **1979:** 1870
  President's support, **1980–81:** 582, 859, 1650,
    1883, 1885
  Reagan, Ronald, position on, **1980–81:** 2306,
    2473
Dawber, Pam, **1980–81:** 1404

Dawidowicz, Lucy S., **1978:** 1973
Dawson, Horace G., Jr., **1979:** 1616, 1679
Day, Clarence C., **1979:** 464
Day, Grace, **1980–81:** 1661n.
Day, James V., **1979:** 1395, 1398
Day, Roger, **1980–81:** 2561
Day care programs, **1977:** 164; **1979:** 1903
Dayan, Moshe, **1977:** 1627, 1728, 1729, 1754, 1755,
    1936; **1978:** 46, 305, 328, 779, 1506, 1516,
    1655, 1662, 1750, 1759, 1771, 1832, 2241
  Camp David agreements, first anniversary re-
    marks, **1979:** 1684, 1685
  Meetings in U.S. with Egyptian Foreign Minister
    Khalil, **1979:** 251, 263, 329
  Mention, **1979:** 1857
Days, Drew S., III.
  See Assistant Attorney General *under* Justice,
    Department of.
Days of Remembrance of Victims of the Holocaust
    (Proc. 4747), **1980–81:** 644
Dayton, Ky., **1977:** 208
Dayton, Ohio, **1980–81:** 2018, 2071
Dayton, Va., **1977:** 529
De Cossio, Felix, **1978:** 965
De Cuellar, Perez, **1977:** 639, 1501
De la Taille, Emmanuel, **1977:** 761
De la Torre Pinkard, Mary, **1980–81:** 3000
De Frantz, Anita, **1978:** 2036
De Freitas, Sir Geoffrey, **1977:** 1163
De la Garza, Repr. E., **1978:** 1696; **1980–81:** 1835,
    1938, 1946
De Guiringaud, Louis, **1978:** 27
De Havilland, Olivia, **1977:** 2042
De Herrera, Laura, **1978:** 1134
De Laboulaye, Francois, **1977:** 2050
De Larosière, Jacques, **1980–81:** 1974n.
De Saint Phalle, Thibaut, **1977:** 1975, 2006
De Varona, Donna, **1978:** 1134; **1979:** 1678
De Vos, Peter Jon, **1980–81:** 1411, 1428
Dealaman, Doris W., **1979:** 886
Dean, Alan L., **1979:** 1670
Dean, David, **1978:** 2003
Dean, James Porter, **1980–81:** 1405
Dean, John Gunther, **1978:** 1513, 1572
Dean, Jonathan, **1978:** 1516; **1979:** 110, 179
Dean, Paul R., **1979:** 271
DeAnda, James, **1979:** 294
Debevoise, Dickinson Richards, **1979:** 1786, 1787
Debris Commission, California, **1980–81:** 237
DeBrun, Anton A., **1980–81:** 2611
DeButts, John D., **1977:** 2106; **1978:** 850, 2238,
    2239; **1980–81:** 1718, 1848, 2074n., 2726,
    2727, 2870, 2874
Dechant, Tony T., **1977:** 595; **1978:** 454
Decio, Arthur C., **1978:** 696; **1980–81:** 2559
Decisive, **1977:** 604
DeConcini, Sen. Dennis, **1977:** 1754; **1978:** 504,
    526, 717, 1926; **1979:** 432, 1849, 2257n.;
    1980–81: 2241, 2381

Deep Seabed Hard Mineral Resources Act, **1980–
    81:** 1284
Deer, Ada E., **1977:** 941
Dees, Maureen, **1977:** 2024, 2037; **1978:** 252, 277
Defense, Department of
  Adviser to the Secretary and Deputy Secretary
    of Defense for NATO Affairs, **1977:** 2068
  Appropriation authorization bill, **1977:** 1693;
    1978: 1438, 1439, 1443, 1447, 1501;
    1980–81: 1667
  Assistant Secretaries, **1977:** 151, 195, 246, 247,
    253, 549, 558, 689, 706, 707, 745, 863,
    1665; **1979:** 269, 294, 1036, 1043, 1678;
    1980–81: 267, 1093, 1111
  Budget
    Cuts due to increased efficiency, **1979:** 1904
    Deferrals and rescissions, **1977:** 352, 931, 1286,
      1357, 2002; **1978:** 2095; **1979:** 200, 603;
      1980–81: 948, 1129, 1440, 2764, 2916
  Consumer Affairs Council membership, **1979:**
    1763
  Contractors indemnification regulations, **1979:**
    1132
  Cuban refugee assistance, **1980–81:** 819, 850
  Defense Research and Engineering, Director,
    1977: 368, 465
  Deputy Assistant Secretary, **1977:** 1823, 1931;
    1978: 2281; **1979:** 1596
  Deputy Secretary, **1977:** 31, 124, 125, 508, 1436,
    1437, 2036, 2089, 2129; **1978:** 239, 1158;
    1979: 906, 1290, 1305, 1319; **1980–81:**
    775, 1740
  Dioxin exposure, health effects study, **1980–81:** 4
  Draft registration for women, consultations with
    the President, **1980–81:** 243
  Earthquake assistance to Italy, **1980–81:** 2746
  Economic adjustment programs, **1978:** 593–595
  Energy crisis, **1977:** 36
  Environmental damage response activities,
    1980–81: 3045
  Export policy, **1978:** 1633
  Gasohol use in motor vehicles, **1980–81:** 2860
  Gasoline allocations for military operations,
    1979: 875
  General Counsel, **1977:** 549, 558; **1978:** 1223;
    1979: 2165, 2187
  Health care programs, **1980–81:** 1251
  Indiantown Gap, Pa., disturbances, investigation
    of, **1980–81:** 1498
  Integrated pest management programs, **1979:**
    1383
  Intelligence activities, **1978:** 202
  Iran, military equipment export suspension,
    1980–81: 717
  Labor-Management Relations Program exemp-
    tions, **1979:** 2146
  Land-based missiles development, **1979:** 696
  Land remote-sensing activities, **1979:** 2150

Defense, Department of — *continued*
    Mention, **1980–81:** 243
    Military Award Program, **1978:** 1345; **1979:** 363;
        1980–81: 474, 2921
    Military installations placement decisions, **1979:**
        906; **1980–81:** 880
    1981 budget
        Allocations recommendations, **1979:** 1629
        Allocations reduction, **1980–81:** 477, 568
    Nuclear arms control responsibilities, **1980–81:**
        451
    Physician shortage, **1980–81:** 456
    Policy Review Director, **1978:** 2056
    President's visit, question-and-answer session,
        1977: 259
    Radiation Policy Council membership, **1980–81:**
        363
    Research Apprenticeship Program, **1979:** 2064
    Sikes Act activities, **1978:** 1250
    Solar energy projects, **1979:** 1100, 1104
    Space program functions, **1978:** 1137
    Special Discharges Review Program, **1977:** 1757,
        1758
    Steel purchases, **1977:** 1435
    Synthetic fuels production responsibilities,
        1980–81: 1972
    Tahoe Federal Coordinating Council member-
        ship, **1980–81:** 2235, 2236
    Task Force on Global Resources and Environ-
        ment, functions, **1980–81:** 1417
    Transfer of certain programs to proposed Energy
        Department, **1977:** 258
    Under Secretary, **1977:** 1824, 1931; **1978:** 1265,
        1279, 1722, 2201, 2209; **1979:** 1774, 1786;
        1980–81: 2195
    Urban noise abatement programs, **1979:** 1371,
        1385
    Urban programs, **1978:** 580, 584
    University research and development programs,
        1979: 543
    Veterans health care legislation, veto recommen-
        dation, **1980–81:** 1563, 1577
    Veterans programs, **1978:**, 1737, 1743
    Weather programs, **1979:** 2150
    See also specific constituent agencies.
Defense, Secretary of (Harold Brown), **1977:** 9, 13,
        85, 86, 248, 259–262, 267, 268, 288, 378,
        476, 508, 553, 556, 557, 596, 641, 662, 743,
        750, 853, 882, 942, 1029, 1030, 1058, 1162,
        1306, 1405, 1436, 1437, 1464, 1465, 1506,
        1532, 1649, 1665, 1749, 1761, 1825, 1884,
        1935, 1963, 1965, 1966, 1983, 2036, 2050,
        2076, 2093, 2129; **1978:** 65, 148, 229, 239,
        302, 355, 415, 456, 530, 534, 570, 596, 749,
        802, 803, 809, 892, 899, 934, 1020, 1034,
        1038, 1039, 1071, 1110, 1130, 1154, 1160,
        1218, 1222, 1278, 1333, 1379, 1380, 1406,

Defense, Secretary of — *continued*
        1457, 1484, 1506, 1516, 1648, 1655, 1668,
        1669, 1722, 1723, 1772, 1879, 2059, 2089,
        2147, 2187, 2270
    Armed Forces benefits recommendations, **1980–**
        81: 969, 972
    Armed Forces physical fitness standards, **1980–**
        81: 262
    Arms export control functions, **1980–81:** 697
    Civil defense programs support for Federal
        Emergency Management Agency, **1979:**
        1279
    Computerized legal research system establish-
        ment, **1979:** 1266
    Courts-martial manual amendments, **1980–81:**
        1627
    Cruise missile development decision, **1980–81:**
        1552
    Defense spending increases recommendations,
        1980–81: 985, 1740
    Draft registration support, **1979:** 249
    Enlistment limitation waivers, **1980–81:** 1668
    Five-year defense program, presentation to Con-
        gress, **1979:** 1630, 2256
    Foreign assistance functions (EO 12163), **1979:**
        1794, 1798
    Foreign policy role, **1980–81:** 876, 2135, 2171
    Government contracts decisions, **1979:** 922
    Interagency Savings Bonds Committee, Chair-
        man, **1979:** 2285
    Iraq-Iran conflict, consultations with the Pres-
        ident, **1980–81:** 1890, 1900, 1902, 1906
    Meetings with the President (Digest), **1979:** 26,
        89, 179, 217, 240, 327, 377, 400, 468, 554,
        618, 732, 787, 842, 957, 983, 1018, 1142,
        1293, 1319, 1397, 1422, 1454, 1604, 1679,
        1705, 1785, 1824, 1882, 2043, 2106, 2139,
        2187, 2207, 2248, 2280; **1980–81:** 25, 104,
        217, 268, 293, 334, 374, 423, 452, 493, 522,
        563, 653, 720, 775, 825, 891, 932, 1013,
        1014, 1050, 1111, 1150, 1376, 1428, 1469,
        1523, 1564, 1598, 1662, 1714, 1846, 1945,
        2070, 2332, 2453, 2726, 2740, 2782, 2823,
        2857, 3049
    Membership on:
        Oil Policy Committee, **1980–81:** 10
        Trade Policy Committee, **1980–81:** 8
    Mentions, **1979:** 831, 902, 1024, 1079, 1155,
        1516; **1980–81:** 90
    Middle East, visit to, **1979:** 302, 312, 350
    Military awards program report, **1980–81:** 475
    Military installations location decisions, **1980–**
        81: 880
    MX missile system basing recommendation,
        1979: 1600, 1605
    National trails designation, **1979:** 1366, 1382
    News conferences (Checklist), **1979:** 843

Defense, Secretary of — *continued*
  Nimitz Battle Group return to U.S., ceremonies attendance, **1980–81:** 976
  Nuclear arms race with Soviet Union, financial cost estimate, **1980–81:** 2249
  Nuclear attack, strategy planning for, **1980–81:** 1553
  Panama Canal functions, **1980–81:** 538, 973–975
  Panama Canal regulations responsibilities (EO 12173), **1979:** 2175
  Permanent American cemetery in Panama responsibilities, **1979:** 82
  Presidential Medal of Freedom recipient, **1980–81:** 2923
  Rapid deployment forces, improvement actions, **1979:** 1804
  SALT II treaty verification statement, **1979:** 749
  Security assistance programs administration (EO 12118), **1979:** 225
  Stealth bomber classification, **1980–81:** 1687, 1688, 1770
  Submarine communications system decision, **1980–81:** 1997
  Synthetic fuels production responsibilities, **1980–81:** 1970, 1971
  Task Force on Global Resources and Environment, duties, **1980–81:** 1417
  Technology and strategic items transfer functions to Soviet Union, **1980–81:** 43, 184
  Titan missile site explosion in Arkansas, evaluation, **1980–81:** 1844
  Transition process, role in, **1980–81:** 2834
  Trident missiles sale, exchange of letters with British Secretary of State, **1980–81:** 1344n.
  United Kingdom-U.S. atomic energy agreement analysis, **1979:** 2164
  Urban noise abatement program development, **1979:** 1385
  Volunteer army, question-and-answer session on, **1980–81:** 1686
  For functions of the Department in general, see Defense, Department of.
Defense appropriation authorization bill.
  See under Defense, Department of.
Defense Civil Preparedness Agency, **1977:** 2062; **1978:** 1128, 1129, 1155; **1979:** 1278
Defense Intelligence Agency, **1978:** 203
Defense Meritorious Service Medal, **1977:** 1959
Defense Mobilization, Office of, **1979:** 1280
Defense and national security
  Administration's accomplishments and goals, **1977:** 2149; **1979:** 561, 719, 830; **1980–81:** 162, 673, 1551
  Arms transfer policy, **1977:** 882, 931
  Budget deferral and rescission, **1978:** 1041; **1980–81:** 2764

Defense and national security — *continued*
  Budget message, **1978:** 187
  Business Council, remarks, **1978:** 2236
  Chemical warfare, **1980–81:** 2021
  Chemical weapons reduction, **1979:** 1711
  Civil defense, **1977:** 540
  Defense spending, **1977:** 217, 222, 289, 389, 750, 1343, 2134; **1978:** 809, 1055, 1061, 1988, 2096, 2206, 2214, 2251
    Congressional reductions of President's budget proposals, **1979:** 1327, 1350
    Disadvantaged persons, effect on, **1979:** 176, 1990
    Gross national product percentage, **1980–81:** 1769, 1887, 2088, 2213, 2269, 2293, 2372
  Increases necessary for:
    Maintenance of world peace, **1979:** 1571, 1905, 1945, 2235
    Strengthening of alliances, **1979:** 116, 299, 695, 1350, 1612, 2018
  Legislation, **1980–81:** 1667
  1980 and 1981 fiscal year budgets, message to Congress, **1979:** 1628
  1981 budget allocations, **1980–81:** 165, 225, 228, 309, 571, 835, 1079, 1274
  1982 budget allocations, **1980–81:** 2893, 2897
  Percentage of gross national product, **1979:** 1904, 1945, 1990, 2018
  Policy comparison with Sen. Kennedy, **1980–81:** 737, 749
  Real rate increases, **1980–81:** 91, 116, 119, 248, 985, 993, 1534, 1554, 1652, 1659, 1682, 1725, 1740, 1742, 1764, 1769, 1871, 1885, 1887, 1893, 1902, 1910, 2011, 2026, 2043, 2088, 2093, 2120, 2125, 2150, 2213, 2261, 2269, 2274, 2292, 2303, 2336, 2373, 2388, 2399, 2405, 2410, 2415, 2421, 2442, 2445, 2471, 2531, 2582, 2597, 2599, 2606, 2624, 2630, 2638, 2668, 2674, 2680
  SALT II treaty passage, effect on, **1979:** 1327, 1350
  Soviet Union-U.S. comparison, **1979:** 176, 1904, 1945, 2018, 2234; **1980–81:** 347, 578, 659
  3-percent real growth in 1980 budget, **1979:** 98, 304, 1612, 1837, 1989, 2234, 2236
  Democratic National Committee, fundraising dinner remarks, **1978:** 1648
  Draft registration.
    See Draft registration *under* Selective Service System.
  Economic adjustment program, **1978:** 594, 595
  Five Year Defense Program, **1979:** 2235, 2236, 2256, 2268; **1980–81:** 197, 347
  Illinois State Legislature, remarks, **1978:** 988
  Intelligence activities, **1977:** 880, 921, 928
  Interview remarks, **1978:** 76, 2017, 2155
  Land remote-sensing activities, **1979:** 2149

Defense and national security — *continued*
  Mention, **1979:** 1485
  Military facilities, **1979:** 906
  MX missile system development, **1979:** 1600
  National Democratic Party Conference, remarks, **1978:** 2194
  National security information, **1979:** 170
  North Atlantic Council, meeting remarks, **1978:** 36
  North Atlantic Treaty Organization defense policy, **1978:** 1019
  Nuclear arms control, relationship with, **1980–81:** 2081
  Nuclear cooperation with European Atomic Energy Community (EO 12193), **1980–81:** 304
  Nuclear submarines, role, **1977:** 1036, 1037
  Oil emergency supplies, **1979:** 937
  Presidential war powers bill, **1977:** 2186, 2187
  President's campaign remarks, **1978:** 1388, 1577, 1581, 1798, 1861, 1867, 1886, 1890, 1939, 1948, 1953
  President's commitment to American strength, **1979:** 106, 155, 636, 1770, 1870, 1875, 2025, 2061; **1980–81:** 109, 541, 578, 874, 1350, 1364, 1562, 1725, 1761, 1855, 1899, 1902, 1995, 2011, 2030, 2043, 2150, 2269, 2388
  Reagan, Ronald, policy differences with the President, **1980–81:** 1662, 1869, 1892, 1909, 1910, 2012, 2037, 2049, 2088, 2126, 2132, 2151, 2201, 2214, 2225, 2249, 2274, 2305, 2324, 2422, 2440, 2446, 2465, 2480, 2498, 2545, 2549, 2555, 2582, 2624, 2643
  Science and technology development, **1979:** 541
  Security assistance programs, **1979:** 225
  State of Union, **1978:** 95, 122
  U.S. defense policy, **1979:** 2232
  Wake Forest University, address, **1978:** 531–535
  War powers resolution, **1977:** 324
  White House briefings for:
    Civic and community leaders, **1980–81:** 367, 452
    Congressional Members, **1980–81:** 333
  See also Armed Forces, United States; Arms and weapons systems.
Defense Policies and Arms Control, National Democratic Conference Workshop on, **1978:** 2198
Defense Program, Long-Term, **1978:** 1021, 1022; **1979:** 156, 1629, 2234, 2268
Defense spending.
  See under National defense and security.
Defense Transportation Day, National, **1979:** 238
Defense Transportation Day and National Transportation Week, National, **1978:** 255; **1980–81:** 506, 783, 930

Defense Transportation Day and Week, National, **1977:** 610
Defreitas, Roger A., **1980–81:** 927
Degnan, June Oppen, **1980–81:** 2871
Dehart, Opal, **1977:** 307
Del Bello, Alfred, **1980–81:** 2889
Del Tufo, Robert J., **1977:** 1613
Delahanty, Thomas Edward, II, **1980–81:** 375
DeLancey, W. J., **1978:** 1725
DeLancey, William, **1980–81:** 2071
Delaney, Gil, **1980–81:** 751n.
Delaney, Repr. James J., **1978:** 1808
Delaney, Patrick J., **1977:** 195, 1916
Delano, Robert B., **1980–81:** 334, 1447
DeLarosiere, Jacques, **1978:** 1629
Delaware
  Gasoline Dealers' Association strike, settlement, **1979:** 1294
  President's visit, **1978:** 385, 386
  U.S. attorney, **1977:** 746
  U.S. marshal, **1978:** 711, 712; **1979:** 1293, 1294
Delaware River Basin Commission, member, **1977:** 251, 2080
Delaware Valley, **1977:** 1794
Delbridge, Brig. Gen. Norman G., **1979:** 43, 91
Delhi Declaration, **1978:** 16, 17, 50
Delinquency Prevention, National Advisory Committee for Juvenile Justice and, **1980–81:** 1097
Dellums, Repr. Ronald V., **1977:** 1059, 1662
Delta Foundation, **1979:** 2276
Delta Queen, **1979:** 1455, 1467n., 1470n., 1471n., 1473, 1474n., 1476n., 1477n., 1491n., 1493n., 1494n., 1508n., 1513n.
DeLuca, John Britt, **1978:** 926
Deluca, John R., **1980–81:** 2609
Demetree, William C., **1978:** 2288
DeMille, Agnes, **1980–81:** 2786
Demirel, Süleyman, **1977:** 847, 869, 882, 1137; **1980–81:** 1398
Democratic Caucus, Asian/Pacific American, **1980–81:** 962
Democratic Congressional Campaign Committee, **1977:** 942; **1980–81:** 1529
Democratic Governors' Caucus, **1979:** 1222
Democratic-Farmer-Labor Party, **1978:** 1826, 1829, 1833
Democratic Mayors, National Conference of, **1978:** 570; **1979:** 1561n., 1973
Democratic National Committee
  Chairman, **1978:** 158, 234, 750, 803, 934, 1110, 1167, 1345, 1578, 1627, 1796, 1826, 1833, 1902, 1954, 2195; **1979:** 89, 376, 571, 966; **1980–81:** 1388, 1541, 1980, 2709; **1980–81:** 1388, 1541, 1980, 2709
  Chairman recommendation, **1977:** 2179, 2223
  Congressional campaign dinner, **1978:** 511; **1980–81:** 538

Democratic National Committee — *continued*
  Executive Committee, **1980–81:** 2806
  Executive Committee and State Chairpersons,
      White House briefing, **1978:** 2092
  Executive Finance Committee, remarks, **1977:** 86
  Finance chairman, **1980–81:** 2872
  Finance council, **1980–81:** 2872
  Fundraising dinners, **1977:** 1153, 1893; **1978:**
      1645; **1979:** 1766
  Fundraising events
    Beverly Hills, Calif., **1980–81:** 1887
    Blountville, Tenn., **1980–81:** 2124
    Boston, Mass., **1980–81:** 2247
    Chicago, Ill., **1980–81:** 2091
    Dallas, Tex., **1980–81:** 1393
    Hollywood, Fla., **1980–81:** 1362
    Houston, Tex., **1980–81:** 1738
    Jacksonville, Fla., **1980–81:** 1360n.
    Modesto, Calif., **1980–81:** 1319
    New Orleans, La., **1980–81:** 2404
    New York City, N.Y., **1980–81:** 2372
    1980 Victory Dinner, **1980–81:** 1977
    Orlando, Fla., **1980–81:** 2397
    Portola Valley, Calif., **1980–81:** 1302
    Robarbs, Ky., **1980–81:** 1388
    Secaucus, N.J., **1980–81:** 2275
  'Get Out the Vote' campaign remarks, **1978:**
      1733
  Max, Peter, donation of Statue of Liberty lith-
      ograph to raise funds, **1980–81:** 2069
  Meeting with the President in New York City,
      1980–81: 1541
  National Finance Council, remarks, **1977:** 734
  National Finance Council breakfast, remarks,
      1978: 2195
  Officials, meetings with the President, **1977:** 9,
      942, 1084, 1161, 1264, 1383, 1436, 1506,
      1612, 1795, 2036; **1978:** 229, 302, 504
  Platform Committee reception, **1980–81:** 1100
  Quarterly meeting remarks, **1977:** 1745
  Special meeting remarks, **1978:** 224
  Spring meeting, **1979:** 948, 958
  Treasurer, **1978:** 158, 1110
  Vice Chairman, **1980–81:** 1541, 1939
  White House receptions
    Executive Group, **1978:** 897
    Finance Council, **1978:** 327
    Members, **1978:** 1071
Democratic Party, **1977:** 147, 1201, 1746, 1896
  Administration's representation of party prin-
      ciples, **1980–81:** 985
  Bangor, Maine, remarks, **1978:** 350
  Campaign funding, **1980–81:** 1363
  Congressional campaign dinner, **1979:** 827;
      1980–81: 538
  Cook County Democratic dinner, remarks, **1978:**
      983, 985

Democratic Party — *continued*
  Dinners and receptions
    Bedford, N.H., **1979:** 714
    Chicago, Ill., **1979:** 1932
    Des Moines, Iowa, **1979:** 804
    Kennedys-King Day, **1979:** 1920
    Los Angeles, Calif., **1979:** 374
    Manchester, N.H., **1979:** 713
    Wausau, Wis., **1979:** 567
  Governors and mayors, meeting with the Pres-
      ident (Digest), **1980–81:** 2872
  Houston, Tex., fundraising dinner remarks,
      1978: 1168
  Interview remarks, **1978:** 2025, 2026
  Jefferson-Jackson Day Dinners
    Indianapolis, Ind., **1979:** 988, 989
    Milwaukee, Wis., **1979:** 573
    Richmond, Va., **1979:** 630
  National Federation of Democratic Women,
      White House reception, **1978:** 797
  New Governors, meeting with the President,
      1979: 376
  News conference remarks, **1978:** 2225
  President's assessment of political principles,
      1979: 2016, 2026; **1980–81:** 541, 542, 938,
      1045, 1304, 1363, 1381, 1388, 1394, 1464,
      1993, 2092, 2525
  President's campaign remarks, **1978:** 1389, 1550,
      1580, 1586, 1621, 1823
  President's commitment to reunify, **1980–81:**
      1024
  President's future role in, **1980–81:** 2706
  Role of the Party, **1978:** 1796, 1797, 1816, 1857,
      1861, 1870, 1899, 1934, 1951, 2189
  Southern Salute to the President Dinner, re-
      marks, **1978:** 156
  State chairmen
    Meetings with the President, **1978:** 1034, 1071;
        1979: 660, 1824, 2280
    White House reception, **1980–81:** 1043
  Support for the President, **1979:** 966
  See also Elections, 1980.
Democratic Party Conference, National, **1978:**
    2189, 2198, 2209, 2222, 2270
Democratic Study Group, **1978:** 286
Democrats of America, Young, **1979:** 1604
Dempsey, Charles L., **1979:** 365, 377
Dempsey, John, Jr., **1978:** 1891
Den Uyl, Johannes, **1977:** 882
Denali National Monument, **1978:** 2121
Deng Xiaoping.
    See China, People's Republic of, Vice Premier.
Denktash, Rauf R., **1977:** 144; **1979:** 998, 1301
Denmark
  Fishery agreement with U.S., **1979:** 1850
  Prime Minister Anker Henrik Jørgensen, **1977:**
      882; **1978:** 276, 389

Denmark — *continued*
    Taxation and fiscal evasion convention with
        U.S., **1980–81:** 1646
    U.S. Ambassador, **1978:** 1008, 1010
    Vice President's visit, **1979:** 221, 639
Dennenberg, Herb, **1980–81:** 2055
Dennin, Joseph F., **1977:** 1533
Dennis, Francis A., **1978:** 1117
Dent, Repr. John H., **1977:** 508, 1232, 1948; **1978:**
    1783
Denton, Harold R., **1979:** 579, 617, 618; **1980–81:**
    744, 1698
DeNunzio, Ralph D., **1978:** 506, 571
Denver, Colo., **1977:** 1861, 1884; **1979:** 183
    Air pollution, **1978:** 853
    Governors' Annual Prayer Breakfast, **1978:** 829
    Haskell, Sen. Floyd K., reception, **1978:** 827
    Leaders, meetings with the President, **1978:** 832,
        881, 882, 1111
    U.S. Mint at, **1979:** 2040, 2044
Denver, John, **1977:** 279; **1978:** 1511; **1980–81:**
    1386, 1388n.
Department.
    See other part of title.
Deposit Insurance Corporation, Federal, **1977:**
        1974, 2006; **1978:** 230, 564, 1059, 2058;
        1979: 91, 930
Depository institutions, regulatory authority, **1977:**
        662
Depository Institutions Deregulation and Mone-
        tary Control Act, **1980–81:** 572, 608
Depuy, Gen. William E., **1977:** 1178, 1179
Derby, Jack, **1979:** 2024
Derian, Patricia M., **1977:** 327, 746, 1085, 1131,
        1795; **1978:** 2188; **1979:** 2010
Derrick, Repr. Butler, **1977:** 1058; **1978:** 303, 2002;
        1979: 942; **1980–81:** 1755, 1762
Derwinski, Repr. Edward J., **1978:** 1318, 1513,
        1762, 1765, 1808; **1979:** 1125, 1777
Des Moines, Iowa, **1977:** 1853, 1855; **1979:** 789,
        804, 843, 2300
Des Pres, Terrence, **1980–81:** 821
Desai, Morarji, **1977:** 2122; **1978:** 2, 3, 11, 16, 42,
        43, 50, 264, 526, 1083, 1085, 1090, 1106;
        1979: 316, 560, 732, 851
Desha, Pilani C., **1978:** 1134
Design Liaison Council, **1980–81:** 3003
Desmond, Chris, **1977:** 895
Detroit, Mich., **1977:** 1829, 1841; **1979:** 1247, 1294,
        1817; **1980–81:** 1556, 2670
Deutch, John M., **1977:** 1585, 1613; **1978:** 950,
        1188; **1979:** 955, 983, 2148, 2204; **1980–
        81:** 335, 849
Developing countries
    Administration's accomplishments and goals,
        1980–81: 2633, 2992
    Aquaculture development, **1980–81:** 1938

Developing countries — *continued*
    Arms sales, **1977:** 539
    Bonn Economic Summit Conference, remarks,
        1978: 1309, 1313, 1314
    Customs Valuation Agreement, **1980–81:** 1463
    Decade of Development, **1980–81:** 561
    Economic relations, **1978:** 1314
    Economic Report, **1978:** 144
    Energy assistance programs, **1978:** 1313; **1980–
        81:** 440
    Environmental concerns, **1977:** 983
    Food Aid Convention, **1978:** 455
    Generalized System of Preferences, **1977:** 255,
        1346, 1671, 1950, 2181; **1978:** 421; **1979:**
        367, 2228; **1980–81:** 429, 549, 703, 1250,
        2911
    Industrialized countries role, **1980–81:** 1218
    Industrialized nations' responsibilities to pro-
        mote, **1979:** 1834
    International assistance, **1977:** 820, 826, 831
    International Chamber of Commerce, remarks,
        1978: 1691
    International health program, **1978:** 816
    Interview remarks, **1978:** 1601
    Nuclear power policy, **1977:** 584
    Oil price increases, impact on, **1980–81:** 1178,
        1186
    OPEC oil price increase, effect on, **1979:** 1191,
        1213
    OPEC oil supplies, **1980–81:** 1578
    State of the Union, **1978:** 119
    Third World debt, **1977:** 502
    United Nations programs, **1978:** 1541; **1980–81:**
        2391
    United Nations Representative Andrew Young,
        role, **1977:** 1108
    United States
        Assistance programs, **1977:** 455, 522; **1979:**
            279, 395, 642, 915, 1230; **1980–81:** 407,
            866, 942, 1207
        Foreign relations, **1980–81:** 579, 869, 870,
            1555, 2366, 2427
        Science and technology assistance programs,
            1979: 540, 680
        Strengthening of ties, **1979:** 355, 1200
        Trade relations, **1977:** 255, 761, 780, 798;
            1980–81: 2208, 2816
        World Bank loans, **1980–81:** 1973
    Venice Economic Summit statement, **1980–81:**
        1189
    West German assistance, **1980–81:** 439
    World Bank Group and International Monetary
        Fund, remarks, **1978:** 1629
    See also Foreign assistance.
Development, Corporations for Innovative, **1980–
        81:** 77
Development assistance programs, **1978:** 932

Development Cooperation Agency, United States International.
See United States International Development Cooperation Agency.
Development Coordination Committee, **1979:** 1796
Development Loan Committee, **1979:** 1796
Devich, Joseph, **1979:** 1468n.
Devine, Frank J., **1977:** 1539, 1568
Devine, Shane, **1977:** 815; **1978:** 935, 936
DeVita, Vincent T., Jr., **1980–81:** 1332
Dew, Bruce Gregory, **1980–81:** 948
DeWaele, Thomas W., **1978:** 968
Dewald, Gretta, **1978:** 1134
Di Bonna, Charles J., **1980–81:** 1405
Diabetes Foundation, Juvenile, **1980–81:** 1051
Diabetes Week, National, **1979:** 1671; **1980–81:** 1519
Diamond, Gustave, **1978:** 571
Diamond, Sidney A., **1979:** 196, 218, 1938, 2081
Diaz, Nelson A., **1977:** 987
Diaz, Patricia O'Reilly, **1979:** 464
Diaz Ordaz, Gustavo, **1979:** 809
Dickerman, Lola, **1977:** 1529
Dickey, James, **1980–81:** 502
Dickey, Robert, III, **1979:** 942
Dickey Lincoln Dam, **1978:** 347
Dickey-Lincoln School Lakes, Maine, **1977:** 208, 490
Dickman, Francois M., **1979:** 1446, 1455
Dickman, Steven G., **1980–81:** 928
Diehl, Mr. and Mrs. Woodward W., **1977:** 1930
Diesel fuel
  Allocations
    Farmers, **1979:** 803, 846, 937, 945, 951, 987, 1135, 1139, 1185, 1242
    Fishermen, **1979:** 846, 937
    Mass transit, **1979:** 1136
    Truckers, **1979:** 1135, 1139, 1185, 1242
  1978 farmers consumption, **1979:** 791
  Prices, **1979:** 1139
Diggs, Repr. Charles C., Jr., **1977:** 784, 785, 1632, 1938
Diggs, Ruth W., **1978:** 2070
Diggs-Taylor, Anna, **1979:** 900
Dik, Carolyn, **1977:** 815
Dille, Roland Paul, **1980–81:** 1332, 1337
Dillman, James J., **1978:** 1721, 1772; **1979:** 23, 46, 90
Dillon, Douglas, **1977:** 1781, 1796; **1979:** 269, 294
Dillon, George S., **1978:** 697
Dillon, Gerald R., **1980–81:** 1672, 1715
DiMaggio, Joe, **1980–81:** 2646
Dimbleby, David, **1977:** 760
Dingell, Repr. John D., **1977:** 7, 1063, 1082, 1092, 1103, 1396, 1978, 1980, 2016; **1978:** 710, 769, 1980, 1982, 2003, **1979:** 840, 2086; **1980–81:** 607, 761, 770
Dinits, Simcha, **1977:** 1127, 2037; **1978:** 2187

Dinneen, Gerald Paul, **1977:** 246, 253
Dion, Jerrold Mark, **1978:** 1406
Dioxin exposure, **1980–81:** 4
Diplomatic Conference on International Humanitarian Law in Armed Conflicts, **1977:** 276
Diplomatic corps, **1977:** 9
Diplomatic hostages, **1980–81:** 1171
Diplomatic Relations Act, **1978:** 1694
DiPrete, Andrew A., **1979:** 981, 984
Dirienzo, Anthony G., Jr., **1977:** 745, 746
Dirks, Leslie C., **1979:** 179
Dirksen, Sen. Everett M., **1978:** 784
Disability insurance system, **1979:** 138
Disability Insurance Trust Fund, **1979:** 1633
Disabled American Veterans, **1978:** 1808
Disabled persons.
  See Handicapped persons.
Disabled Persons, International Year of, **1980–81:** 809
Disabled Persons, National Planning Council for the International Year of, **1979:** 1678
Disabled Veterans Outreach Program, **1978:** 1740
Disadvantaged Business Utilization, Office of Small and, **1980–81:** 73
Disadvantaged Children, National Advisory Council on the Education of, **1979:** 1727; **1980–81:** 257, 1839
Disadvantaged persons
  Administration's accomplishments and goals, **1980–81:** 2944
  Defense budget allocations, effect on, **1979:** 1990
  Democratic Party commitments, **1980–81:** 1887
  Detroit, Mich., forum remarks, **1977:** 1830–1853
  Economic opportunities, **1979:** 1477; **1980–81:** 886
  Educational opportunities, **1979:** 1991
  Employment, **1977:** 1123
  Energy price increases, Federal assistance for, **1979:** 864, 953, 1240, 1244, 1255, 1457, 1485, 1571, 1594, 1632, 1639, 1642, 1746, 1858, 1878, 1900, 1928, 1984, 1993, 2039, 2056, 2057, 2154; **1980–81:** 64, 118, 137, 251, 279, 586, 1118, 1752, 2893, 2948
  Federal programs, **1980–81:** 909
  Food stamp program, **1980–81:** 830, 835
  Fuel bills, assistance, **1977:** 520
  Health coverage, **1979:** 1029, 1633
  Housing programs, **1977:** 136, 137, 310, 646
  Illiteracy correction programs, **1980–81:** 1933
  Inflation, effect on, **1980–81:** 498, 536, 555, 581
  Interview remarks, **1977:** 1343
  News conference remarks, **1977:** 1373
  1981 budget allocations, **1980–81:** 229, 568
  Project Head Start, **1980–81:** 463
  Volunteer service for, **1979:** 2238
  Welfare reform legislation, **1977:** 315; **1979:** 938; **1980–81:** 137

Disadvantaged persons — *continued*
  Youth employment.
    See Employment *under* Children and youth.
Disarmament, Committee on, **1980–81:** 204
Disarmament, Conference of the Committee on,
  1977: 833, 879
Disarmament, Socialist International Study Group
  on, **1979:** 898
Disarmament Agency, United States Arms Control
  and.
    See United States Arms Control and Disar-
      mament Agency.
Disaster assistance, **1978:** 306
  Alabama, **1979:** 1672, 1678; **1980–81:** 1422
  Arkansas, **1980–81:** 1345, 1421
  Foreign, **1980–81:** 943, 2746, 2755, 2804
    Yugoslavia, **1979:** 669
  Georgia, **1980–81:** 1422
  Illinois, **1980–81:** 1422
  Kansas, **1980–81:** 1345, 1421
  Kentucky, **1980–81:** 1422
  Louisiana, **1980–81:** 1345, 1421
  Mississippi, **1979:** 670, 672, 1674, 1678; **1980–81:**
    1422
  Missouri, **1980–81:** 1345, 1421
  Mount St. Helens, Wash., eruption, areas dam-
    aged by, **1980–81:** 950, 956
  Nebraska, **1980–81:** 1090
  Oklahoma, **1980–81:** 1345, 1421
  Tennessee, **1980–81:** 1422
  Texas, **1979:** 665; **1980–81:** 1345, 1421
Disaster Assistance Administration, Federal, **1977:**
  113, 488; **1978:** 1129; **1979:** 1278
Disaster assistance study, **1977:** 1497
Disaster declarations
  Alabama, **1977:** 640; **1978:** 1470; **1979:** 673;
    1980–81: 774
  American Samoa, **1979:** 2105
  Arizona, **1978:** 503, 2281; **1980–81:** 374
  Arkansas, **1978:** 1571; **1979:** 667, 673; **1980–81:**
    720
  California, **1978:** 328, 1771; **1979:** 1319, 2042;
    1980–81: 291, 374, 2070, 2753
  Connecticut, **1979:** 1824
  Florida, **1977:** 35, 85; **1979:** 898, 1675, 1678, 1823
  Georgia, **1977:** 1058, 2005
  Hawaii, **1979:** 402; **1980–81:** 292
  Idaho, **1980–81:** 967
  Illinois, **1979:** 786
  Indiana, **1978:** 640; **1979:** 1396
  Iowa, **1979:** 1222
  Kansas, **1977:** 1649; **1979:** 1043
  Kentucky, **1977:** 596; **1978:** 2269; **1979:** 1293
  Louisiana, **1977:** 805; **1978:** 898, 1571, 2187;
    1979: 787, 1785; **1980–81:** 653, 773, 967
  Maine, **1978:** 329
  Marshall Islands, **1979:** 293, 2205

Disaster declarations — *continued*
  Maryland, **1977:** 31; **1979:** 1679
  Massachusetts, **1978:** 303, 328, 334
  Michigan, **1980–81:** 932, 1714
  Minnesota, **1978:** 801, 1278; **1979:** 786
  Mississippi, **1979:** 731; **1980–81:** 774
  Missouri, **1977:** 881, 1612; **1980–81:** 931
  Montana, **1978:** 1034
  Nebraska, **1978:** 570; **1980–81:** 1050
  New Hampshire, **1978:** 329
  New Jersey, **1977:** 147
  New Mexico, **1979:** 217, 1159
  New York, **1977:** 146, 147; **1980–81:** 967
  North Carolina, **1977:** 2006; **1979:** 1823
  North Dakota, **1978:** 770; **1979:** 732
  Northern Mariana Islands, **1978:** 1458; **1980–81:**
    2753
  Oklahoma, **1979:** 673
  Pennsylvania, **1977:** 1306; **1980–81:** 1564
  Puerto Rico, **1979:** 1603
  Rhode Island, **1978:** 328, 334
  Tennessee, **1977:** 805, 2035; **1979:** 841
  Texas, **1978:** 1381; **1979:** 667, 732, 1043, 1396,
    1785; **1980–81:** 1544, 1946
  Virgin Islands, **1979:** 1704
  Virginia, **1977:** 596, 2035; **1979:** 1293, 1823
  Washington, **1977:** 2129; **1979:** 2300; **1980–81:**
    967
  West Virginia, **1977:** 596; **1978:** 2270; **1980–81:**
    1564
  Wisconsin, **1978:** 1278; **1980–81:** 1428
  Wyoming, **1978:** 1034; **1979:** 1293
  See also Emergency declarations.
Disaster Relief Act amendments, **1977:** 1134
Discount rate increase, **1978:** 1453, 1909
Discrimination
  Civil Rights Act enforcement, **1977:** 1293, 1345
  News conference remarks, **1977:** 1372
  Sex, **1977:** 1502–1505, 2156
Disease Control, Center for, **1979:** 2007, 2036;
  1980–81: 257
Dishart, Michael K., **1980–81:** 929
Disney, Walt, **1980–81:** 350
Dispute Resolution Act, **1980–81:** 303
Dispute Resolution Advisory Board, **1980–81:** 303
Distillate fuels, **1980–81:** 25
Distributive Education Clubs of America, **1978:**
  888
District of Columbia
  Administration anti-inflation briefing for black
    ministers (Digest), **1980–81:** 825
  Administration's accomplishments and goals,
    1980–81: 147, 2963
  Appropriations Act, **1978:** 1531
  Budget deferral, **1979:** 2285
  Congressional representation, **1978:** 1465, 1467

District of Columbia — *continued*
  Court of Appeals
    Associate Judge, **1977:** 940, 944; **1979:** 957
    Chief Judge, **1977:** 377, 1048
  D.C. General Hospital Commission Act, **1977:** 333
  Garnishment of moneys payable to employees, **1978:** 2274
  Home rule, **1978:** 321; **1979:** 1922
    Extension, **1977:** 162
  Housing revenue bonds, **1980–81:** 666
  Judicial nominating panel, **1977:** 1010, 1083
  Metrorail system, **1980–81:** 14, 18
  1978 budget, **1977:** 557
  1979 budget, **1978:** 640
  1980 budget, **1979:** 217
  1981 budget, **1980–81:** 292
  Retirement program, memorandum of disapproval, **1978:** 1961
  State of the Union, **1978:** 113
  Superior Court, Associate Judges, **1977:** 196, 465, 940, 1438, 1439; **1978:** 1533, 1572; **1979:** 46, 91, 665, 667, 980, 984, 1624, 2117; **1980–81:** 458, 1823, 1824, 1847, 2870, 2872
  U.S. attorney, **1979:** 1883
  U.S. circuit judges, **1979:** 733, 787, 957, 958, 983, 1517; **1980–81:** 654, 720
  U.S. district judges, **1977:** 380, 1613, 1614, 1750; **1978:** 571, 1572; **1979:** 93, 378, 402, 2207, 2208
  U.S. marshal, **1977:** 707
  Voting rights, **1980–81:** 224, 830
  Voting rights amendment, **1979:** 143, 144, 298, 1922
District of Columbia, Presidential Task Force on the, **1977:** 784, 1059, 1632, 1651
District of Columbia Commission on Judicial Disabilities and Tenure, **1980–81:** 392
District of Columbia Judicial Nominating Commission, **1980–81:** 1292
District of Columbia Law Revision Commission, **1979:** 2065; **1980–81:** 521
District of Columbia Retirement Reform Act, **1979:** 2144
District Court Organization Act, Federal, **1980–81:** 2241
District judges, U.S.
  See U.S. district judges *under* Appointments and Nominations.
Dixon, Alan J., **1978:** 999; **1980–81:** 1862, 1867
Dixon, Ortense, **1978:** 268, 269
Dixon, Paul Rand, **1977:** 60
Dixon, Sharon, **1979:** 1921
Dixon, William P., **1977:** 1377, 1384
Djerassi, Carl, **1979:** 448
Djibouti
  Refugee assistance, **1978:** 959

Djibouti — *continued*
  U.S. Ambassador, **1980–81:** 1025, 1051
Dobbins Air Force Base, Ga, **1977:** 599; **1978:** 153
Dobbs, Mattiwilda, **1978:** 1789
Dobelle, Edith Huntington Jones, **1978:** 1458
Dobelle, Evan S., **1977:** 101, 272; **1978:** 803, 1110, 1650
Dobry, Anthony, **1980–81:** 770, 771n.
Dobrynin, A. F., **1977:** 86, 100, 560, 603, 641, 1222, 1749, 2037; **1978:** 2267; **1979:** 356, 2008
Docking, Robert B., **1978:** 1813
Doctor of the Year, **1980–81:** 1468
Dodd, Christopher, **1980–81:** 2286
Dodd, Repr. Christopher J., **1978:** 1889
Dodd, Edwin D., **1978:** 1178
Dodson, Christine, **1980–81:** 218
Dogin, Henry S., **1978:** 1538, 1572; **1979:** 268, 294; **1980–81:** 288, 293
Dogoloff, Lee I., **1977:** 92, 148, 378, 1437; **1979:** 618
Doherty, Gerard, **1978:** 1723; **1980–81:** 1679, 1680
Dolan, Joseph, **1977:** 1211, 1212
Dolbeare, Cushing, **1980–81:** 2559
Dole, Sen. Robert, **1979:** 1312; **1980–81:** 2344
Dolland, Franklyn, **1977:** 2050
Dollar, U.S., value, **1978:** 438, 461, 497, 518, 653, 722, 1171, 1254, 1290, 1352, 1411, 1427, 1441, 1487, 1489, 1546, 1628, 1693, 1752, 1839, 1908, 1911, 1913, 1915, 1931, 1934, 1944, 1945, 1955, 2048, 2064, 2153, 2237
  Impact of:
    Energy prices, **1979:** 1183, 1307, 1310
    Inflation, **1979:** 1307, 1310
    International financial markets, **1980–81:** 254
    Trade Agreements Act, **1979:** 1312
    Trade imbalance, **1979:** 953, 1307, 1909
    U.S. export increases, **1980–81:** 254
  International appraisals, **1980–81:** 2262
  Mentions, **1979:** 113, 736, 935; **1980–81:** 499, 541, 558
  1979 rate of exchange statistics, **1980–81:** 400
  Stabilization measures, **1979:** 119, 160, 1840, 2031; **1980–81:** 254, 3005
Dolores, Colo., **1977:** 208
Dolores River, Colo., **1979:** 1813
Dolton, Ill., **1979:** 1940
Dolvin, Jasper, **1980–81:** 1744–1746
Dolvin, Sissy, **1980–81:** 1744
Dolvin, Lt. Gen. Welborn G., **1980–81:** 33
Dombalis, Constantine, **1980–81:** 821
Domenici, Sen. Pete V., **1977:** 1648; **1978:** 769, 933, 1827; **1980–81:** 761, 2106
  Communication from the President, 2257n.
  Legislation passage leadership
    Emergency Energy Conservation Act, **1979:** 2086, 2087
    Energy mobilization board, **1979:** 1819

Domenici, Sen. Peter V. — *continued*
  Legislation leadership — *continued*
    Energy security corporation, **1979:** 1877, 2092, 2102
    Synthetic fuels program, **1979:** 2092, 2102
    Meetings with the President (Digest), **1979:** 1705, 2104
Domestic Council, **1977:** 1257; **1978:** 597
Domestic International Sales Corporation (DISC), **1978:** 160, 172, 332, 346
Domestic policy
  Administration's first-year accomplishments, **1977:** 2136
  Interview remarks, **1977:** 2197
Domestic Policy Review of Solar Energy, **1979:** 1101, 1103–1105
Domestic Policy Review system, **1978:** 892
Domestic Policy Staff, **1978:** 597, 604, 611, 1101, 1223; **1979:** 619, 824, 2007, 2068; **1980–81:** 319, 1429, 2423
Domestic Violence, Interdepartmental Committee on, **1979:** 729
Domestic Volunteer Service Act amendments, **1979:** 2237
Dominica
  Independence celebrations, U.S. delegation, **1978:** 1879
  Trade beneficiary developing country designation, **1980–81:** 550
  U.S. Ambassador, **1979:** 664
  U.S. assistance, **1979:** 2160
  U.S. Special Representative, **1977:** 1530
Dominican Republic
  Ambassador to U.S., **1977:** 806; **1979:** 25, 1882
  Election system, **1980–81:** 626
  Elections, **1978:** 931, 942
  Hurricane David, U.S. assistance, **1979:** 1666
  Inaugural ceremonies, U.S. delegation, **1978:** 1406
  President Joaquín Balaguer, **1977:** 1551, 1568
  Trade with U.S., **1980–81:** 1247
  U.S. Ambassador, **1978:** 567, 641, 1406
  U.S. assistance, **1979:** 2160
Dominick, Charlotte, **1977:** 816
Donahue, Leo C., **1979:** 1023
Donahue, Richard K., **1977:** 815
Donahue, Thomas R., **1978:** 802, 1766; **1980–81:** 1220, 1246, 1412, 1648, 2766ftn., 2870, 2873
Donaldson, Andrew G., **1979:** 1524
Donaldson, Brig. Gen. John, **1978:** 28
Donaldson, Linda M., **1978:** 696
Donaldson, Sam, **1977:** 1467, 1672; **1979:** 744
Dong, Nelson G., **1978:** 1026
Dong Huamin, **1980–81:** 1805, 1806
Donilon, Tom, **1980–81:** 939
Donlon, Sean, **1978:** 1722

Donohoe, Margaret M., **1978:** 1955
Donovan, Hedley W.
  Appointment, **1979:** 1300
  Meetings with the President (Digest), **1979:** 1318, 1455, 1604, 1679, 1705, 1785, 1824, 1882, 1966, 1976, 2043, 2081, 2106, 2139, 2187, 2206, 2207, 2248, 2280; **1980–81:** 25, 63, 104, 217, 268, 293, 334, 374, 452, 493, 521, 654, 719, 825, 893, 931, 932, 967, 1013, 1014, 1111, 1376, 1469, 1523
  Mention, **1979:** 2239
  National agenda development for the eighties, **1980–81:** 2918
  News conference (Checklist), **1979:** 2044
  President's Commission for a National Agenda for the Eighties, responsibilities, **1979:** 2015
  Resignation, **1980–81:** 1509
Donovan, Tom, **1977:** 147
Donsker, Monroe D., **1978:** 408
Doob, Joseph Leo, **1979:** 2289; **1980–81:** 82n.
Dorn, William Jennings Bryant, **1980–81:** 1762
Doron, Shalom, **1980–81:** 1654
Dorsey, Fannie B., **1978:** 702, 711
Dorsey, L. C., **1978:** 709; **1979:** 1447
Dorval, Romeo, **1979:** 720n.
Doty, Paul M., **1978:** 217, 230
Double Eagle II, **1978:** 1449
Dougan, Diana Lady, **1980–81:** 1467, 1524
Douglas, Cathleen, **1979:** 773, 774; **1980–81:** 416
Douglas, Deborah A., **1980–81:** 929
Douglas, Kirk, **1980–81:** 1405, 2341, 2924
Douglas, Rick, **1980–81:** 893
Douglas, William O., **1980–81:** 105, 416
Douglas, Justice William O., Federal Building, **1978:** 1877
Douglas Arctic Wildlife Range, William O., Alaska, **1980–81:** 416, 419
Downey, Mortimer L., III, **1977:** 1752, 1755
Downey, Repr. Thomas J., **1978:** 1380; **1980–81:** 374
Downs, John E., **1977:** 1779, 1795
Downs, Thomas M., **1977:** 987
Doyen, Ross, **1980–81:** 552, 559
Doyle, Joseph A., **1979:** 2232
Drabek, Jaroslav, **1980–81:** 821
Draft evaders.
  See Military Selective Service Act.
Draft registration.
  See under Selective Service System.
Draper, Morris, **1978:** 2288
Drayton, William, Jr., **1977:** 1175, 1212
Dreher, Jennie Taber Clarkson, **1979:** 464
Drinan, Repr. Robert F., **1979:** 666; **1980–81:** 1098, 2218
Driscoll, Margaret C., **1977:** 1713
Driver, Elwood T., **1978:** 223, 232, 1669; **1980–81:** 1975, 2070

Driver, William Joseph, **1980–81:** 12, 25
Drobot, Joseph, **1980–81:** 1851
Drought
  Assistance, Federal coordinator, **1977:** 278
  Legislation, **1977:** 592, 593, 962, 1134
  Message to Congress, **1977:** 487
  Question-and-answer session, remarks, **1977:** 751
  Visits to California
    ˙President, **1977:** 915, 917
    Secretary of Agriculture, **1977:** 705
Drought Assistance Program, Emergency, **1978:** 102
Drozak, Frank, **1980–81:** 719, 1447, 2610
Drug Abuse, National Institute on, **1978:** 1329
Drug Abuse, Strategy Council on, **1977:** 1401; **1979:** 618; **1980–81:** 1440
Drug Abuse Control, United Nations Fund for, **1978:** 1568
Drug Abuse and Drug Traffic Prevention, Federal Strategy for, **1979:** 618, 619
Drug Abuse and Mental Health Administration, Alcohol, **1979:** 1596
Drug Abuse Policy, Office of, **1979:** 824
  Deputy Director, **1977:** 92, 148, 1437
  Director, **1977:** 92, 148, 1046, 1437; **1978:** 1322, 1326, 1329, 1334
  Drug abuse message, **1977:** 1403
  Memorandum specifying responsibilities, **1977:** 378
  Reorganization Plan No. 1 of 1977, **1977:** 1257
  Transfer of functions, **1978:** 597
Drug Abuse Prevention Week, **1978:** 52
Drug Administration, Food and, **1980–81:** 2907
Drug Enforcement Administration, **1977:** 1161, 1401, 1405; **1978:** 205, 1329, 1599; **1979:** 1961, 1977
  Illegal drug traffic prevention on the high seas, **1980–81:** 1443, 1722
  Law enforcement officials, **1980–81:** 413
Drug Policy Office, **1980–81:** 1859
Drug retail chains
  Representatives, meeting with the President, **1980–81:** 607 (Digest), 608
  Voluntary price freeze, **1980–81:** 659, 706
Drugs and narcotics, **1977:** 290, 306, 320, 378, 504, 899, 903, 1399, 1400, 1963, 1976
  Administration's accomplishments and goals, **1980–81:** 2945
  Federal programs, **1980–81:** 1859
  Heroin trafficking, **1980–81:** 413, 1565
  Illegal traffic on the high seas, **1980–81:** 1722, 1848
  Illegal trafficking, **1978:** 873, 1042; **1979:** 135, 236, 1860
  Interview remarks, **1978:** 1779
  News conference remarks, **1978:** 1329, 1599
  Policy functions (EO 12133), **1979:** 824

Drugs and narcotics — *continued*
  Treatment programs, **1980–81:** 2365
  Vietnam veterans abuse treatment, **1978:** 1741
Dubs, Adolph, **1978:** 1022, 1034
  Day honoring (EO 12120), **1979:** 271
  Death statement, **1979:** 269
  Memorial ceremonies, **1979:** 295
  President's remarks, **1979:** 297, 302
Dubs, Marne A., **1978:** 217
Dubuque, Iowa, **1979:** 1474
Duchin, Peter, **1978:** 2228
Duckworth, Sandy L., **1977:** 1243; **1980–81:** 63
Dudley, Dudley, **1979:** 700, 720n.
Dudley, Mary Faye, **1979:** 2076n.
Duenas, Cristobal C., **1978:** 711, 712
Duffey, Joseph D., **1977:** 8, 465, 1398, 1438, 1825; **1978:** 880, 1630, 1669; **1980–81:** 217, 1713, 1847
Duffy, James H., **1979:** 372, 378
Dugan, Francis R., **1977:** 196, 1944, 1966; **1978:** 230; **1980–81:** 941, 968
Duitscher, Annie, **1977:** 2050
Dukakis, Kitty, **1978:** 1973; **1980–81:** 822
Dukakis, Michael J., **1977:** 385, 402; **1978:** 1596, 1893, 2004; **1979:** 947
Duke, Angier Biddle, **1979:** 2077, 2082
Duke, Robin Chandler, **1980–81:** 1713, 1847
Dukes, Hazel N., **1978:** 709; **1979:** 1447
Dukess, A. Carlton, **1980–81:** 2560
Dulles International Airport, Va., **1977:** 322
Duluth, Minn., **1978:** 1949
Duncan, Charles W., Jr.
  See Defense, Department of, Deputy Secretary; Energy, Secretary of.
Duncan, Jack Genair, **1980–81:** 812, 826
Duncan, Repr. John J., **1980–81:** 2344
Duncan, Repr. Robert B., **1978:** 1944; **1980–81:** 318
Duncan, Ruby, **1979:** 1727
Dunfey, Walter J., **1979:** 465
Dunfey, William L., **1979:** 1668, 1680
Dungan, Ralph A., **1977:** 796, 807
Dunham, Daniel B., **1980–81:** 841
Dunham, Richard L., **1977:** 7, 1250
Dunlap, E. T., **1978:** 1208, 2054
Dunlap, James, **1979:** 1442n.
Dunlap, Louise, **1977:** 1408
Dunlop, John, **1979:** 1778, 1859, 1869, 1954
Dunn, George, **1980–81:** 2091n.
Dunn, H. Stewart, **1977:** 1529
Dunn, Jack, **1977:** 31
Dunn, Read P., Jr., **1979:** 598, 619
Dunn, Richard J., **1977:** 1483, 1484
Dunne, George, **1979:** 1933ftn., 1934, 1937; **1978:** 984, 987
Dunne, Steve, **1980–81:** 753
Dupere, Phyllis, **1977:** 303
Duplantier, Adrian G., **1978:** 771, 803

Dupuis, Sylvia L., **1979:** 687
Duran, Alfredo, **1977:** 147, 882; **1978:** 1869
Duran, Maria, **1977:** 78, 90
Durenberger, Sen. David, **1979:** 2257n.
Durham, Ralph V., **1977:** 196; **1979:** 1775
Durham, Willie D., Sr., **1977:** 1650, 1651
Durkin, Sen. John A., **1977:** 1826; **1978:** 366, 421, 549; **1979:** 699, 714, 715, 718
Durkin, Richard, **1978:** 710
Durning, Marvin B., **1977:** 1531, 1534
Duskin, Elizabeth, **1979:** 45, 92
Dutremble, Richard D., **1977:** 1650, 1651
Dutton, Don, **1979:** 1524
Duzak, Thomas F., **1980–81:** 3021
Dyas, Hess, **1978:** 1009
Dyer, David W., **1977:** 1529
Dyess, William J., **1980–81:** 1096, 1428
Dyke, Jim, **1977:** 784, 1633, 1651; **1979:** 1921
Dykman, J. T., **1979:** 931
Dymally, Lt. Gov. Mervyn M., **1978:** 844, 1947
Dymshits, Mark, **1979:** 731
Dyson, Earl Eugene, **1979:** 465

Eads, George C., **1979:** 599, 619, 1222
Eagleburger, Lawrence S., **1977:** 873, 874, 883; **1979:** 669 **1980–81:** 1243
Eagleton, Sen. Thomas F., **1977:** 784, 1084, 1632; **1978:** 1380, 1570, 1667, 1722, 1736, 1754–1757, 1770, 1792, 1794
   Campaign appearances with the President, **1980–81:** 1611, 2552, 2665
   Legislation passage leadership
      Alaska lands, **1980–81:** 1548
      Chrysler Corporation Loan Guarantee Act of 1979, **1980–81:** 27
   Meetings with the President (Digest), **1980–81:** 774, 1523
   Mention, **1980–81:** 1620
Eanes, António dos Santos Ramalho, **1977:** 882; **1978:** 1021; **1980–81:** 1014, 1230, 1231, 1233, 1245
Earle, Ralph, II.
   See United States Arms Control and Disarmament Agency, Director.
Earle, Sylvia A., **1980–81:** 2242
Early, Repr. Joseph D., **1977:** 402
Earned Income Tax Credit, **1978:** 104
Earth Day, **1980–81:** 1, 351, 415
Earth Week, **1977:** 606
Earthquake Hazards Reduction Program, National, **1978:** 1150; **1979:** 537
East Orange, N.J., **1980–81:** 492
East Rutherford, N.J., **1979:** 2024, 2027, 2035
East St. Louis, Ill., **1980–81:** 2664
East-West Foreign Trade Board, **1978:** 2057
Easter egg roll, **1977:** 641

Easter Seal Campaign, **1979:** 377; **1980–81:** 452
Easter Seal Poster Child, **1978:** 457; **1979:** 377
Easter vacation, President's, **1979:** 669
Eastland, Sen. James O., **1977:** 505, 924, 1152, 1323, 1329, 1416, 1745, 1794, 1923, 1941; **1978:** 324, 837, 1383
Eastman, Jorge Mario, **1980–81:** 2807
Eastport, Maine, **1979:** 1017
Eastwood, Mary, **1980–81:** 62
Easum, Donald B., **1980–81:** 1946
Eaton, Cyprus, **1979:** 837
Eberle, W. D., **1978:** 454
Ebert, Robert H., **1980–81:** 1445, 1470
Ecevit, Bulent, **1978:** 555, 1014, 1016, 1018, 1152; **1979:** 192 **1980–81:** 382
Echelman, Shirley, **1979:** 400
Eckart, Dennis, **1980–81:** 1765
Eckerd, Jack M., **1977:** 147, 148; **1978:** 1869
Eckhard, Henry, **1978:** 1627
Eckhardt, Repr. Bob, **1977:** 1930; **1978:** 769; **1980–81:** 303, 2240, 2378, 2603
Eckstine, Billy, **1977:** 557; **1979:** 1015; **1980–81:** 2341
Ecology.
   See Environment.
Ecology Award, Pepperdine University Tyler, **1977:** 642
Economic, Social and Cultural Rights, International Covenant on, **1977:** 1734; **1978:** 395
Economic Adjustment Committee, **1978:** 593, 595
Economic Advisers, Council of, **1980–81:** 1148, 1151, 3004
   Export policy functions, **1978:** 1633
   Members, **1977:** 372, 373, 706; **1979:** 467, 599, 619, 1222, 1233, 1397
   National Productivity Council, **1978:** 1833, 1835
   Reorganization, **1977:** 1258
Economic Advisers, Council of, Chairman (Charles L. Schultze), **1977:** 10, 15, 31, 87, 248, 463, 464, 508, 553, 556, 595, 641, 642, 706, 712, 744, 774, 805, 882, 942, 1030, 1058, 1083, 1111, 1161–1163, 1211, 1221, 1265, 1306, 1382, 1383, 1437, 1506, 1533, 1649, 1690, 1700, 1754, 1761, 1794, 1826, 1966, 2006, 2036, 2076, 2077, 2089, 2102, 2130, 2162; **1978:** 66, 124, 229, 277, 328, 415, 457, 594, 595, 710, 726, 770, 781, 803, 892, 898, 899, 1034, 1072, 1222, 1240, 1333, 1345, 1351, 1381, 1457, 1495, 1669, 1670, 1723, 1725, 1772, 1809, 1849, 1878–1880, 1915, 1954, 1955, 1971, 2031, 2040, 2073, 2147, 2187, 2218, 2238, 2242, 2270
   Agricultural trade development functions, **1980–81:** 1238
   Budget preparation, **1980–81:** 225
   Economic Policy Group member, **1979:** 977
   Inflation rate reduction prediction, **1980–81:** 743
   Inflation task force member, **1979:** 1216

Economic Advisers, Chairman — *continued*
  Meetings with the President (Digest), **1979:** 14, 25, 89, 178, 241, 327, 401, 553, 554, 666, 732, 841, 898, 956, 957, 1018, 1142, 1222, 1604, 1705, 1785, 1824, 1976, 2043, 2187, 2248, 2280; **1980–81:** 24, 63, 267, 292, 374, 423, 452, 493, 607, 719, 892, 932, 1013, 1050, 1469, 1564, 1597, 1846, 2740
  Membership on:
    Oil Policy Committee, **1980–81:** 10
    Trade Policy Committee, **1980–81:** 8
  Mentions, **1979:** 96; **1980–81:** 2834
  News conferences (Checklist), **1979:** 179; **1980–81:** 269, 453, 608, 1429, 3050
Economic Affairs, United States Negotiator for, **1980–81:** 1468, 1470
Economic Community, European.
  See European Economic Community.
Economic Cooperation, Conference on International, **1977:** 612, 820, 824; **1978:** 120
Economic Cooperation and Development, Organization for, **1977:** 11, 63, 965, 1030; **1978:** 49, 1145, 1313, 1314; **1980–81:** 7, 1187, 2218
  Development Assistance Committee, Chairman, **1979:** 224, 241
  International Steel Agreement, **1979:** 7
  Secretary General, **1979:** 787
  Tokyo Summit statement, **1979:** 1198, 1199
  United States Trade Representative, responsibilities of, **1979:** 1731
Economic Development, White House Conference on Balanced National Growth and, **1978:** 53, 66, 265; **1979:** 65, 69
Economic Development Administration, **1977:** 488
  Alcohol fuels production plants loan programs, **1979:** 1502ftn.
  Assistance programs, **1978:** 583, 854, 1002, 2076
  Economic development loan guarantee programs, **1979:** 601
  Hard-core unemployed jobs program, **1979:** 2158
  Hydroelectric power projects loan guarantees, **1979:** 1511
  Jacksonville, Fla., grants, **1980–81:** 1350, 1359
  Miami, Fla., grants, **1980–81:** 1236, 2385
  Minority economic development programs, **1979:** 77
  Oakland, Calif., revitalization program, **1980–81:** 1301
  Philadelphia, Pa., grants, **1980–81:** 726
  Rural development activities, **1980–81:** 1918
  Rural water and sewer services, **1979:** 75
  Solar energy programs, **1979:** 1103
  Steel industry assistance, **1980–81:** 1968, 2353
  Telecommunications minority assistance programs, **1978:** 253, 254
  Urban development programs, **1979:** 1973, 1988; **1980–81:** 1862

Economic Development Admin. — *continued*
  U.S. territories private sector program, **1980–81:** 320
Economic Development Assistance program, **1978:** 834
Economic Development Authority, **1977:** 1573
Economic dislocation early warning system, **1979:** 1384
Economic Opportunity, National Advisory Council on, **1977:** 1030, 1477; **1978:** 709, 1278; **1979:** 1447, 1727, 2042; **1980–81:** 274, 1925
Economic Opportunity Act of 1964, 15th anniversary (Proc. 4675), **1979:** 1477
Economic Opportunity Council, **1977:** 1257; **1978:** 597
Economic Planning Group, **1977:** 463
Economic Policy, Council on International, **1977:** 333, 1012
Economic Policy Board, President's, **1977:** 333
Economic Policy Group, **1977:** 556, 629; **1979:** 977, 1222
  Steering Committee of the, **1978:** 726
Economic Powers Act, International Emergency, **1980–81:** 2772
Economic Regulatory Administration, **1979:** 1654, 2044
Economic Report of the President, **1978:** 123, 129; **1979:** 110, 179; **1980–81:** 245, 269, 3004
Economic Revitalization Board, **1980–81:** 1589, 1650, 1969
Economic and Social Council, Inter-American, **1978:** 1516; **1979:** 1334; **1980–81:** 1428
Economic summit affairs, Ambassador at Large, **1978:** 1704, 1723
Economic summit meeting, international, **1978:** 719, 751
Economic Summits, Special Representative of the President for International.
  See Special Represenive of the President for International Economic Summits.
Economics, 1979 Nobel Prize in, **1979:** 1963
Economy, international, **1977:** 59, 761, 778, 814, 816–819, 825–828, 883, 1669, 2159, 2160
  Administration's accomplishments and goals, **1980–81:** 2991
  Automobile industry competition, **1980–81:** 1329
  Energy strategies, **1980–81:** 174, 253
  Gold prices, **1980–81:** 499
  Impact of:
    Inflation, **1980–81:** 441, 476, 484, 540, 553, 572, 580, 590, 639, 2513, 2691
    Iraq-Iran conflict, **1980–81:** 1900, 1903, 1906, 1922
    Natural rubber prices, **1980–81:** 591
    OPEC oil prices, **1980–81:** 1190, 1206, 1537
    U.S. dollar value, **1980–81:** 254, 499, 558

Economy, international — *continued*
  Monetary policy, **1980–81:** 175
  Multilateral trade agreements, **1980–81:** 254
  United Nations role in, **1980–81:** 1286
  U.S. policy, **1980–81:** 1206
  See also Commerce, international.
Economy, national
  Administration officials, meeting with the President, **1977:** 2162
  Administration's accomplishments and goals, **1980–81:** 199, 481, 498, 513, 541, 734, 2933
  Administration's policies and programs, President's assessment, **1979:** 1841, 1942
  Advisers, meeting with the President (Digest), **1980–81:** 292
  Anti-inflation program, **1978:** 722, 1060, 1839
  Appropriations, bill signing, **1977:** 870
  Business Council
    Question-and-answer session, **1978:** 2236
    Remarks, **1977:** 2108
  Credit controls.
    See Credit controls.
  Democratic National Committee, remarks, **1977:** 1895, 1896
  Democratic workshop on inflation, remarks, **1978:** 2210
  Development assistance legislation, **1980–81:** 118
  Development programs, **1979:** 74, 378
  Dollar, U.S., value of.
    See Dollar, U.S., value of.
  Economic recovery program
    Impact on international economy, **1977:** 64
    Message to Congress, **1977:** 47, 87
    Question-and-answer sessions, **1977:** 599, 601, 618, 631, 633, 761, 920
    News conference remarks, **1977:** 93, 631, 698
    Report to the American people, **1977:** 71
    Summary of arguments for rebate, **1977:** 586
  Economic Report, **1978:** 123, 129
  Emergency declaration, possibility of, **1980–81:** 2834
  Employment.
    See Employment and unemployment.
  Foreign business investors, **1980–81:** 1118
  Free competition, **1977:** 73
  Free enterprise system, **1980–81:** 1569
  Government reports validity, **1980–81:** 2444
  Gross national product.
    See Gross national product.
  Impact of:
    Antitrust laws enforcement, **1979:** 132
    Employment increases, **1980–81:** 110
    Federal budget, **1979:** 96
    International trade agreements, **1979:** 161, 1312
    Oil imports, **1979:** 351, 1212, 1215, 2040, 2108
    Regulatory reform, **1979:** 105

Economy, national — *continued*
  Impact of — *continued*
    Small business sector, **1980–81:** 73
    Soviet trade restrictions, **1980–81:** 184
  Income tax rebate, **1977:** 602
  Industrial innovation initiatives program, **1979:** 2068, 2070
  Inflation.
    See Inflation; Inflation program.
  Interest rates.
    See Interest rates.
  Intergovernmental fiscal assistance, **1979:** 391
  Interview remarks, **1977:** 1275, 1599, 2009, 2010, 2095, 2193, 2194; **1978:** 68, 806, 2040
  Mentions, **1979:** 300, 736
  National Democratic Party Conference, remarks, **1978:** 2191
  National energy plan, impact, **1977:** 1982, 1983, 1999
  National Press Club, question-and-answer session with the President, **1980–81:** 2219, 2333
  National Productivity Council, **1978:** 1833–1836
  Natural resources management, public investment in, **1980–81:** 1143
  News conference
    (Checklist), **1980–81:** 453
    Remarks, **1978:** 331, 497, 2100
    Statement, **1980–81:** 705
  Policy review, **1977:** 1495, 1496
  President's assessment, **1980–81:** 1484
  Productivity growth, **1979:** 103, 111, 113, 935, 1215, 1312
  Productivity per American worker, **1980–81:** 910, 1503, 1678,
  Public works and economic development legislation, **1979:** 600
  Radio address to the Nation, **1980–81:** 2189, 2332
  Recession
    Budget revisions for fiscal year 1981, impact of, **1980–81:** 568
    Inflation and unemployment indicators, **1980–81:** 1066, 1078, 1085, 1832
    Possibility of, **1979:** 1212, 1215, 2030
    Predictions for 1980, **1980–81:** 245, 246, 735, 748, 829
  Relationship with:
    Energy production, **1980–81:** 470, 1197, 2222
    Foreign policy, **1980–81:** 874, 1226
  Renewal program
    Announcement remarks, **1980–81:** 1585, 1599
    Fact sheet and white paper (Checklist), **1980–81:** 1599
  Goals
    Community rebuilding projects, **1980–81:** 1607, 1615, 1631, 1650, 1676, 1986, 1988

Economy, national — *continued*
  Renewal program — *continued*
    Goals — *continued*
      Energy security.
        See National program *under* Energy.
      Industry revitalization.
        See Revitalization program *under* Business and industry.
      Inflation control, **1980–81:** 1504, 1512, 1537, 1675, 1729, 1879, 1896, 1973, 2217, 2433
      Job creation.
        See Job creation *under* Employment and unemployment.
      Mention, **1980–81:** 2119
      President's priority for second term, **1980–81:** 1619
    Research and development program for production increases, **1980–81:** 1963
    Standard of living, President's views on, **1979:** 1992
    State of, President's responsibility for, **1979:** 1713
    State of the Union, **1978:** 91, 92, 119
    Statistical indicators, **1980–81:** 2055, 2205, 2257, 2277, 2362
    Tax message, **1978:** 158
    United Auto Workers, address, **1977:** 887
    White House briefing for community leaders, **1980–81:** 801
    White House Conference on Balanced Growth and Economic Development, **1977:** 1414 1726, 1757, 1884, 2077, 2120, 2166, 2263, 2407
    World Bank Group, remarks, **1977:** 1670
    See also Anti-inflation program; Inflation.
Ecuador
  Ambassador to U.S., **1977:** 194; **1979:** 1882
  President-elect Jaime Roldós, **1979:** 1043, 1044, 1293
  Trade beneficiary developing country designation, **1980–81:** 430, 550
  U.S. Ambassador, **1978:** 1029, 1034
  Vice Adm. Alfredo Povedo Burbano, **1977:** 1549, 1568
Edelman, Edmund D., **1977:** 1058; **1978:** 2269; **1979:** 813n.
Edelman, Marian, **1977:** 316, 489; **1978:** 1190
  National Institute for Building Sciences, report, **1978:** 1154
Edey, Marion, **1977:** 885, 943; **1978:** 302
Edgar, Repr. Robert W., **1977:** 1962; **1980–81:** 563, 1431, 1630, 2042
Edington, Patricia G., **1979:** 465
Edison, Thomas Alva, **1979:** 529; **1980–81:** 274, 2888
Edison and the Centennial of Light, Thomas, **1979:** 197

Editorial Cartoonists, American Association of, **1978:** 1771
Editors, American Society of Newspaper, **1980–81:** 631
Edler, James H., **1980–81:** 2731
Edmo, Maxine R., **1978:** 1419
Edmond, Lester E., **1977:** 795, 807
Edmonds, Oscar H., Jr., **1977:** 2028
Edmondson, William B., **1978:** 745, 750
Edmunds, Mrs. S. Henry, **1979:** 1704
Edmundson, Carole C., **1980–81:** 929
Education
  Administration's accomplishments and goals, **1980–81:** 136, 1295, 2932, 2945
  Aliquippa, Pa., town meeting remarks, **1978:** 1611
  American Federation of Teachers address, **1980–81:** 1557–1563
  Basic Educational Opportunity Grants, **1977:** 2088
  Bilingual programs, **1979:** 1665; **1980–81:** 1459, 1742
  Career Education Incentive Act, **1977:** 2104
  Child food programs, **1978:** 2000
  Church-related organization leaders, meeting with the President, **1977:** 2130
  Congressional Black Caucus, remarks, **1978:** 1681
  Democratic commitment to programs, **1979:** 1935
  Democratic National Committee, fund-raising dinner remarks, **1978:** 1649
  Disadvantaged persons opportunities, **1979:** 1991
  Elementary and secondary, message to Congress, **1978:** 422, 424, 458
  Elementary and secondary reauthorization legislation, **1977:** 2088
  Equal opportunity, **1979:** 884, 885, 909
  European region-U.S. convention, **1980–81:** 2721
  Exchange programs with:
    Japan, **1979:** 767
    Korea, Republic of, **1979:** 1312
  Federal aid, **1979:** 708, 848, 970, 1750, 1768, 1948, 1955, 1969, 2200, 2211
  Federal assistance, **1978:** 288, 304, 423, 425, 986
  Federal funding increases during administration, **1980–81:** 115, 885, 909, 1295, 1351, 1365, 1874, 2026, 2084, 2291, 2360, 2440, 2485, 2573, 2593
  Federal programs, **1979:** 139, 709
  Foreign language studies, **1980–81:** 1297
  Handicapped persons, **1980–81:** 809
  Head Start program, **1980–81:** 1499, 2061, 2617
  Impact aid, **1977:** 1017, 1019
  Indochinese refugee children, emergency assistance to affect school districts, **1979:** 2087
  Interview remarks, **1978:** 1595

Education — *continued*
　International Exchange-of-Persons program,
　　1979: 324
　Materials imports, **1980–81:** 2920
　National Democratic Party Conference, re-
　　marks, **1978:** 2192
　National School Lunch Week, **1980–81:** 1925
　Ohio State Democratic Party, reception remarks,
　　1978: 1626
　Paperwork reduction, **1979:** 2178
　Prayer in public schools, **1978:** 1606; **1979:** 625,
　　655, 1887; **1980–81:** 1621
　President's campaign remarks, **1978:** 1934, 1939,
　　1951
　Private schools.
　　See Private schools.
　Public school system, comments on, **1977:** 326
　Reagan, Ronald, policy differences with the
　　President, **1980–81:** 2078, 2082, 2617
　Research Apprenticeship Program, **1979:** 2064
　Rural area programs, **1980–81:** 2127
　Salute to Learning Day, **1980–81:** 841
　School busing, **1979:** 1946; **1980–81:** 2809
　School desegregation, **1978:** 309
　Spanish-speaking Americans, **1979:** 813; **1980–
　　81:** 859, 1837
　State commissioners, meeting with the President,
　　1978: 66
　State of the Union, **1978:** 104, 111
　Student loans, **1979:** 140, 711
　Teachers, President's comments on, **1980–81:**
　　430, 1297, 1746
　Undocumented alien children, **1980–81:** 1726
　United Negro College Fund, **1977:** 2003
　Urban programs, **1978:** 591
　Veterans programs, **1980–81:** 1121, 2315, 2318
　Vietnam veterans, **1978:** 1740
　Youth employment training programs.
　　See Employment *under* Children and youth.
　See also Colleges and universities.
Education, Advisory Panel on Financing Elemen-
　tary and Secondary, **1979:** 1524
Education, Department of
　Activation (EO 12212), **1980–81:** 818
　Advantages of separation from HEW, **1979:** 127,
　　246, 849, 1414
　Annual report, **1980–81:** 2882
　Assistant Secretaries, **1980–81:** 203, 204, 219,
　　425, 426, 608, 751, 759, 768, 775, 840, 967,
　　1015, 1052, 1133, 1634, 1942
　Bilingual programs, **1980–81:** 1837
　Budget rescission, **1980–81:** 2916
　Classroom teacher to be Secretary, possibility,
　　1979: 1344
　Congress, meetings with the President (Digest),
　　1979: 786, 1785
　Deputy Under Secretaries, **1980–81:** 493
　Fact sheet, **1979:** 242

Education, Department of — *continued*
　General Counsel, **1980–81:** 315
　Handicapped persons programs, **1980–81:** 809,
　　2610
　Inauguration ceremonies, **1980–81:** 523, 850, 855,
　　894
　Inspector General, **1980–81:** 841, 1096, 1112
　Juvenile delinquency programs, **1980–81:** 1273
　Legislation
　　Congressional consideration
　　　House approval, **1979:** 1229, 1776
　　　Mention, **1979:** 711
　　　Senate approval, **1979:** 756, 1728
　　Fact sheet (Checklist), **1979:** 1977
　　Message to Congress transmitting proposal,
　　　1979: 264
　　President's promise to resubmit proposal in
　　　1979, **1979:** 100, 127
　　Signing ceremony, **1979:** 1955
　　Statement on signing, **1979:** 1958
　Libraries and information service programs,
　　1980–81: 1932–1934
　Mentions, **1979:** 2211; **1980–81:** 1328
　1981 budget allocation, **1980–81:** 231
　Office of Libraries and Learning Technologies,
　　1980–81: 1931
　Organization Act, **1979:** 1946, 1955, 1958, 1977
　President's assessment, **1979:** 1946, 2130
　Proposed, **1978:** 423, 425, 1336, 1595, 1611, 1612,
　　1664, 1749, 1754
　Purposes of creation, **1980–81:** 136, 148, 842,
　　1735, 2027, 2052, 2136, 2593
　Reagan, Ronald, position on, **1980–81:** 1995,
　　2091
　Regulatory Council membership, **1980–81:** 1427
　School busing, **1980–81:** 1731, 1734, 1896
　Science and technology programs emphasis,
　　1979: 545; **1980–81:** 81
　Secretary.
　　See Education, Secretary of.
　Under Secretary, **1980–81:** 426, 522
　Youth employment and training programs,
　　1980–81: 1068, 1081, 1706, 1998, 2021,
　　2061, 2133, 2517
　See also specific constituent agencies.
Education, Federal Interagency Committee on,
　1979: 49
Education, Intergovernmental Advisory Council
　on, **1980–81:** 1432
Education, National Advisory Council on Adult,
　1979: 1524; **1980–81:** 267, 844, 2558, 3022
Education, National Advisory Council on Exten-
　sion and Continuing, **1977:** 2063; **1978:**
　913; **1979:** 1023, 1293; **1980–81:** 1669,
　2817
Education, National Advisory Council on Indian,
　1980–81: 849, 2883

Education, National Advisory Council on Vocational, **1980–81:** 2817

Education, National Association for Equal Opportunity in Higher, **1979:** 742

Education, National Institute of.
See National Institute of Education.

Education, Office of, **1979:** 139, 2087; **1980–81:** 25
Commissioner, **1977:** 382, 465

Education, Science and Culture, Inter-American Council on, **1978:** 1516; **1979:** 1334

Education, Secretary of (Shirley M. Hufstedler), **1979:** 2063, 2139, 2199
Bilingual programs promotion, **1980–81:** 1459
Black colleges, Federal program coordinator for, **1980–81:** 329, 1356, 1515, 1516, 1518
Department inauguration ceremonies, **1980–81:** 850, 853, 855
Education Amendments support, **1980–81:** 2063
Handicapped persons program responsibilities, **1980–81:** 809
Meetings with the President (Digest), **1980–81:** 452, 492
Mentions, **1980–81:** 859, 1296, 1427, 1561, 1735, 2027, 2136
President's assessment, **1980–81:** 883, 1874, 2059
President's Council on Spinal Cord Injury, support services, **1980–81:** 2913
Youth employment and education training programs development, **1980–81:** 215
For functions of the Department in general, see Education, Department of.

Education Amendments of 1978, **1978:** 1916, 1918

Education Amendments of 1980, **1980–81:** 2060, 2071

Education Assistance Act, Refugee, **1980–81:** 2152, 2179, 2382

Education Association, National, **1977:** 744; **1978:** 296, 303; **1979:** 1785; **1980–81:** 1295, 2884ftn.

Education Commission of the States Task Force on Responsible Decisions about Alcohol, **1977:** 641

Education and Culture, Inter-American Council for, **1980–81:** 1428

Education Day, U.S.A., **1978:** 756

Education of Disadvantaged Children, National Advisory Council on the, **1979:** 1727; **1980–81:** 257, 1839

Education Institute, Legal, **1979:** 1267

Education Week, American, **1977:** 1694; **1978:** 1651; **1979:** 1698; **1980–81:** 1969

Educational, Scientific and Cultural Organization, United Nations, **1980–81:** 1713, 1847, 2721

Educational, space, and agricultural agreement with China, **1979:** 204

Educational and Cultural Affairs, Bureau of, **1977:** 1765

Educational Programs, National Advisory Committee on Women's, **1979:** 2039, 2044; **1980–81:** 1023, 1051

Educational Progressive Association, Order of the American Hellenic, **1980–81:** 381

Educational Research, National Council on.
See National Council on Educational Research.

Edward, William H., **1980–81:** 3026

Edwards, Bruce, **1977:** 1045; **1979:** 1218

Edwards, Repr. Donald, **1978:** 526, 1267, 1801; **1980–81:** 1098

Edwards, Gov. Edwin W., **1977:** 1335, 1941; **1978:** 1173; **1980–81:** 2401, 2404

Edwards, Harold M., **1977:** 1211, 1213

Edwards, Harry T., **1977:** 526, 1811, 1826; **1978:** 230; **1979:** 2207, 2208

Edwards, Repr. Jack, **1978:** 1379

Edwards, John Saul, **1980–81:** 269

Edwards, Thomas, **1978:** 503

Efferson, John Norman, **1979:** 942

Egan, Michael J., **1977:** 1821, 1826; **1978:** 1652

Eginton, Warren W., **1979:** 1018, 1019

Eglin Air Force Base, Fla., **1980–81:** 834, 850

Egypt
Ambassador to U.S., **1979:** 1684; **1980–81:** 525, 528, 1846
Camp David agreements first anniversary, state officials meeting with the President, **1979:** 1684
Camp David summit meeting.
See Middle East.
Foreign Minister Kamal Hassan Ali, **1977:** 1633, 1651, 1729, 1754; **1978:** 1759, 1772; **1979:** 1684
West Bank and Gaza Strip autonomy negotiations, **1980–81:** 903, 906, 1292, 1303, 1826, 1832, 1846
Interview remarks, **1978:** 1227, 1590, 2020, 2043, 2150, 2173
Ministers, **1978:** 1506, 1554, 1759, 1772
News conference remarks, **1978:** 1179, 2099
Ohio State Democratic Party, reception remarks, **1978:** 1624
Peace negotiations and treaty with Israel.
See under Middle East.
Plane sales, **1978:** 333, 338, 368, 492, 777, 778, 801, 808, 848, 849, 866, 867, 896, 901, 915
President's visit, **1978:** 19; **1979:** 383, 394, 405–415, 430, 440, 441
Soviet relations, **1980–81:** 807
Speaker of the People's Assembly, **1978:** 1154
United States
Financial assistance, **1979:** 1445; **1980–81:** 242
Military facilities, **1980–81:** 391
Relations, **1979:** 1612, 1916, 1992; **1980–81:** 528, 1207, 1364, 2479, 2565
Science and technology cooperation, **1980–81:** 1957

[References are to page numbers except as otherwise indicated]

Egypt — *continued*
  United States — *continued*
    Taxation and fiscal evasion convention,
      1980–81: 2714
    Trade mission, **1979:** 640
    U.S. Ambassador, **1979:** 819, 843, 855; **1980–81:**
      930
    Vice President Muhammad Husni Mubarak,
      1978: 2059, 2061; **1979:** 1023, 1684
    Government democratization role, **1980–81:**
      907
    Visits to U.S., meetings with the President,
      1980–81: 99, 967, 2332, 2764
    War Minister, **1978:** 1071
    See also Middle East.
Egypt, President (Anwar al-Sadat), **1977:** 509, 561,
      567, 595, 601, 1236, 1996, 2037–2042,
      2044, 2050, 2054–2056, 2059, 2091, 2098,
      2107, 2116, 2118, 2126, 2133, 2172–2174,
      2188–2191, 2206; **1978:** 19, 43, 46, 62, 71,
      148, 151, 152, 189, 264, 274, 279, 280, 290,
      291, 305, 368, 370, 441, 493, 494, 779, 992,
      993, 1348, 1393, 1406, 1440, 1442, 1496,
      1497, 1501, 1505, 1506, 1515, 1519–1523,
      1533–1537, 1554, 1566–1568, 1571, 1585,
      1602, 1610, 1646, 1654, 1655, 1658, 1660,
      1672, 1677, 1690, 1746, 1749, 1757, 1758,
      1818, 1825, 1868, 1877, 1887, 1890–1892,
      1901, 1939, 1991, 2220, 2225, 2241, 2253,
      2254
  Camp David agreements anniversary, **1979:**
      1681, 1682n.
  Comprehensive peace negotiations
    Commitment to settlement, **1979:** 751
    Mentions, **1979:** 688, 703, 967
  Egyptian Government democratization, **1980–**
      81: 903, 905
  Egyptian-Israeli peace negotiations
    Direct negotiations with Israeli Prime Minister
      Begin, **1979:** 1752, 2018, 2033
    Jerusalem, status of, **1980–81:** 640
    Mentions, **1979:** 32, 263, 315, 346, 360, 394,
      400, 425, 427, 431, 432, 436, 457, 488, 969
    Personal Representative of the President,
      meeting with, **1980–81:** 2771
    President's trip to Egypt
      Announcement, **1979:** 383
      Meetings, **1979:** 405, 407, 410, 412, 415, 430
    Progress during Carter administration, **1980–**
      81: 1364, 1562, 1614, 1657, 1670, 2376,
      2460
    West Bank and Gaza Strip autonomy nego-
      tiations
      Camp David accords, commitment to,
        1980–81: 378, 469, 679, 714, 879, 1104,
        1624, 1656
      Consultations with the President, **1980–81:**
        511, 521, 523, 694

Egypt, President — *continued*
  Egyptian peace negotiations — *continued*
    West Bank autonomy — *continued*
      Personal Representative of the President,
        meeting with, **1980–81:** 1657, 1832
      Resumption of negotiations support, **1980–**
        81: 903, 1303
      Summit meeting scheduling, **1980–81:** 1614,
        1832
  Egyptian-Israeli peace treaty
    Joint statement, **1979:** 490
    Letters of agreement, **1979:** 516, 517
    Prime Minister Begin's trip to Egypt, **1979:**
      618
    Role, **1980–81:** 525, 632, 687, 1133, 1604, 1660,
      1670, 1767, 2024, 2311, 2371
    Visit to U.S.
      Announcement, **1979:** 467
      Dinner honoring, **1979:** 546
      Mentions, **1979:** 471, 720, 831
      Signing ceremonies, **1979:** 518, 523, 554
  Israeli Prime Minister Begin, meeting with,
      1980–81: 99
  Mentions, **1979:** 1751, 1757, 1857; **1980–81:** 399,
      541, 1005, 1115
  Palestinian question resolution, Camp David
      commitment to, **1979:** 455, 1427
  Relationship with the President, **1980–81:** 181,
      486
  Visit to U.S.
    Meetings with the President, **1980–81:** 622, 623
    Postvisit comments, **1980–81:** 632, 648
    Pre-visit comments, **1980–81:** 579
    State dinner, **1980–81:** 617
Egypt, Prime Minister (Mustafa Kahlil), **1978:**
      2147; **1980–81:** 378, 967
Egypt-U.S. Business Council, dinner attendance,
      1979: 547, 548n.
  Meeting with the President (Digest), **1979:** 553
  Middle East peace negotiations
    Meetings in U.S. with Israeli Foreign Minister
      Dayan, **1979:** 251, 263, 329
    Mentions, **1979:** 347, 408
Ehrenfeld, John R., **1978:** 822
Ehrenfeld, Mikki A., **1978:** 1341
Ehrlich, Dr. S. Paul, **1977:** 806
Ehrlich, Thomas, **1977:** 1178, 1180; **1979:** 1272,
      1293, 1731, 1801, 2248; **1980–81:** 8, 1417
Ehrlichman, John D., **1977:** 2100
Eidenberg, Eugene, **1979:** 1137, 1139
  Advisory Commissions on Intergovernmental
      Relations, member, **1980–81:** 3021
  Assistant to the President for Intergovernmental
      Affairs, appointment, **1980–81:** 1111
  Meetings with the President (Digest), **1980–81:**
      492, 1662
  Miami, Fla., riot assistance actions, **1980–81:**
      1074, 1236

[References are to page numbers except as otherwise indicated]

Eidenberg, Eugene — *continued*
  Neighborhood and community programs involvement, **1980–81:** 2117
  Urban policy development, **1980–81:** 2861
Eighties, President's Commission for a National Agenda for the.
  See President's Commission for a National Agenda for the Eighties.
Eikenberry, Jill, **1978:** 394
Eilburg, Repr. Joshua, **1977:** 1383, 1416, 1919, 1923; **1978:** 59, 246
Eilts, Herman, **1979:** 925
Einstein, Albert, **1979:** 677, 680, 682
Einstein Centennial, Albert, **1979:** 390
Eisele, Albert, **1977:** 58; **1979:** 2054n.
Eisenhower, Dwight D., **1979:** 994, 1012, 1088, 2075; **1980–81:** 852, 1766, 2060, 2343
Eisenhower, Mamie, **1978:** 1239; **1979:** 2074
Eisenhower, U.S.S., **1978:** 538; **1980–81:** 2827n.
Eizenstat, Stuart E., **1977:** 485, 706, 712, 806, 943, 1093, 1162, 1222, 1265, 1296, 1307, 1506, 1533, 1649, 1794, 2036, 2089, 2162; **1978:** 66, 553, 641, 770, 802, 819, 1044, 1072, 1155, 1280, 1469, 1471, 1477, 1478, 1954, 1955, 2092, 2094, 2147, 2226, 2242, 2263
  Carter's Democratic Party platform presentation, **1980–81:** 1101
  Cuban refugee policy news conference, **1980–81:** 914, 932
  Dioxin exposure, health effects study, **1980–81:** 5
  Economic Policy Group member, **1979:** 977
  Handicapped persons program involvement, **1980–81:** 2613
  Industrial innovation initiatives program, **1979:** 2070n., 2082
  Meetings with the President (Digest), **1979:** 14, 25, 178, 240, 327, 467, 553, 554, 666, 732, 842, 898, 956, 983, 1142, 1222, 1453, 1454, 1705, 1785, 1823, 2043, 2081, 2105, 2187, 2206, 2280; **1980–81:** 24, 63, 267, 292, 374, 423, 492, 493, 607, 774, 825, 1050, 1469, 1564, 1597, 1662
  Mentions, **1979:** 708, 1028n., 1138, 1216, 1572, 1649; **1980–81:** 326, 367
  News conferences (Checklist), **1979:** 378, 402, 468, 619, 733, 900, 958, 1028, 1044, 1143, 1144, 1320, 1398, 1706, 1825, 2188; **1980–81:** 25, 64, 65, 104, 219, 293, 335, 1377, 2071, 2332, 3050
  Nuclear energy, question-and-answer session with reporters, **1979:** 2204
  Project Head Start, White House reception attendance, **1980–81:** 462, 466n.
  Steel industry revitalization program responsibilities, **1980–81:** 1960
  Task Force on Global Resources and Environment, duties, **1980–81:** 1416

Eizenstat, Stuart E. — *continued*
  White House task-force on the mushroom industry, chairman, **1980–81:** 2330, 2331
  Woodrow Wilson International Center for Scholars, Board of Trustees, member, **1980–81:** 3023
Eklund, Coy, **1980–81:** 1506
Eklund, Lowell, **1979:** 1023
Ekman, Sheldon V., **1980–81:** 756, 775
El Greco, **1980–81:** 340
El Salvador
  Ambassador to U.S., **1978:** 148; **1980–81:** 775
  Archbishop Oscar Arnulfo Romero, **1980–81:** 534
  Conflict in, **1980–81:** 626
  Honduras, dispute settlement with, **1980–81:** 2734
  President Carlos Humberto Romero, **1977:** 1552, 1568
  Presidential inauguration, head of U.S. delegation, **1977:** 1210
  Slaying of three persons in, **1980–81:** 2859
  Trade with U.S., **1979:** 2255
  U.S. Ambassador, **1977:** 1539, 1568; **1980–81:** 191
  U.S. assistance, **1979:** 2103
  U.S. relations, **1980–81:** 1215, 2734
Elderly persons.
  See Older persons.
Eleanor Roosevelt National Historic Site, **1977:** 1028
Election Campaign Act, Federal, **1977:** 483
Election Campaign Act Amendments of 1979, Federal, **1980–81:** 37
Election Commission, Federal.
  See Federal Election Commission.
Elections
  Campaign financing, **1977:** 1366
  President's support for Democratic candidates, **1977:** 1653–1661
  Reform, **1977:** 221, 224, 481, 509, 893
Elections, 1978
  Campaign appearances
    Connecticut, **1978:** 1887, 1891
    Florida, **1978:** 1865, 1869
    Kansas, **1978:** 1813, 1820
    Maryland, **1978:** 1795
    Massachusetts, **1978:** 1892, 1896
    Minnesota, **1978:** 1828, 1829
    Tennessee, **1978:** 1857, 1862
  Campaign telephone remarks, Mississippi, **1978:** 1963
  'Get Out the Vote' rallies
    Duluth, Minn., **1978:** 1949
    Flint, Mich., **1978:** 1932
    Gresham, Oreg., **1978:** 1942
    New York City, N.Y., **1978:** 1929
    Sacramento, Calif., **1978:** 1946

Elections, 1978 — *continued*
  'Get Out the Vote' rallies — *continued*
    Skokie, Ill., **1978:** 1936
  1978 campaign plans, **1978:** 237
  Public financing, **1978:** 1079, 2046
  Reform, **1978:** 109
  Results remarks, **1978:** 1987, 1991, 2026, 2062,
    2156, 2196
Elections, 1980: announcement of candidacy
  Constituency groups influence, **1979:** 1993
  Friends of Carter/Mondale fundraising dinner,
    1979: 2015
  Kennedy legacy, effect on, **1979:** 1987
  New England primaries, **1979:** 1986
  Possible issues
    Defense spending, **1979:** 2034
    Fiscal responsibility, **1979:** 2034
    President's leadership qualities, **1979:** 2033,
      2051
  President's candidacy
    Announcement remarks, **1979:** 2192, 2193,
      2208
    Preannouncement remarks, **1979:** 40, 172, 563,
      798, 952, 1304, 1307, 1430, 1496, 1582,
      1755, 1840, 1843, 1983
  President's organization, **1979:** 2242
  Vice-presidential running mate, **1979:** 1844
Elections, 1980: caucuses and primaries
  Carter/Mondale Presidential Committee **1980–
    81:** 937, 1024, 1030
  Cuban refugee situation, effect on campaign,
    1980–81: 914
  Debates, possibility of, **1979:** 1840, 1862; **1980–
    81:** 311, 830, 907, 1038
  Democratic candidates debate in Iowa primary,
    1979: 2293
  International interest in, **1980–81:** 1203
  Iranian and Afghan situations, effect on:
    Timing of announcements for political ad-
      vantage, possibility of, **1980–81:** 640, 709,
      799
    Travel plans, **1980–81:** 90, 243, 310, 671, 729,
      730, 746, 762
  Mention, **1980–81:** 93
  Platform presentations, **1980–81:** 1038, 1100
  President's pledge to support Democratic Party
    nominee, **1980–81:** 731, 738, 739, 763
  President's strategy, **1980–81:** 985
  Primary and caucus results
    Alabama primary, **1980–81:** 461
    Alaska caucuses, **1980–81:** 461
    California primary, **1980–81:** 1030
    Connecticut primary, **1980–81:** 534, 538, 564
    Florida primary, **1980–81:** 461
    Georgia primary, **1980–81:** 461
    Hawaii caucuses, **1980–81:** 461
    Iowa caucuses, **1980–81:** 180, 519
    Kansas primary, **1980–81:** 584

Elections, 1980: caucuses — *continued*
  Primary results — *continued*
    Maine caucuses, **1980–81:** 295
    Maryland primary, **1980–81:** 932
    Massachusetts primary, **1980–81:** 428
    Missouri primary, **1980–81:** 762
    Nebraska primary, **1980–81:** 932
    New Hampshire primary, **1980–81:** 399
    New York primary, **1980–81:** 534, 538, 564
    News conference (Checklist), **1980–81:** 894
    Ohio primary, **1980–81:** 992, 995, 1001, 1005
    Oklahoma caucuses, **1980–81:** 461
    Pennsylvania primary, **1980–81:** 729, 739, 762
    Vermont primary, **1980–81:** 428
    Virginia caucuses, **1980–81:** 525
    Washington caucuses, **1980–81:** 461
    Wisconsin primary, **1980–81:** 584, 724
  Reagan, Ronald, President's comments on can-
    didacy, **1980–81:** 729, 739, 763, 939, 1024,
    1029, 1030, 1039, 1046, 1090
Elections, 1980: Democratic National Convention
  Acceptance speech for Presidential nomination,
    1980–81: 1532
  Black delegates, remarks following meeting with,
    1980–81: 1540
  Congressional campaign committee luncheon,
    1980–81: 1529
  Delegates, volunteers, and supporters reception,
    1980–81: 1527
  Informal exchange with reporters, **1980–81:** 1540
  New York State and local officials reception,
    1980–81: 1528
  News conference (Checklist), **1980–81:** 1544
  Nominating and seconding speakers, selection
    announcement, **1980–81:** 1469, 1471
  Open convention, President's position on, **1980–
    81:** 1481, 1491, 1492
  White House receptions for delegates, **1980–81:**
    1380, 1424, 1463
Elections, 1980: Presidential campaign
  Anderson, Repr. John B., President's appeal to
    supporters of, **1980–81:** 2640, 2658, 2663,
    2671, 2676
  Black endorsements, **1980–81:** 2328, 2441
  Debates
    Anderson, Repr. John, President's opposition
      to inclusion, **1980–81:** 1683, 1871, 1873,
      1911, 2272
    Cleveland, Ohio, debate
      Informal exchange with reporters following,
        1980–81: 2502
      Remarks, **1980–81:** 2476–2502
    Importance in voters decision, **1980–81:** 2320
    League of Women Voters proposal for one-
      on-one debate with Ronald Reagan,
      1980–81: 1928
    Mention, **1980–81:** 2432

Elections, 1980: Pres. campaign — *continued*
  Debates — *continued*
    National Press Club debate, President's acceptance, **1980–81:** 1576, 1732, 1829
    Reagan, Ronald
      President's preference for two-man debate with, **1980–81:** 1485, 1559, 1617, 1683, 1701, 1732, 1829, 1872, 1873, 1911, 1978, 2079, 2082, 2092, 2138, 2172, 2334, 2320
      Telephone conversation presenting possibility of, **1980–81:** 1360
  Democratic National Committee events.
    See under Democratic National Committee.
  Issues
    Agricultural programs, **1980–81:** 2601, 2740
    Chrysler Corporation loan.
      See under Chrysler Corporation.
    Civil rights, **1980–81:** 2526, 2530, 2606, 2638
    Cuban and Haitian refugees, **1980–81:** 2156
    Education, **1980–81:** 2078, 2082, 2617
    Energy policy.
      See under Energy.
    Environment, **1980–81:** 2675
    Equal rights amendment, **1980–81:** 2036, 2375
    Fair housing, **1980–81:** 1771
    Food stamps, **1980–81:** 2554
    Iran, American hostages in **1979:** 2194; **1980–81:** 2013, 2397, 2414, 2683, 2690
    Iraq-Iran conflict, **1980–81:** 2126
    Judicial appointments, **1980–81:** 2543
    Kemp-Roth tax bill.
      See Kemp-Roth tax bill.
    Labor policy.
      See under Labor.
    Medicare.
      See under Medicare and Medicaid.
    Minimum wage.
      See under Wages and prices.
    National health plan.
      See National plan *under* Health and medical care.
    New York City.
      See under New York City.
    News conferences (Checklist), **1980–81:** 2332
    Nuclear arms control.
      See under Nuclear weapons.
    OSHA regulations, **1980–81:** 2007, 2473, 2494, 2511, 2554
    Pollution, **1980–81:** 2261, 2415, 2420, 2526, 2582
    Reagan, Ronald, age of, **1980–81:** 2509
    SALT II treaty.
      See under Strategic arms limitation.
    Social security system.
      See under Social security system.
    Soviet invasion of Afghanistan, U.S. retaliatory measures **1980–81:** 641, 1728, 2324, 2470, 2555

Elections, 1980: Pres. campaign — *continued*
  Issues — *continued*
    Stealth bomber, **1980–81:** 1686, 1687, 1770
    Unemployment compensation.
      See under Employment and unemployment.
    Urban areas, **1980–81:** 2196, 2290, 2308, 2543
    War or peace, future possibility of.
      See under Defense and national security.
    Welfare system.
      See under Welfare system.
    Kennedy, Sen. Edward M., support for President.
      See under Kennedy, Sen. Edward M.
    Moral Majority influence, **1980–81:** 1685
    "October surprise," possibility of, **1980–81:** 2168, 2226
    President's campaign style, **1980–81:** 1828, 1978, 2011, 2037, 2049, 2137, 2225
    Public opinion poll statistics, **1980–81:** 2417
    Religious groups role, **1980–81:** 2010
Elections, 1980: Presidential campaign addresses, remarks, etc.
  September 1
    Muscle Shoals, Ala., **1980–81:** 1605n.
    Tuscumbia, Ala., **1980–81:** 1601
  September 2
    Independence, Mo., **1980–81:** 1610
    Kansas City, Mo., **1980–81:** 1610
  September 3, Philadelphia, Pa., **1980–81:** 1629, 1635
  September 9, Perth Amboy, N.J., **1980–81:** 1672, 1677, 1679, 1687
  September 12, Carter/Mondale Reelection Committee, **1980–81:** 1707
  September 15
    Alpharetta, Ga., **1980–81:** 1744
    Corpus Christi, Tex., **1980–81:** 1725
    Houston, Tex., **1980–81:** 1738–1744
    Roswell, Ga., **1980–81:** 1746
  September 16
    Atlanta, Ga., **1980–81:** 1749–1758
    Cleveland, Ohio, **1980–81:** 1762, 1765
    Greer, S.C., **1980–81:** 1762n.
    Lyman, S.C., **1980–81:** 1761
    Startex, S.C., **1980–81:** 1758
  September 20, Niles, Ill., **1980–81:** 1851
  September 22
    Beverly Hills, Calif., **1980–81:** 1887
    Los Angeles, Calif., **1980–81:** 1868, 1883
    Springfield, Ill., **1980–81:** 1862, 1867
    Torrance, Calif., **1980–81:** 1869
  September 23
    Los Angeles, Calif., **1980–81:** 1889
    Portland, Oreg., **1980–81:** 1901
    San Jose, Calif., **1980–81:** 1897, 1900
    Tacoma, Wash., **1980–81:** 1903–1915
  September 25, Congressional Black Caucus, **1980–81:** 1927

Elections, 1980: Pres. addresses — *continued*
  September 26, Hispanic victory dinner, **1980–81:**
    1939
  September 29, New York City, N.Y., **1980–81:**
    1949, 1953
  September 30, 1980 Democratic Victory Dinner,
    1980–81: 1977
  October 1
    Flint, Mich., **1980–81:** 1986, 2009
    Ku Klux Klan, **1980–81:** 1610, 1640, 1750,
      1827, 1833
    Niagara Falls, N.Y., **1980–81:** 2001, 2003
    Wayne, Mich., **1980–81:** 1984
  October 2
    Dayton, Ohio, **1980–81:** 2018
    Lansdowne, Pa., **1980–81:** 2034
    Philadelphia, Pa., **1980–81:** 2043, 2047
  October 6
    Addison, Ill., **1980–81:** 2080
    Chicago, Ill., **1980–81:** 2089, 2091
    Milwaukee, Wis., **1980–81:** 2080
    West Allis, Wis., **1980–81:** 2076
  October 9
    Blountville, Tenn., **1980–81:** 2122
    Clemmons, S.C., **1980–81:** 2145
    Nashville, Tenn., **1980–81:** 2124, 2139
    Tallahassee, Fla., **1980–81:** 2149
    Tri-City Municipal Airport, Tenn., **1980–81:**
      2118
    Winston-Salem, N.C., **1980–81:** 2141
  October 10
    Informal exchange with reporter on departure
      for Camp David, **1980–81:** 2178
    St. Petersburg, Fla., **1980–81:** 2157, 2166
    Tallahassee, Fla., **1980–81:** 2152, 2155
  October 13
    Frankfort, Ill., **1980–81:** 2199
    Marion, Ill., **1980–81:** 2202
    New York City, N.Y., **1980–81:** 2193, 2198
    St. Louis, Mo., **1980–81:** 2204
  October 14, National Press Club's question-
      and-answer session on national economy,
      1980–81: 2219
  October 15
    Boston, Mass., **1980–81:** 2243–2251
    Lyndhurst, N.J., **1980–81:** 2265
    Secaucus, N.J., **1980–81:** 2273,2275
    Yatesville, Pa., **1980–81:** 2251
  October 16
    Hartford, Conn., **1980–81:** 2286
    Hempstead, N.Y., **1980–81:** 2289
    New York City, N.Y., **1980–81:** 2306, 2309
    Newington, Conn., **1980–81:** 2279
    Windsor Locks, Conn., **1980–81:** 2288
  October 19
    Carter/Kennedy Unity Dinner, **1980–81:** 2340
    Foreign policy, radio address to the Nation,
      1980–81: 2336

Elections, 1980: Pres. addresses — *continued*
  October 20
    Beaver Falls, Pa., **1980–81:** 2344
    New York City, N.Y., **1980–81:** 2363–2377
    Nuclear arms control policy, **1980–81:** 2342
    Youngstown, Ohio, **1980–81:** 2347, 2348
  October 21
    Miami, Fla., **1980–81:** 2382, 2394
    New Orleans, La., **1980–81:** 2401
    Orlando, Fla., **1980–81:** 2395
  October 22
    Beaumont, Tex., **1980–81:** 2408, 2409
    Texarkana, Ark., **1980–81:** 2417, 2418
    Waco, Tex., **1980–81:** 2413
  October 23, black ministers, White House re-
      ception, **1980–81:** 2427
  October 24
    Gloucester City, N.J., **1980–81:** 2432
    Grand Rapids, Mich., **1980–81:** 2451
    Wyoming, Mich., **1980–81:** 2441–2451
  October 25
    Toledo, Ohio, **1980–81:** 2455
    Waterville Township, Ohio, **1980–81:** 2466
  October 27, Wayne County, W. Va., **1980–81:**
      2472
  October 28, Cleveland, Ohio, **1980–81:** 2476,
      2502
  October 29
    Newark, N.J., **1980–81:** 2524, 2528
    Pittsburgh, Pa., **1980–81:** 2503, 2520
    Rochester, N.Y., **1980–81:** 2521
  October 30
    New York City, N.Y., **1980–81:** 2542
    Philadelphia, Pa., **1980–81:** 2534, 2542
    Saginaw, Mich., **1980–81:** 2546
    St. Louis, Mo., **1980–81:** 2552
  October 31
    Columbia, S.C., **1980–81:** 2563, 2577
    Houston, Tex., **1980–81:** 2603
    Jackson, Miss., **1980–81:** 2597
    Lakeland, Fla., **1980–81:** 2579, 2586
    Memphis, Tenn., **1980–81:** 2586
  November 1
    Abilene, Tex., **1980–81:** 2627
    Brownsville, Tex., **1980–81:** 2617
    Chicago, Ill., **1980–81:** 2646
    Fort Worth, Tex., **1980–81:** 2635
    Milwaukee, Wis., **1980–81:** 2640–2646
    San Antonio, Tex., **1980–81:** 2622
  November 3
    Akron, Ohio, **1980–81:** 2655–2659
    Detroit, Mich., **1980–81:** 2670
    East St. Louis, Ill., **1980–81:** 2664
    Granite City, Ill., **1980–81:** 2659
    Portland, Oreg., **1980–81:** 2672
    Seattle, Wash., **1980–81:** 2677
    Springfield, Mo., **1980–81:** 2665

[References are to page numbers except as otherwise indicated]

Elections, 1980: Pres. addresses — *continued*
  November 4
    Election outcome, **1980–81:** 2687
    Plains, Ga., **1980–81:** 2682–2685
    Return to White House following campaign,
      1980–81: 2685
  November 5, exchange with reporters on out-
    come, **1980–81:** 2688
Elections, 1980: transition
  Formal efforts initiation, **1980–81:** 2727
  President-elect Reagan, meeting with the Pres-
    ident, **1980–81:** 2739
  Question-and-answer sessions with reporters,
    1980–81: 2702, 2834
Elections, public financing, **1979:** 106, 129
Electoral College, proposed abolishment, **1977:** 484
Electric Cooperative, Inc., Associated, **1978:** 1770
Electric Cooperative Youth Tour, National Rural,
  1977: 1119
Electric utility companies.
  See Utility companies.
Electrical Workers, International Brotherhood of,
  1980–81: 653
Electricity, **1977:** 1839, 1840, 1984; **1978:** 947
Electromagnetic spectrum, **1979:** 541
Electronic communications services, U.S. Postal
  Service, **1978:** 2263
Electronic surveillance, **1977:** 1233; **1979:** 587, 940
Elekdag, Sukru, **1979:** 1454
Elementary and Secondary Education, Advisory
  Panel on Financing, **1979:** 1524
Elementary and Secondary Education Amend-
  ments, **1978:** 426
Eliach, Yaffa, **1978:** 1974
Elias IV, **1977:** 1265
Elisburg, Donald, **1977:** 228, 252; **1979:** 1159
Elizabeth II, Queen, **1977:** 7, 810, 812, 817
Elizandro, David Wayne, **1980–81:** 2107
Elk City, Okla., **1979:** 469, 841
Elkins, Paul H., **1979:** 465
Elkins, W. Va., **1978:** 1729
Elks of the World, Improved Benevolent Protective
  Order of, **1977:** 1482
Ellender, Allen, **1977:** 695
Ellington Air Force Base, Tex., **1978:** 1164
Elliott, John M., **1980–81:** 1644
Ellis, Harry, **1980–81:** 2477
Ellis, Tom, **1979:** 1982
Ellison, James Oliver, **1979:** 1786, 1787
Elmendorf Air Force Base, Alaska, **1979:** 1161;
  1980–81: 1342
Elway, Rita, **1977:** 2025
Embry, Robert Campbell, Jr., **1977:** 367, 373; **1978:**
  1797; **1979:** 1968
Emergency Agricultural Credit Adjustment Act
  Amendments, **1980–81:** 567
Emergency Board to investigate an airline labor
  dispute, **1979:** 89, 293

Emergency Boards to investigate railway labor
  disputes, **1978:** 1654, 1662, 1663, 2270
  American Train Dispatchers Association, **1979:**
    818, 983, 984
  Long Island Rail Road, **1979:** 2246, 2247, 2250;
    1980–81: 103, 104
  Port Authority Trans-Hudson Corp, **1980–81:**
    667, 684, 931
  Rock Island Railroad, **1979:** 1695–1697, 1998
Emergency Broadcast System, **1979:** 567
Emergency building temperature restrictions, **1979:**
  370, 690, 797, 1227, 1246, 1327; **1980–81:**
  685, 2877
Emergency declarations
  Alabama, **1977:** 1306; **1978:** 802
  Arizona, **1977:** 642
  Arkansas, **1978:** 149, 801
  California, **1978:** 1954, 2004
  Colorado, **1977:** 35, 85
  Connecticut, **1978:** 302
  Georgia, **1977:** 1306; **1979:** 440
  Idaho, **1977:** 806
  Illinois, **1979:** 89
  Indiana, **1977:** 86; **1978:** 229
  Iowa, **1977:** 557; **1979:** 618
  Massachusetts, **1978:** 302
  Michigan, **1977:** 147, 279; **1978:** 276
  Mississippi, **1979:** 673
  Missouri, **1979:** 440
  Montana, **1977:** 1506
  Nevada, **1977:** 1126
  New Hampshire, **1979:** 440
  New Mexico, **1977:** 279
  New York, **1977:** 34, 85; **1978:** 1405
  North Carolina, **1977:** 279, 1464
  North Dakota, **1978:** 1278
  Ohio, **1977:** 86; **1978:** 229
  Oregon, **1977:** 805
  Pennsylvania, **1977:** 34, 85
  Rhode Island, **1978:** 302
  South Carolina, **1977:** 1437
  Vermont, **1977:** 1567
  Virgin Islands, **1977:** 1126
  Virginia, **1977:** 31, 1382
  Washington, **1977:** 557; **1979:** 440
  West Virginia, **1977:** 1506, 1507
  Wisconsin, **1977:** 1464; **1979:** 89
  Wyoming, **1977:** 1127
  See also Disaster declarations.
Emergency declarations (Digest)
  Florida, **1979:** 553; **1980–81:** 892
  Maine, **1980–81:** 1945
  New Jersey, **1980–81:** 2453
  Pennsylvania, **1980–81:** 1111
Emergency Drought Assistance Program, **1978:**
  102
Emergency Energy Conservation Act, **1979:** 2085

Emergency management, Federal (EO 12148),
    1979: 1277
Emergency Management Agency, Federal.
    See Federal Emergency Management Agency.
Emergency Management Committee, **1978:** 1130
Emergency Management Council, **1979:** 1280, 1678
Emergency Medical Services Week, **1977:** 1974
Emergency Natural Gas Act of 1977, **1977:** 20, 21,
    66, 68; **1978:** 271
Emergency Preparedness, Office of, **1979:** 1281
Emergency Refugee and Migration Assistance
    Fund, United States, **1977:** 2002, 2125;
    1979: 1925, 2117, 2150
Emergency School Aid Act, **1978:** 427
Emergency weekend gasoline sales restrictions,
    1979: 370, 608
Emerson, Ralph W., **1980–81:** 1926, 1947, 2857,
    2870, 2873
Emerson, Ralph Waldo, **1980–81:** 500
Emery, Repr. David F., **1977:** 1073
Emery, Fred, **1977:** 775; **1978:** 1955; **1980–81:**
    682n.
Emmett, Daniel Decatur, **1980–81:** 502
Emmett, Roger Allan, **1980–81:** 2817
Emminger, Otmar, **1979:** 1840ftn.
Emmitsburg, Md., **1978:** 1239
Emmons, Dale, **1979:** 1604
Emmy Awards program, **1979:** 1615
Emory University, Ga., **1979:** 1561, 1605
Employ the Older Worker Week, National, **1977:**
    155
Employee Benefit Council, Interagency, **1980–81:**
    295, 2864
Employee-Management Relations Commission,
    1977: 2082; **1979:** 606
Employee Retirement Income Security Act of 1974
    (ERISA), **1980–81:** 295, 617
    Transfers, **1978:** 1401, 1407, 1555, 1782, 2290
Employment, Vice President's Task Force on
    Youth, **1980–81:** 124, 815
Employment Act, Federal Employee Part-Time
    Career, **1978:** 1736
Employment and Balanced Growth Act of 1978,
    Full.
    See Full Employment and Balanced Growth Act
        of 1978.
Employment discrimination cases, special panel
    for, **1980–81:** 567
Employment Opportunity Commission, Equal.
    See Equal Employment Opportunity Commis-
        sion.
Employment opportunity, equal, **1978:** 399–406,
    1212, 1714, 2290
Employment Policy, National Commission for,
    1979: 947, 2081; **1980–81:** 1981
Employment and Training Report of the President,
    1978: 1009; **1979:** 1523

Employment and unemployment
    Administration's accomplishments and goals,
        1979: 122, 561, 568, 632, 634, 716, 829,
        991; **1980–81:** 750, 901, 985, 1365, 1485,
        1754, 1951, 2834, 2935
    Age discrimination, **1978:** 698
    Aliquippa, Penn., town meeting remarks, **1978:**
        1604, 1607, 1610
    Anti-inflation program, **1978:** 721, 1839
    Automobile industry.
        See under Automobiles and automobile in-
            dustry.
    Better Jobs and Income program, **1977:** 1443,
        1451, 1844, 2000
    Bonn Economic Summit Conference, remarks,
        1978: 1310
    Business Council, remarks, **1977:** 2107; **1978:**
        2235
    CETA programs.
        See Comprehensive Employment and Train-
            ing Act programs.
    Chrysler Corporation, **1980–81:** 32
    Civil rights reorganization, **1978:** 883
    Coal industry, **1980–81:** 473
    Coal production increase, new job creation,
        1979: 1338
    Columbus, Ohio, Mount Vernon Plaza, dedica-
        tion ceremony remarks, **1978:** 1619, 1620
    Congressional Black Caucus, remarks, **1978:**
        1681
    Construction industry.
        See under Construction industry.
    Cook County Democratic dinner remarks, **1978:**
        984, 985
    Democratic National Committee, fund-raising
        dinner remarks, **1978:** 1649
    Detroit, Mich., public policy forum, **1977:** 1830,
        1833, 1838
    Economic recovery program, **1977:** 51, 71, 72,
        240, 294, 631, 632, 635
    Economic Report, **1978:** 129, 130, 135, 137
    Employment and producer price figures, **1978:**
        1240
    Employment tax credits, **1979:** 77
    Equal employment opportunity, **1977:** 163, 202,
        232, 317, 340, 342, 349
    Federal employment prospects, **1978:** 1374
    Federal procurement policy, **1980–81:** 72
    Federal programs, **1977:** 1272, 1341, 1344, 1610;
        1979: 99, 126, 836; **1980–81:** 878, 919,
        1068
    Full employment and balanced growth bill,
        1977: 1663, 1788, 1995, 2023, 2037
    Hard-core unemployed jobs program, **1979:** 2157
    Handicapped persons, **1980–81:** 809, 1571, 2362
    Illinois State legislature, remarks, **1978:** 988, 994
    Impact of:
        International trade reorganization, **1980–81:** 6

Employment and unemployment — *continued*
  Impact of — *continued*
    Northeast corridor railroad legislation, **1980–81:** 1010
  Imports, U.S., unemployment assistance for workers affected by, **1980–81:** 1999, 2352
  Industrial innovation initiatives program, **1979:** 2067
  Inflation, relationship to, **1980–81:** 124, 244, 250, 472, 582, 798, 802, 1068
  Interview remarks, **1977:** 2198, 2199; **1978:** 691, 1347, 1352, 1410, 1411, 1490, 1493, 1494, 1589, 2067
  Job creation by:
    Economic reveval program, **1980–81:** 1586, 1607, 1676, 1729, 1730, 1734, 1836, 1879, 1885, 1986, 2191, 2205, 2217, 2222, 2253, 2481, 2518
    National energy program, **1980–81:** 1504, 1537, 1560, 1651, 1883, 1898, 2475, 2486, 2568
  Legal bases for discrimination elimination, **1979:** 2137
  Michigan assistance program, **1980–81:** 1992
  Mining jobs in southeastern Ohio, **1979:** 1006
  Minorities.
    See under Minorities; specific group.
  Mountain State Forest Festival, remarks, **1978:** 1732
  National Democratic Party Conference, remarks, **1978:** 2191
  News conference remarks, **1978:** 243, 331, 780, 1660, 2221, 2222
  Nonrubber footwear industry, **1980–81:** 420
  Oakland, Calif., program, **1980–81:** 1301
  Oil imports, effect on.
    See under Oil imports.
  Older persons, **1980–81:** 2280
  Part-time and flextime schedules, **1979:** 1928
  President's campaign remarks, **1978:** 1388, 1552, 1622, 1797, 1816, 1861, 1866, 1885, 1888, 1893, 1894, 1931, 1933, 1938, 1944, 1948, 1950, 1951
  President's commitment to full employment, **1980–81:** 582
  Private sector, job creation, **1977:** 295
  Private Sector Initiative program, **1978:** 959, 1010
  Private sector opportunities, **1980–81:** 124, 2005
  Public sector employers, **1978:** 1215
  Public works programs, **1979:** 1755, 1988, 2049
  Public works and service employment, **1977:** 870, 889, 146
  Relationship with inflation, **1979:** 70, 73, 1249, 1630, 1749, 1869, 1984
  Reorganization Plan No. 1 of 1978, **1978:** 398, 400, 883

Employment and unemployment — *continued*
  Rural areas, **1978:** 2108
  Small business community, **1980–81:** 74
  Solar energy systems, new job creation, **1979:** 1098
  State of the Union, **1978:** 91, 92, 99
  Statistics, **1977:** 1748; **1979:** 104, 112, 117, 126, 299, 568, 716, 829, 970, 1249, 1309, 1507, 1747, 1768, 1866, 1909, 1928, 1936, 1942, 1985, 1988, 2025, 2030, 2122; **1980–81:** 110, 115, 120, 123, 214, 223, 245, 249, 250, 342, 389, 582, 723, 883, 992, 1078, 1301, 1323, 1349, 1503, 1531, 1586, 1613, 1631–1633, 1637, 1681, 1682, 1720, 1730, 1742, 1752, 1762, 1826, 1832, 1867, 1899, 1905, 1913, 1929, 1954, 2009, 2020, 2032, 2047, 2055, 2119, 2192, 2206, 2257, 2298, 2327, 2349, 2352, 2364, 2394, 2402, 2411, 2417, 2420, 2457, 2480, 2516, 2545, 2567, 2581, 2627, 2635, 2655, 2896, 2933, 3005
  Steel industry, **1980–81:** 734, 1827
  Summer and fall urban program, **1980–81:** 1291
  Tax credits, **1978:** 1635
  Tax message, **1978:** 159, 174
  Temporary work permits, **1978:** 906
  Unemployment compensation
    Fiscal year 1982 budget allocations, **1980–81:** 2901
    Payments, **1979:** 1249, 1309
    Reagan, Ronald, policy comparison with the President, **1980–81:** 2026, 2120, 2142, 2149, 2225, 2244, 2252, 2271, 2273, 2296, 2307, 2346, 2348, 2349, 2365, 2384, 2390, 2399, 2403, 2412, 2414, 2419, 2442, 2450, 2473, 2536, 2547, 2553, 2662
  United Steel Workers of America convention, remarks, **1978:** 1545, 1547
  Urban programs, **1978:** 581, 586, 589, 1428–1430
  Welfare reform, effect on, **1979:** 939
  White House Seminar, **1978:** 1341
  Working mothers proclamation, **1980–81:** 1592
  Youth Employment and Demonstration Projects Act of 1977, **1977:** 1427
  Youth programs.
    See Employment *under* Children and youth.
Employment and Unemployment Statistics, National Commission on, **1977:** 1175, 1212; **1978:** 52, 150
Enarson, Harold L., **1980–81:** 96
Encampment River, Colo., **1979:** 1813
Endangered American Wilderness Act, **1978:** 409
Endangered Species, Convention on International Trade in, **1979:** 1364
Endangered Species Act of 1973, **1979:** 1354, 1760; **1980–81:** 416
  Amendments, **1978:** 2002; **1979:** 1994, 2288
Endangered Species Committee, **1979:** 23, 376

Endangered Species of Wild Fauna and Flora, Convention on International Trade in, **1979:** 2288; **1980–81:** 590
Enders, Thomas O., **1979:** 1821, 1824
Energy
  Address to the Nation, **1979:** 1235
    Public reaction, **1979:** 1325
  Administration officials, issues discussions with the President (Digest), **1979:** 1222
  Administration's accomplishments and goals, **1979:** 122, 632, 717, 830, 946; **1980–81:** 1292, 1682, 2932, 2939, 2991, 3006, 3014
  Agricultural programs, **1980–81:** 2468, 2588
  Alaska natural gas transportation system, **1977:** 1212, 1530, 1533, 1620, 1645, 1978, 1980
  Alliance to Save Energy, **1977:** 126, 128, 134
  Alternative sources, **1978:** 373
  Bonn Economic Summit Conference, remarks, **1978:** 1301, 1307, 1309, 1312
  Briefing for Minnesota city officials and citizens (Digest), **1979:** 1454
  Briefing by St. Paul, Minn., citizens, **1979:** 1457
  Briefings, **1978:** 1669, 1723
  Canadian-U.S. relations, **1979:** 381
  Charleston, W. Va., energy panel, **1977:** 402
  Congressional leaders, meeting with the President (Digest), **1979:** 554
  Conservation.
    See Energy conservation.
  Crisis
    Cabinet meeting, **1977:** 34
    Proclamation and Executive order, **1977:** 67, 68
    Statement, **1977:** 6
    Telegram to Governors, **1977:** 37
    Trip to Pittsburgh, Pa., **1977:** 37–45
  Crisis assistance program, **1980–81:** 1421
  Critical facility program, **1979:** 614
  Democratic National Committee, fundraising dinner remarks, **1978:** 1649
  Des Moines, Iowa, Jefferson-Jackson Day dinner remarks, **1977:** 1858
  Emergencies
    Alabama, **1978:** 507
    Florida, **1979:** 637, 817, 1032, 1225
    Indiana, **1978:** 316, 546
    Kentucky, **1978:** 384, 548
    Maryland, **1978:** 471
    Ohio, **1978:** 314, 322, 505
    Oregon, **1979:** 2286
    Pennsylvania, **1978:** 410, 417, 609
  Energy crisis solution
    Cooperation of all Americans, **1979:** 873, 937, 951, 993, 1010
    Public recognition of crisis, **1979:** 912, 933, 936, 993, 1010, 1578, 1770
  Executive order, **1977:** 1299, 1307
  Federal resources management, **1979:** 150

Energy — *continued*
  Forest land resources, **1979:** 670
  Fuel companies.
    See Fuel companies.
  Governors
    Meetings with the President, **1978:** 456, 1480, 1485
    Telephone discussion, **1978:** 1771
  Governors' conference, **1977:** 1225, 1265
  Industrial consumption, relationship with production growth, **1979:** 148
  Initial fuel assurances, **1979:** 326
  Inland impact assistance, **1978:** 834, 882
  International Chamber of Commerce, remarks, **1978:** 1692
  International consumption, relationship with economic growth, **1980–81:** 1197
  International cooperative strategy, **1980–81:** 174, 403, 440, 1400
  International economic summit meeting, **1977:** 819, 823, 825
  Interview remarks, **1977:** 284, 286, 518, 753, 762, 1092, 2187, 2188, 2196, 2197; **1978:** 72, 809, 1349, 1411, 2152
  Japan-U.S. development and research programs, **1979:** 767, 1108, 1145, 1149, 1150
  Legislation.
    See Energy legislation.
  Mentions, **1979:** 902, 948; **1980–81:** 659
  Midwest situation, Congressmen and administration officials, meeting with the President (Digest), **1979:** 956
  National Democratic Party Conference, remarks, **1978:** 2191
  National plan, **1978:** 131, 186, 235, 310, 345, 377, 722, 763, 862, 1158, 1159, 1170–1173, 1253, 1261, 1276, 1324, 1441, 1487, 1489, 1546, 1616, 1625, 1783, 1861, 1914, 1935
    Address to Congress, **1977:** 663, 707
    Addresses to Nation, **1977:** 656, 707, 1981, 2007
    Business Council, remarks, **1977:** 2108
    Congressional action, **1977:** 1082
    Democratic National Committee fundraising dinner, remarks, **1977:** 1896
    Economic and budgetary impact, **1977:** 631, 633, 698, 762
    Fact sheet, **1977:** 672
    Interview remarks, **1977:** 1799, 1806, 2016, 2091
    Legislation, **1977:** 1396
    News conference remarks, **1977:** 1684, 1783, 1908, 1911, 1999, 2057
    Public participation in formulation, **1977:** 274, 363
    White House statement, **1977:** 1945, 2161

Energy — *continued*
National program
Economic renewal program, relationship with, **1980–81:** 1959, 1987, 2222
Evolution during administration, **1980–81:** 1006, 1070, 1739, 1763, 1864, 2005, 2019, 2209, 2297
Goals
Conservation measures development.
See Energy conservation.
Domestic sources development, **1980–81:** 994, 996, 1006, 1070, 1083, 1354, 1365, 1531, 1603, 1633, 1639, 1651, 1973, 2568
New industries creation, **1980–81:** 994, 996, 1070, 1504, 1512, 1537, 1560, 1587, 1606, 1615, 1651, 2191, 2258, 2493
Job creation, **1980–81:** 994, 1504, 1537, 1560, 1651, 1883, 1898, 2475, 2486, 2568
Transportation system modernization, **1980–81:** 1512, 1537, 1639, 2492
Legislation, **1978:** 1978, 1992, 2108
See Crude Oil Windfall Profit Tax Act; Energy Security Act.
Mentions, **1980–81:** 1083, 1721, 2084
Natural resources, **1977:** 97, 117, 123, 136
News conference remarks, **1977:** 197, 222, 224, 631, 633, 635, 699, 702, 703, 1103, 1106, 1783–1785, 1789, 1790, 2117, 2124, 2209
News conference remarks, **1978:** 54–56, 60, 732, 733, 1745, 1752
1980 Presidential election issue, **1979:** 951
1981 budget allocations, **1980–81:** 225, 228
1982 budget allocations, **1980–81:** 2899
Northeast Summit on Energy, **1979:** 2056–2059
Ocean thermal conversion, **1980–81:** 1473
Powerplant conversions and construction restrictions, **1980–81:** 1131, 1151
President's visit to offshore drilling rig, question and-answer session, **1977:** 1334
Prices.
See Energy prices.
Production.
See Energy production.
Public response to administration's efforts, **1979:** 1751
Public works bill, veto, **1978:** 1702, 1707, 1713
Question-and-answer sessions, **1977:** 28, 37, 293, 791, 903, 1144
Reagan, Ronald, policy differences with President, **1980–81:** 1658, 1701, 1865, 1886, 1951, 2007, 2045, 2082, 2091, 2119, 2142, 2165, 2197, 2271, 2307, 2374, 2421, 2493, 2540, 2544, 2568
Research and development.
See Energy research and development.
Rural areas, **1979:** 791, 843
Shortage task force, **1978:** 314

Energy — *continued*
State of the Union, **1978:** 91, 99, 113
Supplies.
See Energy supplies.
United Auto Workers, remarks, **1977:** 890
Utility payments, assistance, **1977:** 1837
Venice Economic Summit Conference declaration, **1980–81:** 1187
Western nation goals, **1980–81:** 1974
White House briefings for community and civic leaders (Digest), **1979:** 862, 2080 ; **1980–81:** 367, 452, 801, 825
See also Alcohol fuels; Biomass energy; Coal; Gasohol; Gasoline; Geothermal energy; Hydroelectric power; Natural gas; Nuclear energy; Oil; Solar energy; Synthetic fuels; Wind energy.
Energy, Alliance to Save, **1979:** 1976
Energy, Department of
Acid rain research programs, **1979:** 1389
Activation date, **1977:** 1581, 1583
Administration, Director of, **1977:** 1585
Alaska Natural Gas Transportation System Project expedition, **1980–81:** 1367
Transfer of functions, **1979:** 594
Alcohol fuels programs, **1979:** 1502ftn.
Annual report, **1979:** 842; **1980–81:** 292
Assistant Secretaries, **1977:** 1584, 1585, 1613, 1646, 1650, 2062, 2077; **1978:** 218, 230–232, 884, 898, 1268, 1279, 1380, 1670; **1979:** 733, 1294, 1652–1654, 1883, 2064, 2065, 2107, 2183, 2187, 2207; **1980–81:** 1377, 1429
Authorization bill, veto, **1977:** 1972
Budget deferral, **1977:** 2002; **1978:** 895
Budget rescission and deferrals, **1979:** 200, 720; **1980–81:** 428, 948, 2916
California gasoline shortages actions, **1979:** 808, 874, 875
Civil land remote-sensing activities, **1979:** 2150
Coal strike, **1978:** 470, 489, 573
Conservation contingency plans regulations, **1979:** 1228
Consumer Affairs Council membership, **1979:** 1763
Controller, **1977:** 1585
Deputy Assistant Secretaries, **1977:** 1585, 1586
Deputy Inspector General, **1978:** 1560, 1572
Deputy Secretary, **1977:** 1584, 1613; **1979:** 1653, 1680, 2135, 2140
Deputy Secretary Lynn R. Coleman **1980–81:** 2841, 2870, 2873
Deputy Secretary John C. Sawhill
International Atomic Energy Agency, General Conference, U.S. Representative, **1980–81:** 1572, 1848, 1859
News conferences (Checklist), **1980–81:** 65, 1377

Energy, Department of — *continued*
  Diesel fuel allocations for farmers, **1979:** 945,
    987, 1135, 1139
  Director, Office of Minority Economic Impact,
    1980–81: 1941
  Division of Naval Reactors
    Associate Director for Surface Ships and Light
      Water Breeder Reactor, **1977:** 2070, 2071
    Deputy Director, **1977:** 2070, 2071; **1978:** 239
  Economic Regulatory Administration, Admin-
    istrator, **1977:** 1584, 1613
  Enabling legislation, **1977:** 1410
  Energy conservation contingency programs,
    1979: 370, 371
  Energy Extension Service program, **1979:**
    1485ftn.
  Energy Information Administration, Adminis-
    trator, **1977:** 2047, 2050
  Energy management in the Federal Government,
    report, **1978:** 1457
  Energy Research, Office of, Director, **1977:** 1585,
    1613; **1978:** 950
  Energy security trust fund, initiatives develop-
    ment for, **1979:** 727
  Energy and water development programs, **1980–
    81:** 1983
  Environmental quality, **1978:** 1414
  Executive order, **1978:** 270
  Executive Secretariat, Director, **1977:** 1586
  Federal energy use reduction responsibilities,
    1979: 219, 647
  Foreign policy role, **1980–81:** 876
  Fossil fuels construction program, **1979:** 720
  Fuel oil management group membership, **1979:**
    2056
  Gasohol use in motor vehicles, duties, **1980–81:**
    2860
  Gasoline allocations responsibilities, **1979:** 968,
    2086
  General Counsel, **1977:** 1646, 1650; **1978:** 231
  Heavy crude oil definition review, **1979:** 2279
  High energy physics agreement with China,
    1979: 207
  Home heating oil prices
    Monitoring, **1978:** 58
    Spot shortage responsibilities, **1979:** 1631,
      1878
  Hydroelectric power projects onsite review,
    1979: 1510, 1511
  Inspector General, **1978:** 760, 771
  Intelligence activities, **1978:** 205
  Interagency Coordinating Council, **1978:** 1434
  Interview remarks, **1978:** 1414
  Labor-Management Relations Program exemp-
    tions, **1979:** 2146
  Low-level radiation activities study, **1979:** 2007
  Magnetic fusion research, development, and
    demonstration program, **1980–81:** 2105

Energy, Department of — *continued*
  Membership on:
    Radiation Policy Council, **1980–81:** 363
    State Planning Council on Radioactive Waste
      Management, **1980–81:** 301
  Mention, **1980–81:** 115
  Military Liaison Committee, Chairman, **1978:**
    1090, 1111
  National Security and Military Applications of
    Nuclear Energy Authorization Act of
    1980, **1979:** 2298
  National security programs, **1979:** 2291
  Natural gas recovery funding, **1979:** 793
  News conference remarks, **1978:** 2102
  Nuclear nonproliferation functions, **1978:** 894
  Nuclear Safety Oversight Committee, support
    services, **1980–81:** 505
  Nuclear waste management responsibilities,
    1980–81: 298, 2002
  Ocean thermal energy conversion programs,
    1980–81: 1375
  Office of Minority Economic Impact, Director,
    1979: 1040, 1044
  Oil
    Decontrol program, **1979:** 721–724
    Import adjustment program responsibilities,
      1980–81: 593
    Imports, **1977:** 2178; **1979:** 629, 630, 1622
    Industry monitoring, **1979:** 872, 1243, 1250,
      1345
    Production expansion, **1977:** 2159
  President's Commission on the Accident at
    Three Mile Island, support services, **1979:**
    659
  President's Commission on the Coal Industry,
    1978: 2244
  Procurement and Contracts Management, Di-
    rector, **1977:** 1586
  Proposal Federal department, **1977:** 163, 204,
    257–259, 280, 286, 410, 518, 660
  Purposes of creation, **1980–81:** 1623
  Radioactivity exposure analysis, **1979:** 182
  Reagan, Ronald, position on, **1980–81:** 1995,
    2045, 2082, 2091, 2119, 2142, 2271, 2307,
    2374, 2421, 2493, 2568
  Reinstatement rights of certain employees, **1977:**
    2080
  Research Apprenticeship Program, **1979:** 2064
  Residual fuel oil and high sulfur fuel oil regu-
    lations, **1978:** 1111, 1112
  Ridesharing programs, **1980–81:** 272
  Secretary.
    See Energy, Secretary of.
  Solar energy projects, **1978:** 826; **1979:** 1100,
    1102–1105
  Special Assistant, **1977:** 1585
  Synthetic fuels production responsibilities,
    1980–81: 1972

Energy, Department of — *continued*
Task Force on Global Resources and Environment, functions, **1980–81:** 1417
Trade Policy Committee membership, **1979:** 1730
Trucking fuel supplies locating mechanism, **1979:** 1624
Under Secretary, **1977:** 1584, 1613; **1979:** 955, 983, 2204; **1980–81:** 335
Uranium enrichment capacity, report preparation, **1979:** 1822
Urban noise abatement programs, **1979:** 1371, 1385
West-to-east crude oil transportation system, report preparation, **1980–81:** 99
Wind energy systems promotion, **1980–81:** 1668
See also specific constituent agencies.
Energy, International Exposition on, **1979:** 1525
Energy, Northeast Summit on, **1979:** 2055
Energy, Secretary of (Charles W. Duncan, Jr.)
Council on Wage and Price Stability, adviser-member, **1980–81:** 967
Crude oil pricing regulations, **1979:** 2290
Emergency building temperature restrictions authority **1980–81:** 686
Emergency Energy Conservation Act, signing ceremony remarks, **1979:** 2086, 2087
Energy conservation
Award presentations, **1980–81:** 791n.
Program development, **1980–81:** 481, 788, 790
Gasohol use authority in motor vehicles, **1980–81:** 2860
Gasoline rationing plan
Functions, **1980–81:** 92, 1099
Proposal preparation, **1979:** 2133
Heavy crude oil price control regulations, **1980–81:** 96
Heavy oil decontrol actions, **1979:** 1450
Home heating oil supplies distribution, **1979:** 1614, 1878, 1879n.
International Energy Agency, U.S. Representative, **1979:** 2243
International nuclear energy agreement analyses, **1980–81:** 782, 1027, 1240, 1281
Iranian oil imports discontinuance actions, **1979:** 2110
Marginal oil wells deregulation functions, **1980–81:** 696
Meetings with the President (Digest), **1979:** 1397, 1678, 2206; **1980–81:** 63, 267, 374
Membership on:
Oil Policy Committee, **1980–81:** 10
Trade Policy Committee, **1980–81:** 8
Mentions, **1979:** 1559, 1561; **1980–81:** 49, 266, 514, 1101, 1740
National energy education policy responsibilities, **1980–81:** 509

Energy, Secretary (Duncan) — *continued*
National Transportation Week, White House ceremony participation, **1980–81:** 930
Natural gas emergency supplies management, **1980–81:** 1628
News conferences (Checklist), **1979:** 1884, 2140
Nomination, **1979:** 1290, 1319
Nuclear waste management, **1980–81:** 298
Ocean thermal energy conversion responsibilities, **1980–81:** 1375, 1473
Oil import adjustment program
Functions, **1980–81:** 594, 599 760
Recommendation to impose conservation fee, **1980–81:** 592
Oil import statistics announcement, **1980–81:** 1681
Oregon energy emergency actions, **1979:** 2286
Petroleum imports and products responsibilities, **1979:** 1622
Powerplant conversions and construction restrictions, **1980–81:** 1132
President's assessment, **1979:** 1305, 1748
President's Awards for Energy Efficiency ceremony participation, **1980–81:** 2877n.
Report receptions
Coal mining safety, **1980–81:** 473
Nuclear Safety Oversight Committee, **1980–81:** 504
State Governors briefing, **1979:** 2135
State Planning Council on Radioactive Waste Management, support services, **1980–81:** 302
Strategic Petroleum Reserve functions, **1980–81:** 1476
Swearing-in ceremony, **1979:** 1514
Synthetic Fuels Corporation, Board of Directors, Advisory Committee Chairman, **1980–81:** 2752
Synthetic fuels production responsibilities, **1980–81:** 1970, 1971
Swearing-in ceremony, **1979:** 1514
Task Force on Global Resources and Environment, duties, **1980–81:** 1417
United Kingdom-U.S. atomic energy agreement analysis, **1979:** 2164
West-to-east crude oil transportation system recommendation, **1980–81:** 100
For functions of the Department in general, see Energy, Department of.
Energy, Secretary of (James R. Schlesinger), **1977:** 1411, 1412, 1437, 1440, 1532, 1569, 1581, 1584, 1613, 1618, 1648, 1761, 1784, 1786, 1930, 1973, 1978, 1979, 1981, 2006, 2069, 2077, 2102, 2124, 2223; **1978:** 55, 248, 311, 313, 327, 352, 414, 509, 594, 595, 641, 770, 811, 826, 846, 892, 950, 1004, 1007, 1112, 1350, 1381, 1453, 1459, 1469, 1471, 1477, 1478, 1644, 1984, 2108, 2185, 2237

Energy, Secretary (Schlesinger) — *continued*
  Alaska natural gas pipeline construction actions, **1979:** 1245
  Alaska Natural Gas Transportation System, Executive Policy Board member, **1979:** 1126
  Conservation contingency plan implementation, **1979:** 1228
  Diesel fuel allocations for farmers, **1979:** 803, 1136
  Energy Coordinating Committee, subcommittee establishment, **1979:** 1106
  High energy physics agreement with China, **1979:** 207
  Iranian oil imports actions, **1979:** 1583
  Meetings with the President (Digest), **1979:** 14, 553, 554, 899, 956, 983, 1222
  Mentions, **1979:** 255, 1155n., 1216
  Mexican energy supplies purchase, **1979:** 58, 185
  National energy supply shortage analysis, **1979:** 1226
  National Security Award, **1979:** 1514
  New England home heating oil inventories, **1979:** 700, 705
  News conferences (Checklist), **1979:** 900, 1019, 1143, 1294
  Oil imports recommendations, **1979:** 628
  Oil and natural gas conservation responsibilities, **1979:** 2262
  President's assessment, **1979:** 1305, 1514, 1748
  President's letter to Sen. DeConcini in support of, **1979:** 432
  Resignation, **1979:** 1290
  Solar energy development bank, board of directors member, **1979:** 1101
  State energy projects management, **1979:** 896
  Urban noise abatement program development **1979:** 1385
  For functions of the Department in general, see Energy, Department of.
Energy Act of 1978, National, **1979:** 1103, 1354, 1622
Energy Administration, Federal.
  See Federal Energy Administration.
Energy Agency, International.
  See International Energy Agency.
Energy conservation, **1977:** 7, 20, 21, 29, 44, 70, 222, 284, 286, 407, 423, 519, 665–668, 1391, 1469, 1599, 1672, 1685, 1784; **1978:** 704, 1172
  Anti-inflation measure, **1980–81:** 570, 580
  Appeal for public support, **1979:** 1240, 1463, 1480, 1487, 1493–1495, 1513, 1568, 1575, 1594, 1652, 1724, 1891, 1894, 1944, 2028, 2054, 2135; **1980–81:** 199, 828, 846, 1006
  Budget allocations, **1980–81:** 1587
  Business and industry measures, **1979:** 1535, 1568, 2051

Energy conservation — *continued*
  Community involvement, **1979:** 1452, 1458, 1480, 1501, 1516, 1576
  Domestic oil prices, effect on, **1979:** 611
  Extension Service program, **1979:** 1485ftn.
  Federal employees ridesharing program, **1980–81:** 271
  Federal programs, **1979:** 1500
    Reports, **1980–81:** 274, 2722
  Food production methods development, **1979:** 1269
  International commitments, **1980–81:** 2810
  Iranian oil imports discontinuance, effect on, **1979:** 2108
  Japanese support, **1979:** 1109
  Legislation, **1979:** 2102, 2155; **1980–81:** 1253, 1318, 1365
  Mandatory measures
    Automobile fuel efficiency improvement, **1979:** 797, 1504, 1549, 1651, 1949
    Contigency plans, **1979:** 370, 608, 612, 690, 797, 1226, 1228, 1327
    Emergency building restrictions, **1980–81:** 685, 2877
    Federal use reduction, **1979:** 219, 613
    55 mile-per-hour speed limit enforcement, **1979:** 613, 864, 876
    Mention, **1980–81:** 121
    Standby gasoline rationing.
      See Standby gasoline rationing plan.
    State goals, **1980–81:** 199
    State goals imposition, proposed, **1979:** 1240, 1243
  Mentions, **1979:** 679, 700, 805, 808, 1097, 1469, 1471, 1496, 1498; **1980–81:** 938, 2630
  National efficiency program, **1980–81:** 1399
  National policy objectives, **1980–81:** 1674
  New Brunswick, N.J., meeting remarks, **1979:** 2020
  1981 budget allocations, **1980–81:** 248, 417
  Oil imports reduction, relationship with, **1980–81:** 71, 314, 461, 509, 512, 585, 802, 846, 920, 938, 977, 984, 993, 1042, 1083, 1351, 1395, 1399, 1448, 1615, 1623, 1651, 1864, 1882, 1897, 1902, 2018, 2033, 2040, 2206, 2410, 2481, 2492, 2568
  President's Award for Energy Efficiency, **1980–81:** 1401
  Public correspondence suggesting measures, **1979:** 1330
  Public and nonprofit enterprises, **1980–81:** 2899
  Public service media instruction, **1980–81:** 368
  Public service and paid advertising instruction, **1979:** 1575
  Research and development, **1980–81:** 1354, 1505
  Ridesharing initiatives, **1979:** 2044

Energy conservation — *continued*
  Rural areas, **1979:** 623
  Science and technology development, **1979:** 533
  State Governors briefing, **1979:** 2133, 2140
  State and local government goals, **1980–81:** 130
  State planning programs, **1979:** 896
  Tax credits, **1980–81:** 130, 1737
    Car and vanpool investment, **1979:** 2022
    Home weatherization, **1979:** 1506, 1632, 1642,
      1993, 2051, 2056
  Unnecessary traffic signs removal, **1979:** 1952
  Voluntary measures
    Automobiles
      Carpools to work, **1979:** 1895, 1949; **1980–
        81:** 802, 1639
      Speed limit observance, **1979:** 1472, 1487,
        1568, 1895, 2032, 2050
      Unnecessary driving reduction, **1979:** 255,
        262, 612, 864, 1470, 1472, 1474, 1475,
        1487, 1500, 1569, 1895; **1980–81:** 802
    Buildings
      Design and construction features, **1979:**
        1537, 1569, 1579
      Insulation, **1979:** 2056
    Homes
      Temperature restrictions, **1979:** 255, 262,
        562, 864, 1470, 1472, 1474, 1475, 1487,
        1568, 1632, 1895, 1992, 2032
      Weatherization, **1979:** 262, 562, 1406, 1413,
        1417, 1463, 1490, 1506, 1632, 1642, 1895,
        1992, 2050, 2056; **1980–81:** 492, 802, 1639,
        3049
    Iraq-Iran conflict, possible impact on, **1980–
      81:** 1891
    Mass transit use increase, **1979:** 255, 613, 960,
      1327, 1369, 1740; **1980–81:** 14, 18, 1639
    Mentions, **1979:** 258, 1892, 1944, 1985, 2021;
      1980–81: 130
    State and local plans, **1979:** 2243
  White House briefings, **1980–81:** 49, 787, 826
  Worldwide efforts, **1980–81:** 1974
Energy Conservation Act, Emergency, **1979:** 2085
Energy Conservation Bank, Solar Energy and.
  See Solar Energy and Energy Conservation
    Bank.
Energy Conservation Days, National, **1980–81:** 783
Energy Conservation Month, International, **1979:**
  1622
Energy Conservation Policy Act, National, **1978:**
  1978
Energy Coordinating Committee, **1978:** 1637, 2281;
  1979: 337, 1106
Energy crisis assistance program, **1979:** 1639
Energy Education Days, National, **1980–81:** 509
Energy Efficiency, President's Award for, **1980–81:**
  1401, 1452, 2875
Energy Efficiency, President's Clearinghouse for
  Community, **1979:** 1453

Energy Efficiency, President's Council for, **1980–
  81:** 1404
Energy Exposition, International, **1978:** 1217
Energy Exposition of 1982, Knoxville Internation-
  al, **1977:** 738; **1978:** 2170; **1979:** 2298;
  1980–81: 1277, 1292, 1577
Energy Extension Service program, **1979:** 1485ftn.
Energy Facility Siting and Evaluation Council,
  Washington State, **1980–81:** 99
Energy Foundation, National, **1980–81:** 1468
Energy Impact Assistance program, **1978:** 834, 882;
  1979: 77, 150
Energy Information Administration, **1979:** 1243
Energy legislation, **1977:** 20, 21, 66, 740, 742, 746,
  1082, 1092, 1103, 1297, 1306, 1648
  Congressional inaction, **1979:** 557, 577, 632, 873,
    951, 1182, 1185, 1219, 1498, 1577, 1901,
    2055, 2058
  Conservation tax credits, **1979:** 1993
  First national plan, 1977, **1979:** 245, 255, 262,
    830, 1219, 1490, 1498, 1622, 1855, 1858,
    1868, 1973, 2034, 2055, 2134; **1980–81:**
    585, 986
  Low-income assistance for price increases, **1979:**
    1632, 1858, 1878
  Meeting with Congressmen (Digest), **1979:** 2080
  Mention, **1979:** 1891
  Second national plan, 1979
    Congressional action, **1979:** 1303, 1577
    Congressional consideration, **1980–81:** 71, 92,
      128, 199, 337, 460, 480, 498, 762, 788, 804,
      829, 846, 986
    Fuel companies, lobbying efforts, **1979:** 1498,
      1577, 1748
    Mentions, **1979:** 830, 1707, 1724, 1855, 1858,
      2023, 2211; **1980–81:** 115
    Message transmittal to Congress, **1979:** 816
    Most difficult challenge of Congress, **1979:**
      2046, 2053
    Passage necessary for:
      American security and freedom, **1979:** 1321,
        1594, 2125, 2155; **1980–81:** 279
      Inflation control, **1979:** 2041, 2047
      Oil import reduction, **1979:** 735, 1997, 2028;
        1980–81: 121, 1113
    United Automobile Workers support, **1979:**
      1498
  State and local areas impact assistance, **1980–81:**
    132
  White House briefing for community and civic
    leaders (Digest), **1979:** 1882
  See also Crude Oil Windfall Profit Tax Act;
      Energy mobilization board; Energy se-
      curity corporation; Energy security trust
      fund; Standby gasoline rationing plan;
      Windfall profits tax.
Energy management partnership act, proposed,
  1979: 895

Energy mobilization board
    Energy projects expedition, **1979:** 1244, 1323,
        1324, 1355, 1570, 1610, 1645, 1854
    Environmental standards waiver, **1979:** 1356,
        1569
    Legislation, **1979:** 1324, 1578, 1691, 1724, 1819,
        2092, 2102, 2155
        Conference Committee consideration, **1980–**
            81: 117, 251, 279, 368, 587, 607, 761, 788,
            1253
        Mentions, **1979:** 1340n., 2283; **1980–81:** 121, 480,
            805, 846, 3014
    Priority of administration, **1980–81:** 129
    Proposed, **1979:** 1240
    Purposes of creation, **1980–81:** 149, 171, 251, 831
Energy National Security and Military Applica-
    tions of Nuclear Energy Authorization
    Act of 1980, Department of, **1979:** 2298
Energy physics agreement with China, **1979:** 207
Energy prices, **1977:** 1320, 2014
    Deregulation, **1980–81:** 788, 2421, 2460
    Future increases inevitability, **1979:** 577, 1496,
        1567
    Future predictions, **1980–81:** 1318, 1639
    Impact on:
        American conservation, **1979:** 262
        Disadvantaged persons.
            See under Disadvantaged persons.
        Inflation rate, **1979:** 1841, 1937, 2028, 2046
        World political stability, **1979:** 2234
    Inflation, relationship with, **1980–81:** 110, 461,
        512, 540, 579, 735, 743, 978
    New England, **1979:** 700, 718, 739
Energy production, **1978:** 1816
    Domestic increase for national security, **1979:**
        1469, 1472, 1474, 1475, 1494, 1495, 1513,
        1574, 1575, 1854, 1868, 2028
    Domestic increases, **1980–81:** 1701, 1737, 1866
    Energy Department programs, **1980–81:** 1623,
        1624
    Environmental standards maintenance in future
        production, **1980–81:** 2589
    Environmental standards in new technologies
        development, **1979:** 1324, 1355
    Future nuclear use, dependence on alternative
        sources development, **1979:** 1504, 2202
    National policy objectives, **1980–81:** 1674
    1981 budget allocations, **1980–81:** 248
    Relationship with:
        Energy Security Trust Fund, **1980–81:** 75, 226,
            251, 279, 448, 585, 1118
        Oil imports reduction, **1980–81:** 50, 71, 314,
            461, 509, 802, 846, 920, 938, 977, 984, 993,
            1043, 1083, 1351, 1395, 1399, 1448, 1615,
            1651, 1682, 1882, 1897, 1902, 2040, 2056,
            2206, 2410, 2481, 2492

Energy Regulatory Commission, Federal, **1977:**
    1585, 1613, 1647, 1650, 1676, 1701; **1978:**
    564; **1979:** 1511, 1879, 1977; **1980–81:**
    813, 1246, 1373, 2807
Energy Research, Office of, **1979:** 1655, 2044
Energy research and development, **1977:** 257, 258,
    304, 306, 582, 1057, 1416, 2097; **1978:** 345,
    352, 473, 947–949, 1172, 1231, 2209
    Agricultural research center, **1979:** 793
    Budget allocations, **1979:** 98, 148, 149, 484, 2021
    Energy Security Trust Fund allocations.
        See Funding purposes *under* Energy Security
        Trust Fund.
    Federal projects, **1980–81:** 664, 1588, 1974
    International commitment, **1979:** 1190, 1199
    U.S. programs size, **1979:** 679
Energy Research and Development Administra-
    tion, **1978:** 272, 273, 1964; **1979:** 1622
    Appropriations, **1977:** 1057
    Budget deferrals, **1977:** 567, 931, 1357
    Division of Naval Reactors, Director, **1977:** 596,
        1033, 1059
    Environmental message, **1977:** 974
    Incorporation into proposed Energy Depart-
        ment, **1977:** 258
Energy Resources, National Student Exposition
    on, **1980–81:** 1468
Energy Resources Council, **1977:** 252, 259, 265,
    280, 1257
Energy Security Act
    Fact sheet (Checklist), **1980–81:** 1292
    Mention, **1980–81:** 1372
    Purposes, **1980–81:** 1326, 1448
    Signing ceremony, **1980–81:** 1252
Energy Security Corporation
    Congressional consideration
        Conference Committee, **1980–81:** 117, 251,
            279, 368, 788
        Mentions, **1980–81:** 121, 480, 846
    Energy bond issuance, **1979:** 1239, 1338
    Independent of Federal Government, **1979:**
        1244, 1338
    Legislation, **1979:** 1578, 1877, 2086, 2092, 2102,
        2207
    Mentions, **1979:** 1340n., 1868, 2283
    New sources development, **1979:** 1244, 1317,
        1323, 1338, 1355, 1644
    Priority of administration, **1980–81:** 129
    Private sector membership, **1980–81:** 1737
    Proposed, **1979:** 1239
    Purposes of creation, **1980–81:** 117, 129, 149,
        251, 832, 1261
    Synthetic fuels projects, **1979:** 1724
Energy security trust fund
    Announcement, **1979:** 610
    Appeal for congressional and public support,
        1979: 612, 613, 633, 679, 790, 830, 865

Energy security trust fund — *continued*
 Congressional consideration, **1979:** 1181, 1212, 1323
 Funding purposes
  Alcohol fuels production plants funding, **1979:** 1501ftn.
  Conservation, **1980–81:** 227, 251, 470, 585, 1639, 2210
  Home weatherization projects, **1979:** 1490, 1493, 1507, 1514, 1570
  Low-income assistance for price increases, **1979:** 624, 632, 649, 679, 700, 718, 735, 816, 848, 865, 953, 961, 986, 993, 1219, 1411, 1425, 1450, 1457, 1469, 1471, 1485, 1493, 1506, 1513, 1567, 1570, 1571, 1632, 1640, 1746, 1878, 1928, 1936, 2029, 2057, 2124, 2155; **1980–81:** 227, 251, 279, 585, 1639, 1752, 2165
  Mass transit improvement, **1979:** 613, 633, 649, 679, 816, 848, 865, 953, 961, 986, 993, 1219, 1411, 1425, 1450, 1457, 1471, 1485, 1493, 1506, 1513, 1567, 1570, 1571, 1623, 1746, 1936, 2029, 2125; **1980–81:** 14, 227, 251, 470, 585, 884, 1639, 1752, 2210, 2485
  Research and development, **1979:** 613, 633, 649, 679, 700, 718, 735, 816, 848, 865, 905, 953, 961, 986, 993, 1102, 1219, 1425, 1457, 1470, 1475, 1479, 1485, 1493, 1495, 1506, 1513, 1567, 1570, 1642, 1868, 1936, 2029, 2057, 2125; **1980–81:** 72, 76, 226, 251, 279, 448, 585, 1733, 1752, 2210, 2492
  Solar programs, **1979:** 1316, 1358, 1570
 Legislative priority of administration, **1979:** 649
 Mention, **1979:** 739
 Message transmitting proposal to Congress, **1979:** 721, 728
 News conference (Checklist), **1979:** 733
 Structure and operation, **1979:** 726, 727
 See also Crude Oil Windfall Profits Tax Act.
Energy Shortages, White House Management Task Force on.
 See White House Management Task Force on Energy Shortages.
Energy supplies
 American percentages of world supplies, **1979:** 1467, 1471, 1472, 2057; **1980–81:** 963, 976, 1615, 1769, 1865, 1995, 2033, 2086, 2119, 2165, 2203, 2206, 2263, 2277, 2294, 2407, 2410, 2587
 Emergency services allocations, **1979:** 1501
 Farmers and fishermen allocations, **1979:** 1496, 1501
 Future American security, relationship with, **1980–81:** 50, 512
 Future guarantees, **1979:** 1242
 Limited American resources, realization of public, **1980–81:** 649, 828, 847, 920, 977

Energy supplies — *continued*
 National shortages
  Cause of fear and division, **1979:** 1241
  Conservation contigency plan implementation, **1979:** 1228
  Effect on:
   Cooperation necessary to overcome, **1979:** 1277
   Future possibilities of, **1979:** 577, 846
   Real income transfers, **1979:** 1199
   Travel and tourism, **1979:** 1580
  Proc. 4667, **1979:** 1226
 World stability, effect on, **1979:** 2234
Energy task force, congressional, **1979:** 1212, 1216
Energy Tax Act, **1978:** 1978
Energy Technology Group, International, **1980–81:** 1188
 Proposed, **1979:** 1199
Energy Technology Seminar, Presidential, **1979:** 1533
Energy and Water Development Appropriation Act, 1980, **1979:** 1760, 1787; **1980–81:** 1983
 See also Public works bill.
Engelberg, Steven L., **1977:** 2101, 2130; **1978:** 89, 232; **1980–81:** 1149, 1246
Engelhard, Mrs. Charles W., **1977:** 2182
Engelhard, Jane R., **1980–81:** 1047, 2117
Enger, Valdik, **1979:** 731
Engineers, Army Corps of.
 See Corps of Engineers, Army.
Engineers, International Association of Operating, **1978:** 880; **1980–81:** 1846
Engineers, National Society of Professional, **1977:** 194
England.
 See United Kingdom.
English, Repr. Glenn, **1978:** 1154
English, Ind., **1979:** 1352n.
English, Joseph T., **1977:** 528
Engram, Irby Dell, Sr., **1980–81:** 845
Enloe, Dr. Cortes F., **1979:** 1603
Ensign, Dale, **1977:** 1059
Enslen, Richard Alan, **1979:** 2188
Enterprise Day, American, **1980–81:** 1519
Environment
 Acid rain, **1980–81:** 1253
 Administration's accomplishments and goals, **1979:** 122, 670, 1354; **1980–81:** 157, 351, 2631, 2756, 2970
 Agricultural conservation, **1979:** 1367, 1382, 1383
 Alaska lands, **1979:** 775, 855, 877
  Protection.
   See Alaska National Interest Lands Conservation Act.
 Alaskan National Monuments, **1978:** 2111–2144
 Budget message, **1978:** 187

Environment — *continued*
   Coal plant conversions to natural gas, effect on,
      1980–81: 1373
   Coal production standards, **1979:** 1325, 1338n.,
      1346; **1980–81:** 473
   Coastal zone management, **1980–81:** 2335
   Conflict with economic growth, **1978:** 266, 588
   Damage responses, **1980–81:** 3043
   Drought in Western and Plains States, **1977:** 487
   Earth Day anniversary, **1980–81:** 1
   Exotic organisms, restrictions, **1977:** 998
   Federal actions, effects abroad, **1979:** 10, 15
   Federal program review, **1977:** 1406, 1437; **1979:**
      75, 147, 150
   Floodplain management, **1977:** 998, 1001
   Global 2000 study, **1980–81:** 1415
   Hazardous waste disposal.
      See Hazardous waste disposal.
   International cooperation to protect, **1980–81:**
      403
   Lake Tahoe region protection, **1980–81:** 2235,
      2237
   Land and resource management, **1979:** 1361,
      1373, 1374, 1376, 1379
   Leaders, meeting with the President, **1978:** 898;
      1980–81: 1714 (Digest)
   Legislation, **1977:** 1961; **1980–81:** 233
   Marine resources protection, **1980–81:** 1592,
      1856
   Meeting with representatives of action groups,
      1977: 1966
   Message to Congress, **1977:** 967, 1031
   Mount St. Helens eruption, effect on, **1980–81:**
      951, 959
   National climate program, **1980–81:** 2723
   National Democratic Party Conference, re-
      marks, **1978:** 2193
   National groups
      Meetings with the President, **1979:** 400, 2105
         (Digest)
      Relationship with the President, **1979:** 1995
   National water policy, **1978:** 1043–1048, 1050
   Nationwide Outdoor Recreation Plan, **1979:**
      2220
   Off-road vehicles, use on public lands, **1977:**
      1002
   Offshore oil drilling, **1977:** 1390
   Pepperdine University Tyler Ecology Award,
      1977: 642
   Priorities and programs, message to Congress,
      1979: 1353, 1398
   Reagan, Ronald, policy differences with the
      President, **1980–81:** 2675
   Science and technology development, **1979:** 537
   Second environmental decade, anniversary cel-
      ebration, **1980–81:** 414
   State standards programs, **1979:** 1643
   State of the Union, **1978:** 115

Environment — *continued*
   Steel industry regulation revision, **1980–81:** 1965,
      2085, 2293
   Strip mining, **1977:** 415, 436, 1507
   Toxic and hazardous substances regulation,
      1977: 1407, 1483
   Urban quality, **1979:** 1369, 1383–1385
   Water resource projects, evaluation, **1977:** 514
   West-to-east crude oil transportation system,
      1980–81: 101
   Wetlands, protection, **1977:** 1003, 1005
   Whale conservation, **1979:** 1359, 1435
   Wilderness resource enlargement, **1979:** 670
   World weather program plan, **1980–81:** 2725
   Worldwide concerns, **1979:** 1371, 1386, 1389
   See also Natural resources; Pollution.
Environment, Panama Canal Joint Commission on
   the, **1980–81:** 35
Environment, United Nations Conference on Hu-
   man, **1980–81:** 1415
Environment Programme, United Nations, **1979:**
   1387, 1389
Environmental evaluation functions, **1978:** 413
Environmental impact statements, **1977:** 1005
Environmental Industry Council, **1980–81:** 414,
   419
Environmental Modification Convention, **1977:**
   1950
Environmental Pesticide Control Act of 1978,
   Federal, **1979:** 1354
Environmental Policy Act, National, **1979:** 121,
   1354; **1980–81:** 351
Environmental Protection Agency
   Acid rain research programs, **1979:** 1389
   Air pollution standards, **1979:** 1360, 1569, 1643
   Air quality standards, enforcement, **1977:** 1460
   Assistant Administrators, **1977:** 1051, 1059, 1175,
      1212, 1531, 1534, 1975, 2006; **1978:** 231;
      1979: 1726, 1785; **1980–81:** 1975, 2070
   Automobile industry, relationship with, **1980–81:**
      2547
   Banned exports task force, membership, **1980–
      81:** 2907
   Budget deferral, **1980–81:** 948
   Civil land remote-sensing activities, **1979:** 2150
   Clean Water Act of 1977, **1977:** 2180
   Coal emission standards, **1979:** 1649; **1980–81:**
      473, 2475
   Denver Air Project, **1978:** 833
   Deputy Administrator, **1977:** 176, 195, 376;
      1979: 1222, 2075
   Dioxin exposure, health effects study, **1980–81:** 4
   Economic Assistance Program, **1979:** 1370
   Economic dislocation early warning system,
      1979: 1384
   Electric powerplants, conversion from fuel oil to
      coal, report, **1979:** 1643
   Environmental message, **1977:** 970–975, 983, 985

Environmental Protection Agency — *continued*
Federal compliance with pollution control standards, **1978:** 1767–1769
Fuel conversion standards, **1980–81:** 1198
Gasoline emission standards, **1979:** 876
Hazardous waste disposal dumpsites analysis, **1979:** 1357
Independent status, **1977:** 259
Inspector General, **1979:** 1691, 1706
Integrated pest management programs, **1979:** 1383
Interagency Coordinating Council, **1978:** 1434
Interview remarks, **1978:** 320, 1414
Love Canal area analysis, **1980–81:** 2430
Low-level radiation protection leadership, **1979:** 2007
Mentions, **1980–81:** 272, 352
National League of Cities, remarks, **1978:** 2077
National water policy functions, **1978:** 1048
News conference remarks, **1978:** 355
Oil spills, prevention, **1977:** 459
Radiation Policy Council memberhip, **1980–81:** 363
Radioactive waste management functions, **1980–81:** 300
Regional Administrator, **1980–81:** 654
Regulatory process streamlining, **1979:** 151, 536, 1361
Regulatory reform, **1980–81:** 59
Research Apprenticeship Program, **1979:** 2064
Rural areas programs, **1979:** 75
Sewage system programs, **1980–81:** 2083
Solid waste exemption rules, **1980–81:** 1844
Steel industry regulations, **1979:** 1641; **1980–81:** 902, 1967, 2085, 2345, 2349, 2354, 2475, 2511, 2660
Steelworkers standards, **1978:** 1725
Tahoe Federal Coordinating Council membership, **1980–81:** 2235, 2237
Three Mile Island, Pa., nuclear accident, environmental protection actions, **1980–81:** 744
Toxic and hazardous substances regulation, **1977:** 1407
Urban area regulation changes, **1980–81:** 1862
Urban noise abatement programs, **1979:** 1371
Urban programs, **1978:** 580, 584
Waste disposal control, **1980–81:** 2054, 2381
West-to-east crude oil transportation system, port facility location recommendation, **1980–81:** 101
Environmental Protection Agency, Administrator (Douglas M. Costle), **1977:** 176, 195, 376, 404, 707, 744, 806, 1072, 1407, 2102, 2179; **1978:** 313, 509, 594, 595, 787, 892, 1725, 1914, 1955
Alaska Natural Gas Transportation System Executive Policy Board member, **1979:** 1126

EPA, Administrator — *continued*
Alaska Natural Gas System — *continued*
Transfer of functions, **1979:** 594
Clean Air Act economic impact study, **1980–81:** 2200
Comprehensive Environmental Response, Compensation, and Liability Act support, **1980–81:** 2800
Damage response activities, **1980–81:** 3044
Economic assistance actions for pollution control, **1979:** 1370, 1384
Energy emergencies, monitoring, **1979:** 637, 817, 1032, 1225, 1998, 2286
Meetings with the President (Digest), **1979:** 327; **1980–81:** 63, 1714, 3044
Mentions, **1979:** 905, 2075
Natural gas emergency supplies functions, **1980–81:** 1629
News conferences (Checklist), **1979:** 1019, 1044
President's assessment, **1980–81:** 59–61, 2054
Radiation Policy Council, Chairman, **1980–81:** 364
Regulatory Council, Chairman, **1979:** 1339n., 1346
Regulatory reform responsibilities, **1979:** 2072
Steel industry revitalization program involvement, **1980–81:** 1960, 1966, 2071
Task Force on Global Resources and Environment, duties, **1980–81:** 1417
Tennessee Valley Authority functions, **1980–81:** 240
Urban noise abatement program development, **1979:** 1385
Environmental Quality, Citizens' Advisory Committee on, **1977:** 1494
Environmental Quality, Council on
Acid rain research programs, **1979:** 1389
Advisory committee review, **1977:** 1012
Annual report, **1979:** 119; **1980–81:** 351, 3018
Banned or significantly restricted substances exports, report evaluation, **1980–81:** 2909
Economic assistance programs, **1979:** 1371
Environmental information exchange with foreign nations, **1979:** 11–13
Environmental Message, **1977:** 969, 972, 976, 977, 983, 985
Floodplain management, **1977:** 1000, 1001
Global 2000 study, **1980–81:** 1415
Integrated pest management programs, **1979:** 1383
Lake Tahoe protection, **1980–81:** 1012
Members, **1977:** 229, 253, 332, 372, 885, 943; **1978:** 1270, 1279; **1979:** 2077, 2082; **1980–81:** 2910
Mentions, **1980–81:** 1, 415
National Productivity Council, **1978:** 1833, 1835
National water policy functions, **1978:** 1044, 1046

Environmental Quality, Council — *continued*
Nonfuel minerals policy, **1977:** 2102
Pollution control, economic assistance programs for, **1979:** 1370
Radiation Policy Council, activities appraisal, **1980–81:** 363
Reorganization Plan No. 1, **1977:** 1258
Report, **1978:** 430
Solar energy estimates, **1978:** 826
Timber harvests, **1978:** 725
Water resource projects, evaluation, **1977:** 207, 490
West-to-east crude oil transportation system, report preparation, **1980–81:** 100
Environmental Quality, Council on, Chairman, **1977:** 375, 806, 1031; **1980–81:** 35, 319n., 1714, 2235, 3044
Environmental Quality, Council on, Chairman (J. Gustave Speth), **1977:** 332, 372; **1980–81:** 335, 419n., 1714, 2236, 3044
Designation to be Chairman, **1979:** 1353
Meetings with the President (Digest), **1979:** 1222, 1454
National trails designation, Federal agencies progress reports reception, **1979:** 1382
News conference (Checklist), **1979:** 1398
Soil conservation incentives study, **1979:** 1382
Urban noise abatement program development, **1979:** 1385
World forest protection duties, **1979:** 1388
Environmental Quality, Council on, Chairman (Charles Warren), **1979:** 872, 876, 960
Environmental Quality, Office of, **1978:** 414
Environmental Response, Compensation, and Liability Act, Comprehensive.
See Comprehensive Environmental Response, Compensation, and Liability Act.
Environmental reviews for U.S. export policy, **1978:** 1634
Environmental Youth awards, President's, **1978:** 787; **1979:** 2075
Episcopal Church, Christian Methodist, **1980–81:** 775
Epstein, Benjamin, **1978:** 1973; **1980–81:** 1438n.
Equal employment opportunity, **1978:** 399–406, 1212, 1714, 2290; **1979:** 847
Equal Employment Opportunity Commission
Employment discrimination, **1977:** 116, 137, 232; **1980–81:** 567
EO 12144, **1979:** 1140
Equal opportunity laws compliance, **1979:** 142
Federal programs coordinator, **1980–81:** 1352, 2682
General Counsel, **1979:** 1157, 1159
Interview remarks, **1978:** 319, 1412
Members, **1978:** 1510, 1517, 1539, 1572; **1979:** 1259, 1293; **1980–81:** 1125, 1150

Equal Employment — *continued*
Reorganization during administration, **1980–81:** 617, 1952
Reorganization Plan No. 1 of 1978, **1978:** 399–406, 2291
State of the Union, **1978:** 111
Vice Chairman, **1977:** 1473
Equal Employment Opportunity Commission, Chair (Eleanor Holmes Norton)
Civil rights enforcement, **1980–81:** 1325, 1501
Commission restructuring, **1980–81:** 223
Interagency Employee Benefit Council, member, **1980–81:** 2864
Mentions, **1977:** 895, 943, 1131, 1345, 1347, 1350; **1978:** 554, 1150, 1681; **1979:** 1159, 1715; **1980–81:** 1004, 1071, 1574, 1632, 2428
Equal Employment Opportunity Coordinating Council, **1978:** 401, 402, 406, 1212
Equal Opportunity in Higher Education, National Association for, **1979:** 742
Equal rights amendment, **1977:** 300, 356, 544, 1502, 1503; **1978:** 363, 553, 839, 939, 989, 1266, 1335, 1406, 1412, 1640, 1643, 1681, 1719, 1725, 1749, 1800, 2193, 2260
Administration's accomplishments and goals, **1980–81:** 2932, 2969
Administration's efforts to secure ratification, **1979:** 144, 1011, 1486, 1897
Biblical basis for, **1979:** 472
Deadline extension for ratification, **1979:** 143; **1980–81:** 118, 154, 2592
Democratic National Convention consideration, **1980–81:** 1381
Fundraising dinner, **1980–81:** 1133
Illinois General Assembly consideration, **1980–81:** 832, 892, 925, 1133
Mention, **1979:** 2198; **1980–81:** 314
President's Advisory Committee for Women, meeting with the President, **1979:** 2042, 2044
President's appeal for public suuport, **1979:** 298, 2018, 2137
President's support, **1980–81:** 118, 154, 830, 880, 1371, 1561, 1652, 2693
Purposes, **1979:** 1476; **1980–81:** 2006, 2036, 2296, 2350, 2591, 2632, 2673
Reagan, Ronald, position comparison with the President, **1980–81:** 1951, 2036, 2044, 2084, 2197, 2250, 2297, 2350, 2373, 2498, 2544, 2549, 2593, 2625
White House briefings, **1980–81:** 333, 921
White House reception for supporters, **1979:** 2008
Women's Equality Day, **1980–81:** 1572, 1575
Equatorial Guinea
Ambassador to U.S., **1980–81:** 1564

[References are to page numbers except as otherwise indicated]

Equatorial Guinea — *continued*
  U.S. Ambassador, **1979:** 2147; **1980–81:** 1107, 1111
Erb, Guy Feliz, **1979:** 1787; **1980–81:** 296, 1446, 1524
Erickson, Richard H., **1979:** 2024
Ericson, Richard A., Jr., **1978:** 1710, 1724
Ericson Society International, Leif, **1979:** 1824
Erikson Day, Leif, **1977:** 1647; **1979:** 1527; **1980–81:** 1509
ERISA.
  See Employee Retirement Income Security Act of 1974.
Erlenborn, Repr. John N., **1978:** 1783
Ernster, Cletus P., **1980–81:** 919
Ertel, Repr. Allen E., **1978:** 1563, 1838; **1979:** 667
Ervin, John B., **1980–81:** 1669
Ervin, Samuel James, III, **1980–81:** 608
Erving, Julius, **1980–81:** 291
Ervis, Leroy, **1980–81:** 1629
Erwin, John R., **1979:** 1448
Erwin, Richard C., **1980–81:** 1111, 1112
Escarcega, Roy Rosavio, **1978:** 697; **1979:** 947; **1980–81:** 2817
Escobar, Ramon, **1977:** 1383
Eskenazi, Jacob V., **1977:** 1613, 1614
Eskind, Jane, **1978:** 1860, 1864
Esparza, Moctesuma Diaz, **1980–81:** 2815
Espinosa, Robert Huertematte, **1980–81:** 33
Espinoza, Leonard G., **1980–81:** 2242
Esquer, Cecilia D., **1977:** 2101, 2130; **1978:** 89, 232; **1980–81:** 1149, 1246
Essex County, N.J., **1979:** 1817
Estevez, Anthony J., **1980–81:** 2074
Estonia, embargo regulations, **1979:** 1657
Estrada, Erik, **1980–81:** 1405
Eteki, William, **1977:** 1825, 1827
Ethical Problems in Medicine and Biomedical and Behavioral Research, President's Commission for the Study of, **1979:** 1263, 1294
Ethical Problems in Medicine and Biomedical and Behavioral Research, President's Special Commission for the Study of, **1979:** 2260
Ethics, Office of Government, **1979:** 1130
Ethics in the Civil Service Commission, Office of, proposed, **1978:** 1645
Ethics in Government Act, **1978:** 1603, 1615, 1622, 1644, 1797, 1854, 1861, 1866, 1880, 1885, 1886, 1890, 1894, 1938, 1966
  Proposed, **1977:** 786, 807
Ethics in Government Act of 1978 amendments, **1979:** 1130
Ethiopia
  Ambassador to U.S., **1977:** 2050
  Cuba, involvement in, **1978:** 1095
  Lt. Gen. Mengistu Haile Mariam, **1978:** 414
  News conference remarks, **1978:** 442, 490
  President's personal emissary, **1978:** 415

Ethiopia — *continued*
  Refugees flight, **1980–81:** 964, 971
  Soviet influence, **1980–81:** 111, 674, 1007
  Trade beneficiary developing country designation withdrawal, **1980–81:** 550
  U.S. Ambassador, **1978:** 1023, 1034
  U.S. policy, **1978:** 121, 324
Ethnic groups, **1979:** 1994
Ethnic organizations, meetings with the President, **1980–81:** 648, 2178
Etienne, Anthony J., **1980–81:** 2076
Etienne, Lizbeth A., **1979:** 2076
Eurocommunism, **1978:** 1302
Europe
  Arms levels, **1979:** 1845
  Communist participation in Western governments, **1977:** 767, 777
  Mutual and balanced force reductions, **1977:** 849, 2210; **1979:** 1845
  President's trip, **1977:** 809–815, 825–818, 840–841, 844, 847, 848, 857, 860, 881
  U.S. delegation's visit, **1979:** 436
  U.S. policy, **1977:** 762, 776
  Vice President's trip, **1977:** 8, 9, 11, 57, 58, 149, 785
  See also specific country.
Europe, Commission on Security and Cooperation in, **1978:** 1340; **1979:** 2184; **1980–81:** 1292
Europe, Conference on Security and Cooperation in, **1977:** 220, 340, 994, 1031, 1085, 1108, 2037, 2038, 2208; **1978:** 453, 2166; **1979:** 979, 1352
  Helsinki Final Act
    Allies review of implementation, **1980–81:** 440, 1215
    Fifth anniversary ceremony, **1980–81:** 1434, 1471
  U.S. delegation, Chairman and Co-chairman, **1980–81:** 848
  U.S. goals, **1980–81:** 1207, 1215, 1659, 1855
Europe, Western
  Interview remarks, **1978:** 1260
  See also North Atlantic Treaty Organization.
European Communities, Commission of the, **1977:** 556, 705; **1978:** 34, 2245; **1979:** 1197; **1980–81:** 189, 1185
European Communities, Council of the, **1977:** 1634
European Economic Community, **1977:** 11, 205, 362; **1978:** 276, 1296, 1310, 1312, 1315
  Afghanistan neutrality proposal, **1980–81:** 439
  Agreement on International Carriage of Perishable Foodstuffs, **1979:** 83
  Atomic Energy Community (EURATOM), **1980–81:** 286, 304
  Geneva Protocol (1979) to the General Agreement on Trade and Tariffs, **1979:** 2223, 2226
  Iran, sanctions against, **1980–81:** 760, 764, 765

European Community — *continued*
   National oil import quotas decision, **1979:** 1184,
      1187, 1198
   Nuclear arms deployment decision, **1979:** 2258,
      2264
   Oil reduction strategy, **1980–81:** 1187
   Parliament, President Simone Veil, **1980–81:** 238
   President, **1979:** 2093, 2097
   Steel industry restructuring, **1980–81:** 1963
   Tokyo Economic Summit attendance, **1979** 550
   Trade with U.S., **1980–81:** 1247, 1824
   U.S. military strength, influence on, **1979:** 2233
   U.S. Representative, **1979:** 1821, 1824
   West Bank and Gaza Strip autonomy negotia-
      tions proposal, **1980–81:** 1114
European Migration, Intergovernmental Commit-
      tee for, **1979:** 2091
European Monetary System (EMS), **1978:** 2245;
      1979: 1200; **1980–81:** 1190
European region-U.S. convention on higher edu-
      cation, **1980–81:** 2721
European Space Organization, **1979:** 539
Evangelista, Lilia, **1980–81:** 2242
Evans, Clifford, **1980–81:** 2430
Evans, Daniel, **1980–81:** 263
Evans, Repr. David W., **1979:** 990
Evans, Doris A., **1980–81:** 1927, 1947
Evans, Elizabeth W., **1980–81:** 273
Evans, John R. **1979:** 1021, 1398
Evans, John V.
   See Governor *under* Idaho.
Evans, Mary Jo, **1978:** 802
Evans, Orinda D., **1979:** 1018, 1019
Evans, Patty, **1979:** 989, 990
Evans, Samuel L., **1978:** 328
Evans, Terrence T., **1979:** 1294, 1319
Everett, Beverly, **1977:** 526
Everett, Robinson O., **1980–81:** 317
Evergone, Inc., **1980–81:** 1402
Evins, William J., Jr., **1977:** 1266, 1307
Evron, Ephraim.
   See Ambassador to U.S. *under* Israel.
Ewing, Oscar, **1980–81:** 535
Excise tax, **1977:** 665
Executive, Legislative, and Judicial Salaries, Com-
      mission on, **1980–81:** 1412, 1947, 2867
Executive agencies, garnishment of moneys pay-
      able to employees, **1978:** 2274
Executive branch
   Affirmative action, **1977:** 1345, 1376
   Reorganization
      Authorization legislation, **1977:** 74, 81–84, 87
      Congressional members, survey, **1977:** 1378
      Displaced employee programs, **1977:** 1463
      Presidential advisory committee, **1977:** 1494,
         1495
      Review studies, **1977:** 1193, 1406, 1495

Executive Committee on Reorganization, **1977:**
      1052
Executive Exchange, President's Commission on,
      1979: 866, 976, 1679; **1980–81:** 272, 1332,
      2533
Executive group to combat fraud and waste in
      government, proposed, **1979:** 780
Executive Interchange Program, President's, **1977:**
      1906
Executive Office of the President, **1979:** 824;
      1980–81: 616
   Office of Administration, **1977:** 2102, 2182
   Presidential Domestic Policy Review System,
      1977: 1589
   Reorganization Plan No. 1 of 1977, **1977:** 1353,
      1355, 1365, 1592
Executive Orders
   ACTION Cooperative Volunteers (EO 12034),
      1978: 51
   Advisory Committee on Small and Minority
      Business Ownership (EO 12190), **1980–81:**
      262
   Agreement on Government Procurement (EO
      12260), **1980–81:** 2854
   Agricultural and trade development (EO 12220),
      1980–81: 1237
   Airport and Airway Development Act functions
      (EO 12079), **1978:** 1532
   Alaska Natural gas Transportation System (EO
      12142), **1979:** 1126
   American prisoners of war (EO 12017), **1977:**
      1958
      (EO 12018), **1977:** 1967
   Anti-inflation program (EO 12161), **1979:** 1778
   Armed Forces promotion and disability separa-
      tion limitations (EO 12082), **1978:** 1541
   Armed Forces promotion and disability separa-
      tion limitations suspensions (EO 12239),
      1980–81: 1857
   Arms export controls administration (EO 12210),
      1980–81: 696
   Bicentennial functions (EO 12001), **1977:** 1190
   Black colleges and universities (EO 12232),
      1980–81: 1518
   Central Intelligence Agency retirement and dis-
      ability system (EO 12023), **1977:** 2066
      (EO 12197), **1980–81:** 431
      (EO 12253), **1980–81:** 2749
      (EO 12273), **1980–81:** 3001
   China-U.S. trade relations (EO 12167), **1979:**
      2007
   Civil service rules
      (EO 12021), **1977:** 2062
      (EO 12043), **1978:** 480
   Civil service status for CETA participants (EO
      12257), **1980–81:** 2820
   Clark, Tom C., death (EO 11996), **1977:** 1102

Executive Orders — *continued*
 Commemorative Presidential proclamations (EO
    12080), **1978:** 1532
 Committee on Selection of the Director of the
    Federal Bureau of Investigation (EO
    11971), **1977:** 144
    (EO 11982), **1977:** 747
 Committee on Selection of Federal Judicial
    Officers (EO 11992) **1977:** 1009
 Competitive status for handicapped Federal em-
    ployees (EO 12125), **1979:** 434
 Consumer Affairs Council (EO 12265), **1980–81:**
    2910
 Courts-martial manual amendments
    (EO 12198), **1980–81:** 493
    (EO 12233), **1980–81:** 1626
 Credit control
    (EO 12201), **1980–81:** 482
    (EO 12225), **1980–81:** 1283
 Critical energy facility program (EO 12129),
    1979: 614
 Cuban and Haitian refugees
    (EO 12244), **1980–81:** 2068
    (EO 12246), **1980–81:** 2183
    (EO 12251), **1980–81:** 2729
    (EO 12256), **1980–81:** 2812
 Defense economic adjustment programs (EO
    12049), **1978:** 593
 Defense Meritorious Service Medal (EO 12019),
    1977: 1959, 1967
 Department of Energy
    (EO 12038), **1978:** 270
    (EO 12156), **1979:** 1621
 Department of Energy Organization Act, effec-
    tuation (EO 12009), **1977:** 1581
 Design Liaison Council (EO 12275), **1980–81:**
    3003
 Domestic Council, Office of Drug Abuse Policy,
    and Economic Opportunity Council (EO
    12045), **1978:** 597
 Drug Enforcement Administration (EO 12230),
    1980–81: 1443
 Drug policy functions (EO 12133), **1979:** 824
 Dubs, Adoph (EO 12120), **1979:** 271
 Education Department activation (EO 12212),
    1980–81: 818
 Educational benefits for veterans and depen-
    dents (EO 12020), **1977:** 1981
 Emergency boards to investigate railway labor
    disputes
    (EO 12085), **1978:** 1662
    (EO 12132), **1979:** 818
    (EO 12159), **1977:** 1696
    (EO 12182), **1979:** 2246
    (EO 12207), **1980–81:** 667
 Emergency Natural Gas Act of 1977, admin-
    istration (EO 11969), **1977:** 68
 Employee Retirement Income Security Act
    transfers (EO 12108), **1978:** 2300

Executive Orders — *continued*
 Energy Coordinating Committee
    (EO 12083), **1978:** 1637
    (EO 12121), **1979:** 337
 Energy policy and conservation (EO 12003),
    1977: 1299, 1307
 Environmental damage responses (EO 12286),
    1980–81: 3043
 Environmental effects abroad of major Federal
    actions (EO 12114), **1979:** 10
 Environmental evaluation functions (EO 12040),
    413
 Environmental impact statements (EO 11991),
    1977: 1005
 Equal employment opportunity
    (EO 12067), **1978:** 1212
    (EO 12086), **1978:** 1714
    (EO 12106), **1978:** 2290
 Equal Employment Opportunity Commission
    (EO 12144), **1979:** 1140
 European Atomic Energy Community-U.S. nu-
    clear cooperaton (EO 12193), **1980–81:**
    304
 Executive development and other personnel
    functions (EO 12027), **1977:** 2080
 Executive Office of the President, Office of
    Administration (EO 12028), **1977:** 2102
 Executive Office of the President, printing ser-
    vices (EO 12134), **1979:** 824
 Executive Schedule
    (EO 11976), **1977:** 363
    (EO 11983), **1977:** 797
    (EO 11986), **1979:** 40
    (EO 11995), **1977:** 1074
    (EO 11999), **1977:** 1180
    (EO 12025), **1977:** 2067
    (EO 12035), **1978:** 126
    (EO 12060), **1978:** 913
    (EO 12069), **1978:** 1220
    (EO 12076), **1978:** 1454
    (EO 12099), **1978:** 2056
    (EO 12111), **1979:** 3
    (EO 12119), **1979:** 270
    (EO 12154), **1979:** 1596
    (EO 12199), **1980–81:** 462
    (EO 12236), **1980–81:** 1645
    (EO 12237), **1980–81:** 1645
 Exotic organisms (EO 11987), **1977:** 998
 Export Administration Act of 1969 (EO 12002),
    1977: 1216
 Export Administration Act of 1979, administra-
    tion (EO 12214), **1980–81:** 823
 Export of banned or significantly restricted sub-
    stances (EO 12264), **1980–81:** 2903
 Export-Import Bank of the United States (EO
    12166), **1979:** 1965
 Fair housing, Federal programs (EO 12259),
    1980–81: 2850

Executive Orders — *continued*
  Federal advisory committees continuation and
      termination
    (EO 12258), **1980–81:** 2849
    (EO 12271), **1980–81:** 2914
  Federal advisory committees (EO 12110), **1978:**
      2301
  Federal anti-inflationary procurement practices
      (EO 12092), **1978:** 1919
  Federal civil service reorganization
    (EO 12107), **1978:** 2292
    (EO 12126), **1979:** 550
  Federal civilian and military pay increases
    (EO 12010), **1977:** 1681
    (EO 12087), **1978:** 1732
    (EO 12165), **1979:** 1848
    (EO 12200), **1980–81:** 467
    (EO 12248), **1980–81:** 2312
  Federal compliance with fuel use prohibitions
      (EO 12217), **1980–81:** 1131
  Federal compliance with pollution control stan-
      dards (EO 12088), **1978:** 1766
  Federal consumer programs (EO 12160), **1979:**
      1762
  Federal cost-of-living allowances (EO 12070),
      1978: 1220
  Federal emergency management (EO 12148),
      1979: 1277
  Federal Emergency Management Agency
    (EO 12127), **1979:** 566
    (EO 12156), **1979:** 1621
  Federal facility ridesharing program (EO 12191),
      1980–81: 271
  Federal Government pension plans (EO 12177),
      1979: 2219
  Federal Labor-Management Relations Program,
      exemptions from (EO 12171), **1979:** 2144
  Federal legal resources management (EO 12146),
      1979: 1264
  Federal pay administration (EO 12004), **1977:**
      1302
  Federal physicians comparability allowance (EO
      12109), **1978:** 2300, 2301
  Federal procurement in labor surplus areas (EO
      12073), **1978:** 1429, 1432
  Federal Property Council, termination (EO
      12030), **1977:** 2124
  Federal Regional Councils (EO 12149), **1979:**
      1288
  Federal space management (EO 12072), **1978:**
      1429, 1430
  Flemming, Arthur S., exemption from manda-
      tory retirement (EO 12000), **1977:** 1190
  Floodplain management (EO 11988), **1977:** 998
  Food Security Wheat Reserve (EO 12266),
      1980–81: 2911
  Food stamps issuance by United States Postal
      Service (EO 12116), **1979:** 83

Executive Orders — *continued*
  Foreign assistance functions
    (EO 12163), **1979:** 1792
    (EO 12178), **1979:** 2220
    (EO 12226), **1980–81:** 1396
  Foreign assistance programs, inspection (EO
      12066), **1978:** 1209
  Foreign duty personnel allowances (EO 12228),
      1980–81: 1420
  Foreign intelligence electronic surveillance (EO
      12139), **1979:** 940
  Foreign Service
    Disability and retirement system (EO 12145),
        1979: 1261
    Employee-management relations (EO 12128),
        1979: 606
    Retirement and disability system (EO 12272),
        1980–81: 3001
    Salary schedule (EO 12249), **1980–81:** 2471
  Garnishment of moneys payable to employees of
      executive agencies and the District of
      Columbia (EO 12105), **1978:** 2274
  Gasohol use in Federal motor vehicles (EO
      12261), **1980–81:** 2860
  Gasoline end-user allocation (EO 12140), **1979:**
      968
    (EO 12162), **1979:** 1779
  Generalized System of Preferences for devel-
      oping countries
    (EO 11974), **1977:** 255
    (EO 12005), **1977:** 1346
    (EO 12032), **1977:** 2181
    (EO 12041), **1978:** 421
    (EO 12124), **1979:** 367
    (EO 12180), **1979:** 2228
    (EO 12181), **1979:** 2229
    (EO 12204), **1980–81:** 549
    (EO 12222), **1980–81:** 1250
    (EO 12267), **1980–81:** 2911
  Government regulations (EO 12044), **1978:** 558
  Heavy crude oil
    (EO 12153), **1979:** 1450
    (EO 12186), **1979:** 2278
    (EO 12189), **1980–81:** 96
  Holiday for Federal employees
    (EO 12179), **1979:** 2222
    (EO 12255), **1980–81:** 2777
  Hostage Relief Act (EO 12268), **1980–81:** 2912
  Imported objects of cultural value (EO 12047),
      1978: 605
  Independent water project review
    (EO 12113), **1979:** 8
    (EO 12141), **1979:** 1000
  India, U.S. export of special nuclear material
    (EO 12055), **1978:** 791
    (EO 12218), **1980–81:** 1137
  Industry and Trade Administration (EO 12096),
      1978: 1924

Executive Orders — *continued*
  Intelligence activities, U.S. foreign
    (EO 11985), **1977:** 880
    (EO 11994), **1977:** 1051
  Interagency Committee for the Purchase of
    United States Savings Bonds (EO 11981),
    1977: 531
  Government regulations improvement (EO
    12221), **1980–81:** 1239
  Interagency Coordinating Council (EO 12075),
    1978: 1429, 1433
  Interagency Employee Benefit Council (EO
    12262), **1980–81:** 2864
  International Communication Agency (EO
    12048), **1978:** 606
  International Convention for the Safety of Life
    at Sea, 1974, enforcement (EO 12234),
    1980–81: 1627
  International Maritime Satellite Organization
    (EO 12238), **1980–81:** 1707
  International organizations entitled to privileges
    and immunities (EO 12033), **1978:** 51
  International Sugar Agreement implementation
    (EO 12224), **1980–81:** 1271
  International trade functions
    (EO 12175), **1979:** 2201
    (EO 12188), **1980–81:** 7
  Iran
    Aliens entry into U.S. (EO 12206), **1980–81:**
      612
    American hostages release agreement imple-
      mentation
      Escrow accounts establishment (EO 12276),
        1980–81: 3027
      Iranian Government's assets transfer (EO
        12277–12281), **1980–81:** 3028, 3030, 3031,
        3033, 3034
      Nonprosecution of hostage claims (EO
        12283), **1980–81:** 3036
      Shah of Iran's property, transfer restrictions
        (EO 12284), **1980–81:** 3037
      Transactions prohibition revocation (EO
        12282), **1980–81:** 3036
    Economic sanctions against
      (EO 12205), **1980–81:** 612
      (EO 12211), **1980–81:** 714
  Iranian aliens (EO 12172), **1979:** 2154
  Iranian Government assets blockage (EO 12170),
    1979: 2118
  Judicial Nominating Commission for the District
    of Puerto Rico (EO 12084), **1978:** 1638
  Kuykendall, Jerome K., exemption from man-
    datory retirement (EO 12031), **1977:** 2157
  Labor dispute in airline industry (EO 12095),
    1978: 1924
  Labor disputes in coal industry (EO 12042),
    1978: 469

Executive Orders — *continued*
  Lake Tahoe region, Federal actions in (EO
    12247), **1980–81:** 2234
  Litigation against public sector employers (EO
    12068), **1978:** 1215
  Management and Budget, Office of, functions of
    Director (EO 12152), **1979:** 1439
  Marginal oil wells decontrol
    (EO 12187), **1979:** 2290
    (EO 12209), **1980–81:** 696
  McCormack, John William (EO 12252), **1980–
    81:** 2743
  Merit selection of United States District Judges
    (EO 12097), **1978:** 1975
  Military pay and allowances (EO 12274), **1980–
    81:** 3001
  Minetti, G. Joseph, exemption from mandatory
    retirement
    (EO 12006), **1977:** 1381
    (EO 12011), **1977:** 1698
    (EO 12016), **1977:** 1946
    (EO 12037), **1978:** 255
    (EO 12056), **1978:** 800
  Multilateral development institutions (EO
    12164), **1979:** 1800
  National Advisory Community Investment
    Board (EO 12254), **1980–81:** 2770
  National Advisory Council for Women
    (EO 12050), **1978:** 680
    (EO 12057), **1978:** 883
  National Commission on the International Year
    of the Child, 1979 (EO 12053), **1978:** 746
  National Commission on the Observance of
    International Women's Year, 1975
    (EO 11979), **1977:** 524
    (EO 11980), **1977:** 527
  National Commission for the Review of Anti-
    trust Laws and Procedures
    (EO 12022), **1977:** 2064
    (EO 12052), **1978:** 707
  National Productivity Council (EO 12089), **1978:**
    1833
  National security information (EO 12065), **1978:**
    1194
  Natural gas emergency supplies management
    (EO 12235), **1980–81:** 1628
  Naturalization based on military service (EO
    12081), **1978:** 1532
  Nondiscrimination laws, leadership and coor-
    dination of (EO 12250), **1980–81:** 2652
  Nuclear nonproliferation (EO 12058), **1978:** 894
  Nuclear power facility accidents (EO 12241)
    1958
  Nuclear Safety Oversight Committee
    (EO 12202), **1980–81:** 504
    (EO 12240), **1980–81:** 1935

Executive Orders — *continued*
    Occupational safety and health programs for
        Federal employees
        (EO 12196), **1980–81:** 393
        (EO 12223), **1980–81:** 1261
    Off-road vehicles on public lands (EO 11989),
        1977: 1002
    Office of Administration
        (EO 12112), **1979:** 4
        (EO 12122), **1979:** 337
    Offshore oil spill pollution (EO 12123), **1979:** 338
    Panama, permanent American cemetery in (EO
        12115), **1979:** 81
    Panama Canal
        (EO 12173), **1979:** 2175
        (EO 12203), **1980–81:** 537
        (EO 12215), **1980–81:** 973
    Papermaking machinery from Finland (EO
        12104), **1978:** 2272
    Paperwork reduction (EO 12174), **1979:** 2176,
        2179
    Peace Corps (EO 12137), **1979:** 877
    Peace Corps Advisory Council (EO 12245),
        1980–81: 2074
    Petroleum and natural gas conservation (EO
        12185), **1979:** 2261
    Presidential Advisory Board on Ambassadorial
        Appointments (EO 11970), **1977:** 89
    Presidential advisory committees (EO 12007),
        1977: 1494, 1495
    Presidential Commission on World Hunger
        (EO 12078), **1978:** 1498
        (EO 12219), **1980–81:** 1139
    Presidential Management Intern Program (EO
        12008), **1977:** 1499, 1500, 1507
    Presidential Scholars (EO 12158), **1979:** 1688
    President's Advisory Committee for Women (EO
        12135), **1979:** 825
    President's award for Federal civilian service
        (EO 12014), **1977:** 1819
    President's Commission on the Accident at
        Three Mile Island (EO 12130), **1979:** 659
    President's Commission on the Coal Industry
        (EO 12062), **1978:** 1006
        (EO 12103), **1978:** 2243
        (EO 12176), **1979:** 2201
    President's Commission on Executive Exchange
        (EO 12136), **1979:** 866
    President's Commission on Foreign Language
        and International Studies
        (EO 12054), **1978:** 766
        (EO 12090), **1978:** 1907
    President's Commission on the Holocaust
        (EO 12093), **1978:** 1920
        (EO 12151), **1979:** 1432
    President's Commission on Hostage Compen-
        sation (EO 12285), **1980–81:** 3039

Executive Orders — *continued*
    President's Commission on Mental Health (EO
        11973), **1977:** 185–189
    President's Commission on Military Compen-
        sation (EO 11998), **1977:** 1176
    President's Commission for a National Agenda
        for the Eighties (EO 12168), **1979:** 2013
    President's Commission on Pension Policy (EO
        12071), **1978:** 1264
    President's Commission on United States-
        Liberian Relations (EO 12195), **1980–81:**
        372
    President's Committee on International Labor
        Organization (EO 12216), **1980–81:** 1127
    President's Committee on Small Business Policy
        (EO 12269), **1980–81:** 2913
    President's Council on Physical Fitness and
        Sports (EO 12098), **1978:** 2036
    President's Council on Spinal Cord Injury (EO
        12270), **1980–81:** 2913
    President's Economic Policy Board (EO 11975),
        1977: 333
    President's Export Council (EO 12131), **1979:**
        784
    President's Foreign Intelligence Advisory Board
        (EO 11984), **1977:** 802
    President's Management Improvement Council
        (EO 12157), **1979:** 1668
    President's Special Commission for the Study of
        Ethical Problems in Medicine and Bio-
        medical and Behavioral Research (EO
        12184), **1979:** 2260
    Privileges, exemptions, and immunities for cer-
        tain public international organizations
        (EO 11977), **1977:** 380
    Quetico-Superior Committee, termination (EO
        12029), **1977:** 2114
    Radiation Policy Council (EO 12194), **1980–81:**
        362
    Refugee admission consultations (EO 12208),
        1980–81: 684
    Regulatory reform, proposed, **1977:** 2034
    Reinstatement rights of certain Energy Depart-
        ment employees (EO 12026), **1977:** 2080
    Rhodesia, trade with U.S. (EO 11978), **1977:** 453
    Science and technology policy functions (EO
        12039), **1978:** 412
    Secretary of State, delegation of functions (EO
        12101), **1978:** 2057
    Security assistance programs, administration of
        (EO 12118), **1979:** 225
    Selective Service Act violations, pardon, facil-
        itation (EO 11967), **1977:** 6
    Sessums, Roy T., exemption from mandatory
        retirement (EO 12077), **1978:** 1455
    Small Business Conference Commission
        (EO 12061), **1978:** 928
        (EO 12091), **1978:** 1919

Executive Orders — *continued*
  Special pay for sea duty (EO 12094), **1978:** 1922
  State Planning Council on Radioactive Waste
      Management (EO 12192), **1980–81:** 301
  Statistical policy functions (EO 12013), **1977:**
      1759
  Strategic and critical materials (EO 12155), **1979:**
      1620
  Strategic Petroleum Reserve (EO 12231), **1980–
      81:** 1476
  Synthetic fuels (EO 12242), **1980–81:** 1970
  Taiwan, U.S. relations (EO 12143), **1979:** 1131
  Taxes, withholding by Federal agencies
      (EO 11968), **1977:** 55, 56
      (EO 11997), **1977:** 1138
  Telecommunications functions (EO 12046),
      1978: 598
  Tin buffer stock, contribution to (EO 12263),
      1980–81: 2869
  Trade committees (EO 12102), **1978:** 2057
  Transfer of certain advisory committee functions
      (EO 12024), **1977:** 2067
  Ugandan imports (EO 12117), **1979:** 224
  United States Circuit Judge Nominating Com-
      mission
      (EO 11972), **1977:** 179
      (EO 11993), **1977:** 1010
      (EO 12059), **1978:** 910
  United States Court of Military Appeals Nom-
      inating Commission (EO 12063), **1978:**
      1038
  United States foreign intelligence activities (EO
      12036), **1978:** 194
  United States Holocaust Memorial Council
      (EO 12169), **1979:** 2040
      (EO 12213), **1980–81:** 820
  United States-Hungary trade relations (EO
      12051), **1978:** 706
  United States International Development Co-
      operation Agency (EO 12147), **1979:** 1272
  United States Sinai Support Mission
      (EO 12150), **1979:** 1298
      (EO 12227), **1980–81:** 1396
  United States Tax Court Nominating Commis-
      sion (EO 12064), **1978:** 1039
  Urban and community impact analyses (EO
      12074), **1978:** 1429, 1433
  Variable housing allowance (EO 12243), **1980–
      81:** 2065
  Wetlands protection (EO 11990), **1977:** 1003
  White House Coal Advisory Council (EO
      12229), **1980–81:** 1433
  White House Fellowships (EO 12012), **1977:**
      1714
  Women's business enterprise (EO 12138), **1979:**
      890
  Work-study program students (EO 12015), **1977:**
      1907

Executive Orders — *continued*
  Zimbabwe-Rhodesia, U.S. trade sanctions revo-
      cation (EO 12183), **1979:** 2251
Executive Schedules, **1977:** 363, 797, 940, 1074,
      1180, 2067; **1978:** 126, 913, 1220, 1454,
      2056; **1979:** 3, 270, 1596; **1980–81:** 462,
      1645
Executive Service, Senior.
  See Senior Executive Service.
Executives, American Society of Association, **1977:**
      706
Executives, Presidential Exchange, **1980–81:** 422
Exon, Gov. J. James, **1977:** 556; **1978:** 1725
Exon, Sen. J. James, **1979:** 956, 2104, 2257n.
Export Administration Act, **1979:** 146, 333, 944
Export Administration Act of 1969, **1977:** 1216
Export Administration Act of 1979, **1980–81:** 403,
      823
Export Administration Amendments of 1977, **1977:**
      1136, 1164
Export Council, President's.
  See President's Export Council.
Export Credits, International Arrangement on,
      1978: 1635; **1979:** 439; **1980–81:** 1191
Export Disincentives, Task Force on, **1980–81:** 402
Export-Import Bank of the United States, **1978:**
      150, 1632
  Advisory committee review, **1977:** 1012
  Board of Directors, members, **1977:** 1751, 1755,
      1975, 2006
  Budget allocations increase, **1979:** 331
  China, People's Republic of, financing agree-
      ment, **1980–81:** 607
  (EO 12166), **1979:** 1965
  Lending authority increase, **1980–81:** 1691
  Mentions, **1979:** 1729; **1980–81:** 942
  Murdoch, Rupert, loan to, **1980–81:** 731
  President, **1977:** 536, 557; **1980–81:**1396
  President and Chairman, **1979:** 1613, 1786
  State trade missions cooperation, **1979:** 332
  U.S. balance of trade and payments, **1977:** 2160
  U.S. export policy support, **1980–81:** 400
  U.S. exports role, **1979:** 439
  Vice President, **1977:** 2128, 2130
Exports.
  See under Commerce, international.

Fabergé, Inc., **1980–81:** 552, 581
Fabiola, Queen, **1980–81:** 757
Fabray, Nanette, **1980–81:** 812, 826
Fabre, Robert, **1978:** 49
"Face the Nation," **1980–81:** 1049
Fahd Bin Abd al-Aziz al-Sa'ud.
  See Saudi Arabia, Crown Prince.
Fahey, Msgr. Charles J., **1980–81:** 816, 826, 1051
Fahmy, Ismail, **1977:** 1633, 1651, 1729, 1754

Fair Housing Act, **1979:** 884
Fair Housing Month, **1978:** 681
Fair Labor Standards Amendments of 1977, **1977:** 1947
Fairfax, Emmett W., **1977:** 1128
Faith, Robert, **1978:** 1543
Fakhruddin, Ali Ahmed, **1977:** 148
Falco, Mathea, **1977:** 8; **1978:** 64; **1979:** 21, 91
Falcon, Walter P., **1978:** 1511
Faletau, 'Inoke, **1979:** 554
Falk, Peter, **1979:** 770
Fallows, James M., **1977:** 30; **1979:** 744, 751
Falwell, Jerry, **1980–81:** 1685, 2218, 2506
Families
    Administration's accomplishments and goals, **1980–81:** 141, 2957
    President's comments, **1980–81:** 650, 2013
Families, interagency task force on, **1979:** 1939
Families, Office of, **1979:** 2136; **1980–81:** 2423
Families, White House Conference on.
    See White House Conference on Families.
Families With Dependent Children, Aid to, **1979:** 940; **1980–81:** 806, 836, 892
Family, American, ceremonies honoring, **1978:** 2084
Family, President's, official dealings with Federal employees, **1980–81:** 1982
Family Grant program, Individual, **1979:** 553
Family life, President's views, **1979:** 138, 1171, 1177, 1288, 1927
Family Practice, American Academy of, **1978:** 934
Family Week, National, **1977:** 1992; **1978:** 1801; **1979:** 2135; **1980–81:** 2749
Fanfani, Amintore, **1980–81:** 1241
Fang Yi, **1979:** 207, 209n.
Fanning, John H., **1977:** 618, 1752, 1755
Fannon, Peter, **1977:** 784
Fanta, Dr. Eugene, **1980–81:** 1468
Faoro, Raymundo, **1978:** 640
Far East
    Soviet military buildup, **1979:** 1148
    U.S. policy, **1979:** 1110
Farber, Eugene M., **1980–81:** 1445, 1470
Farber, Leonard L., **1980–81:** 237, 268
Farber case, New York Times, **1978:** 1591
Farid Mubarak Ali al-Hinai, **1977:** 1754
Farina, Claude, **1980–81:** 1698
Farkas, Gerald M., **1980–81:** 38
Farm Broadcasting, National Association of, **1978:** 1669, 1671
Farm Bureau, American, **1980–81:** 334
Farm Bureau Federation, American, **1979:** 1318
Farm-City Week, National, **1977:** 1821; **1978:** 1636; **1979:** 1999; **1980–81:** 1521
Farm Credit Act Amendment, **1980–81:** 2837
Farm Credit Administration, **1979:** 1418, 1423; **1980–81:** 1291, 2837

Farm Credit Board, Federal, **1977:** 1629, 1650; **1978:** 919, 935
Farm Editors of America, Newspaper, **1977:** 1703
Farm Family of the Year, **1977:** 1700
Farm Safety Week, National, **1977:** 524; **1978:** 545; **1979:** 433; **1980–81:** 683
Farmer, Thomas L., **1977:** 801
Farmers of America, Future, **1978:** 1318, 1994; **1980–81:** 1452
Farmers and farm sector.
    See Agriculture, farmers and farm sector.
Farmers Home Administration, **1977:** 488, 879, 943; **1978:** 102, 1377, 1578, 1852
    Business and industry loan program, **1980–81:** 77; **1979:** 74, 601–603, 1949
    Emergency loan funds, **1980–81:** 567
    Hard-core unemployed jobs program, **1979:** 2158
    Heat- and drought-affected areas, assistance actions, **1980–81:** 1422
    Home mortgage loans, **1980–81:** 2053, 2468
    Mention, **1980–81:** 1279
    North Carolina, rural development cooperation agreement with, **1979:** 77
    Rural development activities, **1980–81:** 1916–1918, 1921
    Rural water services, **1979:** 75
    Solar energy programs, **1979:** 1103
Farmers Organization, National, **1979:** 2206
Farmers Union, National, **1977:** 595; **1980–81:** 1050
Farmers Union, Rocky Mountain, **1977:** 557
Farms and farming.
    See Agriculture and agricultural programs.
Farrell, Robert E., **1977:** 642
Farris, J. Jerome., **1979:** 1232, 1233
Farris, Janie Salinas, **1980–81:** 2609
Fascell, Repr. Dante B., **1978:** 328, 453, 1340, 1695, 1866; **1979:** 666, 1230; **1980–81:** 848, 1328n., 1435, 2152
Fastener Manufacturing Group, United States, **1978:** 299
Father's Day, **1977:** 1067; **1978:** 1068
    (Proc. 4659), **1979:** 747
    (Proc. 4758), **1980–81:** 899
Fatjo, Tom J., Jr., **1980–81:** 1823
Faulk, Richard, **1978:** 2003
Faulkner, William, **1979:** 1772
Fauna and Flora, Convention on International Trade in Endangered Species of Wild, **1979:** 2288; **1980–81:** 590
Fauntroy, Walter E., **1977:** 784, 1632; **1978:** 1467, 1683; **1979:** 1920; **1980–81:** 16
Faust, William, **1980–81:** 775
Faux, Geoffrey, **1978:** 709; **1979:** 1447
Fay, Richard H., **1978:** 1760
Fay, William M., **1980–81:** 683, 720
Fayetteville, N.C., **1977:** 2130, 2133
Fazio, Vic, **1978:** 1947; **1980–81:** 2237

Featherston, C. Moxley, **1980–81:** 683, 720
Federal acid rain assessment program, proposed, **1979:** 1372, 1389
Federal advisory committees, **1977:** 249, 528, 753, 1012, 1494, 1495, 1507, 2067; **1978:** 577, 612, 2301; **1979:** 463, 468; **1980–81:** 507, 2849, 2914
Federal Advisory Council on Occupational Safety and Health, **1980–81:** 395, 396, 2849, 2914
Federal anti-arson program, **1979:** 2249
Federal audiovisual programs, **1978:** 785
Federal audit and investigation functions, reorganization, **1978:** 1570
Federal Aviation Administration, **1977:** 536, 537, 557
Federal buildings, **1977:** 1300
Federal Bureau of Investigation
  Abscam investigation, **1980–81:** 2355
  Agent indictments, **1978:** 733, 734
  Assistant Director and Legal Counsel, **1977:** 1382
  Committee on Selection of the Director of the, **1977:** 182, 251, 747, 901, 1103, 1126, 1128
  Deputy Assistant Director, **1979:** 37, 959
  Director, **1977:** 144, 1238, 1374, 1478, 1479, 1483, 1597, 1701, 2087, 2090; **1978:** 148, 150, 396, 1854; **1979:** 959, 1130, 1143; **1980–81:** 3048
  Enabling legislation, **1977:** 1238, 1374
  Intelligence Division, Director, **1980–81:** 412
  Intelligence Executive order, **1978:** 205, 207, 209, 215
  Intelligence reports legislation, **1980–81:** 119
  Investigation of:
    Billy Carter's activities with Libyan Government, **1980–81:** 1407, 1443
    Ku Klux Klan, **1980–81:** 1640
    Vernon Jordan's shooting, **1980–81:** 1019, 1020
  Puerto Rican terrorist attack on U.S. Navy schoolbus, investigation of, **1979:** 2206
Federal Bureau of Investigation charter act, proposed, **1979:** 1334
Federal cash management, **1977:** 2025; **1978:** 1010
Federal Civil Defense Administration, **1979:** 1281
Federal civil justice reform, **1980–81:** 303
Federal civil justice system, **1979:** 340–346, 378
Federal civil service reform, **1978:** 277, 366, 444, 458, 770, 775, 802, 803, 844, 862, 902, 936, 938, 950, 1073, 1138, 1154, 1175, 1324, 1347, 1348, 1350, 1351, 1361, 1380, 1406, 1412, 1423, 1549, 1551, 1576, 1580, 1590, 1604, 1622, 1648, 1671, 1817, 1831, 1886, 1894, 1935, 1953, 2102, 2231; **1980–81:** 115, 1573, 1697, 2965
  (EO 12126), **1979:** 550
  Federal employee performance, effect on, **1979:** 634, 917, 920

Federal civil service reform — *continued*
  Management improvement program, **1979:** 779
  Mentions, **1979:** 75, 128, 719, 1768
Federal civil service reorganization
  Amendment to Plan No. 2 of 1978, **1978:** 1251
  Congressional actions, **1978:** 1317, 1318, 1346, 1407, 1468, 1512, 1798
  Reorganization Plan No. 2 of 1978, **1978:** 435, 953, 2292
Federal Civilian Service, President's Award for Distinguished, **1980–81:** 86, 2999
Federal Coal Mine Health and Safety Act of 1969, **1977:** 339
Federal Communications Commission, **1977:** 1580, 1612, 1744, 1793, 1826
  Broadcasting regulatory reform, **1979:** 482, 483
  Chairman, **1978:** 564; **1980–81:** 1704, 1706n.
  Commissioner, **1979:** 1921
  First amendment rights protection, **1980–81:** 152
  International Convention for the Safety of Life at Sea, 1974, functions, **1980–81:** 1628
  Members, **1977:** 1580, 1612, 1793, 1826; **1978:** 1719, 1724; **1979:** 46, 91, 1021, 1043;
  Minority programs, **1980–81:** 1352, 1704
  Public broadcasting, **1977:** 1744
  Telecommunications functions, **1978:** 253, 324, 599–601, 603, 605, 611
  Telecommunications industry deregulation, **1979:** 1700–1702
  Regulatory reform, **1980–81:** 152, 1934
Federal consumer programs (EO 12160), **1979:** 1761, 1762, 1783, 1784
Federal Contract Compliance Programs, Office of, **1979:** 142
Federal Coordinating Council for Science, Engineering and Technology, **1978:** 412, 413
Federal Council on the Aging, **1977:** 596, 1066, 1085; **1979:** 1682, 1706, 2043, 2212
  Annual report, **1980–81:** 1291
  Budget allocations, **1980–81:** 536
  Chairman, **1978:** 930
  Legislation, **1978:** 1792, 1794
  Members, **1978:** 702, 711, 1279; **1980–81:** 537, 816, 826, 1051, 1419, 1428, 2533
  Report, **1978:** 818
Federal Council on the Arts and Humanities, **1977:** 1825; **1979:** 956; **1980–81:** 653, 3004
Federal Criminal Code, **1978:** 837
Federal departments and agencies
  Administration's accomplishments and goals, **1979:** 122, 569, 632, 718, 830; **1980–81:** 2901, 2932, 2965
  Affirmative action, **1977:** 1345; **1980–81:** 1502
  Anti-inflation program, **1979:** 308
  Audiovisual activities, memorandum, **1977:** 1112
  Black university programs, **1980–81:** 1515, 1518
  Budget review meetings, **1977:** 1087

Federal departments — *continued*
  Building access for handicapped persons, **1980–81:** 810
  Computer systems, **1977:** 114
  Congressional veto of executive branch actions, ruling, impact on, **1980–81:** 2835
  Consumer programs, **1980–81:** 1054
  Consumer representation plans, **1977:** 1396
  Credit control program, **1980–81:** 2902
  Economic policymaking procedures, **1979:** 978
  Energy shortage task force, **1978:** 314
  Energy use reduction, **1979:** 219
  Environmental impact statements, **1977:** 985, 1005
  Export policy functions, **1978:** 1633
  Fiscal year 1981 continuing appropriations, **1980–81:** 1981, 2015
  Fiscal year 1982 budget allocations, **1980–81:** 2897
  Flexi-time proposal, **1977:** 104, 138
  Fraud and waste elimination, **1978:** 2230–2232, 2270
  Fuel use conversion for powerplants, **1980–81:** 1131, 1151
  Funding simplification legislation, **1980–81:** 2814
  Gasohol use in motor vehicles, **1980–81:** 2860
  Government integrity restoration, **1980–81:** 987, 1875, 1913, 2354
    President's commitment to, **1979:** 561, 569, 715, 829, 991, 1345, 1427, 2027
  Government regulations, public participation programs, **1979:** 867
  Grants-in-aid, **1977:** 1557, 1558, 1569
  Historic buildings, use as offices, **1977:** 976
  Industrial Innovation, Interagency Committee on, **1978:** 892
  Inspectors General offices.
    See Federal Inspectors General offices.
  Installations fuel conversions, **1980–81:** 2702
  Interagency program coordination, **1979:** 1407
  Library and information services, **1980–81:** 1930
  Minority appointments, **1980–81:** 1352, 1633, 1705, 1838
  Minority business enterprise, **1977:** 1579
  Monitoring system, **1978:** 1371
  Nondiscrimination laws, **1980–81:** 2651, 2652
  Nuclear nonproliferation activities, **1979:** 452
  Occupational safety and health activities, **1978:** 1031
  Paperwork reduction, **1977:** 160, 169, 174, 177, 190, 397, 752
  Petroleum and natural gas conservation, financial assistance programs, **1979:** 2261
  Presidential Management Intern Program, **1977:** 1498–1500
  Privacy rights policy, **1979:** 582, 585, 586
  Private sector, relationship with, **1980–81:** 44
  Procurement agreement, **1980–81:** 2854

Federal departments — *continued*
  Reagan, Ronald, position on, **1980–81:** 2008
  Reform and reorganization, **1980–81:** 115, 148, 483, 543, 616, 785, 836, 2024, 2207
  Refugee assistance, **1980–81:** 503
  Regional officials, meeting with the President (Digest), **1980–81:** 217
  Regulatory management, **1979:** 491
  Regulatory reform.
    See Federal regulatory system *under* Regulatory reform.
  Reorganization, **1977:** 163, 169, 190, 258, 302, 394, 571–573, 906, 1094, 1104, 1391, 1582; **1978:** 69, 187, 277, 415
  Reports elimination legislation, **1980–81:** 2344
  Rural development programs managers, **1979:** 2275
  Science and technology activities, **1979:** 531, 545
  Solar energy programs, **1979:** 1100
  Spending programs reduction, **1980–81:** 570
  State and local government, relationship with, **1980–81:** 2958
  State of the Union, **1978:** 94, 108, 110
  Sunshine Act, **1978:** 1068
  Trade functions, **1980–81:** 2828
  Urban policy functions, **1978:** 1428–1431
  Urban and regional development, working policy group, **1977:** 485
  Waste and fraud elimination, **1979:** 129, 780
  Waste paper recycling program, **1977:** 972
  White House Fellowship program, **1977:** 1523
  Zero-base budgeting, **1977:** 154, 160, 169, 190, 214, 232, 239, 394
  See also Memorandums to Federal Agencies; *specific department or agency.*
Federal Deposit Insurance Corporation, **1977:** 1974, 2006; **1978:** 230, 564, 1059, 2058; **1979:** 91, 930
Federal Disaster Assistance Administration, **1977:** 113, 488; **1978:** 328, 1129; **1979:** 1278
Federal District Court Organization Act, **1980–81:** 2241
Federal Election Campaign Act, **1977:** 483
Federal Election Campaign Act Amendments of 1979, **1980–81:** 37
Federal Election Commission, **1977:** 482, 1665, 1700, 1824, 1931; **1980–81:** 2856, 2870, 2873
  Chairman, **1978:** 564
  Members, **1978:** 703, 750, 1418, 1458, 1744, 1773, 1851; **1979:** 45, 46, 90, 91, 757, 788
  President's private airplane flights, **1978:** 276
Federal emergency management (EO 12148), **1979:** 1277
Federal Emergency Management Agency, **1978:** 1128, 1129, 1155, 1572
  Acting Associate Director, **1979:** 599
  Acting Director, **1979:** 567

Federal Emergency Management — *continued*
  Activation, **1979:** 566
    Associate Directors, **1979:** 1601, 1604, 1879, 1977, 2091, 2107, 2126, 2139
    Cuban refugee assistance, **1980–81:** 819, 850
    Deputy Associate Director, **1980–81:** 819
    Director, **1979:** 781, 1044, 1621, 1678
    Disaster preparedness efforts coordination, **1980–81:** 1567
    Fire programs, **1979:** 1438
    Heat- and drought-affected areas, assistance actions, **1980–81:** 1346, 1390, 1423
    Hurricane Frederic, disaster assistance actions, **1979:** 1672, 1769
    Mention, **1980–81:** 617
    Mount St. Helens eruption, disaster assistance actions, **1980–81:** 950
    Nuclear powerplant safety functions, **1980–81:** 131, 505
    Nuclear reactors offsite emergency activities, **1979:** 2203
    Officials, meeting with the President, **1980–81:** 1077n.
    Purposes of creation, **1979:** 537
    Radiation Policy Council membership, **1980–81:** 363
    Regional Director, **1980–81:** 1091
    Regulatory Council membership, **1980–81:** 1427
    Transfer of functions (EO 12148), **1979:** 1278
Federal Emergency Management Agency, Director (John W. Macy, Jr.)
    Environmental damage response activities, **1980–81:** 3044
    Heat- and drought- affected areas, Federal assistance coordinator, **1980–81:** 1346, 1423, 1544
    Memorandum from the President (Digest), **1980–81:** 1427
    Mount St. Helens, Wash., eruption, disaster assistance actions, **1980–81:** 950
    Natural gas emergency supplies management functions, **1980–81:** 1629
    Nuclear powerplant accidents, protection duties, **1980–81:** 1958
Federal Employee Appeals Authority, **1978:** 955
Federal employees
  Anti-inflation program, **1978:** 1841, 1845, 1856
  Blue-collar workers, **1978:** 216
  Civil service positions, **1977:** 2062
  Civil service reform, **1980–81:** 898, 1573, 1697, 2965
  Civilian levels, **1977:** 1273, 1519, 1520, 2084
  College students, summer interns, **1977:** 137
  Combined Federal Campaign, **1977:** 1464; **1978:** 1236; **1979:** 1231; **1980–81:** 1098
  Cost-of-living allowances, **1978:** 1220
  Day care centers, **1977:** 164

Federal employees — *continued*
  Death benefit legislation, **1980–81:** 2830
  Democratic-Farmer-Labor Party rally, remarks, **1978:** 1831
  Displaced Employee Program, **1977:** 1463
  Distinguished service award, **1977:** 1819
  Employment opportunities, **1977:** 163, 202, 232, 241, 323
  Employment for women, **1978:** 1641
  Executive Schedule, **1977:** 797, 940, 1074
  Federal Incentive Awards Program, **1977:** 930
  Foreign duty allowances, **1980–81:** 1420
  Fraud and waste elimination, **1978:** 2231
  Free parking elimination, **1979:** 613, 920, 2022
  Garnishment of moneys, **1978:** 2274
  Handicapped
    Competitive status for, **1979:** 434, 441
    Hiring, **1977:** 1298
  Hatch Act, impact on, **1980–81:** 2567
  Hiring freeze, **1978:** 1841, 1845, 1856, 2081; **1980–81:** 477, 484, 557, 570
  Holiday, Christmas Eve (EO 12179), **1979:** 2222
  Holiday, December 26 (EO 12255), **1980–81:** 2777
  Housing, **1978:** 1430
  Illegal activities, **1977:** 862
  Limitation on hiring, **1977:** 271
  Meetings, nondiscrimination, **1977:** 1053
  Merit pay system, **1980–81:** 73
  Minority appointments, **1980–81:** 1952, 2350, 2485
  National League of Cities budget briefing, remarks, **1978:** 2081
  Occupational safety and health programs, **1977:** 200; **1980–81:** 393, 1261
  Official dealings with President's family, **1980–81:** 1982
  Outstanding contributions, **1977:** 1817; **1978:** 2144
  Part-time employment, **1977:** 1610
  Pay increases, **1977:** 97, 171, 238, 1525, 1630, 1681, 1682; **1978:** 724, 1327, 1423, 1480, 1485, 1732
    5.5 increase in 1980 budget, **1979:** 8, 64, 115
    7 percent increase adjustment, **1979:** 1529, 1530, 1532, 1848
  Pay rates, **1980–81:** 467, 468, 1596, 2315, 2729
  Pay reform legislation, **1979:** 128, 918, 1002, 1019
  Pensions, cost-of-living adjustments, **1977:** 322
  Political activities participation, **1980–81:** 37, 156
  Political rights, **1977:** 484
  President's campaign remarks, **1978:** 1817
  Public officials, standards of conduct, **1978:** 375, 2030, 2031, 2051
  Question-and-answer session with the President, **1979:** 916
  Reagan, Ronald, proposals, **1980–81:** 1377

Federal employees — *continued*
  Retirement and disability system, **1980–81:** 431,
    1727, 2255, 2567
  Retirement systems, **1977:** 1111
  Ridesharing program, **1980–81:** 271
  Salary freeze for senior officials, **1980–81:** 571
  Salary recommendations, **1980–81:** 2865, 2874
  Senior Executive Service.
    See Senior Executive Service.
  Size reduction, **1979:** 1503, 1507, 1841, 1874,
    1892, 1943, 1985; **1980–81:** 389, 1357,
    2035, 2206, 2567, 2710
  Standards of conduct, **1977:** 75, 94, 195, 318
  State of the Union, **1978:** 107
  Taxes, withholding, **1977:** 55, 56, 1138
  Travel credit cards, proposed, **1977:** 170
  Wage control, **1978:** 976, 977, 1613
  Welfare fraud, **1978:** 1657
  See also Armed Forces, United States.
Federal Employees Flexible and Compressed
    Work Schedules Act, **1978:** 1667
Federal Employees Group Life Insurance Act,
    1980–81: 2187, 2831
Federal Employees Part-Time Career Employment
    Act, **1978:** 1736
Federal Employees Pay Council, **1977:** 1525, 1631,
    1682
Federal Energy Administration, **1978:** 271; **1979:**
    1622
  Acting Administrator, **1977:** 16, 35
  Administrator, **1977:** 56, 87, 1299
  Assistant Administrators, **1977:** 590, 597, 939,
    944, 1212, 1250, 1266
  Coal production, loans for small operators, **1977:**
    408
  Deputy Administrator, **1977:** 547, 558
  Energy policy, formation, **1977:** 363
  Gasoline decontrol, **1977:** 16
  Incorporation into proposed Energy Depart-
    ment, **1977:** 258, 259
  Natural gas shortage, **1977:** 7
Federal Energy Regulatory Commission, **1978:**
    564; **1980–81:** 813, 1246, 1367, 2807
  Alaska Natural Gas Transportation System,
    transfer of functions, **1979:** 594
  Chairman, **1979:** 1126
  Commissioner, **1977:** 1676, 1701
  Hydroelectric power projects, loans guarantees,
    1979: 1511
  Members, **1977:** 1585, 1613, 1647, 1650; **1979:**
    1879, 1977
Federal Environmental Pesticide Control Act of
    1978, **1979:** 1354
Federal Farm Credit Board, **1977:** 1629, 1650;
    1978: 919, 935
Federal Government.
  See Federal departments and agencies.
Federal Grain Inspection Service, **1977:** 1079, 1085

Federal grants, **1978:** 1350
Federal grants-in-aid, **1977:** 1557, 1558, 1561, 1563,
    1564
Federal Highway Administration, **1977:** 548, 558,
    879; **1978:** 1357, 1381; **1979:** 75; **1980–81:**
    842, 893
Federal Home Loan Bank Board, **1977:** 1153, 1163,
    2007; **1980–81:** 268, 2149, 2807
  Chairman, **1978:** 564; **1979:** 990, 1336, 1531
  Community Investment Fund program, **1978:**
    1058, 1072
  House financing study, **1979:** 2028, 2050
  Interest rates increase for small savers, **1979:** 930
  Members, **1978:** 703, 711; **1979:** 981, 984, 1336,
    2216
  Redlining regulation, **1978:** 842
  Urban policy functions, **1978:** 589
Federal Home Loan Mortgage Association, **1980–
    81:** 138
Federal Housing Administration, **1980–81:** 2114
Federal Impact Aid Program, Commission on the
    Review of the, **1979:** 1439
Federal Incentive Awards Program, **1977:** 930
Federal Information Centers, **1977:** 165
Federal Information Locator System, **1979:** 2181
Federal Insecticide, Fungicide, and Rodenticide
    Act extension, **1980–81:** 2814
Federal inspector for the Alaska natural gas trans-
    portation system, office of, proposed,
    1979: 591–593, 596, 597
Federal Inspectors General offices
  Coordination of Federal investigative activities,
    1979: 779
  Executive Group to Combat Fraud and Waste in
    Government, membership, **1979:** 780
  Federal fraud and abuse investigations, **1979:**
    300, 308, 462, 719, 917
Federal Insurance Administration, **1977:** 195,
    1000; **1978:** 298, 329, 1129, 1131
Federal Interagency Committee on Education,
    1979: 49
Federal Interagency Committee on Noise, **1979:**
    1386
Federal Interagency Savings Bonds Committee,
    1978: 574
Federal Interagency Task Force on Miami, **1980–
    81:** 1236
Federal Judicial Officers, Committee on Selection
    of, **1977:** 1009, 1528; **1980–81:** 2849
Federal labor-management relations program,
    1979: 2144
Federal Labor Relations Authority, **1980–81:** 84,
    468, 493, 1647
  General Counsel, **1979:** 528, 554
  Members, **1979:** 24, 46, 90, 784, 843
  Proposed, **1978:** 437, 447
  Reorganization Plan No. 2 of 1978, **1978:** 951,
    953, 954, 957–959, 2293, 2298

Federal Labor Relations Council, **1977:** 2081; **1978:** 447, 953, 954, 958
Federal land and resource management, **1979:** 1361, 1374
Federal lands, **1977:** 202, 440, 488
Federal law enforcement assistance programs, **1978:** 1241, 1246, 1280
Federal Legal Council, **1979:** 1264–1266
Federal legal resources management (EO 12146), **1979:** 1264
Federal Magistrates Act of 1979, **1979:** 1849; **1980–81:** 303
Federal Maritime Commission, **1979:** 338, 339, 1395, 1398; **1980–81:** 428, 452, 3045
    Chairman, **1977:** 1437; **1978:** 564
    Commissioners, **1977:** 1358, 1384, 1683, 1701; **1978:** 299, 329, 1211, 1212
    Shipping rebating laws, **1978:** 1962
Federal Mediation and Conciliation Service, **1977:** 616, 642; **1978:** 313, 573; **1979:** 1452, 1467, 1468, 1609; **1980–81:** 2017
Federal Mine Health and Safety Act of 1977, **1979:** 1354, 1445; **1980–81:** 1049; **1977:** 1987, 1989
Federal Mine Safety and Health Review Commission, **1980–81:** 1654, 1715, 2107, 2916
    Members, **1978:** 971, 1010, 1270, 1279, 1343, 1346
Federal National Mortgage Association, **1977:** 706, 934, 1264; **1978:** 920; **1979:** 931; **1980–81:** 911
Federal Paperwork, Commission on, **1977:** 178, 1699; **1979:** 2181
Federal Pay, Advisory Committee on, **1978:** 823, 1457; **1980–81:** 468, 1399, 1596, 2730
Federal Pay, President's Advisory Committee on, **1977:** 1525, 1612, 1630, 1682; **1979:** 64, 1529
Federal Pay Administration, **1977:** 1302
Federal Pesticide Act, **1978:** 1696
Federal physicians comparability allowance, **1978:** 2300, 2301
Federal pipeline inspector, office of the, proposed, **1979:** 381
Federal Power Commission, **1978:** 271, 273
    Alaska natural gas, **1977:** 1212
    Chairman, **1977:** 7, 67, 68, 723, 1250, 1436
    Commissioners, **1977:** 7
    Emergency Natural Gas Act of 1977, administration, **1977:** 66, 68
    Energy crisis, **1977:** 37, 67
    Incorporation into proposed Energy Department, **1977:** 258, 259
    Members, **1977:** 1381, 1384
    Natural gas shortage, **1977:** 7, 66, 68
Federal Preparedness Agency, **1978:** 300, 302; **1979:** 1278

Federal Prevailing Rate Advisory Committee, **1978:** 216; **1980–81:** 1292
Federal Prison Industries, Inc., **1979:** 1961; **1980–81:** 452
Federal Procurement Policy, Office of, **1977:** 1580; **1978:** 254, 1381, 1433, 1847; **1979:** 242, 2072
Federal Procurement Policy Act amendments, Office of, **1979:** 1850
Federal Property Council, **1977:** 1257, 2124
Federal public assistance programs, **1978:** 2232, 2233
Federal Railroad Administration, **1977:** 740, 746; **1979:** 1787
Federal Railroad Safety Act of 1970, **1980–81:** 2872
Federal Regional Councils, **1977:** 1265, 1816; **1978:** 303, 833; **1979:** 81, 269, 1288
Federal regional matters, **1977:** 943
Federal regional offices, **1978:** 310
Federal Register, Office of the, **1978:** 1955
Federal regulatory management, **1978:** 1905
Federal Reserve System
    Anti-inflation program, **1978:** 1872, 2047; **1979:** 114; **1980–81:** 804, 884
    Board of Governors
        Members, **1978:** 230, 1478, 1485; **1979:** 663, 664, 899, 1044, 1921; **1980–81:** 75, 421, 522, 523
        Vice Chairman, **1979:** 1043, 1044; **1980–81:** 2149
    Civil service reform, **1978:** 1374
    Community Investment Fund program, **1978:** 1059
    Credit controls authority, **1980–81:** 478, 482, 485, 497, 513, 571, 666, 961, 1282
    Debt financing, effect on, **1980–81:** 75
    Discount rate increase, **1978:** 1453, 1909
    Dollar, U.S., value, **1978:** 1908, 1954, 1955
    Financial institutions deregulation, effect on, **1980–81:** 573
    Interest rates, **1978:** 781, 1657
        Deposit controls, **1979:** 132, 707, 930
        Prime rate increase, **1979:** 1835, 1840, 1869, 1909
    Money supply responsibilities, **1979:** 1837
    Money supply restrictions, **1980–81:** 254, 570, 2041, 2052, 2128, 2223, 3012
    Relationship with the President, **1978:** 354; **1979:** 2028
    Resignation of Chairman Burns, **1978:** 64
    Seasonal credit loans to farmers, **1980–81:** 702
Federal Reserve System, Board of Governors, Chairman, **1977:** 105, 371, 630, 744, 747, 942, 1162, 1382, 1383, 1699, 1709, 1761. 1909, 1999, 2006, 2011, 2058, 2183–2185, 2192, 2193, 2223; **1978:** 57, 66, 277, 415,

Federal Reserve, Chairman — *continued*
    460, 481, 564, 710, 1222, 1426, 1441, 1489,
    1493, 1723, 1913, 1914, 2237, 2270
Federal Reserve System, Board of Governors,
    Chairman (G. William Miller), **1979:** 401
Federal Reserve System, Board of Governors,
    Chairman (Paul A. Volcker)
  Federal financial institutions deregulation sup-
    port, **1980–81:** 574
  International Monetary Fund, U.S. Alternate
    Governor, appointment, **1979:** 1454, 1519
  Lower American standard of living for inflation
    control, remarks, **1979:** 1992
  Meetings with the President (Digest), **1979:** 1785,
    2248; **1980–81:** 607, 892, 1846
  Mentions, **1979:** 1801, 2289
  Money supply decision, **1980–81:** 2041
  Nomination, **1979:** 1300, 1320
  President's assessment, **1979:** 1307
  Prime interest rate increase action, **1979:** 2051
  Reagan, Ronald, meeting with, **1980–81:** 2833
  Small business financing decision, **1980–81:** 76
  Swearing-in ceremony, **1979:** 1402
Federal Seasonal Loan Program, **1978:** 1399
Federal Service Impasses Panel, **1979:** 23; **1978:**
    411, 954, 957, 958, 2293; **1980–81:** 83,
    1647
Federal space management, **1978:** 1427–1430
Federal and State Laws Relating to Wiretapping
    and Electronic Surveillance, National
    Commission for the Review of, **1979:** 585,
    587–490
Federal-State social services claims, **1978:** 1082
Federal statistical system, **1978:** 891
Federal Strategy for Drug Abuse and Drug Traffic
    Prevention, **1979:** 618, 619
Federal Technology, Center for the Utilization of,
    1979: 2070; **1980–81:** 2379
Federal Trade Commission, **1977:** 486, 510, 691;
    1978: 564, 707, 971, 1010
  Anti-inflation programs, **1979:** 234, 235
  Antitrust policy, **1979:** 2072
  Automobile safety enforcement, **1980–81:** 2049
  Chairman, **1979:** 234, 235, 242; **1980–81:** 281,
    983
  Commissioner, **1979:** 1394, 1397; **1980–81:** 106,
    1111
  Consumer protection activities, **1980–81:** 282
  Interagency Employee Benefit Council member-
    ship, **1980–81:** 2864
  Mentions, **1979:** 1762; **1980–81:** 1352
  Offshore oil spill pollution study, **1979:** 339
  Reauthorization legislation, **1980–81:** 282, 562,
    774, 815
  West-to-east crude oil transportation system,
    report preparation, **1980–81:** 99
Federal Trade Commission Improvements Act,
    1980–81: 982

Federal Wage System, **1979:** 1003
Federal-State Land Use Planning Commission for
    Alaska, **1977:** 1072, 1085
Feed grain program, **1978:** 2011
Feighan, Edward F. **1979:** 1447; **1980–81:** 2610
Feinberg, Abraham, **1978:** 1030
Feinstein, Diane, **1979:** 808ftn.; **1980–81:** 1350n.,
    1438n., 3021
Felder, Allie C., Jr., **1979:** 1022, 1043
Feldman, Harvey J., **1979:** 1228, 1232
Felgehauer, Jack, **1980–81:** 1447
Fell, Bernard, **1980–81:** 268
Fellers, James D., **1977:** 1529
Fellowship Foundation, **1978:** 1668
Fendrick, Mark, **1977:** 293
Fennely, Mr. and Mrs. Robert, **1977:** 194
Fenner, Harold A., Jr., **1977:** 2028
Fenton, Karen Marie Cornelius, **1979:** 1448
Fenton, Ruth P., **1978:** 696
Fenwick, Repr. Millicent, **1978:** 1515
Feragen, Robert, W., **1978:** 1666, 1670
Ferguson, Carr, **1978:** 1711
Ferguson, Ewen, **1977:** 1382
Ferguson, M. Carr, **1977:** 1054, 1059
Ferguson, Warren John, **1979:** 1786, 1787
Fernandes Lopes, Jose Luis, **1980–81:** 1564
Ferraro, Repr. Geraldine A., **1980–81:** 1573, 1662,
    2194, 2807
Ferraro, John, **1978:** 1808
Ferre, Sister M. Isolina, **1979:** 340, 377
Ferre, Maurice, **1977:** 78, 90; **1978:** 1630, 1669;
    1979: 401, 1666; **1980–81:** 1328n.
Ferrell, Carole, **1977:** 404
Ferrell, Joel, Jr., **1980–81:** 1493, 1494n.
Ferren, John, **1977:** 940, 944
Ferrill, Jay R., **1980–81:** 929
Ferris, Charles D., **1977:** 1380, 1412; **1979:** 483,
    485, 1700; **1980–81:** 1704, 1706n.
Ferry, Bob, **1978:** 1070
Ferst, Charlotte, **1977:** 1781, 1796
Fertilizer Development Center, International,
    1977: 381
Fetter, Elizabeth A., **1979:** 914
Fettig, Lester A., **1977:** 607, 642; **1978:** 787; **1979:**
    242
Feynman, Richard Phillips, **1979:** 2289; **1980–81:**
    82n.
Fiedler, Arthur, **1979:** 1226
Field, Irwin S., **1978:** 2269
Fifth Circuit Court of Appeals Reorganization Act,
    1980–81: 2237
55-mile speed limit, **1977:** 1281, 1287
Figueiredo, Gen. Joao Bappispa, **1978:** 632
Figueroa, Julio E., **1977:** 196
Figueroa, Nicholas, **1980–81:** 2815
Fiji
    Ambassador to U.S., **1980–81:** 1598

Fiji — *continued*
  U.S. Ambassador, **1978:** 286, 304, 1668; **1979:**
    1222; **1980–81:** 893, 1107, 1111
Filer, John H., **1977:** 1178, 1179; **1979:** 1976;
    1980–81: 422
Filippine, Edward L., **1977:** 1163, 1164
Film Institute, American, **1977:** 2036, 2041
Finance Corporation, International, **1978:** 1629
Finances, President's, **1980–81:** 968, 1486
Financial institutions deregulation, Federal, **1979:**
    928, 1728, 2079, 2288
Financial Policies, National Advisory Council on
    International Monetary and, **1979:** 1731
Financial reports, President's, **1979:** 983
Finch, Gov. Charles C., **1977:** 1315, 1323, 1507;
    1978: 1383; **1979:** 670, 672, 731, 1674
Finch Raymond L., **1980–81:** 1715
Findley, Repr. Paul, **1978:** 498, 500, 698, 700
Fine Arts, Commission on, **1980–81:** 2701
Fines, Gerald D., **1977:** 1827, 1931
Fink, Stanley, **1980–81:** 303
Finkel, E. Jay, **1977:** 796, 807
Finland
  Ambassador to U.S., **1977:** 2050
  Extradition treaty, **1977:** 655
  Independence anniversary, Presidents personal
    representative, **1977:** 2077
  Papermaking machinery, **1978:** 2271, 2272
  Prime Minister Kalevi Sorsa, **1979:** 898
  U.S. Ambassador, **1977:** 783, 807; **1980–81:** 405,
    423
  Vice President's visit, **1979:** 221, 639
Finley, Murray H., **1978:** 454; **1980–81:** 1048
Finney, Leon, **1980–81:** 2259
Fire Academy, National, **1979:** 1437, 1438
Fire Administration, United States, **1979:** 22, 91,
    566; **1980–81:** 1567, 2266
Fire prevention, **1977:** 488
Fire Prevention and Control, National Academy
    for, **1979:** 566
Fire Prevention and Control Administration, Na-
    tional, **1977:** 118; **1978:** 1129, 1132
Fire Prevention Week, **1977:** 1626; **1978:** 1393
    (Proc. 4672), **1979:** 1438;
    (Proc. 47829), **1980–81:** 1567
Firefighters, Federal, work week reduction, **1978:**
    1133, 1369
Firefighters Memorial Sunday (Proc. 4671), **1979:**
    1437
Firefighters Week, National, **1980–81:** 2266
Fireside chat, **1977:** 69
First Lady, role, **1978:** 2251, 2252
  See also Carter, Rosalynn.
Fiscal assistance legislation, intergovernmental,
    1979: 391, 401–403
Fiscal Assistance legislation, Supplementary, **1978:**
    1406, 1602
Fischer, Carl William, **1980–81:** 204, 219

Fischer, Gotthilf, **1978:** 934
Fish, Repr. Hamilton, Jr., **1980–81:** 1098
Fish, Peter, **1977:** 1243
Fish Fry, Georgia State Society, **1979:** 898
Fish Health Research Laboratory, National, **1979:**
    1042
Fish and wildlife
  International conferences, **1977:** 1220, 1223
  National policy, **1978:** 1045, 1047, 1051
  Sikes Act amendments, **1978:** 1250, 1717
Fish and Wildlife Conservation Act, **1980–81:** 1958
Fish and Wildlife Service, United States, **1978:**
    1051; **1980–81:** 1431
Fisher, Abbi, **1979:** 1226
Fisher, Adrian S., **1977:** 879, 883; **1978:** 919, 935
Fisher, Bernard, **1979:** 2196
Fisher, Carlton, **1977:** 2028
Fisher, Harold, **1979:** 1742
Fisher, Repr. Joseph L., **1978:** 1221, 1362, 1667,
    1695; **1980–81:** 16, 452, 2098, 2178
Fisher, Milton N., **1980–81:** 2117
Fisher, Mr. and Mrs. William, **1979:** 1232, 2104
Fisheries Commission, International North Pacific,
    1978: 216; **1979:** 1001; **1980–81:** 2774
Fishery agreements
  Canada, **1977:** 256; **1978:** 812, 1234; **1979:** 776,
    1420
  Cuba, **1977:** 886
  Denmark, **1979:** 1850
  Japan, **1977:** 205, 1052
  Korea, **1977:** 206
  Mexico, **1977:** 1752
  North Pacific fisheries convention, protocol,
    1978: 1041
  Northwest Atlantic convention, **1979:** 777
  Spain, **1977:** 206
  United Kingdom, **1977:** 1753
Fishery Conservation and Management Act of
    1976, **1977:** 215, 388
  Amendments, **1978:** 1479; **1979:** 1435
Fishing Conservation Zone, **1979:** 1435
Fishing Day, National Hunting and, **1979:** 1626
Fishing industry
  Administration's development policy, **1980–81:**
    160
  Diesel fuel guarantees, **1979:** 846, 937
  Legislation, **1979:** 855; **1980–81:** 2678
  Massachusetts coastline protection, **1979:** 1955
  Mount St. Helens eruption, effect on, **1980–81:**
    951
  Portugal-U.S. agreement, **1980–81:** 2755
  Production increase, **1979:** 754
  Soviet restrictions in American waters
    Announcement, **1980–81:** 23
    President's comments, **1980–81:** 41, 196, 278,
      634, 747, 1193, 1308, 2324, 2470, 2566
  United Kingdom, reciprocal agreement with
    U.S., **1980–81:** 1022

Fishing industry — *continued*
    Vessels, American built requirement, **1979:** 1435
Fishing trips, President's, **1979:** 964, 1042
Financial Management Improvement Program,
    Joint, **1979:** 462
Fitch, Val L., **1980–81:** 2740
Fite, Julian K., **1977:** 1613, 1614
Fithian, Repr. Floyd J., **1978:** 1696; **1979:** 990
Fittipaldi, Joseph R., **1979:** 1448
Fitzgerald, Ernest, **1978:** 1367
Fitzgerald, F. Scott, **1980–81:** 502
FitzGerald, Frances, **1980–81:** 263
FitzGerald, Garret, **1977:** 464
Fitzgerald, Ray V., **1977:** 1228, 1266
Fitzgerald, William, **1978:** 1723, 1934
Fitzmaurice, David J., **1978:** 53
Fitzsimmons, Frank E., **1978:** 1591; **1979:** 1870,
    1954
Flack, Roberta, **1980–81:** 1523
Flag Day and National Flag Week, **1977:** 1097;
    1978: 1014
    (Proc. 4660), **1979:** 817
    (Proc. 4757), **1980–81:** 895
Flaherty, Nancy, **1977:** 78, 90
Flaherty, Peter F., **1977:** 336, 373, 504, 2061, 2085,
    2094; **1978:** 1075
Flaig, Otto, **1977:** 314
Flakus, Gregory Michael, **1980–81:** 2075
Flander, Mervin J., **1980–81:** 931
Flannery, Robert G., **1978:** 1360, 1381
Flawn, Peter T., **1980–81:** 1149, 1246
Fleener, Terre, **1979:** 798
Fleming, J. Carlton, **1977:** 1243
Fleming, Peggy, **1980–81:** 2830
Fleming, Robben W., **1979:** 1954
Flemming, Arthur S., **1977:** 1190; **1979:** 2213;
    1980–81: 537, 2871
Fletcher, Betty Binns, **1979:** 1232, 1233
Fletcher, Willard, **1980–81:** 822
Flexi-time proposal, **1977:** 104, 138
Flint, Andrew P., **1980–81:** 928
Flint, Mich., **1978:** 1932; **1980–81:** 1986, 2009, 2071
Flipper, Cassandra M., **1980–81:** 305
Flooding, **1977:** 42, 86
    Control, **1977:** 645; **1978:** 1043, 1045, 1047, 1048,
    1050
    Insurance, **1978:** 568
Floodplain management, **1977:** 998, 1001; **1980–
    81:** 37
Flora, Convention on International Trade in En-
    dangered Species of Wild Fauna and,
    1979: 2288; **1980–81:** 590
Florence, S.C., **1978:** 503
Flores, Batuel, **1979:** 281n.
Flores, Carlos Thompson, **1978:** 636
Florida
    Cuban refugees.
        See Cuban refugees.

Florida — *continued*
    Democratic caucuses, **1979:** 1838, 1983, 1986,
    1994, 2015, 2044
    Democratic Party primary, **1980–81:** 461
    Disaster declarations, **1977:** 35, 85; **1979:** 893,
    1675, 1678, 1823
    Election prospects of President, **1980–81:** 2157
    Emergency declarations, **1979:** 553; **1980–81:**
    892
    Energy emergency, **1979:** 637, 817, 1032, 1225,
    1998
    Governor Robert Graham, **1978:** 1865, 1869,
    2218, 2269
        Advisory Panel on Financing Elementary and
        Secondary Education, member, **1979:**
        1525
        Anti-inflation program briefing for State and
        local officials (Checklist), **1979:** 328
        Campaign appearance with the President,
        1980–81: 1362, 2148
        Caribbean/Central American Action involve-
        ment, **1980–81:** 624
        Cuban refugee assistance coordination, **1980–
        81:** 820
        Democratic National Convention, nominating
        speaker for President Carter, **1980–81:**
        1469, 1471
        Florida energy emergency actions, **1979:** 637,
        1032, 1225, 1999
        Intergovernmental Advisory Council on Edu-
        cation, member, **1980–81:** 1432
        Meeting with the President (Digest), **1980–81:**
        2069
        Mentions, **1979:** 1578; **1980–81:** 1349
        President's Management Improvement Coun-
        cil, member, **1979:** 1671
        President's support, **1979:** 1590
    Haitian refugees.
        See Haitian refugees.
    Housing and community development projects,
    1980–81: 2112
    Looe Key National Marine Sanctuary, **1980–81:**
    2998
    1980 Presidential campaign, strategic importance
    in, **1979:** 1582, 1591
    Political supporters, White House reception,
    1978: 504
    President's visits, **1977:** 1035–1037; **1978:** 1684–
    1689, 1865, 1869; **1979:** 1566, 1578, 1675,
    2139; **1980–81:** 1066, 1072, 1074, 1322,
    1347, 1349, 1360–1362, 2148–2172, 2382–
    2401, 2579, 2586
    State Democratic officials, meetings with the
    President, **1979:** 1578n., 1588n.
    U.S. attorneys, **1977:** 1613, 1614; **1979:** 241;
    1980–81: 1715

Florida — *continued*
  U.S. district judges, **1977:** 557, 558, 596, 2050,
    2051; **1978:** 1239; **1979:** 242, 957, 1018,
    1019, 1043, 1044, 1232, 1233, 1293, 1294,
    1319, 1423, 1531, 1532; **1980–81:** 1847
  U.S. marshals, **1977:** 1128, 1437, 1438
  White House briefing for civic and community
    leaders (Digest), **1979:** 1679
Florida Power and Light Company, **1979:** 1569
Florida Wildlife Federation, **1979:** 1604
Florio, Repr. James J., **1979:** 468, 2185
  Legislation passage leadership
    Comprehensive Environmental Response,
      Compensation, and Liability Act, **1980–
      81:** 2797, 2798
    Northeast corridor rail system, **1980–81:** 1009,
      1011
    Staggers Rail Act, **1980–81:** 1699, 2226, 2228,
      2230
  Meeting with the President (Digest), **1980–81:**
    1598
Flournoy, Lou, **1980–81:** 1738
Flournoy, Maxine E., **1978:** 1653
Flowerree, Charles C., **1980–81:** 204, 219
Flowers, Repr. Walter, **1978:** 456
Floyd, Sloppy, **1979:** 300
Floyd, William F., III, **1980–81:** 533, 564
Flum, Robert S., Sr., **1980–81:** 1508
Flynt, Larry, **1977:** 234
Fobes, John E., **1980–81:** 1713, 1847
Foege, Dr. William H., **1977:** 806
Foell, Earl, **1979:** 1982
Fogel, David, **1980–81:** 2613
Foley, Repr. Thomas S., **1977:** 508, 1681; **1978:**
    277, 315, 700, 858, 860, 862, 914, 1376,
    1696; **1979:** 943, 2274, 2299
  Legislation passage leadership
    Emergency agricultural credit, **1980–81:** 568
    Farmer-owned grain reserves, **1980–81:** 653
    Food Stamp Act Amendments, **1980–81:** 975
    National Aquaculture Act, **1980–81:** 1938
    Rural Development Policy Act, **1980–81:** 1918
    Small Business Administration authorization,
      1980–81: 1279
  Meeting with the President (Digest), **1980–81:**
    1427
  Mention, **1980–81:** 539
  Mount St. Helens eruption, inspection tour of
    areas damaged by, **1980–81:** 961
Folklife Center, American, **1977:** 2036
Fonda, Henry, **1980–81:** 1718
Fong Eu, March K., **1977:** 526
Fonseca, Wilton, **1980–81:** 1227n.
Fontaine, Lynn, **1980–81:** 2786
Food
  Administration's accomplishments and goals,
    1980–81: 2944, 2973, 2993
  Federal programs, **1979:** 135

Food — *continued*
  Industry representatives, meeting with the Pres-
    ident, **1979:** 1453, 1455
  Mention, **1979:** 935
  Prices, **1977:** 394, 632; **1978:** 1494, 1970; **1979:**
    717, 754, 796, 850, 1413, 1432, 1572;
    1980–81: 453, 504, 2438, 2467
  Processing industry representatives, meeting with
    the President, **1980–81:** 1050, 1052
  Production, development of energy conservation
    techniques, **1979:** 1268
  Programs, **1977:** 1496, 1534, 1679, 1696, 1703,
    1704, 1858; **1978:** 2000
  Retail stores
    Representatives, meeting with the President,
      1980–81: 607 (Digest), 608
    Voluntary prices freeze, **1980–81:** 659, 706
  Security reserves, **1980–81:** 2770, 2911
  Stamps, **1977:** 771, 772, 948, 1345, 1446, 1447,
    1451, 1455, 1679, 1705, 1739; **1978:** 104;
    1979: 83, 188, 480, 1928
    Administration's accomplishments, **1980–81:**
      115, 909
    Authorization legislation, **1980–81:** 830, 835,
      887, 901
    Purchase requirement elimination, **1980–81:**
      115, 1003, 1499, 1951
    Reagan, Ronald, position on, **1980–81:** 2554
  U.S. exports exchange for foreign oil, possibility,
    1979: 791, 802, 1910, 1944
  "War on Hunger" program, **1980–81:** 176
Food and Agricultural Development, Board for
    International, **1978:** 218, 1652; **1979:** 437;
    1980–81: 323
Food and Agricultural Organization, **1980–81:**
    1190
Food and Agricultural Policy, Working Group on,
    1977: 1695
Food and Agriculture Act of 1977, **1977:** 1679,
    1703–1705, 1879; **1978:** 101; **1980–81:** 504
Food Aid Committee, **1979:** 434
Food Aid Convention, **1978:** 455; **1979:** 434, 1625;
    1980–81: 865, 1190
Food Assistance Act, International Development
    and, **1978:** 1721
Food and Commercial Workers International
    Union, United, **1979:** 1008, 1020
Food and Drug Administration, **1977:** 1406, 1407,
    1993; **1979:** 2007; **1980–81:** 2907
Food for Peace program, **1977:** 457; **1978:** 315;
    1979: 1925, 2012, 2103; **1980–81:** 257,
    1333
Food program, United Nations World, **1980–81:**
    257
Food Stamp Act of 1977 amendments, **1979:** 1432;
    1980–81: 975
Foodstuffs, Agreement on International Carriage
    of Perishable, **1979:** 83

Foote, Shelby, **1980–81:** 1604
Footwear industry, American nonrubber, **1977:**
     550–554, 558, 1113, 1148; **1980–81:** 420
Forbes, George, **1980–81:** 1003
Ford, Austin, **1978:** 1190
Ford, Betty, **1977:** 525, 526, 758; **1978:** 963
Ford, Charles R., **1980–81:** 34
Ford, Gerald R., **1977:** 76, 97, 218, 221, 243, 283,
     307, 318, 345, 508, 632, 700, 757, 758, 764,
     765, 780, 943, 1483, 1568, 1749, 1887,
     1936, 2063, 2095; **1978:** 517, 963, 964, 973,
     976, 1688, 2269
  Defense spending recommendations, **1980–81:**
     347
  Kemp-Roth tax bill position, **1980–81:** 1685,
     2023, 2078, 2144, 2420
  Mayaguez incident, **1980–81:** 744
  Meetings with the President (Digest), **1979:** 786,
     2248; **1980–81:** 493
  Mention, **1979:** 1580
  1976 election, **1980–81:** 1492, 1873
  President's comments on:
     Grain embargoes, **1979:** 1710
     Japanese relations, **1979:** 1165
     SALT II negotiations, **1979:** 694
     1976 Presidential election, **1979:** 1713, 1841
Ford, Repr. Harold E., **1979:** 2247
Ford, Henry, II, **1977:** 1059, 2182; **1978:** 759, 1703
Ford, Jineane, **1980–81:** 1469
Ford, John, **1980–81:** 502
Ford, Susan, **1977:** 10
Ford, Sen. Wendell H., **1977:** 744, 1013, 1210,
     1753; **1978:** 457, 512, 769, 1733, 1982;
     1979: 1339, 1340, 1342, 1347; **1980–81:**
     303, 538, 983
Ford, Repr. William D., **1978:** 289, 304, 1917, 1919;
     1980–81: 2064, 2751
Ford Foundation panel on nuclear power, **1977:**
     508
Ford Motor Company, **1979:** 900; **1980–81:** 1984,
     2071
Fordham University, N.Y., **1979:** 984
Ford's Theatre, **1978:** 242
  Country music fundraiser for, **1979:** 1815
Foreign Assets Control, Office of, **1979:** 1656
Foreign assistance
  Administration's accomplishments and goals,
     1980–81: 2980
  Administrative improvement efforts, **1979:** 2088
  Authorization legislation, **1977:** 522
  Development programs, **1978:** 932
  Economic Report, **1978:** 144
  (EO 12226), **1980–81:** 1396
  Food Aid Convention, **1978:** 455
  International Chamber of Commerce, remarks,
     1978: 1691
  International Security Assistance Act of 1977,
     1977: 1431

Foreign assistance — *continued*
  Legislation, **1978:** 1155; **1980–81:** 119, 964
  Message, **1977:** 455
  Nashua, N.H., remarks, **1978:** 380
  News conference remarks, **1978:** 972, 975–977
  Program reorganization, **1979:** 279, 294, 395,
     643, 915, 1230, 1233, 1792
  Religious leaders, meeting with the President,
     1978: 1379
  Security assistance programs administration,
     1979: 225
  Smallpox control, **1979:** 2027
  State of the Union, **1978:** 102
  U.S. policy, **1977:** 239, 313, 1880
  U.S. programs, inspection, **1978:** 1209
  White House briefing for congressional Mem-
     bers, **1980–81:** 941
  See also Developing countries; *specific country or
     area.*
Foreign Assistance Act amendment, **1980–81:** 1522
Foreign Claims Settlement Commission of the
     United States, **1978:** 2095, 2184; **1979:** 46,
     90, 720
  Members, **1980–81:** 534, 564, 1596, 1599, 1926,
     1947, 2857, 2870, 2873
  Reorganization, **1980–81:** 483
Foreign Commercial Service, **1979:** 1732; **1980–81:**
     9
Foreign Corrupt Practices Act, **1980–81:** 1693
Foreign corrupt practices and investment disclo-
     sure bill,**1977:** 2157
Foreign Earned Income Act of 1978, **1980–81:** 1692
Foreign exchange markets, **1978:** 1426
Foreign Intelligence Advisory Board, President's,
     1977: 801, 802
Foreign Intelligence Board, National, **1978:** 197,
     215
Foreign intelligence electronic surveillance (EO
     12139),**1979:** 940
Foreign Intelligence Surveillance Act, **1978:** 1501,
     1853
  Proposed, **1977:** 921, 928, 944
Foreign Investment Disclosure Act, **1978:** 1783
Foreign Language and International Studies, Pres-
     ident's Commission on, **1978:** 766, 1514,
     1907; **1980–81:** 2850
Foreign Military Sales program (FMS), **1978:** 2095
Foreign policy
  Administration advisers, meetings with the Pres-
     ident (Digest), **1979:** 1782, 2105, 2300;
     1980–81: 2332, 2806
  Administration's accomplishments and goals,
     1979: 155, 561, 569, 636, 720, 830, 845,
     950, 1855, 1996; **1980–81:** 162, 326, 1838,
     2692, 2707, 2974
  Administration's first-year accomplishments,
     1977: 2149

Foreign policy — *continued*
  Allies, strengthening of commitments to, **1980–81**: 1007, 1316, 1320, 1391
  Briefing for Members of Congress, **1978**: 1154, 1278
  Briefings, **1977**: 1305, 1306
  China, People's Republic of, diplomatic relations, **1978**: 2264–2268
  Commitments by previous administrations, **1977**: 947
  Diplomatic immunity, **1979**: 2161
  Diplomatic relationships, **1977**: 1109
  Embassy protection, **1980–81**: 2356
  Export controls, **1978**: 1633; **1979**: 2290
  Imperatives, **1980–81**: 632
  Inauguration, remarks to other nations, **1977**: 4
  Intelligence surveillance, **1977**: 880, 921, 928, 1051
  Interview remarks, **1977**: 1173, 1571, 2093, 2201; **1978**: 73, 75, 694, 1255, 1261, 1410, 1590
  Labor groups, influence of, **1980–81**: 1362
  National Democratic Party Conference, remarks, **1978**: 2194
  Negotiations policy, **1977**: 498
  News conference remarks, **1977**: 1469, 1470; **1978**: 1183
  Noninvolvement in other countries' internal affairs, **1979**: 347, 1839
  Policy toward former adversaries, **1977**: 1333
  President's overseas trip accomplishments, **1978**: 41, 44
  President's responsibility to establish policy, **1980–81**: 487, 876, 881, 2135, 2171
  Radio address to the Nation, **1980–81**: 2336, 2453
  Reflection of American ideals, **1979**: 355, 494, 636, 720, 830; **1980–81**: 673, 868, 874, 993, 1164, 1740, 1743, 1855, 2263
  Relationship with:
    Domestic economic situation, **1980–81**: 1226
    Former Soviet allies, **1980–81**: 807
    Military strength, **1980–81**: 1551
  Report to the American people, **1977**: 75
  Southern Legislative Conference, address, **1977**: 1310
  State of the Union, **1978**: 95, 96, 117–123
  Summit meeting, international.
    See Summit meeting, international.
  Terrorism, U.S. position, **1980–81**: 2486
  University of Notre Dame commencement address, **1977**: 954
  U.S. commitment to allies, **1979**: 1989
  U.S. intervention in foreign countries, **1978**: 1303
  U.S. military involvement in foreign countries, **1977**: 769, 782
  U.S. Naval Academy, remarks, **1978**: 1052
  U.S. relations with former Soviet allies, **1979**: 564, 1916, 1992

Foreign policy — *continued*
  U.S. security responsibilities, **1979**: 301
  Wake Forest University address, **1978**: 534
  White House briefings (Digest) with:
    Citizen activists in foreign affairs, **1980–81**: 63
    Congressmen, **1980–81**: 333
  See also specific country or region; Meetings with foreign leaders.
Foreign Policy Association, **1978**: 84, 2281
Foreign Policy Conference, **1979**: 310
Foreign Relations, Council on, **1980–81**: 2574, 2615
Foreign Relations Authorization Act, Fiscal year 1979, **1978**: 1734
Foreign Scholarships, Board of, **1977**: 1766; **1978**: 408, 2264; **1980–81**: 272, 2608
Foreign Service, United States, **1978**: 1209; **1980–81**: 9, 2356, 2471, 3001
  Disability and retirement system, **1979**: 1261
  Employee-management relations, **1979**: 606
  Officers, **1978**: 1735
  Personnel system, **1979**: 760, 1793
  Presidential power of appointment, **1979**: 1434
Foreign Service Act, **1980–81**: 2328
Foreman, Carol Tucker, **1977**: 331, 356, 372, 373, 511; **1979**: 1221, 1223; **1980–81**: 281
Forest Management Act of 1976, National, amendment, **1978**: 384
Forest Products Week, National, **1977**: 1697; **1978**: 1560; **1980–81**: 1645
Forest Service
  Cahaba River, Ala., report preparation, **1979**: 2245
  Federal renewable resources program, **1979**: 1375, 1376, 1381
  Mention, **1979**: 775
  Mount St. Helens eruption, disaster assistance actions, **1980–81**: 951, 953, 958
  National Recreation trails, **1979**: 1366
  Purposes of creation, **1980–81**: 1645
  Secretary of Agriculture's recommended program, **1980–81**: 1141, 1143
Forest System, National.
  See National Forest System.
Forestry Association, American, **1978**: 1234; **1980–81**: 2822
Forestry programs, **1978**: 1234
Forests, **1977**: 978, 1097
  Energy sources development, **1980–81**: 586
  Federal policy statement, **1980–81**: 1141–1146
  International protection efforts, **1979**: 1371, 1386
  Mount St. Helens eruption, effect on, **1980–81**: 951, 956
  New England energy source, **1979**: 701
  U.S. efforts to protect, **1980–81**: 419
Forlani, Orlando, **1980–81**: 1241
Forrestal, Michael, **1978**: 1723
Forrestal, U.S.S., **1980–81**: 1633

Forsht, Donald D., **1977:** 1437, 1438
Forsythe, Repr. Edwin B., **1978:** 2003; **1980–81:** 1938
Fort, W. Howard, **1980–81:** 1823, 1847
Fort Benning, Ga., **1978:** 2286
Fort Chaffee, Ark., **1980–81:** 849, 1053
Fort Devens, Mass., **1977:** 389
Fort Hood, Tex., **1978:** 1176
Fort Wayne, Ind., **1980–81:** 1019
Fort Worth, Tex., **1978:** 1157; **1980–81:** 2635
Fortson, Ben, **1979:** 913
Fortune 500 companies, **1980–81:** 787, 829, 846, 977
Foschio, Leslie G., **1980–81:** 1470, 1471
Foster, Homer, **1977:** 508
Foster Grandparents program, **1978:** 1794; **1979:** 1928
Foundation for International Technological Co-operation, **1978:** 2246; **1979:** 141, 161
Fountain, Repr. L. H., **1978:** 1390, 1570, 1754–1757; **1979:** 2186, 2196
Fountain, Tamara R., **1980–81:** 927
Four Corners Regional Commission, **1977:** 1070, 1085; **1980–81:** 372, 453
Four Power summit meeting, **1977:** 828, 840
4-H Club, National, **1980–81:** 701
Fourth of July, **1978:** 1139
Fouse, Ronald, **1977:** 299
Fowler, Frank E., **1979:** 465
Fowler, Repr. Wyche, Jr., **1978:** 1425
Fox, Eleanor M., **1978:** 1139, 1140
Fox, Renee Claire, **1979:** 1263
Fox, Richard K., Jr., **1977:** 886, 943
Foxx, Robbyn, **1977:** 1084
Foxx, Virginia, **1980–81:** 1203, 1051
Foy, John N., **1978:** 696
France, William C., **1980–81:** 1405
France
    Ambassador to U.S., **1977:** 2050
    Bonn Economic Summit Conference, **1978:** 1310, 1311
    Conventions with U.S.
        Income and property taxes, **1979:** 239
        Taxation and fiscal evasion, **1979:** 238
    Minister of Foreign Affairs, **1979:** 1017
    Nuclear exports, **1977:** 764
    Olympics, 1980 Summer, possibility of boycott, **1980–81:** 676
    President's visits, **1977:** 1649, 1983, 2077, 2188, 2202; **1978:** 20–32, 50
    Prime Minister Raymond Barre, **1977:** 1383, 1590, 1603, 1607, 1609, 1612, 1613
    Summit meeting, international, **1977:** 371
    Terrorist attack on synagogue in Paris, **1980–81:** 2170, 2194
    Tokyo Summit
        Attendance announcement, **1979:** 550

France — *continued*
    Tokyo Summit — *continued*
        Joint statement, **1979:** 1197
        Oil imports ceiling, **1979:** 1198
    U.S. Ambassador, **1977:** 873, 875, 883
    U.S. relations, **1980–81:** 1174
    Vice President's visit, **1977:** 59, 60
    West Bank and Gaza Strip settlements proposal, **1980–81:** 1196
    Zaire, relationship with, **1980–81:** 679
France, President (Valéry Giscard d'Estaing), **1977:** 60, 62, 178, 322, 756, 767, 818, 824, 841, 859, 881, 2122; **1978:** 21, 28, 30, 31, 44, 50 714, 898, 1008, 1308, 1310, 1334, 2187
    Guadeloupe Conference
        Conclusion remarks, **1979:** 17, 20n.
        Meetings with the President and Western European leaders (Digest), **1979:** 14, 25, 26
    Mention, **1979:** 1584; **1980–81:** 674, 2828
    Palestinian autonomy proposal, **1980–81:** 682
    Relationship with the President, **1979:** 1185; **1980–81:** 1174
    Tokyo Summit
        Conclusion remarks, **1979:** 1189, 1197n.
        Meeting with the President, **1979:** 1183n.
        Mention, **1979:** 1212
    Union of Soviet Socialist Republics
        Grain shipments decision, **1980–81:** 42
        President Brezhnev, meeting with, **1980–81:** 1194
        Troop withdrawal from Afghanistan announcement, **1980–81:** 1199
    Venice Economic Summit Conference
        Concluding remarks, **1980–81:** 1175
        Meeting with the President (Digest), **1980–81:** 1243
    West German Chancellor Schmidt, meeting with, **1980–81:** 292, 313
Francis, Leslie C., **1979:** 1976, 1977
Francis, Margaret, **1978:** 1860
Francisco Otero, Joaquin, **1979:** 450
François-Poncet, Jean, **1979:** 1017
Franczyk, Stan, **1978:** 1808
Frank, Irvin, **1980–81:** 822
Frank, John P., **1977:** 816
Frank, Patricia Anne, **1979:** 2042
Frank, Richard A., **1977:** 1196, 1213, 2077
Frankel, Stanley D., **1980–81:** 377, 379
Frankford Arsenal, Pa., **1977:** 305; **1979:** 906; **1980–81:** 877
Franklin, Benjamin, **1979:** 677, 2093; **1980–81:** 81, 526, 924
Franklin, John Hope, **1977:** 78, 90; **1979:** 729, 787; **1980–81:** 1713, 1847
Fraser, Charles E., **1980–81:** 1277, 1292
Fraser, Repr. Donald M., **1978:** 1592, 1593

Fraser, Douglas.
    See United Auto Workers, President.
Fraser, J. Malcolm, **1977:** 1127, 1140; **1979:** 3,
    1231; **1980–81:** 103, 259, 284
Fraser, Jean S., **1980–81:** 926
Fraser, Leila, **1978:** 1630, 1669
Fraternal organization, meeting with the President,
    1980–81: 648
Fratianne, Linda, **1980–81:** 380
Fraud, Abuse and Error, National Conference on,
    1978: 2228, 2270
Fraud and waste in government, executive group to
    combat, proposed, **1979:** 780
Frazier, A. D., Jr., **1977:** 573, 1264, 1265; **1979:**
    232, 242
Frazier, Gregory W., **1980–81:** 2560, 2883
Frazier, Henry B., III, **1979:** 24, 46, 90; **1980–81:**
    468, 493
Frazier, James T., **1977:** 508
Fred, Matthew, **1979:** 773
Fredericks, Thomas W., **1980–81:** 1129, 1151, 2859,
    2870, 2873
Fredericks, Wayne, **1978:** 1514; **1980–81:** 719
Frederickson, Donald S., **1978:** 1188
Fredin, Conrad M., **1980–81:** 269, 273
Free, James C., **1979:** 732, 898
Free Enterprise Day, **1978:** 1225
Freedman, Daniel X., **1977:** 529
Freedom, Presidential Medal of, **1977:** 751, 1057,
    1598, 2922
Freedom of Information Act, **1977:** 244; **1980–81:**
    1932
Freeman, Frankie M., **1979:** 1042, 1044
Freeman, Orville L., **1979:** 214
Freeman, Mrs. Orville L. (Jane), **1978:** 1190
Freeman, Richard M., **1978:** 1449, 1458
Freeman, Rowland G., III.
    See General Services Administration, Adminis-
        trator.
Freeman, S. David, **1977:** 1284, 1307; **1978:** 934,
    946–948; **1979:** 1366, 1382; **1980–81:** 240
Freeport, Ill., **1977:** 208
Freight rail industry.
    See Railroads.
Freitag, Bernard, **1980–81:** 1299n.
French, Philip, **1979:** 993, 1008
Frenzel, Repr. Bill, **1978:** 802; **1979:** 1312; **1980–
    81:** 38
Freund, Paul A., **1977:** 815
Fri, Robert W., **1977:** 1501, 1507
Frias, Auristela, **1980–81:** 1097
Friborg, Donald, **1979:** 1468n.
Friday, William C., **1978:** 537
Fried, Edward R., **1977:** 1067, 1085
Frieder, Bernice S., **1977:** 526
Friedersdorf, Max L., **1978:** 1744, 1773; **1979:** 46,
    91

Friedl, Ernestine, **1978:** 1760, 1773; **1979:** 46, 92
Friedlander, Paul S., **1978:** 1426, 1458; **1979:** 46, 91
Friedman, Clara H., **1980–81:** 684
Friedman, Daniel M., **1978:** 550, 571
Friedman, James M., **1978:** 314, 329; **1980–81:**
    1926, 1947
Friedman, Martin, **1979:** 45, 92
Friedman, Marvin, **1978:** 1500
Friedman, Stephen J., **1980–81:** 235, 564, 2378
Friedricks, K. O., **1977:** 2046
Frieman, Edward Allan, **1979:** 1655, 2044
Friendly, Alfred, **1980–81:** 1203ftn.
Friends of Carter/Mondale, **1979:** 2015
Friendship Force, **1978:** 75, 234, 1296, 1966; **1980–
    81:** 628, 944
Frisbee, Donald C., **1980–81:** 1405
Frisbee, Noland, **1977:** 323
Fritschler, A. Lee, **1979:** 856, 899
Frosch, Robert A., **1977:** 969, 1031, 1699; **1978:**
    1187, 1684; **1979:** 206, 1276, 1277n., 2138;
    1980–81: 563, 1417, 1847, 1876
Fruitland Mesa, Colo., **1977:** 208
Frydenlund, Knut, **1979:** 33n.
Fryman, Patsy L., **1979:** 947
Fuel.
    See specific energy source.
Fuel assurances, initial, **1979:** 326
Fuel companies
    Competition, **1977:** 1320
    Conservation fee on imported oil, effect on,
        1980–81: 497
    Data monitoring, **1977:** 671
    Divestiture, **1977:** 308, 701, 1786
    Domestic production, Federal monitoring, **1979:**
        1242, 1250, 1324, 1345
    Energy legislation, lobbying efforts, **1979:** 1491,
        1499, 1513, 1650, 1743, 1748, 1868, 2056,
        2241
    Federal control of oil imports, possibility of,
        1980–81: 889
    Gasoline shortages, Federal collusion investiga-
        tions, **1979:** 872, 1243, 1585
    Home heating oil programs, **1979:** 1613, 1631,
        1758
    Industry tax, **1977:** 700
    National energy plan, lobbying efforts, **1977:**
        1082, 1092, 1106, 1671, 1685, 1746, 1784,
        1806, 1985; **1978:** 377
    Nationalization, **1977:** 97
    Nationalizaton and divestiture, possibility of,
        1979: 654
    Non-oil supplies, ownership constraints, **1980–
        81:** 883
    Offshore drilling, **1979:** 1549
    Oil price controls, **1979:** 1636
    Pricing decisions, **1977:** 1859, 1882
    Production incentive, **1977:** 754

Fuel companies — *continued*
    Profits, **1979:** 1345, 2039
    Representatives, meeting with the President, **1979:** 983
    Republican Party, position on, **1980–81:** 1886, 1951
    Windfall profits, **1977:** 40, 649, 1397, 1619
    Windfall profits tax.
      See Crude Oil Windfall Profit Tax Act.
Fuel Institute, New England, **1980–81:** 292
Fuel oil management group, **1979:** 2056
Fuentes, Annette Droz, **1980–81:** 258, 1839
Fukuda, Takeo, **1977:** 43, 64, 464, 467, 472, 474, 478, 583, 881, 2093; **1978:** 803, 881, 1287, 1310, 1334; **1979:** 1168n.
Fulbright, Robert, **1977:** 9
Full Employment Action Council, **1978:** 1679, 1871
Full Employment and Balanced Growth Act, **1977:** 295, 1663, 1788, 1995; **1978:** 93, 100, 138, 322, 336, 693, 842, 973, 1457, 1643, 1656, 1678, 1679, 1681, 1719, 1771, 1823, 1871, 1880; **1979:** 116, 126
    Interim goals establishment, **1980–81:** 249, 250
    Mentions, **1980–81:** 115, 124, 1651, 2375, 2932
    Reagan, Ronald, position on, **1980–81:** 2093
Full Employment Council, **1978:** 1679
Fulton, Richard H., **1978:** 1858
Fumich, George M., Jr., **1979:** 1652, 2107
Fungicide, and Rodenticide Act extension, Federal Insecticide, **1980–81:** 2814
Funk, Gerald, **1980–81:** 355, 719
Fuqua, Repr. Don, **1978:** 1009; **1979:** 730; **1980–81:** 1375, 1668, 2380
Furgler, Kurt, **1977:** 881
Fusion Energy Engineering Act, Magnetic, **1980–81:** 2105
Future Farmers of America, **1977:** 1303; **1978:** 1318, 1994; **1979:** 1267; **1980–81:** 1452
Future plans, President's, **1980–81:** 2126, 2705, 2706, 2712
Futures, Trading Act, **1978:** 1696

Gaba, Pierre Toura, **1977:** 822
Gabonese Republic
    Ambassador to U.S., **1978:** 328; **1979:** 25; **1980–81:** 1564
    President El Hadj Omar Bongo, **1977:** 279, 1825, 1827
    U.S. Ambassador, **1978:** 88, 149
Gabor, Peter C., **1980–81:** 928
Gabusi, John B., **1977:** 1262, 1267; **1980–81:** 203, 1942
Gaffney, Edward, **1978:** 819, 821
Gage, Stephen J., **1977:** 1975, 2006; **1978:** 231
Gahe Unit, S. Dak., **1977:** 208
Gairy, Eric M., **1977:** 1566, 1568

Galbreath, Dan, **1980–81:** 371
Galbreath, John, **1980–81:** 995
Galdi, Ernest J., **1978:** 1955
Galindo, Gabriel Lewis, **1977:** 942; **1980–81:** 33
Gallagher, James J., **1978:** 696
Galland, Richard I., **1979:** 1614n.
Gallegos, Herman E., **1978:** 1208; **1980–81:** 263
Gallen, Gov. Hugh, **1979:** 699, 713, 715, 1293; **1980–81:** 2741
Gallop, Donald Philip, **1980–81:** 2614
Galveston, Tex., **1979:** 1817
Galvin, Donald E., **1980–81:** 812, 825
Gambia
    Ambassador to U.S., **1979:** 842
    U.S. Ambassador, **1977:** 1081, 1086; **1978:** 232; **1980–81:** 983, 1014
Gambling, **1977:** 504
    Legalized, **1979:** 246
Gamboa Pascoe, Joaquin, **1978:** 1043
Gammage, Repr. Bob, **1978:** 1164, 1165, 1221
Gammino, Michael A., Jr., **1979:** 435, 441
Gammon, Samuel R., **1978:** 1711, 1724
Gamser, Howard G., **1978:** 411; **1979:** 23
Gandal, Alvin H., **1977:** 2105, 2130; **1978:** 231
Gandhi, Indira Nehru, **1978:** 44
Gandy, Evelyn, **1980–81:** 2613
Gandy, Lt. Gov. Evelyn, **1979:** 731
Gannett newspapers, **1979:** 2239
Garba, Joseph Nanven, **1978:** 645
Garcia, Angelina, **1979:** 926, 927
Garcia, Frances, **1977:** 1667, 1700; **1980–81:** 1942
Garcia, Dr. Hector, **1977:** 816
Garcia, Hipolito Frank, **1979:** 2281
Garcia, Joseph O., **1979:** 1525
Garcia, Matt, **1980–81:** 1149, 1292, 1460
Garcia, Rafael Rivera, **1980–81:** 1445
Garcia, Repr. Robert, **1978:** 415; **1979:** 1664; **1980–81:** 492, 1502, 1835, 2116
Garcia-Palmieri, Mario, **1979:** 1264
Garcia-Rivera, Oscar, **1978:** 1380
Gardner, Andrew E., **1977:** 2050, 2051
Gardner, Carl W., **1977:** 1437, 1438
Gardner, Jim, **1980–81:** 1635
Gardner, John, **1978:** 1766; **1979:** 1012; **1980–81:** 948
Gardner, John W., **1977:** 528, 706, 941, 1142, 1277; **1980–81:** 2823
Gardner, Richard N., **1977:** 280, 462; **1978:** 933; **1979:** 618; **1980–81:** 1162, 1241, 1243
Gardner, Mrs. Richard N., **1980–81:** 1243
Gardner, William C., **1980–81:** 458, 493
Garment Workers Union, International Ladies'.
    See International Ladies' Garment Workers Union.
Garn, Sen. Jake, **1977:** 926; **1978:** 1854; **1980–81:** 573, 2113
Garrahy, Gov. J. Joseph, **1978:** 339, 1808; **1979:** 2061, 2102; **1980–81:** 1010, 1011, 1405

Garret, Thaddeus A., Jr., **1977**: 195
Garrett, Thomas, **1977**: 1532
Garrison, Lorna, **1979**: 2042
Garrison Diversion Unit, N. Dak., S. Dak., **1977**: 208
Garst, David, **1978**: 1652
Garthoff, Raymond L., **1977**: 1220, 1223
Gartner, David G., **1978**: 866, 899, 1096, 1182
Garvin, Clifton C., **1978**: 1539; **1979**: 1614n.
Garvin, James W., Jr., **1977**: 746
Gary, Ind., **1980–81**: 825, 932
Garza, Pedro, **1980–81**: 1981
Garza, Reynaldo G., **1979**: 733, 787; **1980–81**: 2618
Garza, Rodolfo A., **1977**: 883, 884
Gas, natural.
   See Natural gas.
Gas Pipeline, Northern, **1979**: 381
Gaskins, Darius W., Jr., **1979**: 871, 899, 1880; **1980–81**: 1267, 2231, 2240
Gasko, Robert, **1978**: 1543
Gasohol, **1978**: 1616
   Budget allocations increase, **1979**: 484
   Corn mash still project, **1980–81**: 1866n.
   Excise tax exemption, **1979**: 1103, 1317
   Federal motor vehicle use, **1980–81**: 2860
   Increased use, **1979**: 1950
   Legislation, **1979**: 484, 1502ftn., 2155
   Mention, **1979**: 1483
   Production
      Energy legislation allocations, **1980–81**: 586, 1253
      Forest products and crops conversion to, **1979**: 614, 792, 799, 1944, 1950
      Future goals, **1980–81**: 1865, 2468, 2588, 2630
      New initiatives programs, **1980–81**: 61, 229
      Waste products use, **1980–81**: 1748
   Production plants construction, **1979**: 792, 1501
   Research and development, **1979**: 1650
Gasoline
   Administration's price decontrol policy, **1979**: 1975
   California shortages, **1979**: 808, 872, 873, 898, 900, 985
   Conservation fee on imported oil
      Administration's proposal renewal, **1980–81**: 3010, 3014
      Congressional consideration, **1980–81**: 903, 918, 943, 1027
      District Court ruling on constitutionality of fee, **1980–81**: 903, 931, 944
      Letter to congressional leaders, **1980–81**: 1012
      Licensing requirements (Proc. 4762), **1980–81**: 1049
      News conference (Checklist), **1980–81**: 932
      Oil import reduction measure, **1980–81**: 485, 497, 554
      President's promise to not use receipts to balance 1981 budget, **1980–81**: 571

Gasoline — *continued*
   Conservation fee — *continued*
      Proclamation 4744 establishing fee, **1980–81**: 592
         Amendments to Proc. 4744, **1980–81**: 657, 760
      10 cents per gallon proposal, **1980–81**: 485, 497, 571
      Veto of canceling legislation
         Message to Congress, **1980–81**: 1037, 1041
         President's comments, **1980–81**: 1090, 1113
   Consumer and conservation representatives, meeting with the President, **1979**: 983
   Consumption reduction, **1979**: 2243; **1980–81**: 199, 480, 994
   Decontrol, **1977**: 16
   Emergency sales restrictions, **1979**: 370, 608, 689
   End-user allocation, **1979**: 968, 984, 1183, 1185, 1327, 1779, 1787
   Future shortages, **1979**: 1996
   Prices, **1978**: 2220; **1980–81**: 1639
   Rationing, **1977**: 696, 1786
      President's position comparison with Sen. Kennedy, **1980–81**: 750
      Standby plan.
         See Standby gasoline rationing plan.
   State consumption goals, **1980–81**: 481
   Supplies, **1979**: 705
   Tax, **1977**: 284, 665, 674, 695, 750, 1337, 1397
   Western European nations tax per gallon, **1980–81**: 1042
Gasoline Dealers' Association, **1979**: 1294
Gates of the Arctic National Monument, **1978**: 2123
Gatlin, Larry, **1980–81**: 1601
Gatov, Albert W., **1978**: 218
Gatton, T. Harry, **1978**: 2089
Gavin, Gen. James M., **1978**: 2089
Gaydos, Repr. Joseph M., **1980–81**: 369
Gearde, Frank, Jr., **1980–81**: 931
Gebhardt, Joseph D., **1978**: 85
Geeker, Nickolas P., **1980–81**: 1715
Geisel, Ernesto, **1978**: 626, 636, 641
Geller, Henry, **1979**: 619; **1978**: 554, 571, 611, 2263; **1980–81**: 1706
Gellhorn, Walter, **1978**: 1652
General Accounting Office, **1977**: 277, 279, 653, 1498; **1978**: 2296; **1979**: 462, 2182; **1980–81**: 544, 898, 2845
General Accounting Office Act, **1980–81**: 603
General Agreement on Tariffs and Trade (GATT), **1977**: 781; **1978**: 1313
   Customs Valuation Code and Agreement, **1980–81**: 1247, 1251, 1463, 2815
   Geneva Protocol, **1979**: 2223, 2229
   1979 trade agreements acceptance and application, **1979**: 2253
   Schedule modification, **1980–81**: 97

GATT — *continued*
 U.S. efforts to strengthen, **1979:** 1200
 U.S. Trade Representative responsibilities,
  1980–81: 7
 Venice Economic Summit Conference statement,
  1980–81: 1191
General Counsel, Office of the, **1978:** 2293, 2298,
  2299
General Dynamic Shipyard, Quincy, Mass., **1979:**
  1990
General Motors Corporation, **1977:** 917; **1979:** 740,
  786, 1651; **1980–81:** 902
General Pulaski's Memorial Day, **1978:** 1394
 (Proc. 4673), **1979:** 1444
 (Proc. 4787), **1980–81:** 1593
General revenue sharing, **1977:** 54, 72, 889; **1978:**
  2224, 2227; **1979:** 250, 1951
 Administration's legislative priority, **1980–81:**
  116
 5-year extension legislation, **1980–81:** 698, 803,
  832
 President's support, **1980–81:** 142, 555
 Reauthorization proposal, **1980–81:** 25, 118, 122
General Services Administration
 Advisory committee management, **1978:** 612
 Audiovisual programs, **1978:** 786
 Budget rescission, **1977:** 1286
 Civil service rule, **1977:** 2062
 Coal strike, **1978:** 313
 Deputy Administrator, **1978:** 1345, 1446
 Energy functions, transfer, **1978:** 273
 Federal emergency functions (EO 12148), **1979:**
  1278
 Federal Information Centers, **1977:** 165
 Inspector General, **1979:** 198, 378
 Interagency Coordinating Council, **1978:** 1434
 Integrated pest management programs, **1979:**
  1383
 Interview remarks, **1978:** 1674
 Investigation of alleged misconduct, **1978:** 1337,
  1603, 1604
 Labor-Management Relations Program exemp-
  tion, **1979:** 2145
 Labor surplus area goals, **1980–81:** 73
 Labor surplus areas, procurement, **1978:** 1432
 Low-emission vehicles development, **1980–81:**
  484
 Management issues, **1979:** 1670
 Misconduct investigations, **1979:** 719, 924
 National security information functions, **1978:**
  1200, 1202, 1204
 National water policy functions, **1978:** 1049
 Nuclear Safety Oversight Committee, support
  services, **1980–81:** 505
 Occupational safety and health programs, **1980–**
  81: 393, 396

General Services Administration — *continued*
 President's Commission on the Accident at
  Three Mile Island, support services, **1979:**
  659
 Presidential Commission on World Hunger,
  1978: 1499
 Reorganization Plan No. 3 of 1978, **1978:** 1129
 Space management, **1978:** 1431
 Steel purchases, **1977:** 1435
 Telecommunications functions, **1978:** 594, 595,
  603–605
 Transfer of certain advisory committee func-
  tions, **1977:** 2067
 Urban programs, **1978:** 580, 584, 587
 Waste paper recycling program, **1977:** 972
General Services Administration, Administrator,
  1977: 147, 148, 589, 596, 1084, 1300, 2102;
  1978: 306, 594, 595, 898, 1007, 1039, 1040,
  1154, 1165, 1176, 1446, 1505, 1859, 1864,
  1955
General Services Administration, Administrator
  (Rowland G. Freeman, III)
 Automobile purchase, **1980–81:** 2187
 Energy conservation measures, **1980–81:** 790
 Federal Council on the Arts and Humanities,
  member, **1979:** 956
 Federal employees ridesharing program respon-
  sibilities, **1980–81:** 271
 Federal Information Centers location selections,
  1980–81: 1932
 Federal occupational safety and health programs
  study, **1980–81:** 396
 Gasohol use authority in motor vehicles, **1980–**
  81: 2860
 Mentions, **1979:** 2033; **1980–81:** 263, 302, 1433
 Nomination, **1979:** 458, 619
 Nuclear Safety Oversight Committee, support
  services, **1980–81:** 505
 President's Management Improvement Council,
  procedural guidelines establishment,
  1979: 1669
 President's Special Commission for the Study of
  Ethical Problems in Medicine and Bio-
  medical and Behavioral Research, sup-
  port services, **1979:** 2261
 Strategic and critical materials functions (EO
  12155), **1979:** 1621
General Services Administration, Administrator
  (Joel W. Solomon)
 Meetings with the President (Digest), **1979:** 178,
  467
 Resignation, **1979:** 448
 Urban noise abatement program development,
  1979: 1385
Generalized System of Preferences for developing
  countries.
 See under Developing countries.

Genetic Diseases Act, National Sickle Cell Anemia, Cooley's Anemia, Tay-Sachs, and, **1979:** 1705, 2106
Genetic diseases program, **1980–81:** 1049
Geneva (1979) Protocol to the General Agreements on Tariffs and Trade, **1979:** 2223, 2229
Geneva peace conference, **1977:** 497, 600, 722, 1728
Geneva Radio Regulations, 1959, **1980–81:** 225
Geng Biao, **1980–81:** 1013
Genocide, Convention on the Prevention and Punishment of the Crime of, **1977:** 450, 997; **1978:** 2162; **1979:** 162; **1980–81:** 119
Genocide, International Treaty on the Prevention and the Punishment of, **1979:** 684
Genscher, Hans-Dietrich.
    See Foreign Minister and Vice Chancellor *under* Germany, Federal Republic of.
Gentry, John N., **1978:** 469, 2033, 2158; **1980–81:** 292, 374
    Meetings with the President (Digest), **1979:** 25, 467, 1785, 2034
    Under Secretary of Labor, nomination, **1979:** 1836, 1883
Geological Survey, **1978:** 407, 416; **1979:** 373
George's Bank, Mass., **1979:** 1995
Georgia
    Biomass resources, **1979:** 1724
    Democratic Party primary, **1980–81:** 461
    Disaster assistance, **1980–81:** 1422
    Disaster declarations, **1977:** 1058, 2005
    Emergency declarations, **1977:** 1306; **1979:** 440
    Equal rights amendment support, **1980–81:** 924
    Federal recreation and historic sites, **1978:** 1424, 1459
    Friendship Force, **1980–81:** 628
    Gov. George Busbee, **1980–81:** 1423n., 1749, 1756
    Gray's Reef National Marine Sanctuary, **1980–81:** 2997
    1976 campaign volunteers, meeting with the President, **1979:** 618
    President's visits, **1977:** 194, 599, 604, 640, 1033, 1042–1044, 1443, 1459, 2165, 2169–2176; **1978:** 153–158, 228, 538, 539, 945, 1009, 1113, 2285–2287; **1979:** 296–306, 667, 675, 731, 1533, 1561, 1589, 2139; **1980–81:** 1744–1758, 2068, 2682, 2688, 2832, 2839–2841
    U.S. attorneys, **1977:** 1127, 1128, 1211, 1212
    U.S. district judges, **1977:** 1222; **1978:** 1669, 1670; **1979:** 1018, 1019, 1043, 1044, 1293, 1294, 1786, 1787, 2081, 2082
    U.S. marshals, **1977:** 1059, 1507, 1534; **1978:** 416
    White House barbecue for residents, **1980–81:** 1512
Georgia, University of, **1978:** 526
Georgia Institute of Technology, **1979:** 300, 1559
Georgia Lions International, **1979:** 617

Georgia State Society Fish Fry, **1979:** 898
Georgine, Robert A.
    See Building and Construction Trades Department, President *under* AFL-CIO.
Geothermal energy, **1977:** 687; **1979:** 1219, 1575, 1891
Gephardt, Repr. Richard A., **1979:** 942
Gerard, Forrest J., **1977:** 1239, 1266, 1873, 2036
Gerbasi, Salvatore R., **1980–81:** 769
German Democratic Republic
    Ambassador to U.S., **1978:** 1722
    Berlin Wall, **1980–81:** 964, 1007
    Consular convention with U.S., **1980–81:** 783
    Embargo regulations, **1978:** 1505; **1979:** 1657
    Four Power summit meeting, **1977:** 840
    Soviet withdrawal from Afghanistan, U.N. proposal opposition, **1980–81:** 401
    U.S. Ambassador, **1977:** 1218, 1223; **1980–81:** 1025, 1052
    U.S. relations, **1978:** 1283, 1300, 1304
Germany, Federal Republic of
    Ambassador to U.S., **1978:** 934; **1979:** 2162n.
    Basic Law, **1979:** 927
    Bavarian Minister President Franz Josef Strauss, **1980–81:** 470, 518
    Berlin Mayor Dietrich Stobbe, **1980–81:** 644
    Chairman, German Social Democratic Party, **1977:** 371
    Christian Democratic Union/Christian Social Union Chairman, **1978:** 1212
    Coal development project with U.S. and Japan, **1979:** 1150
    Defense Minister, **1978:** 1292
    Diplomatic contacts with Uganda, **1977:** 292, 315
    Exchange rate adjustment with U.S., **1977:** 2160
    Extradition treaty with U.S., **1979:** 85
    Foreign Minister, **1977:** 463; **1978:** 709, 1333
    Foreign Minister Hans-Dietrich Gensecher
        Mention, **1980–81:** 2737
        Vienna Economic Summit Conference attendance, **1980–81:** 1242
        Visits to U.S., meetings with:
            President, **1980–81:** 189, 1292
            Secretary of State Muskie, **1980–81:** 2739
            Secretary of State Vance, **1980–81:** 1202
    Four Power summit meeting, **1977:** 840
    Friendship Force, **1978:** 1966
    Industrial productivity, **1980–81:** 1678
    International Solvent Refined Coal II Agreement with U.S. and Japan, **1980–81:** 1447
    Joint statement, **1980–81:** 438
    Minister of Defense, **1977:** 464
    1980 Summer Olympics, boycott of, **1980–81:** 439, 470, 712, 920
    Nuclear exports, **1977:** 60, 62, 583, 585, 764
    President Walter Scheel, **1978:** 1281, 1284, 1310

Germany, Federal Republic — *continued*
President's Assistant for National Security Affairs, visit, **1978:** 1722
President's visit, **1978:** 1153, 1267, 1281–1316, 1332, 1333
Rescue of hostages in Somalia, **1977:** 1810, 1939
Social security agreement with U.S., **1978:** 1559; **1979:** 362
Summit meeting, international, **1977:** 371
Taxation and fiscal evasion convention with U.S., **1980–81:** 2915
Tokyo Summit
Attendance announcement, **1979:** 550
Joint statement, **1979:** 1197
Oil imports ceiling, **1979:** 1198
Turkey, economic assistance to, **1980–81:** 678
U.S. relations, **1978:** 1262, 1272, 1283, 1284
Vice Chancellor, **1978:** 1292
Vice Chancellor, Hans-Dietrich Genscher, **1977:** 463; **1978:** 709, 1292, 1333; **1979:** 1419
Vice President's trip, **1977:** 43, 60
Vulnerability to East-West tensions, **1980–81:** 675
See also Berlin; Bonn Economic Summit Conference.
Germany, Federal Republic of, Chancellor (Helmut Schmidt), **1977:** 43, 62, 583, 756, 762, 824, 835, 841, 859, 881, 883, 1211, 1241, 1242, 1244–1249, 1251, 1264; **1978:** 720, 1015, 1263, 1272, 1281, 1286, 1289, 1291–1293, 1297, 1298, 1300, 1308, 1310, 1332, 1334, 1360, 1967, 2072, 2187
French President Giscard d'Estaing, meeting with, **1980–81:** 291, 313
Guadeloupe Conference
Conclusion remarks, **1979:** 19, 20n.
Meetings with the President and Western European leaders (Digest), **1979:** 14, 25, 26
International situation comparison with First World War, **1980–81:** 673
Iran and Afghanistan situations, telephone discussion with the President (Digest), **1980–81:** 719
Mentions, **1979:** 1584; **1980–81:** 2828
NATO forces modernization statement, **1979:** 1845
Soviet President Brezhnev, meeting with, **1980–81:** 1194
Tokyo Summit
Conclusion remarks, **1979:** 1191, 1197n.
Meeting with the President, **1979:** 1183n.
Mention, **1979:** 1213
Turkey, economic aid actions for, **1979:** 653
Venice Economic Summit Conference
Concluding remarks, **1980–81:** 1179
Meetings with the President, **1980–81:** 1170, 1200, 1242

Germany, Chancellor — *continued*
Visits to U.S.
Announcement, **1979:** 666; **1980–81:** 103
Meetings with the President, **1979:** 1004, 1005; **1980–81:** 435, 438, 441
Mention, **1979:** 902
Germany, reunification, **1978:** 1263, 1293, 1298
Gershenson, Robert S., **1980–81:** 1334, 1336
Gesell, Gerhard A., **1977:** 380
Getis, Hilary H., **1980–81:** 927
Gettinger, Michael, **1978:** 1974
Gettysburg, Pa., **1978:** 1239, 1515; **1980–81:** 1604
Getzendanner, Susan C., **1980–81:** 1052
Gevirtz, Donald, **1980–81:** 263
Geyer, Paul R., **1980–81:** 927
Ghali, Butrus, **1978:** 1772
Ghana
Ambassador to U.S., **1978:** 710
U.S. Ambassador, **1979:** 1658, 1680; **1980–81:** 1598
Ghandi, Indira, **1979:** 2047
Ghorbal, Ashraf A., **1978:** 2059; **1979:** 1684; **1980–81:** 525, 528, 1846
Ghotzbadeh, Sadegh, **1980–81:** 764, 1203, 1311, 1907
GI bill, **1977:** 306, 307, 317
GI Bill Improvement Act of 1977, **1977:** 2048
GI Forum, **1980–81:** 563, 1725
Giacco, Alexander, **1980–81:** 1718
Giaimo, Repr. Robert N., **1977:** 706; **1978:** 229, 1393, 1888; **1979:** 179, 591n.
Decision to not seek reelection, **1980–81:** 539
Legislation passage leadership
Fiscal year 1981 budget, **1980–81:** 857
Omnibus Reconciliation Act, **1980–81:** 2778, 2779
Mention, **1980–81:** 1718
Giamatti, A. Bartlett, **1980–81:** 1332, 1337
Giannini, Margaret Joan, **1979:** 2089, 2106; **1980–81:** 1718
Giant Foods, **1979:** 850
Gibb, Lois, **1980–81:** 2003
Gibbons, John David, **1980–81:** 931
Gibbons, Repr. Sam, **1978:** 1783
Gibbs, Alan J., **1977:** 591, 596
Gibbs, Todd, **1980–81:** 720
Gibson, Audrey N., **1979:** 925, 927
Gibson, Benjamin F., **1979:** 1232, 1233
Gibson, Carol Saunders, **1979:** 1448
Gibson, Guadalupe, **1980–81:** 1037n.
Gibson, Howard G., **1978:** 1467
Gibson, Hugh, Jr., **1979:** 1397, 1398
Gibson, Kenneth, **1977:** 1100, 1574; **1978:** 2072; **1979:** 402, 942, 2247; **1980–81:** 2889
Gibson, Theodore, **1980–81:** 1328n.
Gierbolini-Ortiz, Gilberto, **1979:** 2188
Gierek, Edward, **1977:** 2203, 2210, 2212; **1978:** 42, 281

Gifts to First Family and administration officials, **1977:** 73
Gignilliat, Thomas, **1978:** 543
Gilbert, Dwayne W., **1978:** 416
Gilbert Islands
  Independence celebrations, President's personal representative, **1979:** 1222, 1223
  Trade beneficiary developing country designation, **1980–81:** 550
Giles, James T., **1979:** 1883
Giles, Jim, **1980–81:** 1633
Gilinsky, Victor, **1979:** 855, 899
Gilford, Meno Vardas, **1977:** 1649
Gilkey, Bertha, **1980–81:** 2559
Gill, Frank, **1980–81:** 1598
Gillespie, James J., **1977:** 1211, 1212
Gilliam, Earl Ben, **1979:** 2207, 2208
Gilliam, Reginald E., Jr., **1979:** 1702, 2249
Gilligan, Gov. John J., **1977:** 240, 337, 372, 533, 1126; **1978:** 932, 1155, 1721; **1979:** 294
Gillotti, Floyd, **1977:** 1855, 1860
Gilman, Repr. Benjamin A., **1978:** 2268
Gilman, Marvin S., **1977:** 934; **1978:** 920; **1979:** 932; **1980–81:** 911
Gilman, Richard Carleton, **1980–81:** 1432
Gilmore, Horace W., **1980–81:** 968
Gilpatric, Roswell, **1979:** 1823
Gimenez-Munoz, Miguel A., **1980–81:** 1470, 1471
Ginn, Repr. Bo, **1977:** 1033; **1978:** 542
Ginsberg, Helen, **1978:** 1974
Ginsburg, Ruth Bader, **1980–81:** 654, 720
Ginzberg, Eli, **1979:** 947, 1963; **1980–81:** 1981
Ginzburg, Alexander, **1977:** 99, 100; **1978:** 1282, 1328; **1979:** 731
Ginzton, Edward L., **1977:** 1944, 1966
Girard, Martha B., **1978:** 1955
Girls Nation, **1980–81:** 1369
Giscard d'Estaing, Valéry.
  See France, President.
Gish, Lillian, **1977:** 2042
Gitlin, Chris, **1977:** 78, 90; **1979:** 465
Glacier Bay National Monument, **1978:** 2125
Gladman, Maury, **1978:** 526
Glaser, Robert D., **1980–81:** 1098, 3022
Glashow, Sheldon L., **1979:** 1963
Glasner, Rabbi Juda, **1978:** 1973
Glasner, Israel Leo, **1980–81:** 1847
Glasser, Melvin Allan, **1980–81:** 2609
Gleason, Ted, **1980–81:** 1648
Gleazer, Edmund J., **1978:** 1514
Glenn, Sen. John H., Jr., **1977:** 595, 744, 1928; **1978:** 498–500, 526, 1221, 1687, 1725
  Campaign appearances with the President, **1980–81:** 992, 2347, 2466, 2502
  General Accounting Office Act, passage leadership, **1980–81:** 603
  Mentions, **1979:** 1646: **1980–81:** 1766

Glenn, Sen. John — *continued*
  Meetings with the President (Digest), **1979:** 178, 617
  Ohio mining jobs preservation actions, **1979:** 1006
  Steel industry task force, member, **1979:** 1640
Glenn, Wayne E., **1978:** 2069
Gleysteen, Mr. and Mrs. William H., **1979:** 1155
Gleysteen, William H., Jr., **1978:** 1023, 1034
Glickman, Repr. Dan, **1978:** 1814, 1819, 1820; **1980–81:** 2807
Glickstein, Howard, **1978:** 416
Global Atmospheric Research Project, **1979:** 539
Global Resources and Environment, Task Force on, **1980–81:** 1415
Global 2000 study, **1980–81:** 1415, 1897
Glomar Explorer, **1979:** 1545, 1549
Gloucester City, N.J., **1980–81:** 2432, 2453
GNP.
  See Gross national product.
Gobbi, Hugo, **1980–81:** 1923, 2740
Goble, Kirk, **1980–81:** 1453
Godbold, Jake, **1980–81:** 1348
Goddard Memorial Trophy, **1980–81:** 563, 564
Godley, Gene E., **1977:** 276, 280
Goheen, Robert F., **1977:** 576, 597, 882; **1978:** 5; **1980–81:** 64
Golatz, Helmut J., **1978:** 913
Gold prices, **1980–81:** 499, 558
Goldberg, Arthur J., **1977:** 2037, 2038; **1978:** 117, 453, 803, 1338, 1339, 1973, 2268; **1980–81:** 1057, 1434
Goldberg, Billy, **1980–81:** 1393n.
Goldberger, Marvin L., **1980–81:** 849
Golden, Colo., **1978:** 824
Goldfeld, Stephen M., **1980–81:** 1148, 1151
Goldhammer, Robert F., **1979:** 465
Goldman, Aaron, **1978:** 1974
Goldman, Leslie Jay, **1977:** 590, 597, 1212; **1979:** 1706, 2183, 2207; **1980–81:** 1377
Goldman, Marvin, **1978:** 933
Goldman, Patricia A., **1979:** 437, 441
Goldman, Nahum, **1977:** 1952, 1957
Goldmark, Peter C., **1977:** 2046; **1979:** 2297
Goldschmidt, Neil.
  See Transportation, Secretary of.
Goldsmith, John, **1979:** 1554
Goldstein, Jonathan, **1977:** 1803
Goldstein, Louis, **1978:** 1799
Goldstein, Sol, **1980–81:** 822
Goldwater, Sen. Barry, **1977:** 1513, 1794; **1979:** 1822; **1980–81:** 1559, 2233
Goldy, Daniel L., **1978:** 454
Gombos, Zoltan, **1980–81:** 2075
Gomes, Constance E., **1979:** 1727
Gomez, Jose, **1980–81:** 1405
Gomez, Joseph N., **1979:** 976

Gonzales, Arnold, **1979:** 401
Gonzalez, Dagoberto, **1978:** 623
Gonzalez, Felipe, **1980–81:** 1244
Gonzalez, Repr. Henry B., **1980–81:** 2622
Gonzalez, Jose A., Jr., **1978:** 1239
González, Raymond E., **1978:** 1029, 1034
Good, Mary Lowe, **1979:** 448; **1980–81:** 1149, 1246
Good Neighbor Fund, **1979:** 2238
Goodby, James Eugene, **1980–81:** 405, 423
Goode, Malvin, **1979:** 319
Gooden, Bennie S., **1980–81:** 1595, 1599
Goodfriend, Isaac, **1978:** 1974; **1980–81:** 822
Goodling, Repr. William F., **1980–81:** 847, 1585
Goodman, June K., **1980–81:** 606
Goodpaster, Andrew J., **1980–81:** 1047
Goodwill Graduate of 1980, National, **1980–81:** 893
Goodwin, Frances H., **1978:** 1564; **1979:** 1776
Gordon, H. Stephan, **1979:** 528, 554
Gordon, Melvin L., **1978:** 481
Gordon, Robert C. F., **1980–81:** 364, 375
Gordy, Tom, **1980–81:** 1385
Gore, Albert, **1977:** 801, 1930; **1978:** 1858
Gore, Repr. Albert, Jr., **1978:** 1860; **1980–81:** 1936, 1937, 2797, 2800
Goren, Shlomo, **1977:** 1127
Gorman, Paddy, **1979:** 1008
Gospel Music Association, **1979:** 1614
Gottbaum, Victor, **1980–81:** 1953
Gottesman, Michael, **1977:** 1083
Gottfredson, Don M., **1980–81:** 2613
Gottschalk, Rabbi Alfred, **1978:** 1973; **1980–81:** 822
Goudsmit, Samuel A., **1977:** 2046
Gould, Harry E., Jr., **1979:** 942
Gover, Margaret L., **1980–81:** 1405
Government departments and agencies.
　　See Federal departments and agencies.
Government Employees, American Federation of, **1978:** 802, 1366, 1765, 1766; **1979:** 2247
Government Financial Operations, Bureau of, **1980–81:** 594
Government National Mortgage Association, **1977:** 591, 596; **1979:** 1316, 1677, 1705; **1980–81:** 138
Government Printing Office, **1977:** 1676; **1978:** 1955; **1980–81:** 1672, 1715
Government Procurement, Agreement on, **1979:** 2253; **1980–81:** 2854
Government purchases, **1978:** 1844, 1847
Government Red Cross Program, **1980–81:** 1292
Government reform and reorganization, **1978:** 457, 542, 543, 584, 1347, 1388, 1409, 1576, 1580, 2190
　Federal Government size, **1979:** 1502
　Federal pay system, **1979:** 919, 1002
　International trade activities, **1979:** 1294

Government reform — *continued*
　Management improvement, **1979:** 1669
　Mention, **1979:** 2044
　1979 proposals, **1979:** 127, 378
　Progress during administration, **1979:** 74, 127
Government regulations, Executive order, **1978:** 556, 558, 561–563, 571, 1024
Governors
　Energy conference, **1977:** 1225, 1265
　Meetings with the President, **1978:** 228, 276, 456
　Relationship with the President, **1978:** 2083
　White House reception, **1978:** 431
Government travel costs, **1978:** 1483
Governors' Association, National.
　See National Governors' Association.
Gowdy, Sharon Kaye, **1979:** 465
Gradison, Repr. Willis D., **1978:** 1668
Grady, Sandy, **1980–81:** 733n.
Graesser, Joy A., **1980–81:** 927
Graham, Adele, **1979:** 1578
Graham, Billy, **1980–81:** 181
Graham, Calvin, **1978:** 899
Graham, Frances Keesler, **1980–81:** 896
Graham, Jim, **1978:** 1392
Graham, Otto, **1980–81:** 607
Graham, Patricia A., **1977:** 1253, 1266
Graham, Gov. Robert.
　See Governor *under* Florida.
Graham, Robert P., **1978:** 409
Graham, Thomas, Jr., **1979:** 1077
Graham-Wheeler, Dorothy, **1980–81:** 2859, 2870, 2873
Grain industry
　Continental Grain Terminal, Tacoma, Wash., **1980–81:** 1904
　Droughts, effect on, **1980–81:** 2438
　Labor dispute, **1979:** 1430, 1452, 1467, 1468, 1708
　Legislation, **1980–81:** 2769
　Prices increase, **1980–81:** 339
　Railroad strike, effect on, **1979:** 1609, 1695
　Reserves storage, **1980–81:** 652, 2224, 2467
　St. Lawrence Seaway transportation system, shipping season extension for, **1979:** 2038
　Storage facility increase, **1979:** 1710
　U.S. embargoes, **1977:** 1857
　　Possibility of, **1979:** 1910, 1945
　U.S. trade
　　Levels increase, **1980–81:** 2205, 2351, 2402
　　U.S. and:
　　　China, People's Republic of.
　　　　See under China, People's Republic of.
　　　Mexico, **1980–81:** 1908, 2203, 2351, 2402, 2407
　　　Union of Soviet Socialist Republics.
　　　　See Trade with U.S. *under* Union of Soviet Socialist Republics.

Grain Inspection Service, Federal, **1977:** 1079, 1085

Grain Millers, American Federation of, **1979:** 1452, 1467, 1468

Grain Reserve program, **1979:** 1497

Gramley, Lyle E., **1977:** 372; **1979:** 467, 1233, 1397; **1980–81:** 421, 522, 523

Grana, Pedro A., **1980–81:** 2117

Grand Island, Nebr., **1980–81:** 1089, 1090

Grand Rapids, Mich., **1980–81:** 2451

Grand Teton National Park, Wyo., **1978:** 1476

Grandmaison, J. Joseph, **1977:** 1071, 1085; **1979:** 270

Grandparents Day, National, **1978:** 1360; **1979:** 1597

Grandparents program, Foster, **1979:** 1928

Grange, National, **1980–81:** 1428

Granger, Carl V., **1980–81:** 1596, 1599

Granite City, Ill., **1980–81:** 2659

Granquist, Wayne E., **1979:** 2207

Grant, Carol A., **1979:** 2191

Grant, George V., **1977:** 1384

Grant, James P., **1978:** 296; **1979:** 2139

Grant, Patrick Allan, **1978:** 454

Grants, Federal, **1978:** 1350

Grants-in-aid, Federal, **1977:** 1557, 1558, 1561, 1563, 1564

Granum, Rex L., **1977:** 290, 610, 942, 943, 1034, 1059; **1979:** 1016n., 1226n., 1583n., 2064n.; **1980–81:** 255, 1347, 1377

Granville, Maurice, **1979:** 1614n.

Grasso, Gov. Ella.
See Governor *under* Connecticut.

Gratch, Serge, **1979:** 1008

Gravel, Sen. Mike, **1977:** 1264, 1979; **1978:** 802, 1786

Graves, Charles E., **1977:** 1211, 1212

Graves, Earl G., **1978:** 1106; **1980–81:** 305

Gravlee, Vendal, **1980–81:** 2560

Gray, Catherine G., **1980–81:** 927

Gray, Charles H., **1978:** 230, 232

Gray, Fred D., **1980–81:** 64, 1846, 1847

Gray, Georgia Neese Clark, **1980–81:** 563

Gray, Hanna Holborn, **1979:** 553

Gray, William B., **1977:** 1266, 1307

Gray, Repr. William H., III, **1979:** 787
  Campaign appearance with the President, **1980–81:** 1629
  Meeting with the President (Digest), **1980–81:** 1469
  President's Commission on United States-Liberian Relations, Chair, **1980–81:** 373, 509
  Zimbabwe independence ceremonies, U.S. delegation member, **1980–81:** 719

Graybeal, Sidney N., **1980–81:** 86

Gray's Reef National Marine Sanctuary, Ga., **1980–81:** 2997

Grayson, C. Jackson, **1980–81:** 263

Grazing fees, public lands, **1978:** 1331, 1876

Great Bear and Bob Marshall Wildernesses, Montana, **1978:** 1902

Great Britain.
  See United Kingdom.

Great Lakes Basin Commission, **1979:** 2248

Great Lakes Fishery Commission, **1978:** 1571, 1986

Great Lakes River Basin Commission, **1978:** 273, 408, 737, 1807

Great Plains coal gasification plant, N. Dak., **1980–81:** 1371, 1448

Greathouse, Pat, **1979:** 942

Greece
  Ambassador to U.S., **1979:** 1882
  Cyprus conflict, **1977:** 143, 144, 638, 1137; **1978:** 361, 1151, 1279, 1333, 2103; **1979:** 191, 1301
  Foreign Minister Constantine Mitsotakis, **1980–81:** 1398
  Mention, **1979:** 846
  News conference remarks, **1978:** 1091, 1097, 1327
  Olympics, proposed permanent summer site, **1980–81:** 107, 108, 383, 520
  President's personal emissary, **1977:** 77, 194, 1966; **1978:** 1110
  Prime Minister Constantine Caramanlis, **1977:** 712, 721, 869, 881, 1137; **1978:** 1025; **1980–81:** 382, 520
  Reintegration into NATO, **1980–81:** 2337, 2342, 2369
  Secretary of State's visit, **1978:** 189
  U.S. Ambassador, **1977:** 1152, 1163; **1978:** 270, 303, 1381
  U.S. arms embargo against Turkey, **1978:** 1337, 1357
  U.S. policy, **1977:** 225; **1979:** 156
  Winter Olympics torch ceremony in Athens (Digest), **1980–81:** 217

Greek Americans, **1980–81:** 2369
  Meeting with the President, **1978:** 1154

Greek Orthodox Church, **1977:** 745; **1979:** 1688

Green, Alexander, **1980–81:** 2875

Green, Archie, **1980–81:** 1610

Green, Bill, **1979:** 2187

Green, Ernest Gideon, **1977:** 228, 252, 944; **1978:** 416, 1773; **1979:** 1976; **1980–81:** 1068, 1071

Green, Frederick C., **1978:** 1190

Green, Harry, **1978:** 2274

Green, Joyce Hens, **1979:** 378, 402

Green, Leslie R., **1980–81:** 1141, 1428

Green, Richard J., **1979:** 2091, 2107

Green, Robert H., **1979:** 2076

Green, Robert L., **1978:** 1190

Green, Wallace O., **1980–81:** 1418, 1428

Green, William.
    See Mayor *under* Philadelphia, Pa.
Green, William J., **1979:** 1042
Green, Repr. William S., **1980–81:** 823
Green, William, Sr., **1980–81:** 2046
Greenberg, Irving, **1980–81:** 822
Greenberg, Maurice R., **1978:** 454; **1980–81:** 1048
Greene, Harold H., **1978:** 571
Greene, James Coffin, **1980–81:** 2731
Greene, W. A. (Nick), Jr., **1978:** 696
Greenough, William C., **1979:** 271
Greensboro, N.C., **1979:** 1453, 2105
Greenwald, Carol Schwartz, **1979:** 2218
Greenwood, Hal, **1980–81:** 2559
Greenwood, Harold W., **1977:** 2153
Greer, Merwyn C., **1977:** 1585
Greer, S.C., **1980–81:** 1762n.
Gregg, Dorothy, **1979:** 1671
Gregg, Frank, **1978:** 223, 232
Gregg, James, **1978:** 1243
Gregory, Karl D., **1978:** 454; **1980–81:** 1048
Grenada
    Ambassador to U.S., **1977:** 2050; **1978:** 1722; **1979:** 1454
    Independence ceremonies, U.S. delegation, **1979:** 2042
    Prime Minister Eric M. Gairy, **1977:** 1566, 1568
    U.S. Ambassador, **1977:** 1189, 1212; **1979:** 664
Grenadines, trade beneficiary developing country designation, **1980–81:** 550
Gresham, Oreg., **1978:** 1942
Grevey, Eileen J. A., **1978:** 506
Greybor Electric Company, **1980–81:** 552, 581
Gribben, Edward P., **1977:** 2050, 2051
Gridiron dinner, **1977:** 507; **1978:** 525
Grier, Roosevelt, **1979:** 2280; **1980–81:** 1405, 2524
Griffin, James D., **1980–81:** 63
Griffin, Marie, **1980–81:** 257
Griffin, Sen. Robert P., **1977:** 1072, 1162, 1699
Griffin, Robert T., **1978:** 1345, 1446
Griffith, George Ashley, **1978:** 1722
Griffiths, Martha, **1977:** 526, 816; **1979:** 271; **1980–81:** 1412
Grigoriv, Konstantin Nickolov, **1978:** 328
Grimes, Glenn, **1978:** 1421
Grinstead, Rear Adm. Eugene A., **1978:** 409
Grisham, Daryl F., **1979:** 1961
Grissom, Betty, **1978:** 1687
Grissom, Lt. Col. Virgil I., **1978:** 1687
Griswold, Erwin, **1977:** 1083
Grits, John, **1978:** 770
Gromyko, A. A., **1977:** 559, 603, 768, 1017, 1043, 1649, 1659, 1689, 1699, 1912, 2206; **1978:** 442, 1033, 1256, 1656, 1672, 1690, 1722, 1724, 1776, 1832, 2253, 2276; **1979:** 1079, 1887; **1980–81:** 878, 1202, 1826, 2080
Gronouski, John A., **1977:** 1073, 1085; **1980–81:** 1376, 1847, 2870, 2872

Groomes, Freddie Lang, **1979:** 2159
Gross, Joan H., **1978:** 920, 935
Gross, Lester, **1980–81:** 2075
Gross national product, **1977:** 241; **1978:** 1311, 1360, 1416, 1845, 2212, 2250
    Business productivity, relationship with energy consumption **1979:** 2049
    Defense spending percentage, **1979:** 1904, 1945, 1989, 2018, 2236; **1980–81:** 347, 1769, 1887, 1909, 2088, 2213, 2216, 2269, 2293, 2373
    Federal budget deficits percentage, **1980–81:** 2327, 2895
    Federal Government spending, percentage reduction, **1979:** 307, 1841, 1892; **1980–81:** 71, 76, 122, 226, 489, 639
    Growth percentage, **1980–81:** 1586, 2834
    Health services percentage, **1979:** 1025, 1030
    National increases of, **1979:** 736, 2040
    New industries investment percentage, **1980–81:** 1973
    1980 decline, President's expectation of, **1980–81:** 227
    World's largest product, **1980–81:** 227
Grosse, George R., **1977:** 1128
Grossman, Grace Cohen, **1978:** 1974
Grotting, Dennis A., **1978:** 216
Grove Lake, Kans., **1977:** 208
Growers Cooperative Warehouse, Inc., **1978:** 1390
Gruber, Peter, **1978:** 1259–1263
Gruening, Clark, **1980–81:** 1945
Grunert, Horst, **1978:** 1722
Grunitzky, Yao, **1979:** 842
Grzywinski, Ronald, **1979:** 1220, 1223
Guadeloupe, President's visit, **1978:** 2171, 2187; **1979:** 14, 17, 25, 26
Guam
    Congressional delegate, meeting with the President, **1977:** 744
    Land claim judgments, **1980–81:** 466
    Proposed constitution, **1978:** 795
    Tax structure, **1978:** 1972
    U.S. attorney, **1977:** 1827, 1931
    U.S. district judge, **1978:** 711, 712
    U.S. marshal, **1977:** 1437, 1438
    U.S. policy, **1980–81:** 317
Guaranteed Student Loans, **1978:** 425, 1918
Guard Day, National, **1978:** 1558
Guatemala
    Ambassador to U.S., **1978:** 148; **1979:** 376, 783, 842
    Gen. Fernando Romeo Lucas Garcia, **1978:** 1111
    President Kjell Eugenio Laugerud, **1977:** 1568
    U.S. Ambassador, **1978:** 1111
Gudger, Repr. Lamar, **1978:** 530, 1575, 1576, 1579
Gudonov, Aleksandr, **1979:** 1590ftn.
Guerin, Elizabeth A., **1980–81:** 928

Guerrero Burciaga, Juan, **1979:** 1293, 1294
Guerrier, Charles, **1979:** 1698
Guertin, Paul, **1977:** 321
Guggenheim Foundation, **1980–81:** 1162
Guidi, Marcello, **1980–81:** 1241
Guillemin, Roger Charles Lewis, **1977:** 2045;
    1980–81: 3023
Guin, Kenneth, **1980–81:** 703n.
Guinea
    Ambassador to U.S., **1977:** 508, 1754; **1979:** 842
    Independence celebrations, U.S. delegation,
        1978: 2072
    President Ahmed Sékou Touré, **1979:** 1417
    U.S. Ambassador, **1977:** 1791, 1796; **1980–81:**
        983, 1015
Guinea-Bissau, U.S. Ambassador, **1977:** 1398,
    1438; **1980–81:** 1411, 1428
Gulf Coast Marine Research Center, **1979:** 1675
Gulley, Warren L. (Bill), **1977:** 1533
Gulliver, Adelaide Cromwell, **1980–81:** 2608
Gun control, **1979:** 652
Gunn, Gladys, **1978:** 1086, 1111
Gunnison River, Colo., **1979:** 1813
Gunter, William B., **1977:** 363, 641, 1265, 1759,
    1935; **1978:** 337, 351, 850, 1076; **1980–81:**
    2157, 2176, 2185, 2397
Guthrie, Janet, **1979:** 1678
Guthrie, Paul N., **1978:** 2033, 2158
Guthrie, Woody, **1978:** 2169
Gutierrez, Alfrédo, **1978:** 53
Gutowsky, Herbert S., **1977:** 2046
Guyana, People's Temple, **1978:** 2068, 2099
Guyana, U.S. Ambassador, **1977:** 1219, 1223; **1979:**
    1617
Guyette, Curtis W., **1979:** 733, 787
Guzmán Fernandez, Silvestre Antonio, **1978:** 932,
    942, 1406
Gwirtzman, Milton S., **1978:** 1721, 1772; **1979:** 23,
    46, 90

Haaland, Jewell, **1979:** 1418, 1423
Haar, Charles, **1980–81:** 2559
Haar, Dan, **1980–81:** 733n.
Haas, James W., **1978:** 1060
Haas, Mr. and Mrs. Walter, **1980–81:** 1444
Habib, Philip C., **1977:** 147, 1021, 1029, 1084
Habyarimana, Juvenal, **1980–81:** 1928
Hackel, Stella B., **1977:** 1907, 1931
Hackerman, Norman, **1979:** 1535, 1538
Hackler, Lloyd, **1978:** 454; **1979:** 832; **1980–81:**
    1048
Hadley, Linda, **1979:** 1447; **1980–81:** 2610
Haener, Dorothy, **1977:** 526
Haffenreffer, Carolyn B., **1979:** 465
Hagans, Theodore R., Jr., **1980–81:** 509
Haggerty, Patrick E., **1979:** 660; **1980–81:** 849

Hahn, Kenneth, **1977:** 882; **1978:** 844; **1979:** 813n.;
    1980–81: 2862
Haig, Gen. Alexander M., Jr., **1978:** 38; **1980–81:**
    2834, 3050
Haines, Dina M., **1980–81:** 926
Haiti
    Ambassador to U.S., **1980–81:** 775
    U.S. Ambassador, **1977:** 1346, 1384; **1980–81:**
        1473, 1524
Haitian refugees
    Administration's plan to ease influx (Checklist),
        1980–81: 1848
    Census statistics, **1980–81:** 2812
    Coast Guard and Navy patrols, **1980–81:** 1989,
        2154, 2211, 2383, 2393, 2458
    Congressional response, **1980–81:** 2156
    Education assistance legislation, **1980–81:** 2152,
        2155, 2382
    Federal assistance program, **1980–81:** 375, 1073
    Florida congressional delegation, meeting with
        the President, **1980–81:** 845, 892
    Mentions, **1980–81:** 901, 971
    President's position on:
        Emergency assistance legislation, **1980–81:**
            2155
        Equitable treatment, **1980–81:** 834, 897, 904,
            914, 916, 1075, 2211
        Immigration laws enforcement, **1980–81:** 990,
            2458
    Reagan, Ronald, position on, **1980–81:** 2156
    Resettlement
        Health and Human Services, Secretary of,
            duties, **1980–81:** 2729
        Private sector sponsorship, **1980–81:** 2387
        Puerto Rico, **1980–81:** 2068, 2117
        Religious group efforts, **1980–81:** 2387
        State, Secretary of, duties, **1980–81:** 2183
        State Department efforts, **1980–81:** 820
        States with low unemployment rates, prefer-
            ence for, **1980–81:** 2387, 2393
    Screening process, **1980–81:** 1091
    U.S. Emergency Refugee and Migration Assis-
        tance Fund allocations, **1980–81:** 1523,
        1945
Hakes, Jay, **1977:** 816
Haldeman, H. R., **1977:** 2100
Hale, Sandra J., **1978:** 734; **1980–81:** 237, 268
Haley, Alex, **1977:** 1661
Halford, Scott, **1978:** 1188
Halibut Fishery, United States-Canada Conven-
    tion on Northern Pacific, **1979:** 1420
Hall, George R., **1977:** 1585, 1613
Hall, Millard W., **1978:** 1837
Hall, Paul, **1978:** 759; **1979:** 942, 943
Hall, Robert H., **1979:** 1786, 1787
Hall, Robert Thallon, **1977:** 280
Hall, Tom T., **1980–81:** 2139, 2140n.
Halleck, Charles W., **1977:** 940

Hallett, William E., **1979:** 1775, 1786

Hallinan, Hazel Hunkins, **1977:** 1502, 1503

Hallmark Cards, Inc., **1980–81:** 1402

Halperin, Samuel, **1980–81:** 2075

Halpern, Paul, **1979:** 465

Halpert, Saul, **1980–81:** 1897n.

Haltom, E. B., Jr., **1980–81:** 64

Hamer, Fanny Lou, **1977:** 544

Hamill, Dorothy, **1978:** 2036

Hamilton, Blake D., **1980–81:** 929

Hamilton, Charles V., **1978:** 1706, 1724, 2150; **1979:** 46, 90

Hamilton, Christopher D., **1980–81:** 927

Hamilton, Frank I., **1979:** 1824; **1980–81:** 344

Hamilton, Repr. Lee H., **1977:** 788, 1136, 1533; **1978:** 504, 2268; **1979:** 666, 990

Hamilton, W. E., **1977:** 196

Hammer, Armand, **1978:** 934; **1980–81:** 341

Hammer, Michael P., **1980–81:** 2859n., 2885

Hammer, Rhea Mojica, **1977:** 526

Hammerschmidt, Repr. John Paul, **1980–81:** 1268

Hammond, Jay S., **1977:** 1084; **1978:** 762; **1980–81:** 1342

Hammond, Jerry, **1978:** 1620

Hamner, Allen, **1977:** 404

Hamzah, Tengku Razaleigh, **1978:** 1629

Hanaford Works Site, Washington, **1980–81:** 664

Handicapped, Committee for Purchase From the Blind and Other Severely, **1979:** 163, 437; **1980–81:** 37, 521, 932

Handicapped, National Council on the.
  See National Council on the Handicapped.

Handicapped, President's Committee on Employment of the, **1978:** 216; **1979:** 463; **1980–81:** 808

Handicapped Employees, Interagency Committee on, **1978:** 406, 2291, 2292

Handicapped Individuals, White House Conference on, **1977:** 464, 988, 1031

Handicapped persons, **1977:** 161, 165, 199, 1298, 1672, 1684; **1978:** 111, 359, 774, 1781

Administration's accomplishments and goals, **1980–81:** 156, 808–812, 2951, 2955

Annual report, **1980–81:** 2726

Competitive status for Federal employees (EO 12125), **1979:** 434, 441

Educational programs, **1980–81:** 1561

Federal facility vendors, **1980–81:** 2518

Federal programs, **1979:** 144; **1980–81:** 2161, 2221, 2284, 2361, 2573

Housing, **1980–81:** 2610

White cane safety, **1979:** 1527; **1980–81:** 1568

Handicapped Research, National Institute of, **1979:** 2089, 2106

Handicapped Week, National Employ the, **1978:** 1502; **1979:** 1660; **1980–81:** 1571

Handler, Philip, **1979:** 682n.

Hankers, Freeman, **1980–81:** 1634

Hanks, Nancy, **1977:** 1522, 1534

Hanley, Repr. James M., **1977:** 1211

Hanley, Joy J., **1979:** 446

Hanley, Mary Ellen, **1978:** 515

Hanlin, Russell L., **1980–81:** 1447

Hanlon, Paul H., **1978:** 1663

Hanmer, Rebecca W., **1980–81:** 654

Hannaford, Repr. Mark W., **1978:** 881, 1112

Hannah, John H., Jr., **1977:** 1222, 1266

Hannibal, Mo., **1979:** 1508

Hannigan, Thomas A., **1977:** 1944, 1966; **1978:** 231

Hansell, Herbert J., **1977:** 471, 509; **1978:** 1340, 2281; **1980–81:** 720

Hansen, Sen. Clifford P., **1978:** 457, 575

Hansen, Kent F., **1977:** 1152, 1163

Hansknecht, Joseph L., **1979:** 1220, 1223

Hansson, Margaret S., **1978:** 1836

Harden, Richard, **1977:** 9, 154, 2182; **1978:** 277; **1979:** 1590

Hardesty, Robert L., **1980–81:** 1432

Hardin, Harold D., **1977:** 1086

Hardy, Charles L., **1980–81:** 608

Hardy, Gladys Change, **1980–81:** 949

Hardy, William E., **1978:** 1117

Harkin, Ruth R., **1980–81:** 293

Harkin, Repr. Thomas R., **1977:** 1855; **1979:** 789, 795n., 805; **1980–81:** 720

Harkin amendment, **1977:** 636

Harkness, Jon L., **1980–81:** 96, 218

Harman, Sidney, **1977:** 465, 691, 1296, 1307, 1579, 1613, 1649, 1930; **1978:** 1753

Harmon, John M., **1977:** 803, 807, 1649; **1978:** 1155

Harnett, William, **1980–81:** 340

Harper, Tom, **1978:** 710

Harper, William L., **1977:** 1128

Harpers Ferry, W. Va., **1978:** 1239

Harriman, Pamela, **1979:** 1603

Harriman, W. Averell, **1977:** 78, 79, 90, 1265; **1978:** 504, 914, 919, 935, 1066, 2058; **1980–81:** 47, 267, 719

Kardelj, Edvard, funeral services for, U.S. delegation head, **1979:** 293

Meetings with the President (Digest), **1979:** 1017, 1823

Mountbatten, Earl, funeral services for, U.S. delegation head, **1979:** 1603

President's assessment, **1979:** 1766

Harriman, Mrs. W. Averell, **1978:** 914; **1979:** 293

Harrington, Edward F., **1977:** 1266, 1307

Harrington, Repr. Michael J., **1978:** 770

Harris, Don, **1978:** 2068; **1979:** 1615

Harris, Emmylou, **1977:** 1533

Harris, Franco, **1980–81:** 291

Harris, Repr. Herbert E., II, **1978:** 1667, 1922

Legislation passage leadership
  Mental Health Systems Act, **1980–81:** 2098

Harris, Repr. Herbert — *continued*
  Legislation leadership — *continued*
    National Capital Transportation Amendments of 1979, **1980–81:** 13, 15, 17
    Meeting with the President (Digest), **1980–81:** 374
Harris, Jean, **1980–81:** 2609
Harris, LaDonna, **1977:** 526, 529
Harris, Laird F., **1980–81:** 1653, 1715, 2164, 2332, 2726, 2727, 2873
Harris, Larnelle, **1980–81:** 183
Harris, Neil, **1977:** 1781, 1796; **1979:** 269, 294
Harris, Patricia Roberts, **1977:** 10, 14, 35, 196, 248, 344, 399, 485, 712, 873, 875, 883, 884, 1342, 1347, 1349, 1383, 1394, 1665, 1728, 1755, 1833, 1837, 1938, 2077; **1978:** 422, 521, 526, 533, 641, 792, 871, 961, 1009, 1010, 1110, 1245, 1429, 1430, 1605, 1681, 2059, 2240; **1979:** 1350, 1383
  See also Health, Education, and Welfare, Secretary of; Health and Human Services, Secretary of; Housing and Urban Development, Secretary of.
Harris, Ralph, **1979:** 746n.
Harris, Maj. Gen. Richard L., **1979:** 44, 92
Harris, Robert, **1980–81:** 2910
Harris, Robert H., **1979:** 2077, 2082
Harris, Robert O., **1977:** 1293, 1307 **1980–81:** 1125, 1150
Harris, Thomas E., **1979:** 757, 788
Harris, William, **1977:** 1817
Harrison, Benjamin, **1979:** 1095
Harrison, Edythe C., **1979:** 465
Harrison, Lt. Jefferey, **1980–81:** 786
Harrison, Pauline L., **1980–81:** 1047
Harrop, William C., **1978:** 2072; **1980–81:** 355, 843, 893
Harry S Truman Scholarship Foundation, **1977:** 2101, 2130; **1978:** 88, 232, 596, 641
Harsha, Repr. William H., **1977:** 744, 2179; **1980–81:** 1147, 1262, 1267, 2240
Hart, Bob, **1980–81:** 1305, 1321
Hart, Sen. Gary, **1977:** 2181; **1978:** 824, 834, 898, 1005; **1979:** 956; **1980–81:** 1257, 1548, 2186
Hart, Sen Philip A., **1980–81:** 281
Harte-Hanks Communicatons, **1980–81:** 761
Hartford, Conn., **1978:** 1887, 1891, 1967; **1979:** 1630, 2280; **1980–81:** 2286
Hartigan, James I., **1977:** 1437, 1438
Hartigan, Neil, **1979:** 401
Hartley, Fred L., **1979:** 1614n.
Hartman, Charles H., **1977:** 2028
Hartman, Frank, **1977:** 196, 1944, 1966; **1978:** 231
Hartman, Hermene D., **1979:** 465
Hartsfield Atlanta International Airport, Ga., **1980–81:** 1755

Harvey, F. Barton, Jr., **1977:** 195
Harvey, Francis J., **1978:** 1026
Harvey, Sgt. John D., **1980–81:** 780n., 864
Harvey Joseph J., **1977:** 943
Harvey, Patricia M., **1979:** 889, 890n.
Harvey, Thomas E., **1977:** 987
Harvin, William, **1977:** 816
Harwood, Stanley, **1980–81:** 2613
Haskell, Sen. Floyd K., **1977:** 557; **1978:** 503, 824, 827, 834, 881, 1111
Haskin, Lynn M., **1977:** 1053
Haslam, Charles Linn, **1977:** 338, 373
Hassan II, King, **1977:** 1966; **1978:** 1808, 2031, 2033, 2055, 2058, 2059
Hassell, John S., Jr., **1980–81:** 842, 893
Hasten, Mark, **1978:** 892
Hastings, Alcee L., **1979:** 1531, 1532
Hastings, Karis A., **1980–81:** 927
Haswell, Anthony, **1977:** 1811, 1826; **1978:** 230, 881
Hatch, Sen. Orrin G., **1978:** 1139, 1140
Hatch Act, **1978:** 108, 1369, 1370; **1979:** 147; **1980–81:** 156, 2567
  Proposed revision, **1977:** 484
Hatcher, Richard, **1979:** 402; **1980–81:** 825, 932, 1432, 2115, 2889, 3021
Hatcher, Richard G., **1978:** 570, 641, 771, 907, 1075, 2151
Hatchett, Joseph W., **1979:** 899, 900, 1809
Hatfield, Dale, **1979:** 1706
Hatfield, Sen. Mark O., **1977:** 1265, 1595; **1978:** 769, 1515; **1979:** 867, 2104
  Federal territorial policy development, **1980–81:** 318
  Legislation passage leadership, **1980–81:** 38, 1548, 1661
  National prayer breakfast attendance, **1980–81:** 275
Hatfield, Sen. Paul, **1978:** 229, 504, 520, 2187
Hatfield, Paul G., **1979:** 441
Hathaway, Dale Ernest, **1977:** 495, 510; **1978:** 2157; **1979:** 217; **1980–81:** 219
Hathaway, Sen. William D., **1977:** 927, 2105; **1978:** 341, 347, 1898
Hatter, Terry J., **1979:** 1786, 1787
Hattiesburg, Miss., **1978:** 82
Hauberg, Robert E., **1978:** 1222, 1223
Hauck, William F., **1977:** 508
Haugerand, Neil S., **1977:** 1917
Haughton, Ronald W., **1979:** 24, 46, 90
Hauser, Rita E., **1977:** 2024, 2037; **1978:** 231
Hawaii
  Democratic Party caucuses, **1980–81:** 461
  Disaster declaration, **1979:** 402; **1980–81:** 292
  President's visit, **1979:** 1217
  U.S. attorney, **1978:** 899
  U.S. district judges, **1980–81:** 423, 424, 2857, 2870, 2873

Hawaii — *continued*
　U.S. marshal, **1977:** 1211, 1212
Hawk, Harry, **1978:** 1878
Hawkins, Repr. Augustus F., **1977:** 1427, 1788,
　　1995, 2023, 2024; **1978:** 416, 693, 698, 842,
　　1679, 1871, 1873; **1979:** 318; **1980–81:**
　　847, 1585
Hawkins, Beverly J., **1977:** 987
Hawkins, Carl S., **1977:** 1055
Hawkins, David G., **1977:** 1531, 1534
Hawkins, Falcon B., **1979:** 1018, 1019
Hawkins, Genta A., **1979:** 1880, 1976
Hawkins, Lawrence R., **1979:** 1448
Hawkins, Michael D., **1977:** 642
Hawley, Philip M., **1979:** 1954
Hawrigan, W. Robert, **1977:** 508
Hay, Betty Jo, **1980–81:** 1395n.
Hay, Jess, **1977:** 86; **1980–81:** 1393, 1395n., 2559
Hayakawa, Sen. S. I., **1978:** 769; **1979:** 2257n.;
　　1980–81: 509, 1455
Hayden, Tom, **1978:** 276
Hayes, Adm. John B., **1980–81:** 932
Hayes, Lawrence, **1978:** 734
Hayes, Miller, **1978:** 1293
Hayes, Robert M., **1979:** 400
Hayes, Spencer T., **1980–81:** 19
Hayne, William A., **1979:** 1042; **1980–81:** 34
Haynes, H. I., **1979:** 1614n.
Haynes, Jim, **1980–81:** 2559
Haynes, Ulric S., Jr., **1977:** 727, 745
Haynes, Mr. and Mrs. Ulric St. Clair, Jr., **1978:**
　　2288
Hays, Gen. Anna Mae, **1978:** 2089
Haytow, Eugene, **1979:** 1603
Hayward, Adm. Thomas B., **1978:** 684, 1219, 1220;
　　1979: 1603
Hazard, Benjamin W., **1977:** 1781, 1796
Hazardous materials, **1980–81:** 2872, 3044
Hazardous Materials Control, Annual Report on,
　　1979: 178
Hazardous waste disposal
　Administration's accomplishments and goals,
　　1980–81: 2972
　Dumpsites, **1979:** 1357, 1429
　Insurance fund for personal property damage,
　　1979: 1351, 1483, 1497
　Legislation, **1979:** 1351, 1357, 1482, 1497
　　See also Comprehensive Environmental Re-
　　　sponse, Compensation, and Liability Act;
　　　Solid Waste Disposal Act Amendments.
　Love Canal, N.Y., accident.
　　See Love Canal, N.Y., accident.
　Nuclear materials.
　　See Nuclear waste disposal.
　Oil, **1980–81:** 116, 158
　Valley of the Drums accident, **1980–81:** 158
Head Start program, **1977:** 1850; **1978:** 1749; **1979:**
　　1903, 1928

Head Start program — *continued*
　Budget allocations, **1980–81:** 1499, 2061, 2617
　15th anniversary ceremony, **1980–81:** 462
　Miami, Fla., program, **1980–81:** 1074
Health, Education, and Welfare, Department of
　Aging, Commissioner on, **1978:** 231; **1979:** 1596
　Appropriations, **1977:** 2087
　Assistant Secretaries, **1977:** 252, 253, 370, 373,
　　465, 1080, 1085, 1665, 1844; **1978:** 971,
　　1681, 1917, 1919; **1979:** 339, 377, 742ftn.,
　　886n., 1143, 1157, 1159, 1319, 1775, 1786
　Black colleges and institutions strengthening,
　　1979: 49
　Budget expenditures, **1978:** 104
　Budget rescission and deferral, **1979:** 200, 1522
　Children's Bureau, Chief, **1977:** 1139, 1163
　Coal mine safety research, **1979:** 1445
　Consumer Affairs Council membership, **1979:**
　　1763
　Department of Education, advantages of sepa-
　　ration from, **1979:** 849, 1956, 1959
　Deputy Inspector General, **1977:** 1195, 1213;
　　1979: 616, 667
　Doctors' fees monitoring, **1979:** 1639
　Education, Commissioner of, **1978:** 1917, 1919;
　　1979: 2276, 2281
　Educational broadcast facilities program, **1977:**
　　1742
　Employment and training program integration
　　into State and local governments, **1979:**
　　1523
　Energy crisis, **1977:** 35
　Environmental effects of advanced technologies,
　　1977: 974
　Families, office of, proposed, **1979:** 1930
　Federal coal mine health activities, **1978:** 576
　Federal paperwork reduction, **1979:** 869
　General Counsel, **1977:** 369, 373; **1979:** 1000,
　　1019, 1960, 1977
　Health research strategy, **1979:** 535
　Healthcare program promotion, **1979:** 1031
　Hospital costs, **1977:** 51
　Inspector General, **1977:** 230, 252; **1978:** 1756,
　　2232
　Integrated pest management programs, **1979:**
　　1383
　Interagency Coordinating Council, **1978:** 1434
　Juvenile justice program, **1977:** 1712
　Low-level radiation analysis, **1979:** 2007
　Medicare, **1977:** 302, 1902
　Mental health demonstration projects, **1979:** 862
　National Conference on Fraud, Abuse and Er-
　　ror, sponsorship, **1978:** 2228
　Office of International Health, Director, **1977:**
　　806
　Officials, meeting with the President, **1977:** 194

Health, Education, Welfare — *continued*
  President's Commission on the Accident at
      Three Mile Island, support services, **1979:**
      659
  President's Special Commission for the Study of
      Ethical Problems in Medicine and Bio-
      medical and Behavioral Research,
      funding support, **1979:** 2261
  President's visit, question-and-answer session,
      1977: 158
  Radioactivity exposure analysis, **1979:** 182
  Reorganization, **1977:** 302
  Reports preparation, **1979:** 103, 362, 1604, 1704,
      1705, 1966, 2035, 2106
  Research guidelines, **1978:** 209
  Rural development programs, **1979:** 75
  School busing authority, **1979:** 1947
  Smallpox control, international, **1979:** 2036
  Under Secretary, **1977:** 252, 706; **1979:** 1851
  U.S.-Federal Republic of Germany social secu-
      rity agreement, **1978:** 1559
  Veteran's Federal Coordinating Committee,
      1978: 1743
  Welfare program administration, **1979:** 940
  Welfare reform, **1977:** 74
  See also specific constituent agencies.
Health, Education, and Welfare, Secretary of (Jo-
      seph A. Califano, Jr.), **1977:** 10, 16, 158,
      159, 164, 194, 200, 230, 248, 315, 328, 356,
      378, 385, 392, 485, 509, 662, 705, 706, 712,
      717, 744, 746, 770, 772, 774, 775, 805, 806,
      838, 898, 990, 1210, 1237, 1325, 1345,
      1348, 1404, 1405, 1436, 1437, 1444, 1447,
      1465, 1665, 1761, 1852, 1963, 2064, 2076,
      2088, 2089, 2130; **1978:** 61, 73, 288, 298,
      304, 309, 356, 357, 362, 423, 458, 536–538,
      553, 594, 595, 607, 710, 748, 766, 767, 770,
      792, 817, 880, 892, 933, 934, 961, 971,
      1034, 1110, 1161, 1186, 1187, 1221, 1235,
      1325, 1344, 1386, 1670, 1724, 1782, 1917,
      1919, 2088, 2146, 2259
  Black colleges and institutions responsibilities,
      1979: 49
  Health information and promotion, report prep-
      aration, **1979:** 467
  Interdepartmental Committee on Domestic Vio-
      lence, Chairman, **1979:** 929
  Meetings with the President (Digest), **1979:** 240,
      898, 1292
  Mentions, **1979:** 246, 386ftn., 691, 886n., 1028n.
  National health plan legislation briefing, **1979:**
      65
  News conferences (Checklist), **1979:** 402, 859,
      958, 1028, 1044
  President's assessment, **1979:** 1350
  Resignation, **1979:** 1270
  Women's educational programs actions, **1979:**
      895

HEW, Secretary — *continued*
  World Health Organization, U.S. Chief Dele-
      gate, **1979:** 815
  For functions of the Department in general, see
      Health, Education, and Welfare, Depart-
      ment of.
Health, Education, and Welfare, Secretary of
      (Patricia Roberts Harris)
  American National Red Cross, Board of Gov-
      ernors, member, **1979:** 1678
  Federal Council on the Aging members, swear-
      ing-in ceremony remarks, **1979:** 2215
  Indochinese refugees emergency assistance, ap-
      propriations requests, **1979:** 2086
  Meetings with the President (Digest), **1979:** 1453,
      1705, 1823, 1975, 2081, 2186
  Mentions, **1979:** 1715, 1921
  News conference (Checklist), **1979:** 2188
  Nomination, **1979:** 1270, 1293
  Office for families, establishment, **1979:** 1930
  President's support, **1979:** 1310, 1350
  Swearing-in ceremony, **1979:** 1391, 1393
  Urban Development Action Grant program,
      second anniversary remarks, **1979:** 1966
  White House Conference on Aging, appointment
      of members, **1979:** 2249
  For functions of the Department in general, see
      Health, Education, and Welfare, Depart-
      ment of.
Health, National Institutes of, **1979:** 544, 2007,
      2064; **1980–81:** 955, 956, 1396, 2806
Health, Physical Education, Recreation and
      Dance, American Alliance for, **1979:** 955
Health, President's, **1979:** 1305
Health Administration, Occupational Safety and.
  See Occupational Safety and Health Adminis-
      tration.
Health Assembly, World, **1977:** 806, 839; **1978:**
      885; **1979:** 815
Health Care Financing Administration, **1979:** 1670
Health Day, Child, **1979:** 1627; **1980–81:** 1520
Health and Human Services, Department of
  Abortion funding, **1980–81:** 2326
  Alcoholic health hazards, report preparation,
      1980–81: 2753
  Assistant Secretaries, **1980–81:** 316, 1942
  Budget rescissions and deferrals, **1980–81:** 235,
      355, 2916
  Dioxin exposure effects study, **1980–81:** 4
  Handicapped persons programs, **1980–81:** 2212,
      2610
  Head Start program.
    See Head Start program.
  Heat- and drought-affected areas, assistance
      functions, **1980–81:** 1421, 1423
  Inauguration ceremonies, **1980–81:** 909

Health and Human Services — *continued*
  Infant nutrition standards monitoring, **1980–81:** 1936, 2051
  Inspector General, **1980–81:** 1494, 1524
  Juvenile deliquency programs, **1980–81:** 1273
  Miami, Fla., assistance program, **1980–81:** 1236
  National Cystic Fibrosis Week functions, **1980–81:** 1396
  Nuclear Safety Oversight Committee, support services, **1980–81:** 505
  Occupational safety and health activities, **1980–81:** 394, 1051
  President's assessment of efficiency, **1980–81:** 2207
  Radiation Policy Council membership, **1980–81:** 363
  Senior citizen programs, **1980–81:** 2212
  Social security
    Agreement with Switzerland, analysis, **1980–81:** 265
    Disability insurance benefits, evaluation, **1980–81:** 1062
  Tahoe Federal Coordinating Council membership, **1980–81:** 2232, 2236
  Task Force on Global Resources and Environment, functions, **1980–81:** 1417
  Urban area programs, **1980–81:** 1862
Health and Human Services, Secretary of (Patricia Roberts Harris)
  Black colleges strengthening efforts, **1980–81:** 329
  Council on Wage and Price Stability, adviser-member, **1980–81:** 967
  Cuban and Haitian refugee assistance, **1980–81:** 780, 2729
  Department inauguration ceremonies, **1980–81:** 908, 911
  Dioxin exposure, legislative requirement for health effects study, **1980–81:** 4
  Environmental damage response activities, **1980–81:** 3044
  Federal mine safety and health, report preparation, **1980–81:** 1049
  Handicapped persons programs support, **1980–81:** 2161, 2284
  Infant formula legislation support, **1980–81:** 1937
  Interagency Employee Benefit Council, member, **1980–81:** 2864
  Interagency Radiation Research Committee, establishment, **1980–81:** 364
  Ku Klux Klan statement, **1980–81:** 1833
  Meetings with the President (Digest), **1980–81:** 267, 492
  Mental health legislation passage leadership, **1980–81:** 2103
  Mentions, **1980–81:** 1004, 1071, 1101, 1510, 1634

Health and Human Services — *continued*
  Nuclear Safety Oversight Committee, report reception, **1980–81:** 504
  President's assessment, **1980–81:** 2059
  Project Head Start responsibilities, **1980–81:** 462, 465, 466n.
  Public Health Service physicians, bonus award authority, **1980–81:** 1252
  Refugee admission functions, **1980–81:** 685
  Rehabilitation Act of 1978, regulations implementation, **1980–81:** 2654
  Task Force on Global Resources and Environment, duties, **1980–81:** 1417
  For functions of the Department in general, see Health and Human Services, Department of.
Health Insurance, National Committee for, **1977:** 1127
Health Insurance Panel, Supplemental, **1980–81:** 2558
Health Maintenance Organizations, **1979:** 134
Health and medical care
  Administration's accomplishments and goals, **1980–81:** 133–136, 2942
  Air pollution, effect, **1977:** 1072
  Alcoholism, **1980–81:** 2753
  American Heart Month, **1978:** 89
  Anti-inflation program, **1978:** 1842
  Black medical students, **1977:** 1575
  Child programs, **1980–81:** 118, 811, 1310, 1355, 2900
  Childhood disease immunization program, **1977:** 605, 892, 896, 2088
  Children's Hospital National Medical Center, **1977:** 327
  Costs, **1977:** 302, 315, 1270, 1321
  D.C. General Hospital Commission Act, **1977:** 333
  Detroit, Mich., public policy forum, **1977:** 1833, 1835, 1840, 1850
  Diabetes control program, **1980–81:** 1520
  Dioxin exposure effects, **1980–81:** 4
  Disabilities, income tax deductions, **1977:** 309, 310, 317
  Disability programs, **1980–81:** 1062
  Disadvantaged persons, **1979:** 1633
  Economic Report, **1978:** 141
  Emergency medical care, **1980–81:** 514
  Emergency Medical Services Week, **1977:** 1974
  Federal employee programs, **1980–81:** 393
  Federal health insurance, **1979:** 898, 925
  Federal mine activities, **1979:** 103, 1445; **1980–81:** 1049
  Federal Mine Safety and Health Amendments Act of 1977, **1977:** 1987, 1989
  Federal physicians comparability allowance, **1978:** 2300
  Federal programs, **1979:** 117, 135

Health and medical care — *continued*
  Food stamps program malnutrition reduction,
    1979: 1433
  Genetic diseases program, **1980–81:** 1049
  Handicapped persons, **1980–81:** 809
  Hazardous waste disposal, **1979:** 1034, 1044
  Health costs review, **1979:** 74
  Health information and promotion, **1980–81:**
    1714
  Heart disease prevention, **1980–81:** 2914
  Herbicides, effect of, **1979:** 2249
  Hospital cost containment legislation.
    See Hospital cost containment legislation.
  Hospital workers in Newington, Conn., Presi-
    dent's remarks to, **1980–81:** 2279, 2286
  Household product warning labels, **1980–81:**
    2051
  Indochinese refugees, screening and care for,
    1979: 2089
  Industry representatives, meeting with the Pres-
    ident, **1980–81:** 563
  Infant mortality, **1980–81:** 3006
  Information and promotion status, report, **1979:**
    467
  International program, **1978:** 816
  Legislation, **1977:** 717, 746, 1778, 1995
  Love Canal area residents, **1980–81:** 2430
  Low-level radiation hazards, **1979:** 2007
  Malpractice insurance, **1978:** 360
  Medic Alert program, **1978:** 612
  Medical research legislation, **1980–81:** 2294
  Medicare-Medicaid Anti-Fraud and Abuse
    Amendments, **1977:** 1902
  Medication, **1977:** 306
  Mental health, **1977:** 185–189, 234, 528, 899;
    1978: 348
  Mental health legislation.
    See Mental Health Systems Act.
  Military physician shortage, **1980–81:** 456
  Mount St. Helens eruption, effect on, **1980–81:**
    951
  National Democratic Party Conference, re-
    marks, **1978:** 2193
  National health insurance, **1977:** 162, 393, 892,
    896, 1327, 1995, 2194
  National plan, **1978:** 348, 369, 710, 876, 1160
    1186, 1325, 1344, 1345, 1492, 1493, 1606,
    2222, 2223
    Administration's proposal, **1980–81:** 117, 133,
      1652, 1875
    Briefing by HEW Secretary Califano, **1979:** 65
    Budget allocation, **1979:** 98
    Congressional consideration, **1979:** 1411, 1595,
      1633, 1634, 1637, 1749
    Congressional leaders, meeting with the Pres-
      ident, **1979:** 1011
    Disadvantaged persons coverage, **1979:** 1633

Health and medical care — *continued*
  National plan — *continued*
    Doctors' fees, public posting, **1979:** 1638
    Mentions, **1979:** 104, 137; **1980–81:** 811, 1990,
      2261
    News conference (Checklist), **1979:** 1044
    Nursing homes long-term care, possibility of,
      1979: 1635
    Objectives, **1980–81:** 1310, 2035, 2160, 2162,
      2361, 2549, 2632
    Older persons benefits, **1979:** 1633
    Phased program implementation, **1979:** 1411,
      1634
    President's support, **1980–81:** 1607, 1619, 1721,
      1886, 2901, 3010
    Proposed legislation, **1979:** 1024, 1028
    Reagan, Ronald, opposition to, **1980–81:** 2142,
      2160, 2253, 2273, 2308, 2360, 2365, 2390,
      2399, 2456, 2496, 2526, 2554, 2581, 2637,
      2662
    1981 budget allocations, **1980–81:** 230, 231,
      1002
  Nurse training programs, **1978:** 2007
  Nurses and physicians' aides, **1977:** 892, 896
  Nursing homes, **1980–81:** 604
  Occupational, **1977:** 979, 1331; **1978:** 1030, 1415,
    1491, 1545
  Occupational safety and health
    Federal employees program, **1980–81:** 1261
    Report, **1980–81:** 1051
  Oil spill damage victims' compensation, **1979:**
    1360
  Older persons, **1979:** 672, 838; **1980–81:** 535
  Paperwork reduction, **1979:** 1636
  Polio immunization, **1980–81:** 811
  Pregnancy, occupational discrimination, **1978:**
    1906
  Regulatory reform, **1979:** 475
  Research and development, **1980–81:** 190
  Rural health clinic services bill, **1977:** 2104
  Rural initiatives, **1979:** 794
  Smallpox eradication, **1979:** 2027
  Spinal cord injuries, **1980–81:** 811
  State of the Union, **1978:** 100, 103
  Tax message, **1978:** 164, 169
  Uniformed services programs, **1980–81:** 1251
  Urban programs, **1978:** 591
  U.S.-Japan Cooperative Medical Science Pro-
    gram, **1977:** 1382
  Veterans programs, **1980–81:** 1121, 1563, 1576
  Vietnam veterans, **1978:** 1741
  See also Hospital cost containment; Mental
    health.
Health Organizaton, World, **1977:** 2037; **1979:**
  2035
Health Planning and Resources Development
  Amendments, **1979:** 1818

Health Professionals Special Pay Act, Uniformed
    Services, **1980–81:** 456, 1251
Health Resources Advisory Committee, National,
    1978: 325
Health and Safety Act of 1968, **1979:** 2043
Health and Safety Act of 1968, Radiation Control
    for, **1978:** 1560
Health Sciences, Uniformed Services University of
    the, **1978:** 1964
Health Service, Public, **1977:** 1080, 1085; **1980–81:**
    456, 908
Health Service award, Public, **1979:** 983; **1979:**
    2036
Health Service Corps, National, **1977:** 2088, 2104;
    1979: 134; **1980–81:** 909
Health Services, Uniformed Services University of
    the, **1980–81:** 1445, 1470, 1927, 1947
Healthcare program, Federal, **1979:** 1024, 1025,
    1028–1031
Healy, Paul, **1977:** 758, 760
Healy, Theresa Ann, **1980–81:** 899, 933
Healy, Timothy S., **1978:** 1514; **1980–81:** 1335,
    1336
Hearing and Speech Month, Better, **1977:** 743;
    1978: 822
Hearst, Patricia, **1978:** 2257; **1979:** 216, 218
Hearst, William Randolph, Jr., **1977:** 80
Heart, Blood Vessel, Lung, and Blood Program,
    National, **1977:** 1209
Heart, Lung, and Blood Institute, National, **1979:**
    178
Heart Association, American, **1980–81:** 190
Heart Month, American, **1978:** 89, 289; **1979:** 21;
    1980–81: 190, 2914
Heath, Josephine W., **1977:** 1055
Heavner, Robert O., **1977:** 987
Hebrew Associaton, Young Men's, **1980–81:** 2537
Hechinger, Fred M., **1978:** 1514
Hechinger, John W., **1978:** 1509, 1516; **1979:** 1921
Heck, L. Douglas, **1977:** 783, 807
Heckert, Richard E., **1978:** 759; **1980–81:** 1048
Heckler, Repr. Margaret, **1977:** 527; **1978:** 1790
Heckman, Richard J., **1980–81:** 304
Hector, Louis J., **1978:** 1706, 1724, 2050; **1979:** 46,
    90
Hedemann, Knut, **1979:** 377
Heen, Walter M., **1978:** 899; **1980–81:** 423, 424,
    2857, 2870, 2873
Heffelfinger, William S., **1977:** 1585
Heffron, Howard A., **1977:** 1961, 1967
Heflin, Sen. Howell, **1979:** 2106
Hefner, Repr. W. G. (Bill), **1977:** 740; **1978:** 530;
    1980–81: 2317
Heftel, Repr. Cecil (Cec), **1979:** 1218
Hegde, K. S., **1978:** 11
Hegner, Anton, **1980–81:** 1598
Heiden, Beth, **1980–81:** 380
Heiden, Eric, **1980–81:** 377, 379

Heidt, James H., **1980–81:** 929
Heidtke, Lisa R., **1980–81:** 928
Height, Dorothy, **1979:** 2135; **1980–81:** 719, 822
Heimann, John G., **1977:** 1025, 1031, 1264; **1978:**
    920
Heine, Walter N., **1977:** 1810, 1826
Heineman, Benjamin W., **1979:** 339, 377
Heinemann, Robert B., **1978:** 2069
Heinz, Sen. H. John, III, **1978:** 303; **1979:** 2257n.
Heir, Rabbi Marvin, **1978:** 1974
Hekman, Capt. Peter, **1978:** 1385
Helen Keller Day (Proc. 4767), **1980–81:** 1147
Helicopter fleet, White House, **1977:** 1162, 1164
Helicopters, President's use of, **1979:** 961
Hellenic Educational Progressive Association,
    Order of the American, **1980–81:** 381
Heller, Helen, **1977:** 302
Heller, Michael A., **1980–81:** 926
Heller, Walter, **1980–81:** 63
Hellring, Bernard, **1977:** 1053
Helman, Gerald B., **1979:** 2147
Helms, Curtis R., **1978:** 952
Helms, Richard, **1977:** 345, 346, 1691, 1912, 1995,
    1998
Help through Industry Retraining and Employ-
    ment (HIRE) program, **1977:** 53, 944,
    1115, 1482, 1611; **1978:** 994, 1739
Helsinki agreement, **1977:** 220, 340
Helsinki Final Act, **1979:** 1835; **1980–81:** 357, 440,
    1434
Hemingway, Ernest, **1979:** 676; **1980–81:** 1441
Hempstead, N.Y., **1980–81:** 2289
Henderson, Albert J., **1979:** 673, 674
Henderson, Donald A., **1979:** 2036
Henderson, Maureen M., **1979:** 686
Henderson, Nicholas, **1979:** 1318
Henderson, Thelton Eugene, **1980–81:** 894
Henderson, Thomas H., Jr., **1980–81:** 62, 374
Hendrie, Joseph M., **1977:** 1189, 1213, 1240; **1980–
    81:** 1848, 1859
Heng Samrin, **1979:** 2197
Hennessey, Jean Lande, **1979:** 1395, 1398
Henning, Jack, **1980–81:** 1884, 1886n.
Henry, Aaron, **1977:** 1437; **1980–81:** 534, 537
    Federal Council on the Aging, member, **1979:**
        317, 323n.
    Mention, **1979:** 2214
    National Caucus on the Black Aged, chairman,
        1979: 1682, 1706
Henry, Bethuel, **1980–81:** 373
Hepburn, Keith, **1978:** 1293
Herbert, Allen Joseph, **1979:** 2159
Herbert, Gary, **1980–81:** 1386, 1388n.
Herbicides, **1979:** 2249
Herbst, Robert L., **1977:** 273, 280; **1978:** 549, 1571
Heritage conservation program, **1979:** 1359
Heritage Conservation and Recreation Service,
    1979: 1380, 1381

Heritage policy act, national, proposed, **1979:** 1359
Heritage Trust, National, **1977:** 979
Herman, Alexis M., **1977:** 366, 373; **1980–81:** 844, 893
Herman, George, **1980–81:** 1049
Hermann, Robert J., **1979:** 1128, 1142
Hermes, Peter, **1979:** 2162n.; **1980–81:** 1449
Hernandez, Anna, **1980–81:** 2559
Hernandez, Richard, **1979:** 811
Hernandez, Rick, **1980–81:** 1942
Herndon, Lillie E., **1980–81:** 1468, 1524
Herndon, Terry, **1977:** 744; **1979:** 1525; **1980–81:** 1299n., 2075, 2884ftn.
Heroin, **1978:** 1329, 1559
Heroin smuggling, **1977:** 290
Herold, John, **1977:** 302
Herrell, Leida Ileana Collado, **1980–81:** 2242
Herrera Campins, Luis, **1979:** 240, 401
Herschler, Gov. Ed, **1978:** 1506; **1979:** 23
Hershey, Lenore, **1977:** 526
Hershey bar prices, **1978:** 1990
Hershow, Russell M., **1980–81:** 928
Herter, Susan, **1977:** 941
Herzog, Ray, **1979:** 2024
Herzstein, Robert E., **1980–81:** 188, 654, 2071
Hesburgh, Rev. Theodore, **1977:** 954, 1751, 1755, 1795
Hesburgh, Theodore M., **1978:** 1222, 1973; **1980–81:** 822, 1837
    See also Select Commission on Immigration and Refugee Policy, Chairman; United Nations Conference on Science and Technology, U.S. delegation head.
Hess, Fran, **1978:** 2110
Hess, Leon, **1979:** 1614n.
Hess, Paul, **1980–81:** 303
Hessler, Curtis Alan, **1980–81:** 434, 453
Heumann, Judith E., **1978:** 1134; **1979:** 464; **1980–81:** 813, 826
Hewitt, Frankie, **1978:** 243
Hewitt, John A., Jr., **1977:** 1952, 1967; **1978:** 231
Hewitt, Ruby, **1977:** 323
Hewitt, William, **1980–81:** 263
Heymann, Philip B., **1978:** 893, 899; **1979:** 619, 1143, 1590
Hezekiah, Lloyd, **1977:** 1780, 1796
Hibernian Society, **1978:** 539
Hickam Air Force Base, Hawaii, **1979:** 1217
Hickey, James B., **1980–81:** 2841
Hickey, Robert C., **1980–81:** 911
Hickman, Curtis, **1978:** 1117
Hicks, Dan P., **1980–81:** 928
Hicks, Jack O., **1980–81:** 2107
Hidaka, Yoshiki, **1979:** 1107
Hidalgo, Edward, **1977:** 550, 558; **1979:** 1659, 1664, 1976; **1980–81:** 1460, 1709, 1943, 3002

Hidalgo y Castilla, Father Miguel, **1979:** 809
Higby, Lynn C., **1979:** 1043, 1044
Higell, Scott, **1978:** 1192
Higginbotham, A. Leon, Jr., **1977:** 463, 1132, 1650, 1651; **1979:** 742, 1403, 1405
Higgins, Regina, **1978:** 1192
Higginson, R. Keith, **1977:** 565
High carbon ferrochromium industry, **1978:** 1940, 1941
High Energy Physics, Committee on, **1979:** 207, 208
High Holy Days, **1980–81:** 1644
Hight, B. Boyd, **1980–81:** 1790–1794
Hightower, Billy O., **1978:** 1808
Highway Administration, Federal, **1977:** 548, 558, 879; **1978:** 1357, 1381; **1980–81:** 842, 893
Highway Safety Act of 1966, **1980–81:** 2880
Highway Safety Advisory Committee, National, **1977:** 2028; **1978:** 1467, 1564; **1979:** 1775; **1980–81:** 1845, 2107, 2815, 3022
Highway Safety and National Motor Vehicle and Traffic Safety Acts of 1966, **1977:** 1210; **1978:** 1237
Highway Safety Report, 1978, **1979:** 1881
Highway Traffic Safety Administration, National, **1977:** 461, 465, 1533; **1980–81:** 281
Highway Trust Fund, **1978:** 222
Highways, **1978:** 106, 220
    Administration's accomplishments and goals, **1980–81:** 2950
    Federal aid, **1977:** 396
    55-mile speed limit, **1977:** 1527; **1979:** 480, 613, 876
    Interstate 75, **1977:** 2165
    Unnecessary traffic signs removal, **1979:** 1952
Hijacking, air, **1980–81:** 1172
Hilberg, Raul, **1978:** 1973; **1980–81:** 822
Hill, B. Harvey, Jr., **1977:** 142
Hill, J. Eldred, Jr., **1978:** 257
Hill, Jesse, Jr., **1977:** 1506; **1978:** 229, 596, 1105, 2146; **1980–81:** 1751
    Communications Satellite Corporation, Board of Directors, member, **1979:** 91, 271, 294
    Mention, **1979:** 33n.
    Pay Advisory Committee, member, **1979:** 1954
Hill, John A., **1977:** 196
Hill, John L., **1978:** 934, 1173
Hill, Kenneth, **1979:** 665
Hill, Roger Gettys, **1980–81:** 2736
Hill, Samuel R., Jr., **1978:** 275, 303
Hill, Steven Richard **1978:** 1026
Hill, Warren G., **1979:** 400
Hilliard, William, **1980–81:** 2477
Hillman, Douglas W., **1979:** 1232, 1233
Himalayan Mountains, American expedition, **1978:** 1558
Hinai, Farid Mubarak Ali al-, **1977:** 1754
Hinds, Albert S., **1977:** 883, 884

Hinerfeld, Ruth J., **1978:** 454; **1979:** 773ftn.; **1980–81:** 589, 836, 1048, 2476
Hines, Earl, **1980–81:** 1405
Hinjose, Jose, **1977:** 508
Hinton, Deane R., **1979:** 2204, 2207; **1980–81:** 521
HIRE.
    See Help Through Industry Retraining and Employment.
Hirohito, Emperor
    Meetings with the President, **1979:** 1164n., 1165, 1167n., 1169
    Mentions, **1979:** 1170, 1190, 1197n., 1218, 1296
    President's assessment, **1979:** 1108, 1112
Hirsche, Sam, **1980–81:** 927
Hispanic Americans.
    See Spanish-speaking Americans.
Hispanic Caucus, Congressional, **1978:** 898; **1979:** 1661; **1980–81:** 1835, 1848
Hispanic Heritage Week, National, **1978:** 1436, 1451; **1980–81:** 1461
    (Proc. 4662), **1979:** 930
Historic Places, National Register of, **1979:** 1359
Historic preservation, **1977:** 979
Historic Preservation, Advisory Council on, **1978:** 228, 1060, 1343; **1979:** 1432, 1704; **1980–81:** 1292, 1935, 2802
Historic Preservation Act Amendments, National, **1980–81:** 2802
Historic Preservation Week, National, **1978:** 887
Historical Association, White House, **1978:** 963, 964
Historical Publications and Records Commission, National, **1978:** 2274; **1980–81:** 1424
Hitachi, Prince and Princess, **1978:** 710
Hitz, Frederick P., **1977:** 1586
Hjort, Howard W., **1977:** 368, 373, 1534; **1978:** 2064; **1980–81:** 219
Ho, Don, **1980–81:** 1405
Hoban, James, **1979:** 2098
Hobbs, Truman McGill, **1980–81:** 218
Hobby, Lt. Gov. William P., **1978:** 1173; **1980–81:** 1393n., 2409
Hobgood, William B., **1980–81:** 1644
Hobgood, William P., **1978:** 1500; **1979:** 1259, 1293
Hoboken, N.J., **1979:** 1817
Hodes, Richard S., **1980–81:** 552, 559, 3021
Hodges, James Alexander, **1979:** 1222
Hodges, Sen. Kaneaster, Jr., **1977:** 2129; **1978:** 457 1405
Hodges, Luther H., Jr., **1980–81:** 25, 43, 73, 521
    Deputy Secretary of Commerce, nomination, **1979:** 2134, 2139, 2149
    Under Secretary of Commerce, nomination, **1979:** 782, 842
Hodges, Winfred, **1978:** 952
Hoese, Frank, **1979:** 1468n.
Hoeveler, William M., **1977:** 597
Hofer, David L., **1980–81:** 183

Hoffman, Ellen Sherry, **1978:** 1086, 1111
Hoffman, John C., **1978:** 1081
Hoffman, Joyce, **1980–81:** 751n.
Hoffman, Terry, **1978:** 1211
Hoffmann, Stanley, **1977:** 78, 90
Hofstede, Albert J., **1980–81:** 1595, 1599
Hogan, Betty, **1977:** 1053
Holahan, Paulette H., **1980–81:** 1445, 1470
Holbrooke, Richard, **1977:** 372, 1029, 1222, 1436; **1979:** 2085
Holcomb, Betty Jeanne, **1978:** 734
Holden, Matthew, Jr., **1977:** 1647, 1650
Holland, Arthur, **1977:** 1576
Holland, Jerome H., **1979:** 552
Holland, Repr. Ken, **1980–81:** 1762
Holleb, Doris B., **1978:** 53; **1980–81:** 1446, 1524
Holliday, Helen, **1980–81:** 893
Hollings, Sen. Ernest F., **1977:** 1264, 1612; **1978:** 1583, 1584, 1879, 1927; **1979:** 1702; **1980–81:** 1755, 1762, 2778, 2780
Holloway, Al, **1980–81:** 552
Holloway, Anne Forrester, **1979:** 1849, 1883
Holloway, Adm. James L., III, **1977:** 1893; **1978:** 2089
Hollywood, Fla., **1980–81:** 1246, 1360
Holman, Carl, **1977:** 941; **1978:** 1706, 1724, 2050; **1979:** 46, 90; **1980–81:** 2559
Holmberg, Ruth, **1977:** 816
Holmes, Cpl. George, Jr., **1980–81:** 780n., 864
Holmes, John Wesley, **1980–81:** 949
Holmes, Larry, **1980–81:** 2453
Holmes, Oliver Wendell, **1980–81:** 2733
Holmes, Peter A., **1980–81:** 1576
Holmes Devise, Permanent Committee for the Oliver Wendell, **1979:** 746
Holmgren, Laton, **1977:** 1612
Holocaust, days of remembrance of victims of the, **1978:** 1529; **1979:** 580, 683, 733; **1980–81:** 644
Holocaust, President's Commission on the.
    See President's Commission on the Holocaust.
Holocaust Memorial Council, United States, **1979:** 2040; **1980–81:** 820, 2106
Holschuh, John David, **1980–81:** 564
Holt, Cleo, **1980–81:** 258, 1839
Holt, Repr. Marjorie S., **1980–81:** 1274
Holton, Thomas L., **1980–81:** 2117
Holtzman, Repr. Elizabeth, **1977:** 527; **1978:** 1902; **1979:** 2085; **1980–81:** 1846
Home Administration, Farmers.
    See Farmers Home Administration.
Home Builders, National Association of, **1978:** 1240; **1979:** 732
Home Loan Bank Board, Federal.
    See Federal Home Loan Bank Board.
Home Mortgage Disclosure Act extension, **1980–81:** 2113

Home Ownership Assistance Plan, **1979:** 74

Honda Motor Company, **1980–81:** 706

Honduras
>   Ambassador to U.S., **1979:** 25, 2162n.; **1980–81:** 2807
>
>   Brig. Gen. Juan Alberto Melgar Castro, **1977:** 1554, 1568
>
>   Dispute settlement with El Salvador, **1980–81:** 2734
>
>   President Policarpo Paz Garcia, **1980–81:** 426
>
>   Trade with U.S., **1979:** 2255
>
>   U.S. Ambassador, **1977:** 1474, 1483; **1980–81:** 1442, 1470
>
>   U.S. assistance, **1979:** 2103

Honolulu, Hawaii, **1980–81:** 720

Hooker, Mrs. James Stewart, **1977:** 2182

Hooks, Benjamin L., **1977:** 1699, 1938; **1978:** 56, 2269; **1980–81:** 164, 1322

Hoopes, Donelson S., **1977:** 2182

Hoopman, H. D., **1979:** 1614n.

Hope, Bob, **1978:** 965–967

Hope, C. C., Jr., **1980–81:** 1405

Hopkins, Teresa Jane, **1977:** 943

Horan, Harold E., **1978:** 1320, 1333

Horan, Hume Alexander, **1980–81:** 1107, 1111

Horbal, Koryne, **1977:** 526, 1176; **1978:** 1134

Hori, Yoshio, **1979:** 1107

Hormats, Robert, **1979:** 2065, 2082; **1980–81:** 25

Hormuz, Straits of.
>   *See* Oil supplies interruption *under* Iraq-Iran conflict.

Hornblower, Ralph, III, **1979:** 2015

Hornby, William, **1980–81:** 643n.

Horner, David B., **1980–81:** 1936

Horner, Vivian M., **1978:** 1514

Horowitz, Herbert E., **1977:** 2182

Horowitz, Vladimir, **1978:** 431, 456; **1980–81:** 2787

Horszowski, Mieczyslaw, **1978:** 284

Horton, Repr. Frank, **1977:** 572, 1411; **1978:** 1755, 1756; **1980–81:** 369, 2795, 2796
>   Department of Education, legislation passage leadership, **1979:** 1230, 1957, 1959
>
>   Federal paperwork reduction actions, **1979:** 2176, 2178, 2182

Horton, Odell, **1980–81:** 423, 424

Horvitz, Wayne L., **1977:** 616, 642; **1979:** 752, 1467, 1468, 1609; **1980–81:** 2017

Hospital Cost Containment Act of 1977, proposed, **1977:** 717, 718, 1778, 1995

Hospital cost containment legislation, **1978:**, 100, 103, 141, 725, 961,1057, 1060, 1061, 1064, 1073, 1326, 1423, 1492, 1548, 1549, 1553, 1587, 1588, 1606, 1607, 1668, 1670, 1842, 1884, 1930, 1970, 2046
>   Administration officials support, **1979:** 2082
>
>   Administration's legislative priority, **1979:** 1855
>
>   Appeal for public support, **1979:** 37, 838, 952

Hospital cost containment — *continued*
>   Congressional consideration, **1979:** 1426, 1633, 1638, 1772, 1919, 2129, 2140
>
>   Congressional inaction, **1979:** 952, 963, 1025
>
>   Inflation control measure, **1979:** 37, 99, 105, 123, 569, 576, 963, 1025, 1392, 1634, 1638
>
>   Letter to House Members, **1979:** 2111
>
>   Meetings with Congressmen (Digest), **1979:** 956, 2043, 2080
>
>   Mentions, **1979:** 111, 134, 926; **1980–81:** 571
>
>   Message transmitting proposals to Congress, **1979:** 383, 386
>
>   National health plan, relationship with, **1979:** 1030; **1980–81:** 231
>
>   News conference (Checklist), **1979:** 402
>
>   Public comments received by White House (Checklist), **1979:** 403, 441
>
>   Purposes, **1980–81:** 117, 133, 1000, 1310, 2162, 2284
>
>   State plans, **1980–81:** 2160
>
>   White House briefing for civic and community leaders, **1979:** 603, 1603 (Digest), 2139

Hospitalized Veterans' Day, National Salute to, **1980–81:** 2888

Hostage Compensation, President's Commission on, **1980–81:** 3039

Hostage Family Liaison Action Group, **1980–81:** 931

Hostage Relief Act, **1980–81:** 2231, 2264, 2912

Hostages, International Convention Against the Taking of, **1980–81:** 1475

Hotel industry, **1980–81:** 967

Hotelling, Joan P., **1980–81:** 926

Houck, C. Weston, **1979:** 1019

Houck, Kenneth L., **1978:** 317

Houdari, Ali El, **1980–81:** 1429

Hourihan, John P., **1980–81:** 813, 826

Housatonic River, Conn., **1979:** 1813

House, Arthur H., **1980–81:** 949

Household Goods Transportation Act, **1980–81:** 2239

Household products, **1980–81:** 2051

Housing
>   Administration's accomplishments and goals, **1980–81:** 138, 2949, 2969
>
>   Black homeowners, **1978:** 842
>
>   Building starts, **1980–81:** 662, 705, 728, 1067, 1081, 1354, 1511, 1632, 1826, 2052, 2128, 2268, 2359
>
>   Community block grant program, **1977:** 889, 904
>
>   Community requirements for Federal aid, **1977:** 344
>
>   Condominium recreation leases, **1980–81:** 2162
>
>   Congressonal Black Caucus, remarks, **1978:** 1681
>
>   Construction costs, **1978:** 725, 1493, 2079
>
>   Construction regulations, **1980–81:** 59
>
>   D.C. revenue bonds, **1980–81:** 666
>
>   Democratic commitment to programs, **1979:** 1935

Housing — *continued*
  Detroit, Mich., forum remarks, **1977:** 1832, 1835, 1837
  Discriminatory practices, **1979:** 884, 911
  Energy-saving measures, **1977:** 136, 286, 408, 521, 666, 675
    Conversion and weatherization programs, **1979:** 1244, 1406, 1413, 1416, 1462, 1490, 1507, 1632, 1642, 2050, 2056
    Heating and cooling restrictions, **1979:** 1471, 1473, 1474, 1476, 1487, 1501, 1569
    New designs and construction features, **1979:** 1537
    Weatherization programs, **1980–81:** 492, 1354, 1587, 1633, 3045
  Fair housing
    Federal programs, **1980–81:** 2850, 2855
    Legislation
      House consideration, **1980–81:** 1071, 1098, 1113, 2426
      Housing and Urban Development Department enforcement authority, **1980–81:** 155
      Leadership Conference on Civil Rights, meeting with the President (Digest), **1980–81:** 720
      Mentions, **1980–81:** 118, 1706
      Reagan, Ronald, position on, **1980–81:** 1771
      Senate consideration, **1980–81:** 1325, 1502, 1754, 1877, 1929
  Federal employees, **1978:** 1430
  Federal mortgage programs, **1979:** 709, 928
  Flood insurance, **1977:** 645
  Handicapped persons, **1980–81:** 810
  Heating oil supplies.
    See Home heating *under* Oil supplies.
  Impact of:
    Federal financial institutions deregulation, **1980–81:** 573
    Inflation, **1980–81:** 723
  Interest rate increases, **1979:** 2027
  Interview remarks, **1977:** 1342, 1373, 1938; **1978:** 806
  Low- and middle-income, **1977:** 47, 136, 137
  Mobile construction and safety standards, **1978:** 880
  Mobile homes, **1977:** 464
  Mortgages
    Federal assistance programs, **1980–81:** 728, 806, 835, 887, 909, 1003, 1499, 2135
    Interest rates, **1980–81:** 806, 890, 978, 994, 2268, 2358, 2437
    Task force on credit, **1980–81:** 2114
  Mortgages, interest rates, **1977:** 310
  Neighborhood revitalization projects, **1979:** 77
  New homes construction, **1979:** 117, 136, 704, 754, 1876, 1909, 1948, 1985, 2028, 2049, 2051

Housing — *continued*
  1980 production report, **1980–81:** 521
  1981 budget allocations, **1980–81:** 230, 536, 540, 555
  Older persons, **1980–81:** 2158, 2163, 2460
  Policy, **1977:** 904, 1326
  Public projects, **1978:** 1242, 1245, 1620
  Spokane, Wash., town meeting remarks, **1978:** 870, 871
  State of the Union, **1978:** 105
  Task force on mortgage credit, **1980–81:** 2114
  Urban homesteading program, **1977:** 976
  Urban programs, **1978:** 590
  Variable allowances for military personnel, **1980–81:** 2065
Housing, Advisory Committee on, **1980–81:** 2559
Housing, President's Commission on Equal Opportunity in, **1980–81:** 2853
Housing Assistance Corporation, **1979:** 2276n.
Housing Benefits Act, Veterans, **1978:** 1791
Housing Benefits Amendments, Veterans' Disability Compensation and, **1980–81:** 2097
Housing Community Development Act of 1974, **1977:** 464; **1980–81:**, 1469
Housing and Community Development Act of 1977, **1977:** 1777, 1787, 1796
Housing and Community Development Act of 1980, **1980–81:** 2112, 2179
Housing for the Eighties, President's Task Force on, **1980–81:** 2179
Housing Goal, National, **1978:** 1723
Housing Month, Fair, **1978:** 681
Housing Partnership, National, **1978:** 1279
Housing Partnerships, National Corporation for, **1978:** 1279, 1500, 1506; **1980–81:** 1048, 1111
Housing Rehabilitation Loan Programs, Assisted, **1978:** 105
Housing and Urban Development, Department of
  Annual reports, **1978:** 1807; **1980–81:** 824, 1714
  Assistant Secretaries, **1977:** 366, 367, 373, 470, 471, 506, 509, 510, 712, 745, 1675, 1834, 1836, 1841, 1848; **1978:**, 1280; **1979:** 42, 61, 93, 1408, 1921, 1972; **1980–81:** 192, 281, 1095, 1941
  Budget rescission, **1979:** 200; **1980–81:** 2916
  Consumer Affairs Council membership, **1979:** 1763
  Defaulted housing projects, **1978:** 106
  Energy crisis, **1977:** 35, 113
  Fair housing, Federal program coordination and leadership, **1980–81:** 2850, 2855
  Federal emergency management, transfer of functions, **1979:** 1278
  Federal paperwork reduction actions, **1979:** 75
  General Counsel, **1977:** 576, 596; **1979:** 1221, 1223

HUD, Department of — *continued*
   Handicapped persons programs, **1980–81:** 2610
   Hard-core unemployed jobs program, **1979:** 2158
   Housing discrimination enforcement, **1979:** 143, 884
   Housing rehabilitation program, **1979:** 77
   Inspector General, **1979:** 365, 377
   Integrated pest management programs, **1979:** 1383
   Interagency Coordinating Council, **1978:** 1434
   Juvenile delinquency programs, **1980–81:** 1273
   Low- and middle-income housing, **1977:** 47
   Membership on:
      Radiation Policy Council, **1980–81:** 363
      Tahoe Federal Coordinating Council, **1980–81:** 2235, 2236
   Mental health demonstration projects, **1979:** 862
   Mobile home construction and safety standards, **1978:** 880
   Mortgage assistance program, **1980–81:** 2113, 2129
   National urban policy report preparation, **1980–81:** 1861
   National water policy functions, **1978:** 1048, 1050
   Neighborhood and community programs, **1980–81:** 2117
   President's visit, question-and-answer session, **1977:** 132
   Public housing projects, **1978:** 1245, 1280
   Regulations, congressional involvement, **1978:** 1227
   Report, **1977:** 744
   Solar energy development bank, **1979:** 1101, 1315, 1316
   Steel industry community assistance, **1980–81:** 1968
   Transfer of certain programs to proposed Energy Department, **1977:** 258
   Under Secretary, **1977:** 275, 280; **1979:** 2078, 2249; **1980–81:** 1460, 1941, 2877n.
   Urban Development Action Grant program.
     See Urban Development Action Grant program.
   Urban homesteading program, **1977:** 976
   Urban noise abatement program, **1979:** 1371, 1385
   Urban programs, **1978:** 584, 586, 598, 590, 592
   See also specific constituent agencies.
Housing and Urban Development, Secretary of (Patricia Roberts Harris), **1977:** 10, 14, 248, 344, 399, 485, 553, 662, 712, 1342, 1347, 1349, 1383, 1394, 1665, 1728, 1755, 1761, 1794, 1833, 1837, 1938, 2077; **1978:** 422, 521, 526, 553, 587, 594, 595, 641, 792, 871, 961, 1009, 1010, 1110, 1245, 1429, 1430, 1605, 1681, 2059, 2240

HUD, Secretary — *continued*
   Federal Council on the Arts and Humanities, member, **1979:** 956
   Federal emergency management functions (EO 12127), **1979:** 566
   Housing discrimination cease and desist authority, **1979:** 884, 911
   President's assessment, **1979:** 1309, 1310
   Solar energy development bank, board of directors chairperson, **1979:** 1315
   For functions of the Department in general, see Housing and Urban Development, Department of.
Housing and Urban Development, Secretary of (Moon Landrieu)
   Council on Wage and Price Stability, adviser-member, **1980–81:** 967
   Economic assistance actions for pollution control, **1979:** 1385
   Energy conservation responsibilities, **1980–81:** 788
   Fair housing, Federal program coordination and leadership duties, **1980–81:** 2850–2854
   Housing and Community Development Act support, **1980–81:** 2115
   Meetings with the President (Digest), **1979:** 1318, 1454, 1823, 1975, 2081, 2187; **1980–81:** 63, 492, 825
   Mention, **1980–81:** 2401
   Nomination, **1979:** 1315, 1320, 1397
   President's assessment, **1979:** 1431, 1748; **1980–81:** 212
   Swearing-in ceremony, **1979:** 1718
   Urban Development Action Grant program, second anniversary remarks, **1979:** 1967
   Urban noise abatement program development, **1979:** 1385
   For functions of the Department in general, see Housing and Urban Development, Department of.
Houston, Tex., **1978:** 1165, 1221; **1980–81:** 29, 1404, 1738–1744, 2603
Howard, George, Jr., **1980–81:** 1015, 1051
Howard, Gerald V., **1977:** 1764
Howard, Repr. James J., **1977:** 1397
   Legislation passage leadership
     Household Goods Transportation Act, **1980–81:** 2240
     Motor Carrier Act, **1980–81:** 1147, 1262, 1265, 1267
   Meetings with the President (Digest), **1979:** 89, 666, 898; **1980–81:** 825
   Trucking industry deregulation, legislation support, **1979:** 1115, 2185
Howard, Joseph C., Sr., **1979:** 957, 958
Howard, Dr. Lee M., **1977:** 806; **1978:** 885; **1979:** 815

Howard, Mark, **1980–81:** 1635
Howe, Harold, II, **1978:** 54, 149; **1979:** 1820
Howe, Kay, **1978:** 2050; **1979:** 46, 90
Howe, Warner, **1980–81:** 533, 564
Howell, Ann, **1980–81:** 893
Howell, Henry, **1977:** 1210, 1653, 1656, 1660, 1987, 2089, 2094
Howlett, Michael, **1979:** 1933ftn.
Hsieh, Paul S., **1980–81:** 927
Hsieh, Thomas, **1980–81:** 1332
Hsu, F. Richard, **1978:** 696
Hua, Guofeng, **1978:** 1445, 2261, 2266; **1979:** 2, 1112; **1980–81:** 1341, 1342n., 1377
Huang, Chen, **1977:** 147, 1203
Huang Hua, **1977:** 1487, 1517, 1520; **1979:** 15, 212n., 248
Hubbard, Repr. Carroll, Jr., **1977:** 1264; **1980–81:** 1388, 1390n.
Hubbard, Howard, **1980–81:** 1168
Hubbell, Ernest, **1978:** 734
Huber, Laura L., **1980–81:** 928
Huberman, Benjamin, **1978:** 232, 1188
Hubert H. Humphrey Fellowship, **1978:** 1011; **1979:** 324
Hubert H. Humphrey North-South Scholarship program, **1978:** 2038, 2158
Hubert Humphrey Institute of Public Affairs, **1980–81:** 935
Hubner, Niko, **1978:** 1283, 1304
Hubschman, Henry A., **1980–81:** 911
Huckel, Claire, **1979:** 377
Huddleston, Sen. Walter, **1977:** 744, 1221; **1978:** 192, 432, 802; **1979:** 1339, 1342; **1980–81:** 268, 1279, 1390n., 2233
Hudson, Elvin, **1978:** 842
Hudson, Thomas H., **1978:** 696
Hudspeth, Harry Lee, **1979:** 1883
Huff, Helen H., **1980–81:** 845
Huffman, Dr. B. Leslie, Jr., **1977:** 1221
Hufstedler, Shirley, **1979:** 2063, 2139, 2199
See also Education, Secretary of.
Hug, Proctor R., Jr., **1977:** 1507, 1534
Huge, Harry, **1978:** 217, 230
Huggins, Charles, **1977:** 196
Hughes, Edward T., **1979:** 1525
Hughes, Frank, **1979:** 1639
Hughes, Harold, **1978:** 1668, 2058; **1980–81:** 2609
Hughes, Harry, **1978:** 1795
Hughes, Gov. Harry, **1980–81:** 303
Hughes, John, **1978:** 727
Hughes, John David, **1980–81:** 813, 1246
Hughes, John T., **1980–81:** 2999
Hughes, Langston, **1980–81:** 56
Hughes, Paula D., **1980–81:** 940, 968
Hughes, Phillip S., **1977:** 1646, 1650
Hughes, Richard, **1977:** 1055
Hughes, Teresa P., **1978:** 2053

Hughes, Repr. William J., **1977:** 1962; **1978:** 1543; **1980–81:** 607
Hull, Ron, **1979:** 465
Hulver, Isaac, **1980–81:** 2846
Human Environment, United Nations Conference on, **1980–81:** 1415
Human rights
    Administration's accomplishments and goals, **1979:** 122, 569, 636, 720, 830, 2122; **1980–81:** 1365, 1682, 1930, 2933
    Bonn Economic Summit Conference, remarks, **1978:** 1298, 1301
    Briefing, **1978:** 2188
    Cambodian violations, **1978:** 767
    Catholic clergy, meeting with the President, **1977:** 1611
    Conventions ratification, **1980–81:** 119
    Democratic National Committee fund-raising dinner remarks, **1977:** 1895, 1896
    District of Columbia congressional representation, **1978:** 1465, 1467
    Domestic
        Administration's accomplishments, **1980–81:** 155
        Blacks, **1979:** 142, 883, 911, 970, 1175, 1563
        Congressional Black Caucus, remarks, **1978:** 1681
        District of Columbia voting rights, **1979:** 143, 144
        Dual prosecution policy, **1978:** 1181
        Federal programs, **1980–81:** 1742
        Freedom of the press, **1979:** 693
        Handicapped, **1979:** 145, 858
        Humphrey, Hubert H., efforts, **1980–81:** 222
        Indians, **1979:** 145, 1914
        Jews, **1979:** 1563, 1173, 2010
        Johnson, Lyndon, efforts, **1980–81:** 463
        Labor laws, **1979:** 108, 146
        Legal assistance, **1978:** 1150
        Legal enforcement, **1980–81:** 1726, 2651, 2652, 2699
        Legal rights advancement, **1979:** 1979
        Los Angeles County Bar Association, remarks, **1978:** 836
        Minorities.
            See Civil rights *under* Minorities; *specific group.*
        National Democratic Party Conference, remarks, **1978:** 2193
        Privacy rights, **1979:** 145
        Reagan, Ronald, differences with the President, **1980–81:** 2526, 2530, 2606, 2625, 2638
        Reorganization Plan No. 1 of 1978, **1978:** 398, 400, 416, 883, 899
        Undocumented aliens, **1979:** 145, 810, 1662, 1664

Human rights — *continued*
  European support, **1980–81:** 1218, 1229
  Foreign
    Administration's accomplishments and goals,
      1980–81: 166, 177, 379, 2933, 2994
    Africa, **1979:** 2033
    Helsinki accords, **1980–81:** 1435, 1659, 1855
    International Labor Organization violations,
      investigation of, **1980–81:** 306
    Korea, Republic of, **1979:** 1154, 1209, 1913
    Namibia, **1980–81:** 1634, 1642
    Panama, **1979:** 575
    Philippines, **1979:** 867, 1913
    Reagan, Ronald, policy differences with the
      President, **1980–81:** 2550
    Rwanda, **1980–81:** 1928
    South Africa, **1980–81:** 1634, 1642
    Third World nations, **1980–81:** 197
    Uganda, **1979:** 867, 1913
    Union of Soviet Socialist Republics.
      See under Union of Soviet Socialist Repub-
        lics.
    U.S. commitment to secure, **1980–81:** 1327,
      1556, 1604, 1619, 1640, 1721, 1765, 1854
    U.S. efforts through United Nations, **1979:** 63
    Women, **1979:** 108, 143, 1011, 2008, 2018
    Worldwide expansion, **1979:** 1312, 1773
    Zimbabwe, **1980–81:** 1581, 1642
  Foreign assistance and loans, **1977:** 522, 636
  Foreign policy, **1977:** 219, 341, 372, 385, 397,
    445, 455, 499, 503, 509, 541, 765, 781, 850,
    913, 947, 958, 1107; **1978:** 986, 1054, 1055
  Hibernian Society dinner, remarks, **1978:** 542
  Human rights treaties, **1978:** 395
  International community, role of, **1979:** 1834
  International covenants, **1977:** 1734
  International labor support, **1980–81:** 1361, 1365
  International support, **1977:** 818, 835, 1950
  Interview remarks, **1977:** 1274, 1323, 1328, 2096,
    2200; **1978:** 237, 323, 695, 907, 1232, 1252,
    1258, 1259, 1273, 1274, 1410, 1598, 2256,
    2257
  Joint communique with Venezuela, **1977:** 1208
  Legislation, **1978:** 1719
  Mentions, **1979:** 640, 830; **1980–81:** 50, 52, 579,
    1071
  Nashua, N.H., town meeting remarks, **1978:** 376
  National Democratic Party Conference, re-
    marks, **1978:** 2193
  News conference remarks, **1977:** 1200, 1205,
    1916, 2115, 2122, 2208, 2209; **1978:** 629,
    633, 973, 1099, 1323, 1325, 1331, 2099
  North Atlantic Alliance Summit, remarks, **1978:**
    1013
  Overseas trips discussions, **1978:** 46, 654
  President's campaign remarks, **1978:** 1388, 1581,
    1624, 1648, 1817, 1832, 1887, 1935, 1943,
    1949, 1953

Human rights — *continued*
  President's commitment to, **1980–81:** 2308, 2535,
    2545
  Progress during administration, **1979:** 162
  Reflection of American ideals, **1979:** 108, 161,
    357, 720, 1011, 1173, 1349, 1769, 2018,
    2125; **1980–81:** 216, 385, 868, 971, 1158,
    1562, 1709, 1854, 1949, 2768, 2892
  Religious groups responsibilities in guaranteeing,
    1979: 1828, 1831
  SALT limitations, **1977:** 100, 540
  Southern Baptist Brotherhood Commission, re-
    marks, **1978:** 1115
  Southern Legislative Conference remarks, **1977:**
    1314
  State of the Union, **1978:** 95, 97, 111, 117
  Travel restrictions on American citizens, remov-
    al, **1977:** 340
  United Nations General Assembly address,
    1977: 444
  United Nations role, **1978:** 1540
  United Steelworkers of America, remarks, **1978:**
    1547
  U.S. foreign policy, relationship with, **1979:** 162,
    627
  World Jewish Congress remarks, **1977:** 1953
Human Rights, American Convention on, **1977:**
    1050; **1978:** 395, 1144; **1980–81:** 2735
Human Rights, Campobello Conference on Peace
    and, **1979:** 1521
Human Rights, Helsinki Agreement on, **1979:** 2184
Human Rights, Inter-American Commission on,
    1978: 1144; **1979:** 162; **1980–81:** 119
Human Rights, International Institute of, **1979:**
    1521
Human Rights, United Nations Commission on,
    1979: 2217; **1980–81:** 495
Human Rights, United Nations High Commis-
    sioner for, proposed, **1977:** 450, 2115
Human Rights, Universal Declaration of, **1978:**
    2161, 2188; **1979:** 2198
Human Rights Award, International, **1979:** 2009
Human Rights Day and Week, **1977:** 2086; **1978:**
    2089
  (Proc. 4705), **1979:** 2198
  (Proc. 4804), **1980–81:** 2724
Humanities.
  See Arts and humanities.
Humanities, National Council on the.
  See National Council on the Humanities.
Humberto Romero, Carlos, **1977:** 1210, 1552, 1568
Humes, David, **1979:** 2276
Hummel, Arthur, W., Jr., **1977:** 964, 1030, 1127
Humphrey, Sen. Hubert H., **1977:** 586, 620, 622,
    650, 882, 1027, 1084, 1155, 1427, 1788,
    1839, 1898–1900, 1995, 2023, 2024, 2073,
    2077, 2089, 2098; **1978:** 78–80, 97, 100,

Humphrey, Hubert — *continued*
  150, 693, 784, 932, 1679, 1713, 1822, 1823,
    1827, 1830, 1871; **1979:** 1036, 1230, 2274
  Civil rights efforts, **1980–81:** 221
  New England tribute, **1980–81:** 935
  1968 election, **1980–81:** 732, 738, 1630, 1648,
    1679, 1755, 1764, 1770, 1956, 1980, 2046,
    2094, 2247, 2250, 2278, 2347, 2395, 2400,
    2416, 2429, 2501, 2528, 2533, 2557, 2603,
    2610, 2622, 2626, 2634, 2640, 2645, 2664,
    2670, 2671, 2676, 2681
  Presidential Medal of Freedom recipient, **1980–
    81:** 752, 1058
  President's assessment, **1980–81:** 1532
  Quoted, **1980–81:** 910
  Rural Development Policy Act of 1972 support,
    1980–81: 1916
Humphrey, Hubert H., Fellowship, **1978:** 1011;
  1979: 324
Humphrey, Hubert H., North-South Scholarship
  program, **1978:** 2038, 2158
Humphrey, Kathleen Elaine, **1978:** 1086, 1111
Humphrey, Sen. Muriel, **1978:** 457, 784, 1771, 1827,
  1873, 2268; **1979:** 2105; **1980–81:** 224,
  935, 1058
Humphrey-Hawkins act.
  See Full Employment and Balanced Growth Act
    of 1978.
Humphrey Institute of Public Affairs, Hubert,
  1980–81: 935
Humphreys, Nancy A., **1979:** 1698
Humphreys, Robert, R., **1977:** 1644, 1650
Hund, Kirsten J., **1980–81:** 929
Hundley, Rebecca B., **1979:** 1034
Hungarian Americans, **1979:** 2024
Hungary
  St. Stephen's Crown, U.S. return of, **1979:** 2024
  Taxation and fiscal evasion convention with
    U.S., **1979:** 822
  Trade with U.S., **1978:** 704–706, 1031–1033;
    1979: 978, 979, 2223; **1980–81:** 980, 982
  U.S. Ambassador, **1977:** 1140, 1163; **1980–81:**
    236, 268
Hungate, William L., **1979:** 899, 900
Hunger, Presidential Commission on World.
  See Presidential Commission on World Hunger.
Hunt, Betsy, **1980–81:** 3023
Hunt, Dale C., **1980–81:** 929
Hunt, Gov. James B., Jr., **1979:** 544, 1766, 2276;
  1978: 457, 529, 537, 1386, 1387, 1580,
    1725, 1782; **1980–81:** 2140, 2145
Hunt, Jeff, **1978:** 1584
Hunter, Larry, W., **1980–81:** 927
Hunt, Pierre, **1979:** 26
Hunter, G. William, **1977:** 1755
Hunter, Helen, **1977:** 816
Hunter, J. Robert, **1977:** 195

Hunting and Fishing Day, National, **1979:** 1626
Huron, Douglas, **1977:** 184; **1979:** 1976
Hurricane Allen, **1980–81:** 1544
Husain, Tabarak, **1978:** 1722
Husayn, Saddam, **1980–81:** 2319
Hussein, King.
  See Jordan, King Hussein.
Hustler magazine, **1977:** 234
Hutcheson, Richard, **1977:** 184
Hutchins, Bob, **1980–81:** 2603
Hutchinson, John, **1977:** 403
Hutchinson, Repr. John, **1980–81:** 1428, 1450
Hutton, Carroll M., **1978:** 1190
Huyser, Gen. Robert E., **1979:** 240
Hwang, Charles, C., **1980–81:** 929
Hyannis, Mass., **1979:** 1908
Hyatt, Clara F., **1977:** 1533
Hyde, Wallace, **1978:** 156, 158, 1582; **1980–81:**
  2781, 2782, 2857
Hydroelectric power, **1977:** 697; **1980–81:** 1617,
  2179
  Mississippi River projects, **1979:** 1506, 1509–
    1511
  New England small-scale production plants,
    1979: 701, 792
  U.S.-Canadian projects, **1979:** 1245
Hydropower Study, National, **1979:** 1511
Hyland, William G., **1977:** 1436, 1464, 1465, 1482
Hylton, Isaac George, **1977:** 1755
Hynes, Thomas C., **1978:** 996

Iacocca, Lee, **1980–81:** 29, 1670
Iakovos, Archbishop, **1977:** 745; **1979:** 1688,
  1980–81: 752, 1059
Ibarguen, Alberto, **1978:** 884, 899
Ibrahim, Hassan, **1977:** 1678, 1701
ICBMs.
  See Intercontinental ballistic missiles.
Iceland
  U.S. Ambassador, **1978:** 1710, 1724
  Vice President's visit, **1979:** 221, 639
Id al-Fitr, **1978:** 1489; **1979:** 1518; **1980–81:** 1527
Idaho
  Disaster declaration, **1980–81:** 967
  Emergency declaration, **1977:** 806
  Gov. John V. Evans, **1978:** 1474, 1725
    Central Idaho Wilderness Act support, **1980–
      81:** 1408
    Mount St. Helens eruption, disaster assistance
      actions, **1980–81:** 950, 952, 957, 959, 960
    State Planning Council on Radioactive Waste
      Management, member, **1980–81:** 303
  Mount St. Helens eruption, areas damaged by,
    1980–81: 957, 958, 991
  President's visit, **1978:** 1471, 1473, 1475, 1485

Idaho — *continued*
  Salmon River and River of No Return, **1980–81:** 416
  U.S. attorney, **1977:** 1569
  U.S. marshal, **1977:** 1569
Idaho Wilderness Act, Central, **1980–81:** 1407 1411
Ideal Basic Industries, **1980–81:** 581
Ikeda, Yoshizo, **1978:** 527
Ilchman, Alice Stone, **1978:** 434, 457
Illinois
  Democratic Party primary, **1980–81:** 538
  Disaster assistance, **1980–81:** 1422
  Disaster declaration, **1979:** 786
  Emergency declaration, **1979:** 89
  Energy crisis, **1977:** 37
  Equal rights amendment consideration, **1980–81:** 833, 892, 924, 1033
  Gov. James R. Thompson, **1980–81:** 1423n.
  Lock and dam project, **1978:** 1673, 1826, 1827
  News conference remarks, **1978:** 973, 974
  President's visits, **1978:** 972, 980, 987, 996, 1009, 1010, 1936 **1979:** 1932, 1940; **1980–81:** 1851, 1862, 1867, 2080, 2089, 2091, 2199, 2202, 2646, 2659, 2665
  U.S. attorneys, **1977:** 943, 1059, 1827, 1931
  U.S. district judges, **1977:** 1307; **1978:** 1407; **1979:** 733, 787, 957, 1397, 1398; **1980–81:** 608, 1015, 1051, 1052
  U.S. marshals, **1977:** 883, 884, 1384, 1755; **1979:** 788
  White House briefings for community and civic leaders (Digest), **1979:** 2081, 2280
Illinois River, Okla., **1979:** 1813
Illinois River, Wild and Scenic River designation, **1978:** 1771
Iloniemi, Jaakko Olavi, **1977:** 2050
Immigration and naturalization, **1977:** 1383
  Administration's accomplishments and goals, **1980–81:** 142
  Admission consultations, **1980–81:** 684
  Cuban refuges.
    See Cuban refugees.
  Haitian refugees.
    See Haitian refugees.
  Iranian aliens, **1979:** 2154; **1980–81:** 615
  Legislation, **1980–81:** 119
  Migration and refugee assistance, **1979:** 2138
  Resettlement grants program, **1980–81:** 2879
  Romanian emigration, **1980–81:** 981
  Undocumented aliens, **1980–81:** 1726
  U.S. policy, **1980–81:** 1312, 1320
  See also Refugees.
Immigration and Naturalization Service, **1978:** 1393
  Commissioner, **1977:** 590, 597, 871, 1416, 1438; **1980–81:** 1149, 1292, 1460
  Cuban refugee assistance actions, **1980–81:** 915, 1075

Immigration Service — *continued*
  Director, **1979:** 1663
  Indochinese refugees in the U.S. actions, **1979:** 2089
  Iranian students in the U.S., visas examination, **1979:** 2109, 2133
  Officials, meeting with the President, **1980–81:** 1077n.
  Undocumented aliens, **1977:** 1417, 1419–1421
  Undocumented aliens responsibilities, **1979:** 806
Immigration and Naturalization Service, Chadha v, **1980–81:** 2836, 2882
Immigration and Refugee Policy, Select Commission on.
  See Select Commission on Immigration and Refugee Policy.
Immunization program for childhood diseases, **1977:** 605, 892, 896, 2088; **1978:** 103
Impact Aid Program, Commission on the Review of the Federal, **1979:** 1439
Impasses Panel, Federal Service, **1980–81:** 83, 1647
Import Bank of the United States, Export-.
  See Export-Import Bank of the United States.
Import Licensing Procedures, Agreement on, **1979:** 2253
Imports U.S.
  See under Commerce, international.
Inaugural Committee, **1978:** 148; **1980–81:** 2727
Inauguration
  Address, **1977:** 1, 10
  Concert, CBS record album, **1977:** 806
  Inaugural Committee reception, **1977:** 1649
  Portfolio, **1977:** 1117
  Receptions, **1977:** 9
  Remarks to other nations, **1977:** 4
Independence, Mo., **1980–81:** 1610, 1663
Independence Day, **1977:** 1209; **1979:** 1127; **1980–81:** 1125
Inderfurth, Karl F., **1980–81:** 1407
India
  Alignment with Soviet Union, **1979:** 316, 1992, 2047
  Ambassador to U.S., **1977:** 1754; **1980–81:** 2752
  Delhi Declaration, **1978:** 16, 17
  Disaster assistance, **1977:** 2077
  Foreign relations
    Pakistan, **1980–81:** 35, 330
    U.S., **1980–81:** 172, 2986
  Import duty reduction, **1978:** 1563
  Minister of External Affairs, **1979:** 732
  Nonaligned status, **1980–81:** 1205
  Nuclear explosive capability, **1977:** 582, 585, 586
  Nuclear fuel shipment from U.S., **1980–81:** 1137, 1138, 1922
  Nuclear material exports from U.S., **1978:** 790, 791; **1979:** 559
  President Fakhruddin Ali Ahmed, death, **1977:** 148

India — *continued*
  President's Personal Emissary, **1980–81:** 188, 217
  President's visit, **1977:** 1649, 1983, 2077, 2188, 2202; **1978:** 1–17, 50
  Prime Minister Morarji Desai, **1977:** 2122; **1978:** 2, 3, 11, 16, 42, 43, 264, 526, 1083, 1085, 1086, 1090, 1106; **1979:** 851
  Trade with U.S., **1980–81:** 2848
  United Nations Industrial Development Organization, Third General Conference site, **1979:** 2187
  U.S. Ambassador, **1977:** 576, 597, 882; **1980–81:** 64
  U.S. relations, **1979:** 1612, 1916, 2045
Indian Affairs, Bureau of, **1977:** 199, 200; **1978:** 1336; **1979:** 1775, 1786
Indian Claims Commission, **1977:** 2157
Indian Claims Settlement Act, Rhode Island, **1978:** 1695
Indian Education, National Advisory Council on, **1978:** 1418; **1979:** 446, 932; **1980–81:** 849, 2883
Indian Ocean
  Demilitarization, **1977:** 497, 1107, 1263, 1721; **1978:** 122
  U.S. military capabilities improvement, **1980–81:** 1555, 1640, 1659, 1686, 1892, 2186, 2304, 2337, 2415, 2447, 2633
  U.S. naval presence in, **1979:** 1804
Indian Religious Freedom Act, American, **1978:** 1417
Indiana
  Administration briefing for community and civic leaders (Digest), **1980–81:** 825
  Disaster declaration, **1978:** 640; **1979:** 1396
  Emergency declaration, **1977:** 86; **1978:** 229
  Energy crisis, **1977:** 37
  Energy emergency, **1978:** 316, 546
  President's visits, **1977:** 954; **1979:** 988, 989, 1017, 1352n.; **1980–81:** 1019
  SALT II treaty briefing by administration officials for civic and community leaders (Digest), **1979:** 2187
  U.S. attorneys, **1977:** 1031, 1131, 1613, 1614
  U.S. district judge, **1979:** 1319, 1320
  U.S. marshals, **1977:** 1163, 1931, 1932
Indianapolis, Ind., **1979:** 988, 989, 1017
Indians, American
  Adminstration's policy, **1979:** 144
  Chippewa Indians, meeting with the President, **1978:** 1344
  Education programs, **1978:** 1336, 1786
  Employment, **1977:** 54, 164, 199
  Irrigation projects, **1977:** 593
  Land claims, **1977:** 1759, 1935; **1978:** 304, 337, 351, 356, 749, 850, 1076
  Maine land claims settlement, **1980–81:** 2176, 2179, 2185

Indians, Americans — *continued*
  Mille Lacs Band of the Minnesota Chippewas, land trusts, **1980–81:** 2189
  Moapa Band of Paiutes, **1980–81:** 2780
  Navajo and Hopi relocation, **1978:** 1925
  Siletz tribes of Oregon, **1980–81:** 1661
  State of the Union, **1978:** 112
  Treaty rights violations, **1979:** 1914
  Water rights, **1977:** 1862, 1873, 1874; **1978:** 1050; **1979:** 1854
  See also Minorities.
Indians in America, National Council of the Associations of, **1979:** 1604
Indiantown Gap, Pa., **1980–81:** 1498
Individual Family Grant program, **1979:** 553
Indochina
  Administration's accomplishments and goals, **1980–81:** 2984
  Missing in action, **1977:** 173, 316, 489, 499
  Premier Phan Van Dong, **1977:** 489
  Refugees, **1977:** 504, 896, 1151, 1744, 1918, 1923, 2161
    International efforts to resettle, **1979:** 765, 971, 1150, 1167, 1173, 1208, 1332
    Mention, **1978:** 473, 2167; **1979:** 1050
    U.S. efforts to resettle, **1979:** 765, 971, 1150, 1173, 1191, 1347, 1497, 1926, 2010, 2081, 2087, 2090
  State of the Union, **1978:** 120
  U.S. assistance, **1977:** 1409
  U.S. policy, **1977:** 173, 489, 499, 1735, 1736; **1979:** 303, 765
  See also specific countries.
Indonesia
  Ambassador to U.S., **1978:** 328, 388
  Natural rubber exports, **1980–81:** 592
  Nuclear energy agreement with U.S., **1980–81:** 1281
  Trade with U.S., **1980–81:** 20, 403, 430, 550, 1247
  Vice President's visit, **1978:** 327
Indo-U.S. Joint Commission, **1979:** 732
Industrial analysis, bureau of, proposed, **1979:** 1733
Industrial Development Organization, United Nations, **1979:** 2187
Industrial innovation, interagency committee on, **1978:** 892
Industrial innovation initiatives program, **1979:** 2067, 2069, 2082
  U.S. Ambassador, **1977:** 1811, 1826
Industrial Launderers, Institute of, **1980–81:** 1403
Industrialization Centers of American, Opportunities, **1980–81:** 1066, 1629n.
Industry.
  See Business and industry, U.S.
Industry, Councils, Private, **1978:** 392, 960
Industry and Trade Administration, **1978:** 1924

Infant Formula Act, **1980–81:** 1936, 1937, 1947, 2051
Inflation, **1978:** 93, 99, 139, 461, 632, 751, 770, 771, 849, 861, 902, 936, 977, 985, 991, 1058, 1073, 1091, 1162, 1169, 1176, 1232, 1240, 1310, 1311, 1327, 1351, 1353, 1381, 1410, 1422, 1441, 1485, 1490, 1495, 1548, 1550, 1552, 1553, 1587, 1591, 1592, 1613, 1650, 1657, 1659, 1660, 1681, 1692, 1748, 1778, 1861, 1862, 1868, 1886, 1894, 1910, 1931, 1932, 1938, 1944, 1952, 1953, 1967, 2026, 2027, 2064, 2077, 2082, 2092–2094, 2110, 2192, 2206, 2236
  Administration's top domestic priority, **1980–81:** 120, 215, 245, 539, 579, 587
  Causes
    Comprehensive energy policy absence of, **1980–81:** 337, 385, 388
    Economic productivity rate decrease, **1980–81:** 215, 476
    Federal budget deficits, **1980–81:** 2029, 2085, 2327
    Food prices, **1979:** 1432; **1980–81:** 2438
    Foreign exchange market prices, **1979:** 125, 474, 487, 736, 1835
    Oil imports.
      See under Oil imports.
    President's assessment of past forces, **1980–81:** 2220, 3008
    Severe winter weather, **1979:** 635, 704, 736, 796
    Small beef herds, **1979:** 635, 705, 736
  Impact on:
    Consumer prices, **1980–81:** 245
    Defense spending, **1979:** 1629, 2236
    Disadvantaged persons, **1980–81:** 536, 540, 798, 1326
    Elderly, **1979:** 111, 113, 122, 796, 838, 912, 1485
    Employment.
      See under Employment and Unemployment.
    Federal taxation, **1979:** 116, 247
    Homebuilding, **1979:** 2049
    Hospital costs, **1979:** 2109
    Interest rates.
      See under Interest rates.
    International economy, **1980–81:** 280, 388, 441
    Investments, **1980–81:** 1503
    Minimum wage, **1980–81:** 115, 572, 580, 590, 637
    Older persons, **1980–81:** 536
    Poor, **1979:** 111, 113, 122, 188, 912, 1485, 1990
    Public confidence, **1979:** 113, 123
    Public role in reduction, **1979:** 1895
    Rate fluctuation, **1979:** 1713
    Tax reduction, **1980–81:** 1613
  Largest threat to American economy, **1979:** 1388, 1530, 1936

Inflation — *continued*
  Mentions, **1979:** 1981, 1991; **1980–81:** 649
  1978 increases in inflation rate, President's assessment, **1979:** 112
  Rate statistics, **1980–81:** 1351, 1354, 1485, 1511, 1585, 1614, 1632, 1637, 1879, 1895, 2055, 2165, 2217, 2433, 2444, 2457, 2480, 2513, 2522, 2567, 2589, 2630, 2655, 3008
  Venice Economic Summit Conference declaration, **1980–81:** 1186
  See also Anti-inflation program.
Inflation, National Democratic Conference Workshop on, **1978:** 2209
Inflation in the Necessities, Consumers Opposed to, **1978:** 2279
Inflation program, **1977:** 497, 621, 622, 629, 642
  Address to the Nation, **1978:** 1839
  Administrative actions, **1978:** 721, 1060, 2010
  Briefings, **1978:** 2028, 2050
  Business Council, question-and-answer session, **1978:** 2238
  Federal procurement practices, **1978:** 1919
  Interview remarks, **1978:** 2039–2041, 2047, 2065, 2176, 2181, 2250, 2251
  Letter to heads of Nation's 500 largest corporations, **1978:** 2054
  Memorandums to Federal heads, **1978:** 927, 1856
  News conference remarks, **1978:** 1989, 2096, 2098
  Private sector support, **1978:** 2188
  State of the Union, **1978:** 100
  White House fact sheet, **1978:** 1845
Inflation task force, congressional, **1979:** 1211, 1216
Information, United States Advisory Commission on, **1977:** 1767, 1770, 1771
Information Act, Freedom of, **1977:** 244; **1980–81:** 1932
Information Agency, United States.
  See United States Information Agency.
Information Centers, Federal, **1977:** 165
Information Coordinating Commitee, **1980–81:** 2686
Information Locator System, Federal, **1979:** 2181
Information Security Committee, Interagency, **1978:** 1205
Information Security Oversight Office, **1978:** 1194–1196, 1199, 1202–1207
Ingersoll, Robert S., **1979:** 1165, 2128
Ingram, G. Conley, **1977:** 942
Ingram, James, **1979:** 959
Ingram, John, **1978:** 1111, 1386, 1579
Inheritance taxes, **1979:** 1912
Iniguez, Guadalupe, **1980–81:** 2614
Inland Navigation Rules Act, **1980–81:** 2836
Inland waterways authorization bill, **1978:** 1826, 1827

Inman, Vice Adm. Bobby R., **1978:** 1854
Innovation and Development, Corporation for, **1979:** 2072; **1980–81:** 77, 2379
Inouye, Sen. Daniel K., **1977:** 221, 345, 1265, 1583, 1794; **1978:** 191, 1808, 2059
　Legislation passage leadership
　　Commission on Wartime Relocation and Internment of Civilians Act, **1980–81:** 1455
　　Intelligence Authorization Act for Fiscal Year 1981, **1980–81:** 2233
　　National Aquaculture Act, **1980–81:** 1938
　　Ocean Thermal Energy Conversion Act, **1980–81:** 1473
　　Meeting with the President (Digest), **1980–81:** 373, 2740
　　Mention, **1980–81:** 962
Inquiry, Board of, **1978:** 469, 488, 489, 504
Insecticide, Fungicide, and Rodenticide Act extension, Federal, **1980–81:** 2814
Inspector General Act, **1978:** 1754, 1757, 1773, 1797, 1998, 2232, 2234
Inspectors General offices, Federal.
See Federal Inspectors General offices.
Installment Sales Revision Act, **1980–81:** 2343
Institute.
See also other part of title.
Institute of Juvenile Development and Research, **1978:** 1249
Institute of Museum Services, **1977:** 2072, 2077; **1978:** 1356; **1979:** 956
Institute for Scientific and Technological Cooperation, **1980–81:** 407
　Congressional consideration, **1979:** 681, 1230
　Establishment (EO 12163), **1979:** 1795
　Reorganization Plan No.2 of 1979, **1979:** 643, 644
　Research and technological innovation in foreign countries, **1979:** 279, 396, 540
Institutionalized Persons Act, Civil Rights of, **1980–81:** 965
Insurance
　Flood, **1978:** 568
　Health, **1977:** 162, 393, 892, 896, 1127, 1327, 1995, 2194; **1978:** 348, 369, 710, 876
Insurance Act, Federal Employees' Group Life, **1980–81:** 2187
Insurance Administration, Federal, **1977:** 195, 1000; **1978:** 298, 329, 1129, 1131
Integrated pest management, **1979:** 1368, 1383
Integrated pest management coordinating committee, proposed, **1979:** 1383
Intelligence activities
　Executive order, **1978:** 66, 189, 194, 214, 232
　Foreign Intelligence Surveillance Act of 1977, **1977:** 944
　News conference remarks, **1978:** 249, 2102
　Proposed legislation, **1977:** 921
　Reorganization, **1977:** 880, 1051, 1104, 1321

Intelligence activities — *continued*
　State of the Union, **1978:** 113
Intelligence Authorization Act for Fiscal Year 1981, **1980–81:** 2232
Intelligence community
　Administration's accomplishments and goals, **1980–81:** 2981
　Budget deferral, **1980–81:** 2916
　Foreign electronic surveillance activities, **1979:** 940
　National security functions, **1980–81:** 167
　New legislative charter, **1980–81:** 155, 167, 1988, 241
　President's assessment, **1977:** 242, 283, 344
　Statutory charters, **1979:** 146
Intelligence and Intelligence-Related Activities Authorization Act, **1978:** 1529
Intelligence Oversight Board, **1978:** 210, 216, 303, 1207
　Chairman and members, **1977:** 801
　Investigation of CIA activities, **1977:** 218, 221, 243, 283, 344
　Meeting with the President, **1977:** 1084
　Reorganization, **1977:** 1258, 1422
Intelligence Surveillance Act, Foreign, **1978:** 1501, 1853
Intelligence Tasking Center, National, **1978:** 197, 215
Interagency Classification Review Committee, **1978:** 1207
Interagency Committee on Emergency Medical Services, **1978:** 1187; **1979:** 2158; **1980–81:** 1936
Interagency Committee on Handicapped Employees, **1978:** 406, 2291, 2292
Interagency Committee for the Purchase of United States Savings Bonds, **1980–81:** 653; **1980–81:** 77, 1569
Interagency Committee on Women's Business Enterprise, **1979:** 891, 892, 894; **1980–81:** 77, 1569
Interagency Coordinating Council
　Chairman, **1979:** 1386
　Establishment, **1978:** 1428, 1429, 1433
　Fact sheet, **1978:** 1459
　Federal Regional Councils policy establishment, **1979:** 1289
　Hard-core unemployed jobs program, **1979:** 2157
　Knoxville International Energy Exposition, **1978:** 1217
　Meeting with the President, **1978:** 934
　President's urban policy progress report, **1979:** 668
　Proposed, **1978:** 585
　State and local development strategies, **1979:** 75, 77
　Title V Regional Commission responsibilities, **1979:** 78–80

Interagency Coordinating Council — *continued*
Urban impact analyses, **1978:** 2084
Interagency Council on Accident Compensation
and Insurance Issues, **1979:** 339
Interagency Council for Minority Business Enter-
prise, **1980–81:** 76
Interagency Drought Coordinating Committe,
1977: 1135
Interagency Employee Benefit Council, **1980–81:**
295, 2864
Interagency Information Security Committee,
1978: 1205
Interagency Radiation Research Committee, **1979:**
2007; **1980–81:** 364
Interagency Regulatory Liaison Group, **1979:** 536
Interagency Review Group, **1978:** 1971
Interagency Review Group on Nuclear Waste
Management, **1979:** 1358, 2298
Interagency Review Group on Radioactive Waste
Management, **1980–81:** 297
Interagency Savings Bonds Committee, **1979:** 2285
Interagency task force on families, **1979:** 1939
Interagency task force on tropical forests, **1979:**
1387; **1980–81:** 1416
Interagency task force on women business owners,
1979: 890
Interagency Trails Council, **1979:** 1366, 1381
Inter-American Board of Agriculture, **1979:** 2120
Inter-American Commission on Human Rights,
1978: 1144
Inter-American Convention on Human Rights,
1979: 162; **1980–81:** 119
Inter-American Council for Education, Science
and Culture, **1978:** 1516; **1979:** 1334;
1980–81: 1428; **1979:** 1454, 1455; **1980–
81:** 2735
Inter-American Development Day (Proc. 4728),
1980–81: 414
Inter-American Economic and Social Council,
1978: 1516; **1979:** 1334; **1980–81:** 1428
Inter-American Foundation, **1978:** 884, 899, 1072;
1980–81: 522, 1446, 1469, 1524
Inter-American Institute of Agricultural Sciences,
1979: 2120
Inter-American Institute for Cooperation on Ag-
riculture, Convention on the, **1979:** 2120
Inter-American Tropical Tuna Commission, **1977:**
1764
Intercontinental ballistic missiles (ICBM's), **1977:**
95; **1978:** 2201; **1980–81:** 1552, 2304
Mobile basing mode, **1979:** 696, 1016
Research and development, **1979:** 155
SALT II treaty provisions, **1979:** 967, 1051, 1059
See also MX missile.
Interdepartment Radio Advisory Committee, **1978:**
601
Interdepartmental Committee on Domestic Vio-
lence, **1979:** 729

Interdepartmental Task Force on Women, **1978:**
2188
Interest rates, **1978:** 57, 781, 1353, 1493, 1494, 1657,
1842
Federal financial institution ceilings, **1980–81:**
573
Federal Reserve Board control, **1979:** 132, 707,
930
Federal Reserve decision, **1980–81:** 2041, 2052,
2223
Housing industry, effect on, **1980–81:** 2128, 2358,
2437
Inflation, relationship with, **1979:** 113, 122, 707,
1892, 1948, 2027, 2051; **1980–81:** 705, 875,
984, 1066, 1083, 2190
Inter-American Development Bank, **1977:** 456,
509, 617, 796, 807, 943
Prime rate increases, **1979:** 1835, 1840, 1869,
1909, 2051
Reform legislation, **1979:** 928
Statistics, **1980–81:** 728, 762, 829, 875, 978, 1046,
1070, 1114, 1118, 1354, 1485, 1504, 1511,
1637, 1879, 2114, 2165, 2270
Intergovernmental Advisory Council on Educa-
tion, **1980–81:** 1432
Intergovernmental Committee for European Migration, **1979:** 2091
Intergovernmental Committee for Science and
Technology for Development, **1980–81:**
408
Intergovernmental fiscal assistance legislation,
1979: 391, 401–403
Intergovernmental Maritime Consultative Organi-
zation, Convention on the, **1979:** 778;
1980–81: 945
Intergovernmental Relations, Advisory Commis-
sion on.
See Advisory Commission on Intergovernmental
Relations.
Intergovernmental Science, Engineering, and Tech-
nology Advisory Panel, **1978:** 412; **1979:**
544
Intergovernmental Task Force on Water Policy,
1978: 2269
Interim Convention on the Conservation of North
Pacific Fur Seals, **1980–81:** 2716
Interior, Department of the
Acid rain research programs, **1979:** 1389
Alaska National Petroleum Reserve, report,
1977: 1127, 1128
Alaska Natural Gas Transportation System,
transfer of functions, **1979:** 594
Alaskan National Monuments, **1978:** 2115–2134,
2138–2143
Appropriations bill, **1979:** 2154
Assistant Secretaries, **1977:** 273, 280, 535, 557,
804, 807, 1104, 1239, 1266, 1790, 1873,

Interior, Department of — *continued*
    2037; **1978:** 549, 1571, 1666, 1670; **1979:**
    46, 91; **1980–81:** 1129, 1151, 1418, 1428,
    2859, 2870, 2873
  Budget deferral, **1977:** 495; **1978:** 407, 895, 1041,
    2183, 2228
  Budget rescission and deferrals, **1979:** 200, 603;
    1980–81: 235, 2917
  California Central Valley Project, San Luis Unit,
    task force, **1977:** 1124
  Canada-U.S. migratory birds protection conven-
    tion, recommendation, **1980–81:** 2744
  Civil land remote-sensing activities, **1979:** 2150
  Coal leasing program, **1980–81:** 2201
  Coal mine health and safety, report preparation,
    1979: 1396
  Consumer Affairs Council membership, **1979:**
    1763
  Dam inspection program, **1977:** 2060, 2072
  Energy crisis, **1977:** 36, 117
  Environmental message, **1977:** 973, 974, 977-980
  Environmental protection activities, **1980–81:**
    352
  Federal water projects assessment, **1980–81:** 239
  Flooding estimates, **1977:** 42
  Hydroelectric power projects, **1979:** 1511
  Indian land claims, **1978:** 351, 1076
  Indian lands, payments, **1977:** 311, 326
  Inspector General, **1979:** 365, 377
  Integrated pest management programs, **1979:**
    1383
  Interagency Coordinating Council, **1978:** 1434
  John Day River in Oregon, wild and scenic river
    study, **1980–81:** 323
  Low-income assistance programs, **1979:** 2188
  National heritage program, **1978:** 116
  National water policy functions, **1978:** 1044,
    1046, 1048–1050
  Paiute Indian Tribe of Utah Restoration Act,
    responsibilities, **1980–81:** 604
  Pinelands National Reserves protection, **1979:**
    1359
  President's visit, question-and-answer session,
    1977: 197
  Public housing projects, recreational facilities,
    1978: 1242
  Public lands grazing fees, **1978:** 1331, 1876
  Reports preparation
    National Petroleum Reserve in Alaska, **1980–**
      81: 63, 232
    West-to-east crude oil transportation system,
      1980–81: 99
  Sikes Act amendments, **1978:** 1250
  Solicitor, **1977:** 227, 252; **1979:** 990; **1980–81:**
    718, 775
  Tahoe Federal Coordinating Council member-
    ship, **1980–81:** 2235, 2236

Interior, Department of — *continued*
  Task Force on Global Resources and Environ-
    ment, functions, **1980–81:** 1417
  Territorial responsibilities, **1980–81:** 319
  Timber harvests, **1978:** 725
  Transfer of certain programs to proposed Energy
    Department, **1977:** 258, 259
  Tuolumne River, Calif., wild and scenic river
    study, **1979:** 1814
  Under Secretary, **1977:** 226, 252; **1979:** 990
  Vietnam veterans memorial operation, **1980–81:**
    1271
  Water project plans, **1980–81:** 88
  Water resource projects, evaluation, **1977:** 207,
    287, 454, 490, 494, 500
  Wild and scenic rivers designation, **1979:** 1380
  Wildlife law enforcement, **1979:** 1364, 1377
  See also specific constituent agencies.
Interior, Secretary of the (Cecil D. Andrus), **1977:**
    9, 13, 36, 114, 197–200, 204, 207, 223, 248,
    251, 269, 287, 288, 403, 408, 488, 490, 500,
    509, 592, 662, 712, 723, 998, 1058, 1125,
    1191, 1221, 1294, 1408, 1612, 1706, 1761,
    1861, 1883, 1926, 1978, 1987, 2076, 2102,
    2162, 2163; **1978:** 272, 273, 509, 549, 575,
    594, 716, 803, 811, 850, 859, 881, 934, 936,
    1043, 1044, 1046, 1072, 1331, 1345, 1418,
    1473–1475, 1674, 1696, 1725, 1921, 2001,
    2111, 2147
  Alaska Natural Gas Transportation System, Ex-
    ecutive Policy Board member, **1979:** 1126
  Alaska national monuments designation, **1979:**
    1356
  Aquaculture research and development func-
    tions, **1980–81:** 1938
  Coal conversion plants sites endorsement, **1979:**
    1610
  Crude oil transportation system, schedule report,
    1979: 2174
  Endangered species scientific authority, **1979:**
    2288
  Environmental damage response activities,
    1980–81: 3047
  Federal emergency management, transfer of
    functions, **1979:** 1280
  George's Bank, Mass., oil drilling leases deter-
    minations, **1979:** 1995
  Land management plans, **1980–81:** 1143
  Legislation support
    African-American historic sites, **1980–81:** 2175
    Alaska National Interest Lands Conservation
      Act, **1980–81:** 1386, 1388n., 2756, 2761
    Idaho wilderness, **1980–81:** 1408
    Vietnam veterans memorial, **1980–81:** 1268
  Marine sanctuaries identification, **1980–81:** 1856
  Meetings with the President (Digest), **1979:** 240,
    386, 773, 1705, 1975, 2105; **1980–81:** 825,
    1714

[References are to page numbers except as otherwise indicated]

Interior, Secretary of — *continued*
  Membership on:
    Oil Policy Committee, **1980–81:** 8
    State Planning Council on Radioactive Waste Management, **1980–81:** 301
    Trade Policy Committee, **1980–81:** 10
  Mentions, **1979:** 246, 386, 773; **1980–81:** 233, 416, 1043
  Mille Lacs Band of the Minnesota Chippewa Indians, land acquisition requirements, **1980–81:** 2189
  Mount St. Helens eruption, disaster assistance responsibilities, **1980–81:** 955, 956
  National Wilderness Preservation System, report preparation, **1979:** 1966
  National trails designation, **1979:** 1366, 1381, 1382
  News conferences (Checklist), **1979:** 402, 900; **1980–81:** 104
  Nonfuel mineral data gathering and analysis, **1980–81:** 2686
  Paiute Indian reservation plan preparation, **1980–81:** 604
  President's assessment, **1980–81:** 2672
  Public lands resources management, **1979:** 1363, 1374
  Recommendations on:
    Water projects, **1980–81:** 89
    West-to-east crude oil transportation system, **1980–81:** 99–101
  Sailors' Snug Harbor, national wild life refuge management, **1980–81:** 1431
  Site establishment to commemorate former Presidents, **1980–81:** 433
  Stanislaus River, Calif., wild and scenic river study, **1980–81:** 1307
  Strategic and critical materials functions, **1979:** 1621
  Synthetic Fuels Corporation, Board of Directors member, **1980–81:** 1717, 1848
  Task Force on Global Resources and Environment, duties, **1980–81:** 1417
  Territorial responsibilities, **1980–81:** 319
  United States Holocaust Memorial Council functions, **1979:** 2041
  Upper Mississippi River, Minn., conceptual master plan development, **1979:** 1365, 1814
  U.S. nuclear test on Northern Marshall Islands, investigation of, **1980–81:** 466
  Ute Mountain Tribe benefits bill, **1980–81:** 1043
  Whale protection, investigation of foreign violations in Fishing Conservation Zone, **1979:** 1435
  Wild and scenic rivers actions, **1979:** 1365, 1381, 1813
  William O. Douglas Arctic Wildlife Range, Alaska, management, **1980–81:** 420

Interior, Secretary of — *continued*
  For functions of the Department in general, see Interior, Department of the.
Internal Revenue Service, **1977:** 470, 509; **1979:** 1962, 1968, 2181; **1980–81:** 20, 289, 322, 2130
International Affairs, Alumni Association of the School for, **1979:** 1787
International air transportation, **1978:** 1462, 1471
International Air Transportation Competition Act, **1980–81:** 332
International Arrangement on Export Credits, **1978:** 1635; **1979:** 439; **1980–81:** 1191
International Association of Lions Clubs, **1978:** 503
International Association of Machinists and Aerospace Workers, **1978:** 229, 299
International Association of Operating Engineers, **1980–81:** 1846
International Atomic Energy Agency, **1978:** 293, 294, 317, 329, 1426, 1458
  Cooperation agreement with U.S., **1980–81:** 266
  General Conference, U.S. Representative and Alternate Representatives, **1977:** 1211, 1501, 1502, 1506, 1507, 1565; **1978:** 1426, 1458; **1980–81:** 1572, 1848, 1859
  Mentions, **1979:** 452, 1048
  Nuclear energy safeguards, **1980–81:** 403, 433, 1188
  Nuclear nonproliferation legislation, **1977:** 729, 731, 732
  Nuclear safeguards agreement, **1978:** 293, 294
  Nuclear safety, international role in ensuring, **1979:** 1199
  U.S. Deputy Representative, **1978:** 317, 329
  U.S. Representative, **1977:** 1182, 1212
  U.S. Representative and Alternate Representatives, **1979:** 2148
  Voluntary safeguards treaty, **1979:** 159
International Bank for Reconstruction and Development, **1978:** 1313, 1314, 1601, 1627; **1979:** 1201, 1454, 1455, 1801, 2104, 2269, 2281; **1980–81:** 2561
  President, **1977:** 641
  U.S. Alternate Executive Director, **1977:** 1377, 1384, 1669
  U.S. Alternate Governor, **1977:** 943
  U.S. Executive Director, **1977:** 1067, 1085
  U.S. Governor, **1977:** 509
  U.S. support, **1977:** 313, 781
International Boundary Commission, United States and Canada, **1977:** 1407; **1979:** 990
International Boundary and Water Commission, **1977:** 723
International broadcasting, **1977:** 478, 1078, 1085
International Broadcasting, Board for, **1977:** 1073, 1085, 2024, 2037; **1978:** 231, 1735; **1979:** 1434, 1659, 1680

International Broadcasting — *continued*
  Chairman, **1980–81:** 1376
  Members, **1980–81:** 56, 218, 1376, 1847, 2870, 2872
International Brotherhood of Electrical Workers, **1980–81:** 653
International Brotherhood of Teamsters, **1978:** 1591
International Centre for the Settlement of Investment Disputes, **1980–81:** 2731
International Chamber of Commerce, **1978:** 1688; **1980–81:** 307, 1127
International Civil Aviation, Convention on, **1980–81:** 3024; **1979:** 449, 1451; **1977:** 1779, 1795
International Clergy Week, **1977:** 33
International Coal Industry Advisory Board, **1980–81:** 1188
International Coffee Study Group, **1978:** 51
International Commission for the Conservation of Atlantic Tunas, **1979:** 436
International Commission for the Northwest Atlantic Fisheries, **1979:** 777
International Committee of the Red Cross, **1979:** 1925, 2011, 2080
International Committee on Telecommunications, **1979:** 270
International Communication, Cultural and Educational Affairs, United States Advisory Commission on, **1977:** 1767, 1770, 1964; **1978:** 510, 571, 1720, 1772; **1979:** 729, 787, 1037, 1044
International Communication Agency, **1977:** 1765, 1768, 1796, 1963, 1964
  Acting Director, **1978:** 2038
  Appropriations, **1978:** 1735
  Appropriations authorization, **1979:** 1434
  Associate Directors, **1978:** 434, 457, 1178, 1222, 1400, 1407; **1980–81:** 236, 452, 1845, 1848
  Budget deferral, **1978:** 895; **1980–81:** 1440
  Budget deferrals and rescission, **1979:** 272, 1801, 2122
  China–U.S. cultural agreement implementation, **1979:** 210
  Deputy Director, **1978:** 277, 303
  Directors, **1978:** 277, 303, 2160; **1980–81:** 1238
  Foreign assistnace functions (EO 12163), **1979:** 1796
  International exchange-of-persons program, **1979:** 324
  Mentions, **1980–81:** 616, 1230n.
  Programs strengthening, **1979:** 142
  Reorganization Plan No. 2 of 1977, **1977:** 1765, 1768, 1796, 1963, 1964
  Telecommunications functions, **1978:** 605–607
International communications policy, **1979:** 240
International Conference of the Red Cross, **1977:** 1795

International Convention Against the Taking of Hostages, **1980–81:** 1475
International Convention on the Elimination of all Forms of Racial Discrimination, **1978:** 395
International Convention on Load Lines, 1966, **1979:** 1954
International Convention on Maritime Search and Rescue, 1979, **1980–81:** 946
International Convention for the Prevention of Pollution from Ships, **1977:** 458
International Convention for the Safety of Life at Sea, 1974 (EO 12234), **1980–81:** 1627
International cooperation on the environment, **1977:** 983, 984
International Court of Justice
  American hostages in Iran
    Attorney General's case presentation, **1979:** 2209, 2240
    Decision regarding, **1979:** 2281, 2287; **1980–81:** 22, 37, 39, 113, 614, 670, 707, 728, 795, 881, 990
    Mention, **1979:** 2278
International Covenant on Civil and Political Rights, **1978:** 395
International Covenant on Economic, Social and Cultural Rights, **1978:** 395
International Dairy Arrangement, **1979:** 2253, 2255
International Development, Agency for
  Administrator, **1977:** 337, 351, 372, 533, 1126, 1402; **1978:** 1155; **1979:** 294, 1271, 1293, 1780
  Appropriations, **1978:** 1721
  Assistant Administrators, **1977:** 739, 746, 804, 807, 933, 943, 944, 1064, 1068, 1081, 1085, 1086; **1978:** 703, 711, 1343, 1346; **1979:** 1664, 1880, 1976; **1980–81:** 1108, 1150
  Civil land remote-sensing activities, **1979:** 2150
  Deputy Administrator, **1977:** 933, 943; **1980–81:** 427, 452
  Development assistance programs, **1978:** 932
  Earthquake assistance to Italy, **1980–81:** 2746
  Environmental message, **1977:** 984
  Foreign assistance functions (EO 12163), **1979:** 1794, 1800
  Labor-Management Relations Program, **1979:** 2146
  Nicaraguan food purchases, **1979:** 1783
  Organization for Rehabilitation through Training, collaboration with, **1980–81:** 561
  Personnel system, **1979:** 760
  Reorganization, **1977:** 243; **1979:** 396, 643, 644, 646, 915, 1230, 1793, 1799
  Science and technology programs, **1979:** 540
  Smallpox vaccination funding, **1979:** 2036
  Solar energy programs, **1979:** 1100, 1105
  Tokyo Summit statement, **1979:** 1266
  World forest preservation programs, **1979:** 1388

International Development Association, **1977:** 456,
    1671; **1978:** 1314, 1629; **1980–81:** 1190
International Development Cooperation Agency,
    United States.
    See United States International Development
    Cooperation Agency.
International Development and Food Assistance
    Act, **1978:** 1721
International Economic Cooperation, Conference
    on, **1977:** 612, 820, 824; **1978:** 120
International Economic Policy, Council on, **1977:**
    333, 1012, 1257, 1760
International economic summit meeting.
    See Summit meeting, international.
International Economic Summits, Special Repre-
    sentative of the President for.
    See Special Representative of the President for
    International Economic Summits.
International Educational and Cultural Affairs,
    United States Advisory Commission on,
    1977: 1767, 1770, 1771
International Emergency Economic Powers Act,
    1980–81: 2772
International emergency wheat reserve, **1980–81:**
    162
International Energy Agency, **1977:** 1784; **1980–81:**
    251, 440, 1187
    Energy conservation commitment, **1979:** 381,
        647, 767, 816, 964, 1623, 2243
    Energy research and development, **1979:** 539
    International Energy Technology Group, **1979:**
        119
International Energy Conservation Month (Proc.
    4681), **1979:** 1622
International Energy Exposition of 1982, Knox-
    ville, **1978:** 1217; **1979:** 1525, 2298; **1980–
    81:** 1577
International Energy Technology Group, **1980–81:**
    1188
    Proposed, **1979:** 1199
International Exchange-of-Persons program, **1979:**
    324
International exhibitions, **1978:** 229
International Federation of Library Associations,
    1980–81: 1933
International Fertilizer Development Center, **1977:**
    381
International Finance Corporation, **1977:** 1669;
    1978: 1629
International Food and Agricultural Development,
    Board for, **1978:** 218, 1652; **1980–81:** 323
International Food Security Reserve, **1980–81:**
    2770
International Fund for Agricultural Development,
    1979: 63; **1980–81:** 1190
International Holocaust Commemoration Day
    (Proc. 4652), **1979:** 581
International Human Rights Award, **1979:** 2009

International Institute of Human Rights, **1979:**
    1521
International Investment, President's Board on,
    1977: 1495
International Joint Commission–United States and
    Canada, **1978:** 681, 711, 761, 803; **1979:**
    1395, 1398
International journalistic freedom, **1979:** 240
International Kiwanis Club, **1978:** 526
International Labor Conference, **1980–81:** 931
International Labor Office, **1980–81:** 931
International Labor Organization, **1977:** 1029,
    1634, 1951, 1965, 1967; **1979:** 63; **1980–
    81:** 306
International Labor Organization, President's
    Committee on the, **1980–81:** 1127, 2849
International Labor Press Association, **1978:** 1457,
    1490
International Ladies Garment Workers Union of
    America, **1977:** 464; **1978:** 276
    Democratic Party rally in New York City,
        1980–81: 2542
    President Sol G. Chaiken, **1977:** 464; **1979:** 2269
    Campaign appearance with the President,
        1980–81: 1949, 1954, 2542
    Conference on Security and Cooperation in
        Europe, Madrid review session, U.S. del-
        egation member, **1980–81:** 1438n.
    Democratic National Convention, seconding
        speaker for the President, **1980–81:** 1469,
        1471
    Triannual convention, **1980–81:** 1949, 2071
International Literacy Day, **1978:** 1461
International Maritime Satellite Organization,
    1980–81: 1707
International Mediation Group for Nicaragua,
    1978: 1694, 2059
International Mediation Medal, **1979:** 1454
International Monetary Fund
    Annual meetings, **1980–81:** 1972, 2071
    Opening session remarks, **1978:** 1627
    Board of Executive Directors, Chairman, **1978:**
        620
    Board of Governors' annual meeting, remarks,
        1977: 1669
    Bonn Economic Summit Conference declara-
        tion, **1978:** 1315
    Developing country loans, **1980–81:** 942, 1190
    Economic Report, **1978:** 144
    Interview remarks, **1978:** 1601
    Mention, **1979:** 1627
    Tokyo Summit statement, **1979:** 1266
    United Nations role in, **1980–81:** 2863
    U.S. Alternate Executive Director, **1977:** 1025;
        1979: 446, 468
    U.S. Alternate Governor, **1978:** 1515, 1517;
        1979: 1455, 1518

International Monetary Fund — *continued*
  U.S. Executive Director, **1977:** 967
  U.S. Governor, **1977:** 509; **1979:** 1454, 1455,
    1543
  U.S. quota increase, **1980–81:** 175, 1190, 2105
  U.S. support, **1979:** 313, 781, 819, 820, 829
International monetary policy, **1978:** 1315
International Natural Rubber Agreement, 1979,
    1980–81: 591
International Navigational Rules Act of 1977,
    1977: 1374
International North Pacific Fisheries Commission,
    1978: 216; **1979:** 1001; **1980–81:** 2774
International Nuclear Fuel Cycle Evaluation, **1977:**
    1718, 1812; **1978:** 114, 501; **1980–81:** 286,
    403, 1188
  Energy needs balance with nonproliferation con-
    cerns, **1979:** 159, 541
  Nonproliferation progress report, **1979:** 452
  Nuclear energy technical studies, **1979:** 767, 1429
International Olympic Committee
  President, **1980–81:** 929
  Rules governing individual representation at
    Games, **1980–81:** 677
  Summer Olympics, 1980
    Decision to hold games in Moscow, **1980–81:**
      305, 311, 356
    U.S. boycott, position presentation to, **1980–
      81:** 106, 108, 356
International organizations, privileges and immu-
    nities, **1978:** 51
International Pacific Salmon Fisheries Commis-
    sion, **1977:** 1485
International Platform Association, **1979:** 1398
International Printing Week, **1978:** 54
International public organizations, privileges, ex-
    emptions, and immunities, **1977:** 380
International Red Cross
  American hostages in Iran, refusal by captors to
    see, **1979:** 2195
  Kampuchean relief efforts, **1979:** 1844, 2037,
    2052, 2113
  Missing persons in Cyprus actions, **1979:** 1302
International Scientific and Technological Coop-
    eration, Council on, **1979:** 1796
International Seabed Authority, **1980–81:** 1284
International Seafarers Convention, **1979:** 1419
International Security Assistance Act of 1977,
    1977: 1431; **1978:** 1471
International Security Assistance Act of 1978,
    1978: 1636
International Security and Development Cooper-
    ation Act, **1980–81:** 2813
International Solvent Refined Coal II Agreement,
    1980–81: 1447, 1471
International Steel Agreement, **1979:** 7
International Study, President's Commission on
    Foreign Language and, **1980–81:** 2850

International Sugar Agreement, **1979:** 153, 161;
    1980–81: 1271; **1978:** 219
International summit conferences, **1978:** 1258
International Telecommunication Union, **1980–81:**
    225
International Telecommunications Convention,
    1979: 541
International Telecommunications Satellite Con-
    sortium, **1980–81:** 705
International Trade Administration, **1980–81:** 2838
International Trade Commission, United States.
    See United States International Trade Commis-
    sion.
International Trade in Endangered Species of Wild
    Fauna and Flora, Convention on, **1979:**
    1364, 2288; **1980–81:** 590
International trade functions (Reorg. Plan No. 3 of
    1979), **1979:** 1729, 1783 (Checklist), 2201
International Trademarks, Nice Agreement on,
    1979: 84
International Transport Workers Federation,
    1980–81: 1360
International Treaty on the Prevention and the
    Punishment of Genocide, **1979:** 684
International Union of Operating Engineers, **1978:**
    880
International Whaling Commission, **1977:** 1135,
    1532, 2077; **1979:** 265, 1359
International Whaling Convention, **1979:** 1435
International Wheat Agreement, **1979:** 434, 1625;
    1980–81: 865
International Wheat Council, **1979:** 434
International Women's Year, 1975, National Com-
    mission on the Observance of, **1977:**
    524–527, 2025; **1978:** 553
International Women's Year Conference, **1977:**
    2130
International Women's Year Plan of Action, **1978:**
    1335, 1640
International Year of the Child, 1979, **1978:** 1191
International Year of the Child, 1979, National
    Commission on the, **1979:** 1445, 2090;
    1980–81: 752
International Year of Disabled Persons, **1980–81:**
    809
Interstate Commerce Act codification, **1978:** 1794
Interstate Commerce Commission, **1977:** 258, 571;
    1978: 564, 1969, 2237
  Appropriations legislation, **1979:** 2185
  Chairman, **1979:** 217, 1880; **1980–81:** 2231, 2240
  Coal hauling actions, **1979:** 1709
  Fuel prices surcharge, **1979:** 1136, 1139, 1624
  Household goods transportation reform propos-
    als, **1980–81:** 2240
  Members, **1979:** 871, 886, 899, 900, 1702, 2249
  Rail industry deregulation, **1979:** 460
  Railroad deregulation, **1980–81:** 584, 1699, 2227,
    2231

Interstate Commerce Commission — *continued*
  Regulatory reform, **1979:** 2181, 2185
  Rock Island Railroad strike actions, **1979:** 1695, 1787, 1999n.
  Trucking industry deregulation, **1979:** 1114, 1118; **1980–81:** 1265
Interstate Commission on the Potomac River Basin, **1978:** 85, 325; **1979:** 399
Interstate Highway System, **1978:** 221
Interstate 75, **1977:** 2165
Inventors' Day, National, **1979:** 196; **1980–81:** 273; **1980–81:** 2887
Investigation, Federal Bureau of.
  See Federal Bureau of Investigation.
Investment, private foreign, **1978:** 1311, 1314
Investment Disputes, International Centre for the Settlement of, **1980–81:** 2731
Investor Protection Corporation, Securities, **1979:** 1022, 1043
Ionatana Ionatana, **1979:** 842
Ionescu, Nicolae, **1978:** 2059
Iowa
  Democratic Party caucuses, **1980–81:** 180
  Democratic Presidential candidates debate, **1979:** 2293
  Disaster declaration, **1979:** 1222
  Emergency declaration, **1977:** 557; **1979:** 618
  Farmers
    Fuel supplies for, **1979:** 791, 803, 862
    Meeting with the President, **1977:** 1930
  Gasohol production, **1979:** 1479, 1651
  Grain sales embargo, **1980–81:** 92
  Political supporters, meeting with the President, **1978:** 148
  President's visits, **1977:** 1607, 1609, 1853, 1855; **1979:** 787, 789, 804, 841, 843, 1473–1476, 1478–1508
  SALT II treaty briefing by administration officials for civic and community leaders (Digest), **1979:** 2187
  U.S. attorneys, **1977:** 1368, 1613, 1614
  U.S. district judge, **1978:** 1670; **1979:** 441
  U.S. marshal, **1977:** 1796; **1978:** 416
  White House briefing for civic and community leaders (Digest), **1979:** 1882
Iowa State Association of Counties, **1979:** 789, 843
Iowa State University, **1979:** 794
Iran
  Airborne Warning and Control System, sale, **1977:** 1377
  Aliens entering U.S. (EO 12172), **1979:** 2154
  American hostage situation
    Address to the Nation, **1980–81:** 22
    Administration officials, meetings with the President (Digest), **1979:** 2105, 2151, 2300
    Advisers, meeting with the President (Digest), **1980–81:** 2698

Iran — *continued*
  American hostages — *continued*
    American Islamic community advice to President on, **1979:** 2206
    American leadership, responsibility for, **1980–81:** 641
    British support, **1979:** 2258, 2267
    Cause for American unity, **1980–81:** 216, 325, 384, 398
    Christmas tape of American hostages, President's comments, **1980–81:** 2840
    Embassy protection before takeover, **1980–81:** 112, 740
    Exchange with reporters, **1980–81:** 1722
    Hostage Family Liaison Action Group, **1980–81:** 931
    Hostage Relief Act, **1980–81:** 2231, 2912
    Impact on:
      Iraq-Iran conflict, **1980–81:** 1881, 1898, 1900, 1907, 1922, 2256, 2289, 2392, 2487
      Presidential campaign.
        See under Elections, 1980.
    International Court of Justice decision.
      See International Court of Justice.
    International Emergency Economic Powers Act invocation, **1980–81:** 2772
    International reaction
      European Communities, **1980–81:** 189, 238, 760, 764, 775, 900
      Germany, Federal Republic of, **1980–81:** 437, 438, 442, 719
      Islamic nations, **1980–81:** 337
      Italy, **1980–81:** 208, 210, 1161
      Kenya, **1980–81:** 355
      Pope John Paul II, **1980–81:** 1165
      Portugal, **1980–81:** 1234
      Spain, **1980–81:** 83, 1229
      Union of Soviet Socialist Republics, **1980–81:** 1851
      United Nations.
        See Iran, American hostages in *under* United Nations.
      U.S. allies, **1980–81:** 338, 638, 662, 668, 707, 712, 728, 882, 897, 987
      Yugoslavia, **1980–81:** 1219
    Iranian Embassy in London, takeover, comparison with, **1980–81:** 845
    Jack Anderson column allegations, **1980–81:** 1545, 1851
    Khomeini statement on conditions necessary for release, **1980–81:** 1712
    Mentions, **1979:** 2210, 2211, 2233, 2263; **1980–81:** 52, 68, 91, 93, 224, 341, 367, 553, 608, 649, 659, 702, 867, 938, 962, 1163, 1211, 1228, 1301, 1327, 1364
    Michael Metrinko's parents, meeting with the President, **1980–81:** 606

Iran — *continued*
  American hostages — *continued*
    National Cathedral in Washington, D.C., service for hostages (Digest), **1979:** 2139
    National Community Christmas Tree ceremony for hostages, **1979:** 2245
    National honor and safety of the hostages, inseparability of, **1980–81:** 729, 745, 765, 1311, 1731, 1992, 2169, 2256, 2266, 2301, 2508, 2833, 2841
    National Unity Day, **1979:** 2252
    News conference, **1979:** 2167
    News conference (Checklist), **1980–81:** 2699
    News conference statements, **1980–81:** 307, 704
    Outside sources, accessibility to hostages, **1980–81:** 2264, 2267
    Possibility of:
      Deadline for release, **1980–81:** 670, 709, 745, 1088
      Food embargo, **1980–81:** 707
      Military measures, **1980–81:** 660, 669, 670, 707–709, 712, 728, 745, 882
      Soviet control of militants, **1980–81:** 637
      Spy trials, **1979:** 2242; **1980–81:** 2833
      Transfer to Iranian Government, **1980–81:** 576, 577
    President's Commission on Hostage Compensation, **1980–81:** 3039
    President's commitment to:
      Peacefully resolve, **1980–81:** 25, 36, 112, 633, 742, 873, 1106, 1225
      Protect lives of hostages, **1980–81:** 25, 36, 88, 112, 345, 875
      Refuse to apoligize for past U.S. actions, **1980–81:** 734
    President's trip cancellations to monitor
      Canada, **1979:** 2099
      Florida, **1979:** 2139
      Georgia, **1979:** 2139
      1980 campaign activities, **1979:** 2192, 2293
      Pennsylvania, **1979:** 2138
    Public support for President's actions, **1980–81:** 90
    Queen, Richard, release of, **1980–81:** 1342, 1381
    Release agreement
      Announcement remarks, **1980–81:** 3019
      Executive orders implementing, **1980–81:** 3027–3039
      Message to Congress, **1980–81:** 3040
      Statements of adherence, **1980–81:** 3026
    Release conditions, **1980–81:** 2649, 2650
    Release efforts
      Advisers, meetings with the President (Digest), **1980–81:** 3049

Iran — *continued*
  American hostages — *continued*
    Release efforts — *continued*
      Algerian Government, intermediary role, **1980–81:** 2683, 2703, 2833, 2840, 2856, 3019
      Carter, Billy, efforts through Libyan Government, **1980–81:** 1406, 1478, 1483, 1488, 1490, 2016
      Direct negotiations with Government, difficulty of, **1980–81:** 1311, 1749, 2169, 2298
      False hopes, danger of American people creating, **1980–81:** 2434, 2448
      Informal exchanges with reporters, **1980–81:** 2288, 2451, 2659, 2833, 2840, 2847, 2868, 2875
      President's comments on past attempts, **1980–81:** 1828, 2255, 2319
      State Department efforts, **1980–81:** 1641, 1749, 2703
    Relocation of hostages, **1980–81:** 888
    Rescue mission
      Address to the Nation, **1980–81:** 772
      Congressional leaders, meeting with the President (Digest), **1980–81:** 775
      Helicopters, mechanical condition of, **1980–81:** 805, 882
      Letter to Speaker of House and Senate President pro tempore, **1980–81:** 777
      News conference, **1980–81:** 792–800
      Nonmilitary mission, **1980–81:** 793, 873, 1426
      Planning, **1980–81:** 889
      President's conviction on rightness of operation, **1980–81:** 787, 860
      Rehearsal of operation in continental U.S., **1980–81:** 882
      Secretary of State Vance's opposition to, **1980–81:** 781, 881
      Servicemen injured during operation, **1980–81:** 756, 793
      Servicemen killed during operation, **1980–81:** 779, 847, 864, 970, 1556
      White House statement, **1980–81:** 771
    State Department briefings for family members, **1980–81:** 2818
    State Department employees, President's remarks to, **1979:** 2205
    State Governors briefing remarks, **1979:** 2132, 2140
    United Nations, Secretary of State Vance's presentation of American case, **1979:** 2287
    U.S. commitment to peacefully resolve, **1979:** 2240
    Venice Economic Summit discussions, **1980–81:** 1235

Iran — *continued*
  American hostages — *continued*
    Vice President's remarks on treatment of hos-
      tages, **1979:** 2194
    Violation of international law, **1979:** 2123,
      2162, 2240
    Violations of religious principles, **1980–81:**
      1858
    White House briefings, **1980–81:** 38, 63
    White House statements, **1979:** 2102, 2141,
      2148, 2239, 2268; **1980–81:** 11
  Ayatollah Ruhollah Khomeini.
    See Iran, Ayatollah Ruhollah Khomeini.
  Canadian delegation, escape assistance to six
    Americans, **1980–81:** 255
  Clark, Ramsey, visit of, **1980–81:** 1087–1089
  Crown Prince Ali Reza Pahlavi, **1978:** 1954
  Economic sanctions against, **1979:** 2277
  Emigration to U.S., **1980–81:** 451
  Foreign Minister Mohammed Ali Rajai, **1980–
    81:** 2288
  Foreign Minister Sadegh Ghotzbadeh, **1980–81:**
    764, 1088, 1203, 1311, 1907
  Government assets blockage in U.S., **1979:** 2118,
    2119, 2123, 2139
  Human rights, **1977:** 766
  Interview remarks, **1978:** 2018–2020, 2172, 2255,
    2256
  Iraq, conflict with.
    See Iraq-Iran conflict.
  Israel, relationship with, **1979:** 359
  Mention, **1979:** 301
  Military capabilities, **1980–81:** 662
  Mission to the U.N., **1979:** 2252
  News conference remarks, **1978:** 1750, 2101,
    2226
  Nuclear agreement with U.S., **1978:** 45, 72
  Oil supplies
    Iraq-Iran conflict, impact on.
      See under Iraq-Iran conflict.
    Levels decrease, **1980–81:** 661
    U.S. imports, **1979:** 51, 171, 255, 347, 352, 661,
      704, 808, 961, 985, 1242, 1324, 1505, 1567,
      1643
      Discontinuance, **1979:** 2109, 2110, 2123,
        2133, 2202; **1980–81:** 685
  President Abol Hassan Bani-Sadr.
    See Iran, President.
  President's visit, **1977:** 1649, 1983, 2077, 2181,
    2202, 2217, 2218
  Prime Minister Mehdi Bazargan, **1979:** 257, 259,
    352
  Pro-Khomeini terrorists in U.S., possibility of,
    1980–81: 1491
  Refugees flight to U.S., **1980–81:** 1881
  Revolutionary Council, **1980–81:** 39, 671, 710,
    724, 741, 742, 745, 764, 794, 2013

Iran — *continued*
  Secretary-General Kurt Waldheim's visit, **1980–
    81:** 39
  Shah Mohammed Reza Pahlavi.
    See Pahlavi, Mohammed Reza.
  Soviet threat of invasion, **1980–81:** 40, 113, 184,
    195, 390, 728
  Students in U.S., visas examination, **1979:** 2109,
    2123, 2133, 2285
  U.S. Ambassador, **1977:** 1030, 1264
  U.S. arms sales, **1979:** 51
  U.S. kerosene sales, **1979:** 1506, 1567, 1583, 1643
  U.S. monitoring stations for SALT II treaty
    verification, **1979:** 56, 934
  U.S. policy, **1980–81:** 1364, 1992, 2359, 2714
  U.S. relations
    American citizens' safety, **1979:** 257
    Bahktiar government, **1979:** 50, 259
    Khomeini government, **1979:** 352
    Noninterference in internal conflict, **1979:**
      159, 171, 255, 302, 312, 313, 365
  U.S. sanctions
    Alien entry restrictions into U.S., **1980–81:** 615
    Diplomatic facility closings in U.S., **1980–81:**
      611, 612, 707, 800
    Economic
      (EO 12205), **1980–81:** 612
      (EO 12211), **1980–81:** 714, 764
      Iranian economy, effect on, **1980–81:** 661
      Mentions, **1980–81:** 800, 1088, 1133
      Messages to Congress reporting U.S. ac-
        tions, **1980–81:** 614, 716
      Purposes, **1980–81:** 670, 707, 882
      International support, **1980–81:** 1194
    Travel prohibition on U.S. citizens, **1980–81:**
      710, 715, 717, 1087, 1088
Iran, Ayatollah Ruhollah Khomeini, **1979:** 51, 352,
  2169
  American hostage situation
    Direct negotiations, U.S. difficulty in holding,
      1980–81: 1311
    Libyan leader Qadhafi's appeal for release,
      1980–81: 1479
    Mentions, **1980–81:** 39, 112, 277, 796, 800,
      2690
    Position on:
      Execution of hostages, **1980–81:** 730, 765
      Release, **1980–81:** 741, 1490, 1712, 1828
      Trials, **1980–81:** 1483
    Responsibility for illegal holding, **1980–81:**
      611
    Transfer to Iranian Government, promise to,
      1980–81: 637, 671, 745, 764
    U.S. Secretary-General Waldheim, refusal to
      see, **1980–81:** 27
  Terminal illness, Assistant to the President's
    remarks on possibility of, **1980–81:** 2534
  United States, feelings toward, **1980–81:** 742

Iran, Central Bank of, **1979:** 2118, 2119; **1980–81:** 614

Iran, President Abol Hassan Bani-Sadr, American hostage situation
    Mentions, **1980–81:** 707, 730, 1311
    Release, position on, **1980–81:** 741, 1088, 1828
    Transfer to Iranian Government, promise to, **1980–81:** 576, 671, 710, 724, 742, 745, 764, 2013

Iran, United Nations commission of inquiry on. *See* United Nations commission of inquiry on Iran.

Iraq
    American citizens safety, **1980–81:** 1906
    Iran, conflict with.
        See Iraq-Iran conflict.
    Oil supplies, impact of Iraq-Iran conflict on.
        See under Iraq-Iran conflict.
    President Saddam Husayn, **1980–81:** 2319

Iraq, U.S. export controls, **1979:** 2291, 2294

Iraq-Iran conflict
    American hostages in Iran, effect on, **1980–81:** 1881, 1890, 1900, 1907, 1922, 1992, 2256, 2289, 2392, 2487
    Mention, **1980–81:** 2691
    National security advisers, meeting with the President (Digest), **1980–81:** 1945
    Oil supplies interruption
        Impact on:
            Allies shipments, **1980–81:** 1903, 1906
            Oil prices, **1980–81:** 1922, 2131
            U.S. energy conservation measures, **1980–81:** 1890, 1900, 1906, 1922, 2025, 2131, 2170, 2268
            Straits of Hormuz, possible U.S. defense of, **1980–81:** 1890, 1900, 1906, 1922, 2025, 2134, 2173, 2267
    Pakistani President Zia-ul-Haq, peacemaking role, **1980–81:** 2056
    Reagan, Ronald, position comparison with the President, **1980–81:** 2126
    Remarks with reporters, **1980–81:** 1900, 1921
    Soviet position, **1980–81:** 2080
    United States
        Efforts to resolve, **1980–81:** 1868, 1890, 1902, 1906, 2024, 2170, 2392
        Position of neutrality, **1980–81:** 1906, 2319, 2487
    White House statement, **1980–81:** 1930

Ireland
    Ambassador to U.S., **1977:** 464; **1978:** 526, 1722
    Foreign Minister, **1977:** 464
    Foreign Minister Brian Lenihan, **1980–81:** 500
    Permanent Secretary, Ministry for Foreign Affairs, **1977:** 464
    Prime Minister John M. Lynch, **1979:** 1976, 2093, 2095, 2097, 2098
    U.S. Ambassador, **1977:** 1132, 1163, 1264

Ireland, Repr. Andy, **1979:** 2143
    Legislation passage leadership
        Regulatory Flexibility Act, **1980–81:** 1509, 1839, 1842, 1844
        Small business, **1980–81:** 2381

Ireland, Northern, international efforts to resolve conflict, **1979:** 1834, 2095, 2265, 2267

Irish-Americans, **1977:** 402; **1980–81:** 502

Irvin, George, **1980–81:** 1670

Irving, Frederick, **1977:** 936, 943

Irving, John J., **1979:** 1976

Irvington, N. J., **1979:** 1817

Irwin, John J., Jr., **1977:** 1103, 1128, 1265

Isaac, William M., **1977:** 1974, 2006; **1978:** 230

Isaiah, **1980–81:** 528

Isbister, James D., **1978:** 1400, 1407

Islamic community, American, **1979:** 2206

Islamic nations
    Response to:
        American hostages in Iran, **1980–81:** 337
        Soviet invasion of Afghanistan, **1980–81:** 88, 284, 325, 329, 390, 398, 459, 579, 642, 1203, 1308, 2292, 2324, 2351, 2835
    U.S. relations, **1980–81:** 283

Israel
    Airbase in the Negev, **1978:** 1655
    Air services agreement with U.S., **1978:** 1462
    Ambassador to Egypt, **1980–81:** 378
    Ambassador to U.S. (Ephraim Evron), **1977:** 1127, 2037; **1978:** 2187; **1979:** 25, 1422, 1684
        Egyptian-Israeli peace treaty, first anniversary reception attendance, **1980–81:** 525, 530
        Meetings with the President (Digest), **1980–81:** 1846, 3049
        Mentions, **1980–81:** 1656, 1661n.
    American prisoner release, **1979:** 798
    Arab boycott, **1977:** 116, 117
    Arab countries, relationship with, **1979:** 1857
    B'nai B'rith Women Children's Home, **1980–81:** 1654
    Bombing incident in Jerusalem, **1978:** 1037
    Border lines, **1977:** 342, 347, 387
    Camp David agreements' first anniversary, state officials meeting with the President, **1979:** 1684
    Camp David summit meeting.
        See Middle East.
    Defense capability, **1978:** 717
    Defense Minister Ezer Weizman, **1978:** 502, 631, 1506, 1554, 1832, 2059, 2061; **1979:** 1684, 1752, 2299; **1980–81:** 825
    Energy Minister Yitzhak Modai, **1980–81:** 2314
    Foreign Minister Moshe Dayan, **1979:** 251, 263, 329, 1684, 1685, 1857
    Foreign Minister Yitzhak Shamir, **1980–81:** 1826, 1832, 1846

Israel — *continued*
Foreign Ministers, **1977:** 836, 1627, 1728, 1729, 1754, 1755, 1936; **1978:** 46, 305, 328, 1506, 1516, 1655, 1662, 1750, 1759, 1771, 1832, 2241
Former Prime Minister Golda Meir, **1978:** 2268
Illinois State legislature, remarks, **1978:** 992
Income tax convention with U.S., **1980–81:** 1285
Interior Minister Yosuf Burg, **1980–81:** 1292, 1303
Interview remarks, **1978:** 1227, 1590, 2020, 2021, 2043, 2044, 2150, 2173
Iran, relationship with, **1979:** 359
Jerusalem, status of.
See under Middle East, Egyptian-Israeli peace negotiations.
Joint statement, **1977:** 1728
Labor Party chairman, meeting with the President (Digest), **1980–81:** 774
Mention, **1980–81:** 91
News conference remarks, **1977:** 1200; **1978:** 1179, 2099
Ohio State Democratic Party, reception remarks, **1978:** 1624
Peace negotiations and treaty with Egypt.
See under Middle East.
Plane sales, **1978:** 333, 335, 368, 492, 777, 778, 782, 801, 807, 808, 848, 849, 857, 866, 867, 896, 901, 915
President's visit, **1979:** 383, 394, 415–430, 440, 441
Romanian emigration, **1979:** 979
Settlements in occupied territories, **1977:** 1393, 1489
Television correspondent Dan Daviv, interview with the President, **1980–81:** 1670
Terrorist attack, **1978:** 505
30th anniversary, White House reception remarks, **1978:** 812
United Nations representation, **1980–81:** 1949, 2195, 2392, 2431, 2461
United States
Air base construction, **1979:** 2220
Financial assistance, **1980–81:** 242, 377, 1535
Military facilities, **1980–81:** 391
Military sales credits, **1979:** 2299
Oil agreement and supplies, **1980–81:** 688, 2313, 2333, 2540
Oil supplies, **1979:** 352
Relations, **1979:** 1752, 1857, 1997; **1980–81:** 527, 1303, 1363, 1655, 2194, 2479, 2531, 2540, 2595
Science and technology cooperation, **1980–81:** 1957
Trade mission, **1979:** 640
U.S. Ambassador, **1977:** 576, 579, 597; **1978:** 1158; **1980–81:** 930

Israel — *continued*
U.S. policy, **1977:** 861, 862, 866, 867, 1954, 1955
Vice President's visit, **1978:** 1090
See also Middle East.
Israel, Prime Minister (Menahem Begin), **1977:** 771, 812, 820, 951, 1011, 1023, 1162, 1200, 1236, 1281, 1283, 1287, 1295, 1306, 1367, 1369, 1370, 1372, 1393, 1489, 2037, 2042–2044, 2050, 2054–2056, 2059, 2107, 2116, 2118, 2124, 2126, 2127, 2131, 2133, 2152, 2163, 2172, 2173, 2176, 2188–2191; **1978:** 20, 43, 71, 151, 152, 189, 246, 264, 305, 328, 335, 368, 370, 440, 456, 493, 494, 505, 525, 544, 545, 547, 550, 551, 570, 631, 779, 808, 813, 865, 866, 992, 993, 1090, 1227, 1348, 1393, 1406, 1440, 1442, 1496, 1497, 1501, 1505–1507, 1515, 1516, 1519, 1521–1523, 1533–1537, 1554, 1566–1568, 1571, 1602, 1609, 1646, 1651, 1654, 1658, 1660–1662, 1672, 1677, 1690, 1746, 1757, 1758, 1818, 1825, 1868, 1877, 1891, 1901, 1932, 1936, 1939, 1940, 1991, 2021, 2043, 2044, 2100, 2173, 2225, 2240, 2253
Camp David agreements anniversary, **1979:** 1681, 1682n.
Comprehensive peace negotiations, **1979:** 251, 688, 703, 967
Egyptian-Israeli peace negotiations
Direct negotiations with Egyptian President Sadat, **1979:** 1752, 2018, 2033
Mentions, **1979:** 32, 263, 329, 352, 394, 406, 408, 413, 416, 425, 427, 432, 436, 459, 969, 995
President's trip to Israel
Announcement, **1979:** 383
Meetings, **1979:** 417, 419, 420, 428, 430
Progress during Carter administration, **1980–81:** 1364, 1562, 1614, 1657, 2460
Visit to U.S.
Announcement, **1979:** 346
Meetings with the President, **1979:** 372, 373, 382, 400
Mentions, **1979:** 360, 375
West Bank and Gaza Strip autonomy negotiations
Camp David accords, commitment to, **1980–81:** 378, 460, 618, 679, 714, 879, 1104, 1115, 1624, 1656
Consultations with the President, **1980–81:** 511, 521, 523, 1115
Personal Representative of the President, meetings with, **1980–81:** 1657, 1832, 2771
Summit meeting scheduling, **1980–81:** 1614, 1832, 2047
Egyptian-Israeli peace treaty
Joint statement, **1979:** 440
Letters of agreement, **1979:** 516, 517

Israel, Prime Minister — *continued*
  Egyptian-Israeli peace treaty — *continued*
    Mentions, **1979:** 1751, 1767, 1857
    Role, **1980–81:** 525, 632, 1133, 1604, 1660,
      1670, 1767, 2024, 2311, 2371
    Trip to Egypt, **1979:** 618
    Visit to U.S.
      Announcement, **1979:** 467
      Mentions, **1979:** 471, 548, 720, 831
      Signing ceremonies, **1979:** 518, 523, 554
  Egyptian President Sadat, meeting with, **1980–
    81:** 99
  Mentions, **1980–81:** 377, 541, 1005, 1115
  Palestinian resolution, Camp David commit-
    ment, **1979:** 455, 1427
  Relationship with the President, **1980–81:** 181,
    486
  Visits to U.S.
    Meetings with the President, **1980–81:** 694,
      700, 2719, 2769
    Pre-visit comments, **1980–81:** 579, 622, 623,
      648
    State dinner, **1980–81:** 686
Israel, Prime Minister (Yitzhak Rabin), **1977:** 225,
  252, 329, 334, 371, 373, 600
Israel Bond Organization, State of, **1980–81:** 2766,
  2782
Italian-American Foundation, National, **1980–81:**
  208, 1718, 1848
Italian-American Heritage Week (Proc. 4800),
  1980–81: 2198, 2199
Italian-American Sports Hall of Fame, **1980–81:**
  2646
Italian Migration, American Committee on, **1980–
  81:** 1063
Italy
  Ambassador to U.S., **1978:** 710; **1980–81:** 1241
  Bonn Economic Summit Conference, **1978:**
    1310, 1311
  Chief of Protocol, **1980–81:** 1241
  Earthquake assistance from U.S., **1980–81:** 2746,
    2755, 2804, 2807, 2889
  Foreign Affairs Minister, **1980–81:** 1110
  Former Prime Minister Aldo Moro, **1978:** 515,
    885, 933, 1020
  Grain imports, **1980–81:** 2469
  Joint statements, **1980–81:** 210, 1160
  NATO role, **1980–81:** 679
  Nonrubber footwear exports, **1980–81:** 421
  Political party members, meetings with the Pres-
    ident (Digest), **1980–81:** 1241
  Pope John Paul I
    Funeral, U.S. delegation, **1978:** 1722, 1724
    Inaugural ceremonies, **1978:** 1478
  Pope John Paul II, investiture, U.S. delegation,
    1978: 1808
  Pope Paul VI, funeral, U.S. delegation, **1978:**
    1393, 1457

Italy — *continued*
  President's visit
    American Embassy in Rome, **1980–81:** 1162
    Announcement, **1980–81:** 1014
    Daily schedule (Digest), **1980–81:** 1241–1243
    Germany, Federal Republic of, meeting with
      Chancellor Schmidt, **1980–81:** 1170
    News conference (Checklist), **1980–81:** 1246
    Pre-visit comments, **1980–81:** 1102
    State dinner, **1980–81:** 1153, 1246
  Reporters, interview with the President, **1980–81:**
    1102
  Social security agreement with U.S., **1978:** 429
  Summit meeting, international, **1977:** 371
  Tokyo Summit
    Announcement of attendance, **1979:** 550
    Joint statement, **1979:** 1197
    Oil imports ceiling, **1979:** 1198
  U.S. Ambassador, **1977:** 280, 462; **1978:** 933;
    1979: 618; **1980–81:** 1162, 1241, 1243
  U.S. relations, **1979:** 1414
  Venice Economic Summit Conference.
    See Venice Economic Summit Conference.
  Vice President's trip, **1977:** 63
  See also Vatican City.
Italy, President (Alessandro Pertini)
  Earthquake assistance from U.S., message from
    the President, **1980–81:** 2746
  President's assessment, **1980–81:** 1156
  President's state visit
    Meetings with the President, **1980–81:** 1160,
      1163, 1241
    Pre-visit comments, **1980–81:** 1102
    State dinner, **1980–81:** 1153
Italy, Prime Minister (Giulio Andreotti), **1977:** 767,
  824, 881, 884, 1264, 1353, 1358, 1363,
  1383; **1978:** 1019, 1310, 1334; **1979:** 1193,
  1197n., 1415
Italy, Prime Minister (Francesco Cossiga)
  Mention, **1980–81:** 1102
  President's state visit, meetings with the Pres-
    ident, **1980–81:** 1157, 1160, 1163, 1241,
    1242
  Venice Economic Summit Conference
    Attendance announcement, **1980–81:** 1014
    Conclusion remarks, **1980–81:** 1174
    Joint statements issuance, **1980–81:** 1171–1173
  Visit to U.S.
    Announcement, **1980–81:** 24
    Joint press statement, **1980–81:** 210
    State dinner, **1980–81:** 207
    Welcoming ceremony, **1980–81:** 200
Italy in America, Sons of, **1979:** 1408
Itani, Khalil, **1978:** 2059
Itkoff, Dr. Phillip, **1978:** 897
Ito, Masayoshi, **1980–81:** 1339
Iturralde Ballivian, Carlos, **1978:** 710
Ives, George S., **1978:** 1701, 1724

Ivie, Robert M., **1978:** 454; **1980–81:** 1048
Ivory Coast
    Ambassador to U.S., **1977:** 710
    U.S. Ambassador, **1979:** 1617
Iwo Jima Commemoration Day (Proc. 4724),
    1980–81: 350
Izard, John, **1978:** 1139, 1140

Jabaley, Michael E., **1980–81:** 927
Jackman, Oliver H., **1977:** 942
Jackson, Alphonse, Jr., **1980–81:** 2751
Jackson, Andrew, **1979:** 992; **1980–81:** 1347, 1349,
    2122, 2124, 2125, 2402
Jackson, H. L., **1979:** 1479
Jackson, Sen. Henry M., **1977:** 592, 593, 943, 1127,
    1294, 1408, 1411, 1427, 1568, 1700, 1794,
    1978, 1980, 2000, 2057, 2130; **1978:** 55,
    310, 409, 410, 415, 519, 769, 862, 1278,
    1443, 1531, 1644, 1654, 1823, 1980
    Campaign appearances with the President,
        1980–81: 1903, 2677
    Communications from the President, **1980–81:**
        63, 233n., 1100n., 2471
    Energy mobilization board legislation support,
        1980–81: 761
    Israel, support for, **1980–81:** 2193
    Legislation passage leadership
        Alaska National Interest Lands Conservation
            Act, **1980–81:** 2756, 2760
        Alaska public lands, **1979:** 2068
        Emergency Energy Conservation Act, **1979:**
            2086
        Energy mobilization board, **1979:** 1691, 1819
        Energy Security Act, **1980–81:** 1254
        Energy security corporation, **1979:** 1877, 2092,
            2102
        Standby gasoline rationing plan, **1979:** 840
        Synthetic fuels program, **1979:** 2092, 2102
        Wind Energy Systems Act, **1980–81:** 1668
    Meeting with the President (Digest), **1979:** 178
    Mentions, **1979:** 865, 1212
    1976 Presidential campaign, Pennsylvania pri-
        mary, **1979:** 1304, 1994
    United States Holocaust Memorial Commission,
        member, **1980–81:** 823
    U.S. territorial policy development, **1980–81:** 318
Jackson, Hobart C., Sr., **1978:** 702, 711, 1279
Jackson, Jesse, **1978:** 1333; **1980–81:** 933, 1946
    Meetings with the President (Digest), **1979:** 618,
        1422
    Middle East, meetings with leaders, **1979:** 1838,
        1997
    SALT II treaty support, **1979:** 1328
Jackson, Maxie C., **1979:** 1524; **1980–81:** 2559
Jackson, Maynard.
    See Mayor *under* Atlanta, Ga.

Jackson, Miss., **1977:** 1315; **1978:** 1963; **1979:** 670,
    673; **1980–81:** 2597
Jackson, Otis, **1980–81:** 1744n.
Jackson, Pazell, **1980–81:** 2559
Jackson, Reggie, **1980–81:** 291
Jacksonville, Fla., **1980–81:** 1246
Jacob, John, **1977:** 1083; **1980–81:** 1506
Jacobs, Arthur I., **1980–81:** 1927, 1947
Jacobs, Repr. Andrew, Jr., **1979:** 990
Jacobs, Franklin A., **1978:** 759; **1980–81:** 1048
Jacobson, Charlotte, **1978:** 2269
Jacobson, Lele G., **1979:** 465
Jacovides, Andreas J., **1979:** 1318
Jadot, Archbishop Jean, **1977:** 596; **1980–81:** 1714
Jadwin, Linda J., **1979:** 465
Jaffe, Celia P., **1980–81:** 928
Jagoda, Barry, **1977:** 30, 1699, 1756
Jahn, Marie, **1977:** 1855, 1860
Jamaica
    First Lady's trip, **1977:** 1045
    Prime Minister Michael Manley, **1977:** 2128;
        1978: 1119, 1122, 1123
    Taxation and fiscal evasion convention with
        U.S., **1980–81:** 1476
    U.S. Ambassador, **1977:** 936, 943; **1979:** 220, 241
    U.S. economic assistance, **1980–81:** 3025
Jamal, Amir H., **1980–81:** 1974n.
Jamasi, Muhammad 'Abd al-Ghani al-, **1978:** 1071,
    1506, 1554
James, Clarence L., Jr., **1977:** 1667, 1700
James, Gen. Daniel (Chappie), **1978:** 229
James, Daniel "Chappie," Jr., Airmen and Indus-
    trial Museum, **1977:** 1485
James, Gov. Fob, **1979:** 842, 1672
James, Gov. Forrest H., Jr., **1980–81:** 1423n.
Janis, Jay, **1977:** 275, 280; **1979:** 1336, 1531;
    1980–81: 2153
Japan
    Agreement on Trade in Civil Aircraft exception,
        1979: 2255
    Ambassador to U.S., **1977:** 464; **1978:** 802;
        1980–81: 422, 775
    American troops in, **1979:** 1905
    Bonn Economic Summit Conference, **1978:**
        1310, 1311, 1314
    Business leaders, meeting with the President,
        1977: 595
    China, trade with, **1979:** 334, 1150
    China-U.S. civil air route services, **1980–81:** 1784
    Coal imports from U.S., **1979:** 1643
    Diet members, meeting with the President, **1979:**
        786
    Economic policies, **1977:** 60, 836
    Emperor Hirohito.
        See Hirohito, Emperor.
    Energy development and research programs with
        U.S., **1979:** 767, 1108, 1145, 1149, 1150
    Exchange rate adjustment with U.S., **1977:** 2160

Japan — *continued*
  Extradition treaty with U.S., **1979:** 598
  Fishery agreements with U.S., **1977:** 205, 1052
  Foreign Minister Saburo Okita, **1980–81:** 1184
  Former Prime Minister Nobusuke Kishi, **1977:** 1602
  Industrial productivity, **1980–81:** 1678
  International Solvent Refined Coal II Agreement with U.S. and West Germany, **1980–81:** 1447
  Interview remarks, **1978:** 1254, 1256, 1262
  Japanese Broadcasting Corporation, interview with the President, **1979:** 1107
  Joint statement, **1979:** 763
  Medical science program, **1977:** 1382
  Minister for External Economic Affairs, **1977:** 2130
  Oil imports ceiling, **1979:** 1197, 1198
  Oil sales from U.S., **1978:** 810, 878
  President's Assistant for National Security Affairs, visit, **1978:** 803
  President's visit, **1980–81:** 1339
    Departure from White House, **1979:** 1154, 1159
    Exchange with reporters, **1979:** 1167
    Japanese Diet reception, **1979:** 1168
    Luncheon toast, **1979:** 1162
    OPEC oil price increase, exchange with reporters, **1979:** 1181
    President's summary of trip, **1979:** 1217
    Shimoda town meeting, **1979:** 1169
    State dinner, **1979:** 1165, 1223
  Prince and Princess Hitachi, **1978:** 710
  Relationship with the Western world, **1979:** 1205
  Reporters, interview with the President, **1980–81:** 1339
  Steel exports, **1978:** 1661
  Summit meeting, international, **1977:** 371
  Television exports to U.S., **1977:** 43, 644, 755, 937–939, 944, 1158
  Television receivers exports, **1979:** 167, 168
  Tokyo Economic Summit Conference.
    See Tokyo Economic Summit Conference.
  Trade missions visit to U.S., **1978:** 527
  Train systems research and development, **1980–81:** 664
  Under Secretary of State and Chairman, Joint Chiefs of Staff, visit, **1977:** 1084
  United States
    Relations, **1980–81:** 169, 1304, 1743, 2983
    Science and technology cooperation, **1980–81:** 407, 816, 826
    Trade, **1978:** 67; **1979:** 1147
      Automobiles, **1980–81:** 1734, 1826, 1904, 1908, 1915, 1990, 2187, 2222
      Grain, **1980–81:** 392, 2469
  U.S. Ambassador, **1977:** 576, 579, 597, 1030; **1978:** 302, 504, 1879; **1979:** 1155, 1162

Japan — *continued*
  U.S. defense expenditures, **1979:** 1147, 1149
  U.S. policy, **1977:** 792
  U.S. relations, **1979:** 156, 1146, 1174, 1211, 1218
  Vice President's visit, **1977:** 8, 9, 11, 57, 58, 149
  Withdrawal of U.S. ground forces from Korea, **1977:** 64
Japan, Prime Minister (Takeo Fukuda), **1977:** 464, 467, 472, 474, 478, 508, 583, 824, 881, 2093; **1978:** 803, 881, 1287, 1310, 1334
Japan, Prime Minister (Masayoshi Ito), **1980–81:** 1339
Japan, Prime Minister (Masayoshi Ohira)
  Death, **1980–81:** 1096, 1339, 1340
  Mentions, **1979:** 745, 1108–1110, 1145, 1146; **1980–81:** 1150
  President's visit
    Meetings with the President, **1979:** 1162, 1164n., 1168n., 1169
    Mentions, **1979:** 1167, 1211
  Tokyo Economic Summit Conference, conclusion remarks, **1979:** 1187, 1197n.
  Visit to U.S.
    Announcement, **1979:** 468; **1980–81:** 607
    Meetings with the President, **1979:** 761, 763, 768
    Mention, **1980–81:** 806
  Science and technology agreement, signing ceremony remarks, **1980–81:** 816, 817
Japan, Prime Minister (Zenko Suzuki), **1980–81:** 2560
Japan-U.S. Cooperative Medical Science Program, **1978:** 1278; **1979:** 732; **1980–81:** 493
Japan-U.S. Economic Relations Group, **1979:** 1165, 2127, 2248
Japanese-American Citizens League, **1980–81:** 1455
Japanese Americans, **1978:** 1569
Jaques, Milton, **1980–81:** 733n.
Jaramillo, Mari-Luci, **1977:** 1474, 1483
Jardine, James S., **1977:** 987
Jarrett, Vernon, **1978:** 688
Jasinowski, Jerry Joseph, **1977:** 248, 253, 1649
Jatti, B. D., **1978:** 11
Javits, Sen. Jacob K., **1977:** 882, 1949; **1978:** 416, 897, 1139, 1140, 1667, 1782, 2268; **1980–81:** 1859, 1946, 2002
  Hospital cost containment legislation support, **1979:** 385, 386
  Meeting with the President (Digest), **1979:** 240
  President's Export Council, member, **1979:** 943
  SALT II treaty support, **1979:** 2101
  United Nations Pleding Conference on Refugee Relief, members, **1979:** 2085
Javits, Marian B., **1980–81:** 264
Jaworski, Leon, **1980–81:** 1977
Jay, Peter, **1977:** 1382, 1383; **1978:** 415, 1034

Jaycees, U.S., **1977:** 1612; **1978:** 1669; **1979:** 1723
Jeffers, Dean, **1980–81:** 995, 996n.
Jefferson, Andrew L., Jr., **1979:** 1883
Jefferson, Edward, **1979:** 1533, 1535
Jefferson, Thomas
    Education, **1979:** 2130
    Educational philosophy, **1980–81:** 852, 856, 2060
    Legal administration, **1979:** 759
    Louisiana Purchase, **1980–81:** 2402
    Mentions, **1980–81:** 81, 924, 1853
    Quoted, **1979:** 832, 993; **1980–81:** 646, 1064, 2062
    Scientific endeavors, **1979:** 677, 2053
Jefferson-Jackson Day dinners, **1979:** 573, 630, 988
Jeffords, Repr. James M., **1980–81:** 847, 1585
Jeffrey, Mildred, **1977:** 526; **1978:** 1134
Jellinek, Steven D., **1977:** 1531, 1534
Jen Hsin-min, **1979:** 206
Jenkins, Bruce S., **1978:** 1485
Jenkins, Repr. Ed, **1979:** 841
Jenkins, George L., **1979:** 947
Jenkins, Howard, Jr., **1978:** 1468, 1471
Jenkins, Ray, **1979:** 1518, 1519; **1980–81:** 990ftn., 1443n., 1471
Jenkins, Roy H., **1977:** 556, 705; **1978:** 34, 36, 1293, 2245; **1979:** 1197; **1980–81:** 189, 1185
Jenkins, Timothy L., **1980–81:** 940, 968
Jenkins, Wilbur, **1977:** 252
Jennings, Peter, **1979:** 410n.
Jenrette, Repr. John W., Jr., **1977:** 1084
Jenrette, Richard H., **1978:** 228
Jestrab, Frank F., **1978:** 734, 971, 1010
Jewett, Alan, **1977:** 382, 402
Jewish Americans, **1978:** 491
    Chassidic rabbis, meeting with the President (Digest), **1979:** 2279
    Relationship with blacks, **1979:** 1564, 1860, 1997, 2009
Jewish Appeal, United, **1980–81:** 377, 931
Jewish Cadet Chapel, United States Military Academy, **1977:** 1125
Jewish Committee, American, **1977:** 788, 1136
Jewish Congress, American, **1977:** 788, 1136
Jewish Congress, World, **1977:** 1952; **1979:** 1706
Jewish Documentation Center, **1980–81:** 1495
Jewish Heritage Week (Proc. 4752), **1980–81:** 768
Jewish High Holy Days, **1977:** 1476; **1978:** 1565; **1979:** 1627
Jewish Organizations, Conference of Presidents of Major American, **1980–81:** 1714, 2372n.
Jewish Press Association, American, **1980–81:** 1113
Jewry, National Conference on Soviet, **1980–81:** 1662
Jews
    Arab boycott of American businesses, **1977:** 116
    Campaign issues, news conference by the Vice President, **1980–81:** 2333
    Community leaders, meeting with the President, **1977:** 1221

Jews — *continued*
    Emigration from Soviet Union, **1977:** 100
    High Holy Days, **1980–81:** 1644, 1670
    Oganization for Rehabilitation through Training, foundation of, **1980–81:** 561
    President's meetings with:
        New York Board of Rabbis (Digest), **1980–81:** 2453
        New York community leaders, **1980–81:** 2370
        St. Louis Federation (Digest), **1980–81:** 217
    Soviet emigration, **1980–81:** 116, 1659, 2194, 2472, 2540
    Young Men's Hebrew Association, President's remarks to, **1980–81:** 2537
Jews, National Conference of Christians and, **1980–81:** 343
Jiminez, Gloria Cusumano, **1978:** 298, 329; **1979:** 559, 1601, 1604
Jimmy Carter Personal Assets Trust, **1977:** 140–143
Job, Glenn, **1980–81:** 380
Job Corps, **1977:** 349, 2088; **1979:** 1960
    Budget allocations increase, **1980–81:** 1003, 1074, 1324, 1499
    Miami, Fla., program, **1980–81:** 2900
Jobs.
    See Employment and unemployment.
Jobs Demonstration program, Targeted, **1979:** 2148
Joe, Thomas C., **1980–81:** 813, 826
Joffrey, Robert, **1980–81:** 1440, 1470
Joffrian, Brian P., **1980–81:** 1292
Jogging Day, National, **1978:** 1770
Jogging habits, President's, **1979:** 737, 1151; **1980–81:** 2132
John Day River in Oregon, **1980–81:** 323
John F. Kennedy Center for the Performing Arts, **1977:** 508, 709, 987; **1978:** 2186, 2269; **1979:** 23, 464, 2015
    Advisory Committee on the Arts, members, **1980–81:** 273, 304
    Board of Trustees, members, **1980–81:** 2871, 3023
    "Elephant Man" performance, President's attendance, **1980–81:** 399n.
    Kennedy Center Honors, award ceremony, **1980–81:** 2785
John F. Kennedy International Airport, N.Y., **1977:** 178, 322
John F. Kennedy Library, Boston, Mass., **1977:** 1028; **1979:** 1979, 2044
John Paul I, Pope.
    See Pope John Paul I.
John Paul II, Pope.
    See Pope John Paul II.
Johnson, Andrew, **1980–81:** 2124, 2125
Johnson, Bruce P., **1978:** 1069, 1072; **1980–81:** 1443, 1470
Johnson, Daniel, Sr., **1979:** 774

Johnson, Staff Sgt. Dewey L., **1980–81:** 780n., 864
Johnson, Eddie Bernice, **1977:** 816
Johnson, Francis Severin, **1979:** 1619, 1680
Johnson, Frank M., Jr., **1977:** 1478, 1479, 1483,
    1494, 1597, 1701, 2087, 2090; **1979:** 555,
    619
Johnson, Gloria T., **1979:** 1448
Johnson, Repr. Harold T. (Bizz), **1977:** 963, 2179;
    1978: 229, 1278, 1407, 1563, 1669, 1827,
    1838, 1947; **1979:** 1115, 2185
  Legislation passage leadership
    Comprehensive Environmental Response,
      Compensation, and Liabilities, **1980–81:**
      2797
    Household Goods Transportation Act, **1980–
      81:** 2240
    International Air Transportation Competition
      Act, **1980–81:** 333
    Motor Carrier Act, **1980–81:** 1147, 1262, 1263,
      1267
    Meeting with the President (Digest), **1980–81:**
      825
    National Highway Safety Advisory Committee,
      member, **1980–81:** 3022
Johnson, Mrs. Harold T., **1979:** 376
Johnson, Harvey N., Jr., **1977:** 1384
Johnson, J. Ken, **1978:** 1998
Johnson, J. Leonard, **1979:** 1639
Johnson, Jack B., **1978:** 952
Johnson, Jeffalyn, **1977:** 526; **1978:** 1134
Johnson, John H., **1980–81:** 1405
Johnson, Keith, **1980–81:** 2560
Johnson, Lady Bird, **1977:** 941, 1543; **1979:** 2008;
    1980–81: 463, 466n., 1059, 2413
Johnson, Lyndon B., **1977:** 865
  Civil rights leadership, **1980–81:** 1631, 1726, 2420
  Economic Opportunity Act of 1964, sponsorship,
    1979: 1477
  Education legislation support, **1980–81:** 852,
    2060
  Federal aid for education position, **1979:** 1414
  Head Start program establishment, **1980–81:** 463
  Medicare and Medical support, **1979:** 1028
  Mentions, **1979:** 828, 2016; **1980–81:** 766, 1532
  1964 election, **1980–81:** 1559
  Percentage of proposed legislation passed, **1979:**
    1855, 2017, 2033, 2054
  Presidential Medal of Freedom recipient, **1980–
    81:** 752, 1059
  President's assessment, **1980–81:** 2412
  Quoted, **1980–81:** 910
  SALT negotiations, **1979:** 694, 1088
  U.S.S. *Pueblo* incident, **1980–81:** 744
  Vietnam war policy, **1979:** 1996
  White House Fellowships establishment, **1979:**
    1397
Johnson, Marilyn P., **1978:** 1451, 1458

Johnson, Marsha A., **1979:** 914
Johnson, Mary Joanne, **1978:** 2036
Johnson, Michael C., **1980–81:** 928
Johnson, Murray L., **1979:** 2116
Johnson, Nicholas, **1979:** 400
Johnson, Norma Holloway, **1980–81:** 423, 424
Johnson, Ollin D., **1980–81:** 1758
Johnson, Robin K., **1980–81:** 926
Johnson, Samuel D., Jr., **1979:** 1423
Johnson, W. Thomas, **1977:** 941
Johnson, Rev. William D., Jr., **1977:** 1163
Johnson and Johnson Co., **1979:** 2022
Johnston, Sen. J. Bennett, **1977:** 1335, 1339; **1978:**
    769, 1669
  Federal territorial policy development, 318
  Legislation passage leadership
    Emergency Energy Conservation Act, **1979:**
      2086
    Energy mobilization board, **1979:** 1691, 1819;
      1980–81: 761
    Energy security corporation, **1979:** 1877, 2092,
      2102
    Northern Mariana Islands, military service for
      citizens of, **1980–81:** 1723
    Synthetic fuels program, **1979:** 2092, 2102
  Meeting with the President (Digest), **1979:** 2104
  1976 Presidential election, Louisiana State chair-
    man for President, **1980–81:** 2404
  Social security system support, **1980–81:** 2402
Johnston, William B., **1979:** 2125, 2138
Johnstone, Edward H., **1977:** 1507
Joint Chiefs of Staff, **1979:** 533, 1043
  Atomic weapons, limitations, **1977:** 345, 496
  Chairman, **1977:** 85, 1021, 1029, 1084, 1221,
      1473, 1526, 2036, 2089; **1978:** 684, 1071,
      1110, 1218, 1669; **1980–81:** 1014, 1015,
      1667, 2159
  Chief of Naval Operations, **1978:** 684, 1218
  Chief of Staff of the Air Force, **1978:** 684, 1218
  Cruise missile development decision, **1980–81:**
    1552
  Defense spending levels recommendation,
    1980–81: 985, 1740
  Meetings with the President, **1977:** 508, 1437,
      1464, 2129; **1978:** 898, 2281
  Panama Canal treaties, **1977:** 1462, 1749, 1884,
    1887
  Relationship with the President, **1977:** 2100
  Submarine communications system decision,
    1980–81: 1997
Joint Financial Management Improvement Pro-
    gram, **1979:** 462
Joint Statements
  Bangladesh, **1980–81:** 1579
  Brazil, **1978:** 636
  Camp David meeting on the Middle East, **1978:**
    1501

Joint Statements — *continued*
Canada, **1977:** 1546; **1979:** 381
China, People's Republic of, **1979:** 213; **1978:** 2264
Egyptian-Israeli peace treaty, **1979:** 490
Four Power summit meeting, **1977:** 840
Germany, Federal Republic of, **1980–81:** 438
India, **1978:** 17, 1106
International economic summit meeting, **1977:** 819; **1978:** 719
International terrorism, **1978:** 1308
Israel, **1977:** 1728
Italy, **1980–81:** 210, 1160
Japan, **1977:** 478; **1979:** 763, 2127
Korea, Republic of, **1979:** 1207
Mexico, **1977:** 178; **1979:** 287, 1703, 1789
Morocco, **1978:** 2055
Multilateral meetings in Panama, **1978:** 1123
New Zealand, **1977:** 1991
Nigeria, **1978:** 661, 664
Poland, **1977:** 2216
Portugal, **1980–81:** 1233
Romania, **1978:** 743, 753
Spain, **1980–81:** 1228
Thailand, **1979:** 230
Treaty Concerning the Permanent Neutrality and Operation of the Panama Canal, statement of understanding, **1977:** 1793
Tunisia, **1978:** 2144
Union of Soviet Socialist Republics, **1979:** 1081
Venezuela, **1977:** 1207, 1208; **1978:** 623
Venice Economic Summit Conference
Afghanistan, Soviet invasion of, **1980–81:** 1170
Diplomatic hostages, **1980–81:** 1171
Hijacking, **1980–81:** 1172
Refugees, **1980–81:** 1172
Yugoslavia, **1978:** 485; **1980–81:** 1216
Joint U.S.-U.S.S.R. Commercial Commission, **1979:** 1453
Jolaoso, Olujimi, **1977:** 1754
Jones, Anne P., **1978:** 1719, 1724; **1979:** 46, 91
Jones, Boisfeuillet, **1977:** 941
Jones, C. Fred, **1979:** 1008
Jones, Clara S., **1978:** 920, 935
Jones, Repr. Ed, **1978:** 457, 1376, 1860
Jones, Gen. David C., **1978:** 684, 1071, 1218, 1220, 1669; **1979:** 436; **1980–81:** 1014, 1015, 1667, 2195
Jones, Edward H., **1980–81:** 2117
Jones, Edward Vason, **1977:** 2182
Jones, Frank, **1977:** 1439, 1458; **1980–81:** 1074, 1236
Jones, Herbert, **1977:** 403
Jones, J. Albert, **1977:** 1222, 1266
Jones, James E., Jr., **1978:** 411; **1979:** 23; **1980–81:** 567, 1051
Jones, James P., **1979:** 899, 900

Jones, Repr. James R., **1977:** 251; **1979:** 956
Jones, Johnny J., **1979:** 1727
Jones, Kenneth A., **1979:** 914
Jones, Lois Mailou, **1980–81:** 602
Jones, Mary Gardiner, **1978:** 1878
Jones, Milton, **1979:** 306n.
Jones, Nathaniel R., **1979:** 885, 1531, 1532
Jones, Peter T., **1978:** 884, 899
Jones, Reginald H., **1979:** 942, 943; **1980–81:** 2827
Jones, Robert T., **1980–81:** 2999
Jones, Mrs. Robert Trent, **1980–81:** 1438n.
Jones, Shirley B., **1979:** 957
Jones, Thomas D., **1977:** 2068
Jones, Thomas R., **1978:** 1187
Jones, William B., **1977:** 1356, 1384
Jones amendment, **1978:** 1185, 1230, 1323, 1354
Jonsen, Albert Rupert, **1979:** 1264
Joplin, George, **1977:** 1928
Jordan
Ambassador to U.S., **1980–81:** 1051
Camp David summit meeting, **1978:** 1524, 1535, 1610
Chief of the Royal Court and Foreign Minister, meeting with the President, **1977:** 1678, 1701
Egyptian-Israeli peace negotiation role, **1980–81:** 1116, 1122
Interview remarks, **1978:** 1590
King Hussein.
See Jordan, King Hussein.
Middle East peace settlement position, **1979:** 350
Palestinians, **1977:** 601
Queen Alia, death, **1977:** 147
Queen Noor, **1980–81:** 1126
Secretary of Defense's visit, **1979:** 453, 454, 456
U.S. Ambassador, **1978:** 1397, 1407
U.S. delegation's visit, **1979:** 436
West Bank and Gaza Strip settlements, law enforcement responsibilities, **1980–81:** 618
See also Middle East.
Jordan, Repr. Barbara C., **1978:** 394, 1139, 1140, 1683; **1979:** 553
Jordan, Charles O., **1978:** 802
Jordan, Emma Coleman, **1980–81:** 949
Jordan, Hamilton, **1977:** 9, 99; **1978:** 49, 229, 277, 303, 327, 328, 443, 504, 525, 526, 540, 570, 710, 750, 769, 802, 803, 880, 897, 898, 934, 1009, 1034, 1071, 1154, 1221, 1222, 1278, 1333, 1344, 1345, 1379, 1380, 1406, 1411, 1457, 1484, 1506, 1515, 1668, 1719, 1722, 1723, 1772, 1879, 1954, 1955, 2004, 2058, 2059, 2073, 2146, 2147, 2187, 2269, 2281
Cocaine use investigation, **1979:** 1845; **1980–81:** 984, 1015, 1487, 2355, 2690
Deputy Chairman of the Carter/Mondale Presidential Committee, Inc., appointment, **1980–81:** 1110

Jordan, Hamilton — *continued*
  Foreign policy role, **1980–81:** 708
  Meetings with the President (Digest), **1979:** 26,
      89, 178, 179, 217, 241, 293, 327, 401, 467,
      468, 553, 618, 666, 732, 787, 842, 898, 899,
      956, 957, 982, 983, 1017, 1018, 1043, 1142,
      1319, 1397, 1422, 1454, 1455, 1607, 1679,
      1705, 1824, 1882, 1975, 2043, 2106, 2248,
      2280; **1980–81:** 24, 25, 63, 103, 217, 267,
      268, 293, 334, 374, 423, 452, 522, 563, 654,
      775, 825, 892, 893, 933, 967, 1014, 1050,
      1110, 1111
  White House chief of staff
      Appointment, **1979:** 1292
      President's assessment, **1979:** 1306
Jordan, King Hussein, **1977:** 147, 641, 710, 720,
      722, 744, 2060, 2119, 2174, 2189–2191,
      2206; **1978:** 46, 49, 71, 305, 1537, 1554,
      1610, 1746, 1780; **1979:** 454, 456
  Egyptian-Israeli peace negotiations, role in,
      1980–81: 1116
  Lebanese conflict settlement actions, **1980–81:**
      2025
  Visit to U.S.
      Announcement, **1980–81:** 1014
      Meetings with the President, **1980–81:** 1123,
          1129, 1130
      Mentions, **1980–81:** 1105, 1671
      State dinner, **1980–81:** 1125
      Welcoming ceremony, **1980–81:** 1121
Jordan, McClaran, **1979:** 1614n.
Jordan, Robert G., Jr., **1978:** 407; **1980–81:** 2242
Jordan, Shirley, **1980–81:** 1001, 1019
Jordan, Vernon E., Jr.
  See President *under* National Urban League.
Jørgensen, Anker Henrik, **1977:** 882; **1978:** 276,
      389
Jorling, Thomas C., **1977:** 1051, 1059; **1979:** 1044;
      1980–81: 264
Joseph, Geri M., **1978:** 1100, 1111
Joseph, James Alfred, **1977:** 226, 252; **1979:** 990;
      1980–81: 344, 2614
Journalistic freedom, international, **1979:** 240
Journalistic work products, protection, **1978:** 2234
Juan Carlos I, King.
  See Spain, King.
Juarez, Rafael E., **1977:** 1613
Judge, Gov. Thomas L., **1978:** 1506
Judges, National Association of Women, **1980–81:**
      2057, 2071
Judicial Councils Reform and Judicial Conduct
      and Disability Act, **1980–81:** 2240
Judicial Disabilities and Tenure, District of Co-
      lumbia Commission on, **1980–81:** 392
Judicial Nominating Commission, District of Co-
      lumbia, **1980–81:** 1292

Judicial Nominating Commission for the District
      of Puerto Rico, **1978:** 1638; **1980–81:**
      2849
Judicial Officers, Committee on Selection of Fed-
      eral, **1977:** 1009, 1528; **1980–81:** 2849
Judicial Salaries, Commission on Executive, and,
      1980–81: 1412, 2867
Judiciary, U.S.
  See Courts, U.S.
Jun-Ching Lin, **1980–81:** 927
Juneau, W. Stanley, **1980–81:** 849
Jung, Francis L., **1980–81:** 534, 564, 1595, 1599
Junior Achievement Program, **1977:** 86; **1979:** 179
Justice, Department of
  Antitrust laws guide for industrial firms, **1979:**
      2071
  Appropriations, **1977:** 1409; **1978:** 1735; **1980–
      81:** 2774, 2809
  Assistant Attorney General Drew S. Days III,
      1977: 156, 195; **1978:** 1181, 1182, 1681;
      1979: 1159
  Civil rights enforcement, **1980–81:** 1325, 1501
  Ku Klux Klan activities investigation, **1980–
      81:** 233, 1640
  Mentions, **1980–81:** 1004, 1071, 1877
  Miami, Fla., court system investigation,
      1980–81: 1075
  President's assessment, **1980–81:** 1634
  Assistant Attorneys General, **1977:** 155, 195, 803,
      807, 1054, 1059, 1217, 1222, 1280, 1649,
      1971; **1978:** 707, 893, 899, 1098, 1155,
      1181, 1182, 1681; **1979:** 234, 235, 242, 619,
      975, 976, 983, 984, 1044, 1143, 1159, 1590,
      2038, 2044, 2175, 2188
  Associate Attorneys General, **1977:** 1821, 1826,
      2067; **1979:** 2038, 2044
  Attorneys General, **1977:** 6, 9, 19, 195, 234, 242,
      248, 266, 311, 378, 662, 712, 882, 922, 924,
      1009, 1103, 1126, 1210, 1238, 1280, 1293,
      1305, 1345, 1347, 1383, 1399, 1403, 1406,
      1416, 1438, 1442, 1465, 1504, 1533, 1649,
      1691, 1761, 1803, 1912, 1963, 1996, 1998,
      2077, 2130, 2161, 2177; **1978:** 58, 59, 61,
      65, 66, 77, 148, 150, 190, 211, 215, 245,
      314, 363, 397, 470. 488, 489, 594, 599, 695,
      734, 841, 892, 1068, 1098, 1147, 1155,
      1181, 1182, 1206, 1207, 1215, 1223, 1230,
      1242, 1328, 1610, 1854, 2165
  See also under Attorney General.
  Budget deferrals, **1978:** 2095; **1979:** 200, 1299,
      2122
  Budget rescission, **1977:** 1647
  Budget rescission and deferrals, **1980–81:** 235,
      899, 948, 2916
  Bureau of Justice Statistics, Director, **1980–81:**
      1290
  Carter, Billy, investigation of activities with
      Libyan Government, **1980–81:** 1406,

Justice, Department of — *continued*
  Carter, Billy, investigation — *continued*
    1439, 1443, 1467, 1468, 1479, 1486, 1487,
    1489, 2017, 2554, 2647
  Carter family peanut warehouse investigations,
    1979: 1954
  Competition policy in fighting inflation author-
    ity, **1979:** 234, 235
  Congressional veto of executive branch actions,
    position on, **1980–81:** 2836, 2882
  Consumer rights, **1977:** 575
  Criminal code reform, **1980–81:** 156
  Criminal justice programs, **1978:** 837
  Cuban and Haitian refugees
    Immigration violations prosecution, **1980–81:**
      1032, 1053
    Indiantown Gap, Pa., disturbances, investi-
      gation of, **1980–81:** 1498
    Processing in Puerto Rico, appeal expedition,
      1980–81: 2178
  Deputy Attorneys General, **1977:** 336, 373, 504,
    2061, 2083, 2085, 2090; **1978:** 231, 460,
    1280, 1505; **1979:** 1221, 1293, 2148;
    1980–81: 1412, 2788
  Director of Public Information, **1979:** 1591
  Ethics in Government Act of 1978, amendment
    recommendation, **1979:** 1130
  Export policy functions, **1978:** 1633, 1634
  Federal Bureau of Investigation, legislative pro-
    posals development, **1979:** 1335
  Federal civil justice system, **1979:** 344–346
  Federal legal resources, transfer of functions,
    1979: 1364
  Foreign Claims Settlement Commission, transfer
    to, **1980–81:** 483
  Foreign Corrupt Practices Act enforcement,
    1980–81: 402, 1694
  Fraud and waste elimination in Government
    programs, **1978:** 2232, 2234
  Freedom of Information Act administration,
    1980–81: 1932
  Fuel companies non-oil supplies ownership,
    monitoring, **1980–81:** 883
  Government regulations, public participation
    funding programs authority, **1979:** 868
  Hazardous waste disposal prevention duties,
    1980–81: 2381
  Hearst, Patricia, sentence commutation recom-
    mendation, **1979:** 216
  Hulver, Isaac, case consideration, **1980–81:** 2846
  Independent truckers strike actions, **1979:** 1130,
    1139
  Indian land claims, **1978:** 850, 1076
  Interagency Coordinating Council, **1978:** 1434
  International trade investigations, **1980–81:** 402
  Investigation of Korean agents activity in the
    U.S., **1977:** 1969
  Iranian assets blockage rulings, **1980–81:** 2773

Justice, Department of — *continued*
  Labor-Management Relations Program exemp-
    tions, **1979:** 2146
  Minority-owned businesses protection, **1980–81:**
    1705
  National Commission for the Review of Anti-
    trust Laws and Procedures, **1977:** 2064
  Nondiscrimination laws enforcement, **1980–81:**
    2651, 2653
  Office of Professional Responsibility, Counsel,
    1980–81: 2557
  Oil industry monitoring, **1979:** 1130, 1139, 1243,
    1250, 1345
  Privacy protection guidelines, **1980–81:** 2218
  Puerto Rican terrorist attack on U.S. Navy
    schoolbus, investigation of, **1979:** 2206
  Racial harassment investigations, **1980–81:** 1640
  Radiation Policy Council membership, **1980–81:**
    363
  Railroad merger jurisdiction, **1979:** 460
  Reorganization Plan No. 1 of 1978, **1978:** 399,
    401
  Rodriguez case, Dallas, **1978:** 1181, 1328
  School busing enforcement, **1980–81:** 1896
  Solicitor General, **1977:** 155, 195, 1345; **1978:**
    322
  State and local dispute resolution programs,
    1980–81: 303
  Task Force on Global Resources and Environ-
    ment, functions, **1980–81:** 1417
  Trucking industry deregulation, report respon-
    sibilities, **1979:** 1124
  Undocumented aliens, **1977:** 1416–1418
    Fair treatment investigations, **1979:** 807
  U.S. attorney Herman Sillas, Jr., investigation of,
    1980–81: 1346, 1412, 1661
  U.S. attorneys, **1977:** 1498
  U.S. district judges, merit selection, **1978:** 1975
  Veterans, upgraded discharges, benefits, **1977:**
    1758
  Veterans' Federal Coordinating Committee,
    1978: 1743
  Welfare fraud, **1978:** 1657
  West-to-east crude oil transportation system,
    1980–81: 100
  Wildlife law enforcement, **1979:** 1364, 1378
  Wilmington 10, **1978:** 1331
  Wiretapping and electronic surveillance review
    system, **1979:** 587, 589
  Women's business enterprises, **1979:** 888, 891
  See also specific constituent agencies.
Justice, International Court of.
  See International Court of Justice.
Justice, National Institute of, **1979:** 131; **1980–81:**
    2612, 2701, 2875
  Proposed, **1978:** 1242, 1249
Justice Assistance, Research, and Statistics, Office
  of, **1980–81:** 288, 293

Justice Assistance, Office of — *continued*
    Proposed, **1978:** 1249
Justice Statistics, Bureau of, proposed, **1978:** 1242, 1249
Justice system, Federal civil, **1979:** 340–346, 378
Juvenile Development and Research, Institute of, proposed, **1978:** 1249
Juvenile Diabetes Foundation, **1980–81:** 1051
Juvenile Justice, Office of, **1980–81:** 1273
Juvenile Justice Amendments, **1980–81:** 2787
Juvenile Justice Amendments of 1977, **1977:** 1711, 1755
Juvenile Justice and Delinquency Prevention, Co-ordinating Council on, **1980–81:** 1273
Juvenile Justice and Delinquency Prevention, National Advisory Committee for, **1977:** 1713; **1978:** 1193; **1980–81:** 1097, 3022

Kaasa, Olaf J., **1980–81:** 1405
Kabbani, Najati, **1978:** 795
Kahlil, Mustafa, **1978:** 2147
Kahn, Alfred E., **1977:** 758, 766, 933, 944, 1134, 1365, 1669, 2223; **1978:** 471, 1139, 1140, 1837, 1849, 1850, 1879, 1880, 1914, 1915, 1954, 1971, 2031, 2041, 2050, 2092, 2094, 2176, 2188, 2218, 2238, 2242, 2279
    Anti-inflation accords with labor leaders, meeting with reporters, **1979:** 1778, 1787
    Anti-inflation program actions, **1979:** 234, 309n., 621, 752
    Council on Wage and Price Stability, Chairman, resignation, **1980–81:** 2726
    Meetings with the President (Digest), **1979:** 14, 25, 178, 241, 327, 467, 554, 732, 842, 898, 899, 956, 1222, 1453, 1785, 2043, 2106, 2206, 2248; **1980–81:** 24, 292, 374, 493, 607, 774, 892, 893, 1050, 1469, 1564, 1847
    Mentions, **1979:** 657n., 745; **1980–81:** 59, 61
    News conferences (Checklist), **1979:** 620, 668, 843, 1455, 1706
    President's assessment, **1979:** 651
    Voluntary energy conservation, comments on, **1979:** 561
    Voluntary wage and price guidelines, telegram to Fortune 500 companies (Checklist), **1980–81:** 453
Kahn, Eve M., **1980–81:** 926
Kaiser, Philip M., **1977:** 1140, 1163; **1980–81:** 191
Kaiser Aluminum & Chemical Corp., **1980–81:** 892
Kamel, Mohamed Ibrahim, **1978:** 46, 1506
Kaminer, Peter H., **1980–81:** 2731
Kamm, Linda Heller, **1977:** 84, 148
Kampelman, Max M., **1978:** 2269; **1979:** 2117, 2248; **1980–81:** 848, 1434

Kampuchea
    American Legion relief support, **1980–81:** 1554
    Embargo regulations, **1978:** 1505; **1979:** 1656
    First Lady's trip, **1979:** 2090, 2112
    Geneva relief conference, **1980–81:** 931
    Human rights violations, **1978:** 767
    Refugees, **1980–81:** 964, 971, 1165
    Relief efforts
        International, **1979:** 1844, 1925, 2197
        Religious groups, **1979:** 2113
        U.S.
            Food for Peace appropriation, **1979:** 2011
            Mentions, **1979:** 2126, 2244
            News conferences (Checklist), **1979:** 2044, 2189
            Pledge announcements, **1979:** 1924, 1927, 2011, 2052, 2117
            Proc. 4700, **1979:** 2080
            White House meeting remarks, **1979:** 2112
    Senatorial delegation's visit, **1979:** 2036, 2044
    Soviet influence, **1980–81:** 674
    United Nations refugee assistance role, **1980–81:** 1286
    U.S. export controls, **1979:** 2292, 2295
    U.S. food assistance, **1980–81:** 1333
    Vietnamese invasion, **1979:** 303, 348, 765, 1348
    Vietnamese occupation, **1980–81:** 1579, 2021, 2863
Kanazawa, Shimeji, **1980–81:** 816, 826
Kane, John L., Jr., **1977:** 1967
Kane, Larry, **1980–81:** 2055
Kane, Robert.
    See United States Olympic Committee, President.
Kang Shi'en, **1979:** 982
Kansas
    Democratic Party primary, **1980–81:** 584
    Disaster assistance, **1980–81:** 1345, 1421
    Disaster declaration, **1977:** 1649; **1979:** 1043
    Federal recreation and historic sites, **1978:** 1424, 1459
    Gov. John Carlin, **1980–81:** 1423n.
    President's visit, **1978:** 1813–1820
    U.S. attorney, **1977:** 1128
    U.S. district judge, **1979:** 1786, 1787; **1980–81:** 720
Kansas City, Mo., **1978:** 1986, 1994; **1979:** 1241, 1294, 1925, 1931; **1980–81:** 1610
Kantor, Michael, **1978:** 1753, 1772; **1979:** 46, 91
Kanuk, Leslie L., **1978:** 299, 329
Kaplan, Deborah, **1977:** 2028
Kapnick, Harvey E., Jr., **1978:** 454; **1979:** 271
Karamanlis, Constantine, **1980–81:** 382, 520
Karatjas, Rita, **1977:** 299
Kardelj, Edvard, **1977:** 1649, 1700; **1979:** 293
Karim, Abdul Wahid, **1977:** 1383
Kariuki, Godfrey G., **1980–81:** 355
Karl, Max, **1980–81:** 2560

Karlton, Lawrence K., **1979:** 1018, 1019
Karmel, Roberta S., **1977:** 1395, 1438
Karpatkin, Rhoda, **1980–81:** 264
Karunaratne, W. S., **1978:** 1070
Kasha, Michael, **1979:** 196, 218
Kaslow, Audrey A., **1977:** 1824, 1931
Kassebaum, Sen. Nancy Landon, **1979:** 956;
    1980–81: 584, 1009
Kassot, Allen H., **1978:** 1514
Kastenmeier, Repr. Robert W., **1977:** 926; **1978:**
    1854; **1979:** 1849
  Legislation passage leadership
    Dispute Resolution Act, **1980–81:** 303
    Federal District Court Organization Act,
      1980–81: 2242
    Judicial Councils Reform and Judicial Con-
      duct and Disability Act, **1980–81:** 2241
    Privacy Protection Act, **1980–81:** 2218
    Small business, **1980–81:** 2381
Kateri Takakwitha, **1980–81:** 1168, 1242
Katmai National Monument, **1978:** 2127
Katterhagen, J. Gale, **1980–81:** 911
Katz, Abraham, **1980–81:** 48, 374
Katz, Julius L., **1977:** 8, 805
Katz, Leon, **1977:** 1053
Katz, Nancy, **1979:** 842
Katzenbach, Nicholas, **1979:** 1823
Kauffman, Howard, **1980–81:** 2748
Kaufman, Robert E., **1980–81:** 606
Kaunda, Kenneth D., **1978:** 771, 917, 920, 924, 934,
    940, 976
Kavanaugh, Daniel P., **1978:** 1467
Kavanaugh, Paul F., **1980–81:** 237
Kazarian, Dennis, **1978:** 1947
Kazen, Repr. Abraham, Jr., **1980–81:** 2622
Kazen, George P., **1979:** 402, 403
Keane, Benjamin, **1979:** 2251
Kearns, David T., **1980–81:** 1332
Kearse, Amalya L., **1977:** 1529; **1979:** 788
Keatley, Anne, **1978:** 1188
Kee, Esther G., **1979:** 553
Kee, Norman, **1980–81:** 1438n.
Keefe, Robert, **1979:** 401
Keeley, Robert V., **1980–81:** 717, 720
Keenan, Burt H., **1980–81:** 2242
Keene, Joseph Ransdell, **1979:** 667, 668
Keeny, Spurgeon M., Jr., **1977:** 733, 745
Keep, Judith Nelsen, **1980–81:** 894
Keep America Beautiful, Inc., **1978:** 771
Keeton, Robert E., **1979:** 179, 180
Kefauver, Estes, **1978:** 1858
Kehoe, James W., **1979:** 1293, 1294
Keil, Alfred A. H., **1978:** 217
Keim, Robert P., **1980–81:** 1405
Keiser, Dick, **1977:** 942
Keiser, Mr. and Mrs. Edward, **1980–81:** 1428
Keith, Damon J., **1977:** 1701
Keith, William D., **1978:** 1468

Keliikoa, Edward N., **1977:** 1211, 1212
Keller, Helen, **1980–81:** 1147
Keller, Oliver James, Jr., **1978:** 1083, 1111
Kelley, Clarence M., **1977:** 182, 900; **1978:** 397,
    1854
Kelley, James F., **1979:** 465
Kelley, Lucille, **1978:** 420
Kelley, Michael R., **1979:** 1001, 1019
Kelley, Peter, **1980–81:** 1541
Kelly, Bernard, **1977:** 1817; **1979:** 270
Kelly, Patrick F., **1980–81:** 720
Kelly, Peter, **1978:** 2288
Kelly, Bishop Thomas, **1977:** 1611; **1978:** 2059
Kelly, Thomas C., **1980–81:** 2841
Kelm, Doug, **1979:** 270
Kemeny, John G.
  See President's Commission on the Accident at
    Three Mile Island, Chairman.
Kemp, Bob, **1978:** 843
Kemp, John, **1977:** 1817; **1979:** 270
Kemp-Roth tax bill, President's opposition to,
    1980–81: 1327, 1354, 1505, 1511, 1531,
    1537, 1586, 1640, 1659, 1674, 1684, 1729,
    1880, 1886, 1895, 1911, 1951, 1977, 2007,
    2023, 2046, 2144, 2220, 2254, 2291, 2326,
    2363, 2420, 2428, 2433, 2434, 2450, 2462,
    2480, 2544, 2568, 2607
Kemper, James S., Jr., **1980–81:** 2609
Kenai Fjords National Monument, **1978:** 2129
Kenen, Isaiah L., **1978:** 2269
Kennedy, Agnes, **1980–81:** 1369
Kennedy, Cornelia G., **1979:** 620, 667
Kennedy, Sen. Edward M., **1977:** 40, 389, 394, 396,
    402, 485, 923, 928, 988, 1134, 1416, 1649,
    1826, 1837, 1920, 1923, 1941, 2162; **1978:**
    348, 400, 710, 762, 781, 792, 837, 1038,
    1139, 1140, 1221, 1243, 1247, 1345, 1393,
    1413, 1467, 1493, 1668, 1838, 1854, 1893,
    2223, 2225, 2226, 2249, 2250
  Chrysler Corporation, Federal assistance sup-
    port, **1980–81:** 311
  Democratic National Convention
    Address, **1980–81:** 1528, 1532
    Delegates commitment, **1980–81:** 1383, 1426
    Open convention proposal, **1980–81:** 731, 737,
      739, 1481
    Platform presentation, **1980–81:** 1100
    President's acceptance speech attendance,
      1980–81: 1540
    President's appeal for support, **1980–81:** 1532
  Democratic Presidential campaign
    Debate with the President, Sen. Byrd's ad-
      vocacy of, **1980–81:** 907
    Policy differences with the President, **1980–81:**
      736, 749, 750
    Primary and caucus results, **1980–81:** 180, 295,
      399, 429, 525, 534, 762

Kennedy, Sen. Edward — *continued*
  Presidential campaign — *continued*
    U.S. Conference of Mayors, speech cancellation, **1980–81:** 1086
    Withdrawal, possibility of, **1980–81:** 491, 729
    Employment legislation sponsorship, **1980–81:** 1085
    Fair housing legislation support, **1980–81:** 1754, 1878
    Federal civil justice system, reform proposals, **1979:** 341
    Iran and Afghanistan situation positions, **1980–81:** 308
    Legislation passage leadership
      Dispute Resolution Act, **1980–81:** 303
      Federal Magistrate Act, **1979:** 1849
      Hospital cost containment, **1979:** 385
      Judicial reform, **1980–81:** 2241
      Mental health systems, **1979:** 857
      Mental Health Systems Act, **1980–81:** 1976, 2099, 2101, 2361
      Motor Carrier Act, **1980–81:** 281, 1262, 1264, 1267
      Privacy protection, **1980–81:** 2218
      Trucking industry deregulation, **1979:** 1116
    Massachusetts fishing industry protection, support for, **1979:** 1996
    Meetings with the President, **1980–81:** 1028, 1031, 1038, 1050, 1598
    Mentions, **1979:** 170, 1978; **1980–81:** 631
    National health plan legislation
      Comparisons with administration's proposal, **1979:** 1411, 1635, 1637
      Cooperation with administration, **1979:** 1011, 1392, 1411, 1637
      Major legislative goal, **1979:** 1749
    1980 budget recommendation, **1979:** 187
    1980 Presidential campaign
      Campaign appearances with the President, **1980–81:** 1548, 1887, 2243, 2251, 2273, 2276, 2363
      Carter/Kennedy unity dinner, **1980–81:** 2340
      Florida caucus results, **1979:** 1983, 1986
      Impact of:
        Chappaquiddick incident, **1979:** 1839
        Kennedy legacy, **1979:** 1986
      President's precandidacy remarks on, **1979:** 848, 904, 966, 1582, 1750
      Public opinion polls ratings, **1979:** 2241
      Support for the President's candidacy, **1980–81:** 1631, 1635, 1678, 1679, 1755, 1762, 1912, 2094, 2163, 2396
    Political philosophy, differences with President, **1979:** 2034
    Relationship with the President, **1979:** 1982, 1987; **1980–81:** 1529, 1557
    Windfall profits tax position, **1979:** 753, 865
Kennedy, Ethel, **1980–81:** 2099

Kennedy, George Alexander, **1980–81:** 1332, 1337
Kennedy, Henry H., Jr., **1979:** 1624, 1680
Kennedy, John C., **1977:** 1626, 1650
Kennedy, John F.
  Assassination, **1979:** 1237, 1992
  Business investment proposals, **1980–81:** 2434
  Civil rights efforts, **1980–81:** 1631
  Cuban missile crisis, **1979:** 1804; **1980–81:** 2594
  Dinner honoring, **1979:** 1920
  Knights of Columbus involvement, **1980–81:** 2434
  Medicare and Medicaid enactment, **1979:** 1028
  Mental health legislation, **1980–81:** 2099
  Mentions, **1979:** 828, 2016
  National impact, **1979:** 1982
  1960 election, **1980–81:** 1741 1765, 1770, 1956, 2089, 2094, 2247, 2278, 2310, 2395, 2400, 2404, 2416, 2429, 2501, 2527, 2535, 2557, 2562, 2603, 2622, 2634, 2640, 2645, 2664, 2670, 2671, 2676, 2681
  Nuclear explosives test ban agreement with Soviet Union, **1979:** 694, 1088
  Political philosophy, **1979:** 1978, 1986, 2034
  President's assessment, **1980–81:** 1532, 2341
  Quoted, **1979:** 678, 693, 2018; **1980–81:** 502, 867, 2244, 2311, 2383, 2536, 2551, 2554, 2581, 2599, 2604, 2620, 2623, 2628, 2636, 2642, 2656, 2661, 2666, 2679
  Trade agreements legislation, **1979:** 1312, 1713
Kennedy, Mrs. Joseph P., **1978:** 1033
Kennedy, Louisa, **1980–81:** 972
Kennedy, Richard T., **1977:** 1501, 1507
Kennedy, Sen. Robert F., **1978:** 1051; **1979:** 1237, 1920, 1980, 1992; **1980–81:** 1838, 2364, 2367, 2528, 2626, 2659, 2664, 2670, 2677, 2682
Kennedy, Rose, **1980–81:** 2243
Kennedy, William, **1978:** 1878
Kennedy, William J., III, **1980–81:** 305
Kennedy Center Honors, **1978:** 2186
Kennedy Center for the Performing Arts, John F. *See* John F. Kennedy Center for the Performing Arts.
Kennedy Space Center, Fla., **1978:** 1684, 1724
Kennedy-Minott, Rodney O., **1977:** 1356, 1384
Kennedys-King Day dinner, **1979:** 1920, 1977
Kenney, Sandra R., **1977:** 1944, 1966; **1978:** 231
Kenny, Nick, **1978:** 539
Kenopensky, Andrew H., **1977:** 196; **1978:** 484, 504
Kentucky
  Civic and community leaders, meeting with administration officials, **1978:** 2146
  Coal supplies, **1979:** 1341
  Democratic Party fundraiser, President's attendance cancellation, **1979:** 1222
  Disaster assistance, **1980–81:** 1422
  Disaster declaration, **1977:** 596; **1978:** 2269; **1979:** 1293

Kentucky — *continued*
  Energy crisis, **1977:** 37
  Energy emergency, **1978:** 384, 548
  Gov. John Y. Brown, **1980–81:** 422, 1388, 1390n., 1423
  High-sulfur coal plants, **1979:** 1644
  President's visit, **1979:** 1337, 1340, 1398; **1980–81:** 1388
  State officials, meeting with the President (Digest), **1980–81:** 422
  Telephone service in Bullitt County, **1979:** 1343
  U.S. attorneys, **1977:** 1059, 1222, 1266
  U.S. district judges, **1977:** 1507, 1700, 1701; **1979:** 1531, 1532, 1883, 2281
  U.S. marshals, **1977:** 943, 1163
Kenya
  Ambassador to U.S., **1977:** 508
  Delegation, meeting with the President, **1978:** 449
  President Jomo Kenyatta, **1978:** 1467
  President Daniel T. arap Moi, **1980–81:** 334, 335, 352, 354, 357
  U.S. Ambassador, **1977:** 576, 597; **1980–81:** 843, 893
  U.S. military bases, **1980–81:** 35, 391
Kenyatta, Imze Jomo, **1980–81:** 353, 357
Kenyatta, Jomo, **1978:** 1467
Kenyon, David Vreeland, **1980–81:** 1151
Keppel, Francis, **1979:** 196, 218
Kerr, Louise Año Nuevo, **1980–81:** 1332, 1337
Kerry, Henry E., Jr., **1977:** 1486
Kessler, Gladys, **1977:** 465
Kessler, Joan F., **1978:** 457, 458
Kester, John G., **1979:** 435
Ketchum, Repr. William M., **1978:** 1178
Ketelson, James L., **1979:** 1614n.
Kettle River, Minn., **1979:** 1813
Keyes, Daniel M., Jr., **1977:** 815
Keys, Repr. Martha, **1978:** 1814
Keys, Martha E., **1980–81:** 840, 967
Keyserling, Leon, **1978:** 1871
Khaddam, Abd al-Halim, **1977:** 704, 1677
Khalid bin Abd al-Aziz Al-Sa'ud, **1978:** 18, 1537, 1554, 1876
Khalid Bin Abdul Aziz, **1977:** 1825, 2120; **1979:** 456
Khalil, Mustafa.
  See Egypt, Prime Minister.
Khan, Sultan Muhammad, **1979:** 376
Khomeini, Ayatollah Ruhollah.
  See Iran, Ayatollah Ruhollah Khomeini.
Khorshed, Omar, **1979:** 527
Kidd, Adm. I. C., **1978:** 1385
Kidd, William Matthew, **1979:** 2188
Kiereini, Jeremiah G., **1980–81:** 355
Kiker, John W., **1980–81:** 19
Kildee, Repr. Dale E., **1978:** 458
Killanin, Lord, **1980–81:** 929

Killeen, James R., **1979:** 687
Killen, Denis James, **1980–81:** 422
Killgore, Andrew I., **1977:** 1355, 1384
Killy, Jean Claude, **1980–81:** 380
Kilpatrick, James J., **1977:** 1513
Kilpatrick, Norman, **1977:** 404
Kim, Bok-Lim C., **1978:** 1190
Kim, Yong Shik, **1977:** 882
Kim Chaekyu, **1979:** 2054n.
Kim Yong Sam, **1979:** 1913ftn., 1919
Kimball, Spencer W., **1977:** 372; **1978:** 2088
Kimball, Tom, **1979:** 444
Kimble, Kerry, **1977:** 324
Kimbrough, William A., Jr., **1977:** 1128
Kimche, Lee, **1979:** 956
Kimche, Leila I., **1977:** 2072, 2077
Kimelman, Henry L., **1979:** 465; **1980–81:** 1473, 1524
Kindt, Donald J., **1977:** 2130, 2131
King.
  See specific forename.
King, Alice, **1979:** 1851
King, Bill G., **1978:** 2165
King, Gov. Bruce, **1979:** 1851, 1863; **1980–81:** 303
King, Colbert I., **1979:** 2269, 2281
King, Coretta Scott, **1977:** 526, 1210, 1230, 1545, 1626, 1650; **1978:** 64, 398, 1679, 1703, 1871, 1874, 2219; **1979:** 33n., 909, 1920
  African American historic sites legislation, signing ceremony remarks, **1980–81:** 2174
  Democratic National Convention, seconding speaker for President, **1980–81:** 1469, 1471
  Martin Luther King, Jr., national holiday efforts, **1980–81:** 890
  Mentions, **1980–81:** 84, 1500, 1930
  Peace efforts, **1980–81:** 2915
  White House Conference on Families, Deputy Chair, **1980–81:** 1037n.
King, David S., **1979:** 2269, 2281
King, Edward, **1978:** 1893, 1896
King, Gov. Edward, **1979:** 1785; **1980–81:** 1549
King, Evelyn (Champagne), **1979:** 1015
King, James B., **1977:** 1286, 1307; **1978:** 277, 303; **1980–81:** 493
King, Rev. Martin Luther, Jr., **1977:** 1215, 1230; **1978:** 64, 1780
  Assassination, **1979:** 1237, 1992
  Birthday, message of the President, **1979:** 22
  Birthday anniversary statement, **1980–81:** 61, 296
  Civil rights efforts, **1979:** 970, 972, 2009; **1980–81:** 84, 223, 887
  Dinner honoring, **1979:** 1920, 1968
  Dream for America, **1979:** 909
  Federal Bureau of Investigation's surveillance, **1979:** 1335

King, Rev. Martin Luther — *continued*
  Mentions, **1979:** 912; **1980–81:** 1750, 1752, 2249, 2426, 2530
  National holiday
    Legislation, **1980–81:** 155, 890, 1751, 2969
    President's support, **1979:** 34, 145
  Presidential Medal of Freedom recipient, **1980–81:** 1057
  Quoted, **1979:** 913; **1980–81:** 1002, 1071, 1326, 1502, 1581, 1751
King, Martin Luther, Jr., Center for Social Change, **1978:** 1702; **1979:** 33n.
King, Martin Luther, Jr., national historic site, **1980–81:** 2172, 2179, 2184
King, Martin Luther, Jr. Nonviolent Peace Award, **1979:** 27
King, Rev. Martin Luther, Sr., **1977:** 1230; **1978:** 1703; **1979:** 33n., 319; **1980–81:** 1001, 1750, 2174, 2427
King, Mrs. Martin Luther, Sr., **1980–81:** 1001
King, Martin Luther, III, **1980–81:** 1946
King, Mary E., **1977:** 216, 253, 376, 608, 1048
King, Patricia, **1977:** 1083; **1979:** 1264
King, Robert R., **1977:** 987, 1163
King, Susan B., **1978:** 84, 149, 1208; **1980–81:** 281, 1050
King, Yolanda, **1980–81:** 2075
Kingsland, Robert D., **1977:** 1650, 1651
Kingston, Maxine Hong, **1980–81:** 2075
Kingston, Gen. Robert C., **1979:** 1201
Kinney, Harry E., **1977:** 196
Kinstler, Everett Raymond, **1978:** 965
Kirbo, Charles H., **1977:** 221, 1044; **1978:** 1329, 2179; **1979:** 1422; **1980–81:** 1747, 1749n.
Kirby, R. E., **1979:** 976
Kirby, Robert, **1977:** 2070; **1980–81:** 1405
Kirchschläger, Rudolph, **1979:** 1047, 1142
Kiribati
  Friendship treaty with U.S., **1980–81:** 206
  Trade beneficiary developing country designation, **1980–81:** 550
  U.S. Minister, **1980–81:** 1107, 1111
Kirillin, V. A., **1977:** 1222
Kirk, Elise Kuhl, **1979:** 465
Kirk, Roger, **1978:** 317, 329, 1426, 1458; **1979:** 2148; **1980–81:** 1572
Kirkland, J. Lane, **1977:** 31, 508, 1529, 1825, 1965
Kirkland, Lane.
  See AFL-CIO, Secretary-treasurer; AFL-CIO President.
Kirkpatrick, Thomas B., Jr., **1980–81:** 1440
Kirschenbaum, Bruce, **1977:** 184
Kirtland Air Force Base, N. Mex., **1979:** 1851
Kissinger, Henry A., **1977:** 10, 100, 507, 538, 540, 647, 764, 974, 1173, 1211, 1482, 1493, 1543, 1749, 1808, 1887, 2011, 2195; **1978:** 2268

Kissinger, Henry — *continued*
  Egyptian-Israeli peace negotiations, role, **1980–81:** 2834
  Meeting with the President (Digest), **1979:** 1823
  Mention, **1980–81:** 631
  Nigeria, refusal of admittance to, **1979:** 1349, 1917; **1980–81:** 2147, 2300, 2366, 2406, 2428, 2565
  SALT II treaty opposition, **1979:** 1350
  Palestine Liberation Organization position, **1979:** 1579
  Shah of Iran, role in admittance to U.S., **1979:** 2170
  Soviet troops in Cuba recommendations, **1979:** 1838
Kiwanis Club, International, **1978:** 526; **1979:** 467; **1980–81:** 930
Klabunde, Lloyd, **1977:** 1700
Klaus, Ida
  Emergency Boards to investigate railway labor disputes, member, **1979:** 819, 1697, 2247
  Mention, **1979:** 1999
Klein, Joan Dempsey, **1980–81:** 2057
Klein, Lawrence, **1980–81:** 2309
Klemperer, William, **1979:** 1619, 1680
Klerman, Gerald L., **1977:** 1779, 1796
Klima, Otta, **1978:** 218
Kline, Mark D., **1980–81:** 927
Klineman, Alan I., **1980–81:** 2615
Kling, Lee, **1977:** 1013
Kling, S. Lee, **1978:** 1915, 1971, 2184, 2188; **1979:** 92
Klonoski, Jim, **1978:** 1946
Klopf, Gordon J., **1978:** 1190
Klos Visessurakarn, **1978:** 1380
Klotz, Bobi, **1980–81:** 377, 379
Klutznick, Philip M., **1977:** 1952
  See also Commerce, Secretary of.
Klyberg, Albert T., **1980–81:** 2859, 2870, 2873
Knap, Ted, **1980–81:** 733n.
Knauer, Virginia H., **1977:** 196
Knauss, John A., **1978:** 218; **1979:** 2187
Kneip, Richard F., **1978:** 821, 881
Kneip, Gov. Richard F., **1977:** 147, 1476
Kniska, Nick, **1977:** 295
Knoche, E. Henry, **1977:** 31, 85
Knowles, Marjorie Fine, **1979:** 365, 377
Knox, Marcy, **1980–81:** 824
Knox, Patricia J., **1978:** 968
Knox, William D., **1978:** 759; **1980–81:** 1048
Knoxville, Tenn., **1977:** 738; **1978:** 945, 1217; **1979:** 1525
Knoxville International Energy Exposition of 1982, **1978:** 2170; **1979:** 2298; **1980–81:** 1277, 1292, 1577
Knuth, Donald E., **1979:** 2289; **1980–81:** 82n.
Kobayashi, K. Jessie, **1980–81:** 1023, 1051

Kobrine, Arthur I., **1980–81:** 3026
Kobuk Valley National Monument, **1978:** 2130
Koch, Charles, **1979:** 1614n.
Koch, Edward I., **1978:** 270, 440, 1397, 1399, 1723, 1929, 1930; **1979:** 240, 1742, 1745, 2297; **1980–81:** 1527, 1954, 2310, 2377
Koch, Repr. Edward I., **1977:** 1699, 1729, 1805, 1826
Kocoras, Charles P., **1980–81:** 1015, 1051
Koff, Robert H., **1979:** 1727; **1980–81:** 1839
Koger, Ira McKissick, **1979:** 465
Kohl, Dr. Helmut, **1978:** 1212
Kohler, Saul, **1980–81:** 751n.
Kolberg, William, **1980–81:** 422
Koleda, Michael S., **1977:** 1415; **1978:** 66, 1500
Koliševski, Lazar, **1980–81:** 828
Kollek, Teddy, **1979:** 417n.
Komer, Odessa, **1978:** 1134; **1980–81:** 813, 826
Komer, Robert W., **1979:** 1774, 1786; **1980–81:** 2195
Kontos, C. William, **1980–81:** 843, 893
Konyha, Bill, **1980–81:** 1648
Koole, Florine, **1978:** 1134
Koontz, Elizabeth, **1978:** 1134; **1979:** 827
Kopman, Marlene, **1980–81:** 192
Korcak, Jerome, **1978:** 2110
Korea, People's Republic of
　Embargo regulations, **1978:** 1505
　Mention, **1979:** 187
　Trade restrictions with U.S., **1979:** 1656, 2292, 2295
　U.S. Army helicopter, downing, **1977:** 1250, 1263
　U.S. reassessment of military strength, **1979:** 1148, 1275
　U.S. relations, **1979:** 1153, 1209
Korea, Republic of
　Acting President Choi Kyu Ha, **1979:** 2053
　Activity of agents in the U.S., **1977:** 1280, 1969
　Ambassador to U.S., **1977:** 882
　Arms transfers, conventional, **1979:** 1154
　Exports to U.S., **1977:** 644, 755, 1114
　Fishery agreement with U.S., **1977:** 206
　Foreign Minister, **1977:** 343, 372
　Generalized System of Preferences, **1979:** 2230
　Human rights violations, **1979:** 1913
　Interview remarks, **1978:** 67
　Mention, **1979:** 187
　Joint statement, **1979:** 1207
　Nonrubber footwear exports, **1980–81:** 420
　President's Assistant for National Security Affairs, visit, **1978:** 803
　President's meeting with opposition party leaders, possibility of, **1979:** 1148, 1151
　President's visit
　　Arrival, **1979:** 1201
　　Departure from White House, **1979:** 1154, 1159

Korea, Republic of — *continued*
　President's visit — *continued*
　　President's summary of trip, **1979:** 1217
　　State dinner, **1979:** 1202, 1223
　Television receiver exports, **1979:** 167, 168
　Trade with U.S., **1980–81:** 1258, 2588, 2601, 2607
　Transfer of certain defense articles, **1977:** 1822
　Under Secretary of State and Chairman, Joint Chiefs of Staff, visit, **1977:** 1021, 1029, 1084
　U.S. Ambassador, **1977:** 1970; **1978:** 1023, 1034
　U.S. policy, **1977:** 372
　U.S. relations, **1979:** 156, 1152, 1205, 1349; **1980–81:** 169, 1618
　U.S. troops, withdrawal, **1977:** 64, 343, 1018, 1822; **1978:** 122, 768
　U.S. troops in, **1979:** 247, 764, 1148, 1153, 1218, 1275, 1294; **1980–81:** 2447
　Whaling operations, **1979:** 266–268
Korea, Republic of, President (Park Chung Hee), **1977:** 1018; **1978:** 1330
　Assassination, **1979:** 2054
　Invitation to President Carter to visit, **1979:** 673
　Meetings with the President, **1979:** 1202, 1207, 1217n.
　Mentions, **1979:** 1111, 1148, 1216, 1218
Korenko, Michael Karl, **1980–81:** 949
Korman, Edward R., **1978:** 1333, 1334
Kornberg, Arthur, **1979:** 2289; **1980–81:** 82n.
Kornegay, Francis Albert, **1980–81:** 237
Kosciuszko, Thaddeus, **1980–81:** 1853
Koski, Sherill, **1978:** 1190
Koskinen, John A., **1979:** 1671
Kostelanetz, Andre, **1978:** 944
Kourouma, Daouda, **1977:** 508
Koury, E. G., **1980–81:** 1446
Kovacevic, Zivorad, **1980–81:** 1244
Kovats de Fabricy, Col. Michael, **1979:** 2024
Kovelant, Kevin E., **1979:** 2075
Kowal, Sheila, **1978:** 829
Kozaren, Robert, **1980–81:** 292
Kraft, Timothy E., **1977:** 441; **1978:** 803; **1980–81:** 939, 1707, 1708n., 1744
　Carter-Mondale Committee, Inc., campaign manager appointment, **1979:** 1422
　Ethnic and minority groups, discussions with, **1979:** 245
　Mentions, **1979:** 880, 1865, 1976
Kramer, Clarence, **1978:** 2158
Kravitch, Phyllis A., **1979:** 93
Kreeger, Bill, **1980–81:** 412
Kreidler, Robert L., **1980–81:** 928
Kreisky, Bruno, **1977:** 463, 785; **1979:** 1047, 1142, 2036
Krents, Harold Eliot, **1980–81:** 949
Kreps, Allyn, **1977:** 2181
Kreps, Juanita M., **1980–81:** 47
　See also Commerce, Secretary of.

Kriangsak Chomanan.
  See Thailand, Prime Minister.
Krick, Harold J., **1980–81:** 1508
Krieger, Richard, **1978:** 1974
Krim, Arthur, **1977:** 1154; **1978:** 217, 1932; **1980–81:** 2340
Krim, Mathilde, **1978:** 1630, 1669; **1979:** 1264
Krimsky, George A., **1977:** 100
Kroeze, Henry, **1977:** 1944, 1966; **1978:** 230
Krol, John Cardinal, **1980–81:** 1168
Kroll, Bernard, **1979:** 306n.
Kronheim, Milton S., **1980–81:** 2883
Krsul, John C., **1977:** 1308
Krueger, Robert, **1979:** 1134, 1143; **1980–81:** 756n.
Krueger, Repr. Robert, **1977:** 1162, 1389; **1978:** 1723, 2073
Krulak, Lt. Gen. Victor H., **1977:** 1432
Krulitz, Leo M., **1977:** 227, 252, 266, 1759; **1979:** 990
Krumhansl, James A., **1977:** 1929, 1931
Krumholtz, Fred J., **1979:** 607
Krumholz, Norman, **1977:** 2153
Krupsak, Mary Ann, **1977:** 526
Krupsak, Lt. Gov. Mary Anne, **1978:** 1808
Kruse, Bob, **1980–81:** 1413, 1415n.
Kryder, Charles (Chuck) and Genie, **1977:** 921
Kryza, E. Gregory, **1977:** 1792, 1796
Ku Klux Klan, **1979:** 1712
  Justice Department investigation, **1980–81:** 223
  President's opposition, **1980–81:** 1501, 1601, 1640, 1753
  Reagan, Ronald, statement on, **1980–81:** 1610, 1640, 1750
  Secret training camps, **1980–81:** 1997
  Truman, Harry, 1924 incident with, **1980–81:** 1612
Kubisch, Jack B., **1980–81:** 1860, 1947
Kucinich, Dennis J., **1978:** 229
Kulas, Julian E., **1980–81:** 822
Kulongoski, Ted, **1980–81:** 2672
Kunene, Musa Simon, **1977:** 508
Kuntz, Marcia B., **1980–81:** 928
Kurose, Aki, **1980–81:** 258
Kurtz, Jerome, **1977:** 470, 509; **1978:** 1711
Kushner, Rose, **1980–81:** 911
Kusielewicz, Eugene, **1978:** 1808
Kutak, Robert J., **1978:** 1753, 1772; **1979:** 46, 92
Kuwait
  Abstention from voting on sanctions against Iran, **1980–81:** 39
  Oil supplies, **1980–81:** 2025
  U.S. Ambassador, **1979:** 1446, 1455
Kuykendall, Crystal A., **1978:** 913
Kuykendall, Jerome K., **1977:** 2157
Kuznetsov, Edward, **1979:** 731
Kyprianou, Spyros Achilles, **1977:** 1501, 1754; **1978:** 1151–1153, 1719; **1979:** 998, 1301, 2163; **1980–81:** 382

LaBerge, Walter B., **1977:** 1174, 1212
Labor
  Administration's renewal program, **1980–81:** 1587
  AFL-CIO, President's addresses to organizations of, **1980–81:** 1647, 1883
  Anti-inflation accords with administration, **1980–81:** 71, 76, 121, 248, 497, 581
    Announcement, **1979:** 1772, 1787
    Fact sheet (Checklist), **1979:** 1787
    President's remarks, **1979:** 1859, 1869, 1908, 1937, 1942, 2017, 2049
  Anti-inflation program, **1978:** 1843, 1844, 1846, 1880
  Common situs picketing bill, **1977:** 516
  Fair Labor Standards Amendments of 1977, **1977:** 1947
  Federal arbitration of strikes, **1980–81:** 2358, 2411, 2457, 2514
  Human rights efforts, **1980–81:** 1361
  Industrial innovation initiatives program, **1979:** 2067, 2072
  Law reform, **1980–81:** 156, 1883
    Legislation, **1977:** 1277, 1332, 1924, 1925; **1978:** 990, 993, 1070, 1079, 1496, 1547
  Leaders, meetings with the President, **1977:** 595, 642, 706
  Leaders, White House dinner honoring, **1980–81:** 2883
  Legal rights protection, **1980–81:** 1951
  Legislation, **1979:** 146, 1870; **1980–81:** 582
  Low-level radiation hazards, **1979:** 2007
  Metropolitan Opera dispute, **1980–81:** 2017
  Minimum wage, **1977:** 516
  National presidents, meeting with the President, **1977:** 1611
  Occupational safety and health programs, **1977:** 200, 1430; **1979:** 135
  Occupational safety report, **1980–81:** 1051
  Ocean mining legislation cooperation, **1980–81:** 1284
  Organization representatives, White House picnic for, **1979:** 1593, 1605; **1980–81:** 1605–1610
  Pension funds, **1980–81:** 2166
  President's meetings with leaders of:
    New Jersey, **1980–81:** 2273
    New York, **1980–81:** 451, 2306, 2333
  Reagan, Ronald, policy differences with the President, **1980–81:** 2007, 2167, 2273, 2306, 2536, 2671
  Relationship with the President, **1977:** 775; **1979:** 1994
  Representatives, meetings with the President, **1978:** 897, 898
  Retirement, **1977:** 911
  Right-to-work laws, **1978:** 1993
  Situs picketing, **1980–81:** 1883

[References are to page numbers except as otherwise indicated]

Labor — *continued*
   State of the Union, **1978:** 109
   Surplus areas procurement, **1978:** 1428, 1429, 1432
   Surplus procurement program, **1980–81:** 1427
   Trade unionism, **1979:** 1252
   Undocumented aliens, **1977:** 632, 644, 901, 1030, 1101
   Unions, relationship with Labor Department, **1977:** 106, 107
   United Auto Workers, address, **1977:** 887, 944
   United Mine Workers strike, **1978:** 469, 488
   Voluntary wage and price controls, **1978:** 1327, 1352, 1423, 1910, 1912, 2066, 2239; **1979:** 48, 307, 935, 1252, 1258, 1841
   Wage increases, voluntary prior notice, **1977:** 51, 219
   Windfall profits tax support, **1980–81:** 586
   See also Wages and prices.
Labor, Department of
   Appropriations, **1977:** 2087
   Assistant Secretaries, **1977:** 228, 252, 364, 365, 373, 944, 1407, 2109; **1978:** 218, 230, 416, 447, 820, 953, 954, 958, 1492, 1773, 2298, 2299; **1979:** 1159, 1259, 1293, 1976; **1980–81:** 1071
   Budget deferral, **1979:** 200; **1980–81:** 2916
   Budget rescissions, **1978:** 1321, 1652
   CETA program administration, **1980–81:** 909
   Commissioner of Labor Statistics, **1979:** 528, 554
   Consumer Affairs Council membership, **1979:** 1763
   Deputy Assistant Secretary, **1977:** 1065, 1085; **1979:** 339, 377, 974
   Deputy Under Secretary, **1979:** 1596
   Director, Office of Federal Contract Compliance Programs, **1980–81:** 1502
   Employee retirement cooperative agreements, **1980–81:** 295
   Employment programs, **1977:** 53, 54, 390, 983
   Energy crisis, **1977:** 35, 113
   Equal employment enforcement, transfer of functions (EO 12144), **1979:** 1140, 1529
   Equal employment opportunity functions, **1978:** 1714
   Executive Assistant and Counselor to the Secretary, **1979:** 1596
   Fastener workers employment, **1978:** 300, 301
   Federal Mine Safety and Health Amendments Act of 1977, **1977:** 1987, 1989
   Frances Perkins Building dedication, **1980–81:** 629
   Handicapped persons programs, **1980–81:** 2610
   Hard-core unemployed jobs program, **1979:** 2158
   Industry relocation, programs for workers affected by, **1980–81:** 1968
   Inspector General, **1979:** 365, 377

Labor, Department of — *continued*
   Integrated pest management programs, **1979:** 1383
   Interagency Coordinating Council, **1978:** 1434
   Juvenile delinquency programs, **1980–81:** 1273
   Labor surplus areas procurement, **1978:** 1432
   Mention, **1979:** 1609
   Miami, Fla., training and job programs, **1980–81:** 1236
   Miners benefits, **1978:** 432
   National Productivity Council, **1978:** 1833, 1835, 1836
   Opportunities Industrialization Centers programs, **1980–81:** 1068
   Paperwork reduction, **1979:** 2181
   President's Commission on the Coal Industry, **1978:** 2244
   President's Visit, question-and-answer session, **1977:** 102
   Radiation Policy Council membership, **1980–81:** 363
   Reorganization, **1977:** 106
   Reorganization Plan No. 1 of 1978, **1978:** 399, 401, 404, 405
   Reorganization Plan No. 4 of 1978, **1978:** 1401–1405
   Rural wastewater treatment training programs, **1979:** 75
   Solicitor, **1977:** 227, 252, 1306
   Telecommunications minority assistance programs, **1978:** 253, 254
   Toxic and hazardous substances regulation, **1977:** 1407
   Trade adjustment assistance determination, **1980–81:** 823
   Under Secretary, **1977:** 227, 252, 1930; **1979:** 1836, 1883; **1980–81:** 292, 374
   Undocumented aliens investigations, **1977:** 1418; **1979:** 806
   United Mine Workers strike, **1978:** 328, 573
   U.S. competition in world markets, study preparation, **1980–81:** 1695
   Veterans programs, **1978:** 1740, 1743; **1980–81:** 1550
   Welfare programs, **1980–81:** 2133
   Welfare reform, **1977:** 74
   Youth employment and training programs, **1980–81:** 125, 312, 337, 1081, 1706, 1874, 1998, 2021, 2061, 2133, 2517
   See also specific constituent agencies.
Labor, Secretary of (F. Ray Marshall), **1977:** 10, 26, 32, 87, 93, 105, 109, 151, 198, 227, 248, 252, 269, 378, 419, 464, 485, 551–554, 641, 646, 662, 676, 712, 744, 774, 775, 806, 944, 1169, 1222, 1273, 1277, 1306, 1348, 1383, 1405, 1406, 1416, 1421, 1438, 1444, 1465, 1482, 1532, 1648, 1690, 1754, 1801, 1833, 1952, 1966, 1967, 1987, 2001, 2076. 2089,

Labor, Secretary of — *continued*
  2109, 2162, 2198; **1978:** 313, 316, 320, 327,
  328, 331, 333, 336, 366, 379, 414–416, 419,
  489, 553, 574, 594, 595, 641, 682, 770, 897,
  933, 960, 1004, 1007, 1010, 1070, 1158,
  1333, 1344, 1407, 1492, 1544, 1545, 1674,
  1872, 1875, 1915, 1971
  Alaska Natural Gas Transportation System, Ex-
    ecutive Policy Board member, **1979:** 1126
  Auto Industry Committee, Executive Committee
    member, **1980–81:** 1670
  Coal mining safety report reception, **1980–81:**
    473
  Economic assistance actions for pollution con-
    trol, **1979:** 1385
  Environmental damage response activities,
    1980–81: 3046
  Federal civilian and military pay increase rec-
    ommendations, **1979:** 64, 1530; **1980–81:**
    468
  Federal Council on the Humanities, member,
    1980–81: 653
  Frances Perkins Building, dedication ceremony
    attendance, **1980–81:** 629
  Grain industry labor dispute actions, **1979:** 1430,
    1452, 1708
  Import relief determinations, **1980–81:** 3, 4, 532,
    533
  Interagency Employee Benefit Council, Chair-
    man, **1980–81:** 2864
  Labor/Technology Forecasting System devel-
    opment, **1979:** 2073
  Meetings with the President (Digest), **1979:** 467,
    1454, 1823, 2081, 2187; **1980–81:** 63, 374,
    825, 932
  Mentions, **1979:** 752, 1008, 1595; **1980–81:** 808,
    1510, 2401
  News conference (Checklist), **1979:** 1143
  Occupational safety and health programs for
    Federal employees, **1980–81:** 393
  President's assessment, **1979:** 1866, 2122; **1980–
    81:** 1609, 1647, 2885
  President's Committee on the International La-
    bor Organization, Chairman, **1980–81:**
    1127
  Rock Island Railroad strike actions, **1979:** 1696
  Steel industry revitalization program responsi-
    bilities, **1980–81:** 1960
  Venezuela inauguration ceremonies, U.S. dele-
    gation head, **1979:** 401
  White House Coal Advisory Council, support
    services, **1980–81:** 1433
  Youth employment and education program ac-
    tions, **1980–81:** 64, 215
  For functions of the Department in general, see
    Labor, Department of.
Labor Conference, International, **1980–81:** 931

Labor Council for Latin American Advancement,
  1980–81: 857
Labor Day, **1977:** 1530; **1978:** 1483; **1979:** 1528,
  1593, 1605; **1980–81:** 1474, 1605
Labor Intensive Public Works program, **1978:** 1010
Labor-Management Relations Program, Federal,
  1979: 2144
Labor Office, International, **1980–81:** 932
Labor Organization, International, **1977:** 1029,
  1634, 1951, 1965, 1967; **1979:** 63; **1980–
  81:** 306
Labor Organization, President's Committee on the
  International, **1980–81:** 1127, 2849
Labor Press Association, International, **1978:** 1490
Labor Relations Act amendments, National,
  1980–81: 2856
Labor Relations Authority, Federal.
  See Federal Labor Relations Authority.
Labor Relations Board, National.
  See National Labor Relations Board.
Labor Relations Council, Federal, **1978:** 447, 952,
  953, 957
Labor Statistics, Bureau of, **1977:** 1665, 1700;
  1980–81: 2055, 2901, 3010
Labor Surplus Area Outreach Program, **1979:** 1680
Labor/Technology Forecasting System, **1979:** 2073
Lacaya, Carmela, **1980–81:** 1541, 1939
Lacey, George W., **1978:** 919, 935
Lackey, Gerald B., **1980–81:** 1599
Ladd, Don, **1977:** 1059
Ladies' Garment Workers Union, International.
  See International Ladies' Garment Workers
    Union.
Laetrile, **1977:** 307
LaFalce, Rep. John J., **1978:** 1808, 1885; **1980–81:**
  2003, 2381
Laffoon, James R., **1980–81:** 269
LaFontaine, Herman, **1979:** 1448
Lagather, Robert B., **1978:** 218, 230
Lagomarsino, Repr. Robert F., **1980–81:** 318, 433
Laingen, Lowell Bruce, **1977:** 195, 714, 745; **1980–
  81:** 2264, 2267
Laird, Melvin, **1977:** 1018, 1749, 1887
Laise, Carol C., **1977:** 8; **1979:** 553
Laitin, Joseph, **1977:** 547, 557
Lakas, Demetric B., **1978:** 1118, 1122, 1153
Lake, Meno Truman, **1980–81:** 1332
Lake, W. Anthony, **1980–81:** 891
Lake Clark National Monument, **1978:** 2132
Lake County, Ind., **1980–81:** 966
Lake Placid Olympic Organizing Committee,
  1980–81: 268
Lake Tahoe Compact, Truckee, Carson and Walk-
  er Rivers, **1978:** 1466
Lake Tahoe Federal Coordinating Council, **1980–
  81:** 1012
Lake Tahoe protection, **1980–81:** 1012, 1015, 2234,
  2236

Lake Tahoe Regional Planning Agency, **1980–81:** 1946

Lakeland, Fla., **1980–81:** 2579–2586

Laker Airways, **1977:** 1112

Lalanne, Bernard Loustau, **1978:** 2059

Lamb, Lawrence, **1980–81:** 261

Lamine Conde, Mamady, **1979:** 842

Lamm, Rabbi Norman, **1978:** 1973; **1980–81:** 822

Lamm, Gov. Richard D., **1977:** 1863, 1883; **1978:** 824, 828, 829, 1750; **1979:** 2085, 2132, 2133ftn.

Lamport Rodil, Jorge, **1978:** 148

Lance missile, **1978:** 702

Land Management, Bureau of, **1977:** 980; **1978:** 223, 232

   Federal renewable resources program, **1979:** 1374, 1376

   Public lands management, **1979:** 1363, 1364

Land and resource management, Federal, **1979:** 1361, 1374

Land and Water Conservation Fund, **1977:** 1097; **1978:** 2002

Landa, Esther, **1978:** 1134

Landau, George W., **1977:** 1588

Landau, William M., **1979:** 783, 842, 899

Landen, John C., **1979:** 1776

Landers, Ann, **1980–81:** 911

Landgraf, Tana, **1979:** 2076

Landmann, Robert S., **1977:** 1262, 1267

Landon, Robert W., **1980–81:** 2107

Landow, Nathan, **1980–81:** 1859, 1946, 2070, 2726, 2727

Landrieu, Moon.
   See Housing and Urban Development, Secretary of.

Landrieu, Phyllis, **1978:** 1380

Landry, Mr. and Mrs. Paul, **1977:** 1084

Lands Conservation Act, Alaska National Interest.
   See Alaska National Interest Lands Conservation Act.

LANDSAT program, **1979:** 2149

Lane, Edward E., **1977:** 1653, 1656, 1660

Lane, George M., **1978:** 1266, 1279

Lane, Lyle Franklin, **1979:** 1131, 1143; **1980–81:** 1290

Lane, Wesley D., **1977:** 1266, 1307

Laney, James T., **1979:** 1561, 1565n.

Langenberg, Donald N., **1980–81:** 1022, 1051

Langlotz, Bennet K., **1980–81:** 927

Lanphere, Phyllis, **1978:** 269

Lansdowne, Pa., **1980–81:** 2034

Lanzillo, Jay G., **1980–81:** 2243

Laos, **1977:** 489

Lapin, Raymond H., **1977:** 934; **1978:** 920; **1979:** 932; **1980–81:** 911

Laredo, Tex., **1979:** 1817

LaRoche, Robert P., **1977:** 1613, 1614

Larry, R. Heath, **1977:** 2036; **1979:** 957, 1954

Larson, Douglas, **1979:** 1468n.

Las Vegas, Nev., **1979:** 932

Laskin, Carol, **1980–81:** 1936

Lasorda, Tommy, **1980–81:** 2646

Latimer, George, **1979:** 1458; **1980–81:** 1405

Latin America

   American Convention on Human Rights, **1977:** 1050

   Caribbean community, cooperation with, **1979:** 2161

   Cuban influence, **1980–81:** 173, 626, 1017, 1216, 1712

   First Lady's visit, **1977:** 1041–1046, 1089, 1098

   Inter-American Development Bank, role in, **1980–81:** 414

   Interview remarks, **1978:** 1597–1602

   Organization of American States, **1977:** 465, 611, 642, 984, 1542–1544, 1720

      Address, **1978:** 1141

   Secretary of State's visit, **1980–81:** 2690

   Spain, relations with, **1980–81:** 1214, 1215

   Treaty for Prohibition of Nuclear Weapons, **1978:** 962, 1143

   Treaty of Tlatelolco, **1977:** 1027; **1980–81:** 2734

   United States

      Assistance legislation, **1980–81:** 1017

      Exchange programs, **1980–81:** 628

      Foreign relations, **1980–81:** 173, 626, 944, 1215, 2339, 2734, 2789

      Nongovernmental volunteer programs, **1980–81:** 64

   U.S. assistance, **1979:** 2103

   U.S. policy, **1978:** 120, 908; **1979:** 160, 1665

   See also Caribbean; *specific country.*

Latin American Advancement, Labor Council for, **1980–81:** 857

Latin American Citizens, League of United, **1980–81:** 563, 1725

Latter-day Saints, Church of Jesus Christ of, **1977:** 1059; **1978:** 2088

Latvia, embargo regulations, **1979:** 1657

Lau, John Raymond, **1977:** 321

Lauder, Ronald S., **1979:** 465

Laue, James Howard, **1979:** 2196

Lauredo, Luis J., **1978:** 1380; **1979:** 401

Laurence, Margaret Muth, **1980–81:** 237, 268

Laurent, Ronald P., **1979:** 1677, 1705

Laureta, Alfred, **1978:** 712, 750

Laurie, Scott M., **1979:** 2075

Lautenberg, Frank, **1978:** 1973; **1980–81:** 822

Law Day, U.S.A., **1977:** 607; **1978:** 773

   (Proc. 4649), **1979:** 527, 757

   (Proc. 4733), **1980–81:** 457

Law Enforcement Assistance Administration, **1977:** 1079, 1085, 1712

   Administrator, **1978:** 1538, 1572; **1979:** 268; **1980–81:** 288, 293

Law Enforcement Assistance — *continued*
 Associate Administrator, **1979:** 2183, 2207
 Deputy Administrators, **1978:** 1538, 1572
 Federal civil justice system, **1979:** 344
 Foreign intelligence activities, **1978:** 209
 Legislative proposals, **1979:** 131
 Miami, Fla., programs, **1980–81:** 1236
 Prison program funding, **1980–81:** 2283
 Reform legislation, **1980–81:** 154
 Reorganization, **1978:** 1241, 1246, 1280
 State of the Union, **1978:** 113
 Urban programs, **1978:** 592
 Vietnam-era veterans programs, **1978:** 1742
Law enforcement and crime
 Administration's accomplishments and goals,
  1979: 1859
 Civil disorders, **1977:** 346
 Criminal justice system, **1978:** 837, 838, 841, 873
 Detroit, Mich., public policy forum, **1977:** 1835
 Electronic surveillance, **1977:** 928
 Federal criminal code, **1979:** 146; **1980–81:** 156,
  2969
 Federal justice system, **1977:** 1498
 Federal reorganization, **1978:** 1241, 1246, 1280
 Institutionalized persons civil rights, **1980–81:**
  965
 International, **1977:** 825, 826, 834
 Juvenile Justice Amendments of 1977, **1977:**
  1711
 Organized crime, **1977:** 504
 Prison sentences, **1977:** 156, 234
 State attorneys general, district attorneys, and
  police chiefs, White House reception,
  1980–81: 412
 State of the Union, **1978:** 112
 Urban programs, **1978:** 592
 White-collar crime, **1977:** 504
 Wiretapping and electronic surveillance, **1979:**
  587
Law Enforcement and Criminal Justice, National
 Institute for, **1978:** 1249
Law of the Sea Conference, **1980–81:** 1284, 2073
 Deputy Special Representative, **1977:** 1667, 1795,
  1826
 Special Representative, **1977:** 17, 252
Lawing, Karlin, **1977:** 1055
Lawrence, Jacob, **1978:** 252, 277; **1977:** 1118, 2024,
  2037; **1980–81:** 602, 1609
Lawrence, Loren E., **1979:** 220, 241
Lawson, A. E., **1978:** 971, 1010
Lawson, Louise Quarles, **1980–81:** 305
Lawson, Marjorie M., **1979:** 24, 1921
Lawson, Russell, **1977:** 317
Lawson, William, **1979:** 974
Lawton, Okla., **1979:** 1817
Lawyers' Committee for Civil Rights Under Law,
 1978: 1149

Lax, Peter David, **1980–81:** 1149, 1246
Laxalt, Sen. Paul, **1979:** 2271; **1980–81:** 1013, 1509
Lazarow, Joseph, **1978:** 1543
Lazarus, Emma, **1979:** 1409
Lazarus, Ralph, **1978:** 455
Le Carpentier, Jean Louis, **1978:** 30
Le Melle, Wilbert John, **1977:** 576, 597
Leach, Daniel E., **1977:** 1473; **1979:** 1259, 1293
Lead products, **1980–81:** 1723, 3000
Leadership Conference on Civil Rights, **1980–81:**
 221, 720
Leadership qualities, President's, **1979:** 2033, 2053
League.
 See also other part of title.
League of Conservation Voters, **1978:** 302
League of Postmasters, **1977:** 1084
League of Women Voters of the United States,
  1979: 771
Leahy, Sen. Patrick J., **1977:** 784, 1632, 2105; **1978:**
  1696, 1808, 2003; **1979:** 1143, 2042, 2275,
  2280; **1980–81:** 1918, 1936
Learning Day, Salute to, **1980–81:** 841
Leath, Repr. Marvin, **1980–81:** 2413
Leather wearing apparel industry, **1980–81:** 531,
  532
Lebanon
 Ambassador to U.S., **1978:** 795, 2059
 Camp David summit meeting, **1978:** 1526, 1537
 Conflict in, **1978:** 1239, 1678, 1687, 1688
 Foreign Minister, **1977:** 1730, 1754
 News conference remarks, **1978:** 1658
 Palestinian terrorists, **1980–81:** 390
 Relationship with Israel, **1979:** 1857
 United Nations role, **1980–81:** 1286
 U.S. Ambassador, **1977:** 81, 87; **1978:** 1513, 1572
Leber, George, **1977:** 464
Lebron, Lolita, **1979:** 1597
Lecht, Daniel, **1979:** 465
LeCuyer, Jack A., **1977:** 987
Ledbetter, Brownie, **1978:** 1134
Leddy, Thomas B. C., **1977:** 1025, 1031
Lederberg, Joshua, **1979:** 2196
Lederberg, Victoria, **1979:** 1525
Lederman, Leon M., **1979:** 448
Lee, Bert D., **1980–81:** 1595, 1599
Lee, Acting Gov. Blair, III, **1978:** 1057, 1795
Lee, Edward M., **1980–81:** 1570
Lee, Eileen Meany, **1980–81:** 1609
Lee, Eugene H., **1980–81:** 927
Lee, Frances Snow, **1980–81:** 1445
Lee, Jimmy, **1978:** 2036
Lee, Linda J., **1979:** 827
Lee, Myrra Lenore, **1977:** 477
Lee, Robert E., **1980–81:** 864
Lee, Shepard, **1978:** 1836
Lee, W. Spencer, **1977:** 816; **1979:** 1592
Lee Kuan Yew, **1977:** 1699, 1754, 1756

Leeke, William Dent, **1980–81:** 2613
Leet, Mildred Robbins, **1980–81:** 1946
Leetown, W. Va., **1979:** 1042
Leffall, Lasale D., Jr., **1980–81:** 911
Leffall, Ruth McWilliams, **1979:** 465
LeFlore, Ron, **1978:** 1193
Legal Council, Federal, **1979:** 1264–1266
Legal Defense Fund, **1977:** 942
Legal Education Institute, **1979:** 1267
Legal Services Corporation, **1977:** 1409, 2101, 2130; **1979:** 46, 91, 92; **1980–81:** 1149, 1246
   Appropriations, **1978:** 839
   Board of Directors, members, **1978:** 88, 232, 1753, 1772
Legal system, President's assessment of, **1978:** 835–841, 856, 857, 864
Leggett, Isiah, **1978:** 1026
Leggett, Repr. Robert L., **1978:** 2003
Legionville National Historic Site, **1978:** 1926
Legislative, and Judicial Salaries, Commission on Executive, **1980–81:** 1412, 2867
Legislative vetoes, **1978:** 1146, 1155
LeGrand, Keech, **1979:** 473ftn., 1574
Lehman, Justus F., **1980–81:** 3026
Lehman, Repr. William, **1977:** 194; **1978:** 1866; **1980–81:** 823, 1362
Leif Ericson Society International, **1979:** 1824
Leif Erikson Day, **1977:** 1647; **1978:** 1497
   (Proc. 4677), **1979:** 1527
   (Proc. 4777), **1980–81:** 1509
Leighton, David Trent, **1977:** 2070, 2071
Leinsdorf, Erich, **1980–81:** 1440, 1470
Leiter, Avi, **1980–81:** 2311, 2539
Leith, Emmett Norman, **1979:** 2289; **1980–81:** 82n.
Leland, Repr. Mickey, **1980–81:** 1469
LeMelle, Wilbert John, **1980–81:** 355
Lemle, J. Stuart, **1977:** 987
Lemmond, William Park, Jr., **1980–81:** 757
Lena, Sam, **1979:** 947
Lenihan, Brian, **1980–81:** 500
Lennon, John, **1980–81:** 2788
Leogh, Dennis, **1977:** 34
Leon Bejarano, Armando, **1979:** 281n.
Leonard, James F., Jr., **1977:** 505, 510, 1625, 1650; **1978:** 919, 935, 1509, 1516; **1979:** 852, 1706
Leonard, Rodney E., **1978:** 2280
Leonard, Walter J., **1979:** 730
Leone, Antoinette L., **1980–81:** 814
Leone, Giovanni, **1978:** 515
Leone, Richard C., **1979:** 2027, 2154
Lerman, Miles, **1978:** 1974; **1980–81:** 822
Lerner, Gerda, **1980–81:** 412
Lerner, Louis A., **1977:** 1206, 1213; **1980–81:** 333, 1438n.
Lerner, Mrs. Louis A., **1980–81:** 333

Lesher, Richard L., **1977:** 1048; **1979:** 548n.
Leslie, John Oliver, **1980–81:** 2614
Lesotho
   Ambassador to U.S., **1977:** 195, 714, 745; **1979:** 554, 1446, 1455; **1980–81:** 775
L'Esperance, Francis A., **1978:** 325
Leszkiewicz, Ted, **1978:** 1879
Letters, Messages, Telegrams
   Air service with China and United Kingdom, letter to Civil Aeronautics Board Chairman, **1980–81:** 2651
   Air services with United Kingdom, letter to Civil Aeronautics Board Chairman, **1977:** 1365; **1978:** 471
   Alaska natural gas transportation system, letter to Prime Minister Pierre Elliott Trudeau of Canada, **1980–81:** 1367
   Albert Einstein Centennial, message, **1979:** 390
   Aliens, undocumented, letter to State Governors, **1979:** 806
   American Embassy fire in Moscow, message to Ambassador Toon, **1977:** 1519
   Anhydrous ammonia industry, letter to USITC Chairman, **1980–81:** 102
   Anti-inflation program, letter to heads of Nation's 500 largest corporations, **1978:** 2054
   Apollo 11 anniversary, message, **1979:** 1259
   Armed Forces benefits, letter to Defense Secretary, **1980–81:** 969
   Atlantic Treaty Organization, letter to President Mommer, **1977:** 1520
   Automobile industry, letter to United States International Trade Commission Chairman, **1980–81:** 1330
   Better Hearing and Speech Month, messages, **1977:** 743; **1978:** 822
   Bolt, nut, and large screw industry, letter to Secretary of the Treasury, **1978:** 300
   Camp David summit meeting agreements
      Israeli approval, letter to Prime Minister Begin, **1978:** 1651
      Letters accompanying documents, **1978:** 1566
   Campobello Conference on Peace and Human Rights, message accepting human rights award medal, **1979:** 1521
   China, People's Republic of-U.S. relations, New Year's messages, **1979:** 2
   Chinese New Year, messages, **1978:** 257; **1979:** 109
   Christmas, messages, **1977:** 2171; **1978:** 2274
   Civil Rights, Commission on, message on 20th anniversary, **1977:** 1629
   Coal industry labor dispute, letter to Attorney General, **1978:** 488
   Conflict of interest and financial guidelines exceptions, letters to Navy Secretary-designate and Deputy Secretary of Defense-designate, **1977:** 124

Letters, Messages, Telegrams — *continued*
  Country Music Month, messages, **1977:** 1679;
      1978: 1653; **1979:** 1728; **1980–81:** 1927
  Daniel "Chappie" James, Jr., Airmen and In-
      dustrial Museum, telegram to Charles
      Wallace, **1977:** 1485
  Democratic National Committee, telegram to
      members on recommendation for chair-
      man, **1977:** 2179
  Dominican Embassy in Bogota, Colombia, re-
      lease of hostages
    Letter to Colombian President, **1980–81:** 780
    Letter to U.S. Ambassador, **1980–81:** 781
  Earthquake in southern Italy, message to Pres-
      ident Alessandro Pertini, **1980–81:** 2746
  Eisenhower Battle Group return to U.S., mes-
      sage to officers and men, **1980–81:** 2827
  Emergency assistance to Romania, letter to Pres-
      ident Nicolae Ceausescu, **1977:** 327
  Energy conservation, community involvement,
      letter to city officials, **1979:** 1452
  Fair Housing Month, message, **1978:** 681
  Farm program, exchange of letters with Mrs.
      Eston Luke, **1977:** 2166
  Federal Trade Commission reauthorization leg-
      islation, **1980–81:** 815
  Foreign-produced alcohol fuel, letter to Treasury
      Secretary, **1980–81:** 2560
  Germany, Federal Republic of, Basic Law, mes-
      sage to President Walter Scheel, **1979:** 927
  Government regulations, letter to heads of in-
      dependent regulatory agencies, **1978:** 563
  Grain industry labor dispute
    Telegram to Governors Al Quie of Minnesota
        and Arthur A. Link of North Dakota,
        1979: 1468
    Telegram to industry and union leaders, **1979:**
        1467
  Heat and drought conditions, telegram to Gov-
      ernors of affected States, **1980–81:** 1423
  Himalayan Mountains, American expedition,
      message to team members, **1978:** 1558
  Home heating oil, telegrams to heads of major
      oil companies, **1979:** 1613
  Id al-Fitr, message, **1979:** 1518; **1980–81:** 1527
  Independence Day, message, **1979:** 1127; **1980–
      81:** 1125
  International Printing Week, message, **1978:** 54
  Iran, rescue attempt of American hostages, me-
      morial service message for eight service-
      men, **1980–81:** 779
  Jewish High Holy Days, messages, **1977:** 1476;
      1979: 1627; **1980–81:** 1644
  Kidnaping of Aldo Moro, letter to Italian Pres-
      ident Leone, **1978:** 515
  King, Martin Luther, Jr., birthday
    Messages, **1979:** 22; **1980–81:** 61
    Letter to Coretta Scott King, **1978:** 64

Letters, Messages, Telegrams — *continued*
  Korea, Republic of, death of President Park
      Chung Hee, letter to acting President
      Choi Kyu Ha, **1979:** 2054
  Korean and East Asian issues, questions and
      answers for Orient Press, **1979:** 1151
  Labor Day, messages, **1977:** 1530; **1978:** 1483;
      1980–81: 1474
  Meir, Golda, letter to former Israeli Prime Min-
      ister, **1978:** 543
  Metropolitan Opera labor dispute, telegram to
      principal parties, **1980–81:** 2017
  Mississippi disaster emergency, telegrams to
      Gov. Finch and Mayor Danks of Jack-
      son, **1979:** 670, 672
  Monnet, Jean, letter on 90th birthday, **1978:**
      1985
  National Afro-American (Black) History Month,
      messages, **1978:** 224; **1980–81:** 85
  National Architectural Barrier Awareness Week,
      letter to members of National Association
      of Theater Owners, **1978:** 933
  National Brotherhood Week, messages, **1978:**
      326; **1980–81:** 343
  National Newspaper Week, messages, **1979:**
      1807; **1980–81:** 2188
  National Nursing Home Week, messages, **1978:**
      823; **1979:** 549; **1980–81:** 604
  Natural gas emergency, telegram to Governors
      of 12 States, **1977:** 37
  Neave, Airey, death, message to British Prime
      Minister Callaghan, **1979:** 567
  Newspaper Carrier Day, message, **1980–81:** 2188
  1978 Nobel Peace Prize, message to President
      Sadat of Egypt and Prime Minister Begin
      of Israel, **1978:** 1877
  Nobel Prizes, 1979, messages to winners, **1979:**
      1962, 1963
  Nomination withdrawals
    Civil Aeronautics Board, Vice Chairman,
        1977: 1714
    Federal Bureau of Investigation, Director,
        1977: 2087
  Olympics, 1980 Summer, U.S. Olympic Com-
      mittee President
    Letter, **1980–81:** 106
    Mailgram, **1980–81:** 616
  Pan American World Airways-National Airlines
      Merger, letter to Civil Aeronautics Board
      Chairman, **1979:** 2283
  Pope John Paul I, message, **1978:** 1478
  Presidential campaign debates, letter to National
      Press Club board of directors chairman,
      1980–81: 1576
  Presidential Scholars, mailgram, **1977:** 725;
      1978: 763
  Reagan, Ronald, telegram following Republican
      Presidential nomination, **1980–81:** 1347

[References are to page numbers except as otherwise indicated]

Letters, Messages, Telegrams — *continued*
St. Patrick's Day, messages, **1977:** 402; **1978:** 516; **1979:** 432
Secretary of Energy, letter to Sen. Dennis DeConcini, **1979:** 432
Service Corps of Retired Executives, 15th anniversary message, **1979:** 1816
Skylab, message to Australian Prime Minister Fraser, **1979:** 1231
Small businesses and regulatory programs, letter to heads of regulatory agencies, **1979:** 2143
Stewart, Bill, telegram to American Broadcasting Company, **1979:** 1158
Sugar industry and imports, letter to Secretary of Agriculture, **1977:** 799
Terrorist attack in Israel, letter to Israeli Prime Minister Begin, **1978:** 505
Thirtieth World Health Assembly, message, **1977:** 839
Thomas Edison and the Centennial of Light, message, **1979:** 197
Transatlantic air fares, letter to Civil Aeronautics Board Chairman, **1977:** 1669
Transatlantic balloon crossing, telegram to Ben Abruzzo, Max Anderson, and Larry Newman **1978:** 1449
Trident I missile sale to United Kingdom, exchange of letters with Prime Minister Margaret Thatcher, **1980–81:** 1343
Tris in sleepwear, Government ban, letter to Small Business Administrator, **1978:** 1977
Truckers' strikes, independent, letter to State Governors, **1979:** 1138
United States Military Academy Board of Visitors, letter to chairman, **1977:** 1397
United States Naval Academy Board of Visitors, letter to chairman, **1977:** 1432
Wichita Falls, Tex., tornado disaster, telegram to Mayor Hill, **1979:** 665
Yugoslavia, earthquake, letter to President Tito, **1979:** 669
See also Congress, Communications to; Resignations and Retirements.
Letters to Members of Congress.
See under Congress, Communications to.
Leval, Pierre N., **1977:** 1826, 1827
Levenson, Frances, **1979:** 1220, 1223
Levesque, Anna Doyle, **1979:** 340, 377
Levi, Arrigo, **1980–81:** 1102
Levi, Edward H., **1978:** 1854
Levi Strauss Co., **1980–81:** 1444
Levin, Betsy, **1978:** 896, 935; **1980–81:** 315
Levin, Carl, **1978:** 1932, 1933, 2268
Levin, Sen. Carl, **1979:** 1777
Frances Perkins Building dedication ceremony attendance, **1980–81:** 631n.

Levin, Sen. Carl — *continued*
Legislation passage leadership
Alaska lands, **1980–81:** 1548
Chrysler Corporation Loan Guarantee Act of 1979, **1980–81:** 27, 30
Michigan army missile plant conveyance, **1980–81:** 769, 770
Small business, **1980–81:** 2381
Mention, **1980–81:** 1658
Levin, Sander Martin, **1977:** 804, 807
Levinson, David, **1980–81:** 1405
Levis, Ray Marie, **1980–81:** 2817
Levitan, Sar A., **1977:** 1175, 1212
Levitas, Repr. Elliott H., **1977:** 1134, 1210; **1978:** 1425; **1979:** 33n.
Levitt, Arthur, Jr.
See Chairman *under* White House Conference on Small Business.
Levy, Elizabeth A., **1980–81:** 926
Lewis, Carolyn, **1979:** 856
Lewis, Claude, **1978:** 688
Lewis, Franklin L., **1979:** 1439
Lewis, Gabriel, **1977:** 1383; **1978:** 759; **1979:** 837
Lewis, Capt. Harold, **1980–81:** 780n., 849, 864
Lewis, Helen A., **1980–81:** 19
Lewis, Jean P., **1977:** 933, 943
Lewis, Jerry, **1978:** 1221
Lewis, John, **1979:** 912
Lewis, John P., **1979:** 224, 241
Lewis, John R., **1977:** 1243, 1266
Lewis, Paul, **1978:** 1974
Lewis, Robert E., **1978:** 1955
Lewis, Ronald B., **1980–81:** 1146, 2801
Lewis, Rufus A., **1977:** 1755
Lewis, Samuel W., **1977:** 576, 579, 597, 1283; **1978:** 1158, 2268; **1980–81:** 930
Lewis, Mrs. Samuel W., **1978:** 2268
Lewis, Sir William Arthur, **1979:** 1963, 2160
Lewis, William Walker, **1979:** 1654, 1883
Leyland, Mary F., **1977:** 1243, 1266
Lezak, Sidney I., **1978:** 881, 882
Li Xiang, **1979:** 2005
Liang, Louis L., **1977:** 987
Libassi, Frank Peter S., **1977:** 369, 373
Liberia
Ambassador to U.S., **1978:** 1117; **1980–81:** 268
President's visit, **1978:** 416, 417, 671, 675, 709
President William R. Tolbert, Jr., **1979:** 1806; **1980–81:** 373
Trade with U.S., **1979:** 2255
U.S. Ambassador, **1979:** 579, 619
Liberian Relations, President's Commission on United States-, **1980–81:** 372, 373, 503, 2850
Libertarian Party, **1980–81:** 1636
Libraries and Information Science, National Commission on, **1978:** 919, 935, 1454, 1458;

Libraries — *continued*
    1979: 196, 218, 2277, 2281; **1980–81:**
       1445, 1470, 1933
Libraries and information services, **1980–81:** 1930
Libraries and Information Services, White House
    Conference on, **1979:** 400, 746, 2129;
    1980–81: 1930
Libraries and library sciences, **1979:** 2129
Library Association, International Federation of,
    1980–81: 1933
Library of Congress, **1977:** 1235; **1979:** 2130, 2145;
    1980–81: 1047, 1933, 2883
Library of Medicine, National, **1977:** 196
Libya.
    Carter, Billy, activities with.
       See under Carter, Billy.
    Col. Mu'ammar al-Qadhafi, **1980–81:** 1479, 1484
    Diplomatic Mission in Washington, D.C., **1980–**
       81: 1429
    Oil exports to U.S., **1980–81:** 1681
    U.S. export controls, **1979:** 2291, 2294
    U.S. policy, **1980–81:** 1477
Lichtenstein, Roy, **1977:** 1117
Liddy, G. Gordon, **1977:** 609, 1914
Liepold, Nathan, **1979:** 2076
Lievano Aguirre, Indalecio, **1978:** 1146
Light, Ed, **1977:** 403
Lighting restrictions, advertising, **1979:** 370
Limbs, Lee A., Jr., **1977:** 1086
Lin Zheng, **1980–81:** 1788, 1790–1793
Linakis, Yorka C., **1980–81:** 218
Limited Test Ban Treaty, **1979:** 1038
Lincoln, Abraham, **1980–81:** 851, 890, 1121, 1383,
    2060
    Mention, **1979:** 908
    National Academy of Sciences establishment,
       1979: 677
    Quoted, **1979:** 728, 1806, 2194
Lincoln Heights, Ohio, **1979:** 1817
Lincoln Land Community College, **1980–81:** 1862,
    1947
Lindbergh, Charles A., **1977:** 939
Linden, Henry, **1979:** 1534, 1536
Lindenbaum, Abraham M., **1978:** 696
Linder, Rev. Eileen W., **1978:** 1190
Linder, P. Scott, **1979:** 942
Linder, Robert D., **1977:** 273, 512
Lindley, Elizabeth A., **1980–81:** 926
Linehan, John A., **1977:** 986, 1030
Link, Gov. Arthur, **1977:** 595; **1979:** 1452, 1468;
    1980–81: 1372
Linowes, David, **1979:** 619
Linowitz, Sol M., **1977:** 101, 148, 279, 1383, 1463–
    1465, 1483, 1493, 1525, 1544, 1796, 1844;
    1978: 1511, 1712, 1725
    See also Middle East, Egyptian-Israeli peace
       negotiations, Personal Representative of

Linowitz, Sol M. — *continued*
    See also — *continued*
       the President; Presidential Commission
       on World Hunger, Chairman.
Linton, Ron M., **1979:** 465
Lions International, **1977:** 1161; **1978:** 503; **1979:**
    240, 1178
Lipman, Walter, **1977:** 320
Lippmann, Walter, **1980–81:** 200, 1298
Lippold, Herbert R., Jr., **1980–81:** 1432, 1470
Lipshutz, Robert J., **1977:** 148, 279, 346, 347, 1265,
    1480, 1533, 1642, 1649; **1978:** 65, 749,
    802; **1979:** 1159, 1422, 1823, 1825
Lipton, John M., **1979:** 1448
Lissit, Robert, **1978:** 786
List, Gov. Robert, **1980–81:** 303, 422, 606, 904
Literacy Day, International, **1978:** 1461
Lithuania, embargo regulations, **1979:** 1657
Litt, David G., **1980–81:** 928
Littell, Franklin, **1978:** 1974; **1980–81:** 822
Little, John Russell, Jr., **1978:** 1466
Litvack, Sanford M., **1979:** 2175, 2188
Livable Cities and Neighborhood Self-Help De-
    velopment programs, **1979:** 136
Livable Cities program, **1978:** 1010
Livestock industry, feed assistance, **1977:** 251, 487
Lizarraga, David C., **1977:** 2153; **1979:** 401
Llado, Jose, **1980–81:** 1244
Llado y Fernandez-Urrutia, José, **1978:** 1380
Llewellyn, J. Bruce, **1978:** 1701, 1724; **1979:** 1786
Lloyd, Frank, **1977:** 1756
Lloyd, Jack, **1977:** 404
Lloyd, Repr. James F., **1977:** 1211
Lloyd, Repr. Marilyn, **1978:** 526
Lloyd, Melinda L., **1979:** 976
Load Lines, 1966, International Convention on,
    1979: 1954
Lobby law reform, **1979:** 129
Lobbying reform, **1978:** 110, 781, 784, 838, 1079
Lockard, Frank R., **1978:** 1986
Loehr, Al G., **1978:** 1341
Lof, George, **1978:** 826
Loff, Deborah, **1980–81:** 291
Loftus, Bud and Margaret, **1980–81:** 2080
Logan, James K., **1977:** 1967
Logue, Frank, **1978:** 1974
Lohfeldt, Heinz, **1978:** 1272
Lomax, Charles, **1979:** 293
Loncar, Budimir, **1979:** 2162n.; **1980–81:** 892
Long, Beverly, **1977:** 530
Long, Repr. Clarence, **1979:** 2085
Long, Repr. Gillis W., **1979:** 942, 1143
Long, Sen. Russell B., **1977:** 464, 650, 706, 962,
    1335, 1339, 1371, 1437, 1448, 1449, 1583,
    1612, 1789, 1825, 1942, 2000, 2016, 2057,
    2064, 2154, 2155, 2157; **1978:** 148, 311,
    432, 503, 504, 512, 720, 934, 1154, 1349,
    1674, 1772, 1827, 1980

Long, Sen. Russell B. — *continued*
  Campaign appearance with the President, **1980–81:** 2401
  Legislation passage leadership
    Adoption Assistance and Child Welfare Act, **1980–81:** 1124
    Crude Oil Windfall Profit Tax Act, **1980–81:** 542, 580, 588
    Installment Sales Revision Act, **1980–81:** 2344
    Omnibus Reconciliation Act, **1980–81:** 2778
    Railroad deregulation, **1979:** 2185
    Social Security Disability Amendments, **1980–81:** 1063
    Staggers Rail Act, **1980–81:** 584, 2226, 2230
    Trade Agreements Act, **1979:** 1312, 1313
  Meetings with the President (Digest), **1979:** 217, 1017
  Mention, **1979:** 1609
  National health plan legislation support, **1979:** 1011, 1026, 1411, 1634, 1637
Long Beach, Calif., **1980–81:** 1877
Long Island Rail Road, N.Y., **1979:** 2246, 2247, 2250; **1980–81:** 103, 104, 668
Long-Term Defense program, **1978:** 1020, 1021, 1025; **1979:** 156, 1629, 2268
Longfellow, Henry, **1979:** 2278
Longley, Gov. James B., **1978:** 1506
Longo, Pietro, **1980–81:** 1241
Longworth, Alice Roosevelt, **1980–81:** 362
Looe Key National Marine Sanctuary, Fla., **1980–81:** 2997
Loomis, Philip A., Jr., **1979:** 1022, 1398
Lopez, Alfredo, **1979:** 837
López, Bernard B., **1979:** 45, 92
Lopez, Franklin Delano, **1977:** 1127; **1979:** 401, 1664; **1980–81:** 305
Lopez, Jose A., **1979:** 899, 900
Lopez, Nancy, **1980–81:** 1405
Lopez, Raul A., **1977:** 1781, 1796
Lopez, Rose Marie, **1979:** 400
Lopez De Bird, Sandra, **1980–81:** 1713
Lopez-Doriga, Joaquin, **1979:** 252
Lopez Escobar, Mario Anibal, **1977:** 942
Lopez Guevara, Carlos Alfredo, **1979:** 377
Lopez Michelsen, Alfonso, **1977:** 1401, 1537, 1567; **1978:** 1119, 1122, 1123, 1600
López Portillo, Mrs. Carmen, **1979:** 281ftn.
López Portillo, José.
  See Mexico, President.
Lopez Valdez, Abelardo, **1978:** 1406
Lora Gonzales, Francisco Augusto, **1979:** 25
Loren, Sophia, **1980–81:** 267
Lorenz, John G., **1978:** 2274
Lorenz, Peter, **1978:** 1306
Loring Air Force Base, Maine, **1977:** 1935; **1978:** 355

Los Angeles, Calif., **1977:** 887, 895, 915, 1893; **1978:** 834, 841, 882; **1979:** 374, 809, 843, 875, 2206; **1980–81:** 1510, 1868, 1883, 1889
Los Angeles, U.S.S., **1977:** 1036–1037, 1059
Los Angeles Times, **1979:** 813; **1980–81:** 1469
Loughlin, Martin F., **1979:** 241, 242
Louisell, Brig. Gen. William Charles, **1980–81:** 2609
Louisiana
  Black leaders, meeting with the President, **1979:** 841
  Civic leaders, meeting with the President, **1978:** 1457
  Disaster assistance, **1980–81:** 1345, 1421
  Disaster declarations, **1977:** 805; **1978:** 898, 1571, 2187; **1979:** 787, 1785; **1980–81:** 65, 773, 967
  Gov. David C. Treen, **1980–81:** 1423n.
  Livestock feed assistance, **1977:** 251
  President's visit, **1980–81:** 2401
  U.S. attorneys, **1977:** 1222, 1266, 1569; **1978:** 66, 149; **1979:** 667, 668
  U.S. district judges, **1977:** 1307, 1967; **1978:** 231, 771, 803; **1979:** 957, 958, 1018, 1019, 1043, 1044, 1883; **1980–81:** 608
  U.S. marshal, **1978:** 329, 330; **1980–81:** 1292
Louisville, Ky., **1979:** 1337, 1398, 1570
Louisville Gas and Electric Company, **1979:** 1337, 1339n.
Louisville University basketball team, **1980–81:** 607
Loutfi, Ali, **1979:** 548n.
Love, Ruth B., **1977:** 530, 642; **1979:** 947
Love Canal chemical waste landfill, N.Y., accident, **1978:** 1405; **1979:** 1034, 1357
  Area residents, health effects on, **1980–81:** 1353
  Emergency declaration, **1980–81:** 967
  Environmental damage, **1980–81:** 352
  Federal assistance legislation, **1980–81:** 2001, 2054, 2430
  Federal Government response, **1980–81:** 158
  Mention, **1980–81:** 2381
Lovelace, Alan M., **1979:** 242
Lovins, Amory, **1977:** 1825
Low, Harry W., **1980–81:** 757
Low, James, **1980–81:** 1405
Low, James Patterson, **1979:** 976
Low, Stephen, **1979:** 1451, 1519
Low-Emission Vehicle Certification Board, **1980–81:** 483
Low-income energy assistance program, **1979:** 1639
Low-income persons.
  See Disadvantaged persons.
Lowe, Maj. Gen. Dewey K. K., **1978:** 409
Lowe, George H., **1978:** 771, 803
Lowe, Mary Johnson, **1978:** 898, 899
Lowe, Richard B., III, **1979:** 616, 667; **1980–81:** 1494, 1524

Lowell, Mass., **1979:** 1817
Lowell, Stanley, **1978:** 2269; **1980–81:** 1439n.
Lowell National Historical Park, Mass., **1978:** 1037
Lowen, Robert J., **1980–81:** 509
Lowenstein, Allard Kenneth, **1977:** 1252, 1266, 1626, 1650; **1980–81:** 495
Lowenstein, James G., **1977:** 873, 875, 883
Lowenthal, Abraham F., **1978:** 1406
Lower Wisconsin River, Wis., **1979:** 1813
Lowery, Joseph E., **1977:** 641
Lowinson, Joyce H., **1977:** 1963
Lowry, Peter M., **1980–81:** 1599
Loy, Frank E., **1980–81:** 217
Loyalty Day, **1977:** 486; **1978:** 793
	(Proc. 4657), **1979:** 662
	(Proc. 4734), **1980–81:** 457
Lubar, Sheldon B., **1979:** 230
Lubbers, Jan Hendrik, **1980–81:** 1598
Lubbers, William A., **1979:** 2166, 2300; **1980–81:** 217, 218
Lubensky, Earl H., **1977:** 1210
Lubick, Donald C., **1978:** 569, 641; **1979:** 733
Lucas, Aubrey, **1978:** 82, 84
Lucas, Larry, **1980–81:** 1946
Lucas, Sandra Kay, **1980–81:** 1432
Lucas, William, **1977:** 1103, 1128, 1264
Lucas, William S., **1980–81:** 926
Lucas Garcia, Gen. Fernando Romeo, **1978:** 1111
Lucey, Patrick J., **1977:** 589, 943; **1979:** 278, 574, 1472, 1846
Ludsin, Stephen, **1978:** 1974; **1980–81:** 822
Ludwig, Ruby B., **1979:** 446
Luehring, Dale W., **1979:** 2024
Luers, William H., **1978:** 1465, 1471
Lugar, Sen. Richard G., **1977:** 2181; **1978:** 1696; **1980–81:** 31, 2378
Lugovino, Francisco, **1980–81:** 2559
Luhrs, Caro M., **1980–81:** 1445, 1470
Luis, Gov. Juan F., **1978:** 1333
Lujan, Repr. Manuel, Jr., **1980–81:** 1835
Lukash, Dr. William M., **1978:** 276
Lukash, Rear Adm. William M., **1980–81:** 104
Luke, Mrs. Eston, **1977:** 2166
Luken, Repr. Thomas A., **1978:** 1668
Lukfata Lake, Okla., **1977:** 208
Lumber industry, **1978:** 725, 750, 806, 845, 846; **1979:** 1044; **1980–81:** 1144, 1145
Luna, Charles, **1977:** 1811, 1826; **1978:** 230; **1980–81:** 1969, 2070
Lunch Week, National School, **1978:** 1503
Lundine, Repr. Stanley N., **1980–81:** 2001, 2002
Lung, Heart, and Blood Institute, National, **1980–81:** 190
Luns, Joseph M. A. H., **1977:** 641, 642, 852; **1978:** 38, 1014, 1033; **1980–81:** 892
Lupus Week, National, **1977:** 1527; **1978:** 1456; **1980–81:** 2183
	(Proc. 4680), **1979:** 1620

Lusk, Robert F., **1979:** 465
Lutz, Genevieve Meany, **1980–81:** 1609
Lutz, Theodore C., **1979:** 1742, 1744, 2139
Luxembourg
	Prime Minister Gaston Thorn, **1977:** 882, 1754, 1789
	U.S. Ambassador, **1977:** 873, 876, 883
Lyall, Katherine, **1980–81:** 2560
Lydon, Christopher, **1979:** 1982
Lydon, Thomas E., Jr., **1977:** 557, 558
Lyet, J. Paul, **1979:** 942
Lykins, Billie, **1977:** 1163
Lyman, Ralph A., **1979:** 240
Lyman, S. C., **1980–81:** 1761
Lynch, Amos, **1978:** 1620
Lynch, John M., **1979:** 1976, 2093, 2095, 2097, 2098
Lyndhurst, N.J., **1980–81:** 2265
Lynn, Loretta, **1980–81:** 850, 2075
Lynn, Mass., **1978:** 1892, 1896
Lyons, Charles, **1980–81:** 1514
Lyons, Jack, **1980–81:** 1372
Lyons, John H., **1978:** 53; **1979:** 271, 1868, 1954
Lythcott, Dr. George I., **1977:** 806; **1978:** 318

Mabry, Guy O., **1979:** 44, 92
MacArthur, Gen. Douglas, **1979:** 1905; **1980–81:** 1604
Macchiarola, Frank J., **1979:** 1439
MacCready, Paul, **1979:** 2079
MacDonald, Donald G., **1977:** 1081, 1086
MacDonald, Peter, **1980–81:** 303
Machel, Samora Moises, **1977:** 1723, 1754, 1755; **1978:** 976
Machinery industry, **1980–81:** 1050
Machinists and Aerospace Workers, International Union of, **1978:** 229, 299
Mack, P. A., Jr., **1979:** 1041, 1044
MacLaughlin, Harry H., **1977:** 1438, 1439
MacLeish, Archibald, **1980–81:** 1438
MacNaughton, Donald S., **1977:** 988; **1979:** 23, 46, 90
MacNeil, Robert, **1977:** 2187
Macy, John W., Jr.
	See Federal Emergency Management Agency, Director.
Madagascar, U.S. Ambassador, **1980–81:** 1577, 1599
Madden, Eugene, Jr., **1978:** 1222, 1223
Madden, Mary Helen, **1978:** 1134
Madden, Thomas, **1978:** 1280
Maddox, Lester G., **1980–81:** 829
Madfa, Hamad Abdel Rahman al, **1977:** 822
Madigan, Repr. Edward R.
	Legislation passage leadership
		Northeast corridor rail system, **1980–81:** 1009

Madigan, Repr. Edward R. — *continued*
  Legislation leadership — *continued*
    Staggers Rail Act, **1980–81:** 1699, 2226, 2230
    Meeting with the President (Digest), **1980–81:** 1598
Madison, Dolley, **1979:** 2264
Madison, James, **1979:** 759
Madison, Tamara, **1980–81:** 1369
Maduff, Michael L., **1978:** 1879
Maestrone, Frank E., **1980–81:** 1547
Magazine Publishers Association, **1977:** 1087
Magistrate Act, Federal, **1979:** 1849
Magistrates Act of 1979, Federal, **1980–81:** 303
Magnetic Fusion Energy Engineering Act, **1980–81:** 2105
Magnus, Christopher J., **1980–81:** 3023
Magnuson, Anna, **1980–81:** 928
Magnuson, Catherine J., **1980–81:** 928
Magnuson, Sen. Warren G., **1977:** 1134, 1916; **1978:** 229, 315, 858, 860, 862, 1110; **1979:** 591n., 1435
  Campaign appearance with the President, **1980–81:** 2677
  Communication from the President, **1980–81:** 777
  Mount St. Helens, Wash., eruption, emergency funds decision, **1980–81:** 960
  National Aquaculture Act, passage leadership, **1980–81:** 1938
  President's assessment, **1980–81:** 1903, 1914
Magnuson Clinical Center, Warren Grant, **1980–81:** 2806
Maguire, Repr. Andrew, **1977:** 1930
Maguire, Archbishop John J., **1980–81:** 2309
Mahaffey, Maryann, **1980–81:** 1037n.
Mahan, Joseph B., Jr., **1978:** 1343
Maher, Robert W., **1979:** 377, 378, 842, 956
Mahler, Dr. Halfdon T., **1977:** 839, 2037
Mahmoud, Dr. Abdul Halim, **1977:** 2076
Mahon, Repr. George H., **1977:** 505, 1152, 1700, 1703, 1745, 1901; **1978:** 472, 1379
Mahoney, Florence, **1977:** 530
Mahoney, Margaret, **1977:** 528
Mahony, John A., **1979:** 2024
Mahre, Phil, **1980–81:** 380
Maier, Henry W., **1978:** 570, 641, 2269; **1979:** 402, 573, 1970; **1980–81:** 2560
Maine
  Democratic Party caucuses, **1980–81:** 295
  Disaster declaration, **1978:** 329
  Emergency declaration, **1980–81:** 1945
  Indian land claims, **1977:** 363, 1265, 1759, 1935; **1978:** 304, 337, 351, 356, 749, 850, 1076
  Potato growers, task force to consider Federal policies affecting, **1980–81:** 608
  President's visits, **1978:** 341, 344, 414, 1897
  U.S. attorney, **1977:** 597; **1980–81:** 375

Maine — *continued*
  U.S. district judge, **1979:** 1397, 1398; **1980–81:** 1599
  U.S. marshal, **1977:** 1650, 1651
  Water resources project, **1977:** 490
  White House briefing by administration officials for civic and community leaders (Digest), **1979:** 2186
Maine Indian Claims Settlement Act, **1980–81:** 2176, 2179, 2185
Majerus, Raymond E., **1978:** 1809
Makarios, Archbishop, III, **1977:** 144, 1409
Makela, Marcelyn, **1978:** 897
Malawi, U.S. Ambassador, **1978:** 1320, 1333; **1980–81:** 1860, 1946
Malaysia
  Natural rubber trade, **1980–81:** 592
  Prime Minister Datuk Hussein bin Onn, **1977:** 1612, 1699
  U.S. Ambassador, **1977:** 873, 876, 883; **1980–81:** 1334, 1336
Malchon, Jeanne, **1978:** 762
Malcolm, Benjamin J., **1977:** 1644, 1650
Maldives, U.S. Ambassador, **1977:** 1196, 1212; **1978:** 231; **1979:** 2097, 2107
Maldonado, Juan J., **1980–81:** 2610
Malek, Redha, **1979:** 2162n.
Mali
  Ambassador to U.S., **1978:** 2059
  U.S. Ambassador, **1979:** 1849, 1883
Mallory, William L., **1979:** 1776
Malmquist, Walter, **1980–81:** 380
Maloney, Thomas, **1977:** 1817; **1979:** 270
Malta
  Income tax treaty with U.S., **1980–81:** 756
  U.S. Ambassador, **1977:** 195, 714, 745; **1979:** 215, 241
Mambouka, Jean-Daniel, **1978:** 328
Management and Budget, Office of
  Acting Director, **1977:** 1649, 1698, 1700, 1706, 1754, 1794, 1825, 1930, 1963, 1966, 2005, 2036, 2037, 2050, 2059, 2076, 2088, 2089, 2113, 2129, 2162, 2176, 2223; **1978:** 125, 149, 229, 276, 302, 328, 414, 416, 457, 503, 509, 525
  Advisory committee review, **1977:** 1012, 1162
  Anti-inflation program, **1978:** 927, 1856
  Associate Directors, **1977:** 1162; **1979:** 378, 733, 2207
  Audiovisual activities, memorandum, **1977:** 1112; **1978:** 786
  Briefings for administration executives, **1977:** 604
  Budget spending estimates, evaluation, **1977:** 215
  Civil rights reorganization, **1978:** 416
  Computer systems, **1977:** 115
  Cuban and Haitian refugees assistance assessment, **1980–81:** 1075

Management and Budget, Office — *continued*
  Deputy Director, **1977:** 157, 371, 511, 689, 706,
      745, 805, 1482, 1665; **1978:** 225, 1665,
      1772, 1921; **1980–81:** 292, 293, 607, 774,
      1377
  Domestic assistance plans, review, **1977:** 1285
  Employee Retirement Income Security Act of
      1974, report preparation, **1980–81:** 295
  Energy security trust fund responsibilities, **1979:**
      727
  Executive Assistant for Budget, **1978:** 1596
  Executive Associate Directors, **1977:** 573, 943;
      1978: 1280, 1573, 2082–2084; **1980–81:** 25
  Export development programs, **1978:** 1632
  Federal civil service reform, **1978:** 2300
  Federal consumer programs, **1979:** 1761
  Federal energy use reduction monitoring, **1979:**
      647
  Federal facility ridesharing program, **1980–81:**
      271
  Federal grants-in-aid review, **1977:** 1560
  Federal information policy development, **1980–
      81:** 1932
  Federal personnel ceilings, **1979:** 925
  Federal Procurement Policy, Administrator,
      1977: 607, 642; **1980–81:** 371, 375
  Federal procurement policy monitoring, **1980–
      81:** 73
  Federal Regional Councils functions, **1979:** 1289
  Fraud and waste elimination in Government
      programs, **1978:** 2232, 2234
  Government contract decisions, **1979:** 922
  Government regulations, **1978:** 557
  Government reorganization, **1977:** 74, 129, 573,
      1193, 1211, 1258, 1495–1498, 1507, 1612
  Government travel costs, **1978:** 1483
  Independent water project review, **1979:** 9, 10
  Joint Financial Management Improvement Pro-
      gram, **1979:** 462
  Low-level radiation, research program funding,
      1979: 2007
  National climate program, **1978:** 1908
  National Productivity Council, **1978:** 1833, 1835,
      1836
  National water policy functions, **1978:** 1044,
      1046, 1047, 1050
  1980 fiscal budget preparation, **1979:** 95
  1981 budget revisions role, **1980–81:** 569
  Occupational safety and health programs for
      Federal employees, **1980–81:** 394
  Paperwork reduction, **1979:** 494, 2178, 2181,
      2182; **1980–81:** 2795
  Physicians comparability allowance, **1978:** 2301
  Pollution control standards, Federal compliance,
      1978: 1767, 1769
  President's Commission for a National Agenda
      for the Eighties, oversight responsibilities,
      1979: 2015

Management and Budget, Office — *continued*
  President's Reorganization Project, **1980–81:** 483
  Privacy Act of 1974, implementation, **1978:** 1481
  Privacy rights policy implementation, **1979:** 586
  Radiation effects review, **1980–81:** 364
  Regulatory management, **1978:** 1905
  Reorganization Plan No. 4 of 1978, **1978:** 1402,
      1405
  Small businesses and regulatory reform, imple-
      mentation of administration policy, **1979:**
      2142, 2143
  Space management, **1978:** 1431
  Statistical policy functions, **1977:** 1759
  Sunshine Act implementation, **1978:** 1068
  Telecommunications functions, **1978:** 254, 600–
      602, 604, 611
  Transfer of certain advisory committee func-
      tions, **1977:** 2067
  Transfer of certain executive development and
      other personnel functions, **1977:** 2080,
      2081
  United States International Development Co-
      operation Agency, budget submittal re-
      ception, **1979:** 395, 644, 646
  Urban and community impact analyses, **1978:**
      1433
  Urban programs, **1978:** 585
  Veterans' Federal Coordinating Committee,
      1978: 1743
  Water resource policy, **1977:** 207, 287, 490, 976
  Women's business enterprises, **1979:** 888
  Zero-base budgeting, **1977:** 105, 106, 207, 289,
      490, 976; **1978:** 753, 815
Management and Budget, Office of, Deputy Di-
      rector (John P. White)
  American Red Cross, Board of Governors mem-
      ber, **1979:** 376
  Meetings with the President (Digest), **1979:** 1142,
      1785
  News conferences (Checklist), **1979:** 294, 1019,
      1532
  Nomination, **1979:** 46, 89
Management and Budget, Office of, Director
      (Thomas Bertram Lance), **1977:** 10, 14,
      31, 36, 85, 154, 177, 248, 251, 252, 271,
      279, 287, 371, 378, 464, 508, 509, 532, 549,
      608, 641, 642, 705, 706, 712, 744, 745, 882,
      942, 1030, 1049, 1052, 1058, 1083, 1095,
      1127, 1162, 1193, 1211, 1221, 1254, 1265,
      1300, 1305, 1377, 1382, 1396, 1436, 1445,
      1471, 1480–1483, 1489–1494, 1506, 1512,
      1518, 1532, 1567, 1581, 1595, 1596, 1611,
      1616, 1617, 1635–1643, 1648, 1691, 1692,
      1698, 1699, 1761, 1771, 1966, 2102, 2104,
      2112, 2113, 2125, 2165; **1978:** 155, 156,
      158, 273, 406, 412–414, 568, 594–596, 607,
      710, 750, 769, 770, 880, 892, 897, 958,

Management and Budget, Director — *continued*
    1110, 1128, 1154, 1155, 1207, 1221, 1222,
    1345, 1380, 1405, 1407, 1573, 1668–1670,
    1723, 1725, 1765, 1772, 1807, 1878, 1954,
    1999, 2004, 2058, 2073, 2146, 2226, 2261,
    2270; **1979:** 968
For functions of the Office in general, see Man-
    agement and Budget, Office of.
Management and Budget, Office of, Director
    (James T. McIntyre, Jr.)
  Agricultural trade development functions,
    1980–81: 1238
  Alaska Natural Gas Transportation System,
    transfer of functions, **1979:** 597
  Black university program responsibilities, **1980–
    81:** 1518
  Budget message remarks, **1979:** 96
  Budget preparation
    1981, **1980–81:** 225, 226, 569, 608
    1982, **1980–81:** 2893
  Critical energy facility program establishment
    (EO 12129), **1979:** 614
  Economic growth policy for State and local
    governments, **1979:** 77, 80
  Economic Policy Group, member, **1979:** 917
  Education Department establishment, transfer
    functions, **1980–81:** 819
  Environmental damage response fund alloca-
    tions, **1980–81:** 3046
  Equal employment enforcement, transfer of
    functions (EO 12144), **1979:** 1141
  Federal civilian and military pay increases rec-
    ommendations, **1979:** 64, 1530; **1980–81:**
    468
  Federal emergency management functions, **1979:**
    566, 1278
  Federal Legal Council, member, **1979:** 1265
  Foreign assistance administration functions (EO
    12163), **1979:** 1793, 1794, 1797
  Interagency Employee Benefit Council, member,
    1980–81: 2864
  Juvenile delinquency programs implementation,
    1980–81: 1274
  Management improvement and waste and fraud
    elimination, **1979:** 779
  Meetings with the President (Digest), **1979:** 14,
    25, 89, 178, 217, 240, 241, 327, 376, 401,
    467, 553, 554, 618, 666, 732, 786, 841, 842,
    898, 955, 956, 1142, 1222, 1318, 1422,
    1454, 1678, 1705, 1785, 1975, 2043, 2081,
    2105, 2138, 2139, 2186, 2206, 2248, 2279,
    2280; **1980–81:** 24, 63, 103, 268, 374, 422,
    423, 492, 563, 607, 774, 825, 892, 966,
    1050, 1150, 1469, 1564, 1597, 1662, 1846,
    2782, 2822
  Mention, **1980–81:** 2654
  National trail designation, Federal agencies
    progress reports reception, **1979:** 1382

Management and Budget, Director — *continued*
  News conferences (Checklist), **1979:** 242, 378,
    1233, 1294; **1980–81:** 23, 64, 1429, 2071
  Paperwork reduction responsibilities, **1979:** 2180
  Peace Corps functions (EO 12137), **1979:** 881,
    882
  Pension plan functions (EO 12177), **1979:** 2219
  Petroleum and natural gas conservation respon-
    sibilities, **1979:** 2261
  Powerplant conversion and construction restric-
    tions responsibilities, **1980–81:** 1132
  Presidential Management Improvement Award
    presentation, **1980–81:** 1507
  President's Commission for a National Agenda
    for the Eighties, functions (EO 12168),
    1979: 2014
  President's Management Improvement Council,
    Cochairman, **1979:** 1668–1670
  Printing service functions (EO 12134), **1979:** 825
  Radiation Policy Council, activities appraisal,
    1980–81: 363
  Research Apprenticeship Program development,
    1979: 2064
  Task Force on Global Resources and Environ-
    ment, duties, **1980–81:** 1416
  Trade policy functions, **1980–81:** 6–8, 11
  Transfer of functions (EO 12152), **1979:** 1439
  Urban noise abatement program development,
    1979: 1385
For functions of the Office in general, see Man-
    agement and Budget, Office of.
Management Improvement Awards, Presidential,
    1977: 1818; **1980–81:** 18, 19, 1507
Management Improvement Council, President's,
    1979: 780, 1668–1670, 2154; **1980–81:**
    2850
Management Initiatives Program, Presidential,
    1977: 112
Management Intern Program, Presidential, **1977:**
    1498–1500, 1507
Manatos, Andrew E., **1977:** 2025, 2037
Manatos, Michael, **1980–81:** 218
Manatt, Charles T., **1980–81:** 1541, 2872
Manchester, N.H., **1979:** 713
Manes, Donald R., **1979:** 1760n.; **1980–81:** 2560
Manfredo, Fernando, **1979:** 2074
Manilow, Lewis, **1978:** 1720, 1772; **1979:** 729, 787
Manley, Joan D., **1980–81:** 272
Manley, Michael, **1977:** 1045, 2128; **1978:** 1119,
    1122, 1123
Mann, Carol, **1979:** 1678
Mann, David Emerson, **1977:** 472, 509
Mann, Repr. James R., **1978:** 394, 1855
Mann, Theodore, **1978:** 2269; **1979:** 1861; **1980–81:**
    1439n., 2372n., 2537
Manning, Bayless Andrew, **1980–81:** 2731
Manning, Frank, **1980–81:** 2243
Manoogian, Richard A., **1978:** 916, 1500

[References are to page numbers except as otherwise indicated]

Manpower Policy, National Commission on, **1978:** 391, 697

Mansfield, Harry D., **1977:** 1931, 1932

Mansfield, John Kenneth, **1978:** 760, 771

Mansfield, Michael J., **1977:** 86, 316, 489, 576, 597, 1030; **1978:**, 302, 504, 1879; **1979:** 316, 1155, 1162

Mansfield, Mrs. Michael J., **1979:** 1155

Manshel, Warren Demian, **1978:** 1008, 1010

Mantle, Mickey, **1980–81:** 2646

Manufacturers, National Association of, **1977:** 2036; **1979:** 957; **1980–81:** 292

Maoui, Abdelaziz, **1977:** 1163

Marane, A. Russell, **1980–81:** 752, 775

March of Dimes, **1980–81:** 645

March of Dimes Birth Defects Prevention Month, **1978:** 2273

March of Dimes Foundation, **1979:** 1410

March of Dimes Poster Child, **1978:** 2274; **1979:** 2248

Marcos, Ferdinand E., **1978:** 2257; **1980–81:** 720

Marcos, Imelda, **1977:** 1754

Marcus, Daniel, **1979:** 980, 984

Marcus, Edward L., **1978:** 1037, 1071; **1980–81:** 1926, 1947

Mardigan, Edward, **1980–81:** 1439n.

Marei, Sayed, **1978:** 1154

Mareschalchi, Antonello, **1980–81:** 682n.

Mariam, Lt. Gen. Mengistu Haile, **1978:** 414

Mariana Islands, Northern.
   See Northern Mariana Islands.

Marietta, Ga., **1977:** 2165

Marijuana, **1977:** 1400, 1404; **1978:** 804, 1329, 1779

Marine Corps, United States, **1978:** 697, 1507, 1929; **1979:** 671; **1980–81:** 350, 780n., 1710n., 1857

Marine Corps Memorial Commission, United States, **1980–81:** 483

Marine Living Resources, Convention on the Conservation of Arctic, **1980–81:** 2765

Marine Mammal Commission, **1979:** 2116

Marine Pollution, Convention on the Prevention of, **1979:** 224

Marine pollution protocol, **1977:** 1352

Marine protection and research legislation, **1980–81:** 1592

Marine Safety Information System, U.S., **1977:** 459

Marine sanctuaries, **1977:** 977

Marine Sanctuaries, National, **1980–81:** 2997

Marion, Ill., **1980–81:** 2202

Maritime Administration, **1980–81:** 1473, 2239

Maritime Commission, Federal, **1977:** 1358, 1384, 1437, 1683, 1701; **1978:** 299, 329, 564, 1211, 1222, 1962, 1963; **1979:** 338, 339, 1398; **1980–81:** 428, 452, 3045

Maritime Consultative Organization Convention, Intergovernmental, **1979:** 778; **1980–81:** 945

Maritime Day, National, **1977:** 640; **1978:** 515; **1979:** 606; **1980–81:** 469

Maritime industry.
   See Ships and shipping.

Maritime Satellite Organization, International, **1980–81:** 1707

Maritime Search and Rescue, 1979, International Convention on, **1980–81:** 946

Mark, Hans M., **1977:** 966, 1031; **1979:** 1127, 1142

Mark, Herman F., **1979:** 2289; **1980–81:** 82n.

Markey, Repr. Edward J., **1977:** 1930

Markle, Roger A., **1978:** 1269, 1279; **1980–81:** 1644

Markoe, Frank, Jr., **1977:** 2024, 2037; **1978:** 231

Marks, Al, **1978:** 1543

Marks, Edward, **1977:** 1398, 1438

Marks, Paul A., **1979:** 660

Marlin, Fred, **1979:** 676

Marmor, Theodore, **1980–81:** 264

Marotta, Vincent G., **1980–81:** 1005, 1718

Marquette University, Wis., **1979:** 572, 573

Marquez, Alfred C., **1980–81:** 1015, 1051

Marrero, Victor, **1979:** 2078, 2249; **1980–81:** 1460, 1941, 2877n.

Marrett, Cora B., **1979:** 661

Marsaro, Tom, **1979:** 1972

Marsey, Charles, **1978:** 2274

Marsh, Henry L., III, **1977:** 1243; **1980–81:** 1946

Marsh, Milan, **1977:** 1210

Marshall, Consuelo B., **1980–81:** 1151

Marshall, Danny Kevin, **1980–81:** 2883

Marshall, F. Ray.
   See Labor, Secretary of.

Marshall, Harry H., **1977:** 1755

Marshall, Mary A., **1978:** 702, 711; **1980–81:** 2534

Marshall, Ray.
   See Labor, Secretary of.

Marshall, Maj. Gen. Robert C., **1977:** 1375, 1384, 1462

Marshall, Thurgood, **1977:** 47; **1979:** 1393

Marshall Islands
   Disaster declarations (Digest), **1979:** 293, 2205
   Health care and environmental benefits monitoring, **1980–81:** 466
   Self-government agreement with U.S., **1980–81:** 2611

Marshals, U.S.
   See U.S. marshals *under* Appointments and Nominations.

Marston, Christine Pratt, **1979:** 1447

Marston, David W., **1978:** 57, 59, 61, 77, 150, 245, 246, 460, 497, 524

Martens, Patricia, **1980–81:** 19

Marthinsen, Charles E., **1980–81:** 718, 720

Martin, Arthur E., **1980–81:** 19

Martin, Boyce F., Jr., **1979:** 1018, 1019

Martin, Charles Arthur, **1978:** 1026

Martin, Edwin W., Jr., **1980–81:** 759, 841, 1052

Martin, Gordon A., Jr., **1978:** 2269; **1980–81:** 2613

Martin, Guy Richard, **1977:** 273, 280
Martin, John B., **1979:** 1682, 1706, 2214
Martin, John S., Jr., **1980–81:** 523, 564
Martin, Louis Emanuel, **1978:** 1407, 1682, 1719, 2288; **1979:** 39, 49, 886n., 2064; **1980–81:** 908, 1750ftn.
Martin, Red, **1977:** 917–920
Martin, Vernon, **1979:** 1853
Martin, W. F., **1979:** 1614n.
Martin Luther King, Jr., national historic site, **1980–81:** 2172, 2179, 2184
Martin Luther King, Jr. Center for Social Change, **1978:** 1702; **1979:** 33n.
Martin Luther King, Jr. Nonviolent Peace Award, **1979:** 27
Martindell, Anne Clark, **1977:** 78, 90; **1979:** 1040, 1043
Martinez, Arabella, **1977:** 253, 1844; **1979:** 1143
Martinez, Bennie A., **1977:** 1222, 1266
Martinez, Elena, **1980–81:** 814
Martinez, Vilma, **1977:** 78, 90
Martinsburg, W. Va., **1979:** 1232
Marty, Martin, **1980–81:** 264
Martz, Clyde O., **1980–81:** 718, 775
Marutani, William M., **1980–81:** 2871
Maryland
 Administration anti-inflation briefing for black ministers (Digest), **1980–81:** 825
 Democratic primary, **1980–81:** 934
 Disaster declaration, **1977:** 31; **1979:** 1679
 Energy emergency, **1978:** 471
 Gov. Harry Hughes, **1980–81:** 303
 Metrorail system, **1980–81:** 14, 18
 President's visits, **1978:** 1795; **1979:** 1406, 1975; **1980–81:** 1722n.
 State police department, **1980–81:** 403
 U.S. attorney, **1978:** 935, 936
 U.S. district judges, **1979:** 957, 958; **1980–81:** 1428, 1429
 U.S. marshal, **1980–81:** 269
 White House briefing on administration's programs for community and civic leaders (Digest), **1979:** 2081
Mashingaidze, Elleck K., **1980–81:** 1598
Mashpee, Mass., **1977:** 641
Mason, Barbara Roberts, **1979:** 1439
Mason, Christopher T., **1980–81:** 926
Mass transit, **1977:** 697, 908, 949
 Administration's accomplishments and goals, **1980–81:** 2950
 Budget allocations increase during administration, **1980–81:** 1082, 1673
 District of Columbia metro system, **1979:** 1922; **1980–81:** 13, 17
 Energy conservation measure, **1979:** 255, 613, 960, 1327, 1369, 1740
 Handicapped persons programs, **1980–81:** 810

Mass transit — *continued*
 Los Angeles system, **1979:** 875, 953, 1327
 Mention, **1980–81:** 555
 National system improvement
  Energy security trust fund allocations. *See under* Energy security trust fund.
  Federal assistance programs, **1979:** 1355, 1369, 1384, 1744, 1745; **1980–81:** 215, 909
  Mention, **1980–81:** 14, 1537
 Philadelphia, Pa., system, Federal grants for, **1980–81:** 726
 Reagan, Ronald, policy comparison with the President, **1980–81:** 2196
Massachusetts
 Democratic Party primary, **1980–81:** 399, 428
 Disaster declaration, **1978:** 303, 328, 334
 Emergency declaration, **1978:** 302
 Gov. Edward King, **1980–81:** 1549
 President's visits, **1977:** 382; **1978:** 1892, 1896; **1979:** 1979, 1982; **1980–81:** 1548, 1549, 2243–2251
 U.S. attorney, **1977:** 1266, 1307
 U.S. district judges, **1977:** 2050, 2051; **1978:** 231; **1979:** 179, 180
 U.S. marshal, **1977:** 1437, 1438
 White House briefing for civic and community leaders by administration officials (Digest), **1979:** 468
Massachusetts Institute of Technology, **1979:** 1326; **1980–81:** 664
Massell, Sam, **1980–81:** 1756
Massey, Alyne Queener, **1979:** 465
Massey, Walter E., **1978:** 1760, 1773; **1979:** 46, 92
Massillon, Ohio, **1980–81:** 1846
Masters, Billie Nave, **1978:** 1135
Masters, Edward E., **1977:** 1811, 1826
Masuck, Joan, **1977:** 78, 90
Masvidal, Paul, **1980–81:** 2560
Mather, Barbara, **1977:** 1053
Matheron, Richard C., **1979:** 2062, 2081
Matheson, Gov. Scott M., **1978:** 936, 2088; **1980–81:** 422
Mathias, Sen. Charles McC., Jr., **1977:** 784, 925, 1084, 1632, 2181; **1978:** 193, 549, 919, 935, 1695
 Legislation passage leadership
  Alaska National Interest Lands Conservation Act, **1980–81:** 1548
  Intelligence Authorization Act for Fiscal Year 1981, **1980–81:** 2233
  National Capital Transportation Amendments of 1979, **1980–81:** 15
  Vietnam veterans memorial, **1980–81:** 1268, 1270
Mathis, Repr. Dawson, **1977:** 1507
Matlock, Jack F., Jr., **1980–81:** 1926, 1947
Matsui, Bob, **1978:** 1947
Matsui, Repr. Robert T., **1980–81:** 962, 1455, 2226

Matsunaga, Sen. Spark M., **1977:** 1506; **1979:** 1155, 1217, 1219
    Asian/Pacific American Democratic Caucus dinner attendance, **1980–81:** 962
    Federal territorial policy development, **1980–81:** 318
    Legislation passage leadership
        Commission on Wartime Relocation and Internment of Civilians Act, **1980–81:** 1455, 1456
        Ocean Thermal Energy Conversion Research, Development, and Demonstration Act, **1980–81:** 1375
        Wind Energy Systems Act, **1980–81:** 1668
Matsunaga, Mrs. Spark M., **1979:** 1155, 1217
Matthews, Martha A., **1980–81:** 926
Mattison, Dorothy L., **1979:** 1525
Mattson, Gerald, **1979:** 1468n.
Mauksch, Ingeborg G., **1980–81:** 822
Maurer, Lucille, **1980–81:** 1432
Mauritania
    Ambassador to U.S., **1979:** 376; **1980–81:** 2751
    U.S. Ambassador, **1977:** 1792, 1796; **1980–81:** 1289
Mauritius, U.S. Ambassador, **1978:** 1711, 1724; **1980–81:** 364, 375
Mavrinack, Albert A., **1980–81:** 1439n.
Max, Peter, **1980–81:** 2069
Maxwell, Marcella, **1980–81:** 2751
Mayaguez, SS, incident, **1980–81:** 744
Mayer, Jean, **1978:** 1511
Mayer, Regina Meany, **1980–81:** 1609
Maynard, Libby, **1979:** 401
Maynes, C. William, **1977:** 8, 510; **1979:** 2085
Maynor, Dorothy, **1979:** 320
Mayo, Sgt. Joe C., **1980–81:** 780n., 864
Mayors, National Council of, **1978:** 229
Mayors, United States Conference of, **1977:** 1100; **1980–81:** 212, 1078, 1662
Mayors Conference, Democratic, **1978:** 570
Mays, Benjamin R., **1980–81:** 1514, 1517
    Living Legacy Award recipient, **1979:** 320
    Mentions, **1979:** 33n., 60
    Presidential Advisory Board on Ambassadorial Appointments, member, **1979:** 553
    President's assessment, **1979:** 1958
Mays, William O., **1977:** 2028
Mazewski, Aloysius A., **1978:** 1809; **1980–81:** 822, 1439n., 1851
Mazzei, Philip, **1980–81:** 1064
Mazzoli, Repr. Romano L., **1979:** 1339
Mazzone, A. David, **1977:** 2050, 2051; **1978:** 231
Mbogua, John Peter, **1977:** 508; **1980–81:** 355
McAdams, Francis H., **1978:** 795, 881
McAdams, Harry, **1977:** 31
McAfee, Jerry, **1979:** 1614n.
McAuliffe, Lt. Gen. Dennis P., **1978:** 1406, 1723; **1979:** 1333, 1786

McBee, Susanna B., 1157, 1159, 1319
McBride, Gerald, **1980–81:** 521
McBride, Lloyd, **1977:** 1541, 1796; **1978:** 762, 1544, 1545, 1725; **1979:** 661, 1705, 1954; **1980–81:** 1510, 1670, 2071, 2345
McBride, Thomas F., **1979:** 366, 377
McCain, Betty, **1978:** 1578
McCall, Cecil M., **1977:** 1644, 1650
McCall, H. Carl, **1979:** 2196; **1980–81:** 1860, 1946, 2070, 2726, 2727
McCall, Richard Lee, Jr., **1980–81:** 991, 1015
McCalpin, F. William, **1978:** 1753, 1772; **1979:** 46, 92
McCart, John A., **1979:** 1671
McCarthy, Eugene, 1968 election, **1980–81:** 732, 738, 2366, 2395, 2429, 2533, 2645, 2676, 2681
McCarthy, George D., **1977:** 1071, 1085
McCarthy, Leo, **1979:** 876, 1034
McCarthy, Leo T., **1978:** 53, 1949
McCarty, Virginia Dill, **1977:** 1031
McClaughry, John, **1977:** 2153
McCleary, Joel, **1977:** 86, 1612; **1978:** 156, 158
McClellan, Sen. John L., **1977:** 505, 924, 1152, 1745, 2053, 2129; **1978:** 837
McClelland, Col. Lester C., **1980–81:** 654
McClintock-Hernandez, Kenneth, **1978:** 1193
McClone, John, **1979:** 1822
McClory, Repr. Robert, **1977:** 927; **1978:** 1139, 1140; **1980–81:** 1455, 1456
McCloskey, Robert J., **1978:** 270, 303, 1381
McCloy, John J., **1979:** 1042, 1823
McClure, Dorothy Watson, **1979:** 465
McClure, Sen. James A., **1978:** 769, 1473, 1477; **1980–81:** 318
McColough, C. Peter, **1978:** 1502
McCone, John, **1979:** 1823
McConn, James, **1978:** 1165, 1173
McConnell, Barnett W., **1980–81:** 19
McConnell, Joseph H., **1980–81:** 1412
McCord, Larry R., **1977:** 2006, 2007
McCormack, John, **1980–81:** 501
McCormack, John William, **1980–81:** 2743
McCormack, Repr. Mike, **1977:** 1211; **1980–81:** 2106
McCormally, John, **1979:** 1508n.
McCormick, Brooks, **1978:** 1031
McCowen, Alec, **1978:** 2070; **1979:** 60
McCree, Wade H., Jr., **1977:** 155, 195, 254, 1345; **1978:** 322
McCullah, Grace D., **1980–81:** 2075
McCullough, David, **1978:** 262
McCullough, Glendon, **1977:** 877; **1978:** 1117, 1469
McCullough, John, **1980–81:** 2080
McCullough, Veronica J., **1980–81:** 928
McCurn, Neal P., **1979:** 1786, 1787
McDade, Clinton L., **1980–81:** 926

McDaniel, Gary L., **1979:** 868, 870
McDaniel, Virginia, **1979:** 870
McDermott, Albert L., **1980–81:** 1405
McDermott, James, **1980–81:** 1903, 1914, 2677
McDermott, James A., **1979:** 1525
McDevitt, Justin H., **1979:** 400
McDonagh, Robert, **1977:** 464
McDonald, Alden, **1980–81:** 2559
McDonald, Alice Coig, **1979:** 827; **1980–81:** 2753, 2870, 2872, 2873
McDonald, Alonzo L., Jr., **1977:** 1305, 1308
  Acting Special Representative for Trade Negotiations, nomination, **1979:** 1418
  Assistant to the President, nomination, **1979:** 1423
  Meetings with the President (Digest), **1979:** 1823, 2081, 2187, 2206; **1980–81:** 268, 292, 374, 423, 492, 607, 825, 1469, 1564, 2822
  Multilateral trade negotiations role, **1980–81:** 6
  News conference (Checklist), **1980–81:** 1429
  Trade Agreements Act, passage leadership, **1979:** 1808
McDonald, Charles R., **1979:** 1954
McDonald, Gabrielle K., **1977:** 816; **1978:** 1879; **1979:** 377, 378
McDonald, Marshall, **1980–81:** 1405
McDonald, Mary Jane, **1977:** 816
McDonald, Walter J., **1979:** 1000, 1018
McDonnel, Sanford Noyes, **1980–81:** 1405
McDonnell Douglas Aircraft, **1980–81:** 1403
McDougal, Myers Smith, **1980–81:** 2731
McDuffie, Rudolph, **1979:** 920, 927
McElligott, Joseph P., **1979:** 1727
McFadden, Frank H., Jr., **1980–81:** 926
McFarland, Robert H., **1978:** 1154, 1155
McGahn, Patrick T., Jr., **1979:** 2042
McGarigal, John T., **1980–81:** 1299n.
McGarry, John W., **1977:** 1665, 1700; **1978:** 703, 750, 1851; **1979:** 45, 90
McGee, Gale W., **1977:** 465; **1978:** 1516
McGee, James H., **1980–81:** 509
McGee, Thomas, **1980–81:** 292, 2247
McGee, Thomas W., **1978:** 1896
McGiffert, David E., **1977:** 247, 253, 1085; **1980–81:** 267
McGill, Dan M., **1978:** 1760
McGill, William J., **1979:** 200, 2014, 2044; **1980–81:** 2822, 2917, 2919
McGovern, Sen. George, **1977:** 706, 861, 864; **1978:** 919, 935; **1979:** 956; **1980–81:** 1548, 1920, 1921
McGowan, William L., **1980–81:** 2004, 2242
McGrail, William T., **1977:** 398
McGranahan, LeAnn J., **1980–81:** 509
McGrath, C. Peter, **1980–81:** 323
McGrath, Mike, **1977:** 301, 307
McGregor, Ian, **1978:** 1694

McGregor, Jack, **1980–81:** 1490
McGregor, Iowa, **1979:** 1473
McGrew, Jane, **1979:** 1221, 1223
McGuire, Alfred J., **1978:** 2036; **1980–81:** 260, 262, 1440, 1662
McGuire, Chester Crawford, Jr., **1977:** 506, 510
McGuire, Frank J., **1978:** 696
McGuire, John R., **1979:** 1044
McGuire, Willard, **1980–81:** 1296
McHenry, Donald F.
  See United Nations, U.S. Representative.
McIntosh, Capt. Lynn D., **1980–81:** 780n., 864
McIntyre, James T., Jr., **1977:** 157, 195, 372, 511, 596, 805, 1482, 1612, 1649, 1698, 1700, 1706, 1754, 1794, 1825, 1930, 1963, 1966, 2005, 2036, 2037, 2050, 2088, 2089, 2113, 2129, 2162, 2176, 2177, 2223; **1978:** 125, 149, 229, 276, 302, 328, 414, 416, 457, 503, 525, 568, 710, 748, 750, 769, 770, 815, 880, 897, 1110, 1128, 1154, 1155, 1221, 1222, 1345, 1380, 1405, 1407, 1573, 1668–1670, 1723, 1725, 1765, 1772, 1807, 1954, 2004, 2058, 2073, 2146, 2226, 2232, 2270
  See also Management and Budget, Office of, Director.
McIntyre, Maureen, **1980–81:** 273
McIntyre, Thomas J., **1979:** 699, 714, 715
McIntyre, Sen. Thomas J., **1978:** 364, 414, 421, 1237, 1278
McIsaac, George S., **1977:** 2062, 2077; **1978:** 231
McKay, Repr. Gunn, **1977:** 372; **1980–81:** 422
McKay, Monroe G., **1977:** 1967
McKee, Jean, **1979:** 1037, 1044
McKee, Vice Adm. Kinnaird, **1978:** 1057
McKelvey, Jean T., **1978:** 411; **1979:** 23; **1980–81:** 84
McKenna, Margaret, **1977:** 184; **1978:** 1652; **1980–81:** 493
McKenna, Robert J., **1980–81:** 2812
McKenzie, Floretta, **1977:** 1083
McKeown, Mary Margaret, **1980–81:** 949
McKernan, Donald L., **1978:** 217
McKevitt, James D., **1977:** 196
McKhann, Guy M., **1980–81:** 192
McKinley, Francis, **1980–81:** 849
McKinney, Alice Greene, **1979:** 465
McKinney, Robert H., **1977:** 1153, 1163, 2007; **1978:** 1058, 1072; **1979:** 990; **1980–81:** 912, 2560
McKinney, Repr. Stewart B., **1977:** 784, 1632; **1980–81:** 31
McKnew, Louis Bouscaren, **1980–81:** 3026
McKnight, Rev. Albert Joseph, **1979:** 1220, 1223
McLaughlin, Earle B., **1977:** 1266, 1307
McLaughlin, Peter J., **1978:** 711, 712
McLaurin, Philip W., **1979:** 1447
McLaurin, W. Philip, **1978:** 709

McLean, John J., Jr., **1977:** 1053
McLernon, James W., **1980–81:** 770, 771, 1670
McLin, C. J., Jr., **1980–81:** 2175
McLin, Rhine Lana, **1980–81:** 1023, 1051
McLoughlin, Joseph M., **1978:** 503
McManus, Lewis, **1977:** 403
McMillan, Bill, **1978:** 1082
McMillan, Capt. Charles T., II, **1980–81:** 780n., 864
McMillian, John G., **1977:** 1979
McMillian, Theodore, **1978:** 1381
McMullen, William Patrick, Jr., **1980–81:** 218
McMurtrie, Mrs. William Gerald, **1977:** 2183
McNamara, Margaret C., **1979:** 400; **1980–81:** 2925
McNamara, Robert S., **1977:** 641, 1671; **1978:** 1629; **1980–81:** 1973, 1974n.
McNaught, John J., **1979:** 179, 180
McNaughton, Donald S., **1977:** 509
McNeil, Francis J., **1980–81:** 900, 932
McNeil, Robert L., Jr., **1977:** 2183
McNichols, Robert J., **1979:** 2106, 2107
McNichols, William H., **1978:** 2080; **1979:** 328; **1980–81:** 808
McPhedran, Winifred, **1980–81:** 258
McPherson, Harry C., Jr., **1979:** 661
McPherson, Tom, **1978:** 1178
McPhetres, Agnes Manglona, **1980–81:** 344
McQuillen, William F., **1977:** 367, 465
McReal, Jerry J., **1977:** 196
McSweeney, Dorothy Pierce, **1979:** 465
McSweeney, William F., **1979:** 976
McWherter, Ned R., **1978:** 948, 1406; **1980–81:** 2122
Mead, Bill O., **1977:** 2183
Mead, Margaret, **1978:** 2036; **1979:** 87
Meade, Edward J., Jr., **1979:** 400
Meador, Daniel J., **1977:** 195; **1979:** 340–342
Meadows, Marion E., **1980–81:** 19
Meadows, Oliver E., **1978:** 2089
Mealey, Margaret J., **1977:** 526
Meals on Wheels
	Mention, **1980–81:** 2212
	1981 budget allocation, **1980–81:** 536, 540, 806, 836, 892, 998
Meals on Wheels Week, National, **1979:** 1693
Meany, George, **1977:** 31, 219, 508, 516, 595, 621, 629, 865, 1210, 1947, 1949, 1965; **1978:** 66, 236, 710, 802, 1344, 1591, 1912, 1989
	Civil rights award presentation, **1980–81:** 222
	Commemorative stamp ceremony, **1980–81:** 1608
	Death statement, **1980–81:** 56
	Mention, **1980–81:** 2766
	President's assessment, **1980–81:** 1362, 1648
	Proc. 4712, **1980–81:** 67
	Requiem Mass at St. Matthews Cathedral (Digest), **1980–81:** 103
	See also AFL-CIO, President.

Mears, Walter, **1980–81:** 1049
Meat, Arrangement Regarding Bovine, **1979:** 2253
Meat industry, **1980–81:** 10, 2467, 2753, 2801
	Imports, **1978:** 1236, 1988, 2009, 2011, 2212; **1979:** 336, 2299
	Prices, **1979:** 1572
Meatcutters, Amalgamated, **1979:** 1008
Medal of Freedom, Presidential, **1977:** 1215, 1228; **1979:** 87; **1980–81:** 751, 1057, 1598
Medal of Honor, Congressional, **1980–81:** 1379, 1708
Medal of Science, National, **1977:** 2044; **1980–81:** 80
Medberry, C. J., **1978:** 455
Medearis, Donald N., **1979:** 1264
Mediation Board, National, **1977:** 1293, 1307; **1978:** 1701, 1723; **1979:** 1319, 1696; **1980–81:** 103, 667, 1125, 1150
Mediation and Conciliation Service, Federal, **1977:** 616, 642; **1978:** 313; **1979:** 1452, 1467, 1468, 1609; **1980–81:** 2017
Mediation Medal, International, **1979:** 1454
Medic Alert program, **1978:** 612
Medic Alert Week, National, **1980–81:** 514
Medicaid and Medicare, **1977:** 75, 302, 1449, 1458, 2105; **1978:** 103
	Ball, Robert, transcript remarks, **1980–81:** 2615
	Child health program, **1979:** 117, 134, 862
	Consolidation under national health plan, **1979:** 1024
	Cost form regulations, **1979:** 2111
	Establishment, **1980–81:** 535
	Fiscal year 1982 budget allocations, **1980–81:** 2900
	Hospital costs coverage, **1979:** 838
	Infant mortality prevention program, **1980–81:** 3006
	Insurance program, **1980–81:** 1878
	Legislation, **1980–81:** 1063
	Mentally ill outpatient services, **1979:** 857
	Mentions, **1979:** 1028; **1980–81:** 1990
	1981 budget allocations, **1980–81:** 540, 555
	Older persons coverage, **1979:** 1029, 1633, 1635
	President's commitment to, **1980–81:** 1763
	Reagan, Ronald, position on, **1980–81:** 1994, 2007, 2142, 2149, 2159, 2161, 2166, 2197, 2225, 2244, 2271, 2274, 2282, 2296, 2308, 2348, 2361, 2390, 2398, 2403, 2409, 2412, 2414, 2419, 2456, 2496, 2526, 2531, 2543, 2556, 2577, 2582, 2585, 2605, 2625, 2636, 2662, 2667, 2673
Medical care.
	See Health and medical care.
Medical Center, National Naval, **1980–81:** 104
Medical information act, privacy of, proposed, **1979:** 583
Medical Science program, Japan-U.S. Cooperative, **1980–81:** 493

Medical Services, Interagency Committee on Emergency, **1979:** 2158; **1980–81:** 1936

Medical Services Week, Emergency, **1977:** 1974

Medicare-Medicaid Anti-Fraud and Abuse Amendments, **1977:** 1902

Medicare renal disease program, **1978:** 1086

Medicine, National Library of, **1977:** 196; **1978:** 275, 303

Medicine, 1979 Nobel Prize in, **1979:** 1962

Medicine and Biomedical and Behavioral Research, President's Commission for the Study of Ethical Problems in, **1979:** 1263, 1294; **1980–81:** 896, 1723

Medicine and Biomedical and Behavioral Research, President's Special Commission for the Study of Ethical Problems in, **1979:** 2260

Medicine and Dentistry of New Jersey, College of, **1977:** 1574

Medina, William A., **1977:** 600, 622, 712; **1980–81:** 1941

Meed, Benjamin, **1978:** 1974; **1980–81:** 822

Meeds, Repr. Lloyd, **1977:** 592, 593, 1427; **1978:** 1786

Meehan, Francis J., **1979:** 383, 402; **1980–81:** 1703

Meese, Edwin, **1980–81:** 2708

"Meet the Press", **1980–81:** 107

Meetings With Foreign Leaders

    Argentina, President Jorge Rafael Videla, **1977:** 1552, 1568

    Australia, Prime Minister J. Malcolm Fraser, **1977:** 1140; **1979:** 3; **1980–81:** 259

    Austria, President Rudolph Kirchschläger, **1979:** 1047, 1142, 2036

    Bahamas, Prime Minister Lynden O. Pindling, **1977:** 1568

    Bangladesh, Prime Minister Ziaur Rahman, **1980–81:** 1577, 1579

    Belgium

        King Baudouin I, **1978:** 32, 33

        King Baudouin I and Queen Fabiola, **1980–81:** 757

        Prime Minister Leo Tindemans, **1977:** 882, 1814, 1818

    Bermuda, Prime Minister John David Gibbons, **1980–81:** 932

    Bolivia, President Hugo Banzer Suarez, **1977:** 1550, 1568

    Brazil

        President Ernesto Geisel, **1978:** 626, 627, 636, 641

        Vice President Adalberto Pereira dos Santos, **1977:** 1567

    Canada

        Prime Minister Joe Clark, **1979:** 1181, 1195

        Prime Minister Pierre Elliott Trudeau, **1979:** 379, 381; **1977:** 208, 210, 223, 1568; **1978:** 1310

Meetings With Foreign Leaders — *continued*

    Chile, President Augusto Pinochet Ugarte, **1977:** 1538, 1567

    China, People's Republic of, Vice Premier Deng Xiaoping, **1979:** 189, 191n., 192, 195, 200, 213

    Columbia, President Alfonso Lopez Michelsen, **1977:** 1537, 1567; **1978:** 1119, 1122, 1123

    Costa Rica

        President Rodrigo Carazo Odio, **1978:** 1119, 1122, 1123; **1980–81:** 2781

        President Daniel Oduber Quirós, **1977:** 1566, 1568

    Cyprus, President Spyros Kyprianou, **1977:** 1754

    Denmark, Prime Minister Anker Henrik Jørgensen, **1977:** 882; **1978:** 389

    Dominican Republic, President Joaquín Balaguer, **1977:** 1551, 1568

    Ecuador, Vice Adm. Alfredo Poveda Burbano, **1977:** 1549, 1568

    Egypt, President Anwar al-Sadat, **1977:** 561, 567, 595; **1978:** 19, 274, 279, 290, 291, 1505, 1506, 1515, 1519–1523, 1571; **1979:** 405, 407, 410, 412, 415, 430, 518, 522n., 523, 548n.; **1980–81:** 623

    El Salvador, President Carlos Humberto Romero, **1977:** 1552, 1568

    European Parliament, President Simone Veil, **1980–81:** 238

    Finland, Prime Minister Kalevi Sorsa, **1979:** 898

    France

        President Valéry Giscard d'Estaing, **1977:** 881; **1978:** 20, 21, 27, 28, 30, 31, 1008, 1308, 1310; **1979:** 14, 17, 25, 26, 1183n., 1187

        Prime Minister Raymond Barre, **1977:** 1590, 1603, 1607, 1613

    Gabon, President El Hadj Omar Bongo, **1977:** 1825

    Germany, Federal Republic of

        Bavarian Minister President Franz Josef Strauss, **1980–81:** 470

        Chancellor Helmut Schmidt, **1977:** 881, 1241, 1242, 1244–1249, 1251; **1978:** 1015, 1281, 1286, 1289, 1292, 1293, 1308, 1310, 1332; **1979:** 14, 17, 25, 26, 1183n., 1187; **1980–81:** 435, 438, 441, 1170, 2736, 2738

        Foreign Minister Hans-Dietrich Genscher, **1980–81:** 189

        President Walter Scheel, **1978:** 1286, 1289, 1310

    Greece, Prime Minister Constantine Caramanlis, **1977:** 881; **1978:** 1025

    Grenada, Prime Minister Eric M. Gairy, **1977:** 1556, 1568

    Guatemala, President Kjell Eugenio Laugerud, **1977:** 1568

    Guinea, President Ahmed Sékou Touré, **1979:** 1417

[References are to page numbers except as otherwise indicated]

Meetings With Foreign Leaders — *continued*
  Honduras
    Brig. Gen. Juan Alberto Melgar Castro, **1977:** 1554, 1568
    President Policarpo Paz Garcia, **1980–81:** 426
  India
    President N. S. Reddy, **1978:** 1, 11
    Prime Minister Morarji Desai, **1978:** 2, 3, 5, 16, 1083, 1085, 1086, 1090, 1106
  Iran
    Crown Prince Ali Reza Pahlavi, **1978:** 1954
    Shah Mohammad Reza Pahlavi, **1977:** 2026, 2028, 2029, 2033
  Ireland, Prime Minister John M. Lynch, **1979:** 2091, 2094, 2095, 2097
  Israel
    Prime Minister Menahem Begin, **1977:** 1281, 1283, 1287, 1295, 1306, 2127, 2131, 2152, 2163; **1978:** 544, 547, 550, 570; **1979:** 372, 373, 382, 400, 417, 419, 428, 430n., 518, 522n., 523; **1980–81:** 686, 694, 700, 2719
    Prime Minister Yitzhak Rabin, **1977:** 329, 334, 371, 373
  Italy
    President Alessandro Pertini, **1980–81:** 1153, 1160, 1241
    Prime Minister Giulio Andreotti, **1977:** 881, 1353, 1358, 1363, 1383; **1978:** 1019, 1310
    Prime Minister Francesco Cossiga, **1980–81:** 210, 1157, 1160, 1241, 1242
  Jamaica, Prime Minister Michael Manley, **1977:** 2128; **1978:** 1119, 1122, 1123
  Japan
    Prime Minister Takeo Fukuda, **1977:** 467, 472, 478, 508, 881; **1978:** 1310
    Prime Minister Masayoshi Ohira, **1979:** 761, 763, 768, 1162, 1168n., 1187
  Jordan, King Hussein I, **1977:** 710, 720, 722, 744; **1980–81:** 1123, 1129, 1130
  Kenya, President Daniel T. arap Moi, **1980–81:** 352, 354, 357
  Korea, Republic of, President Park Chung Hee, **1979:** 1202, 1207
  Liberia, President William R. Tolbert, Jr., **1978:** 671, 675, 709; **1979:** 1806
  Luxembourg, Prime Minister Gaston Thorn, **1977:** 882, 1754
  Mexico, President José López Portillo, **1977:** 178, 194; **1978:** 1119; **1979:** 272, 273, 277, 279n., 280, 281, 284, 287, 294, 1781, 1787, 1789
  Morocco
    King Hassan II, **1978:** 2031, 2033, 2058, 2059
    Prime Minister Ahmed Osman, **1977:** 2079
  Mozambique, President Samora Moises Machel, **1977:** 1754
  Netherlands
    Prime Minister Andreas van Agt, **1979:** 2201

Meetings With Foreign Leaders — *continued*
  Netherlands — *continued*
    Prime Minister Johannes den Uyl, **1977:** 882
  New Zealand, Prime Minister Robert D. Muldoon, **1977:** 1989, 1991
  Nigeria
    Lt. Gen. Olusegun Obasanjo, **1977:** 1762, 1772, 1781; **1978:** 643, 654, 661, 664, 709
    President Alhaji Shehu Shagari, **1980–81:** 2095, 2104, 2108
  Norway, Prime Minister Odvar Nordli, **1977:** 882; **1979:** 2201
  Pakistan, President Mohammad Zia ul-Haq, **1980–81:** 2055
  Panama
    Brig. Gen. Omar Torrijos Herrera, **1977:** 1535, 1567, 1593; **1978:** 1118, 1120, 1122, 1123, 1153
    President Aristides Royo, **1979:** 836
  Paraguay, President Alfredo Stroessner, **1977:** 1537, 1567
  Peru, President Francisco Morales Bermudez Cerruti, **1977:** 1536, 1567
  Portugal, President António dos Santos Ramalho Eanes, **1977:** 882; **1978:** 1021; **1980–81:** 1230, 1231, 1233
  Rhodesia, Bishop Abel Tendekai Muzorewa, **1979:** 1230
  Romania, President Nicolae Ceausescu, **1978:** 734, 738, 743, 753
  Saudi Arabia
    Crown Prince Fahd bin Abd al-Aziz Al-Sa'ud, **1977:** 991, 1006, 1010; **1978:** 19
    King Khalid bin Abd al-Aziz Al-Sa'ud, **1978:** 18, 1876
  Senegal, President Léopold Sédar Senghor, **1978:** 1071; **1980–81:** 653
  Sierra Leone, President Siaka Stevens, **1980–81:** 1945
  Singapore, Prime Minister Lee Kuan Yew, **1977:** 1754
  Spain
    King Juan Carlos I, **1980–81:** 334, 1220, 1228
    Prime Minister Adolfo Suárez, **1980–81:** 82, 1223, 1228
  Sudan, President Gaafar Muhammed Nimeiri, **1978:** 1561
  Sweden, Prime Minister Ola Ullsten, **1979:** 89
  Switzerland, President Kurt Furgler, **1977:** 881
  Syria, President Hafiz al-Asad, **1977:** 835, 841, 842, 844
  Tanzania, President Julius K. Nyerere, **1977:** 1412, 1423, 1433, 1434, 1437
  Thailand, Prime Minister Kriangsak Chomanan, **1979:** 221, 226, 230
  Tunisia, Prime Minister Hedi Nouira, **1978:** 2090

Meetings With Foreign Leaders — *continued*
  Turkey
    Prime Minister Süleyman Demirel, **1977:** 847, 882
    Prime Minister Bulent Ecevit, **1978:** 1016, 1018
  Union of Soviet Socialist Republics, President L. I. Brezhnev, **1979:** 1048, 1049, 1051, 1079, 1081, 1143
  United Kingdom
    Prime Minister James Callaghan, **1977:** 353, 359, 371; **1978:** 564, 566, 1034, 1221, 1308, 1310; **1979:** 14, 17, 25, 26
    Prime Minister Margaret Thatcher, **1979:** 1181, 1183n., 1187, 2259, 2264, 2267
  Uruguay, President Aparicio Méndez Manfredini, **1977:** 1556, 1568
  Vatican City, Pope John Paul II, **1979:** 1827, 1830, 1834, 1881; **1980–81:** 1164
  Venezuela, President Carlos Andrés Pérez, **1977:** 1180, 1183, 1188, 1190, 1211; **1978:** 613–619, 623, 641, 1119, 1122, 1123
  Yugoslavia
    President Cvijetin Mijatovic, **1980–81:** 1208, 1210, 1212, 1216
    President Josip Broz Tito, **1978:** 473, 475, 485
  Zambia, President Kenneth D. Kaunda, **1978:** 771, 917, 920, 934
  Zimbabwe, Prime Minister Robert Mugabe, **1980–81:** 1579, 1584
Meguid, Abdel-, **1979:** 548n.
Mehta, Jagat, **1978:** 50
Meierotto, Larry E., **1978:** 1666, 1670; **1979:** 46, 91
Meir, Golda, **1977:** 2005; **1978:** 543, 2185, 2268; **1980–81:** 1488, 2767
Meissner, Charles F., **1980–81:** 1468, 1470
Mekler, Arlen, **1977:** 1053
Melamu, Moteane John, **1980–81:** 2807
Melara, Sonia E., **1980–81:** 1098, 3023
Melcher, Sen. John, **1978:** 303
Melfi, John, **1977:** 313
Melgar Castro, Brig. Gen. Juan Alberto, **1977:** 1554, 1568
Melkonian, Marilyn, **1980–81:** 2559
Melley, Ken, **1980–81:** 1299n.
Mellody, Katherine A., **1978:** 1955
Mellon, Paul, **1978:** 1028
Melone, Harry Roberts, **1979:** 1726, 1785
Melones Dam, Calif., **1980–81:** 1307
Melton, Howell M., **1977:** 557, 558
Memorandums of disapproval.
  See under Congress, Communications to.
Memorandums to Federal Agencies
  Acid rain research program, **1979:** 1389
  Advisory committee review, **1977:** 1012, 1495
  Affirmative action, **1977:** 1376; **1978:** 1320
  Alternative approaches to regulation, **1980–81:** 1109

Memorandums to Agencies — *continued*
  Anhydrous ammonia industry, **1979:** 2221
  Anti-inflation program, **1978:** 927, 1856
  Artificial baits and flies industry, **1978:** 2071
  Audit plans, **1977:** 1563
  Barbados, defense sales to, **1979:** 1133
  Bicycle tire and tube industry, **1978:** 1904
  Black colleges and universities, **1979:** 48
  Bolt, nut, and large screw industry, **1978:** 299, 2284
  Cash management, **1977:** 2025
  Childhood diseases immunization program, **1977:** 605
  China-U.S. trade relations, **1979:** 2005
  Citizens band radio transceivers, **1978:** 608
  Civil Rights Act, Title VI, enforcement, **1977:** 1293
  Civil Service Reform Act, **1978:** 1972
  Clothespin industry, **1978:** 1698; **1979:** 232–234
  Combined Federal Campaign, **1977:** 1464; **1978:** 1235, 1236; **1979:** 1231; **1980–81:** 1098
  Conference on Security and Cooperation in Europe, Final Act implementation, **1978:** 2166
  Consumer affairs, **1978:** 789
  Consumer Affairs Council, designation of Chairperson, **1979:** 1766
  Copper industry, **1978:** 1805
  Customs Valuation Code implementation, **1980–81:** 2815
  Dam safety, **1977:** 723
  Defense economic adjustment programs, **1978:** 594
  Domestic assistance plans, review, **1977:** 1285, 1307
  Economic policymaking, **1979:** 977
  Embargo regulations under the Trading With the Enemy Act, **1979:** 1655
  Employment of women, **1977:** 2034
  Energy use reduction, **1979:** 219, 647
  Equality for women, **1978:** 1335
  Executive branch reorganization studies
    Administrative services delivery, **1977:** 1195
    Disaster preparedness, **1977:** 1497
    Economic analysis and political machinery, **1977:** 1495
    Federal justice system, **1977:** 1498
    Food and nutrition policy, **1977:** 1496
    Human services, **1977:** 1194
    Law enforcement, **1977:** 1193
    Legal representation system, **1977:** 1497
    Local development programs, **1977:** 1193
    Natural resources and environmental programs, **1977:** 1406
  Federal aid system, administration, **1977:** 1564
  Federal employees, outstanding contributions, **1978:** 2144

Memorandums to Agencies — *continued*
　Federal employment of the handicapped, **1977:** 1298
　Federal legal resources management, **1979:** 1266
　Federal pay and the anti-inflation program, **1979:** 8
　Federal personnel manual, **1977:** 1053
　Federal Trade Commission, reauthorization legislation, **1980–81:** 815
　Florida energy emergency, **1979:** 817, 1032, 1225, 1998
　Footwear industry, American non-rubber, **1977:** 552, 553
　General Services Administration, **1978:** 1337
　Government regulations, public participation, **1979:** 867
　Government reorganization, **1977:** 1463
　Government in the Sunshine Act, **1978:** 1068
　High carbon ferrochromium industry, **1978:** 1941
　Independent water project review, **1979:** 10
　Indochinese refugees, **1978:** 2167
　Inspector General Act, **1978:** 1998
　Integrated pest management, **1979:** 1383
　Interagency Committee for the Purchase of U.S. Savings Bonds, **1977:** 532
　Interagency Task Force on Occupational Safety and Health, **1977:** 1430
　Interdepartmental Committee on Domestic Violence, **1979:** 729
　International trade agreements, **1979:** 6
　Iran, diplomatic relations with, **1980–81:** 612
　Joint Financial Management Improvement Program, **1979:** 462
　Kampuchean relief efforts, **1979:** 2117
　Leather wearing apparel industry, import relief determination, **1980–81:** 531
　Liaison with State and local leaders, **1977:** 1602
　Management improvement and waste and fraud elimination, **1979:** 779
　Military education for Yugoslav officers in U.S., **1980–81:** 1077
　Minority bank deposit program, **1977:** 593
　Multilateral trade negotiations, **1979:** 2253
　Multi-year budget planning, **1978:** 62
　Mushroom industry, import relief determination, **1980–81:** 2331
　National climate program, **1978:** 1907
　National coastal protection, **1979:** 1373
　National Hispanic Heritage Week, **1978:** 1451
　National Productivity Council, **1978:** 1835
　National Volunteer Week, **1980–81:** 695
　Neighborhood and community programs, **1980–81:** 2116
　Nicaragua, procurement of grain in, **1979:** 1780
　Nonfuel minerals, domestic policy review on, **1980–81:** 2686

Memorandums to Agencies — *continued*
　Nuclear Waste Management Task Force, **1978:** 509
　Office of Drug Abuse Policy, **1977:** 378
　Official dealings between Federal employees and the President's family, **1980–81:** 1982
　Offshore oil spill pollution, **1979:** 338
　Oil portraits of Cabinet Secretaries, **1977:** 662
　Olympics, 1980 Summer, **1980–81:** 559
　Oregon energy emergency, **1979:** 2286
　Outstanding contributions by Federal employees, **1977:** 1817
　Paperwork reduction, **1977:** 177
　Part-time employment, **1977:** 1610
　Peace Corps, **1979:** 881
　Peanut imports control, **1980–81:** 2772
　Pollution control, economic assistance, **1979:** 1384
　Pollution control standards, compliance, **1978:** 1769
　Porcelain-on-steel cookware industry, import relief determination, **1980–81:** 3
　Power failure in New York metropolitan area, **1977:** 1250
　Presidential domestic policy review system, **1977:** 1589
　Presidential Management Improvement Awards, **1980–81:** 18
　President's Executive Interchange Program, **1977:** 1906
　President's Management Improvement Council, **1979:** 1669
　Privacy Act of 1974, executive branch administration, **1978:** 1481
　Private consultation services, use by Federal Government, **1977:** 878
　Procurement policy, **1980–81:** 72
　Public assistance programs, **1978:** 2233
　Public land resources, **1979:** 1374
　Red Cross Month, **1977:** 250; **1978:** 285; **1979:** 215; **1980–81:** 193
　Refugee assistance to Somalia and Djibouti, **1978:** 959
　Regional commissions, **1979:** 79
　Regulations, Government, **1978:** 562
　Regulatory management, **1978:** 1905
　Romania, Hungary, and the People's Republic of China, trade with U.S., **1980–81:** 982
　Romania and Hungary, trade with U.S., **1979:** 979
　Senior Executive Service
　　Conversion rights, **1979:** 392
　　Pay schedule, **1979:** 393
　　Selection and development, **1979:** 1692
　Sex discrimination, **1977:** 1504, 1505
　Small Business Administration, **1979:** 2074
　Small business regulatory programs, **1979:** 2142

Memorandums to Agencies — *continued*
Soil conservation incentives, **1979:** 1382
Spending, Government, **1978:** 1318
Stainless steel table flatware industry, **1978:** 1216
State and local officials, involvement in administration policies and programs, **1977:** 274
Statistical system, **1978:** 891
Steel, Government purchases and industry study, **1977:** 1435, 1436
Sugar industry and imports, **1977:** 799
Supply purchasing, control, **1977:** 1113
Survey of congressional constituent problems, **1977:** 1966
Taiwan, U.S. relations, **1979:** 1
Task Force on Global Resources and Environment, **1980–81:** 1416
Task Force on Women Business Owners, **1977:** 1429
Television industry and imports, **1977:** 936
Toxic and hazardous substances regulation, **1977:** 1407
Trade agreement with Romania, **1977:** 1057
Trade with Hungary and Romania, **1978:** 1032
Trading With the Enemy Act, embargo regulations, **1978:** 1504
Transportation policy, **1979:** 1383
Travel costs, Government, **1978:** 1483
Uganda
Refugee assistance from U.S., **1979:** 2150
Trade with U.S., **1979:** 867
Undocumented aliens, **1979:** 1667
Union of Soviet Socialist Republics
Agricultural commodities shipment termination, **1980–81:** 32
Technology and other strategic item exports, **1980–81:** 43
United Kingdom-U.S. Agreement for Cooperation on the Uses of Atomic Energy for Mutual Defense Purposes, **1979:** 216
United States Savings Bonds program, **1978:** 574; **1979:** 309, 2284
United States-Turkish military cooperation, **1978:** 1636
Urban noise program, **1979:** 1385
Urban and regional development policies, **1977:** 485
Veterans' Federal Coordinating Committee, **1978:** 1743
Veterans readjustment and career-conditional appointment program, **1978:** 1742
Waste, fraud, and error in Government programs, **1978:** 2233
White House Conference on Families, **1979:** 1939
White House Conference on Small Business, **1978:** 1101
Wild and scenic rivers, **1979:** 1379

Memorandums to Agencies — *continued*
Wildlife law enforcement, **1979:** 1376
Women's business enterprise, **1979:** 894
Working Group on Food and Agricultural Policy, **1977:** 1695
World forests, **1979:** 1386
World Hunger Working Group, **1977:** 1696
Youth summer employment program, **1978:** 315; **1979:** 836; **1980–81:** 815
Zaire, security assistance, **1978:** 930
Zero-base budgeting, **1978:** 753
Executive branch, **1977:** 154, 728
Zimbabwe-Rhodesia, trade sanctions against, **1979:** 2120
Memorial Day, **1977:** 716; **1978:** 931; **1980–81:** 813, 970, 972
(Proc. 4651), **1979:** 550
Memphis, Tenn., **1978:** 2189–2218; **1979:** 1817; **1980–81:** 2586
Menard, H. William, **1978:** 407, 416, 1188; **1979:** 1544
Menario, John E., **1979:** 376, 1017
Mendelsohn, Robert H., **1977:** 804, 807, 1104, 1790, 2037
Mendez, Jose F., **1979:** 465
Méndez Manfredini, Aparicio, **1977:** 1556, 1568
Menninger, Karl, **1980–81:** 2926
Men's apparel industry, **1978:** 1808
Mental health, **1978:** 348, 878
Administration's accomplishments and goals, **1980–81:** 2944
Administration's commitment to improvement, **1979:** 1350
Legislation, **1979:** 135, 857, 859, 861, 862
Mental Health, President's Commission on.
See President's Commission on Mental Health.
Mental Health Administration, Alcohol, Drug Abuse and, **1979:** 1596
Mental Health Association, National, **1980–81:** 785, 1091
Mental Health Centers, Community, **1979:** 860
Mental Health Month, **1980–81:** 784
Mental Health System, Community, **1979:** 135
Mental Health Systems Act
Congressional approval of Conference report, **1980–81:** 1976
Fact sheet (Checklist), **1980–81:** 2179
Mentions, **1980–81:** 118, 2004, 2035, 2281, 2361
Signing ceremony, **1980–81:** 2098
Mental Retardation, President's Committee on.
See President's Committee on Mental Retardation.
Mentschikoff, Soia, **1980–81:** 2731
Menuhin, Mr. and Mrs. Yehudi, **1977:** 596
Menzies, Sir Robert, **1978:** 913
Meramec Park Lake, Mo., **1977:** 208, 494
Mercado, Judith, **1979:** 914

Mercersburg, Pa., **1978:** 1239
Merchant Marine, United States, **1977:** 640; **1980–81:** 469
Merchant Marine Academy, United States, **1980–81:** 2235
Mercure, Alex P., **1977:** 535, 557, 745, 2036; **1978:** 506; **1979:** 1865; **1980–81:** 1938, 1941, 2453, 2726, 2727, 2870, 2873
Meredith, Joseph Nelson, **1978:** 2288
Merino Rabago, Francisco, **1979:** 281n.
Merit Pay System, **1978:** 1365
Merit Systems Protection Board, **1980–81:** 62, 374, 567, 617
    Chair, **1979:** 3, 90, 1921
    Civil service reform, roundtable discussion, **1978:** 1363, 1366
    Members, **1979:** 46, 90, 1019, 1302, 1319
    Proposed, **1978:** 437, 445
    Reorganization Plan No. 2 of 1978, **1978:** 951, 953–955, 957, 2292–2294, 2296
    Special Counsel, **1979:** 3, 46
Merkel, John C., Jr., **1977:** 883, 884
Merritt, Doris H., **1978:** 275, 303
Merritt, Gilbert C., **1977:** 1507
Merseburger, Peter, **1978:** 1258, 1260–1263
Merson, Alan, **1978:** 833
Mesquita, Julio, **1978:** 640
Messages to Congress.
    See under Congress, Communications to.
Mestre, Luis E., **1979:** 465
Metal industry, **1980–81:** 775
Metcalf, Andrew L., Jr., **1978:** 1346
Metcalf, Sen. Lee, **1978:** 63, 97, 575, 1902
Metcalfe, Repr. Ralph H., **1977:** 2077; **1978:** 1743
Methodist Conference, United, **1980–81:** 774
Methodist Episcopal Church, Christian, **1980–81:** 775
Metric Board, United States, **1977:** 196, 1944, 1966; **1978:** 230, 484, 504, 1069, 1072; **1980–81:** 940, 967, 1443, 1470
Metrinko, Mr. and Mrs. Harry, **1980–81:** 606
Metrinko, Michael J., **1980–81:** 606
Metropolitan Opera, New York City, labor dispute, **1980–81:** 2017
Mettler, Ruben, **1978:** 710; **1979:** 1976
Metzenbaum, Sen. Howard M., **1977:** 509, 744, 1826; **1978:** 229, 1139, 1140; **1979:** 1006
    Campaign appearances with the President, **1980–81:** 1766, 2466
    Legislation passage leadership, **1980–81:** 303, 1936, 1937
Mexican-American Legal Defense and Educational Fund, **1978:** 2059
Mexican border patrol, **1978:** 61
Mexico
    Aliens, undocumented.
        See Aliens, undocumented.

Mexico — *continued*
    Armed Forces physical fitness requirements, **1980–81:** 262
    Commemoration of the victory at Puebla, **1978:** 880
    Consultative mechanism with U.S., **1979:** 1667, 1787, 1790
    Drug control, **1978:** 1329, 1599
    Fishery agreement, **1977:** 1752
    Foreign Minister, **1979:** 791, 802
    Generalized System of Preferences, **1979:** 2230
    Illegal drug trafficking, **1977:** 290, 306, 1399, 1401; **1979:** 564
    Interview remarks, **1978:** 904, 2062, 2179
    Joint statement, **1979:** 1789
    Mention, **1979:** 809
    Mexican television, interviews with the President, **1979:** 235, 252
    Oil and natural gas, transfer to U.S., **1977:** 67; **1979:** 58, 612, 736, 791, 802, 813, 1245, 1327, 1413, 1569
    Oil spill, **1979:** 1497
    Penal sentences, treaty with U.S., **1977:** 156, 899
    President's visit, **1978:** 2058
        Dinner honoring President López Portillo, **1979:** 281, 294 (Checklist)
        Ixtlilco el Grande, town square remarks, **1979:** 280
        Joint communique, **1979:** 287
        Luncheon honoring President Carter, **1979:** 273
        Mexican Congress address, **1979:** 284, 294 (Checklist)
        Postvisit comments, **1979:** 331
        Previsit comments, **1979:** 181, 243
        Return, **1979:** 293
        U.S. Embassy visit, **1979:** 277
        Welcoming ceremony, **1979:** 272
    Prisoner transfers with U.S., **1977:** 1919
    Science and technological cooperation with U.S., **1979:** 539; **1980–81:** 407
    Secretary of Foreign Relations, **1977:** 179
    Trade with U.S., **1979:** 2223
        Agricultural products, **1979:** 791
        Grain, **1980–81:** 392, 1908, 2203, 2351, 2402, 2407, 2469, 2619, 2632, 2638
        Lead products, **1980–81:** 1723, 3000
        Levels increase, **1980–81:** 1734, 1743, 1748, 1769, 1915, 1943, 2587, 2601, 2607, 2828
    Treaties with U.S.
        Extradition, **1979:** 450
        Maritime boundary, **1979:** 86
    U.S. Ambassador, **1977:** 589, 943; **1979:** 1473, 1846
    U.S. Ambassador Julian Nava
        Meeting with the President, **1980–81:** 755
        Nomination, **1980–81:** 434, 452
        President's assessment, **1980–81:** 1838, 1943

Mexico — *continued*
  U.S. border States, relationship with, **1979:** 335
  U.S. grain exchange for Mexican oil, possibility, **1979:** 791, 802
  U.S. Interparliamentary Conference, reception for delegates, **1978:** 1042
  U.S.-Mexican border fence, **1979:** 563
  U.S. relations, **1979:** 1667; **1980–81:** 1312, 1995
  Vice President's visit, **1977:** 2073
Mexico, President (José López Portillo), **1977:** 30, 67, 149, 151, 178, 194, 290, 900; **1978:** 873, 904, 1042, 1119, 1329, 1599, 2058, 2179; **1980–81:** 407
  Mention, **1979:** 2129
  Natural gas sales to U.S., decision, **1979:** 1413
  President's visit to Mexico
    Meetings with the President, **1979:** 272, 273, 277, 279n., 280, 281, 284, 287, 294
    Previsit comments, **1979:** 58, 237
  Relationship with the President, **1979:** 181, 235, 243, 252, 253, 736
  Undocumented aliens, negotiations with U.S., **1979:** 184, 185, 236, 253, 564, 806, 812, 907
  Visit to U.S.
    Announcement, **1979:** 1604
    Departure from U.S., **1979:** 1790
    Meetings with the President, **1979:** 1787, 1789
    Postvisit comments, **1979:** 1846, 1874
    Previsit comments, **1979:** 1664, 1666
    State dinner, **1979:** 1781
Mexico-United States Interparliamentary Conference, **1980–81:** 892
Mexico-U.S. Agreement on Natural Gas, **1979:** 1703, 1706
Meyer, Gen. Edward C., **1980–81:** 1686
Meyer, Lt. Gen. Edward C., **1979:** 763
Meyer, Helen, **1979:** 746
Meyer, Jennifer, **1980–81:** 927
Meyer, Paul R., Jr., **1980–81:** 3026
Meyer, Robert Haldeman, **1977:** 505, 510, 1705, 1906
Meyers, Gerald, **1980–81:** 1670
Meyers, Ishmael A., **1978:** 899
Mezvinsky, Edward M., **1977:** 1252
M.I.A. Recognition Day, National P.O.W.-, **1980–81:** 1282
Miami, Federal Interagency Task Force on, **1980–81:** 1236
Miami, Fla., **1980–81:** 850, 913, 915, 916
  Federal assistance for riot-damaged areas, **1980–81:** 1236, 1492, 2332
  President's visits, **1980–81:** 1066, 1072, 1074, 1085, 2382, 2394
  Urban Development Action Grant program, **1980–81:** 2112
Miami Beach, Fla., **1978:** 1865, 1869

Miami Conference on the Caribbean, **1979:** 2159
Mica, Repr. Dan, **1979:** 667
Michael, Don, **1979:** 989, 990
Michael, James Harry, Jr., **1980–81:** 654
Michaelson, Julius, **1980–81:** 1439n.
Michaux, Henry M., Jr., **1977:** 1127, 1128
Michelson, Gertrude G., **1978:** 697; **1980–81:** 305
Michigan
  Army missile plant legislation, **1980–81:** 769, 776
  Department of transportation, **1980–81:** 1403
  Disaster declarations, **1980–81:** 932, 1714
  Drought assistance, **1977:** 279
  Emergency declaration, **1977:** 147, 279; **1978:** 276
  Officials, labor leaders and Democratic citizens, briefing, **1978:** 1723
  President's visits, **1977:** 1829; **1978:** 1932; **1979:** 1247, 1294; **1980–81:** 1329, 1356, 1984, 1986, 2009, 2441–2452, 2567, 2670
  Project Seafarer, **1979:** 1710
  SALT II treaty briefing by administration officials for civic and community leaders (Digest), **1979:** 2187
  State Senate leader, meeting with the President (Digest), **1980–81:** 775
  U.S. attorneys, **1977:** 1031, 1755
  U.S. district judges, **1978:** 1345, 1346; **1979:** 899, 900, 1232, 1233, 2188; **1980–81:** 968
  U.S. marshals, **1978:** 1111, 1346
Michigan, U.S.S., **1980–81:** 1552
Micik, Sylvia H., **1978:** 1187
Mickel, Buck, **1978:** 759
Mickey Mouse birthday party, **1978:** 2059
Micronesia
  Appropriations legislation, **1980–81:** 467
  President, **1980–81:** 373
  Self-government agreement with U.S., **1980–81:** 2611
  Speaker of the Congress, **1980–81:** 373
Midcontinent Farmers Association, **1978:** 1419
Middle East
  Administration's accomplishments and goals, **1980–81:** 2633, 2984
  Administration's progress toward comprehensive settlement, **1979:** 1857, 1871, 1966, 2047
  Air Force One, question-and-answer sessions, **1978:** 43, 44, 46, 151
  American military bases, **1979:** 350
  Arab boycott of American businesses, **1977:** 116
  Border lines, **1977:** 342, 347, 386, 387
  Business Council remarks, **1977:** 2106, 2107
  Cairo conference, U.S. participation, **1977:** 2054
  Camp David agreements, first anniversary of, **1979:** 1681, 1684
    Egyptian-Israeli peace treaty negotiations, **1978:** 1660–1662
  Camp David Summit meeting
    Conclusion remarks, **1978:** 1519

Middle East — *continued*
  Camp David Summit meeting — *continued*
    Interview remarks, **1978:** 1602
    Israeli approval of Camp David agreements,
      1978: 1651, 1653
    Israeli settlements, **1978:** 1609, 1654, 1655
    Joint Session of Congress, address, **1978:** 1533
    Joint statement, **1978:** 1501
    Letters accompanying documents agreed to at
      Camp David, **1978:** 1566
    Meetings, **1978:** 1484, 1506, 1515, 1516, 1571
    News conference remarks, **1978:** 1440, 1442,
      1660, 1661
    President's departure from the White House,
      1978: 1496
    President's comments on, **1980–81:** 1604, 1660,
      1670, 1767, 2259, 2311, 2539
    Text of documents agreed to at Camp David,
      1978: 1523
    White House Press Secretary's announcement
      of meeting, **1978:** 1393
  Commitments of previous administrations, **1977:**
    947
  Comprehensive peace negotiations, **1980–81:**
    338, 345, 878, 986, 1195, 1888, 2025, 2046
    Mentions, **1979:** 1005, 1024, 1050
    OPEC oil production increase, effect on, **1979:**
      1584
    U.S. Mission Chief, **1979:** 1706
    U.S. role, **1979:** 703, 967, 1834, 1857
  Cook County Democratic dinner remarks, **1978:**
    986
  Democratic National Committee, remarks, **1978:**
    2197
  Drug trafficking, **1980–81:** 2365
  Egyptian-Israeli peace negotiations
    Administration advisers, meeting with the
      President (Digest), **1980–81:** 930
    Business Council, remarks, **1978:** 2240–2242
    Deputy to the Personal Representative of the
      President, **1979:** 852
    Direct negotiations between Israeli Prime
      Minister Begin and Egyptian President
      Sadat, **1979:** 1752, 1997, 2017, 2033, 2047
    Egyptian Prime Minister Khalil and Israeli
      Foreign Minister Dayan, visit to U.S.,
      1979: 263, 303, 329, 331
    Future commitments, **1980–81:** 2769, 2834
    International support, **1980–81:** 1161, 1219,
      1229
    Interview with Israeli television, **1979:** 453
    Israeli settlements, **1978:** 1887, 1890–1892,
      1895
    Jerusalem, status of, **1980–81:** 487, 1086, 1087,
      1625, 1657, 2195, 2301, 2357, 2372, 2461,
      2541
    Jordan, role of, **1980–81:** 1116, 1122, 1126,
      1129, 1130, 1196

Middle East — *continued*
  Egyptian-Israeli negotiations — *continued*
    Meetings with Egyptian-Israeli delegations,
      1978: 1808, 1832, 1833
    Mentions, **1979:** 1751, 2053; **1980–81:** 91, 579,
      622, 623, 648, 659, 702, 807, 896
    Opening ceremony remarks, **1978:** 1757
    Personal Representative of the President (Sol
      M. Linowitz)
      Designation, **1979:** 2105, 2107
      Meetings with the President, **1979:** 1823,
        2104, 2206; **1980–81:** 293, 930, 3048
      Mention, **1980–81:** 2834
      Nomination for rank of Ambassador, **1979:**
        2159, 2187
      West Bank and Gaza Strip settlements,
        autonomy negotiations, **1980–81:** 378,
        459, 527, 861, 870, 906, 1093, 1614, 1652,
        1657, 1832, 2196, 2771
    Personal Representative of the President
      (Robert S. Strauss)
      American blacks-Jews relationship respon-
        sibilities, **1979:** 1861
      Appointment, **1979:** 687
      Jesse Jackson's trip to Middle East, report
        reception, **1979:** 1836, 1998
      Mention, **1979:** 703, 852
      Middle East, visit to, **1979:** 1519
      Nomination for rank of Ambassador, **1979:**
        1706
    President's campaign remarks, **1978:** 1818,
      1861, 1868, 1939, 1940
    President's trip to Egypt
      Announcement, **1979:** 383
      Departure from U.S., **1979:** 394
      Dinner honoring President Carter, **1979:**
        410
      Meetings with President Sadat, **1979:** 407,
        410, 415, 430
      People's Assembly address, **1979:** 412
      Return to U.S., **1979:** 430
      Trip from Cairo to Alexandria, exchange
        with reporters, **1979:** 407
      Welcoming ceremony, **1979:** 405
    President's trip to Israel
      Announcement, **1979:** 383
      Cabinet action approving negotiations pro-
        posals, **1979:** 432
      Departure from Israel, **1979:** 428
      Dinner honoring President Carter, **1979:**
        419
      Knesset address, **1979:** 424
      Meeting with Prime Minister Begin, **1979:**
        417
      Welcoming ceremony, **1979:** 415
    Prime Minister Begin's visit to U.S.
      Meetings with the President, **1979:** 372, 373,
        382, 400

Middle East — *continued*
  Egyptian-Israeli negotiations — *continued*
    Prime Minister Begin — *continued*
      Mentions, **1979:** 346, 360, 375
      Progress during administration, **1980–81:**
        1389, 1562, 1656, 1657, 1767, 2024, 2131,
        2196, 2339, 2370, 2375, 2460, 2771, 2932
      Secretary of Defense's visit, **1979:** 302, 312
      United Nations involvement, **1979:** 1332
      U.S. delegation's visit to Saudi Arabia and
        Jordan, **1979:** 436
      U.S. role, **1979:** 107, 159, 251, 302, 313, 315,
        357, 360; **1980–81:** 673, 869, 870, 1018,
        1888
      Venice Economic Summit discussions, **1980–**
        81: 1195
      West Bank and Gaza Strip settlements au-
        tonomy
        Camp David accord goals, **1980–81:** 197,
          378, 427, 618, 679, 680, 714, 1087, 1624,
          1656
        Egyptian and Israeli delegations, meetings
          in U.S., **1980–81:** 1086, 1093, 1303, 1826,
          1832, 1846
        Egyptian President Sadat and Israeli Prime
          Minister Begin, discussions with the Pres-
          ident, **1980–81:** 511, 521, 527, 679, 908,
          1114
        European proposal, **1980–81:** 1017, 1104,
          1114, 1197
        Israeli security posts at specified locations,
          1980–81: 1115, 1119, 1120
        Mention, **1980–81:** 797, 861
        Middle East security, crucial to, **1980–81:**
          486, 511, 876
        Palestinian and refugee representation,
          1980–81: 1117, 1196, 1624
        Resumption of negotiations, **1980–81:** 1670
        Self-governing transition period proposal,
          1980–81: 460, 526
        Senior Adviser to the U.S. Representative,
          1980–81: 720
        Summit conference scheduling, **1980–81:**
          1614, 1888, 2047, 2704
        West German support, **1980–81:** 440
      White House Statement following meetings
        with Egyptian-Israeli delegations, **1978:**
        1789, 1806
  Egyptian-Israeli peace treaty
    Egyptian Cabinet approval, **1979:** 436
    First anniversary, White House reception,
      1980–81: 525
    Implementation
      Honoring of commitments, **1980–81:** 211,
        337, 541, 618, 632, 687, 700, 879, 1018,
        1397, 1535
      U.S. economic assistance, **1980–81:** 943

Middle East — *continued*
  Egyptian-Israeli treaty — *continued*
    Implementation — *continued*
      U.S. monitoring responsibilities, **1980–81:**
        697
      Israeli Knesset approval, **1979:** 439
      Israeli settlement policy, **1979:** 755
      Japanese support, **1979:** 765
      Joint letter of agreement, **1979:** 516
      Major foreign policy achievement, **1980–81:**
        2400, 2449
      Mentions, **1979:** 490; **1980–81:** 89, 109, 116,
        459
      Postsigning remarks, **1979:** 1752, 1769, 2244
      Prime Minister Begin's visit to Egypt, **1979:**
        1005
      Texts of treaty and related documents, **1979:**
        495
      U.S. financial assistance, authorizing legisla-
        tion, **1979:** 471, 590, 638
      U.S. monitoring of Sinai area, **1979:** 756
  Energy sources, **1978:** 1301
  Geneva Conference, **1977:** 497, 600, 722, 1728
  Illinois State legislature, remarks, **1978:** 989
  International Exchange-of-Persons program,
    1979: 324
  Interview remarks, **1977:** 1800, 1804, 2010, 2091,
    2098, 2099, 2133, 2188–2191; **1978:** 68, 70,
    305, 1227, 1348, 1672, 1780, 2020–2022,
    2042–2044, 2150, 2173, 2252–2255
  Iranian situation, effect on U.S. policy in, **1979:**
    2169, 2171
  Mention, **1979:** 1936
  Military sales, **1978:** 245, 333, 335, 338, 359, 368,
    777, 778, 782, 801, 806, 807, 848, 849, 857,
    866, 867, 896, 901, 910, 915
  National Democratic Party Conference, re-
    marks, **1978:** 2194
  News conference remarks, **1977:** 1236, 1368,
    1470, 1623, 1686–1688, 1996, 1997, 2054–
    2056, 2059, 2116–2120, 2206, 2210; **1978:**
    62, 245–247, 333, 335, 338, 440, 491, 492,
    494, 628, 631, 777–779, 782, 1179, 1746,
    1749, 1990, 2099, 2220, 2255
  Ohio State Democratic Party, reception remarks,
    1978: 1624
  Palestinians.
    See Palestinians.
  Peace prospects, **1977:** 203, 225, 386, 457, 513,
    702, 721, 723, 768, 836, 845, 858, 1011
  Persian Gulf area.
    See Persian Gulf area.
  President's visit, **1978:** 1655
  Remarks with reporters, **1977:** 1781, 2172–2176
  Secretary of State Vance's trip, **1977:** 17, 289,
    330; **1978:** 189
  Spokane, Wash., town meeting remarks, **1978:**
    865

[References are to page numbers except as otherwise indicated]

Middle East — *continued*
    State of the Union, **1978:** 96, 121
    Terrorism, **1978:** 1676
    Terrorist attacks, **1979:** 656
    United Nations General Assembly address,
        1977: 1720, 1721
    U.S. arms sales, **1979:** 656
    U.S. economic assistance, **1980–81:** 2813
    U.S. military strength, influence on peace set-
        tlement, **1979:** 2233
    U.S. policy, **1977:** 1136, 1201, 1515, 1747, 1897;
        1979: 1857; **1980–81:** 170, 1551, 1555,
        1614, 2170
    United States Sinai Support Mission, **1977:** 734,
        1820; **1978:** 773; **1979:** 64, 1821; **1980–81:**
        1396, 1547, 1957
    U.S.-Soviet joint statement, **1977:** 1935, 2062
    Vice President's trip, **1978:** 1227, 1239
    Visit of Egyptian President Anwar al-Sadat to
        Israel, **1977:** 2042–2044, 2050
    World Jewish Congress remarks, **1977:** 1954–
        1957
Middle Income Student Assistance Act, **1978:**
    1916, 1918
Middle Income Student Assistance program, **1979:**
    264
Middleton, Austin H., **1980–81:** 2847
Middleton, Blue, **1977:** 316
Middletown, Pa., **1979:** 578
Mier, Mariano J., **1979:** 977
MIG-23's in Cuba, **1978:** 2101, 2176
Mighell, Kenneth J., **1977:** 211, 1212
Migrant workers, **1977:** 54, 1831, 1840
Migratory Birds, United States-Soviet Union Con-
    vention on, **1977:** 1279
Migratory birds protection convention, U.S.-Can-
    ada, **1980–81:** 2743
Migratory species, diplomatic conference on the
    protection of,**1979:** 1042
Miguel Barros, Jose, **1978:** 1070
Mijatovic, Cvijetin, **1980–81:** 1208, 1213n., 1216,
    1220, 1243
Mike, Joseph C., **1980–81:** 2558
Mikulski, Repr. Barbara A., **1977:** 544, 546; **1978:**
    1809
Mikva, Abner J., **1979:** 958, 983; **1980–81:** 45
Mikva, Repr. Abner J., **1977:** 1930; **1978:** 1936,
    1940
Milano, Anthony Vincent, **1980–81:** 2614
Milativic, Veljko, **1979:** 669
Milewski, Rev. Stanley E., **1978:** 1808
Milford, Repr. Dale, **1978:** 457
Military, U.S.
    See Armed Forces, United States.
Military Academy, United States, **1977:** 1125,
    1397; **1978:** 510; **1979:** 687

Military aircraft
    Passengers, **1977:** 1306
    White House passenger lists, **1979:** 240
Military Appeals, United States Court of, **1979:**
    1452; **1980–81:** 317
Military Appeals Nominating Commission, United
    States Court of, **1978:** 1038; **1979:** 1451;
    1980–81: 2850
Military Applications of Nuclear Energy Author-
    ization Act of 1982, Department of En-
    ergy National Security and, **1979:** 2298
Military Assistance program (MAP), **1978:** 2095
Military Command Center, National, **1978:** 276
Military Compensation, President's Commission
    on, **1977:** 1176, 1178; **1978:** 749, 751
Military Construction Authorization Act, **1980–81:**
    2185
Military installations, **1978:** 973, 974
Military Personnel and Compensation Amend-
    ments, **1980–81:** 1665, 1715
Military Sales program, Foreign (FMS), **1978:** 2095
Military Selective Service Act of 1967 amendments,
    1980–81: 339, 1274
Military Selective Service Act violations, pardon,
    1977: 5, 6, 266, 321, 1409
Military service, naturalization based on, **1978:**
    1532
Milk, Harvey, **1978:** 2088
Milk price supports, **1977:** 635; **1979:** 2163
Millan, Robert Q., **1980–81:** 3023
Mille Lacs Band of the Minnesota Chippewa
    Indians, **1980–81:** 2189
Miller, Anita, **1978:** 703, 711; **1980–81:** 2560
Miller, Anita M., **1978:** 596, 641
Miller, Arnold, **1977:** 403, 882; **1978:** 308, 1006,
    1787
Miller, Betty, **1978:** 833; **1979:** 270
Miller, Betty J., **1977:** 1817
Miller, Elizabeth, **1977:** 1587
Miller, Col. F. Donald, **1980–81:** 104
Miller, G. William, **1977:** 944, 1117, 1482, 1611,
    2183–2186, 2193; **1978:** 57, 230, 354, 460,
    481, 710, 1059, 1222, 1426, 1441, 1515,
    1517, 1723, 1908, 1913, 1914, 1954, 1955,
    2237, 2270
    See also Federal Reserve System, Board of
        Governors, Chairman; Treasury, Secre-
        tary of the.
Miller, Repr. George, **1980–81:** 1124
Miller, George L., **1977:** 1796
Miller, Harry John, II, **1978:** 926
Miller, Rabbi Israel, **1978:** 2269
Miller, Jeffrey G., **1980–81:** 1975, 2070
Miller, Joyce D., **1977:** 1944, 1966; **1978:** 231,
    1135; **1979:** 942; **1980–81:** 1648
Miller, Leonard, **1979:** 44, 92
Miller, Mike, **1979:** 1468n.

Miller, Paul G., **1980–81:** 305
Miller, Robert H., **1977:** 873, 876, 883
Miller, Shirley C., **1978:** 2070
Miller, William, **1980–81:** 264
Miller, William G., **1979:** 2104
Miller, Lt. Gov. Zell, **1977:** 1534
Millhone, John P., **1979:** 44, 92, 607, 619
Milliken, Gov. William G., **1978:** 934, 1485; **1979:** 1809, 2085
Millonzi, Robert I., **1979:** 465, **1980–81:** 1047
Mills, Billy M., **1978:** 2280
Mills, James R., **1977:** 1811, 1826; **1978:** 230; **1980–81:** 296
Mills, Raymond T., **1977:** 508
Mills, Thomas H., **1978:** 952
Millstein, Ira M., **1978:** 1652
Milwaukee, Wis., **1979:** 572, 573, 1973; **1980–81:** 2080, 2640, 2646
Milwaukee Area Technical College, **1980–81:** 2076, 2179
Mindlin, Jose, **1978:** 640
Mindlin, Raymond D., **1979:** 2289; **1980–81:** 82n.
Mine Enforcement Safety Administration, **1978:** 803
Mine Health and Safety Act of 1977, Federal, **1979:** 1354, 1445
Mine Health and Safety Act of 1969, Federal Coal, **1978:** 1271
Mine Health and Safety Administration, **1978:** 1006; **1979:** 1354
Mine Safety and Health Amendments Act of 1977, Federal, **1977:** 1987, 1989
Mine Safety and Health Review Commission, Federal, **1978:** 970, 1009, 1270, 1279, 1343, 1346; **1980–81:** 1654, 1715, 2107, 2916
Mine Workers, United.
  See United Mine Workers.
Mines, Bureau of, **1977:** 259, 706; **1978:** 803, 1269, 1279; **1980–81:** 1065, 1111, 2686
Mines and mining
  Alaska claims, **1979:** 855
  Energy resources development, **1980–81:** 1144
  Environment message, **1977:** 974, 978
  Federal health and safety activities, **1980–81:** 564, 1049, 1433
  National policy, **1977:** 1058
  Nonfuel data gathering and analysis, **1980–81:** 2686
  Nonfuel energy sources, **1979:** 533
  Nonfuel mineral policy study, **1977:** 2102
  Ocean capabilities development, **1980–81:** 1284
  Ohio jobs preservation, **1979:** 1006
  Old Ben Coal Mine No. 25, President's remarks to employees, **1980–81:** 2199
  Phosphate shipments suspension to Soviet Union, **1980–81:** 560, 2470

Mines and Mining — *continued*
  Safety and health, **1979:** 1445, 1642
  Surface Mining Control and Reclamation Act of 1977, **1977:** 1407
Mineta, Repr. Norman Y., **1978:** 526, 1947; **1979:** 942; **1980–81:** 962, 1455, 1456, 1668
Minetti, G. Joseph, **1977:** 1381, 1698, 1946; **1978:** 255, 277, 800; **1979:** 2015
Minimum wage.
  See under Wages and prices.
Minimum Wage, Coalition for a Fair, **1977:** 942
Minimum Wage Study Commission, **1977:** 1948
Mining Control and Reclamation Act of 1977, Surface, **1980–81:** 416
Mining Enforcement Safety Administration, **1977:** 706
Mining law reform, **1978:** 116
Mining Reclamation and Enforcement, Office of Surface, **1980–81:** 2201
Mink, Pasty T., **1977:** 412, 1408
Minneapolis, Minn., **1977:** 1898; **1978:** 1826, 1828, 1829; **1979:** 1817
Minnesota
  Disaster declarations, **1978:** 801, 1278; **1979:** 786
  Editors and broadcasters, interview with the President, **1979:** 2047
  Election results, **1978:** 2156
  Grain industry labor dispute, **1979:** 1430, 1452, 1467, 1468
  Mille Lacs Band of Chippewa Indians, **1980–81:** 2189
  President's visits, **1977:** 1898–1900; **1978:** 1822, 1826, 1828, 1829, 1949; **1979:** 1454, 1457, 1468, 1471
  State Democratic party, **1978:** 1592
  U.S. attorney, **1979:** 2281; **1980–81:** 25
  U.S. district judges, **1977:** 1438, 1439; **1979:** 2188, 2189
  U.S. marshal, **1977:** 1266, 1307
  White House briefing by administration officials for civic and community leaders (Digest), **1979:** 2138
Minnesota City, Minn., **1979:** 1471
Minnesota Mining and Manufacturing Company, **1979:** 1472
Minorities
  Administration's accomplishments, **1979:** 561, 888
  Administration's accomplishments and goals, **1980–81:** 1312, 1492, 2932
  Administration's relationship with, **1977:** 1938
  Affirmative action programs, **1980–81:** 115
  Bank deposit program, **1977:** 593
  Business assistance, **1979:** 145, 847, 888
  Business enterprises, **1977:** 117, 118, 1322, 1429, 1437, 1438, 1579; **1978:** 111, 319, 588, 843, 1103; **1979:** 847, 1842

Minorities — *continued*
  Business enterprises — *continued*
    Administration's accomplishments and goals,
      1980–81: 2938
    Airport construction contracts, **1980–81:** 1756
    Federal contracts, **1980–81:** 70, 76, 127, 1280,
      1324, 1352, 1459, 1502, 1840
    Legislation, **1980–81:** 76, 127, 2380
    Telecommunications programs, **1980–81:**
      1704, 2021
  Civil rights
    Economic opportunities, **1980–81:** 1631
    Laws enforcement, **1980–81:** 1836, 2058
    Leadership Conference on Civil Rights, Pres-
      ident's address, **1980–81:** 222
    Republican Party position, **1980–81:** 1952
    Voting and Civil Rights Acts importance,
      1980–81: 1500
    See also Human rights, domestic.
  Civil rights prosecutions, **1978:** 1181
  Cultural heritage, **1977:** 166
  Democratic Party commitments, **1980–81:** 1381
  Detroit, Mich., public policy forum, **1977:** 1832,
    1835, 1838, 1842, 1848
  District and circuit judges, additional appoint-
    ments, **1978:** 1803
  Economic development program, **1979:** 77
  Economic recession, impact on, **1980–81:** 798
  Employment, **1977:** 164, 202, 232, 241, 317, 902,
    1532, 1533, 1663, 1938; **1978:** 92, 99, 137,
    972, 994, 1162, 1342, 1607, 1608, 1635,
    1739
    Federal programs, **1980–81:** 805, 1069, 2019
    Opportunities, **1979:** 34, 116, 813, 847, 1842
    Private sector opportunities, **1980–81:** 2426
    Statistics, **1980–81:** 805, 878, 1069, 1985
    Youth initiatives program.
      See Employment *under* Children and youth.
  Federal appointments, **1980–81:** 1352, 1633, 2485
  Federal programs, **1980–81:** 489, 886
  Interview remarks, **1978:** 318, 688
  Judicial appointments.
    See under Courts, United States.
  Leaders, meetings with the President, **1977:** 1533,
    2130
  National Black Network interview, **1977:** 1340
  National Urban League remarks, **1977:** 1347
  News conference remarks, **1978:** 731
  Prison sentences, **1977:** 234
  Public broadcasting programs, **1977:** 1497, 1742,
    1743
  Publishing firms, Government loans, **1979:** 35
  Research Apprenticeship Program, **1979:** 2064
  Reverse discrimination, **1978:** 692
  Science and technology participation program,
    1980–81: 2804
  Small businesses, **1977:** 117, 118
  Small business assistance, **1978:** 1848

Minorities — *continued*
  Telecommunications assistance program, **1978:**
    252, 277
  See also specific group.
Minority business development agency, proposed,
  1980–81: 77
Minority Business Enterprise, Interagency Council
  for, **1977:** 1579, 1611, 1613; **1980–81:** 76
Minority Business Enterprise, Office of, **1977:** 517,
  1580
Minority Business Ownership, Advisory Commit-
  tee on Small and, **1980–81:** 262, 305, 2849
Minority Economic Impact, Office of, **1979:** 1040,
  1044
Minority Enterprise, Advisory Council for, **1977:**
  1494
Minority Purchasing Council, **1980–81:** 1281
Minority Purchasing Council, National, **1979:** 1975
Minot, Chuck, **1977:** 1013
Minow, Newton, **1978:** 1940
Mint, Bureau of the, **1978:** 325, 329, 390, 408, 416,
  569; **1979:** 2040, 2044; **1980–81:** 483
Minter, Steven A., **1978:** 1190; **1980–81:** 426, 522
Minter, Thomas Kendall, **1980–81:** 426, 608, 841,
  1634
Mintz, John A., **1977:** 1382
Minuteman missiles, **1979:** 695, 1601, 2235; **1980–
  81:** 1909, 2337
Minuteman III missile, **1977:** 1693
Miranda, Rafael Cancel, **1979:** 1597
MIRV missiles (multiple independently targetable
  reentry vehicles), **1977:** 538, 1199, 1807,
  1912; **1978:** 2205; **1979:** 1052, 1062;
  1980–81: 2322
Mishkin, Chase Mitchell, **1979:** 465
Mishkin, Paul J., **1979:** 746
Miss Universe, **1980–81:** 1469
Miss U.S.A., **1980–81:** 1469
Missing in action, **1977:** 85, 147, 173, 316, 377, 499
Missing and Unaccounted for in Southeast Asia,
  Presidential Commission on Americans,
  1977: 316, 377, 489, 499
Mississippi
  Disaster assistance, **1980–81:** 1422
  Disaster declaration, **1980–81:** 774
  Emergency declaration, **1978:** 802
  Flood disaster, **1979:** 670, 672, 673, 731, 956
  Gov. William F. Winter, **1980–81:** 422, 1423n.
  Livestock feed assistance, **1977:** 251
  President's visits, **1977:** 1316; **1979:** 1674, 1678
  U.S. attorney, **1978:** 1222, 1223
  U.S. district judge, **1979:** 1883
  U.S. marshal, **1977:** 2037, 2038; **1978:** 1572
  White House Briefings by administration offi-
    cials for community leaders (Digest),
    1979: 1604, 2081
Mississippi, U.S.S., **1978:** 1383, 1388

Mississippi River
  Hydroelectric power projects, **1979:** 1506, 1509, 1510
  President's trip, **1979:** 1455, 1467–1476, 1478–1513, 1518
Mississippi River Basin Commission, Upper, **1978:** 273, 737, 1807, 1828; **1979:** 2248
Mississippi River Commission, **1977:** 1375, 1384, 1542, 1569; **1978:** 511, 898, 1279, 1455; **1979:** 44, 92, 1129, 1143
  Members, **1980–81:** 1432, 1470, 2070, 2916, 3050
Missouri
  Disaster assistance, **1980–81:** 1345, 1421
  Disaster declarations, **1977:** 881, 1612; **1980–81:** 931
  Emergency declaration, **1979:** 440
  Gov. Joseph P. Teasdale, **1980–81:** 1423n., 2665
  President's visits, **1978:** 1419, 1986, 1994, 2075, 2080; **1979:** 1241, 1294, 1508, 1511, 1925, 1931; **1980–81:** 1610, 2103, 2552, 2665
  U.S. attorneys, **1977:** 1163, 1164, 1650, 1651
  U.S. district judges, **1977:** 372, 1127, 1128, 1163, 1164; **1979:** 899, 900, 957, 958; **1980–81:** 608
  U.S. marshals, **1977:** 1128, 1483, 1484
  White House briefing for community and civic leaders (Digest), **1980–81:** 719
Missouri River Basin Commission, **1978:** 273, 737, 1807, 1837; **1979:** 2248
Misty Fiords National Monument, Alaska, **1978:** 2134; **1979:** 855
Mitchell, Bob, **1977:** 305
Mitchell, Clarence, III, **1980–81:** 1946
Mitchell, Clarence J., **1977:** 1949
Mitchell, Clarence M., Jr., **1978:** 1429, 1430, 1683; **1979:** 377; **1980–81:** 222, 752, 1059
Mitchell, Don, **1978:** 696
Mitchell, George J., **1977:** 597; **1979:** 1397, 1398
Mitchell, Sen. George J., **1980–81:** 966, 2177
Mitchell, Martha M., **1977:** 357, 530, 784, 1059, 1633, 1651; **1978:** 321, 1682; **1979:** 1921
Mitchell, Repr. Parren J., **1977:** 1306, 1323, 1348, 1533, 1662, 1938; **1978:** 1571, 1679, 1684, 1848, 1871; **1980–81:** 1280, 1324, 2069, 2381
Mitchell, Susan, **1980–81:** 2558
Mitchell-Bateman, Mildred, **1977:** 530
Mitsotakis, Constantine, **1980–81:** 1398
Mitterrand, Francois, **1978:** 49
Mize, Dwight W., **1980–81:** 272
Mizell, M. Hayes, **1979:** 1727
Mmahat, Arlene Montgomery, **1979:** 465
Moakley, Thomas F., **1977:** 1683, 1701; **1978:** 1211, 1222
Moapa Band of Paiutes, **1980–81:** 2781
Mobil Oil Corporation, **1980–81:** 552, 581, 707, 776
Mobile, Ala., **1979:** 1672

Mobutu, Sese Seko, **1977:** 502; **1979:** 1627
Modai, Yitzhak, **1980–81:** 2314
Moffett, Repr. Anthony Toby, **1977:** 1930; **1978:** 1889; **1979:** 2086
Moffett, Walter L., **1978:** 702, 711
Moi, Daniel T. arap, **1978:** 449; **1980–81:** 334, 335, 352, 354, 357
Mojsov, Lazar, **1977:** 1715
Moldonado, Juan Jose, **1979:** 1447
Moline, Ill., **1979:** 1491n.
Molloy, John G., **1977:** 464; **1978:** 526
Molloy, Patrick H., **1977:** 1059
Momjian, Joan Reed, **1979:** 465
Momjian, Set Charles, **1978:** 1509, 1516; **1980–81:** 822
Mommer, Karl, **1977:** 1520
Mondale, Joan, **1977:** 1781, 1796, 2076; **1978:** 276, 1357, 1478, 2059; **1979:** 221n., 401; **1980–81:** 397, 754, 1333, 3023
Mondale, Walter F.
  See Vice President.
Mondale, William, **1978:** 1478
Mondjo, Nicholas, **1979:** 25
Monetary and Financial Policies, National Advisory Council on International, **1979:** 440, 1731
Monetary Fund, International.
  See International Monetary Fund.
Mongiardo, Victoria M., **1977:** 2153
Monnet, Jean, **1978:** 1985
Monroe, Bill, **1980–81:** 107, 2124
Montana
  Absaroka-Beartooth Wilderness, **1978:** 575
  Department of Highways, **1980–81:** 1403
  Disaster declaration, **1978:** 1033
  Emergency declaration, **1977:** 1506
  Great Bear and Bob Marshall Wildernesses, **1978:** 1902
  Mount St. Helens eruptions, areas damaged by, **1980–81:** 957, 991
  U.S. attorney, **1977:** 1701
  U.S. district judge, **1979:** 441
  U.S. marshal, **1977:** 1308
Montemurro, Frank J., Jr., **1979:** 1417n.
Monterroso Miranda, Felipe Doroteo, **1979:** 376
Montgomery, Repr. G. V. (Sonny), **1977:** 85, 1323, 1333; **1978:** 1965
Montoya, Joe, **1977:** 816
Montoya, Joseph B., **1980–81:** 2754
Montoya, Sen. Joseph M., **1978:** 1040
Moody, Tom, **1978:** 1620, 2080, 2082
Mookodi, Bias, **1977:** 194
Moon landing, Apollo 11, anniversary, **1979:** 1259, 1276; **1978:** 1322
Moore, Bessie B., **1979:** 196, 218
Moore, Calvin C., **1979:** 448
Moore, Cory, **1977:** 347

Moore, Frank B., **1977:** 31, 86, 312, 705, 805, 1083, 1198, 1264, 1533, 1930, 2089, 2124, 2162; **1978:** 66, 277, 302, 303, 327, 328, 414, 415, 456, 457, 503, 504, 525, 526, 570, 710, 749, 750, 769, 770, 801–803, 880, 881, 897, 898, 933, 934, 1009, 1071, 1110, 1154, 1221, 1222, 1278, 1279, 1332, 1333, 1344, 1345, 1380, 1405, 1406, 1457, 1484, 1505, 1571, 1644, 1668, 1669, 1722, 1723, 1771, 1772, 1879, 2003, 2187

Ayatollah Ruhollah Khomeini's health, remarks on, **1980–81:** 2534

Meetings with the President (Digest), **1979:** 89, 179, 216, 217, 239–241, 293, 327, 376, 377, 401, 440, 467, 468, 553, 554, 617, 618, 666, 731, 732, 786, 787, 841, 842, 898, 899, 955–957, 982, 983, 1017, 1018, 1042, 1043, 1142, 1292, 1293, 1318, 1319, 1396, 1397, 1422, 1454, 1455, 1603, 1604, 1784, 1785, 1823, 1824, 1882, 1975, 1976, 2042, 2043, 2081, 2105, 2106, 2138, 2139, 2186, 2206, 2207, 2247, 2279, 2280; **1980–81:** 22, 63, 64, 103, 217, 267, 268, 291–293, 333, 334, 374, 422, 423, 451, 452, 492, 493, 521, 563, 607, 719, 720, 774, 775, 824, 825, 868, 869, 932, 933, 966, 967, 1013, 1014, 1049, 1050, 1110, 1111, 1150, 1291, 1377, 1427, 1428, 1468, 1469, 1523, 1564, 1598, 1662, 1714, 1846, 1945, 2070, 2117, 2726, 2740, 2752, 2781, 2782, 2806, 2807, 2822, 2823, 2841, 2872, 3048, 3049

Mention, **1979:** 2210

News conference (Checklist), **1979:** 1825; **1980–81:** 2071

Moore, John Lovell, Jr., **1977:** 536, 557; **1978:** 2288; **1979:** 1613, 1786

Moore, Kathleen A., **1980–81:** 926

Moore, Marvin J., **1979:** 2159

Moore, Mary Tyler, **1980–81:** 1405, 2075

Moore, Wenda, **1980–81:** 1432

Moore, William T., Jr., **1977:** 1127, 1128

Moorer, Joseph P., Jr., **1979:** 1603

Moorhead, Repr. Carlos J., **1979:** 1212

Moorhead, Repr. William S.

Legislation passage leadership

Chrysler Corporation Loan Guarantee Act of 1979, **1980–81:** 28, 30

Housing and Community Development Act, **1980–81:** 2113, 2115

Meeting with the President (Digest), **1980–81:** 22

Moorman, James W., **1977:** 803, 807; **1979:** 1044

Moose, Richard M., **1977:** 280, 1054, 1059; **1978:** 526; **1980–81:** 719

Mora, Roland R., **1977:** 1065, 1085

Moral Majority, **1980–81:** 2505

Morales, Ana Marta, **1979:** 466

Morales, Jimmy L., **1980–81:** 926

Morales, Lupe, **1979:** 2213; **1980–81:** 534, 537

Morales Bermudez Cerruti, Francisco, **1977:** 1536, 1567

Moran, David A., **1980–81:** 928

Moran, James B., **1979:** 957

Moran, W. Dean, **1978:** 2281

More, Sir Thomas, **1980–81:** 207

Morehead, C. G., **1977:** 1210

Moreland, Thomas D., **1977:** 2166

Moreno, Richard, **1980–81:** 2875

Moret, Louis F., **1979:** 811, 1040, 1044; **1980–81:** 1941

Morgan, Charles, Jr., **1977:** 182

Morgan, Lee L., **1980–81:** 2611

Morgan, Sen. Robert B., **1977:** 1568; **1978:** 457, 529, 537, 1016, 1139, 1140, 1386, 1390, 1576, 1579; **1979:** 1101, 1396; **1980–81:** 2140, 2145, 2381

Morgan, Thomas E., **1978:** 453

Morgenthau, Henry, **1980–81:** 2075

Morgenthau, Ruth S., **1977:** 1587

Mori, Jun, **1979:** 942

Morial, Ernest, **1978:** 276, 1723; **1980–81:** 303

Morita, Akio, **1979:** 2127

Moro, Aldo, **1978:** 515, 885, 933, 1020; **1980–81:** 208, 1241

Morocco

Ambassador to U.S., **1977:** 1163

Joint statement, **1978:** 2055

King Hassan II, **1977:** 1966; **1978:** 1808, 2031, 2033, 2058, 2059

Nuclear energy agreement with U.S., **1980–81:** 1026

Prime Minister Ahmed Osman, **1977:** 2079

Taxation and fiscal evasion convention, **1978:** 818

U.S. Ambassador, **1978:** 1700, 1724; **1979:** 2077, 2082

U.S. relations, **1980–81:** 173

Moroz, Valentyn, **1979:** 731

Morris, Alvin R., **1978:** 325

Morris, Charles J., **1978:** 411; **1979:** 23

Morris, Lt. Gen. J. W., **1977:** 371, 2076

Morris, Ken, **1978:** 257

Morris, Norval, **1978:** 1538, 1572

Morris, Thomas D., **1977:** 230, 252; **1978:** 1756, 2232

Morrison, Alan, **1980–81:** 264

Morrison, Lydia, **1980–81:** 2312n.

Morrison, Toni, **1980–81:** 1440, 1470

Morrison, Truman A., III, **1979:** 980, 984

Morse, Kathryn, **1978:** 699

Morse, Phoebe Diane, **1980–81:** 949

Morse, Mrs. Wayne, **1980–81:** 2672

Mortgage Association, Federal Home Loan, **1980–81:** 138

Mortgage Association, Federal National, **1977:** 706, 934, 1264; **1978:** 920; **1979:** 931; **1980–81:** 911

Mortgage Association, Government National, **1977:** 591, 596; **1979:** 1316, 1677, 1705; **1980–81:** 138

Mortgage programs, Federal, **1979:** 709

Mortola, Edward J., **1980–81:** 845

Morton, Mrs. Ardis, **1978:** 802

Morton, Azie Taylor, **1977:** 1066, 1085; **1978:** 1809

Morton, Rogers C. B., **1979:** 672

Moscone, George, **1978:** 2088; **1979:** 807, 808ftn., 843

Moseley, David Herron, **1980–81:** 1098, 3023

Moser, Leo J., **1978:** 1668

Moses, Alfred H., **1980–81:** 651, 1467, 1976n.

Moses, Lincoln E., **1977:** 2047, 2050

Moses, Win, **1980–81:** 1019

Moskow, Michael H., **1978:** 52, 150

Moslem nations.
  See Islamic nations.

Mosley, Lenora, **1980–81:** 1369

Moss, Ambler H., Jr., **1978:** 1512, 1517, 1723; **1979:** 837; **1980–81:** 34

Moss, Eunice Lockhart, **1980–81:** 509

Moss, Repr. John E., **1977:** 98; **1978:** 393, 1946

Moss, Otis, **1980–81:** 1001, 1005

Most Favored Nations legislation, **1979:** 358, 359

Mota, Manny, **1979:** 1882

Moten, Rashey, **1979:** 1929

Mother Teresa of Calcutta, **1979:** 1962

Mother's Day, **1977:** 690; **1978:** 890
  (Proc. 4646), **1979:** 438
  (Proc. 4743), **1980–81:** 583

Mothers' Day, Working, **1980–81:** 1592

Motion picture industry, **1977:** 1700, 2041, 2042

Motley, Archibald, Jr., **1980–81:** 602

Motley, Tony, **1978:** 2158

Motor Carrier Act
  Congressional consideration
    Conference committee, **1980–81:** 252
    House of Representatives approval, **1980–81:** 1147
    President's appeal for action, **1980–81:** 78, 150, 498
    Senate approval, **1980–81:** 693, 918
    Senate Commerce Committee action, **1980–81:** 461
    Senators Hart and Kennedy, leadership roles, **1980–81:** 281
  Mentions, **1980–81:** 118, 121, 215, 573, 1358, 1537
  Signing ceremony, **1980–81:** 1261, 1265

Motor Carrier Ratemaking Study Commission, **1980–81:** 2731

Motor Carrier Safety, Bureau of, **1979:** 1625

Motor vehicle safety, **1978:** 1237

Motor Vehicle Safety Act of 1966, National Traffic and, **1980–81:** 2880

Motor Vehicle Safety Report, 1978, **1979:** 1881

Mott, Lucretia, **1980–81:** 412

Mottl, Repr. Ronald M., **1980–81:** 1936, 1937

Motulsky, Arno G., **1979:** 1264

Mount St. Helens, Wash., eruption
  Disaster declaration (Digest), **1980–81:** 967
  Federal assistance, **1980–81:** 991, 1084n., 1092
  President's comments, **1980–81:** 1002, 1903
  President's inspection tour
    Portland, Oreg., **1980–81:** 950
    Spokane, Wash., **1980–81:** 956
    Vancouver, Wash., **1980–81:** 967

Mountain State Forest Festival, **1978:** 1729

Mountbatten, Lord Louis, **1979:** 1522, 1603

Moxley, John Howard, II, **1979:** 1036, 1043

Moyer, Homer E., Jr., **1979:** 2231

Moyers, Bill, **1978:** 2014

Moyers, Judith D., **1978:** 1190

Moynihan, Sen. Daniel Patrick, **1977:** 23, 1233, 1306, 1499; **1978:** 246, 440, 504, 1071, 1772, 1885, 1929, 1930, 2268; **1979:** 240, 898, 1746, 2106
  Campaign appearances with the President, **1980–81:** 2194, 2377
  Legislation passage leadership
    Adoption Assistance and Child Welfare Act, **1980–81:** 1124
    West Valley Demonstration Project Act and Love Canal Agreement, **1980–81:** 2001, 2002

Mozambique
  President Samora Moises Machel, **1977:** 1723, 1754, 1755; **1978:** 976
  Relationship with Western nations, **1979:** 316
  U.S. Ambassador, **1980–81:** 1699

Ms. United Teenager, **1978:** 1333

Mt. Hood Community College, **1978:** 1946

Mubarak, Muhammad Husni.
  See Vice President *under* Egypt.

Muellenberg, Kurt W., **1979:** 198, 378

Mueller, Erwin W., **1977:** 2046

Mueller, Leah Poulos, **1980–81:** 380

Muftic, Dr. Michael, **1979:** 293

Mugabe, Robert.
  See Zimbabwe, Prime Minister.

Muhammed, Matthews Saad, **1980–81:** 1523

Muir, Colleen, **1977:** 314

Mulcrone, Richard T., **1978:** 1503, 1506

Muldawer, Paul, **1979:** 2191; **1980–81:** 2731

Muldoon, Robert D., **1977:** 1649, 1989, 1991, 2007

Mulhern, Francis J., **1979:** 923, 924, 927

Muller, Steven, **1977:** 941; **1978:** 1511

Mulligan, William Hughes, **1980–81:** 2309

Mulroy, John, **1980–81:** 2889

Multifiber Trade Agreement, extension, **1977:** 123

Multilateral Development Banks, **1979:** 279, 396;
    1980–81: 942
Multilateral development institutions (EO 12164),
    1979: 1800
Multilateral Export Controls, report, **1978:** 1278
Multilateral trade agreements
    Administration's legislative priority, **1979:** 944
    Cheese and chocolate crumb import limitations,
        1979: 2228
    Customs Valuation Agreement amendment,
        1980–81: 95
    Enforcement and monitoring of MTN codes,
        1979: 1729
    European Council, U.S. consultations with,
        1979: 2097
    Mentions, **1979:** 1100, 1147; **1980–81:** 322, 2228
    Message transmittal to Congress of agreements
        and implementing legislation, **1979:** 1092,
        1143 (Checklist)
    Presidential determination on acceptance and
        application of agreements, **1979:** 2253
    Purposes of agreements, **1979:** 125, 331, 1488;
        1980–81: 126, 175, 254, 1689, 1904
    Statement by the President, **1979:** 662
    Steel imports antidumping claims, **1980–81:** 902
    Textile arrangements, **1980–81:** 2038
    Tokyo Summit support statement, **1979:** 1200
Multilateral trade negotiations (MTN), **1978:** 144,
    1272, 1309, 1313, 1319, 1333, 1635, 1663,
    2245
    Canadian support, **1979:** 382
    Congressional support, President's appeal for,
        1979: 107, 118, 125, 331
    Countervailing duties waiver, **1979:** 46
    Progress during administration, **1980–81:** 126,
        254, 400, 1545
    Strauss, Robert, role in completion of Tokyo
        Round, **1980–81:** 6, 175
Multiple Sclerosis Mother and Father of the Year,
    1978: 897
Multiple Sclerosis Society, National, **1979:** 842;
    1980–81: 893
Multi-State Regional Action Planning Commis-
    sions, **1979:** 602
Mulvey, Mary C., **1979:** 1682, 1706, 2214
Mund, Vernon A., **1978:** 88; **1980–81:** 1700
Mundheim, Robert H., **1977:** 1119, 1128; **1978:**
    1711
Muñoz Marín, Gov. Luis, **1980–81:** 808
Muramoto, Shuza, **1979:** 2127
Murase, Jiro, **1980–81:** 1048
Muratti, Jose A., Jr., **1979:** 2186
Murdoch, Rupert, **1980–81:** 731
Murelaga, Diana S., **1980–81:** 927
Murie, Mardy, **1980–81:** 1386, 1388n.
Murie, Olaus, **1980–81:** 1386
Murnaghan, Francis D., Jr., **1979:** 843

Murphy, Repr. Austin J., **1980–81:** 369
Murphy, Christopher Jay, III, **1979:** 466
Murphy, Diana E., **1979:** 2188
Murphy, Evelyn F., **1978:** 218; **1979:** 1628
Murphy, Harold L., **1977:** 1222
Murphy, James C., Jr., **1977:** 1059
Murphy, Repr. John M., **1977:** 1962; **1978:** 315,
    1531, 2003; **1979:** 89, 1125, 1777; **1980–
    81:** 318, 1938
Murphy, Mrs. John M., **1979:** 89
Murphy, Repr. Morgan F., **1978:** 193, 1854
Murphy, Patrick Vincent, **1980–81:** 2613
Murphy, Richard W., **1978:** 888, 899
Murphy, Stephen P., **1980–81:** 2731
Murphy, Thomas A., **1977:** 1162; **1978:** 771, 850;
    1979: 786, 1651; **1980–81:** 902, 1670
Murphy, Thomas F., **1980–81:** 95
Murphy, William, **1980–81:** 2889
Murphy Oil Company, **1980–81:** 581
Murray, Paul F., **1978:** 1035, 1071
Murray, Robert J., **1980–81:** 98
Murray, Mr. and Mrs. Robert, **1978:** 364
Murray, Russell, II, **1977:** 549, 558
Muscar, Jakie, Jr., **1980–81:** 1508
Muscatine, Iowa, **1979:** 1492
Muscle Shoals, Ala., **1980–81:** 1605n.
Muscular Dystrophy Association, **1978:** 1221;
    1980–81: 492
Muscular Dystrophy Poster Child, **1977:** 1483
Museum of African Art, **1978:** 1712
Museum Day, National, **1979:** 897
Museum Services, Institute of, **1977:** 2072, 2077;
    1978: 1356; **1979:** 956
Museum Services Board, National.
    See National Museum Services Board.
Mushroom industry, **1980–81:** 2829, 2331, 2562
Mushroom industry, White House task force on
    the, **1980–81:** 2330, 2331
Mushrooms, canned, imports, **1977:** 362
Music Association, Country, **1978:** 769
Music Corporation of America, Inc., **1980–81:** 2806
Music Month, Country, **1978:** 1653; **1980–81:** 1927
Muskie, Sen. Edmund S., **1977:** 40, 650, 706, 1072,
    1460, 1825, 1837, 2162, 2179; **1978:** 282,
    344, 347, 700, 1194, 1808, 2003; **1979:** 179,
    591n., 898, 1609
    See also State, Secretary of.
Musto, David F., **1977:** 1963
Musto, Repr. Raphael, **1980–81:** 2251
Mutual and balanced force reductions, **1977:** 849,
    2210; **1978:** 38, 122, 875, 1013, 1183, 1256,
    1283, 1516; **1979:** 110, 179, 1845
Mutual Educational and Cultural Exchange Act of
    1961, **1978:** 229
Mutuale, Kasongo, **1977:** 1754
Muzorewa, Bishop Abel Tendekai, **1979:** 1014,
    1230
MX missile, **1977:** 1692; **1978:** 123, 533, 2098, 2205

MX missile — *continued*
  Congressional consideration of production pro-
      gram, **1980–81:** 2442
  Missile system basing, **1979:** 1599, 1605, 1607,
      1612, 2235
  Mobile system development, **1980–81:** 348, 1552,
      1725, 1740, 1871, 1909, 2011, 2126, 2213,
      2307, 2337, 2639
  Nevada deployment sites, **1980–81:** 901
  President's decision to deploy, **1979:** 1016
  SALT II treaty provisions, **1979:** 966, 1090, 2235
  Silo missile defense, **1980–81:** 2415
  Solid propellant use, **1980–81:** 1909
Myer, Rashish, **1980–81:** 1048
Myers, Dale D., **1977:** 1584, 1613; **1978:** 1426, 1458
Myers, Frank, **1977:** 142
Myers, Jim, **1979:** 1615
Myers, Maurice, **1978:** 1176
Myers, Samuel L., **1978:** 1514
Myers, Sondra Gelb, **1980–81:** 2701
Myerson, Bess, **1977:** 1699; **1978:** 1511
Myricks, Noel, **1978:** 913

NAACP.
  See National Association for the Advancement
      of Colored People.
Nabisco, Company, **1979:** 2022
Nachmanoff, Arnold, **1978:** 884, 899
Nadao, Hirokichi, **1979:** 1169n.
Naden, Kenneth D., **1978:** 455; **1980–81:** 1048
Nader, Ralph, **1977:** 60
Naess, Michael R., **1978:** 217; **1979:** 2116
Naftalin, Frances H., **1978:** 920, 935
Naill, John D., Jr., **1978:** 919, 935
Nailor, George, **1979:** 956
Najoma, Sam, **1977:** 1433
Nakayama, Tosiwo, **1980–81:** 373
Nam, Byung H., **1980–81:** 774
Namath, Joe, **1980–81:** 2344
Namibia
  Democratic National Committee, remarks, **1978:**
      2197
  Interview remarks, **1978:** 940, 1257, 1348, 1410,
      2178
  Jefferson-Jackson dinner, remarks, **1978:** 1900
  Majority government rule, **1977:** 1720, 1724;
      1979: 39, 357
  News conference remarks, **1978:** 2221
  Peace settlement negotiations, **1980–81:** 1219,
      1585, 1634, 1642, 2096, 2109, 2301
  SWAPO and Western five contact group agree-
      ment, **1978:** 1271
  United Nations involvement, **1979:** 1333; **1980–
      81:** 1286
  U.S. export controls, **1979:** 2291, 2293

Namibia — *continued*
  U.S. policy, **1977:** 646, 913, 1090; **1978:** 121, 629,
      653; **1980–81:** 1929
  U.S. relations, **1979:** 2137, 2264
Naparstek, Arthur J., **1977:** 2153
Naples, Samuel F., **1980–81:** 423, 424
Narayanan, K. R., **1980–81:** 2752
Narcotics.
  See Drugs and narcotics.
Narita, Hiroshi, **1978:** 1254, 1257
NASA.
  See National Aeronautics and Space Adminis-
      tration.
Nasher, Ray, **1980–81:** 2560
Nashua, N. H., **1978:** 364, 414
Nashville, Tenn., **1978:** 1857, 1862; **1980–81:** 2124,
      2139
Nason, Marshall, **1978:** 85, 87
Natcher, Repr. William H., **1977:** 784, 1632; **1979:**
      2156
Natchez Trace National Scenic Trail, **1979:** 1367,
      1814
Nathan, Richard, **1978:** 507
Nathan, Robert, **1979:** 1954
Nathan, Ronald G., **1977:** 1811, 1826; **1978:** 230
National Academy for Fire Prevention and Con-
      trol, **1979:** 566
National Academy of Peace and Conflict Reso-
      lution, Commission for the, **1979:** 2195
National Academy of Sciences, **1979:** 676–682,
      733; **1980–81:** 473
National Advisory Committee for Juvenile Justice
      and Delinquency Prevention, **1977:** 1713;
      1978: 1193; **1980–81:** 1097, 3022
National Advisory Committee on Oceans and
      Atmosphere, **1978:** 217; **1979:** 1628, 2118,
      2187; **1980–81:** 1023, 2242
National Advisory Committee for Women, **1978:**
      680, 883, 1134
National Advisory Committee for Women
  Acting Chairperson, **1979:** 88, 217
  Chairperson, **1979:** 26
  Relationship with the President, **1979:** 52
  White House statement, **1979:** 27
National Advisory Community Investment Board,
      1979: 1815; **1980–81:** 2613, 2770, 2882
National Advisory Council on Adult Education,
      1978: 570; **1979:** 1524; **1980–81:** 267, 844,
      2558, 3022
National Advisory Council on Economic Oppor-
      tunity, **1977:** 1030, 1477 **1978:** 709, 1278;
      1979: 1447, 1727, 2042; **1980–81:** 274,
      1925, 2672
National Advisory Council on the Education of
      Disadvantaged Children, **1979:** 1727;
      1980–81: 257, 1839

National Advisory Council on Extension and Con-
    tinuing Education, **1977:** 2063; **1978:** 913;
    1979: 1023, 1293; **1980–81:** 1669, 2817
National Advisory Council on Indian Education,
    1978: 1418; **1979:** 446, 932; **1980–81:** 849,
    2883
National Advisory Council on International Mon-
    etary and Financial Policies, **1979:** 439,
    1731
National Advisory Council on Vocational Educa-
    tion, **1979:** 1447; **1980–81:** 2817
National Advisory Council on Women's Educa-
    tional Programs, **1978:** 1086, 1111; **1979:**
    339, 377, 2039, 2044; **1980–81:** 508, 1023,
    1051, 1569
National Aeronautics and Space Administration,
    1977: 965, 1031, 1699; **1978:** 892, 1137,
    1165, 1684; **1980–81:** 563, 1417
  Administrator, **1979:** 1276, 1277n., 2138
  Inspector General, **1979:** 398, 402
  LANDSAT program, **1979:** 2149
  Research Apprenticeship Program, **1979:** 2064
  Rockwell International, contract with, **1979:** 242
  Solar energy programs, **1979:** 1105
  U.S.-People's Republic of China science and
    technology agreements, **1979:** 201, 206
  Weather programs, **1979:** 2150
National Afro-American (Black) History Month,
    1980–81: 84
National Agenda for the Eighties, President's Com-
    mission for a.
  See President's Commission for a National
    Agenda for the Eighties.
National Agriculture Day, **1980–81:** 2145n.
National Airlines, **1979:** 2283
National Alcohol Fuels Commission, **1979:** 1007,
    1445; **1980–81:** 235, 899
National Alliance of Business, Inc., **1978:** 1772;
    1980–81: 422
National Alliance of Businessmen, **1977:** 1611;
    1978: 961, 973, 994; **1979:** 1976
National Alliance for the Prevention and Treat-
    ment of Child Abuse and Maltreatment,
    1980–81: 267
National Anthem, **1978:** 2221
National Aquaculture Act, **1980–81:** 1937
National Architectural Barrier Awareness Week,
    1978: 774, 933
  (Proc. 4656), **1979:** 641
National Architectural and Transportation Com-
    pliance Board, **1978:** 933
National Archives and Records Service, **1978:**
    1200, 1202, 1955
National Armed Forces Museum Advisory Board,
    1980–81: 1047
National Association for the Advancement of
    Colored People (NAACP), **1977:** 1699;

National Association (NAACP) — *continued*
    1978: 56, 2269; **1979:** 38; **1980–81:** 1281,
    1322
National Association of Broadcasters, **1978:** 254;
    1979: 482, 490; **1980–81:** 1050
National Association of Community Health Cen-
    ters, **1979:** 983
National Association of Counties, **1977:** 1794;
    1979: 1241, 1294; **1980–81:** 1846
National Association for Equal Opportunity in
    Higher Education, **1979:** 742
National Association of Farm Broadcasting, **1978:**
    1669, 1671
National Association of Home Builders, **1978:**
    1240; **1979:** 732
National Association of Manufacturers, **1977:**
    2036; **1979:** 957; **1980–81:** 292
National Association of State Departments of
    Agriculture, **1979:** 240; **1980–81:** 492
National Association of State Attorneys General,
    1977: 251; **1979:** 618
National Association of Theater Owners, **1978:** 933
National Association of Wheat Growers, **1978:** 525
National Association of Women Judges, **1980–81:**
    2057, 2071
National Athletic Boosters Week (Proc. 4764),
    1980–81: 1131
National Audubon Society, **1980–81:** 415
National Aviation Facilities Experimental Center,
    1978: 1542
National Aviation Year and Wright Brothers Day,
    1978: 1396
National Bankers Association, **1977:** 744
National Basketball Association, **1978:** 1070;
    1980–81: 268
National Bible Week, **1978:** 2070; **1980–81:** 2747
National Bicycling Day (Proc. 4741), **1980–81:** 562
National Black Caucus of State Legislators, **1980–
    81:** 333
National Black Radio Network, **1977:** 1340
National Broadcasting Company (NBC), **1979:**
    1678; **1980–81:** 34, 561, 1246, 2233
National Brotherhood Week, **1978:** 326; **1980–81:**
    343
National Bureau of Standards, **1977:** 1300, 2001,
    2006; **1978:** 231
National Business League, **1980–81:** 63, 1281
National Cable Television Association, **1978:** 254;
    1979: 932; **1980–81:** 483, 1403
National Cancer Advisory Board, **1979:** 673, 686,
    1975, 2151; **1980–81:** 911
National Cancer Institute, **1977:** 1378; **1980–81:**
    1332
National Cancer Program, **1977:** 556, 706; **1979:**
    673, 2105
National Capital Planning Commission, **1979:** 687;
    1980–81: 1412
National Capital Transportation Amendments of
    1979, **1980–81:** 13, 17

[References are to page numbers except as otherwise indicated]

National Captioning Institute, **1980–81:** 811
National Cathedral, Washington, D.C., **1979:** 2139
National Cattlemen's Association, **1980–81:** 521
National Caucus on the Black Aged, **1979:** 317
National Center of Economic Education for Children, **1979:** 842
National Center for Productivity and Quality of Working Life, **1978:** 1835
National Championship Chess Team, **1979:** 787
National Child Abuse Prevention Month (Proc. 4704), **1979:** 2153
National Citizen's Coalition for the Windfall Profits Tax, **1979:** 1705, 2043; **1980–81:** 586
National climate program, **1978:** 1907; **1980–81:** 2723
National Coal Mining Museum, **1980–81:** 2199
National coastal protection, **1979:** 1362, 1373
National Commission on Air Quality, **1978:** 762, 1178; **1979:** 1353; **1980–81:** 508
National Commission on Alcoholism and Other Alcohol-Related Problems, **1980–81:** 2609, 2801
National Commission on Employment Policy, **1979:** 947, 2081; **1980–81:** 1981
National Commission on the International Year of the Child, 1979, **1979:** 229, 1445, 2090; **1980–81:** 752
  Chairman, **1978:** 815
  Establishment, **1978:** 746
  Legislation, **1978:** 963
  Members, **1978:** 1190
  U.S. participation, **1978:** 1191
National Commission on Libraries and Information Science, **1978:** 919, 935, 1454, 1458; **1979:** 196, 218, 2277, 2281; **1980–81:** 1445, 1470, 1933
National Commission on Manpower Policy, **1978:** 391, 697
National Commission on Neighborhoods, **1977:** 1905, 1931, 2153; **1979:** 618; **1980–81:** 1094, 2117
National Commission on the Observance of International Women's Year, 1975, **1977:** 524–527, 2025; **1978:** 553
National Commission for the Review of Antitrust Laws and Procedures, **1977:** 2064, 2177; **1979:** 132, 178, 875; **1980–81:** 2850
  Business Panel on Antitrust Export Issues, members, **1978:** 1878
  Executive order, **1978:** 707
  Members, **1978:** 1139, 1140
  State of the Union, **1978:** 112
National Commission for the Review of Federal and State Laws Relating to Wiretapping and Electronic Surveillance, **1979:** 585, 587–590

National Commission on Social Security, **1978:** 1720, 1772; **1980–81:** 2900
  Budget deferrals, **1979:** 1522, 2285
  Members, **1979:** 23, 45, 46, 90, 92
National Commission on Student Financial Assistance, **1980–81:** 2751, 2812
National Commission on Unemployment Compensation, **1978:** 174, 257, 1051
National Committee for an Effective Congress, **1978:** 770
National Committee for Health Insurance, **1977:** 1127
National Communications System, **1978:** 602, 604
National Community Christmas Tree, **1979:** 2244; **1980–81:** 2817
National Conference of Artists, **1980–81:** 600
National Conference of Black Mayors, **1977:** 1945; **1980–81:** 720
National Conference of Catholic Bishops, **1977:** 1611; **1978:** 2059; **1979:** 1925, 1977
National Conference of Christians and Jews, **1979:** 969; **1980–81:** 343
National Conference of Democratic Mayors, **1979:** 1561n.
National Conference on Fraud, Abuse and Error, **1978:** 2228, 2270
National Conference on Physical Fitness and Sports for All, **1980–81:** 259
National Conference on Soviet Jewry, **1980–81:** 1662
National Conference of State Legislatures, **1979:** 1705, 2150; **1980–81:** 552
  Representatives, meeting with the President, **1977:** 252
National Conference of State Societies, **1977:** 546
National Consumer Cooperative Bank
  Board of Directors, members, **1979:** 1220, 1223, 1317, 1319; **1980–81:** 605, 608, 844, 893, 2614
  Budget allocations increase, **1980–81:** 146
  Budget deferral, **1979:** 2285; **1980–81:** 2961
  Congressional approval, **1979:** 136
  Office of Self-Help Development and Technical Assistance, Director, **1980–81:** 1419, 1428
National Consumer Education Week (Proc. 4746), **1980–81:** 621
National Corporation for Housing Partnerships, **1978:** 1279, 1500, 1506; **1980–81:** 1048, 1111
National Council on the Arts, **1977:** 1264, 2024, 2037; **1978:** 252, 277; **1980–81:** 237, 268, 452
  Annual report, **1979:** 2280
  Members, **1979:** 45, 92, 435, 441
National Council of the Associations of Indians in America, **1979:** 1604

National Council of Churches of Christ of America, **1978:** 415
National Council of Churches Full Employment Mobilization Group, **1978:** 1154
National Council on Educational Research, **1978:** 54, 149, 895, 935; **1979:** 44, 91, 1820
  Members, **1980–81:** 96, 218, 508, 522, 1335, 1336, 2752, 2870, 2872, 2873
National Council on the Handicapped, **1979:** 2089
  Chairman, **1980–81:** 810
  Members, **1980–81:** 812, 826, 1596, 1599
National Council on the Humanities, **1978:** 1706, 1724, 2049; **1980–81:** 264, 269
  Members, **1979:** 45, 46, 90, 91, 232, 242
National Council of Mayors, **1978:** 229
National Council of Negro Women, **1979:** 2136
National Council of Senior Citizens, **1978:** 1062
National Credit Union Administration, **1977:** 744, 1375, 1376, 1384; **1978:** 1059, 1772
  Interest rate increase for small savers, **1979:** 930
  National Credit Union Board, members, **1979:** 397, 402, 1041, 1044, 1299, 1319
National crime index, **1977:** 1976
National Cystic Fibrosis Poster Child, **1980–81:** 720
National Cystic Fibrosis Week (Proc. 4775), **1980–81:** 1395
National Day of Prayer, **1977:** 1792; **1978:** 1482
  (Proc. 4690), **1979:** 1694
  (Proc. 4795), **1980–81:** 1858
National defense and security.
  See Defense and national security.
National Defense Transportation Day (Proc. 4639), **1979:** 238
National Defense Transportation Day and National Transportation Week, **1977:** 610; **1978:** 255
  (Proc. 4737), **1980–81:** 506, 930
National Democratic Party Conference, **1978:** 2073, 2189, 2198, 2209, 2222, 2270
National Development Bank, **1979:** 99, 117, 137
  Proposed, **1978:** 580, 581, 587, 2193
National Diabetes Week
  (Proc. 4686), **1979:** 1671
  (Proc. 4779), **1980–81:** 1519
National Earthquake Hazards Reduction program, **1979:** 537
National Education Association, **1977:** 744; **1978:** 296, 303; **1979:** 1785; **1980–81:** 1295, 2884ftn.
National Employ the Handicapped Week, **1977:** 1672; **1978:** 1502
  (Proc. 4685), **1979:** 1660
  (Proc. 4784), **1980–81:** 1571
National Employ the Older Worker Week, **1977:** 155
National Endowment for the Arts, **1979:** 142, 2280; **1978:** 590

National Endowment for the Arts — *continued*
  Annual report, **1977:** 1264; **1980–81:** 452, 1428
  Chairman, **1977:** 1522, 1534, 1946, 1966
  Challenge grants increase, **1980–81:** 601
  National Council on the Arts, members, **1980–81:** 1439, 1470, 1927, 1947
  Public broadcasting, **1977:** 1744
National Endowment for the Humanities, **1977:** 556, 1398, 1438, 1465, 1744; **1978:** 880; **1979:** 142; **1980–81:** 521, 774, 1332, 1337
National Energy Act of 1978, **1979:** 1103, 1354, 1622
National Energy Conservation Days (Proc. 4753), **1980–81:** 783
National Energy Conservation Policy Act, **1978:** 1978
National Energy Education Day (Proc. 4738), **1980–81:** 509, 510
National Energy Foundation, **1980–81:** 1468
National energy supply shortage (Proc. 4667), **1979:** 1227
National Environmental Policy Act of 1970, **1980–81:** 351, 415
National Environmental Policy Act of 1978, **1979:** 121, 1354
National Family Week, **1977:** 1992; **1978:** 1801
  (Proc. 4703), **1979:** 2134
  (Proc. 4806), **1980–81:** 2749
National Farm-City Week, **1977:** 1821; **1978:** 1636
  (Proc. 4696), **1979:** 1999
  (Proc. 4781), **1980–81:** 1521
National Farm Safety Week, **1977:** 524; **1978:** 545
  (Proc. 4645), **1979:** 433
  (Proc. 4749), **1980–81:** 683
National Farmers Organization, **1979:** 2206
National Farmers Union, **1977:** 595; **1980–81:** 1050
National Federation of Democratic Women, **1978:** 797, 803
National Fire Academy, **1979:** 1437, 1438
National Fire Prevention and Control Administration, **1977:** 118; **1978:** 1129, 1132
National Firefighters Week, **1980–81:** 2266
National Fish Health Research Laboratory, **1979:** 1042
National Foreign Intelligence Board, **1978:** 197, 213, 215
National Forest Management Act of 1976, amendment, **1978:** 384
National Forest Products Week, **1977:** 1697; **1978:** 1560
  (Proc. 4687), **1979:** 1686
  (Proc. 4790), **1980–81:** 1645
National Forest Service, **1979:** 775
National Forest System, **1979:** 151, 669, 670
  Additional lands designation, **1980–81:** 159, 1410, 1646
  Lands conveyance legislation, **1980–81:** 2845
  Timber supply source, **1980–81:** 1145

National Forest System — *continued*
 Wood residue utilization, **1980–81:** 2821
National Foundation on the Arts and Humanities,
   1978: 2059; **1980–81:** 754
National 4-H Club, **1980–81:** 701
National Gallery of Art, **1978:** 606, 1027; **1980–81:**
   340
National Good Neighbor Day, **1978:** 1569
National Goodwill Graduate of 1980, **1980–81:** 893
National Governors' Association, **1978:** 934, 936;
   1980–81: 397
 Chairman, **1979:** 1222
 Committee on international trade and foreign
   relations, question-and-answer session
   with the President, **1979:** 330
 Foreign trade and export development seminars,
   sponsorship, **1979:** 897, 900
 Independent truckers' strikes recommendations,
   1979: 1138
 Rural development recommendations, **1979:**
   2276
 Space program board, membership, **1979:** 2150
 Winter session meeting, White House dinner for
   members attending, **1979:** 354
National Governors' Conference, **1977:** 268, 279,
   280, 1211, 2162; **1978:** 431, 1480
National Grandparents Day, **1978:** 1360
   (Proc. 4679), **1979:** 1597
National Grange, **1978:** 1345; **1980–81:** 1428
National Guard Day, **1978:** 1558
National Guard and Reserve, **1977:** 1694
National Gypsum Co., **1980–81:** 581
National health insurance, **1977:** 162, 393, 892, 896,
   1327, 1995, 2194
National Health Insurance, Committee for, **1977:**
   1127
National Health Resources Advisory Committee,
   1978: 325
National Health Service Corps, **1977:** 2088, 2104;
   1978: 102; **1979:** 134; **1980–81:** 909
National Heart, Lung, and Blood Institute, **1979:**
   178; **1980–81:** 190
National heritage policy act, proposed, **1979:** 1359;
   1980–81: 418
National Heritage Trust, proposed, **1977:** 979
National Highway Safety Advisory Committee,
   1977: 2028; **1978:** 1467, 1564; **1979:** 1775;
   1980–81: 1845, 2107, 2815, 3022
National Highway Traffic Safety Administration,
   1977: 461, 465, 1533; **1980–81:** 281
National Hispanic Heritage Week, **1977:** 1521,
   1600; **1978:** 1436, 1451
   (Proc. 4662), **1979:** 930
   (Proc. 4776), **1980–81:** 1461
National Historic Preservation Act Amendments,
   1980–81: 2802
National Historic Preservation Week, **1978:** 887

National Historical Publications and Records
   Commission, **1978:** 2274; **1980–81:** 1424
National Housing Goal, **1978:** 1723
National Housing Partnership, **1978:** 1279
National Hunting and Fishing Day (Proc. 4682),
   1979: 1626
National Hydropower Study, **1979:** 1511
National Institute of Building Sciences, **1978:** 1154
 Annual report, **1979:** 982; **1980–81:** 422
 Board of Directors, members, **1979:** 44, 92, 607,
   619; **1980–81:** 533, 564
 Members, **1980–81:** 1595, 1599
National Institute of Corrections, **1978:** 1249
National Institute of Education, **1977:** 1253, 1266,
   1780
 Deputy Director, **1980–81:** 949
 Director, **1980–81:** 651, 825
 National Council on Educational Research,
   members, **1980–81:** 1335, 1336
National Institute of Handicapped Research, **1979:**
   2089, 2106
National Institute of Justice, **1979:** 131; **1980–81:**
   2612, 2701, 2875
 Proposed, **1978:** 1242, 1249
National Institute for Law Enforcement and Crim-
   inal Justice, proposed, **1978:** 1249
National Institute for Occupational Safety and
   Health, **1980–81:** 395
National Institutes of Health, **1979:** 544, 2007,
   2064; **1980–81:** 955, 956, 1396
National Intelligence Tasking Center, **1977:** 1422;
   1978: 197, 215
National Inventors' Day
   (Proc. 4635), **1979:** 196
   (Proc. 4721), **1980–81:** 273
   (Proc. 4814), **1980–81:** 2887
National Issue Forum, **1979:** 1630
National Italian-American Foundation, **1980–81:**
   1718, 1848
National Jogging Day, **1978:** 1770
National Labor Relations Act amendments, **1980–**
   81: 2856
National Labor Relations Board, **1977:** 618, 1277,
   1666, 1700, 1752, 1755; **1978:** 109, 564,
   1468, 1471; **1979:** 1976, 2166, 2300
 Chairman, **1980–81:** 2856
 General Counsel, **1980–81:** 217, 218
 Interagency Employee Benefit Council, member-
   ship, **1980–81:** 2864
 Members, **1980–81:** 1026, 1052, 1494, 1524, 2453,
   2726, 2727, 2870, 2873
National League of Cities, **1978:** 2075, 2080, 2188;
   1980–81: 103, 495, 523
National League of Families of American Prisoners and Missing in Southeast Asia,
   1977: 147

National Library of Medicine, **1977:** 196; **1978:** 275, 303

National Lupus Week, **1977:** 1527; **1978:** 1456 (Proc. 4680), **1979:** 1620 (Proc. 4779), **1980–81:** 2183

National Main Street Center, **1980–81:** 932

National Marine Sanctuaries, **1980–81:** 2997

National Maritime Day, **1977:** 640; **1978:** 515 (Proc. 4653), **1979:** 606 (Proc. 4736), **1980–81:** 469

National Meals on Wheels Week (Proc. 4689), **1979:** 1693

National Medal of Science, **1977:** 2044; **1979:** 2289; **1980–81:** 80

National Medal of Science, President's Committee on the, **1980–81:** 2849, 3023

National Mediation Board, **1977:** 1293, 1307; **1978:** 1701, 1724; **1979:** 1299, 1319, 1696; **1980–81:** 103, 667, 1125, 1150

National Medic Alert Week (Proc. 4739), **1980–81:** 514

National Mental Health Association, **1980–81:** 785, 1091

National Military Command Center, **1978:** 276

National Minority Purchasing Council, **1979:** 1975

National Mortgage Association, Federal, **1980–81:** 911

National Mortgage Association, Government, **1980–81:** 138

National Multiple Sclerosis Society, **1979:** 842

National Museum Day (Proc. 4661), **1979:** 897

National Museum Services Board, **1977:** 1780, 1796; **1980–81:** 2859, 2870, 2873
  Chairman, **1979:** 956
  Members, **1979:** 269, 294, 1157, 1159

National Naval Medical Center, **1980–81:** 104

National Newspaper Association, **1977:** 1921

National Newspaper Publishers Association, **1977:** 1126; **1979:** 440

National Newspaper Week, **1979:** 1807; **1980–81:** 2188

National Nursing Home Week, **1978:** 823; **1979:** 549; **1980–81:** 604

National Oceanic and Atmospheric Administration, **1977:** 983, 1196, 1213; **1978:** 285, 304, 576, 641; **1979:** 1363, 2149
  Administrator, **1980–81:** 3047
  Budget deferral, **1980–81:** 1577
  Commissioned Officer Corps, Director, **1980–81:** 2746, 2782
  Environmental protection activities, **1980–81:** 352
  Mention, **1980–81:** 415
  National Ocean Survey, Director, **1980–81:** 1432, 1470
  Ocean thermal energy conversion industry, licensing program, **1980–81:** 1473

National Oceans Week, **1978:** 756

National Panama Canal Citizens Committee, **1977:** 2037

National Park Service, **1979:** 1366
  Channel Islands Marine Sanctuary designation, **1980–81:** 1856
  Co-founder Horace Albright, **1980–81:** 1598
  Mount St. Helens, Wash., eruption, disaster assistance actions, **1980–81:** 951, 953, 958

National Park System, **1979:** 1354, 1365; **1980–81:** 433, 1411, 2756

National Parks and Recreation Act of 1978, **1978:** 1999; **1979:** 1354, 1359; **1980–81:** 416
  Amendments, **1980–81:** 432

National Patriotism Week (Proc. 4810), **1980–81:** 2832

National Petroleum Reserve, Alaska, **1978:** 1345; **1980–81:** 63

National Planning Council for the International Year of Disabled Persons, **1979:** 1678

National Poison Prevention Week, **1977:** 145; **1978:** 281 (Proc. 4638), **1979:** 232 (Proc. 4719), **1980–81:** 238

National Porcelain Art Month (Proc. 4772), **1980–81:** 1277

National Port Week, **1978:** 1513 (Proc. 4695), **1979:** 1835 (Proc. 4798), **1980–81:** 2066

National P.O.W.-M.I.A. Recognition Day, **1978:** 1453 (Proc. 4664), **1979:** 999 (Proc. 4774), **1980–81:** 1282

National Prayer Breakfast, **1977:** 24; **1978:** 263; **1979:** 58; **1980–81:** 275

National Press Club, **1977:** 22, 642; **1980–81:** 1576, 1732, 1829, 2219, 2333

National Productivity Council, **1978:** 1833–1835; **1979:** 532, 2072

National Public Radio, **1977:** 1738; **1979:** 1518, 1885

National public works and economic development act, proposed, **1979:** 599, 601, 602

National Radio Broadcasters Association, **1978:** 254

National Railroad Passenger Corporation (Amtrak), **1977:** 1810, 1826
  Board of Directors, members, **1978:** 230, 881, 1512, 1517, 2184; **1979:** 92, 397, 402; **1980–81:** 296, 1010, 1823, 1847, 1969, 2070
  Legislation, **1978:** 1718
  President's commitment to improvement, **1979:** 1408
  Schedule modifications, **1979:** 1326

National Railway Labor Conference, **1979:** 818, 819

National Recreation and Parks Week (Proc. 4760), **1980–81:** 936
National recreation trails, **1979:** 1366
National and Regional Intergovernmental Audit Forums, **1977:** 1563
National Register of Historic Places, **1979:** 1359
National Register of Natural Areas, **1979:** 1359
National Religious Broadcasters, **1980–81:** 180
National Retired Teachers Association, **1979:** 1630
National Rural Electric Cooperative Association, **1977:** 1119, 1965; **1978:** 1101; **1980–81:** 1110, 1714
National Rural Water Association, **1980–81:** 1429
National Safe Boating Week, **1977:** 1080
National Salute to Hospitalized Veterans' Day (Proc. 4815), **1980–81:** 2888
National School Board Association, **1979:** 1018
National School Lunch Week, **1977:** 1643; **1978:** 1503
  (Proc. 4691), **1979:** 1694
  (Proc. 4796), **1980–81:** 1925
National Science Board, **1977:** 2002, 2006; **1978:** 128, 1358, 1760, 1773
National Science Foundation, **1978:** 412, 892, 1378
  Acid rain research program, **1979:** 1389
  Annual reports, **1979:** 1272; **1980–81:** 1287
  Appropriations legislation, **1980–81:** 2804
  Assistant Directors, **1977:** 1475, 1483, 1529, 1534, 1929, 1931; **1979:** 1619
  Budget deferral, **1977:** 2002
  Deputy Director, **1977:** 1475, 1483; **1980–81:** 1022, 1051
  Director, **1977:** 689, 707, 1046, 2102; **1979:** 205, 1388, 1389; **1980–81:** 1238, 1289, 1292, 1417
  Environment message, **1977:** 983
  Industrial innovative initiatives programs, **1979:** 2071, 2072
  National Science Board
    Members, **1979:** 46, 92, 93, 196, 218, 529, 554; **1980–81:** 1149, 1246
    Report, **1979:** 2156
  Public broadcasting, **1977:** 1744
  Radiation Policy Council membership, **1980–81:** 363
  Report, **1977:** 1475, 1476
  Research Apprenticeship Program, **1979:** 2064
  Science and technology programs, **1979:** 531, 544, 545
  Small business assistance program, **1980–81:** 77
  World forest preservation responsibilities, **1979:** 1388
National Science and Technology Policy Organization and Priorities Act of 1976, **1978:** 1639
National security.
  See Defense and national security.

National Security Agency, **1978:** 203, 1854
National Security Award, **1979:** 1515
National Security Council
  Arms control, **1977:** 380
  B-1 bomber, assessment, **1977:** 224
  Civil defense planning oversight, **1979:** 1279
  Daily intelligence reports submittal to President, **1979:** 676
  Intelligence activities, **1978:** 195, 214, 232
  Iran, American hostages in, consultations with the President, **1980–81:** 11, 577, 1490
  Kampuchean relief efforts recommendations, **1979:** 2112, 2113
  Meetings with the President (Digest), **1977:** 9, 31, 111, 251, 279, 508, 1464, 1465, 1482, 1567; **1978:** 415, 2280; **1979:** 2105, 2206; **1980–81:** 607, 2806
  National security information functions, **1978:** 1194, 1199, 1202, 1204, 1205
  News conference remarks, **1978:** 1183
  Organization, **1977:** 8
  Policy Review Committee, **1978:** 1135
  Press Officer, **1980–81:** 1203
  Reorganization, **1977:** 1104, 1258, 1421
  Reorganization Plan No. 3 of 1978, **1978:** 1130
  Soviet troops in Cuba review, **1979:** 1704
  Special Coordination Committee, **1978:** 881
  Staff members, **1979:** 984, 1045, 1522n., 1787, 2183n., 2189
  State Department, relationship with, **1980–81:** 797, 877, 881
  Telecommunications functions, **1978:** 601–604, 607, 611
National security information, **1978:** 1193, 1207, 1223; **1979:** 170, 585
National Security Medal, **1979:** 179
National Security and Military Applications of Nuclear Energy Authorization Act of 1980, Department of Energy, **1979:** 2298
National Sickle Cell Anemia, Cooley's Anemia, Tay-Sachs, and Genetic Diseases Act, **1978:** 897; **1979:** 1705, 2106
National Small Business Person of the Year, **1978:** 819; **1979:** 868
National Society of Professional Engineers, **1977:** 194
National Solar User Information Program, **1979:** 1102
National Space Club, **1980–81:** 563
National Student Association, **1978:** 769
National Student Exposition on Energy Resources, **1980–81:** 1468
National Student Lobby, **1978:** 769
National Task Force on Ridesharing, **1979:** 2022, 2023
National Teacher of the Year, **1978:** 546

National Technical Information Service, **1979:** 2070; **1980–81:** 1932

National Telecommunications and Information Administration, **1978:** 786; **1979:** 586; **1980–81:** 1706n.

National toxicology program, **1979:** 536

National Traffic and Motor Vehicle Safety Act of 1966, **1980–81:** 2880

National Trails System, **1979:** 1354, 1366, 1380–1382, 1813

National Trails System Act of 1968, **1979:** 1366, 1380, 1382

National Transportation Policy Study Commission, **1978:** 930

National Transportation Safety Board, **1977:** 1217, 1286, 1307; **1980–81:** 493, 1975, 2070
  Chairman and members, **1978:** 223, 232, 277, 303, 795, 881, 1669
  Members, **1979:** 437, 441, 1007, 1019, 1964, 2043
  Vice Chairman, **1978:** 1669

National Transportation Week
  (Proc. 4639), **1979:** 238
  (Proc. 4753), **1980–81:** 783, 931

National Unity Day (Proc. 4709), **1979:** 2252

National Urban Coalition, **1980–81:** 563

National Urban League, **1977:** 1347, 1384
  Annual conference, **1980–81:** 1499, 1524
  President Vernon E. Jordan, Jr., **1977:** 1347, 1348, 1373, 1938, 1963
    Annual conference attendance, **1980–81:** 1499, 1506
    President's past relationship with, **1980–81:** 1001
    Shooting of
      Mention, **1980–81:** 1049
      President's comments, **1980–81:** 1001
      Statement by the President, **1980–81:** 991
      Visit to Fort Wayne, Ind., hospital, remarks following, **1980–81:** 1019–1022

National Voluntary Action program, **1979:** 880

National Volunteer Organizations, Conference of, **1979:** 1679

National Volunteer Week, **1980–81:** 695

National Weather Service, **1980–81:** 1050

National Wild and Scenic Rivers System, **1978:** 1771, 1999; **1979:** 1364, 1813, 1815, 2245
  Alaska additions, **1980–81:** 2758
  Birch River, W. Va., **1980–81:** 433
  John Day River, Oreg., **1980–81:** 323
  Salmon River, Idaho, **1980–81:** 1408, 1410
  Stanislaus River, Calif., **1980–81:** 1307

National Wilderness Preservation System, **1979:** 240, 669, 1975; **1980–81:** 1142, 1411, 2756

National Wildlife Federation, **1979:** 443

National Wildlife Refuge, **1980–81:** 1411, 1431

National Women's Conference, **1978:** 2069

National Women's History Week, **1980–81:** 412

National Women's Political Caucus, **1977:** 544

National YMCA Youth Governors Conference, **1978:** 1210

National Youth Conservation Corps, proposed, **1977:** 349

Nationwide Insurance Co., **1980–81:** 995n.

Nationwide Outdoor Recreation Plan, **1979:** 2220

NATO.
  See North Atlantic Treaty Organization.

Natural Areas, National Register of, **1979:** 1359

Natural gas
  Alaska transportation system, **1977:** 1242, 1530, 1533, 1620, 1645, 1978, 1980; **1978:** 114
  Business and industry representatives, legislation briefing, **1978:** 1484
  Coal plants conversion to, **1980–81:** 1372
  Commercial exploration in Alaska, **1980–81:** 233, 234
  Conservation, **1977:** 348, 519, 680, 1515
  Conservation (EO 12185), **1979:** 2261
  Deregulation, **1977:** 43, 222, 284, 699, 1082, 1092, 1235, 1389, 1397, 1672, 1685, 1724, 1881, 1925, 1940, 1985; **1978:** 497, 941
  Drilling equipment export suspension to Soviet Union, **1980–81:** 41
  Emergency, **1977:** 67, 555
  Emergency supplies management (EO 12335), **1980–81:** 1628
  Extraction from coal and shale, **1979:** 793
  Farm organizations representatives, meeting with the President, **1978:** 1484
  Federal leases, **1977:** 1395
  Governors, meeting with the President, **1978:** 1480, 1485
  Imports, **1979:** 236
  Imports from Canada, **1977:** 283, 534
  Increased domestic production, **1980–81:** 480, 889
  Industrial users, **1978:** 1488
  Industry tax, **1977:** 700
  Interview remarks, **1978:** 1349, 1490, 1589, 1671, 1672
  Legislation, **1977:** 20, 21, 32, 66, 68; **1978:** 768, 967, 1452, 1459, 1469, 1471, 1476, 1487–1489, 1542, 1644, 1653, 1654
  Mexican supplies, **1979:** 58, 182, 185, 612, 737, 791, 813, 1413, 1569
  News conference remarks, **1978:** 1444, 1745
  New England home heating use, **1979:** 1327
  Pipeline safety, **1980–81:** 2869
  Presidents visit to offshore drilling rig, question-and-answer session, **1977:** 1334
  Price decontrol, **1979:** 1482, 1586, 2056; **1980–81:** 92, 250, 762, 1733, 1737, 2406, 2410, 2417, 2601
  Prices, **1977:** 283, 703, 906, 1172, 1911; **1978:** 56, 2048

Natural gas — *continued*
  Production, **1979:** 175, 1316, 1724
  Shortage, **1977:** 6, 32, 34, 37–45, 259, 1514, 1600
  Supplies, **1977:** 222, 223
  Undiscovered U.S. supplies, **1979:** 1575
  United Steelworkers of America Convention, remarks, **1978:** 1546
  U.S.-Canadian pipeline agreement, **1977:** 1546, 1547, 1569
  Utility companies use reduction, **1980–81:** 448, 472
  Well drillings, 1980 statistics, **1980–81:** 1603, 1675, 1721, 1743, 1763, 1768, 1827, 1864, 1870, 1882, 1884, 1888, 1898, 1902, 1915, 1974, 2005, 2045, 2047, 2082, 2119, 2142, 2166, 2204, 2277, 2297, 2353, 2406, 2410, 2416, 2421, 2457, 2481, 2531, 2539, 2589, 2601, 2607, 2630
  World Bank Group and International Monetary Fund, remarks, **1978:** 1628
Natural Gas, U.S.-Mexico Agreement on, **1979:** 1703, 1706
Natural Gas Pipeline Safety Act of 1968, **1977:** 1699; **1980–81:** 291
Natural Gas Policy Act of 1978, **1978:** 1978; **1979:** 1097
Natural Gas Transportation System, Alaska.
  See Alaska Natural Gas Transportation System.
Natural resources, **1977:** 1406, 1437
  Administration's accomplishments and goals, **1980–81:** 157, 2969
  Alaska lands legislation.
    See Alaska National Interest Lands Conservation Act.
  Conservation, **1980–81:** 1143, 1145, 2891
  Federal policy statement, **1980–81:** 1141
  U.S. productivity asset, **1980–81:** 1206
  See also Environment.
Natural resources, department of, proposed, **1979:** 378, 444, 534
Natural Rubber Agreement, 1979, International, **1980–81:** 591
Natural rubber industry, **1980–81:** 2992
Naturalization Service, Immigration and.
  See Immigration and Naturalization Service.
Nauru
  Ambassador to U.S., **1980–81:** 1051
  U.S. Ambassador, **1977:** 873, 876, 883; **1978:** 231; **1979:** 46, 91
Nautilus, U.S.S., **1980–81:** 2286
Nava, Julian.
  See U.S. Ambassador *under* Mexico.
Navajo and Hopi relocation bill, memorandum of disapproval, **1978:** 1925
Navajo Tribe, **1980–81:** 1043
Naval Academy, United States, **1977:** 1432; **1978:** 515, 1052, 1057, 1072; **1979:** 730; **1980–81:** 769, 875, 2613, 2847

Naval Medical Center, National, **1980–81:** 104
Navarro, Ana, **1978:** 407
Navon, Yitzhak, **1979:** 415, 419n.
Navy, Department of the
  Assistant Secretaries, **1977:** 472, 509, 550, 558, 1779, 1795; **1979:** 2232
  Budget, **1978:** 809, 1055
  Chief of Naval Operations, **1979:** 1603
  Commander in Chief, U.S. Pacific Fleet, **1977:** 372
  Cuban refugee patrols, **1980–81:** 780, 1072, 1880, 1989, 2154, 2383, 2393, 2458
  Eisenhower Battle Group, return to United States, **1980–81:** 2827
  Labor-Management Relations Program exemptions, **1979:** 2145
  Long Beach, Calif., commissaries, **1980–81:** 1877
  Maritime industry, relations with Federal officials, **1978:** 1926
  Merchant marine coordination, **1980–81:** 2239
  Military personnel promotion and disability separation limitations, suspension, **1980–81:** 1857
  National Petroleum Reserve in Alaska, exploration, **1980–81:** 233
  Naval Sea Systems Command, Deputy Commander for Nuclear Propulsion, **1977:** 1707, 2037, 2068; **1978:** 949, 1052, 1067, 1385, 1446
  Persian Gulf area presence, **1980–81:** 233, 970, 973
  President's cruise on nuclear submarine, **1977:** 1024
  Printing services functions, **1979:** 824
  Secretary, **1977:** 90, 930; **1978:** 809; **1979:** 1280, 1659, 1664, 1976; **1980–81:** 1460, 1709, 1943, 3002
  Ship refitting projects, **1980–81:** 1633, 2043
  Shipbuilding programs, **1980–81:** 167, 475
  Supreme Allied Commander, Atlantic, **1978:** 1407
  Under Secretary, **1977:** 207, 252; **1980–81:** 98, 218
  See also specific constituent agencies.
Navy, United States.
  See United States Navy.
NBC.
  See National Broadcasting Company.
Ndegwa, Philip, **1980–81:** 355
Ne Win, **1977:** 1401
Neal, Homer A., **1980–81:** 1149, 1246
Neal, Repr. Stephen L., **1977:** 2181; **1978:** 529, 535, 537, 771; **1979:** 1101; **1980–81:** 2141, 2146
Nease, Marian P., **1978:** 971, 1010
Neave, Airey, **1979:** 567
Nebraska
  Democratic Party primary, **1980–81:** 934

Nebraska — *continued*
  Disaster declaration, **1978:** 570; **1980–81:** 1050
  President's visits, **1977:** 1860, 1861; **1980–81:** 1090
  U.S. attorney, **1977:** 1650, 1651
  U.S. marshals, **1979:** 468; **1980–81:** 755, 1715
Nederlander, Robert E., **1980–81:** 508, 522
Nedzi, Repr. Lucien N., **1978:** 1009, 1713, 1809
  Legislation passage leadership
    Michigan army missile plant conveyance, **1980–81:** 769, 771
    Military Construction Authorization Act, 1981, **1980–81:** 2186
    Vietnam veterans memorial, **1980–81:** 1268, 1270
    Poznan International Technical Fair, U.S. Representative, **1980–81:** 1049
Neel, Alice, **1979:** 217
Neel, Frank, **1977:** 1811, 1826; **1978:** 230; **1980–81:** 296
Negley, Nancy, **1977:** 1781, 1796
Negro Affairs, American Foundation for, **1978:** 328
Negro College Fund, United, **1977:** 2003; **1978:** 1457; **1980–81:** 53, 1561
Negro Women, National Council of, **1979:** 2135
Negroponte, John D., **1977:** 1220, 1223
Nehring, Richard W., **1978:** 416
Neighbor Day, National Good, **1978:** 1569
Neighborhood Commercial Reinvestment Centers, **1978:** 589
Neighborhood development.
  See Community development.
Neighborhood rehabilitation, **1979:** 1406
Neighborhood Self-Help Development programs, Livable Cities and, **1979:** 136
Neighborhood Self-Help program, **1978:** 1010
Neighborhoods, National Commission on, **1977:** 1905, 1931, 2153; **1979:** 618; **1980–81:** 1094, 2117
Neil, Kay E., **1979:** 2191
Nelson, Repr. Bill, **1980–81:** 2397
Nelson, David S., **1979:** 179, 180
Nelson, Dorothy W., **1979:** 271, 1786, 1787
Nelson, Sen. Gaylord, **1977:** 1427, 1930, 2154, 2157; **1978:** 303, 695, 710, 711, 820, 1493, 1667, 1736, 1851, 1852, 1966
  Campaign appearances with the President, **1980–81:** 2076, 2641
  Federal paperwork reduction support, **1979:** 2178
  Hospital cost containment legislation support, **1979:** 384, 385, 569, 576
  Legislation passage leadership
    Alaska public lands, **1980–81:** 1548
    Regulatory Flexibility Act, **1980–81:** 1509, 1839, 1844

Nelson, Sen. Gaylord — *continued*
  Legislation leadership — *continued*
    Small business development, **1980–81:** 1278, 2378, 2381
    Social Security Disability Amendments, **1980–81:** 1063
  Mention, **1979:** 992
  National health plan support, **1979:** 1027
  Small business regulatory reform legislation sponsorship, **1979:** 2143
  White House Conference on Small Business Involvement, **1980–81:** 68, 74, 917
  Sponsorship, **1979:** 369
Nelson, Helen Ewing, **1979:** 942
Nelson, Robert L., **1977:** 934, 944
Nelson, Willie, **1977:** 1533; **1978:** 999, 1002; **1980–81:** 1722n., 2414
Nemirow, Samuel B., **1979:** 1036, 1044; **1980–81:** 1805, 1806
Nepal
  Ambassador to U.S., **1980–81:** 1598
  Trade with U.S., **1979:** 2255
  U.S. Ambassador, **1977:** 783, 807; **1980–81:** 843, 893
  U.S. relations, **1980–81:** 172
Netherlands
  Ambassador to U.S., **1980–81:** 1598
  Attorney General's trip, **1979:** 2209
  Prime Minister Andreas van Agt, **1979:** 2201
  Prime Minister Johannes den Uyl, **1977:** 882
  Resistance fighters during World War II, meeting with the President, **1978:** 1009
  U.S. Ambassador, **1978:** 1100, 1111
  Vice President's visit, **1979:** 221, 639
Neto, Angostinho, **1977:** 647; **1978:** 851, 1185
Netsch, Walter A., **1980–81:** 2701
Neugarten, Bernice L., **1978:** 702, 711; **1979:** 2213; **1980–81:** 534, 537, 2534
Neuharth, Allen H., **1979:** 699n., 2241n.
Neuman, Nancy, **1978:** 1135
Neusner, Jacob, **1978:** 1706, 1724; **1979:** 46, 90
Neustadt, Richard M., **1977:** 1756; **1978:** 1223; **1979:** 619, 1706
Neutron bomb.
  See Radiation weapons, enhanced.
Nevada
  Emergency declaration, **1977:** 1126
  Gov. Robert List, **1980–81:** 303, 422, 606, 901
  Lake Tahoe region legislation, **1980–81:** 2235, 2264
  MX missile site, **1980–81:** 904
  Radioactivity exposure, **1979:** 182
  U.S. attorney, **1977:** 1931, 1932
  U.S. district judge, **1978:** 1346; **1979:** 667, 668
  U.S. marshal, **1977:** 1483, 1484
Nevelson, Louise, **1979:** 217
New Brunswick, N.J., **1979:** 2020

New Coalition, **1979:** 1678
New Community Development Corporation, **1977:** 575, 596; **1980–81:** 752, 775
New England Basins Commission, **1979:** 2248
New England Fuel Institute, **1980–81:** 292
New England Regional Commission, **1977:** 1071, 1085
New England River Basins Commission, **1978:** 273, 737, 822, 1807
New England Telephone Co., Southern, **1980–81:** 1404
"New Foundation", **1979:** 172
New Hampshire
    Democratic Party primary, **1980–81:** 399
    Disaster declaration, **1978:** 329
    Emergency declaration, **1979:** 440
    Political supporters, White House reception, **1978:** 420
    President's visit, **1978:** 364, 414; **1979:** 699–720, 733
    U.S. attorney, **1977:** 1266, 1307
    U.S. district judge, **1978:** 935, 936; **1979:** 241, 242
    U.S. marshal, **1977:** 1384
    White House briefing by administration officials for civic and community leaders (Digest), **1979:** 2186
    White House briefings for civic and community leaders, **1980–81:** 334
New Jersey
    Civic leaders, meeting with the President, **1978:** 1380
    Disaster declaration, **1977:** 147
    Economic compact with New York, **1979:** 2297
    Election prospects of President, **1980–81:** 2047
    Emergency declaration, **1980–81:** 2453
    Energy crisis, **1977:** 37
    Gov. Brendan T. Byrne, **1977:** 1264, 1571, 1574, 1936, 1962, 2007; **1978:** 415
        Advisory Committee on Housing, member, **1980–81:** 2560
        Campaign appearances with the President, **1980–81:** 1672, 1677, 1680, 2276, 2525, 2529
        Energy conservation measures, **1979:** 2022
        Industrial and economic development actions, **1979:** 2297
        Meetings with the President (Digest), **1979:** 898, 1705; **1980–81:** 2752
    Mention, **1979:** 2101
    National Citizens' Coalition for Windfall Profits Tax, cochairperson, **1980–81:** 586, 588
    National Governors' Association, winter session attendance, **1980–81:** 397
    News conference (Checklist), **1979:** 402
    1976 gubernatorial election, **1979:** 2020, 2025, 2032; **1980–81:** 2048
    Northeast corridor rail transportation, legislation support, **1980–81:** 1009, 1011

New Jersey — *continued*
    Gov. Brendan Byrne — *continued*
        Water shortage actions, **1980–81:** 2267
    President's visits, **1977:** 1571, 1574, 1576; **1978:** 1542–1555; **1979:** 2020, 2024, 2027; **1980–81:** 1672, 1677, 1679, 1687, 2265, 2275, 2432, 2524, 2528
    SALT II treaty briefing for community and civic leaders by administration officials (Digest), **1979:** 2106
    U.S. attorney, **1977:** 1613
    U.S. district judges, **1979:** 1786, 1787
New Mexico
    Disaster declarations (Digest), **1979:** 217, 1159
    Emergency declaration, **1977:** 279
    Gov. Bruce King, **1980–81:** 303
    Navajo-Ute Mountain Ute Tribe boundary dispute, **1980–81:** 1043
    President's visit, **1979:** 1851, 1853, 1863
    U.S. attorney, **1978:** 899
    U.S. district judge, **1978:** 1034, 1035; **1979:** 1293, 1294
    U.S. marshal, **1977:** 1222, 1266
New Orleans, La., **1977:** 1334; **1979:** 1817; **1980–81:** 2401, 2848n.
New Partnership, **1978:** 581, 582
New Year's Day, 1981, **1980–81:** 2847
New York
    Board of Rabbis, meeting with the President (Digest), **1980–81:** 2453
    Business/Labor Committee for Carter/Mondale, **1980–81:** 1953, 2071
    Democratic Party primary, **1980–81:** 534, 538, 564
    Disaster declaration, **1977:** 146; **1980–81:** 967
    Economic compact with New Jersey, **1979:** 2297
    Emergency declaration, **1977:** 34, 85; **1978:** 1405
    Energy crisis, **1977:** 37
    Gov. Hugh L. Carey, **1977:** 263, 322, 1154, 1754; **1978:** 440, 1393, 1399, 1883, 1929; **1979:** 240, 1745, 2297; **1980–81:** 1954, 2002, 2365, 2377
    Labor leaders, meeting with the President (Digest), **1980–81:** 451
    Lt. Gov. Mario Cuomo, **1980–81:** 821, 1037n., 2807
    President's visits, **1977:** 1715–1737; **1978:** 1883, 1929, 2160; **1980–81:** 2001, 2003, 2289, 2521
    State and local officials, meeting with the President, **1980–81:** 1528
    U.S. attorneys, **1977:** 1211, 1212, 1569; **1978:** 771, 803, 1333, 1334; **1980–81:** 523, 564, 1470, 1471
    U.S. district judges, **1977:** 1483, 1484, 1826, 1827; **1978:** 329, 330, 711, 712, 898, 899; **1979:** 93, 1786, 1787; **1980–81:** 1015, 1051, 1847

New York — *continued*
  U.S. marshals, **1977:** 1384; **1978:** 1072, 1222, 1223
  White House briefing for civic and community leaders, **1980–81:** 458
New York, Public Employees Federation of, **1980–81:** 374
New York City, N.Y.
  Brzezinski, Zbigniew, visit to, **1979:** 788
  Federal aid, **1977:** 263, 264, 1730, 1755
  Financing legislation, **1978:** 101, 440, 782, 1062, 1098, 1109, 1208
  Mayor Edward I. Koch, **1979:** 240, 1742, 1745, 2297
  Mention, **1979:** 1972
  Metropolitan Opera labor dispute, **1980–81:** 2017
  Port Authority, **1977:** 178, 765
  Power failure, **1977:** 1250, 1330, 1384, 1394
  President's visits, **1977:** 1153; **1978:** 1397; **1979:** 217, 328, 693, 1739, 1745, 1746; **1980–81:** 1499, 1506, 1527–1544, 1949, 1953, 2193, 2198, 2306–2312, 2333, 2363–2377, 2542
  Statement following meeting with Mayor Koch, **1978:** 270
  Urban Parks and Recreation Recovery program, **1979:** 1817
  Welfare program, **1977:** 1449
New York City Loan Guarantee Act, **1978:** 1397
New York Municipal Assistance Corporation, **1980–81:** 1714
New York Times, Farber case, **1978:** 1591
New Zealand
  Ambassador to U.S., **1978:** 710; **1980–81:** 1598
  Cook Islands-U.S. maritime boundary treaty, **1980–81:** 1626
  Deputy Prime Minister, **1980–81:** 422
  Joint statement, **1977:** 1991
  Prime Minister Robert D. Muldoon, **1977:** 1649, 1989, 1991, 2007
  U.S. Ambassador, **1979:** 1040, 1043
  U.S. relations, **1980–81:** 169, 2983
  Vice President's visit, **1978:** 327
Newark, N.J., **1977:** 1102, 1571; **1979:** 2247; **1980–81:** 2524, 2528
Newblatt, Stewart A., **1979:** 899, 900
Newcastle-Upon-Tyne, England, **1977:** 809–813, 869, 881
Newell, Barbara W., **1979:** 1819, 1824; **1980–81:** 1713, 1847
Newell, Wayne A., **1979:** 446
Newhouse, John, **1977:** 1135, 1163
Newhouse, Samuel I., **1979:** 1526
Newhouse Newspapers, **1980–81:** 984
Newington, Conn., **1980–81:** 2279
Newkirk, Donald R., **1977:** 1055
Newman, Jon O., **1979:** 733, 787

Newman, Joseph H., **1979:** 44, 92
Newman, Larry, **1978:** 1449
Newman, Paul, **1979:** 919, 935
Newman Drug Abuse Prevention Award, Scott, **1980–81:** 1715
Newport Jazz Festival, **1978:** 1153
Newport News, Va., **1979:** 906; **1980–81:** 500
News Conferences
  1977
    February 8 (No. 1), **1977:** 92
    February 23 (No. 2), **1977:** 216
    March 9 (No. 3), **1977:** 340
    March 24 (No. 4), **1977:** 496
    April 15 (No. 5), **1977:** 629
    April 22 (No. 6), **1977:** 695
    May 12 (No. 7), **1977:** 860
    May 26 (No. 8), **1977:** 1016
    June 13 (No. 9), **1977:** 1103
    June 30 (No. 10), **1977:** 1197
    July 15 (No. 11), **1977:** 1231
    July 28 (No. 12), **1977:** 1366
    August 6 (No. 13), **1977:** 1443
    August 23 (No. 14), **1977:** 1486
    September 21 (No. 15), **1977:** 1635
    September 29 (No. 16), **1977:** 1684
    October 13 (No. 17), **1977:** 1783
    October 27 (No. 18), **1977:** 1908
    November 10 (No. 19), **1977:** 1994
    November 30 (No. 20), **1977:** 2053
    December 15 (No. 21), **1977:** 2115
    December 30 (No. 22), **1977:** 2205
  1978
    January 12 ((No. 23), **1978:** 54
    January 30 (No. 24), **1978:** 243
    February 17 (No. 25), **1978:** 331
    March 2 (No. 26), **1978:** 438
    March 9 (No. 27), **1978:** 489
    March 30 (No. 28), **1978:** 627
    April 11 (No. 29), **1978:** 727
    April 25 (No. 30), **1978:** 775
    May 4 (No. 31), **1978:** 844
    May 25 (No. 32), **1978:** 972
    June 14 (No. 33), **1978:** 1091
    June 26 (No. 34), **1978:** 1178
    July 20 (No. 35), **1978:** 1322
    August 17 (No. 36), **1978:** 1438
    September 28 (No. 37), **1978:** 1653
    October 10 (No. 38), **1978:** 1745
    November 9 (No. 39), **1978:** 1986
    November 30 (No. 40), **1978:** 2096
    December 12 (No. 41), **1978:** 2219
  1979
    January 17 (No. 42), **1979:** 50
    January 26 (No. 43), **1979:** 170
    February 12 (No. 44), **1979:** 255
    February 27 (No. 45), **1979:** 346
    March 25 (No. 46), **1979:** 482

News Conferences — *continued*
  1979 — *continued*
    April 10 (No. 47), **1979:** 648
    April 30 (No. 48), **1979:** 747
    May 4 (No. 49), **1979:** 795
    May 29 (No. 50), **1979:** 959
    July 25 (No. 51), **1979:** 1303
    October 9 (No. 52), **1979:** 1836
    November 28 (No. 53), **1979:** 2167
  1980
    February 13 (No. 54), **1980–81:** 307
    March 14 (No. 55), **1980–81:** 484
    April 17 (No. 56), **1980–81:** 704
    April 29 (No. 57), **1980–81:** 792
    August 4 (No. 58), **1980–81:** 1477
    September 18 (No. 59), **1980–81:** 1826
News Conferences Other Than Presidential
  Vice President Mondale's trip to Europe and Japan, Vice President, **1977:** 58
News media
  Black representation at news conferences, **1978:** 321
  Coverage of:
    Interviews with the President, **1979:** 1863
    Pope John Paul II, **1979:** 1867
  Coverage of the President, **1977:** 701, 1171; **1978:** 313, 1228, 2027
  Federal access to files, **1979:** 585
  First amendment privileges, **1979:** 485
  Frequency of meetings with the President, **1979:** 1856
  Influence on American society, **1980–81:** 896
  Interview remarks, **1978:** 2258, 2259
  Interviews
    ABC News, **1977:** 1467
    "Conversation With the President" television interview, **1977:** 1467
    Editors, publishers, and broadcasters, **1977:** 1165, 1269, 1387, 1509, 1615, 1799, 1933, 2009, 2091
    European journalists, **1977:** 760, 775
    Magazine Publishers Association, **1977:** 1087
    National Black Network, **1977:** 1340
    National Newspaper Association, **1977:** 1921
    Newspaper Farm Editors of America, **1977:** 1703
    Radio-Television News Directors Association, **1977:** 747, 1594
    See also under Addresses and Remarks.
  Journalists' overseas trips, **1979:** 628
  Middle East negotiations, **1978:** 152
  New Orleans, La., question-and-answer session with reporters, **1977:** 1334
  Panama Canal treaties, **1978:** 306
  Public broadcasting system, **1977:** 1737
  Relationship with the President, **1979:** 1306
  White House News Photographers Association, **1977:** 557

News media — *continued*
  White House press corps, meeting with the President, **1977:** 194
  See also Addresses and Remarks, interviews with the news media.
Newsom, Barbara, **1980–81:** 1860, 1946, 2070, 2726, 2727
Newsom, David D., **1977:** 1673, 1700, 1931; **1978:** 508, 571; **1979:** 2043; **1980–81:** 891
Newspaper Association, National, **1977:** 1921
Newspaper Carrier Day, **1980–81:** 2188
Newspaper Editors, American Society of, **1977:** 789; **1979:** 788; **1980–81:** 631
Newspaper Farm Editors of America, **1977:** 1703
Newspaper industry, **1978:** 1591
Newspaper Publishers Association, American, **1979:** 440, 693, 733; **1980–81:** 720
Newspaper Publishers Association, National, **1977:** 1126
Newspaper Week, National, **1979:** 1807; **1980–81:** 2188
Ngonda, Putteho Muketoi, **1977:** 1383
Niagara Falls, N.Y., **1980–81:** 2001, 2003, 2071
Nicaragua
  Ambassador to U.S., **1979:** 2162n.; **1980–81:** 2752
  Democratic National Committee, remarks, **1978:** 2197
  International Mediation Group, **1978:** 1694, 2059
  Interview remarks, **1978:** 1599, 2177
  Junta, meeting with the President, **1979:** 1722
  News conference remarks, **1978:** 1993, 2221
  Revolution anniversary celebrations, U.S. delegation, **1980–81:** 1377
  U.S. Ambassador, **1977:** 1219, 1223; **1979:** 685, 733, 1318
  U.S. assistance, **1979:** 1317, 2103
  U.S. economic assistance, **1980–81:** 1017, 1215, 1712
  U.S. grain procurements, **1979:** 1780
  U.S. policy, **1980–81:** 2734
  U.S. relations, **1979:** 160, 1307, 1790
Nice Agreement on International Trademarks, **1979:** 84
Niceville, Fla., **1980–81:** 780n.
Nicholas, James A., **1978:** 2036
Nichols, Repr. Bill, **1980–81:** 1665
Nichols, Gregory Scott, **1978:** 1208
Nichols, Mildred T., **1979:** 1524
Nicholson, James M., **1978:** 1139, 1140
Nicholson, Mrs. Richard, **1977:** 300
Nickerson, Eugene H., **1977:** 1483, 1484; **1980–81:** 1599
Nickinello, Louis R., **1979:** 2024
Niederlehner, Leonard, **1980–81:** 87
Niekro, Joe, **1980–81:** 2603

Nies, Helen Wilson, **1980–81:** 866, 894
Nieto, Consuelo, **1978:** 1514
Niger
    U.S. Ambassador, **1979:** 979, 984
    Vice President's trip, **1980–81:** 1333
Nigeria
    Ambassador to U.S., **1977:** 1754
    Lt. Gen. Olesugun Obasanjo, **1977:** 1611, 1762, 1772, 1781, 1796, 1809
    President Alhaji Shehu Shagari, **1980–81:** 1945, 2095, 2104, 2108
    President's visit, **1977:** 1649, 1983, 2077; **1978:** 416, 417, 643–664, 709, 711
    Soviet Union relations, **1980–81:** 807
    United States
        Relations improvement during administration, **1980–81:** 897, 1207, 2147, 2277, 2301, 2366, 2406, 2428, 2565
        Trade, **1980–81:** 2587, 2601, 2607
    U.S. Ambassador, **1979:** 1451, 1519
    U.S. policy, **1978:** 374, 688, 694
    U.S. relations, **1979:** 355, 1917
    U.S. Representative to United Nations, trip, **1977:** 33
    Vice President's trip, **1980–81:** 1333, 1502
Nigh, Gov. George, **1980–81:** 1423n., 2421
Nigh, Gov. and Mrs. George, **1979:** 217
Niles, Ill., **1980–81:** 1851, 1947
Nimeiri, Gaafar Muhammed, **1978:** 1561; **1980–81:** 1291
Nimitz, Matthew, **1977:** 509; **1978:** 1340; **1980–81:** 219, 1398
    Kampuchean relief efforts, news conferences (Checklist), **1979:** 2139, 2187
    Mention, **1979:** 2183n.
    Under Secretary of State, nomination, **1979:** 2270
    United Nations Pledging Conference on Refugee Relief, member, **1979:** 2085
Nimitz, U.S.S., **1980–81:** 882, 969, 972, 976, 1013
Nimmons, Ralph W., Jr., **1980–81:** 1847
Nims, Arthur L., III, **1979:** 820, 843
1936 Summer Olympics, **1980–81:** 518, 635
1959 Geneva Radio Regulations, **1980–81:** 225
1976 Presidential campaign supporters, White House reception, **1978:** 1668
1976 upland cotton program, **1978:** 1571
1979 White House Conferences on the Arts and Humanities, **1978:** 823
1980 Olympics, **1978:** 1327
1980 Presidential campaign.
    See Elections, 1980.
1980 Summer Olympics.
    See Olympics, 1980 Summer.
1980 Winter Olympics.
    See Olympics, 1980 Winter.
1981 Inaugural Committee, **1980–81:** 2727
Nishimura, Glenn, **1977:** 1944, 1966; **1978:** 231

Nissan Motor Company, **1980–81:** 706
Nitze, Paul H., **1977:** 1749
Nix, Repr. Robert N. C., **1977:** 1699; **1978:** 1138, 1318, 1513, 1667, 1683, 1736, 1762, 1765
Nixon, John T., **1980–81:** 423, 424
Nixon, Richard M., **1977:** 129, 130, 500, 632, 758, 867, 868, 942, 948, 1205; **1978:** 343, 2098
    Chinese Vice Premier Deng, White House invitation to dinner for, **1979:** 54, 175
    1968 election, **1980–81:** 738, 1755, 1764, 2250, 2347, 2366, 2395, 2429, 2528, 2603, 2622, 2626, 2634, 2646
    President's comments on
        Grain embargoes, **1979:** 1710
        Israel, commitment to, **1979:** 1580
        Mandatory wage and price controls, **1979:** 849
        SALT negotiations, **1979:** 694, 1088
        Shanghai Communique of 1972, **1980–81:** 1772
        Supreme Court appointments, **1980–81:** 1325
Njonjo, Charles, **1980–81:** 355
Noatak National Monument, **1978:** 2136
Nobel Peace Prize, **1978:** 1877; **1979:** 1962, 1963
Nobel Peace Prize winners, American, **1980–81:** 2740
Noble, Carol, **1980–81:** 703n.
Nobusuke Kishi, **1977:** 1602
Nogales, Luis Guerrero, **1980–81:** 1446, 1524
Noise, Federal Interagency Committee on, **1979:** 1386
Nolan, Kathleen, **1978:** 1426, 1458; **1979:** 46, 91; **1980–81:** 1713, 1847
Noll, Roger, **1980–81:** 264
Nonfuel minerals, **1980–81:** 2686
Non-Proliferation Matters, U.S. Special Representative for, **1977:** 1182, 1211, 1212, 1506
Non-Proliferation Treaty Review Conference, **1979:** 685; **1980–81:** 930
Nonrubber footwear industry, **1977:** 550–554, 558, 1113, 1128, 1148; **1980–81:** 420
Noor, Noor Ahmad, **1978:** 1380
Noor, Queen, **1980–81:** 1126
Nooter, Robert H., **1977:** 933, 943
Nordhaus, Robert Riggs, **1977:** 372, 373, 939, 944
Nordhaus, William D., **1977:** 373, 706
Nordli, Odvar, **1977:** 882; **1979:** 1042, 2201
Norfolk, Va., **1977:** 1656; **1978:** 1383; **1980–81:** 969, 972
Norland, Donald R., **1977:** 195, 714, 745
Norman, Lindsay D., Jr., **1980–81:** 1065, 1111
Norris, Bob, **1980–81:** 1508; **1979:** 1676, 1705
Norris, John M., **1980–81:** 928
Norris, William Albert, **1980–81:** 423
Norris, William C., **1978:** 53
Norrish, Merwyn, **1978:** 710
North, Jerrold Martin, **1980–81:** 1025, 1051 **1980–81:** 1258
North American Affairs, Coordination Council for, **1979:** 640, 1133, 2223; **1980–81:** 1258

North Atlantic Alliance Summit.
  See under North Atlantic Treaty Organization.
North Atlantic Assembly, **1977:** 1163
North Atlantic Treaty Organization
  Administration's accomplishments and goals,
    1980–81: 2932, 2980, 2982
  Bonn Economic Summit Conference, remarks,
    1978: 1283, 1288, 1289, 1297, 1316
  Business Council, remarks, **1978:** 2236, 2237
  Committee on the Challenges of Modern Society
    Alternate U.S. Representative, **1980–81:** 493
    U.S. Representative and Alternate Represen-
      tative, **1977:** 744
  Cook County Democratic dinner, remarks, **1978:**
    986
  Coordinating Committee (COCOM), **1980–81:**
    44
  Creation, purposes of, **1980–81:** 195
  Defense policy, **1978:** 1019
  Defense spending, **1980–81:** 168, 348, 673, 712,
    986, 2711
  Force reductions, **1977:** 496
  Foreign Ministers meeting, **1980–81:** 2807
  Greek re-integration, **1980–81:** 169, 383, 2337,
    2342, 2369
  Infrastructure program, **1980–81:** 2184
  Interview remarks, **1977:** 1809; **1978:** 937, 1075,
    1272, 2251
  Italian support, **1980–81:** 210, 1157
  Long-Term Defense Program, **1979:** 156, 1629,
    2234, 2268; **1980–81:** 168, 439, 1554, 2213,
    2440, 2566
  Mentions, **1979:** 1904, 2260; **1980–81:** 338, 642,
    758
  Military capabilities improvement, **1979:** 156,
    314, 316, 1349, 1613, 1802, 1989, 1996,
    2264; **1980–81:** 806, 807, 869, 1103, 1160,
    1208
  Ministerial meeting, **1977:** 848, 852
  News conference remarks, **1977:** 1233, 2122;
    1978: 777, 1091, 1097, 1326, 1439, 1446,
    1448, 1988
  North Atlantic Alliance Summit, **1978:** 1011,
    1014, 1024, 1034
  North Atlantic Council, remarks, **1978:** 36, 38
  Nuclear force modernization program
    British forces, **1980–81:** 1343, 1344
    Deployment modernization, **1979:** 1845, 2234,
      2236, 2268
    Intermediate- and long-range missile deploy-
      ment, **1980–81:** 168, 197, 211, 348, 440,
      2126
    Mention, **1980–81:** 986
    Sites location, **1980–81:** 1165
    Soviet SS-20 missile development, effect on,
      1980–81: 109, 168, 348, 442, 1195, 1554,
      1686

North Atlantic Treaty Organization — *continued*
  Nuclear forces — *continued*
    Stockpile streamlining, **1980–81:** 168
    Unanimous support of allies, **1980–81:** 168,
      673, 1554, 1686
    Portuguese support, **1980–81:** 1225, 1232, 1233
    SALT II treaty, effect on, **1979:** 695, 903, 1806,
      2237
    Secretary General, **1977:** 641, 642, 852; **1978:**
      1014, 1033; **1980–81:** 892
    Soviet invasion of Afghanistan, effect on, **1980–
      81:** 1224
    State of the Union, **1978:** 123
    Supreme Allied Commander, Atlantic fleet,
      1978: 1407
    Supreme Allied Commander, Europe, and Com-
      mander in Chief of U.S. Forces in Eu-
      rope, **1979:** 363, 378, 1043, 1882; **1980–81:**
      2369
  Troop strength, **1980–81:** 660
  Turkey
    Economic strengthening responsibilities, **1979:**
      845; **1980–81:** 169
    U.S. arms embargo, **1978:** 1337
  United Kingdom, nuclear forces commitment to,
    1979: 2164
  United States
    Military assistance, **1980–81:** 91, 109, 116, 166,
      248, 345, 477, 672, 1535, 1640, 1659, 1740
    Role of, **1980–81:** 712
  U.S. defense spending, **1979:** 98, 106, 1629
  U.S. efforts to strengthen, **1979:** 2033, 2047, 2258
  U.S. Naval Academy, remarks, **1978:** 1056
  U.S. Permanent Representative, **1977:** 589, 597
  U.S. policy, **1977:** 776, 1520, 2134
  Vice President's trip, **1977:** 11, 58
  Wake Forest University, address, **1978:** 533
  Weapons transfers, **1977:** 556
  West German support, **1979:** 1005; **1980–81:** 437
North Carolina
  Disaster declaration, **1977:** 2006; **1979:** 1823
  Emergency declarations, **1977:** 279, 1464
  Federal-State partnership in rural development,
    1978: 1573
  Gov. James B. Hunt, Jr., **1980–81:** 2140, 2145
  President's visits, **1977:** 2094, 2130, 2133; **1978:**
    529, 535, 1386, 1390, 1575, 1579; **1980–81:**
    2140, 2145
  Shooting of demonstrators in Greensboro, **1979:**
    2105
  State legislature members, meeting with the
    President, **1979:** 1396
  U.S. attorneys, **1977:** 1127, 1128, 1211, 1213;
    1980–81: 1715
  U.S. district judges, **1979:** 554, 555; **1980–81:**
    654, 720, 1111, 1112, 1598, 1599
  U.S. marshals, **1977:** 1138, 1550, 1804, 1805

[References are to page numbers except as otherwise indicated]

North Country National Scenic Trail, **1980–81:** 432
North Country Trail, **1979:** 1814
North Dakota
    Disaster declaration, **1978:** 770; **1979:** 732
    Emergency declaration, **1978:** 1278
    Gov. Arthur A. Link, **1980–81:** 1372
    Grain industry labor dispute, **1979:** 1452, 1468
    Great Plain coal gasification plant, **1980–81:** 1372
    U.S. attorney, **1977:** 883
    U.S. marshal, **1977:** 883, 884
North Pacific Fisheries Commission, International, **1979:** 1001
North Pacific Fisheries Convention, **1978:** 1041
North Pacific Fur Seals, Interim Convention on Conservation of, **1980–81:** 2716
North Umpqua River, Oreg., **1979:** 1814
North Yemen, trade with U.S., **1979:** 2255
Northeast corridor rail transportation, **1980–81:** 1009, 1052
Northeast Corridor Railroad Improvement Program, **1978:** 106
Northeast Summit on Energy, **1979:** 2055
Northeastern Governors, Coalition of, **1979:** 2060
Northeastern States, economic development assistance, **1980–81:** 1680
Northern, Richard, **1979:** 914
Northern Gas Pipeline, **1979:** 381
Northern Ireland, U.S. policy, **1977:** 1524
Northern Mariana Islands
    Constitution, **1977:** 1904
    Disaster declaration, **1978:** 1458; **1980–81:** 2753
    Trusteeship agreement with U.S., **1980–81:** 2612
    U.S. attorney, **1978:** 149, 150
    U.S. district judge, **1978:** 712, 750
    U.S. laws, application, **1978:** 885; **1980–81:** 365
    U.S. marshal, **1978:** 149, 150
    U.S. military service for citizens, **1980–81:** 1722
    U.S. policy, **1980–81:** 317
Northern Mariana Islands Commission on Federal Laws, **1980–81:** 343, 930
Northern Marshall Islands.
    See Marshall Islands.
Northern Pacific Halibut Fishery, United States-Canada Convention on, **1979:** 1420
Northern Tier Pipeline Co., **1980–81:** 99, 1912
Northwest Alaska Pipeline Company, **1979:** 591
Northwest Atlantic Fisheries, International Commission for, **1979:** 777
Northwest Atlantic Fisheries Convention, **1979:** 777
Northwest Energy Company, **1980–81:** 100
Norton, Eleanor Holmes, **1977:** 528, 544, 885, 943, 1131, 1345, 1347, 1350; **1978:** 319, 554, 1150, 1412, 1681; **1979:** 912, 1159, 1715, 2138
    See also Equal Employment Opportunity Commission, Chair.

Norton, James A., **1978:** 269
Norton, Mary Beth, **1978:** 1706, 1724, 2050; **1979:** 46, 90
Norway
    Ambassador to U.S., **1979:** 377
    Extradition treaty with U.S., **1979:** 1420
    Foreign Minister, **1979:** 33n.
    Prime Minister Odvar Nordli, **1977:** 882; **1979:** 1042, 2201
    Taxation convention with U.S., **1980–81:** 2763
    U.S. Ambassador, **1977:** 1206, 1213; **1979:** 2217; **1980–81:** 333, 1438n.
    Vice President's visit, **1979:** 221, 639
Norwood, Janet L., **1979:** 528, 554
Nosenzo, Louis V., **1977:** 1501, 1507
Notre Dame, University of, **1977:** 954, 1031
Nouira, Hedi, **1978:** 2073, 2090, 2144
Novotny, Josepn N., **1977:** 1931, 1932
Nowak, Repr. Henry J., **1978:** 1809, 1885; **1980–81:** 2002
Noyce, Robert N., **1979:** 2289; **1980–81:** 82n.
Nuclear energy
    Administration's accomplishments and goals, **1980–81:** 131, 2941
    Australian-U.S. nonproliferation agreement, **1979:** 1314
    Breeder reactor technology financing, **1979:** 1324
    Clinch River breeder reactor plant.
        See Clinch River breeder reactor plant.
    Democratic National Committee, fundraising dinner remarks, **1978:** 1648
    European Atomic Energy Community-U.S. cooperation (EO 12193), **1980–81:** 304
    Exports, **1977:** 60–62, 769, 779; **1978:** 1309, 1312; **1979:** 559; **1980–81:** 286, 403
    Federal programs, **1979:** 149
    Ford Foundation panel, **1977:** 508
    Fort Worth Civic Organizations, remarks, **1978:** 1161
    Fusion research, **1980–81:** 664
    Increased production, **1979:** 1190, 1199
    India, export of U.S. materials to, **1980–81:** 1137, 1922
    India, U.S. export of special materials, **1978:** 790, 791
    Industry shutdown, possibility of, **1980–81:** 582
    Initial fuel assurances, **1979:** 326
    International agreements
        Canada, **1980–81:** 782
        Colombia, **1980–81:** 2878
        Indonesia, **1980–81:** 1281
        Morocco, **1980–81:** 1026
        Peru, **1980–81:** 1239
    International fuel bank, proposal, **1977:** 1813
    Interview remarks, **1978:** 72, 238, 939, 1231
    Legislation, **1980–81:** 418
    Low-level radiation, **1979:** 2207

Nuclear energy — *continued*
  Meetings with the President (Digest)
    Administration officials and environmental and community leaders, **1979:** 841
    Energy Secretary Schlesinger and Congressmen, **1979:** 553
  Mention, **1979:** 1245
  National Democratic Party Conference, remarks, **1978:** 2195
  News conference remarks, **1977:** 2211; **1978:** 248, 630, 2096
  Nonproliferation activities, Federal, **1980–81:** 403
  Nonproliferation functions, Executive order, **1978:** 894, 1309, 1886, 1895, 1900, 1945, 1949, 1953, 2199
  Nonproliferation of nuclear weapons, **1977:** 540, 582–586, 613, 728, 730, 763, 779, 817, 818, 825—834, 960, 1027, 1145, 1716, 1717, 1856, 1895, 1954, 1972, 2012, 2096; **1978:** 388, 498, 500, 961, 986, 1053, 1056
  North Atlantic Treaty Organization defense policy, **1978:** 1020
  Ombudsman for administration, **1979:** 1648
  Physical protection in international transport, **1980–81:** 867
  Policy, **1977:** 587, 764, 903
  Powerplant safety, **1980–81:** 744, 1958, 2438
  Powerplants.
    See Nuclear powerplants.
  President's Commission on the Accident at Three Mile Island, final report, **1979:** 2062
  President's cruise on nuclear submarine, **1977:** 1024
  President's position on future use, **1979:** 799, 1109, 1647, 1906, 2202
  Production, **1980–81:** 440
  Radiation protection program, **1980–81:** 364
  Research and development, **1978:** 949, 950, 2109
  Safeguards agreement, **1978:** 293, 294
  Safety, **1977:** 259, 686, 836
  South Africa, explosion in, **1979:** 2048
  State of the Union, **1978:** 96, 114, 117, 122
  Test ban, **1978:** 96, 122, 875, 1075
  Test ban treaty, **1977:** 61, 96, 358, 496, 539, 1107, 1366, 1659, 1717, 1800, 1954, 2010, 2092, 2191
  Three Mile Island nuclear plant, Pa.
    See Three Mile Island nuclear plant, Pa.
  United Kingdom-U.S. atomic energy agreement, **1979:** 2164
  Uranium enrichment capacity, **1979:** 1822
  Venice Economic Summit Conference statement, **1980–81:** 1188, 1197
  Waste disposal.
    See Nuclear waste disposal.

Nuclear energy — *continued*
  Weapons.
    See Nuclear weapons.
    See also Arms and weapons; Nuclear weapons.
Nuclear Energy Authorization Act of 1982, Department of Energy National Security and Military Applications of, **1979:** 2298
Nuclear Fuel Cycle, International.
  See International Nuclear Fuel Cycle.
Nuclear Material, Convention on the Physical Protection of, **1980–81:** 434, 867
Nuclear Non-Proliferation Act, **1978:** 498, 500
Nuclear Non-Proliferation Act of 1977, **1979:** 452, 1354
  Proposed, **1977:** 728, 730
Nuclear Non-Proliferation Act of 1978, **1980–81:** 403
Nuclear Planning Group, **1978:** 1020
Nuclear powerplants, **1977:** 949, 1167, 1170, 1706; **1978:** 335, 373, 770, 847
  Construction, **1979:** 712, 741
  Safety
    Federal Government role, **1979:** 702
    President's Commission on the Accident at Three Mile Island, final report recommendations, **1979:** 2061, 2206
    Public concern, effect on, **1979:** 706
    Three Mile Island, Pa., accident, reassessment due to, **1979:** 558, 577, 681, 702, 712, 798, 1428, 1503, 1537, 1753, 1906
Nuclear Regulatory Commission
  Annual report, **1980–81:** 2722
  Appropriations, **1978:** 1971
  Appropriations authorization legislation, **1980–81:** 1257
  Chairman, **1977:** 1240, 1266; **1978:** 564; **1980–81:** 301, 504, 1331, 1377
  Export of special nuclear material to India, **1978:** 790, 791
  Exports licensing, **1980–81:** 403
  India, export recommendation of U.S. nuclear materials to, **1980–81:** 1137
  India, U.S. nuclear materials export approval, **1979:** 559
  International agreement recommendations, **1980–81:** 266, 782, 1027, 1281, 2879
  Low-level radiation protection issuances, **1979:** 2007
  Members, **1977:** 1152, 1163, 1189, 1213, 1240, 1266; **1978:** 929, 935; **1979:** 855, 899; **1980–81:** 1240
  Office of Nuclear Reactor Regulation, Director, **1979:** 579, 617, 618; **1980–81:** 1698
  Powerplant licensing, **1980–81:** 2438
  Radiation Policy Council membership, **1980–81:** 363

Nuclear Regulatory Commission — *continued*
    Reorganization, **1977:** 259
        Amendment to Plan No. 1, **1980–81:** 836
        Congressional consideration, **1980–81:** 617,
            744
        Plan No. 1 of 1980, **1980–81:** 543, 564
        President's commitment to submit plan,
            1980–81: 116, 118, 131, 149
    Safety responsibilities, **1980–81:** 504
    Seabrook, N.H., nuclear plant, **1978:** 334
    Three Mile Island, Pa., accident study, **1979:**
        702, 741, 798, 1504, 1753, 2202–2204
    Waste disposal regulation, **1979:** 2298
    Waste disposal review, **1980–81:** 240, 300, 2002
Nuclear Safety Oversight Committee, **1980–81:**
    504, 849, 1935
Nuclear waste disposal, **1978:** 846, 949; **1979:** 588,
    706, 1351, 1358, 1428, 1482, 2298
    Federal management program, **1980–81:** 296,
        335
    International safety efforts, **1980–81:** 404
    Legislation.
        See Comprehensive Environmental Response,
            Compensation, and Liability Act.
    Republican Party platform position, **1980–81:**
        1865
    Research and development, **1980–81:** 2002
    State Planning Council on Radioactive Waste
        Management, establishment, **1980–81:**
        301
Nuclear Waste Management, Interagency Review
    Group on, **1979:** 1358, 2298
Nuclear Waste Management Task Force, **1978:** 509
Nuclear weapons
    Alert systems, **1980–81:** 1226
    Budget allocations reduction, **1980–81:** 1622
    Control and disarmament
        Administration's accomplishments and goals,
            1980–81: 178, 451, 1304, 1562, 1604, 1659,
            2633, 2891, 2996
        American Legion support, **1980–81:** 1551
        Overall military strength, relationship with,
            1980–81: 2081
        Western nations priority, **1980–81:** 442
    Fail-safe devices, **1980–81:** 1894
    First strike capability, **1980–81:** 1553, 1830
    NATO forces modernization.
        See under North Atlantic Treaty Organization.
    Nonproliferation
        Export controls, **1979:** 2292
        Indian Ocean deployment limits, **1979:** 158
        Japanese support, **1979:** 767
        Mentions, **1979:** 106, 541, 681, 719, 795, 1594
        President's commitment to, **1979:** 1493
        Transfer limit of conventional arms, **1979:**
            158, 171, 357
        U.S. leadership role, **1979:** 590, 694, 1828,
            1831, 1834

Nuclear weapons — *continued*
    Production, **1979:** 559
    Reagan, Ronald, policy differences with the
        President, **1980–81:** 1534, 1617, 1622,
            1755, 1764, 1767, 1910, 1956, 1994, 2011,
            2030, 2038, 2044, 2050, 2081, 2088, 2093,
            2121, 2138, 2150, 2197, 2214, 2248, 2305,
            2322, 2338, 2342, 2346, 2348, 2350, 2373,
            2399, 2408, 2413, 2421, 2445, 2453, 2487,
            2491, 2497, 2507, 2523, 2532, 2545, 2550,
            2555, 2583, 2644, 2668, 2674
    Strategic arms limitation.
        See Strategic arms limitation.
    Test ban treaty, **1979:** 216, 1038
    Titan missile silo explosion in Arkansas, **1980–
        81:** 1844, 1894
    Treaty of Tlatelolco, **1980–81:** 2734
    U.S. exports, **1980–81:** 401
    See also specific weapons system; Strategic arms
        limitation.
Nuclear Weapons, Treaty on the Non-Proliferation
    of, **1980–81:** 403, 433
Nuclear Weapons in Latin America, Treaty for the
    Prohibition of, **1978:** 962
Nugent, Mrs. Patrick J., **1978:** 1808
Nuñez, Louis, **1978:** 2219; **1979:** 91
Nunn, Sen. Sam, **1977:** 1568, 1794, 2130; **1978:** 415,
    540, 542, 1278, 1333, 1425, 1848, 2208;
    1979: 178, 2257n.
    Legislation passage leadership
        Judicial Councils Reform and Judicial Con-
            duct and Disability Act, **1980–81:** 2241
        Military Personnel and Compensation
            Amendments, **1980–81:** 969, 972, 1665,
            1667
        Small Business Administration authorization,
            1980–81: 1279
    Meeting with the President (Digest), **1980–81:**
        893
Nunn Amendment, **1978:** 2212
Nurse training programs, **1978:** 2007, 2011
Nursing Home Week, National, **1978:** 823; **1979:**
    549; **1980–81:** 604
Nvono Nca Menene Oluy, Don Carmelo, **1980–81:**
    1564
Nyachae, Simon, **1980–81:** 355
Nye, Joseph Samuel, Jr., **1977:** 8, 1502, 1507
Nyere, Julius K., **1977:** 1264, 1412, 1423, 1433,
    1434, 1437; **1978:** 695, 976, 1095
Nze Abuy, Rafael M., **1978:** 1471

Oak Ridge, Tenn., **1978:** 948
Oakar, James, **1980–81:** 1001n.
Oakar, Repr. Mary Rose, **1980–81:** 999, 1000, 1257,
    1765
Oakley, Robert B., **1979:** 1848, 1883

OAS.
See American States, Organization of.
Obasanjo, Lt. Gen. Olesugun, **1977:** 1611, 1762, 1772, 1781, 1796, 1809; **1978:** 643, 651, 654, 661, 664, 668, 709, 711
Oberdorfer, Louis F., **1977:** 1613, 1614
Oberstar, Repr. James L., **1979:** 293
Obey, Repr. David R., **1978:** 148; **1979:** 567, 666; **1980–81:** 857
Obledo, Mario, **1978:** 1723
O'Brien, Donald E., **1978:** 1670
O'Brien, James R., **1978:** 257
O'Brien, Jim, **1980–81:** 1635
O'Brien, Larry, **1978:** 1070
O'Brien, Timothy, **1979:** 1591
O'Callaghan, Michael, **1979:** 435
O'Callaghan, Gov. Michael, **1978:** 1725
Occupational Safety and Health, Federal Advisory Council on, **1980–81:** 385, 396, 2849, 2914
Occupational Safety and Health, Interagency Task Force on, **1977:** 1430
Occupational Safety and Health, National Institute for, **1980–81:** 395
Occupational safety and health activities, Federal, **1978:** 1030
Occupational Safety and Health Administration
Assessment, **1977:** 122, 200, 1430
Business Council, remarks, **1978:** 2237
Cotton dust regulations, **1978:** 1061, 1674
Director, **1977:** 104, 105, 108
Environmental message, **1977:** 967
Interview remarks, **1978:** 1491, 1594
Paperwork reduction, **1977:** 1273, 1330
Reagan, Ronald, position on, **1980–81:** 1951, 2306, 2473, 2494, 2511, 2554
Regulatory reform, **1979:** 795, 869, 1346, 1361, 1936, 2181; **1980–81:** 59, 70, 281
Occupational safety and health programs (EO 12223), **1980–81:** 1261
Occupational Safety and Health Review Commission, **1977:** 1529, 1541, 1569; **1978:** 231, 564; **1979:** 552, 619, 841
Ocean Thermal Energy Conversion Act, **1980–81:** 1473
Ocean Thermal Energy Conversion Research, Development, and Demonstration Act, **1980–81:** 1375
Oceanic and Atmospheric Administration, National.
See National Oceanic and Atmospheric Administration.
Oceans, **1977:** 17, 465, 1962
Margin drilling program, **1980–81:** 269
Mining capabilities development, **1980–81:** 1284
Oceans and Atmosphere, National Advisory Committee on, **1978:** 217; **1979:** 1628, 2118, 2187; **1980–81:** 1023, 2242

Oceans Week, National, **1978:** 756
Ochenrider, Elizabeth R., **1979:** 466
Ochi, Rose Matsui, **1979:** 450
Ochoa, Ralph M., **1979:** 1447
Ochoa, Severo, **1979:** 2289; **1980–81:** 82n.
O'Connell, Brian, **1977:** 528
O'Connor, Edwin, **1980–81:** 502
O'Connor, Flannery, **1980–81:** 502
O'Connor, Francis J., **1978:** 1809
O'Connor, Patrick J., **1979:** 466
O'Connor, Robert, **1980–81:** 2560
Odeen, Philip A., **1977:** 1178, 1179
Odom, Col. William, **1979:** 436
Oduber, Quirós, Daniel, **1977:** 1566, 1568
Odum, Eugene P., **1977:** 642, 2165
Odum, Vernon, **1980–81:** 1635
Oei, Paul, **1980–81:** 1468
O'Farrall, McLain T., Jr., **1980–81:** 2614
Office.
See other part of title.
Officer, Carl, **1979:** 2105
Officers' Training Corps, Reserve, **1980–81:** 2292
Off-road vehicles, use on public lands, **1977:** 979, 1002
Offutt Air Force Base, Nebr., **1977:** 1860, 2089
O'Grady, Col. Lawrence R., **1980–81:** 374
O'Hara, Clifford B., **1980–81:** 33
Ohio
Air quality standards, **1978:** 1625
Civic leaders, briefing with administration officials, **1978:** 1808
Emergency declaration, **1977:** 86; **1978:** 229
Energy crisis, **1977:** 37
Energy emergency, **1978:** 314, 322, 505
Farm bureau presidents, meeting with the President (Digest), **1980–81:** 493
Mining jobs, **1979:** 1006
President's visits, **1978:** 1619, 1620; **1979:** 1640; **1980–81:** 992, 995, 997, 1001, 1005, 1762, 1765, 2018, 2347, 2348, 2455, 2466, 2476, 2502, 2655–2659
State Democratic leaders, meeting with the President, **1979:** 1652n.
Urban parks system, **1980–81:** 1681
U.S. attorneys, **1978:** 416, 457, 458
U.S. district judges, **1980–81:** 564, 654, 720, 1599
U.S. marshals, **1977:** 1569, 2130, 2131
Ohio, U.S.S., **1980–81:** 1552
Ohio River Basin Commission, **1978:** 273, 737, 1807; **1979:** 607, 2248
Ohio River Valley Water Sanitation Commission, **1977:** 1486; **1978:** 556; **1980–81:** 654
Ohira, Masayoshi.
See Japan, Prime Minister.
Ohlin, Lloyd Edgar, **1980–81:** 2613
Ohrt, Alvin, **1979:** 795n.

Oil
    Alaska National Petroleum Reserve, report,
        1977: 1127, 1128
    Alternative energy sources, replacement with,
        1980–81: 1198
    Alternative fuel sources, **1977:** 659, 660
    Canadian production, **1979:** 381, 2050
    Conservation, **1977:** 519, 680, 1515
    Conservation (EO 12185), **1979:** 2261
    Conversion from:
        Coal, **1979:** 1255, 1575
        Shale rock, **1979:** 1185, 1190, 1255, 1327, 1575
        Tar sands, **1979:** 1185, 1190
    Crude oil equalization tax, **1978:** 968, 1490
    Crude oil transportation system, **1979:** 2174
    Domestic production, **1977:** 910
    Embargo, possibility, **1978:** 363
    Federal leases, **1977:** 1395
    High sulfur crude and residual fuel, **1978:** 1112
    Home heating
        Price monitoring, **1978:** 58
        Rebates, **1977:** 1397
    Imports.
        See Oil imports.
    International transaction register, **1979:** 1198
    Interview remarks, **1978:** 716
    Israel, supplies to, **1979:** 352, 427, 428
    Israel-U.S. agreement, **1980–81:** 2313, 2333
    Legislation.
        See Oil legislation.
    Marginal wells, **1980–81:** 696
    News conference remarks, **1978:** 2223
    Offshore drilling, **1977:** 520, 1390
    Offshore pollution, **1979:** 338, 1035, 1360, 1496
    Pipelines, **1977:** 283
    President's visit to offshore drilling rig, ques-
        tion-and-answer session, **1977:** 1334
    Prices.
        See Oil prices.
    Production.
        See Oil production.
    Research and development, **1980–81:** 233
    Sales to Japan, **1978:** 810
    Shortages, **1977:** 1514
    Small royalty owners tax exemptions, **1980–81:**
        2421
    Spills, **1977:** 387, 458, 465
    Strategic reserve, **1980–81:** 1476
    Supplies.
        See Oil supplies.
    Surplus, **1978:** 877, 878
    Tanker spills, **1978:** 116, 1296
    Tankers, **1977:** 29, 387, 458, 465
    U.S. drilling equipment exports suspension to
        Soviet Union, **1980–81:** 41
    Utilities use reduction.
        See under Utilities.

Oil — *continued*
    Venice Economic Summit statement, **1980–81:**
        1187
    Waste disposal, **1980–81:** 119, 158
    Well drillings, 1980 statistics, **1980–81:** 1603,
        1675, 1721, 1748, 1763, 1768, 1827, 1864,
        1870, 1882, 1884, 1888, 1898, 1902, 1915,
        1974, 2005, 2045, 2047, 2082, 2119, 2142,
        2166, 2204, 2277, 2297, 2353, 2406, 2410,
        2416, 2421, 2457, 2481, 2531, 2539, 2540,
        2589, 2601, 2607, 2630
    West-to-east crude oil transportation system,
        1980–81: 99, 104
    See also Fuel companies; OPEC.
Oil, hazardous substances and hazardous waste
    response, liability and compensation act,
    proposed, **1979:** 1360
Oil companies.
    See Fuel companies.
Oil imports, **1977:** 283, 422, 534, 656, 658, 819,
        1172, 1368, 1514, 1515, 1599, 1672, 1685,
        1784, 1789, 1799, 1908, 1982, 2017, 2061,
        2108, 2159, 2178; **1978:** 55, 56, 119, 132,
        438, 763, 776, 824, 862, 985, 1003, 1158,
        1159, 1170, 1171, 1253, 1261, 1276, 1307,
        1312, 1409, 1410, 1424, 1442, 1469, 1487–
        1489, 1494, 1546, 1616, 1625, 1628, 1630,
        1914, 1993, 2051, 2153, 2185
    Adjustment program, **1980–81:** 592, 657, 760,
        1140, 1151
    Federal control, possibility of, **1980–81:** 889
    Foreign nations sales to U.S., political uses of,
        1979: 2241
    Gasoline conservation fee.
        See under Gasoline.
    Iranian supplies.
        See under Iran.
    Iraq-Iran conflict, effect on, **1980–81:** 1890,
        1900, 1903, 1906, 1921, 1974, 2025, 2131,
        2191, 2199, 2206, 2268, 2410
    Libyan supplies, **1980–81:** 1681
    Licensing requirements (Proc. 4762), **1980–81:**
        1049
    Mentions, **1979:** 796, 1981
    Mexican supplies, **1979:** 58, 612, 736, 791, 802,
        813, 1245, 1327, 1413, 1569
    Reduction
        Administration's program, **1979:** 1294, 1316
        International Energy Agency support, **1980–
        81:** 251
        International Energy Agency's commitment
        to, **1979:** 2243
        Mentions, **1979:** 2018; **1980–81:** 626
        National energy policy, relationship with,
        1980–81: 70, 75, 121, 128, 242, 251, 279,
        314, 367, 461, 480, 499, 509, 512, 829, 846,
        875, 977, 993, 1083, 1301, 1303, 1307,

Oil imports — *continued*
  Reduction — *continued*
    National policy — *continued*
        1351, 1389, 1395, 1399, 1448, 1603, 1615,
        1651, 1897, 1902, 2040, 2086, 2410, 2481,
        2492, 2810
      National quotas, **1979:** 1145, 1183, 1184, 1190,
        1198, 1218, 1239, 1243–1245, 1337, 1355,
        1475, 1607, 1646, 1748, 1869, 1936; **1980–
        81:** 199, 251, 369, 480, 512, 540, 846, 1681
    Relationship with:
      Energy conservation, **1979:** 1169, 1242,
        1470, 1472, 1480, 1493, 1495, 1575, 1594,
        1891, 1942, 1944, 2023
      Increased domestic production, **1979:** 245,
        1095, 1169, 1242, 1337, 1449, 1470, 1472,
        1474, 1480, 1493, 1495, 1502ftn., 1575,
        1594, 1854, 1942, 1944
      Windfall profits tax, **1979:** 1449, 1457, 1475,
        1566, 2283
    Statistics, **1980–81:** 71, 92, 829, 875, 918, 977,
        986, 992, 994, 1006, 1070, 1083, 1253,
        1349, 1389, 1392, 1503, 1536, 1560, 1587,
        1603, 1606, 1615, 1623, 1633, 1650, 1658,
        1675, 1733, 1739, 1748, 1760, 1763, 1768,
        1827, 1884, 1888, 1898, 1902, 1974, 2000,
        2005, 2045, 2053, 2077, 2082, 2119, 2130,
        2142, 2189, 2190, 2204, 2217, 2222, 2277,
        2298, 2353, 2374, 2481, 2492, 2531, 2539,
        2568, 2589, 2630, 2876
    U.S. efforts for international cooperation,
        1980–81: 640
    Venice Economic Summit commitment,
        1980–81: 1178, 1187, 1235
    Western allies support, **1979:** 1182
  Relationship with:
    Employment, **1980–81:** 71, 580, 787, 829, 846,
        860, 977, 993, 1235, 1252, 1301, 1504,
        1739, 1760, 1768, 1863, 1869, 2057, 2077,
        2190, 2834, 2876
    Inflation, **198081:** 58, 71, 75, 89, 110, 199, 245,
        246, 280, 388, 399, 461, 472, 476, 480, 487,
        496, 553, 580, 665, 685, 735, 787, 801, 829,
        846, 859, 919, 977, 993, 1235, 1252, 1301,
        1504, 1720, 1739, 1760, 1768, 1863, 1869,
        2029, 2053, 2077, 2084, 2129, 2165, 2190,
        2358, 2834, 2896, 3008
    Inflation and employment, **1979:** 1340, 1457,
        1481, 1492, 1512, 1566, 1630, 1723, 1770,
        1841, 1852, 1865, 1873, 1891, 1931, 1937,
        2021, 2028, 2055, 2125, 2155
  Trade balance, **1980–81:** 126, 1696
  Saudi Arabian supplies, **1979:** 1226, 1246, 1766
  Tariff suspension, **1979:** 628
  Threat to national security, **1979:** 678, 1337,
        1472, 1479, 1480, 1493, 1495, 1740, 1861,
        1865, 1868, 1893, 1896, 2028, 2055

Oil imports — *continued*
  U.S. food exchange for, possibility, **1979:** 791,
        802, 1910, 1944
Oil legislation, congressional inaction, **1979:** 611,
        632, 1185, 1498, 2034, 2055
Oil Pipeline Corporation, Trans Mountain, **1980–
        81:** 99
Oil Policy Committee, **1980–81:** 10
Oil portraits of Cabinet Secretaries, **1977:** 662
Oil prices, **1977:** 698, 1203, 1881; **1978:** 1324, 1349,
        2048, 2063, 2064, 2226, 2227, 2271
  Decontrol
    Base period control level, **1979:** 722
    Completion schedule, **1980–81:** 2899
    Congress, consultations with the President,
        1979: 56, 149
    Crude, **1980–81:** 128, 233, 250, 470, 762, 1733,
        1737, 2406, 2410, 2417, 2601
    Heavy crude, **1979:** 1449, 1450, 1455, 1479,
        2278, 2279; **1980–81:** 96, 233
    Legislation extending controls, **1979:** 801, 931,
        963
    Marginal wells, **1979:** 2290; **1980–81:** 696
    Mentions, **1979:** 236, 700, 1586, 2056
    Purposes
      Conservation measure, **1979:** 721, 873, 985,
        2124
      Domestic production increase, **1979:** 600,
        721, 748, 816, 873, 876, 961, 985, 1079,
        1336, 1482, 2125
      Import reduction, **1979:** 622, 649, 816, 873,
        960, 985
      Inflation control measure, **1979:** 988
    Statement by the President, **1979:** 981
    Windfall profits tax, relationship with, **1979:**
        721, 735, 748, 801, 816, 864, 953, 961,
        1316, 2283
  Domestic levels equal to world market, **1979:**
        1199
  Federal controls, President's opposition to,
        1980–81: 314, 417, 583
  Future prices, President's assessment, **1979:**
        1255, 1758; **1980–81:** 314, 369, 1639, 2492
  Inflation, relationship with, **1980–81:** 120, 245,
        280, 1354, 1452, 1613, 1637
  Iraq-Iran conflict, effect on, **1980–81:** 1892
  Marketing and delivery increase, **1979:** 1190
  Past increases percentage, **1980–81:** 553, 639,
        846, 976, 998, 1070, 1082, 2018, 2081, 2257
  Purchase certification for producing countries,
        1979: 1199
  West German Chancellor Schmidt, review of
        increases with the President, **1980–81:** 440
  See also OPEC.
Oil production, **1980–81:** 50, 233, 368, 480, 1701,
        1974
  Heavy crude, **1979:** 1498

Oil production — *continued*
  Independent oilmen, tax exemption, **1979:** 1309, 1320, 1426
  New sites exploration, **1979:** 1544, 1995
  Recovery from immobile sources, **1979:** 1538
  Refineries operating capacity, **1979:** 1324
  U.S. levels, increase, **1979:** 175, 1190, 1724, 1942
Oil supplies
  Defense emergency allocations, **1979:** 937
  Domestic priorities allocations, **1979:** 1185, 1242, 1858
  Home heating
    Disadvantaged persons, Federal assistance for, **1979:** 1256, 1758, 1878, 1903, 1993, 2030, 2056
    Energy Department's allocation responsibilities, **1979:** 1878
    Fuel companies programs, **1979:** 1613, 1758
    Heating oil management group, **1979:** 1631
    New England, **1979:** 739, 862, 1324, 1410, 1416, 1431, 1631, 1901, 1983, 2030
    Reserve stocks buildup, **1979:** 848, 987, 1256, 1324, 1431, 1631, 1858, 1877, 1911, 1983, 2056
  Impact of:
    Iraq-Iran conflict.
      See under Iraq-Iran conflict.
    Soviet invasion of Afghanistan, **1980–81:** 26, 35, 108, 111, 183, 197, 346, 976
  Undiscovered U.S. sources, **1979:** 1575
Oil Windfall Profit Tax Act, Crude.
  See Crude Oil Windfall Profit Tax Act.
Okawara, Yoshio, **1980–81:** 775, 1499
O'Keefe, Georgia, **1979:** 217
O'Keeffe, Charles B., Jr., **1977:** 1963
Okita, Saburo, **1980–81:** 522, 1184
Oklahoma
  Black leaders, meeting with the President, **1979:** 841
  Democratic Party caucuses, **1980–81:** 461
  Disaster assistance, **1980–81:** 1345, 1421
  Disaster declaration, **1979:** 673
  Gov. George Nigh, **1980–81:** 1423n., 2421
  President's visit, **1979:** 469
  State legislature and officials, meetings with the President, **1979:** 217, 841
  U.S. attorneys, **1977:** 1266, 1307, 1613, 1614, 1931, 1932; **1978:** 231
  U.S. district judges, **1979:** 1786, 1787
  U.S. marshals, **1977:** 1437, 1438, 1569, 2089, 2090; **1978:** 231
Oksenberg, Michel, **1978:** 1188
Okun, Arthur, **1980–81:** 533
Okun, Herbert S., **1978:** 1697, 1723; **1980–81:** 1025, 1052
O'Laughlin, Michael, **1980–81:** 2003
Old Age and Survivors Insurance Trust Fund, **1979:** 1633

Old West Regional Commission, **1977:** 1071, 1085
Oldendorf, William H., **1980–81:** 2999
Older American Community Service Employment program, **1978:** 1794
Older Americans Act, **1980–81:** 620
Older Americans Act, Comprehensive, **1979:** 1633
Older Americans Act Amendments, Comprehensive, **1978:** 1792, 1793
Older Americans Month, **1977:** 605; **1978:** 761
  (Proc. 4658), **1979:** 671
  (Proc. 4745), **1980–81:** 620
Older persons, **1977:** 136, 155, 302, 1836, 1847; **1978:** 105, 930, 1062, 1614, 1792, 1793
  Administration's accomplishments and goals, **1980–81:** 141, 620, 998, 999, 1990, 2951, 2956
  Disability programs, **1980–81:** 1062
  Employment, **1980–81:** 2280
  Energy prices, Federal assistance for, **1979:** 2154; **1980–81:** 1345, 1421
  Federal budget allocations, **1980–81:** 767
  Federal programs, **1980–81:** 2212, 2456
  Food stamps, **1979:** 480
  Health and medical care, **1980–81:** 2281
  Health costs assistance, **1979:** 387, 1432
  House-Senate bipartisan intern program, **1979:** 837
  Housing, **1980–81:** 2460
  Housing costs assistance, **1979:** 1432
  Interest rates, effect on, **1979:** 928
  Leaders, meeting with the President (Digest), **1980–81:** 1945
  Legislation, **1979:** 139
  Mandatory retirement age, **1980–81:** 1000
  Mental health services funding, **1979:** 862
  National health plan provisions, **1979:** 1029
  National Issue Forum with the President, **1979:** 1630
  President's remarks to groups at:
    Boston, Mass., **1980–81:** 2243
    St. Petersburg, Fla., **1980–81:** 2157
  Rural housing program, **1979:** 218, 843
  White House Conference on Aging, reception remarks, **1980–81:** 534
  See also Medicaid and Medicare; Social security system.
O'Leary, Charles J., **1980–81:** 2817
O'Leary, Jean, **1978:** 1135
O'Leary, John F., **1977:** 35, 56, 87, 526, 1092, 1584, 1613
O'Leary, Robert T., **1977:** 1701
Olivarez, Graciela (Grace), **1977:** 564, 596, 872, 1127, 1837, 1844, 1852; **1978:** 1094; **1979:** 1317, 1319, 1865; **1980–81:** 281, 1460
Oliveira, Elmar, **1978:** 1356
Oliver, Earl, **1977:** 1239, 1266; **1978:** 1438, 1720, 1724
Oliver, R. Spencer, **1978:** 1340

Oliver Wendell Holmes Devise, Permanent Committee for the, **1979:** 746
Oliveria, Arnulfo, **1980–81:** 2617
Olmsted, Mary S., **1978:** 1188, 1222
Olney, Warren, **1980–81:** 1897n.
Olson, Jack B., **1977:** 195
Olson, Paul and Janet, **1978:** 857, 870
Olson, William C., **1980–81:** 928
Olympic Committee, International.
   See International Olympic Committee.
Olympic Committee, United States.
   See United States Olympic Committee.
Olympic Organizing Committee, Lake Placid, **1980–81:** 268
Olympic Sports, President's Commission on, **1978:** 1976
Olympics, 1936 Summer, **1980–81:** 518, 635
Olympics, 1980, **1978:** 1327
Olympics, 1980 Summer
   International boycott
      African leaders, consulations with Muhammad Ali, **1980–81:** 333
      Effectiveness of, **1980–81:** 1727
      France, **1980–81:** 676
      Germany, Federal Republic of, **1980–81:** 439, 470, 712, 920
      Kenya, **1980–81:** 353, 358
      Mentions, **1980–81:** 1193, 1308
      Soviet people, impact on, **1980–81:** 747
      United Kingdom, **1980–81:** 676, 677
      U.S. efforts to secure, **1980–81:** 796, 804, 989, 1103, 1173, 2351
   International Olympic Committee
      Decision to hold games in Moscow, **1980–81:** 305
      President Killanin, meeting with the President, **1980–81:** 929
   Permanent site in Greece, possibility of, **1980–81:** 107, 108, 383
   Soviet troop withdrawal from Afghanistan, effect on, **1980–81:** 1174
   U.S. boycott
      Administration officials meeting with U.S. Olympic Committee executives (Digest), **1980–81:** 104
      Alternative games, possibility of, **1980–81:** 108, 260, 380, 388
      Effectiveness, **1980–81:** 1435, 1727
      Mention, **1980–81:** 889
      News conference (Checklist), **1980–81:** 219
      Olympic athletes' support, **1980–81:** 388
      President's comments, **1980–81:** 23, 107, 196, 259, 311, 312, 346, 635, 663, 675, 747, 989
      Prohibition on Olympic-related exports to Soviet Union, **1980–81:** 559, 560, 565
      Reagan, Ronald, opposition to, **1980–81:** 1530, 1535

Olympics, 1980 Summer — *continued*
   U.S. boycott — *continued*
      Special medal ceremony for athletes, **1980–81:** 1315
      U.S. Olympic Committee response.
         See under United States Olympic Committee.
      Vice President's address to U.S. Olympic Committee House of Delegates, announcement (Digest), **1980–81:** 653
      White House briefing for U.S. team representatives, **1980–81:** 517
      White House statement officially announcing withdrawal, **1980–81:** 356
      U.S. team, **1980–81:** 1440, 1444, 1470, 1493
Olympics, 1980 Winter
   Lake Placid Olympic Organizing Committee, chairman, **1980–81:** 268
   Mentions, **1980–81:** 260, 377
   Olympic torch ceremony in Athens, Greece, U.S. representatives, **1980–81:** 217
   U.S. team, White House reception, **1980–81:** 379
Olympics, 1984 Summer, **1979:** 2206
Olyphant, Pa., **1980–81:** 606
Olzak, Greg, **1980–81:** 1319
O'Malley, Carlon M., Jr., **1977:** 2089, 2090; **1979:** 93
Oman
   Ambassador to U.S., **1977:** 1754; **1979:** 1453
   Foreign Affairs Minister, **1980–81:** 452
   U.S. Ambassador, **1978:** 1557, 1572
   U.S. military bases, **1980–81:** 35, 391
Omenn, Gilbert S., **1980–81:** 3026
Omnibus Reconciliation Act, **1980–81:** 2778, 2782
O'Neal, A. Daniel, **1977:** 571; **1978:** 2237; **1979:** 217, 1624, 1787
O'Neal, Lacey, **1979:** 1678
O'Neill, Eugene, **1980–81:** 502
O'Neill, Mildred A., **1978:** 242; **1980–81:** 500
O'Neill, Millie, **1979:** 2211
O'Neill, Repr. Thomas P., Jr.
   See Speaker of the House of Representatives.
O'Neill, Mrs. Thomas P., Jr., **1978:** 1808
O'Neill, Lt. Gov. Thomas P., III, **1978:** 2209, 2218
Onek, Joseph, **1979:** 1976; **1980–81:** 104, 518
Onn, Datuk Hussein bin, **1977:** 1612, 1699
Onyonka, Zacharia T., **1980–81:** 355
OPEC (Organization of Petroleum Exporting Countries), **1977:** 1203, 1783, 1983, 2170, 2197; **1978:** 363, 461, 2063, 2226, 2271
   December, 1979, discussions in Caracas, Venezuela, **1980–81:** 570
   Decontrol of U.S. oil prices, effect on, **1979:** 982
   Developing countries
      Appeal for lower prices, **1980–81:** 1178, 1186, 1578
      Energy production assistance, **1980–81:** 441
   Export reduction, **1979:** 2243

OPEC — *continued*
  June price increase
    Announcement, **1979:** 1181, 1183n.
    Developing nations, effect on, **1979:** 1212
    Mention, **1979:** 1439
    Tokyo Summit statements, **1979:** 1190, 1199, 1200
    U.S. energy crisis and inflation, cause for, **1979:** 1219, 1239, 1242, 1485, 1636, 1641, 1748, 1837, 1841, 1865, 1874, 1891, 1942, 1984, 1994, 2028, 2057
    U.S. energy technologies development, effect on, **1979:** 1647
  Libyan role in, **1980–81:** 1477
  Mentions, **1979:** 721, 736, 1146, 2031; **1980–81:** 499
  1973 embargo, **1980–81:** 875, 1392, 1681, 2045
  Past price increases, **1979:** 611, 717, 944, 964
  Price increases
    Impact on:
      Disadvantaged persons, **1980–81:** 587
      International economy, **1980–81:** 1206, 1537
      U.S. automobile industry, **1980–81:** 1984, 1987, 2009, 2048
      U.S. inflation rates, **1980–81:** 58, 71, 75, 110, 120, 199, 250, 388, 713, 735, 743, 801, 881, 938, 1042, 1066, 1069, 1082, 1354, 1504, 1869, 1879, 1895, 2029, 2090, 2119, 2130, 2165, 2190, 2204, 2219, 2327, 2345, 2349, 2352, 2374, 2433, 2444, 2457, 2480, 2513, 2547, 2553, 2567, 2589, 2630, 2834, 2896
    Relationship with:
      U.S. national energy policy development, **1980–81:** 128, 1392, 1760
      U.S. wage and price structure, **1980–81:** 280
  Price structure, **1979:** 245
  Production, **1979:** 1584, 1741, 2241
  Production increases to maintain stable prices, **1980–81:** 943
  Profits investment in U.S., **1980–81:** 1118
  U.S. agricultural products exchange for oil, possibility, **1979:** 802, 1910, 1944
  U.S. dollar, value increase in, **1979:** 1840
  U.S. oil boycott, possibility, **1979:** 1583
  U.S. relations, **1979:** 1896
  World supplies percentage, **1979:** 1471, 1473; **1980–81:** 368, 461, 514, 847, 963, 976, 1615, 1678, 1769, 1865, 1995, 2033, 2086, 2119, 2165, 2203, 2206, 2263, 2277, 2294, 2407, 2410, 2589
Operation of the Automotive Products Trade Act of 1965, **1979:** 178; **1980–81:** 653
Operation PUSH (People United to Save Humanity), **1978:** 1333; **1979:** 1422; **1980–81:** 932, 1946
Opheim, Edwin O., **1980–81:** 813, 826
Oplinger, Gerald G., **1979:** 1045

Oppedahl, David B., **1980–81:** 928
Oppenheimer, Jesse H., **1979:** 2118; **1980–81:** 2732
Opportunities Industrialization Centers of America, **1980–81:** 1066, 1629n.
Order of the American Hellenic Educational Progressive Association, **1980–81:** 381
Ordin, Andrea M. Sheridan, **1977:** 1613, 1614
Oregon
  Civic leaders, meeting with the President, **1978:** 1571
  Emergency declaration, **1977:** 805
  Energy emergency, **1979:** 2286
  John Day River, **1980–81:** 323
  Mount St. Helens eruption, areas damaged by, **1980–81:** 750, 958, 991
  President's visits, **1978:** 844, 853, 855, 1942; **1979:** 2186; **1980–81:** 950, 1901, 2672
  SALT II treaty briefing for community and civic leaders by administration officials (Digest), **1979:** 2106
  Siletz Indian tribes, **1980–81:** 1661
  U.S. attorney, **1978:** 881, 882
  U.S. district judge, **1979:** 2207
  U.S. marshal, **1977:** 1437, 1438
  Yaguina Head Outstanding Natural Area, **1980–81:** 433
O'Reilly, Jacqueline D., **1979:** 466
Orfila, Alejandro, **1977:** 1542, 1544; **1978:** 570, 1146
Organization.
  See other part of title.
Orlando, Fla., **1978:** 1687–1689; **1980–81:** 2397
Orlov, Yuri, **1978:** 938
O'Rourke, Larry, **1977:** 758, 760
Orr, Roy, **1980–81:** 1393n., 1770, 1846, 2889
Ortega, Daniel, **1979:** 1722
Ortique, Revius O., Jr., **1978:** 1753, 1772; **1979:** 46, 92
Ortiz, Alba A., **1980–81:** 192
Ortiz, Frank V., Jr., **1977:** 1189, 1212, 1530; **1978:** 1879; **1979:** 293, 783, 842
Ortiz, Mrs. Frank V., Jr., **1979:** 293
Osborn, Mary Jane, **1980–81:** 1149, 1246, 3023
Oser, Marie M., **1978:** 1190
O'Shei, Col. Donald M., **1977:** 1553, 1569
Osman, Ahmed, **1977:** 2079
Ostrander, Nancy, **1978:** 760, 771
Oswald, Rudolph A., **1978:** 52, 150; **1980–81:** 2609
Otero, Alejandro, **1977:** 1184
Otero, Joaquin F., **1978:** 1514; **1979:** 812
Otlowski, George J., **1980–81:** 1672
Ottawa Tribe, **1977:** 311, 326
Ottinger, Betty Ann, **1977:** 741
Ouko, Robert J., **1980–81:** 355
Ould Daddah, Abdallah, **1980–81:** 2752
Ourso, Laurence P., **1980–81:** 2107
Ouse, Clifford M., **1978:** 506

Outdoor Life magazine, **1979:** 2186
Outer Continental Shelf, **1977:** 973; **1978:** 114;
    1980–81: 233
Outer Continental Shelf Lands Act Amendments,
    1978: 1530
Ovel, Gerald L., **1978:** 696
Overseas Private Investment Corporation, **1977:**
    805
Overseas Development Corporation, **1979:** 2012n.
Overseas Development Council, **1979:** 2138
    Board of Directors, members, **1978:** 314, 329,
        1037, 1071; **1979:** 783, 842, 899, 1022,
        1043; **1980–81:** 521, 1446, 1522, 1926,
        1947
    Executive Vice President, **1980–81:** 605, 608
    President, **1978:** 1701, 1724; **1979:** 1786
    Reorganization, **1979:** 279, 396, 643, 1230
    United States Trade Representative responsibil-
        ities, **1979:** 1731
Overton, William Ray, **1979:** 402, 403
Oveson, Mr. and Mrs. Clarence, **1980–81:** 2839,
    2840
Owen, David, **1977:** 646, 647, 1382, 1487
Owen, David A. L., **1978:** 495, 504
Owen, Henry, **1977:** 332, 827, 829, 852; **1978:** 751,
    758, 1704, 1723
Owen, Henry D.
    See Special Representative of the President for
        International Economic Summits.
Owen, Roberts B., **1979:** 1697, 1706, 2210
Owens, Brian, **1979:** 2042
Owens, Edris (Soapy), **1977:** 1855, 1860
Owens, Hugh F., **1977:** 2183; **1978:** 150
Owens, Jesse, **1979:** 322; **1980–81:** 380, 574
Owens, Judith M., **1980–81:** 1432
Owens, Ray, **1978:** 526
Owings, Nathaniel, **1978:** 2050
Owyhee River, Idaho-Oregon, **1979:** 1814
Oxman, Stephan A., **1979:** 436
Ozar, I. I., **1979:** 293
Ozarks Regional Commission, **1977:** 1070, 1085
Ozores, Carlos, **1979:** 837

Pace, Clyde W., Jr., **1979:** 1451
Pace, Norma, **1979:** 1954
Pace, Steve, **1980–81:** 2405
Pacheco, Donald, **1977:** 1055
Pachios, Harold, **1978:** 1902
Pacific American Heritage Week, Asian/ (Proc.
    4727), **1980–81:** 405
Pacific Fisheries Commission, International North,
    1980–81: 2774
Pacific Islands, Trust Territory of the, **1977:** 705,
    745, 1294, 1303, 1308; **1980–81:** 301, 319,
    466

Pacific nations.
    See specific country.
Pacific Northwest Regional Commission, **1977:**
    1071, 1085
Pacific Northwest River Basins Commission, **1978:**
    272, 481, 737; **1979:** 2248
Pacific Salmon Fisheries Commission, Interna-
    tional, **1977:** 1485
Packard, Beth, **1977:** 816
Packard, David, **1979:** 1823
Packer, Arnold H., **1977:** 365, 373; **1978:** 416
Packwood, Sen. Bob, **1978:** 2003; **1979:** 1435
    Legislation passage leadership
        Household Goods Transportation Act, **1980–
            81:** 2240
        Motor Carrier Act, **1980–81:** 461, 589, 694,
            1262, 1267
        Staggers Rail Act, **1980–81:** 2226, 2230
Padilla, James Jerome, **1978:** 1026
Padron, Eduardo J., **1979:** 466
Page, Richard Stephen, **1977:** 1061, 1100, 1127
Page, Walter N., **1977:** 1178, 1180
Pahlavi, Ali Reza, **1978:** 1954
Pahlavi, Shah Mohammad Reza, **1977:** 1825, 2026,
    2028, 2029, 2033, 2042, 2217, 2218; **1978:**
    47, 1515, 1750, 2101, 2172, 2226, 2255,
    2256
    Departure from U.S., **1979:** 2251
    Entry into U.S.
        President's decision to allow, **1979:** 2169, 2171
        Wilford Hall Air Force Hospital, San
            Antonio, Tex., departure to recuperate,
            1979: 2191
    Financial holdings investigations, possibility of,
        1979: 2174
    Medical treatment in U.S., **1980–81:** 112
    Overthrow as Iranian leader, **1980–81:** 741
        President's comments on, **1979:** 50, 259, 313,
            565
    Political criminal trial, U.S. refusal of, **1979:**
        2205, 2240, 2242
    U.S. property transfer restrictions, **1980–81:** 3037
    U.S. support of regime, **1980–81:** 307, 341, 742
Paine, James C., **1979:** 1232, 1233
Paintsville Lake, Ky., **1977:** 208, 490
Paiute Indians, **1980–81:** 604, 2781
Pak Tong-chin, **1977:** 372
Pakistan
    Afghan refugees migration, **1980–81:** 256, 663,
        964
    Ambassador to U.S., **1979:** 376
    American Embassy, terrorist attack on, **1979:**
        2150, 2151; **1980–81:** 2356
    Foreign affairs adviser Agha Shahi, **1980–81:** 67
    Foreign relations
        India, **1980–81:** 330
        U.S., **1980–81:** 390, 2986
    Nuclear reprocessing plants, **1977:** 764

[References are to page numbers except as otherwise indicated]

Pakistan — *continued*
    President Mohammad Zia-ul-Haq, **1979:** 2151;
        1980–81: 34, 40, 1945, 2055, 2356
    Soviet invasion of Afghanistan, effect on, **1980–
        81:** 24, 184
    U.S. Ambassador, **1977:** 576, 581, 597, 807, 964,
        1031, 1127
    U.S. food assistance, **1980–81:** 1333
    U.S. military assistance, **1980–81:** 24, 34, 91, 109,
        119, 172, 198, 439
    West German assistance, **1980–81:** 439
Pakistan, Himalayan Mountains, American expe-
    dition, **1978:** 1558
Palade, George Emil, **1978:** 739
Palano, Christopher John, **1978:** 926
Palestine Liberation Organization (PLO), **1977:**
    1687, 1688, 2059, 2120; **1978:** 1612
    Arab countries endorsement, **1980–81:** 879
    European recognition, **1980–81:** 682, 1115
    Israel, refusal to recognize autonomy of, **1979:**
        454, 456, 623, 907, 1428, 1579, 1845
    Jackson, Jesse, meeting with leaders, **1979:** 1997
    Libyan position on, **1980–81:** 1477
    Mention, **1979:** 453
    United Nations observer, **1979:** 1591ftn.
    U.S. refusal to recognize, **1980–81:** 379, 460, 527,
        682, 688, 879, 1115, 1657, 2194, 2371,
        2434, 2462, 2489, 2541, 2596
Palestinians, **1977:** 387, 600, 722, 861, 862, 1011,
    1236, 1459, 1623, 1624, 1687, 1688, 1783,
    1804, 1915, 1936, 1956, 2010, 2011, 2055,
    2116, 2117, 2173, 2189, 2190, 2206; **1978:**
    44, 247, 292, 305, 494, 1524, 1534, 1535,
    1590, 1609, 1610, 1746
    Arab commitment to independent state, **1979:**
        1585
    Camp David accords commitment to self-de-
        termination, **1980–81:** 338, 526, 618, 682,
        870, 879, 1129, 1196
    Camp David agreement to resolve settlement of,
        1979: 455, 1867, 2047
    Mentions, **1979:** 427, 488, 703, 911, 1005
    President's opposition to separate state, **1979:**
        1427; **1980–81:** 378, 390, 527, 1656, 2194,
        2430, 2461, 2541
    Right to autonomy, **1979:** 408, 413, 455, 623, 967,
        1427, 1752
    Soviet tanks delivery to terrorists, **1980–81:** 390
    West Bank and Gaza Strip settlements, auton-
        omy negotiations.
        See under Middle East, Egyptian-Israeli peace
        negotiations.
Paletta, Len J., **1978:** 711, 712, 1010
Palkhivala, N. A., **1977:** 1754
Palmer, Darlene, **1980–81:** 1706n.
Palmer, John L., **1980–81:** 316
Palmer, Russell E., **1979:** 1671

Palmer, Wayman D., **1980–81:** 1419, 1428
Palmieri, Victor H., **1977:** 941
    See also State, Department of, Coordinator for
        Refugee Affairs.
Palumbo, Benjamin L., **1980–81:** 2807
Pan American Day and Pan American Week,
    1977: 469; **1978:** 566
    (Proc. 4644), **1979:** 390
    (Proc. 4732), **1980–81:** 455
Pan American Railway Congress Association,
    1978: 898
Pan American World Airways, **1979:** 2283
Panama
    Ambassador to U.S., **1977:** 942, 1383; **1978:** 759;
        1979: 377
    Brig. Gen. Omar Torrijos Herrera, **1977:** 1535,
        1544, 1567, 1787, 1788, 1793, 1796, 1885,
        1886, 2196; **1978:** 82, 86, 120, 517, 717,
        758, 759
    Inaugural ceremonies, U.S. delegation, **1978:**
        1723
    Jefferson-Jackson dinner, remarks, **1978:** 1900
    Penal sentences treaty with U.S., **1979:** 1329
    Permanent American cemetery, **1979:** 81
    President Aristides Royo, **1979:** 683, 836, 1628,
        2251
    President's visit, **1978:** 1118–1127, 1153, 1155
    Shah Mohammed Reza Pahlavi of Iran, resi-
        dency acceptance of, **1979:** 2251
    U.S. Ambassador, **1978:** 1512, 1517, 1723
    U.S. relations, **1979:** 1349
    Vice President's visit, **1979:** 1628; **1980–81:** 1564
Panama Canal
    Ambassador at Large, **1977:** 148
    Functions delegation, **1980–81:** 537, 973
    Negotiations, **1977:** 148, 225, 279, 325, 614, 1326,
        1383
    Second canal, possibility, **1977:** 1326, 1338, 1487,
        1492, 1493
    Special Representative of the President for the
        Panama Canal negotiations, **1977:** 101,
        147
    Treaties.
        See Panama Canal treaties.
    Treaty Affairs, deputy to Ambassador Bunker,
        1977: 1581
Panama Canal Act, **1979:** 1776
Panama Canal Commission, **1979:** 1333, 1786,
    2074, 2175; **1980–81:** 32, 974, 1522
Panama Canal Company, **1979:** 102
Panama Canal Consultative Committee, **1980–81:**
    33
Panama Canal Joint Commission on the Envi-
    ronment, **1980–81:** 34
Panama Canal treaties
    Address to the Nation, **1978:** 258, 277
    Administration's accomplishment, **1980–81:** 579,
        870, 1365, 2933

Panama Canal treaties — *continued*
  Agreement in principle, **1977:** 1462, 1465
  Briefings, **1977:** 1507, 1513, 1525, 1568, 1612,
      1648, 1649, 1699, 1794, 2005, 2006, 2077,
      2089; **1978:** 229, 276, 415
  Citizens' committees, **1977:** 1825, 2037
  Congressional Members, meeting with the Pres-
      ident, **1978:** 302
  Council of the Americas, meeting with the Pres-
      ident, **1978:** 148
  Denver, Colo., briefing, **1977:** 1884
  Entry into force ceremonies, U.S. representa-
      tives, **1979:** 1628
  Foreign relations with Latin America, effect on,
      1980–81: 870, 1652
  Implementing legislation
    Congressional consideration, **1979:** 901, 963,
        1125, 1665, 1698
    Congressmen, administration briefings for
        (Digest), **1979:** 841, 1042
    Mention, **1979:** 2017
    Statement on signing, **1979:** 1776
  Interview remarks, **1977:** 1512, 1513, 1597, 2195,
      2196; **1978:** 68, 306, 520, 717, 718, 1590,
      1598
  Letter to Sen. Richard Stone, **1978:** 227, 232
  Mentions, **1979:** 2033, 2160
  Most difficult political challenge of President,
      1979: 1996, 2018, 2053
  Nashua, N.H., forum remarks, **1978:** 378, 383
  National Education Association, remarks, **1978:**
      297
  News conference remarks, **1977:** 1488, 1787,
      1788
  1977 treaty and related agreements, **1979:** 102,
      160, 836, 1349, 1611
  Ohio State Democratic Party, reception remarks,
      1978: 1623
  Panama Canal regulations, continuing applica-
      bility of (EO 12173), **1979:** 2175
  Protocol of Exchange of Instruments of Rati-
      fication, signing ceremony, **1978:** 1118
  Purposes, **1980–81:** 345, 2734
  Ratification process, President's comments on,
      1980–81: 2707
  Senate ratifications
    Neutrality Treaty, **1978:** 516
    Panama Canal Treaty, **1978:** 758, 802
  Signing ceremony, **1977:** 1542, 1544
  State of the Union, **1978:** 96, 97, 120
  Statement of understanding, **1977:** 1793, 1796
  Support of ratification, **1977:** 1752
  Telephone question-and-answer sessions
    Albuquerque, N. Mex., **1978:** 85
    Hattiesburg, Miss., **1978:** 82
  Transmittal to Senate, **1977:** 1625
  United Nations address, **1977:** 1722

Panama Canal treaties — *continued*
  U.S. human rights policy, impact on, **1979:** 585
  U.S. public opinion poll, **1979:** 1712, 1751
  U.S. relations with Latin America, **1977:** 2093
Panetta, Repr. Leon E., **1978:** 1515; **1980–81:** 2778
Pangelinan, Edward DLG, **1980–81:** 344, 1723
Panner, Owen M., **1979:** 2207
Panofsky, Wolfgang K. H., **1978:** 217, 230
Pansa Cedronio, Paolo, **1978:** 710
Pantoja, Antonia, **1980–81:** 2075
Panupong, Arun, **1977:** 822
Papanek, Mrs. Betka, **1980–81:** 1439n.
Papermaking machinery, **1978:** 2271, 2272
Paperwork, Commission on Federal, **1977:** 178,
    1699
Paperwork reduction, **1977:** 160, 169, 174, 177, 178,
    190, 752, 1273, 1285, 1557, 1558, 1564,
    2015, 2016, 2109; **1978:** 94, 108, 269, 1223,
    1226, 1247, 1350, 1422, 1594
  Administration's accomplishments and goals,
      1980–81: 2967
  Broadcasting industry, **1979:** 483
  Employee Retirement Income Security Act
      forms, **1980–81:** 295
  Environmental reports, **1979:** 1346
  EO 12174, **1979:** 2176, 2179
  Federal Government, **1979:** 129, 494, 869, 935,
      1935, 1943; **1980–81:** 75, 153, 215, 1357,
      2344, 2629
  HEW forms, **1979:** 869, 1346
  Legislation, **1979:** 2177
  Medicare forms, **1979:** 1636
  Message to Congress on administration's
      progress, **1979:** 2180, 2189
  News conference (Checklist), **1979:** 2207
  OSHA regulations, **1979:** 868, 1346, 1936
  Small businesses, **1979:** 1346
Paperwork Reduction Act
  Congressional consideration, **1980–81:** 78, 153
  Fact sheet (Checklist), **1980–81:** 2807
  Signing ceremony, **1980–81:** 2794
Pappas, Jographia, **1979:** 466
Papua New Guinea
  Ambassador to U.S., **1980–81:** 2807
  U.S. Ambassador, **1979:** 1228, 1232
Paraguay
  Ambassador to U.S., **1977:** 942
  Inaugural ceremonies, U.S. delegation, **1978:**
      1406
  President Alfredo Stroessner, **1977:** 1537, 1567
  Trade with U.S., **1979:** 2255
  U.S. Ambasssador, **1977:** 1763, 1795; **1978:**
      1406; **1980–81:** 1290
Paraquat, **1978:** 1329
Pardon, violations of Military Selective Service
    Act, **1977:** 5, 6, 266, 321
Park Chung Hee.
  See Korea, Republic of, President.

Park Service, National.
See National Park Service.
Parker, Alan A., **1979:** 975, 983
Parker, Barrington, **1979:** 1717
Parker, Brenda, **1978:** 1135
Parker, Cindi, **1979:** 2076
Parker, Dave, **1980–81:** 291
Parker, Earl R., **1979:** 2289; **1980–81:** 82n.
Parker, Edna Gaynell, **1980–81:** 757, 775
Parker, George, **1977:** 1383
Parker, Jack S., **1979:** 977
Parker, John V., **1979:** 957, 958
Parker, Joseph O., **1978:** 1154
Parker, Richard B., **1977:** 81, 87; **1978:** 1700, 1724
Parker, Robert M., **1979:** 241, 242
Parkinson, Nicholas F., **1979:** 2162n.
Parks, Paul, **1978:** 1086, 1111
Parks, Rosa, **1978:** 1683; **1979:** 321, 2009; **1980–81:** 2426
Parks, national, **1977:** 1073, 1097
    Alaskan National Monuments, **1978:**2111–2144
Parks, urban, **1978:** 590
Parks and Recreation Act, National, **1978:** 1999
Parks and Recreation Act of 1978, National, **1979:** 1354, 1359; **1980–81:** 416
Parks and Recreation Act of 1978 amendments, National, **1980–81:** 432
Parks and Recreation Recovery Program, Urban, **1979:** 1817, 2220
Parks Week, National Recreation and, **1980–81:** 936
Parma, Ohio, **1980–81:** 997
Parmer, Hugh, **1978:** 1164
Parole Commission, United States, **1977:** 1644, 1650, 1824, 1931; **1978:** 1083, 1111, 1503, 1506; **1980–81:** 1411, 1428
Parris, O. B., **1977:** 308
Partington, John J., **1979:** 2249
Partners of the Americas, **1980–81:** 628
Parton, Dolly, **1979:** 1815
Partridge, Robert, **1980–81:** 1405
Pascagoula, Miss., **1979:** 1674, 1817
Passmore, William A., **1979:** 2191
Passover, **1978:** 766
Pastor, Robert A., **1978:** 1406; **1979:** 189, 837
Pastore, Sen. John, **1979:** 2059
Patel, Marilyn Hall, **1980–81:** 894
Patent Appeals, United States Court of Customs and, **1980–81:** 866, 870
Patent system, **1979:** 2069, 2071
Patent and Trademark Office, **1979:** 196, 218, 1938, 2071, 2081; **1980–81:** 237, 2803
Patent and trademark system
    Counsels for small and minority business, **1980–81:** 78
    Foreign sale of American patents, **1980–81:** 2263, 2277, 2294

Patent and trademark system — *continued*
    Reform legislation, **1980–81:** 154
    Technological advancement, role in, **1980–81:** 273, 2888
Patino, Lorenzo E., **1980–81:** 2613
Patlan, Juan J., **1979:** 1221, 1223
Patolichev, N. A., **1977:** 2006
Patrick, Gerald H., **1980–81:** 1644
Patrick, Hugh T., **1979:** 2128
Patridge, Robert D., **1977:** 1965
Patriotism Week, National, **1980–81:** 2832
Patten, Repr. Edward J., **1980–81:** 1672, 1673, 1677
Patterson, Eugene C., **1978:** 727
Patterson, Gardner, **1980–81:** 1975, 2070
Patterson, Repr. Jerry M., **1978:** 1947
Patterson, Liz, **1980–81:** 1758
Patterson, Mary Jean, **1977:** 78, 90
Patton, Larry D., **1977:** 1931, 1932; **1978:** 231
Paul, Alice, **1977:** 1503; **1980–81:** 412
Pauling, Linus, **1980–81:** 1405
Paulsen, Gordon W., **1980–81:** 2837
Paulucci, Jeno, **1980–81:** 208, 1718, 2807
Pavarotti, Luciano, **1980–81:** 2198
Pawlikowski, John T., **1980–81:** 822
Pawlings, Steven, **1980–81:** 2822
Pay Advisory Committee, **1980–81:** 479, 1650
    Chairman and members, **1979:** 1953
    Establishment, **1979:** 1778, 1779
    Functions, **1979:** 1859
    Meeting with the President (Digest), **1979:** 1975
    Mention, **1979:** 1869
Pay Agent, President's, **1980–81:** 1596, 2729
Pay Comparability Alternative Plan, Federal, **1979:** 1529
Payne, Franklin, **1977:** 1483, 1484
Payne, Kenneth R., **1978:** 1955
Payne, Roger S., **1979:** 2116
Payne, Seth T., **1980–81:** 1576
Payton, Carolyn R., **1977:** 1540, 1568, 1699, 1701; **1978:** 884, 899, 1682, 2072
Paz Garcia, Policarpo, **1980–81:** 426
Peace, Food for, **1980–81:** 257
Peace, President's commitment to, **1979:** 1207, 1220, 1312, 1341, 1485, 1493, 1595, 1751, 1769, 1802, 1828, 1831, 1905, 1989, 2026, 2033, 2047, 2061, 2122, 2233, 2236, 2237; **1980–81:** 111, 195, 344, 541, 579, 632, 637, 673, 871, 941, 993, 1302, 1308, 1320, 1392, 1394, 1426, 1530, 1535, 1550, 1562, 1603, 1607, 1619, 1652, 1682, 1721, 1743, 1760, 1762, 1868, 1887, 1892, 1899, 1902, 1910, 2044, 2088, 2120, 2269, 2435, 2505, 2577, 2582, 2587, 2624, 2639, 2662, 2668, 2675, 2680
Peace, White House Conference on Religion and, **1979:** 1598

Peace and Conflict Resolution, Commission on Proposals for the National Academy of, **1979:** 2195

Peace Corps, **1977:** 272, 1699, 1701; **1978:** 484, 1682, 2072
  Carter, Lillian, service in, **1979:** 1982
  Deputy Director, **1979:** 1692, 1706
  EO 12137, **1979:** 877
  Establishment as autonomous agency within ACTION, **1979:** 881
  Founding, **1979:** 1980
  1980 budget allocations, **1980–81:** 942
  Programs, organizational review, **1979:** 396
  Shriver, Sargent, role in, **1980–81:** 464
  Voluntary service effectiveness, **1980–81:** 328
  Volunteer Deborah Loff, meeting with the President (Digest), **1980–81:** 291
  Volunteer Richard Starr, release by Colombian terrorists, **1980–81:** 306
  See also ACTION.
Peace Corps, Director (Richard F. Celeste), **1980–81:** 291, 774, 1396, 2823
  Functions, **1979:** 877, 881
  Nomination, **1979:** 551, 554
  Swearing in, **1979:** 956
Peace Corps Advisory Council, **1979:** 878, 879; **1980–81:** 1240, 2074, 2849
Peace and Human Rights, Campobello Conference on, **1979:** 1521
Peace Prize, 1979 Nobel, **1979:** 1962
Peacock, Andrew S., **1980–81:** 422
Peacock, William E., **1977:** 1586; **1980–81:** 304
Peanut Brigade, **1977:** 1795
Peanuts
  Imports, **1980–81:** 2772, 2775
  Legislation, **1978:** 1675
Peapples, George A., **1977:** 1779, 1795
Pearlman, Mark David, **1980–81:** 2859n.
Pearson, James B., **1979:** 942
Pearson, Sen. James B., **1978:** 229, 762, 1509, 1516, 2187
Pease, Repr. Donald J., **1979:** 867
Pechota, Terry Lee, **1979:** 1883, 1884
Peden, Katherine G., **1978:** 53.
Pedeway, Clyde, **1977:** 882
Pedro, Erasmo Martins, **1978:** 635, 636
Peek, Linda K., **1979:** 742n.
Pei, I. M., **1978:** 1028; **1980–81:** 1440, 1470
Pell, Sen. Claiborne, **1977:** 1084, 1612; **1978:** 289, 304, 339, 453, 823, 1340, 1695, 1713, 1917, 1919; **1979:** 2085
  Conference on Security and Cooperation in Europe, U.S. delegation vice-chairman, **1980–81:** 848
  Legislation passage leadership
    Education Amendments, **1980–81:** 2064
    Federal Election Campaign Act Amendments of 1979, **1980–81:** 38

Pell, Sen. Claiborne — *continued*
  Legislation leadership — *continued*
    Northeast corridor rail system, **1980–81:** 1009
    United States Holocaust Memorial Council, member, **1980–81:** 823
Pellegrino, Edmund, **1980–81:** 264, 1718
Pelletreau, Robert H., Jr., **1979:** 101, 179
Pelosi, Nancy, **1980–81:** 2807
Pence, Alfred M., **1977:** 1055
Penn, John G., **1979:** 93
Penn, William, **1980–81:** 2538
Pennington, John, **1980–81:** 2743
Pennino, Martha V., **1980–81:** 1405
Pennsylvania
  Civic leaders, meeting with the President, **1978:** 1406
  Democratic Party primary, **1980–81:** 729, 739
  Disaster declarations, **1977:** 1306; **1980–81:** 1564
  Emergency declarations, **1977:** 34, 85; **1980–81:** 1111
  Energy crisis, **1977:** 37
  Energy emergency, **1978:** 410, 417, 609
  Gasoline Dealers' Association strike, settlement, **1979:** 1294
  Gov. Dick Thornburgh, **1980–81:** 727, 736
  Indiantown Gap, disturbances at, **1980–81:** 1498
  Legionville National Historic Site, **1978:** 1926
  News media, interviews with the President, **1980–81:** 723, 742
  President's visit, **1977:** 37–45; **1978:** 1603, 1617; **1979:** 578, 1232, 2138; **1980–81:** 67, 874, 893, 894, 1629, 1635, 2034, 2043, 2047, 2251, 2344, 2503, 2520, 2534–2542
  U.S. attorneys, **1977:** 2089, 2090; **1978:** 57, 59, 61, 77, 150, 245, 246, 899, 1222, 1223; **1979:** 93
  U.S. district judges, **1977:** 463, 1132, 2050, 2051; **1978:** 231, 571, 711, 712, 1010, 1071, 1072, 1381; **1979:** 958, 983, 1398, 1883
  U.S. marshals, **1977:** 1438, 1439, 1483, 1484; **1979:** 733, 787
Pennsylvania Avenue Development Corporation, **1978:** 2001, 2050; **1980–81:** 95, 1346, 1981, 2916
Pensacola, Fla., **1979:** 1675
Pension Benefit Guaranty Corporation, **1978:** 317, 898, 1760; **1979:** 781, 1586; **1980–81:** 2789, 3021
Pension plans (EO 12177), **1979:** 2219
Pension Policy, President's Commission on, **1978:** 1264, 1502, 1507, 2056; **1979:** 138, 271, 2122; **1980–81:** 2861, 2900
Pensions, **1980–81:** 2164, 2830
Peoples, Clinton T., **1978:** 1222, 1223
People's Republic of China.
  See China, People's Republic of.
People's Temple, **1978:** 2068; **1979:** 35

Peperno family, Vincent, **1980–81:** 2823
Pepper, Repr. Claude, **1977:** 1712; **1978:** 698, 699,
    1063, 1865, 1869
    Campaign appearances with the President,
        1980–81: 1362, 2157, 2397
    Legislation passage leadership
        Refugee Education Assistance Act, **1980–81:**
        2154
        Social Security Disability Amendments,
            1980–81: 1063
        Mandatory age retirement removal support,
            1980–81: 1000
    Mention, **1980–81:** 1328n.
Pepperdine University Tyler Ecology Award, **1977:**
    642
Perales, Cesar A., **1980–81:** 316, 1942
Percy, Sen. Charles H., **1977:** 147, 527, 595, 1411,
    1567, 1595; **1978:** 498, 499, 500, 897, 1329,
    1468, 1755, 1756, 1763, 1765, 1855, 1966;
    1979: 1115, 1116, 1143, 1959
Perdue, Jean Jones, **1979:** 1682, 1706, 2214
Pereira dos Santos, Adalberto, **1977:** 1567
Pereira Lopez, Ernesto, **1980–81:** 945
Perelman, S. J., **1979:** 1964
Peres, Shimon, **1980–81:** 774
Perez, Carlos Andrés, **1978:** 613–619, 623, 641,
    1119, 1122, 1123
Perez, Frank H., **1977:** 1485, 1507
Perez de Cuellar, Gen. Javier, **1979:** 1301
Perez-Chiriboga, Marcial, **1979:** 1318
Perez-Gimenez, Juan M., **1979:** 2044
Pericles, **1980–81:** 779
Periis, Leo, **1979:** 2085
Perito, Robert, **1978:** 2110
Perkins, Repr. Carl D., **1977:** 1232, 1427, 1428,
    1948, 1987, 1989; **1978:** 289, 304, 432, 458,
    698, 700, 1917, 1919; **1979:** 1957ftn.,
    2238; **1980–81:** 847, 1390n., 1585, 2726
Perkins, Frances, **1980–81:** 629
Perkins, James A., **1978:** 1514
Perkins, Lucian, **1980–81:** 1460
Perlman, Itzhak, **1979:** 527
Permanent Committee for the Oliver Wendell
    Holmes Devise, **1979:** 746
Permanent Joint Board on Defense-United States
    and Canada, **1978:** 453
Pernell, Ruby B., **1980–81:** 2075
Perpich, Gov. Rudy, **1978:** 1824, 1828
Perrero, Sergio, **1980–81:** 1073
Perry, Evelyn, **1980–81:** 2075
Perry, Jack Richard, **1979:** 1262, 1293
Perry, Matthew J., Jr., **1979:** 1223, 1452
Perry, Tom, **1977:** 997
Perry, William J., **1977:** 368, 465, 1824, 1931; **1978:**
    1722, 2201, 2209
Persian Gulf area
    Administration's accomplishments and goals,
        1980–81: 2985

Persian Gulf area — *continued*
    Heroin trafficking, **1980–81:** 1565
    Iraq-Iran conflict.
        See Iraq-Iran conflict.
    Oil supplies, **1980–81:** 2131
    Soviet invasion of Afghanistan, effect on:
        Stability of region, **1980–81:** 673, 685
        U.S. military capabilities improvement, **1979:**
            2240; **1980–81:** 35, 91, 171, 241, 289, 348,
            391, 634, 1555, 1640, 1659, 1892, 2126,
            2186, 2213, 2337, 2447, 2633
        U.S. security interests, **1980–81:** 183, 241, 511,
            616, 1545, 1554
    U.S. naval presence, **1980–81:** 973, 976, 980
    U.S. policy toward outside intervention, **1980–**
        81: 197, 346, 579, 871, 2132, 2479
    World oil supplies, **1980–81:** 108, 171, 728, 803
    See also specific country.
Persinger, Mildred E., **1977:** 526
Perskie, Stephen, **1978:** 1543
Personal Representatives of the President.
    See under Middle East, Egyptian-Israeli peace
    negotiations.
Personnel Interchange, President's Commission on,
    1977: 1907; **1978:** 968, 1466; **1979:** 866
Personnel Management, Office of
    Annual report, **1980–81:** 1569
    Deputy Director, **1979:** 3, 46, 90
    Federal consumer programs, **1979:** 1765
    Federal employees protection, **1979:** 922
    Federal pay system reform actions, **1979:** 1003
    Federal physicians comparability allowance,
        1978: 2300, 2301
    Mention, **1980–81:** 617
    Occupational safety and health programs for
        Federal employees, **1980–81:** 394
    Office of Government Ethics, Director, **1979:** 41,
        2153
    Opportunities Industrialization Centers pro-
        grams, **1980–81:** 1068
    President's Commission on Executive Exchange,
        staff services, **1979:** 867
    Proposed, **1978:** 437, 445, 446
    Reorganization Plan No. 2 of 1978, **1978:** 951,
        953–957, 959, 1363, 2292–2300
    Senior Executive Service review, **1979:** 393
Personnel Management, Office of, Director (Alan
    K. Campbell)
    Appointment and nomination, **1979:** 3, 46, 90
    Award presentations
        Presidential Management Improvement
            Awards, **1980–81:** 1507
        Presidential Rank Awards for the Senior Ex-
            ecutive Service, **1980–81:** 1697, 1699n.
    Civil service reform implementation, **1980–81:**
        898
    Civil service regulations for CETA participants,
        1980–81: 2820, 2821

Personnel Management, Director — *continued*
Drug Enforcement Administration, regulations prescription, **1980–81:** 1443
Federal civilian and military pay increase responsibilities, **1979:** 8, 1530, 1532
Federal emergency management functions, **1979:** 1281
Federal Government employees, question-and-answer session, **1979:** 917
Federal legal resources management functions, **1979:** 1265, 1267
Federal pay increase recommendations, **1980–81:** 468
Federal summer employment program guidance, **1980–81:** 815
Foreign assistance functions, **1979:** 1796
Investigative and audit training improvement responsibilities, **1979:** 779
News conference (Checklist), **1979:** 1019; **1980–81:** 1377
President's Management Improvement Council, Cochairman, **1979:** 1668–1670
Senior Executive Service selection and development programs criteria, **1979:** 1693
Summer youth employment program, **1979:** 1836
Taiwan relations functions (EO 12143), **1979:** 1132
Perth Amboy, N.J., **1979:** 1817; **1980–81:** 1672, 1677, 1679, 1687
Pertini, Alessandro.
See Italy, President.
Pertschuk, Michael, **1977:** 486, 510, 692; **1978:** 1139, 1140, 1652; **1979:** 234, 235, 242; **1980–81:** 281, 983
Peru
Ambassador to U.S., **1977:** 806; **1979:** 554; **1980–81:** 2807
Cuban refugees in Havana Embassy, asylum for, **1980–81:** 626, 642, 682, 913, 915
Nuclear energy agreement with U.S., **1980–81:** 1239
Penal sentences treaty with U.S., **1979:** 2272
President Francisco Morales Bermudez Cerruti, **1977:** 1536, 1567
Science and technology cooperation with U.S., **1980–81:** 407
U.S. Ambassador, **1977:** 873, 876, 883; **1980–81:** 1711, 1715
Whaling operations, **1979:** 266–268
Pesqueira, Richard E., **1978:** 968
Pest management, integrated, **1979:** 1368, 1383
Pest management coordinating committee, integrated, proposed, **1979:** 1383
Pesticide Act, Federal, **1978:** 1696
Pesticides, **1977:** 792, 972, 982, 1710
Petchler, Christopher R., **1979:** 2075
Peters, James J., **1980–81:** 3026
Peters, Roberta, **1980–81:** 2863

Peterson, Ellie, **1979:** 2008, 2009n.
Peterson, Esther, **1977:** 565, 572, 575, 597, 1048, 1396; **1978:** 789, 804, 1066, 1418, 1915, 1971, 2002, 2218
Anti-inflation program actions, **1979:** 234
Auto Industry Committee, member, **1980–81:** 1670
Banned or significantly restricted substance exports, study preparation, **1980–81:** 2910
Consumer Affairs Council chairperson, **1979:** 1766
Federal consumer programs coordination, **1979:** 1761, 1787; **1980–81:** 1055, 1056
Meeting with the President (Digest), **1979:** 1453
Mentions, **1979:** 621, 838
News conferences (Checklist), **1979:** 242, 620; **1980–81:** 453
Potofsky, Jacob, funeral services attendance, **1979:** 1421n.
Presidential Medal of Freedom recipient, **1980–81:** 2927
President's assessment, **1980–81:** 281
Public participation in Federal agency proceedings, **1979:** 867
Peterson, Roger Tory, **1980–81:** 752, 1059
Peterson, Rudolph A., **1977:** 1529
Peterson, Russell, **1979:** 661
Peterson, Sharon L., **1979:** 1008
Peterson, Rev. Thomas R., **1977:** 815
Peterson, Viola G., **1978:** 1419
Petree, Richard W., **1978:** 1509, 1516, 1528, 1572; **1979:** 1668, 1680, 2038, 2044, 2085
Petrie, Elizabeth, **1979:** 466
Petrilli, Lisa A., **1980–81:** 927
Petrilli, Richard W., **1980–81:** 1860, 1946, 2070, 2726, 2727
Petroleum.
See Oil.
Petroleum Exporting Countries, Organization of.
See OPEC.
Petroleum Reserve of Alaska, National, **1980–81:** 63
Petroleum Reserve program, Strategic, **1979:** 147, 720; **1980–81:** 251, 1476
Petruska, John, **1980–81:** 997
Petterson, Donald K., **1978:** 1562, 1572
Pettigrew, Richard A., **1977:** 147, 1052, 1379, 1960; **1979:** 378
Pettis, Repr. Shirley N., **1978:** 394
Pettit, Joseph M., **1977:** 2002, 2006; **1979:** 306n., 1559
Petty, Maj. Leslie, **1980–81:** 786
Peyser, Repr. Peter A., **1980–81:** 1502
Pezzullo, Lawrence A., **1977:** 1206, 1213; **1979:** 685, 733, 1318
Pfaelzer, Mariana R., **1978:** 1407
Pfeiffer, Jane Cahill, **1977:** 941; **1978:** 1706, 1724

Pfeiffer, Jane P., **1977:** 1178, 1179
Pfenninger, Leslie, **1977:** 323
Pforzheimer, Carl H., Jr., **1978:** 896, 935
Pham Van Dong, **1977:** 489
Philadelphia, Pa., **1979:** 787, 906
    Economic Development Administration grants, **1980–81:** 726, 736
    Government employment, **1980–81:** 877
    Mayor William Green
        Campaign appearances with the President, **1980–81:** 1629, 2046
        Kennedy, Sen. Edward M., endorsement of, **1980–81:** 729, 736
        President's assessment, **1980–81:** 874, 1642
        President's visits, **1980–81:** 867, 874, 893, 894, 933, 1629, 1635, 1663
Philippines
    Foreign Minister, **1977:** 1754; **1978:** 1379
    Generalized System of Preferences, **1979:** 2230
    Human rights violations, **1979:** 1913
    President Ferdinand E. Marcos, **1978:** 2257; **1980–81:** 720
    Trade with U.S., **1980–81:** 1251, 2912
    U.S. Ambassador, **1977:** 1673, 1700, 1931; **1978:** 888, 899
    U.S. naval bases, **1979:** 626
    U.S. policy, **1979:** 156
    U.S. relations, **1980–81:** 169
    Vice President's visit, **1978:** 327
Phillips, Bernadette Pardo, **1979:** 1524
Phillips, Craig, **1980–81:** 1432
Phillips, H. Brooks, **1978:** 1572
Phillips, James Dickson, Jr., **1978:** 1334
Phillips, Mr. and Mrs. Joseph, **1980–81:** 2043n.
Phillips, Capt. Mark, **1977:** 1127
Phillips, Rufus, **1978:** 1878
Phillips, Val, **1980–81:** 1439n.
Phillips Petroleum Company, **1980–81:** 721
Phosphate shipments to Soviet Union, **1980–81:** 560, 2470
Photographers Association, White House News, **1977:** 557
Photovoltaic cells, **1979:** 1104, 1219
Physical Fitness Award, Presidential, **1979:** 955
Physical Fitness and Sports, President's Council on.
    See President's Council on Physical Fitness and Sports.
Physical Fitness and Sports for All, National Conference on, **1980–81:** 259
Physicians comparability allowance, Federal, **1978:** 2300, 2301
Physics, 1979 Nobel Prize in, **1979:** 1963
Picasso, Pablo, **1980–81:** 1540
Piccoli, Flaminio, **1980–81:** 1241
Piccolo, Joy, **1980–81:** 2646
Picker, Arnold, **1978:** 1973
Pickering, Thomas R., **1978:** 1509, 1516

Pickle, Repr. J. J., **1978:** 1783; **1980–81:** 1063
Picott, J. Rupert, **1980–81:** 84
Pierce, D. Laverne, **1978:** 1193
Pierce, Timatha S., **1980–81:** 1405
Pierre, Henri, **1977:** 776
Pierre, Percy A., **1977:** 712, 745
Pigford, Thomas, **1979:** 661
Pike, Repr. Otis G., **1978:** 393
Pillard, Charles H., **1978:** 216, 455; **1979:** 1868; **1980–81:** 653, 1048
Pilot, Lynn, **1980–81:** 1936
Pimentel, George C., **1977:** 1475, 1483
Pinder, Frank E., **1980–81:** 509
Pindling, Lynden O., **1977:** 1568
Pine Creek, Pa., **1979:** 1813
Pinelands National Reserve, N.J., proposed, **1979:** 1359
Pinochet Ugarte, Augusto, **1977:** 1538, 1567; **1978:** 2257
Pipeline inspector, office of the Federal, proposed, **1979:** 381
Pipeline Safety Act of 1968, Natural Gas, **1980–81:** 291
Piper, H. C., Jr., **1977:** 196
Piper, Larry Gordon, **1980–81:** 983, 1014
Pippert, Wes, **1979:** 748
Pirie, Robert B., Jr., **1979:** 269, 294, 1678
Pitofsky, Robert, **1978:** 971, 1010; **1980–81:** 2726
Pitot, Henry C., **1979:** 686
Pitt, William E., **1978:** 1407
Pittle, R. David, **1977:** 1945, 1966; **1978:** 85, 149
Pittsburgh, Pa., **1977:** 37–45; **1980–81:** 726, 734, 2503, 2517
Pittsburgh Pirates, **1979:** 1975
Pittsburgh Pirates and Steelers, **1980–81:** 369
Pittston Company, **1979:** 376, 1017
Plainfield, N.J., **1979:** 1817
Plains, Ga., **1977:** 194, 304, 1044, 1437, 1443, 1467, 2163, 2169–2175; **1978:** 228, 945, 1009, 2286, 2302; **1979:** 731, 1589, 1603; **1980–81:** 2682–2685, 2832, 2839–2841, 2868
Plant enforcement task force, proposed, **1979:** 1377–1379
Plants, restrictions on exotic species, **1977:** 998
Platform Association, International, **1979:** 1398
Plauche, A. Lane, **1977:** 816
Plaza, Galo, **1978:** 942
PLO.
    See Palestine Liberation Organization.
Plotkin, Manuel D., **1977:** 617, 642; **1979:** 240
Plunkett, Connie, **1977:** 526
Plutonium, **1977:** 588, 779
Poage, Bob, **1980–81:** 2413
Poage, Repr. W. R., **1977:** 1680
Point Reyes-Farallon Islands National Marine Sanctuary, Calif., **1980–81:** 2997
Poison Prevention Week, National, **1977:** 145; **1978:** 281; **1979:** 232; **1980–81:** 238

Poland
  Agricultural commodity credit guarantees from
    U.S., **1980–81:** 1711, 1715, 1905, 2537
  Airplane crash near Warsaw, **1980–81:** 482, 517,
    564
  Ambassador to U.S., **1978:** 710
  Clothespin exports, **1979:** 233
  First Secretary Edward Gierek, **1977:** 2203, 2210,
    2212; **1978:** 42, 281
  Foreign Minister, **1977:** 1754
  Joint communique, **1977:** 2216
  News conference remarks, **1977:** 2207–2211
  Poznan International Technical Fair, **1978:**
    1009; **1980–81:** 1049
  President's visit, **1977:** 1649, 1983, 2077, 2188,
    2202, 2203, 2205, 2212
  Soviet troop buildup on borders of, **1980–81:**
    2771, 2785
  U.S. Ambassador, **1978:** 87, 149; **1980–81:** 1703
  U.S. relations, **1980–81:** 1854, 2537, 2978
  Worker strikes
    AFL-CIO support, **1980–81:** 1649, 2885
    New Polish President, honoring of agreements
      by, **1980–81:** 1680
    President's support, **1980–81:** 1605, 1606, 1642,
      1679, 1765, 1853
Policy Review Committee, **1979:** 1704, 2149
Polio vaccine, Salk, **1980–81:** 645, 811
Polish Americans, **1978:** 281; **1979:** 1397, 1444;
  1980–81: 2534
Polish National Alliance, **1980–81:** 1852, 1947
Political contributions, **1978:** 164
Political philosophy, President's, **1979:** 2034
Political prisoners, **1978:** 1325, 1328
Politz, Henry A., **1979:** 788
Polk, James K., **1980–81:** 2124, 2125, 2146, 2299,
  2402
Polk, Louis F., **1977:** 196, 1944, 1966; **1978:** 230
Pollack, Stuart, **1979:** 1451
Pollak, Louis H., **1978:** 1071, 1072
Pollak, Stephen J., **1980–81:** 1406, 1467
Polland, Rebecca R., **1979:** 437
Pollard, Anderson W., **1978:** 407; **1980–81:** 2242
Pollard, Joseph M., **1977:** 882
Pollin, Abe, **1978:** 1070
Polls, public opinion.
  See Public opinion polls.
Pollution
  Administration's accomplishments and goals,
    1980–81: 2972
  Air, **1978:** 832, 833, 853, 1415; **1979:** 183, 349,
    539, 1569, 1900, 1998
  Automobile emissions, **1977:** 86, 286
  Chemical, **1977:** 172
  Clean Air Act amendments, **1977:** 1072, 1082
  Energy production standards, **1980–81:** 831,
    1198, 1865, 2201, 2262, 2493, 2511, 2590

Pollution — *continued*
  Environmental message, **1977:** 967
  Federal economic assistance for control pro-
    grams, **1979:** 1370, 1384
  Industrial facility standards, **1980–81:** 352
  Industrial investment in control devices, **1977:**
    2113
  Marine protocol, **1977:** 1352, 1460, 2113
  Noise, **1977:** 322; **1979:** 1370
  Oil spills, **1977:** 387, 458; **1978:** 1296; **1979:** 338,
    1497
  Reagan, Ronald, policy comparisons with the
    President, **1980–81:** 2261, 2415, 2420,
    2526
  Ship prevention legislation, **1980–81:** 2378
  Steel industry standards, **1980–81:** 2085
  Water, **1977:** 240, 440, 2179, 2180; **1978:** 1415;
    1979: 224, 349; **1980–81:** 2290
  See also Environment.
Pollution control standards, Federal compliance,
    1978: 1766, 1769
Pollution from Ships, Convention on, **1979:** 85
Pollution from Ships, International Convention for
    the Prevention of, **1977:** 458, 476
Polozola, Frank J., **1980–81:** 608
Pomerleau, Donald D., **1977:** 1963
Pompa, Gilbert G., **1978:** 784, 803
Ponomarev, B. N., **1978:** 220
Poole, Cecil F., **1979:** 1883
Poorman, Robert L., **1980–81:** 1866n.
Pope, John M., **1978:** 2089
Pope John Paul I, **1978:** 1478, 1665, 1722, 1724
Pope John Paul II, **1978:** 1785, 1808
  Kampuchean relief efforts, **1979:** 1925
  President's state visit
    Announcement, **1980–81:** 1014
    Meetings with the President, **1980–81:** 1164,
      1168, 1242
    Pre-visit comments, **1980–81:** 1102
  Visit to U.S.
    Meeting with the President (Digest), **1979:**
      1881
    Postvisit comments, **1979:** 1839, 1852, 1864,
      1867, 1872, 1925, 1932, 1935, 1938, 1940,
      2061, 2126, 2244
    President's comments, **1980–81:** 181, 1163,
      1609, 1853, 1876, 2535
    Previsit comments, **1979:** 1322
    Welcoming ceremony, **1979:** 1827, 1883
      (Checklist)
    White House reception, **1979:** 1830, 1883
      (Checklist)
    White House statement, **1979:** 1834
Pope Paul VI, **1977:** 11, 58; **1978:** 1392, 1407, 1457
Popkin, Samuel L., **1978:** 52, 150
Popper, David H., **1977:** 1581; **1978:** 86, 87;
  1980–81: 34

Population concentrations, **1977:** 514
Population growth, world, **1977:** 983
Porcelain Art Month, National, **1980–81:** 1277
Porcelain-on-steel cookware industry, **1980–81:** 2, 3, 97
Pork industry, **1979:** 754
Port Authority Trans-Hudson Corporation, **1980–81:** 667, 684, 930
Port Canaveral, Fla., **1977:** 1035–1037
Port Week, National, **1978:** 1513; **1979:** 1835; **1980–81:** 2066
Porter, Donald James, **1979:** 441
Porter, Elsa Allgood, **1977:** 381, 465
Porter, Keith R., **1977:** 2046
Porter, Paul C., **1978:** 2072; **1979:** 466
Porter, Robert, **1977:** 1222
Porter, Walter A., **1977:** 816, 941
Porterfield, Mr. and Mrs. Marvin, **1979:** 1232, 2104
Portis, Daniel F., **1979:** 1776
Portland, Maine, **1978:** 1897
Portland, Oreg., **1978:** 844, 853, 855, 881, 882; **1979:** 1452, 1817; **1980–81:** 950, 1402, 1901, 2672
Portsmouth, N.H., **1979:** 699, 733
Portsmouth, Ohio, uranium enrichment facility, **1977:** 744
Portsmouth, Va., **1979:** 1817
Portugal
  African relations, **1980–81:** 1234
  Ambassador to U.S., **1980–81:** 1245
  ANOP news agency, interview with the President, **1980–81:** 1223
  Democratic process development, **1980–81:** 1224, 1232, 1233
  Fishery agreement with U.S., **1980–81:** 2755
  North Atlantic Treaty Organization, role in, **1980–81:** 1225
  President Antonio dos Santos Ramalho Eanes, **1977:** 882; **1978:** 1021; **1980–81:** 1230, 1231, 1233, 1245
  President's visit
    Announcement, **1980–81:** 1014
    Arrival, **1980–81:** 1230, 1246
    Daily schedule (Digest), **1980–81:** 1245
    Meeting with President Eanes and Government officials, **1980–81:** 1233
    State luncheon, **1980–81:** 1231, 1246
  Prime Minister Francisco Sá Carneiro, **1980–81:** 1234, 1245
  Prime Minister Mario Soares, **1977:** 556, 706
  Socialist Party leader, meeting with the President (Digest), **1980–81:** 1245
  U.S. Ambassador, **1977:** 252, 2161; **1978:** 149; **1980–81:** 1245
  U.S. policy, **1979:** 156
  Vice President's visit, **1977:** 785
Poseidon submarines, **1979:** 108

Post, Donald E., **1980–81:** 2075
Postal policy, **1977:** 1924; **1978:** 309
Postal Rate Commission, **1977:** 1352, 1384, 2105, 2130; **1978:** 231, 564; **1979:** 372, 378, 856, 899; **1980–81:** 979, 1015
Postal reform legislation, **1978:** 1596
Postal Service, United States.
  See United States Postal Service.
Postmasters, League of, **1977:** 1084
Poston, Ersa, **1977:** 526, 794, 807
Posvar, Wesley Wentz, **1980–81:** 606
Potato growers in Maine, task force to consider Federal policies affecting, **1980–81:** 608
Potofsky, Jacob, **1979:** 1421
Potomac Heritage Trail, **1979:** 1814
Potomac River Basin, Interstate Commission on the, **1978:** 85, 325; **1979:** 399
Potter, Bill, **1978:** 1620
Poujol, Federico Edmundo, **1980–81:** 2807
Poveda Burbano, Vice Adm. Alfredo, **1977:** 1549, 1568
P.O.W.-M.I.A. Recognition Day, National, **1978:** 1453; **1979:** 999; **1980–81:** 1282
Powell, Jody, **1977:** 8, 32, 178, 268, 281, 290, 463, 556, 692, 759, 760, 773, 1082, 1105, 1250, 1263, 1518, 1595, 1642, 1691, 1800, 2007, 2053, 2091; **1978:** 42, 48, 50, 150, 671, 1029, 1097, 1330, 1334, 1337, 1393, 1471, 1476, 1477, 1496, 1674, 1724, 2039, 2068, 2180–2182, 2188, 2268, 2282
  American hostages in Iran, release negotiation activities, **1980–81:** 3019
  Announcements (Checklist), **1980–81:** 25, 608, 721, 1471
  Announcements to the press, **1979:** 218, 383, 1221, 1270, 1272, 1273, 1285, 1290, 1300, 1315, 1418, 1455, 1691, 1787, 2107, 2129, 2189, 2251, 2281
  Bugging of U.N. Representative Young's apartment, advisal to ABC News to cancel story, **1979:** 1591
  Carter, Billy, press briefings on activities with Libyan Government, **1980–81:** 2016
  Democratic Party primary and caucus results, question-and-answer session (Checklist), **1980–81:** 494
  Meetings with the President (Digest), **1980–81:** 2070
  Mentions, **1979:** 621, 743, 744, 1286; **1980–81:** 1086, 1202, 1439, 2323, 2441
  News conferences, **1979:** 658n., 843, 1143
  News conferences (Checklist), **1980–81:** 219, 564, 775, 826, 894, 932, 1246, 1377, 1429, 1524, 2332, 2699
  Notice issuance to the press, **1979:** 1183ftn.
  Secretary of State Cyrus R. Vance, resignation letter reading, **1980–81:** 782n.

Powell, Jody — *continued*
White House statements reading, **1979:** 310, 609, 731, 1125, 2102, 2268; **1980–81:** 11, 12, 28, 258, 461, 534, 584, 668, 760, 1053, 1092, 1123, 1420, 1466, 1498, 1770, 1771, 2649, 2859
Power, Joseph T., **1980–81:** 533, 564
Power, Sarah G., **1978:** 1630, 1669
Power Commission, Federal.
See Federal Power Commission.
Powerplant and Industrial Fuel Use Act, **1978:** 1978
Powerplants.
See Nuclear powerplants.
Powers, Mary Elizabeth, **1980–81:** 1405
Powers, Roger, **1978:** 771
Powers, William E., **1980–81:** 911
Poznan International Technical Fair, **1978:** 1009; **1980–81:** 1049
Representative of the President, **1977:** 936
Prairie du Chien, Wis., **1979:** 1472, 1475n.
Prasad, Rajendra, **1979:** 1604; **1980–81:** 2817
Pratt, Carlisle, **1977:** 1438, 1439
Pratt, Edmund T., Jr., **1980–81:** 3022
Pravda, **1977:** 692
Prayer, National Day of, **1977:** 1792; **1978:** 1482; **1979:** 1694; **1980–81:** 1858
Prayer Breakfast, National, **1977:** 24; **1978:** 263; **1979:** 58; **1980–81:** 275
Prayer for Peace, Memorial Day, **1977:** 716; **1978:** 931
(Proc. 4651), **1979:** 550
(Proc. 4754), **1980–81:** 813
Prayer in public schools, President's views on, **1979:** 625, 655, 1887; **1980–81:** 1621
Prebisch, Raul, **1977:** 612
Precht, Henry, **1980–81:** 1289
Prechtl, Fritz, **1980–81:** 1360
Preciado, Cecelia DeBurciago, **1977:** 526
Predator control, **1978:** 1674
Pregerson, Harry, **1979:** 1531, 1532
Pregnancy, occupational discrimination, **1978:** 1906
Pregnancy disability act, **1978:** 1643
Prentiss, Maj. Gen. Louis W., **1979:** 44, 92
Preparedness Agency, Federal, **1978:** 300, 302; **1979:** 1278
Presidency, views on, **1977:** 952, 1168, 1323, 1370, 1467, 1468, 2200; **1978:** 74, 357, 382, 518, 543, 691, 728, 729, 979, 1355, 1415, 1614, 1615, 1997, 2014–2016, 2022, 2023, 2027, 2247, 2248, 2258, 2262, 2263
Best job in America, **1979:** 1895
Constitutional powers, **1980–81:** 2519, 2890
Daily schedule, **1980–81:** 766
Experiences gained during first term, **1980–81:** 2041

Presidency, views on — *continued*
Incumbency, advantages and disadvantages of, **1980–81:** 938
Length of term, **1980–81:** 242, 2696
Loneliness of job, **1980–81:** 1913, 2041
Management of:
Controversial issues, **1979:** 789, 949, 1010; **1980–81:** 1739, 1741, 1748, 1764, 1766, 1867, 1872, 1901, 1913, 2031, 2089, 2890
Crises, **1980–81:** 888, 2012, 2088, 2122, 2168, 2215, 2325, 2500
Personal assessment, **1980–81:** 742, 906
Responsibilities of position, **1979:** 475, 962, 1242, 1484, 2020; **1980–81:** 397, 710, 1553, 2125
Second-term goals, **1980–81:** 2014
Spokesman for people, **1979:** 1235, 1256, 1305, 1321; **1980–81:** 1616
State legislature experience, relationship with, **1979:** 296, 2053
President of the Senate.
See Vice President.
Presidential Advisory Board on Ambassadorial Appointments, **1977:** 78, 86, 89, 90, 148, 576; **1979:** 552, 2042
Presidential campaign, 1980.
See Elections, 1980: campaign.
Presidential Commission on Americans Missing and Unaccounted for in Southeast Asia, **1977:** 316, 377, 489, 499
Presidential Commission on World Hunger, **1978:** 1782; **1980–81:** 777, 1139, 2850
Chairman, **1978:** 1725; **1979:** 147, 2012
Establishment, **1978:** 1498
International role, **1978:** 1712
Members, **1978:** 1511, 2069; **1979:** 214
Officials, meeting with the President, **1978:** 277
Preliminary report, **1979:** 2247, 2249
Study to alleviate worldwide needs, **1979:** 147, 2011
Presidential domestic policy review system, **1977:** 1589
Presidential Energy Technology Seminar, **1979:** 1533
Presidential Exchange Executives, **1980–81:** 422
Presidential Management Improvement Awards, **1977:** 1818; **1978:** 950; **1980–81:** 18, 19, 1507
Presidential Management Initiatives Program, **1977:** 112
Presidential Management Intern Program, **1977:** 1498–1500, 1507
Presidential Medal of Freedom, **1977:** 1215, 1228; **1978:** 1338; **1979:** 87; **1980–81:** 751, 1057, 1598, 2922
Presidential papers, **1977:** 1205
Presidential Physical Fitness Award, **1979:** 955
Presidential proclamations, commemorative, **1978:** 1532

Presidential Records Act, **1978:** 1965
Presidential Scholars, **1977:** 725, 1074; **1978:** 763,
    968; **1979:** 852, 1668; **1980–81:** 925
Presidential Scholars, Commission on, **1977:** 478;
    1978: 696, 970; **1979:** 598, 853, 1034;
    1980–81: 606, 774, 1444, 2815
Presidential Task Force on the District of Colum-
    bia, **1977:** 784, 1059
Presidential term of office, **1977:** 1924; **1979:** 738,
    1898
Presidential transition.
    See Elections, 1980: transition.
Presidential vetoes, **1977:** 93, 919, 1019; **1978:** 1659
Presidential war powers bill, **1977:** 2186, 2187
President's Advisory Board on Ambassadorial Ap-
    pointments, **1980–81:** 1420, 2849
President's Advisory Board on International In-
    vestment, **1977:** 1495
President's Advisory Committee for Women,
    1980–81: 63, 814, 2822, 2849, 2914
    Chair, **1979:** 825
    Meeting with the President (Digest), **1979:** 2042
    Members, **1979:** 826, 1697, 2159
    News conference (Checklist), **1979:** 2044
    Vice-Chairs, **1979:** 825
President's Award for Distinguished Federal Civil-
    ian Service, **1980–81:** 86, 2999
President's Award for Energy Efficiency, **1980–81:**
    1401, 2875
President's campaign airplane flights, **1978:** 276
President's Cancer Panel, **1977:** 1587; **1979:** 2196;
    1980–81: 1292
President's Clearinghouse for Community Energy
    Efficiency, **1979:** 1453
President's Commission on the Accident at Three
    Mile Island
    Establishment, **1979:** 657, 659
    Final Report
        Actions in response to, remarks announcing,
            1979: 2202, 2208
        Announcement remarks, **1979:** 2062
        Preparation, **1979:** 1245, 1358, 1428, 1482,
            1505, 1537, 1647, 1753, 1906, 1907
        Recommendations
            Nuclear Regulatory Commission reorgani-
                zation, **1980–81:** 118, 544, 617, 744
            Nuclear safety improvement, **1980–81:** 131,
                364, 504, 1257
    Meetings with the President, **1979:** 690, 2080
        (Digest)
    Members, **1979:** 660, 856
    Mentions, **1979:** 701, 702, 713, 798
    Termination of (EO 12258), **1980–81:** 2850
President's Commission on the Accident at Three
    Mile Island, Chairman (John G.
    Kemeny), **1980–81:** 118, 131, 544, 1257
    Appointment, **1979:** 660

President's Commission — *continued*
    Commission establishment, remarks, **1979:** 658
    Final report recommendations, **1979:** 2062, 2202
    Mentions, **1979:** 701, 702, 706
    Nuclear powerplant safety, immediate recom-
        mendation authority, **1979:** 703
    President's meeting with Commission, remarks,
        1979: 692
President's Commission on the Coal Industry,
    1978: 573; **1980–81:** 471, 1649
    Chairman, **1979:** 293, 684
    Coordinator of Labor Relations, **1978:** 1500
    Environmental standards maintenance recom-
        mendations in future production, **1979:**
        1325, 1346
    EO 12176, **1979:** 2201
    Establishment, **1978:** 1002, 1006, 1010
    Interview remarks, **1978:** 1349
    Members, **1978:** 1500
    Reestablishment, **1978:** 2243
    Report, **1979:** 1302
    Staff Director, **1978:** 1500
    Utility companies conversion to coal recommen-
        dations, **1979:** 1327, 1643, 1650
President's Commission on Equal Opportunity in
    Housing, **1980–81:** 2853
President's Commission on Executive Exchange,
    1979: 866, 976, 1679; **1980–81:** 272, 1332,
    2533
President's Commission on Foreign Language and
    International Studies, **1978:** 766, 1514,
    1907; **1980–81:** 2850
President's Commission on the Holocaust, **1978:**
    1530, 1920, 1973; **1980–81:** 148, 687, 2194,
    2542
    Chairman, **1979:** 293, 684
    Final report, **1979:** 1432, 1773
    Progress since establishment, **1979:** 147
President's Commission on Hostage Compensa-
    tion, **1980–81:** 3039
President's Commission on Mental Health, **1978:**
    103, 349, 791; **1979:** 857, 859–861; **1980–
    81:** 784, 811, 1976, 2099
    Chairperson, **1977:** 234, 899
    Establishment, **1977:** 185, 187
    Members, **1977:** 528, 556
    Report, **1977:** 1612
    Vice Chairman, **1977:** 642
President's Commission on Military Compensa-
    tion, **1977:** 1176, 1178; **1978:** 749, 751
President's Commission for a National Agenda for
    the Eighties, **1979:** 2013, 2014, 2044
    Chairman, **1980–81:** 2822
    Economic revitalization recommendations,
        1980–81: 481
    Final report, **1980–81:** 2917
    Global 2000 study, consideration, **1980–81:** 1416
    Members, **1980–81:** 263

President's Commission on Olympic Sports, **1978:**
1976
President's Commission on Pension Policy, **1978:**
1264, 1502, 1507, 2056; **1979:** 138, 271,
2122; **1980–81:** 2862, 2900
President's Commission on Personnel Interchange,
1977: 1907; **1978:** 968, 1466; **1979:** 866
President's Commission for the Study of Ethical
Problems in Medicine and Biomedical
and Behavioral Research, **1979:** 1263,
1294; **1980–81:** 896, 1723
President's Commission on United States-Liberian
Relations, **1980–81:** 372, 373, 508, 2850
President's Commission on White House Fellow-
ships, **1977:** 941, 1143; **1978:** 149, 737;
1979: 931; **1980–81:** 949, 1823, 2849
President's Committee on Employment of the
Handicapped, **1978:** 216; **1979:** 493;
1980–81: 808
President's Committee on HIRE, **1977:** 1115
President's Committee on the International Labor
Organization, **1980–81:** 1127, 2849
President's Committee on Mental Retardation,
1978: 407, 2070
  Continuance (EO 12258), **1980–81:** 2849
  Meeting with the President (Digest), **1980–81:**
  217
  Members, **1980–81:** 192, 2004, 2242
President's Committee on the National Medal of
Science, **1979:** 448; **1980–81:** 2849, 3023
President's Committee on Science and Technology,
1978: 412
President's Committee on Small Business Policy,
1980–81: 2913
President's Council for Energy Efficiency, **1980–
81:** 1404
President's Council on Physical Fitness and Sports,
1978: 1341, 1345, 2036, 2059, 2280; **1979:**
955, 1226, 1815
  Chairman, **1980–81:** 262n., 1440, 1662
  Continuance (EO 12258), **1980–81:** 2849
  Executive director, **1980–81:** 262n.
  Members, **1980–81:** 1823, 2883
  School programs, **1980–81:** 261
President's Council on Spinal Cord Injury, **1980–
81:** 811, 2914, 3025
President's economic advisers, **1978:** 2242
President's Economic Policy Board, abolishment,
1977: 333
President's Environmental Youth awards, **1978:**
787; **1979:** 2075
President's Executive Interchange Program, **1977:**
1906
President's Export Council, **1978:** 892; **1979:** 784,
942, 943, 1727
  Continuance (EO 12258), **1980–81:** 2849
  Export policy review, **1980–81:** 401, 1690
  Final report, **1980–81:** 2827

President's Export Council — *continued*
  Members, **1980–81:** 1570, 2610, 2736
President's family, official dealings with Federal
employees, **1980–81:** 1982
President's finances, **1977:** 296; **1978:** 846, 1097,
1112, 1329, 2151; **1979:** 983; **1980–81:**
719, 968, 1486
President's first 100 days, **1977:** 775, 789
President's first-year accomplishments, **1977:** 2136,
2200, 2201
President's Foreign Intelligence Advisory Board,
abolishment, **1977:** 801, 802
President's future plans, **1980–81:** 2126, 2705, 2706,
2712
President's goals.
  See Administration's accomplishments and
  goals.
President's jogging habits, **1980–81:** 2132
President's leadership qualities, **1979:** 2033, 2053
President's Management Improvement, **1980–81:**
2850
President's Management Improvement Council,
1979: 780, 1668–1670, 2154
President's 1976 campaign, **1978:** 2261
President's 1978 campaign plans, **1978:** 465, 717,
847
President's 1978 Employment and Training Re-
port, **1978:** 1009
President's 1978 National Urban Policy Report,
1978: 1430
President's 1980 candidacy plans, **1978:** 1413, 2016,
2223, 2224, 2248, 2249
President's openness with the American people,
1977: 1174, 1394, 1469, 1470, 1514; **1978:**
110
President's Pay Agent, **1977:** 1525, 1630, 1682;
1979: 1529, 1530; **1980–81:** 1596, 2729
President's plans following term of office, **1977:**
1021; **1978:** 70, 249
President's policymaking procedures, **1979:** 261
President's political philosophy, **1979:** 2034
President's popularity in polls, **1978:** 439, 466, 523,
810, 851, 852, 978, 979, 1474, 1655, 2024
President's popularity in western States, **1978:** 1750
President's relationship with the American people,
1977: 2013, 2134, 2135, 2199; **1978:** 463,
715, 807, 810, 811, 855, 1228, 2151, 2258
President's religious convictions, **1977:** 2207; **1978:**
370, 378, 1113, 1993; **1979:** 472, 1827,
1830, 1839
President's schedule, **1977:** 2097
President's Special Commission for the Study of
Ethical Problems in Medicine and Biomedical and Behavioral Research (EO
12184), **1979:** 2260
President's Special Summit Representative, **1978:**
758
President's style, **1977:** 864

President's Task Force on Housing for the Eighties,
    1980–81: 2179
President's tax return, **1977:** 1111, 1163, 1204
President's travel
  Domestic
    Alabama, **1979:** 1672; **1980–81:** 1601
    Alaska, **1979:** 1161; **1980–81:** 1342
    Arkansas, **1980–81:** 2417, 2418
    California, **1977:** 887, 895, 915, 917, 1893;
      1978: 834, 841, 1946; **1979:** 787, 807, 809,
      810, 841, 843, 1866, 1872, 1876; **1980–81:**
      1295–1322, 1868–1900
    Colorado, **1977:** 1861, 1884; **1978:** 824, 827,
      829, 832
    Connecticut, **1978:** 1887, 1891; **1979:** 1630;
      1980–81: 2279–2287
    Delaware, **1978:** 385, 386
    Florida, **1977:** 1035–1037; **1978:** 1684–1689,
      1865, 1869; **1979:** 1566, 1578, 1675;
      1980–81: 1066, 1072, 1322, 1347, 1349,
      1360–1362, 2148–2172, 2382–2402, 2579–
      2586
    Georgia, **1977:** 194, 640, 1033, 1042–1044,
      1143, 1459, 1467, 2165, 2169–2176; **1978:**
      153–158, 228, 538, 539, 945, 1009, 1113,
      2285–2287; **1979:** 296–306, 675, 731, 1533,
      1561, 1589, 1603; **1980–81:** 1744–1758,
      2068, 2682–2685, 2832, 2839–2841, 2868
    Hawaii, **1979:** 1217
    Idaho, **1978:** 1473, 1475
    Illinois, **1978:** 972, 980, 987, 996, 1009, 1010,
      1936; **1979:** 1932, 1940; **1980–81:** 1851,
      1862, 1867
    Indiana, **1977:** 954; **1979:** 988, 989, 1017,
      1352n.; **1980–81:** 1019
    International crises, effect on, **1980–81:** 803
    Iowa, **1977:** 1853, 1855; **1979:** 787, 789, 804,
      841, 843, 1473–1476, 1478–1508
    Kansas, **1978:** 1813–1820
    Kentucky, **1979:** 1337, 1398; **1980–81:** 1388
    Louisiana, **1977:** 1334; **1980–81:** 2401
    Maine, **1978:** 341, 344, 414, 1897
    Maryland, **1978:** 1795; **1979:** 1406, 1975;
      1980–81: 1722n.
    Massachusetts, **1977:** 382; **1978:** 1892, 1896;
      1979: 1979, 1982; **1980–81:** 1548, 1549,
      2243–2251
    Michigan, **1977:** 1829; **1978:** 1932; **1979:** 1247,
      1294; **1980–81:** 1329, 1556, 1984, 1986,
      2009, 2442–2452, 2546, 2670
    Minnesota, **1977:** 1898–1900; **1978:** 1822–
      1829, 1949; **1979:** 1457, 1468, 1471
    Mississippi, **1977:** 1315; **1979:** 1674; **1980–81:**
      2597
    Missouri, **1978:** 1419, 1986, 1994, 2075, 2080;
      1979: 1241, 1294, 1508, 1511, 1925, 1931;
      1980–81: 1610, 2103, 2552, 2665
    Nebraska, **1977:** 1860, 1861; **1980–81:** 1090

President's travel — *continued*
  Domestic — *continued*
    New Hampshire, **1978:** 364, 414; **1979:** 699–
      720, 733
    New Jersey, **1978:** 1542–1555; **1979:** 2020,
      2024, 2027, 2035; **1980–81:** 1672, 1677,
      1679, 1687, 2275, 2432, 2453, 2524, 2528
    New Mexico, **1979:** 1851, 1853, 1863
    New York, **1977:** 1153, 1715–1737; **1978:** 1883,
      1929, 2160; **1979:** 217, 327, 328, 693, 1739,
      1745, 1746; **1980–81:** 1499, 1506, 1527–
      1544, 1949, 1953, 2001, 2003, 2193, 2198,
      2289–2312, 2363, 2377, 2521, 2542
    North Carolina, **1977:** 2094, 2130, 2133; **1978:**
      529, 535, 1386, 1390, 1575, 1579; **1980–81:**
      2140, 2145
    Ohio, **1978:** 1619, 1620; **1979:** 1640; **1980–81:**
      992, 995, 997, 1001, 1005, 1762, 1765,
      2018, 2347, 2348, 2453–2471, 2476–2502,
      2655, 2659
    Oklahoma, **1979:** 469
    Oregon, **1978:** 844, 853, 855, 1942; **1980–81:**
      950, 1901, 2672
    Pennsylvania, **1977:** 37–45; **1978:** 1603, 1617;
      1979: 578, 1232; **1980–81:** 873, 880, 1629,
      1635, 2034, 2043, 2047, 2251, 2344, 2503,
      2520, 2534–2542
    Rhode Island, **1978:** 331, 339, 414; **1979:** 2055,
      2059
    South Carolina, **1977:** 1309; **1978:** 1582;
      1980–81: 1758, 1761, 2563, 2577
    Tennessee, **1978:** 945, 948, 1008, 1857, 1862,
      2187, 2189–2219; **1980–81:** 2118, 2140,
      2586
    Texas, **1978:** 1157, 1164, 1165, 1173, 1176;
      1979: 482; **1980–81:** 786, 1390, 1391,
      1393, 1725, 1738–1744, 2408, 2417, 2603,
      2617–2640
    Utah, **1978:** 2084
    Virginia, **1977:** 1653, 1656, 1659; **1978:** 1383;
      1979: 630; **1980–81:** 969, 972, 2060
    Washington, **1978:** 857, 860; **1980–81:** 956,
      1078, 1903–1915, 2677
    West Virginia, **1977:** 402; **1978:** 999, 1002,
      1009, 1729; **1979:** 1232; **1980–81:** 2472
    Wisconsin, **1979:** 567, 572, 573, 1471, 1472,
      1475n.; **1980–81:** 2076, 2080, 2640, 2646
    Wyoming, **1978:** 1476
  Foreign
    Announcements, **1977:** 1649, 1825, 1983, 2077,
      2078, 2122, 2188
    Austria, **1979:** 1038, 1045–1047, 1081
    Belgium, **1978:** 32–39
    Brazil, **1978:** 626–636
    Departure remarks, **1977:** 2202
    Egypt, **1978:** 19; **1979:** 394, 405–415, 430
    England, **1977:** 809–815, 840, 881
    France, **1978:** 20–32

President's travel — *continued*
  Foreign — *continued*
    Germany, Federal Republic of, **1978:** 1267, 1281–1316, 1332, 1333
    Guadeloupe, **1978:** 2188; **1979:** 14, 17, 25, 26
    India, **1978:** 1–17
    Iran, **1977:** 2217, 2218
    Israel, **1979:** 394, 415–430
    Italy, **1980–81:** 1153–1204, 1241–1243
    Japan, **1979:** 1154, 1162–1169, 1181–1187, 1211, 1223; **1980–81:** 1339
    Korea, Republic of, **1979:** 1154, 1200, 1202, 1223
    Liberia, **1978:** 671, 675, 709
    Mexico, **1979:** 272, 273, 277, 280, 281, 284
    Nigeria, **1978:** 643–664, 709
    Panama, **1978:** 793, 1118–1127, 1153, 1155
    Poland, **1977:** 2203, 2205, 2212
    Portugal, **1980–81:** 1230–1234, 1245
    Saudi Arabia, **1978:** 18
    Spain, **1980–81:** 1220–1223, 1227–1230, 1244
    Switzerland, **1977:** 809, 825–828, 841, 844, 881
    Vatican City, **1980–81:** 1164, 1168, 1242
    Venezuela, **1978:** 613–623
    Yugoslavia, **1980–81:** 1208–1213, 1216–1220, 1243
  Trip cancellations to monitor Iranian situation, **1979:** 2106, 2138, 2139, 2186, 2192
President's travel plans, **1978:** 631, 634, 811
Presley, Dewey, **1978:** 1004
Presley, Elvis, **1977:** 1478
Presley, Rex O., **1977:** 1569
Press, Frank.
  See Science and Technology Policy, Office of, Director.
Press Club, National, **1977:** 22, 642; **1980–81:** 1576, 1732, 1829, 2219, 2333
Pressler, Sen. Larry, **1979:** 2257n.
Pressly, William L., **1978:** 697, 968, 971
Prestage, Jewel Limar, **1980–81:** 1023, 1051
Preston, Robert F., **1979:** 720n.
Preus, David, **1980–81:** 1439n.
Preyer, Repr. Richardson, **1978:** 530, 1194, 1644, 1855, 1966; **1980–81:** 303
Price, Albert, **1980–81:** 719
Price, Ed H., Jr., **1977:** 816
Price, Edward Dean, **1979:** 2081, 2082
Price, Leontyne, **1978:** 1771; **1979:** 527, 1015; **1980–81:** 1405, 2787
Price, Repr. Melvin, **1980–81:** 1666, 2186, 2660
Price Advisory Committee, **1979:** 1778, 1779, 2218, 2248; **1980–81:** 121, 246, 249
Prices.
  See Wages and prices.
Priest River, Idaho, **1979:** 1813
Primack, Sam, **1978:** 826
Princeton University, **1980–81:** 664

Principe, U.S. Ambassador, **1978:** 88, 149
Printing Industries of America, Inc., **1978:** 1223
Printing Week, International, **1978:** 54
Prison Industries, Inc., Federal, **1979:** 1961; **1980–81:** 452
Prisoner transfers with Bolivia and Mexico, **1978:** 748, 1600
Prisoner transfers with Canada and Mexico, **1977:** 1919
Prisoners of war, **1977:** 1958, 1959
Prisons, **1978:** 836
Prisons, Bureau of, **1979:** 1299, 1598
Privacy Act of 1974, **1977:** 1211; **1979:** 586, 1446; **1980–81:** 1462
  Report, **1978:** 1321, 1481
Privacy of medical information act, proposed, **1979:** 583
Privacy policy, national, **1980–81:** 2969
Privacy Protection Act, **1980–81:** 156, 2218, 2333
Privacy Protection Study Commission, **1977:** 1264; **1979:** 582, 619
Privacy of research records acts, proposed, **1979:** 584
Privacy rights, **1978:** 1098; **1979:** 581, 619
Private Industry Councils, **1978:** 392, 960; **1979:** 126
Private schools, **1978:** 349, 428, 868, 1444, 1609, 2181; **1979:** 848, 1414
  Federal assistance, President's position on, **1980–81:** 1735
  Reagan, Ronald, proposals for, **1980–81:** 2221
Private Sector Initiative program, **1978:** 391, 392, 959, 1010, 1872; **1979:** 74, 100, 126, 601, 2158
Privileges, exemptions, and immunities for certain public international organizations, **1977:** 380
Probst, Raymond, **1980–81:** 1564
Proclamations
  Admiralty Island National Monument (Proc. 4611), **1978:** 2112
  Afghanistan Relief Week (Proc. 4765), **1980–81:** 1139
  Alloy tool steel imports
    (Proc. 4509), **1977:** 1121
    (Proc. 4559), **1978:** 682
  American Education Week
    (Proc. 4529), **1977:** 1694
    (Proc. 4603), **1978:** 1651
    (Proc. 4692), **1979:** 1698
    (Proc. 4797), **1980–81:** 1969
  American Enterprise Day (Proc. 4778), **1980–81:** 1519
  American Heart Month
    (Proc. 4546), **1978:** 89
    (Proc. 4633), **1979:** 21
    (Proc. 4716), **1980–81:** 190

Proclamations — *continued*
  American Heart Month — *continued*
    1981 (Proc. 4816), **1980–81:** 2914
  Anhydrous ammonia industry (Proc. 4714),
    1980–81: 101
  Aniachak National Monument (Proc. 4612),
    1978: 2114
  Anniversary of the adoption of the Articles of
    Confederation (Proc. 4540), **1977:** 2027
  Argentina-U.S. trade relations (Proc. 4694),
    1979: 1791
  Armed Forces Day
    (Proc. 4492), **1977:** 476
    (Proc. 4571), **1978:** 912
  Asian/Pacific American Heritage Week
    (Proc. 4650), **1979:** 549
    (Proc. 4727), **1980–81:** 405
  Becharof National Monument (Proc. 4613),
    1978: 2116
  Bering Land Bridge National Monument (Proc.
    4614), **1978:** 2117
  Bill of Rights Day, Human Rights Day and
    Week
    (Proc. 4542), **1977:** 2086
    (Proc. 4609), **1978:** 2089
    (Proc. 4705), **1979:** 2198
    (Proc. 4804), **1980–81:** 2724
  Black Press Day (Proc. 4507), **1977:** 1099
  Bolt, nut and large screw industry (Proc. 4632),
    1979: 4
  Cancer Control Month
    (Proc. 4490), **1977:** 338
    (Proc. 4552), **1978:** 509
    (Proc. 4643), **1979:** 389
    (Proc. 4731), **1980–81:** 450
  Cape Krusenstern National Monument (Proc.
    4615), **1978:** 2119
  Captive Nations Week
    (Proc. 4513), **1977:** 1292
    (Proc. 4578), **1978:** 1251
    (Proc. 4666), **1979:** 1141
    (Proc. 4761), **1980–81:** 940
  Census 1980 (Proc. 4701), **1979:** 2088
  Ceramic tableware imports (Proc. 4604), **1978:**
    1699
  Cheese and chocolate crumb imports (Proc.
    4708), **1979:** 2227
  Cheese imports (Proc. 4811), **1980–81:** 2846
  Child Health Day
    (Proc. 4522), **1977:** 1631
    (Proc. 4587), **1978:** 1450
    (Proc. 4683), **1979:** 1627
    (Proc. 4780), **1980–81:** 1520
  China-U.S. trade relations (Proc. 4697), **1979:**
    2000
  Citizens band radio transceivers (Proc. 4561),
    1978: 707

Proclamations — *continued*
  Citizenship Day and Constitution Week
    (Proc. 4517), **1977:** 1521
    (Proc. 4579), **1978:** 1317
    (Proc. 4670), **1979:** 1297
    (Proc. 4773), **1980–81:** 1279
  Clothespin imports (Proc. 4640), **1979:** 325
  Color television receiver imports
    (Proc. 4511), **1977:** 1157
    (Proc. 4759), **1980–81:** 920
    (Proc. 4679), **1980–81:** 1257
  Columbus Day
    (Proc. 4527), **1977:** 1675
    (Proc. 4586), **1978:** 1437
    (Proc. 4676), **1979:** 1526
    (Proc. 4788), **1980–81:** 1593
  Constantino Brumidi Day (Proc. 4794), **1980–81:**
    1834
  Constitution of the Northern Mariana Islands
    (Proc. 4534), **1977:** 1904
  Country Music Month (Proc. 4531), **1977:** 1697
  Customs Valuation Code
    (Proc. 4768), **1980–81:** 1247
    (Proc. 4809), **1980–81:** 2815
  Days of remembrance of victims of the Holo-
    caust
    (Proc. 4652), **1979:** 580
    (Proc. 4747), **1980–81:** 644
  Denali National Monument (Proc. 4616), **1978:**
    2121
  Disney, Walt, honoring the memory of (Proc.
    4725), **1980–81:** 350
  Douglas, William O. (Proc. 4715), **1980–81:** 105
  Drug Abuse Prevention Week (Proc. 4544),
    1978: 52
  Earth Day (Proc. 4710), **1980–81:** 1
  Earth Week (Proc. 4498), **1977:** 606
  Economic Opportunity Act of 1964, 15th anni-
    versary (Proc. 4672), **1979:** 1477
  Education Day, U.S.A. (Proc. 4562), **1978:** 756
  Emergency building temperature restrictions
    (Proc. 4750), **1980–81:** 685
    (Proc. 4813), **1980–81:** 2877
  Emergency Medical Services Week (Proc. 4535),
    1977: 1974
  European Communities, duty increase for textile
    articles from (Proc. 4793), **1980–81:** 1824
  Father's Day
    (Proc. 4505), **1977:** 1067
    (Proc. 4574), **1978:** 1068
    (Proc. 4659), **1979:** 747
    (Proc. 4758), **1980–81:** 899
  Fire Prevention Week
    (Proc. 4521), **1977:** 1626
    (Proc. 4581), **1978:** 1393
    (Proc. 4672), **1979:** 1438
    (Proc. 4782), **1980–81:** 1567

Proclamations — *continued*
  Firefighters' Memorial Sunday (Proc. 4671),
    1979: 1437
  Flag Day and National Flag Week
    (Proc. 4508), **1977:** 1097
    (Proc. 4573), **1978:** 1014
    (Proc. 4660), **1979:** 817
    (Proc. 4757), **1980–81:** 895
  Free Enterprise Day (Proc. 4576), **1978:** 1225
  Gates of the Arctic National Monument (Proc.
    4617), **1978:** 2123
  General Pulaski's Memorial Day
    (Proc. 4520), **1977:** 1606
    (Proc. 4582), **1978:** 1394
    (Proc. 4673), **1979:** 1444
    (Proc. 4787), **1980–81:** 1593
  Geneva (1979) Protocol to the General Agree-
    ment on Tariffs and Trade (Proc. 4707),
    1979: 2223
  Glacier Bay National Monument (Proc. 4618),
    1978: 2125
  Helen Keller Day (Proc. 4767), **1980–81:** 1147
  High carbon ferrochromium imports (Proc.
    4608), **1978:** 2037
  Humphrey, Sen. Hubert H. (Proc. 4545), **1978:**
    80
  India, imports (Proc. 4589), **1978:** 1563
  India, temporary tariff concessions to (Proc.
    4812), **1980–81:** 2848
  Inter-American Development Bank Day (Proc.
    4728), **1980–81:** 414
  International Clergy Week (Proc. 4484), **1977:** 33
  International Energy Conservation Month (Proc.
    4681), **1979:** 1622
  International Literacy Day (Proc. 4589), **1978:**
    1461
  Iranian oil imports (Proc. 4702), **1979:** 2110
  Italian-American Heritage Week (Proc. 4800),
    1980–81: 2199
  Iwo Jima Commemoration Day (Proc. 4724),
    1980–81: 350
  Jewish Heritage Week (Proc. 4752), **1980–81:** 768
  Kampucheans, aid for (Proc. 4700), **1979:** 2080
  Kitmai National Monument (Proc. 4619), **1978:**
    2127
  Kenai Fjords National Monument (Proc. 4620),
    1978: 2129
  Knoxville International Energy Exposition of
    1982 (Proc. 4628), **1978:** 2170
  Kobuk Valley National Monument (Proc. 4621),
    1978: 2130
  Lake Clark National Monument (Proc. 4622),
    1978: 2132
  Law Day, U.S.A.
    (Proc. 4499), **1977:** 607
    (Proc. 4565), **1978:** 773
    (Proc. 4649), **1979:** 527
    (Proc. 4733), **1980–81:** 457

Proclamations — *continued*
  Lead product imports
    (Proc. 4792), **1980–81:** 1723
    (Proc. 4817), **1980–81:** 3000
  Leif Erikson Day
    (Proc. 4524), **1977:** 1647
    (Proc. 4592), **1978:** 1497
    (Proc. 4677), **1979:** 1527
    (Proc. 4777), **1980–81:** 1509
  Live cattle imports (Proc. 4808), **1980–81:** 2801
  Loyalty Day
    (Proc. 4493), **1977:** 486
    (Proc. 4567), **1978:** 793
    (Proc. 4657), **1979:** 662
    (Proc. 4734), **1980–81:** 457
  Meany, George (Proc. 4712), **1980–81:** 67
  Meat imports
    (Proc. 4577), **1978:** 1236
    (Proc. 4642), **1979:** 336
  Military Selective Service Act registration (Proc.
    4771), **1980–81:** 1275
  Military Selective Service Act violations, pardon
    (Proc. 4483), **1977:** 5
  Misty Fjords National Monument (Proc. 4623),
    1978: 2134
  Mother's Day
    (Proc. 4503), **1977:** 690
    (Proc. 4570), **1978:** 890
    (Proc. 4646), **1979:** 438
    (Proc. 4743), **1980–81:** 583
  Mushroom industry import relief (Proc. 4801),
    1980–81: 2562
  National Architectural Barrier Awareness Week
    (Proc. 4566), **1978:** 774
    (Proc. 4656), **1979:** 641
  National Athletic Boosters Week (Proc. 4764),
    1980–81: 1131
  National Aviation Year and Wright Brothers
    Day (Proc. 4584), **1978:** 1396
  National Bicycling Day (Proc. 4741), **1980–81:**
    562
  National Child Abuse Prevention Month (Proc.
    4704), **1979:** 2153
  National Consumer Education Week (Proc.
    4746), **1980–81:** 621
  National Cystic Fibrosis Week (Proc. 4775),
    1980–81: 1395
  National Day of Prayer
    (Proc. 4532), **1977:** 1792
    (Proc. 4591), **1978:** 1482
    (Proc. 4690), **1979:** 1694
    (Proc. 4795), **1980–81:** 1858
  National Defense Transportation Day and Na-
    tional Transportation Week
    (Proc. 4500), **1977:** 610
    (Proc. 4548), **1978:** 255
    (Proc. 4639), **1979:** 238
    (Proc. 4737), **1980–81:** 506

[References are to page numbers except as otherwise indicated]

Proclamations — *continued*
  National Diabetes Week
    (Proc. 4686), **1979:** 1671
    (Proc. 4779), **1980–81:** 1519
  National Employ the Handicapped Week
    (Proc. 4526), **1977:** 1672
    (Proc. 4593), **1978:** 1502
    (Proc. 4685), **1979:** 1660
    (Proc. 4784), **1980–81:** 1571
  National Employ the Older Worker Week (Proc.
    4487), **1977:** 155
  National Energy Conservation Days, National
    Transportation Week (Proc. 4753), **1980–
    81:** 783
  National Energy Education Day (Proc. 4738),
    1980–81: 509
  National energy supply shortage (Proc. 4667),
    1979: 1226
  National Family Week
    (Proc. 4536), **1977:** 1992
    (Proc. 4606), **1978:** 1801
    (Proc. 4703), **1979:** 2135
    (Proc. 4806), **1980–81:** 2749
  National Farm-City Week
    (Proc. 4533), **1977:** 1821
    (Proc. 4602), **1978:** 1636
    (Proc. 4694), **1979:** 1999
    (Proc. 4781), **1980–81:** 1521
  National Farm Safety Week
    (Proc. 4494), **1977:** 524
    (Proc. 4556), **1978:** 545
    (Proc. 4645), **1979:** 433
    (Proc. 4749), **1980–81:** 683
  National Forest Products Week
    (Proc. 4530), **1977:** 1697
    (Proc. 4599), **1978:** 1560
    (Proc. 4687), **1979:** 1686
    (Proc. 4790), **1980–81:** 1645
  National Good Neighbor Day (Proc. 4601),
    1978: 1569
  National Grandparents Day
    (Proc. 4580), **1978:** 1360
    (Proc. 4679), **1979:** 1597
  National Guard Day (Proc. 4598), **1978:** 1558
  National Hispanic Heritage Week
    (Proc. 4516), **1977:** 1521
    (Proc. 4585), **1978:** 1436
    (Proc. 4662), **1979:** 930
    (Proc. 4776), **1980–81:** 1461
  National Historic Preservation Week (Proc.
    4569), **1978:** 887
  National Hunting and Fishing Day (Proc. 4682),
    1979: 1626
  National Inventors' Day
    (Proc. 4635), **1979:** 196
    1980 (Proc. 4721), **1980–81:** 273
    1981 (Proc. 4814), **1980–81:** 2887
  National Jogging Day (Proc. 4605), **1978:** 1770

Proclamations — *continued*
  National Lupus Week
    (Proc. 4518), **1977:** 1527
    (Proc. 4588), **1978:** 1456
    (Proc. 4680), **1979:** 1620
    (Proc. 4779), **1980–81:** 2183
  National Maritime Day
    (Proc. 4502), **1977:** 640
    (Proc. 4555), **1978:** 515
    (Proc. 4653), **1979:** 606
    (Proc. 4736), **1980–81:** 469
  National Meals on Wheels Week (Proc. 4689),
    1979: 1693
  National Medic Alert Week (Proc. 4739), **1980–
    81:** 514
  National Museum Day (Proc. 4661), **1979:** 897
  National Oceans Week (Proc. 4563), **1978:** 756
  National Patriotism Week (Proc. 4810), **1980–81:**
    2832
  National Poison Prevention Week
    (Proc. 4486), **1977:** 145
    (Proc. 4550), **1978:** 281
    (Proc. 4638), **1979:** 232
    (Proc. 4719), **1980–81:** 238
  National Porcelain Art Month (Proc. 4772),
    1980–81: 1277
  National Port Week
    (Proc. 4596), **1978:** 1513
    (Proc. 4695), **1979:** 1835
    (Proc. 4798), **1980–81:** 2066
  National P.O.W.-M.I.A. Recognition Day
    (Proc. 4664), **1979:** 999
    (Proc. 4774), **1980–81:** 1282
  National Recreation and Parks Week (Proc.
    4760), **1980–81:** 936
  National Safe Boating Week (Proc. 4506), **1977:**
    1080
  National Salute to Hospitalized Veterans' Day
    (Proc. 4815), **1980–81:** 2888
  National School Lunch Week
    (Proc. 4523), **1977:** 1643
    (Proc. 4594), **1978:** 1503
    (Proc. 4691), **1979:** 1694
    (Proc. 4796), **1980–81:** 1925
  National Unity Day (Proc. 4709), **1979:** 2252
  Natural gas emergency
    (Proc. 4485), **1977:** 67
    (Proc. 4495), **1977:** 555
  Noatak National Monument (Proc. 4624), **1978:**
    2136
  Nonrubber footwear imports (Proc. 4510), **1977:**
    1148
  Northern Mariana Islands
    (Proc. 4568), **1978:** 885
    (Proc. 4726), **1980–81:** 365
  North Atlantic Treaty Organization, 30th an-
    niversary (Proc. 4648), **1979:** 451

Proclamations — *continued*
Older Americans Month
  (Proc. 4497), **1977:** 605
  (Proc. 4564), **1978:** 761
  (Proc. 4658), **1979:** 671
Older Americans Month and Senior Citizens
  Day (Proc. 4745), **1980–81:** 620
Organization for Rehabilitation through Train-
  ing Centennial Day (Proc. 4740), **1980–
  81:** 561
Pan American Day and Pan American Week
  (Proc. 4491), **1977:** 469
  (Proc. 4557), **1978:** 566
  (Proc. 4644), **1979:** 390
  (Proc. 4732), **1980–81:** 455
Papermaking machinery from Finland (Proc.
  4630), **1978:** 2271
Peanut imports (Proc. 4807), **1980–81:** 2775
Petroleum import adjustment program
  (Proc. 4744), **1980–81:** 592
  (Proc. 4748), **1980–81:** 657
  (Proc. 4751), **1980–81:** 760
  (Proc. 4766), **1980–81:** 1140
Petroleum import licensing requirements (Proc.
  4762), **1980–81:** 1049
Petroleum imports (Proc. 4543), **1977:** 2178
Petroleum imports and products
  (Proc. 4629), **1978:** 2185
  (Proc. 4655), **1979:** 628
Porcelain-on-steel cookware industry (Proc.
  4713), **1980–81:** 97
Prayer for Peace, Memorial Day
  (Proc. 4504), **1977:** 716
  (Proc. 4572), **1978:** 931
  (Proc. 4651), **1979:** 550
  (Proc. 4754), **1980–81:** 813
Red Cross Month
  (Proc. 4489), **1977:** 249
  (Proc. 4551), **1978:** 284
  (Proc. 4636), **1979:** 214
  (Proc. 4717), **1980–81:** 193
Salute to Learning Day (Proc. 4755), **1980–81:**
  841
Save Your Vision Week
  (Proc. 4488), **1977:** 157
  (Proc. 4549), **1978:** 257
  (Proc. 4637), **1979:** 220
  (Proc. 4718), **1980–81:** 234
Scouting Recognition Week (Proc. 4706), **1979:**
  2209
Servicemen, tribute to eight American (Proc.
  4756), **1980–81:** 847
Small Business Week
  (Proc. 4501), **1977:** 616
  (Proc. 4553), **1978:** 514
  (Proc. 4641), **1979:** 335
  (Proc. 4723), **1980–81:** 349

Proclamations — *continued*
Steel imports
  (Proc. 4665), **1979:** 1032
  (Proc. 4668), **1979:** 1228
Sugar, sirups, and molasses imports
  (Proc. 4538), **1977:** 2019
  (Proc. 4539), **1977:** 2021
  (Proc. 4547), **1978:** 145
  (Proc. 4610), **1978:** 2104
  (Proc. 4631), **1978:** 2288
  (Proc. 4663), **1979:** 946
  (Proc. 4720), **1980–81:** 265
  (Proc. 4770), **1980–81:** 1272
Sun Day (Proc. 4558), **1978:** 574
Teacher Day, USA (Proc. 4730), **1980–81:** 430
Television receiver imports (Proc. 4634), **1979:**
  166
Thanksgiving Day
  (Proc. 4537), **1977:** 2004
  (Proc. 4607), **1978:** 1802
  (Proc. 4693), **1979:** 1780
  (Proc. 4803), **1980–81:** 2723
Trade with Indonesia, Trinidad, Tobago, and
  countries forming Cartegena Agreement
  (Proc. 4711), **1980–81:** 20
United Nations Day
  (Proc. 4525), **1977:** 1664
  (Proc. 4597), **1978:** 1539
  (Proc. 4684), **1979:** 1657
  (Proc. 4789), **1980–81:** 1594
United States Space Observance
  (Proc. 4512), **1977:** 1227
  (Proc. 4669), **1979:** 1260
University Press Centennial Observance (Proc.
  4575), **1978:** 1100
Upland cotton imports
  (Proc. 4742), **1980–81:** 575
  (Proc. 4805), **1980–81:** 2745
U.S.-Hungary trade relations (Proc. 4560), **1978:**
  706
Veterans Administration's 50th anniversary
  (Proc. 4763), **1980–81:** 1120
Veterans Day
  (Proc. 4519), **1977:** 1586
  (Proc. 4595), **1978:** 1510
  (Proc. 4688), **1979:** 1687
  (Proc. 4791), **1980–81:** 1702
Vietnam Veterans Week (Proc. 4647), **1979:** 445
Vinson, Carl (Proc. 4735), **1980–81:** 468
White Cane Safety Day
  (Proc. 4528), **1977:** 1684
  (Proc. 4583), **1978:** 1395
  (Proc. 4678), **1979:** 1527
  (Proc. 4783), **1980–81:** 1568
Will Rogers Day (Proc. 4698), **1979:** 2078
William O. Douglas Arctic Wildlife Range (Proc.
  4729), **1980–81:** 419

[References are to page numbers except as otherwise indicated]

Proclamations — *continued*
  Women's Equality Day
    (Proc. 4515), **1977:** 1503, 1504
    (Proc. 4590), **1978:** 1470
    (Proc. 4674), **1979:** 1476
    (Proc. 4785), **1980–81:** 1575
  Working Mothers' Day (Proc. 4786), **1980–81:** 1592
  World Law Day (Proc. 4514), **1977:** 1481, 1482
  World Trade Week
    (Proc. 4496), **1977:** 594
    (Proc. 4554), **1978:** 514
    (Proc. 4654), **1979:** 616
    (Proc. 4722), **1980–81:** 322
  Wrangell-St. Elias National Monument (Proc. 4625), **1978:** 2138
  Wright Brothers Day
    (Proc. 4541), **1977:** 2048
    (Proc. 4699), **1979:** 2079
    (Proc. 4802), **1980–81:** 2717
  Yukon-Charley National Monument (Proc. 4626), **1978:** 2140
  Yukon Flats National Monument (Proc. 4627), **1978:** 2142
Proctor, George Washington, **1979:** 1786, 1787
Procurement, Agreement on Government, **1980–81:** 2854
Procurement policy, Federal, **1980–81:** 72
Procurement Policy, Office of Federal, **1979:** 2072
Procurement Policy Act amendments, Office of Federal, **1979:** 1850
Procurement practices, Federal, **1979:** 308
Producer Price Index, **1979:** 717
  Annual increases, **1980–81:** 496
  April statistics, **1980–81:** 869, 875, 884
  February statistics, **1980–81:** 453, 512
  May statistics, **1980–81:** 1046
  September statistics, **1980–81:** 2055
Product Safety Commission, Consumer, **1980–81:** 281
Productivity Council, **1980–81:** 127
Productivity Council, National, **1978:** 1833–1835; **1979:** 532
Productivity and Quality of Working Life, National Center for, **1978:** 1835
Productivity rates, U.S., **1978:** 1415
Project Head Start, **1980–81:** 462, 494
Project Integrity, **1978:** 2230
Project Match, **1978:** 2230
Project Seafarer, **1978:** 239, 464; **1979:** 1710
Prok Amaranand, **1980–81:** 1564
Prokop, Ruth T., **1977:** 576, 596, 706, 934; **1978:** 920; **1979:** 3, 46, 90, 1019, 1921
Property Council, Federal, **1977:** 1257, 2124
Propst, Robert B., **1980–81:** 64, 65
Prostitution, **1977:** 504
Prothro, Johnnie W., **1978:** 218
Providence, R. I., **1978:** 331, 339, 414; **1979:** 2055

Proxmire, Sen. William, **1977:** 788, 1136, 1491, 1628, 1835; **1978:** 148; **1979:** 1728, 2078; **1980–81:** 573, 1548, 2113, 2378
Prudential Insurance Company, **1979:** 2022; **1980–81:** 1403
Pryor, Sen. David, **1980–81:** 1050, 1938
Pryor, Gov. David H., **1978:** 2187
Pryor, Malcolm D., **1980–81:** 2614
Pryor, William Cornet, **1979:** 957
Psychotropic Substances, Convention on, **1977:** 1402
Psychotropic Substances Act, **1978:** 2003
Public assistance programs, Federal, **1978:** 2232, 2233
Public broadcasting, **1977:** 1699, 1737, 1756; **1978:** 110; **1980–81:** 913
  Administration's priorities, **1979:** 141
  First amendment privileges, **1979:** 486
  Industry deregulation, **1979:** 483, 485
  Legislation, **1979:** 488
  Worldwide impact, **1979:** 482
Public Broadcasting, Carnegie Commission on the Future of, **1977:** 1739; **1979:** 199
Public Broadcasting Service, **1977:** 327, 1738; **1978:** 2014
Public debt limit extension bill, **1980–81:** 1037, 1041
Public Diplomacy, United States Advisory Commission on, **1980–81:** 1445, 1470, 1846
Public employee strikes, **1978:** 1326
Public Employees Federation of New York, **1980–81:** 374
Public Health Service, **1977:** 1080, 1085; **1979:** 2036, 2090, 2091, 2112; **1980–81:** 456, 908, 1252
Public Health Service Award, **1979:** 983
Public Housing Authority, **1977:** 1728
Public international organizations, privileges, exemptions, and immunities, **1977:** 380
Public lands, roadless areas review and evaluation, **1979:** 669, 670
Public lands grazing fees, **1978:** 1331, 1876
Public officials, standards of conduct, **1977:** 396
Public opinion polls, **1977:** 409, 602, 1914
  Approval ratings of the President, **1980–81:** 89, 1643
  Elections, effect on, **1979:** 1712, 1751
  1977 national energy address, President's loss due to, **1979:** 1893, 2032, 2054, 2059
  Presidential candidate preference ratings, **1980–81:** 1831, 2417, 2688
  President's decisions, effect on, **1980–81:** 740
  President's rating in, **1979:** 1918, 2241
Public Papers of the Presidents, **1978:** 1955
Public Radio, National, **1977:** 1738
Public Rangelands Improvement Act, **1978:** 1875
Public sector employers, **1978:** 1215

Public service employment program, **1978:** 99, 138, 392, 506, 586

Public Telecommunications Financing Act, **1978:** 1927

Public Transit Association, American, **1979:** 1739, 1787

Public Utility Regulatory Policies Act, **1978:** 1978

Public works bill, **1978:** 1659, 1702, 1706, 1713, 1724, 1725

Public works and economic development act, national, proposed, **1979:** 599, 601, 602

Public works and service employment, **1977:** 97, 240, 290, 294, 870, 889, 1461, 1833, 1838, 1938, 2001

Publications and Records Commission, National Historical, **1978:** 2274

Publishing firms, minority, Government loans, **1979:** 35

Pucinski, Roman, **1979:** 1448

Puckett, Paul J., **1977:** 1483, 1484

Pueblo, U.S.S., incident, **1980–81:** 744

Puerto Rico
   Cuban and Haitian refugees resettlement, **1980–81:** 1944, 1989, 2069, 2178
   Cuban influence in internal affairs, **1979:** 1943
   Disaster declaration, **1979:** 1603
   Economic report, **1980–81:** 291, 293
   Former Gov. Luis Muñoz Marín, **1980–81:** 808
   Future statehood, President's support for, **1980–81:** 1838
   Gasoline production, import conservation fee waiver, **1980–81:** 596, 598, 657
   Governor Carlos Romero-Barcelo, **1977:** 279
   Hurricane David, assistance to Dominican Republic, **1979:** 1666
   Interview remarks, **1977:** 1620
   Judicial nominating commission, **1978:** 1638
   Leaders, meeting with the President, **1978:** 934
   Nationalists, commutation of prison sentences, **1979:** 1597, 1608, 1663
   President's assessment of future opportunity for statehood, **1979:** 1664
   Resident Commissioner, **1978:** 458
   SALT II treaty briefing for community and civic leaders by administration officials (Digest), **1979:** 2106
   Secretary of State, **1980–81:** 1939, 1944
   Submerged land jurisdiction, **1980–81:** 466
   Terrorist attack on U.S. Navy schoolbus, **1979:** 2206
   26th anniversary of the Commonwealth, **1978:** 1336
   U.S. attorney, **1980–81:** 269
   U.S. district judges, **1979:** 2044, 2188; **1980–81:** 933, 934, 1470, 1471
   U.S. marshal, **1979:** 899, 900
   U.S. policy, **1980–81:** 319

Puerto Rico, Judicial Nominating Commission for the District of, **1980–81:** 2849

Pulaski, Casimir, **1980–81:** 1593, 1853

Pulaski's Memorial Day, General, **1977:** 1606; **1978:** 1394; **1979:** 1444

Pulitzer, Emily Rauh, **1979:** 1157, 1159

Pungan, Vasile, **1977:** 251

Purcell, Arthur H., **1978:** 697

Purcell, Edward Mills, **1979:** 2289; **1980–81:** 82n.

Purcival, Ralph, **1980–81:** 930

Purks, James H., III, **1979:** 1017

Pursch, Joseph A., **1980–81:** 2609

Purushottam, S. V., **1978:** 50

PUSH (People United to Save Humanity), Operation, **1979:** 1422; **1980–81:** 932, 1946

Putnam, Peter B., **1978:** 927

Pye, A. Kenneth, **1979:** 1451

Pym, Francis, **1980–81:** 1344n.

Qadhafi, Col. Mu'ammar al-, **1980–81:** 1479, 1484

Qatar
   Ambassador to U.S., **1980–81:** 1564
   U.S. Ambassador, **1977:** 1355, 1384; **1980–81:** 718, 720

Quackenbush, James H., **1980–81:** 930

Quackenbush, Justin L., **1980–81:** 894

Quadripartite Agreement, **1977:** 840; **1978:** 1283, 1294, 1296–1300, 1304

Quainton, Anthony C. E., **1979:** 1158, 1159

Quaison-Sackey, Alex, **1978:** 710

Quandt, William, **1977:** 1283

Quandt, William B., **1978:** 2288

Quandt, William E., **1980–81:** 1407

Queen.
   See specific forename.

Queen, Richard, release by Iranian captors
   Meeting with the President, **1980–81:** 1380, 1427, 2508
   President's comments, **1980–81:** 1342, 2264
   Telephone conversation with the President, **1980–81:** 1376

Queen, Thomas, **1980–81:** 509

Quetico-Superior Committee, **1977:** 2114

Quie, Gov. Albert H., **1979:** 1452, 1468

Quilligan, Edward J., **1978:** 2070

Quincy, Mass., **1979:** 1990

Quinn, Cheryl, **1977:** 317

Quinn, Archbishop John R., **1978:** 2059

Quinn, Thomas H., **1979:** 1659, 1680

Quinonez Meza, Roberto, **1978:** 148

Raatz, Gretchen E., **1977:** 816

Rabbis, New York Board of, **1980–81:** 2453

Rabbit, President's fishing encounter with, **1979:** 1579, 1592

Rabbit meat inspection, **1977:** 1993

Rabin, Yitzhak, **1977:** 225, 252, 311, 329, 334, 373, 600; **1979:** 1752

Racial Discrimination, Convention on, **1979:** 162; **1980–81:** 119

Racial Discrimination, International Convention on the Elimination of all Forms of, **1978:** 395

Racial Discrimination, Treaty for the Elimination of All Forms of, **1977:** 450

Racism and Racial Discrimination, World Conference to Combat, **1978:** 1456

Racker, Efraim, **1977:** 2046

Radiation, low-level, **1979:** 2007

Radiation Control for Health and Safety Act, **1977:** 609; **1980–81:** 1014

Radiation Control for Health and Safety Act of 1968, **1978:** 1560

Radiation Control for the Health and Safety Act of 1968, Administration of the, **1979:** 2043

Radiation Policy Council, **1979:** 2007 (EO 12194), **1980–81:** 362, 364

Radiation protection program, **1980–81:** 364

Radiation Research Committee, Interagency, **1979:** 2007; **1980–81:** 364

Radiation weapons, enhanced, **1977:** 1231, 1331; **1978:** 536, 702, 709, 776, 874, 875, 1283

Radio, "Ask President Carter," CBS telephone call-in program, **1977:** 291

Radio, National Public, **1979:** 1518

Radio Advisory Committee, Interdepartment, **1978:** 601

Radio Broadcasters Association, National, **1978:** 254

Radio Conference, Worldwide Administrative, **1979:** 541, 1334

Radio Free Europe/Radio Liberty, **1977:** 478

Radio Regulations, 1959 Geneva, **1980–81:** 225

Radio stations, **1978:** 598, 599

Radio and Television Correspondents Association, **1978:** 504

Radio-Television News Directors Association, **1977:** 747, 1594

Radio transceivers, citizens band, **1978:** 707

Radioactive Waste Management, Interagency Review Group on, **1980–81:** 297

Radioactive Waste Management, State Planning Council on, **1980–81:** 297, 301, 303

Radioactivity exposure, **1979:** 182

Radioactivity exposure in Utah, **1978:** 2088

Radix, Bernard Kendrick, **1979:** 1454

Rafael Echeverria, Jose, **1978:** 1070

Rafshoon, Gerald M., **1977:** 1914; **1978:** 934; **1979:** 1678; **1980–81:** 2871

Ragone, David V., **1978:** 1760, 1773; **1979:** 46, 92

Rahall, Repr. Nick J., II, **1977:** 1163; **1980–81:** 1450, 1598, 1699, 2226

Rahn, Betsy F., **1977:** 2028

Raiche, Robert E., **1977:** 1384

Raikes, Ralph, **1980–81:** 1291

Rail Public Counsel, Office of, **1977:** 1961, 1967

Railroad Administration, Federal, **1977:** 740, 746; **1979:** 1787

Railroad Improvement Program, Northeast Corridor, **1978:** 106

Railroad Investments, Branch Line, **1979:** 76

Railroad Passenger Corporation, National. *See* National Railroad Passenger Corporation (Amtrak).

Railroad rehabilitation, **1978:** 516

Railroad Retirement Board, **1978:** 231, 1438, 1720, 1724; **1980–81:** 1547
  Annual report, **1977:** 84
  Budget deferral, **1979:** 2122
  Members, **1977:** 1239, 1266, 1644, 2079, 2089; **1979:** 1037, 1044
  Report, **1979:** 1683, 1772

Railroad Safety Act of 1970, **1977:** 1465; **1980–81:** 292, 2872

Railroad Safety Report, **1978:** 1772

Railroads
  Administration's accomplishments and goals, **1980–81:** 2951
  Alaska Railroad, **1980–81:** 2726, 2845
  Coal transportation costs, **1979:** 1709
  Distillate fuel supplies, **1979:** 1416
  Federal control, **1980–81:** 1357
  Industry deregulation
    Freight industry, proposed legislation, **1979:** 459
    President's appeal for congressional support, **1979:** 1409, 1696, 2186
    President's commitment to reform in 1979, **1979:** 105, 114, 128, 130
    See also Staggers Rail Act.
  Japanese train system, **1980–81:** 664
  Northeast corridor legislation, **1980–81:** 1009
  Retirement benefits, **1977:** 47
  Strike, effect on grain industry, **1979:** 1609
  Worker pension benefits, **1980–81:** 2830

Railsback, Repr. Thomas, **1979:** 1849; **1980–81:** 303, 1098, 2217, 2241

Railway Association, United States, **1978:** 1269, 1333, 1360, 1381; **1979:** 43, 93; **1980–81:** 392, 1824, 1847

Railway Carmen of the United States and Canada, Brotherhood of, **1980–81:** 667, 684, 931

Railway Labor Conference, National, **1979:** 818, 819

Railway labor disputes, Emergency Boards to investigate. *See* Emergency Boards to investigate railway labor disputes.

Raines, Franklin D., **1980–81:** 1824, 1847
Raitt, John, **1980–81:** 2887
Rajai, Mohammed Ali, **1980–81:** 2288
Rajoppi, Joanne, **1979:** 1034
Ralls, William R., **1979:** 2191; **1980–81:** 2731
Ramadan, **1979:** 1518
Rambo, Sylvia H., **1979:** 958, 983
Ramee, Mark, **1979:** 1143
Ramey, Estelle, **1979:** 1698
Ramirez, Blandina Cárdenas, **1980–81:** 605, 968
Ramirez, Dr. Mario E., **1978:** 934
Ramirez, Raul A., **1979:** 2249
Ramirez, Sergio, **1979:** 1722
Ramo, Simon, **1979:** 2289; **1980–81:** 82n.
Rampey, D. Lee, Jr., **1977:** 1211, 1212
Ramphal, Sir Shridath, **1980–81:** 334
Ramsay, Ann S., **1978:** 737; **1979:** 827
Ramsay, Walter, **1978:** 2110
Ramsbotham, Peter, **1977:** 31
Ramsey, Norman P., **1980–81:** 1428, 1429
Rand, Sidney Anders, **1979:** 2217
Randall, Carolyn D., **1979:** 787, 788
Randall, Claire, **1977:** 526; **1978:** 1135
Randolph, A. Philip
  Death statement, **1979:** 882
  Living Legacy Awards recipient, **1979:** 321
  Memorial services, **1979:** 996, 1015
  President's assessment, **1979:** 883, 911
Randolph, Sen. Jennings, **1977:** 403, 1073, 1161,
    1409, 1410, 1649, 1947, 1962, 1988, 2105,
    2179; **1978:** 265, 302, 432, 433, 999, 1002,
    1005, 1729–1732, 1827, 2003, 2154; **1979:**
    65, 68, 293
  Campaign appearance with the President, **1980–
    81:** 2472
  Handicapped programs support, **1980–81:** 808
  International Solvent Refined Coal II Agree-
    ment support, **1980–81:** 1450
  Legislation passage leadership
    Alaska National Interest Lands Conservation
      Act, **1980–81:** 1548
    Comprehensive Environmental Response,
      Compensation, and Liability Act, **1980–
      81:** 2797–2799
  News conference (Checklist), **1980–81:** 2071
Range, M. Athalie, **1978:** 1512, 1517; **1979:** 397,
    402
Range, Mertie Helen, **1980–81:** 1390
Range, Mr. and Mrs. Olen, **1980–81:** 1390, 2782
Rangel, Repr. Charles B., **1978:** 282, 284, 503, 1452,
    2268; **1980–81:** 1469, 1502, 2363
  Hospital cost containment legislation support,
    1979: 384–386
  Meetings with the President, **1979:** 293 (Digest),
    1017, 2187
  National health plan support, **1979:** 1011, 1025
  Welfare reform legislation, passage leadership,
    1979: 2092

Rangel, Irma, **1977:** 816
Rangelands Improvement Act, **1978:** 1875
Ranis, Beatrice, **1980–81:** 1713, 1847
Rankin, Samuel, **1977:** 315
Rankow, Dan, **1980–81:** 1405
Ranney, Sally, **1980–81:** 1386, 1388n.
Rape victims, protection, **1978:** 1902
Rappaport, Paul, **1978:** 824, 826
RARE.
  See Roadless area review and evaluation lands.
Raritan River Steel Plant, N.J.
  Dedication ceremonies, **1980–81:** 1672, 1715
    (Checklist)
  Exports to China, **1980–81:** 1674, 1678, 1697,
    1740, 1749, 1753, 1769, 2039, 2142, 2205,
    2294, 2406, 2411
  Highest productivity per steelworker in world,
    1980–81: 1697, 1753, 1769, 2039, 2142,
    2205, 2294, 2406, 2411
  Mentions, **1980–81:** 1677, 1679
Rashish, Myer, **1978:** 759
Raskas, Rabbi Bernard, **1978:** 1974; **1980–81:** 822
Rasmuson, Elmer E., **1979:** 1001
Rasmussen, Karen L., **1980–81:** 928
Rassias, John A., **1978:** 1514
Ratchford, Bill, **1978:** 1889
Rattley, Jessie, **1978:** 2080; **1980–81:** 103, 495, 1432
Rau, Violet E., **1979:** 446
Raullerson, Calvin H., **1978:** 1343, 1346
Rauschenberg, Robert, **1977:** 1117
Raven, Peter H., **1977:** 1780, 1796
Ravenel, Charles, **1978:** 1582; **1980–81:** 25
Raviv, Dan, **1980–81:** 1670
Rawls, Byron, **1980–81:** 1453
Rawls, Nancy V., **1979:** 1617, 1679
Ray, Gov. Dixy Lee.
  See Governor *under* Washington.
Ray, James Earl, **1978:** 1780
Ray, Gov. Robert D., **1979:** 2085
Rayburn, Sam, **1980–81:** 2604
Raynor, John P., **1979:** 573n.
Raynor, Shari K., **1980–81:** 926
Re, Edward D., **1977:** 372
Reactor Safeguards, Advisory Committee on,
    1980–81: 504, 547, 549, 837–840
Read, Benjamin H., **1977:** 1353, 1384; **1980–81:**
    891
Read, Sister Joel, **1978:** 1706, 1724, 2050; **1979:** 46,
    90
Read, Brig. Gen. William Edgar, **1977:** 1542, 1569
Read, Maj. Gen. William Edgar, **1980–81:** 2916,
    3050
Reader's Digest, **1977:** 1127
Ready, David T., **1977:** 1613, 1614
Reagan, Barbara B., **1978:** 54
Reagan, Nancy, **1980–81:** 2739

Reagan, Ronald
  Meeting with the President (Digest), **1980–81:** 3049
  Presidential campaign.
    See Elections, 1980: campaign.
  President's former relationship with, **1980–81:** 987
  Republican Presidential nomination
    Telegram from the President, **1980–81:** 1347, 1377
    Telephone conversation with the President, **1980–81:** 1360, 1377
Real estate, foreign ownership of U.S., **1980–81:** 1924
Real wage insurance, **1978:** 1843, 1847, 1912
  Anti-inflation policy, **1979:** 74, 105, 951
  Mention, **1979:** 111
  President's appeal for congressional support, **1979:** 256, 951
  Tax credit feature, **1979:** 74, 115, 124, 307, 951
Reasoner, Harry, **1977:** 1467
Reavley, Thomas M., **1979:** 899, 900
Recession.
  See under Economy, national.
Reclamation, Bureau of, **1977:** 208, 288, 454, 488, 490, 494, 565; **1978:** 1044, 1045, 1049; **1979:** 1510, 1511
Reclamation Safety of Dams Act, **1978:** 1928
Reconstruction and Development, International Bank for.
  See International Bank for Reconstruction and Development.
Recording for the Blind, Inc., **1978:** 925
Recording Industry Association, **1977:** 1612; **1979:** 446
Recreation, **1977:** 1080, 1097
Recreation, forest land allocation, **1979:** 670
Recreation Act of 1978, National Parks and, **1980–81:** 416, 432
Recreation and Parks Week, National, **1980–81:** 936
Recreation Plan, Nationwide Outdoor, **1979:** 2220
Recreation Recovery program, Urban Park and, **1978:** 2000; **1979:** 2220
Recreation Trails, National, **1979:** 1366
Rector, John M., **1977:** 1079, 1085
Recycling, **1977:** 972
Red Cross, American National, **1977:** 210, 249, 250, 1665; **1978:** 770; **1979:** 376, 552, 1678; **1980–81:** 951, 1292
Red Cross, International.
  See International Red Cross.
Red Cross, International Committee of the, **1979:** 1925, 2011, 2080
Red Cross, International Conference of the, **1977:** 1795
Red Cross Bloodmobile, **1977:** 252

Red Cross Month, **1977:** 210, 249, 250; **1978:** 284, 285; **1979:** 214, 215; **1980–81:** 193
Red Cross Program, Government, **1980–81:** 1292
Red River Compact Commission, **1977:** 1462
Redbird, Helen Marie, **1980–81:** 849
Redden, James Anthony, **1979:** 2207
Reddy, N. S., **1978:** 1, 11; **1979:** 732
Redford, Lola, **1978:** 1191
Redlich, Fritz C., **1979:** 1264
Redmond, William A., **1978:** 996
Redstone, Sumner Murray, **1979:** 466
Redwood National Park, **1977:** 983; **1978:** 116, 575, 641
Reece, Mamie, **1977:** 816
Reed, Antoinette E., **1980–81:** 927
Reed, Carolyn, **1978:** 1135
Reed, Edward C., Jr., **1979:** 667, 668
Reed, Joe, **1979:** 2104
Reed, Robert G., **1979:** 1614n.
Reed, Ronald S., Jr., **1977:** 1163, 1164
Reed, Scott E., **1979:** 1531, 1532
Reese, Claude H., **1980–81:** 1440
Reeves, Caroline B., **1980–81:** 928
Refugee Act, **1980–81:** 503, 892
Refugee Education Assistance Act, **1980–81:** 2152, 2179, 2382
Refugee and Migration Assistance Fund, United States Emergency, **1979:** 1925, 2117, 2150
Refugee Policy, Select Commission on Immigration and.
  See Select Commission on Immigration and Refugee Policy.
Refugee Relief, United Nations Pledging Conference on, **1979:** 2085
Refugees
  Administration's accomplishments and goals, **1980–81:** 2995
  Afghanistan.
    See Refugees *under* Afghanistan.
  Ethiopia, **1980–81:** 946, 971, 1317, 1880, 2211
  Kampuchea, **1980–81:** 964, 971, 1165, 1317, 1320, 1393, 1880, 2211
  U.S. assistance, **1980–81:** 1333
  Venice Economic Summit Conference statements, **1980–81:** 1172
  Yugoslavian assistance, **1980–81:** 1219
  See also Immigration and naturalization.
Refugees, United Nations High Commission for, **1980–81:** 256, 1139
Regan, Ann K., **1979:** 2015
Regional Action Planning Commissions, Multi-State, **1979:** 602, 1288, 1289
Regional Commissions, Title V.
  See Title V Regional Commissions.
Regional Councils, Federal, **1977:** 1265, 1816; **1978:** 303; **1979:** 81, 1288
Register, Richard A., **1980–81:** 927

Regulatory Analysis Review Group, **1978:** 1905,
1906; **1979:** 74, 128, 492
Regulatory Calendar, **1979:** 128, 492, 536, 1361
Regulatory Council, **1978:** 1845, 1905, 1914, 1955
Alternative regulatory approaches development,
1980–81: 1109, 2227, 2230
Banned and significantly restricted substance
exports, regulations review, **1980–81:** 2908
Chairman, **1980–81:** 59, 63, 1110
Coal production regulations review, **1979:** 1339n.
Education Department and Federal Emergency
Management Agency membership,
1980–81: 1427
Federal agencies coordination, **1980–81:** 75, 252,
1055
Meeting with the President (Digest), **1980–81:**
1111
Mention, **1980–81:** 2932
Proposed regulations, review, **1979:** 74
Regulating agencies coordination, **1979:** 2072
Regulation calendar preparation, **1979:** 128, 492,
536, 1361
Report on reforms since 1978, **1980–81:** 785
Small Business Administration membership,
1979: 2074, 2142, 2143; **1980–81:** 78, 127
Vice Chairman, **1980–81:** 1050
Regulatory Flexibility Act
Fact sheet (Checklist), **1980–81:** 1848
House of Representatives approval, **1980–81:**
1697
Proposed, **1980–81:** 127
Senate approval, **1980–81:** 1508
Signing ceremonies, remarks and statement,
1980–81: 1839, 1843
Regulatory Liaison Group, Interagency, **1979:** 536
Regulatory management, Federal, **1978:** 1905
Regulatory reform, **1977:** 74, 160, 258, 389, 397,
626–628, 633, 752, 1069, 1085, 1379, 1561,
1562, 1564, 2034, 2095; **1978:** 70, 94, 100,
108, 140, 269, 724, 820, 840, 985, 1024,
1175, 1226, 1388, 1422, 1492, 1578, 1593,
1594, 1648, 1798, 1841, 1842, 1845, 1846,
2078, 2231
Administration's program proposals to Congress,
1979: 491
Airline industry.
See under Aircraft and aviation.
Anti-inflation measure, **1980–81:** 120, 215, 573,
604
Bus industry, **1979:** 105, 128
Drug laws, **1979:** 135
Federal regulatory system, **1977:** 160, 258, 389,
397, 626–628, 633, 752, 2034; **1979:** 111,
114, 127, 484, 634, 719, 1115, 1346, 1361,
1768, 1841, 1951, 2072
Alternative approaches to regulation, **1980–81:**
1109
EO 12221, **1980–81:** 1239

Regulatory reform — *continued*
Federal regulatory system — *continued*
Legislation, **1980–81:** 118, 121, 151, 498, 604
Private sector, effect on, **1980–81:** 215, 226,
281, 920
Financial institutions.
See under Banks and banking.
Legislation, **1979:** 493, 2271
Medical care, **1979:** 475
Occupational safety and health regulations,
1979: 634, 834, 1936
Presidential oversight of regulation, **1980–81:**
152
Progress during administration, **1980–81:** 252,
785, 1537, 1586, 1684, 1737, 1740, 1768,
2077, 2082, 2190, 2208, 2227, 2230, 2375,
2400, 2406, 2411, 2417, 2499, 2514, 2532,
2629, 2932, 2966, 3007
Railroad industry.
See Railroads; Staggers Rail Act.
Small businesses.
See under Small businesses.
State and local governments regulations, **1979:**
72, 100
Sunset review, **1979:** 2182; **1980–81:** 118, 153
Telecommunications industry.
See under Communications and telecommu-
nications.
Trucking industry.
See under Trucking industry.
See also Paperwork reduction.
Regulatory Reform, White House Conference on,
1980–81: 57
Rehabilitation Act of 1973, **1980–81:** 2654, 2726
Rehabilitation Services Administration, **1977:**
1644, 1650
Rehabilitation through Training, Organization for,
1980–81: 561
Reich, Jay A., **1979:** 914
Reichart, Lou, **1978:** 1558
Reiche, Frank P., **1979:** 757, 788
Reichl, Eric, **1977:** 404
Reid, Inez Smith, **1979:** 1691, 1706
Reilly, William Kane, **1980–81:** 1405
Reinhardt, John E., **1977:** 372, 512; **1978:** 277, 303,
1514, 1630, 1669, 2160
Reinhardt, Stephen R., **1979:** 2188, 2189
Reischauer, Edwin O., **1978:** 1515
Reiser, Carolyn S., **1980–81:** 926
Religion
Black ministers, White House reception, **1980–
81:** 2425
Leaders, U.S. meetings with the President, **1978:**
1669; **1980–81:** 49, 217 (Digest)
National Bible Week, **1980–81:** 2747
Political influence, **1980–81:** 1685, 2010

Religion — *continued*
    President's views on, **1979:** 1827, 1830, 1839;
        1980–81: 181, 1612, 2311, 2386, 2505,
        2590, 2628
    Separation of church and state, **1980–81:** 2386
Religion and Peace, White House Conference on,
    1979: 1598
Religious Broadcasters, National, **1980–81:** 180
Relocation Commission, **1978:** 1925
Renal disease program, **1978:** 1086
Rencher, Ronald E., **1977:** 1569
Renegotiation Board, **1977:** 337, 367, 465; **1979:**
    374, 402
Renfrew, Charles B., **1979:** 2148; **1980–81:** 2788
Renfrow, R. Todd, **1980–81:** 1845
Renner, Robert G., **1979:** 2188, 2189
Renouf, Alan Philip, **1977:** 194
Renouf, Clem, **1978:** 2073
Reorganization, Executive Committee on, **1977:**
    1052
Reorganization Act of 1977, **1977:** 571, 597; **1980–
    81:** 616
Reorganization Plans
    Alaska Natural Gas Transportation System (No.
        1 of 1979), **1979:** 591
    Employee Retirement Income Security Act
        transfers (No. 4 of 1978), **1978:** 1401,
        1407, 1555, 1782
    Equal employment opportunity enforcement
        (No. 1 of 1978), **1978:** 398, 400, 416, 883
    Executive Office of the President
        Amendments, **1977:** 1592
        No. 1 of 1977, **1977:** 1252, 1255
    Federal civil service reform (No. 2 of 1978),
        1978: 953, 1251, 1317, 2292
    Federal Emergency Management Agency (No. 3
        of 1978), **1978:** 1128, 1129, 1155
    International Communication Agency
        Amendments, **1977:** 1963, 1964
        No. 2 of 1977, **1977:** 1765
    International trade functions (No. 3 of 1979),
        1979: 1729
    Nuclear Regulatory Commission (No. 1 of 1980),
        1980–81: 543
        Amendment, **1980–81:** 836
    United States International Development Co-
        operation Agency (No. 2 of 1979), **1979:**
        642
        Amendments, **1979:** 915
Reports to Congress.
    See under Congress, Communications to.
Reports elimination act, proposed, **1979:** 2182
Reports to the President
    Boy Scouts of America, **1977:** 194
    Emergency Board to investigate an airline in-
        dustry dispute, **1979:** 293
    Energy management in the Federal Government,
        1978: 1457

Reports to the President — *continued*
    Federal Strategy for Drug Abuse and Drug
        Traffic Prevention, **1979:** 618
    National Commission on Neighborhoods, **1979:**
        618
    National Commission for the Review of Anti-
        trust Laws and Procedures, **1979:** 178
    Privacy Protection Study Commission, **1977:**
        1264
    United States Military Academy Board of Vis-
        itors, **1977:** 1397
    United States Naval Academy Board of Visitors,
        1977: 1432
    U.S. steel industry, **1977:** 2083, 2090
Republic Steel Corporation, **1978:** 1725; **1980–81:**
    2071
Republican Party, **1979:** 1396
    Campaign remarks on, **1980–81:** 1542, 1616,
        1754, 1766, 1886
    Historical differences with Democrats, **1980–81:**
        1425, 1994, 2296, 2390, 2398, 2403, 2416
    National Convention, **1980–81:** 1381
    Platform, **1980–81:** 1304, 1534
    See also Elections, 1980.
Research Apprenticeship Program, **1979:** 2064
Research and development, **1979:** 140, 141, 529,
        1251, 2064; **1980–81:** 229, 2086
    Agriculture, **1977:** 170, 1710, 2097
    Breeder reactors, **1977:** 1462
    Budget message, **1978:** 187
    Business and industry production, **1980–81:** 1963
    Employment, **1977:** 910
    Energy.
        See Energy research and development.
    Federal budget allocations increase, **1980–81:**
        2086
    Federal funding, **1979:** 99, 678
    Federal programs, **1978:** 1842, 1914
    Health and medical care, **1978:** 349; **1980–81:**
        190, 2294
    Natural resources management, **1980–81:** 1144
    Pollution, **1977:** 172
    Science and technology.
        See Science and technology.
    State of the Union, **1978:** 116
    Submarines, **1978:** 239
Research records acts, privacy of, proposed, **1979:**
    584
Reserve Officers' Association, **1978:** 710; **1980–81:**
    374
Reserve Officers Training Corps, **1980–81:** 2292
Resignations and Retirements
    Agriculture Department, Assistant Secretary,
        1977: 1906
    Ambassadors, U.S., Mexico, **1979:** 1846
    Civil Aeronautics Board, Chairman, **1978:** 1850
    Commerce Department
        Bureau of the Census, Director, **1979:** 240

Resignations and Retirements — *continued*
  Commerce Department — *continued*
    Secretary, **1979:** 1818
    Under Secretary, **1978:** 1753
  Council on Wage and Price Stability, Chairman,
    1980–81: 2726
  Energy Department, Secretary, **1979:** 1290
  Federal Reserve System, Board of Governors,
    Chairman, **1978:** 64
  General Services Administrator, **1979:** 448
  Health, Education, and Welfare Department,
    Secretary, **1979:** 1270
  Justice Department
    Attorney General, **1979:** 1272, 1401
    Deputy Attorney General, **1977:** 2085
  Law Enforcement Assistance Administrator,
    1979: 294
  Management and Budget, Office of, Director,
    1977: 1635, 1636
  National Endowment for the Arts, Chairman,
    1977: 1522, 1534
  National Labor Relations Board, General Coun-
    sel, **1979:** 1976
  Peace Corps, Director, **1978:** 2072
  Presidential Advisory Board on Ambassadorial
    Appointments, Chairman, **1979:** 2034
  Special Representative for Trade Negotiations,
    1979: 1418
  State Department
    Ambassadors at Large, **1980–81:** 2073, 2718
    Coordinator for Refugee Affairs, **1979:** 2066
    Secretary, **1980–81:** 781
  Transportation Department, Secretary, **1979:**
    1285; **1979:** 1273
  United Nations, U.S. Representative, **1979:**
    1436, 1455
  United States Arms Control and Disarmament
    Agency
    Director, **1979:** 2270
    Director and SALT Negotiator, **1978:** 1744
  U.S. district judges
    District of Columbia, **1977:** 1750
    Missouri, **1977:** 372
  White House staff
    Assistant to the President, **1979:** 1422
    Assistant to the President for Public Liaison,
      1978: 1358
    Assistant Special Counselor on Inflation,
      1978: 2184
    Correspondence, Chief, **1977:** 1533
    Counsels to the President, **1979:** 1422, 1823;
      1980–81: 2750
    Deputy to the Chief of Staff, **1979:** 1976
    Messenger Service, Chief, **1977:** 1383
    Military Office, Director, **1977:** 1533
    Senior Adviser to the President, **1980–81:** 1509
    Telegraph and Transportation Services, Chief,
      1977: 1211

Resignations and Retirements — *continued*
  Wien Air Alaska emergency board, chairman,
    1978: 2158
Resor, Stanley R., **1978:** 1265, 1279, 1516
Resources Conservation Act, **1979:** 1382
Resources Planning Act, **1979:** 1375, 1376, 1382
Retail Federation, American, **1979:** 832
Retired Executives, Service Corps of, **1979:** 1816
Retired People, American Association of, **1979:**
  1630; **1980–81:** 589
Retired Senior Volunteers, **1978:** 1794
Retired Teachers Association, National, **1979:** 1630
Retirement Income Security Act of 1974, Employ-
  ee, **1980–81:** 295, 617
Retirement Income Security Act transfers, Em-
  ployee, **1978:** 1782, 2300
Retirement Reform Act, District of Columbia,
  1979: 2144
Retirement systems, **1977:** 911, 1094, 1109, 1111,
  1847, 2156
Rettgers, Forrest I., **1979:** 957; **1980–81:** 292
Reuss, Repr. Henry S., **1977:** 1628, 1699; **1978:**
  803; **1980–81:** 573, 2113
Reuther, Walter, **1980–81:** 2549
Revelle, Roger, **1980–81:** 1713, 1847
Revenue Act of 1978, **1978:** 1989, 2024; **1979:** 2072
Revenue sharing, general.
  See General revenue sharing.
Rexed, Dr. Bror, **1978:** 1569
Reyes, Ben, **1978:** 1328
Reyes, Tony G., **1979:** 942
Reynolds, Allan L., **1979:** 367, 377
Reynolds, Burt, **1980–81:** 1405
Reynolds, Charles McKinley, Jr., **1980–81:** 1405
Reynolds, David P., **1980–81:** 892
Reynolds, Hobson R., **1977:** 1482
Reynolds, James J.
  Emergency Boards to investigate railway labor
    disputes, Chairman, **1979:** 819, 1697, 2247
  Mention, **1979:** 1999
Reynolds, James M., **1977:** 1613, 1614
Reynolds Electric and Engineering Co., **1980–81:**
  1403
Reynolds Metals Co., **1980–81:** 892
Reynoso, Cruz, **1977:** 182; **1979:** 450, 812
Rezende, Enrico, **1978:** 635, 636
Rhett, John T., **1979:** 1016, 1019
Rhoades, Dennis K., **1980–81:** 1591
Rhoads, James B., **1978:** 1955
Rhode Island
  Disaster declaration, **1978:** 328, 334
  Emergency declaration, **1978:** 302
  President's visit, **1978:** 331, 339, 414; **1979:** 2055,
    2059
  U.S. attorney, **1978:** 1035, 1071
  U.S. district judge, **1977:** 807
  U.S. marshal, **1979:** 2249

Rhode Island Indian Claims Settlement Act, **1978:** 1695

Rhoden, Thomas Arny, **1977:** 2037, 2038

Rhodes, Repr. John J., **1977:** 251, 1280, 1912; **1978:** 148, 1530; **1980–81:** 966, 2797, 2822

Rhodes, Milford, **1978:** 952

Rhodesia.
  See Zimbabwe.

Rhome, Frances Dodson, **1980–81:** 1332, 1337

Rhyne, Genitha, **1979:** 1408

Ribicoff, Sen. Abraham, **1977:** 99, 1411, 1491, 1567, 1825; **1978:** 399, 498, 500, 526, 897, 934, 1468, 1509, 1516, 1570, 1665, 1667, 1736, 1754, 1755, 1757, 1763, 1765, 1782, 1855, 1889–1892, 1966, 2268; **1980–81:** 483, 616, 2283, 2286
  Legislation passage leadership
    Department of Education, **1979:** 756, 1728, 1776, 1957, 1959
    Ethics in Government Act of 1978 amendments, **1979:** 1130
    Trade Agreements Act, **1979:** 1312
    U.S. foreign assistance programs reorganization, **1979:** 1230
  Meeting with the President (Digest), **1979:** 178
  National health plan support, **1979:** 1011, 1027, 1411, 1635
  Reelection, decision not to seek, **1979:** 782
  Regulatory reform legislation support, **1979:** 2178, 2272

Ribicoff, Lois M., **1979:** 24

Ricco, Felix, **1979:** 1468n.

Rice, Donald B., **1980–81:** 1149, 1246

Rice, Emmett J., **1979:** 663, 899, 1921

Rice, Lois D., **1978:** 1208

Rice, Stuart A., **1980–81:** 1149, 1246

Rice, Walter Herbert, **1980–81:** 654, 720

Richard B. Russell Project, Ga., **1977:** 208, 1394

Richards, Ann, **1978:** 1135; **1979:** 2044

Richards, Deborah D., **1977:** 1776

Richardson, Archie G., Jr., **1978:** 1468

Richardson, Elliot L., **1977:** 17, 252; **1980–81:** 2073

Richardson, Mary, **1979:** 1982

Richardson, Robert E., **1980–81:** 929

Richburg, Tyree A., **1978:** 1407

Richley, J. Phillip, **1977:** 2028

Richman, Harold, **1977:** 530

Richmond, Repr. Frederick W., **1977:** 2181

Richmond, Dr. Julius B., **1977:** 530, 1080, 1085, 1665; **1978:** 885; **1979:** 815, 2090, 2112; **1980–81:** 261

Richmond, Va., **1979:** 630, 1817

Richter, Walter H., **1979:** 2191

Rickover, Adm. Hyman G., **1977:** 146, 303, 596, 949, 1024, 1707, 2037, 2068; **1978:** 239, 283, 949, 1052, 1067, 1385, 1446; **1980–81:** 752, 1060, 2248, 2287

Riddell, Tom H., Jr., **1973:** 2054

Ridesharing, National Task Force on, **1979:** 2022, 2023

Ridesharing program, Federal facility, **1980–81:** 271

Ridgway, Gen. Matthew B., **1977:** 1893

Ridgway, Rick, **1978:** 1558

Ridgway, Rozanne L., **1977:** 783, 807; **1979:** 2270; **1980–81:** 334

Riegle, Sen. Donald W., Jr., **1977:** 1072, 1628; **1978:** 416, 1933, 2110; **1979:** 956, 2081; **1980–81:** 27, 770

Riehl, Jack B., **1979:** 1448

Rietze, Harry L., **1979:** 1002

Riffle, Nancy L., **1978:** 802

Right-to-work laws, **1978:** 1993

Riles, Wilson C., **1978:** 896, 935

Riley, Col. Leonard J., **1977:** 1058

Riley, Richard W., **1977:** 1477; **1978:** 1586, 2198, 2209; **1979:** 463

Riley, Gov. Richard W., **1980–81:** 297, 303, 1762, 2563

Rinker, Doug, **1980–81:** 1453, 1454

Rinzler, Ralph C., **1980–81:** 1513, 1514n.

Rios, Richard J.
  See Community Services Administration, Director.

Riperton, Minnie, **1977:** 566

Ritchey, Craig S., **1978:** 1026

Ritchey, Mrs. John, **1977:** 311, 326

Ritter, Patricia K., **1978:** 1500, 1506

River of No Return, Idaho, **1980–81:** 416, 1408–1411

River of No Return Wilderness, **1978:** 2279

Rivera, José A., **1979:** 435, 441

Rivera, Tomas, **1978:** 408; **1980–81:** 264

Rivers, Richard R., **1979:** 1678; **1980–81:** 1447

Rivers, preservation of wild and scenic, **1977:** 980

Rivers System, National Wild and Scenic.
  See National Wild and Scenic Rivers System.

Rives, Richard, **1980–81:** 2238

Rizzo, Frank L., **1980–81:** 726, 736

Rizzutto, Phil, **1980–81:** 2646

RKO General Broadcasting, **1980–81:** 2430

Roach, Archbishop John R., **1978:** 2059

Roadless area review and evaluation (RARE) lands, **1979:** 151, 669, 670; **1980–81:** 159, 1142

Roanoke, Va., **1977:** 1653

Robb, Charles S., **1977:** 1653, 1657, 1660

Robb, Lt. Gov. Charles S., **1978:** 969; **1979:** 631; **1980–81:** 17

Robb, Lynda Johnson, **1978:** 398, 970, 971; **1979:** 826, 2008, 2044

Robbins, Warren, **1978:** 1713

Robelo, Alfonso, **1979:** 1722

Roberts, David G., **1980–81:** 1599

Roberts, George B., Jr., **1979:** 1617, 1679

Roberts, Hope M., **1980–81:** 2817

Roberts, J. Milnor, **1980–81:** 374
Roberts, Joseph L., Jr., **1979:** 33n.
Roberts, Louise R., **1980–81:** 928
Roberts, Oral, **1977:** 251
Roberts, Repr. Ray, **1977:** 2179; **1978:** 229, 1965;
  1980–81: 2315
Robertson, Cliff, **1978:** 394
Robertson, Reuben B., III, **1980–81:** 1146, 1147,
  1150
Robins, Eva, **1978:** 469; **1980–81:** 1399
Robinson, Benjamin B., **1980–81:** 928
Robinson, David, **1980–81:** 1867
Robinson, Douglas G., **1977:** 98
Robinson, Gilbert, **1980–81:** 2748n.
Robinson, Glen E., **1978:** 711, 712
Robinson, Glen O., **1979:** 1334
Robinson, Gregory, **1978:** 2068
Robinson, Harold Frank, **1980–81:** 323
Robinson, Hugh Granville, **1980–81:** 2070
Robinson, Repr. J. Kenneth, **1980–81:** 2233
Robinson, James K., **1977:** 1031
Robinson, Mary Lou, **1979:** 327, 328
Robinson, Olin, **1980–81:** 1846
Robinson, Prezell R., **1980–81:** 509
Robinson, Randall M., **1980–81:** 509
Robison, Olin C., **1978:** 510, 571; **1979:** 730, 787
Robustelli, Andy, **1980–81:** 2646
Roche, Mr. and Mrs. Phillip, **1977:** 309, 310
Roche, William J., **1978:** 455; **1980–81:** 1048
Rochester, Minn., **1978:** 1822
Rochester, N.Y., **1980–81:** 2521
Rochlin, Robert S., **1977:** 1565
Rock Island Railroad, **1980–81:** 1010, 2227, 2231
Rock Island Railroad labor dispute
  Agreement announcement, **1979:** 1999
  Emergency Board establishment, **1979:** 1695
  News conferences (Checklist), **1979:** 1706, 1787
  President's decision to intervene, **1979:** 1708
Rockefeller, David, **1977:** 502; **1978:** 770
Rockefeller, Gov. John D., IV, **1977:** 404; **1978:** 54,
  66, 265, 415, 416, 1004, 1005, 1349, 1729–
  1731; **1980–81:** 471, 1644, 2472
  Coal production increase actions, **1979:** 648, 905,
    1346, 1643
  White House Conference on Balanced National
    Growth and Economic Development,
    State representative chairman, **1979:** 65,
    67
Rockefeller, Nelson A., **1977:** 10, 1931; **1979:** 189,
  217
Rockefeller, Sharon Percy, **1977:** 1509, 1713, 1755
Rockwell International, **1979:** 242
Rocky Mountain Farmers Union, **1977:** 557
Roddy, Mary Jane, **1979:** 2076
Rodenticide Act extension, Federal Insecticide,
  Fungicide, and, **1980–81:** 2814
Roderick, David M., **1980–81:** 732, 736, 1405
Roderick, Lee, **1977:** 1059

Rodgers, David H., **1978:** 1721, 1772; **1979:** 23, 46,
  90
Rodgers, George, **1980–81:** 2563
Rodgers, Richard, **1977:** 1249
Rodham, Hillary, **1977:** 2101, 2130; **1978:** 89, 232;
  1980–81: 1149, 1246
Rodino, Repr. Peter W., Jr., **1977:** 505, 923, 928,
  1152, 1383, 1416, 1574, 1675, 1745, 1919,
  1923; **1978:** 1139, 1140, 1243, 1244, 1247,
  1267, 1554, 1854
  Campaign appearance with the President, **1980–
    81:** 2276
  Federal civil justice system, **1979:** 340, 341
  Legislation passage leadership
    Economic compact between New Jersey and
      New York, **1979:** 2297
    Fair Housing Amendment, **1980–81:** 1098
    Federal Magistrates Act, **1979:** 1849
    Judicial Councils Reform and Judicial Con-
      duct and Disability Act, **1980–81:** 2241
    Motor Carrier Act, **1980–81:** 1267
    Privacy Protection Act, **1980–81:** 2218
  Letter to the President, **1980–81:** 1468
  Meeting with the President (Digest), **1980–81:**
    492
  Mentions, **1979:** 1410; **1980–81:** 1718
Rodino, Peter W., III, **1979:** 1776
Rodriguez, Alexander R. H., **1980–81:** 949
Rodriguez, Armando M., **1978:** 1510, 1517
Rodriguez, Irving Flores, **1979:** 1597
Rodriguez, Reymundo, **1977:** 530
Rodriguez, Ricardo A., **1980–81:** 33
Rodriguez, Mr. and Mrs. Stephen, **1979:** 808n.
Rodriguez case, Dallas, Tex., **1978:** 1181, 1328
Rody, Frederick A., Jr., **1979:** 1961, 1977
Roe, David, **1979:** 1468n.
Roe, John A., **1977:** 1796
Roe, Repr. Robert A., **1978:** 1278; **1979:** 666;
  1980–81: 2276
Roel, Santiago, **1979:** 281n., 791, 802, 812
Rogalski, Bernard, **1980–81:** 1851
Rogers, Barbara B., **1979:** 466
Rogers, Gen. Bernard W., **1977:** 1021; **1979:** 363,
  378, 1043, 1882; **1980–81:** 2369
Rogers, Bill, **1979:** 738, 770; **1980–81:** 259
Rogers, Coy W., **1977:** 2089, 2090; **1978:** 231
Rogers, Harold E., Jr., **1978:** 1879; **1979:** 1439
Rogers, Lida, **1980–81:** 1440, 1470
Rogers, Michael V., **1979:** 977
Rogers, Paul, **1980–81:** 264
Rogers, Repr. Paul G., **1977:** 185, 1460, 1778, 1903,
  2105; **1978:** 769, 792, 1034; **1979:** 385
Rogers, Phyllis, **1977:** 306
Rogers, William, **1979:** 1823
Rogers, William D., **1977:** 1543
Rogers, William J., **1977:** 508, 1749, 1887
Rogers Day, Will (Proc. 4698), **1979:** 2078
Rogoff, Martin A., **1977:** 815

Rohatyn, Felix, **1980–81:** 1714
Roldós, Jaime, **1979:** 1293
Rolett, Danny, **1979:** 1705
Rollins, Hazel R., **1977:** 1250, 1266; **1979:** 1654, 2044
Romania
  Ambassador to U.S., **1978:** 2059
  Clothespin exports, **1979:** 233
  Emigration to Israel and U.S., **1979:** 979
  Emigration to U.S., **1980–81:** 981
  Joint statement, **1978:** 743, 753
  President Nicolae Ceausescu, **1977:** 251, 327; **1978:** 570, 734, 735, 738, 740, 743, 753
  Secretary of the Treasury's visit, **1978:** 2187
  Trade agreement, **1977:** 1055, 1057
  Trade with U.S., **1978:** 1031–1033; **1979:** 978, 979, 2223; **1980–81:** 980, 982
  U.S. Ambassador, **1977:** 1673, 1700
  U.S. disaster assistance, **1977:** 327
Romanian Orthodox Church, Patriarch Justin, meeting with the President, **1979:** 842
Romanian-U.S. Joint Economic Commission, **1980–81:** 981
Romero, Edward L., **1980–81:** 1439n., 1447, 1939
Romero, Archbishop Oscar Arnulfo, **1980–81:** 534
Romero-Barcelo, Gov. Carlos, **1977:** 279; **1978:** 934; **1979:** 1666; **1980–81:** 291
Romney, Marion G., **1978:** 2088
Romulo, Carlos P., **1977:** 1754; **1978:** 1379
Roncalio, Repr. Teno, **1977:** 1978, 1980; **1978:** 409
Rondon, Fernando E., **1980–81:** 1577, 1599, 2752
Ronstadt, Linda, **1979:** 745
Rooney, Art, **1980–81:** 371
Rooney, Fred, **1980–81:** 2228
Roosevelt, Eleanor, **1979:** 1521
Roosevelt, Eleanor, National Historic Site, **1977:** 1028
Roosevelt, Franklin D.
  Automobile industry revitalization, **1980–81:** 1986, 1988
  Blind persons legislation, **1980–81:** 808
  Channel Islands National Park, Calif., establishment, **1980–81:** 432
  Environmental protection leadership, **1980–81:** 416
  GI bill approval, **1980–81:** 851
  Great Depression, **1979:** 2025
  Human rights position, **1979:** 1521
  Influence on President's life, **1980–81:** 2390
  Mentions, **1979:** 2016; **1980–81:** 397, 766, 1532
  New Deal programs, **1980–81:** 538, 583, 630, 1603, 1994, 2142, 2149, 2159, 2245, 2273, 2282, 2295, 2307, 2342, 2346, 2390, 2398, 2403, 2409, 2416, 2419, 2441, 2466, 2504, 2530, 2536, 2544, 2548, 2553, 2564, 2581, 2598, 2599, 2604, 2625, 2628, 2635, 2661, 2667
  1944 Presidential campaign, **1980–81:** 992

Roosevelt, Franklin D. — *continued*
  Power of fear philosophy, **1979:** 995, 1012
  Quoted, **1980–81:** 280, 1506, 2192, 2535, 2551, 2554, 2581, 2599, 2604, 2623, 2628, 2636, 2642
  Veterans programs, **1980–81:** 1383
Roosevelt, Franklin D., Jr., **1979:** 24
Roosevelt, James, **1977:** 464; **1979:** 977, 1604
Roosevelt, Theodore, **1979:** 775, 1995; **1980–81:** 415, 1142, 1683
Roosevelt, Theodore, IV, **1979:** 774
Ropp, Theodore, **1980–81:** 1047
Rose, Repr. Charles, **1979:** 982
Rose, Repr. Mary, **1980–81:** 1001
Rose, Mason H. V., **1979:** 2192
Rose, Pete, **1978:** 1668; **1980–81:** 653, 2251
Rosen, Howard T., **1979:** 1668, 1680
Rosen, Nathaniel, **1978:** 1356
Rosenberg, Henry A., Jr., **1979:** 1614n.
Rosenberg, Maurice, **1979:** 976, 984
Rosenblatt, Peter R., **1977:** 1303, 1308; **1980–81:** 2614
Rosenblith, Walter A., **1978:** 2264
Rosenquist, James A., **1979:** 435, 441
Rosensaft, Hadassah, **1978:** 1974; **1980–81:** 822
Rosenthal, Repr. Benjamin S., **1977:** 644, 788, 1136; **1978:** 1530; **1979:** 666, 1668, 1680; **1980–81:** 2194
Rosenthal, Merilyn Carol, **1978:** 926
Rosh Hashanah, **1979:** 1627; **1980–81:** 1670
Roskelley, John, **1978:** 1558
Rosow, Jerome M., **1978:** 823
Ross, David Gray, **1980–81:** 1098
Ross, Diana, **1979:** 375
Ross, Stanford G., **1978:** 1468, 1471
Ross, Thomas B., **1977:** 195
Rosser, James M., **1980–81:** 1443, 1470
Rossi, Alice S., **1977:** 526
Rossie, J. Richard, **1978:** 1086, 1111, 1135
Rossini, Frederick D., **1977:** 2046
Rossman, Mike, **1978:** 1878
Rostenkowski, Repr. Dan, **1977:** 147, 936, 1210, 1778, 1825, 1903, 1931, 2105; **1978:** 282, 328, 770, 802, 983–985, 1809; **1979:** 943, 1935, 1937, 2081; **1980–81:** 1852, 2344, 2780
Rostker, Bernard Daniel, **1979:** 1419, 1604; **1980–81:** 1277, 1653
Rostow, Elspeth D., **1978:** 455; **1980–81:** 1447
Roswell, Ga., **1980–81:** 1746
Roszkowski, Stanley J., **1977:** 1307
Rotary International, **1977:** 1506; **1978:** 2073; **1980–81:** 334
ROTC.
  See Reserve Officers' Training Corps.
Roth, Sen. William V., Jr., **1979:** 1312, 1882; **1980–81:** 1548, 2829

Rothbein, Ludwig, **1978:** 407
Rothberg, Sam, **1978:** 2269
Rothchild, Kennon V., **1978:** 1500, 1506; **1980–81:** 1048, 1111
Rothstein, Barbara J., **1979:** 2207
Rougeau, Weldon J., **1980–81:** 1502
Rouillard, John C., **1979:** 932
Roupe, Diane S., **1978:** 2069
Rousakis, John P., **1978:** 543, 748, 2080, 2082, 2188; **1979:** 402
Rouse, Jim, **1980–81:** 2560
Rowan, Carl T., **1980–81:** 107
Rowlett, John D., **1979:** 1448
Rowley, Janet D., **1979:** 686
Roy, Bill, **1978:** 1813, 1820
Roy, Elsijane Trimble, **1977:** 1827, 1931
Roy, William R., **1980–81:** 1445, 1470
Roybal, Repr. Edward R., **1977:** 1427; **1978:** 1947; **1980–81:** 1835
Roybal, Repr. and Mrs. Edward R., **1979:** 1662
Royer, Charles T., **1980–81:** 108n., 1405, 2560
Royer, Robert L., **1979:** 1339n.
Royo, Aristides, **1977:** 1383; **1979:** 683, 836, 1628, 2251
Rubal, Marina, **1979:** 466
Rubber Agreement, 1979, International Natural, **1980–81:** 591
Rubber industry, **1979:** 161, 752
Rubber industry, natural, **1980–81:** 2992
Rubenstein, David, **1980–81:** 1101
Rubin, Al, **1979:** 1678
Rubin, Alvin B., **1977:** 1483, 1484
Rubin, Florence, **1977:** 816
Rubin, Julia S., **1980–81:** 929
Rubin, Robert E., **1980–81:** 2117
Rubin, Seymour Jeffrey, **1980–81:** 2731
Ruckelshaus, Jill, **1978:** 1135; **1980–81:** 605, 608
Rudd, Joe, **1978:** 2158
Ruder, William, **1980–81:** 1405
Rudolph, Susanne H., **1978:** 2264
Rudolph, Wilma, **1979:** 25
Ruff, Charles F. C., **1977:** 1195, 1213; **1979:** 1883; **1980–81:** 521
Ruff, S. Eugene, **1980–81:** 533, 564
Running schedule, President's, **1979:** 1747
Runnion, Marjorie B., **1979:** 466
Rupple, Brenton H., **1978:** 506, 571; **1979:** 1022, 1043
Rural areas
  Administration's accomplishments and goals, **1980–81:** 144, 2952, 2960
  Development policies and initiatives
    Administration's policy, **1979:** 2273, 2281
    Communication systems, **1979:** 270
    Energy
      Conservation, **1979:** 623
      Development, **1979:** 843
    Health care, **1979:** 75, 77, 154, 794

Rural areas — *continued*
  Development policies — *continued*
    Housing, **1979:** 74, 77, 136, 154, 218, 794, 843
    Loans and grants, **1979:** 74, 75, 600–602
    Training and employment, **1979:** 75, 154, 600, 602
    Transportation, **1979:** 75, 77, 154, 1143
    Water and sewer services, **1979:** 75, 77, 154, 733, 795
  Educational programs, **1980–81:** 2127
  Federal initiatives, **1978:** 2106, 2147
  Federal policy
    Comprehensive program, **1979:** 154, 794
    Review, **1979:** 73, 77
  Income, **1979:** 600, 602
  Legislation, **1979:** 77, 153, 599
  National Main Street Center, **1980–81:** 932
  National policy, **1978:** 1782
  President's comments on attitudes and values, **1979:** 792
  Private investment, **1979:** 600, 602
  Progress during administration, **1979:** 154, 570
  Transportation legislation, **1978:** 222
  Women representatives, meeting with the President, **1980–81:** 774 (Digest), 775 (Checklist)
  See also Agriculture.
Rural Coalition, **1979:** 1824, 2276
Rural Development Policy Act, **1980–81:** 1916, 1920, 1947
Rural Development, Working Group on, **1979:** 75
Rural Development Council, **1979:** 2275
Rural Electric Cooperative Association, National, **1977:** 1119, 1965; **1978:** 1101; **1980–81:** 1110, 1714
  Rural Electric Cooperative Youth Tour, National, **1977:** 1119
Rural Electrification Administration, **1977:** 258; **1978:** 1666, 1670, 2107, 2109; **1979:** 1511
  Loans, **1980–81:** 1917
  Roosevelt, Franklin, establishment by, **1980–81:** 539, 583, 630, 1603, 2142, 2149, 2390, 2398, 2403, 2409, 2416, 2530, 2548, 2553, 2564, 2581, 2597, 2598, 2605, 2625, 2628, 2635, 2662
Rural health clinic services bill, **1977:** 2104
Rural Telephone Bank, **1978:** 506; **1980–81:** 293
Rural Water Association, National, **1980–81:** 1429
Rusher, Albert H., **1978:** 515
Rushing, Byron, **1980–81:** 2175
Rusk, David, **1979:** 1851, 1863
Rusk, Dean, **1977:** 78, 79, 90, 1534, 1749, 1787; **1979:** 1823; **1980–81:** 720
Rusk, Howard A., **1979:** 2089; **1980–81:** 810, 813, 826
Russell, Harold J., **1979:** 464; **1980–81:** 808

Russell, Herman J., **1977:** 1506; **1978:** 1500, 1506; **1980–81:** 1756

Russell, R. Robert.
   See Wage and Price Stability, Council on, Director.

Russell, Richard B., Project, Ga., **1977:** 208, 1394

Russo, Repr. Martin A., **1980–81:** 2782
   Airline deregulation legislation support, **1979:** 1951
   China, People's Republic of, visit to, **1979:** 667
   Meeting with the President (Digest), **1979:** 731
   Mention, **1979:** 1940
   Small business regulatory reform legislation support, **1979:** 2143

Rustin, Bayard, **1978:** 1974; **1979:** 321, 996; **1980–81:** 822

Ruth, Henry, **1980–81:** 1406, 1467

Rutherford, Edgar C., **1977:** 1629, 1650

Rutherford, F. James, **1977:** 1475, 1483; **1980–81:** 425, 608, 841

Ruttenberg, Stanley, **1979:** 2218

Ruvin, Harvey, **1980–81:** 1405

Rwanda
   President Juvenal Habyarimana, **1980–81:** 1928
   U.S. Ambassador, **1979:** 1726, 1785

Ryan, Cleve, **1977:** 1506

Ryan, E. H., **1979:** 1468n.

Ryan, Repr. Leo J., **1978:** 2068, 2099

Ryor, John, **1977:** 744

Rzepca, Fred, **1979:** 466

Sá Carniero, Francisco, **1980–81:** 1234, 1245

Saadi, Elias T., **1978:** 794

Sabimbona, Simon, **1980–81:** 268

Sabine River Compact Administration, **1978:** 1466

Sabo, Martin O., **1977:** 1477

Sachar, Abraham, **1980–81:** 822

Sachs, Howard F., **1979:** 899, 900; **1980–81:** 1470, 1471

Sachs, Steven, **1978:** 1799

Sacks, Howard R., **1978:** 1753, 1772; **1979:** 46, 92

Sacramento, Calif., **1978:** 1946

Sadat, Anwar al-.
   See Egypt, President.

Sadat, Mrs. Anwar al-, **1979:** 522n.

Saeki, Kiichi, **1979:** 2128

Safe Boating Week, National, **1977:** 1080

Safe Drinking Water Act, **1979:** 1360

Safety and Health Administration, Occupational, **1979:** 2181

Safety Reactor Experimental Facility (SAREF), **1977:** 2012

Saffels, Dale Emerson, **1979:** 1786, 1787

Sagan, Carl, **1980–81:** 264

Saginaw, Mich., **1980–81:** 2546

Sagner, Alan, **1979:** 2297

Sailors' Snug Harbor, N.Y., **1980–81:** 1431

St. Christopher-Nevis-Anguilla, U.S. Special Representative, **1977:** 1530; **1979:** 980

St. George, Joseph I., **1978:** 1072

St. Germain, Repr. Fernand J., **1977:** 1058; **1978:** 1695; **1980–81:** 573

St. Germaine, Richard D., **1980–81:** 258, 1839

St. Joseph, Mo., **1979:** 1817

St. Lawrence Seaway, **1979:** 2037

Saint Lawrence Seaway Development Corporation, **1977:** 1306; **1978:** 1333; **1979:** 1319; **1980–81:** 237, 1418

St. Louis, Mo., **1978:** 1910, 2075, 2080; **1979:** 1455, 1511; **1980–81:** 2103, 2552

St. Louis Airport, Mo., **1977:** 286

Saint Lucia
   Ammbassador to U.S., **1980–81:** 775
   Independence celebrations, U.S. delegation, **1979:** 293
   Trade beneficiary developing country designation, **1980–81:** 550
   U.S. Ambassador, **1980–81:** 1860, 1947
   U.S. Minister, **1979:** 664
   U.S. Special Representative, **1977:** 1530

St. Marie, Satenig S., **1977:** 196, 1944, 1966; **1978:** 231

St. Patrick's Day, **1977:** 464; **1978:** 516; **1979:** 432; **1980–81:** 474, 500

St. Paul, Minn., **1979:** 1455, 1457

St. Petersburg, Fla., **1980–81:** 893, 2157, 2166

St. Simons Island, Ga., **1978:** 228, 570

Saint Stephen's Crown, **1979:** 2024

Saint Vincent
   Independence ceremonies, U.S. delegation, **1979:** 2042
   Trade beneficiary developing country designation, **1980–81:** 550
   U.S. Special Representative, **1979:** 980; **1977:** 1530

Sakharov, Andrei, **1980–81:** 194, 357, 1437

Sakharov, Mrs. Andrei, **1980–81:** 357

Salaries, Commission on Executive, Legislative, and Judicial, **1980–81:** 1947, 2867

Saldana, Lupe, **1980–81:** 563

Saldise, Teresa, **1977:** 816

Sales, Eugenio de Arauio Cardinal, **1978:** 640

Saletic, William G., **1979:** 1001

Salij, Elena A., **1980–81:** 927

Salisbury, Harrison E., **1980–81:** 2608

Salk, Dr. Jonas E., **1977:** 1215, 1228; **1980–81:** 645, 1057, 1405

Salmon, Thomas P., **1979:** 43, 93

Salmon fisheries, sockeye, **1977:** 548

Salmon River, Idaho, **1978:** 1471, 1475, 1485; **1979:** 1813; **1980–81:** 416, 1408–1410

Saloom, Kaliste J., **1977:** 2028

Salpeter, Edwin E., **1978:** 1760, 1773; **1979:** 46, 93

SALT.
See Strategic arms limitation.
Salt Lake City, Utah, **1978:** 2084
Salter, Hugh, **1977:** 1384
Salute to Learning Day (Proc. 4755), **1980–81:** 841
Salzman, Herbert, **1977:** 965, 1030
Sambito, Joe, **1980–81:** 2603
Samoa, American, disaster assistance, **1979:** 2106
Samoa, Western, U.S. Ambassador, **1979:** 1040, 1043
Sample, Winona E., **1978:** 1191
Sampson, Robert G., **1979:** 464, 2192
Samuels, Howard, **1980–81:** 264
Samuels, Sheldon W., **1979:** 686
San Antonio, Tex., **1979:** 2191; **1980–81:** 452, 786, 2622
San Diego, Calif., **1979:** 1866, 1872, 1876, 1883
San Francisco, Calif., **1979:** 807, 1817; **1980–81:** 432, 931, 1402
San Jose, Calif., **1979:** 1817; **1980–81:** 1897, 1900
Sanchez, Delores G., **1978:** 1051
Sanchez, Manuel, **1979:** 466
Sanchez, Manuel A., Jr., **1978:** 390, 416
Sanchez, Archbishop Robert F., **1979:** 1863
Sanchez, Yolanda, **1980–81:** 2075
Sand, Leonard B., **1978:** 711, 712
Sandborn, Mark, **1979:** 1270
Sanders, Carl, **1980–81:** 1512
Sanders, Edward, **1978:** 1457, 1458, 2269; **1979:** 1861, 2009ftn.; **1980–81:** 822
Sanders, Harold Barefoot, Jr., **1979:** 241, 242
Sandison, Gordon, **1977:** 1485
Sandler, Bernice, **1978:** 1086, 1111
Sandler, Marian, **1980–81:** 2559
Sandler, Marion O., **1979:** 1671
Sandstrom, Eric G., **1978:** 1669
Sang, Bahk, **1980–81:** 305
Santamaria, Sarah I., **1978:** 1515
Santini, Repr. Jim, **1977:** 372; **1980–81:** 1013, 2237
Santos, Lucille L., **1980–81:** 258, 1839
Sao Tome, U.S. Ambassador, **1978:** 88, 149
Sapelo Island, Ga., **1979:** 675, 2138; **1980–81:** 1376
Saragat, Giuseppe, **1980–81:** 1241
Sarasin, Repr. Ronald A., **1978:** 416
Saratoga, U.S.S., **1979:** 906; **1980–81:** 726, 878, 1633, 2043, 2437
Sarauskas, R. George, **1979:** 914
Sarbanes, Repr. Paul S., **1978:** 802, 1695
Sarbanes, Sen. Paul S., **1980–81:** 15, 383, 2113, 2378
Sarkis, Elias, **1978:** 1537, 1678
Sarokin, H. Lee, **1979:** 1786, 1787
Sarros, Peter, **1978:** 1723, 1808
Sasser, James Franklin, **1979:** 977
Sasser, Sen. James R., **1978:** 526, 802, 897, 1859, 1862, 2147; **1979:** 2036, 2044, 2085, 2110; **1980–81:** 333, 616, 2118, 2122
Satellite Corporation, Communication, **1978:** 2146; **1979:** 271

Sato, Frank S., **1979:** 398, 402
Saud al-Faisal, **1977:** 1826, 1903, 1932
Saudi Arabia
Ambassador to U.S., **1979:** 1318
Crown Prince Fahd Bin Abd al-Aziz al-Saud. *See* Saudi Arabia, Crown Prince.
Foreign Minister, **1977:** 1826, 1903, 1932
Crude oil production, **1979:** 1226, 1246, 1766
Interview remarks, **1978:** 1590, 1779, 1780
King Khalid bin Abd al-Aziz Al-Sa'ud, **1977:** 1825, 2120; **1978:** 1537, 1554, 1876
Middle East peace settlement position, **1979:** 456
Oil supplies, **1980–81:** 2025
Plane sales, **1978:** 333, 339, 492, 777, 778, 782, 801, 807, 808, 848, 849, 866, 867, 896, 899, 901, 915; **1980–81:** 2170, 2431, 2542
President's visit, **1977:** 1825, 1983, 2077, 2188, 2202; **1978:** 18
U.S. Ambassador, **1977:** 993, 1031, 1162, 1826; **1978:** 526; **1979:** 983, 1585, 2105
U.S. delegation's visit, **1979:** 436
U.S. military bases, **1979:** 350
U.S. relations, **1979:** 1585
Saudi Arabia, Crown Prince (Fahd Bin Abd al-Aziz Al-Sa'ud), **1977:** 991, 1006, 1010, 1825, 2043, 2190; **1978:** 19, 264, 1554
Crude oil production increase commitment, **1979:** 1226
Palestinian problem position, **1979:** 456, 1585
Visit to U.S., **1979:** 182, 240, 242
Saug, Wilton S., **1978:** 1974
Saunders, Frank A., **1980–81:** 305
Saunders, Harold H., **1977:** 8; **1978:** 452, 458, 2059, 2268; **1980–81:** 87, 930
Saunders, Louise H., **1979:** 230
Savage, Frank, **1980–81:** 1717, 1848, 2074n., 2726, 2727, 2870, 2874
Savannah, Ga., **1978:** 538, 539; **1979:** 1817, 1884; **1980–81:** 501
Save Your Vision Week, **1977:** 157; **1978:** 257
(Proc. 4637), **1979:** 220
(Proc. 4718), **1980–81:** 234
Savery-Pot Hook, Colo., Wyo., **1977:** 208
Savimbe, Jonas, **1978:** 851
Savings Bonds, Interagency Committee for the Purchase of United States, **1977:** 531, 532; **1980–81:** 653
Savings Bonds, United States, **1978:** 574; **1979:** 309, 2284
Savings Bond Campaign, **1980–81:** 653
Savings Bonds Committee, Federal Interagency, **1978:** 574; **1979:** 2285
Savings and loan associations, interest rates, **1979:** 929
Sawhill, John C.
See Energy, Department of, Deputy Secretary; Synthetic Fuels Corporation, Board of Directors, Chairman.

Saxon, John David, **1978:** 1026
Sayed, Ali al, **1979:** 548n.
Sayre, Robert M., **1978:** 295, 304
Scannell, Francis X., **1977:** 196
Scarr, Harry Alan, **1980–81:** 1290
Schachter, Oscar, **1980–81:** 2731
Schaefer, Allan, **1977:** 1222
Schaefer, Philip, **1977:** 816; **1980–81:** 1332, 1337
Schaefer, William, **1978:** 1797
Schaefer, William Donald, **1979:** 1406, 1413
Schaeffer, Edward D., **1977:** 1438, 1439
Schaeffer, Milton T., **1979:** 466
Schaeffer, Philip A., **1980–81:** 377, 379
Schafer, Maj. James, **1980–81:** 786
Schaffer, Beverly K., **1978:** 411; **1979:** 23
Schaffer, Gloria, **1978:** 1270, 1279
Schaller, Don and Carolyn, **1980–81:** 2466
Schapiro, Ruth, **1978:** 1711
Scharansky, Anatoly, **1977:** 1110
Scharf, Helen M., **1979:** 687
Scharlau, Winifred, **1980–81:** 682n.
Schatz, Julius, **1980–81:** 822
Schaufele, William E., Jr., **1977:** 1152, 1163; **1978:** 87, 149
Schecter, Jerrold L., **1977:** 1613, 1614, 1651, 1755, 1756, 1796, 1827, 1932, 2007; **1979:** 436, 768, 1143, 1787
Schector, Jay, **1978:** 1974
Scheel, Walter, **1978:** 1153, 1281, 1284, 1289, 1310; **1979:** 927
Scheidt, Cindy M., **1980–81:** 927
Schell, Orville, **1980–81:** 1439n.
Scheuer, Repr. James H., **1978:** 2003; **1980–81:** 303, 983, 2378
Schieffer, Bob, **1977:** 2187
Schifter, Richard, **1978:** 1974; **1980–81:** 822
Schine, Leonard A., **1979:** 1353
Schirmer, Kitty, **1980–81:** 1429
Schlaudeman, Harry W., **1980–81:** 1710, 1715
Schlesinger, James R., **1977:** 7, 14, 22, 32, 37, 41, 67, 70, 86, 98, 113, 114, 123, 134, 136, 163, 199, 204, 223, 252, 257, 274, 280, 283, 352, 371, 403, 408, 463, 508, 519, 556, 557, 706, 744, 746, 944, 1058, 1072, 1143, 1221, 1225, 1265, 1306, 1336, 1411, 1412, 1437, 1438, 1441, 1532, 1569, 1582, 1584, 1613, 1618, 1648, 1749, 1784, 1786, 1930, 1978, 1979, 1981, 2006, 2069, 2077, 2124, 2223; **1978:** 55, 248, 311, 327, 352, 414, 641, 770, 811, 826, 846, 950, 1112, 1350, 1381, 1453, 1459, 1469, 1471, 1477, 1478, 1644, 1984, 2108, 2237
  See also Energy, Secretary of.
Schlossberg, Stephen I., **1977:** 90
Schmeling, Max, **1978:** 1967
Schmidt, Bob, **1979:** 937, 938n.
Schmidt, Helmut.
  See Germany, Federal Republic of, Chancellor.

Schmidt, Mr. and Mrs. William E., **1977:** 1264
Schmitt, Sen. Harrison H., **1978:** 86, 87; **1979:** 2257n.
Schmitt, John, **1979:** 1468n.
Schmoke, Kurt, **1977:** 784
Schneider, David T., **1977:** 1977, 2006; **1978:** 231
Schneider, Howard A., **1978:** 1511
Schneider, J. Glenn, **1980–81:** 1432
Schneider, Pauline, **1979:** 1921
Schneider, Stanley E., **1977:** 1649
Schneiderman, Leonard, **1979:** 1524
Schneiders, Gregory S., **1977:** 9, 205; **1978:** 330
Schneidman, Harold F., **1978:** 1400, 1407
Schnuhl, Mrs. Harlan, **1977:** 298
Schober, Karl Herbert, **1977:** 508
Schoen, Kenneth F., **1978:** 1193
Schoenberg, Eric A., **1980–81:** 926
Scholars, Commission on Presidential, **1980–81:** 2815
Scholars, Presidential, **1980–81:** 927
Scholars, Woodrow Wilson International Center for, **1979:** 2118, 2248; **1980–81:** 2732, 3023
Scholarships, Board of Foreign, **1980–81:** 272, 2608
School Board Association, National, **1979:** 1018
School Lunch Week, National, **1977:** 1643; **1978:** 1503; **1979:** 1694; **1980–81:** 1925
Schooley, Edna, **1980–81:** 2451n.
Schools.
  See Education.
Schorr, Daniel, **1980–81:** 1017, 1246
Schoumaker, Raoul, **1979:** 1882
Schreiber, Ellen F., **1980–81:** 928
Schreiber, Lt. Gov. Martin J., **1978:** 1952
Schreiber, William M., **1977:** 1407; **1979:** 990
Schricker, Henry, **1979:** 990
Schrier, Morris M., **1979:** 686
Schroeder, Mary M., **1979:** 788
Schroeder, Repr. Patricia, **1978:** 834, 1644, 1667, 1736, 1855; **1980–81:** 1573
Schropp, Jill L., **1979:** 827
Schueler, Ruth, **1979:** 942
Schuler, Harold, **1979:** 1468n.
Schultz, Franklin M., **1980–81:** 1146
Schultz, Frederick H., **1978:** 54, 149; **1979:** 664, 1043, 1044; **1980–81:** 2149
Schultz, James C., **1978:** 1468
Schultz, Theodore W., **1979:** 1963
Schultze, Charles L.
  See Economic Advisers, Council of, Chairman.
Schulz, Charles, **1979:** 2042
Schumacher, E. F., **1977:** 508
Schuman, Adolph P., **1978:** 1483, 1485
Schwab, Mrs. Richard, **1977:** 2046
Schwabe, John and Jean, **1980–81:** 1901
Schwalb Lopez Aldana, Fernando, **1980–81:** 2807
Schwartz, Frederick August Otto, **1977:** 182
Schwartz, Harry K., **1977:** 471, 509

Schwartz, Ira M., **1979:** 2183, 2207
Schwartz, Milton Lewis, **1979:** 1786, 1787
Schwartz, Teresa M., **1978:** 1026
Schwartz, Theodore A., **1979:** 1008
Schwartz, William B., Jr., **1977:** 1475, 1483
Schwartz, William B., III, **1978:** 1380; **1979:** 977
Schweiker, Sen. Richard S., **1977:** 595; **1978:** 525;. **1980–81:** 2099
Schwelb, Frank E., **1979:** 1624, 1680
Schwinden, Lt. Gov. Ted, **1980–81:** 1523
Scianna, Kerin Rodgers, **1979:** 466
Science, Engineering, and Technology Advisory Panel, Intergovernmental, **1979:** 544
Science, National Medal of, **1977:** 2044; **1979:** 2289; **1980–81:** 80
Science, President's Committee on the National Medal of, **1979:** 448; **1980–81:** 2849, 3023
Science, Weizmann Institute of, **1980–81:** 646
Science Board, National, **1977:** 2002, 2006; **1978:** 128, 1358, 1760, 1773
Science Foundation, National.
See National Science Foundation.
Science and technology
Administration's accomplishments and goals, **1980–81:** 146, 2961
Administration's policy, **1979:** 676
Agreement with China, **1979:** 202, 540
Agreement with Soviet Union, **1977:** 1222
Annual reports, **1980–81:** 2702, 3024, 3049
Communications and telecommunications, **1980–81:** 1934
Economic and social role, **1979:** 2146
Egypt and Israel cooperation agreement with U.S., **1980–81:** 1957
Fiscal Year 1982 budget allocations, **1980–81:** 2899
Japan-U.S. agreement, **1980–81:** 816, 826
Legislation, **1980–81:** 2379
Materials imports, **1980–81:** 2920
Minority participation, **1980–81:** 2804
Nuclear waste disposal investigations, **1980–81:** 299
Research and development, **1977:** 2045; **1978:** 2237, 2246; **1979:** 229, 816, 825
Soviet trade restrictions
Letter to Speaker of the House and President of Senate, **1980–81:** 184
Memorandum to Department Secretaries, **1980–81:** 43
Mentions, **1980–81:** 560, 2566
President's comments, **1980–81:** 23, 36, 41, 278, 634, 747
State of the Union, **1980–81:** 196
Validated export licenses suspension, **1980–81:** 63
Space program, **1980–81:** 1620, 2726
Technological information dissemination, **1979:** 2070

Science and technology — *continued*
U.S. international programs, **1980–81:** 406
Science and Technology, United States-Soviet Joint Commission on, **1979:** 539
Science and Technology for Development, Intergovernmental Committee for, **1980–81:** 408
Science and Technology for Development, United Nations Conference on, **1979:** 541; **1980–81:** 408
Science and Technology Policy, Office of, **1979:** 204, 207, 545, 2007; **1980–81:** 364, 1416
Emergency preparedness functions, **1978:** 1129
National Productivity Council, **1978:** 1833, 1835
Science and technology policy functions, **1978:** 412, 413
Telecommunications functions, **1978:** 601–603, 611
Science and Technology Policy, Office of, Director (Frank Press), **1977:** 459, 465, 556, 1046, 1222, 1258, 2045, 2072, 2102; **1978:** 66, 289, 509, 950, 1135, 1187, 1207, 1278, 1669, 1908
Federal emergency management functions (EO 12148), **1979:** 1278
Industrial innovative initiatives, news conference, **1979:** 2070n., 2082
International research and development promotion, **1980–81:** 2087
Latin America and Caribbean, visit to, **1980–81:** 407
Meetings with the President (Digest), **1979:** 899; **1980–81:** 2823
Mention, **1979:** 544
Mount St. Helens eruption, disaster assistance actions, **1980–81:** 952, 956, 959
National Medal of Science, presentation ceremony attendance, **1980–81:** 80
News conferences (Checklist), **1979:** 900; **1980–81:** 335
Nigeria, visit to, **1980–81:** 2108
Nuclear energy, news conference on future uses, **1979:** 2204
Policy Review Committee on Space, Chairman, **1979:** 2149
Presidential Energy Technology Seminar, remarks, **1979:** 1533
Research Apprenticeship Program development, **1979:** 2064
Science and technology regulatory reform responsibilities, **1979:** 536
Space, agriculture, and education agreement with China, **1979:** 204, 206n.
Steelmaking technology research program, development, **1980–81:** 1964
Water research responsibilities, **1979:** 534
Science and Technology Policy, Organization, and Priorities Act of 1976, **1978:** 1639

Sciences, National Academy of, **1979:** 676, 733; **1980–81:** 473
Scientific and Cultural Organization, United Nations Educational, **1980–81:** 2721
Scientific and Technological Cooperation, Institute for.
   See Institute for Scientific and Technological Cooperation.
Scientific and Technological Cooperation, United States-People's Republic of China, Joint Commission on, **1979:** 203
Scitovsky, Anne A., **1979:** 1264
SCORE.
   See Service Corps of Retired Executives.
Scott, Anne Firor, **1979:** 2118
Scott, Basil Y., **1977:** 2028
Scott, Gloria, **1977:** 526
Scott, James E., **1977:** 882
Scott, James Henry, **1978:** 1026
Scott, Jim, **1979:** 1982
Scott, Robert, **1978:** 1006
Scott, Ulric, **1978:** 1826, 1833
Scott, Robert McCance, **1977:** 196, 465
Scott, Robert W., **1977:** 1026, 1031
Scott Newman Drug Abuse Prevention Award, **1980–81:** 1715
Scott Paper Company, **1980–81:** 552, 581
Scouting Recognition Week (Proc. 4706), **1979:** 2209
Scowcroft, Brent, **1978:** 217, 230; **1979:** 1823
Scrader, George R., **1979:** 1671
Scranton, William W., **1977:** 78, 79, 90, 464, 801, 941
Scranton, Pa., **1980–81:** 726
Scripps-Howard National Spelling Bee, **1980–81:** 1008
Scroggin, Fred, **1979:** 443
Scruggs, Jan C., **1980–81:** 1268
Sea, Convention for the Safety of Life at, **1979:** 86
Sea, 1974, International Convention for the Safety of Life at, **1980–81:** 1627
Sea Conference, Law of the, **1977:** 17, 252, 1667, 1795, 1826; **1980–81:** 2073
Sea duty, special pay, **1978:** 1922
Sea Wolf, U.S.S., **1980–81:** 2287
Seabed Arms Control Treaty Review Conference, **1977:** 1162
Seabed Authority, International, **1980–81:** 1284
Seabed Hard Mineral Resources Act, Deep, **1980–81:** 1284
Seabrook, N.H., **1978:** 334, 372
Seafarers Convention, International, **1979:** 1419
Seafarers Union, **1979:** 943
Seaga, Edward, **1980–81:** 3025
Seals, Interim Convention on the Conservation of North Pacific Fur Seals, **1980–81:** 2716
Sears Roebuck and Company, **1979:** 850; **1980–81:** 552, 581

Seasonal Loan Program, Federal, **1978:** 1399
Seattle, Wash., **1979:** 1817; **1980–81:** 1078, 1403, 2677
Seaver, Tom, **1977:** 1155
Seay, Frank Howell, **1979:** 1786, 1787
Sebastian, Frank, **1980–81:** 414
Sebelius, Sen. Keith G., **1978:** 549
Sebo, Katherine A., **1977:** 1243; **1979:** 914
Secaucus, N.J., **1980–81:** 2273, 2275
Seckinger, Allen, **1977:** 744
Secret Service, United States, **1977:** 10, 942, 1263; **1978:** 2280; **1979:** 2280; **1980–81:** 612, 2829
Securities and Exchange Commission, **1978:** 564; **1979:** 339, 1021, 1022, 1398
   Foreign Corrupt Practices Act enforcement, **1980–81:** 402
   Fuel regulation and distribution, **1977:** 258
   Interagency Employee Benefit Council, membership, **1980–81:** 2864
   Members, **1977:** 195, 537, 557, 691, 1395, 1438; **1980–81:** 235, 564, 1434, 1470
   Small business legislation support, **1980–81:** 2378
Securities Investor Protection Corporation, **1979:** 1022, 1043
   Directors, **1977:** 195, 2183; **1978:** 150, 506, 571, 1483, 1485
Security, national.
   See Defense and national security.
Security Assistance Act of 1977, International, **1978:** 1471
Security Assistance Act of 1978, International, **1978:** 1636
Security assistance programs, **1977:** 522
Security and Cooperation in Europe, Commission on, **1978:** 1340
Security and Cooperation in Europe, Conference on, **1978:** 453; **1979:** 1352
Security Council, National.
   See National Security Council.
Security Medal, National, **1979:** 179
Seder, Arthur, **1980–81:** 1372
Seelye, Talcott W., **1978:** 1252, 1279
Segovia, Andres, **1979:** 447
Segui, Jacques, **1978:** 1253, 1255, 1257
Seibel, Laurence, **1978:** 2158
Seiberling, Repr. John F., **1978:** 1139, 1140; **1980–81:** 2756, 2759, 2803
Seidenberg, Jacob, **1978:** 1663
Seidman, Bert, **1978:** 1051
Seidman, Herta Lande, **1979:** 942; **1980–81:** 255, 522
Seigel, Stuart Evan, **1977:** 803, 807
Seigenthaler, John, **1977:** 816
Seigman, Rabbi Henry, **1978:** 2269
Seignious, George M., II, **1977:** 1651; **1978:** 1807, 2053; **1979:** 45, 90, 2270; **1980–81:** 25
Seith, Alex, **1977:** 78, 90; **1978:** 983, 984, 1009, 1937

Seko, Mobutu Sese, **1979:** 1604
Sela, Michael, **1980–81:** 646, 648
Selander, Kelsey Phipps, **1980–81:** 949
Select Commission on Immigration and Refugee
    Policy, **1979:** 450; **1980–81:** 1837
Select Commission on Immigration and Refugee
    Policy, Chairman (Reubin O'D. Askew)
    Appointment, **1979:** 450
    Undocumented aliens, permanent solution ef-
      forts, **1979:** 564, 812, 907
    Venezuelan and Brazilian inaugural ceremonies,
      U.S. delegation member, **1979:** 401
Select Commission on Immigration and Refugee
    Policy, Chairman (Theodore M.
    Hesburgh)
    Appointment, **1979:** 1876
    Kampuchean relief efforts, **1979:** 2012n., 2044,
      2114, 2139
    United Nations Pledging Conference on Refugee
      Relief, Senior Adviser, **1979:** 2085
Selective Service Act, Military, violations, pardon,
    1977: 5, 6, 266, 321
Selective Service Act of 1967 amendments, Mili-
    tary, **1980–81:** 339
Selective Service System, **1977:** 267; **1979:** 1419,
    1604
    Director, **1980–81:** 1277, 1653
    Draft imposition, President's opposition to im-
      mediate, **1980–81:** 327, 340, 346, 2028,
      2030, 2213, 2448
    Draft registration and reinstatement, **1979:** 249,
      472, 654
      Military strength, relationship with, **1980–81:**
        680
      Possible reinstatement, **1977:** 267, 314, 388,
        399
      Proclamation 4771 enacting registration,
        1980–81: 1275
      Proclamation signing ceremony, **1980–81:**
        1274
      Proposed legislation, **1980–81:** 333
      Public reaction, **1980–81:** 312, 328
      Purposes, **1980–81:** 1392, 1414
      Registration success, **1980–81:** 1653, 1686,
        1728, 1875, 2260, 2387, 2446
      Soviet invasion of Afghanistan, response to,
        1980–81: 312, 330, 340, 346, 1530, 1535
      Women, **1980–81:** 243, 313, 342, 880
    Revitalization, **1980–81:** 198, 243, 289, 293
Self-Help Development and Technical Assistance,
    Office of, **1980–81:** 1419, 1428
Selikoff, Irving J., **1979:** 686
Selkregg, Lidia L., **1978:** 54
Sellers, Dorothy, **1980–81:** 1823, 1847, 2871, 2872
Sellers, Robert V., **1979:** 1614n.
Selvidge, Shannon, **1980–81:** 1453
Senate Youth Program, United States, **1977:** 79

Sender, Stanton P., **1978:** 1360, 1381; **1980–81:**
    1824, 1847
Senegal
    President Léopold Sédar Senghor, **1978:** 1071;
      1980–81: 653
    U.S. Ambassador, **1977:** 1081, 1086; **1980–81:**
      1148, 1246
    Vice President's trip, **1980–81:** 1333
Senghor, Léopold Sédar, **1978:** 1071; **1980–81:** 653
Senior citizens.
    See Older persons.
Senior Citizens, National Council of, **1978:** 1062
Senior Citizens Day (Proc. 4745), **1980–81:** 620
Senior Companions, **1978:** 1794
Senior Executive Service
    Civil service reorganization roundtable, remarks,
      1978: 1362–1365, 1374
    Conversion rights of career appointees to Pres-
      idential appointments, **1979:** 392
    Establishment, **1978:** 1765
    Executives approval of Service, **1980–81:** 898,
      1569
    Federal implementation, **1978:** 1972
    Pay schedule rates, **1979:** 393, 1530, 1848; **1980–
      81:** 467, 1597
    Performance bonus system, **1980–81:** 1289
    Presidential Rank Awards, **1980–81:** 1697, 1715
    Procurement goals, **1980–81:** 73
    Proposed, **1978:** 436, 445, 446
    Selection and development programs, **1979:** 1692
    Senior executives approval of Service, **1979:** 917,
      926
Senter, L. T., Jr., **1979:** 1883
Sequoia, **1977:** 557
Serio, James V., Jr., **1978:** 329, 330
Serna, Carl E., **1979:** 1776
Serrano, Jose E., **1980–81:** 1433
Service Corps of Retired Executives (SCORE),
    1979: 1816
Service Employees International Union, **1980–81:**
    2453
Sessions, Lee M., Jr., **1979:** 1222
Sessums, Roy T., **1978:** 511, 1279, 1455
Sewell, Duane C., **1978:** 884, 898
Seybolt, George C., **1977:** 1780, 1796; **1979:** 956
Seychelles
    Ambassador to U.S., **1978:** 2059
    U.S. Ambassador, **1977:** 576, 578, 597; **1980–81:**
      843, 869
Seymour, Stephanie K., **1979:** 1531, 1532
Shadur, Milton Irving, **1980–81:** 608
Shafer, Kimberly, **1979:** 2076
Shagari, Alhaji Shehu, **1980–81:** 1945, 2095, 2104,
    2108
Shah of Iran.
    See Pahlavi, Mohammad Reza.
Shaheen, Edward L., **1977:** 1569
Shaheen, Michael E., Jr., **1980–81:** 2558

Shaheen, William H., **1977**: 1266, 1307
Shakespeare, William, **1979**: 997
Shakow, Alexander, **1977**: 1068, 1085
Shalala, Donna Edna, **1977**: 470, 509
Shallbetter, Clarence, **1979**: 2024
Shamir, Yitzhak, **1979**: 428n.; **1980–81**: 1826, 1832, 1846
Shanahan, Eileen, **1977**: 465
Shanghai Communique, **1977**: 863; **1978**: 942
Shanker, Albert, **1977**: 1222; **1979**: 1525; **1980–81**: 1558
Shanklin, John, **1977**: 372
Shannon, Clyde Frederick, Jr., **1979**: 2281
Shannon, William V., **1977**: 1133, 1163, 1264
Shapell, Nathan, **1978**: 1974
Shapiro, Irving S., **1980–81**: 1589, 1650, 2797
Shapiro, Jonathan, **1980–81**: 1414, 1415n.
Shapiro, Norma Levy, **1978**: 1381
Shapiro, Peter, **1979**: 956; **1980–81**: 2559
Shapiro, Samuel H., **1978**: 999
Shapp, Gov. Milton J., **1977**: 37, 45; **1978**: 415, 416, 1506
Sharaf, Sherif Fawaz, **1980–81**: 1051
Sharif, Carl, **1979**: 1525
Sharif Abdul Hamid Sharaf, **1977**: 1678, 1701
Sharp, Repr. Philip R., **1978**: 769; **1979**: 990
Sharpe, Lois K., **1979**: 399
Sharpsburg, Md., **1978**: 1239
Sharry, Ann R., **1980–81**: 2559
Shaw, John M., **1979**: 1018, 1019
Shaw, Leslie N., **1977**: 195
Shaw, Robert L., **1979**: 45, 92
Shcharanskiy, Anatoly, **1978**: 1099, 1252, 1282, 1328
Shea, William A., **1980–81**: 1433
Sheafe, Larry B., **1977**: 1263
Sheahan, John, **1979**: 2218
Shearer, Derek N., **1979**: 1221, 1223
Sheehan, John J., **1980–81**: 508
Sheen, Bishop Fulton, **1979**: 58
Sheeran, Dick, **1980–81**: 742n.
Sheffield, James Edward, **1980–81**: 654
Sheldon, Georgiana, **1977**: 1381, 1384, 1585, 1613; **1980–81**: 2807
Shelley, Percy Bysshe, **1980–81**: 381
Shelton, Sally Angela, **1979**: 665, 667, 980, 2042; **1980–81**: 1860, 1947
Shelton, Stephen, **1979**: 913
Shemtov, Abraham, **1980–81**: 1433
Shemya Air Force Base, Alaska, **1980–81**: 1403
Shenefield, John H., **1977**: 1217, 1222; **1978**: 1139, 1140; **1979**: 178, 234, 242, 2038, 2044
Shenoula III, Pope, **1977**: 706
Shepard, Rear Adm. Alan, **1978**: 1687
Shepard, Macler C., **1977**: 2153
Shepaug River, Conn., **1979**: 1813
Shepherd, Mark, Jr., **1979**: 942
Sheppard, Harold L., **1980–81**: 718

Sheps, Cecil G., **1978**: 275, 303
Sherar, Archie P., **1977**: 1701
Sherburne, Neil C., **1979**: 730, 787
Sherer, Albert W., Jr., **1977**: 1031
Sherrad, Robert, Jr., **1980–81**: 703n.
Sherwood, David J., **1979**: 2024
Shestack, Jerome J., **1979**: 2217
Shevchenko, Arkady, **1978**: 1746
Shevin, Robert L., **1978**: 1869
Shields, Joseph C., **1980–81**: 927
Shik Kim, Yong, **1977**: 882
Shilon, Dan, **1979**: 453
Shinn, David H., **1978**: 2049
Shipp, John E., Jr., **1980–81**: 1335, 1336
Shipping, American Bureau of, **1980–81**: 1628
Shipping rebating laws, **1978**: 1962
Shippingport, Pa., light water breeder reactor, **1977**: 1707, 2068
Ships, Convention on Pollution from, **1979**: 85
Ships and shipping, **1978**: 1926
  Administration's accomplishments and goals, **1980–81**: 1652, 2952
  Administration's proposals, **1979**: 130
  China-U.S. agreement, **1980–81**: 1772, 1801
  Containerized shipping development, **1980–81**: 1300
  Fishing vessels, American built requirement, **1979**: 1435
  International conventions, **1980–81**: 945, 946, 1627
  International training requirements for seafarers, **1979**: 1419
  Iran, prohibition on business with, **1980–81**: 612
  Maritime training legislation, **1980–81**: 2238
  National Port Week, **1980–81**: 2066
  Navy building programs, **1980–81**: 475
  Pollution prevention legislation, **1980–81**: 2378
  Ports improvement, **1979**: 1836
  Quality standards, **1977**: 29
Shirley, John William, **1980–81**: 1845, 1848
Shiskin, Julius, **1977**: 1665, 1700
Shlaudeman, Harry W., **1977**: 883
Shoe industry and imports, **1977**: 283, 550–554, 558, 644, 755, 1113, 1128, 1148, 1296, 1307
Shoob, Marvin H., **1979**: 1018, 1019
Shore, Dinah, **1978**: 2036
Shore, Herbert H., **1980–81**: 2434
Shorenstein, Carole J., **1979**: 466
Shorenstein, William H., **1977**: 2183
Shores, Arthur D., **1977**: 816
Shornstein, Walter, **1980–81**: 1305n.
Short, D. Clive, **1979**: 468; **1980–81**: 775
Shorter, Frank, **1980–81**: 259
Shrimp industry, **1977**: 1033, 1058
Shriver, Eunice Kennedy, **1978**: 407; **1980–81**: 2099
Shriver, Sargent, **1980–81**: 464
Shriverdecker, Wallace T., **1978**: 1471
Shubin, Marilyn, **1978**: 1974

Shuker, Robert Alan, **1977:** 196, 465
Shulevitz, Judith A., **1980–81:** 927
Shulman, Marshall O., **1977:** 1222
Shulman, Polly, **1980–81:** 928
Shulman, Rebecca, **1978:** 2269
Shump, Ramona Toledo, **1978:** 1753, 1772; **1979:** 46, 92
Shumway, Jean, **1977:** 1055
Shurtliff, M. Karl, **1977:** 1569
Shuster, Repr. Bud, **1980–81:** 1147, 1262, 1267, 2240
Shwe, U Hla, **1978:** 1380
Sick, Gary, **1979:** 436
Sickle cell anemia, **1977:** 1649; **1978:** 897
Sickle Cell Anemia, Cooley's Anemia, Tay-Sachs, and Genetic Diseases Act, National, **1979:** 1705, 2106
Sickle Cell Anemia Poster Child, **1980–81:** 1946
Sidell, Bill, **1979:** 1868
Sidell, William, **1980–81:** 33
Sidles, Sheila D., **1978:** 1468
Sidlin, Murry, **1978:** 697
Siebert, Horst-Alexander, **1977:** 778
Sieff, Lord, **1980–81:** 646, 648
Siefken, Mary Ethel, **1977:** 816
Siegel, Mark, **1977:** 184
Siegel, Mark A., **1978:** 496
Siegel, Stanley, **1978:** 734
Siemer, Deanne C., **1977:** 549, 558; **1978:** 1223; **1979:** 1451
Sierra Leone
    Ambassador to U.S., **1978:** 1380
    President Siaka Stevens, **1980–81:** 1928, 1945
    U.S. Ambassador, **1977:** 986, 1030; **1980–81:** 899, 932
Sievering, Nelson F., Jr., **1977:** 1502, 1507
Sifton, Charles P., **1977:** 1483, 1484
Siggard, Karin, **1980–81:** 929
Sights, Dale, **1979:** 230
Sights, Dale and Margaret Ann, **1980–81:** 1388, 1390n.
Sikes Act Amendments, **1978:** 1250, 1717
Sikorski, Gerry, **1978:** 1822, 1824
Silberman, Richard, **1977:** 816
Silbert, Mimi Halper, **1980–81:** 2613
Silcott, T. George, **1980–81:** 1098, 3023
Siletz Indian tribes of Oregon, **1980–81:** 1661
Sillas, Herman, Jr., **1977:** 1796; **1980–81:** 1346, 1412, 1661
Sillin, Lelan F., Jr., **1978:** 54
Sills, Beverly, **1978:** 432; **1979:** 447; **1980–81:** 264, 752, 1060
Silva, Manuel (Cal), **1977:** 921, 1264
Silver, Charles H., **1980–81:** 2309
Silver Buffalo award, **1978:** 328
Silver prices, **1980–81:** 558
Silverman, Saul, **1978:** 569, 641
Silvers, Anita, **1980–81:** 1332, 1337

Silvers, Jack, **1979:** 1448
Silverstein, Leonard L., **1979:** 730, 787; **1980–81:** 1445, 1470
Silvestro, Gayton, **1980–81:** 1508
Simcox, David E., **1980–81:** 1699
Simmons, Adele Smith, **1978:** 1511
Simmons, J. J., III, **1978:** 968; **1980–81:** 2533
Simmons, Paul A., **1977:** 2050, 2051; **1978:** 231
Simmons, Sherwin, **1978:** 1711
Simmons, William, **1979:** 1525
Simms, Margaret C., **1979:** 1525
Simon, Dorothy M., **1979:** 448
Simon, Neil, **1980–81:** 1405
Simon, Repr. Paul, **1978:** 919, 935, 1515
Simon, Paul, **1980–81:** 2200
Simon, Ted, **1979:** 466
Simonet, Henri, **1978:** 32
Simons, Florence K., **1978:** 407
Simons, Lawrence B., **1977:** 366; **1978:** 1280
Simpson, Sen. Alan K., **1979:** 2104, 2257n.
Simpson, Charles R., **1980–81:** 683, 720
Simpson, George L., Jr., **1979:** 306n.
Simpson, William
    Deputy Assistant to the President, appointment, **1979:** 7
    Mention, **1979:** 1674
    Mississippi flood disaster actions, **1979:** 670, 672, 673, 956
Sinai Support Mission, United States, **1977:** 734, 1820; **1978:** 773; **1979:** 64, 756, 1298, 1821; **1980–81:** 697, 1396, 1547, 1957
Sindjelic, Vladimir, **1980–81:** 1023
Sinfelt, John H., **1979:** 2289; **1980–81:** 82n.
Singapore
    Natural rubber trade, **1980–81:** 592
    Prime Minister Lee Kuan Yew, **1977:** 1699, 1754, 1756
    U.S. Ambassador, **1978:** 821, 881; **1980–81:** 1834, 1847
Singer, Isaac Bashevis, **1978:** 1974
Singlaub, Maj. Gen. John, **1977:** 1018, 1020, 1021, 1030
Singletary, Raymond C., Jr., **1978:** 1511
Sirica, John J., **1977:** 1675, 1750; **1978:** 264; **1979:** 1410, 1417n.
Sisco, Jean H., **1978:** 455; **1980–81:** 1048
Sister Cities program, **1980–81:** 628
Sizemore, Charlene F., **1980–81:** 533, 564
Skelton, Repr. Ike, **1979:** 1247
Skinner, James F., **1979:** 2076
Skokie, Ill., **1978:** 249, 1936
Skopil, Otto R., Jr., **1979:** 1043, 1044
Skoro, Anton T., **1977:** 1569
Skylab, **1979:** 1231
"Skytrain" airline service, **1977:** 1112
Slack, Repr. John M., **1978:** 1003, 1005; **1980–81:** 506

Slade, Roy, **1977:** 546
Slaughter, Constance I., **1978:** 697
Slaughter, John B., **1977:** 1529, 1534; **1979:** 448;
    1980–81: 1289, 1292
Slepak, Vladimir, **1978:** 1099
Slichter, Charles P., **1978:** 1760, 1773; **1979:** 46, 93
Sloan, Edith B., **1978:** 85, 149; **1979:** 1921
Sloane, Harvey I., **1977:** 1963
Sloss, Leon, **1977:** 1162
Slovik, Antoinette, **1978:** 282, 284
Sloviter, Dolores K., **1979:** 619
Small Business, White House Commission on,
    1980–81: 916
Small Business, White House Conference on.
    See White House Conference on Small Business.
Small Business Act and Small Business Investment
    Act amendments, **1978:** 1851
Small Business Administration
    Advisory Committee on Small and Minority
        Business Ownership, support services,
        1980–81: 263
    Appropriations, **1977:** 1409
    Appropriations authorization legislation, **1980–
        81:** 1277, 1292
    Automobile dealership loans, **1980–81:** 1329
    Budget deferral, **1980–81:** 2916
    Budget rescission, **1979:** 433
    Budget rescission and deferrals, **1977:** 352
    Businesswomen loan programs, **1979:** 894
    Chief Counsel for Advocacy, **1978:** 451, 457
    Deputy Administrator, **1979:** 890
    Deputy Administrator-designate, **1977:** 1438
    Disaster loans, **1978:** 472
    Drought assistance, **1977:** 488
    Energy loan programs, **1978:** 1237
    Export policy functions, **1978:** 1632
    Export promotion programs, **1980–81:** 400, 1691,
        2380
    Home heating oil, credit assistance for small
        suppliers, **1979:** 1878
    Independent truckers' strikes actions, **1979:** 1625
    Inspector General, **1979:** 399, 402
    Interagency Coordinating Council, **1978:** 1434
    Legislation, **1979:** 141
    Lending activity expansion, **1980–81:** 75
    Loan guarantee programs, **1980–81:** 1840
    Mention, **1979:** 35
    Miami, Fla., assistance programs, **1980–81:** 1075,
        1236, 2385
    Minority assistance programs, **1978:** 253, 319,
        1848
    Minority business programs, **1977:** 1322, 1516,
        1580
    Minority-owned business loans, **1980–81:** 127
    National Conference on Fraud, Abuse and Er-
        ror, remarks, **1978:** 2230
    Philadelphia, Pa., grants, **1980–81:** 726

Small Business Administration — *continued*
    Pollution control, economic assistance programs,
        1979: 1385
    Procurement Automated Source System, **1979:**
        894
    Public works and economic development pro-
        grams, **1979:** 601–603
    Regulatory Council membership, **1979:** 2074,
        2142, 2143
    Reorganization, **1977:** 1410
    Small business initiatives, **1980–81:** 78
    Solar energy programs, **1979:** 1103
    State of the Union, **1978:** 102
    Targeted Jobs Demonstration program, **1979:**
        2158
    Tris in sleepwear, Government ban, **1978:** 1977
    Women's Business Ownership Campaign, **1977:**
        1437, 1438
Small Business Administration, Administrator (A.
        Vernon Weaver), **1977:** 475, 510, 691, 996,
        1438, 1580; **1978:** 302, 319, 594, 595, 696,
        711, 819–821, 1101, 1919, 1977
    Advisory Committee on Small and Minority
        Business Ownership, support services,
        1980–81: 263
    Communication from the President, **1979:** 2073
    Federal procurement policy functions, **1980–81:**
        73
    Interagency Committee on Women's Business
        Enterprise, support services, **1979:** 891
    Interagency Employee Benefit Council, member,
        1980–81: 2864
    Meeting with the President (Digest), **1980–81:** 64
    Mention, **1979:** 868
    Pollution control, economic assistance actions,
        1979: 1385
    President's assessment, **1979:** 369
    President's Committee on Small Business Policy
        support services, **1980–81:** 2913
    Regulatory Flexibility Act support, **1980–81:**
        1842
    Small Business Persons awards, **1980–81:** 919
    Small Business Week ceremony attendance,
        1980–81: 916, 919
    White House Conference on Small Business
        Attendance, **1980–81:** 68, 72n.
        Discussions with the President, **1979:** 869
Small Business Conference Commission, **1979:** 230,
        368; **1978:** 928, 1836, 1919; **1980–81:** 2850
Small Business Energy Loan Act, **1978:** 1237
Small Business Innovation Research Program,
        1979: 2071
Small Business Investment Incentive Act, **1980–81:**
        2377, 2380
Small Business Person of the Year, National, **1978:**
        819; **1979:** 868

Small Business Policy, President's Committee on, **1980–81:** 2913
Small Business Week, **1977:** 616; **1978:** 514
(Proc. 4641), **1979:** 335
(Proc. 4723), **1980–81:** 349, 918
Small businesses, **1978:** 102, 162, 175, 863, 1452
Administration's accomplishments, **1979:** 141
Administration's accomplishments and goals, **1980–81:** 2937
Catastrophic health insurance coverage, **1979:** 1029
Export promotion policies, **1980–81:** 1691
Federal regulatory programs, **1979:** 1347, 2142, 2143, 2181
Innovative firms development, **1979:** 2072
Leaders, meeting with the President, **1980–81:** 515
Legislation, **1980–81:** 126, 127
Message to Congress, **1980–81:** 73–79, 104
Minority enterprises, **1980–81:** 127
Patent ownership, **1979:** 2069
Regulatory reform, **1979:** 2073, 2142, 2143
Administration's accomplishments and goals, **1980–81:** 70, 74, 517
Legislation.
See Regulatory Flexibility Act.
Women's enterprises, **1980–81:** 128
Small and Disadvantaged Business Utilization, Office of, **1980–81:** 73
Small and Minority Business Ownership, Advisory Committee on, **1980–81:** 262, 305, 2849
Smallpox eradication, **1979:** 2035
Smeal, Eleanor, **1977:** 526; **1978:** 1135
Smerling, Louis R., **1980–81:** 2558
Smith, Albert P., **1979:** 2231; **1980–81:** 1644
Smith, Alfred E., **1980–81:** 2404
Smith, Alfred E., Memorial Dinner, **1980–81:** 2309
Smith, Allie, **1977:** 2172; **1978:** 2287; **1980–81:** 2839, 2840n.
Smith, Dennis R., **1978:** 484, 504; **1980–81:** 1443, 1470
Smith, Don S., **1977:** 1676, 1701
Smith, Ed, **1977:** 404
Smith, Edward S., **1978:** 1218, 1222
Smith, Elbert B., **1978:** 408
Smith, Gerald C., **1979:** 2148
Smith, Gerald D.
See Special Representative of the President for Nonproliferation Matters *under* State, Department of.
Smith, Gerard C., **1977:** 1182, 1211, 1212, 1502, 1506, 1507; **1978:** 1426, 1458
Smith, Gorman C., **1977:** 16
Smith, Herman, **1980–81:** 2560
Smith, Howard K., **1980–81:** 2477
Smith, Ian, **1977:** 1089; **1978:** 668, 1747, 1777
Smith, Irvin B., Jr., **1979:** 1293, 1294
Smith, J. Clay, Jr., **1978:** 1539, 1572

Smith, J. Stanford, **1978:** 455; **1980–81:** 1447
Smith, Jace L., **1980–81:** 1846
Smith, Jack F., **1977:** 464
Smith, James Cloudis, **1980–81:** 2613
Smith, James Robert, **1980–81:** 1419, 1428
Smith, John, **1980–81:** 1853
Smith, Joseph B., **1978:** 2036
Smith, Karen L., **1980–81:** 927
Smith, Col. Leo W., **1980–81:** 1319
Smith, Lillian, **1980–81:** 2819
Smith, Lynne, **1977:** 2028
Smith, Marilyn, **1980–81:** 1439n.
Smith, Mark A., Jr., **1980–81:** 930
Smith, Michael B., **1978:** 1809; **1979:** 2066, 2082
Smith, Monica Herrara, **1979:** 1961
Smith, Repr. Neal, **1977:** 1855; **1978:** 504, 1851, 1852
Legislation passage leadership
Regulatory Flexibility Act, **1980–81:** 1509, 1839, 1844
Small Business Administration authorization, **1980–81:** 1278
Small businesses, **1980–81:** 2381
Legislation sponsorship
Small business regulatory reform, **1979:** 2142
Trucking industry, **1979:** 1137
Mentions, **1979:** 789, 795n., 805
Mexican oil, proposal to exchange U.S. corn for, **1979:** 791, 802
White House Conference on Small Business Involvement, **1980–81:** 68, 74, 916, 917
Sponsorship, **1979:** 369
Smith, Orma R., Jr., **1977:** 816
Smith, Otis M., **1978:** 1652, 1878
Smith, P. R. (Bobby), **1978:** 326, 416, 457, 458
Smith, Robert Charles, **1978:** 277
Smith, Robert N., **1977:** 1263, 1267
Smith, Robert P., **1979:** 579, 619
Smith, Roy A., **1977:** 1569
Smith, T. Eugene, **1980–81:** 1412
Smith, Thomas W. M., **1979:** 1658, 1680
Smith, Tim, **1978:** 1140
Smith, Verne, **1980–81:** 1762
Smith, Warren J., **1977:** 1210
Smith, William K., **1978:** 1269, 1333
Smith, William Lee, **1979:** 2276, 2281; **1980–81:** 25
Smith, Zane G., **1980–81:** 1946
Smithsonian Institution, **1978:** 606, 1712; **1980–81:** 1513, 1514n.
Smoking, **1978:** 61, 536
Smoking, Surgeon General's report on, **1979:** 55
Smorodsky, Myroslaw, **1980–81:** 1439n.
Smyrnis, Nick, **1980–81:** 218, 383
Smythe, Mabel Murphy, **1977:** 713, 745; **1979:** 2147
Sneider, Richard L., **1977:** 1970
Snelling, Richard A., **1977:** 1476

Snelling, Gov. Richard A., **1978:** 1506; **1979:** 2085; **1980–81:** 1335

Snepp, Frank, **1978:** 441

Snodgrass, Charles William, **1980–81:** 449, 453

Snowden, Judy Glissen, **1979:** 466

Snug Harbor Cultural Center, Inc., **1980–81:** 1431

Snyder, Elizabeth, **1977:** 670

Snyder, John W., **1977:** 2101, 2130; **1978:** 89, 232

Snyder, Paul W., **1979:** 23

Soares, Mario, **1977:** 706; **1980–81:** 1245

Sobral, Joao Fernando, **1977:** 1161

Social Security, National Commission on.
   See National Commission on Social Security.

Social Security Administration, **1978:** 1468, 1471
   Commissioner, **1980–81:** 12, 25, 217, 218
   Disability benefit laws evaluation, **1980–81:** 1062
   Draft registration, computer support, **1980–81:** 289

Social Security Amendments of 1977, **1977:** 2153, 2155

Social Security Disability Amendments, **1980–81:** 1062

Social security system, **1977:** 47, 171, 322, 836, 891, 907, 1112, 1917, 1926, 1940, 2016, 2063, 2089, 2091, 2109, 2219, 2130; **1978:** 161, 312, 429, 443, 522, 720, 731, 783, 867, 991, 1063, 1545, 1559, 1868, 1950, 1989
   Administration's accomplishments, **1979:** 122, 569, 1633, 1769, 2026
   Administration's accomplishments and goals, **1980–81:** 115, 138, 620, 1682, 1990, 2026, 2158, 2166, 2402, 2932, 2947
   Antimarriage features removal, **1979:** 1928
   Benefits, **1980–81:** 2384, 2435, 2456, 2460
   Civil service retirement system, **1979:** 918
   Democratic program commitment, **1979:** 1935
   Federal employee system, **1980–81:** 2255
   Federal Republic of Germany-U.S. agreement, **1979:** 362
   Income tax increases, **1980–81:** 1590, 1675, 1729, 1734, 1840, 2024, 2255, 2434, 2897
   Inflation, effect on, **1980–81:** 555
   Mentions, **1980–81:** 535, 539, 783, 1763
   1981 budget allocations, **1980–81:** 536, 540, 806, 835, 887, 998, 1499
   1982 budget allocations, **1980–81:** 2900
   Payments increase, **1979:** 796, 838, 1485; **1980–81:** 389, 999, 1871, 2158, 2504
   President's commitments to, **1980–81:** 2363, 2456
   Proposed legislation, **1980–81:** 138
   Reagan, Ronald, position on, **1980–81:** 1632, 1994, 2142, 2159, 2166, 2221, 2245, 2253, 2271, 2273, 2282, 2346, 2348, 2390, 2398, 2412, 2414, 2419, 2436, 2456, 2473, 2495, 2496, 2504, 2526, 2531, 2556, 2578, 2581, 2584, 2605, 2615, 2637
   Reform, **1979:** 99, 137, 173

Social security system — *continued*
   Supplemental Security Income program.
      See Supplemental Security Income program.
   Tax credits, **1980–81:** 1590

Social services, **1977:** 1852
   Federal-State claims, **1978:** 1082
   Interview remarks, **1978:** 2250, 2251
   Urban policy, **1978:** 591

Social welfare reform amendments, proposed, **1979:** 938

Socialist International Study Group on Disarmament, **1979:** 898

Society.
   See other part of title.

Sockeye salmon fisheries, **1977:** 548

Socrates, **1980–81:** 2444

Sofaer, Abraham D., **1979:** 93

Sofia, Queen, **1980–81:** 334, 335, 1244, 1245

Soft Drink Interbrand Competition Act, **1980–81:** 1334

Sohn, Michael N., **1979:** 886

Soil conservation, **1979:** 1382

Soil Conservation Service, **1978:** 1044, 1046, 1048, 1051

Solar energy, **1977:** 258, 304, 306, 520, 687, 903, 2209; **1978:** 807, 824, 828, 829, 853, 868, 869, 881, 2209
   Administration's proposals, **1979:** 148, 1095, 1097, 1143
   Biomass conversions, **1979:** 1541, 1724
   Budget allocations increase, **1980–81:** 1832, 1898, 1931
   Energy security trust fund, future development funds from, **1979:** 614
   Federal funding increases, **1979:** 1245, 1355
   Future national goals, **1980–81:** 130, 1864, 1882, 1898
   Home installation tax credit, **1979:** 1316, 1489, 1894
   Increased use, **1979:** 1181, 1185, 1190, 1327, 1482, 1570, 1575, 1891, 1894, 1896, 1944, 2056; **1980–81:** 470, 586, 664, 1733, 1748, 1769, 1884, 1888, 1898, 1915, 2630
   Legislation, **1979:** 2155; **1980–81:** 1307
   Meetings with Congressmen and solar groups representatives (Digest), **1979:** 327, 553
   Mentions, **1979:** 792, 2038
   Photovoltaic cells, **1979:** 712, 1219, 1554
   Research and development, **1979:** 1169, 1239, 1358, 1573, 1896; **1980–81:** 417, 1537, 1898
   Swine and poultry houses heating, **1979:** 194
   Urban heating units installation, **1979:** 1408
   Water heating, **1979:** 533

Solar Energy, Domestic Policy Review of, **1979:** 1101, 1103–1105

Solar Energy Caucus, **1979:** 1095

Solar Energy Centers, Regional, **1979:** 1102
Solar energy development bank
  Home and commercial installation financing,
    1979: 1096, 1101, 1358, 1894
  Mentions, **1979:** 1239, 1245
  Proposed legislation transmittal, **1979:** 1315,
    1320
Solar Energy and Energy Conservation Bank
  Legislation, **1980–81:** 131, 418, 1253
  President, **1980–81:** 2046, 2782, 2856, 2870, 2873
Solar Energy Research Institute, **1978:** 824, 882;
    1979: 148, 149, 1102, 1105
Solar Energy Research Institute, Center for the,
    1977: 520
"Solar Memphis" program, **1979:** 1103
Solar Photovoltaic Energy Research, Development,
    and Demonstration Act, **1978:** 1964
Solar User Information Program, National, **1979:**
    1102
Solarz, Repr. Stephen J., **1977:** 2181; **1978:** 1667,
    2268; **1979:** 2280; **1980–81:** 719, 823
Solaun, Mauricio, **1977:** 1219, 1223
Solberg, Hilmar L., **1979:** 467
Sole, Donald Bell, **1977:** 942
Solid Waste Disposal Act Amendments, **1980–81:**
    2381
Sollars, Frank B., **1980–81:** 605, 608
Solomon, Anthony Morton, **1977:** 280, 1690, 1790,
    1801, 2083, 2090; **1978:** 1910, 1954, 1955
Solomon, Arthur K., **1978:** 1630, 1669
Solomon, Deene S., **1980–81:** 2789
Solomon, Joel W. (Jay), **1977:** 589, 596, 872, 1084;
    1978: 306, 898, 1154, 1165, 1176, 1337,
    1446, 1505, 1604, 1859, 1864, 1955; **1979:**
    178, 448, 467
Solomon Islands
  Ambassador to U.S., **1979:** 554
  Independence ceremonies, President's personal
    representative and U.S. delegation, **1978:**
    1221, 1223
  U.S. Ambassador, **1978:** 1188, 1222; **1979:** 1228,
    1232
Solzhenitsyn, Aleksandr, **1977:** 100
Somalia
  Ambassador to U.S., **1980–81:** 1598
  Ethiopian refugees migration, **1980–81:** 964
  Refugee assistance, **1978:** 959
  U.S. Ambassador, **1978:** 1562, 1572
  U.S. military bases, **1980–81:** 35, 391
  U.S. policy, **1978:** 121, 324, 442, 490
  West German rescue of hostages, **1977:** 1810,
    1939
Somerville, Richard, **1979:** 2024
Sommers, Albert T., **1979:** 2218
Somoza-Debayle, Anastasio, **1978:** 2177; **1979:**
    1307
Sonnenberg, Maurice, **1979:** 942
Sorensen, Gillian N., **1977:** 1713, 1755

Sorensen, Theodore, **1978:** 455
Sorenson, Roger A., **1977:** 806
Sorokin, H. Lee, **1979:** 1783, 1784
Sorsa, Kalevi, **1979:** 898
Sorum, Judith Ann, **1978:** 1026
Soscia, Louis J., **1977:** 1437, 1438
Soto, Ricardo Midence, **1979:** 2162n.
South, The, **1977:** 1309, 1315, 1328
South, President's views on the, **1980–81:** 1601,
    1749, 1760
South Africa
  Ambassador to U.S., **1977:** 447, 508
  Arms embargo, **1978:** 652
  Chief Gatsha Buthelezi, **1977:** 371
  Democratic National Committee, remarks, **1978:**
    2197
  Foreign Minister, **1978:** 2146, 2147
  Interview remarks, **1978:** 940, 1410, 1776, 2047,
    2178
  Majority rule government, **1979:** 38, 357
    International support, **1980–81:** 1219
    U.S. policy, **1980–81:** 172, 1502, 1634, 1642
  News conference remarks, **1977:** 1910, 1911,
    1914–1916; **1978:** 2221
  Nuclear explosive tests, **1977:** 1487; **1979:** 2048
  Prime Minister B. J. Vorster, **1977:** 785, 913,
    1089, 1922
  Raid in Angola, **1978:** 851, 855
  United Nations role, **1977:** 1725
  U.S. Ambassador, **1978:** 745, 750
  U.S. business investments, **1980–81:** 2300
  U.S. export controls, **1979:** 2291, 2293
  U.S. policy, **1977:** 225, 451–453, 913, 953, 1088,
    1922; **1978:** 121, 374
South Bronx, N.Y., **1977:** 1787
South Carolina
  Emergency declaration, **1977:** 1437
  Energy crisis, **1977:** 37
  Gov. Richard W. Riley, **1980–81:** 297, 303, 1762,
    2563
  President's visits, **1978:** 1582; **1980–81:** 1758,
    1761, 2563–2577
  U.S. attorney, **1977:** 557, 558
  U.S. district judges, **1979:** 1018, 1019, 1223,
    1452; **1980–81:** 721
  U.S. marshal, **1977:** 596
South Carolina, U.S.S., **1980–81:** 2827n.
South Dakota
  U.S. attorney, **1977:** 746; **1979:** 1883, 1884
  U.S. district judge, **1979:** 441
  U.S. marshal, **1977:** 2050, 2051
  Water supplies legislation, **1980–81:** 1920, 1921
South East Asian Nations, Association for, **1980–
    81:** 169, 170
South Pacific Commission, **1978:** 88, 898, 1266;
    1980–81: 893, 1700
Southeast Asia.
  See Indochina.

Southeast Asia, Presidential Commission on Americans Missing and Unaccounted for in, **1977:** 316, 377, 489, 499
Southeast Asia Treaty Organization, **1978:** 51
South-East Asian Nations, Association of, **1978:** 1378; **1979:** 303, 304
Southern Baptist Brotherhood Commission, **1978:** 1113
Southern Baptist Convention, **1977:** 877; **1979:** 1422
Southern Baptist Convention Mission Service Corps, **1978:** 881
Southern Baptist leaders, meeting with the President, **1977:** 1084
Southern Baptist Radio and Television Commission, **1980–81:** 333
Southern Christian Leadership Conference, **1977:** 641; **1980–81:** 2453
Southern Legislative Conference, **1977:** 1309, 1384
Southern Rhodesia
    Chrome legislation, **1977:** 451–453
    Majority rule in Zimbabwe, **1977:** 1720, 1723
    Peace negotiations, **1977:** 1487
    United Nations role, **1977:** 1725
    U.S. policy, **1977:** 646
    See also Zimbabwe.
Southwest Africa.
    See Namibia.
Southwest Asia.
    See Persian Gulf area; *specific country.*
Southwest Border Commission, **1979:** 1665
Southwest Border Regional Commission, **1977:** 1069, 1085
Southwestern Power Administration, **1977:** 488; **1978:** 1770
Soviet Jewry, National Conference on, **1980–81:** 1662
Soviet Union.
    See Union of Soviet Socialist Republics.
So-Whon Hyon, **1979:** 1154
Space, agricultural, and educational agreement with China, **1979:** 204
Space, Policy Review Committee on, **1979:** 2149
Space Administration, National Aeronautics and.
    See National Aeronautics and Space Administration.
Space Club, National, **1980–81:** 563
Space management, Federal, **1978:** 1427–1430
Space Medal of Honor Awards, Congressional, **1978:** 1684
Space observance, United States (Proc. 4669), **1979:** 1260
Space Organization, European, **1979:** 539
Space program, **1977:** 303, 948, 1227; **1978:** 519, 1135, 1303, 1322, 1684, 1773, 1776; **1980–81:** 1620, 1934, 2726, 2899
    Apollo 11 anniversary ceremony, **1979:** 1277
    Federal activities, **1979:** 1421, 1911

Space program — *continued*
    National policy, **1979:** 536, 2149
    1980 budget allocations, **1979:** 141
    Private industries research and development, **1979:** 712, 1251
    Purposes of program, **1979:** 681
    Space Shuttle, **1979:** 141, 536, 681, 712, 1250
Space Transportation System, **1978:** 1137
Spadolini, Giovanni, **1980–81:** 1241
Spaeth, Merrie, **1980–81:** 949
Spain, James W., **1979:** 1298, 1319, 2238
Spain
    Ambassador to U.S., **1978:** 1380; **1980–81:** 1244
    Constitutional referendum, **1978:** 2183
    Democratic process development, **1980–81:** 1213, 1224
    EFE news agency, interview with the President, **1980–81:** 1213
    Fishery agreement with U.S., **1977:** 206
    Friendship and cooperation treaty with U.S., **1980–81:** 1860, 1947
    Human rights support, **1980–81:** 1229
    Latin America, relations with, **1980–81:** 1214, 1215
    President Adolfo Suarez Gonzalez, **1977:** 464, 745, 748
    President's visit
        American Embassy in Madrid, **1980–81:** 1227
        Announcement, **1980–81:** 1014
        Daily schedule (Digest), **1980–81:** 1244
        Meeting with Prime Minister Suárez and Government officials, **1980–81:** 1223
        State luncheon, **1980–81:** 1220
    Queen Sofia, **1980–81:** 334, 335, 1244, 1245
    Socialist Workers' Party head, meeting with the President (Digest), **1980–81:** 1244
    U.S. Ambassador, **1978:** 887, 899; **1980–81:** 1227
    U.S. relations, **1980–81:** 1214
    Vice President's visit, **1977:** 785
Spain, King Juan Carlos I
    Democratic process development, **1980–81:** 1213
    President's state visit, meetings with the President, **1980–81:** 1222n., 1228, 1244, 1245
    Visit to U.S., **1980–81:** 334, 335
Spain, Prime Minister Adolfo Suárez, **1977:** 464, 745, 748
    President's state visit, meeting with the President, **1980–81:** 1223, 1228, 1244, 1245
    Visit to U.S., **1980–81:** 64, 82
Spalding, George Thomas, **1980–81:** 920
Spangenberg, Craig, **1978:** 1139, 1140
Spanish-speaking Americans, **1977:** 86, 99, 233, 242, 279, 1521, 1600, 1848
    Brownsville, Tex., President's remarks at, **1980–81:** 2617–2622
    Civil rights, **1980–81:** 224, 1877
    Congressional Hispanic Caucus dinner, **1979:** 1661; **1980–81:** 1835

Spanish-speaking Americans — *continued*
  Democratic victory dinner, **1980–81:** 1939
  Discrimination, **1979:** 237, 813
  Economic briefing, **1978:** 415
  Employment, **1979:** 813
    Federal Government, **1978:** 1372; **1980–81:**
      1459
    Federal initiatives program.
      See Employment *under* Children and youth.
    Statistics, **1980–81:** 249, 859, 1531, 1726, 1730,
      1742, 1752, 1836, 2484
  Federal appointments, **1980–81:** 1325
  Federal Government representation, **1979:** 811,
    847
  Federal programs, **1980–81:** 859, 1312
  Heritage week proclamation, **1980–81:** 1461
  Interview with media representatives, **1978:** 901
  Judicial appointments, **1979:** 131, 759, 847;
    1980–81: 1726
  Leaders, meeting with the President (Digest),
    1980–81: 775
  Mexican immigration, **1979:** 812, 907
  Ministers, meeting with the President, **1980–81:**
    333
  Representatives of Houston, Tex., meeting with
    the President, **1978:** 1221
  White House briefing by administration officials
    for community and civic leaders (Digest),
    1979: 1422
  White House ceremony honoring, **1980–81:** 1457
  See also Minorities.
Spanogle, Bob, **1980–81:** 1413, 1415n.
Sparkman, Sen. John J., **1977:** 505, 882, 1136, 1152,
    1745, 1794, 1920, 1940, 1972; **1978:** 449,
    500, 517, 758, 899
Spasowski, Romuald, **1978:** 710
Spaulding, Asa, **1979:** 322
Speaker of the House of Representatives (Thomas
    P. O'Neill, Jr.), **1977:** 78, 90, 98, 99, 359,
    508, 522, 523, 619, 672, 742, 800, 882,
    1016, 1058, 1063, 1162, 1396, 1444, 1530,
    1694, 1786, 1823, 1972, 2016, 2064, 2154,
    2178; **1978:** 98, 148, 286, 302, 449, 452,
    511, 512, 608, 700, 704, 720, 897, 963,
    1321, 1345, 1505, 1513, 1548, 1553, 1563,
    1588, 1644, 1647, 1723, 1754, 1771, 1785,
    1805, 1808, 1854, 1855, 1871, 1892–1894,
    1904, 1941, 1979–1981, 2071, 2280, 2284
  Communications from the President, **1979:** 102,
    232, 461, 895, 997, 1034, 1301, 1315, 1316,
    1446, 1522, 1656, 1738, 2006, 2162, 2174,
    2221, 2290
  Congressional energy and inflation task forces,
    membership recommendations to Presi-
    dent, **1979:** 1216
  Democratic congressional campaign dinner at-
    tendance, **1980–81:** 538

Speaker of the House — *continued*
  Legislation passage leadership
    Chrysler Corporation Loan Guarantee Act of
      1979, **1980–81:** 28
    Crude Oil Windfall Profit Tax Act, **1980–81:**
      588
    Department of Education, **1979:** 1230, 1776
    Omnibus Reconciliation Act, **1980–81:** 2780
  Letters from the President.
    See under Congress, Communications to.
  Meeting with the President (Digest), **1980–81:**
    267
  Mentions, **1979:** 103, 109n., 745, 1092n., 1745,
    1768, 1976, 2005, 2006, 2098; **1980–81:** 28,
    39, 200n., 569, 1977
  O'Neill Chair at Boston College, fundraising
    dinner for, **1979:** 2210
  President's assessment, **1979:** 829
  St. Patrick's Day celebration, **1980–81:** 501
  Standby gasoline rationing plan support, **1979:**
    840, 1213
  United States Holocaust Memorial Commission,
    membership designation authority, **1980–**
    81: 820
  Welfare cash assistance reform support, **1979:**
    2092
Spears, Nancy, **1978:** 1191
Special Central American Assistance Act of 1979,
    1980–81: 1017
Special Conservation Award of the Florida Wild-
    life Federation, **1979:** 1604
Special Counsel, Office of the, **1978:** 2292, 2293,
    2296
Special Country Music Association Award, **1979:**
    898
Special education programs, **1977:** 1850
Special interest groups, **1978:** 2046
Special Panel on Appeals, **1980–81:** 1051
Special Panel for employment discrimination cases,
    1980–81: 567
Special Prosecutor, legislation, **1977:** 788
Special Representative of the President for Inter-
    national Economic Summits (Henry D.
    Owen), **1980–81:** 219, 867, 1192
  Kampuchean relief efforts, **1979:** 2012n., 2044
  Meeting with the President (Digest), **1979:** 1222
  Mentions, **1979:** 1185, 2183n., 2189
  News conferences (Checklist), **1979:** 294, 2140
Special Representative for Trade Negotiations,
    Office of the.
    See United States Trade Representative, Office
    of the.
Special Representative for Trade Negotiations
    (Reubin O'B. Askew).
    See United States Trade Representative.
Special Representative for Trade Negotiations
    (Robert S. Strauss), **1977:** 125, 370, 373,
    412, 533, 551–554, 558, 595, 641, 644, 712,

Special Representative, Trade — *continued*
    755, 798, 799, 801, 806, 807, 936, 944,
    1114, 1128, 1210, 1258, 1506, 1690, 1795,
    1796, 1930, 2006, 2102; **1978:** 153, 511,
    527, 726, 750, 770, 771, 892, 1003, 1034,
    1035, 1062, 1072, 1111, 1155, 1158, 1166,
    1167, 1207, 1222, 1223, 1240, 1333, 1670,
    1673, 1808, 1849, 1878, 1915, 1971, 2066,
    2073, 2198, 2210
  Import functions
    Steel, **1979:** 1034, 1229
    Sugar, **1979:** 946
    Television receivers, **1979:** 167–169
  Japan, visit to, **1979:** 1167, 1211
  Meetings with the President (Digest), **1979:** 467,
    2104
  Mentions, **1979:** 490n., 746, 768, 827, 1024, 1767,
    2015
  Multilateral trade negotiations, Tokyo Round
    negotiator, **1979:** 6, 47, 331, 834, 944,
    1093, 1311, 1808
  News conference (Checklist), **1979:** 1294
  Resignation, **1979:** 1418
  Steel industry task force, member, **1979:** 1640
  Trade Agreements Act, signing ceremony re-
    marks, **1979:** 1313
  U.S. trade mission to Egypt and Israel, dele-
    gation head, **1979:** 640
Special Supplemental Food Program for Women,
  Infants, and Children (WIC), **1978:** 2000
Speech Month, Better Hearing and, **1977:** 743
Speer, Edgar, **1977:** 1796
Speer family, **1980–81:** 1601
Speilberger, Adele D., **1979:** 1776
Speilman, Phyllis, **1980–81:** 2789
Spelling Bee, Scripps-Howard National, **1980–81:**
    1008
Spellman, Eugene P., **1979:** 1294, 1319
Spellman, Repr. Gladys Noon, **1977:** 744; **1978:**
    1667; **1980–81:** 13, 15, 16, 2188
Spencer, Edson W., **1979:** 2127
Spencer, Samuel R., **1980–81:** 272
Spencer, Vaino, **1980–81:** 2057
Spero, Joan Edelman, **1980–81:** 507, 522, 1860,
    1946
Speth, J. Gustave.
  See Environmental Quality, Council on, Chair-
    man.
Spiegel, Abraham, **1978:** 1974
Spiegel, S. Arthur, **1980–81:** 654, 720
Spiegel Magazine, **1978:** 1272
Spielman, Phyllis R., **1979:** 781
Spiers, Ronald I., **1977:** 617, 642
Spieth, Robert E., **1980–81:** 928
Spinal Cord Injury, President's Council on, **1980–
    81:** 811, 2914, 3025
Spiro, Robert Harry, Jr., **1980–81:** 98
Spirou, Christos C., **1979.** 700, 720n.

Spitz, Mark, **1980–81:** 380
Spitzer, Jack, **1978:** 1809; **1980–81:** 1654, 1661n.
Spitzer, Lyman, Jr., **1979:** 2289; **1980–81:** 82n.
Spivack, Gordon B., **1978:** 1139, 1140
Spokane, Wash., **1978:** 857, 860; **1980–81:** 956
Spong, William, **1977:** 1243
Sports, President's Council on Physical Fitness
    and.
  See President's Council on Physical Fitness and
    Sports.
Sports Act, Amateur, **1978:** 1976
Sports for All, National Conference on Physical
    Fitness and, **1980–81:** 259
Sports Hall of Fame, Italian-American, **1980–81:**
    2646
Sprague, Irvine H., **1978:** 2058; **1979:** 91
Sprague, Philip A., **1979:** 196, 218
Sprik, Dale, **1980–81:** 2441, 2451
Springfield, Ill., **1978:** 987, 996; **1980–81:** 1862,
    1867, 1947
Springfield, Mo., **1980–81:** 2665
Springfield, Va., **1980–81:** 868
Springs, Carol C., **1980–81:** 928
Sprizzo, John E., **1980–81:** 1015, 1051
Sprouse, James M., **1979:** 1223
Spurrier, John W., **1980–81:** 269
Sri Lanka
  Ambassador to U.S., **1978:** 1070
  U.S. Ambassador, **1977:** 1196, 1212; **1979:** 2097,
    2107
SS missiles, **1979:** 1844
SS-20 missiles, **1977:** 2211; **1980–81:** 1195
SST (Supersonic Transport), **1977:** 321
Staats, Elmer B., **1977:** 1498; **1979:** 1671; **1980–81:**
    898
Stabler, Ken, **1980–81:** 1738n.
Stacey, Virginia Allred, **1979:** 1439
Stack, Repr. Edward J., **1980–81:** 1362, 2152
Stacy, Charles B., **1977:** 1243
Stadtman, Earl Reece, **1979:** 2289; **1980–81:** 82n.
Stafford, Bishop J. Francis, **1980–81:** 1037n.
Stafford, Sen. Robert T., **1977:** 1073, 2179; **1978:**
    458; **1980–81:** 2797, 2799
Staggers, Repr. Harley O., **1977:** 943, 1396, 1825,
    1978, 1980, 2000, 2006, 2106, 2036, 2105;
    1978: 769, 802, 1005, 1729–1732, 1927,
    1980, 1981
  Communication from the President, **1980–81:**
    1100n.
  Energy mobilization board support, **1980–81:**
    761
  Hospital cost containment legislation support,
    1979: 385, 1772
  International coal agreement support, **1980–81:**
    1450
  Legislation passage leadership
    Railroad industry deregulation, **1979:** 2185

Staggers, Repr. Harley O. — *continued*
  Legislation leadership — *continued*
    Small Business Investment Incentive Act,
      1980–81: 2378
    Meetings with the President (Digest), **1979:** 293;
      1980–81: 1598
    National health plan support, **1979:** 1026
Staggers Rail Act
  Congressional consideration, **1980–81:** 252, 573,
    1261, 1699
  Fact sheet (Checklist), **1980–81:** 2333
  Legislative commitment for 1980, **1980–81:** 118,
    121
  Mentions, **1980–81:** 215, 920, 1537
  Purposes, **1980–81:** 150
  Senate approval, **1980–81:** 584
  Signing ceremony, **1980–81:** 2226, 2229
Stahl, Angelique O., **1978:** 1509, 1516
Stahl, Lesley, **1980–81:** 1049
Stainless steel table flatware industry, **1978:** 1215,
  1216
Staker, Robert J., **1979:** 1044
Stalnaker, John M., **1978:** 697
Stamberg, Susan, **1979:** 1518, 1885
Stamford Daily case, **1978:** 1591
Standards, National Bureau of, **1977:** 1300, 2001,
  2006; **1978:** 231; **1980–81:** 483, 1403
Standby gasoline rationing plan
  Conditions necessary for implementation, **1979:**
    748, 797, 863, 1343; **1980–81:** 92
  Congressional plan, **1979:** 1213, 1240, 1243,
    1311, 1323, 1691
  Mention, **1980–81:** 279
  President's commitment to propose legislation,
    1980–81: 116, 117, 129
  President's plan
    Congressional actions, **1979:** 706, 748, 823,
      840, 845, 936, 951
    Message transmitting proposals to Congress,
      1979: 371, 402
      Amendments, **1979:** 813, 820
    President's appeal for congressional approval,
      1979: 655, 690, 1997, 2155
  Progress report on plan development, **1980–81:**
    1099
  Secretary of Energy's plan preparation, **1980–81:**
    92
Standing Consultative Commission, U.S.-U.S.S.R.,
  1979: 1056, 1057
Stanislaus River, Calif., **1980–81:** 1307
Stanley, Michelle, **1977:** 325
Stanton, Elizabeth Cady, **1980–81:** 412
Stanton, J. William, **1980–81:** 573, 2113
Stanton, Robert L., **1978:** 506
Stapleton, Jean, **1977:** 527
Stapleton, Ruth Carter, **1977:** 2137
Stapleton, Col. Samuel L., **1978:** 1515

Stapleton, Sydney Scott, **1977:** 2130
Star, Tamataiti Willie, **1980–81:** 1051
Starbuck, Dorothy L., **1979:** 1671; **1980–81:** 87
Stark, Arthur, **1978:** 411; **1979:** 23; **1980–81:** 684
Stark, Repr. Fortney H. (Pete), **1978:** 1947
Stark, Nathan J., **1979:** 1851
Stark, Steven D., **1977:** 1713
Starr, Richard, **1980–81:** 306
Startex Mills, S.C.
  Modernization efforts, **1980–81:** 1769, 2039,
    2142, 2205, 2407
  President's visit, **1980–81:** 1758
State, County, and Municipal Employees, Amer-
  ican Federation of, **1980–81:** 1662
State, Department of
  Acid rain research programs, **1979:** 1389
  Ambassadors at Large, **1978:** 494, 1066; **1979:**
    42, 91, 364, 377, 1134, 1143, 1221, 1222,
    2182, 2189; **1980–81:** 219, 891, 1192
  Appropriations, **1977:** 1409; **1978:** 1735; **1979:**
    1434; **1980–81:** 2774, 2809
  Assistant Secretaries, **1977:** 8, 280, 372, 465, 510,
    804, 807, 884, 1029, 1030, 1046, 1059,
    1222, 1436, 2054, 2181; **1978:** 189, 280,
    305, 434, 441, 452, 457, 458, 494, 526,
    1060, 1072, 1380, 1406, 1509, 1516, 2188;
    1979: 21, 91, 1292, 1294, 1524, 1531, 1603,
    1960, 2083, 2151, 2204, 2207; **1980–81:**
    719, 930, 991, 1015, 1096, 1398, 1428
  Banned or significantly restricted substance ex-
    ports, duties, **1980–81:** 2905, 2909
  Beef imports, **1978:** 1074
  Budget deferrals, **1978:** 2095, 2183; **1979:** 1522,
    2120; **1980–81:** 235, 2916
  Bureau of Intelligence and Research, Director,
    1977: 8
  Bureau of Security and Consular Affairs, Ad-
    ministrator, **1977:** 510
  Career Ministers, **1978:** 230
  Carter, Billy, record of activities with Libyan
    Government, **1980–81:** 1443, 1467
  Chief of Protocol, **1977:** 101, 272, 273; **1980–81:**
    1461, 1941
  Civil land remote-sensing activities, **1979:** 2150
  Consumer Affairs Council membership, **1979:**
    1763
  Coordinator for Mexican Affairs, **1979:** 1134,
    1143; **1980–81:** 756n.
  Coordinator for Population Affairs, **1979:** 377,
    378
  Coordinator for Refugee Affairs (Dick Clark)
    Kampuchean relief efforts, **1979:** 2037
    Meeting with the President (Digest), **1979:**
      1142
    Mentions, **1979:** 789, 795n.
    Nomination, **1979:** 364, 377
    Resignation, **1979:** 2066

State, Department of — *continued*
  Coordinator for Refugee Affairs (Matthew Nim-
    itz), **1979:** 2138, 2183n., 2189
  Coordinator for Refugee Affairs (Victor H.
    Palmieri), **1979:** 2183, 2189, 2249
    Afghan refugees in Pakistan, assistance ac-
      tions, **1980–81:** 257
    Cuban refugee actions, **1980–81:** 819, 933
    Refugee admission functions, **1980–81:** 684,
      685
    Resettlement grants program study, **1980–81:**
      2879
  Coordinator for State and Local Governments,
    1979: 2083
  Counselor, **1977:** 509; **1978:** 1340; **1979:** 2083,
    2270; **1980–81:** 334
  Cuban refugee assistance, **1980–81:** 820
  Cyprus conflict negotiations, **1980–81:** 552
  Cyprus conflict settlement actions, **1979:** 461
  Deputy Assistant Secretaries, **1978:** 2072; **1980–**
    81: 892, 893, 1790–1794
  Deputy Coordinator for Refugee Affairs, **1980–**
    81: 217
  Deputy Secretary.
    See State, Deputy Secretary of.
  Deputy Under Secretary, **1977:** 280, 1353, 1384
  Director, Office of Research and Analysis for
    East Asia and the Pacific, **1977:** 2181
  Embargo regulations, **1978:** 1504
  Environmental effects abroad of Federal actions,
    responsibilities for, **1979:** 11–13
  Environmental message, **1977:** 983, 984
  Executive Secretary, **1977:** 8; **1980–81:** 892
  Export development programs, **1978:** 1632, 1633
  Financial transaction audits, **1980–81:** 603
  Foreign assistance programs reorganization,
    1979: 279, 395, 643, 976
  Foreign policy role, **1980–81:** 876, 2833
  Foreign Service, Director General, **1977:** 8
  Foreign technical information dissemination,
    1979: 2070
  Germany, Federal Republic of, social security
    agreement with U.S., **1978:** 1559
  Global 2000 study, **1980–81:** 1415
  Human Rights and Humanitarian Affairs, Co-
    ordinator, **1977:** 195, 746, 1131
  Indochina refugees, health medical screening
    responsibilities, **1979:** 2091
  Intelligence activities, **1978:** 202, 208
  Intelligence and Research, Director, **1980–81:**
    933
  Interagency task force on tropical forests, **1979:**
    1387
  International trade functions, **1979:** 1731
  Investigation of Korean agents activity in the
    United States, **1977:** 1969

State, Department of — *continued*
  Iran
    American hostages release negotiation, **1980–**
      81: 1311, 1490
    Briefings for American hostage family mem-
      bers, **1980–81:** 2818
    Christmas tape reception of American hos-
      tages, **1980–81:** 2840
    President's remarks to Department employees,
      1979: 2205
    Travel prohibitions on U.S. citizens, **1980–81:**
      710
  Kampuchean relief efforts, **1979:** 2037
  Legal Adviser, **1977:** 471, 509; **1978:** 1340; **1979:**
    1697, 1706, 2210
  Mention, **1979:** 362
  National Airlines merger recommendation,
    1979: 1587
  National Security Council, relationship with,
    1980–81: 876, 881
  Nuclear nonproliferation functions, **1978:** 894
  Office for Liaison With State and Local Gov-
    ernments, **1978:** 2049
  Panama Canal Treaty Affairs, Deputy for, **1978:**
    86, 87
  Policy Planning Staff, Director, **1980–81:** 891
  President's Commission on United States-
    Liberian Relations, support services,
    1980–81: 373
  President's visit, question-and-answer session,
    1977: 235
  Refugee resettlement grants programs, **1980–81:**
    2879
  Report preparations
    International science and technology activi-
      ties, **1980–81:** 406
    1959 Geneva Radio Regulations, partial revi-
      sion, **1980–81:** 225
  SALT representative, **1977:** 1485, 1507
  Senior Adviser for foreign policy, **1978:** 1457,
    1458
  Senior Adviser to the Secretary, **1979:** 1596,
    2009ftn.
  Shipping rebating laws, **1978:** 1962, 1963
  Soviet U.N. Mission bombing, statement to
    Chargé d'Affaires, **1979:** 2232
  Special Adviser for Soviet Affairs, **1977:** 1222,
    1376, 1384
  Special Representative of the President for:
    Law of the Sea Conference, **1980–81:** 2073
    Nonproliferation Matters (Gerald C. Smith)
      International Atomic Energy, General Con-
        ference, U.S. Alternative Representative,
        1980–81: 1572, 1848, 1859
      Presidential Medal of Freedom recipient,
        1980–81: 2927
      Resignation, **1980–81:** 2718

State, Department of — *continued*
  Telecommunications functions, **1978:** 599, 600, 603
  Treaty and international agreement reports, **1979:** 84–87, 224, 238, 239, 434, 449, 450, 776, 778, 882, 1155, 1390, 1391, 1420, 1625, 1954, 2120, 2272; **1980–81:** 206, 590, 591, 756, 783, 865, 867, 925, 946, 1285, 1475, 1476, 1625, 1646, 2763, 2765, 2915, 2920, 3019
  Turkish-U.S. military cooperation, **1978:** 1636
  Under Secretaries, **1977:** 86, 147, 557, 1021, 1029, 1084, 2089, 2162; **1978:** 508, 571, 1351; **1979:** 2043, 2270; **1980–81:** 219, 775, 876, 1398
  Undocumented aliens, **1977:** 1419; **1979:** 1667
  United States Emergency Refugee and Migration Assistance Fund, monitoring functions, **1979:** 2117
  Uranium enrichment capacity, report preparation, **1979:** 1822
  Vance, Cyrus R., reception honoring, **1980–81:** 2732
  Whale conservation programs, **1979:** 267
  World forest protection support, **1979:** 1388
  Zaire, U.S. assistance, **1978:** 930
  See also specific constituent agencies.
State, Deputy Secretary of (Warren M. Christopher), **1977:** 148, 1029, 1464, 2130; **1978:** 526, 1034, 1110, 1340, 1799, 1832, 2281
  Acting Secretary of State announcement, **1980–81:** 782n.
  American hostages in Iran, release efforts, **1980–81:** 2649, 2703, 2868, 2875, 3019
  Cuban refugee assistance actions, **1980–81:** 780
  Cyprus conflict negotiations, **1979:** 192; **1980–81:** 382
  Foreign policy role, **1980–81:** 877
  Geneva Conference on Kampuchean relief, U.S. delegation head, **1980–81:** 933
  Kampuchean relief role, **1980–81:** 931
  Meetings with the President (Digest), **1979:** 957, 983, 1422, 1454, 1824, 2106, 2248; **1980–81:** 64, 267, 654, 775, 825, 891, 893, 930, 936, 1112, 1372, 1427, 1523, 1564, 1598, 1662, 1846, 1945, 2070, 2332, 2726, 2740, 2782, 2804, 2823
  Mentions, **1980–81:** 359, 791, 861
  Middle East and European leaders, meetings with, **1979:** 436
  News conference (Checklist), **1979:** 1706
  Panama, meeting with President Royo, **1979:** 837
  Presidential Medal of Freedom recipient, **1980–81:** 2924
  Soviet invasion of Afghanistan
    Meeting with European leaders, **1979:** 2287
    Meetings with U.S. allies, **1980–81:** 11, 80

State, Secretary of (Edmund S. Muskie)
  Agricultural trade development functions, **1980–81:** 1237, 1239
  China-U.S. Consular Convention representative, **1980–81:** 1821, 1822
  Clark, Ramsey, position on prosecution of, **1980–81:** 1087, 1089
  Cuban and Haitian refugee assistance actions, **1980–81:** 913, 1073, 2183
  Cyprus conflict settlement efforts, **1980–81:** 1398
  Demarcation lines between high seas and inland waters, determination, **1980–81:** 1522
  Egyptian-Israeli peace negotiations, **1980–81:** 1086, 1087, 1104, 1113, 1198
  Export administration functions, **1980–81:** 824
  Foreign policy role, **1980–81:** 2135, 2171
  Hostage Relief Act functions, **1980–81:** 2912
  International Convention for the Safety of Life at Sea, functions, **1980–81:** 1628
  International nuclear energy agreements analysis, **1980–81:** 1027, 1240, 1281
  Iran, American hostage situation, release efforts, **1980–81:** 1641, 1749, 3019
  Iraq-Iran conflict, consultations with the President, **1980–81:** 1890, 1900, 1902, 1906, 1930
  Israel-U.S. oil agreement signatory, **1980–81:** 2314
  Latin America, visit to, **1980–81:** 2690
  Maine Indian and claims settlement efforts, **1980–81:** 2177
  Meetings with:
    ASEAN nation Foreign Ministers, **1980–81:** 1228
    European Foreign Ministers, **1980–81:** 1228
    Soviet Foreign Minister Gromyko, **1980–81:** 872, 898, 1202, 2080
    West German Foreign Minister Genscher, **1980–81:** 1242, 2739
    Zimbabwean Prime Minister Mugabe, **1980–81:** 1580
  Meetings with the President (Digest), **1980–81:** 825, 891, 893, 930, 966, 967, 1013, 1014, 1050, 1110, 1111, 1150, 1291, 1376, 1427, 1469, 1564, 1598, 1662, 1714, 1846, 1945, 2070, 2332, 2726, 2740, 2823, 2857, 3049
  Mentions, **1980–81:** 1101, 1434, 1510, 1852
  Military education for Yugoslav officers in U.S., **1980–81:** 1077
  NATO meetings attendance, **1980–81:** 896, 900, 941, 2807
  Nomination, **1980–81:** 791, 826, 893
  Nuclear attack, strategy planning for, **1980–81:** 1553
  Nuclear weapons control in Europe, meeting with Soviet Minister Gromyko, **1980–81:** 1826

State, Secretary of (Muskie) — *continued*
  Omnibus Reconciliation Act support, **1980–81:** 2778
  Overseas personnel functions, **1980–81:** 1421
  Panama Canal functions, **1980–81:** 975
  Presidential Medal of Freedom recipient, **1980–81:** 2926
  President's assessment, **1980–81:** 800, 877, 881, 2251
  President's Commission on Hostage Compensation, functions, **1980–81:** 3040
  President's Committee on the International Labor Organization, member, **1980–81:** 1127
  President's Export Council, participation, **1980–81:** 2829
  Relationship with the President, **1980–81:** 1488, 2080
  Romania, Hungary, and the People's Republic of China, trade with the U.S., **1980–81:** 982
  SALT II treaty ratification efforts, **1980–81:** 2322
  Sugar import functions, **1980–81:** 1271, 1272
  Swearing-in ceremony, **1980–81:** 861, 862
  Transition process, role in, **1980–81:** 2830
  United Nations General Assembly address, **1980–81:** 2434
  Vance, Cyrus R., honorary ceremony attendance, **1980–81:** 2732
  For functions of the Department in general, see State, Department of.
State, Secretary of (Cyrus R. Vance), **1977:** 8, 9, 13, 17, 31, 46, 62, 76, 85, 86, 89, 179, 203, 225, 235–237, 239, 242–245, 248, 378, 380, 451, 464, 496, 507, 538, 553, 559, 576, 584, 595, 603, 628–636, 641, 648, 662, 712, 743, 768, 769, 785, 883, 1010, 1017, 1043, 1057, 1084, 1089, 1107, 1137, 1168, 1203, 1210, 1216, 1222, 1265, 1283, 1295, 1305, 1306, 1369, 1382, 1383, 1402, 1421, 1433, 1434, 1436, 1459, 1482, 1487, 1489, 1516, 1519, 1520, 1532, 1534, 1612, 1649, 1665, 1723, 1728, 1729, 1748, 1754, 1795, 1826, 1885, 1931, 1963, 1966, 1971, 2006, 2036, 2076, 2077, 2092, 2098, 2102, 2118, 2124, 2130, 2152, 2161, 2162, 2172, 2173, 2176, 2189; **1978:** 45, 50, 62, 68, 151, 189, 229, 277, 303, 328, 361, 374, 415, 441, 495, 504, 509, 526, 556, 570, 606, 607, 610, 667, 710, 714, 801–804, 872, 903, 934, 950, 959, 972, 1029, 1032, 1033, 1071, 1110, 1154, 1159, 1163, 1209, 1222, 1235, 1256, 1278, 1333, 1348, 1379, 1380, 1393, 1406, 1440, 1457, 1484, 1506, 1515, 1516, 1537, 1538, 1554, 1571, 1656, 1668, 1672, 1678, 1690, 1722–1724, 1744, 1747, 1751, 1760, 1772, 1776, 1799, 1817, 1832, 1868, 1879, 1893, 1932, 1936, 1940, 1955, 2004, 2057–2059, 2103,

State, Secretary of (Vance) — *continued*
  2147, 2167, 2173, 2187, 2188, 2197, 2220, 2241, 2242, 2253, 2255, 2270, 2276, 2285–2287
  Afghan refugee assistance, report preparation, **1980–81:** 257
  British Government, consultations with new administration, **1979:** 803, 965
  Brzezinski, Zbigniew, relationship with, **1980–81:** 876
  Canadian-U.S. nuclear energy agreement analysis, **1980–81:** 782
  China
    Consular Relations and Consulates General agreement, **1979:** 212
    New Year's message to Huang Hua, **1979:** 15
    Trade relations, memorandums transmittal to Congress, **1979:** 2005
  Credit application functions (EO 12166), **1979:** 1965
  Cypriot President Kyprianou, meeting with, **1979:** 2163
  Cyprus conflict settlement actions, **1979:** 998; **1980–81:** 382, 552
  Dubs, Adolph, commemorative service remarks, **1979:** 295
  Egyptian-Israeli peace negotiations, **1979:** 251, 263, 303, 329n., 408, 688, 852, 969
  Embargo regulations authorities, **1979:** 1655
  Environmental effects abroad of Federal actions, responsibilities for, **1979:** 11–13
  Foreign assistance functions (EO 12163), **1979:** 1793, 1795, 1796, 1798, 1799
  Foreign policy role, **1980–81:** 881
  Foreign Service review, **1979:** 925
  Guinea, meeting with President Touré, **1979:** 1417
  Hungary and Romania, visit to, **1979:** 157
  International science and technology activities evaluation, **1980–81:** 408
  International trade functions, **1979:** 1731
  Iran
    Alien immigration restrictions, **1979:** 2154
    Diplomatic exchange reports, **1980–81:** 257
    Khomeini government, meeting with emissaries of, **1979:** 352
    Oil imports discontinuance actions (Proc. 4702), **1979:** 2108
    Sanctions responsibilities, **1980–81:** 611, 612, 716, 717
    Situation resolution actions, **1979:** 2124, 2205, 2287
  Kampuchean aid actions, **1979:** 2117
  Korean President Park Chung Hee, U.S. funeral delegation head, **1979:** 2054n.
  Meetings with the President (Digest), **1979:** 26, 89, 179, 217, 240, 293, 327, 377, 400, 468, 554, 618, 732, 787, 842, 899, 1018, 1142,

State, Secretary of (Vance) — *continued*
  Meetings with the President — *continued*
        1293, 1319, 1397, 1604, 1679, 1705, 1785,
        1882, 1976, 2043, 2105, 2106, 2138, 2139,
        2187, 2207, 2105, 2106, 2138, 2139, 2187,
        2207, 2248, 2280; **1980–81:** 25, 64, 104,
        217, 268, 291, 293, 334, 423, 452, 493, 522,
        563, 720, 775, 824
  Mentions, **1979:** 332, 333, 676, 768, 798, 831,
        837n., 847, 1014, 1024, 1155n., 1861, 1997,
        2010, 2052, 2169; **1980–81:** 90, 266, 307,
        460, 640
  Middle East peace negotiations, **1980–81:** 487
  News conferences (Checklist), **1979:** 843, 1020,
        1223, 1519
  1980 Summer Olympics, meeting with U.S.
        Olympic Committee President, **1980–81:**
        107
  Oil imports consultations, **1980–81:** 598
  Panama
    Permanent American cemetery negotiations,
        1979: 81
    Visit to, **1979:** 1628
  President's Commission on United States-
        Liberian Relations, final report reception,
        1980–81: 372
  Puerto Rican Nationalists, prison sentences
        commutation recommendation, **1979:**
        1598
  Refugee admission functions, 684, 685
  Resignation, **1980–81:** 781, 791, 797, 798, 826,
        881
  Security assistance program administration,
        1979: 225
  Soviet Union
    Backfire bomber statement, **1979:** 1079
    Political prisoners, consultations to secure re-
        lease of, **1979:** 1887
    Technology and strategic items transfer to,
        1980–81: 43
    Troops in Cuba, actions, **1979:** 1589, 1602,
        1714
  State Governors briefing, **1979:** 2135
  Sugar imports actions, **1979:** 946
  Taiwan relations responsibilities, **1979:** 1131
  Trade policy functions, **1980–81:** 8, 10
  Uganda
    Refugee assistance actions, **1979:** 2150
    Trade actions, **1979:** 225, 867
  United Kingdom-U.S. atomic energy agreement,
        amendment implementation, **1979:** 2165
  United Nations
    General Assembly session activities, **1979:**
        1855
    Role in, **1979:** 62
    U.S. Representative nominee recommenda-
        tion, **1979:** 1589

State, Secretary of (Vance) — *continued*
  United Nations Pledging Conference on Refugee
        Relief, U.S. Representative, **1979:** 2085
  U.S. Ambassador to Mexico, meeting remarks,
        1980–81: 756
  U.S. Consulates closings recommendations,
        1979: 1434
  Whale protection, negotiations of foreign vio-
        lations in Fishing Conservation Zone,
        1979: 1435
  World forest preservation responsibilities, **1979:**
        1386, 1388
  Zimbabwe independence talks, role in, **1980–81:**
        1706, 1929
  Zimbabwe-Rhodesia trade functions (EO 12183),
        1979: 2252
  For functions of the Department in general, see
        State, Department of.
State Attorneys General, National Association of,
        1977: 251
State Community Conservation and Development
        Act, proposed, **1978:** 1010
State Incentive Grant program, **1978:** 586
State of Israel Bond Organization, **1980–81:** 2766
State Legislatures, National Conference of, **1977:**
        252; **1979:** 1705, 2150; **1980–81:** 552
State and Local Energy Task Force, **1979:** 1678
State and local governments
  Administration's accomplishments and goals,
        1980–81: 142
  Anti-inflation program, **1978:** 2079; **1979:** 124,
        308
  Better Jobs and Income program, **1977:** 1444,
        1451
  Coastal zone management, **1980–81:** 2335
  Corporations for Innovation and Development
        program, **1980–81:** 2379
  Crime reduction, **1977:** 504
  Dam inspection program, **1977:** 2071, 2099
  Domestic assistance plans, **1977:** 1285, 1307
  Economic growth and development activities,
        1979: 66, 70, 71, 78
  Economic Report, **1978:** 136
  Education, department of, effects on, **1979:** 1414
  Educational programs, **1978:** 424, 426; **1979:**
        2200
  Emergency management, **1979:** 1672, 1674, 1675
  Employment discrimination, **1978:** 404
  Energy conservation
    Citizens' initiatives, **1979:** 1452, 1500
    Extension service program, **1979:** 1479,
        1485ftn.
    Mandatory goals, **1979:** 1243, 1244
    Mentions, **1979:** 2054, 2058
    President's letter to officials citing successful
        programs, **1979:** 1458, 1515, 1576
    State laws assessment, **1979:** 2134
    Voluntary measures, **1979:** 2243

State and local governments — *continued*
  Energy program, **1977:** 34, 37, 86, 679, 1225
  Energy shortage task force, **1978:** 314
  Environment, **1977:** 440, 985
  Environmental laws enforcement, **1979:** 1643
  Equal rights amendment, **1977:** 300; **1979:** 2008
  Export trade services, **1980–81:** 400
  Federal aid, **1979:** 250
  Federal assistance programs reassessment, **1980–81:** 554
  Federal funding, **1977:** 399
  Federal funding simplification legislation, **1980–81:** 2814
  Federal Government, relationship with, **1979:** 130, 1864, 1969, 2021; **1980–81:** 213, 275, 987, 1045, 1074, 1366
  Federal grants-in-aid, **1977:** 1557, 1558, 1563, 1564; **1980–81:** 495, 1323, 1862, 2006, 2021, 2958
  Federal law enforcement assistance, **1978:** 1241, 1246
  Federal officials for liaison with State and local leaders, **1977:** 1602
  Federal program funds, allocation, **1978:** 307
  Fish and wildlife inventories, **1980–81:** 1959
  Flood control projects, **1979:** 2048
  Floodplain management programs, **1980–81:** 37
  General revenue sharing.
    See General revenue sharing.
  Government regulations, **1978:** 562
    Regulatory reform, **1980–81:** 58
  Governors and legislators, meeting with the President on 1981 budget (Digest), **1979:** 2207
  Health planning programs, **1979:** 1819
  Heat and drought conditions, assistance role, **1980–81:** 1345, 1423
  Home heating oil management, **1979:** 1631
  Hospital care expenditures, **1979:** 387
  Innovative development corporations, **1979:** 2072
  Intergovernmental fiscal assistance legislation, **1979:** 391, 401, 2196
  Involvement of officials in administration policies and programs, **1977:** 274
  Judicial dispute resolution grant programs, **1980–81:** 303
  Labor Department functions, **1977:** 109
  Law enforcement responsibilities, **1979:** 1860
  Legislature salary increases, **1978:** 2152
  Low-income energy assistance program, **1979:** 1640
  National agenda for the eighties involvement, **1979:** 2014
  National water policy functions, **1978:** 1043–1051
  Neighborhood development groups, **1980–81:** 1094

State and local governments — *continued*
  Nuclear energy programs, **1980–81:** 297, 302, 505
  Nuclear powerplant construction decisions, **1979:** 1753
  Officials
    Meetings with the President, **1977:** 641; **1980–81:** 2872 (Digest)
    White House dinner, **1980–81:** 2861
  Officials' responsibilities, **1979:** 1853
  Pay increases, **1978:** 724
  Privacy protection legislation, **1980–81:** 2218
  Privacy rights policy, **1979:** 583
  Radiation activities study, **1979:** 2007
  Reagan, Ronald, proposals for, **1980–81:** 2143, 2290
  Refugee assistance, **1980–81:** 503
  Regional commissions, **1979:** 79
  Residential mortgage loans availability, **1979:** 2288
  Science and technology programs, **1979:** 544
  Small business programs, **1980–81:** 77
  Social services claims settlement, **1977:** 1732
  Solar energy programs, **1979:** 1100
  State of the Union, **1978:** 101, 104
  Tax message, **1978:** 164, 170
  Transportation legislation, **1978:** 221
  Truck size and weight regulations, **1979:** 1137, 1140, 1624
  Urban communities aid, **1979:** 2238
  Urban programs, **1978:** 581, 585, 1430, 1431
  Urban and regional development, policy formation, **1977:** 485
  Vanpooling laws, **1979:** 2022
  Voter registration, **1977:** 482
  Wage rate comparability surveys, **1979:** 1003
  Water allocation systems, **1979:** 1854
  Welfare reform programs, **1979:** 117
  White House Conference on Balanced Growth and Economic Development, remarks, **1978:** 266
  Youth training and employment, **1977:** 52
State Planning Council on Radioactive Waste Management, **1980–81:** 297, 301, 303
State Societies, National Conference of, **1977:** 546
State of the Union Address, **1978:** 90, 150; **1979:** 103, 179; **1980–81:** 194, 219 (Checklist)
  Congressional reaction, **1978:** 153
  Message to Congress, **1978:** 98; **1979:** 121; **1980–81:** 114, 2931
  News conference (Checklist), **1980–81:** 3050
Statements by the President
  Administration's first-year accomplishments, **1977:** 2136
  Afghanistan, Soviet invasion of, **1980–81:** 2835
  Air quality standards in Ohio, **1979:** 1006
  Air services agreement with United Kingdom, **1977:** 1137, 1346
  Airline deregulation legislation, **1978:** 762, 1562

Statements by the President — *continued*
  Airplane crash near Warsaw, Poland, **1980–81:**
    482
  Alaska
    Airplane crash, **1978:** 2158
    National monuments, designation, **1978:** 2111
    Natural Gas Transportation System, **1980–81:**
      1368
    public lands, **1979:** 887, 2067; **1980–81:** 1548,
      2718
  Alcohol fuels programs, **1980–81:** 61
  Alliance to Save Energy, formation, **1977:** 126
  Anti-inflation program, **1977:** 622; **1978:** 2010
  Arms transfer policy, **1977:** 931
  Bourne, Dr. Peter G., **1978:** 1322
  Cambodia, human rights violations, **1978:** 767
  Camp David agreements, first anniversary, **1979:**
    1681
  Camp David agreements, Israeli approval, **1978:**
    1653
  Carnegie Commission on the Future of Public
    Broadcasting, **1979:** 199
  Carter, Billy, activities with Libyan Government,
    1980–81: 1407, 1477
  Chadha v. *Immigration and Naturalization Serv-
    ice,* **1980–81:** 2836
  Channel Islands Marine Sanctuary, Calif.,
    1980–81: 1856
  China, People's Republic of, diplomatic rela-
    tions, **1978:** 2266
  Chinese New Year, **1980–81:** 257
  Christmas, **1979:** 2245; **1980–81:** 2764
  Civil Service Reform Act of 1978 implementa-
    tion, **1980–81:** 898
  Clinch River breeder reactor, **1979:** 730, 795, 887
  Coal strike, **1978:** 313, 331, 489, 539, 573
  Commemoration of the victory at Puebla, Mex-
    ico, **1978:** 880
  Comprehensive Employment and Training Act,
    1978: 506
  Conference on Security and Cooperation in
    Europe, fourth anniversary of signing of
    Final Act, **1979:** 1352
  Consumers Opposed to Inflation in the Neces-
    sities, **1978:** 2279
  Continuing budget appropriations for fiscal year
    1981, **1980–81:** 1981
  Conventional arms transfer policy, **1978:** 256
  Cuban refugees, transport to U.S., **1980–81:** 1031
  Dam inspection program, **1977:** 2071
  Deaths
    Allen, Repr. Clifford R., **1978:** 1133
    Allen, Sen. James B., **1978:** 1029
    Bartlett, Sen. Dewey, **1979:** 372
    Bayh, Marvella, **1979:** 690
    Bolin, Gov. Wesley, **1978:** 468
    Boumediene, Houari, **1978:** 2288
    Brown, Gen. George S., **1978:** 2165

Statements by the President — *continued*
  Deaths — *continued*
    Bruce, David K. E., **1977:** 2083
    Byron, Repr. Goodloe E., **1978:** 1761
    Clark, Tom C., **1977:** 1102
    Clay, Gen. Lucius D., **1978:** 757
    Crosby, Bing, **1977:** 1794
    Crowley, Steven J., **1979:** 2150
    Douglas, William O., **1980–81:** 105
    Dubs, Adolph, **1979:** 269
    Eaton, Cyrus, **1979:** 837
    Eisenhower, Mamie, **1979:** 2074
    Fiedler, Arthur, **1979:** 1226
    Fortson, Ben, **1979:** 913
    Humphrey, Sen. Hubert H., **1978:** 78
    Ketchum, Repr. William M., **1978:** 1178
    Lennon, John, **1980–81:** 2788
    Longworth, Alice Roosevelt, **1980–81:** 362
    Lowenstein, Allard K., **1980–81:** 495
    Makarios, Archbishop, III, **1977:** 1409
    McClellan, Sen. John L., **1977:** 2053
    McCormack, John William, **1980–81:** 2743
    McCulloch, Rev. Glendon, **1978:** 1469
    Mead, Margaret, **1978:** 2036
    Meany, George, **1980–81:** 56
    Meir, Golda, **1978:** 2185
    Menzies, Sir Robert, **1978:** 913
    Metcalf, Sen. Lee, **1978:** 63
    Metcalfe, Repr. Ralph H., **1978:** 1743
    Milk, Harvey, **1978:** 2088
    Montoya, Sen. Joseph N., **1978:** 1040
    Moro, Aldo, **1978:** 885
    Morton, Rogers C. B., **1979:** 672
    Moscone, George, **1978:** 2088
    Mountbatten, Lord Louis, **1979:** 1522
    Muñoz Marín, Luis, **1980–81:** 808
    Newhouse, Samuel I., **1979:** 1526
    Ohira, Masayoshi, **1980–81:** 1096
    Okun, Arthur, **1980–81:** 533
    Owens, Jesse, **1980–81:** 574
    Pennington, John, **1980–81:** 2743
    Perelman, S. J., **1979:** 1964
    Pope John Paul I, **1978:** 1665
    Pope Paul VI, **1978:** 1392
    Potofsky, Jacob, **1979:** 1421
    Presley, Elvis, **1977:** 1478
    Randolph, A. Philip, **1979:** 882
    Rockefeller, Nelson A., **1979:** 189
    Romero, Archbishop Oscar Arnulfo, **1980–81:**
      534
    Ryan, Repr. Leo J., **1978:** 2068
    Slack, Repr. John M., **1980–81:** 506
    Steiger, Repr. William A., **1978:** 2157
    Stewart, Bill, **1979:** 1113
    Tito, Josip Broz, **1980–81:** 827
    Von Braun, Wernher, **1977:** 1125
    Wayne, John, **1979:** 1031

Statements by the President — *continued*
  Deaths — *continued*
    Wood, John H., Jr., **1979:** 959
    Woodworth, Lawrence N., **1977:** 2084
  D.C. General Hospital Commission Act, **1977:** 333
  Defense Department appropriation authorization bill
    House of Representatives' action to sustain veto, **1978:** 1501
    Veto, **1978:** 1438
  Democratic Party primaries and caucuses
    Connecticut and New York primaries, **1980–81:** 534
    Iowa caucuses, **1980–81:** 180
    Maine caucuses, **1980–81:** 295
    Massachusetts and Vermont primaries, **1980–81:** 428
  District of Columbia, congressional representation, **1978:** 1465, 1467
  Domestic airline industry, **1977:** 1961
  Domestic programs, **1978:** 243
  Dominican Republic, election, **1978:** 931
  Earthquake in southern Italy, **1980–81:** 2755
  Economy, national, **1978:** 331
  Education, Secretary of, nomination, **1979:** 2063
  Education Department legislation, **1980–81:** 1664
    Congressional actions, **1979:** 1229, 1728, 1776
    Proposed, **1979:** 756
  Egyptian-Israeli peace negotiations, **1979:** 346, 432, 436, 449
  Employee Retirement Income Security Act transfers, **1978:** 1782
  Employment tax credit legislation, **1978:** 1635
  Energy conservation contingency plans, **1979:** 689
  Energy crisis, **1979:** 648, 747, 959
  Energy emergencies
    Alabama, **1978:** 507
    Indiana, **1978:** 316, 546
    Kentucky, **1978:** 384, 548
    Maryland, **1978:** 471
    Ohio, **1978:** 314, 505
    Pennsylvania, **1978:** 410, 609
  Energy legislation, **1978:** 1783
  Energy mobilization board, **1979:** 1819
  Energy security corporation, **1979:** 2092, 2102
  Enhanced radiation weapons, **1978:** 702
  Equal rights amendment, **1978:** 1719
  Ethics in Government legislation, **1978:** 1644
  Export of banned or significantly restricted substances, Executive order signing, **1980–81:** 2909
  Export policy, United States, **1978:** 1631
  Federal civil service reform, congressional actions on Reorganization Plan No. 2 of 1978, **1978:** 844, 1317, 1318, 1468, 1512

Statements by the President — *continued*
  Federal grants-in-aid, **1977:** 1558
  Federal programs in fair housing, Executive order signing, **1980–81:** 2855
  55-mile speed limit, **1977:** 1527
  Financial institutions deregulation legislation, **1979:** 1728
  Floodplain management, **1977:** 1001
  Footwear industry, American nonrubber import relief, **1977:** 550
  Foreign assistance programs, **1978:** 971
  Foreign boycott legislation, **1977:** 688
  Foreign intelligence surveillance legislation, **1978:** 1501
  Fourth of July, **1978:** 1139
  Freight rail industry deregulation legislation, **1980–81:** 584
  Full employment and balanced growth bill, **1977:** 2033
  Gasoline shortages in California, **1979:** 808, 873
  Geological Survey, 100th anniversary, **1979:** 373
  Global 2000 study, **1980–81:** 1415
  Government regulations, **1978:** 561, 1024
  Grain industry labor dispute, **1979:** 1452
  Grasso, Ella, resignation as Connecticut Governor, **1980–81:** 2772
  Hospital cost containment legislation, **1978:** 1057; **1979:** 1772
  Human rights, **1977:** 2115
  Humphrey-Hawkins full employment legislation, **1978:** 1678, 1719
  Hungarian Americans, **1979:** 2024
  Hydroelectric power projects, **1979:** 1510
  Id al-Fitr, **1978:** 1489
  Independence Day, **1977:** 1209
  Indian education programs, **1978:** 1336
  Inflation, **1979:** 255
  Inflation and Federal spending, **1977:** 1091
  Intelligence Oversight Board, **1977:** 801
  International air transportation negotiations, **1978:** 1462
  International health program, **1978:** 816
  International Labor Organization, **1977:** 1029, 1951; **1980–81:** 306
  Iran, American hostages in,
    Release agreement, **1980–81:** 3026
    Request for special prayers, **1979:** 2141
  Islamic nations, relations with, **1980–81:** 283
  Israel
    Income tax convention, **1980–81:** 1285
    Terrorist attack, **1978:** 505
  Israel settlements and status of Jerusalem, **1980–81:** 427
  Jewish High Holy Days, **1978:** 1565
  Jobs Corps, 15th anniversary, **1979:** 1960
  Johnson, Frank M., Jr., nomination to be Federal Bureau of Investigation Director, **1977:** 1479

Statements by the President — *continued*

Jordan, Hamilton, cocaine use investigation, **1980–81:** 984

Jordan, Vernon E., Jr., shooting of, **1980–81:** 991

Journalistic work products, protection, **1978:** 2234

Kampuchea, international relief efforts, **1979:** 1924

Kennedy, Sen. Robert F., **1978:** 1051

King, Martin Luther, Jr., birth anniversary, **1980–81:** 2915

Korea, Republic of, withdrawal of U.S. troops, **1978:** 768; **1979:** 1275

Labor Day, **1979:** 1528

Lake Tahoe region, Federal actions in, Executive order signing, **1980–81:** 2236

Lebanon, fighting in, **1978:** 1239, 1678

Legislation in the 95th Congress, **1978:** 1745

Lindbergh, Charles A., 50th anniversary of trans-Atlantic flight, **1977:** 939

Lobbying legislation, public disclosure of, **1978:** 784

Love Canal area residents, health and medical care for, **1980–81:** 2430

Low-income energy assistance program, proposed legislation, **1979:** 1639

March of Dimes Birth Defects Prevention Month, **1978:** 2273

Medic Alert program, **1978:** 612

Medicare and social security, policy differences with Ronald Reagan, **1980–81:** 2577

Mental Health Month, **1980–81:** 784

Mental health systems legislation, **1980–81:** 1976

Middle East arms sales, **1978:** 910, 915

Minority business enterprise, **1977:** 1579

Moon landing, ninth anniversary, **1978:** 1322

Multilateral trade negotiations agreements, **1979:** 662

National energy plan, **1977:** 742, 1396, 1945

National Forest System, **1979:** 669

National goals, **1979:** 1302

National Guard and Reserve, **1977:** 1694

National Marine Sanctuaries, **1980–81:** 2297

National Petroleum Reserve, Alaska, proposed legislation, **1980–81:** 233

National Productivity Council, **1978:** 1834

National security information, Executive order signing, **1978:** 1193

National Women's Conference, **1978:** 2069

National Women's History Week, **1980–81:** 412

Natural gas deregulation, **1977:** 1724

Natural gas legislation, **1978:** 768, 967, 1542, 1654

Natural gas shortage, **1977:** 6

New York City, **1977:** 1730
  Financing legislation, **1978:** 1062, 1109, 1208
  Meeting with Mayor Koch, **1978:** 270

1980 fiscal year budget, **1979:** 50, 947

Statements by the President — *continued*

1981 fiscal year budget, **1980–81:** 857

95th Congress, **1978:** 1784

Nondiscrimination laws, leadership and coordination of, **1980–81:** 2651

North Atlantic Treaty Organization, **1979:** 363

Northern Ireland, U.S. policy, **1977:** 1524

Nuclear power policy, **1977:** 587

Oil prices, phased decontrol of domestic, **1979:** 981

Olympic boycott by West Germans, **1980–81:** 920

Panama Canal treaties, implementing legislation, **1979:** 1125

Passover, **1978:** 766

Peace Corps, 17th anniversary, **1978:** 484

Peace Corps volunteer Richard Starr Colombian terrorists release of, **1980–81:** 306

Poland, situation in, **1980–81:** 2771

Pollution control standards, Federal compliance, **1978:** 1769

Pope John Paul II, **1978:** 1785

Presidential Commission on World Hunger, **1978:** 1712; **1980–81:** 777

President's Commission on the Coal Industry, **1979:** 1302

President's Commission for a National Agenda for the Eighties, final report reception, **1980–81:** 2919

Public works bill, **1978:** 1713

Puerto Rico, 26th anniversary of Commonwealth, **1978:** 1336

Radioactivity exposure in Utah, **1978:** 2088

Railroad deregulation legislation, **1980–81:** 1699

Regulatory reform, **1979:** 483; **1980–81:** 604, 785

Ribicoff, Sen. Abraham, reelection decision, **1979:** 782

Richardson, Elliott L., nomination to be U.S. Representative for Law of the Sea Conference, **1977:** 17

St. Patrick's Day, **1980–81:** 474

Salk polio vaccine, 25th anniversary, **1980–81:** 645

Selective Service System revitalization, **1980–81:** 289

Senior Executive Service, **1980–81:** 1289

Shcharanskiy, Anatoly, sentence, **1978:** 1281

"Skytrain" airline service, **1977:** 1112

Small business regulatory flexibility legislation, **1980–81:** 1508, 1697

Somalian-Ethiopian conflict, **1978:** 490

Soviet Cosmos satellite, **1978:** 244

Spain, constitutional referendum, **1978:** 2183

Standby gasoline rationing plan, **1979:** 689, 823

Steel industry revitalization program, **1980–81:** 1960

Sugar, sirups, molasses imports, proclamation signing, **1978:** 145

Statements by the President — *continued*
  Sunset review legislation, **1979:** 941
  Supplementary Fiscal Assistance legislation, **1978:** 1602
  Synthetic fuels and conservation programs legislation, **1979:** 2092, 2102
  Synthetic Fuels Corporation, Board of Directors, members nomination, **1980–81:** 1717
  Tax reduction, **1978:** 1178
  Telecommunications functions, Executive order signing, **1978:** 611
  10-4 Day, **1978:** 1697
  Treaty on the Non-Proliferation of Nuclear Weapons, 10th anniversary, **1980–81:** 433
  Trucking industry deregulation, **1980–81:** 161, 693, 1147
  Trucking industry labor dispute, **1979:** 657
  Turkey, U.S. arms embargo, **1978:** 1091, 1357
  Uganda, human rights, **1979:** 867
  United Kingdom, air services agreement with U.S., **1978:** 525
  United Nations Children's Fund, **1977:** 954
  United Nations Day, **1978:** 1540
  United Nations Decade for Women, World Conference for the, **1980–81:** 1335
  United Nations Fund for Drug Abuse Control, **1978:** 1568
  United Nations sponsorship of week devoted to disarmament, **1978:** 1851
  U.S. arms transfer levels, **1978:** 2094
  U.S. balance of trade and payments, **1977:** 2159
  U.S. Commission on Security and Cooperation in Europe, report, **1979:** 2184
  U.S. export policy, **1980–81:** 400
  U.S. foreign intelligence activities, **1978:** 214
  U.S. Military Academy, Jewish Cadet Chapel, **1977:** 1125
  Veterans Administration health care legislation, **1980–81:** 1576
  Vice President's trips
    Canada, **1977:** 2073
    China, People's Republic of, **1979:** 1125
    Europe, **1977:** 785
    Israel, **1978:** 1090
    Mexico, **1977:** 2073
    Nordic countries and the Netherlands, **1979:** 221
    Pacific area, **1978:** 327
    Senegal, Niger, and Nigeria, **1980–81:** 1333
  Visit of Egyptian President Anwar al-Sadat to Israel, **1977:** 2042
  Voyager spacecraft, **1979:** 1379
  Water resource projects, **1977:** 651; **1979:** 1854
  Welfare cash assistance reform legislation, **1979:** 1661, 2092
  Wetlands protection, **1977:** 1005
  White House Conference on Families, **1978:** 251; **1980–81:** 2422

Statements by the President — *continued*
  Windfall profits tax legislation, **1979:** 1964, 2283
  Wireless communications, 75th anniversary, **1978:** 87
  Youth employment and education legislation, **1980–81:** 847, 1585
  Yugoslavia, departure from, **1980–81:** 1220
  See also Bill Signings.
Statements Other Than Presidential
  Afghanistan, development and military assistance programs, White House Press Secretary, **1979:** 310
  American hostages in Iran, White House Press Secretary, **1979:** 2239; **1980–81:** 11, 2649
  Australia, meeting with Prime Minister J. Malcolm Fraser, White House Press Secretary, **1980–81:** 259
  Camp David meeting on the Middle East, White House Press Secretary, **1978:** 1393
  Carter, Billy, activities with Libyan Government, White House Press Secretary, **1980–81:** 1466
  Concorde, aircraft, landing rights, White House Press Secretary, **1977:** 178
  Cuban refugees
    Vice President, **1980–81:** 780
    White House Press Secretary, **1980–81:** 1053
  Democratic Party primaries and caucuses, White House Press Secretary, **1980–81:** 461, 584
  Domestic issues, White House Press Secretary, **1979:** 1221
  El Salvador, slaying of three persons in, White House Press Secretary, **1980–81:** 2859
  Energy program, White House Press Secretary, **1977:** 1082
  Guyana, death of three newsmen, White House Press Secretary, **1978:** 2068
  Hospital cost containment legislation, White House Press Secretary, **1979:** 2129
  Indiantown Gap, Pa., disturbances at, White House Press Secretary, **1980–81:** 1498
  Iran, European Community sanctions against, White House Press Secretary, **1980–81:** 760
  Jordan, meeting with King Hussein, White House Press Secretary, **1980–81:** 1123, 1130
  Korea, downing of U.S. Army helicopter, White House Press Secretary, **1977:** 1250, 1263
  Middle East arms sales, White House Press Secretary, **1978:** 801
  MX missile deployment, White House Deputy Press Secretary, **1979:** 1016
  National health plan, Secretary of Health, Education, and Welfare, **1978:** 1344
  National Security Council organization, White House Press Secretary, **1977:** 8
  Olympics, 1980 Summer, White House Press Secretary, **1980–81:** 668

[References are to page numbers except as otherwise indicated]

Statements, Other — *continued*
Reagan, Ronald, position on fair housing, **1980–81:** 1771
SALT II treaty delay request, White House Press Secretary, **1980–81:** 12
Shah Mohammed Reza Pahlavi of Iran, departure from U.S., White House Press Secretary, **1979:** 2251
Soviet invasion of Afghanistan, White House Press Secretary, **1980–81:** 11
Soviet press comments on President's economic programs, White House Press Secretary, **1977:** 586
Stealth bomber leaks, charges against the administration by Adm. Zumwalt, White House Press Secretary, **1980–81:** 1770
Turkey, U.S. arms embargo, **1978:** 1337
United Nations, meeting with Secretary-General Waldheim, White House Press Secretary, **1980–81:** 27
Urban aid program funds, White House Press Secretary, **1979:** 609
Vice President's trip to Europe and Japan, White House Press Secretary, **1977:** 8
See also White House Statements.
Station Program Cooperative **1977:** 1741
Statistical Policy Coordinations Committee, **1977:** 1759
Statistical system, Federal, **1978:** 891
Statistics, Bureau of, **1980–81:** 1290
Statler, Stuart M., **1979:** 1041, 1044
Steade, Susan G., **1980–81:** 926
Stealth bomber, **1980–81:** 1686, 1687, 1770
Stebbins, George Ledyard, Jr., **1979:** 2289; **1980–81:** 82n.
Steed, Repr. Tom, **1979:** 2182
Steel, alloy tool, **1977:** 1121
Steel, White House Conference on, **1977:** 1795, 1796
Steel Agreement, International, **1979:** 7
Steel Caucus, Congressional, **1979:** 1018
Steel Corporation, United States.
See United States Steel Corporation.
Steel industry, **1977:** 1320, 1435, 1436, 1690, 1754, 1789, 1801, 1831, 1930, 2083, 2090; **1978:** 632, 633, 682, 1545, 1546, 1604, 1613, 1625, 1626, 1661, 1725, 2153
Administration's accomplishments and goals, **1980–81:** 723, 734, 750
Employment, **1980–81:** 1827
Federal assistance, **1980–81:** 1676
Federal task force, **1979:** 1640
Imports, **1979:** 1032, 1228, 1429
Statistics, **1980–81:** 665, 2039
Trigger price mechanism.
See Trigger price mechanism.
Ohio mill project loan programs, **1980–81:** 2353

Steel industry — *continued*
Raritan River Steel Plant, N.J.
See Raritan River Steel Plant, N.J.
Revitalization program
Announcement remarks, **1980–81:** 1959
Environmental regulations revision, **1980–81:** 2085, 2293, 2345, 2349, 2354, 2475, 2511, 2660
Fact sheet (Checklist), **1980–81:** 2071
Investment tax credits, **1980–81:** 2039, 2045, 2085, 2293, 2345, 2349
Mentions, **1980–81:** 1607, 1619, 2005, 2047, 2437
News conference (Checklist), **1980–81:** 2071
Research and development, **1980–81:** 2087
Statement by the President, **1980–81:** 1960
Trigger price mechanism
Administrative improvement, **1980–81:** 1964
Reinstatement, **1980–81:** 1964, 2045, 2293, 2345, 2349, 2512
U.S. Steel Corporation's antidumping suits withdrawal, relationship with reinstatement, **1980–81:** 732, 735, 905, 1961
Wage settlement, **1980–81:** 725
Steel table flatware industry, stainless, **1978:** 1215, 1216
Steel Tripartite Advisory Committee, **1980–81:** 1650, 1960
Steelworkers of America, United, **1978:** 299, 1544, 1725; **1980–81:** 1510, 2071, 2345
Steering Committee of the Economic Policy Group, **1978:** 726; **1979:** 977
Steiger, Janet Dempsey, **1980–81:** 979, 1015
Steiger, Repr. William A., **1978:** 1223, 2157
Steiger amendment, **1978:** 1178, 1181, 1185, 1230, 1323, 1354, 1416
Stein, Eileen, **1977:** 1243
Stein, Leon, **1978:** 1706, 1724, 2050; **1979:** 46, 90
Steinbock, Irving, **1979:** 1720
Steinem, Gloria, **1977:** 527
Stelson, Thomas, **1979:** 1541, 2065, 2207; **1980–81:** 1429
Stembridge, William Ashbury, Sr., **1979:** 1448
Stenholm, Charles, **1980–81:** 2627
Stennis, Sen. John C., **1977:** 218, 1323, 1329, 1568, 1700, 1794; **1978:** 472, 525, 935, 1071, 1278, 1383, 2208; **1980–81:** 539, 1666, 2186
Meetings with the President (Digest), **1979:** 89, 786, 898
Panama Canal Act of 1979, passage leadership, **1979:** 1777
Pascagoula, Miss., inspection tour following Hurricane Frederic, **1979:** 1674
Stephens, Betty J., **1979:** 466
Stephens, Dorothy C., **1978:** 1341
Stephenson, Judy, **1977:** 403

Sterling, Va., **1980–81:** 2060
Sterling Heights, Mich., **1980–81:** 770
Stern, Alfred L., **1978:** 2264
Stern, Mrs. Isaac, **1978:** 2269
Stern, Lawrence H., **1979:** 1776
Stern, Paula, **1978:** 1453, 1458; **1980–81:** 1446, 1524
Sterner, Michael, **1979:** 436
Sternstein, Rabbi Joseph P., **1977:** 2085
Stetson, John C., **1977:** 474, 510; **1979:** 1280
Stetson Junior High School, West Chester, Pa., **1977:** 27
Steubenville, Ohio, **1979:** 1640, 1817
Stevens, Elizabeth G., **1978:** 1668
Stevens, Paul M., **1977:** 195
Stevens, Paul, **1979:** 490n.
Stevens, Robert C., **1980–81:** 950
Stevens, Roger, **1977:** 508, 710
Stevens, Siaka, **1980–81:** 1928, 1945
Stevens, Sen. Ted, **1977:** 1506, 1794, 1979; **1978:** 302, 1345, 1808, 2158; **1980–81:** 318, 1456, 2755, 2760
Stevens, Mrs. Ted, **1978:** 2158
Stevenson, Adlai, **1980–81:** 1044, 2089
Stevenson, Sen. Adlai E., **1977:** 7, 788, 1136; **1978:** 974, 983–985, 1009, 1772, 1827; **1979:** 943, 948, 1935; **1980–81:** 2381, 2404
Stevenson Wydler Technology Innovation Act, **1980–81:** 2379
Stewart, Repr. Bennett M., **1980–81:** 1469
Stewart, Bill, **1979:** 1113, 1158, 1615
Stewart, Carleton M., **1980–81:** 509
Stewart, Donald, **1977:** 78, 90
Stewart, Sen. Donald, **1979:** 1397; **1980–81:** 1938
Stewart, Mary Anne B., **1980–81:** 3023
Stewart, Milton D., **1978:** 451, 457
Stewart, Sharron, **1978:** 217; **1980–81:** 2243
Stibravy, William J., **1978:** 2157
Stills, Stephen, **1980–81:** 1405
Stimpson, Catherine C., **1978:** 896, 935
Stingel, Donald E., **1977:** 1751, 1755
Stith, Ann Carter, **1978:** 734
Stobbe, Dietrich, **1978:** 1293, 1295, 1306; **1980–81:** 644
Stock Exchange, American, **1980–81:** 64
Stock market, **1977:** 1234
Stockwell, Eugene I., **1978:** 1511
Stokey, Stan, **1979:** 2024
Stoll, Edward, **1980–81:** 1050
Stone, Charles, **1977:** 310
Stone, Edward Durrell, Jr., **1980–81:** 2701
Stone, Galen L., **1977:** 1502, 1507; **1978:** 295, 304
Stone, George W., **1980–81:** 1050, 1447
Stone, James M., **1979:** 41, 93
Stone, Lawrence, **1978:** 1711
Stone, Lucy, **1980–81:** 412
Stone, Marvin, **1980–81:** 2477
Stone, Patsy S., **1979:** 466

Stone, Sen. Richard, **1977:** 882, 1127; **1978:** 227, 229, 232, 2003; **1979:** 217, 2257n.; **1980–81:** 823, 1938, 2152, 2157
Stonewall, Tex., **1980–81:** 465
Stover, Christopher R., **1980–81:** 929
Strachlitz, Sigmund, **1980–81:** 822
Straits of Hormuz.
    See Oil supplies interruption *under* Iraq-Iran conflict.
Strategic Air Command, **1977:** 1860, 2089
Strategic arms limitation
    Administration's policy statement, **1979:** 693–699
    Chemical weapons reduction, **1979:** 1711
    Effect on overall U.S.-Soviet relations, **1979:** 305, 317, 348, 851, 1091, 1611, 1770, 2256
    International support, **1979:** 382, 764, 1004, 1005
    Major foreign policy objective of administration, **1980–81:** 869
    MX missile deployment, **1979:** 1016, 1600
    SALT (Strategic Arms Limitation Talks), **1977:** 66, 95, 96, 345, 348, 358, 447, 498, 502, 538, 558, 603, 634, 648, 740, 746, 859, 942, 959, 1017, 1038, 1107, 1199, 1202, 1313, 1485, 1507, 1651, 1659, 1689, 1700, 1716, 1718, 1782, 1800, 1808, 1856, 1894, 1895, 1912, 2010, 2017, 2018, 2092, 2106, 2191, 2192, 2205; **1978:** 37, 95, 122, 442, 457, 459, 533, 852, 875, 974, 1013, 1029, 1053–1057, 1075, 1160, 1184, 1256, 1260, 1273, 1274, 1282, 1288, 1656, 1658, 1672, 1722–1724, 1744, 1747, 1748, 1776, 1832, 1857, 1860, 1861, 1867, 1886, 1895, 1900, 1945, 1949, 1953, 1987, 2045, 2097, 2149, 2156, 2180, 2195, 2197, 2202, 2204, 2219, 2220, 2257, 2268, 2276, 2278, 2279, 2285–2287
    SALT I, **1980–81:** 196, 434, 488
    SALT II negotiations, **1980–81:** 906
        Chief Negotiator, **1979:** 1077
        Mentions, **1979:** 158, 356, 543, 637, 652, 683, 772, 902, 966
        News conference (Checklist), **1979:** 843
        Soviets negotiating in good faith, **1979:** 170
        Strengths of U.S. position, **1979:** 1091
        White House statement, **1979:** 329
    SALT II treaty, **1980–81:** 12, 26
        Addesss to Congress, **1980–81:** 1087
        Address to the Nation, **1979:** 1803, 1805
        Appeal for public support, **1979:** 637, 719, 805, 831, 839, 952, 1012, 1492, 2137
        Briefings by administration officials (Digest), **1979:** 898, 955, 956, 983, 1017, 1042, 1454, 1678, 1679, 1704, 1723, 1824, 1882, 2043, 2081, 2106
        British support, **1979:** 2258, 2259, 2268
        Japanese leaders, discussions with, **1979:** 1167
        Labor organizations support, **1979:** 1595

Strategic arms limitation — *continued*
　SALT II treaty — *continued*
　　Legislative priority of administration, **1979:**
　　　1855
　　Mentions, **1979:** 1995, 2047; **1980–81:** 434,
　　　1226, 1652, 1766
　　Message to Senate, **1979:** 1155
　　Military and administration leaders support,
　　　1979: 1350
　　Minority groups support, **1979:** 1328
　　NATO weapons deployment decision, effect
　　　of, **1979:** 1845
　　New missile systems development terms, **1979:**
　　　966
　　President's commitment to abide by terms
　　　until ratification, **1980–81:** 872
　　Purposes
　　　Alliances, strengthening of, **1979:** 32, 845,
　　　　851, 903, 1770, 1837, 1871, 1875, 1889
　　　Defense spending increases for convention-
　　　　al forces, **1980–81:** 179, 345, 2569
　　　Developing nations, example of peaceful
　　　　intentions of U.S., **1979:** 32, 559, 845, 851,
　　　　994, 1875, 1889; **1980–81:** 196
　　　Human rights expansion, **1979:** 1871
　　　National security enhancement, **1979:** 107,
　　　　694, 835, 994, 1611, 1770, 1837, 1862,
　　　　1889, 2018; **1980–81:** 179, 345, 348, 1159,
　　　　1619
　　　Nuclear nonproliferation strengthening,
　　　　1980–81: 345, 2569, 2880, 2996
　　　Reapportionment of defense funds for so-
　　　　cial needs, **1979:** 1327, 1871, 1916
　　　Soviet-U.S. relations improvement, **1979:**
　　　　32, 845, 851, 903, 944, 1611
　　　Western nations leadership maintenance,
　　　　1979: 1837, 1871
　　　World peace contributor, **1979:** 32, 107, 576,
　　　　694, 835, 851, 903, 966, 994, 1522, 1566,
　　　　1611, 1770, 1837, 1871, 1889, 1980; **1980–**
　　　　81: 196, 345, 1553, 1619, 2337
　　Reagan, Ronald, position comparison with
　　　President, **1980–81:** 1304, 1994, 2011,
　　　2030, 2044, 2081, 2121, 2137, 2150, 2225,
　　　2249, 2278, 2304, 2322, 2338, 2347, 2374,
　　　2445, 2490, 2507, 2523, 2532, 2570, 2674,
　　　2703
　　Senate ratification
　　　Committee on Foreign Relations report,
　　　　1980–81: 451
　　　Final vote in 1979, possibility of, **1979:** 751
　　　Foreign Relations Committee approval,
　　　　1979: 2101
　　　Mentions, **1979:** 1321, 1425, 1707, 1905
　　　President's appeal for, **1979:** 750, 831, 845,
　　　　852, 1493, 1751, 1937, 2237
　　　President's letter to Members, **1979:** 2256

Strategic arms limitation — *continued*
　SALT II treaty — *continued*
　　Senate ratification — *continued*
　　　President's request for delay in considera-
　　　　tion, **1980–81:** 12, 23
　　　Reconsideration, possibility of, **1980–81:**
　　　　831, 1208, 1212, 2880
　　　Select Committee on Intelligence report,
　　　　1979: 1822
　　　Treaty amendments, possibility of, **1979:**
　　　　903, 1587
　　　Soviet combat troops in Cuba, effect on, **1979:**
　　　　1611, 1757, 1802, 1805, 1809
　　　Soviet invasion of Afghanistan, effect on,
　　　　1980–81: 26, 119, 180, 451, 636, 831, 1105,
　　　　1620, 2322, 2880
　　　Soviet military capability, effect on ratifica-
　　　　tion, **1979:** 56
　　　Text of treaty and related documents, **1979:**
　　　　1051
　　　Verification of terms, **1979:** 107, 305, 749, 934,
　　　　994; **1980–81:** 345, 488, 2571
　　　West German support, **1980–81:** 440
　　　Yugoslavian support, **1980–81:** 1218
　　SALT III negotiations, **1979:** 682, 683, 903, 1091,
　　　1600, 2237; **1980–81:** 440, 831, 1208, 1620
　　Soviet-U.S. relations, impact on overall, **1980–**
　　　81: 2088, 2323
　　Theater nuclear weapons in Europe, **1980–81:**
　　　1826
　　U.S. military strength, effect on, **1979:** 2237
　　Vienna Summit Meeting.
　　　See Vienna Summit Meeting.
Strategic and critical materials (EO 12155), **1979:**
　1620
Strategic Offensive Arms, United States-Soviet
　Union Treaty on the Limitation of, **1979:**
　1051, 1155
Strategic Petroleum Reserve, **1977:** 2178, 2180;
　1978: 60; **1979:** 147, 720; **1980–81:** 251,
　593, 1476
Strategy Council, **1977:** 378, 1963, 1976
Strategy Council on Drug Abuse, **1979:** 618; **1980–**
　81: 1440
Strategy for Drug Abuse and Drug Traffic Pre-
　vention, Federal, **1979:** 618
Stratton, Repr. Samuel S., **1978:** 1855
Straub, Gov. Robert W., **1977:** 1965; **1978:** 854,
　881, 1725, 1943
Straub, Terrence D., **1979:** 990
Straus, R. Peter, **1977:** 1211; **1978:** 1178, 1222
Strauss, Annette, **1980–81:** 2871
Strauss, Adm. Elliott Bowman, **1979:** 1604
Strauss, Franz Josef, **1980–81:** 470, 518
Strauss, Henry L., **1978:** 1879
Strauss, Leon Richter, **1980–81:** 2614
Strauss, Robert S., **1977:** 192, 370, 464, 533, 551–
　554, 558, 595, 641, 644, 712, 755, 798, 799,

Strauss, Robert S. — *continued*
  801, 806, 807, 936, 944, 1114, 1128, 1210,
  1506, 1690, 1754, 1795, 1806, 1930, 2006;
  1978: 153, 224, 511, 527, 726, 750, 770,
  771, 805, 850, 898, 936, 1003, 1034, 1035,
  1062, 1072, 1111, 1155, 1157, 1158, 1166,
  1167, 1222, 1223, 1240, 1333, 1670, 1673,
  1808, 1849, 1878, 1915, 1971, 2066, 2073,
  2198, 2210
  Campaign appearances with the President,
    1980–81: 1977, 2340
  Carter/Mondale Presidential Committee, Inc.,
    chairman, **1980–81:** 937, 995, 1005, 1030,
    1031, 1544
  Carter/Mondale Re-election Committee, chair-
    man, **1980–81:** 1707, 1708n.
  Dinners honoring, **1980–81:** 2790, 2791
  Mention, **1980–81:** 2502
  Multilateral trade negotiations, role in, **1980–81:**
    6, 2828
  News conference (Checklist), **1980–81:** 932
  Presidential Medal of Freedom recipient, **1980–
    81:** 2928
  Steel imports antidumping suits investigation,
    1980–81: 732, 736
  See also Special Representative for Trade Ne-
    gotiations; Middle East, Egyptian-Israeli
    peace negotiations, Personal Representa-
    tive of the President.
Strickland, John, **1977:** 325
Strikes, President's views on, **1978:** 1326
Stringum, Guy, **1978:** 802
Strip mining, **1977:** 415, 436, 1407
Strobbe, Deitrich, **1977:** 1506
Strochlitz, Sigmund, **1978:** 1974; **1980–81:** 822
Stroessner, Alfredo, **1977:** 1537, 1567; **1978:** 1406
Strong, Henry, **1980–81:** 2871
Stroud, Joe, **1980–81:** 2009
Struthers, Sally, **1977:** 641
Student Assistance program, Middle Income, **1979:**
  264
Student Association, National, **1978:** 769
Student Exposition on Energy Resources, Nation-
  al, **1980–81:** 1468
Student Financial Assistance, National Commis-
  sion on, **1980–81:** 2751, 2812
Student Loan Marketing Association, **1978:** 1208,
  2053
Student Loans, Guaranteed, **1978:** 425
Student Lobby, National, **1978:** 769
Stults, Walter, **1980–81:** 516
Suárez, Adolfo.
  See Spain, Prime Minister.
Submarines, **1978:** 239, 464; **1979:** 558, 695
  Communications systems, **1980–81:** 1996
  President's cruise, **1977:** 1024, 1033–1041, 1059
  Project Seafarer, **1977:** 1171

Submarines — *continued*
  Trident.
    See under Trident weapons systems.
Sudan
  President Gaafar Muhammed Nimeiri, **1978:**
    1561; **1980–81:** 1291
  U.S. Ambassador, **1977:** 873, 874, 883; **1980–81:**
    843, 893
Sugahara, Kay, **1980–81:** 218
Sugar, sirup, and molasses imports, **1980–81:** 265,
  1272
Sugar Agreement, International, **1979:** 153, 161;
  1980–81: 1271
Sugar Bowl football game, **1980–81:** 2848n.
Sugar industry and imports, **1977:** 797–801, 807,
  1622, 1705, 2019, 2021; **1978:** 102, 145,
  219, 1154, 1675, 2104, 2288; **1980–81:**
  2992
  Domestic program, **1979:** 153
  Imports, **1979:** 153, 946
Sugarman, Jule M., **1977:** 793, 807; **1978:** 968;
  1979: 3, 46, 90, 977
Sugarman, Robert J., **1978:** 681, 711
Suher, Sidney, **1980–81:** 1240, 2075
Suhler, Carl G., **1979:** 914
Suisman, Richard, **1980–81:** 1570
Sulaiman, Sadek Jawad, **1979:** 1453
Sulfur dioxide pollution, **1977:** 406, 407, 429, 439
Sullivan, Austin P., Jr., **1979:** 947
Sullivan, George M., **1978:** 217
Sullivan, Grace, **1980–81:** 1629
Sullivan, James B., **1978:** 217
Sullivan, John H., **1977:** 804, 807
Sullivan, John L., **1979:** 2097
Sullivan, John McGrath, **1977:** 246, 253, 707, 740,
  746; **1978:** 898; **1979:** 977, 1787
Sullivan, Lawrence A., **1978:** 1139, 1140
Sullivan, Leon H., **1978:** 54; **1979:** 1042; **1980–81:**
  1066, 1629, 1634, 1981
Sullivan, Mary, **1977:** 1053; **1980–81:** 927
Sullivan, Paul D., **1977:** 1264, 1506, 1612, 2036
Sullivan, Roger W., **1978:** 1188, 2281
Sullivan, Thomas P., **1977:** 943
Sullivan, William H., **1977:** 576, 580, 597, 1030
Sullivan, William J., **1978:** 24, 46, 90
Sulsona, Herman, **1979:** 466
Sultanik, Kalman, **1980–81:** 822
Summer Olympics, 1980.
  See Olympics, 1980 Summer.
"Summer on the White House Lawn" picnic, **1977:**
  805
Summers, James C., **1980–81:** 1669
Summit conferences, international, **1978:** 719, 751,
  1258
  Invitation to countries, **1977:** 371
  Meetings, **1977:** 755, 761, 762, 779, 814, 816–819,
    825–828, 883

Summit conferences — *continued*
  Preparations, President's personal representative, **1977:** 332, 852
  Vice President's news conference, **1977:** 59, 61, 63
Summit Representative, President's Special, **1978:** 758
Sun Day, **1978:** 574; **1979:** 1097
"Sunset legislation," **1977:** 395; **1979:** 129, 494, 941
Sunset review legislation, **1980–81:** 118, 153
Sundlun, Bruce G., **1978:** 569
Sunley, Emil M., **1978:** 936
Sunshine Act, **1978:** 1068
Suomi, Verner E., **1977:** 2047
"Superman" film, **1978:** 2269
Supplemental Appropriations Act, **1978:** 472
Supplemental Appropriations and Rescissions Act, **1980–81:** 1333
Supplemental Fiscal Assistance program, **1978:** 590, 1406
Supplemental Health Insurance Panel, **1980–81:** 2558
Supplemental Security Income (SSI) program, **1977:** 47, 1451, 1455; **1978:** 104
  Disabled person programs, **1980–81:** 1062, 2212
  1981 budget allocations, **1980–81:** 536, 540, 806, 836, 887, 998
Supplementary Fiscal Assistance legislation, **1978:** 1406, 1602
Supplementary Security Income, **1979:** 940
Supreme Court of the United States, **1979:** 1441, 2201n.
  Abortion decision, **1980–81:** 2257, 2354
  Associate Justices, **1977:** 17, 47, 1700
  Chadha v.*Immigration and Naturalization Service* opinion review, possibility of, **1980–81:** 2835, 2836
  Chief Justice, **1977:** 4, 13, 15, 19, 26, 27, 396, 1700
  Future judge selection criteria, **1980–81:** 2059
  Members, meeting with the President, **1977:** 147
  Minority business set-aside provision ruling, **1980–81:** 1280
  Navaho-Ute boundary dispute ruling, **1980–81:** 1043
  Nixon appointees, **1980–81:** 1325
  Reagan, Ronald, promise to name woman to, **1980–81:** 2233, 2250
  Statute of limitations ruling, **1980–81:** 2846
  Zurcher v. *Stamford Daily* decision, **1980–81:** 2218
Surface Mining Control and Reclamation Act of 1977, **1977:** 1407; **1978:** 115; **1980–81:** 416
Surface Mining Reclamation Act of 1977, **1979:** 1354
Surface Mining Reclamation and Enforcement, Office of, **1977:** 1810, 1826; **1980–81:** 2201

Surface transportation legislation, **1978:** 1573
Surgical Care–Blue Shield of Wisconsin, **1978:** 1155
Surinam, U.S. Ambassador, **1978:** 760, 771; **1980–81:** 1108, 1111
Survivors Insurance Trust Fund, Old Age and, **1979:** 1633
Susan B. Anthony coin authorization bill, **1978:** 1737
Susquehanna River Basin Commission, **1977:** 251, 1916
Sutherland, Peter Adams, **1980–81:** 1106, 1112
Suzuki, Zenko, **1980–81:** 2560
Sviridoff, Mitchell, **1978:** 52, 150
Swabb, Lawrence, **1979:** 1538
Swan, Robert J., **1979:** 446
Swann, Richard R., **1978:** 314, 329
Swanstrom, Bishop Edward E., **1980–81:** 1065
Swaziland
  Ambassador to U.S., **1977:** 195, 508, 714, 745
  U.S. Ambassador, **1979:** 2062, 2081
Swearing-in ceremonies.
  See under Addresses and Remarks.
Swearingen, John E., **1979:** 1614n.
Sweden
  Ambassador to U.S., **1980–81:** 2740
  Prime Minister Ola Ullsten, **1979:** 33, 89
  U.S. Ambassador, **1977:** 1356, 1384
  Vice President's visit, **1979:** 221, 639
Sweeney, John, **1980–81:** 1648
Sweeney, Paul W., Jr., **1979:** 914
Sweet, Robert W., **1978:** 329, 330
Swett, Pernell, **1980–81:** 2559
Swibel, Howard J., **1978:** 1406
Swift, Repr. Al, **1980–81:** 306
Swinburn, Charles, **1980–81:** 1698
Swing, William, **1979:** 580, 619
Switzerland
  Ambassador to U.S., **1980–81:** 1564, 1598
  President Kurt Furgler, **1977:** 881
  President's visit, **1977:** 809, 841, 844, 881
  Social security agreement with U.S., **1980–81:** 264
  Trade with U.S., **1980–81:** 1247
  U.S. Ambassador, **1977:** 1026, 1031; **1979:** 1618
Swygert, H. Patrick, **1979:** 3, 46
Sykes, James T., **1978:** 702, 711; **1980–81:** 2534
Sykes, Richard, **1978:** 2158
Sykes, William G., **1979:** 1692, 1706
Sylvester, Barbara T., **1977:** 1713; **1980–81:** 3023
Symon, Mary Louise, **1980–81:** 303
Synagogue Council of America, **1979:** 2009
Synar, Repr. Michael Lynn, **1980–81:** 1098
Synthetic fuels
  Congressional actions on legislation, **1979:** 2092, 2102
  Conversion from:
    Coal, **1979:** 1538, 1575, 1640; **1980–81:** 883,

Synthetic fuels — *continued*
    Conversion from — *continued*
        Coal — *continued*
            1882, 2040, 2086, 2258
            Oil and natural gas, **1979:** 1849
            Oil shale and tar sands, **1980–81:** 1882
            Shale rock, **1979:** 1575
        Domestic production, **1979:** 1138, 1185, 1190, 1341
        Facilities modernization, **1980–81:** 2200, 2474
        Increased use, **1979:** 2020
        Industry creation, **1980–81:** 1587
        Legislation, **1979:** 1181, 2154; **1980–81:** 1318
        Plant installations, **1979:** 1540
        Production
            Environmental standards, **1980–81:** 417
            EO 12242, **1980–81:** 1970, 1971
            Federal budget allocations, **1980–81:** 1974, 2086
            Mention, **1980–81:** 1354
            U.S. energy independence, relationship with, **1980–81:** 470, 2086
        Research and development, **1980–81:** 1769, 2192
Synthetic Fuels Corporation
    Board of Directors
        Advisory Committee, Chairman and Vice Chairman, **1980–81:** 2752
        Members, **1980–81:** 1717, 1848, 2071, 2074, 2179, 2726, 2727, 2870, 2874
        Production responsibilities, **1980–81:** 1970, 1972, 2200, 2899, 3014
Synthetic Fuels Corporation, Board of Directors, Chairman (John C. Sawhill)
    Nomination, **1980–81:** 1700, 1715, 2726, 2727, 2870, 2873
    Recess appointment, **1980–81:** 2074n.
Syracuse, N.Y., **1979:** 1817
Syria
    Camp David summit meeting, **1978:** 1526
    Deputy Prime Minister, **1977:** 704
    Foreign Minister, **1977:** 704, 1677
    Lebanese situation, **1978:** 1658
    Middle East peace settlement role, **1979:** 453, 456
    Oil imports, **1980–81:** 1681
    President Hafiz al-Asad, **1977:** 835, 841, 842, 844, 884, 1433, 1434, 2044, 2059, 2098, 2119, 2120, 2172, 2175, 2189, 2190, 2206; **1978:** 46, 71, 1554, 1678
    U.S. Ambassador, **1978:** 1252, 1279
    U.S. export controls, **1979:** 2291, 2294
Syrkin, Marie, **1978:** 2269
Syvrud, Donald E., **1979:** 446, 468
Szanton, Peter L., **1979:** 294
Szego, Dr. George C., **1980–81:** 1405
Szymanowicz, Helen, **1980–81:** 1852

Tabenken, Gerald M., **1979:** 293, 466; **1980–81:** 2533
Tackett, Gene, **1980–81:** 2075
Tacoma, Wash., **1979:** 1817; **1980–81:** 1903, 1905, 1914, 1947
Taft, Julia V., **1977:** 941
Taft, William Howard, **1980–81:** 1852
Taft-Hartley Act, invocation in grain industry labor dispute, **1979:** 1430
Taggart, Capt. Kelly E., **1980–81:** 2746, 2782
Tahoe Federal Coordinating Council, **1980–81:** 2235, 2236
Taiwan
    American Institute in, **1979:** 2223
    China, agreement to peacefully resolve differences with, **1979:** 53, 257
    EO 12143, **1979:** 1131
    Nonrubber footwear exports, **1980–81:** 420
    Shoe exports to U.S., **1977:** 644, 755, 1113, 1128, 1148
    Television receivers exports, **1979:** 167, 168
    Trade with U.S., **1979:** 158, 331, 334, 1111, 2224
        Levels increase, **1980–81:** 963, 987, 1300, 1304, 1904, 2147, 2469, 2531, 2828
        Mentions, **1980–81:** 1908, 1915
    U.S. policy, **1977:** 863
    U.S. relations
        Continuation of commercial and cultural relations, **1979:** 1, 170, 248, 257, 356, 576, 1111
        Impact of U.S.-People's Republic of China normalization, **1980–81:** 91, 338, 345, 399, 579, 906, 963, 987, 1322, 1740, 1743, 1904, 2277, 2368, 2440
        Legislation, **1979:** 165, 170
        Memorandum to Federal agencies, **1979:** 1
        Mentions, **1979:** 2033, 2047
Taiwan Relations Act, **1979:** 640
Talarico, Sam, **1979:** 1008
Talboys, Brian E., **1980–81:** 422
Talisman, Mark, **1978:** 1974; **1980–81:** 823
Tall, Macky Koreissi Aguibou, **1978:** 2059
Tallahassee, Fla., **1980–81:** 2148, 2157
Talley, Mae Sue, **1979:** 730, 787
Talmadge, Sen. Herman E., **1977:** 508, 557, 950, 1689, 1778, 1833, 1903, 2105; **1978:** 235, 315, 530, 540, 542, 700, 914, 934, 1425, 1696, 1965; **1979:** 33n., 384, 2274, 2299
    Legislation passage leadership
        Emergency Agricultural Credit Adjustment Act extension, **1980–81:** 568
        Farmer-owned grain reserve, **1980–81:** 653
        Food Stamp Act Amendments, **1980–81:** 975
        National Aquaculture Act, **1980–81:** 1938
        Rural Development Policy Act, **1980–81:** 1916
        Small Business Administration authorization, **1980–81:** 1279

Talmadge, Sen. Herman E. — *continued*
  Meeting with the President (Digest), **1980–81:**
    1427
Tamez, Diana M., **1977:** 1713
Tamoyo, Marcos, **1978:** 640
Tampa, Fla.,,, **1979:** 1566, 1578
Tandem Mortgage Assistance program, **1978:** 584
Tang, Thomas, **1977:** 1507, 1534
Tanimoto, Lawrence G., **1980–81:** 927
Tankers, oil, **1977:** 387, 458, 459, 465
Tanner, Jack E., **1978:** 149, 150
Tanner, Joe, **1977:** 1033
Tannenbaum, Rabbi Marc, **1978:** 1974
Tanner, N. Eldon, **1978:** 2088
Tanzania
  Alignment with Soviet Union, **1979:** 316
  Finance Minister, **1980–81:** 1974n.
  President Julius K. Nyerere, **1977:** 1264, 1412,
    1423, 1433, 1434, 1437; **1978:** 695, 976,
    1095
  U.S. Ambassador, **1979:** 1618
  U.S. Representative to the United Nations, trip,
    1977: 33
Tapa, Dr. Sione, **1977:** 840
Tapper, George G., **1978:** 1809; **1980–81:** 2243
Taracido, M. D. (Lita), **1980–81:** 1439n.
Targeted Jobs Demonstration program, **1979:** 2158
Targeted Employment Tax Credit, **1978:** 586
Taras Shevchenko, **1977:** 604
Tariff Schedules of the United States, **1977:** 255
Tariffs and Trade, General Agreement on.
  See General Agreement on Tariffs and Trade.
Tarjan, George, **1977:** 530
Tarnoff, Peter, **1980–81:** 892
Tashima, A. Wallace, **1980–81:** 894
Tashjian, Michael J., **1977:** 1586
Tasi, Lila C., **1980–81:** 2559
Task Force on Export Disincentives, **1980–81:** 402
Task Force on Global Resources and Environ-
  ment, **1980–81:** 1415
Task Force on Women Business Owners, **1978:**
  1188; **1979:** 894, 895
Task Force on Youth Employment, Vice Presi-
  dent's, **1980–81:** 124
Tate, Albert, Jr., **1979:** 1397, 1398
Tate, Danny C., **1977:** 2181; **1978:** 1154
  Meetings with the President (Digest), **1979:** 467,
    553, 618, 666, 732, 786, 842, 898, 1142
Tate, Horace, **1977:** 1210; **1978:** 920, 935
Tate, S. Shepherd, **1979:** 760n.
Tatum, Miltum T., **1980–81:** 929
Tau, Cecelia Mildred Nana, **1980–81:** 775
Taub, Henry, **1980–81:** 1439n.
Taube, Henry, **1977:** 2047
Taube, Stanley, **1980–81:** 2560
Tauzin, Repr. Bill, **1980–81:** 1050
Tax Court, United States, **1979:** 820, 843; **1980–81:**
  683, 720, 756, 775

Tax Court Nominating Commission, United States,
  1978: 1039, 1711; **1980–81:** 2849
Tax Reduction and Simplification Act of 1977,
  1977: 962
Tax Reform, Ad Hoc Committee on, **1978:** 769
Taxation
  Administration's accomplishments and goals,
    1980–81: 3010
  Anti-inflation program, **1978:** 1841
  Automobile industry investment credits, **1980–
    81:** 2187
  Better Jobs and Income program, **1977:** 1443,
    1451
  Business investment credits, **1979:** 601; **1980–81:**
    1587
  Business tax credit proposals, **1977:** 618–622,
    642, 695
  Campaign financing, **1977:** 483
  Capital gains tax, **1978:** 1178, 1185
  Capital investment, **1980–81:** 253
  Carryover basis reform, **1979:** 132
  College tuition credits, **1980–81:** 2019
  Conventions with U.S.
    Bangladesh, **1980–81:** 2762
    Canada, **1980–81:** 2715
    Cyprus, **1980–81:** 925
    Denmark, **1980–81:** 1646
    Egypt, **1980–81:** 2714
    France
      Income and property taxes, **1979:** 239
      Taxation and fiscal evasion, **1979:** 238
    Germany, Federal Republic of, **1980–81:** 2915
    Hungary, **1979:** 822
    Israel, **1980–81:** 1285
    Jamaica, **1980–81:** 1476
    Malta, **1980–81:** 756
    Morocco, **1978:** 818
    Norway, **1980–81:** 2763
    United Kingdom, **1977:** 1066; **1979:** 663, 778
  Disability deductions, **1977:** 309, 310, 317
  Economic recovery program, **1977:** 54, 72
  Economic Report, **1978:** 134
  Employment tax credit, **1978:** 1635, 1872; **1979:**
    99, 601
  Energy credits and exemptions
    Alcohol fuels excise exemption, **1979:** 1317,
      1503ftn.
    Conservation credits
      Home weatherization, **1979:** 1507, 1632,
        1642, 1993, 2049, 2056
      Solar installation, **1979:** 1102, 1103, 1316,
        1490, 1894
      Vanpools, **1979:** 2022
      Woodburning stoves, **1979:** 1102, 1317
      Gasohol investment credits, **1979:** 792
    Independent oilmen, daily production exemp-
      tion, **1979:** 1309, 1320, 1426

Taxation — *continued*
  Energy credits — *continued*
    Shale oil and natural gas production credits, **1979:** 1316
    Synthetic fuels conversion credits, **1979:** 1503ftn.
  Excise tax, **1977:** 665
  Export policy, **1978:** 1633
  Federal expenditures review, **1979:** 942
  Federal policy, **1978:** 899
  Financial capital, **1978:** 1416
  Gasoline, **1977:** 674, 750, 1337
  Income tax analysis, **1977:** 385, 397
  Income tax surcharge, **1979:** 651
  Income taxes reduction and reform
    Interest and dividend payments withholding, **1980–81:** 571
    Marriage penalty elimination, **1980–81:** 1590, 1620, 1729, 2024, 2083, 2254, 2363, 2434, 2460
    1978 tax cut, **1980–81:** 112, 253
    1980 tax cut, President's rejection of, **1980–81:** 122, 247, 558, 1351, 1613, 1826, 2190, 2363
    1981 tax cut, possibility of, **1980–81:** 724, 1351, 1729, 1911, 2024, 2326, 2363, 2704, 2897
    System improvement efforts, **1980–81:** 389, 888, 987
  Industrial innovation incentives, **1979:** 2072
  Industrial investment credits, **1980–81:** 1963, 1968, 2023, 2077, 2084, 2293, 2462, 2514, 2547, 2568, 2897, 3011
  Inheritance taxes, **1979:** 1912
  Installment sales revision, **1980–81:** 2343
  Interview remarks, **1978:** 311, 524
  Kemp-Roth proposed legislation.
    See Kemp-Roth tax bill.
  Legislation, **1978:** 1745, 1751, 2097; **1979:** 2034; **1980–81:** 639
  Message to Congress, **1978:** 124, 158
  Morocco, taxation and fiscal evasion convention, **1978:** 818
  News conference remarks, **1978:** 59, 243, 250, 332, 338
  President's tax return, **1977:** 1111, 1163
  Private school exemptions, **1980–81:** 2130
  Property, **1978:** 1613, 1614
  Proposition 13, effect, **1978:** 1077, 1093, 1096
  Rebates
    Proposal, **1977:** 200, 240, 301, 520, 581, 586, 602, 1618, 1693
    Withdrawal, **1977:** 618–622, 635, 637, 642, 650, 790
  Reduction and reform, **1979:** 188, 962, 1215, 1249, 1759, 1886, 1936, 2026; **1978:** 369, 494, 710, 754, 755, 770, 778, 783, 802, 863, 987, 1061, 1064, 1178, 1181, 1185, 1223, 1229, 1230, 1323, 1354, 1407, 1548, 1649,

Taxation — *continued*
  Reduction and reform — *continued*
    1752, 1861, 1868, 1885, 1890, 1894, 1934, 1939, 1951, 1968, 1969, 2192
  Reform, **1977:** 74, 292, 299, 310, 315, 515, 867, 889, 892, 907, 942, 1111, 1264, 1330, 1533, 1619, 1621, 1747, 1785, 1908, 1909, 1939, 2001, 2060, 2109, 2112, 2123, 2155, 2193, 2194
  Relationship with inflation, **1979:** 247
  Savings account interest and stock dividends, **1977:** 299
  Small business investment credits, **1980–81:** 75, 127
  Small oil royalty owners exemptions, **1980–81:** 2421
  Standard deductions, increase, **1977:** 171, 296, 301, 310
  State of the Union, **1978:** 92, 98, 100
  Sunset review for tax expenditures, **1979:** 2182
  Targeted employment credit, **1978:** 936
  Targeted jobs credit, **1980–81:** 124
  Tax base incomes policy, **1980–81:** 884
  Territorial revenues, **1980–81:** 317
  United States territories, structure, **1978:** 1971
  U.S. citizens living abroad, **1979:** 1523; **1980–81:** 1692
  Wellhead tax, **1977:** 668, 698, 751, 1618
  Windfall profits tax.
    See Crude Oil Windfall Profit Tax Act.
  Withholding by Federal agencies, **1977:** 55, 56, 1138
Tay-Sachs disease, **1978:** 897
Tay-Sachs and Genetic Diseases Act, National Sickle Cell Anemia, Cooley's Anemia, **1979:** 1705, 2105
Taylor, Charlotte A., **1978:** 1190
Taylor, Daniel B., **1980–81:** 751, 1015, 3022
Taylor, Eldon D., **1979:** 398, 402
Taylor, Ethel, **1977:** 527
Taylor, Gardner, **1980–81:** 2363
Taylor, Harriett R., **1979:** 665, 667
Taylor, Hobart, Jr., **1979:** 977
Taylor, Hubert T., **1977:** 1211, 1212
Taylor, John, **1977:** 110, 111, 127, 133
Taylor, John D., **1978:** 841
Taylor, Kenyon Y., **1977:** 196
Taylor, L. David, **1978:** 952
Taylor, Michael A., **1978:** 506, 571
Taylor, Paul, **1980–81:** 733n.
Taylor, Quentin St. Clair, **1977:** 537, 557
Taylor, Susanne Dabney, **1979:** 466
Taylor, Telford, **1978:** 1974
Taylor, Theodore B., **1979:** 661
Taylor, Tom, **1978:** 2169
Taylor, Woody, **1977:** 942
Tchaikovsky Competition, **1978:** 1356

Teacher Day, USA (Proc. 4730), **1980–81:** 430
Teacher of the Year, National, **1978:** 546
Teachers, American Federation of, **1977:** 1222;
     1980–81: 1549, 1556
Teague, Barry E., **1977:** 1613, 1614
Teamsters, International Brotherhood of, **1978:**
     1591; **1979:** 48, 560, 740, 745, 752, 850;
     1980–81: 1999
Teasdale, Gov. Joseph P., **1977:** 557; **1978:** 1506;
     1980–81: 1423n., 2665
Technical and Cultural Interchange Between East
     and West, Inc., Center for, **1977:** 1766
Technical Information Service, National, **1979:**
     2070; **1980–81:** 1932
Technological Cooperation, Foundation for Inter-
     national, **1978:** 2246; **1979:** 141, 161
Technological Cooperation, Institute for Scientific
     and.
     See Institute for Scientific and Technological
     Cooperation.
Technology, Center for Utilization of Federal,
     1979: 2070; **1980–81:** 2379
Technology Assessment, Office of, **1980–81:** 5
Technology Innovation Act, Stevenson-Wydler,
     1980–81: 2379
Tedder, Cooper, **1978:** 503
Teeters, Nancy Hays, **1978:** 1478, 1485
Teige, Peter N., **1980–81:** 428, 452
Tejeda, Frank M., **1979:** 1222
Telecommunication Union, International, **1980–
     81:** 225
Telecommunications.
     See Communications and telecommunications.
Telecommunications, International Committee on,
     1979: 270
Telecommunications Convention, International,
     1979: 541
Telecommunications Financing Act, Public, **1978:**
     1927
Telecommunications industry, regulatory reform,
     1979: 1699, 1706
Telecommunications and Information Administra-
     tion, National, **1978:** 786; **1979:** 586;
     1980–81: 1706n.
Telecommunications Policy, Office of, **1977:** 1257,
     1756
     Federal audiovisual programs, **1978:** 786
     Telecommunications functions, **1978:** 253, 598–
     602, 604, 605, 611
Telecommunications Satellite Consortium, Inter-
     national, **1980–81:** 705
Telephone Bank, Rural, **1980–81:** 292
Telephone call-in, "Ask President Carter," **1977:**
     291
Telephone industry, service rates, **1979:** 1701
Telephone services, **1978:** 173

Telephone and Telegraph Company, American,
     1980–81: 653
Television
     Industry, **1977:** 1690
     Receivers, imports from Japan, **1977:** 644, 755,
          944, 1158; **1979:** 166; **1980–81:** 920, 1257
     Visual aids for hearing-impaired, **1977:** 199
Television Arts and Sciences, Academy of, **1979:**
     1615
Television Association, National Cable, **1978:** 254
Teller, Adam J., **1980–81:** 926
Tellico Dam, Fla., **1979:** 1570, 1760, 1995
Telling, Edward R., **1980–81:** 581
Telmon, Sergio, **1978:** 1253, 1256; **1980–81:** 1102
Temperature restrictions, emergency building,
     1979: 1227, 1246, 1327
Temple University, Pa., **1980–81:** 874
Templer, Mark, **1980–81:** 926
Templeton, Robert, **1979:** 297
Temporary work permits, **1978:** 906
10-4 Day, **1978:** 1697
Teng Hsiao-p'ing.
     See Deng Xiaoping.
Tennessee
     Disaster assistance, **1980–81:** 1422
     Disaster declarations, **1977:** 805, 2035; **1979:** 841
     Energy crisis, **1977:** 37
     Gov. Lamar Alexander, **1980–81:** 1423n.
     President's visits, **1978:** 945, 948, 1008, 1857,
          1862, 2187, 2189–2209; **1980–81:** 2118–
          2140, 2586
     U.S. attorneys, **1977:** 373, 1086, 2037
     U.S. district judge, **1978:** 1381
     U.S. marshals, **1977:** 1266, 1307, 1931, 1932
Tennessee Valley Authority
     Board of Directors
          Chairman, **1979:** 1366, 1382
          Chairman and members, **1978:** 934, 1449, 1458
          Members, **1977:** 1284, 1307; **1979:** 877, 957
     Budget deferral, **1979:** 200
     Budget deferral and rescission, **1980–81:** 2764,
          2916
     Dam safety, **1977:** 723
     Energy-saving projects, **1977:** 411, 521, 1169
     Energy and water development program, **1980–
          81:** 1983
     Knoxville, Tenn., remarks to employees, **1978:**
          945
     Interview remarks, **1978:** 939
     National water policy functions, **1978:** 1044,
          1046
     Partisan politics involvement, possibility of,
          1980–81: 240
     Roosevelt, Franklin, establishment by, **1980–81:**
          539, 583, 630, 1603, 2597, 2598, 2605,
          2625, 2635, 2662
     Solar energy programs, **1979:** 1096, 1100, 1103,
          1105

Tennessee Valley Authority — *continued*
  Water resource projects, **1977:** 495
Tenorio, Pedro Agulto, **1980–81:** 344
Teresa of Calcutta, Mother, **1979:** 1962
Terrorism, **1977:** 60, 1939
  International, **1978:** 1308, 1676
  U.S. policy, **1980–81:** 2486
Terrorism, Negotiations for Combating, **1979:**
    1158, 1159
Terry, Claude E., **1978:** 2036
Terzi, Fehdi Labib, **1979:** 1591ftn.
Test Ban Negotiations, Comprehensive, **1979:** 216,
    1129, 1143
Test Ban Treaty, Limited, **1979:** 1038
Texaco, Inc.
  Chief executive officer, **1979:** 1614n.
  Home heating oil program, **1979:** 1613, 1631,
    1636, 1758
Texarkana, Ark., **1980–81:** 2417, 2418
Texas
  Black leaders, meeting with the President, **1979:**
    841
  Disaster assistance, **1980–81:** 1345, 1421
  Disaster declarations, **1978:** 1381; **1979:** 667,
    732, 1396, 1785; **1980–81:** 1544, 1946
  Ft. Worth community and civic leaders, meeting
    with the President (Digest), **1980–81:** 1427
  Gov. William P. Clements, Jr., **1980–81:** 1423n.
  Interview remarks, **1977:** 1922
  Lt. Gov. William Hobby, **1980–81:** 1399n., 2409
  1976 political supporters reception, **1978:** 1221
  President's visits, **1978:** 1157, 1164, 1165, 1173,
    1176, 1221; **1979:** 482; **1980–81:** 786,
    1390, 1391, 1393, 1727, 1738–1744, 2408–
    2417, 2603, 2617–2640
  U.S. attorneys, **1977:** 883, 884, 1211, 1212, 1222,
    1266
  U.S. circuit judge, **1979:** 1423
  U.S. district judges, **1977:** 944; **1979:** 241, 242,
    294, 327, 328, 377, 378, 402, 403, 1397,
    1398, 1883, 2281; **1980–81:** 104, 218, 1599
  U.S. marshals, **1977:** 883, 884, 943, 1222, 1266,
    1650, 1651; **1978:** 1222, 1223
  White House briefing by administration officials
    for civic and community leaders (Digest),
    1979: 1454
Texas, U.S.S., **1980–81:** 972, 976
Textile and apparel industry, **1978:** 2008, 2011,
    2067
  Multifiber agreement, **1977:** 755
  Representatives, meeting with the President,
    1979: 467
  Startex Mills, S.C.
    See Startex Mills, S.C.
  Trade unions, **1977:** 641
  U.S. trade
    China-U.S. agreement, **1980–81:** 1772, 1794

Textile and apparel industry — *continued*
  U.S. trade — *continued*
    European Communities, duty increases for
      articles from, **1980–81:** 1824
    Statistics, **1980–81:** 1769, 1951, 2039, 2142,
      2205, 2257, 2328, 2407
Textile Manufacturers Institute, American, **1977:**
    120
Textile matters, U.S. negotiator, **1978:** 1809; **1980–
    81:** 2751
Textile Workers, Amalgamated Clothing and,
    1978: 750; **1980–81:** 563
Thahane, Timothy, **1979:** 554
Thailand
  Ambassador to U.S., **1977:** 822; **1978:** 1380;
    1980–81: 1564
  Drug traffic, **1977:** 1399, 1401, 1402
  Joint statement, **1979:** 230–232
  Kampuchean relief efforts, **1979:** 2081, 2112
  Military equipment airlift from U.S., **1980–81:**
    1267
  Natural rubber trade, **1980–81:** 592
  Rosalynn Carter's visit, **1979:** 2090, 2100, 2112
  Senatorial delegation's visit, **1979:** 2036
  Trade with U.S., **1980–81:** 1251, 2912
  U.S. Ambassador, **1978:** 1030, 1034; **1980–81:**
    2999
  U.S. assistance, **1979:** 2126
  U.S. relations, **1979:** 53
  Vice President's visit, **1978:** 327
Thailand, Prime Minister (Kriangsak Chomanan)
  Kampuchean relief efforts, **1979:** 2090
  Visit to U.S.
    Announcement, **1979:** 178, 179
    Meetings with the President, **1979:** 221, 226,
      242 (Checklist)
    President's previsit comments, **1979:** 54, 182
Thaler, Daisy W., **1980–81:** 1433
Thanin, Trakraivixin, **1977:** 1401
Thanksgiving Day, **1977:** 2004, 2049; **1978:** 1802
  (Proc. 4693), **1979:** 1780
  (Proc. 4803), **1980–81:** 2723
Thapa, Bhekh Bahadur, **1980–81:** 1598
Thatcher, Margaret, **1977:** 881, 1611
  See also United Kingdom, Prime Minister.
Thatcher, Richard, **1980–81:** 933
Thaxton, Carlton J., **1979:** 400
Thayer, Harry E. T., **1980–81:** 1834, 1847
Thayer, Robert H., **1977:** 710
Theater Owners, National Association of, **1978:**
    933
Themido, Joao Hall, **1980–81:** 1245
Theodore Roosevelt Association, **1977:** 1382
Thibodaux, La., **1980–81:** 893
Third World, debt, **1977:** 502
Third World countries.
  See Developing countries.

Thomas, Barbara R., **1980–81:** 1434, 1470
Thomas, Charles Walker, **1980–81:** 84
Thomas, Dylan, **1977:** 1014
Thomas, Edward K., **1980–81:** 849
Thomas, Esther, **1977:** 292
Thomas, Francena, **1977:** 816
Thomas, Harold Lafayette, **1980–81:** 1423, 1469, 2432, 2726, 2727, 2870, 2873
Thomas, James Bert, **1980–81:** 1096, 1112
Thomas, John M., **1977:** 8
Thomas, Lewis, **1980–81:** 264
Thomas, Marlo, **1978:** 1135, 1191
Thomas, Nasha L., **1980–81:** 928
Thomas, O. Pendleton, **1979:** 1658
Thometz, Michael C., **1980–81:** 2731
Thompson, Anne Elise, **1979:** 1786, 1787
Thompson, Bradbury, **1980–81:** 2748
Thompson, Mr. and Mrs. Edward, **1977:** 402
Thompson, Repr. Frank, Jr., **1977:** 485, 1931; **1978:** 289, 304, 432, 434, 525, 1966; **1980–81:** 38
Thompson, Rear Adm. Gerald J., **1980–81:** 1292
Thompson, Harold G., **1980–81:** 929
Thompsom, Herbert B., **1980–81:** 1428
Thompson, Jeff, **1977:** 2133
Thompson, John D., **1977:** 934; **1978:** 920; **1979:** 932
Thompson, Lea, **1980–81:** 1936, 1937n.
Thompson, Marilyn Berry, **1980–81:** 3022
Thompson, Gov. Meldrim, Jr., **1978:** 382
Thompson, Myron B., **1980–81:** 344, 1700, 1847
Thompson, Brig. Gen. Nathaniel R., Jr., **1979:** 163
Thompson, Robert M., **1977:** 2077
Thompson, Roosevelt L., **1980–81:** 926
Thompson, Rufus E., **1978:** 899
Thompson, Sandra Joan, **1980–81:** 2107
Thompson, Wayne E., **1979:** 1671
Thomson, Meldrim, **1979:** 720n.
Thomson, Robert, **1979:** 467, 732
Thomson, Robert N., **1978:** 2110
Thomson, Scott D., **1980–81:** 1445
Thomson, Vernon, **1980–81:** 2856, 2870, 2873
Thomson, Vivienne S., **1980–81:** 1595, 1599
Thone, Charles, **1980–81:** 1090
Thorn, Gaston, **1977:** 882, 1754, 1789
Thornburg, Greg W., **1980–81:** 928
Thornburgh, Gov. Richard, **1979:** 578, 579; **1980–81:** 727, 736
Thorndike, Nicholas S., **1980–81:** 927
Thorne, Robert D., **1977:** 1502, 1507, 1584; **1978:** 232
Thornton, Barbara, **1977:** 816
Thorpe, Earl E., **1980–81:** 84
Thorpe, Jim, **1980–81:** 380
Thorstenson, Robert M., **1979:** 1001
3M Company, **1980–81:** 1404
Three Mile Island, Pa., nuclear plant accident, **1980–81:** 726, 743, 2438

Three Mile Island — *continued*
Federal monitoring, **1979:** 558, 577, 625
Mention, **1979:** 795
President's meetings with Federal officials (Digest), **1979:** 617, 618
Results of accident
Federal administration investigations, **1979:** 741
Nuclear energy reassessment, **1979:** 624, 681, 712, 798, 1428, 1505, 1537, 1753, 1906
White House statement, **1979:** 617
See also President's Commission on the Accident at Three Mile Island.
Three Mile Island, President's Commission on the Accident at.
See President's Commission on the Accident at Three Mile Island.
Thrower, Julius B., **1979:** 947
Thucydides, **1980–81:** 382
Thurmond, Sen. Strom, **1977:** 924; **1979:** 1444n., 1849; **1980–81:** 2218, 2788
Thurow, Lester C., **1978:** 697
Thurston, Don, **1979:** 482
Tice, Carol H., **1978:** 1191
Tickner, Charlie, **1980–81:** 380
Tidwell, G. Ernest, **1979:** 1018, 1019
Tiegs, Cheryl, **1980–81:** 1405
Tienken, Arthur T., **1978:** 88, 149
Tillich, Paul, **1979:** 972
Tilove, Robert, **1978:** 318; **1980–81:** 2789
Timber harvests.
See Lumber industry.
Timberlake, Constance H., **1980–81:** 2817
Timberlake, Robert, **1978:** 771
Timilty, Joseph F., **1977:** 182, 1905, 1931
Timmons, William E., **1978:** 759
Timpane, P. Michael, **1977:** 1780; **1980–81:** 651, 825
Tin buffer stock (EO 12263), **1980–81:** 2869
Tin industry, **1979:** 161
Tin Myaing Thein, **1978:** 1135
Tindemans, Leo, **1977:** 882, 1506, 1532, 1533, 1634, 1814, 1818, 1827; **1978:** 32, 34
Tinicum National Environmental Center, **1977:** 1962; **1980–81:** 1431
Tinker, Irene, **1977:** 1243, 1266
Tinsley, Jack, **1978:** 1164
Tipps, Paul, **1978:** 1620, 1621, 1627
Tirana, Bardyl, **1978:** 1128, 1155
Titan missiles
Phase-out, possibility of, **1980–81:** 1895, 1909
Silo explosion in Arkansas, **1980–81:** 1844, 1894
Title V Regional Commissions
Federal growth policy implementation, **1979:** 72
Proposed legislation, **1979:** 78
Regional growth policy process, **1979:** 79, 81
State cooperation efforts, **1979:** 66

Tito, Josep Broz.
  See Yugoslavia, President.
Titus, Allan, **1978:** 432
Tlateloco, Treaty of, **1977:** 613, 1027, 1812; **1978:**
    961, 1143, 1597; **1979:** 159, 835; **1980–81:**
    2734
Tobacco industry, **1977:** 1273, 2133, 2134; **1978:**
    72, 1386, 1390, 1392; **1979:** 55; **1980–81:**
    2144
Tobago
  Ambassador to U.S., **1977:** 806
  Trade with U.S., **1980–81:** 20
  U.S. Ambassador, **1977:** 886, 943; **1979:** 1156,
    1159
Tobin, Francis X., **1980–81:** 1091
Tobin, Joan F., **1978:** 1380, 2146; **1979:** 91; **1980–
    81:** 515, 894
Tobin, Maurice B., **1980–81:** 1031, 2533
Tobin, Mrs. Maurice B., **1980–81:** 1031
Toccoa, Ga., **1977:** 1997
Tocqueville, Alexis de, **1980–81:** 2061
Todd, Frank, **1978:** 1578
Todd, Brig. Gen. Harold, **1979:** 436
Todman, Terence A., **1977:** 373, 806, 1046; **1978:**
    887, 899; **1980–81:** 848, 1227
Togo, Fumihiko, **1977:** 464; **1978:** 802; **1980–81:**
    422
Togo
  Ambassador to U.S., **1979:** 842
  U.S. Ambassador, **1978:** 1451, 1458
Tokyo Economic Summit Conference, **1980–81:** 95
  Announcement, **1979:** 550
  Canadian and British Prime Ministers, meeting
    with the President, **1979:** 1181
  Conclusion remarks, **1979:** 1187
  Joint declaration, **1979:** 1197
  Postconference remarks, **1979:** 1211, 1218, 2055,
    2058, 2258
  Preconference remarks, **1979:** 1004, 1108, 1109,
    1145
  President's remarks with reporters, **1979:** 1183,
    1187
  Tokyo Round of Multilateral Trade Negotia-
    tions, **1977:** 819, 822
Tolbert, William R., Jr., **1978:** 671, 675, 709; **1979:**
    1806; **1980–81:** 373
Toledo, Ohio, **1980–81:** 2455
Toma, Iulai, **1978:** 328
Tomayko, John F., **1978:** 1760
Tomich, Rosemary, **1979:** 942
Tomlin, Lillie, **1979:** 1287
Tompkins, Rachel B., **1979:** 1727
Tone, Philip W., **1980–81:** 1976n., 2647
Toner, Brig. Gen. Francis J., **1980–81:** 37
Toner, Joseph, **1979:** 402
Tonga
  Ambassador to U.S., **1979:** 554

Tonga — *continued*
  U.S. Ambassador, **1979:** 1523, 1531; **1980–81:**
    893, 1107, 1111
Tongsun Park, **1977:** 1969; **1978:** 67, 1078
Toohey, William D., **1980–81:** 1405
Toon, Malcolm, **1977:** 195, 715, 745, 1030, 1519;
    1978: 1722
Tootle, Bill, **1980–81:** 786
Topande-Makambo, Jacques, **1980–81:** 1051
Topeka, Kans., **1980–81:** 563
Topel, Henry, **1980–81:** 2614
Topel, Sidney, **1980–81:** 3023
Torrance, Calif., **1980–81:** 1869, 1947
Torres, Estaban E., **1977:** 1540, 1568; **1978:** 1630,
    1669; **1979:** 1422, 1664, 2064; **1980–81:**
    1461, 1705ftn., 1939
Torres, Julio, **1979:** 466
Torres-Gil, Fernando Manuel, **1978:** 702, 711, 1026
Torrijos Herrera, Brig. Gen. Omar, **1977:** 1535,
    1544, 1567, 1787, 1788, 1793, 1796, 1885,
    1886, 2196; **1978:** 82, 86, 120, 517, 717,
    758, 759, 1118, 1120, 1122, 1123, 1153
Touhy, Jack, **1978:** 984, 987
Touhy, John, **1980–81:** 2091n.
Touré, Ahmed Sékou, **1979:** 1417
Tourism, **1980–81:** 2838
Toussaint, Donald R., **1979:** 2097, 2107
Towe, Peter Milburn, **1977:** 1383, 1978, 1980
Tower, Sen. John, **1980–81:** 2378
Towles, Dr. Jeffrey, **1980–81:** 1001, 1019
Toxic chemicals, **1977:** 969
Toxic Substances Control Act, **1979:** 1360
Toxic waste disposal.
  See Hazardous waste disposal.
Toxicology program, national, **1979:** 536
Toynbee, Arnold, **1979:** 1564; **1980–81:** 2747
Toyota, Tricia, **1980–81:** 1897n.
Trabulsi, Richard, **1978:** 2072
Tracy, Thomas M., **1979:** 1524, 1531
Trade
  Adjustment assistance program, **1977:** 1296,
    1307
  Agricultural exports, **1977:** 1921
  Anti-inflation program, **1977:** 628
  Balance of payments, **1977:** 289, 819, 1896, 1908,
    2017, 2061, 2159
  Barriers, **1977:** 755, 780
  China, People's Republic of, **1977:** 1708, 1994
  Customs convention, **1977:** 1357
  Foreign boycotts, **1977:** 788, 1136
  Generalized System of Preferences, **1977:** 255,
    1346, 1671, 1950, 2181
  Open international system, **1977:** 819, 820, 825,
    835
  Poznan International Technical Fair, **1977:** 936
  Romanian agreement, **1977:** 1055, 1057
  Small businesses, **1977:** 398

Trade — *continued*
  Tariffs, **1977:** 2109
  See also Commerce; Imports.
Trade, Agreement on Technical Barriers to, **1979:** 2253
Trade, General Agreement on Tariffs and.
  See General Agreement on Tariffs and Trade.
Trade, U.S.
  See Commerce, international.
Trade Act, Agricultural, **1978:** 1818
Trade Administration, International, **1980–81:** 2838
Trade Agreement, Multifiber, extension, **1977:** 123, 124
Trade Agreements Act, **1979:** 1092, 1311
  Trade Agreements Program, **1977:** 1163
Trade Board, East-West Foreign, **1978:** 2057
Trade in Civil Aircraft, Agreement on, **1979:** 2224, 2225, 2227, 2253, 2255
Trade Commission, Federal.
  See Federal Trade Commission.
Trade Commission, United States International
  See United States International Trade Commission.
Trade Complaint Center, **1979:** 1733
  Trade and Development, United Nations Conference on, **1977:** 522, 612; **1979:** 1731; **1980–81:** 7
Trade and Economic Council, U.S.-U.S.S.R., **1978:** 1723
Trade in Endangered Species of Wild Fauna and Flora, Convention on International, **1979:** 2288
Trade Negotiating Committee, **1979:** 1731; **1980–81:** 7
Trade Negotiations, Advisory Committee for.
  See Advisory Committee for Trade Negotiations.
Trade negotiations, multilateral.
  See Multilateral trade negotiations.
Trade Negotiations, Office of the Special Representative for.
  See Special Representative for Trade Negotiations, Office of the; United States Trade Representative, Office of the.
  Trade Negotiations, Tokyo Round of Multilateral, **1977:** 819, 822
Trade Policy Committee, **1978:** 2057; **1979:** 168, 169, 1730, 2256; **1980–81:** 8, 1259, 1695, 2330
Trade Policy Staff Committee, **1978:** 1563
Trade Representative, Office of the United States.
  See United States Trade Representative, Office of the
Trade unions, **1979:** 1252
Trade Week, World, **1977:** 594; **1978:** 514; **1979:** 616; **1980–81:** 322
Trademark Office, Patent and, **1980–81:** 237, 2803

Trademark system.
  See Patent and trademark system.
Trademarks, Nice Agreement on International, **1979:** 84
Trading Act, Futures, **1978:** 1696
Trading with the Enemy Act, **1979:** 1655, 1656
  Embargo regulations, **1978:** 1504
Traffic and Motor Vehicle Safety Act of 1966, National, **1980–81:** 2880
Traffic safety, **1978:** 1237
Traffic Safety Administration, National Highway, **1980–81:** 281
Tragen, Irving G., **1978:** 1515, 1516; **1979:** 1334
Trail, North Country National Scenic, **1980–81:** 432
Trails, designation and preservation of recreational and scenic, **1977:** 981
Trails Council, Interagency, **1979:** 1366, 1381
Trails System, National, **1979:** 1354, 1366, 1380–1382, 1813
Trails System Act of 1968, National, **1979:** 1366, 1380–1382
Train, Vice Adm. Harry D., II, **1978:** 1407
Train, Adm. Harry D., II, **1980–81:** 972n.
Train Dispatchers Association, American, **1979:** 818, 984
Trans-Alaska Oil Pipeline, **1979:** 592
Trans Mountain Oil Pipeline Corporation, **1980–81:** 99
Transatlantic air service, **1977:** 1668, 1669, 1952, 2158
Transatlantic balloon crossing, **1978:** 1449
Transition, Presidential.
  See Elections, 1980: transition.
Transport Workers Federation, International, **1980–81:** 1360
Transportation
  Administration's accomplishments and goals, **1980–81:** 140, 2950
  Concorde aircraft, landing rights, **1977:** 178
  Deregulation of industry, **1977:** 389
  Energy conservation measures, **1980–81:** 787, 826, 1399
  Energy crisis, **1977:** 35
  Federal programs, **1980–81:** 1588
  Hazardous materials, **1980–81:** 2872
  Industries deregulation, **1979:** 128, 130, 459
  Interstate 75, **1977:** 2165
  Mass transit, **1977:** 697, 908
  Message to Congress, **1978:** 220, 232
  National system modernization, **1980–81:** 1512, 1537, 1639, 1676, 1986, 1988, 2492
  Public trasnportation and parking, **1978:** 1431
  State of the Union, **1978:** 106
  Urban Mass Transportation Act of 1964 amendments, **1977:** 2033
  Urban programs, **1978:** 590

Transportation — *continued*
Urban programs to improve environmental qual-
ity, **1979:** 1369, 1383–1385
See also Aircraft and aviation; Authomobiles
and automobile industry; Mass transit;
Railroads; Ships and shipping; Trucking
industry.
Transportation, Department of
Acting Secretary, **1979:** 1285
Alaska Natural Gas Transportation System,
transfer of functions, **1979:** 594
Alaska Railroad, annual report, **1977:** 1030
Annual reports, **1978:** 1345; **1979:** 786; **1980–81:**
423
Assistant Secretaries, **1977:** 84, 148, 1752, 1755,
1794; **1979:** 2089, 2107, 2126, 2139
Automobile industry assistance, **1980–81:** 1330
Automobile safety enforcement, **1980–81:** 2049
Budget deferrals, **1977:** 352; **1979:** 200, 272,
1780, 2122; **1980–81:** 235, 1129, 2764
China-U.S. civil air transport agreement author-
ity, **1980–81:** 1774
Civil land remote-sensing activities, **1979:** 2150
Commuter and mass transit development, **1979:**
2022
Consumer Affairs Council membership, **1979:**
1763
Deputy Secretary, **1977:** 84, 744; **1980–81:** 25,
2877n.; **1979:** 2039, 2044
Diesel fuel shortages responsibilities, **1979:** 945
Energy conservation and transportation effi-
ciency observance, **1980–81:** 784
Environmental protection programs, **1979:** 1369
55-mile per hour speed limit enforcement, **1979:**
876
Food transportation system, **1977:** 2168
Fuel oil management group membership, **1979:**
2056
General Counsel, **1977:** 84, 148; **1980–81:** 643,
775
Grain supplies shipment, **1979:** 1609
Handicapped persons programs, **1980–81:** 810,
2610
Hard-core unemployed jobs program, **1979:** 2158
Heating oil management group, **1979:** 1631
Highway and motor vehicle safety, reports prep-
aration, **1979:** 1881
Inspector General, **1979:** 398, 402
Interagency Coordinating Council, **1978:** 1434
Marihuana, effects on driving, **1977:** 1404
Mass transit assistance, **1979:** 727, 875
Military Award Program, **1978:** 1345; **1979:** 363;
1980–81: 474, 2921
Nuclear waste disposal regulations, **1980–81:** 300
Offshore oil spill pollution prevention, **1979:** 338,
1361
Outer Continental Shelf development, **1977:** 974

Transportation, Department of — *continued*
Pipeline safety responsibilities, **1980–81:** 2869
Planning and air quality agreement, **1979:** 75
President's visit, question-and-answer session,
1977: 231
Price index for hauling of exempt commodities,
1979: 1136, 1139
Providence, R.I., station complex relocation
project, **1979:** 2061
Radiation Policy Council membership, **1980–81:**
363
Railroad industry study, **1979:** 459
Ridesharing programs, **1980–81:** 272
Tahoe Federal Coordinating Council member-
ship, **1980–81:** 2235, 2236
Task Force on Global Resources and Environ-
ment, functions, **1980–81:** 1417
Transfer of certain programs to proposed Energy
Department, **1977:** 258
Trucking fuel supplies locating mechanism,
1979: 1624
Urban area assistance, **1980–81:** 1358, 1862
Urban noise abatement programs, **1979:** 1371,
1385
Urban programs, **1978:** 584
Water user fees, **1978:** 1828
Westway Interstate Highway, **1977:** 1731
See also specific constituent agencies.
Transportation, Secretary of (Brock Adams), **1977:**
10, 14, 31, 86, 231–234, 248, 279, 286, 378,
389, 396, 458, 476, 485, 508, 662, 745, 748,
806, 949, 989, 1084, 1134, 1210, 1306,
1527, 1533, 1648, 1668, 1731, 1761, 1916,
2036, 2165; **1978:** 221, 232, 509, 516, 553,
594, 595, 1297, 1471, 1573, 1669, 1718,
1827, 1839, 2077, 2146, 2147, 2269
Alaska Natural Gas Transportation System, Executive Policy Board member, **1979:** 1126
Environmental protection actions, **1979:** 1383
Federal Council on the Arts and the Humanities,
member, **1979:** 956
Meetings with the President (Digest), **1979:** 786,
899, 1293
News conferences (Checklist), **1979:** 468, 900,
1143
Oil tanker inspection requirements, **1979:** 1360
Resignation, **1979:** 1285
Trucking industry deregulation, **1979:** 1117,
1124, 1125, 1137
Urban noise abatement program development,
1979: 1385
For functions of the Department in general, see
Transportation, Department of.
Transportation, Secretary of (Neil Goldschmidt),
1978: 854
Alaska Railroad land rental duties, **1980–81:**
2845

Transportation, Secretary of — *continued*
  Alaska Railroad report preparation, **1979:** 1785
  Appointment, **1979:** 1423
  Auto Industry Committee, Executive Committee member, **1980–81:** 1670
  Campaign appearance with the President, **1980–81:** 2672
  D.C. Metrorail system financing agreement, **1980–81:** 18
  Energy conservation efforts, **1980–81:** 788–791
  Environmental damage response activities, **1980–81:** 3044
  High seas and inland waters, demarcation lines establishment, **1980–81:** 1521
  Illinois highway problems investigation, **1980–81:** 1863
  Independent truckers' strike progress reports, **1979:** 1624
  Meetings with the President (Digest), **1979:** 1319, 1705, 1823, 1975, 2081, 2187; **1980–81:** 63, 267, 423, 492, 825, 931
  Membership on:
    State Planning Council on Radioactive Waste Management, **1980–81:** 301
    Trade Policy Committee, **1980–81:** 8
  Mentions, **1979:** 1324, 1500; **1980–81:** 1901
  Military awards program report, **1980–81:** 475
  News conferences (Checklist), **1979:** 1706; **1980–81:** 1337
  Nomination, **1979:** 1317, 1320, 1397, 1679
  President's assessment, **1979:** 1323, 1742, 1749
  President's Energy Efficiency Awards presentation, **1980–81:** 1401
  Rail system restructuring duties, **1980–81:** 2231
  Ridesharing program implementation, **1979:** 2022
  Rock Island Railroad strike actions, **1979:** 1696
  Ship pollution prevention, regulations preparation, **1980–81:** 2378
  Swearing-in ceremony, **1979:** 1718
  Task Force on Global Resources and Environment, duties, **1980–81:** 1417
  United Auto Workers, consultations with, **1980–81:** 1989
  Unnecessary stop signs removal, **1979:** 1952
  West-to-east crude oil transportation system recommendation, **1980–81:** 100
  Zimbabwe-Rhodesia trade functions (EO 12183), **1979:** 2252
  For functions of the Department in general, see Transportation, Department of.
Transportation Amendments of 1979, National Capital, **1980–81:** 13, 17
Transportation Barriers Compliance Board, Architectural and, **1979:** 2191; **1980–81:** 2730

Transportation Day, National Defense, and National Transportation Week, **1977:** 610; **1978:** 255; **1979:** 238; **1980–81:** 506, 783, 930
Transportation legislation, surface, **1978:** 1573
Transportation Policy Study Commission, National, **1978:** 930
Transportation and Related Agencies Appropriations Act, 1980, Department of, **1979:** 2185
Transportation Safety Board, National.
  See National Transportation Safety Board.
Trantham, Roy, **1978:** 1578
Trantum, Thomas A., **1979:** 871, 899
Travel costs, Government, **1978:** 1483
Travel restrictions, removal, **1977:** 340, 385, 782
Travel Service, United States, **1979:** 1850; **1980–81:** 2838
Travel and tourism administration, United States, proposed, **1980–81:** 2838
Travel and tourism advisory board, proposed, **1980–81:** 2838
Travis, J. Glennon, **1980–81:** 1596
Travis, Roger E., **1977:** 1944, 1966; **1978:** 231
Travolta, John, **1978:** 1829
Treasury, Department of the
  Alaska Natural Gas Transportation System, transfer of functions, **1979:** 596
  Alcoholic health hazards report preparation, **1980–81:** 2753
  American Indian Religious Freedom Act, implementation, **1978:** 1418
  Antiboycott programs, **1980–81:** 402
  Asset depreciation range system, **1978:** 175
  Assistant General Counsel (Chief Counsel for the Internal Revenue Service), **1977:** 803, 807; **1979:** 1977
  Assistant Secretaries, **1977:** 86, 181, 252, 377, 460, 465, 547, 557; **1978:** 126, 569, 641, 1155, 1682; **1979:** 240, 733, 1000, 1018, 1233; **1980–81:** 434, 453
  Automobile industry assistance, **1980–81:** 1329
  Budget deferrals, **1977:** 739, 2125; **1978:** 1041, 2183; **1979:** 200, 272, 2285; **1980–81:** 355, 2764
  Cash management policies review, **1979:** 462
  Comptroller of the Currency, **1977:** 1025, 1031, 1264, 1445, 1480, 1481, 1490–1492, 1494, 1617, 1637
  Comptroller General, **1979:** 1531, 2186, 2219
  Consumer Affairs Council membership, **1979:** 1763
  Counselor on Legislative and Intergovernmental Policy, **1979:** 270
  Deputy Assistant Secretary, **1979:** 890
  Deputy Secretary, **1977:** 485, 487, 510, 1930; **1980–81:** 374, 774

Treasury, Department of — *continued*
  Deputy Under Secretary, **1977:** 148, 280
  Director of the Mint, **1977:** 1907, 1931
  Dollar U.S., value, **1978:** 1908, 1954, 1955
  Embargo regulations functions, **1979:** 1656
  Employee retirement cooperative agreements,
    1980–81: 295
  Energy security trust fund responsibilities, **1979:**
    727
  Energy tax credit legislation, **1979:** 1102
  Export policy functions, **1978:** 1634, 1635
  Federal cash management, **1977:** 2025
  Fraud and waste elimination in Government
    programs, **1978:** 2234
  General Counsel, **1977:** 1119, 1128; **1978:** 1039
  Intelligence activities, **1978:** 202
  Interagency Coordinating Council, **1978:** 1434
  Interest rate controls review, **1979:** 928
  International trade functions, **1979:** 1731
  Iran, travel prohibitions on U.S. citizens to,
    1980–81: 710
  Labor-Management Relations Program exemp-
    tions, **1979:** 2145
  Minority businesses, **1977:** 1580
  Multilateral trade negotiations, **1978:** 1663
  National Productivity Council, **1978:** 1833, 1835
  Paperwork reduction, **1979:** 2181
  President's visit, question-and-answer session,
    1977: 126
  Reorganization Plan No. 4 of 1978, **1978:** 1401–
    1405
  Seasonal financing loans, **1977:** 1731
  Short-term cash balances, **1977:** 1932
  Steel antidumping suits investigation, **1980–81:**
    2512
  Sugar, sirups, and molasses imports, **1978:** 2106,
    2289
  Susan B. Anthony dollar coin, **1978:** 1737
  Tax courts reform responsibilities, **1979:** 345
  Taxes, withholding of District of Columbia,
    State, and city income or employment,
    1977: 1138
  Treasurer of the United States, **1977:** 1068, 1085;
    1978: 1809
  Under Secretaries, **1977:** 275, 280, 1690, 1790,
    1801, 2083, 2090; **1978:** 1407, 1910
  Wildlife law enforcement, **1979:** 1364, 1379
  See also specific constituent agencies.
Treasury, Secretary of the (W. Michael Blumen-
    thal), **1977:** 9, 13, 31, 55, 56, 194, 248, 279,
    311, 333, 378, 381, 453, 463, 485, 532, 549,
    553, 595, 621, 628–636, 641, 642, 662, 705,
    712, 744, 774, 805, 806, 883, 942, 1083,
    1162, 1222, 1265, 1306, 1382, 1464, 1491,
    1533, 1648, 1699, 1709, 1761, 1794, 1796,
    1826, 1963, 2005, 2006, 2050, 2076, 2089,
    2102, 2162; **1978:** 66, 124, 126, 270, 300,

Treasury, Secretary (Blumenthal) — *continued*
    301, 303, 415, 440, 588, 710, 726, 769, 770,
    782, 802, 892, 961, 1040, 1098, 1222, 1334,
    1380, 1399, 1407, 1426, 1441, 1495, 1504,
    1723, 1772, 2059, 2063, 2147, 2153, 2187,
    2237, 2242, 2270, 2288
  Alaska Natural Gas Transportation System,
    transfer of functions, **1979:** 596
  China, People's Republic of, visit to, **1979:** 174,
    331, 348
  Color television receiver imports functions (Proc.
    4634), **1979:** 168
  Countervailing duties' waiver, **1979:** 46
  Economic Policy Group, Chairman, **1979:** 977
  Electronic surveillance orders review, **1979:** 585,
    589
  Export financing negotiations, **1979:** 439
  Hungary and Romania, visit to, **1979:** 157
  Investigative and audit training program im-
    provement, **1979:** 779
  Meetings with the President (Digest), **1979:** 25,
    178, 240, 327, 401, 467, 554, 732, 841, 956,
    1142, 1222, 1293
  Mentions, **1979:** 96, 157, 865, 1155, 1216
  Multilateral development banks arrangements,
    1979: 396
  1980 budget preparation, **1979:** 96
  Oil price decontrol adjustments, **1979:** 724, 725
  Resignation, **1979:** 1273
  Solar energy development bank, board of direc-
    tors member, **1979:** 1101
  Ugandan import actions, **1979:** 225, 867
  Whaling conservation responsibilities, **1979:** 266
  For functions of the Department in general, see
    Treasury, Department of the.
Treasury, Secretary of the (G. William Miller)
  Agricultural trade development functions,
    1980–81: 1238, 1239
  Alcohol fuels foreign production tax exemption
    action, **1980–81:** 2560
  Anti-inflation accords with labor actions, **1979:**
    1778, 1787
  Automobile companies, meeting with chief ex-
    ecutives (Digest), **1980–81:** 932
  Budget 1981 preparation, **1980–81:** 225, 569, 608
  Chrysler Corporation, Federal assistance ac-
    tions, **1979:** 1430; **1980–81:** 27
  Color television receiver import functions,
    1980–81: 1259
  Crude Oil Windfall Profit Tax Act, signing
    ceremony remarks, **1980–81:** 589
  Embargo regulations authorities, **1979:** 1655
  Environmental damage response activities,
    1980–81: 3045
  Federal agency consumer programs analysis,
    1980–81: 1056
  Federal financial institutions deregulation ef-
    forts, **1980–81:** 572

Treasury, Secretary (Miller) — *continued*
Foreign assistance administration functions (EO 12163), **1979:** 1793, 1795, 1796
Foreign policy role, **1980–81:** 876
Interagency Employee Benefit Council, member, **1980–81:** 2864
Inter-American Development Bank, U.S. Governor, **1980–81:** 414
Iran
American hostage release agreement, implementation functions, **1980–81:** 3027–3031, 3033–3038
American hostage release negotiations, **1980–81:** 3019
Assets blockage functions (EO 12170), **1979:** 2118
Oil imports discontinuance actions (Proc. 4702), **1979:** 2110
Sanction against, duties, **1980–81:** 611–613, 715, 717
Meetings with the President (Digest), **1979:** 1785, 2043, 2110, 2206; **1980–81:** 292, 493, 607, 931, 1050, 1469, 1564, 1597, 1846
Membership on:
Advisory Commission on Intergovernmental Relations, **1980–81:** 104
Oil Policy Committee, **1980–81:** 10
Trade Policy Committee, **1980–81:** 8
Mentions, **1979:** 1307, 1429, 2289; **1980–81:** 1974n., 2833
Mortgage money survey, **1979:** 2028, 2050
News conference (Checklist), **1979:** 2139; **1980–81:** 1337
Nomination to be Secretary, **1979:** 1273, 1294
Nominations to assume positions in international organizations, **1979:** 1454
Oil imports adjustment program responsibilities, **1980–81:** 592, 598
Oveson, Mr. and Mrs. Clarence, claims settlement, **1980–81:** 2839
Pension plan reports (EO 12177), **1979:** 2219
State Governors briefing, **1979:** 2134
Swearing-in ceremony, **1979:** 1402
Synthetic Fuels Corporation, Board of Directors, Advisory Committee Vice Chairman, **1980–81:** 2752
Synthetic fuels production responsibilities, **1980–81:** 1971
Taxation reports on U.S. citizens living abroad, **1979:** 1523; **1980–81:** 207
Voluntary wage and price guidelines, telegram to Fortune 500 companies, **1980–81:** 453
Zimbabwe-Rhodesia trade functions (EO 12183), **1979:** 2252
For functions of the Department in general, see Treasury, Department of the.

Treaties and other international agreements.
See under Congress, Communications to; Panama Canal treaties.
Tree, Marietta, **1979:** 977
Treen, Gov. David C., **1980–81:** 1423n.
Trees, John S., **1978:** 1468
Trencher, Carol W., **1978:** 318, 898
Trenton, N.J., **1977:** 1576
Tribally Controlled Community College Assistance Act, **1978:** 1786
Tribbitt, Sherman W., **1977:** 2080
Tri-City Municipal Airport, Tenn., **1980–81:** 2118
Trident weapons systems
Lawsuits filing, **1980–81:** 2304, 2439
Missiles sale to United Kingdom, **1980–81:** 1343, 1344
President's commitment to develop, **1980–81:** 1535, 1725, 1740, 1871, 1909
Production schedule, **1980–81:** 2011, 2415, 2439
Submarines, **1978:** 123, 533, 809, 2199; **1979:** 155, 1612, 2235
Construction program, **1980–81:** 348, 475
Sea trials, **1980–81:** 1552, 2125, 2213, 2304, 2415
Trilateral Commission, **1978:** 1110
Trimble, Phillip R., **1980–81:** 843, 893
Trinidad
Ambassador to U.S., **1977:** 806, 886, 944
Trade with U.S., **1980–81:** 20
U.S. Ambassador, **1977:** 886, 943;, **1979:** 1156,1159
Tripp, Dwight L., Jr., **1978:** 919, 935; **1979:** 1418, 1423
Trippie, Charlie, **1980–81:** 2251
Tris in sleepwear, Government ban, **1978:** 1977
Tropical Forests, Interagency Task Force on, **1979:** 1387; **1980–81:** 1416
Trowbridge, Alexander, **1980–81:** 292, 1405
Truax, Anne Thorsen, **1980–81:** 1569
Truck and Bus Fuel Economy Advisory Committee, **1980–81:** 1404
Truckee, Carson, and Walker Rivers and Lake Tahoe Compact, **1978:** 1466
Trucking Associations, American, **1980–81:** 1402
Trucking competition and safety act, proposed, **1979:** 1114
Trucking industry, **1977:** 389; **1978:** 109
Deregulation
President's commitment to reform in 1979, **1979:** 105, 114, 128, 130, 459
Proposed legislation, **1979:** 1114, 1117, 1143, 2186
Independent truckers' strikes, **1979:** 1129, 1135, 1143, 1144, 1159, 1624
Labor dispute, **1979:** 657, 668
Legislation.
See Motor Carrier Act.

Trucking industry — *continued*
  Deregulation — *continued*
    Representatives, meeting with the President,
      1979: 178
    Special working groups for independent truck-
      ers' problems, **1979:** 1223
  Household goods transportation, **1980–81:** 2239
Trudeau, Pierre Elliott.
  See Canada, Prime Minister.
Trudell, Richard Allan, **1977:** 2101, 2130; **1978:** 89,
  232; **1980–81:** 1149, 1246
Truesdale, John C., **1977:** 1666, 1700; **1980–81:**
  1494, 1524, 2453, 2726, 2727, 2870, 2873
Trujillo, Rupert, **1979:** 1023
Truman, Bess, **1980–81:** 1610
Truman, Harry S
  American citizens' seizure in Mongolia, **1980–81:**
    744
  Democratic Party principles, **1979:** 1766, 1932
  Education, **1979:** 2130
  Franklin D. Roosevelt's death, reaction to,
    1980–81: 1616
  GI bill signing, **1980–81:** 2060
  Health care program, **1979:** 1024, 1028
  Japanese military requirements, **1979:** 1905
  Medicare support, **1980–81:** 2403
  Mentions, **1979:** 1038, 1515, 2016, 2242
  1948 election, **1980–81:** 2395, 2557, 2598, 2603,
    2608, 2622, 2626, 2634, 2645, 2663, 2664,
    2670, 2671, 2676, 2681
  Nuclear control efforts, **1979:** 1087
  Political philosophy, **1979:** 1931, 1932
  President's assessment, **1980–81:** 1532, 1611
  Public opinion polls' importance, **1979:** 1932,
    2059
  Puerto Rican nationalists assasination attempt,
    1979: 1664
  Quoted, **1979:** 1010; **1980–81:** 282, 349, 1571,
    1625, 1649
  U.S.S. *Nautilus* christening, **1980–81:** 2287
Truman, Margaret, **1980–81:** 1611
Trunk, Ann, **1979:** 662
Trust Agreement, President Carter's personal as-
  sets, **1977:** 140–143
Trust Territory of the Pacific Islands, **1980–81:** 301,
  319, 466
  High Commissioner, **1977:** 705, 745
  Postsecondary education, report, **1977:** 1294
  U.S. Representative, **1977:** 1303, 1308
Trusteeship Council, United Nations, **1980–81:** 495
Truth, Sojourner, **1980–81:** 412
Tso, Harold W., **1978:** 762
Tsongas, Repr. Paul E., **1977:** 402; **1978:** 229, 1038,
  1893, 1896
Tsongas, Sen. Paul E., **1979:** 1996, 2068
  Campaign efforts for the President, **1980–81:**
    1549, 2106

Tsongas, Sen. Paul E. — *continued*
  Legislation passage leadership
    Alaska National Interest Lands Conservation
      Act, **1980–81:** 1386, 2719, 2756
    Magnetic Fusion Energy Engineering Act,
      1980–81: 2106
    United Nations General Assembly, U.S. Rep-
      resentative, **1980–81:** 1859, 1946
Tubman, Harriet, **1980–81:** 412
Tuchman, Barbara, **1980–81:** 774
Tucker, Benjamin M., **1979:** 466
Tucker, Donald L., **1977:** 355, 1124, 1128, 1622,
  1714, 1755; **1978:** 1406
Tucker, Gordon, **1979:** 914
Tucker, Jim Guy, **1980–81:** 1032, 2423
Tucker, Repr. Jim Guy, **1977:** 1930, 2154; **1979:**
  667, 668, 1286
Tucker, Marna, **1977:** 1083
Tucker, Sterling, **1977:** 789, 1632; **1979:** 61, 93,
  1921
Tucker, William H., **1978:** 930
Tucson, Ariz., **1979:** 1817
Tuerkheimer, Frank F., **1977:** 707
Tull, David, **1978:** 1193
Tullio, Lois J., **1980–81:** 369, 2889
Tuna Commission, Inter-American Tropical, **1977:**
  1764
Tunas, International Commission for the Conser-
  vation of Atlantic, **1979:** 436
Tunisia
  Joint statement, **1978:** 2144
  Prime Minister Hedi Nouira, **1978:** 2073, 2090
  Special Representative Bourguiba, **1980–81:** 423
  U.S. Ambassador, **1979:** 101, 179
Tuolumne River, Calif., **1979:** 1815
Turay, Mohamed Morlai, **1978:** 1380
Turbay Avala, Julio Cesar, **1978:** 1380; **1980–81:**
  780
Tureen, Tom, **1980–81:** 2177
Turkey
  Ambassador to U.S., **1979:** 1454
  Cyprus conflict, **1977:** 143, 144, 638, 1137; **1978:**
    361, 1151, 1279, 1333, 1481, 2103; **1979:**
    191, 461, 998, 1301
  Mentions, **1979:** 845, 1006
  President's personal emissary, **1977:** 77, 194,
    1966; **1978:** 1110
  Prime Minister Bulent Ecevit, **1978:** 555, 1014,
    1016, 1017, 1019
  Prime Minister Šleyman Demirel, **1977:** 847, 869,
    882, 1137; **1980–81:** 382, 1398
  Secretary of State's trip, **1978:** 189
  Treaties with U.S.
    Extradition and mutual assistance in criminal
      matters, **1979:** 1390
    Penal judgments, **1979:** 1391
  U.S. Ambassador, **1977:** 617, 642; **1979:** 2238

[References are to page numbers except as otherwise indicated]

Turkey — *continued*
  U.S. arms embargo, **1978:** 1091, 1097, 1110,
    1326, 1337, 1357, 1590, 1636
  U.S. assistance, **1979:** 647, 653; **1980–81:** 439
  U.S. policy, **1977:** 225, 847
  U.S. relations, **1979:** 156; **1980–81:** 390
  West German economic assistance, **1980–81:**
    439, 678, 679
Turner, J., **1980–81:** 1372
Turner, J. C., **1978:** 880; **1980–81:** 1644
Turner, Howard J., Jr., **1977:** 1482, 1484
Turner, Irby, Jr., **1977:** 1817, 1826, 2000
Turner, Jay, **1979:** 1868
Turner, Adm. Stansfield, **1977:** 91, 194, 218, 344,
    350, 371, 464, 508, 641, 649, 706, 744, 745,
    806, 882, 942, 943, 1030, 1059, 1084, 1126,
    1162, 1163, 1210, 1222, 1264, 1265, 1306,
    1383, 1436, 1506, 1533, 1568, 1649, 1691,
    1699, 1754, 1794, 1825, 1930, 1966, 1998,
    2005, 2036, 2050, 2076, 2088, 2162; **1978:**
    65, 66, 148, 190, 276, 327, 372, 415, 456,
    525, 710, 750, 769, 802, 897, 934, 1009,
    1034, 1071, 1110, 1185, 1221, 1278, 1333,
    1344, 1380, 1435, 1436, 1457, 1571, 1722,
    1747, 1772, 1807, 1854, 1954, 2004, 2058,
    2073, 2146, 2187, 2269, 2281
  See also Central Intelligence Agency, Director.
Turner, Ted, **1977:** 1544; **1980–81:** 1405
Tuscumbia, Ala., **1980–81:** 1601, 1663
Tuskeegee, Ala., **1977:** 1485
Tuttle, Elbert, **1980–81:** 2238, 2929
Tuvalu
  Ambassador to U.S., **1979:** 842
  Friendship treaty with U.S., **1979:** 822
  Independence ceremonies, U.S. delegation, **1978:**
    1668
  Trade beneficiary developing country designa-
    tion, **1980–81:** 550
  U.S. Ambassador, **1979:** 1523, 1531; **1980–81:**
    893, 1107, 1111
Twain, Mark, **1979:** 1508, 1596
Tydings, Joseph, **1977:** 1083; **1979:** 1921
Tyree, Randell L., **1978:** 948
Tyson, Remer, **1980–81:** 2009
Tzounis, John, **1979:** 1882

UAW.
  See United Auto Workers.
Udall, Alice, **1978:** 1193
Udall, Repr. Morris K., **1977:** 1127, 1294, 1408,
    1978, 1980; **1978:** 148, 409, 1278, 1318,
    1513, 1762, 1765, 1926; **1979:** 776
  Communication from the President, **1980–81:**
    233

Udall, Repr. Morris K. — *continued*
  Legislation passage leadership
    Alaska National Interest Lands Conservation
      Act, **1980–81:** 2719, 2756, 2759
    Nuclear Regulatory Commission appropria-
      tions authorization, **1980–81:** 1257
Udall-Anderson act, proposed, **1979:** 855, 877
Udwin, Gerald E., **1980–81:** 742n.
Uehling, Barbara S., **1980–81:** 96, 218
Uganda
  Ambassador to U.S., **1979:** 1882
  Human rights violations, **1979:** 867, 1913
  President Idi Amin, **1977:** 220, 269, 292, 315
  Trade beneficiary developing country designa-
    tion, **1980–81:** 430, 550
  Trade with U.S., **1979:** 224, 867
  U.S. aid for refugees, **1979:** 2150
  U.S. Ambassador, **1980–81:** 629, 720
  U.S. policy, **1977:** 220, 292, 315
Uhlenbeck, George E., **1977:** 2047
Uhlman, Wesley C., **1978:** 702, 711; **1980–81:** 2534
Ujvagi, Peter Sandor, **1977:** 2153
Ullman, Repr. Al, **1977:** 31, 194, 962, 964, 1063,
    1082, 1092, 1103, 1371, 1396, 1436, 1447,
    1533, 1825, 2036, 2064, 2105, 2154, 2155,
    2157; **1978:** 148, 250, 432, 504, 720, 770,
    1772, 1783, 1827, 1980
  Home mortgage legislation sponsorship, **1980–
    81:** 662
  Legislation passage leadership.
    Beef and veal imports, **1979:** 2299
    Crude Oil Windfall Profit Tax Act, **1980–81:**
      470, 585, 588
    Installment Sales Revision Act, **1980–81:** 2344
    Social Security Disability Amendments,
      1980–81: 1063
    Trade Agreements Act, **1979:** 1312, 1313, 1808
    Welfare reform, **1979:** 1661
  Meeting with the President (Digest), **1979:** 217
  National health plan support, **1979:** 1011, 1637
  Windfall profits tax consideration, **1979:** 982
Ullman, Mrs. Al, **1978:** 1340
Ullman, Claire F., **1980–81:** 928
Ullsten, Ola, **1979:** 33, 33n., 89
Ulman, Lloyd, **1979:** 1954
Umpqua Indian Tribe, **1980–81:** 980
Undocumented aliens, **1977:** 632, 644, 901, 1030,
    1101, 1415, 1416, 1438, 1802, 1923; **1980–
    81:** 1726
Unemployment Compensation, National Commis-
  sion on, **1978:** 174, 257, 1051
UNESCO.
  See United Nations Educational, Scientific and
    Cultural Organization.
UNESCO, U.S. National Commission for, **1978:**
  1380
UNICEF.
  See United Nations Children's Fund.

Uniformed Services, Civilian Health and Medical Program for the, **1980–81:** 972, 1355
Uniformed Services Health Professionals Special Pay Act, **1980–81:** 456, 1251
Uniformed Services University of the Health Sciences, **1978:** 1964; **1980–81:** 1445, 1470, 1927, 1947
Union of Soviet Socialist Republics
  Afghanistan, invasion of.
    See Afghanistan, Soviet invasion.
  Africa, involvement in, **1978:** 56, 442, 871, 903, 905, 940, 941, 974, 977, 978, 1056, 1094, 1275
  Ambassador to U.S., **1977:** 86, 100, 560, 603, 641, 768, 1222, 1749, 2037
  American Embassy, fire, **1977:** 1519
  Anhydrous ammonia exports to U.S., **1979:** 2221, 2222
  Arms control and disarmament, **1977:** 28, 93–96, 849
  Arms sales from U.S., **1979:** 184
  Bolshoi Ballet, dancers defection in New York City, **1979:** 1590
  Broadcasting, international, **1977:** 478
  Chemical warfare, **1980–81:** 2021
    Negotiations with U.S., **1978:** 122
  Conference on Security and Cooperation in Europe, **1978:** 453
  Convention on International Civil Aviation, **1979:** 449
  Cosmos satellite, **1978:** 228, 232, 238, 241, 244, 248
  Cuba, combat troops in.
    See under Cuba.
  Defense spending, **1979:** 1904, 1989, 2233; **1980–81:** 347, 578, 659, 680, 869, 993
  Democratic Party Conference workshops, remarks, **1978:** 2202, 2214
  Exchange of Soviet citizens with U.S., **1979:** 731, 751, 965
  Far East, military buildup in, **1979:** 1148
  Fishing vessel, seizure by U.S. Coast Guard, **1977:** 604
  Foreign Minister A. A. Gromyko, **1977:** 545, 559, 603, 1649, 1659, 1689, 1699, 1912, 2206; **1978:** 442, 1033, 1282, 1656, 1672, 1690, 1722, 1724, 1832, 2253; **1979:** 1079, 1887; **1980–81:** 872, 1202, 1826, 2080
  Foreign policy, **1980–81:** 633, 641, 674, 964, 1316
  Foreign relations
    Angola, **1980–81:** 108, 674, 1105, 1225
    China, People's Republic of, **1978:** 2267; **1979:** 57; **1980–81:** 1995
    Cuba, **1979:** 1754, 1943; **1980–81:** 93, 625, 642, 2594
    Ethiopia, **1980–81:** 94, 108, 111, 674, 1007, 1225

U.S.S.R. — *continued*
  Foreign relations — *continued*
    Former allies, **1979:** 565, 1612, 1916, 1992, 2045; **1980–81:** 807, 2565
    Japan, **1979:** 764
    Kampuchea, **1980–81:** 674, 1105
    United States.
      See U.S. relations.
  Fort Worth Civic Organizations, remarks, **1978:** 1159, 1160
  Grain imports from U.S., **1977:** 1708, 1921, 2014; **1978:** 1819
  Grain production, **1980–81:** 2438
  Human rights issue, **1977:** 99, 100, 540, 541, 765, 766, 1107; **1978:** 453, 938, 973, 1054, 1099, 1100, 1252, 1258, 1259, 1273, 1274, 1282
  Human rights violations
    Helsinki accords honoring, **1980–81:** 379, 1116, 1207, 1435–1437, 1642, 2472
    International Labor Organization investigation, **1980–81:** 306
    Jewish emigration.
      See Jewish emigration.
    Sakharov, Mr. and Mrs. Andrei, internal exile of, **1980–81:** 194, 357
  International Year of Disabled Persons sponsorship, **1980–81:** 809
  Interview remarks, **1978:** 2017, 2018, 2045, 2276
  Iran
    Abstention from voting on U.S. sanctions against, **1980–81:** 39, 79, 611, 615, 669, 990
    American hostage situation, reaction to, **1980–81:** 637, 1851
    Involvement in, **1978:** 2255
    Trade with, **1980–81:** 712
  Iraq-Iran conflict, position on, **1980–81:** 1907, 2080
  Jewish emigration, **1980–81:** 1116, 1437, 1659, 2194, 2472, 2540
  Kampuchean relief efforts, lack of support for, **1979:** 2197
  Middle East role, **1977:** 1935, 2056
  MIG-23's in Cuba, **1978:** 2176
  Military capability, **1978:** 37, 123, 875, 1012, 1275
  Military strength comparison with U.S., **1980–81:** 660
  Minister of Foreign Trade, **1977:** 2006
  Mutual and balanced force reductions, **1977:** 2210; **1978:** 1182, 1183
  Neutron bomb, **1978:** 776
  News conference remarks, **1977:** 1198, 1235, 1238, 1239, 2119, 2205, 2206; **1978:** 1180, 1184, 1323, 1330, 1443, 1748, 2101
  Oil
    Afghanistan invasion, threat to world supplies, **1980–81:** 108, 111, 183

U.S.S.R. — *continued*
  Oil — *continued*
    Imports, **1980–81:** 35
  Olympics, 1980 Summer.
    See Olympics, 1980 Summer.
  Orlov, Yuri, trial, **1978:** 938
  Poland, troop buildup on borders of, **1980–81:** 2771, 2785
  Political prisoners, U.S. efforts to secure release of, **1979:** 1887
  Pravda comments on President Carter, **1977:** 692
  Principles compared with U.S., **1979:** 1838, 1916
  Quadripartite Agreement, **1978:** 1299
  Science and technology
    Agreement, **1977:** 1222
    Cooperation with U.S., **1980–81:** 406
    Repressive system, effect on development, **1980–81:** 81, 1554, 1686, 1895, 1909
  Secretary of State's visit, **1977:** 380, 496, 538, 559
  Space activities, **1979:** 1912
  SS missile development, **1980–81:** 1195, 1554, 1686, 1895, 1909
  SS-20 missile development, **1979:** 2234
  Strategic arms limitation.
    See Strategic arms limitation.
  Supreme Soviet Parliamentarians, meeting with delegation head, **1978:** 220
  Tchaikovsky Competition in Moscow, **1978:** 1356
  Trade with U.S., **1978:** 2224, 2225; **1979:** 331, 358, 359, 749, 2292, 2296
    Agricultural products.
      See Soviet trade suspension *under* Agricultural trade.
    Anhydrous ammonia exports, **1980–81:** 102
    Fishing rights suspension.
      See under Fishing industry.
    Phosphate shipments suspension, **1980–81:** 560, 2470
    Summer Olympics articles prohibition, **1980–81:** 559, 560, 565
    Technology and other strategic items suspension.
      See under Science and technology.
  U.S. legislation amendment, **1980–81:** 2471
  United Nations Mission, bombing of, **1979:** 2231
  U.S. Ambassador, **1977:** 195, 715, 745, 1030, 1519; **1978:** 1722; **1979:** 1284, 1293, 1824; **1980–81:** 11, 23, 1050
  U.S. Naval Academy, address, **1978:** 1052
  U.S. policy, **1977:** 220, 447, 502, 630, 648, 766, 781, 959, 1107
  U.S. relations, **1978:** 1256, 1258, 1260, 1263, 1273, 1275, 1276, 1288, 1301
    Administration's accomplishments and goals, **1980–81:** 2977
    Afghanistan invasion, effect on, **1980–81:** 36, 108, 111, 164, 346, 673, 674, 1105

U.S.S.R. — *continued*
  U.S. relations — *continued*
    Détente maintenance, **1979:** 158; **1980–81:** 442, 872, 1105, 1157, 1159, 1207, 2336
    Impact of:
      SALT II treaty, **1979:** 305, 317, 348, 851, 1019, 1611, 1770, 2256
      Soviet troops in Cuba, **1979:** 1805
      U.S.-Chinese normalization, **1979:** 172
      Peaceful competition policy, **1979:** 260, 693, 903, 1805
    Post-World War II relationship, **1980–81:** 195
    President's second-term goals, **1980–81:** 1619
    Worldwide influence, Soviet-U.S. comparison, **1979:** 1612
  Verification of agreements with U.S., **1977:** 1202
  Vienna Summit Meeting.
    See Vienna Summit Meeting.
  Wake Forest University, address, **1978:** 531
  Union of Soviet Socialist Republics, President (L. I. Brezhnev), **1977:** 100, 496, 498, 502, 540, 603, 634, 859, 1107, 1198, 1314, 1912, 1954, 2010, 2037, 2192; **1978:** 776, 852, 872, 903, 940, 974, 1180, 1184, 1260, 1776, 1832, 2180, 2202, 2253, 2255, 2276
    Arms reduction offer to European nations, **1979:** 1844
    Backfire bomber negotiations, **1979:** 1587
    Invitation to visit U.S., **1979:** 158
    Iraq-Iran conflict, exchange of letters with the President, **1980–81:** 2080, 2132
    Mention, **1979:** 1521
    Nuclear weapons nonproliferation support, **1979:** 1838, 1905
    Soviet dissidents' exchange approval, **1979:** 751
    Soviet invasion of Afghanistan, position on troops withdrawal, **1980–81:** 674, 1194, 1199, 1202
    Trade with U.S., position on, **1979:** 331, 356
    U.S. arms sale to China, warning against, **1979:** 184
    Vienna Summit Meeting.
      See Vienna Summit Meeting.
United Arab Emirates
  Ambassador to U.S., **1977:** 822
  Oil supplies, **1980–81:** 2025
  U.S. Ambassador, **1979:** 1300, 1319
United Auto Workers, **1977:** 86, 489, 887, 944, 1892, 1966, 1967; **1978:** 303, 710, 898; **1979:** 740, 752, 1252, 1499, 1652, 1705, 1954
  Chrysler Corporation Loan Guarantee Act of 1979, negotiations, **1980–81:** 28
  Industry revitalization involvement, **1980–81:** 1985, 2010
  Mention, **1980–81:** 770
  Presidential endorsement, **1980–81:** 1680

United Auto Workers, President (Douglas Fraser)
  Auto Industry Committee, member, **1980–81:** 1670
  Chrysler Corporation Loan Guarantee Act of 1979 support, **1980–81:** 28
  Industry revitalization efforts, **1980–81:** 1330
  Meeting with the President (Digest), **1980–81:** 931
  Mentions, **1977:** 816, 895, 1541, 1966, 1967; **1978:** 217, 230, 303, 710; **1980–81:** 1986n., 1989, 2884ftn.
United Automobile, Aerospace & Agricultural Implement Workers of America, **1980–81:** 1598
United Food and Commercial Workers International Union, **1979:** 1008, 1020
United Garment Workers, **1977:** 464
United Jewish Appeal, **1980–81:** 377, 931
United Kingdom
  African policy, **1977:** 1089
  Air service with U.S., **1980–81:** 2651
  Ambassador to U.S., **1977:** 31, 1382, 1383; **1978:** 415; **1979:** 1318
  Atomic energy for mutual defense purposes agreement with U.S., **1979:** 2164
  Bilateral air services agreement, **1978:** 442, 471, 525, 527; **1977:** 256, 508, 748, 757, 1137, 1346, 1365, 1482
  Bonn Economic Summit Conference, **1978:** 1310, 1311
  Conservative Party leader, **1977:** 1610
  Convention on taxation and fiscal evasion, **1977:** 1066
  Cyprus conflict resolution support, **1979:** 191, 998
  Elections, **1979:** 803
  Fishery agreement, **1977:** 1753
  Foreign Minister, **1977:** 646, 647, 1487; **1979:** 2259, 2264
  Foreign Minister Lord Carrington, **1980–81:** 868
  Foreign Secretary, **1977:** 251; **1978:** 495, 504
  Former Prime Minister James Callaghan, **1980–81:** 63, 2828
  Iranian Embassy takeover, **1980–81:** 845
  Mountbatten, Lord Louis, death, **1979:** 1522, 1603
  Northern Ireland, efforts to resolve conflict in, **1979:** 2097
  Nuclear arms control, **1980–81:** 434
  Nuclear test ban, **1979:** 902
  Olympics, 1980 Summer, possibility of boycott, **1980–81:** 676
  President's visit, **1977:** 809–815, 881
  Princess Anne, **1977:** 1127
  Queen Elizabeth II, **1977:** 810, 812, 817
  Reciprocal fisheries agreement with U.S., **1980–81:** 1022
  Secretary of State Francis Pym, **1980–81:** 1344n.

United Kingdom — *continued*
  Summit meeting, international, **1977:** 371
  Taxation and fiscal evasion convention with U.S., **1979:** 663, 778
  Tokyo Summit
    Attendance announcement, **1979:** 550
    Joint statement, **1979:** 1197
    Oil imports ceiling, **1979:** 1198
  Trident I missiles sale from U.S., **1980–81:** 1343, 1344
  U.S. Ambassador, **1977:** 597, 811, 942, 1382; **1979:** 1603
  Vice President's visit, **1977:** 785
  Zimbabwe, final settlement agreement, **1980–81:** 541, 679, 807
  Zimbabwe-Rhodesia conflict
    Final settlement agreement, **1979:** 2262, 2264, 2267
    Negotiations, **1979:** 357, 755, 1013, 1230, 2121, 2137, 2258, 2259
United Kingdom, Prime Minister (James Callaghan), **1977:** 178, 353, 359, 371, 584, 748, 756, 757, 809–815, 825, 826, 841, 881; **1978:** 34, 526, 564, 566, 1017, 1034, 1221, 1308, 1310, 1334, 2187
  Guadeloupe Conference
    Conclusion remarks, **1979:** 17, 20n.
    Meetings with the President and Western European leaders, **1979:** 25, 26
United Kingdom, Prime Minister (Margaret Thatcher)
  Secretary of State Vance, meetings with, **1979:** 803, 965
  Tokyo Summit
    Conclusion remarks, **1979:** 1194, 1197n.
    Meetings with the President, **1979:** 1181, 1183n.
    Mention, **1979:** 1185
  Trident I missiles sale from U.S., **1980–81:** 1343, 1344
  Venice Economic Summit Conference
    Concluding remarks, **1980–81:** 1180
    Meeting with the President (Digest), **1980–81:** 1243
    Mention, **1980–81:** 1193
  Visit to U.S.
    Announcement, **1979:** 1976
    Meetings with the President, **1979:** 2257, 2259, 2264, 2267
United Methodist Conference, **1980–81:** 774
United Mine Workers of America, **1977:** 403, 882, 1169
  Officials, meetings with the President, **1978:** 328, 1006; **1979:** 905, 1650
  President's Commission on the Coal Industry, **1978:** 2243
Strike.
  See under Coal.

United Mine Workers of America, President (Sam Church, Jr.)
Mentions, **1980–81:** 2201, 2475, 2511
President's Council for Energy Efficiency, member, **1980–81:** 1404
White House Coal Advisory Council, member, **1980–81:** 1644
United Nations
Afghanistan, responses to Soviet invasion of
General Assembly vote, **1980–81:** 106, 108, 189, 244, 520, 541, 560, 578, 634, 673, 796, 989, 1105, 1308, 1309, 1530, 2056, 2835
Moslem nations, **1980–81:** 643, 2324
Multinational petition to condemn action, **1980–81:** 22, 40
Third World nations, **1980–81:** 224
African issues, **1978:** 1095
African nations luncheon, **1977:** 1723
African role, **1977:** 647
Alternate U.S. Representative for Special Political Affairs, **1977:** 1252, 1266; **1978:** 1528, 1572
Asian nations luncheon, **1977:** 1735
Commission on the Status of Women, U.S. Representative, **1977:** 1176
Conference on Science and Technology, U.S. Ambassador, **1978:** 1222
Conference on Science and Technology Development, Coordinator, **1977:** 1230, 1266
Congressional Black Caucus, remarks, **1978:** 1682
Cuban Mission bombing, **1979:** 2231
Cuban refugee assistance, **1980–81:** 914
Cyprus conflict, **1977:** 143
Negotiations, **1980–81:** 205, 1397, 1923, 2740, 3020
Resolution actions, **1979:** 191, 461, 648
Deputy U.S. Representative, **1977:** 505, 510, 527, 557; **1979:** 1298, 1319, 1396, 1725, 2043, 2083
Developing countries role, **1980–81:** 2391
Developmental programs, **1979:** 1794
Disarmament week sponsorship, **1978:** 1851
Drug abuse control, **1977:** 1402
Drug abuse control fund, **1978:** 1568
Economic and Social Council
Commission on Narcotic Drugs, U.S. Representative, **1978:** 64
Commission for Social Development U.S. Representative, **1977:** 1587
U.S. Deputy Representative, **1977:** 1587
U.S. Representative, **1977:** 994, 1031
Deputy U. S. Representative, **1980–81:** 606
Kampuchean relief, **1980–81:** 931
U.S. Deputy Representative, **1978:** 2157
U.S. Representative, **1980–81:** 507, 522
Egyptian-Israeli peace treaty implementation, **1979:** 497, 499, 501, 504, 507, 517, 518

United Nations — *continued*
Environment program, **1980–81:** 590
European nations dinner, **1977:** 1727
European Office, U.S. Representative, **1977:** 1123, 1128; **1979:** 2147
General Assembly
Addresses, **1977:** 444, 465, 1715, 1755
Secretary of State's activities in session of, **1979:** 1855
Special Session on Disarmament
Special Adviser, **1978:** 757
U.S. Representatives and Alternate Representatives, **1978:** 919, 935, 1110
Vice President's address, **1978:** 928
U.S. Representative and Alternate Representatives, **1977:** 527, 557, 1437, 1625, 1626, 1650; **1978:** 1185, 1509, 1516; **1979:** 1667, 1680; **1980–81:** 1859, 1946, 2070, 2726, 2727
Genocide Convention, **1977:** 450
Global 2000 study, **1980–81:** 1415
High Commissioner for Human Rights, proposed, **1977:** 450, 2115
High Commissioner for Refugees, **1979:** 765, 2150
Human Environment Conference, **1980–81:** 1415
Human Rights Commission, **1978:** 768
U.S. Representative, **1977:** 1252
Human rights treaties, **1978:** 395
International covenants on human rights, **1977:** 1734; **1979:** 162; **1980–81:** 119
Interview remarks, **1978:** 1410
Iran, responses to American hostages in
Diplomatic sanctions, possibility of, **1980–81:** 669, 670
Economic sanctions
Imposition, **1979:** 2277
Mentions, **1980–81:** 91, 113
Security Council approval, **1980–81:** 79, 611, 614, 669, 670, 707, 764
Soviet veto, **1980–81:** 79, 669, 674, 990
U.S. proposal, **1980–81:** 40
Release efforts, **1980–81:** 22, 39, 79, 794
Unanimous condemnation, **1980–81:** 36, 39, 224, 728, 763, 795, 882, 2863
Iranian Mission, **1979:** 2252
Iraq-Iran conflict settlement efforts, **1980–81:** 1906, 1921
Israeli representation, **1980–81:** 1949, 2195, 2392, 2431, 2461
Israeli settlements and status of Jerusalem vote, **1980–81:** 427, 640
Kampuchean relief efforts, **1979:** 2037, 2052, 2113
Latin American nations reception, **1977:** 1754
Middle East conference, proposed, **1977:** 2055
Outer Space Conference, **1980–81:** 1846, 1847
Peacekeeping role, **1980–81:** 1218

United Nations — *continued*
  Reform, report to Congress, **1978:** 449
  Resolutions 242 and 338, **1978:** 491, 1523–1527
  Science and Technology for Development, Conference on, **1977:** 1751, 1755
  Secretariat, U.S. delegation, **1977:** 1725
  Security Council, **1980–81:** 638
    Deputy U.S. Representative, **1979:** 2038, 2044
    Iranian situation consideration, **1979:** 2124, 2133, 2168, 2195, 2240, 2287
    U.S. Deputy Representative, **1978:** 1185
  Soviet Mission bombing, **1979:** 2231
  Special Political Affairs, Alternate U.S. Representative, **1979:** 2196
  Trusteeship Council, U.S. Representative, **1978:** 895
  Under Secretary General, **1979:** 1301
  U.S. foreign assistance programs, **1979:** 279, 396, 644
  U.S. Naval Academy, remarks, **1978:** 1056
  U.S. 1979 dues payment, **1979:** 1434
  U.S. participation, **1977:** 1950; **1979:** 62; **1980–81:** 1286, 2391, 2863
  World Food program, **1980–81:** 257
United Nations, Secretary-General (Kurt Waldheim), **1977:** 77, 245, 444, 638, 1715, 1734, 1950, 2055; **1978:** 450, 555, 1151–1153, 1482, 1541, 1687–1689, 2221
  Cyprus conflict settlement actions, **1979:** 191, 461, 998, 1738, 2163; **1980–81:** 205, 382, 551, 947, 1397
  Geneva Conference on Kampuchean relief, convening of, **1980–81:** 931
  Indochinese refugee assistance actions, **1979:** 1188ftn.
  Iran, efforts to negotiate release of American hostages, **1980–81:** 39, 79, 307, 356, 386, 455, 612, 614
  Iraq-Iran conflict settlement negotiations, **1980–81:** 1921
  Kampuchean relief efforts, **1979:** 1925, 2029
  Meetings with the President, **1979:** 1332; **1980–81:** 27
  Mention, **1979:** 62
  1959 Geneva Radio Regulations, partial revision, **1980–81:** 225
United Nations, U.S. Representative (Donald F. McHenry)
  Developing countries, relationship with, **1980–81:** 224, 1501, 2366, 2427
  General Assembly, U.S. Representative nomination, **1980–81:** 1859, 1946, 2070, 2726, 2727
  Iran, opposition to discussions in Security Council of, **1979:** 2124
  Meetings with the President (Digest), **1979:** 2280; **1980–81:** 966
  Mentions, **1980–81:** 861, 1634

UN, U.S. Representative — *continued*
  Nomination to be U.S. Representative, **1979:** 1588, 1679
  Nomination to be U.S. Representative to the General Assembly, **1979:** 1667, 1680
  President's assessment, **1979:** 1589, 1590
  Soviet dancers' defection, recommendation on, **1979:** 1590ftn.
  Soviet U.N. Mission bombing, apology statement to Soviet Representative, **1979:** 2232
  Swearing-in ceremony, **1979:** 1715
  United Nations Pledging Conference on Refugee Relief, member, **1979:** 2085
  U.S. delegation head for:
    Nicaraguan revolution anniversary celebrations, **1980–81:** 1376
    World Conference for the United Nations Decade for Women, **1980–81:** 1336
  Zimbabwe independence talks, role in, **1980–81:** 1580, 1581, 1706
United Nations, U.S. Representative (Andrew J. Young), **1977:** 10, 31, 33, 46, 76, 85, 220, 245, 248, 378, 451, 595, 647, 709, 710, 913, 1021, 1084, 1108, 1347, 1382, 1471, 1472, 1487, 1723, 1726, 1727, 1737, 1748, 1809, 1938, 2201; **1978:** 374, 456, 526, 871, 1105, 1325, 1330, 1406, 1668, 1682, 1703, 1723, 2072, 2197, 2219
  African nations, relationship with, **1979:** 38
  Australian-American Week, U.S. Representative, **1979:** 376
  Bugging of New York City apartment, possibility, **1979:** 1586, 1590
  Future plans, **1979:** 1613
  Meetings with the President (Digest), **1979:** 14, 1454
  Mentions, **1979:** 883, 886ftn., 909, 912
  News conference (Checklist), **1979:** 1786
  President's assessment, **1979:** 31, 62, 1564, 1613
  Recommendation for successor, **1979:** 1589
  Resignation, **1979:** 1436, 1455
  Swearing in of U.N. Representative Donald F. McHenry, remarks, **1979:** 1717
United Nations Association of the U.S.A., **1979:** 1658
United Nations Children's Fund, **1977:** 954; **1978:** 296, 318, 746
  Executive Board, U.S. Representatives, **1979:** 1602, 2083
  Kampuchean relief efforts, **1979:** 1925, 2011, 2052, 2080, 2113, 2117
United Nations Commission on Human Rights, **1979:** 2217; **1980–81:** 495
United Nations commission of inquiry on Iran
  Establishment, **1980–81:** 356
  Meeting with Iranian leaders, **1980–81:** 386
  Suspension of activities, **1980–81:** 455, 458
  U.S. support, **1980–81:** 1828

United Nations Conference on Science and Technology for Development, **1977:** 1950; **1980–81:** 408
    U.S. delegation head, **1979:** 541
United Nations Conference on Trade and Development, **1977:** 522, 612, 1950; **1979:** 1731; **1980–81:** 7
United Nations Day, **1977:** 1059, 1664; **1978:** 1539, 1540; **1979:** 1657; **1980–81:** 653, 1594
United Nations Decade for Action to Combat Racism and Racial Discrimination, **1978:** 1456
United Nations Decade for Women, Equality, Development and Peace, **1979:** 825
United Nations Decade for Women, **1980–81:** 1335
United Nations Development Program, **1977:** 456
United Nations Economic Commission for Latin America, **1977:** 612
United Nations Educational, Scientific, and Cultural Organization, **1977:** 1486, 1540, 1568; **1978:** 1630, 1669; **1979:** 1422, 1665, 1819, 1824; **1980–81:** 1713, 1847, 2721
United Nations Environment Programme, **1979:** 1387, 1388
United Nations High Commission for Refugees, **1980–81:** 256
United Nations Industrial Development Organization, **1979:** 2187
United Nations Joint Inspection Unit, **1979:** 1531, 2186
United Nations Pledging Conference on Refugee Relief, **1979:** 2085
United Nations Trusteeship Council, **1980–81:** 495
United Negro College Fund, **1977:** 2003; **1978:** 1457; **1980–81:** 53, 1561
United Press International Newspaper Advisory Board, **1979:** 735
United Service Organizations, Inc., **1978:** 965, 1340, 1653
United States Advisory Commission on Information, **1977:** 1767, 1770, 1771
United States Advisory Commission on International Communication, Cultural and Educational Affairs, **1977:** 1767, 1770, 1964; **1978:** 510, 1720, 1772; **1979:** 729, 787, 1037, 1044
United States Advisory Commission on International Educational and Cultural Affairs, **1977:** 1767, 1770, 1771
United States Advisory Commission on Public Diplomacy, **1980–81:** 1445, 1470, 1846
United States Air Force, **1980–81:** 780n.
United States Air Force Academy, **1978:** 569; **1978:** 435; **1980–81:** 606, 757, 2802
United States amateur boxing team, **1980–81:** 482, 517, 564

United States Arms Control and Disarmament Agency
    Annual reports, **1979:** 682; **1980–81:** 450, 2110
    Appropriation authorization, extension, **1977:** 358; **1978:** 451
    Assistant Directors, **1977:** 1135, 1163, 1528, 1534, 1676, 1680; **1979:** 685; **1980–81:** 428, 452, 866, 894, 930
    Deputy Director, **1977:** 745
    General Advisory Committee
        Members, **1977:** 217, 230, 1706, 1724; **1980–81:** 25, 217, 218
        Meeting with the President, **1978:** 2270
        Chairman, **1979:** 1820
    General Counsel, **1979:** 1077
    Indonesia-U.S. nuclear agreement analysis, **1980–81:** 1281
    Member, **1979:** 45, 90
    Reports, **1978:** 549, 1029
    Special Representative for Arms Control and Disarmament Negotiations, **1977:** 1607
    Uranium enrichment capacity, report preparation, **1979:** 1822
United States Arms Control and Disarmament Agency, Director (Ralph Earle II), **1977:** 66, 87, 93, 358, 379, 740, 743, 1107, 1127, 1263, 1607; **1978:** 457, 594, 595, 1722, 1744, 1747, 1807, 1857, 1879, 2053; **1979:** 1107, 1143, 2270
    International nuclear energy agreements analysis, **1980–81:** 782, 1027, 1240, 2878
    Nomination, **1980–81:** 217, 219
    Nuclear proliferation assessment statement, **1980–81:** 266
    Recess appointment, **1980–81:** 25
United States Army.
    See Army, Department of the.
United States Assay Offices, **1978:** 390, 416, 569, 641
United States Catholic Conference, **1980–81:** 2841
United States Chamber of Commerce, **1980–81:** 1281
    Officials, meeting with the President, **1977:** 251, 1048
United States Circuit Judge Nominating Commission, **1977:** 179, 815, 1010, 1053, 1055, 1127, 1242; **1978:** 910; **1980–81:** 2849
United States Circuit Judge Nominating Panel for the Eighth Circuit, **1978:** 734
United States Civil Service Commission, **1979:** 8, 64, 1882; **1980–81:** 617
    Anti-inflationary program, **1978:** 1856
    Board of Directors, **1977:** 264
    Briefings for administration executives, **1977:** 604
    Chairman, **1977:** 570, 596, 1053, 1499, 1532; **1978:** 316, 594, 595, 802, 897, 953, 1138, 1158, 1362, 1407, 1765, 1773, 1972

U.S. Civil Service Commission — *continued*
  Civil service rules amendment, **1978:** 480
  Commissioners, **1977:** 570, 596, 793, 794, 807,
      871
  Discrimination, **1977:** 115, 116, 264
  Displaced employee program, **1977:** 1463
  Equal employment opportunity programs, **1978:**
      1213
  Federal personnel manual, **1977:** 1053
  Fraud and waste elimination in Government
      programs, **1978:** 2234
  Government reorganization, **1977:** 164
  Hiring practices, **1977:** 271, 323
  National Productivity Council, **1978:** 1833, 1835,
      1836
  Office of Ethics, proposed, **1977:** 787
  President's award for distinguished Federal ci-
      vilian service, **1977:** 1819
  Reorganization, **1978:** 399, 401, 403, 405, 437,
      445, 447, 953–956, 958, 1363, 2291, 2292
  Reports, **1977:** 566, 1162
  Transfer of certain executive development and
      other personnel functions, **1977:** 2080,
      2081
  Veterans programs, **1978:** 1742, 1743
  Vice Chairman, **1977:** 793
  Work-study program students, **1977:** 1907
United States Coast Guard, **1977:** 388, 458, 604;
      1979: 1360, 1361, 1631, 2057
  Commandant, **1980–81:** 932
  Cuban refugees
    Patrols to stop influx, **1980–81:** 1880, 1989,
        2154, 2211, 2383, 2393, 2458
    Radio communications to U.S. boats attempt-
        ing illegal transport, **1980–81:** 913, 915
    Rescue attempts, **1980–81:** 780, 819, 1072
  Drug trafficking prevention, **1980–81:** 1722
  Environmental damage response activities,
      1980–81: 3044
  International Convention for the Safety of Life
      at Sea, enforcement functions, **1980–81:**
      1628
  Officials, meeting with the President, **1980–81:**
      1077n.
  Unified navigation rules, **1980–81:** 2837
United States Coast Guard Academy, **1980–81:** 607
United States Commission on Security and Co-
      operation in Europe, **1979:** 2184
United States Conference of Mayors, **1977:** 1100;
      1980–81: 212, 1078, 1662
United States Conference on Science and Tech-
      nology Development, **1977:** 1795
United States Court of Claims, **1980–81:** 980
United States Court of Customs and Patent Ap-
      peals, **1980–81:** 866, 894
United States Court of Military Appeals, **1980–81:**
      317

United States Court of Military Appeals Nomi-
      nating Commission, **1978:** 1038; **1979:**
      1451; **1980–81:** 2850
United States Customs Service
  Commissioner of Customs, **1980–81:** 98, 102,
      1260
  Cuban refugee boat seizures, **1980–81:** 917
  Drug traffic prevention, **1980–81:** 1722
  Officials, meeting with the President, **1980–81:**
      1077n.
United States Emergency Refugee and Migration
      Assistance Fund, **1979:** 1925, 2117, 2150
United States Fastener Manufacturing Group,
      1978: 299
United States Fire Administration, **1979:** 22, 91,
      566; **1980–81:** 1567, 2266
United States Fish and Wildlife Service, **1980–81:**
      1431
United States Foreign Service, **1978:** 1209
United States Foreign Claims Settlement Commis-
      sion, **1979:** 46, 90
United States Holocaust Memorial Council, **1979:**
      2040; **1980–81:** 820, 2106
United States Information Agency, **1978:** 606
  Assistant Director, **1977:** 1211
  Deputy Director, **1977:** 732, 745
  Director, **1977:** 372, 512
  Reorganization Plan No. 2 of 1977, **1977:** 1765,
      1770
United States International Development Coop-
      eration Agency
  Agricultural trade development functions,
      1980–81: 1237, 1239
  Associate Director, **1980–81:** 51, 218
  Deputy Director, **1980–81:** 296
  Director, **1979:** 1272, 1293, 1731, 1801, 2248;
      1980–81: 8
  Establishment (EO 12163), **1979:** 1792, 1800
  Independent agency in executive branch, **1979:**
      395
  Reorganization Plan No. 2 of 1979
    Administration's proposal announcement,
        1979: 279
    Amendment, **1979:** 915
    Congressional approval, **1979:** 1230
    Message transmitting plan to Congress, **1979:**
        642
    Sections 2, 3, 4 enactment, **1979:** 1272
  Task Force on Global Resources and Environ-
      ment, duties, **1980–81:** 1417
  See also specific constituent agencies.
United States International Trade Commission
  Anhydrous ammonia imports, **1979:** 2221, 2222
  Appropriations, **1977:** 1479, 1480
  Artificial baits and flies industry, **1978:** 2071
  Bicycle tire and tube industry, **1977:** 1903, 1904
  Bolt, nut, and large screw industry and imports,
      1978: 299, 301, 2283, 2284; **1979:** 4, 5

U.S. International Trade — *continued*
Chairman, **1979:** 2285; **1980–81:** 102, 948
Chairman and Vice Chairman, **1978:** 1154
Citizens band radio transceivers, **1978:** 607–609, 707
Clothespin industry and imports, **1978:** 1698; **1979:** 233, 234, 325
Copper industry, **1978:** 1804, 1805
Customs duty determination, **1980–81:** 1249
High carbon ferrochromium industry, **1978:** 1941, 2037
Import duties decreases, **1979:** 2225
Import relief determination, **1977:** 937–939
Anhydrous ammonia, **1980–81:** 102
Automobiles, **1980–81:** 1330, 1985, 1991, 2222
Color television receivers, **1980–81:** 1258
India, imports from **1978:** 1563
Leather wearing apparel, **1980–81:** 531, 532
Mushrooms, **1980–81:** 2329, 2331, 2562
Nonrubber footwear, **1980–81:** 420
Porcelain-on-steel cookware, **1980–81:** 2, 3, 97
Members, **1977:** 1666, 1700; **1978:** 1453, 1458; **1979:** 2161, 2188; **1980–81:** 1975, 2070, 2071
Mushroom imports, **1977:** 362
Peanut price support program investigations, **1980–81:** 2776
Stainless steel table flatware industry, **1978:** 1216
Steel industry and imports, **1978:** 682, 802; **1979:** 1033
Sugar industry and imports, **1977:** 2019, 2021; **1978:** 145, 146
Television receiver imports, **1977:** 1157; **1979:** 166, 167
Vice Chairman, **1980–81:** 1150
United States-Japan Cooperative Medical Science Program, **1978:** 1278
United States-Japan Economic Relations Group, **1979:** 2127, 2248
United States Jaycees, **1978:** 1669; **1979:** 1723
United States-Liberian Relations, President's Commission on, **1980–81:** 508
United States Marine Corps, **1978:** 697; **1979:** 671; **1980–81:** 350, 780n., 1710n., 1857
United States Marine Corps Memorial Commission, **1980–81:** 483
United States Marine Safety Information System, **1977:** 459
United States Merchant Marine, **1980–81:** 469
United States Merchant Marine Academy, **1980–81:** 2239
United States Metric Board, **1977:** 196, 1944, 1966; **1978:** 230, 484, 504, 1069, 1072; **1980–81:** 940, 967, 1443, 1470
United States-Mexico Agreement on Natural Gas, **1979:** 1703, 1706
United States Military Academy, **1977:** 1125, 1397; **1978:** 510; **1979:** 687

United States Naval Academy, **1977:** 1432; **1978:** 515, 1052, 1057, 1072; **1979:** 730; **1980–81:** 769, 880, 2613, 2847
United States Navy
Ku Klux Klan activities, **1979:** 1712
Modernization of forces, **1979:** 2236
President's service in, **1979:** 1872
Shipbuilding contracts and programs, **1979:** 1990, 2235
See also Navy, Department of.
United States Negotiator for Economic Affairs, **1980–81:** 1468, 1470
United States Office of Consumer Affairs, **1979:** 1765; **1980–81:** 83
United States Olympic Committee
Budget appropriations, **1980–81:** 893
Executive director, **1980–81:** 104
Fundraising drive, **1980–81:** 966
Mention, **1980–81:** 196
Support activities for Olympic teams, **1980–81:** 381
U.S. boycott of 1980 Summer Olympics
House of Delegates vote, **1980–81:** 668
Position presentation to International Olympic Committee, **1980–81:** 108, 305, 356
Support of President's decision, **1980–81:** 259, 676, 989, 1315, 1441, 1493
Vice President's address to House of Delegates, announcement (Digest), **1980–81:** 653
United States Olympic Committee, President (Robert Kane)
Meeting with administration officials (Checklist), **1980–81:** 104
Mention, **1980–81:** 381
National Conference on Physical Fitness and Sports for All, attendance, **1980–81:** 259, 261n.
U.S. boycott of 1980 Summer Olympics
Acceptance of President's decision, **1980–81:** 356
Communications from the President, **1980–81:** 106, 616
United States Parole Commission, **1977:** 1644, 1650, 1824, 1931; **1978:** 1083, 1111, 1503, 1506; **1980–81:** 411, 1428
United States-People's Republic of China Joint Commission on Scientific and Technological Cooperation, **1979:** 203
United States-People's Republic of China Joint Economic Committee, **1979:** 1453
United States Postal Service, **1978:** 504, 934, 2263
Board of Governors, members, **1979:** 24, 46, 90, 215, 241; **1980–81:** 940, 968, 2781, 2782, 2857
Budget rescission, **1980–81:** 2916
Deputy Postmaster General, **1979:** 972
Draft registration assistance, **1980–81:** 289
Food stamps issuance, **1979:** 83

[References are to page numbers except as otherwise indicated]

U.S. Postal Service — *continued*
  George Meany commemorative stamp issuance,
      1980–81: 1607
  Inspector General, **1977:** 1084
  Interview remarks, **1977:** 905, 1091, 1170, 1511,
      1512, 1927
  Low-emission fuel vehicles, **1980–81:** 484
  News conference remarks, **1977:** 1204
United States Railway Association, **1978:** 1269,
      1333, 1360, 1381; **1979:** 43, 93; **1980–81:**
      392, 423, 1824, 1847
United States Savings Bonds, **1978:** 574; **1979:** 309,
      2284
United States Savings Bonds, Interagency Com-
      mittee for the Purchase of, **1977:** 531, 532;
      1980–81: 653
United States Secret Service, **1977:** 10, 942, 1263;
      1978: 208, 2280; **1979:** 2280; **1980–81:**
      612, 2829
United States Sinai Support Mission, **1977:** 734,
      1820; **1978:** 773; **1979:** 64, 756, 1298,
      1821; **1980–81:** 697, 1396, 1547, 1957
United States-Soviet Joint Commission on Science
      and Technology, **1979:** 539
United States-Soviet Standing Consultative Com-
      mission, **1978:** 63, 149
United States-Soviet Union Treaty on the Limi-
      tation of Strategic Offensive Arms, **1979:**
      1051, 1155
United States space observance (Proc. 4669), **1979:**
      1260
United States Steel Corporation
  Antidumping suit filing against foreign manu-
      facturers, **1980–81:** 732, 735, 903, 1961,
      1964, 2512
  President, **1980–81:** 735
United States Tax Court, **1979:** 820, 843; **1980–81:**
      683, 720, 756, 775
United States Tax Court Nominating Commission,
      1978: 1039, 1711; **1980–81:** 2849
United States Trade Representative (Reubin O'D.
      Askew)
  Agreement on Government Procurement inter-
      pretation, **1980–81:** 2854
  Council on Wage and Price Stability, member,
      1980–81: 967
  Customs Valuation Agreement, consultations
      with Congress on, **1980–81:** 95
  European Communities, duty increase determi-
      nation for textile articles from, **1980–81:**
      1825
  Exports
    Promotion policies review, **1980–81:** 1689,
        1692, 1694
    Trade balance examination, **1980–81:** 401
  General Agreement on Tariffs and Trade mod-
      ifications, **1980–81:** 1250
  Import relief determinations, **1980–81:** 3, 98, 102,
      421, 531, 1259, 2330, 2331

U.S. Trade Representative — *continued*
  International Sugar Agreement implementation
      functions, **1980–81:** 1271, 1272
  Japanese automobile imports study, **1980–81:**
      1991
  Meeting with the President (Digest), **1980–81:**
      967
  Mentions, **1980–81:** 1328n.,1330, 2149
  Peanut import duties, **1980–81:** 2772, 2775
  President's assessment, **1980–81:** 2400
  Steel industry revitalization program involve-
      ment, **1980–81:** 1960, 1965, 2071
  Trade policy functions, **1980–81:** 6–11
  See also Special Representative for Trade Ne-
      gotiations (Robert S. Strauss).
United States Trade Representative, Office of the
  Banned exports task force, membership, **1980–**
      81: 2907
  Deputy U.S. Trade Representative, **1980–81:** 25
  EO 12188, implementing Reorganization Plan
      No. 3 of 1979, **1980–81:** 7
  European Communities, duty increase hearings
      for textile articles from, **1980–81:** 1825
  Export promotion policies, **1980–81:** 1546, 1690
  Lead products, tariff concessions on, **1980–81:**
      1724
  Mention, **1980–81:** 617
  Special Representative for Trade Negotiations,
      Office of the
    Acting Special Representative, **1979:** 1418,
        1423, 1678
    Artificial baits and flies industry, **1978:** 2071
    Bicycle tire and tube industry, **1978:** 1904
    Bolt, nut, and large screw industry, **1978:** 299,
        2284
    Citizens band radio transceivers, **1978:** 608
    Clothespin industry, **1978:** 1698
    Copper industry, **1978:** 1805
    Deputy Special Representatives, **1977:** 795,
        807, 1305, 1308; **1979:** 2065, 2066, 2082
    India, import duty reduction, **1978:** 1563
    Multifiber Trade Agreement, **1977:** 123
    High carbon ferrochromium industry, **1978:**
        1941
    National Productivity Council, **1978:** 1833,
        1835
    Redesignation as Office of United States
        Trade Representative, **1979:** 1729
    Special Assistant to the Special Representa-
        tive, **1979:** 1596
    Stainless steel table flatware industry, **1978:**
        1216
    Strauss, Robert S.
      See Special Representative for Trade Ne-
          gotiations.
    Television imports, **1977:** 1159
    Textile and apparel industry, **1978:** 2008

U.S. Trade Representative, Office — *continued*
  Special Representative for Trade Negotiations
      (Reubin O'D. Askew)
    Anhydrous ammonia industry study, **1979:**
        2221
    General Agreement on Tariffs and Trade,
        consultations with Congress, **1979:** 2224
    International trade functions, **1979:** 1730
    Meeting with the President (Digest), **1979:**
        1422
    Mention, **1979:** 2034
    Multilateral trade negotiations, transmittal of
        Presidential determinations to Congress,
        1979: 2253, 2256
    Nomination, **1979:** 1418, 1423, 1680
    Redesignation as United States Trade Rep-
        resentative, **1979:** 1729
    Swearing-in ceremony, **1979:** 1807
  See also United States Trade Representative.
United States Travel Service, **1979:** 1850; **1980–81:**
    2838
United States travel and tourism administration,
    proposed, **1980–81:** 2838
United Steelworkers of America, **1978:** 299, 1544,
    1725; **1980–81:** 1510, 1670, 2071, 2345
Unity Day, National, **1979:** 2252
Universal Declaration of Human Rights, **1978:**
    2161, 2188; **1979:** 2198
Universal Voter Registration Act of 1977, pro-
    posed, **1977:** 509
Universe, Miss, **1980–81:** 1469
University of California v. *Bakke* , **1977:** 1345; **1978:**
    111, 322, 1223, 1230
University Press Centennial Observance, **1978:**
    1100
Unruh, Jesse M., **1977:** 279; **1980–81:** 1299n., 2534
Unseld, Wesley, **1978:** 1070
Unthank, G. Wix, **1979:** 2281
Upland cotton imports program, **1979:** 786; **1980–
    81:** 575, 2745
Upper Great Lakes Regional Commission, **1977:**
    1070, 1085
Upper Mississippi River, Minn., **1979:** 1365, 1814
Upper Mississippi River Basin Commission, **1977:**
    1917; **1978:** 273, 737, 1807, 1828; **1979:**
    2248
Upper Volta, U.S. Ambassador, **1978:** 1109, 1111
Upton, Arthur C., **1977:** 1378
Uranium
  Enrichment, **1977:** 588, 744
  Enrichment capacity report, **1979:** 1822
  U.S. supplies, **1979:** 1647
Urban, Lt. Col. Matt, **1980–81:** 1379, 1380
Urban areas
  Administration's accomplishments and goals,
      1980–81: 115, 143, 1080, 1082, 1658, 1681,
      1682, 1721, 2484, 2933, 2959

Urban areas — *continued*
  Administration policy, **1977:** 485, 908, 948, 1023
  Administration's rebuilding efforts, **1979:** 122,
      1935, 1936, 2122
  Alternate transportation methods, **1979:** 864
  Community Investment Fund, **1978:** 1058
  Employment, **1977:** 646, 889, 948
  Environmental message, **1977:** 975
  Environmental programs, **1979:** 1369, 1383–1385
  Federal assistance programs, **1977:** 263, 399, 899,
      1095, 1392, 1729; **1980–81:** 495, 555, 832,
      1323, 2004, 2020, 2427
  Frostbelt migration, **1980–81:** 2920
  Housing, **1977:** 646, 889, 976, 1777
  Impact analyses, **1978:** 1428, 1429, 1433; **1979:**
      72, 77, 609, 1972
  Interview remarks, **1978:** 75, 521, 689
  Legislation, **1980–81:** 2112
  Mass transit.
    See Mass transit.
  National Democratic Party Conference, re-
      marks, **1978:** 2193
  National Main Street Center, **1980–81:** 933
  National policy, **1978:** 577–581, 641, 853, 854,
      986, 994, 1010, 1427, 1434, 1459, 1782,
      1797, 2076, 2084; **1979:** 1934, 1935
  National policy report, **1980–81:** 1861
  National water policy, **1978:** 1043, 1045, 1048,
      1049
  Neighborhood development, **1980–81:** 139, 1094
  News conference remarks, **1977:** 1787
  Park systems, **1980–81:** 1673, 1681
  Public works and economic development, **1979:**
      600, 668
  Reagan, Ronald, policy differences with the
      President, **1980–81:** 2196, 2290, 2308,
      2543
  Renewal, **1978:** 1605
  Revenue sharing, **1977:** 72
  Revitalization, **1977:** 1833, 1835
  State of the Union, **1978:** 100
  Summer job programs, **1980–81:** 1291
  Transportation legislation, **1978:** 221
  United States Conference of Mayors, **1977:** 1100
  Volunteer service programs, **1979:** 2238
  Water system programs, **1980–81:** 2083
Urban Coalition, National, **1980–81:** 563
Urban Development Action Grant program, **1977:**
    1731; **1978:** 100, 579, 583, 588, 2076
  Chicago, Ill., grants, **1979:** 1935
  City eligibility requirements, **1980–81:** 1358
  Fact sheet, **1979:** 1977
  Increased funding, **1979:** 74, 601
  Legislation, **1979:** 600; **1980–81:** 2112
  Long Beach, N.Y., grant, **1980–81:** 2295
  New job creation, **1979:** 136, 1988
  New York City, N.Y., grant, **1980–81:** 2543

Urban Development Grant — *continued*
  Newark, N.J., grant, **1980–81:** 2525
  1981 budget allocations, **1980–81:** 555, 727
  Oakland, Calif., projects, **1980–81:** 1300
  Private investments in, **1979:** 136
  Private sector involvement, **1980–81:** 213, 1862
  San Antonio, Tex., grant, **1980–81:** 2623
  Second anniversary ceremony, **1979:** 1965
Urban League, National.
  See National Urban League.
Urban Mass Transportation Act of 1964 amendments, **1977:** 2033
Urban Mass Transportation Administration, **1977:** 1100, 1127; **1979:** 75, 1744, 2139, 2158; **1980–81:** 1236
Urban Park and Recreation Recovery program, **1978:** 2000; **1979:** 1817, 2220
Urban Policy Group, **1979:** 1972
Urban Policy Report, President's 1978 National, **1978:** 1430
Urban Volunteer Corps, **1978:** 581, 582, 592; **1979:** 2238
Urbina, Ricardo M., **1980–81:** 1824, 1847, 2870–2873
Uruguay
  Ambassador to U.S., **1980–81:** 1051
  President Aparicio Méndez Manfredini, **1977:** 1556, 1568
  U.S. Ambassador, **1977:** 1206, 1213; **1980–81:** 1334, 1336; **1979:** 1131, 1143
U.S. aquaculture bill, memorandum of disapproval, **1978:** 1799
U.S. National Commission for UNESCO, **1978:** 1380
U.S. productivity rates, **1978:** 1415
U.S.A. Miss, **1980–81:** 1469
Ushiba, Nobuhiko, **1977:** 2130; **1979:** 1165, 2126
U.S.S.
  See specific name of United States ship.
U.S.S.R.-U.S. Commercial Commission, Joint, **1979:** 1454
U.S.-U.S.S.R. Trade and Economic Council, **1978:** 1723
Utah
  Paiute Indian Tribe, **1980–81:** 604
  President's visit, **1978:** 2084
  Radioactivity exposure, **1978:** 2088; **1979:** 182
  U.S. district judge, **1978:** 1485; **1979:** 2081, 2082
  U.S. marshal, **1978:** 1407
Utah project, Central, **1978:** 520
Ute Mountain Ute Tribe benefits bill, **1980–81:** 1043
Utica, N.Y., **1979:** 1817; **1980–81:** 2822
Utilities, conversion to nonoil fuels, **1979:** 1239, 1244, 1327, 1338, 1643, 1650
  Legislation
    Energy Department development of proposal, **1980–81:** 129

Utilities, conversion — *continued*
  Legislation — *continued*
    Mentions, **1980–81:** 883, 1587, 2040, 2349
    Priority of administration, **1980–81:** 116
    Proposal transmittal to Congress, **1980–81:** 448
    Purposes, **1980–81:** 117, 129, 472
  Plant selections, **1980–81:** 2438
Utility companies
  Costs increase, **1979:** 479
  Legislation, **1979:** 479
  Low-cost loan programs for customers, **1979:** 1244, 1338
  Powerplant safety guidelines, **1979:** 2203
Utke, Roy, **1978:** 455

Vagts, Detley Frederick, **1980–81:** 175, 2731
Vaira, Peter F., Jr., **1978:** 899
Vaisnys, Elona Marijosius, **1978:** 1515
Vajpayee, Atal Bihari, **1979:** 732
Vaky, Viron P., **1978:** 1060, 1072, 1380, 1406; **1979:** 837
Valdez, Alaska, **1978:** 802
Valdez, Albelardo L., **1977:** 933, 943; **1979:** 1659, 1664, 1976; **1980–81:** 217, 1461, 1941
Valente, Vittorio, **1980–81:** 1242
Valenti, Jack, **1978:** 1878; **1980–81:** 1405
Valentine, Roy, **1980–81:** 264
Valge, Viia E., **1980–81:** 927
Valuchek, Andrew, **1979:** 293
Van Agt, Andreas, **1979:** 2201
Van Cleve, Harry R., **1977:** 367, 465
Van Dam, Philip, **1977:** 1803
Van de Kamp, John K., **1977:** 1103, 1128, 1265
Van Deerlin, Repr. Lionel, **1978:** 1927; **1979:** 1702, 1874
Van Derzee, James, **1979:** 322
Van Doren, Charles N., **1977:** 1528, 1534; **1979:** 685; **1980–81:** 930
Van Dyk, Frederick T., **1977:** 739, 746
Van Gorkom, J. W., **1977:** 196
Van Lennep, Emile, **1978:** 49; **1979:** 787
Van Lopik, Jack R., **1978:** 217; **1979:** 2118
Van Ness, Stanley, **1977:** 1053
Vance, Cyrus R.
  See State, Secretary of.
Vance, Mrs. Cyrus R., **1978:** 2268; **1979:** 1155
Vance, Estil, **1980–81:** 1393n.
Vance, Gay, **1980–81:** 2732
Vance, Kay, **1977:** 1041
Vance, Robert S., **1977:** 1967
Vance, Susan Margaret, **1979:** 340, 377
Vancouver, Wash., **1980–81:** 967
Vanden Heuvel, William J., **1977:** 1123, 1128; **1978:** 885; **1979:** 1725, 2043, 2085; **1980–81:** 1859, 1946, 2070, 2726, 2727

Vander Jagt, Repr. Guy, **1978:** 1530; **1980–81:** 275
Vanik, Charles, **1980–81:** 1765
Vanik, Repr. Charles A., **1979:** 1312
Vanlare, Paula J., **1980–81:** 928
Vann, David, **1978:** 641
VanNatta, Ralph, **1978:** 1468
Varipapa, Andy, **1980–81:** 2646
Varner, Nellie Mae, **1980–81:** 2614
Varon, Silvio S., **1980–81:** 3026
Vaschenko family, **1978:** 1748
Vasquez, Manuel, **1978:** 697
Vasquez, Patricia M., **1979:** 1448
Vasquez, Pedro, **1980–81:** 1939, 1944
Vatican, President's Personal and Deputy Personal
        Representatives, **1977:** 1215; **1978:** 1795,
        1808
Vatican City
    Apostolic Delegate to U.S., **1980–81:** 1714
    Envoy of the President, **1980–81:** 1242
    Pope John Paul II.
        See Pope John Paul II.
    President's visit
        Announcement, **1980–81:** 1014
        Beatification of Kateri Takakwitha, **1980–81:**
            1168
        Daily schedule (Digest), **1980–81:** 1242
        Pre-visit comments, **1980–81:** 1102
        Welcoming ceremony, **1980–81:** 1164
Vaughan, Patrick J., **1977:** 1071, 1085
Vaughn, Jack Hood, **1980–81:** 1108, 1150
Vaughn, Sarah, **1980–81:** 1405, 1946
Vaux Junior High School, Pa., **1979:** 787
Vavasis, Stephen A., **1980–81:** 928
Veal imports, **1979:** 2299
Vega, Marta Moreno, **1979:** 466
Vehicle Certification Board, Low-Emission, **1980–
        81:** 483
Veil, Simone, **1980–81:** 238
Vela, Filemon B., **1980–81:** 104
Vela, Xavier M., **1977:** 965, 1031
Velarde, Edwin Fabrega, **1980–81:** 33
Velde, Richard W., **1979:** 294
Veliotes, Nicholas A., **1978:** 1397, 1407
Venable, Abraham S., **1980–81:** 1405
Venezuela
    Ambassador to U.S., **1979:** 1318
    Inaugural ceremonies, U.S. delegation, **1979:**
        240, 242, 401
    Joint communiques, **1977:** 1207, 1208
    Maritime boundary treaty with U.S., **1979:** 86
    OPEC meeting in Caracas, **1980–81:** 570
    President Carlos Andrés Pérez, **1977:** 640, 1098,
        1180, 1183, 1188, 1190, 1207, 1208, 1211,
        1542, 1568; **1978:** 1119, 1122, 1123
    President's visit, **1977:** 1649, 1983, 2077; **1978:**
        416, 417, 613–623
    Science and technology cooperation with U.S.,
        1980–81: 407

Venezuela — *continued*
    Trade beneficiary developing country designa-
        tion, **1980–81:** 430, 550
    Trade with U.S., **1979:** 2255
    U.S. Ambassador, **1978:** 1465, 1471
Venice Economic Summit Conference
    Announcement of President's attendance, **1980–
        81:** 1014
    Canadian energy projects, discussions with
        Prime Minister Trudeau, **1980–81:** 1368
    Concluding statements, **1980–81:** 1174
    Daily schedule (Digest), **1980–81:** 1243
    Exchange with reporters following first two ses-
        sions, **1980–81:** 1173
    Final declaration, **1980–81:** 1186
    Interview with reporters following conclusion of
        Conference, **1980–81:** 1191
    Joint statements
        Afghanistan, Soviet invasion of, **1980–81:** 1170
        Diplomatic hostages, **1980–81:** 1171
        Hijacking, **1980–81:** 1172
        Refugees, **1980–81:** 1172
    Mentions, **1980–81:** 1018, 1113
    Multinational commitments, **1980–81:** 1304,
        1400, 1415, 1693
    News conference (Checklist), **1980–81:** 1246
    Pre-summit comments on agenda, **1980–81:** 440,
        681, 777, 794, 870, 1135
Veraa, Richard P., **1980–81:** 3026
Verburg, Jeffrey L., **1980–81:** 20
Verity, C. William, Jr., **1978:** 455, 1723; **1979:** 942;
        1980–81: 522, 1048
Vermont
    Administration briefing for community and civic
        leaders, **1980–81:** 334
    Democratic Party primary, **1980–81:** 428
    Emergency declaration, **1977:** 1567
    Gov. Richard A. Snelling, **1980–81:** 1335
    U.S. attorney, **1977:** 1266, 1307
    U.S. marshal, **1977:** 1266, 1307
    White House briefing by administration officials
        for civic and community leaders (Digest),
        1979: 2186
Veron, Earl E., **1977:** 1307
Verrett, Shirley, **1977:** 2183
Vesco, Robert, **1979:** 1590, 1592; **1980–81:** 904
Vessey, Gen. John W., Jr., **1977:** 343; **1979:** 1206
Vest, George S., **1977:** 576, 581, 597, 804, 807;
        1979: 1603
Veterans
    Administration's accomplishments and goals,
        1980–81: 142, 2159, 2957
    Agent Orange victims, **1980–81:** 2464, 2509
    Benefits, **1980–81:** 2464
    Benefits, cost-of-living adjustments, **1977:** 322
    Benefits to U.S. citizens living abroad, **1979:**
        1522

Veterans — *continued*
   Civil service reform preference, **1978:** 448, 799,
      1138, 1351, 1361, 1372, 1373
   Cpl. Anthony Casamento, Congressional Medal
      of Honor presentation, **1980–81:** 1708
   Education programs, **1977:** 391, 1981
   Employment, **1977:** 32, 52, 53, 72, 73, 391, 944,
      1115
   Employment preference, **1978:** 2165
   Employment and training services, **1979:** 1523
   GI bill, **1977:** 301, 306, 307, 317, 1901, 2048, 2049
   Health care legislation, **1980–81:** 1563, 1576
   Legislation, **1979:** 139
   Low-level radiation hazards, **1979:** 2007
   Military Selective Service Act violations, pardon,
      1977: 5, 6
   Organization leaders, meeting with the President,
      1977: 1126
   Readjustment and career-conditional appoint-
      ments program, **1978:** 1742
   Representatives, meeting with the President,
      1978: 935
   State of the Union, **1978:** 107
   Tax reform, **1977:** 301
   Vietnam.
      See Vietnam veterans.
Veterans Administration
   Dioxin exposure, study of effects on Vietnam-era
      veterans, **1980–81:** 4
   50th anniversary, **1980–81:** 1120, 1383, 1388
   Handicapped employment programs, **1980–81:**
      2362
   Health care legislation, **1980–81:** 1563, 1576
   Home loan program, **1978:** 1791
   Hulver, Isaac, case consideration, **1980–81:** 2846
   Inspector General, **1979:** 367, 377
   Overseas personnel allowances, **1980–81:** 1420
   Pay schedules, **1979:** 1848
   Radiation Policy Council membership, **1980–81:**
      363
   Rehabilitation and education programs, **1980–
      81:** 2315, 2318
   Upgraded discharge benefits, **1977:** 1757
   Vietnam-era veterans, **1978:** 1738
      Memorial legislation sponsorship, **1980–81:**
         1268
      Service programs, **1980–81:** 1550; **1979:** 1040
   Water conservation programs, **1978:** 1048
Veterans Administration, Administrator (Max
      Cleland), **1977:** 192, 252, 272, 273, 299,
      300, 378, 391, 991, 1115, 1162, 1405, 1900,
      1901, 1963, 1981; **1978:** 263, 935, 1743,
      1773, 2014; **1979:** 974, 2182
   Agent Orange investigation, **1980–81:** 2464, 2509
   Dioxin exposure study provision, **1980–81:** 5
   Mention, **1980–81:** 275

Veterans Administration — *continued*
   National Commission on Alcoholism and Other
      Alcohol-Related Problems, member,
      1980–81: 2609
   Overseas personnel allowance functions, **1980–
      81:** 1421
   President's assessment, **1980–81:** 1550, 2573
   Rehabilitation programs leadership, **1980–81:**
      2160, 2362
   Veterans Administration's 50th anniversary cel-
      ebration, remarks, **1980–81:** 1384
   Veterans legislation support, **1980–81:** 1268,
      1269, 2315, 2316
Veterans Day, **1977:** 1586, 1900; **1978:** 1510, 2012
   (Proc. 4688), **1979:** 1687
   (Proc. 4791), **1980–81:** 1702
Veterans' Day, National Salute to Hospitalized,
      1980–81: 2888
Veterans' Disability Compensation and Housing
      Benefits Amendments, **1980–81:** 2097
Veterans' Disability Compensation and Survivor
      Benefits Act of 1977, **1977:** 1712; **1978:**
      1789, 1791; **1979:** 2165
Veterans' Federal Coordinating Committee, **1978:**
      1743; **1979:** 974; **1980–81:** 1591
Veterans of Foreign Wars, **1978:** 1669
Veterans' Health Care Amendments, **1979:** 1039
Veterans' Housing Benefits Act, **1978:** 1789, 1791
Veterans' Readjustment Appointment Authority,
      1978: 1138
Veterans' Rehabilitation and Education Amend-
      ments, **1980–81:** 2315, 2318, 2434
Veterans' and Survivors' Pension Improvement
      Act, **1978:** 1965
Veto messages.
   See under Congress, Communications to.
Vetoes, legislative, **1978:** 1146, 1155
Vianna, Marcos, **1978:** 640
Vice President, Office of the, **1977:** 1257
Vice President, role, **1977:** 1689, 2100, 2101
Vice President (Walter F. Mondale)
   Africa, visit to, **1980–81:** 1333, 1501
   American hostages in Iran, remarks on, **1979:**
      2194
   Auto industry, economic assistance actions,
      1980–81: 1989
   Brock, Lou, ceremony attendance for, **1979:**
      1784
   Campaign efforts for the President, **1979:** 1986,
      2194; **1980–81:** 391, 1024, 1541
   Congressional August recess remarks (Check-
      list), **1979:** 1398
   Cuban refugees statement, **1980–81:** 780
   Cyprus conflict negotiations, **1980–81:** 382
   District of Columbia task force organization,
      1979: 1921
   Economic Policy Group, *ex officio* member,
      1979: 977

Vice President — *continued*
  Energy situation management in President's absence, **1979:** 1142
  Equal rights amendment activities, **1980–81:** 833
  Federal anti-arson program announcement, **1979:** 2249
  Foreign policy role, **1980–81:** 2168
  Hospital cost containment, remarks (Checklist), **1979:** 2138
  Hubert H. Humphrey tribute in New England, attendance, **1980–81:** 935
  Inauguration ceremonies in Brazil and Venezuela, U.S. delegation head, **1979:** 242
  Kentucky Democratic Party fundraiser attendance, **1979:** 1223
  Labor leaders, White House dinner remarks to, **1980–81:** 2883
  Meetings with the President (Digest), **1979:** 14, 25, 26, 89, 178, 179, 216, 217, 239–241, 293, 327, 376, 377, 400, 401, 467, 553, 554, 731, 732, 786, 787, 841, 842, 898, 956, 957, 1017, 1042, 1043, 1142, 1222, 1318, 1319, 1396, 1397, 1453, 1454, 1603, 1604, 1679, 1704, 1785, 1823, 1824, 1882, 1975, 2043, 2080, 2081, 2105, 2106, 2138, 2139, 2186, 2206, 2207, 2247, 2280; **1980–81:** 63, 103, 217, 267, 268, 292, 293, 333, 374, 422, 423, 451, 452, 492, 493, 521, 563, 653, 720, 774, 775, 825, 892, 893, 930, 931, 966, 1013, 1050, 1110, 1150, 1428, 1469, 1523, 1564, 1598, 1714, 1945, 2726, 2782, 2807, 2823, 2857
  Mentions, **1977:** 8, 9, 11, 23, 30, 57, 58, 76, 80, 86, 147, 149, 251, 269, 279, 305, 324, 344, 356, 359, 371, 463, 464, 467, 481, 508, 522, 523, 586, 595, 596, 609, 640, 646, 650, 700, 705, 706, 742, 743, 748, 758, 759, 784, 785, 801, 805, 809, 882, 887, 893, 913, 925, 953, 1030, 1052, 1059, 1083, 1089, 1126, 1154, 1161–1163, 1210, 1221, 1225, 1263–1265, 1283, 1305, 1306, 1382, 1383, 1436, 1437, 1506, 1530, 1532, 1567, 1611, 1648, 1649, 1689, 1699, 1745, 1754, 1794, 1823, 1825, 1826, 1900, 1930, 1931, 1965, 1966, 1972, 1998, 2005, 2007, 2036, 2050, 2053, 2076, 2077, 2088–2090, 2100, 2101, 2129, 2130, 2162, 2178, 2203, 2223; **1978:** 39, 65, 66, 190, 229, 276, 277, 296, 302, 303, 327, 414–416, 423, 452, 456, 458, 503, 504, 511, 513, 525, 526, 568, 570, 608, 610, 678, 704, 710, 749, 750, 785, 802, 803, 898, 928, 934, 936, 961, 963, 1034, 1071, 1090, 1110, 1153, 1221, 1222, 1227, 1239, 1267, 1278, 1315, 1321, 1332, 1333, 1344, 1345, 1379, 1380, 1457, 1465, 1477, 1478, 1484, 1495, 1505–1507, 1516, 1644, 1647, 1668, 1669, 1722–1724, 1771–1773, 1805, 1808, 1822, 1825, 1827, 1831, 1854, 1904, 1941,

Vice President — *continued*
  Mentions — *continued*
    1950, 1954, 1955, 2004, 2059, 2068, 1071–2073, 2146, 2147, 2187, 2190, 2269, 2270, 2280, 2284; **1979:** 370n., 375, 548n., 827, 1008, 1182, 1412, 1844, 1861, 1955, 1997, 2066n., **1980–81:** 391, 397, 569, 732, 738, 763, 939, 995, 999, 1039, 1101, 1102, 1381, 1382, 1424
  News conferences (Checklist), **1979:** 378, 1787; **1980–81:** 1337, 2333
  Philadelphia, Pa., visit to, **1980–81:** 2043
  President of the Senate, communications from the President, **1979:** 102, 233, 897, 1035, 1446, 1656, 1999, 2006, 2162, 2174, 2221, 2290
  See also Congress, Communications to.
  President's assessment, **1979:** 39; **1980–81:** 1295, 1463, 1527, 1528, 1532, 1558, 1708, 1950, 2093, 2215, 2655, 2687, 2707
  President's decision to renominate in 1980 campaign, **1979:** 2192; **1980–81:** 1045
  President's departure to Europe, remarks, **1980–81:** 1135
  President's trip to Middle East, departure and return remarks, **1979:** 394, 430
  Relationship with the President, **1979:** 2015
  Trips to foreign countries
    China, People's Republic of, **1979:** 1112
    Nordic countries and Netherlands, **1979:** 221, 691
    Panama, **1979:** 1628
  United States Holocaust Memorial Council, membership designation authority, **1980–81:** 820
  United States Olympic Committee address (Digest), **1980–81:** 653
  Youth employment and training task force, chairman, **1979:** 911
  Yugoslavian President Tito's funeral services, U.S. delegation head, **1980–81:** 827n.
Vice President's Task Force on Youth Employment, **1980–81:** 124, 1503
Vickery, Gordon, **1979:** 22, 91, 567
Vidal, David Jonathan, **1980–81:** 949
Videla, Jorge Rafael, **1977:** 1555, 1568
Vienna Summit Meeting
  Announcement, **1979:** 1038
  Meetings, **1979:** 1048, 1049, 1051, 1079, 1081, 1143
  Postsummit comments, **1979:** 2055, 2244
  Presummit comments, **1979:** 772, 805, 831, 902, 1002
  SALT II treaty, **1979:** 1079
    Signing ceremony, **1979:** 1143
    Soviet backfire bomber statement, **1979:** 1079
    Texts of treaty and related documents, **1979:** 1051

Vienna Summit Meeting — *continued*
  SALT II treaty — *continued*
    U.S.S.R.-U.S. joint statement, **1979:** 1081
    Welcoming ceremony, **1979:** 1047, 1143
    Working dinners
      Soviet Embassy, **1979:** 1049, 1143
      U.S. Ambassador's residence, **1979:** 1048, 1143
Viera, José Rodolfo, **1980–81:** 2859n.
Vietnam
  Embargo regulations, **1978:** 1505
  Kampuchea, involvement in, **1979:** 303, 314, 348,
    765, 2051, 2197; **1980–81:** 2021, 2863
  Missing in action, **1977:** 85, 147, 173, 316, 377,
    489, 499
  Premier Van Dong, **1977:** 489
  Soviet influence, **1980–81:** 674
  Thailand, invasion of, **1980–81:** 1267
  U.S. policy, **1977:** 173, 489, 499, 501, 1333
  U.S. trade restrictions, **1979:** 1656, 2292, 2295
Vietnam veterans, **1978:** 463, 973, 994, 1379, 1737,
    1773, 2013; **1979:** 973–975, 984, 1011
  Memorial legislation, **1980–81:** 1268
  Services and benefits, **1980–81:** 1550
Vietnam Veterans Memorial Fund, Inc., **1980–81:**
    1268
Vietnam Veterans Week (Proc. 4647), **1979:** 445,
    972
Vietnamese refugees.
  See Indochina.
Vietor, Harold Duane, **1979:** 441
Viets, Richard N., **1979:** 1618, 1679
Vigil, Juan R., **1979:** 914
Vilas, Franklin E., Jr., **1977:** 530
Vilella, Edward, **1980–81:** 1406
Villaescusa, Louis G., Jr., **1977:** 2090
Vilus, Ranko, **1980–81:** 1243
Vincent, Robert D., **1977:** 1644, 1650
Vine, Richard David, **1979:** 1618, 1679
Vining, Robert L., Jr., **1979:** 1043, 1044
Vins, Georgi, **1979:** 731, 758n.
Vinson, Carl, **1980–81:** 468
Violence, Interdepartmental Committee on Do-
    mestic, **1979:** 729
Virgil, **1980–81:** 208
Virgin Islands
  Delegation, meeting with the President, **1978:**
    1333
  Disaster declaration, **1979:** 1704
  Gasoline production, import conservation fee
    waiver, **1980–81:** 593, 596, 598
  Oil imports, **1980–81:** 467
  Proposed constitution, **1978:** 1556
  Tax structure, **1978:** 1972
  U.S. attorney, **1978:** 899
  U.S. district judge, **1978:** 66, 149; **1980–81:** 1715
  U.S. policy, **1980–81:** 317

Virginia
  Campaign for Democratic candidates, **1977:**
    1653–1661
  Democratic Party caucuses, **1980–81:** 525
  Disaster declarations, **1977:** 596, 2035; **1979:**
    1293, 1823
  Emergency declarations, **1977:** 31, 1126, 1382
  Energy crisis, **1977:** 37
  Federal judge appointments, **1978:** 2175
  Gov. John H. Dalton, **1980–81:** 268, 303
  Metrorail system, **1980–81:** 14, 18
  President's visits, **1978:** 1383; **1979:** 630; **1980–
    81:** 969, 972, 2060
  U.S. attorney, **1980–81:** 269
  U.S. district judges, **1979:** 667, 668, 899, 900;
    1980–81: 654
  U.S. marshals, **1977:** 1483, 1484, 1755
  White House briefing by administration officials
    for civic and community leaders (Digest),
    1979: 2207
Virginia, U.S.S., **1980–81:** 2827n.
Virginia Beach, Va., **1979:** 897
Viscardi, Henry, Jr., **1977:** 464
Visentini, Bruno, **1980–81:** 1241
Vision Week, Save Your, **1977:** 157; **1978:** 257;
    1979: 220; **1980–81:** 234
VISTA (Volunteers in Service to America), **1977:**
    272; **1978:** 484; **1979:** 2237, 2280
Vladivostok agreement, **1977:** 498, 538, 540–542
Vlasova, Lyudmila, **1979:** 1590ftn.
Vocational Education, National Advisory Council
    on, **1979:** 1447; **1980–81:** 2817
Voice of America
  Director, **1977:** 1211, 1766
  Message to Congress, **1977:** 478
Volcker, Paul A.
  See Federal Reserve System, Board of Gover-
    nors, Chairman.
Volkswagen of America, **1980–81:** 706, 770, 1991,
    2039
Volpe, John, **1980–81:** 1718
Voluntary Action program, National, **1979:** 880
Volunteer Organizations, Conference of National,
    1979: 1679
Volunteer Service Act Amendments of 1979, Do-
    mestic, **1979:** 2237
Volunteer Week, National, **1980–81:** 695
Volunteer work, **1980–81:** 2279, 2285
Volz, John P., **1978:** 66, 149
Von Braun, Wernher, **1977:** 1125
Von Staden, Berndt, **1978:** 934, 1967
Voorde, Frances M., **1978:** 893; **1979:** 990n.
Vorster, B. J., **1977:** 785, 913, 1089, 1922
Voss, Gordon, **1980–81:** 303
Votaw, Carmen Delgado, **1977:** 527; **1978:** 1135
Voter registration, **1977:** 30, 481, 509

Voting rights, **1979:** 911
Voting Rights Act of 1965, **1980–81:** 1500
Voyager spacecraft, **1977:** 1379
Voyageurs National Park, **1980–81:** 2839
Vriesman, Wayne, **1977:** 1594
Vrooman, David V., **1977:** 746
Vuley, Brig. Gen. Ernest A., Jr., **1978:** 409

Wabasha, Minn., **1979:** 1468
Wachman, Marvin, **1980–81:** 874, 891n.
Wachtmeister, Wilhelm H., **1980–81:** 2740
Waco, Tex., **1980–81:** 2413
Waddell, James M., Jr., **1979:** 2116
Wade, James Paul, Jr., **1978:** 1090, 1111
Wade, Larry, **1979:** 481n.
Wade, Mrs. Paul R., **1979:** 481n.
Wade, Stephen, **1979:** 1596
Wadley, Ellen, **1977:** 24
Wage and Hour Administration, **1977:** 965, 1031
Wage insurance, real.
　See Real wage insurance.
Wage and Price Stability, Council on
　Anti-inflation programs, **1977:** 623, 626; **1979:**
　　125, 1779; **1980–81:** 121, 552; **1978:** 725,
　　726, 1327, 1847, 1848, 2054
　Appropriations legislation, **1980–81:** 2789
　Business and industry regulation, **1977:** 2112
　Chairman
　　Kahn, Alfred E.
　　　See Kahn, Alfred E.
　　Schultze, Charles L.
　　　See Schultze, Charles L.
　Deputy Adviser for Labor-Management, **1980–
　　81:** 462
　Deputy Advisers, **1979:** 25, 467, 1596, 1782, 2043
　Director.
　　See Wage and Price Stability, Council on,
　　　Director.
　Federal anti-inflationary procurement practices,
　　1978: 1920
　Industry analysis, **1977:** 51
　Interview remarks, **1978:** 1495
　Members, **1977:** 712; **1979:** 1454
　Members and adviser-members, **1980–81:** 967,
　　1427
　National Productivity Council, **1978:** 1833, 1835
　Pay standards recommendations, **1980–81:** 479
　Quarterly reports, **1977:** 706, 1771; **1978:** 252,
　　422, 701; **1980–81:** 645, 1446, 2701, 2992
　Reports, **1978:** 1559; **1979:** 178, 393, 815, 1683,
　　2272
　Steel industry prices, study, **1977:** 1189, 1190
　Voluntary wage and price standards compliance
　　review, **1980–81:** 581, 707
　Wage increase standards, **1979:** 1529, 1531, 1859
　Wage and price monitoring, **1979:** 256, 471, 560,
　　752, 850

Wage and Price Stability, Council on, Chairman.
　See Kahn, Alfred E.; Schultze, Charles L.
Wage and Price Stability, Council on, Director
　　(Barry P. Bosworth), **1977:** 1220, 1223,
　　1259; **1978:** 726, 1111, 1327, 1494, 1495,
　　1879
　Meetings with the President (Digest), **1979:** 14,
　　25, 241, 327, 467, 554, 732, 842, 956, 1142
　Mentions, **1979:** 252, 752, 1122
　Resignation, **1979:** 1333
Wage and Price Stability, Council on, Director (R.
　　Robert Russell), **1979:** 1333, 1604, 1787,
　　2043
　Meetings with the President (Digest), **1980–81:**
　　24, 292, 374, 774, 1050, 1469
　Oil companies wage and price compliance re-
　　view, **1980–81:** 552, 721
Wage System, Federal, **1979:** 1003
Wages and prices
　Anti-inflation program, **1978:** 1843, 1844, 1846,
　　1847, 2176; **1979:** 1779
　Blue-collar workers, **1978:** 216
　Business Council, remarks, **1978:** 2238
　Control, **1978:** 1353, 1495, 1592, 1613, 1886,
　　1912, 1968, 2040, 2066
　Democratic workshop on inflation, remarks,
　　1978: 2212
　Energy price increases, effect on pay structure,
　　1980–81: 249
　Federal anti-inflationary procurement practices,
　　1978: 1919, 1920
　Federal civilian and military pay increase, **1979:**
　　1481, 1529, 1530; **1980–81:** 467, 468, 1596
　Legislation, **1978:** 2252
　Mandatory controls, **1979:** 849, 1942, 2030
　　President's opposition to, **1980–81:** 387, 389,
　　　479, 485, 555, 582, 725
　　Sen. Kennedy's position comparison with
　　　President, **1980–81:** 737, 750, 1040
　Military physicians, **1980–81:** 456
　Minimum wage, **1977:** 516, 1232, 1947, 2016;
　　1978: 2240
　　Increases during administration, **1980–81:** 115
　　Legislation, **1979:** 2122
　　Reagan, Ronald, policy differences with the
　　　President, **1980–81:** 1381, 1950, 2120,
　　　2141, 2149, 2159, 2225, 2244, 2252, 2271,
　　　2273, 2307, 2346, 2348, 2365, 2390, 2398,
　　　2403, 2405, 2412, 2414, 2419, 2436, 2442,
　　　2450, 2473, 2483, 2536, 2544, 2554, 2582,
　　　2605, 2662, 2671
　News conference remarks, **1978:** 729, 730, 849,
　　2224
　Price standards, **1979:** 1859
　Real wage insurance.
　　See Real wage insurance.
　Voluntary business control, **1978:** 93, 100, 141,
　　235, 723, 902

Wages and prices — *continued*
  Voluntary guidelines
    Administration's update of standards, **1980–81:** 246, 479, 485, 497, 513, 517
    Business and industry, **1980–81:** 120, 247, 248, 581
    Chemical industry, **1980–81:** 658
    Corporations, **1979:** 124, 256, 486, 560, 622, 635, 650, 740, 752, 833, 850, 935; **1980–81:** 453
    Effectiveness, **1980–81:** 3013
    Fortune 500 companies, **1980–81:** 453
    Labor, **1979:** 477, 635, 752, 850, 1252, 1254, 1258
      See also Anti-inflation accord with administration *under* Labor.
    Mentions, **1979:** 74, 115, 307, 650, 704, 714, 736, 962; **1980–81:** 570
    Mobil Oil Corporation, **1980–81:** 552, 581, 707, 776
    Phillips Petroleum Company, **1980–81:** 721
    President's commitment to, **1979:** 1739
    Price Advisory Committee, pay increase review, **1979:** 1778
    Progress since 1978, **1979:** 1942, 2049
    Real wage insurance proposal, **1980–81:** 884
    Violations of guidelines, **1979:** 471, 560, 740, 752
  Wage increases for 1979, **1980–81:** 244, 248, 497
  White House officials, **1980–81:** 571
  Women, **1980–81:** 1952
Waggoner, Repr. Joe D., Jr., **1978:** 148, 770
Wagner, Annice McBryde, **1977:** 196, 465
Wagner, Aubrey J., **1978:** 946–948
Wagner, James, **1980–81:** 1009
Wagner, Robert F., **1978:** 1795, 1808; **1980–81:** 1242
Wagner, Rabbi Stanley M., **1978:** 503
Wahl, Constance, **1979:** 466
Wahwassuck, Brigitte T., **1980–81:** 927
Wake Forest University, **1978:** 529
Walcott, Jersey Joe, **1977:** 1578
Wald, Jeff, **1978:** 1653
Wald, Patricia McGowan, **1977:** 156, 195; **1979:** 733, 787, 1516; **1980–81:** 2613
Walden, Bobbie L., **1979:** 1524
Walden, Omi G., **1978:** 218, 230, 1380, 1670
Walden, Philip M., **1977:** 2183; **1979:** 447
Waldheim, Kurt.
  See United Nations, Secretary-General.
Waldie, Jerome, **1978:** 1343, 1346; **1979:** 2213; **1980–81:** 534, 537
Wales, Ross, **1980–81:** 1493
Walesa, Stanley, **1980–81:** 2534
Walgren, Repr. Doug, **1980–81:** 369
Walker, A. Maceo, Sr., **1979:** 230
Walker, Charles J., **1979:** 1264
Walker, Dan, **1978:** 999

Walker, Hershel, **1980–81:** 2563
Walker, John, **1978:** 1028
Walker, Lannon, **1980–81:** 1946
Walker, LeRoy T., **1978:** 2036
Walker, Gen. Samuel S., **1978:** 1446
Walker, Valida Smith, **1980–81:** 2242
Walker, Wallace Earl, **1980–81:** 949
Walker, Wesley M., **1977:** 1242
Wall, James M., **1977:** 941; **1980–81:** 509
Wall, James and Mary Eleanor, **1978:** 987
Wall, Mary Eleanor, **1977:** 182; **1980–81:** 273
Wallace, Dave, **1980–81:** 1938
Wallace, George, **1980–81:** 1683, 2250, 2395, 2429
Wallace, Gov. George, **1977:** 279, 1597, 1940
Wallace, Phyllis, **1979:** 1954
Wallace and Wallace Enterprises, Inc., **1977:** 1485
Wallenberg, Raoul, **1979:** 1887
Waller, Patricia F., **1979:** 1776; **1980–81:** 2017, 3026
Wallis, Col. Charles R., **1978:** 1406
Wallop, Sen. Malcolm, **1978:** 2003
Walsh, Don, **1979:** 2118
Walsh, Ethel Bent, **1980–81:** 1125, 1150
Walsh, James P., **1978:** 285, 304
Walsh, Jeremiah Thomas, **1980–81:** 533, 564
Walsh, Julia M., **1977:** 1083; **1980–81:** 272, 1981
Walsh, Michael H., **1977:** 941, 1967
Walter, J. Jackson, **1979:** 2153
Walters, Barbara, **1977:** 2187; **1978:** 2247; **1980–81:** 2137, 2477
Walters, David, **1977:** 1215; **1978:** 1393
Walters, Raymond L., **1977:** 1586
Wampler, Atlee W., III, **1980–81:** 1715
Wampler, William D., **1980–81:** 1291
War powers resolution, **1977:** 324
Ward, Daniel P., **1978:** 996
Ward, Horace T., **1979:** 2081, 2082
Ward, Kevin, **1979:** 2076
Ward, Marty, **1979:** 1868
Ward, Robert E., **1978:** 1515
Warden, Margaret S., **1979:** 2277, 2281
Warden, Richard D., **1977:** 370, 373
Ware, Keren K., **1980–81:** 930
Warhol, Andy, **1977:** 1118
Warin, Edward G., **1977:** 1650, 1651
Warner, Carolyn, **1979:** 1525
Warner, Sen. John W., **1979:** 2257n.; **1980–81:** 969, 972, 1268, 1665
Warner, Marvin L., **1977:** 1026, 1031
Warner, Rawleigh, Jr., **1979:** 1614n.
Warner-Lambert Co., **1980–81:** 552, 581
Warner Robins Air Force Base, Ga., **1977:** 2175
Warnke, Paul C., **1977:** 66, 87, 93, 96, 345, 379, 743, 1107, 1127, 1263; **1978:** 457, 1029, 1722, 1744, 1747, 1879
Warns, Carl A., **1978:** 469
Waronker, Cecile C., **1979:** 1034

Warren, Charles Hugh, **1977:** 9, 229, 253, 375, 806, 1031; **1979:** 872, 876, 960; **1980–81:** 2243
Warren, Dave, **1979:** 45, 91
Warren, Earl, **1979:** 884, 885; **1980–81:** 2929
Warren, Harold C., **1977:** 883, 884
Warren, Jack, **1980–81:** 1738
Warren, Richard, **1980–81:** 2731
Warren, Robert Penn, **1980–81:** 752, 1060
Warren, Ohio, **1979:** 1817
Warren Grant Magnuson Clinical Center, **1980–81:** 2806
Warsame Ali, Mohamed, **1980–81:** 1598
Warsaw Pact, **1977:** 1233; **1978:** 37, 38, 875, 1012, 1013, 1276, 1297
Wartime Relocation and Internment of Civilians Act, Commission on, **1980–81:** 1455, 2870
Washington, Bob, **1979:** 1921
Washington, George, **1979:** 2053, 2136; **1980–81:** 556, 856, 890, 924, 1385
Washington, Robert B., Jr., **1979:** 1727
Washington, Walter E., **1977:** 333, 784, 1632; **1980–81:** 16
Washington, Warren M., **1978:** 217; **1980–81:** 2243
Washington
    Democratic Party caucuses, **1980–81:** 461
    Disaster declaration, **1977:** 2129; **1979:** 2300; **1980–81:** 967
    Emergency declaration, **1977:** 557; **1979:** 440
    Gov. Dixy Lee Ray
        Mount St. Helens eruption, disaster assistance actions, **1980–81:** 950, 952, 953, 957, 959, 1903, 1914
        State Planning Council on Radioactive Waste Management, member, **1980–81:** 303
    Mount St. Helens eruption.
        See Mount St. Helens, Wash., eruption.
    President's visits, **1978:** 857, 860; **1979:** 2186; **1980–81:** 950, 956, 967, 1078, 1903–1915, 2677
    U.S. attorneys, **1977:** 883, 884, 1211, 1212
    U.S. district judges, **1978:** 149, 150; **1979:** 2105, 2106, 2207; **1980–81:** 894
    U.S. marshals, **1977:** 943, 1701
    White House briefing on administration's programs for civic and community leaders (Digest), **1979:** 2043
Washington, D.C.
    See District of Columbia.
Washington Bullets basketball team, **1978:** 1069
Washington Metropolitan Area Transit Authority, **1980–81:** 18
Washington Old Hall, Washington, England, **1977:** 881
Washington Post, **1980–81:** 728
Washington Press Club, **1977:** 22
Washington State Energy Facility Siting and Evaluation Council, **1980–81:** 99

Wasilewski, Vincent T., **1979:** 490n.
Wasserman, Lew R., **1979:** 375n.; **1980–81:** 2806, 2871
Wasserman, Mrs. Lew R., **1980–81:** 2806
Wasserman, Mr. and Mrs. Lew R., **1977:** 1894, 2031, 2041, 2183
Waste disposal, hazardous.
    See Hazardous waste disposal.
Waste Disposal Act Amendments, Solid, **1980–81:** 2831
Waste Isolation Pilot Plant, Carlsbad, N. Mex., proposed, **1979:** 2298; **1980–81:** 298, 299
Waste Management, Interagency Review Group on Radioactive, **1980–81:** 297
Waste Management, State Planning Council on Radioactive, **1980–81:** 297, 301
Water Act Amendments of 1978, Clean, **1980–81:** 416
Water Association, National Rural, **1980–81:** 1429
Water Conservation Fund, Land and, **1977:** 1097
Waste treatment and disposal, **1977:** 972
Watanabe, Ruth K., **1979:** 293
Water Development Appropriation Act, 1980, Energy and, **1979:** 1760, 1787; **1980–81:** 1983
Water Policy, Intergovernmental Task Force on, **1978:** 2269
Water Research and Development Act, **1978:** 1786
Water Research and Technology, Office of, **1978:** 1786
Water Resources Council, **1977:** 975, 976, 999–1001; **1978:** 1044, 1046, 1049, 1709; **1979:** 9, 10, 1760, **1980–81:** 36, 1983
Water and waterways
    Administration's accomplishments and goals, **1980–81:** 2951
    Aquaculture legislation, **1980–81:** 1937
    Clean Water Act of 1977, **1977:** 2179
    Coal slurry pipeline, **1977:** 2093
    Coastal zone management, **1979:** 1362, 1373
    Conservation, **1977:** 302, 488, 751, 754, 912
    Dam and water projects, **1979:** 1914
    Demarcation lines dividing the high seas and inland water, **1980–81:** 1521
    Denver, Colo., panel discussion, **1977:** 1861
    Energy sources development, **1980–81:** 586
    Environmental message, **1977:** 971, 976, 980
    EO 12141, **1979:** 1000
    Floodplain management, **1977:** 998, 1001; **1980–81:** 36
    International treaties and agreements, **1980–81:** 1625
    Interview remarks, **1978:** 307, 308, 715, 943, 944
    Legislation, **1979:** 150, 2049; **1980–81:** 159, 239, 275, 280, 417
    Long Island, N.Y., system pollution, **1980–81:** 2290
    Marine protection, **1980–81:** 1592, 1856

Water and waterways — *continued*
  Meeting with Congressmen, **1977:** 372
  National Forest land quality goals, **1980–81:** 1144
  National policy, **1978:** 848, 1043, 1044, 1072, 2109
  News conference remarks, **1978:** 1092
  New Jersey shortages, **1980–81:** 2267, 2453
  Pollution, **1977:** 440
  Pollution control programs, **1979:** 1359
  Project review, **1979:** 8–10
  Public works bill, **1978:** 1702, 1707–1710, 1713
  Resource projects, **1977:** 207, 287, 425, 435, 453, 490, 500, 514, 517, 586, 637, 651, 751, 754, 790, 919, 1017, 1019, 1030, 1276, 1329, 1461, 2050
  Resources management, **1980–81:** 419
  Resources policy, **1979:** 1358, 1854
  Rural areas programs, **1979:** 75, 675, 733, 794, 795
  Rural systems, **1980–81:** 1429
  Science and technology development, **1979:** 534
  Sewage grants, **1978:** 2108
  South Dakota supplies legislation, **1980–81:** 1920, 1921
  Southwest projects, **1980–81:** 88
  State of the Union, **1978:** 107, 115
  Unified navigation rules, **1980–81:** 2836
  Urban area systems, **1980–81:** 2083
  Waste treatment grants, **1978:** 472, 1376
  Water policy costsharing legislation, **1979:** 900
  Water users fees, **1978:** 976, 1673
  Westeern State Governors, meetings with the President, **1978:** 934, 936
  Wetlands, protection, **1977:** 1003, 1005
  Wild and scenic rivers, **1979:** 1354, 1364, 1379
Watergate, **1977:** 94. 867, 1914
Waters, Maxine, **1978:** 844, 1135
Waterville Township, Ohio, **1980–81:** 2466, 2615
Waterways authorization bill, inland, **1978:** 1826, 1827
Watkins, Robert, **1977:** 1083
Watkins, Ted, **1978:** 844
Watkins, Repr. Wesley W., **1977:** 1127; **1978:** 842; **1979:** 2276; **1980–81:** 1919
Watson, Barbara M., **1977:** 510; **1980–81:** 1334, 1336
Watson, Bernard C., **1980–81:** 96
Watson, Billy, **1977:** 1391
Watson, George, **1980–81:** 1017
Watson, Jack H., Jr., **1977:** 34–37, 86, 226, 278, 485, 943, 944, 1100, 1162, 1222, 1254, 1557, 1930, 2162; **1978:** 595, 690, 1110, 1217, 1218, 1350, 1428, 1429, 1605, 1725, 2083, 2084
  Assistant to the President and White House Chief of Staff, nomination, **1980–81:** 1110

Watson, Jack H., Jr. — *continued*
  Cuban refugees assistance responsibilities, **1980–81:** 819, 834, 914, 932
  Federal anti-arson program announcement, **1979:** 2249
  Federal procurement policy monitoring, **1980–81:** 73
  Hurricane Frederic relief responsibilities, **1979:** 1674
  Independent truckers' strike actions, **1979:** 1159, 1624
  Interagency Coordinating Council, Chairman, **1979:** 2157
  Meetings with the President (Digest), **1979:** 178, 240, 1454, 1705, 1823, 1975, 2187, 2280; **1980–81:** 63, 267, 463, 825, 1376, 1427, 1469, 1523, 1564, 1598, 1662, 1714, 1945, 1946
  Mentions, **1979:** 67, 658n., 794, 888, 1853; **1980–81:** 2401
  Miami, Fla., racial violence, President's representative, **1980–81:** 1074
  News conferences (Checklist), **1979:** 1143, 1159; **1980–81:** 25
  Oil reserves buildup monitoring, **1979:** 1324
  President's representative to Wichita Falls, Tex., tornado disaster, **1979:** 665, 668
  Rural Development Policy Act, signing ceremony remarks, **1980–81:** 1920n.
  Rural development responsibilities, **1979:** 2275
  State and local governments, White House liaison for, **1980–81:** 213
  Transition team head, **1980–81:** 2689, 2699, 2708
  Urban Development Action Grant program, second anniversary remarks, **1979:** 1965, 1974
  Urban policy development, **1980–81:** 2861
  White House Management Task Force on Energy Shortages, Chairman, **1979:** 1137, 1139
Watson, Thomas J., Jr., **1978:** 217, 230; **1979:** 1284, 1293, 1824; **1980–81:** 11, 25, 1050
Watson, Mrs. Thomas J., Jr., **1979:** 1824
Watt, Coral, **1980–81:** 752
Wattenburg, Ben J., **1977:** 78, 90; **1980–81:** 1439n.
Wattleton, Faye, **1980–81:** 2075
Watts, Evelyn, **1979:** 1447; **1980–81:** 2610
Watts, Glenn E., **1977:** 530, 1013; **1978:** 686, 1974, 2264; **1979:** 1247, 1252, 1258; **1980–81:** 823, 2609
Watts Labor Community Action Committee, **1978:** 841
Wausau, Wis., **1979:** 567
Waxman, Repr. Henry A.
  Hospital cost containment legislation support, **1979:** 384, 385, 1772
  Legislation passage leadership, **1980–81:** 1936, 1937, 1976, 2099, 2102

Waxman, Repr. Henry A. — *continued*
  Meeting with the President (Digest), **1979:** 293
  Mental health legislation sponsorship, **1979:** 857
Waycross, Ga., **1979:** 1615
Wayne, John, **1979:** 813n., 959, 1031, 2098; **1980–81:** 502, 752, 1061
Wayne, Mrs. John, **1980–81:** 1061
Wayne, Mich., **1980–81:** 1984, 2071
Wayne County, W. Va., **1980–81:** 2472
Wayson, Billy L., **1980–81:** 2613
Weapons.
  See Arms and weapons systems.
Weather Program, World, **1977:** 1957; **1980–81:** 2725
Weather Service, National, **1980–81:** 1050
Weatherly, Shawn, **1980–81:** 1469
Weaver, A. Vernon, Jr.
  See Small Business Administration, Administrator.
Weaver, Adrian G., **1977:** 196, 1944, 1966; **1978:** 231
Weaver, Repr. James, **1977:** 2181; **1978:** 409; **1980–81:** 2672
Weaver, Robert, **1979:** 322; **1980–81:** 2114, 2559
Webb, Henry Reiter, Jr., **1980–81:** 2753
Webb, J. David, **1980–81:** 813, 826
Webb, Marcia, **1979:** 466
Webber, E. Leland, **1977:** 1781, 1796
Webber, Paul Rainey, III, **1977:** 465
Weber case, **1979:** 847, 1159
Weber, Isabelle P., **1980–81:** 1406
Webster, James C., **1979:** 1779, 1824
Webster, William H., **1978:** 66, 148, 150, 1854; **1979:** 959, 1130, 1143, 1335; **1980–81:** 3048
Weddington, Sarah C., **1977:** 1252, 1266; **1978:** 506, 1484, 1485, 1725, 1801, 2288; **1980–81:** 833, 1336, 2476
  Meetings with the President (Digest), **1979:** 553, 1422
  Mention, **1979:** 772ftn.
  Women's business enterprises responsibilities, **1979:** 888
  Women's judicial appointments responsibilities, **1979:** 773
Wedemeyer, A., **1979:** 1604
Wegman, Richard A., **1980–81:** 264
Wegner, William, **1977:** 2070, 2071
Weicker, Sen. Lowell P., Jr., **1979:** 867
Weiden, Ron, **1980–81:** 2672
Weil, Frank Alan, **1977:** 229, 252, 805, 1085
Weiler, Lawrence D., **1978:** 757
Weinberg, Philip, **1980–81:** 1847
Weinberg, Steven, **1979:** 448, 1968; **1980–81:** 3023
Weinberger, Caspar W., **1980–81:** 2834
Weiner, Leon, **1980–81:** 2560
Weinshienk, Zita L., **1979:** 984
Weinstein, Steven E., **1978:** 1836

Weisberg, Frederick, **1977:** 1438, 1439
Weisman, Marcia Simon, **1979:** 466
Weisner, Jerome, **1979:** 1326
Weisner, Adm. Maurice, **1977:** 372
Weiss, Aileen A., **1978:** 2070
Weiss, Carl, **1977:** 761
Weiss, Paul A., **1979:** 2289; **1980–81:** 82n.
Weiss, Michael A., **1978:** 697
Weiss, Repr. Ted, **1978:** 458
Weisskopf, Victor F., **1980–81:** 82n.
Weissman, Marvin, **1977:** 935, 943; **1980–81:** 287, 293
Weizman, Ezer, **1978:** 502, 631, 779, 866, 1506, 1554, 1832, 2043, 2059, 2061; **1979:** 1684, 1752, 2299; **1980–81:** 825
Weizmann Institute of Science, **1980–81:** 646
Welch, Nathaniel, **1978:** 1360, 1381
Welch, Neil John, **1977:** 1103, 1128, 1211
Welfare Act, Adoption Assistance and Child, **1980–81:** 1124
Welfare system
  Administration's accomplishments, **1979:** 122
  Family planning, **1977:** 392
  Fraud, **1978:** 1657
  Funding, **1977:** 698
  Message to Congress, **1977:** 1451
  News conference remarks, **1977:** 1371
  State of the Union, **1978:** 104
  Welfare and food stamp consolidation report, **1979:** 2181
Welfare system reform, **1977:** 74, 159, 173, 315, 385, 770, 863, 892, 951, 1023, 1344, 1383, 1443, 1465, 1732, 1747, 1844; **1978:** 133, 986, 2232
  Administration's accomplishments and goals, **1980–81:** 910, 1607, 1619, 2948
  Child programs, **1980–81:** 1355
  Legislation
    Cash assistance, **1979:** 2092
    Child programs, **1979:** 138
    Countercyclical aid for State and local governments, **1979:** 258
    Effective in 1982, **1979:** 117
    House approval, **1980–81:** 118, 137
    House Ways and Means Committee action, **1979:** 1661, 1746, 1928
    Mentions, **1979:** 1342, 2034
    Message to Congress transmitting proposals, **1979:** 938, 958 (Checklist)
    President's appeal for support, **1980–81:** 1652, 1886, 2006
    President's commitment to legislative proposal in 1979, **1979:** 76
    Purposes, **1980–81:** 137, 1310, 1730, 2133
    Senate consideration, **1980–81:** 118, 2133
    Senate Finance Committee consideration, **1979:** 1746

Welfare system reform — *continued*
    Reagan, Ronald, position on, **1980–81:** 1955, 2078, 2082, 2093, 2376
Wellford, W. Harrison, **1977:** 573, 943, 1193, 1211, 1507, 1612; **1978:** 416, 1280; **1979:** 378; **1980–81:** 25
Wellhead tax, **1977:** 668, 698, 751, 1618, 1692; **1978:** 135
Wells, James Lesene, **1980–81:** 602
Wells, Melissa F., **1977:** 994, 1031, 1626, 1650; **1978:** 1509, 1516
Welsh, Matt, **1979:** 990
Welsh, William B., **1979:** 42, 1775, 1786
Welty, Eudora, **1980–81:** 752, 1061
Wenz, Russ, **1977:** 324
Werner, Dean, **1980–81:** 2503
Wertheim, Ronald P., **1979:** 1302, 1319
Wesley, Charles, **1979:** 322, 1565
Wesley, Charles H., **1980–81:** 84
Wesley, John, **1979:** 1565
West, John C., **1977:** 641, 993, 1031, 1162, 1826; **1978:** 526; **1979:** 983, 1585, 2105; **1980–81:** 2575
West, Kelly M., **1978:** 275, 303
West, Lee R., **1977:** 806; **1979:** 1786, 1787
West, Togo D., Jr., **1979:** 2165, 2187
West Allis, Wis., **1980–81:** 2076, 2179
West Chester, Pa., students, **1977:** 27
West Frankfort, Ill., **1980–81:** 2199
"West Side Story" cast, White House dinner, **1980–81:** 291
West Valley Demonstration Project Act, **1980–81:** 2001, 2071
West Virginia
    Birch River, **1980–81:** 433
    Coal industry, **1980–81:** 471, 1448
    Disaster declaration, **1977:** 596; **1978:** 2270; **1980–81:** 1564
    Emergency declaration, **1977:** 1506, 1507
    Energy crisis, **1977:** 37
    Housing program, **1977:** 434
    President's visits, **1977:** 402; **1978:** 999, 1002, 1009, 1729; **1979:** 1232; **1980–81:** 2472
    Strip mining, **1977:** 436
    U.S. attorney, **1977:** 1163
    U.S. district judges, **1979:** 1044, 2188
    U.S. marshals, **1977:** 1211, 1212, 1438, 1439
West Virginia Coal Association, **1978:** 1006
West Virginia State Society, **1978:** 924
Western Governors' Policy Office, **1979:** 1852
Western and Plains States Governors, meeting with the President, **1977:** 1222
Western Samoa
    Ambassador to U.S., **1978:** 328
    U.S. Ambassador, **1979:** 1040, 1043
Western States
    President's relationship, **1978:** 715, 807, 810, 811, 855

Western States — *continued*
    White House briefing for community leaders (Digest), **1980–81:** 932
Western State Governors, meeting with the President, **1979:** 1854, 1864
Westinghouse Broadcasting Co., Inc., **1980–81:** 733
Westinghouse National Science Talent Search, **1978:** 503
Weston, Paul, **1980–81:** 1591
Wetlands, protection, **1977:** 976, 1003, 1005
Wexler, Anne, **1978:** 770, 771, 1719, 2188
    Meetings with the President (Digest), **1979:** 544, 666, 1453, 2105; **1980–81:** 1662
    Mentions, **1979:** 245; **1980–81:** 1086
    News conferences (Checklist), **1979:** 1294; **1980–81:** 1429, 2333
    Olympic torch ceremony in Athens, Greece, U.S. delegation head, **1980–81:** 217
    Women's business enterprises responsibilities, **1979:** 888
Whalen, Repr. Charles W., Jr., **1977:** 788,1136, 1626, 1650, 2181; **1978:** 394, 919, 935
Whalen, William, **1977:** 2036
Whales, protection, **1977:** 984; **1979:** 1359, 1435
Whaling Commission, International, **1977:** 1135, 1532, 2077; **1979:** 265, 1359
Whaling Convention, International, **1979:** 1435
Wharton, Clifton R., Jr., **1978:** 1511; **1980–81:** 323
Wharton, T. Girard, **1977:** 1053
Wheat Agreement, International, **1980–81:** 865
Wheat Agreement of 1971, International, **1979:** 434, 1625
Wheat Council, International, **1979:** 434
Wheat reserves and exports, **1978:** 915; **1979:** 153, 1251; **1980–81:** 162, 2911
Wheat Growers, National Association of, **1978:** 525
Wheat Trade Convention, **1979:** 434, 1625
Wheeler, Gerridee, **1977:** 527
Wheeler, Joseph C., **1977:** 1064; **1980–81:** 427, 452
Wheeler, Michael Orvan, **1978:** 1027
Wheller, Albert, **1978:** 641
Whinnery, John R., **1979:** 448
Whistle-blowers, Federal Government, **1979:** 917
White, Alton M., **1979:** 1815
White, Barbara M., **1977:** 78, 90
White, Charles, **1980–81:** 602
White, George, **1980–81:** 1004
White, George M., **1978:** 770
White, George Washington, **1980–81:** 564
White, Howard A., **1978:** 1744, 1772; **1979:** 46, 91; **1980–81:** 1468, 1524
White, Hugh, **1977:** 813
White, John C., **1977:** 339, 373, 508, 557, 1534, 2179, 2223; **1978:** 234, 302, 504, 511, 556, 750, 803, 934, 1110, 1158, 1167, 1345, 1578, 1627, 1650, 1733, 1796, 1826, 1833, 1902, 1954, 2195, 2196, 2198

White, John C. — *continued*
    See also Democratic National Committee, Chairman.
White, John P.
    See Management and Budget, Deputy Director.
White, Kevin, **1980–81:** 2889
White, Lee, **1977:** 7
White, Linda D., **1980–81:** 928
White, Nellie, **1978:** 2269
White, Robert E., **1977:** 1763, 1795; **1978:** 1406;
    1980–81: 191
White, Robert M., **1979:** 2116
White, William, **1978:** 1117
White, William J., **1977:** 575, 596
White, Wynelle Watson, **1979:** 1604
White Cane Safety Day, **1977:** 1684; **1978:** 1395
    (Proc. 4678), **1979:** 1527
    (Proc. 4783), **1980–81:** 1568
White House, Committee for the Preservation of
    the, **1977:** 2182; **1977:** 1500; **1979:** 782;
    1980–81: 1047, 1935, 2849
White House, solar energy system, installation,
    1978: 1670; **1979:** 1143
White House authorized military aircraft, **1978:**
    327
White House Coal Advisory Council, **1980–81:**
    473, 1433, 1643
White House Commission on Small Business,
    1980–81: 64, 916
White House Communications Agency, **1977:** 1058
White House Conference on Aging, **1978:** 1792,
    1794; **1979:** 1445, 2212, 2249; **1980–81:**
    462, 534, 539, 2280
White House Conference on Balanced National
    Growth and Economic Development,
    1977: 1414; **1978:** 53, 66, 265; **1979:** 65, 69
White House Conference on Coal Exports, **1980–
    81:** 2810
White House Conference on Families, **1978:** 251,
    748; **1980–81:** 224, 1032, 1052, 2422
    Chairperson, **1979:** 667, 668
    Memorandum from the President, **1979:** 1939
    Mention, **1979:** 2136
    Purposes, **1979:** 1929
    White House reception, **1979:** 1286
White House Conference on Handicapped Individuals, **1977:** 464, 988, 1031
White House Conference on Libraries and Information Services, **1979:** 400, 746, 2129;
    1980–81: 1930
White House Conference on Regulatory Reform,
    1980–81: 57
White House Conference on Religion and Peace,
    1979: 1598
White House Conference on Small Business, **1978:**
    695, 820, 928, 1101, 1852
    Advisory group, **1979:** 639
    Chairman, **1979:** 811

White House Conference — *continued*
    Chairman Arthur Levitt, Jr., **1978:** 1836
        Final report recommendations, **1980–81:** 916,
        918, 920, 1598, 1840
        Meeting with the President (Digest), **1980–81:**
        64
        Opening session attendance, **1980–81:** 68
        President's Council on Energy Efficiency,
        member, **1980–81:** 1405
    Mentions, **1979:** 370, 1608, 2143
    Opening session, **1980–81:** 68, 104
    Pre-conference meeting with administration officials (Digest), **1980–81:** 64
    Preconference preparation, **1979:** 142, 335
    Purposes, **1980–81:** 74, 126
    Recommendations, **1980–81:** 1277, 1587, 1598,
    1840
White House Conference on Steel, **1977:** 1795,
    1796
White House Conferences on the Arts and Humanities, **1978:** 823
White House conferences on national energy policy, **1977:** 363
White House Correspondents Association, **1977:**
    758; **1978:** 2039, 2171; **1979:** 743
White House Fellows, **1977:** 986, 1143, 1523; **1978:**
    1026, 1381; **1979:** 914, 1397; **1980–81:**
    948, 966
White House Fellowships, **1977:** 941, 1143, 1714
White House Fellowships, President's Commission
    on, **1978:** 149, 737; **1979:** 931; **1980–81:**
    948, 949, 1823, 2849
White House Forum on Inflation, **1977:** 1910, 1967
White House Halloween party, **1978:** 1954
White House helicopter fleet, **1977:** 1162, 1164
White House Historical Association, **1978:** 964, 965
White House Management Review Committee,
    1977: 942
White House Management Task Force on Energy
    Shortages
    Establishment, **1979:** 1137
    Independent truckers' strike actions, **1979:** 1139,
    1159, 1233
    Members, meeting with the President, **1979:** 1222
White House Military Office, **1979:** 170
White House News Photographers Association,
    1977: 557
White House News Summary, **1978:** 906
White House passenger lists for military aircraft,
    1978: 1406; **1979:** 240
White House press corps, **1978:** 2281
White House Promenade, **1978:** 944
White House Rural Development Initiatives program, **1979:** 270
White House staff
    Administrative Officer, **1977:** 252
    Adviser to the President on Inflation.
        See Kahn, Alfred E.

White House staff — *continued*
Annual report, **1980–81:** 2782
Appointments Secretary to the President, **1978:** 892; **1979:** 1577; **1980–81:** 1406, 2698ftn.
Assistant to the President for Communications, **1979:** 1678
Assistant to the President for Congressional Liaison, **1978:** 66, 277, 302, 303, 327, 328, 414, 415, 456, 457, 503, 504, 525, 526, 570, 710, 749, 750, 769, 770, 801–803, 880, 881, 897, 898, 933, 934, 1009, 1071, 1110, 1154, 1221, 1222, 1278, 1279, 1332, 1333, 1344, 1345, 1350, 1380, 1405, 1406, 1457, 1484, 1505, 1571, 1644, 1668, 1669, 1722, 1723, 1771, 1772, 1879, 2003, 2187
See also Moore, Frank B.
Assistant to the President for Domestic Affairs and Policy, **1978:** 321, 509, 641, 690, 770, 802, 819, 1044, 1072, 1155, 1280, 1433, 1469, 1471, 1477, 1478, 1743, 1954, 1955, 2092, 2094, 2147, 2226, 2242, 2263
See also Eizenstat, Stuart E.
Assistant to the President for energy policy, **1977:** 7, 14, 22, 32, 37, 41, 67, 70, 86, 98, 114, 123, 134, 136, 163, 199, 204, 223, 252, 257, 274, 280, 283, 371, 403, 408, 463, 519, 556, 557, 706, 744, 746, 1058, 1072, 1143, 1221, 1225, 1265, 1306, 1336
Assistant to the President for Intergovernmental Affairs, **1978:** 595, 1110, 1217, 1218, 1350, 1428, 1429, 1605, 1725, 2083, 2084
See also Eidenberg, Eugene; Watson, Jack H., Jr.
Assistant to the President for National Security Affairs, **1977:** 8, 15, 30, 46, 85, 86, 243, 248, 251, 252, 279, 371, 463, 464, 508, 555–558, 595, 596, 640, 705, 706, 743–745, 805, 806, 882–884, 942, 943, 951, 1029, 1030, 1058, 1083, 1084, 1126, 1127, 1137, 1161–1163, 1210, 1211, 1221, 1263–1265, 1283, 1305, 1306, 1382, 1383, 1436, 1437, 1482, 1506, 1532, 1567, 1611, 1612, 1648, 1649, 1651, 1699, 1753, 1754, 1794, 1795, 1825, 1826, 1884, 1930, 1931, 1965, 1966, 1998, 2005, 2006, 2035, 2036, 2050, 2076, 2077, 2088, 2089, 2102, 2129, 2130, 2162, 2207, 2223; **1978:** 45, 50, 65, 66, 148, 149, 215, 229, 232, 276, 277, 281, 302, 303, 327, 328, 414, 415, 456, 457, 503, 504, 509, 525, 526, 570, 610, 641, 710, 711, 749, 750, 769, 770, 801–803, 880, 881, 892, 897, 898, 933, 934, 936, 1034, 1070, 1071, 1110, 1153, 1154, 1159, 1160, 1183, 1207, 1221, 1222, 1278, 1279, 1332, 1333, 1379, 1380, 1405, 1406, 1457, 1459, 1484, 1485, 1505, 1506, 1515, 1516, 1538, 1571, 1668, 1669, 1722, 1723, 1771, 1772, 1807–1809, 1879, 1954, 1955, 2004, 2058, 2059, 2072, 2073, 2146,

White House staff — *continued*
Assistant for National Security — *continued*
2147, 2156, 2186, 2187, 2269, 2270, 2280, 2281
See also Brzezinski, Zbigniew.
Assistant to the President for Public Liaison, **1978:** 459, 464, 533, 771, 1335, 1336, 1338
Assistant Press Secretary, **1979:** 1017
Assistant Special Counsel on Inflation, **1978:** 1915, 1971
Assistants to the President, **1977:** 31, 37, 85, 86, 268, 279, 281, 290, 357, 485, 705, 706, 712, 805, 943, 944, 1052, 1083, 1119, 1162, 1198, 1222, 1254, 1264, 1265, 1296, 1303, 1307, 1379, 1396, 1399, 1437, 1438, 1506, 1533, 1557, 1649, 1794, 1930, 1960, 2036, 2089, 2124, 2162; **1978:** 229, 277, 443, 525, 526, 570, 710, 750, 769, 802, 803, 897, 898, 934, 1034, 1071, 1154, 1221, 1222, 1278, 1333, 1344, 1345, 1379, 1380, 1406, 1411, 1457, 1484, 1506, 1515, 1516, 1668, 1719, 1722, 1723, 1772, 1879, 1954, 1955, 2004, 2058, 2059, 2073, 2146, 2147, 2187, 2188, 2269, 2281
Jordan, Hamilton.
See Jordan, Hamilton.
Kraft, Timothy E.
See Kraft, Timothy E.,
McDonald, Alonzo L., Jr.,
See McDonald, Alonzo L., Jr.,
Reorganization, **1979:** 378
Weddington, Sarah C., **1980–81:** 834, 1336, 2476
Wexler, Anne.
See Wexler, Anne.
Associate Assistant, **1977:** 184
Associate Counsels, **1977:** 184; **1979:** 1976
Associate Press Secretaries, **1977:** 1614, 1651, 1755, 1756, 1796, 1827, 1932; **1978:** 1496, 1596
Bario, Patricia Y.
See Bario, Patricia Y.
Schecter, Jerrold, **1979:** 768, 1143, 1787
Camp David meetings, **1978:** 755, 769
Chief Executive Clerk, **1977:** 273, 512
Chief of Protocol, **1979:** 1659, 1664, 1976
Chief Speechwriter, **1977:** 30
Chief of Staff.
See Jordan, Hamilton.
Christmas receptions, **1978:** 2280, 2281; **1979:** 2248
Correspondence, Chief, **1977:** 1533
Counsel, **1977:** 148, 279, 346, 347, 1265, 1480, 1533, 1642, 1649; **1978:** 65, 749, 802
See also Cutler, Lloyd N.
Counselor, **1977:** 1066
Counselor to the President on Aging, **1978:** 819, 930, 933, 1062, 1066, 1067, 1793; **1979:**

White House staff — *continued*
 Counselor on Aging — *continued*
  1633, 1635, 2081; **1980–81:** 534, 718
 Counsels to the President
  Cutler, Lloyd N.
   See Cutler, Lloyd N.
  Lipshutz, Robert J., **1979:** 1159, 1422, 1823,
   1835
 Deputy Adviser on Inflation and Counselor on
  Labor-Management Relations, **1979:** 25,
  467
 Deputy Appointments Secretary, **1978:** 893;
  1979: 990n.
 Deputy Assistant for National Security Affairs,
  1978: 232, 415, 503, 934, 1008, 1009, 1110,
  1154, 1344, 1345, 1571, 1668, 1722, 1723,
  1878, 2209
 Deputy Assistant for Policy Analysis, **1978:** 496
 Deputy to the Assistant to the President, **1980–**
  81: 1466
 Deputy Assistants, **1977:** 86, 184, 806, 1126,
  1210, 1382, 1699, 1930, 1965, 2005, 2036,
  2049, 2130
  Butler, Landon, **1979:** 1785, 2043
  Congressional Liaison, **1980–81:** 2071
  Congressional Liaison (House).
   See Cable, William H.
  Congressional Liaison (Senate).
   See Tate, Danny C.
  Domestic Affairs and Policy, **1979:** 1294
  Eidenberg, Eugene, **1979:** 1137, 1139
  National Security Affairs.
   See Aaron, David L.
  Simpson, William.
   See Simpson, William
 Deputy Associate for Congressional Affairs,
  1977: 2181
 Deputy to the Chief of Staff, **1979:** 1976, 1977
 Deputy Counsels, **1977:** 184; **1978:** 1652; **1979:**
  1976; **1980–81:** 104, 518, 3050
 Deputy Press Secretaries, **1977:** 290, 610, 942,
  943, 1034, 1059, 1808; **1978:** 313, 325, 719
  812, 908, 944, 1080, 1081, 1233, 1355,
  1417, 1678, 1782, 2068
  Bario, Patricia Y.
   See Bario, Patricia Y.
  Granum, Rex, **1979:** 1016n., 1226n., 1583,
   2062n., 2082; **1980–81:** 255, 1347, 1377
  Wurfel, Walt W., **1979:** 566, 628
 Deputy Special Assistant, **1977:** 1756
 District of Columbia liaison, **1977:** 784
 Georgians in the administration, **1977:** 2058
 Limousine service, **1977:** 30, 73
 Members, meetings with the President, **1977:** 85,
  147, 251, 463, 596, 640, 641, 705, 744, 882,
  1030, 1084, 1126, 1127, 1161, 1210, 1221,
  1263, 1305, 1436, 1506, 1611, 1699, 1753,

White House staff — *continued*
 Members, meetings — *continued*
  1825, 1965, 2005, 2036, 2050, 2088, 2129;
  1978: 276
 Messenger Service, Chief, **1977:** 1383
 Military Office, Director, **1977:** 1533
 Officials, selection, **1978:** 2258
 Physician, **1977:** 296; **1978:** 276
 Presidential Personnel Office
  Briefings for administration officials, **1977:**
   604
  Director, **1978:** 1787
 Press Secretary, **1977:** 8, 32, 178, 268, 290, 463,
  556, 692, 759, 760, 773, 1082, 1105, 1250,
  1263, 1595, 1642, 1691, 1800, 2053, 2091;
  1978: 42, 48, 50, 150, 671, 1030, 1097,
  1330, 1334, 1337, 1393, 1471, 1476, 1477,
  1485, 1496, 1674, 1724, 2039, 2068, 2180–
  2182, 2188, 2268, 2282
  See also Powell, Jody.
 Reduction, **1977:** 73, 637, 1254, 1259
 Salaries, **1977:** 746, 866
 Science and Technology Policy Advisor, **1977:**
  459, 465, 556, 723, 1222; **1978:** 892
 Secretary to the President, **1980–81:** 1466
 Senior Adviser for foreign policy, **1978:** 1457
 Senior Adviser to the President.
  See Donovan, Hedley W.,
 Senior Associate Counsel, **1979:** 1976
 Senior members, **1980–81:** 2726, 2822
  Meeting with the President, **1978:** 1405
 Senior officials, meeting with the President (Di-
  gest), **1979:** 1292
 South Grounds picnic, **1978:** 1071
 Special Advisor on Women, **1977:** 216
 Special Assistants to the President, **1977:** 9, 30,
  86, 154, 290, 306, 357, 565, 575, 595, 597,
  840, 954, 1048, 1059, 1383, 1633, 1651,
  1696, 1699, 1756, 1963, 1976, 2037; **1978:**
  906, 1407, 1484, 1485, 1682, 1719, 1724,
  1801
  Administration, **1978:** 1670
  Appointments, **1978:** 803
  Budget and Organization, **1978:** 277
  Congressional Liaisons (House)
   Beckel, Robert G.
    See Beckel, Robert G.
   Free, James C., **1979:** 732, 898
   Maher, Robert W., **1979:** 377, 378, 842, 956
   Straub, Terrence D., **1979:** 990
  Congressional Liaison (Senate), **1979:** 467, 732
  Consumer Affairs, **1978:** 789, 804, 1066, 1915,
   1971, 2002, 2218
   See also Peterson, Esther.
  Ethnic Affairs, **1980–81:** 13
  Health Issues, **1978:** 277, 770, 873, 1322, 1326,
   1329, 1334

White House staff — *continued*
  Special Assistants — *continued*
    Hispanic Affairs, **1980–81:** 1461, 1705ftn., 1939
    Information Management, **1979:** 1590ftn.
    Jenkins, C. Ray, **1979:** 1518, 1519; **1980–81:** 990ftn., 1443n., 1471
    Martin, Louis E., **1979:** 39, 49, 886n., 2064; **1980–81:** 908, 1705ftn.
    Special Projects, **1978:** 1682
    Torres, Esteban, **1979:** 1664, 2064
    Weddington, Sarah.
      See Weddington, Sarah.
  Special Coordinator for International Disaster Assistance, **1977:** 1126
  Special Counsel to the President, **1980–81:** 1976n.
  Staff Secretary, **1977:** 184
  Telegraph and Transportation Services, Chief, **1977:** 1211
  White House Projects, Director, **1977:** 9; **1978:** 330
White House Statements
  Airborne Warning and Control System, sale, **1977:** 1377
  Anti-inflation program, **1978:** 1845
  Association of South-East Asian Nations, **1978:** 1378
  August Consumer Price Index, **1979:** 1739
  Australia, meeting with Prime Minister J. Malcolm Fraser, **1979:** 3
  Austria, meeting with Chancellor Bruno Kreisky, **1979:** 2036
  Belgium, visit of Prime Minister Tindemans, **1977:** 1818
  Bombing incident in Jerusalem, **1978:** 1037
  Bonn Economic Summit Conference, **1978:** 1360
  Canada, Prime Minister Joe Clark, meeting with, **1979:** 1181
  Carter, Billy, activities with Libyan Government
    Justice Department investigation, **1980–81:** 1406, 2557, 2647
    Senate Judiciary Committee inquiry, **1980–81:** 1420, 1976, 2016
    State Department cables, **1980–81:** 1443
  Carter family peanut warehouse, **1979:** 1954
  Chadha v. *Immigration and Naturalization Service,* **1980–81:** 2282
  China, People's Republic of, Chief of the Liaison Office, **1978:** 1538
  China, People's Republic of—U.S. grain agreement, **1980–81:** 2433
  Commission of the European Communities, meeting with President Jenkins, **1978:** 2245
  Commission on European Communities, meeting with President Roy Jenkins, **1980–81:** 189

White House statements — *continued*
  Conference on Security and Cooperation in Europe, Belgrade Review Conference, **1978:** 453
  Consultative Group on U.S.-Japan Economic Relations, **1979:** 1165
  Cuban refugee policy, **1980–81:** 682, 914
  Cyprus
    Varosha, administration, **1978:** 1331
    Visit of President Kyprianou, **1978:** 1719
  Deep Seabed Hard Mineral Resource Act, **1980–81:** 1284
  Denmark, visit of Prime Minister Jorgensen, **1978:** 389
  Discount rate increase, **1978:** 1453
  Egypt
    Foreign Minister Fahmy, visit of, **1977:** 1633
    President Anwar al-Sadat, meetings with, **1978:** 279, 291; **1979:** 407, 410; **1980–81:** 623
    Vice President Muhammad Hasni Mubarak, meeting with, **1979:** 1023; **1980–81:** 99
  Egyptian-Israeli peace negotiations, **1978:** 1789, 1806
  Energy legislation, **1979:** 1691
  Energy mobilization board legislation, **1980–81:** 761
  Energy security corporation, Senate action, **1979:** 1877
  European Parliament, meeting with President Simone Veil, **1980–81:** 238
  Fair housing legislation, **1980–81:** 1098
  Federal Reserve System
    Board of Governors anti-inflation actions, **1979:** 1835
    Credit controls moderation, **1979:** 961
  Financial institutions deregulation legislation, **1979:** 2078
  Foreign exchange markets, **1978:** 1426
  France
    Visit of President Giscard d'Estaing, **1978:** 1008
    Visit of Prime Minister Barre, **1977:** 1609
  Germany, Federal Republic of
    Bavarian Minister President Franz Josef Strauss, meeting with, **1980–81:** 470
    Berlin Mayor Dietrich Stobbe, meeting with, **1980–81:** 644
    Chancellor Schmidt, meetings with, **1977:** 1251; **1978:** 1015; **1979:** 1005; **1980–81:** 2738
    Dr. Kohl, visit, **1978:** 1212
    Foreign Minister Hans-Dietrich Genscher, meeting with, **1980–81:** 189
    Vice Chancellor Hans-Dietrich Genscher, meeting with, **1979:** 1419
  Greece, visit of Prime Minister Caramanlis, **1978:** 1025

White House statements — *continued*
Guinea, President Ahmed Sékou Touré, meeting with, **1979:** 1417
Heavy crude oil price controls amendments, **1979:** 2279
Honduras, President Policarpo Paz Garcia, meeting with, **1980–81:** 426
India
Nuclear fuel shipment from U.S., **1980–81:** 1922
Prime Minister Desai, visit, **1978:** 1085, 1090
International Olympic Committee President, meeting with, **1980–81:** 929
Iran
American hostages in, **1979:** 2102, 2141, 2148, 2268
Ayatollah Khomeini's health, Assistant to the President for Congressional Liaison's remarks, **1980–81:** 2534
Rescue attempt for American hostages, **1980–81:** 771
Shah Pahlavi, visit, **1977:** 2028, 2033
U.S. policy, **1980–81:** 1851
Iranian student visas, court decision, **1979:** 2285
Iraq-Iran conflict, **1980–81:** 1930
Ireland, meeting with Prime Minister John M. Lynch, **1979:** 2097
Israel
Defense Minister Weizman, visit, **1978:** 502
Foreign Minister Dayan, visit of, **1977:** 1627
Prime Minister Begin, visits, **1977:** 1283, 2127, 2131, 2152, 2163; **1978:** 547
Prime Minister Menahem Begin, meetings with, **1979:** 372, 373, 382; **1980–81:** 700
U.S. foreign military sales credits, **1979:** 2299
Italy, Prime Minister Andreotti, visits, **1977:** 1363; **1978:** 1019
Jamaica
Prime Minister Manley, visit, **1977:** 2128
U.S. economic assistance to, **1980–81:** 3025
Japan, meeting with Prime Minister Zenko Suzuki, **1980–81:** 2560
Jordan, meeting with Chief of Royal Court and Foreign Minister, **1977:** 1678
Kampuchea, international aid, **1979:** 2197
Kenya
Meeting with delegation, **1978:** 449
Meeting with President Daniel T. arap Moi, **1980–81:** 354
Kenyatta, President Jomo, death, **1978:** 1467
Lake Tahoe protection, **1980–81:** 1012
Liberia, meeting with President William R. Tolbert, Jr., **1979:** 1806
Middle East, Secretary of State Vance's trip, **1978:** 189
Minority business public works contracts, **1980–81:** 1280

White House statements — *continued*
Morocco, Prime Minister Osman, visit, **1977:** 2079
Namibia, agreement, **1978:** 1271
National Advisory Committee for Women, **1979:** 27
National economy data, **1980–81:** 2055
National energy plan, **1977:** 2161
National health plan legislation, **1979:** 65
Natural gas legislation, **1978:** 1469
Netherlands, Prime Minister Andreas van Agt, meeting with, **1979:** 2201
Nicaragua, meeting with the Junta, **1979:** 1722
Nigeria, President Alhaji Shehu Shagari, meeting with, **1980–81:** 2104
Norway, Prime Minister Odvar Nordli, meeting with, **1979:** 2201
Oil price decontrol, **1979:** 931
Olympics, 1980 Summer, **1980–81:** 305, 356, 560
OPEC (Organization of Petroleum Exporting Countries), **1978:** 2271
Pahlavi, Shah Mohammed Reza, **1979:** 2191
Pakistan, meeting with Agha Shahi, **1980–81:** 67
Panama, visit of Brig. Gen. Torrijos Herrera, **1977:** 1535
Panama Canal treaties implementing legislation, House of Representatives disapproval, **1979:** 1698
Persian Gulf area security, **1980–81:** 1545
Poland, situation in, **1980–81:** 2785
Portugal, President António dos Santos Ramalho Eanes
Meeting with, **1980–81:** 1233
Visit, **1978:** 1021
President's Personal Emissary to India, **1980–81:** 188
Regulatory reform legislation, **1979:** 2271
Rock Island railraod labor dispute, **1979:** 1999
SALT II treaty
Senate Foreign Relations Committee approval, **1979:** 2102
Senate Select Committee on Intelligence report, **1979:** 1822
Saudi Arabia
Foreign Minister, meeting with, **1977:** 1903
King Khalid, visit, **1978:** 1876
Saudi Arabian crude oil production, **1979:** 1226, 1766
Smallpox eradication, **1979:** 2035
Social security financing legislation, **1977:** 1917; **1978:** 720
Soviet citizens' exchange with U.S., **1979:** 731
Soviet Mission to United Nations, bombing of, **1979:** 2231
Spain, meetings with Prime Minister Adolfo Suárez, **1980–81:** 82, 1223

White House statements — *continued*
State and local governments fiscal assistance, Government Operations Committee report, **1979:** 2196
State Governors, meeting with the President, **1978:** 1480
Strategic arms limitation, **1979:** 329
Sudan, visit of President Nimeiri, **1978:** 1561
Summer Olympics, 1980, decision to boycott, **1980–81:** 972
Supplemental Appropriations and Rescissions Act, Food for Peace provision, **1980–81:** 1333
Supreme Soviet parliamentarians, meeting with delegation head, **1978:** 220
Syria, Foreign Minister, meetings with, **1977:** 704, 1677
Tanzania, President Nyerere, visit, **1977:** 1434
Three Mile Island, Pa., nuclear plant, **1979:** 617
Trade negotiations in Geneva, Switzerland, **1978:** 1271
Trident I missile sale to United Kingdom, **1980–81:** 1344
Truckers' strikes, independent, **1979:** 1135
Turkey, Prime Minister Ecevit, visit, **1978:** 1018
Union of Soviet Socialist Republics
Iran, veto of economic sanctions against, **1980–81:** 79
Sakharov, Mr. and Mrs. Andrei, internal exile of, **1980–81:** 194, 357
United Kingdom
Prime Minister Callaghan, visit, **1978:** 566
Prime Minister Margaret Thatcher, meeting with, **1979:** 1181, 2267
United Mine Workers strike, **1978:** 508
United Nations, meetings with Secretary General Waldheim, **1978:** 1687; **1979:** 1332
United Nations commission of inquiry on Iran, **1980–81:** 356, 455
United States International Development Cooperation Agency, **1979:** 1230
United States-Japan trade agreement, **1978:** 67
U.S. Attorney Herman Sillas, Jr., **1980–81:** 1346, 1412, 1661
Vatican City, Pope John Paul II, meeting with, **1979:** 1834
Veterans' preference in employment, **1978:** 2165
Virginia Democratic Party caucuses, **1980–81:** 525
Water projects legislation, **1980–81:** 275
West German rescue of hostages in Somalia, **1977:** 1810
West-to-east crude oil transportation system, **1980–81:** 99
Windfall profits tax legislation, **1980–81:** 470
World Conference to Combat Racism and Racial Discrimination, **1978:** 1456

White House statements — *continued*
Yugoslavia, President Cvijetin Mijatovic, meeting with, **1980–81:** 1210
Yugoslavian diplomat's home, bombing of, **1980–81:** 1023
Zaire
President Sese Seko Mobutu, meeting with, **1979:** 1627
Prime Minister Mugabe, meeting with, **1980–81:** 1584
Zimbabwe-Rhodesia
Bishop Abel Tendekai Muzorewa, meeting with, **1979:** 1230
Conflict settlement, **1979:** 2262
White House task force on the mushroom industry, **1980–81:** 2330, 2331
White House visitors, **1978:** 1186
Whitefield, George, **1979:** 1565
Whitehead, Charlie, **1980–81:** 1362
Whitehouse, Alton W., Jr., **1979:** 1614n.
Whitehurst, Dan, **1977:** 917
Whitly, Repr. Charles, **1978:** 530
Whitman, Marina v.N., **1980–81:** 264
Whitman, Samuel, **1978:** 407
Whitman, Walt, **1979:** 2265
Whitney, Hassler, **1977:** 2046
Whitten, Repr. Jamie L., **1979:** 240, 591n., 2156
Wholberuck, Aliceann Fritchler, **1979:** 1854
Wholesale Price Index.
See Producer Price Index.
Wichita, Kans., **1978:** 1813–1820
Wichita Falls, Tex., **1979:** 665, 668
Wicker, Veronica D., **1979:** 1018, 1019
Wickwire, James, **1978:** 1558
Widener, Mary, **1980–81:** 2560
Widnall, Sheila, **1978:** 569
Wien Air Alaska, Inc., **1978:** 1924, 2033, 2158; **1979:** 89, 293
Wiesel, Elie, **1978:** 1973; **1979:** 293, 684, 1773, 1861; **1980–81:** 823
Wiesenthal, Simon, **1980–81:** 1495
Wiesner, Adm. Maurice, **1978:** 2281
Wiesskopf, Victor F., **1979:** 2289
Wigder, Howard J., **1978:** 1468
Wiggins, Repr. Charles E., **1978:** 394, 1139, 1140
Wilberforce University, **1980–81:** 2173
Wilcox, Maj. Gen. Howard S., **1977:** 1397
Wilcox, William H., **1979:** 2127, 2139
Wild and Scenic Rivers System, National.
See National Wild and Scenic Rivers System.
Wilderness Preservation System, National, **1979:** 240, 669, 1975; **1980–81:** 1142, 1411, 2756
Wilderness and wildlife, **1978:** 409, 2111–2144; **1979:** 151
Alaskan protection, **1980–81:** 233, 234, 419
Federal programs, **1980–81:** 1144
Legislation, **1980–81:** 1408–1411

Wilderness and wildlife — *continued*
  Wilderness preservation, **1977:** 593, 979, 981,
    998, 1073, 1097, 1264
  Wildlife protection, **1979:** 1435
Wildlife, Sikes Act amendments, **1978:** 1250
Wildlife Conservation Act, Fish and, **1980–81:**
  1958
Wildlife law enforcement, **1979:** 1364, 1376
Wildlife law enforcement coordinating committee,
  1979: 1364, 1377–1379
Wildlife Refuge, National, **1980–81:** 1411, 1431
Wildlife Service, United States Fish and, **1980–81:**
  1431
Wildman, Jerry, **1977:** 315
Wiles, Ed, **1978:** 1006
Wiley, Marshall W., **1978:** 1557, 1572
Wilkes, Peter J., **1979:** 788
Wilkins, Roy, **1979:** 323
Wilkins, Mr. and Mrs. Roy, **1977:** 1306
Wilkowski, Jean M., **1977:** 1230, 1266
Will Rogers Day (Proc. 4698), **1979:** 2078
Willens, Harold, **1977:** 941
William O. Douglas Arctic Wildlife Range, Alaska,
  1980–81: 416, 419
Williams, Bathrus B., **1977:** 2153
Williams, Carolyn Antonides, **1980–81:** 1723
Williams, Charlotte, **1978:** 268, 269; **1979:** 1241
Williams, Harold M., **1977:** 537, 557, 692; **1980–81:**
  2378
Williams, Sen. Harrison A., Jr., **1977:** 509, 988,
    1427, 1428, 1575, 1948, 1987, 1989; **1978:**
    289, 304, 432, 698, 699, 1425, 1543, 1667,
    1782, 1917, 1919, 2110; **1980–81:** 1009,
    2113, 2114
  Comprehensive energy plan support, **1979:** 2039
  Financial institutions deregulation, legislation
    passage leadership, **1979:** 2288
  Hospital cost containment legislation support,
    1979: 385, 386
  Meeting with the President (Digest), **1979:** 898
  Mention, **1979:** 2021
  President's Export Council, member, **1979:** 943
  Urban Action Development Grant program,
    second anniversary remarks, **1979:** 1972
Williams, Henry, **1980–81:** 813, 826
Williams, Hubert, **1980–81:** 2613
Williams, Lt. Gov. J. H., **1978:** 2155
Williams, James F., II, **1978:** 275, 303
Williams, James H.
  See Agriculture, Department of, Deputy Secre-
    tary.
Williams, James R., **1978:** 416
Williams, Jeannette, **1979:** 2024
Williams, Jerre S., **1978:** 1663; **1980–81:** 654, 720
Williams, Jim.
  See Deputy Secretary *under* Agriculture, De-
    partment of.

Williams, Vice Adm. Joe, Jr., **1977:** 1041
Williams, Karen Hastie, **1980–81:** 371, 375
Williams, Lorraine, **1977:** 1083
Williams, Richard L., **1979:** 667, 668
Williams, Samuel L., **1978:** 841
Williams, Stanton, **1978:** 1766
Williams, Susan J., 2089, 2107
Williams, Susan K., **1980–81:** 929
Williams, Tennessee, **1980–81:** 752, 1061
Williams, Wesley, **1977:** 1083
Williams, William E., **1979:** 919, 927
Williamsburg, Va., **1977:** 1659
Williamson, Thomas S., Jr., **1978:** 1560, 1572
Willie, Charles V., **1977:** 531
Willis, William, **1979:** 23
Willman, Joseph, **1977:** 292
Wills, Joan L., **1978:** 52, 150
Wilmington, Del., **1978:** 385, 386
Wilmington 10, **1977:** 1105, 2123; **1978:** 323, 537,
  695, 1098, 1328, 1330
Wilson, Repr. Bob, **1978:** 193
Wilson, Carrol L., **1980–81:** 930
Wilson, Repr. Charles H., **1977:** 1533; **1978:** 769
Wilson, Edward O., **1977:** 2046
Wilson, Genevieve H., **1977:** 1714
Wilson, George, **1980–81:** 1770
Wilson, Hal, **1979:** 2276n.
Wilson, Ida Marie, **1977:** 816
Wilson, James C., **1980–81:** 1644
Wilson, James M., Jr., **1977:** 195
Wilson, Lionel, **1980–81:** 1299
Wilson, Gen. Louis H., **1978:** 1383, 2089; **1979:**
  1222
Wilson, Margaret Bush, **1978:** 217, 230; **1979:** 931;
  1980–81: 1322
Wilson, Rosine McFaddin, **1979:** 466
Wilson, Theresa A., **1980–81:** 928
Wilson, Wade, **1979:** 742, 911, 913
Wilson, Woodrow, **1979:** 832; **1980–81:** 222, 324,
  1852
Wilson, N.C., **1978:** 1386, 1390
Wilton, Conn., **1980–81:** 893
Wilzig, Siggi, **1978:** 1975; **1980–81:** 823
Wimer, Connie, **1979:** 466
Winberry, Charles B., Jr., **1979:** 554, 555; **1980–81:**
  1599
Wind energy systems, **1979:** 1104; **1980–81:** 586
Wind Energy Systems Act, **1980–81:** 1668
Winder, David K., **1979:** 2081, 2082
Windfall profits tax
  Announcement, **1979:** 610, 611
  Appeal for congressional and public support,
    1979: 653, 718, 753, 790, 801, 830, 912,
    982, 1303, 1309, 1339, 1410, 1425, 1457,
    1470, 1473, 1479, 1489, 1490, 1492, 1493,
    1513, 1567, 1743
  Comprehensive energy plan, dependence on pas-
    sage of tax, **1979:** 1338, 1342, 1411, 1425,

Windfall profits tax — *continued*
  Comprehensive energy plan — *continued*
    1450, 1475, 1495, 1506, 1513, 1570, 1571,
      1610, 1632, 1644, 1646, 1725, 1743, 1828,
      2029, 2055
  Congressional amendments to President's pro-
      posal, possibility, **1979:** 749, 753, 790
  Congressional consideration
    Conference Committee action, **1979:** 2281
    House approval, **1979:** 1182, 1303, 1309, 1323,
      1426, 1577, 1609, 2029, 2048, 2056, 2155
    Inaction, **1979:** 1212, 1410, 1469, 2283
    Mentions, **1979:** 1321, 1450, 1632, 1640, 1642,
      1646, 2092, 2102
    Senate action, **1979:** 1339, 1342, 1426, 1450,
      1577, 1609, 1964, 2029, 2048, 2056, 2155
  Congressmen, meeting with the President, **1979:**
      732
  Energy security corporation funding, **1979:** 1338,
      1868
  Fuel companies, lobbying efforts, **1979:** 1309,
      1338, 1342, 1491, 1498, 1513, 1577
  Heavy crude oil, exemption from tax, **1979:** 1317
  Mentions, **1979:** 802, 805, 848, 873, 905, 933,
      1340n., 1463, 1715, 1758, 1936, 2125
  Message to Congress transmitting proposal,
      1979: 721, 728
  News conference (Checklist), **1979:** 733
  White House briefings for community and civic
      leaders (Digest), **1979:** 1882, 2042
  See also Energy security trust fund; Crude oil
      windfall profits tax act.
Windfall Profits Tax, National Citizens' Coalition
      for, **1979:** 1705, 2043; **1980–81:** 586
Windsor Locks, Conn., **1980–81:** 2288
Winfield, David, **1980–81:** 2075
Wing, Michael H., **1980–81:** 926
Wingreen, Ned S., **1980–81:** 926
Winkel, Adrian P., **1977:** 705, 745
Winn, Joan T., **1980–81:** 2075
Winn, Larry, Jr., **1979:** 1668, 1680
Winn, William, **1978:** 2269
Winship, Thomas, **1980–81:** 643n.
Winstead, Thomas W., **1978:** 952
Winston, Ellen, **1979:** 2213; **1980–81:** 537
Winston, Morton M., **1979:** 1614n.
Winston-Salem, N.C., **1978:** 529, 535; **1980–81:**
      2140
Winter, Gov. William F., **1980–81:** 422, 1423n.
Winter Olympics, 1980.
  See Olympics, 1980 Winter.
Wireless communications, 75th anniversary, **1978:**
      87
Wiretapping, **1979:** 585, 587
Wiretapping and Electronic Surveillance, National
      Commission for the Review of Federal
      and State Laws Relating to, **1979:** 585,
      587–590

Wirth, Repr. Timothy E., **1978:** 824, 834, 881, 882;
      1979: 2086
Wirtz, Willard, **1978:** 1004
Wisconsin
  Dairy farms, **1977:** 298
  Democratic Party primary, **1980–81:** 584, 724
  Disaster declaration, **1978:** 1278; **1980–81:** 1428
  Emergency declaration, **1977:** 1464; **1979:** 89
  Grain industry labor dispute, **1979:** 1468, 1469
  Indian land claims, **1977:** 311, 326
  President's visits, **1979:** 567, 572, 573, 1470, 1472,
      1475n.; **1980–81:** 2076, 2080, 2640, 2646
  U.S. attorney, **1977:** 707; **1978:** 457, 458
  U.S. district judges, **1979:** 1294, 1319
  U.S. marshals, **1977:** 1569, 2078
  White House briefing for civic and community
      leaders, **1980–81:** 268
Wisconsin, Surgical Care—Blue Shield of, **1978:**
      1155
Wise, Billy M., **1979:** 1820, 1824
Wise, Phillip J., Jr., **1978:** 892; **1979:** 1577; **1980–
      81:** 1406
Wiseman, Thomas A., Jr., **1978:** 1381
Wisner, Frank George, II, **1979:** 1263, 1293
Witt, Michael E., **1979:** 2040, 2044
Witteveen, H. Johannes, **1977:** 1671; **1978:** 620
Wittner, Loran, **1977:** 1817
Wittstock, Laura, **1980–81:** 2801
Woerner, John, **1979:** 2075
Wogan, Gerald N., **1979:** 686
Wojtaszek, Emil, **1977:** 1754
Wojtylo, John, **1978:** 1809
Wolf, Milton A., **1977:** 1124, 1128; **1979:** 1048;
      1980–81: 1765, 1770n., 2883
Wolf, Peter Henry, **1978:** 1533, 1572; **1979:** 46, 91
Wolfe, Thomas, **1980–81:** 1562, 1605
Wolff, Alan W., **1977:** 795, 807; **1979:** 1808;
      1980–81: 1447
Wolff, Lester L., **1977:** 1625, 1650; **1978:** 1154;
      1979: 2085; **1980–81:** 522
Wolle, William D., **1979:** 1300, 1319
Womach, Emily H., **1980–81:** 272
Women
  Ad hoc coalition, **1977:** 355
  Administration's accomplishments and goals,
      1979: 888; **1980–81:** 140, 2954
  Affirmative action programs, **1980–81:** 115
  Business enterprises, **1979:** 887, 890, 894
  Discrimination, **1977:** 1502–1505; **1978:** 111
  District and circuit judges, appointments, **1978:**
      1803
  Draft registration, **1980–81:** 289, 243, 313, 333,
      342
  Employment, **1977:** 99, 114, 115, 117, 137, 138,
      232, 242, 317, 2034; **1978:** 1412; **1979:**
      126, 890, 1507; **1980–81:** 123, 830, 2020
  Equal rights amendment.
    See Equal rights amendment.

Women — *continued*
  Equality, memorandum, **1978:** 1335
  Federal appointments, **1980–81:** 1325, 1952, 2350
  Federal equal opportunity programs, **1979:** 143
  Federal executive employment, **1978:** 354
  Federal programs, **1980–81:** 1499
  Judicial appointments, **1979:** 131, 759, 772, 847; **1980–81:** 223
  Military draft, inclusion, **1977:** 314
  Military service, **1980–81:** 2448
  Occupational discrimination based on pregnancy, **1978:** 1906
  Organizations' representatives, meeting with the President, **1979:** 2248; **1980–81:** 268, 423, 774
  Prison programs, **1980–81:** 2282
  Rape victims, **1978:** 1902
  Small business activities, **1980–81:** 70, 77, 127, 128
  Social security discrimination, **1977:** 2156
  Special Advisor on Women, **1977:** 216
Women, Citizens' Advisory Council on the Status of, **1977:** 1494
Women, Convention on the Elimination of All Forms of Discrimination Against, **1980–81:** 2476, 2715
Women, Equality, Development and Peace, United Nations Decade for, **1979:** 825
Women, Infants, and Children, Special Supplemental Food Program for, **1978:** 2000
Women, Interdepartmental Task Force on, **1978:** 2188
Women, National Advisory Committee on. *See* National Advisory Committee on Women.
Women, National Federation of Democratic, **1978:** 797, 803
Women, President's Advisory Committee for. *See* President's Advisory Committee for Women.
Women, U.N. Commission on the Status of, **1977:** 1176
Women, World Conference for the United Nations Decade for, **1980–81:** 1335
Women Business Owners, Interagency Task Force on, **1979:** 890, 894, 895
Women Business Owners, Task Force on, **1977:** 1429; **1978:** 1188
Women Judges, National Association of, **1980–81:** 2057, 2071
Women Voters of the United States, League of, **1979:** 771
  Biennial national convention, **1980–81:** 828
  President, **1980–81:** 589, 2476
  Presidential debates organizer, **1980–81:** 1702, 1928, 2138, 2173, 2272, 2320
Women's Business Enterprise, Interagency Committee on, **1979:** 891, 892, 894; **1980–81:** 77, 1569

Women's Business Ownership Campaign, **1977:** 1437, 1438
Women's Caucus for Art awards, **1979:** 217
Women's Conference, National, **1978:** 2069
Women's Educational Equity Act, **1978:** 429
Women's Educational Programs, National Advisory Council on, **1979:** 339, 377, 2039, 2044; **1978:** 1086, 1111; **1980–81:** 508, 1023, 1051, 1569
Women's Equality Day, **1977:** 1502–1504; **1978:** 1470; **1979:** 1476; **1980–81:** 1572, 1575, 1599
Women's History Week, National, **1980–81:** 412
Women's Political Caucus, National, **1977:** 544
Women's Sport Foundation, **1979:** 1678
Women's Year, 1975, International, **1978:** 1335, 1640
Women's Year, 1975, National Commission on the Observance of International, **1977:** 524–527, 2025; **1978:** 553
Women's Year Conference, International, **1977:** 2130
Won Pat, Del. Antonio Borja, **1980–81:** 318, 1723
Wong, France Yanai, **1980–81:** 2075
Wood, David T., **1977:** 1827, 1931; **1978:** 149, 150
Wood, Harlington A., Jr., **1977:** 1103, 1128, 1211
Wood, John H., Jr., **1979:** 959
Wood, Reginald Lightbourn, **1980–81:** 775
Wood Residue Utilization Act, **1980–81:** 2821
Woodburning stoves
  Installation tax credit, **1979:** 701, 1102, 1317
  Mentions, **1979:** 1894, 1900
  New designs, **1979:** 793
  White House installation, **1979:** 793, 801
Woodcock, Leonard, **1977:** 78, 79, 316, 377, 489, 500, 863, 887, 888, 892, 894, 1132, 1163, 1222; **1978:** 302, 1445, 2267; **1980–81:** 1013
  See also China, U.S. Ambassador.
Woodrow Wilson International Center for Scholars, **1977:** 2036; **1978:** 1011, 1602; **1979:** 2116, 2248; **1980–81:** 2732, 3023
Woodruff, Arthur H., **1980–81:** 1700
Woodruff, Hale, **1980–81:** 603
Woodruff, Judy, **1980–81:** 107
Woods, Eloise A., **1977:** 1375, 1384
Woods, Henry, **1979:** 2249
Woods, James A., **1979:** 1524
Woods, Jessie A., **1979:** 45, 92
Woods, Noah, **1980–81:** 849
Woods, Rilla Moran, **1980–81:** 1569
Woods, Shawn, **1980–81:** 1453
Woodson, G. Carter, **1980–81:** 85
Woodson, Howard, **1980–81:** 2524
Woodward, C. Vann, **1978:** 880
Woodward, Don A., **1978:** 455
Woodworth, Laurence N., **1977:** 181, 252, 1794, 2084; **1978:** 124, 125

Woodyard, William, **1980–81:** 2558
Woolsey, R. James, **1977:** 207, 252
Woolsey, Suzanne H., **1977:** 1162
Woolston, Lionel L., **1980–81:** 1508
Wooten, James T., **1977:** 759
Worcester, Mass., **1980–81:** 935
Work permits, temporary, **1978:** 906
Work-study program students, **1977:** 1907
Word and training opportunities act, proposed, **1979:** 938
Workers' Viewpoint Organization, **1979:** 2104
Working Group on Food and Agricultural Policy, **1977:** 1695
Working Group on Rural Development, **1979:** 75
Working Mothers' Day (Proc. 4786), **1980–81:** 1592
World Administrative Radio Conference, 1979, **1979:** 541, 1334
World Bank
 Annual meeting of Board of Governors, **1980–81:** 1972, 2071
 Energy resources development, **1980–81:** 1189
 Grain storage initiatives, **1980–81:** 1190
 Latin American involvement, **1980–81:** 2735
 U.S. allocations, **1980–81:** 941, 1206
 See also International Bank for Reconstruction and Development.
World Coal Study, **1980–81:** 930
World Conference to Combat Racism and Racial Discrimination, **1978:** 1456
World Congress of Postal, Telegraph and Telephone International, **1978:** 1808
World Food program, United Nations, **1980–81:** 257
World forests, **1979:** 1371, 1386
World Health Assembly, **1977:** 806, 839; **1978:** 885; **1979:** 815
World Health Organization, **1977:** 2037; **1979:** 2035, 2091
World Hunger, Presidential Commission on. *See* Presidential Commission on World Hunger.
World Hunger Working Group, **1977:** 1696
World Jewish Congress, **1977:** 1952, 1967; **1979:** 1706
World Law Day, **1977:** 1481, 1482
World Trade Week, **1977:** 594; **1978:** 514
 (Proc. 4654), **1979:** 616
 (Proc. 4722), **1980–81:** 322
World Weather Program, **1977:** 1957; **1980–81:** 2725
Worthington, Charles, **1978:** 1543; **1980–81:** 2889
Worthy, Josephine, **1977:** 1882, 2101, 2130; **1978:** 89, 232; **1980–81:** 1149, 1246
Wrangell-St. Elias National Monument, **1978:** 2138
Wriggins, W. Howard, **1977:** 1196, 1212; **1978:** 231
Wright, Danny A., **1980–81:** 1508
Wright, Repr. James C., Jr., **1977:** 24, 26, 371, 595, 1016, 1030, 1163; **1978:** 1157, 1530, 1571, 1647, 1854; **1979:** 1125, 1212, 2086

Wright, Repr. James C., Jr. — *continued*
 Campaign appearance with the President, **1980–81:** 2635
 Energy Security Act, passage leadership, **1980–81:** 1255
 Meetings with the President (Digest), **1980–81:** 825, 1427
 National prayer breakfast attendance, **1980–81:** 275
Wright, Martha Sinnard, **1979:** 466
Wright, Robert L., **1977:** 943
Wright, Scott O., **1979:** 957, 958
Wright Brothers Day, **1977:** 2048
 (Proc. 4699), **1979:** 2079
 (Proc. 4802), **1980–81:** 2717
Wright Brothers Day, National Aviation Year and, **1978:** 1396
Wruble, Bernhardt R., **1979:** 41
Wunnicke, Esther C., **1977:** 1072, 1085
Wurf, Jerry, **1980–81:** 1647, 2004
Wurfel, Walter W., **1977:** 290, 1808; **1978:** 313, 325, 719, 812, 908, 944, 1080, 1081, 1233, 1355, 1417, 1678, 1782, 2068; **1979:** 189, 566, 628, 2239
Wyant, Dennis R., **1979:** 339, 377, 974
Wyatt, Addie, **1977:** 527; **1978:** 1135; **1980–81:** 264, 1439n.
Wyatt, Oscar S., Jr., **1979:** 1614n.
Wyatt, Wilson W., **1977:** 816
Wydler, Repr. John W., **1980–81:** 2379
Wyeth, Jamie, **1977:** 27, 1118; **1980–81:** 2341
Wylie, Repr. Chalmers P., **1977:** 1628
Wyman, Rosalind W., **1979:** 45, 92; **1980–81:** 1439n.
Wyman, Thomas H., **1978:** 2069
Wynde, Yvonne J., **1978:** 697
Wynn, William H., **1979:** 1008, 1009, 1671, 1954
Wyoming
 Disaster declaration, **1978:** 1033; **1979:** 1293
 Emergency declaration, **1977:** 1127
 Federal oil and gas leases, **1977:** 1395
 President's visit, **1978:** 1476
 U.S. attorney, **1977:** 1211, 1212
 U.S. marshal, **1977:** 745, 746
Wyoming, Mich., **1980–81:** 2441–2451
Wyszynski, Stefan Cardinal, **1977:** 2207; **1978:** 45, 281

Xerox Education Publications, **1977:** 1211
Ximenes, Vincente T., **1977:** 941

Yaguina Head Outstanding Natural Area, Oreg., **1980–81:** 433
Yamani, Sheik Ahmed Zaki, **1978:** 849

Yamashita, Hiroshi, **1980–81:** 1433
Yamashita, Satsuki, **1980–81:** 929
Yancey, James W., **1978:** 511, 898
Yankovich, Margaret, **1980–81:** 1369
Yapczenski, Lorrie, **1980–81:** 2055
Yarborough, Cale, **1980–81:** 1406
Yarborough, Ralph W., **1978:** 2033; **1980–81:** 2409
Yarborough, Richard W., **1978:** 2184; **1979:** 46, 90
Yarn, Jane Hurt, **1978:** 1270, 1279
Yarnall, D. Robert, Jr., **1980–81:** 867, 874n.
Yastrzemski, Carl, **1978:** 1893; **1979:** 1824
Yasui, Ken, **1979:** 1169n.
Yates, Repr. Sidney R., **1977:** 1211; **1978:** 415, 2268; **1980–81:** 318, 823
Yatesville, Pa., **1980–81:** 2251
Yatesville Lake, Ky., **1977:** 208
Yatron, Repr. Gus, **1978:** 1406
Yazoo City, Miss., **1977:** 1316
Yazurlo, John C., **1980–81:** 841
Ybarrando, Lawrence, **1979:** 1534, 1537
Ycaza Borja, Gustavo, **1977:** 194
Yemen
    Prime Minister 'Abd al-'Aziz 'Abd al-Ghani, **1978:** 1485
    Trade with U.S., **1979:** 2229, 2291, 2294
    U.S. Ambassador, **1978:** 1266, 1279
Yeongchi Wu, **1980–81:** 1508
Yidan, Yigael, **1979:** 428n.
Ylvisaker, Paul N., **1978:** 267, 269
YMCA Youth Governors Conference, National, **1978:** 1210
Yokich, Stephen P., **1980–81:** 2610
Yokota, Shari H., **1980–81:** 927
York, E. T., **1980–81:** 323, 628
York, Herbert F., **1977:** 1178, 1179; **1979:** 216, 1129, 1143
York, Pa., **1980–81:** 824
Yost, Robert L., **1977:** 489; **1978:** 567, 641, 1406
Youghiogheny River, Pa.-Md., **1979:** 1813
Young, Andrew J., **1977:** 10, 31, 33, 46, 76, 85, 194, 220, 245, 248, 451, 595, 600, 647, 709, 710, 913, 1021, 1084, 1108, 1347, 1382, 1471, 1472, 1487, 1625, 1650, 1662, 1723, 1726, 1727, 1737, 1748, 1809, 1938, 2201; **1978:** 374, 456, 526, 871, 919, 935, 1105, 1325, 1330, 1406, 1410, 1509, 1516, 1668, 1682, 1703, 1723, 2072, 2197, 2219
    Developing countries, relationship with, **1980–81:** 224, 1501, 2366, 2427
    Mentions, **1980–81:** 538, 1004, 1071, 1499, 1752
    Peace Corps Advisory Council, member, **1980–81:** 2075
    Presidential Medal of Freedom recipient, **1980–81:** 2930
    Zimbabwe
        Independence ceremonies, U.S. delegation cochairman, **1980–81:** 719, 1327

Young, Andrew J. — *continued*
    Zimbabwe — *continued*
        Independence talks, role in, **1980–81:** 1580, 1581, 1634, 1706, 1753, 1929
    See also United Nations, U.S. Representative.
Young, Mrs. Andrew J., **1979:** 376
Young, Bryant L., **1977:** 987
Young, Repr. C. W. (Bill), **1979:** 2085
Young, Coleman A., **1977:** 816, 1162, 1835, 1841; **1978:** 229, 641; **1979:** 948, 954n.; **1980–81:** 27, 1330, 1541, 2862
Young, Jean C., **1978:** 815, 1191; **1979:** 1613, 2090, 2112; **1980–81:** 752
Young, Kenneth, **1980–81:** 1823
Young, Margaret Buckner, **1978:** 510, 596
Young, Rebecca C., **1977:** 2028
Young, Repr. Robert A., **1980–81:** 492
Young Adult Conservation Corps, **1977:** 349, 1427
Young Democrats of America, **1979:** 1604
Young Men's Hebrew Association, **1980–81:** 2537
Young Presidents' Organization, Inc., **1977:** 1795
Youngstown, Ohio, **1980–81:** 2347, 2348
Youth.
    See Children and youth.
Youth camps, **1978:** 1778
Youth Employment, Vice President's Force on, **1980–81:** 124, 815, 1503
Youth Employment and Demonstration Projects Act of 1977, **1977:** 1427, 1438; **1978:** 138
Yugoslavia
    Ambassador to U.S., **1979:** 2162n.; **1980–81:** 892
    Chief of Protocol, **1980–81:** 1243
    Earthquake, U.S. assistance, **1979:** 669, 1679
    Joint statements, **1978:** 485; **1980–81:** 1216
    Member of the Presidency, **1977:** 1649, 1700
    Military officers education in U.S., **1980–81:** 1077
    Minister-Counselor at Embassy in D.C., bombing of home, **1980–81:** 1023
    Nonaligned status, **1980–81:** 1205
    President Cvijetin Mijatovic, **1980–81:** 1208, 1213n., 1216, 1220, 1243
    President Lazar Kolisevski, **1980–81:** 827
    President's visit
        Announcement, **1980–81:** 1014
        Arrival in Belgrade, **1980–81:** 1208
        Daily schedule (Digest), **1980–81:** 1243
        Departure statement, **1980–81:** 1220
    Kalemegdan Park tour, **1980–81:** 1210
        Meeting with President Mijatovic and Government officials, **1980–81:** 1210
        State dinner, **1980–81:** 1211, 1246
    Reporters, interview with the President, **1980–81:** 1204
    U.S. Ambassador, **1977:** 873, 874, 883; **1980–81:** 1243
    U.S. policy, **1980–81:** 315, 827
    Vice President's visit, **1977:** 785

Yugoslavia, President (Josip Broz Tito), **1977:** 785, 786; **1978:** 302, 473–476, 485; **1979:** 669
   Death statement, **1980–81:** 827
   Funeral services, President's absence at, **1980–81:** 1199
   Gravesite visit by the President, **1980–81:** 1244
   Invitation to President to visit Yugoslavia, **1980–81:** 1208
   Mentions, **1980–81:** 1210, 1220
   Nonaligned movement organizer, **1980–81:** 1211, 1216
   Past visit to U.S., **1980–81:** 315, 1204
Yukon-Charley National Monument, **1978:** 2140
Yukon Flats National Monument, **1978:** 2142

Zablocki, Repr. Clement J., **1977:** 505, 788, 1136, 1152, 1533, 1745, 1972; **1978:** 315, 498–500, 897, 1809, 2268
   Campaign appearance with the President, **1980–81:** 2076
   Carter, Billy, activities with Libyan Government, letter requesting information from President (Digest), **1980–81:** 1468
   Communication from the President, **1979:** 590
   Foreign assistance programs reorganization support, **1979:** 643, 1230
   Kampuchean relief legislation sponsorship, **1979:** 2012
   Legislation passage leadership
      Intelligence Authorization Act for Fiscal Year 1981, **1980–81:** 2233
      Small business, **1980–81:** 2381
   Mention, **1980–81:** 1852
   Reception for, President's remarks at, **1979:** 572
   United Nations Pledging Conference on Refugee Relief, member, **1979:** 2085
Zabludovsky, Jacobo, **1979:** 235
Zagoria, Samuel D., **1977:** 1824, 1931; **1978:** 703, 750, 1418, 1458, 1666, 1670
Zaire
   Ambassador to U.S., **1977:** 1754
   France, relationship with, **1980–81:** 679
   News conference remarks, **1978:** 1092
   President Mobuto Sese Seko, **1977:** 502; **1979:** 1604, 1627
   Tank sale, **1977:** 700
   U.S. Ambassador, **1979:** 1848, 1883
   U.S. assistance, **1978:** 930, 937, 944, 945, 971, 972
   U.S. policy, **1977:** 502, 703, 782
Zake, Joshua Luyimbazi, **1979:** 1882
Zaldumbide, Ricardo Crespo, **1979:** 1882
Zambia
   Ambassador to U.S., **1977:** 1383
   President Kenneth D. Kaunda, **1978:** 771, 917, 920, 924, 934, 940, 976
   Presidential Adviser, **1977:** 2089

Zambia — *continued*
   U.S. Ambassador, **1979:** 1263, 1293
Zamorano, Eluid Hector, **1979:** 1727
Zamyatin, Leonid, **1979:** 1143
Zannoni, Stella, **1977:** 816
Zanone, Valerio, **1980–81:** 1241
Zariski, Daniel A., **1980–81:** 927
Zavala County Economic Development Corporation, **1978:** 1094
Zawawi, Qais Abdul Munim Al-, **1980–81:** 452
Zborowski, Eli, **1980–81:** 823
Zeferetti, Repr. Leo C., **1978:** 1809; **1980–81:** 451
Zeidman, Philip F., **1978:** 968; **1980–81:** 2533
Zemel, Richard S., **1980–81:** 928
Zengerle, Joseph Charles, III, **1979:** 2271, 2281
Zerbe, John A., **1980–81:** 928
Zero-base budgeting, **1977:** 112, 131, 135, 154, 160, 169, 174, 190, 214, 232, 239, 394, 728, 1030, 1087; **1978:** 125, 133, 187, 753, 815, 882, 1422; **1979:** 75, 97, 100; **1980–81:** 115, 1357, 2902
Zhao Zhongxiang, **1979:** 163
Zhulev, Stoyan Iliev, **1980–81:** 2752
Zia-ul-Haq, Mohammad, **1979:** 2151; **1980–81:** 34, 40, 1945, 2056, 2356
Ziaur Rahman, **1980–81:** 1564, 1577, 1579
Zidek, Anthony, **1978:** 457
Ziegler, Donald E., **1978:** 571
Zielinski, Helen, **1980–81:** 1852
Ziff, Irvin, **1978:** 1975
Zigler, Edward, **1980–81:** 193
Zimbabwe
   Ambassador to U.S., **1980–81:** 1598
   Independence ceremonies, U.S. delegation cochairmen, **1980–81:** 719
   Majority rule
      British support, **1980–81:** 541, 679, 2428
      Free elections, **1980–81:** 355, 807
      Major U.S. foreign policy accomplishment, **1980–81:** 870, 1501, 2147
      Mention, **1980–81:** 2096
      Reagan, Ronald, policy differences with the President, **1980–81:** 2325
      U.S. support, **1980–81:** 1327, 1535, 1642, 1753, 1929, 2109, 2123, 2301
      Young, Andrew, role in, **1980–81:** 1634, 2366, 2428
   Question-and-answer session with reporters, **1978:** 653
   Trade with U.S., **1980–81:** 401, 430, 550
   U.S. Ambassador, **1980–81:** 717, 720
   U.S. policy, **1978:** 121, 495
   U.S. relations, **1980–81:** 896
   Yugoslavian relations, **1980–81:** 1219
Zimbabwe, Prime Minister (Robert Mugabe)
   Relationship with U.S., **1980–81:** 807

Zimbabwe, Prime Minister — *continued*
  Visit to U.S.
    Meetings with the President, **1980–81:** 1579,
      1584
    Postvisit remarks, **1980–81:** 1634, 1706, 1753,
      1929
Zimbabwe-Rhodesia
  Air Force One briefing, **1978:** 667, 668
  Bishop Abel Tendekai Muzorewa, **1979:** 1230
  Conflict settlement, **1979:** 2258, 2259, 2262, 2264,
    2267
  Democratic National Committee, remarks, **1978:**
    2197
  Elections
    Comments on, **1979:** 737, 755
    President's assessment, **1979:** 1013
  Interview remarks, **1978:** 1257, 1348, 1410, 1777,
    2178
  Jefferson–Jackson dinner, remarks, **1978:** 1900
  Majority rule, U.S. policy, **1979:** 39, 357, 755
  Mention, **1979:** 902, 1006, 2244
  News conference remarks, **1978:** 1747, 1751
  Trade sanctions
    Comments on, **1979:** 755, 847, 965, 2137
    Legislative authority, **1979:** 1434
    Meeting with congressional leaders (Digest),
      1979: 1018
    News conference (Checklist), **1979:** 1020

Zimbabwe-Rhodesia — *continued*
  Trade sanctions — *continued*
    President's decisions
      Continuation, **1979:** 1013, 2119
      Revocation, **1979:** 2251
    U.S. policy, **1978:** 121, 374, 495
  See also Zimbabwe; Southern Rhodesia.
Zimmerman, Don Alan, **1980–81:** 1026, 1052
Zimmerman, Harriet M., **1978:** 1706, 1724, 2050,
    2269; **1979:** 46, 90
Zionism, **1978:** 1456
Zionist Organization of America, **1977:** 2085
Zobel, Rya W., **1979:** 179, 180
Zook, Ray M., **1977:** 1211
Zorinsky, Sen. Edward, **1978:** 303, 526; **1979:** 956,
    2257n.
Zucconi, Vittorio, **1977:** 777
Zukas, Hale J., **1979:** 2192; **1980–81:** 2731
Zukerman, Pinchas, **1979:** 527
Zumas, Nicholas H.
  Emergency Boards to investigate railway labor
    disputes, member, **1979:** 819, 1697, 2247
  Mention, **1979:** 1999
Zumwalt, Adm. Elmo R., Jr., **1977:** 2141; **1980–81:**
    1770
Zurcher v. *Stamford Daily*, **1980–81:** 2218
Zwick, Charles J., **1977:** 1178, 1179, 1706; **1978:** 751
Zynstein, Solomon, **1978:** 1975.